ELEMENTS OF LITERATURE

FIRST COURSE

ANNOTATED TEACHER'S EDITION

LTX
7-05-016
Teacher

DISCARDED

HOLT, RINEHART AND WINSTON, INC.
AUSTIN NEW YORK SAN DIEGO CHICAGO TORONTO MONTREAL

Lamar University Library

Acknowledgments

For permission to reprint copyrighted sources, grateful acknowledgment is made to the following sources:

Arte Publico Press: From "Ghosts and Voices: Writing from Obsession" by Sandra Cisneros, Copyright © 1986 by Sandra Cisneros.

Edward Field: Comment by Edward Field on "Daisy." Copyright © 1989, by Edward Field.

Gale Research Inc.: From Nicholasa Mohr in *Something About the Author,* vol. 8, edited by Anne Commire. Copyright © 1976 by Gale Research Company.

Harcourt Brace Jovanovich, Inc: "Little Girl, Be Careful What You Say" from *New Section* by Carl Sandburg. Copyright 1934, 1938, 1940, 1941, 1943, 1945, 1946, 1947 by Carl Sandburg. From *Bygones* by Louis Untermeyer. Copyright © 1965 by Louis Untermeyer.

Harvard University Press on behalf of the Publishers and the Trustees of Amherst College: "There is no Frigate like a Book" from *The Poems of Emily Dickinson,* edited by Thomas H. Johnson. Copyright © 1951, 1955, 1979, 1983 by the President and Fellows of Harvard College. Published by the Belknap Press of Harvard University Press, Cambridge, MA.

Evelyn Tooley Hunt: "Mama Is a Sunrise" by Evelyn Tooley Hunt from *The Lyric.* Copyright © 1972 by Evelyn Tooley Hunt.

Alfred A. Knopf, Inc.: From "Madam's Past History" in *Selected Poems of Langston Hughes.* Copyright © 1959 by Langston Hughes.

Macmillan Publishing Company: From *The Young Writer at Work* by Jessie Rehder. Copyright © 1962 by the Bobbs-Merrill Company, Inc.

Estate of Phyllis McGinley: From "Telltale Hearth," an interview with Phyllis McGinley which appeared in *Time,* June 18, 1965.

William Morrow and Company: "Because" by Nikki Giovanni from *Cotton Candy on a Rainy Day.* Copyright © 1978 by Nikki Giovanni.

The New Yorker Magazine Inc.: From the obituary of James Thurber by E. B. White in *The New Yorker,* November 11, 1961. Copyright © 1961 by The New Yorker Magazine, Inc.

O Estado de S. Paulo: From an interview-article about Robert Frost from *O Estado de S. Paulo,* August 18, 1954.

Omni Publications International, Ltd.: From "The Poet as Anti-Specialist" by May Swenson in *Saturday Review* Magazine, January 30, 1965. Copyright © 1965 by Saturday Review Magazine.

Gale Sayers: From Gale Sayers's acceptance speech for the George S. Halas Award for Courage. Copyright © 1969 by Gale Sayers.

Rosemary Thurber, Attorney-in-Fact for Helen W. Thurber: "The Little Girl and the Wolf" from *Fables for Our Time* by James Thurber. Copyright 1940 by James Thurber; copyright © 1968 by Helen Thurber. Published by Harper & Row, Publishers, Inc.

Twayne Publishers, a division of G. K. Hall & Company, Boston, MA: From *Ursula K. Le Guin* by Charlotte Spivack. Copyright © 1984 by G. K. Hall & Company.

University of Florida Press / Gainesville: From *Selected Letters of Marjorie Kinnan Rawlings,* edited by Gordon E. Bigelow and Laura V. Monti. Copyright © 1983 by the Board of Regents of the State of Florida.

Copyright © 1989 by Holt, Rinehart and Winston, Inc.

All rights reserved. No part of this publication may be reproduced or transmitted in any form or by any means, electronic or mechanical, including photocopy, recording, or any information storage and retrieval system, without permission in writing from the publisher.

Requests for permission to make copies of any part of the work should be mailed to: Permissions, Holt, Rinehart and Winston, Inc., 1627 Woodland Avenue, Austin, Texas 78741

Printed in the United States of America

ISBN 0-03-029599-8

90123456 071 98765432

The *Elements of Literature* Program

> English belongs to all those all over the world who speak and write it, who read its literature, and who treasure it. They are the ones who are its tomorrow.
>
> —John Algeo, Sixth Course

Elements of Literature is a new literature program that has been written by professional creative writers and academic experts, and reviewed by panels of junior and senior high-school teachers.

Elements has been called the program with a distinctive "voice." Carefully crafted instructional materials on the elements of literature are provided by a poet, novelist, dramatist, nonfiction writer, and mythologist (all of whom are also teachers). This means that your students will hear John Malcolm Brinnin tell them what poetry is and why it is important. They will hear Robert Anderson tell them about the "bare bones" of drama and John Leggett discuss the age-old elements of storytelling. They will hear Janet Burroway and Susan Allen Toth present the techniques of nonfiction writing. They will hear David Leeming discuss the connections between ancient myth and modern literature and life. At the eleventh and twelfth grade levels, students will hear the authoritative voices of academic experts: John Algeo, Gary Arpin, Donald Gray, Harley Henry, and C. F. Main. Following current scholarship, these teachers have taken a fresh approach to the author biographies and the historical and cultural introductions to American and British literature.

The aim of all the writers in this program has been to provide instructional material that will invite students to become active, imaginative participants in the reading process. Students will see literature as an art form exhibiting certain structural and thematic features that can be recognized and analyzed. But they will also see literature as an invitation to participate in a search for meaning. In this program, students will respect each work of literature and its authority. But they will also be encouraged to discover and formulate their own unique and creative responses to the literature in this book and thus to the world they live in.

The selections in *Elements of Literature* have been chosen with equal care by our team of writers, academics, and classroom teachers. Each anthology includes representative classics of our tradition as well as those fresh, new selections which will possibly form the canon of tomorrow.

Thus, in *Elements of Literature* you can be sure of three things: first, that the instructional material from grades seven through twelve allows a student to hear the voices of experts in their fields; second, that all of the instructional material is accessible to junior or senior high-school students; third, that the selections will have strong appeal to your students and will provide you with the materials for a sound course of study.

Elements of Literature is not a textbook series written by anonymous "hack" writers; *Elements* has been written with care by people who know their craft well and who can communicate what they know to young students.

Writers, academics, classroom teachers, editors: our job has been a collaboration, and our intent has been to supply you with the very best teaching materials possible. *Elements of Literature:* There is no other high-school literature program like it.

Supplementary Materials for the *Elements of Literature* Program

Supplementary materials for the program include the following components:

Teacher Materials

- *Annotated Teacher's Edition* for each level
- *Teacher's Manual* for each level, which provides further commentary, complete lesson plans, specific objectives for each selection, reteaching alternatives, complete answers to the text questions and language and vocabulary questions, and strategies for evaluating the composition assignments
- *Elements of the Novel* booklets, which provide study guides to selected novels not included in the student text but commonly taught at the grade level

Testing Materials

- *Test Book* for each level, which provides a test for every selection (or, in the case of shorter works, group of selections), tests for the introductions, unit review tests using new material, tests on critical thinking and writing, and word analogy tests
- *Reading Check Test* blackline masters for each level, which provide quick, factual quizzes on every selection (except for short lyric poems)
- *Test Generators* for each level

Student Enrichment Materials

- *Vocabulary Activity Worksheets* for each level, which provide preteaching and mastery strategies for all the words included on the vocabulary portion of the selection tests in the *Test Book*
- *Workbooks* for each level, featuring lessons to accompany all selections
- *Study and Reinforcement Worksheets* (SRW) for each level, featuring worksheets on literary types and terminology
- *Connections Between Reading and Writing* workbooks for each level, which provide activities for further self-directed work on certain key selections
- *Instructional Overhead Transparencies* for each level, which include various charts and diagrams for organizing information, as well as a set of *Elements of Poetry* transparencies with overlays, which provide aids for teaching and interpreting poetry
- *Reader's Response Journals*, illustrated response activities for First and Second Courses only

Audiovisual Materials

- *Audiocassettes*, which offer three hours of professional readings of poems, short stories, dramas, and essays for each level
- *Posters* for each level
- *Video Series*, featuring five VHS format videos on the following topics: *A Sense of Wonder—From Myth to Science Fiction; The Epic Hero; Theatercraft; American Dreamers; The Victorian Novelist*

Features of the *Annotated Teacher's Edition* for *Elements of Literature*

The annotations in this text have been prepared to help you plan your lessons and your class discussions, and to help you evaluate student achievement. The following types of annotations are featured:

1. The Introductions and Author Biographies

The unit introductions are annotated at all grade levels; author biographies are annotated at grades eleven and twelve. At times these annotations extend information. These notes allow you to adapt your lectures or discussions to classes of varying abilities.

The End of the Civil War
Winston Churchill describes tersely Cromwell's achievements: "By the end of 1648 all was over. Cromwell was Dictator. The Royalists were crushed; Parliament was a tool; the Constitution was a figment; the Scots were rebuffed, the Welsh back in their mountains; the Fleet was reorganized, London overawed. King Charles, at Carisbrooke castle, where the donkey treads the water wheel, was left to pay the bill. It was mortal."

ATE Sixth Course

2. The Selections

The first annotations for each selection help you prepare the student for reading. In grades 7–10 these annotations are called **Prereading**; in grades 11 and 12 they are called **Preparation**. At all levels, these annotations include one or all of these notes:

a. Building on Prior Knowledge. Though the headnotes in the *Elements* texts are extremely thorough, in almost every case students can benefit from more prereading information, which will ease their entrance into the selection and make their reading more meaningful.

Building On Prior Knowledge
"Focusing on Background" (text page 186) is an excellent introduction both to the rite-of-passage genre and to this particular story. Discuss with students some of the tasks that are involved in an American youth's passage: creating an identity separate from family, choosing a career, leaving home, and so on. Although some details in the story are specific to the Russian setting, other aspects will be familiar to many students: the extended family, the life of a factory town, the necessity for teenagers to accept responsibility.

ATE Third Course

b. Establishing a Purpose. Other notes suggest purposes that can be set for reading.

Establishing a Purpose
Reinforce the headnote's comments about the title, alerting students to pay special attention to events and descriptions related to the bridge. To discourage the notion that a story is simply a set of ideas, ask students to put themselves in Kostya's place. Would you feel as he does? Act as he does? Change as he does?

ATE Third Course

c. Prereading Journal. This is an optional note and is used when a selection suggests a particularly interesting topic for free writing. Often these suggestions are tied in to a composition activity at the end of the selection.

Prereading Journal
Have students make two columns in their journals, headed "Future" and "Bridges." Under "Future," tell them to list or describe any personal desires they have for the rest of their high school years or adult life—tangible ones like careers or intangible ones like qualities of character. Then direct them to describe, in the second column, what might be a "bridge" for each entry: What will take them to their goals?

ATE Third Course

d. Closure. To close your lesson—to review for students the main thrust of the instruction—you need to provide closure. Every selection is provided with a suggestion for closure. The closure activities should take only from five to ten minutes; many of them call for oral activities.

> **Closure**
> As a class activity, or with students divided into three groups, have the students compose orally three brief summaries: what Kostya is like at the beginning of the story, what he *does* in the story (his actions), and what he is like at the end of the story. Have students then use the three summaries to prepare a class statement of theme.
>
> ATE Third Course

e. Supplementary Support Materials. For a quick review of the extra materials available to you in the *Elements of Literature* program, a list of supplementary support materials is provided for every selection.

> **Supplementary Support Materials**
> - Vocabulary Activity Sheet
> - Reading Check Test blackline master
> - Selection Test
> - Audiocassette recording
> - Author photograph on *A Gallery of Authors* poster
> - Worksheet: *Connections Between Reading and Writing*
>
> ATE Third Course

f. Developing Vocabulary. Lists are provided of words from each selection that are tested on in the *Test Book* selection tests. For quick access to the way each word is used in context, the words are underscored on the student pages in this text. Note that an activity worksheet is provided for every one of these words. This activity worksheet is a preteaching tool that should be used *before* the selection test is administered. For most selections, ten words have been selected for the vocabulary test.

> **Developing Vocabulary**
> The following words appear on a test in the *Test Book,* page 39. (See also the Vocabulary Activity Sheet.)
>
> | | |
> |---|---|
> | hoisting | crest |
> | translucent | impetus |
> | compounded | scaffolding |
> | tributaries | hampered |
> | remnants | grandiose |
>
> ATE Third Course

g. Reading Check Test. For every prose selection and for longer narrative poems, a quick check-up test is provided. This test poses only simple recall questions. These quizzes can help you determine quickly whether everyone in class has read the selection. You will probably want to use these quizzes before you discuss the questions at the end of the selection, which call for higher-level thinking skills. Each of these Reading Check Tests is also available on a blackline transparency master.

> **Reading Check Test**
> **1.** The boy tries to snatch a purse from a very old and frail woman. (F)
> **2.** Mrs. Jones makes the boy pick up her purse; then she drags him home with her. (T)
> **3.** Roger admits that he tried to steal Mrs. Jones's purse because he needed money to buy food. (F)
> **4.** After Mrs. Jones and Roger eat, she gives him the money he wants. (T)
> **5.** Roger and Mrs. Jones become life-long friends who visit each other often. (F)
>
> ATE Third Course

h. Selection Annotations. The selection annotations are of several types. They might suggest ways to guide students' reading of a selection; they might provide ideas for enrichment. The annotations that contain a question for the student are signalled by a question mark. Except for questions calling for individual student responses, the questions posed to students are answered on the page. The most common annotations highlight a literary element or a reading technique.

> **Flashback/Inferring**
> ? Where are we now? (Flashed back to the war, in the Liberator, Leon Crane's plane) What sentence marks a break in the narrative, and what do we infer happened during this time? (The break occurs between "Leon's" and "The Liberator." What happened is a lot: The reporter has located Crane and heard his story.)
>
> ATE Third Course

Other annotations include expansion of a concept in the text, a note on vocabulary, a close reading note, and a responding question, among others. The label in boldface will identify the nature of each annotation.

ELEMENTS OF LITERATURE

FIRST COURSE

HOLT, RINEHART AND WINSTON, INC.

AUSTIN NEW YORK SAN DIEGO CHICAGO TORONTO MONTREAL

Candy Carter wrote the Exercises in Critical Thinking and Writing. She is English Department Chair at Tahoe Truckee Junior-Senior High School in California. Ms. Carter has served on the editorial committee of the NCTE and has been an editor of the *California English Magazine*. She has edited books and journal articles for the NCTE and was selected to participate in the Summer 1987 NCTE/MLA invitational institute on the teaching of English. She lives in Truckee, California.

Sandra Cisneros has served as Consultant for the program. A graduate of the Writer's Workshop at the University of Iowa, she has written a novel, *The House on Mango Street*, and several collections of poems, including *My Wicked, Wicked Ways*. She has taught at the California State University, Chico, and now makes her home in Texas.

Nancy E. Wiseman Seminoff has served as Consultant in Reading and Questioning Strategies for the program. Dr. Seminoff is Dean of the School of Education and Professional Studies at the Central Connecticut State University, New Britain. She has served as a reading consultant and as a classroom teacher. She has published widely in national and state educational periodicals.

Copyright © 1989 by Holt, Rinehart and Winston, Inc.

All rights reserved. No part of this publication may be reproduced or transmitted in any form or by any means, electronic or mechanical, including photocopy, recording, or any information storage and retrieval system, without permission in writing from the publisher.

Requests for permission to make copies of any part of the work should be mailed to: Permissions, Holt, Rinehart and Winston, Inc., 1627 Woodland Avanue, Austin, Texas 78741.

Printed in the United States of America

ISBN 0-15-717500-6

890123456 041 98765432

Acknowledgments

Grateful acknowledgment is made to the teachers who reviewed materials in this book, in manuscript or in classroom tests.

Bea Cassidy
Miami Springs Junior High School
Miami Springs, Florida

Bernice Causey
Mobile County Public Schools
Mobile, Alabama

Charles Crawford
Radnor Middle School
Wayne, Pennsylvania

Jean Heller
Williamsport Schools
Williamsport, Pennsylvania

Anamae Hill
Henrico County Schools
Highland Springs, Virginia

Karen Libby
Hamilton Junior High School
Denver, Colorado

Kathryn McMillan
Stratford, Connecticut

Sandra Prillaman
Wicomico Board of Education
Salisbury, Maryland

Sylvia Skarstad
Cleveland High School
Portland, Oregon

Grateful acknowledgment is also made to the following teachers who assisted in the planning of the instructional apparatus and in its preparation:

Sally Borengasser
Bentonville, Arkansas

Marie C. Brown
Sterling Heights, Michigan

Mary Beth Lorsbach
Marquette, Michigan

Craig Minbiole
Rochester Hills, Michigan

vi

For permission to reprint copyrighted material, grateful acknowledgment is made to the following sources:

Louise Hardeman Abbot/Conde Nast Publications, Inc.: "The Lost Beach" by Louise Hardeman. Copyright © 1954 and renewed 1984 by The Conde Nast Publications, Inc. Courtesy *Mademoiselle.*

Jack Anderson: "Going to Norway" from *City Joys* by Jack Anderson. Copyright © 1975 by Jack Anderson. Published by Release Press.

Isaac Asimov: "The Fun They Had" by Isaac Asimov.

Beatriz Badikian: "elements for an autobiographical poem:" by Beatriz Badikian. Published in *Imagine, International Chicano Poetry Journal,* Vol. I, No. 2, Winter 1984.

Elizabeth Barnett, as Executor of the Literary Estate of Norma Millay Ellis: From "Recuerdo" in *Collected Poems* by Edna St. Vincent Millay. Copyright © 1922, 1928, 1950, 1955 by Edna St. Vincent Millay and Norma Millay Ellis. Published by Harper & Row, Publishers, Inc.

Susan Bergholz Literary Services: "Eleven" by Sandra Cisneros. Copyright © 1987 by Sandra Cisneros. Comment by Sandra Cisneros. Copyright © 1987 by Sandra Cisneros.

The Bodley Head: "Narcissus" and "The First Anemones" from *Tales the Muses Told* by Roger Lancelyn Green.

Charles Boer: "Demeter" from *The Homeric Hymns,* Revised Edition, translated by Charles Boer. Published by Spring Publications, 1979.

Brandt & Brandt Literary Agency, Inc.: From "Little Test for Mothers" by Shirley Jackson. First published in *Good Housekeeping,* October 1960. Copyright © 1960 by the Hearst Corporation.

Curtis Brown Group, Ltd.: Lassie Come-Home by Eric Knight. Copyright © 1938 by The Curtis Brown Publishing Company; copyright 1940 by Jere Knight; copyright renewed © 1968 by Jere Knight, Betty Noyes Knight, Winifred Mewborn, and Jennie Knight Moore. Originally published in *The Saturday Evening Post,* December 17, 1938. From Eric Knight's foreward to *Song on Your Bugles.* Copyright 1937 by Eric M. Knight; renewed © 1965 by Jere Knight, Betty Noyes Knight, Winifred Knight Mewborn, and Jennie Knight Moore. From "Johanna" in *Shape Shifters* by Jane Yolen. Copyright © 1978 by Jane Yolen.

Curtis Brown Group, Ltd., on behalf of the Estate of Rex Warner: "Ceres and Proserpine" from *Men and Gods* by Rex Warner. Copyright 1950 by Rex Warner.

Capitol Cities Communications, Inc./Ed Friendly: From "Here Come the Brides" by John T. Dugan from the *Little House on the Prairie* television series, based on the novels by Laura Ingalls Wilder. Copyright © 1977 by Capitol Cities Communications, Inc./Ed Friendly.

Arthur Cavanaugh: "Miss Awful" by Arthur Cavanaugh. Copyright © 1969 by Arthur Cavanaugh. Comment on "Miss Awful" by Arthur Cavanaugh. Copyright © 1989 by Arthur Cavanaugh.

Laura Cecil, Literary Agent for the James Reeves Estate: "Giant Thunder" from *James Reeves: The Complete Poems.* Copyright © by the James Reeves Estate.

Checkerboard Press, a division of Macmillan, Inc.: "Young Ladies Don't Slay Dragons" from *The Princess Book* by Joyce Hovelsrud. Copyright © 1974 by Checkerboard Press, a division of Macmillan, Inc.

Columbia Pictures and William Blinn: Adapted from *Brian's Song* by William Blinn.

Don Congdon Associates, Inc.: "The Naming of Names" from *The Martian Chronicles* by Ray Bradbury. Copyright © 1950, renewed 1977 by Ray Bradbury. Published by Doubleday & Company. From the introduction to *Mars and the Mind of Man* by Ray Bradbury. Copyright © 1973 by Ray Bradbury.

Davis Publications, Inc. and Isaac Asimov: From "Hints" by Isaac Asimov from *Isaac Asimov's Science Fiction Magazine.* Copyright © 1979 by Davis Publications.

Dodd, Mead & Company, Inc.: "Wine on the Desert" from *Wine on the Desert and Other Stories* by Max Brand. Copyright 1936 by Frederick Faust; copyright renewed 1964 by Jane F. Easton, Judith Faust, and John Frederick Faust. "The Story of the Fisherman" from *The Arabian Nights* published by Dodd, Mead & Company, Inc. "The Cremation of Sam McGee" from *The Collected Poems of Robert Service.* From the Introduction to *Max Brand's Best Western Stories,* edited by William F. Nolan. Copyright © 1981 by William F. Nolan.

Doubleday, a division of Bantam, Doubleday, Dell Publishing Group, Inc.: "The Tom-Cat" from *Poems & Portraits* by Don Marquis. Copyright 1917; renewed 1945 by The Sun Printing and Publishing Association. "You Can't Just Walk On By" from *The Least One* by Borden Deal. Copyright © 1967 by Borden Deal. From *Wanda Hickey's Night of Golden Memories and Other Disasters* by Jean Shepherd. Copyright © 1971 by Jean Shepherd. From *Tell Me How Long the Train's Been Gone* by James Baldwin. Copyright © 1968 by James Baldwin. From "Forgotten Dreams" by Edward Silvera in *The Poetry of the Negro 1746–1970,* edited by Langston Hughes and Arna Bontemps. From *The Best of Don Marquis.* Copyright © 1946 by Doubleday & Company, Inc.

E. P. Dutton, a division of NAL Penguin, Inc.: "The Flower-Fed Buffaloes" from *Going-To-The-Stars* by Vachel Lindsay. Copyright 1926 by D. Appleton & Co.; copyright renewed 1954 by Elizabeth C. Lindsay. A Hawthorn book.

Esquire Associates: "Three Skeleton Key" by George G. Toudouze from *Esquire.*

Farrar, Straus & Giroux, Inc.: "Charles" from *The Lottery* by Shirley Jackson. Copyright © 1948, 1949 by Shirley Jackson; copyright renewed © 1976, 1977 by Lawrence Hyman, Barry Hyman, Mrs. Sarah Webster, and Mrs. Joanne Schnurer. From *Annie John* by Jamaica Kincaid. Copyright © 1983, 1984, 1985 by Jamaica Kincaid.

Edward Field: "Daisy" from *Variety Photoplays* by Edward Field. Copyright © 1967 by Edward Field.

Feinman & Krasilvosky: From *Ploughman of the Moon* by Robert Service. Copyright © 1945 by Dodd, Mead and Company. Inc.

The Free to Be Foundation, Inc.: "Southpaw" by Judith Viorst from *Free to Be . . . You and Me* by Marlo Thomas. Copyright © 1974 by the Free to Be Foundation, Inc.

Richard Garcia: "The Clouds Pass" by Richard Garcia. Copyright © 1979 by Richard Garcia.

vii

Harcourt Brace Jovanovich, Inc.: "The Boy and the Wolf" from *The Magic Circle,* edited by Louis Untermeyer. Copyright 1952 by Harcourt Brace Jovanovich, Inc.; renewed 1980 by Bryna Ivens Untermeyer, Lawrence S. Untermeyer, and John F. Moore. "The Fifty-Yard Dash" from *My Name Is Aram* by William Saroyan. Copyright 1938, 1966 by William Saroyan. "The Saddest Day the Summer Had" from *Raymond and Me That Summer* by Dick Perry. Copyright © 1963, 1964 by Dick Perry. "A Loud Sneer for Our Feathered Friends" from *My Sister Eileen* by Ruth McKenney. Copyright 1938, 1966 by Ruth McKenney. From *"O Beloved Kids,"* by Rudyard Kipling, edited by Elliot L. Gilbert. Copyright © 1983 by the National Trust for Places of Historic Interest or Natural Beauty. From *1984* by George Orwell. Copyright 1949 by Harcourt Brace Jovanovich, Inc.; copyright renewed 1977 by Sonia Brownell Orwell.

Harper & Row, Publishers, Inc.: Slight adaptation from pp. 175–178 of *A Tree Grows in Brooklyn* by Betty Smith. Copyright 1943 by Betty Smith. "Princess" (pp. 97–115) and the Introduction from *El Bronx Remembered: A Novella and Stories* by Nicholasa Mohr. Copyright © 1975 by Nicholasa Mohr. "Hector the Collector" from *Where the Sidewalk Ends: The Poems and Drawings of Shel Silverstein.* Copyright © 1974 by Snake Eye Music, Inc. From *Two Worlds for Memory* by Alfred Noyes. Copyright © 1953 by Alfred Noyes.

Hart-Davis: "The Shepherd's Hut" from *Collected Poems* by Andrew Young.

Harvard University Press on behalf of the publishers and the Trustees of Amherst College: "There is no frigate" from *The Poems of Emily Dickinson,* edited by Thomas H. Johnson.

Henry Holt and Company, Inc.: "The Objection to Being Stepped On" and "The Pasture" from *The Poetry of Robert Frost,* edited by Edward Connery Lathem, copyright 1939, © 1967, 1969, by Holt, Rinehart and Winston, Inc.; copyright © 1962 by Robert Frost. Excerpt from *Survive the Savage Sea* by Dougal Robertson. Copyright © 1973 by Dougal Robertson. "Christmas" from *Homecoming: An Autobiography* by Floyd Dell. Copyright 1933, © 1961 by Floyd Dell.

Hill & Wang, a division of Farrar, Straus & Giroux, Inc.: From *The Big Sea* by Langston Hughes. Copyright © 1940 by Langston Hughes; copyright renewed © 1968 by Arna Bontemps and George Houston Bass.

Horn Book, Inc.: "An Interview with Robert Cormier" by Anita Silvey from *Horn Book Magazine,* May–June 1985. Copyright © 1985 by Horn Book, Inc.

Houghton Mifflin Company: "Rhyming Riddle" from *The Children Sing in the Far West* by Mary Austin. Copyright 1928 by Mary Austin; copyright renewed 1956 by Kenneth Mc. Chapman and Mary C. Wheelwright. *A Wizard of Earthsea* by Ursula K. Le Guin. Copyright © 1968 by Ursula K. Le Guin. A Parnassus Press Book. "The Mysteries of Dionysus" from *Greek Myths* by Olivia Coolidge. Copyright 1949, renewed 1977 by Olivia E. Coolidge. From *Randall Jarrell's Letters, an Autobiographical and Literary Selection,* edited by Mary Jarrell. Copyright © 1985 by Mary Jarrell. From *The Hobbit* by J. R. R. Tolkien. Copyright © 1937, 1938, and 1966 by J. R. R. Tolkien.

Daniel Keyes and his agent, Richard Curtis Associates, Inc.: "Flowers for Algernon" by Daniel Keyes from *The Magazine for Science Fiction.* Copyright © 1959 by Mercury Press, Inc.

Alfred A. Knopf, Inc.: "Madam and the Rent Man" reprinted from *Selected Poems of Langston Hughes.* Copyright 1948 by Alfred A. Knopf, Inc.

Felicia Lamport: "Eggomania" by Felicia Lamport. Published in the *Boston Globe.* Copyright © 1983 by Felicia Lamport.

Mrs. Allison Lawbury, Executrix of the estate of Andrew Young: "The Shepherd's Hut" from *Collected Poems* by Andrew Young.

Little, Brown & Company, Inc.: From *Mythology* by Edith Hamilton. Copyright 1942 by Edith Hamilton. Copyright renewed © 1969 by Dorian Fielding Reid and Doris Fielding Reid. "The Tale of Custard the Dragon" from *Family Reunion* by Ogden Nash. Copyright 1936 by Ogden Nash. "The Kitten" and "The Dog" from *Custard and Company* by Ogden Nash. Copyright 1940; renewed 1962 by Ogden Nash. "The Kitten" first appeared in *The Saturday Evening Post,* August 3, 1940. "The Germ," "The Octopus," and "The Porcupine" from *Verses from 1929 On* by Ogden Nash. Copyright 1933, 1942 by Ogden Nash. "The Germ" and "The Octopus" first appeared in *The New Yorker.* "The Porcupine" first appeared in *The Saturday Evening Post.*

Macmillan Publishing Company: "Bats" from *The Bat Poet* by Randall Jarrell. Copyright © 1963, 1964 by Macmillan Publishing Company. From "A Coat" in *The Collected Poems of W. B. Yeats* by W. B. Yeats. "The Horse" by José Maria Eguren from *The Yellow Canary Whose Eye Is So Black,* edited and translated by Cheli Durán. Copyright © 1977 by Cheli Durán Ryan.

Macmillan of Canada, a division of Canada Publishing Corporation: "Aeneas," "The Creation," "Deucalion's Flood," "The Golden Age," "Pandora's Box," "Prometheus," and "War in Heaven," from *Four Ages of Man* by Jay Macpherson. Copyright © 1962, 1965 by Jay Macpherson.

New American Library: From "A Marriage Proposal" by Anton Chekov, translated by Joachim Neugroschev in *The Mentor Book of Short Plays,* edited by Richard H. Goldston and Abraham Lass. Copyright © 1969 by Joachim Neugroschev.

The New York Times Company: From "Immortal Mortal" by Betty Smith in *The New York Times Magazine,* May 28, 1987. Copyright © 1987 by The New York Times Company. "O. Henry's New Yorkers—And Today's" by Gilbert Millstein from *The New York Times,* September 9, 1962. Copyright © 1962 by The New York Times Company.

The New Yorker: "Rolls for the Czar" by Robin Kinkead. Copyright © 1937; renewed © 1965 by *The New Yorker.* "Phaethon" by Morris Bishop from *The Best of Bishop: Light Verse From The New Yorker and Elsewhere* (Cornell). Originally published in *The New Yorker,* August 27, 1955. Copyright © 1955 by The New Yorker.

Harold Ober Associates, Inc.: "The Quiet Heart" from *Under the Boardwalk* by Norman Rosten. Copyright © 1968 by Norman Rosten.

Oxford University Press: "Conversation with a Giraffe at Dusk in the Zoo" from *Eyes Closed Against the Sun* by Douglas Livingstone. Copyright © 1970 by Oxford University Press.

Pantheon Books, a division of Random House, Inc.: "The Moustache" and "Guess What? I Almost Kissed My Father Goodnight" from *Eight Plus One* by Robert Cormier. Copyright © 1971 by Robert Cormier. From "The Water of Life" in *The Complete Grimm's Fairy Tales* by the Grimm Brothers, based on a translation by Margaret Hunt, revised, corrected,

viii

and completed by James Stern. Copyright 1944 by Pantheon Books, Inc.; copyright renewed 1972 by Random House, Inc. From "Depot in Rapid City" by Roberta Hill in *A Book of Women Poets from Antiquity to Now,* edited by Aliki and Willis Barnstone.

Murray Pollinger: From the Introduction by James Cameron to *The Best of Roald Dahl.* Copyright © 1965 by Roald Dahl.

Random House, Inc.: "The 1st" from *Good Times* by Lucille Clifton. Copyright © 1969 by Lucille Clifton.

Saturday Review: "The Dinner Party" by Mona Gardner from *Saturday Review of Literature,* 25:15–16, January 31, 1942. Copyright 1941 by Saturday Review Magazine.

Gale Sayers and Al Silverman: From "The Short Courageous Life of Brian Piccolo" from *I Am Third,* by Gale Sayers and Al Silverman, published by Viking Penguin, Inc. First published in *Look* Magazine, September 25, 1970. Copyright © 1970 by Gale Sayers and Al Silverman.

Charles Scribner's Sons: "A Mother in Mannville" from *When the Whippoorwill* by Marjorie Kinnan Rawlings. Copyright 1936 The Curtis Publishing Company; copyright renewed © 1964 by Nortin Baskin.

Charles Scribner's Sons, an imprint of Macmillan Publishing Company: Marjorie Kinnan Rawlings, Introduction by Julia Scribner Bigham from the *Marjorie Rawlings Reader.* Copyright © 1956 by Charles Scribner's Sons; copyright renewed.

Robert Silverberg/Agberg, Ltd.: "Collecting Team" by Robert Silverberg. Copyright © 1956, 1984 by Agberg, Ltd. Comment from Robert Silverberg. Copyright © 1989 by Robert Silverberg.

Simon & Schuster, Inc.: From "The Third Level" in *About Time* by Jack Finney. Copyright © 1976 by Jack Finney. From *Webster's New World Dictionary of the English Language,* edited by David B. Guralnik.

The Society of Authors as representatives for Walter de la Mare: "The Listeners" by Walter de la Mare.

Song Press: From "The Blacksmiths" in *Curses and Laments,* retold by Wesli Court. Copyright © 1978 by Song Press.

Lloyd Sarett Stockdale: "Requiem for a Modern Croesus" from *Slow Smoke* and published by Henry Holt & Company. Copyright 1925 by Henry Holt & Company.

May Swenson: "Cat & the Weather" by May Swenson. Copyright © 1963 by May Swenson.

Rosemary A. Thurber, Attorney-in-Fact for Helen W. Thurber: "The Dog That Bit People" from *My Life and Hard Times* by James Thurber. Copyright 1933, 1961 by James Thurber. Published by Harper & Row, Publishers, Inc. "The Scotty Who Knew Too Much" from *Fables for Our Time* by James Thurber. Copyright © 1940 by James Thurber. Copyright © 1968 by Helen Thurber. Published by Harper & Row, Publishers, Inc. From *Selected Letters of James Thurber,* edited by Helen Thurber and Edward Weeks, published by Atlantic-Little Brown.

Viking Penguin Inc.: "Strange Tree" from *Under the Tree* by Elizabeth Madox Roberts. Copyright 1922 by B. W. Huebsch, Inc., copyright renewed 1950 by Ivor S. Roberts. Copyright 1930 by The Viking Press, Inc., copyright renewed 1958 by Ivor S. Roberts and The Viking Press, Inc. "A Choice of Weapons" from *Times Three* by Phyllis McGinley. Copyright 1954 by Phyllis McGinley; copyright renewed © 1982 by Phyllis Hayden Blake. Originally published in *The New Yorker.*

Watkins/Loomis Agency, Inc.: "Beware of the Dog" from *Over to You, Ten Stories of Flyers and Flying* by Roald Dahl. Copyright © 1945 by Roald Dahl.

A.P. Watt, Ltd., on behalf of the Executors of the Estate of Robert Graves: "Daedalus," "King Midas's Ears," "The Palace of Olympus," and from "Phaethon Story" in *Greek Gods and Heroes* by Robert Graves. "Paris and Queen Helen" from *The Siege and Fall of Troy* by Robert Graves.

The Writer: From "Letter to a Son Who Has Declared His Ambition to Become a Writer" by Borden Deal. Appeared in *The Writer,* November 1974. Copyright © 1974 by The Writer, Inc.

Design: Kirchoff/Wohlberg, Inc.
Art Development and Picture Research: Photosearch, Inc.
Cover: *Under the Falls, The Grand Discharge* by Winslow Homer (1895). Watercolor. The Brooklyn Museum. Bequest of Helen B. Sanders.
Page v: *The Blank Signature* (detail) by René Magritte (c. 1956). Oil. National Gallery of Art, Washington, D.C. Collection of Mr. and Mrs. Paul Mellon.

ix

SUPPLEMENTARY SUPPORT MATERIAL
Previewing the Anthology:
1. Using the Table of Contents (page 1 of Workbook)
2. Genres (page 5 of Workbook)
3. Previewing the Unit (page 7 of Workbook)
4. Previewing a Selection (page 9 of Workbook)

CONTENTS

UNIT THREE: DISCOVERIES

UNIT FOUR: THE ELEMENTS OF A SHORT STORY

UNIT FIVE: THE ELEMENTS OF POETRY

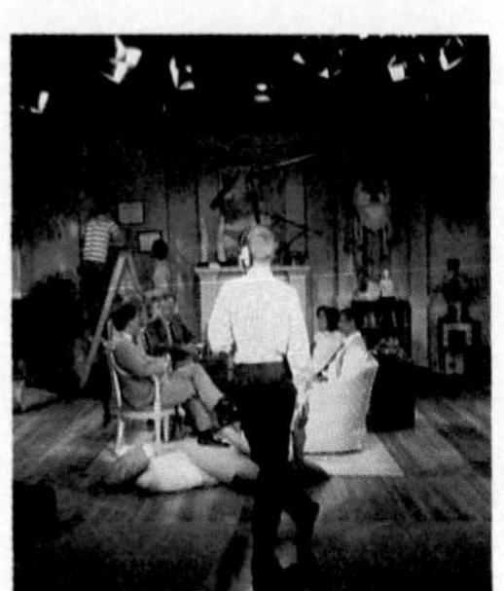

UNIT SIX: THE ELEMENTS OF DRAMA

UNIT SEVEN: FANTASY AND SCIENCE FICTION

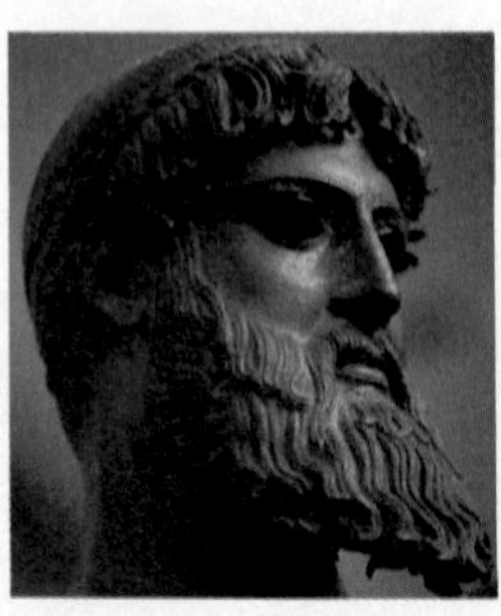

UNIT EIGHT: THE MYTHS OF GREECE AND ROME

CONFLICTS

Seeking Shelter by Roger Brown (1983). Oil. Courtesy of the Phyllis Kind Galleries. Chicago/New York.

UNIT ONE **John Leggett**

Humanities Connection: Discussing the Fine Art

? What is happening in the painting? (A tornado is striking.) What does the title of the painting tell you? (It tells what the people are doing.) How do you think the people in the painting feel? (Scared, panicky) Point out to students the relative sizes of the tornado, the trees, the houses, and the people. What do you think the artist is trying to convey by painting the tornado so big? (It makes the smaller elements in the picture seem weaker and more vulnerable to the power of the tornado.) Do you think this painting was a good choice to begin a unit entitled "Conflicts"? Why?

Teaching Conflicts

Before focusing specifically on conflicts, discuss with students the art and value of storytelling. You may want to discuss briefly the fact that storytelling seems to be a part of human nature; certainly people have been telling stories since the dawn of time.

What is a story? What is a good story? What is the difference between a true-life story and a made-up story? What true-life stories do we see and hear every day? How do we use these stories in our own lives? Why do people like true-life stories? Where do storytellers get ideas for made-up stories? Why do we like them? Before most people knew how to read, how were stories transmitted? What new methods of storytelling have been developed in this century? What are the advantages of each mode: hearing a story told, reading a story, seeing it performed?

This discussion may sensitize students to how storytelling pervades their lives. When they realize this, they may be more receptive to reading and writing stories, which they are already making up every day, anyway. Most students, of course, like stories and will read those in this unit with pleasure. You can use students' enthusiasm to develop a sense of wonder and enjoyment for the whole class.

Objectives of the Unit on Conflicts

1. To improve reading proficiency
2. To identify external and internal conflicts
3. To identify suspense
4. To identify foreshadowing
5. To increase awareness of vocabulary and word choice
6. To respond to stories in oral and written expression
7. To use reading to stimulate creative writing
8. To use the following critical thinking skills:
   - **a.** Comparing and contrasting characters
   - **b.** Interpreting a passage
   - **c.** Describing a character
   - **d.** Analyzing a character
   - **e.** Analyzing a relationship

SUPPLEMENTARY SUPPORT MATERIAL: UNIT ONE

1. Introduction/Understanding Conflict Test (page 1 of Test Book)
2. Word Analogies Test (page 15 of Test Book)
3. Reading Check Test blackline master
4. Unit Review Test (page 17 of Test Book)
5. Critical Thinking and Writing Test (page 21 of Test Book)
6. Instructional Overhead Transparencies

Unit Outline
CONFLICTS

A. Discussing the Quotation
In the quotation, Janet Burroway makes the point that stories, especially heroic and suspenseful ones, have been a popular form of entertainment from earliest times.

? Why do you enjoy stories?

> *It seems likely that the earliest storytellers—in the tent or around the campfire or on the Viking ship—told stories out of an impulse to tell stories. They made themselves popular by distracting their listeners from a dull or dangerous evening with heroic exploits and a skill at creating suspense: What happened next? And after that? And then what happened?*
>
> —Janet Burroway

SRW p. 13

A

Conflict

B

Illustration for *Treasure Island* by N. C. Wyeth (1911).

Why do certain stories catch our attention instantly, draw us in, and make us care about what's going on? It is as if each of these stories has a motor that keeps us reading, or that makes us read faster and faster.

Conflict: The Energy of a Story

An interesting story creates an energy that attracts us. Where does this energy come from? It comes from conflict. **Conflict** is a struggle between opposing forces. A conflict results when a person disturbs the balance of things, because of desire or dread. In a conflict, a character may struggle with another person, with a whole army, with a hungry tiger, or with a troublesome aspect of his or her own personality. Conflict is found in true stories as well as fictional stories.

When a baby wants a rattle but cannot reach it, there is conflict. When a girl wishes that the boy with freckles—who never notices her—would ask her to the picnic, there is conflict. When a pinch hitter picks up a bat and starts toward the plate, or when a doctor frowns at the laboratory report, or when a political candidate learns that his opponent has taken the lead, a conflict has been started. A story begins.

Each of us knows about conflict. We encounter it and try to resolve it every day. From the moment we wake in the morning, we must deal with conflict. The conflict might involve guilt over the homework we didn't finish. It might involve anger at the traffic jams on the way to school. It might involve some big guy who bumps us in the hall. If we don't overcome the conflict, we feel frustrated and angry. If we do overcome it, we feel great.

Two Kinds of Conflict: External and Internal

In daily life, as in literature, there are two basic types of conflict. **External conflict** is a struggle between a character and some outside force. It may take place when one person threatens another. An example might be a bully who waits for a smaller child on the way home. An external conflict may also take place between one person

B. Discussing the Illustration
N. C. Wyeth (1882–1945) was an American mural painter and illustrator noted primarily for his illustrations of such classics of Western literature as the novels of Robert Louis Stevenson, Daniel Defoe's *Robinson Crusoe,* Homer's *Odyssey,* the Robin Hood tales, and many others. N. C. Wyeth was father and teacher to the famous American painter Andrew Wyeth.

You can tell students that *Treasure Island,* the well-known novel by Robert Louis Stevenson, is about a search for buried treasure that pits young Jim Hawkins against two evil villains, Long John Silver and Blind Pew.

? Are the men in this picture involved in an external conflict or an internal conflict?

A. Responding to the Photograph
Discuss with students how external conflict often leads to internal conflict.

? How might the external conflict depicted in the photograph lead to internal conflict?

Responding to a Story
As an alternative to the instructions suggested in the student text, have student volunteers read the selection aloud as the balance of the class follows along silently. Then instruct students to go back through the excerpt, this time paying attention to the side comments and jotting down on a separate sheet of paper any notes that occur to them. When everyone has finished reading and writing, lead a discussion on the importance of formulating key questions while reading.

B. Suspense and Foreshadowing

? Tell about an incident from a TV show you have seen or a story you have read in which foreshadowing heightened suspense.

C. Active Reading
The reading strategy reflected by the sidenotes is an interactive one; it demonstrates that the reader has combined his or her existing knowledge with the information presented in the story. By questioning, predicting, monitoring comprehension, and confirming and revising predictions along the way, the reader becomes actively involved in the reading process. This involvement leads not only to increased comprehension but also to greater enjoyment of the story.

D. Pronunciation
attachés
(at′ə·shāz′)

★ **Texas Essential Elements/(a) English Language Arts: 4H** Point of view. **(c) Reading: 1A** Context clues; **1C** Dictionaries; **3A** Main ideas/details; **3F** Purpose/point of view/opinion; **3H** Predict

A

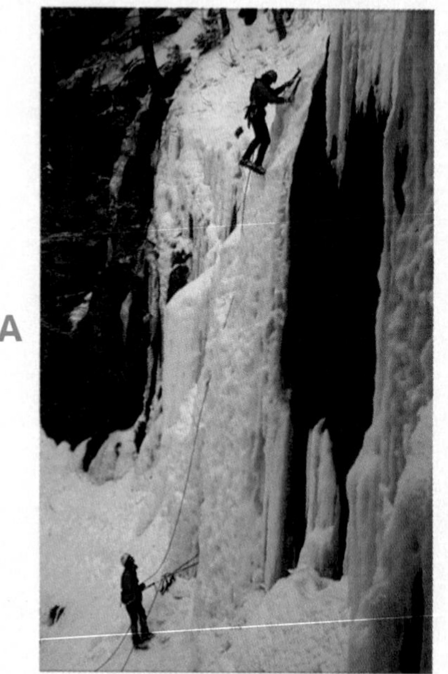

and a group of people. For instance, an outlaw in a Western story may struggle with a sheriff and his deputies. An external conflict also may take place when a person is challenged or threatened by nature. This kind of conflict might involve a mountain climber struggling to reach the peak of a steep, ice-covered mountain. It could also involve a storm at sea that keeps a sailor from the safety of the harbor.

The second basic type of conflict takes place within our minds or hearts. **Internal conflict** is a struggle between opposing desires or emotions in a person. Suppose a desire to pass the test tempts Miranda to glance at Alice's paper. At the same time, Miranda doesn't want to lose the respect of her teacher and classmates, who disapprove of cheating. As she decides whether or not to look at Alice's answer, Miranda is enduring an internal conflict.

Suspense: Exciting Uncertainty

In literature, once a conflict begins we want to know what happens next. Once Miranda realizes she could see Alice's paper if she turned her head slightly, or once the batter faces the pitcher, or once the climber starts up that mountain, we begin to wonder what is going to happen. This anxious curiosity is called **suspense.** Suspense usually begins to build as soon as a conflict begins.

B Sometimes suspense is increased by hints or clues about what will happen later. Such hints or clues are called **foreshadowing.** Say a character about to dive into the ocean hears someone remark that sharks were once sighted near shore. As you read, you suspect the sharks will appear again—and you feel that tingle of fear and excitement that keeps you turning the pages.

Responding to a Story

C The following short short story has notes in the right-hand margin. These notes are the thoughts of one reader who was reading the story for the first time. Notice that the reader doesn't always understand every reference in the story. Notice how the reader uses context clues to try to figure out unfamiliar words. Notice how the reader looks for the conflict in the story and responds to it.

The Dinner Party

D The country is India. A colonial official and his wife are giving a large dinner party. They are seated with their guests—army officers and government attachés and their wives, and a visiting American naturalist—in their spacious dining room, which has a bare marble floor, open rafters, and wide glass doors opening onto a veranda.

A spirited discussion springs up between a young girl who insists that women have outgrown the jumping-on-a-chair-at-the-

What do I know about dinner parties? Well, they're usually full of people talking and having fun.
What's "colonial India"? (India was once a British colony.)

What is a naturalist? Must have something to do with nature.

Reading Check Test

1. A struggle between two opposing forces is called a conflict. *(True)*
2. There are three basic types of conflict. *(False)*
3. Internal conflict is a struggle between a character and some outside force. *(False)*
4. Anxious curiosity about a story is called suspense. *(True)*
5. Hints or clues that increase suspense are called foreshadowing. *(True)*

sight-of-a-mouse era and a colonel who says that they haven't.

"A woman's unfailing reaction in any crisis," the colonel says, "is to scream. And while a man may feel like it, he has that ounce more of nerve control than a woman has. And that last ounce is what counts."

I see a conflict right away between the girl and this stuffy old colonel. A

The American does not join in the argument but watches the other guests. As he looks, he sees a strange expression come over the face of the hostess. She is staring straight ahead, her muscles contracting slightly. With a slight gesture she summons the native boy standing behind her chair and whispers to him. The boy's eyes widen: He quickly leaves the room.

I already dislike this colonel. I predict that he is going to get it at the end. Remember, the *writer* is a woman. B

Something's happening! (No clues.)

Of the guests, none except the American notices this or sees the boy place a bowl of milk on the veranda just outside the open doors.

What's the milk for? A cat? Is it important that it's put outside the doors?

The American comes to with a start. In India, milk in a bowl means only one thing—bait for a snake. He realizes there must be a cobra in the room. He looks up at the rafters—the likeliest place—but they are bare. Three corners of the room are empty, and in the fourth the servants are waiting to serve the next course. There is only one place left—under the table.

A snake! I didn't know they drank milk!

His first impulse is to jump back and warn the others, but he knows the commotion would frighten the cobra into striking. He speaks quickly, the tone of his voice so arresting that it sobers everyone.

Isn't this what the colonel said women do? I wonder if he *will* jump?

"I want to know just what control everyone at this table has. I will count to three hundred—that's five minutes—and not one of you is to move a muscle. Those who move will forfeit fifty rupees. Ready!"

Why doesn't he just tell them the truth? What is he trying to do? Rupees must be Indian money.

The twenty people sit like stone images while he counts. He is saying ". . . two hundred and eighty . . ." when, out of the corner of his eye, he sees the cobra emerge and make for the bowl of milk. Screams ring out as he jumps to slam the veranda doors safely shut.

"You were right, Colonel!" the host exclaims. "A man has just shown us an example of perfect control."

But *who* ordered the milk?

"Just a minute," the American says, turning to his hostess. "Mrs. Wynnes, how did you know that cobra was in the room?"

A faint smile lights up the woman's face as she replies: "Because it was crawling across my foot."

—Mona Gardner

Great twist! I like it! So what does the colonel say to all of this? I can think of a better title for this story: "The Uninvited Guest."

A. Conflict
Remind students to look always for conflicts in the stories they read, for it is usually the conflict, be it external or internal, that is at the heart of the plot.

B. Making Predictions
Remind students of the importance of making predictions and of confirming and revising them as they read. Most good readers do it automatically.

Thinking Over the Story

If you had this story read by ten different readers, you'd have ten different responses. You'd also find that not every reader picked up on all the story's important details.

Suppose now that you wanted to use your response notes to write about the story. You'd have a great deal of material to start with. You'd see two things at once: (1) You were so gripped by the problem in the story that you kept wanting to know what happened next. (2) You got interested in the conflict—the argument between the stuffy old-fashioned colonel and the girl. At the end of the story, you might even have made an unconscious prediction about what happens next: Does the colonel apologize? What does he say?

PREREADING

1. **BUILDING ON PRIOR KNOWLEDGE.** Before they read, ask students what they know about lighthouses and their keepers. Lighthouses, whose purpose is to provide the seafarer with an aid to position and a means of safe coastal navigation, have been in existence for centuries. The first man-made lighthouse was erected by the ancient Egyptians. The development of modern lighthouses started in 1700 with the advent of improved structures and lighting equipment. To provide an identification signal to mariners, most lighthouses emit an intense beam of light whose visibility depends upon atmospheric conditions and elevation. This light is flashed at regular intervals in a manner that is agreed to by an international association.

2. **ESTABLISHING A PURPOSE.** Before students begin reading, you might have them read question 9 on page 15. This will help establish a purpose for their reading. You may wish to review with students the many purposes for which authors write: to persuade, to inform, to entertain.

Responding to the Photograph

You might want to lead a discussion on lighthouses and lighthouse keepers (see Building on Prior Knowledge above).

? Imagine that you are a lighthouse keeper. Where are your living quarters in this lighthouse, and what do the rooms look like? What would your average day at the lighthouse be like?

3. **Prereading Journal.** Before they read, have students write a brief paragraph in which they tell how they would react if they suddenly found themselves surrounded by rats.

Supplementary Support Material

1. Vocabulary Activity Sheet
2. Reading Check Test blackline master
3. Selection Test (page 3 of Test Book)
4. Reader's Response Journal
5. Workbook (page 11)

Developing Vocabulary

The following words appear on a test in the Test Book, page 4. (See also the Vocabulary Activity Sheet.)

key	fathom
treacherous	incessant
maneuver	vivid
maritime	derisive
clannish	incendiary

Texas Essential Elements/(a) English Language Arts: 1B Purpose and audience; **3A** Plot/character; **4F** Generalizations; **4G** Fact/nonfact; **4H** Point of view

THREE SKELETON KEY

George G. Toudouze

On an isolated island off the coast of French Guiana, in South America, three men in a lighthouse struggle against an invading army. It is not a *human* army, however. Pause after the third paragraph. Who is the narrator—the person telling the story? Write down any hints dropped by the narrator which suggest that something weird and frightening might happen in this story.

For a detailed lesson plan on this story, see Teacher's Manual pages 1–2.

A biography of George G. Toudouze appears on text page 16.

My most terrifying experience? Well, one does have a few in thirty-five years of service in the Lights, although it's mostly monotonous routine work—keeping the light in order, making out the reports.

A When I was a young man, not very long in the service, there was an opening in a lighthouse newly built off the coast of Guiana,[1] on a small rock twenty miles or so from the mainland. The pay was high, so in order to reach the sum I had set out to save before I married, I volunteered for service in the new light.

Three Skeleton Key, the small rock on which the light stood, bore a bad reputation. It earned its name from the story of the three convicts who, escaping from Cayenne[2] in a stolen dugout canoe, were wrecked on the rock during the night, managed to escape the sea but eventually died of hunger and thirst. When they were discovered, nothing remained but three heaps of bones, picked clean by the birds. The story was that the three skeletons, gleaming with phosphorescent light, danced over the small rock, screaming. . . .

But there are many such stories and I did not give the warnings of the old-timers at the *Isle de Sein*[3] a second thought. I signed up, boarded ship, and in a month I was installed at the light.

Picture a gray, tapering cylinder, welded to the solid black rock by iron rods and concrete, rising from a small island twenty-odd miles from land. It lay in the midst of the sea, this island, a small, bare piece of stone, about one hundred fifty feet long, perhaps forty wide. Small, barely large enough for a man to walk about and stretch his legs at low tide.

This is an advantage one doesn't find in all lights, however, for some of them rise sheer from the waves, with no room for one to move save within the light itself. Still, on our island, one must be careful, for the rocks were treacherously smooth. One misstep and down you would fall into the sea—not that the risk of drowning was so great, but the waters about our island swarmed with huge sharks that kept an eternal patrol around the base of the light. B

Still, it was a nice life there. We had enough provisions to last for months, in the event that the sea should become too rough for the supply ship

Context Clues. A few words in this story may be unfamiliar to you. A few are defined in footnotes. You can probably figure out others by looking at their context. The *context* is made up of the words and sentences surrounding a word. Each time you come across a word you don't recognize, examine the word's context for clues to its meaning.

1. **Guiana** (gē·ä′nə): French Guiana, an overseas department, or administrative district, of France, located on the northeast coast of South America.
2. **Cayenne** (kī·en′): capital of French Guiana. There really was an old convict settlement there.
3. ***Isle de Sein*** (ēl·də·sen).

A. "What I Know So Far"
At this point in their reading, ask the students to answer the questions posed in the headnote. (The narrator was a lighthouse keeper for thirty-five years. When he was young, he took a job off Guiana to save some money before he got married. The place's name suggests something frightening. The story of the convicts' skeletons is weird.)

B. Responding
? Would you volunteer for service in this lighthouse? Why or why not?

A. Character

? Based on what you have read so far, how would you describe the narrator's character? (Practical, somewhat of a loner, sensible) Cite details to support your answer. (He needed money to get married so he took a high-paying job; he doesn't mind living with only a few other people on an isolated rock; he doesn't believe fantastic stories about screaming skeletons.)

B. Geography

Paramaribo is the capital of Surinam, formerly Dutch Guiana, a nation on the north central coast of South America. Surinam is bordered on the east by French Guiana, where "Three Skeleton Key" is located.

C. Character

? What does the fact that Itchoua laughs at Le Gleo suggest about Itchoua's character? (It suggests that Itchoua can be insensitive to other people's fear.)

★ **Texas Essential Elements/(c) Reading: 1A** Context clues; **1C** Dictionaries; **3A** Main ideas/details; **3D** Generalizations; **3E** Fact/fictional details; **3F** Purpose/point of view/opinion; **3I** Draw conclusions

to reach us on schedule. During the day we would work about the light, cleaning the rooms, polishing the metalwork and the lens and reflector of the light itself, and at night we would sit on the gallery and watch our light, a twenty-thousand-candle-power lantern, swinging its strong, white bar of light over the sea from the top of its hundred-twenty-foot tower. Some days, when the air would be very clear, we could see the land, a threadlike line to the west. To the east, north, and south stretched the ocean. Landsmen, perhaps, would soon have tired of that kind of life, perched on a small island off the coast of South America for eighteen weeks, until one's turn for leave ashore came around. But we liked it there, my two fellow-tenders and myself—so much so that, for twenty-two months on end with the exception of shore leaves, I was greatly satisfied with the life on Three Skeleton Key. A

I had just returned from my leave at the end of June, that is to say mid-winter in that latitude, and had settled down to the routine with my two fellow-keepers, a Breton[4] by the name of Le Gleo and the head keeper Itchoua, a Basque[5] some dozen years or so older than either of us.

Eight days went by as usual; then on the ninth night after my return, Itchoua, who was on night duty, called Le Gleo and me, sleeping in our rooms in the middle of the tower, at two in the morning. We rose immediately and, climbing the thirty or so steps that led to the gallery, stood beside our chief.

Itchoua pointed, and following his finger, we saw a big three-master, with all sail set, heading straight for the light. A queer course, for the vessel must have seen us; our light lit her with the glare of day each time it passed over her.

Now, ships were a rare sight in our waters, for our light was a warning of treacherous reefs, barely hidden under the surface and running far out to sea. Consequently we were always given a wide berth, especially by sailing vessels, which cannot maneuver as readily as steamers.

No wonder that we were surprised at seeing this three-master heading dead for us in the gloom of early morning. I had immediately recognized her lines, for she stood out plainly, even at the distance of a mile, when our light shone on her.

She was a beautiful ship of some four thousand tons, a fast sailer that had carried cargoes to every part of the world, plowing the seas unceasingly. By her line she was identified as Dutch-built, which was understandable, as Paramaribo and Dutch Guiana are very close to Cayenne. B

Watching her sailing dead for us, a white wave boiling under her bows, Le Gleo cried out:

"What's wrong with her crew? Are they all drunk or insane? Can't they see us?"

Itchoua nodded soberly, looked at us sharply as he remarked: "See us? No doubt—if there *is* a crew aboard!"

"What do you mean, chief?" Le Gleo had started, turned to the Basque. "Are you saying that she's the *Flying Dutchman*?"[6]

His sudden fright had been so evident that the older man laughed: C

"No, old man, that's not what I meant. If I say that no one's aboard, I mean she's a derelict."[7]

Then we understood her queer behavior. Itchoua was right. For some reason, believing her doomed, her crew had abandoned her. Then she had righted herself and sailed on, wandering with the wind.

The three of us grew tense as the ship seemed about to crash on one of our numerous reefs, but she suddenly lurched with some change of the wind, the yards swung around and the derelict came clumsily about and sailed dead away from us.

In the light of our lantern she seemed so sound, so strong, that Itchoua exclaimed impatiently:

"But why the devil was she abandoned? Nothing is smashed, no sign of fire—and she doesn't sail as if she were taking water."

Le Gleo waved to the departing ship:

"*Bon voyage!*" he smiled at Itchoua and went

---

4. **Breton** (bret''n): person from Brittany, a region of northern France.
5. **Basque** (bask): member of a people in France and Spain who speak the Basque language.
6. **Flying Dutchman:** fabled Dutch ghost ship whose captain is said to be condemned to sail the seas until Judgment Day. Seeing the Flying Dutchman supposedly brings bad luck.
7. **derelict** (der'ə·likt'): ship abandoned by those who were on board.

The Seducer by René Magritte (1950). Oil.

Virginia Museum of Fine Arts, Richmond.
Collection of Mr. and Mrs. Paul Mellon.

on. "She's leaving us, chief, and now we'll never know what——"

"No, she's not!" cried the Basque. "Look! She's turning!"

As if obeying his words, the derelict three-master stopped, came about and headed for us once more. And for the next four hours the vessel played around us—zigzagging, coming about, stopping, then suddenly lurching forward. No doubt some freak of current and wind, of which our island was the center, kept her near us.

Then suddenly, the tropic dawn broke, the sun rose and it was day, and the ship was plainly visible as she sailed past us. Our light extinguished, we returned to the gallery with our glasses and inspected her.

The three of us focused our glasses on her poop, saw standing out sharply, black letters on the white background of a life-ring, the stenciled name: A

Cornelius de Witt, Rotterdam.

We had read her lines correctly, she was Dutch. Just then the wind rose and the *Cornelius de Witt* changed course, leaned to port and headed straight for us once more. But this time she was so close that we knew she would not turn in time.

"Thunder!" cried Le Gleo, his Breton soul aching to see a fine ship doomed to smash upon a reef. "She's going to pile up! She's gone!"

I shook my head:

"Yes, and a shame to see that beautiful ship wreck herself. And we're helpless."

Humanities Connection: Discussing the Fine Art
Belgian-born artist René Magritte (1898–1967) was one of the most prominent painters of the Surrealist school of art, which tried to discover the "more than real world behind the real." The Surrealists often used the kind of imagery we associate with dreams (and nightmares). Like many of Magritte's paintings, this one changed a subject's substance and boundaries. Fellow Surrealist Salvador Dali called Magritte "one of the most ambiguous painters of our time."

? Do you think this is a real ship, or is it a mirage (or illusion)? What is odd about the ship? (It is made of waves, just like the sea it is supposed to be floating on—or is it rising out of the water?) Why do you think it is called *The Seducer*? (Maybe it is a mirage and is luring sailors to follow it—where?)

A. Expansion
The *poop* is a raised deck at the front of a sailing ship.

A. Mood

? By describing the rats in the way that he does, what mood, or feeling, does the author create? (Horror, revulsion, awe) Cite details to support your answer. (The author says the rats are fierce, bold, large, strong, and more intelligent than the best mariners. He tells of the rats' sharp cry and of their movement in hordes. He says that the rats swarm over people and tear at their flesh until there is only bone left.)

B. Drawing Inferences

? How does he know the ship hasn't been abandoned, and what does this imply about the crew? (None of the lifeboats were used; the crew had been eaten by the rats.)

C. Foreshadowing

? What could this foreshadow? (That the rats will eat them too)

D. Figurative Language

? To what does the author compare the sounds of the rats? (To the sound of sawing iron) Why is this a good comparison?

★ **Texas Essential Elements/(c) Reading (continued): 4D** Diagrams/graphs

There was nothing we could do but watch. A ship sailing with all sail spread, creaming the sea with her forefoot as she runs before the wind, is one of the most beautiful sights in the world—but this time I could feel the tears stinging in my eyes as I saw this fine ship headed for her doom.

All this time our glasses were riveted on her and we suddenly cried out together:

"The rats!"

Now we knew why this ship, in perfect condition, was sailing without her crew aboard. They had been driven out by the rats. Not those poor specimens of rats you see ashore, barely reaching the length of one foot from their trembling noses to the tip of their skinny tails, wretched creatures that dodge and hide at the mere sound of a footfall.

No, these were ships' rats, huge, wise creatures, born on the sea, sailing all over the world on ships, transferring to other, larger ships as they multiply. There is as much difference between the rats of the land and these maritime rats as between a fishing smack and an armored cruiser.

A

The rats of the sea were fierce, bold animals. Large, strong, and intelligent, clannish and seawise, able to put the best of mariners to shame with their knowledge of the sea, their uncanny ability to foretell the weather.

And they are brave, the rats, and vengeful. If you so much as harm one, his sharp cry will bring hordes of his fellows to swarm over you, tear you, and not cease until your flesh has been stripped from the bones.

The ones on this ship, the rats of Holland, are the worst, superior to other rats of the sea as their brethren[8] are to the land rats. There is a well-known tale about these animals.

A Dutch captain, thinking to protect his cargo, brought aboard his ship—not cats—but two terriers, dogs trained in the hunting, fighting, and killing of vicious rats. By the time the ship, sailing from Rotterdam, had passed the Ostend light, the dogs were gone and never seen again. In twenty-four hours they had been overwhelmed, killed, and eaten by the rats.

At times, when the cargo does not suffice, the rats attack the crew, either driving them from the ship or eating them alive. And studying the *Cornelius de Witt,* I turned sick, for her small boats were all in place. She had not been abandoned. B

Over her bridge, on her deck, in the rigging, on every visible spot, the ship was a writhing mass—a starving army coming toward us aboard a vessel gone mad! C

Our island was a small spot in that immense stretch of sea. The ship could have grazed us, passed to port or starboard with its ravening[9] cargo—but no, she came for us at full speed, as if she were leading the regatta at a race, and impaled herself on a sharp point of rock.

There was a dull shock as her bottom stove in, then a horrible crackling as the three masts went overboard at once, as if cut down with one blow of some gigantic sickle. A sighing groan came as the water rushed into the ship; then she split in two and sank like a stone.

But the rats did not drown. Not these fellows! As much at home in the sea as any fish, they formed ranks in the water, heads lifted, tails stretched out, paws paddling. And half of them, those from the forepart of the ship, sprang along the masts and onto the rocks in the instant before she sank. Before we had time even to move, nothing remained of the three-master save some pieces of wreckage floating on the surface and an army of rats covering the rocks left bare by the receding tide.

Thousands of heads rose, felt the wind and we were scented, seen! To them we were fresh meat, after possible weeks of starving. There came a scream, composed of innumerable screams, sharper than the howl of a saw attacking a bar of iron, and in the one motion, every rat leaped to attack the tower! D

We barely had time to leap back, close the door leading onto the gallery, descend the stairs and shut every window tightly. Luckily the door at the base of the light, which we never could have reached in time, was of bronze set in granite and was tightly closed.

The horrible band, in no measurable time, had swarmed up and over the tower as if it had been a tree, piled on the embrasures of the windows,

8. **brethren:** brothers; here, the other rats of the sea.

9. **ravening** (rav''ning): greedily searching for prey.

scraped at the glass with thousands of claws, covered the lighthouse with a furry mantle, and reached the top of the tower, filling the gallery and piling atop the lantern.

Their teeth grated as they pressed against the glass of the lantern room, where they could plainly see us, though they could not reach us. A few millimeters of glass, luckily very strong, separated our faces from their gleaming, beady eyes, their sharp claws and teeth. Their odor filled the tower, poisoned our lungs, and rasped our nostrils with a pestilential, nauseating smell. And there we were, sealed alive in our own light, prisoners of a horde of starving rats.

That first night, the tension was so great that we could not sleep. Every moment, we felt that some opening had been made, some window given away, and that our horrible besiegers were pouring through the breach. The rising tide, chasing those of the rats which had stayed on the bare rocks, increased the numbers clinging to the walls, piled on the balcony—so much so that clusters of rats clinging to one another hung from the lantern and the gallery.

With the coming of darkness we lit the light and the turning beam completely maddened the beasts. As the light turned, it successively blinded thousands of rats crowded against the glass, while the darkside of the lantern room gleamed with thousands of points of light, burning like the eyes of jungle beasts in the night.

All the while we could hear the enraged scraping of claws against the stone and glass, while the chorus of cries was so loud that we had to shout to hear one another. From time to time, some of the rats fought among themselves and a dark cluster would detach itself, falling into the sea like a ripe fruit from a tree. Then we would see phosphorescent streaks as triangular fins slashed the water—sharks, permanent guardians of our rock, feasting on our jailers.

The next day we were calmer, and amused ourselves teasing the rats, placing our faces against the glass which separated us. They could not fathom the invisible barrier which separated them from us, and we laughed as we watched them leaping against the heavy glass.

But the day after that, we realized how serious our position was. The air was foul; even the heavy smell of oil within our stronghold could not dominate the fetid odor of the beasts massed around us. And there was no way of admitting fresh air without also admitting the rats.

The morning of the fourth day, at early dawn, I saw the wooden framework of my window, eaten away from the outside, sagging inward. I called my comrades and the three of us fastened a sheet of tin in the opening, sealing it tightly. When we had completed the task, Itchoua turned to us and said dully:

"Well—the supply boat came thirteen days ago, and she won't be back for twenty-nine." He pointed at the white metal plate sealing the opening through the granite. "If that gives way"—he shrugged—"they can change the name of this place to Six Skeleton Key."

The next six days and seven nights, our only distraction was watching the rats whose holds were insecure fall a hundred and twenty feet into the maws of the sharks—but they were so many that we could not see any diminution in their numbers.

Thinking to calm ourselves and pass the time, we attempted to count them, but we soon gave up. They moved incessantly, never still. Then we tried identifying them, naming them.

One of them, larger than the others, who seemed to lead them in their rushes against the glass separating us, we named "Nero"[10]; and there were several others whom we had learned to distinguish through various peculiarities.

But the thought of our bones joining those of the convicts was always in the back of our minds. And the gloom of our prison fed these thoughts, for the interior of the light was almost completely dark, as we had to seal every window in the same fashion as mine, and the only space that still admitted daylight was the glassed-in lantern room at the very top of the tower.

Then Le Gleo became morose and had nightmares in which he would see the three skeletons dancing around him, gleaming coldly, seeking to grasp him. His maniacal, raving descriptions were so vivid that Itchoua and I began seeing them also.

10. **Nero:** emperor of Rome (54–68), known for his cruelty.

A. Suspense

How does this long passage create suspense? (It provides vivid descriptive details that make the reader wonder if and when the rats will break into the lighthouse and attack the lighthouse keepers, and if and how the lighthouse keepers will be able to save themselves.)

B. Descriptive Details

What descriptive details increase suspense and make you feel you "are there" by appealing to your senses of sight, hearing, and smell? (There are several.)

C. Characters' Actions

What does the fact that the lighthouse keepers named one of the rats indicate about how they have come to view their situation? (It indicates that the lighthouse keepers have become used to seeing the rats, that the rats have become a part of their lives.)

Humanities Connection: Discussing the Fine Art

American naturalist and artist John James Audubon (1785–1851) is best known for his illustrations of all known species of North American birds. His meticulous attention to detail and to the violence in nature are apparent in this watercolor showing the American black rat raiding a hen's nest.

? What mood does this painting create? Cite details to support your answer. Do the rats in the painting make you think of the rats in the story? Why or why not?

American Black Rat (detail) by John James Audubon (1842). Watercolor.

It was a living nightmare, the raging cries of the rats as they swarmed over the light, mad with hunger; the sickening, strangling odor of their bodies——

True, there is a way of signaling from lighthouses. But to reach the mast on which to hang the signal we would have to go out on the gallery where the rats were.

A There was only one thing left to do. After debating all of the ninth day, we decided not to light the lantern that night. This is the greatest breach of our service, never committed as long as the tenders of the light are alive; for the light is something sacred, warning ships of danger in the night. Either the light gleams, a quarter hour after sundown, or no one is left alive to light it.

Well, that night, Three Skeleton Light was dark, and all the men were alive. At the risk of causing ships to crash on our reefs, we left it unlit, for we were worn out—going mad!

At two in the morning, while Itchoua was dozing in his room, the sheet of metal sealing his window gave way. The chief had just time enough to leap to his feet and cry for help, the rats swarming over him.

But Le Gleo and I, who had been watching from the lantern room, got to him immediately, and the three of us battled with the horde of maddened rats which flowed through the gaping window. They bit, we struck them down with our knives—and retreated.

We locked the door of the room on them, but before we had time to bind our wounds, the door was eaten through, and gave way and we retreated up the stairs, fighting off the rats that leaped on us from the knee-deep swarm.

I do not remember, to this day, how we ever managed to escape. All I can remember is wading through them up the stairs, striking them off as they swarmed over us; and then we found ourselves, bleeding from innumerable bites, our clothes shredded, sprawled across the trapdoor in the floor of the lantern room—without food or drink. Luckily, the trapdoor was metal set into the granite with iron bolts.

The rats occupied the entire light beneath us, and on the floor of our retreat lay some twenty of their fellows, who had gotten in with us before the trapdoor closed, and whom we had killed with our knives. Below us, in the tower, we could hear the screams of the rats as they devoured everything edible that they found. Those on the outside squealed in reply, and writhed in a horrible curtain as they stared at us through the glass of the lantern room.

Itchoua sat up, stared silently at his blood trickling from the wounds on his limbs and body, and running in thin streams on the floor around him. Le Gleo, who was in as bad a state (and so was I, for that matter), stared at the chief and me vacantly, started as his gaze swung to the multitude of rats against the glass, then suddenly began laughing horribly:

"Hee! Hee! The Three Skeletons! Hee! Hee! The Three Skeletons are now *six* skeletons! *Six* skeletons!" B

He threw his head back and howled, his eyes glazed, a trickle of saliva running from the corners of his mouth and thinning the blood flowing over his chest. I shouted to him to shut up, but he did not hear me, so I did the only thing I could to quiet him—I swung the back of my hand across his face.

The howling stopped suddenly, his eyes swung around the room, then he bowed his head and began weeping softly, like a child.

Our darkened light had been noticed from the mainland, and as dawn was breaking the patrol was there, to investigate the failure of our light. Looking through my binoculars, I could see the horrified expression on the faces of the officers and crew when, the daylight strengthening, they saw the light completely covered by a seething mass of rats. They thought, as I afterward found out, that we had been eaten alive.

But the rats had also seen the ship, or had scented the crew. As the ship drew nearer, a solid phalanx[11] left the light, plunged into the water and, swimming out, attempted to board her. They would have succeeded, as the ship was hove to,[12] but the engineer connected his steam to a hose on the deck and scalded the head of the attacking C

11. **phalanx** (fā'langks): large, closely packed group.
12. **hove to:** stopped by taking in sail and turning the ship into the wind.

A. Interpreting
? Why did they decide not to light the lantern? (The darkness would alert people on the mainland that something was wrong in the lighthouse. See the paragraph beginning "Our darkened light" in the next column.)

B. Characters' Actions
? How would you explain Le Gleo's and the narrator's behavior? (Both Le Gleo and the narrator are in pain and under extreme tension, fighting for their lives. Le Gleo's laughter and howling shows he is cracking under the tension. The narrator knows that for even one man to lose control as Le Gleo has done is to lose the battle for survival. He tries to restore control by slapping Le Gleo to bring him back to his senses.)

C. Plot and Complication
? How does the rats' awareness of the ship complicate the situation? (If the rats board the ship, it might be difficult if not impossible for the ship to rescue the men.)

READING CHECK TEST

1. The narrator's most terrifying experience takes place in a lighthouse off the coast of Guiana. (*True*)
2. Ships are rare off the coast of Three Skeleton Key because the waters contain treacherous reefs. (*True*)
3. The lighthouse is attacked by wolves. (*False*)
4. As a signal that they are in trouble, the lighthouse keepers do not light the lantern. (*True*)
5. After the experience with the rats, the narrator quits his job as a lighthouse keeper. (*False*)

Critical Comment

About horror stories, writer Isaac Asimov has said, "When I was a lad . . . I found myself fearfully attracted to stories that scared me. Don't ask why—I hate being scared, but I didn't mind, as long as I knew in my heart that I was safe."

When they have read this story, have students apply this statement to their discussion of question 10 on page 15.

A. Predicting

? How do you predict the ship's crew will rescue the men?

B. Conflict and Resolution

? How is the conflict between the men and the rats resolved? (A tug lures the rats to a barge filled with meat. When the rats board the barge, they are doused with gasoline and burned. A whaleboat removes the men from the island. Le Gleo's and Itchoua's fates are described in the next paragraph.)

column, which slowed them up long enough for the ship to get underway and leave the rats behind.

Then the sharks took part. Belly up, mouths gaping, they arrived in swarms and scooped up the rats, sweeping through them like a sickle through wheat. That was one day that sharks really served a useful purpose.

The remaining rats turned tail, swam to the shore and emerged dripping. As they neared the light, their comrades greeted them with shrill cries, with what sounded like a derisive[13] note predominating. They answered angrily and mingled with their fellows. From the several tussles that broke out, it seemed as if they resented being ridiculed for their failure to capture the ship.

But all this did nothing to get us out of our jail. The small ship could not approach, but steamed around the light at a safe distance, and the tower must have seemed fantastic, some weird, many-mouthed beast hurling defiance at them.

Finally, seeing the rats running in and out of the tower through the door and the windows, those on the ship decided that we had perished and were about to leave when Itchoua, regaining his senses, thought of using the light as a signal. He lit it and, using a plank placed and withdrawn before the beam to form the dots and dashes, quickly sent out our story to those on the vessel.

Our reply came quickly. When they understood our position, how we could not get rid of the rats, Le Gleo's mind going fast, Itchoua and myself covered with bites, cornered in the lantern room without food or water, they had a signalman send us their reply.

His arms swinging like those of a windmill, he quickly spelled out:

A "Don't give up, hang on a little longer! We'll get you out of this!"

Then she turned and steamed at top speed for the coast, leaving us little reassured.

She was back at noon, accompanied by the supply ship, two small coast guard boats, and the fireboat—a small squadron. At twelve-thirty the battle was on.

After a short reconnaissance,[14] the fireboat picked her way slowly through the reefs until she was close to us, then turned her powerful jet of water on the rats. The heavy stream tore the rats from their places, hurled them screaming into the water where the sharks gulped them down. But for every ten that were dislodged, seven swam ashore, and the stream could do nothing to the rats within the tower. Furthermore, some of them, instead of returning to the rocks, boarded the fireboat and the men were forced to battle them hand-to-hand. They were true rats of Holland, fearing no man, fighting for the right to live!

Nightfall came, and it was as if nothing had been done, the rats were still in possession. One of the patrol boats stayed by the island; the rest of the flotilla departed for the coast. We had to spend another night in our prison. Le Gleo was sitting on the floor, babbling about skeletons; and as I turned to Itchoua, he fell unconscious from his wounds. I was in no better shape and could feel my blood flaming with fever.

Somehow the night dragged by, and the next afternoon I saw a tug, accompanied by the fireboat, come from the mainland with a huge barge in tow. Through my glasses, I saw the barge was filled with meat.

Risking the treacherous reefs, the tug dragged the barge as close to the island as possible. To the last rat, our besiegers deserted the rock, swam out, and boarded the barge reeking with the scent of freshly cut meat. The tug dragged the barge about a mile from shore, where the fireboat drenched the barge with gasoline. A well-placed incendiary shell from the patrol boat set her on fire. The barge was covered with flames immediately and the rats took to the water in swarms, but the patrol boat bombarded them with shrapnel[15] from a safe distance, and the sharks finished off the survivors. B

A whaleboat from the patrol boat took us off the island and left three men to replace us. By nightfall we were in the hospital in Cayenne. What became of my friends?

13. **derisive** (di·rī′siv): ridiculing.

14. **reconnaissance** (ri·kän′ə·səns): exploratory survey or examination.

15. **shrapnel:** exploding shells filled with small metal balls.

CLOSURE

Working in pairs, students should explain external conflict. Have them give examples of external conflicts that could take place in a school, outdoors, or at home.

Additional Speaking Assignment

Have students work in groups of three, and imagine that they are literary critics for their school newspaper. As such, have them summarize "Three Skeleton Key," tell if they enjoyed it and why, and tell whether or not and for whom they would recommend the story and why.

ANALYZING THE STORY

Identifying Facts

1. Three Skeleton Key is a very small island, one hundred fifty feet long and forty feet wide, about twenty miles off the coast of Guiana. Nothing grows on the island, and there is no fresh water. One must not slip off the rocks, for sharks roam the waters.

2. The narrator enjoys his job because the pay is excellent, the provisions are plentiful, his duties are light, he likes the spot, and his companions are compatible.

3. At first the three men believe the ship's crew abandoned her. When they spot the rats, they reason that the lifeboats are still in place; the crew did not abandon the vessel, but were eaten by the rats.

4. The rats threaten the men's minds and their bodies. Before they break into the lighthouse, their presence—enormous numbers, disgusting appearance, horrible odor, terrible cries—creates nine days of horror. Once the rats break into the lighthouse the men face real physical danger from the rats' numerous bites and from possible infection.

5. When the men leave the light off at night, it is noticed on the mainland. The first patrol boat is not enough: The crew must drive the rats away from their own ship with steam. Even four boats and a fireboat are insufficient. The fireboat *(Answers continue on page 16.)*

Well, Le Gleo's mind had cracked and he was raving mad. They sent him back to France and locked him up in an asylum, the poor devil. Itchoua died within a week; a rat's bite is dangerous in that hot, humid climate, and infection sets in rapidly.

As for me—when they fumigated[16] the light and repaired the damage done by the rats, I resumed my service there. Why not? No reason why such an incident should keep me from finishing out my service there, is there?

Besides—I told you I liked the place—to be truthful, I've never had a post as pleasant as that one, and when my time came to leave it forever, I tell you that I almost wept as Three Skeleton Key disappeared below the horizon.

16. **fumigated** (fyo͞o′mə·gāt′id): sprayed with chemical vapors to drive out pests.

Responding to the Story

Analyzing the Story

Identifying Facts

SRW p. 79

1. Describe the **setting,** or place where the story occurs. Where is Three Skeleton Key located? What are some of its physical features? (You might want to add a sketch of the island.)
2. Why does the narrator enjoy his job at the lighthouse?
3. Explain how the narrator figures out the fate of the crew of the *Cornelius de Witt.*
4. How do the rats threaten the narrator and his two companions?
5. Describe how the three men receive aid. What finally happens to the rats?

Interpreting Meanings

6. **Conflict** involves a struggle between opposing forces. An **external conflict** can involve a person struggling against another person, against a group of people, or against nature. What is the external conflict in this story? Describe the opposing forces. Who is the winner in the conflict?
7. Early in the story the narrator explains how Three Skeleton Key got its name. How does this explanation **foreshadow**—or hint at—the danger later faced by the narrator and his companions? SRW p. 43
8. Do you think this is, or could be, a true story? Give reasons for your opinion. (You might wish to do some research on sea rats before you answer the question.)
9. In your opinion, is the author's **purpose** merely to scare you, or does he have a message for you? Support your answer with evidence from the story.

Applying Meanings

10. Describe how you felt as you read about the attack on the lighthouse. Why do you think so many people enjoy horror stories and movies?

Writing About the Story

A Creative Response

1. **Describing a Conflict.** In a paragraph or two, write about a terrifying **conflict,** or struggle. Describe the opposing forces. Give details that make your description both horrifying and exciting. Be sure to tell who wins the struggle.
2. **Writing a Radio Script.** In 1949 a drama called "Three Skeleton Key" was broadcast on a radio series called *Escape,* a half-hour program of horror-adventure stories. Write your own radio script of the part of the story you feel is most exciting. You will have to include lines for a narrator who sets the scene. You will also have to provide **dialogue,** or conversation, for the characters. Your script should not change anything in the story. Since sound effects are important in a radio drama, put necessary sound effects in parentheses right where you want them heard. If you or your teacher wishes, present your dramatization to the class.

(Answers begin on page 150.)
knocks many rats off the lighthouse, but most swim back while some climb onto the fireboat. Finally, a tug hauls out a meat-filled barge that lures the ravenous rats aboard. The barge is towed away and set on fire, and the rats that are not burned take to the water, but are killed by gunfire and sharks.

Interpreting Meanings

6. The story involves a human-versus-nature conflict. On one side are the three men, whose only weapons are their ingenuity and their ability to endure. On the other side are the rats, whose strength lies in their numbers, their ability to terrify, and their sharp teeth and claws. Although all three men make it off the island, only the narrator is not defeated; he survives and returns to Three Skeleton Key. Itchoua dies from infection, and Le Gleo goes insane.

7. The legend involves three men who die of hunger and thirst on the island. All that is left of them are three skeletons that magically dance and scream. This foreshadows the threat to the lighthouse keepers. They are trapped without food

(Answers continue in left-hand column.)

(Continued from top.)
and water, and if the rats get in, their bones will be picked clean.

8. The story is possible, but unlikely. Could rats become so numerous on one ship as to overcome the crew? A small group could be directed to the library for a factual report on sea rats.

9. The author's main purpose seems to be to relate a terrifying story. But by describing how each of the men reacts to the crisis, he also shows that someone with luck, ingenuity, and a strong mind can survive an experience that destroys others.

10. Some students will enjoy this kind of delicious fear, while others will be repulsed. They may suggest that people like to feel afraid when they're really safe, that they like to see others sharing their own nightmares, or that the suspense keeps interest high.

A Critical Response

3. Contrasting Characters. Each of the three **characters** in the lighthouse responds differently to the rat invasion. For example, one is more frightened than the others, and one is calmer. In the first of two paragraphs, describe each character. Use details from the story in your descriptions. In the second paragraph, contrast the reactions of the three characters to the invasion of the rats. Before you start, you may want to organize your data by filling out a chart like the following one.

	Details About Characters	Reactions to Rat Invasion
Narrator		
Le Gleo		
Itchoua		

For answers, see Teacher's Manual page 3.

Analyzing Language and Vocabulary

Context Clues

When you read, you will come across new words. Sometimes you can figure out a new word's meaning by its **context**—the words and sentences surrounding it. For example, a word may be coupled with a **synonym**, or word that has about the same meaning. Look at the following sentence from the story: "His maniacal, raving descriptions were so vivid that Itchoua and I began seeing them also." *Maniacal* might puzzle you. Because it is used with the word *raving,* you can make an educated guess that it has a similar meaning—"mad," or "crazy."

You may also be able to figure out a new word because it is the **antonym** (that is, has roughly the opposite meaning) of another word or phrase in the context. In the following excerpt, *maritime* may be new to you: "There is as much difference between the rats of the land and these *maritime* rats as between a fishing smack and an armored cruiser." The words "rats of the land" suggest that *maritime* has an opposite meaning—of the sea.

A sentence may also offer or suggest a definition of an unfamiliar word. In the following sentence, *derelict* will probably be a new word for you. "If I say that no one's aboard, I mean she's a derelict." By looking at the context, you can figure out that a *derelict* is an abandoned ship.

For each quote below, use context clues to try to figure out the meaning of the italicized word. Tell what clues helped you in each case. Then check your accuracy by looking up the word in a dictionary.

1. "The air was foul; even the heavy smell of oil within our stronghold could not dominate the *fetid* odor of the beasts massed around us."
2. "She was back at noon, accompanied by the supply ship, two small coast guard boats, and the fireboat—a small *squadron.*"
3. "One of the patrol boats stayed by the island; the rest of the *flotilla* departed for the coast."
4. "To the last rat, our besiegers deserted the rock, swam out, and boarded the barge *reeking* with the scent of freshly cut meat."
5. "A well-placed *incendiary* shell from the patrol boat set her on fire."

For answers, see Teacher's Manual page 4.

Reading About the Writer

George G. Toudouze (b. 1877) was born in France and had many literary interests—he was a playwright, an essayist, and an illustrator. He also had a great interest in the sea, and he worked on a history of the French Navy. One critic says of his storytelling style: "It has the impact of a powerful man at a fair who, for the fun of it, takes the hammer and at one blow sends the machine to the top, rings the bell, and walks off." "Three Skeleton Key" first appeared in *Esquire* magazine.

PREREADING

1. BUILDING ON PRIOR KNOWLEDGE. Before they read, ask students what stories they already know about people adrift at sea or who have suffered from other natural disasters and are left to survive without enough food, water, or means of navigation. Examples of such stories are *Robinson Crusoe,* about a sailor who is marooned on a desert island; *Alive,* the gripping true story (and movie) of survivors of a plane crash; and *The Swiss Family Robinson,* a tale of a shipwrecked family's struggle for survival. List with them all the problems they think they would encounter, including hunger, thirst, skin exposure, danger of fierce animals, conflicts arising from the cramped quarters, fear, hallucinations, etc.

2. ESTABLISHING A PURPOSE. Suggest to students that as they read, they think about how they would have responded to this perilous situation. What conflicts spring up on the Robertsons' boat? What conflicts would students feel if they were one of the survivors? Would they be external or internal conflicts, or both?

SURVIVE THE SAVAGE SEA

Dougal Robertson

3. PREREADING JOURNAL. Before they read, have students write a brief paragraph in which they tell what personal qualities would help a person to survive a disaster. Refer back to their responses after the story is over. See also question 7.

Responding to the Photograph

? What is the subject of the photograph? (A shark) What do you know about sharks? (Some sharks are man-eaters. They often travel in groups. They even attack ships.) What do you think this selection might be about, given its title and the subject of the photograph?

SUPPLEMENTARY SUPPORT MATERIAL

1. Vocabulary Activity Sheet
2. Reading Check Test blackline master
3. Selection Test (page 5 of Test Book)
4. Reader's Response Journal
5. Workbook (page 13)

DEVELOPING VOCABULARY

The following words appear on a test in the Test Book, page 6. (See also the Vocabulary Activity Sheet.)

retrieve	copious
debris	scanty
transparent	deteriorate
abandon	heed
incision	illuminated

A. Journal
Remind students that a journal is a chronological account of daily events.

 **Texas Essential Elements/(a) English Language Arts: 3A** Plot/character; **4H** Point of view

The passages that follow are taken from a sea journal which was later made into a book called *Survive the Savage Sea.* On June 15, 1972, the sailing ship *Lucette* was attacked by killer whales in the Pacific Ocean. The boat sank in sixty seconds. The *Lucette* was sailed by Dougal Robertson, an ex-farmer, and his family: his wife Lyn, their eighteen-year-old son Douglas, their twelve-year-old twin sons Neil and Sandy, and a young family friend Robin. Set adrift with a rubber raft and a fiberglass dinghy, Robertson and his crew begin their struggle to survive. They are without maps, compass, or instruments of any kind. They have emergency rations of food and water for only three days. Steering their course by the sun and stars, they make for the coast of Costa Rica, a thousand miles away.

The narrator is Robertson himself. He wrote his journal on bits of paper from the instruction booklet and on pieces of sail. As you read, see if you can't help wondering whether you could have survived this conflict against the savage sea.

Jargon. *Jargon* is made up of specialized words relating to a particular activity or group of people. Baseball jargon, for instance, includes words and phrases like *steal, force out,* and *double play.* This story contains jargon relating to boating and the sea. As you read, make a list of such words. The first example of jargon—the word *flotsam*—is in the first sentence of the story.

A

First Day

We sat on the salvaged pieces of flotsam[1] lying on the raft floor, our faces a pale bilious color under the bright yellow canopy, and stared at each other, the shock of the last few minutes gradually seeping through to our consciousness. Neil, his teddy bears gone, sobbed in accompaniment to Sandy's hiccup cry, while Lyn repeated the Lord's Prayer; then, comforting them, sang the hymn "For Those in Peril on the Sea." Douglas and Robin watched at the doors of the canopy to retrieve any useful pieces of debris which might float within reach and gazed with dumb longing at the distant five-gallon water container, bobbing its polystyrene lightness ever further away from us in the steady trade wind. The dinghy[2] *Ednamair* wallowed, swamped, nearby with a line attached to it from the raft, and our eyes traveled over and beyond to the heaving undulations of the horizon, already searching for a rescue ship even while knowing there would not be one. Our eyes traveled fruitlessly across the limitless waste of sea and sky, then once more ranged over the scattering debris. Of the killer whales which had so recently shattered our very existence, there was no sign. Lyn's sewing basket floated close and it was brought aboard followed by a couple of empty boxes, the canvas raft cover, and a plastic cup.

I leaned across to Neil and put my arm round him, "It's all right now, son, we're safe and the whales have gone." He looked at me reproachfully. "We're not crying cos we're frightened," he sobbed, "we're crying cos Lucy's gone." Lyn gazed at me over their heads, her eyes filling with tears. "Me too," she said, and after a moment added, "I suppose we'd better find out how we stand. . . ."

We cleared a space on the floor and opened the survival kit, which was part of the raft's equipment, and was contained in a three-foot-long polyethylene cylinder; slowly we took stock:

Vitamin fortified bread and glucose[3] for ten men for two days.

Eighteen pints of water, eight flares (two parachute, six hand).

One bailer, two large fishhooks, two small, one spinner and trace, and a twenty-five-pound breaking strain fishing line.

A patent knife which would not puncture the raft (or anything else for that matter), a signal

1. **flotsam:** wreckage of a ship and its cargo.

2. **dinghy** (diŋ'gē): small boat carried on a larger boat, often as a lifeboat.

3. **glucose** (glo͞o'kōs): kind of sugar providing quick energy.

For a detailed lesson plan on this selection, see Teacher's Manual pages 4-6. A biography of Dougal Robertson appears on text page 27.

★ Texas Essential Elements/(c) Reading: **1A** Context clues; **1C** Dictionaries; **2A** Word meaning; **3A** Main ideas/details; **3F** Purpose/point of view/opinion; **3G** Compare/contrast; **3I** Draw conclusions

mirror, torch, first aid box, two sea anchors, instruction book, bellows, and three paddles.

In addition to this there was the bag of a dozen onions which I had given to Sandy, to which Lyn had added a one-pound tin of biscuits and a bottle containing about half a pound of glucose sweets, ten oranges, and six lemons. How long would this have to last us? As I looked around our meager stores my heart sank and it must have shown on my face for Lyn put her hand on mine; "We must get these boys to land," she said quietly. "If we do nothing else with our lives, we must get them to land!" I looked at her and nodded, "Of course, we'll make it!" The answer came from my heart
A but my head was telling me a different story. . . .

In the next twelve days, the family survives on a small amount of water collected from rain showers, on the meager food supplies found on the raft, and on the few fish they catch. They battle
B *seasickness and skin boils, which develop from over-exposure to the seawater. They catch sight of one ship a few miles from the raft, but they cannot catch its attention.*

Fourteenth Day

The beautiful starlit night shone sparkles of stars on the quiet swells of the now distant trade winds, and seemed to mock our feeble struggle for existence in the raft; to become one with the night
C would be so easy. We blew, and bailed the forward section continually, and when Sandy found the hole which leaked into the after section, surrounded by transparently thin fabric, I felt that this was the beginning of the end of the raft. I knew that it was unlikely that I would be able to plug this one, and yet if I left it, it would certainly split open in the next heavy sea. I made a plug and inserted it into the hole, tape ready to bind it if it held. The hole split across and water flooded into the after compartment; I rammed the plug home in disgust and stopped enough of the water to bail the compartment dry but the raft would now need constant bailing at both ends. Apart from discomfort, my only real opposition to abandoning the raft was because it would mean abandoning the shelter afforded by the canopy, so I decided to think of a way of fastening the canopy on the dinghy to give us continuing shelter from the sun if we had to abandon.

We had a sip of water for breakfast with no dried food to detract from its value, after which I crossed to the dinghy to try for a dorado.[4] The heat of the sun's rays beat on my head like a club and my mouth, dry like lizard skin, felt full of my tongue; the slightest exertion left me breathless. I picked up the spear; the dorado were all deep down as if they knew I was looking for them. A bump at the stern of the raft attracted Sandy's attention. "Turtle!" he yelled. This one was much smaller than the first, and with great care it was caught and passed through the raft—with Douglas guarding its beak, and the others its claws, from damaging the fabric—to me on the dinghy where I lifted it aboard without much trouble. I wrapped a piece of tape around the broken knife blade and made the incision into its throat. "Catch the blood," Lyn called from the raft. "It should be all right to drink a little." I held the plastic cup under the copious flow of blood, the cup filled quickly and I stuck another under as soon as it was full, then raising the full cup to my lips, tested it cautiously. It wasn't salty at all! I tilted the cup and drained it. "Good stuff!" I shouted. I felt as if I had just consumed the elixir of life.[5] "Here, take this," and I passed the bailer full of blood, about a pint, into the raft for the others to drink. Lyn D
said afterward she had imagined that she would have to force it down us and the sight of me, draining the cup, my mustache dripping blood, was quite revolting. I don't know what I looked like, but it certainly tasted good, and as the others followed my example it seemed they thought so too. I passed another pint across and though some of this coagulated before it could be drunk, the jelly was cut up and the released serum collected and used as a gravy with the dried turtle and fish.

I set to cutting my way into the turtle much refreshed, and even with the broken knife, made faster work of it than the first one, both because

4. **dorado** (də·rä′dō): brightly colored fish.
5. **elixir** (i·lik′sər) **of life:** mythical substance said to allow a person to live forever.

A. Interpreting
? What is the significance of this remark? (His intellect tells him that their chances of survival are slim. In fact, he doesn't believe they'll make it.)

B. Expansion
Tell students that the passages in italics are bridge passages whose purpose is to fill in the gaps in the narrative.

C. Interpretation
? What do you think the narrator means when he says, "to become one with the night would be so easy"? (He means that it would be easy to stop struggling and die.) Note that this is a conflict: The narrator has to struggle to keep his will to fight and live.

D. Plot and Character
? What does this incident tell you about the Robertson family? (They are resourceful people who will do whatever they have to do in order to survive.) Do you think you could have drunk the turtle's blood? Why or why not?

Responding to the Photograph

What overall impression does the photograph convey, and how does it make you feel? If you had to provide a title for the photograph, what would it be? Why?

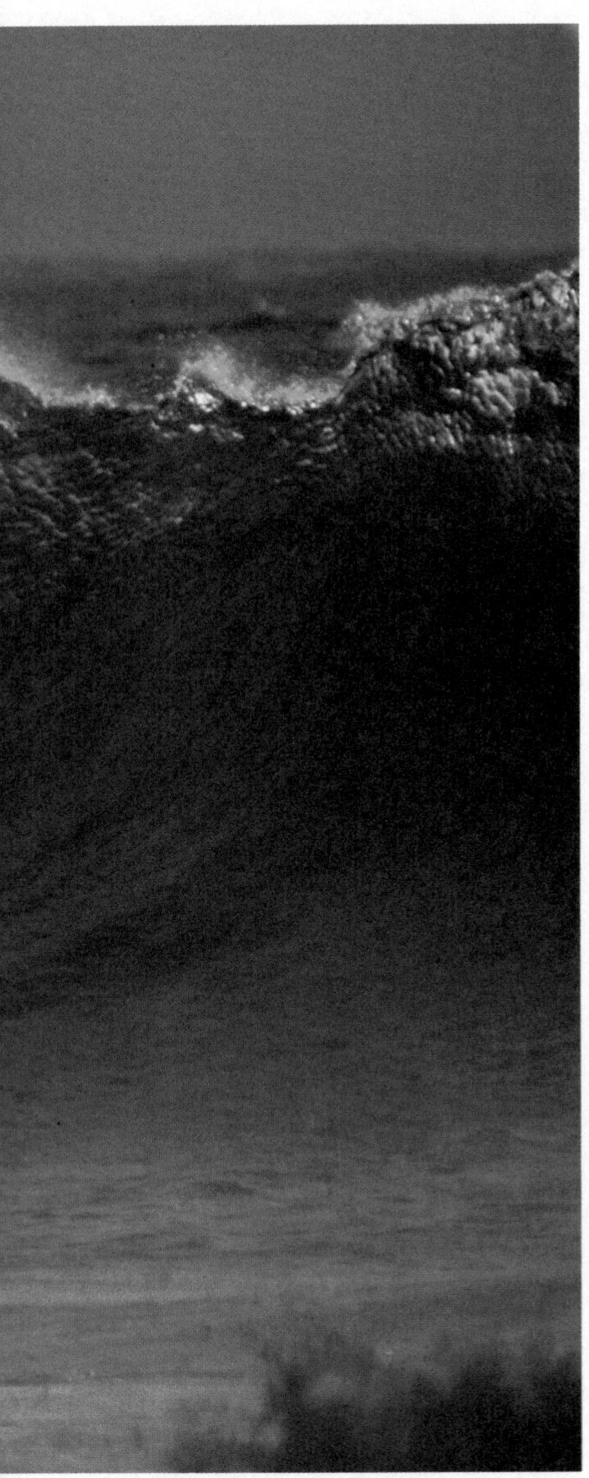

it was smaller, and being younger the shell was not so tough; the fact that I now knew my way around inside a turtle helped a lot too.

The sky was serenely blue that afternoon and with our position worked out at 5° 00′ north, 250 miles west of Espinosa, we had arrived at the official limits of the Doldrums.[6] Was this, then, Doldrums weather? Was "The Rime of the Ancient Mariner"[7] right with its "Nor any drop to drink?" We had four tins of water left, one of them half sea water, and if any of the other three contained short measure, well, there might come another turtle. I looked around the raft at the remains of Robin and the Robertson family, water-wrinkled skin covered with salt-water boils and raw red patches of rash, lying in the bottom of the raft unmoving except to bail occasionally, and then only halfheartedly, for the water was cooling in the heat of the day. Our bones showed clearly through our scanty flesh; we had become much thinner these last few days and our condition was deteriorating fast. The raft was killing us with its demands on our energy. Douglas looked across at me, "Do you think it'll rain tonight, Dad?" I looked at him and shrugged, looked at the sky, not a cloud. "I suppose it could do," I said. "Do you think it will?" he insisted. "For heaven's sake, Douglas, I'm not a prophet," I said testily. "We'll just have to wait it out." His eyes looked hopeless at the blue of the sea from the deep cavities under his brow; how could I comfort him when he knew as well as I that it might not rain for a week and that we'd be dead by then. I said, "Fresh turtle for tea, we can suck something out of that." We could live on turtles, maybe. A

We took no water that evening, only a little for the twins. We talked of the dishes we'd like to eat in the gathering twilight and I chose fresh fruit salad and ice cream; Lyn, a tin of apricots; Robin, strawberries and ice cream with milk; Douglas,

A. Responding

? With whom do you sympathize more in this exchange, Douglas or his father? Why?

---

6. **Doldrums** (däl′drəmz): ocean regions near the equator, noted for dead calms and light changing winds.

7. "**The Rime of the Ancient Mariner**": long poem by Samuel Taylor Coleridge. The poem is about a mariner, or sailor, punished by God for killing an albatross (a kind of bird). At one point the Mariner, stopped without wind in the middle of the ocean, laments, "Water, water everywhere,/Nor any drop to drink."

A. Character
What does Douglas's response to his father tell you about Douglas? (That he is sensitive to his father's feelings and that he does not want to add to the strain his father is under by pressuring him for reassurance)

B. Suspense
How does the narrator create suspense in this passage? (Though we know he survives—or he couldn't have written the book—we worry about what might happen next. The mention of sharks and of his belly crawling increases our tension.)

C. Interpretation
What is the significance of this remark? (If they hadn't been full of food, the sharks would have attacked him.)

the same as me; Neil, chocolate chip ice cream; Sandy, fresh fruit, ice cream, and milk—gallons of ice-cool milk. Later that night as I took the watch over from Douglas, he described in detail the dish he had dreamed up during his watch. "You take a honeydew melon," he said. "Cut the top off and take out the seeds; that's the dish. Chill it and drop a knob of ice cream in, then pile in strawberries, raspberries, pieces of apple, pear, orange, peach, and grapefruit, the sweet sort, then cherries and grapes until the melon is full; pour a lemon syrup over it and decorate it with chips of chocolate and nuts. Then," he said with a dreamy expression on his face, "you eat it!" "I'll have one too," I said, taking the bailer from his boil-covered hand. I looked at the sky; to the northeast a faint film of cirrostratus cloud dimmed the stars; "You know, I think it might rain by morning." I could feel him relax in the darkness; his voice
A came slowly, "I'll be all right if it doesn't, Dad." he said.

I started to bail mechanically. We would have to abandon the raft, soon, I thought, and that meant ditching all the unnecessary stuff overboard; in the dinghy there was only room for food, water, flares, and us. We'd start to sort things out in the morning.

Fifteenth Day

I watched the cloud develop slowly and drift across the night sky, blotting out the stars one by one. Was it another occluded front?[8] I watched the fish surge out from under the raft, touched one as I tried to grab it; then, the memory of the shark strong in my mind, drew back. I bailed and blew until Lyn took over; I pointed to the thickening cloud: "Maybe we'll get something to drink out of that."

It rained at dawn, beautiful, gorgeous rain. We saved three and a half gallons and drank our fill besides; the wind, from the south, freshened a little and as the weather cleared we lay back and enjoyed the sensation of being without thirst, bailing and blowing unheeded for the moment. We talked of the ship that didn't see us, for that had happened after the last rain, and argued whether it would have seen us better if it had been night time. The twins were talking when Douglas, on watch, his voice desperate with dismay, called, "Dad, the dinghy's gone!" I was across the raft in an instant. I looked at the broken end of wire trailing in the water, the broken line beside it. The dinghy was sixty yards away, sailing still and our lives were sailing away with it. I was the fastest swimmer, no time for goodbyes, to the devil with sharks; the thoughts ran through my head as I was diving through the door, my arms flailing into a racing crawl even as I hit the water. I heard Lyn cry out but there was no time for talk. Could I swim faster than the dinghy could sail, that was the point. I glanced at it as I lifted my head to breathe, the sail had collapsed as the dinghy B yawed, I moved my arms faster, kicked harder, would the sharks let me, that was another point. My belly crawled as I thought of the sharks, my arms moved faster still; I glanced again, only thirty yards to go but she was sailing again, I felt no fatigue, no cramped muscles, my body felt like a machine as I thrashed my way through the sea only one thought now in mind, the dinghy or us. Then I was there; with a quick heave I flipped over the stern of the dinghy to safety, reached up and tore down the sail before my knees buckled and I lay across the thwart trembling and gasping for breath, my heart pounding like a hammer. I lifted my arm and waved to the raft, now two hundred yards away, then slowly I untied the paddle from the sail and paddled back to the raft; it took nearly half an hour. The long shapes of two sharks circled curiously twenty feet down; they C must have had breakfast. . . .

Sixteenth Day

The rain continued all night long, and as we bailed the warm sea water out of the raft we were glad not to be spending this night in the dinghy at least. I went over to the dinghy twice in the night to bail out, for the rain was filling her quite quickly, and I shivered at the low temperature of the rain water.

8. **occluded** (ə·klo͞o′did) **front:** shift in air masses that can result in rain or snow.

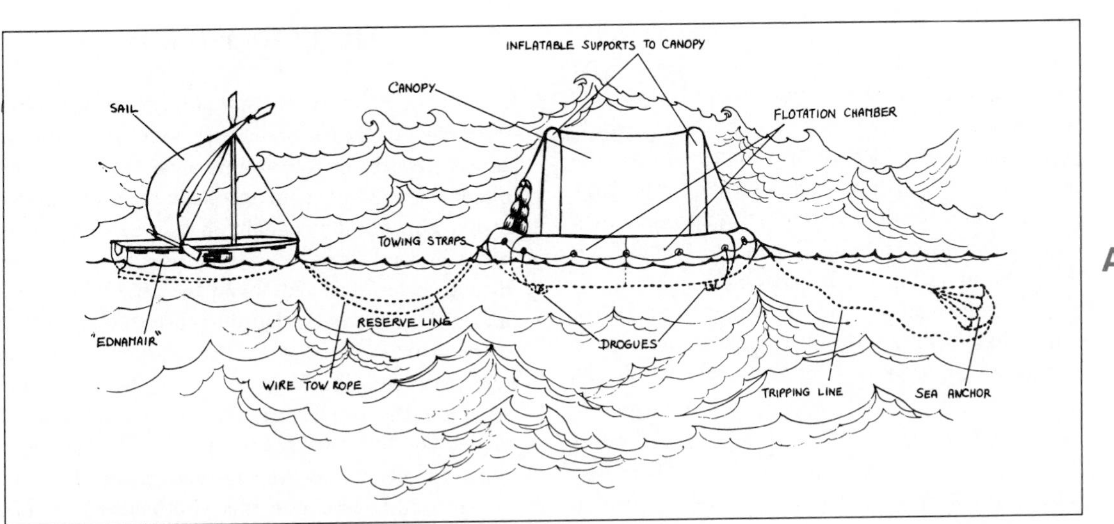

A drawing of the Robertson's raft and the *Ednamair.*

The raft canopy offered grateful warmth when I returned, and the puddles of salt water in the bottom of the raft seemed less hostile after the chill of the dinghy. We all huddled together on top of the flotation chambers, our legs and bottoms in the water, and although we did not sleep, we rested, for the work of blowing and bailing now went on around the clock, the bailer passing back and forth between the two compartments. Our sores stung as we knocked them against the raft and each other, our eyes were suppurating,[9] our limbs permanently wrinkled and lumpy with boils. My backside was badly blistered from sunburn acquired on my turtle-dressing expeditions, which made it necessary for me to lie on my stomach all the time, a painful piece of carelessness.

B

The rain continued to beat on the calm sea till midmorning, when after a few desultory bursts of sunshine, the weather closed in again and it drizzled for the rest of the day. I had decided to postpone the evacuation of the raft until the weather improved a little and I detected a feeling of relief among the others. (It wasn't until much later that I learned that my propaganda about trim had been so effective that they were frightened to go into the dinghy at all!) We had enough problems without adding cold to them so we ate our dried turtle and fish, drinking plenty of water with it and feeling much better for it.

C

We had made no progress in the windless weather so I entered our noon position the same as the day before and during the afternoon we talked at length about what we should have to do when the time came to get into the dinghy, which pieces of the raft we would cut out and which pieces of essential equipment we would take, and where they would be stowed. As evening closed in the drizzle eased a little and the air became much warmer. We bailed and blew in the darkness until Douglas suddenly said, "Quiet!" We listened, holding our breath. "Engines," he whispered. I could hear the faint beat of what might have been a propeller blade; it grew louder. I climbed into the dinghy with a torch[10] but could neither see nor hear anything from there. I flashed SOS around the horizon in all directions for a couple of minutes but there was no answering light, and after a further round of flashes returned to the raft. We speculated on the possibility of its being a submarine bound for the atomic testing grounds at Tahiti where a test was shortly to take place, and then took it a little further and wondered what spy submarine would pick up survivors and if it did, what then?

9. **suppurating** (sup′yoo·rā′ting): discharging pus.

10. **torch:** here, flashlight.

A

A. Responding to the Drawing
? Based on the drawing, can you see why the Robertsons stayed in the raft? (It's larger and the canopy can protect them from the sun.)

B. Vivid Description
? What effect does the vivid description of the family's physical condition have on you? (Probably horror and disgust. It also helps us share the family's sufferings because the details help us imagine precisely what their physical condition is, and how it feels. With this picture of suffering in our minds, we also see the family's real courage.)

C. Vocabulary
To *trim* a boat is to balance it by moving around cargo.

A. Responding
? Do you agree or disagree with the narrator's preference for moving into the dinghy as opposed to remaining in the raft? Give reasons to support your opinion.

B. Vocabulary
Thole pins are made of metal or wood and are set in the upper edge of a boat to support the oars.

C. Responding
? In what ways has the family's sense of values been altered? (They once, for example, took water for granted.) What other kinds of experiences might cause someone to alter his or her sense of values?

The twins talked quietly in a corner about the sort of cat they were going to have when we returned to England, where they could keep it and what they would feed it on, and how they would house train it. Neil loved furry animals and could talk for hours on the subject. Douglas was back on roast rabbit and Robin was in rhapsodies over oatmeal porridge and milk. Lyn and I thanked our destinies for water; it was so good!

That night will live in our memories as one of utter misery. Our mouths were raw with the rough surface of the bellows tube; our lungs and cheeks ached with the effort of keeping the raft inflated. Because of the sea water on the floor of the raft we tried to lie with our bodies on top of the flotation chambers, and because we lay on the flotation chambers we squeezed the air out of them more quickly. Lyn was terrified in case one of the twins should fall asleep face downward in the after compartment and drown, for we now bailed only in the forward section, and even then we could not bail quickly enough to keep it dry; the after section was flooded to a depth of three inches. I estimated that we could probably keep the raft afloat for a few days more, but the effort involved was depriving us of all bodily stamina; our limbs, almost hourly, suffered extensions of boil-infested areas, and we were pouring our lives away in this struggle to keep afloat. Our evacuation to the dinghy had to come, and soon. Death in the dinghy would come as a result of an error of judgment, a capsize perhaps, or through being swamped in heavy weather; either of these in my estimate was preferable to the deterioration of our physical and mental state, through sheer exhaustion, into submission and death. . . . A

The next day, the family is forced to move into the dinghy. They sing and tell stories to keep up their spirits. But even so, arguments and flare-ups of temper reveal the strain they are under. Once, they come close to death as they battle a fierce twelve-hour thunder and lightning storm. However, after surviving thirty-seven days at sea, they feel that they will be able to survive until they reach land—which the narrator estimates is fifteen days away.

Thirty-Eighth Day

Lyn bathed the twins that afternoon and after their daily exercises and a half-hour apiece on the center thwart to move around a bit, they retreated under the canopy again as a heavy shower threatened. The dorado, caught in the morning, now hung in wet strips from the forestay while the drying turtle meat festooned the stays and cross lines which had been rigged to carry the extra load of meat from two turtles. We worked a little on the thole pins, binding canvas on them to save B wear on the rope, then realizing that we were neglecting the most important job of making a flotation piece, took the unused piece of sleeve and started to bind one end with fishing line. The clouds grew thicker as the afternoon advanced; it was going to be a wet night again and perhaps we would be able to fill the water sleeve. Seven gallons of water seemed like wealth beyond measure C in our altered sense of values.

I chopped up some dried turtle meat for tea, and Lyn put it with a little wet fish to soak in meat juice. She spread the dry sheets for the twins under the canopy, then prepared their "little supper" as we started to talk of Dougal's Kitchen and if it should have a wine license. As we pondered the delights of Gaelic coffee, my eye, looking past the sail, caught sight of something that wasn't sea. I stopped talking and started; the others all looked at me. "A ship," I said. "There's a ship and it's coming toward us!" I could hardly believe it but it seemed solid enough. "Keep still now!" In the sudden surge of excitement, everyone wanted to see. "Trim her! We mustn't capsize now!" All sank back to their places.

I felt my voice tremble as I told them that I was going to stand on the thwart and hold a flare above the sail. They trimmed the dinghy as I stood on the thwart. "Right, hand me a flare, and remember what happened with the last ship we saw!" They suddenly fell silent in memory of that terrible despondency when our signals had been unnoticed. "O God!" prayed Lyn, "please let them see us." I could see the ship quite clearly now, a Japanese tuna fisher. Her gray and white paint stood out clearly against the dark cross swell. "Like a great

Critical Comment

In the foreword to the 1984 edition of *Kon-Tiki,* the famous Norwegian biologist and adventurer Thor Heyerdahl writes: "The *Kon-Tiki* expedition opened my eyes to what the ocean really is. It is a conveyor and not an isolator."

Would Dougal Robertson agree with Heyerdahl's assessment of the ocean?

Reading Check Test

1. In order to conserve water, the family drinks the blood of a turtle. (*True*)
2. The name of the Robertsons' ship is the *Robin.* (*False*)
3. When the dinghy breaks away from the raft, the narrator risks his life to retrieve it. (*True*)
4. The narrator uses a torch to send signals to the approaching ship. (*False*)
5. The Robertsons are rescued by a fishing boat. (*True*)

white bird,'' Lyn said to the twins, and she would pass within about a mile of us at her nearest approach. I relayed the information as they listened excitedly, the tension of not knowing, or imminent rescue, building like a tangible, touchable, unbearable unreality around me. My eye caught the outlines of two sharks, a hundred yards to starboard. ''Watch the trim,'' I warned. ''We have
A two man-eating sharks waiting if we capsize!''

Then, ''I'm going to light the flare now, have the torch ready in case it doesn't work.''

I ripped the caps off, pulled out the striker and struck the primer. The flare smoked then sparked into life, the red glare illuminating *Ednamair* and the sea around us in the twilight. I could feel my index finger roasting under the heat of the flare and waved it to and fro to escape the searing heat radiating outward in the calm air; then unable to

A. Suspense

? Why does this remark create suspense? (Even now, the sharks are waiting to see if the people will end up in the water, and they might get one of the family yet.)

Responding to the Photograph

? Can you identify the survivors in this photograph? If you were to show this photograph to the narrator now, what do you think his first reaction would be? What might the first reactions of the other survivors be?

The rescue, after thirty-eight days adrift.

CLOSURE

Working in pairs, students should define suspense and explain how it adds to the enjoyment of a story. Ask them to cite one other story they have read or seen on TV in which suspense was a key element.

Additional Writing Assignment

Have students imagine that they are copywriters in the advertising department of the publishing company that is releasing the paperback version of the book *Survive the Savage Sea.* As such, tell them to write a blurb of no more than twenty-five words that will get people to buy the book.

ANALYZING THE STORY

Identifying Facts

1. They salvage a survival kit (vitamin-fortified bread and glucose, some water, flares, bailer, fishing equipment, dull knife, signal mirror, torch [flashlight], first-aid box, two sea anchors, bellows, three paddles), a sewing kit, a canvas cloth, a plastic cup, and a few onions, biscuits, glucose sweets, oranges, and lemons.

bear the heat any longer, I dropped my arm, nearly scorching Lyn's face, and threw the flare high in the air. It curved in a brilliant arc and dropped into the sea. "Hand me another, I think she's altered course!" My voice was hoarse with pain and excitement and I felt sick with apprehension that it might only be the ship cork-screwing in the swell, for she had made no signal that she had seen us. The second flare didn't work. I cursed it in frustrated anguish as the priming substance chipped off instead of lighting. "The torch!" I shouted, but it wasn't needed, she had seen us, and was coming toward us.

I flopped down on the thwart. "Our ordeal is over," I said quietly. Lyn and the twins were crying with happiness; Douglas with tears of joy in his eyes, hugged his mother. Robin laughed and cried at the same time, slapped me on the back and shouted "Wonderful! We've done it. Oh! Wonderful!" I put my arms about Lyn feeling the tears stinging my own eyes: "We'll get these boys to land after all." As we shared our happiness and watched the fishing boat close with us, death could have taken me quite easily just then, for I knew that I would never experience another such pinnacle of contentment.

Responding to the Story

Analyzing the Story

Identifying Facts

1. When the Robertsons' ship sinks, they are left with a limited supply of food and other bare necessities for survival. List the items they are able to salvage from their sinking boat.
2. What does the family eat and drink to stay alive for thirty-eight days?
3. The inflatable raft is leaking, yet the family is reluctant to abandon it until the last possible moment. Why don't they want to transfer to the dinghy?
4. One way the family members keep up their spirits is by thinking and talking about some of the pleasures they will enjoy when they are back on land. What are some of these pleasures?
5. Describe how, on the thirty-eighth day of their ordeal, the family is rescued.

Interpreting Meanings

6. The main **conflict,** or struggle, in this story is the most basic conflict of all—between people and nature. Explain what animals and natural forces present dangers. Describe the physical needs and discomforts that also threaten the Robertsons.
7. Even though the odds are against them, the family wins its struggle at sea. Their survival is partly due to Mr. Robertson's exceptional personal qualities. For example, his comments to his son and his wife just after the shipwreck show cheerfulness in the face of disaster. Describe some other personal qualities Mr. Robertson displays during the struggle.
8. This story and "Three Skeleton Key" (page 7) involve struggles between people and nature. Did you enjoy one more than the other, or did you enjoy them equally? Did you perhaps not enjoy either one? Give several reasons for your opinion.

Applying Meanings

9. What other true stories do you know of, in which people struggle against nature to survive? What do you think helps some people to survive such ordeals, while others perish?

Writing About the Story

A Creative Response

SRW p. 69

Writing from Another Point of View. The Robertsons' story is told by Mr. Robertson. Therefore, you don't learn much about the other characters' thoughts. Write a paragraph in which you tell what one of the other characters in the raft is thinking during the first hours after the boat was wrecked. Use the first-person pronoun *I*.

See Teacher's Manual page 6.

2. They live on rainwater, which they collect in improvised containers, and on fish and turtle (including turtle blood). They either dry the meat, or eat it with congealed blood and other body juices.
3. The raft has a canopy under which the family is protected from the sun; it is also roomier and more stable than the dinghy, which is vulnerable to wind and wave.
4. Primarily, their dreams involve food, with ice cream and fruit high on the list. They also talk of a restaurant they could open called Dougal's Kitchen. The twins dream about the cat they will have.
5. When Dougal spots a ship, a Japanese tuna fisher, he stands on the thwart and waves, and then throws into the air a lighted flare. A second flare doesn't work, but the ship sees the first one.

Interpreting Meanings

6. The killer whales that wrecked the *Lucette* and the sharks that swim near the raft threaten the family. Other natural forces that threaten them are the searing sun, waves that could swamp them, and winds that could overturn them. They also face extreme discomfort: lack of fresh water, sunburn, saltwater boils, skin rashes, suppurating eyes, and constantly wet skin.
7. Mr. Robertson has courage, as shown when he retrieves the dinghy. He also shows courage in drinking turtle blood, something he never imagined himself doing. He has great self-control, and can comfort his family when he must. He is committed to survival, keeping the family in the safer raft longer.
8. Encourage students to be specific in their responses—not "It was gross, and I like gross stories," but, "The vivid description of their skin problems let me really see the family's suffering."

Applying Meanings

9. Responses will probably be tied to where students live—being lost in the desert, trapped in a blizzard, caught in a flood, etc. This assignment, along with question 7, can lead to a discussion of the personal qualities that help a person survive no matter what the conflict.

Analyzing Language and Vocabulary

Jargon

SRW p. 59

The narrator of the story used **jargon,** or specialized vocabulary, of sailing and the sea. Careful reading can give you an idea what many of these technical terms mean, even though they are probably new to you. From your reading of the story, match each specialized word below with the appropriate definition.

1. yaw
2. thwart
3. trim
4. forestay
5. swamp
6. swell

a. rower's seat placed across a boat
b. boat's balanced position in the water
c. strong rope supporting a boat's foremast
d. to swerve from its course, as when struck by a wave
e. large wave
f. to sink by filling with water

Check a dictionary to make sure you correctly matched the words and definitions. Then use each word in a sentence of your own.

For answers, see Teacher's Manual page 27.

Reading About the Writer

Dougal Robertson (1924-　　) was born in Edinburgh, Scotland. After attending Leith Nautical College, Robertson joined the British Merchant Navy. He then took a leave from maritime life to raise a family and to become a dairy farmer. In 1970 Robertson bought the *Lucette* to take his wife and children on an educational tour of the world. Since 1973, Robertson has primarily worked as a writer. Besides *Survive the Savage Sea*, he has also written *Sea Survival: A Manual*. Robertson's other interests are rugby, music, and French.

Focusing on Background

What Happened Next?

After they are rescued, the Robertsons spend four days aboard the Japanese ship before they reach land. The following is taken from the book's last chapter, called "Safety."

"I staggered back to the foredeck where the family and Robin were seated with their backs against the hatch coaming,[1] in their hands tins of cool orange juice, and a look of blissful content on their faces. I picked up the tin that was left for me, smiled my thanks to the Japanese who grinned broadly back at me, then lifting my arm said 'Cheers.' I shall remember the taste of that beautiful liquid to the end of my days. . . . The Japanese crew carried the twins to the large four-foot deep, hot seawater bath, Robin and Douglas tottering along behind on uncertain legs. There was also a fresh water shower (we had to readjust our ideas to the notion that fresh water could be used for other things besides drinking!) where they soaped and lathered and wallowed in luxury, scrubbing at the brown scurf which our skins had developed (but which took days to disappear). . . . On our return to the foredeck, there on the hatch stood a huge tray of bread and butter and a strange brown sweet liquid called coffee. Our eyes gleamed as our teeth bit into these strange luxuries and in a very short space of time the tray was empty, the coffee pot was empty, and our stomachs were so full that we couldn't squeeze in another drop. It felt rather like having swallowed a football. . . . In the days that followed we indulged in the luxury of eating and drinking wonderful food, the meals growing in quantity and sophistication. The familiar figure of the cook, Sakae Sasaki, became the symbol round which our whole existence revolved as he bore tray after tray up the foredeck to us. . . .

"It took four days for *Toka Maru II* to reach Balboa [seaport in Panama], by which time we had to some extent learned to use our legs again; in four days Captain Kiyato Suzuki and his wonderful crew brought the milk of human kindness to our tortured spirits and peace to our savage minds."

—Dougal Robertson

1. **coaming:** raised border around the opening of the hatch, which keeps out water.

PREREADING

1. **BUILDING ON PRIOR KNOWLEDGE.** Before they read, have students discuss the role pets play in people's lives. Recently scientists have found that, in addition to being just pets, animals actually contribute to people's well-being. Researchers have discovered that people are more relaxed with pets, with the result that stress is reduced and blood pressure is lowered. In addition, interaction with pets helps people get involved with things other than themselves. Pets give them the opportunity to form relationships, to alleviate loneliness, and to learn responsibility.

2. **ESTABLISHING A PURPOSE.** Before students begin reading, you might have them read question 7 on page 37.

3. **PREREADING JOURNAL.** Before they read, have students write a brief paragraph in which they try to persuade a person who does not have a pet to get one.

A. Humanities Connection: Discussing the Fine Art

Twentieth-century Dutch painter Kees van Dongen (1877–1968) was a member of the Fauve movement, which was known primarily for its spontaneity in texture, pattern, and color.

? Imagine that you must describe the painting to someone who had never seen it. What would you say? Include details about the painting's color, objects, and emotional effect. Be sure to explain that patch of red on the dog's coat.

★ **Texas Essential Elements/(a) English Language Arts: 1B** Purpose and audience; **3A** Plot/character; **3C** Literary traditions; **4F** Generalizations

PRINCESS

For a detailed lesson plan on this story, see Teacher's Manual pages 6–9. A biography of Nicholasa Mohr appears on text page 38.

Nicholasa Mohr

Judy can't have a pet of her own. But she becomes attached to a dog named Princess, who belongs to the owners of a neighborhood store. This leads to complications—and to a conflict involving life and death. Before you read the story, think of why pets are important to people. Then, as you read, notice how Princess affects the lives of the people who love her.

A

Fancy Dog by Kees Van Dongen (1920). Oil.

Virginia Museum of Fine Arts, Richmond. Collection of Mr. and Mrs. Paul Mellon.

Post-it™ routing request pad 7664
ROUTING - REQUEST
Please
READ
HANDLE
APPROVE
and
FORWARD
RETURN
KEEP OR DISCARD
REVIEW WITH ME
To
From
Date

DEVELOPING VOCABULARY
The following words appear on a test in the Test Book, page 8. (See also the Vocabulary Activity Sheet.)

dote	persist
allergy	convulsion
retrieve	trepidation
inferior	adjoining
exasperation	unkempt

meaning; **3D** Generalizations; **3G** Compare/contrast

Judy … valdo … '' He … gainst … uarter … f fat- … r him to pack the groceries. "Sit . . . sit up, Princess. That's a good girl. Nice. Now shake hands. Give me your paw. Right paw! Left paw! Good. Good." The little dog wagged her tail and licked Judy's hand.

"O.K., Judy, I got everything your Mama ordered here in the bag."

"Thank you, Don Osvaldo; put it on our bill."

"I already did," he said, closing a large thick ledger. The gray binding on the ledger was worn, frayed, and filthy with grease spots from constant use. Don Osvaldo would jot down whatever his
A credit customers bought, including how much it cost. Every name was there in the book, in alphabetical order; a clear record for all to see. At the end of each month, before any more credit was extended, customers were obliged to settle accounts according to the ledger.

"Can I come back and take Princess for a walk?" Judy asked again.

"All right," he said.

"I'm coming back to take you for a walk later," she said to the little dog, and patted her on the head.

Princess began to whine and bark after Judy. Don Osvaldo looked at the dog and smiled. "Nereida, Nereida," he called into the back of the store.

Spanish Words. The characters in this story live in the Bronx, a section of New York City. They are of Hispanic background. You'll notice the use of some Spanish words. For example, the Spanish words *Don* and *Doña* (dôn′yə) are spoken before a person's first name to show respect. *Don* means "sir" and *Doña,* "madam."

"What is it?" his wife asked.

"Princess is crying—she wants to go with Judy for a walk."

"She's too smart for her own good," his wife said, coming into the store. "Give her something to make her feel better. . . . Go on."

Don Osvaldo went over to the meat counter and removed a hunk of boiled ham. Taking a sharp knife, he cut off a small piece and fed it to the dog. Amused, they watched Princess as she chewed the piece of ham, then sat up begging for more.

"She's so clever," said Doña Nereida, and patted the dog affectionately.

Five years ago a customer had given them the white fluffy-haired puppy, which Doña Nereida had decided to call Princess. Princess was loving and friendly, and showed her gratitude by being obedient. Osvaldo and Nereida Negrón lavished all their affection on the little dog and doted on her. They had no children, hobbies, or interests other than their store, Bodega[2] Borinquén, a grocery specializing in tropical foods, which they kept open seven days a week; and Princess. The dog shared the small, sparsely furnished living quarters in the back of the store with her owners. There, she had her own bed and some toys to play with. Doña Nereida knitted sweaters for Princess and shopped for the fanciest collars and leashes she could find. A child's wardrobe unit had been B
purchased especially for her.

Customers would comment among themselves:

"That dog eats steak and they only eat tuna fish."

"Princess has better furniture than they have."

"I wish my kids ate as well as that mutt. It's not right, you know. God cannot justify this." And C
so on.

Despite all the gossip and complaints about the dog, no one dared say anything openly to Don Osvaldo or Doña Nereida.

Customers had to agree that Princess herself was a friendly little animal, and pleasant to look at. When children came into the store to shop they would pet her, and she was gentle with them, accepting their attention joyfully.

1. **fatback:** salted fat from the back of a hog.

2. **Bodega** (bō·dä′gə): Spanish word for a small grocery store.

A. Character
? Based on this paragraph, how would you characterize Don Osvaldo? (Don Osvaldo is a good but tough businessman. He sees to it that his credit customers pay up before he extends further credit. Note that the words "filthy with grease spots" put Don Osvaldo in an unsavory light.)

B. Interpretation
? What details in this paragraph suggest that Princess is treated like the child the Negróns never had? (The dog shares their living quarters, has her own bed and toys, wears sweaters knit by Dõna Nereida, and has a "child's wardrobe unit"—a kind of closet.)

C. Character
? How would you characterize the customers? (Jealous, resentful, fearful of the shopkeepers)

A. Characters' Actions

? Why do you suppose the Negróns do not like to leave the store? (Perhaps they are interested only in business—in making money.)

B. Making an Inference

? How old is Judy now? (Eleven)

C. Plot

? What do you learn about Judy and Princess from this paragraph? (Judy and Princess are very close. Princess trusts Judy and follows her commands, behaving as though she were Judy's dog.)

Princess was especially fond of Judy, who frequently took her out and taught her tricks. At first, Don Osvaldo and Doña Nereida were worried about letting Judy take Princess for walks. "Hold on to that leash. You mustn't let her get near other dogs; especially those male dogs," they warned. But several months had gone by and Judy and the dog always returned safe and sound. Actually, neither owner liked to leave the store, and they were silently grateful that Judy could take Princess out for some air. A

"Mami, can I go back downstairs and take Princess for a walk?" Judy asked her mother.

Her mother had emptied the brown grocery bag and was checking the items.

"Look at that! Fifteen cents' worth of fatback and look at the tiny piece he sends. Bendito!"[3] She shook her head. "I have to watch that man, and she's no better. Didn't I tell you to check anything that he has to weigh?" Judy looked at her mother, expecting her to complain as always about Don Osvaldo and Doña Nereida. "Because we have to buy on credit, they think they can cheat us. When I have cash I will not buy there. I cannot trust them. They charge much more than any other store, but they can get away with it because we buy on credit. I would like to see him charge a cash-paying customer what he does me!"

"Mami, can I go to walk Princess now?" Judy asked again.

"Why do you want to walk that dog? You are always walking that dog. What are you, their servant girl, to walk that stupid dog?"

"I'm the one who wants to walk her. . . . I love Princess. Please may I—"

"Go on!" her mother interrupted, waving her hands in a gesture of annoyance.

Before her mother could change her mind, Judy quickly left the apartment. Her little brother, Angel, had had another asthma attack today, and she knew her mother was in a lousy mood. After her father's death, Judy had moved into this neighborhood with her family: her mother, older sister Blanca, older brother William, and little brother Angel. That was three years ago, when she was just eight. B The family had been on public assistance since almost immediately after her father had died. Her mother was always worried about making ends meet, but she was especially hard to live with whenever Angel got sick.

She ran toward the grocery store, anxious to take Princess for her walk. Judy had wanted to have a pet ever since she could remember. It was the one thing that she had always prayed for at Christmas and on her birthday, but her mother absolutely refused. Once she had brought home a stray cat and her little brother Angel had had a severe asthma attack. After that, she was positive that she could never ever have a pet. No matter how she had reasoned, her mother could not be persuaded to change her mind.

"I could give the cat my food, Mami. You don't have to spend no money. And during the day I could find a place to keep it until I got home from school."

"No. We cannot make ends meet to feed human beings, and I am not going to worry about animals. Besides, there's Angel and his allergies." Her mother always won out.

If Papi had lived, maybe things would be different, Judy often thought. But since she could play with Princess and take her out, that was almost like having her own dog, and she had learned to be content with that much.

When Judy arrived at the store, Doña Nereida had Princess all ready.

"See, Judy," Doña Nereida said, "she's got a new leash—pale-blue with tiny silver studs. She looks good in blue, don't you think so?" she asked. "It goes with her coloring. Her fur is so nice and white."

The little dog ran, tugging at the leash, and Judy followed, laughing.

Outside in the street, Judy shouted, "Ready, get set . . . go!" Quickly, Judy and Princess began to run, as usual, in the direction of the schoolyard. Once they got there, Judy unleashed Princess and she ran freely, chasing her and some of the other children.

They were all used to Princess, and would pet her, run with her, and sometimes even play a game of ball with the little dog. They watched as Princess followed Judy's commands: She could sit up, C

3. **Bendito** (ben·dē'tō): exclamation meaning "blessed."

roll over, play dead, retrieve, and shake hands. Everyone at the schoolyard treated Princess as if she belonged to Judy and asked her permission first before they played or ran with the little dog. And Princess behaved as if she were Judy's dog. She listened and came obediently when Judy called her. After they had finished playing, Judy leashed Princess and they walked back to the store.

"Did you have a good time?" Doña Nereida asked when they returned. "Come inside with Mama. . . . She has a little something for you," she said to Princess.

Judy handed the leash to Doña Nereida. She had never been invited inside where Princess lived. Whenever she came back from her walks she waited around, hoping they would ask her in as well, but they never did. No one was invited into the back rooms where Don Osvaldo, Doña Nereida, and Princess lived.

"Before you leave—Judy, here, have a piece of candy." Doña Nereida opened the cover of a glass display case and removed a small piece of coconut candy that sold for two cents apiece or three for a nickel. She handed it to Judy.

"Thank you," Judy said, taking the candy. She didn't much like it, but she ate it anyway.

"Osvaldo . . . Osvaldo," Doña Nereida called, "come out here; I have to take Princess inside." Turning to Judy, she said, "Goodbye, Judy, see you later."

Judy smiled and left the store. She wished she could see where Princess lived. Shrugging her shoulders, she said to herself, "Maybe tomorrow they'll ask me in."

A "There's something wrong with these beans. Smell!" her mother said, handing the can of pork and beans to her children.

"Whew, yeah!" said Blanca. "They smell funny." She handed the can to William, who agreed, and then to Judy.

"They smell funny." Judy nodded.

"Can I smell too?" asked Angel. Judy handed him the can.

"Peeoowee . . . ," he said, making a face. They all laughed.

"It's not funny," her mother said. "If these beans are rotten we could die." She held up the can. "Look—see that? The can is dented and swollen. Sure, he always gives us inferior merchandise. That no-good louse!" She shook her head. "We have to return them, that's all. You go, Judy, bring them back and tell him we want another can that's not spoiled." B

"I have to walk Princess, Mami; send somebody else."

"You have to walk to the store and back here. Never mind Princess. Go on!"

"But I'll be too late then," Judy protested, thinking about her friends in the schoolyard.

"How would you like not to walk that mutt at all? What if I say that you cannot walk her anymore?" her mother said, looking severely at Judy.

Quietly, Judy got up and took the can of beans. "Mami, they are already opened."

"Of course. How would I know otherwise if they are rotten? Here is the cover—just place it on top." She put the tin lid back on the opened can. "There . . . don't spill them and come right back here. I have to start supper."

"Can I walk Princess after I come back?"

"Yes," her mother said with exasperation. "Just come back with another can of beans!"

Judy rushed as quickly as she could, at the same time making sure that she did not spill the contents of the can.

"Here she is," said Doña Nereida when she saw Judy, "ready to take you out, Princess." As she fastened the leash, the dog barked and jumped, anxious to go out.

"Doña Nereida, I have to give you something first," Judy said.

"What?"

"Here is a can of beans that my brother William brought home before, and they are rotten." She put the can on the counter. "So my mother says could you please give us another can that is not spoiled."

Doña Nereida picked up the can and lifted the lid, sniffing the contents. "What's wrong with them?" she asked.

"They are rotten."

"Who says? They smell just fine to me. Wait a minute. Osvaldo! Osvaldo, come out here please!" Doña Nereida called loudly.

A. Reading Aloud
You may wish to call on volunteers to read aloud the various characters' parts, starting with the line "There's something wrong with these beans" and ending with the line ". . . back in a little while" in the left-hand column on page 32. Remind students to read the dialogue in a lively manner, clearly, and with expression.

B. Expansion
The food could be contaminated with harmful bacteria that causes botulism—a deadly form of food poisoning. This bacteria can cause the can or container to swell because of gas production. Even when they are treated, people and animals who get botulism usually die.

A. Responding

? Do you think the Negróns are treating Mrs. Morales fairly? Why or why not? How would you have handled the situation?

"What do you want? I'm busy." Don Osvaldo came out.

"Smell these beans. Go on." She handed her husband the opened can.

Don Osvaldo sniffed the contents and said, "They are fine. What's wrong?"

"Judy brought them—her mother wants another can. She says they are spoiled, that they are rotten."

"Tsk . . . ," Don Osvaldo sighed and shook his head. "They are fine. They don't smell spoiled to me, or rotten. Besides, the can is opened. I can't exchange them if she opened the can already." He put the can back on the counter and covered it with the lid. "Here, take it back to your mother and tell her that there is nothing wrong with those beans. I can't change them."

Judy stood there and looked at the couple. She wanted to say that they smelled bad to her, too, but instead she said, "OK, I'll tell her." She picked up the can of beans and returned home.

"What? Do you mean to tell me that he told you that there is nothing wrong with this can of beans?" Her mother's voice was loud and angry. "I don't believe it! Did he smell them?" she asked Judy.

"Yes," Judy said. "They both did."

Her mother shook her head. "I'm not putting up with this anymore. This is the last time that thieving couple do this to me. Come on, Judy. You come with me. I'm taking back the beans myself. Let's see what he will tell me. You too, William; you come with us, since you were the one that bought the beans."

"Can I come too?" asked Angel.

"No," his mother answered, "stay with Blanca till I get back. I don't want you going up and down the stairs. And you, Blanca, start the rice. I'll be back in a little while."

Her mother walked in first, holding the can of beans. Judy and William followed.

"Don Osvaldo, I would like to return this can of beans," her mother said. Don Osvaldo was seated behind the counter, looking through his ledger. He put the book down.

"Mrs. Morales, there is nothing wrong with them beans," he said.

"Did you take a good smell? I sent Judy down before; and I cannot believe that after smelling them, you could refuse to exchange them for another can that is not spoiled!" She put the can on the counter.

Doña Nereida walked in, followed by Princess. When the dog saw Judy, she began to bark and jump up. "Shh . . . ," said Doña Nereida. "Down! Get down, Princess, you are not going out right now. Maybe later. Down!" Princess sat down obediently, wagging her tail and looking at Judy. "What's happening here, Mrs. Morales?" she asked.

"It's about these beans. I refuse to accept them. That can is dented and swollen, that's how it got spoiled. Surely you don't expect me to feed this to my children."

"Why not?" said Doña Nereida. "They smell and look perfectly fine to me."

"Look, Mrs. Morales," said Don Osvaldo, "you probably opened the can and left it open a long time, and that's why they smell funny to you. But they are not spoiled, and I cannot give you another one or any credit for this."

"How could I know they are rotten unless I open up the can? Besides, I did not leave them open a long time. William just bought it here this afternoon," Mrs. Morales said and turned to her son. "Isn't that so, William?"

"Yes. I got them here and the can was already dented," said William.

"That doesn't mean anything," said Don Osvaldo. "You people opened them. There's nothing we can do."

Mrs. Morales looked at Don Osvaldo and Doña Nereida and smiled, remaining silent. After a moment, she asked, "You expect me to eat this and to feed this to my children?"

"You can do what you want with those beans," said Don Osvaldo. "It's not my affair."

"Will you at least give us some credit?" asked Mrs. Morales. A

"We already told you, no!" said Doña Nereida. "Listen, you are making a big thing over a can of beans when there is nothing wrong with them."

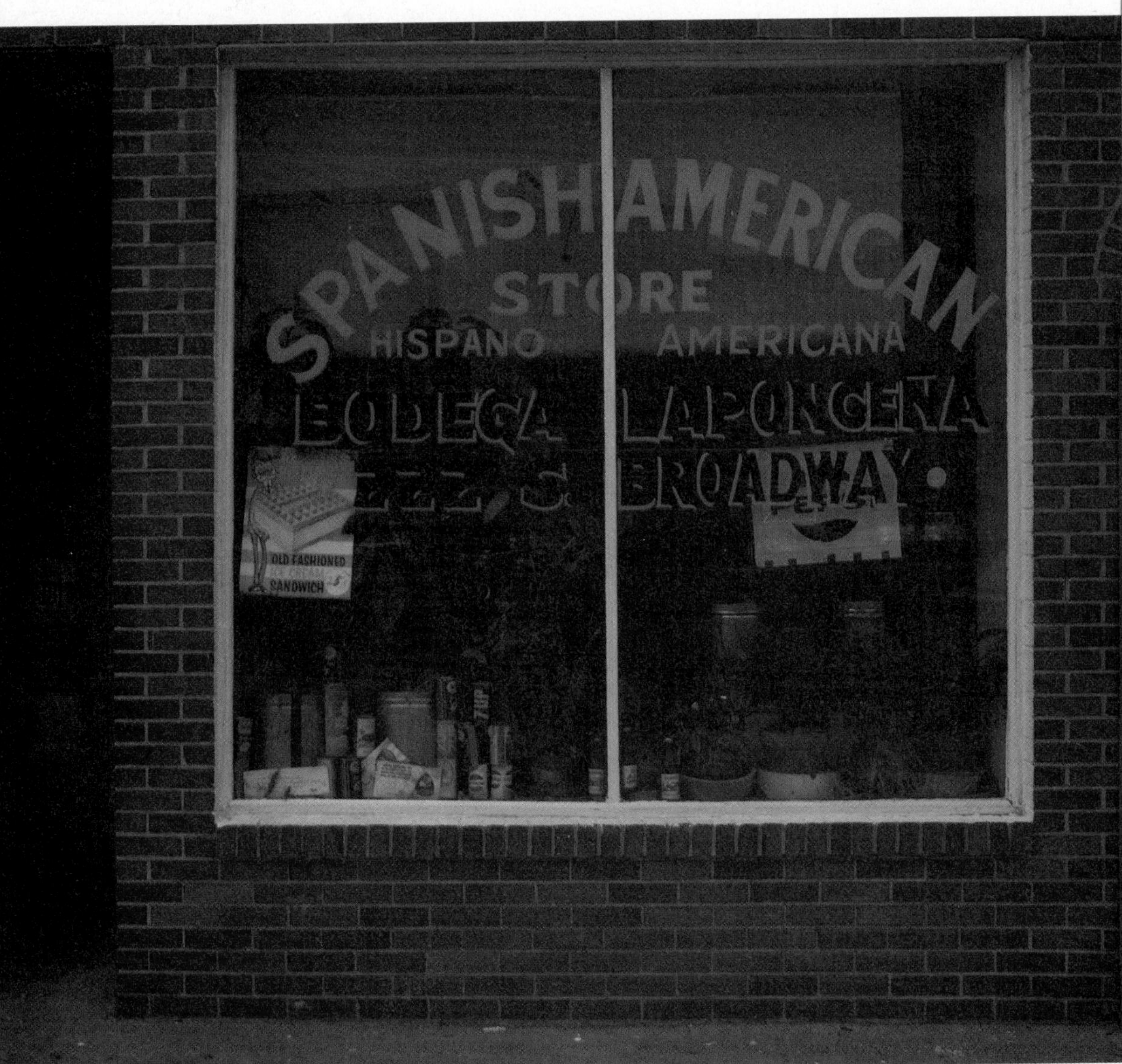

"Would you eat this, then?" asked Mrs. Morales.

"Of course," said Don Osvaldo.

"Certainly!" Doña Nereida nodded in agreement.

"O.K.," said Mrs. Morales, smiling, "I'll tell you what: You take them. A present from me to you. Eat them and enjoy them."

"All right." Don Osvaldo shrugged his shoulders. "If that's how you feel. It will be your loss. This can is not spoiled."

"Well then, I'll tell you what," said Mrs. Morales. "Why don't you feed it to Princess? Let Judy give it to her—a little present from us."

Don Osvaldo looked at his wife and she returned his glance, shrugging her shoulders. A

"We are not going to eat them anyway, so why should they go to waste?" said Mrs. Morales. "Go

Responding to the Photograph

? What would you expect to see, hear, and smell if you were to enter this store? Does this store remind you of one in your neighborhood? If so, describe that store.

A. Characters' Actions and Thoughts

? What do the Negróns' actions, their glances at each other, and Doña Nereida's shrugging, reveal about their thoughts? (Their actions reveal that while they are unsure of Mrs. Morales's proposal, they feel that they have no choice but to go along with it. Unless they go back on their word that nothing is wrong with the beans, they have to test them on Princess.)

A. Irony
There are several examples of irony here—the difference between what one expects to be true and what is actually true. Doña Nereida's statement "There! Nothing was wrong with them" is ironic because the beans are, in fact, spoiled. The fact that Judy is the person who gives Princess the food that will kill her is ironic because she loves Princess very much and would never knowingly do anything to harm her. The picture of the happy white poodle on Princess's bowl and the Negróns' laughter make us feel irony later, because actually sadness and tears are about to follow.)

B. Foreshadowing
Judy's mother's refusal to let Judy walk Princess "now or later" foreshadows Princess's death. Neither Judy nor anyone else will ever walk Princess again.

C. Character's Actions
? Are you surprised at Doña Nereida's behavior?

on, Judy, take the beans and feed them to Princess." Turning toward Doña Nereida, she asked, "Perhaps you could give Judy a little dish?" Doña Nereida did not answer, and looked with uncertainty at her husband. Mrs. Morales continued; this time she spoke to Don Osvaldo. "Why not? Don Osvaldo, if there is nothing wrong with the beans, then let's give them to Princess. She would probably enjoy them. It would be a treat."

"OK," he nodded, "sure. Nereida, get her blue dish from inside. If there is something wrong with the beans, Princess will not eat them."

His wife went into the back and returned, holding a bright-blue bowl with a happy white poodle on it.

"Here, Judy, you do it," said Mrs. Morales, looking at her daughter. "You give it to the dog. She'll take it from you."

Doña Nereida emptied the contents of the can into the bowl and gave it to Judy. Judy set it down on the floor near Princess.

"Here, girl, here's some beans for you," she said. Quickly, the little dog went over to the bowl
A and began to eat the beans, wagging her tail.

"See? Mrs. Morales, Princess is eating them beans. . . . There! Nothing was wrong with them. So you gave them away for nothing."

"That's all right, Don Osvaldo," Mrs. Morales responded. "It's not for nothing. Princess is enjoying the beans."

"Do you want another can of pork and beans?" asked Don Osvaldo, laughing. "I'm afraid I'll have to charge you, though!" His wife joined him in laughter as they both watched Princess finish the beans.

"No, thanks. I'll make do with what I have at home." Mrs. Morales turned to leave the store.

"Mami," said Judy, "can I walk Princess now?"

"No," her mother said, "you may not walk her
B now or later." As Judy followed her mother and brother out of the store, Don Osvaldo and Doña Nereida could still be heard laughing and commenting.

"How about tomorrow, Mami? Can I walk Princess tomorrow?" Judy persisted.

"We'll see . . . tomorrow," her mother answered.

At two the next morning, Osvaldo and Nereida Negrón were awakened by low whining sounds and grunts. When they got up to investigate, they found that Princess was having convulsions. Frightened, they tried to comfort the little dog by giving her water and then warm milk to drink. They even placed a hot-water bottle in her bed, but nothing seemed to help. The whining became softer and lower, until there was no sound at all. Princess lay in her small bed quietly, her eyes wide open, staring. The only visible sign of life was when her body jumped involuntarily, as if she had hiccups.

Don Osvaldo tried to calm his wife; she cried and wrung her hands, on the verge of hysteria. After a while, they decided the best thing to do was to take Princess to a veterinarian. Don Osvaldo found the names of several animal hospitals in the Yellow Pages, and after some telephone calls found one that would take Princess at this time of the morning. They wrapped the dog in a blanket and took a cab to the animal hospital. The doctor examined Princess and told them that her chances of surviving were slim. Whatever she had eaten was already digested and in her bloodstream. However, he promised to do his best and call them, no matter what happened.

The Negróns returned to their store at six A.M., and at six-thirty A.M. they received a phone call from the hospital informing them that Princess was dead. For a small fee they offered to dispose of the remains, and Don Osvaldo agreed.

Doña Nereida took to her bed, refusing to get up. Don Osvaldo opened his store a little late that day. Many of his credit customers had been patiently waiting outside; they had no place else to shop.

No one seemed to notice that Princess was not C
in the store. Don Osvaldo waited on his customers in silence, checking the back rooms every once in a while to see how his wife was. She remained in her bed, moaning softly and crying quietly.

As usual, that afternoon Judy went to the store to see Princess before going home. She entered and looked around for the little dog. Don Osvaldo was working behind the meat counter.

Comment from the Writer
Writing about her work, Nicholasa Mohr says, "My work as a writer is expressed through the creative medium of fiction with the intent of reaching all people. It incorporates a strong social statement; the plight and constant struggle of the Puerto Ricans on the mainland, to receive their basic human rights. Using art, the universal language of humanity, I bring forth the point of view of a subculture in America."

Ask students to discuss books, movies, or TV shows that depict people from different cultures who have come to the United States to live. Ask students what they like or dislike about these stories. What do the characters in these stories seem to have in common? What problems do they face?

"Hi, Don Osvaldo," she said. "Where's Princess?"

"She's not here."

"Is she inside with Doña Nereida?" Judy asked and waited for a response. Don Osvaldo continued his work behind the meat counter, not speaking. Judy felt awkward and stepped up a little closer to the counter so that she could see Don Osvaldo. He was carefully cutting small, neat slices from a large side of beef and stacking them evenly on the other side of the chopping block.

After a short while, she said, "I'll be back, then, to walk her later. Goodbye, see you later," and turned to leave.

A "Judy," Don Osvaldo said, "please tell your mother that when she sends for her groceries today, she should come herself." He paused. "Did you hear? Tell your mother to come for her groceries herself!"

"Yes," Judy replied, and went home.

Mrs. Morales entered Don Osvaldo's store accompanied by William and Judy.

"Be right with you, Mrs. Morales," Don Osvaldo said, and continued his work on the ledger.

The store was empty, and Judy looked around for Princess. In spite of her concern, she dared not ask Don Osvaldo about the little dog. Her mother's solemn attitude and Don Osvaldo's request this afternoon frightened her. For once, she wished her mother had not asked her to come along.

Don Osvaldo closed the ledger and looked at Mrs. Morales, staring at her without speaking. Finally, he asked, "Do you want anything? Can I get you something?"

"No, thank you," Mrs. Morales answered.

"Nothing?" he asked. "How about you, Judy? Do you want to take Princess for a walk?"

Judy looked at her mother, who reached out and pulled her daughter close to her.

"Do you want me to get her for you, Judy?" Don Osvaldo continued raising his voice loudly. "Do you want to take Princess for a little stroll? Well, answer! Answer!" he yelled.

Judy could feel her mother's body tensing up and trembling slightly.

"What do you want? You sent for me—what is it?" her mother asked.

"Do you know where she is? Where Princess is? She's dead. Dead. You killed her, that's what you did. You, too, Judy, both of you . . . all of you." Don Osvaldo's voice was angry. "She never did anything to you, to any of you. But you!" He pointed at Mrs. Morales. "You had to give that innocent animal, who never harmed you, something that would kill her, on spite! And you knew it—you knew it!"

"What do you want?" Mrs. Morales asked in a loud voice. "You have business with me? Tell me, or I'll leave!"

"Here . . . ," Don Osvaldo said and pushed a white sheet of paper across the counter. "I don't want to touch you. Here is your bill. Pay up by the end of the week, or I'll take you to court. You get no more credit here!"

Mrs. Morales picked up the bill and examined it carefully. "I see, Don Osvaldo, that you have charged me for the beans." Her voice was shaking and she paused, clearing her throat. "I'm glad, real glad you did. It's a small price to pay for the life of my children. As God will judge!" Mrs. Morales made the sign of the cross. "You will get your money, don't worry, Don Osvaldo. It will be my pleasure."

In a moment, Mrs. Morales and her two children left the store.

Judy cried that night and on many other nights whenever she remembered Princess. She wished she had never given the beans to Princess. She stopped going to the schoolyard; she didn't know what to tell the kids there. B

Her mother found a grocery store that sold to credit customers. It was farther away—an extra fifteen-minute walk. They had two cats that Judy enjoyed playing with, but it was not the same.

Very often, she would pass by Don Osvaldo's grocery and glance inside, wondering if it had all been a dream and Princess were really in there waiting for her to come and play. She had spoken to several of the kids that shopped there, and all of them told her that the little dog was definitely not in the store. Still, there were times she would walk by and imagine Princess barking and wagging her tail, asking to be taken out to the schoolyard.

A. Character's Motivation
? Why do you suppose Don Osvaldo insists on having Judy's mother come to the store herself? (He wants to blame her and make her feel guilty for Princess's death.)

B. Responding
? With which character do you sympathize the most: Don Osvaldo, Doña Nereida, Mrs. Morales, or Judy? The least? Why?

Reading Check Test

1. Princess is Judy's dog. *(False)*
2. Judy's mother likes the Negróns very much. *(False)*
3. Judy's mother believes the beans are spoiled. *(True)*
4. Doña Nereida feeds the beans to Princess. *(False)*
5. After the death of Princess, Judy becomes closer to the Negróns. *(False)*

Closure

Working with a partner, students should define external and internal conflict and explain how the former can lead to the latter.

Analyzing The Story

Identifying Facts

1. The story takes place in a Hispanic neighborhood in a city.

Answers will vary. Judy Morales is a young, friendly girl, whose major concern seems to be playing with Princess. Mrs. Morales is a stern mother who fights for every penny so her family will survive. Mr. Negrón is a hard businessman with a

A. Character's Motivation

Why does Don Osvaldo want his wife to give away Princess's things? (He probably feels that Doña Nereida will get over Princess's death if she is not constantly reminded of her. He might be selfish, believing that the sooner Doña Nereida recovers from the loss of Princess the sooner his life will get back to normal.)

B. Character

? Based on Judy and Doña Nereida's conversation and on the description of Princess's room, how would you describe the relationship between the woman and the little dog? (Doña Nereida and Princess had a mother-child relationship.)

C. Plot

? Why is the episode of Judy's visit with Doña Nereida an important part of the story? (It allows the reader to see the true relationship between Doña Nereida and Princess. It causes Judy to change as she recognizes the sadness of the Negróns' lives and the loneliness of Doña Nereida.)

Two months went by, and one day, as Judy walked by Don Osvaldo's store on the way home, she heard someone call her name.

"Judy . . . psst, Judy . . . come over here."

She saw Doña Nereida calling her. "Come over here, Judy. . . . I want to talk to you." Judy moved slowly, with some trepidation. "Come on," Doña Nereida insisted. "I just want to see you a minute."

She followed the woman into the store. It was the first time she had set foot inside since the day that Don Osvaldo had spoken to her mother. She could hear her heart pounding, and she wondered what they wanted.

Don Osvaldo was busy waiting on a customer, and did not look in her direction.

"Come on with me," Doña Nereida whispered. "Come on!" Judy followed as she led her behind the counter and over to the back of the store.

They entered a medium-sized room with an old gas stove, a sink, a small refrigerator, and several kitchen cabinets. The room was furnished with an old armchair in need of upholstering and a kitchen table with four chairs.

"Sit . . . sit down, Judy." They both sat down.

"I suppose you are wondering why I asked you in," she said. Judy nodded. "It's that . . . I just want to talk to you. About . . . Princess." Doña Nereida lowered her eyes and sighed. "You miss her too, I'll bet." Judy blushed. Being here with Doña Nereida embarrassed her. "Don't you?"

"Yes . . . ," Judy said.

"She was so good; such a fine little dog. Almost like a person. We had her for five years. She was so obedient." Doña Nereida paused and, choking back the tears, wiped her eyes. "It's not the same anymore, you know. And he . . ." She gestured into the store. "He doesn't understand and expects me to forget! I can't. You understand, don't you?"

Judy nodded.

A "See—I knew it. I told him. Judy—Judy knows. She loved Princess. She'll understand. I don't want another dog. You see, it wouldn't be fair to Princess. I have all her things, and he wants me to give them away!" She paused. "Would you like to see them? Would you?"

Judy shrugged her shoulders, feeling uncomfortable.

"Don't be shy. I know you want to see where Princess slept. Come on, now." Doña Nereida stood up and took Judy into a small adjoining room. It had a large double bed and a dresser. Over in a corner was a child's colorful yellow-and-blue wardrobe unit. Next to it, on the floor, was what appeared to Judy to be a flat kind of wicker basket with a pillow. Inside were a rubber ball, a teething ring, and a toy telephone. "That's her little bed. We bought it at the pet shop on Third Avenue." B

The room was stuffy and unkempt. Judy tried not to show her displeasure at the way the room smelled.

"Its been very hard on me." Judy wished that Doña Nereida would stop talking.

"Doña Nereida," Judy said, "I have to go home now. My mother is waiting."

"Of course. What will you think of me?" She led Judy back out through the front. Don Osvaldo was busy looking at his ledger. "Here, Judy. . . ." Doña Nereida reached into the glass display case and took a piece of white coconut candy. "Here."

"Thank you," said Judy.

"I know how you used to like this candy." She smiled.

"Goodbye," said Judy.

"Tomorrow. Come back tomorrow, Judy, and we'll talk some more!" She smiled.

"OK," Judy said, leaving the store. She put the candy in her mouth and decided that she definitely did not like it.

As she walked home, she felt strange about what had just happened. The back of the store didn't seem to have anything to do with the Princess she remembered—barking wildly, jumping, running, playing in the schoolyard, and chasing all the kids.

Judy made sure that on her way home from school, she did not pass by Don Osvaldo's store the next day, or any other day. C quick temper. Mrs. Negrón is emotional, and treats her dog as if she were a child. Princess is a pleasant dog who loves to play.

2. Judy can't have a pet because her family can't support a pet and her brother has asthma. She takes Princess for a walk because she loves her and her tricks, and likes the attention that Princess brings her at the schoolyard.

3. "That dog eats steak and they only eat tuna fish"; "Princess has better furniture than they have"; "I wish my kids ate as well as that mutt."

4. Mrs. Morales demands replacement or credit for the can of spoiled beans. The Negróns say it is not spoiled and refuse to take it back.

Mrs. Morales challenges the Negróns to give the beans to Princess to prove that they are good. The Negróns agree; but since the beans are bad, Princess dies.

5. Judy at first feels guilty about giving Princess the beans. She misses Princess and the attention of the other kids in the schoolyard. Later, when Mrs. Negrón shows Judy the back rooms of the store, Judy is uncomfortable with this memorializing of Princess.

Responding to the Story

Analyzing the Story

Identifying Facts

SRW p. 79

1. Describe the story's **setting**—where it takes place. Then list the main characters and describe each in a sentence or two.
2. Explain why Judy can't have a pet of her own. Why does she take the Negróns' dog, Princess, for a walk almost every day?
3. The people who shop at the grocery store are outraged at the way the Negróns treat Princess. List three remarks people make about how Princess is treated.
4. Judy's mother and the Negróns have an argument over a can of beans. Tell what they argue about. Then explain how the argument leads to the death of Princess.
5. List three ways Judy's life changes after the dog dies.

Interpreting Meanings

6. **Conflict** involves a struggle between opposing forces. A conflict is **external** when it takes place between a character and some outside force, another person or group of persons, or a force of nature, such as a mud slide or wolves. Stories usually contain more than one conflict. Identify what you consider the main external conflict in "Princess." Describe the opposing forces. Does one of the forces win out by the end of the story?
7. A conflict is **internal** when it exists in the mind or heart of a character. The character may be torn by the desire to do two conflicting things. Describe Doña Nereida's internal conflict when Mrs. Morales suggests that the beans be fed to Princess.
8. Mrs. Morales is very sure about the condition of the beans. Why, then, does she want to feed them to Princess? Why doesn't Judy object?
9. At the end of the story, Doña Nereida shows Judy the back of the store, where Princess once lived. "The back of the store didn't seem to have anything to do with the Princess she remembered—barking wildly, jumping, running, playing in the schoolyard, and chasing all the kids." Explain why Judy felt the living quarters didn't fit the personality of Princess.

Applying Meanings

10. How did you feel about Don Osvaldo and his wife, who lavished care on a pet when neighborhood children were going hungry?
11. What would you do if a store sold you an unsafe or spoiled product and refused to take it back? Discuss ways you have to obtain justice.

Writing About the Story

A Creative Response

1. **Writing a Diary Entry.** Imagine you are Judy, and that Judy keeps a diary. Write the entry for the day Judy decides never again to pass by the Negróns' store. Have Judy give specific reasons for her decision. She might also give her opinion of other characters in the story. Remember that a diary is usually written in the first person, using the pronoun *I*. Write one or two paragraphs.

A Critical Response

2. **Comparing and Contrasting Characters.** In a paragraph or two compare and contrast the personalities of Doña Nereida and Don Osvaldo. How are they similar? How are they different? Before you write, think about the following questions.

   a. How does each treat Princess?
   b. How does each treat Judy? Other customers?
   c. How does each react when Mrs. Morales suggests the beans be fed to Princess?
   d. How does each feel about the death of Princess?
   e. How do they treat each other?

   The first part of your composition should talk about the characters' similarities. The second part should discuss their differences.

See Teacher's Manual page 8.

Analyzing Language and Vocabulary

English Words with Spanish Origins

All languages borrow words from other languages. German contains words borrowed from French, Russian contains words borrowed from English, Chinese contains words borrowed from Japanese. When people speaking different languages come

Interpreting Meanings

6. The main external conflict is between the Negróns and Mrs. Morales—the Negróns are a powerful economic force, whereas Mrs. Morales is a powerful moral force. Some students may say that Mrs. Morales wins because the death of Princess shows that she is right, and the Negróns deserve what they get. Others will maintain that nobody wins; the Negróns lose Princess, and Mrs. Morales does not get credit for the beans and now has to shop in another store that is farther away.

7. Doña Nereida's conflict is between standing by her husband against Mrs. Morales and refusing to feed Princess food that is possibly spoiled.

8. Answers will vary. Mrs. Morales's first objective is to get credit for the beans. Suggesting that the beans be fed to Princess may just be a strategy to get the Negróns to take back the can. Mrs. Morales doesn't care about Princess the way Judy *(Answers continue on page 38.)*

(Answers begin on page 37.)
and Doña Nereida do. Judy doesn't object out of obedience to her mother.
9. Since Judy's memory of Princess is of a loving, happy, active dog, the stuffy, unkempt area behind the store does not seem to have any relation to Princess.
10. Answers will vary. Some students will say that it was all right to give Princess such care, since she was like the child the Negróns never had. Others will say that the Negróns could have been more responsive to their neighbors.
11. Ask students to tell about times they or their families faced this problem, and how they handled it. Some students may know about newspaper or radio consumer hotlines, the Better Business Bureau, and local or state consumer protection agencies. You could direct individuals or small groups to research these avenues and report about them to the class.

Additional Writing Assignment
Have students write the next episode in the story "Princess." To help students get started, offer the following suggestions as settings for what happens next: Judy's home, another store in which she meets Doña Nereida, in the schoolyard.

A. Writing a Report
You might want to have students write a report on Puerto Rico. Suggest that their reports answer questions pertaining to the geographic, economic, political, and cultural aspects of the island and its people. Help students with reference materials if necessary. When their reports are finished, allow students who wish to do so to read them to the class.

FURTHER READING FOR STUDENTS
If students are interested in reading more about Spanish-speaking people in the United States, they might try the other stories in Nicholasa Mohr's *El Bronx Remembered.* They might also read Ernesto Galarza's autobiography set in California, *Barrio Boy,* and Piri Thomas's autobiography set in New York, *Down These Mean Streets.* Sandra Cisneros's stories about Hispanic life are found in *The House on Mango Street.*

into contact, they often borrow each others' words. It is no surprise, therefore, that English contains many words borrowed from Spanish (as well as from other languages). The words below are examples of Spanish words that have been adopted into the English language. Define as many of the words as you can, using a sentence or two for each word. Then check the definitions of all the words in a dictionary. Notice how the dictionary indicates each word should be pronounced. Finally, use each word in a sentence.

rodeo	plaza	siesta	mosquito
fiesta	patio	canyon	cafeteria

For answers, see Teacher's Manual page 9.

Reading About the Writer

Nicholasa Mohr (1939–), who was born in New York City, writes stories and novels that take place in her old neighborhoods. She is also a painter and she often illustrates her own books. Mohr has taught art, creative writing, and Puerto Rican Studies in several schools and colleges. She won the *New York Times* outstanding book award in teenage fiction for *El Bronx Remembered,* from which the story "Princess" is taken. She also won awards for her novel *Nilda,* which traces a young Puerto Rican girl's coming of age. One reviewer of *El Bronx Remembered* said, "If there is any message at all in these stories, any underlying theme, it is that life goes on. But Nicholasa Mohr is more interested in people than in messages. Essentially, she is an old-fashioned writer, a meat-and-potatoes writer, whose stories stick to your ribs. . . . *Qué fenomenal!*"

A

Focusing on Background
El Bronx

The following is Nicholasa Mohr's introduction to *El Bronx Remembered:*

"There have been Puerto Ricans living in the mainland U.S.A. since the middle of the last century. But it was after the second World War, when traveling became cheaper and easier, that the greatest influx began. In 1946, Puerto Ricans could purchase, for a small amount of money, a one-way ticket to the mainland. As citizens they did not face immigration laws or quotas . . . and so they arrived by the tens of thousands, first by freighter and later by airplane.

"A small percentage went to work as migrant workers in the rural areas of the country. The majority settled in New York City. Many went to live in Spanish Harlem, known as El Barrio, an older community of Spanish-speaking people, on Manhattan's Upper East Side. There they joined family and friends. Others moved into congested neighborhoods inhabited by the children of earlier immigrant groups. Thus, they formed new neighborhoods in Brooklyn and Manhattan's Lower East Side. One area in particular was heavily populated by these newcomers, and became an extension or suburb of Spanish Harlem. This was the South Bronx, known to the Puerto Ricans as 'El Bronx.'

"These migrants and their children, strangers in their own country, brought with them a different language, culture, and racial mixture. Like so many before them they hoped for a better life, a new future for their children, and a piece of that good life known as the 'American dream.'

"This collection of stories is about the Puerto Rican migrants and their everyday struggle for survival, during that decade of the promised future 1946 through 1956, in New York City's 'El Bronx.' "

—Nicholasa Mohr

PREREADING

1. **BUILDING ON PRIOR KNOWLEDGE.** Before they read, ask students what they know about India. India, which is the seventh largest and second most populous nation in the world, is located in southern Asia, separated from its neighbors to the north by the Himalayas. Three seasons govern the country: the cold-weather season, the hot-weather season, and the rainy season. Because of its great latitudinal spread, India produces many types of vegetation, and it is home to a varied wildlife population, including animals as large as the bear and the elephant and as small as the mongoose and the cobra. To enhance their appreciation of the story, be sure students understand the concept of natural enemies.

2. **ESTABLISHING A PURPOSE.** Before students begin reading, you might have them read question 7 on page 50. This will help establish a purpose for their reading.

3. **PREREADING JOURNAL.** Before they read, have students write at least two sentences describing the way they feel about snakes and why they feel that way. Refer back to their responses after the story is over. See also question 8.

★ **Texas Essential Elements/(a) English Language Arts: 1B** Purpose and audience; **3A** Plot/character; **3B** Figurative language; **3C** Literary traditions; **4E** Predict; **4F** Generalizations

A

Illustration by Kipling's father, J. L. Kipling.

Courtesy of Rare Books and Manuscripts Division, The New York Public Library.

For a detailed lesson plan on this story, see Teacher's Manual pages 9–11.
A biography of Rudyard Kipling appears on text page 51.

A. Responding to the Illustration
John Lockwood Kipling (1837–1911) was an architectural sculptor who is best known today for the illustrations he did for several books written by his son Rudyard.

? What has just happened in the illustration? What creatures can you find in the picture? (Mongoose, snake, parrot, muskrat, bird, birds in nest) What do you think is the connection between the illustration and the title of the selection?

RIKKI-TIKKI-TAVI

Rudyard Kipling

The conflict in this exciting story involves a mongoose living in India. A mongoose is a small animal that resembles a weasel and a ferret. Today, India is an independent country, but at the time of the story it was ruled by Great Britain. Many British people like the family in this story lived in India. As you read, notice how Kipling helps you to enter the animals' world.

This is the story of the great war that Rikki-tikki-tavi fought single-handed, through the bathrooms of the big bungalow in Segowlee cantonment.[1] Darzee, the tailor bird, helped him, and Chuchundra, the muskrat, who never comes out into the middle of the floor, but always creeps round by the wall, gave him advice; but Rikki-tikki did the real fighting.

He was a mongoose, rather like a little cat in his fur and his tail, but quite like a weasel in his head and his habits. His eyes and the end of his restless nose were pink; he could scratch himself anywhere he pleased with any leg, front or back, that he chose to use; he could fluff up his tail till it looked like a bottle brush, and his war cry as he scuttled through the long grass was: *Rikk-tikk-tikki-tikki-tchk!*

One day, a high summer flood washed him out of the burrow where he lived with his father and mother, and carried him, kicking and clucking, down a roadside ditch. He found a little wisp of grass floating there, and clung to it till he lost his

Onomatopoeia. Rikki-tikki's name is an example of *onomatopoeia* (än′ə·mat′ə·pē′ə). This means the mongoose's name imitates a sound associated with it. If you named a canary Tweety (for its song), or a dog Ruff (for its bark), you'd also be using onomatopoeia. Many familiar words, such as *buzz, crackle,* and *hiss,* are examples of onomatopoeia (you might use them to describe the sounds of a fly, autumn leaves, and an angry snake). Watch for other words in this story that are onomatopoeic. They will help you to hear as well as see Rikki-tikki's story.

SRW p. 63

1. **Segowlee** (sē·gou′lē) **cantonment:** British army post in Segowlee, India.

SUPPLEMENTARY SUPPORT MATERIAL

1. Vocabulary Activity Sheet
2. Reading Check Test blackline master
3. Selection Test (page 9 of Test Book)
4. Author photograph on *A Gallery of Authors* poster
5. Connections Between Reading and Writing worksheet
6. Reader's Response Journal
7. Workbook (page 17)

DEVELOPING VOCABULARY

The following words appear on a test in the Test Book, page 10. (See also the Vocabulary Activity Sheet.)

ferret	fledgling
wisp	gait
draggled	coiled
cowered	consolation
spectacle	cunningly

A. Character

? Based on this passage, how would you characterize the boy's parents? How do you know? (His parents are compassionate, generous, and gentle people. Their traits are revealed by their actions and words.)

B. Foreshadowing

Teddy's father's words foreshadow Rikki-tikki-tavi's rescue of Teddy from a snake attack later in the story.

C. Vivid Description

? What details does Kipling provide to help his readers clearly picture the garden setting? (He says the garden is big and only half cultivated; he describes the bushes as being as big as houses; he tells what kinds of flowers, trees, and grasses are in the garden; he tells about the birds who live in the garden and he describes their nest.)

★ **Texas Essential Elements/(c) Reading: 1C** Dictionaries; **3A** Main ideas/details; **3D** Generalizations; **3H** Predict

senses. When he revived, he was lying in the hot sun on the middle of a garden path, very draggled indeed, and a small boy was saying: "Here's a dead mongoose. Let's have a funeral."

"No," said his mother; "let's take him in and dry him. Perhaps he isn't really dead."

They took him into the house, and a big man picked him up between his finger and thumb and said he was not dead but half choked; so they wrapped him in cotton-wool, and warmed him over a little fire, and he opened his eyes and sneezed.

"Now," said the big man (he was an Englishman who had just moved into the bungalow), "don't frighten him, and we'll see what he'll do."

It is the hardest thing in the world to frighten a mongoose, because he is eaten up from nose to tail with curiosity. The motto of all the mongoose family is, "Run and find out"; and Rikki-tikki was a true mongoose. He looked at the cotton-wool, decided that it was not good to eat, ran all round the table, sat up and put his fur in order, scratched himself, and jumped on the small boy's shoulder. A

"Don't be frightened, Teddy," said his father. "That's his way of making friends."

"Ouch! He's tickling under my chin," said Teddy.

Rikki-tikki looked down between the boy's collar and neck, snuffed at his ear, and climbed down to the floor, where he sat rubbing his nose.

"Good gracious," said Teddy's mother, "and that's a wild creature! I suppose he's so tame because we've been kind to him."

"All mongooses are like that," said her husband. "If Teddy doesn't pick him up by the tail, or try to put him in a cage, he'll run in and out of the house all day long. Let's give him something to eat."

They gave him a little piece of raw meat. Rikki-tikki liked it immensely, and when it was finished he went out into the veranda[2] and sat in the sunshine and fluffed up his fur to make it dry to the roots. Then he felt better.

"There are more things to find out about in this house," he said to himself, "than all my family could find out in all their lives. I shall certainly stay and find out."

He spent all that day roaming over the house. He nearly drowned himself in the bathtubs; put his nose into the ink on a writing table, and burnt it on the end of the big man's cigar, for he climbed up in the big man's lap to see how writing was done. At nightfall he ran into Teddy's nursery to watch how kerosene lamps were lighted, and when Teddy went to bed Rikki-tikki climbed up too; but he was a restless companion, because he had to get up and attend to every noise all through the night, and find out what made it. Teddy's mother and father came in, the last thing, to look at their boy, and Rikki-tikki was awake on the pillow. "I don't like that," said Teddy's mother; "he may bite the child." "He'll do no such thing," said the father. "Teddy's safer with that little beast than if he had a bloodhound to watch him. If a snake came into the nursery now——" B

But Teddy's mother wouldn't think of anything so awful.

Early in the morning Rikki-tikki came to early breakfast in the veranda riding on Teddy's shoulder, and they gave him banana and some boiled egg; and he sat on all their laps one after the other, because every well-brought-up mongoose always hopes to be a house-mongoose some day and have rooms to run about in; and Rikki-tikki's mother (she used to live in the General's house at Segowlee) had carefully told Rikki what to do if ever he came across white men.

Then Rikki-tikki went out into the garden to see what was to be seen. It was a large garden, only half cultivated, with bushes, as big as summer houses, of Marshal Niel roses; lime and orange trees, clumps of bamboos, and thickets of high grass. Rikki-tikki licked his lips. "This is a splendid hunting ground," he said, and his tail grew bottle-brushy at the thought of it, and he scuttled up and down the garden, snuffing here and there till he heard very sorrowful voices in a thornbush. It was Darzee, the tailor bird, and his wife. They had made a beautiful nest by pulling two big leaves together and stitching them up the edges with fibers, and had filled the hollow with cotton and downy fluff. The nest swayed to and fro as they sat on the rim and cried. C

2. **veranda:** open porch with a roof along the outside of a building.

"He came to breakfast riding on Teddy's shoulder."

Illustration by W. H. Drake.

Discussing the Illustration

American illustrator William Henry Drake (1856–1926) is noted particularly for his black-and-white drawings of gold and silver antiquities and old armor. His book illustrations include those that appear in Kipling's *The Jungle Book.* Call students' attention to the artist's rendering of the boy and the mongoose, noting particularly the way in which the boy holds his left arm and his old-fashioned clothing.

? What do you think the boy is saying to the mongoose? If the mongoose could speak, how do you think it would reply?

A. Conflict
Do you think a conflict will develop between Rikki-tikki and Nag? Why? What type of conflict would this be? (A conflict will develop between Rikki-tikki and Nag. The author says that it is a mongoose's business to fight snakes. This will be an external conflict.) What do you think it means that Nag's heart is "cold"? (Snakes are cold-blooded, meaning that their body temperature alters with the temperature of their environment. But "cold" here could also mean cruel, pitiless, unfeeling.)

B. Foreshadowing
This passage foreshadows the death of the cobra and his family.

C. Responding
Why do you suppose that if Rikki-tikki were older he would know better how to kill Nagaina? (He'd have had experience.)

D. Vocabulary
A *snakeling* is a small snake. *Karait* is an Indian word for an extremely poisonous, small snake.

"What is the matter?" asked Rikki-tikki.

"We are very miserable," said Darzee. "One of our babies fell out of the nest yesterday and Nag ate him."

"H'm!" said Rikki-tikki, "that is very sad—but I am a stranger here. Who is Nag?"

Darzee and his wife only cowered down in the nest without answering, for from the thick grass at the foot of the bush there came a low hiss—a horrid cold sound that made Rikki-tikki jump back two clear feet. Then inch by inch out of the grass rose up the head and spread hood of Nag, the big black cobra, and he was five feet long from tongue to tail. When he had lifted one third of himself clear off the ground, he stayed balancing to and fro exactly as a dandelion tuft balances in the wind, and he looked at Rikki-tikki with the wicked snake's eyes that never change their expression, whatever the snake may be thinking of.

"Who is Nag," said he. "*I* am Nag. The great God Brahm[3] put his mark upon all our people, when the first cobra spread his hood to keep the sun off Brahm as he slept. Look, and be afraid!"

He spread out his hood more than ever, and Rikki-tikki saw the spectacle-mark on the back of it that looks exactly like the eye part of a hook-and-eye fastening. He was afraid for the minute; but it is impossible for a mongoose to stay frightened for any length of time, and though Rikki-tikki had never met a live cobra before, his mother had fed him on dead ones, and he knew that all a grown mongoose's business in life was to fight and eat snakes. Nag knew that too and, at the bottom of his cold heart, he was afraid. A

"Well," said Rikki-tikki, and his tail began to fluff up again, "marks or no marks, do you think it is right for you to eat fledglings out of a nest?"

Nag was thinking to himself, and watching the least little movement in the grass behind Rikki-tikki. He knew that mongooses in the garden meant death sooner or later for him and his family; B but he wanted to get Rikki-tikki off his guard. So he dropped his head a little, and put it on one side.

"Let us talk," he said. "You eat eggs. Why should not I eat birds?"

"Behind you! Look behind you!" sang Darzee.

Rikki-tikki knew better than to waste time in staring. He jumped up in the air as high as he could go, and just under him whizzed by the head of Nagaina, Nag's wicked wife. She had crept up behind him as he was talking, to make an end of him; and he heard her savage hiss as the stroke missed. He came down almost across her back, and if he had been an old mongoose he could have known that then was the time to break her back C with one bite; but he was afraid of the terrible lashing return-stroke of the cobra. He bit, indeed, but did not bite long enough, and he jumped clear of the whisking tail, leaving Nagaina torn and angry.

"Wicked, wicked Darzee!" said Nag, lashing up as high as he could reach toward the nest in the thornbush; but Darzee had built it out of reach of snakes, and it only swayed to and fro.

Rikki-tikki felt his eyes growing red and hot (when a mongoose's eyes grow red, he is angry), and he sat back on his tail and hind legs like a little kangaroo, and looked all round him, and chattered with rage. But Nag and Nagaina had disappeared into the grass. When a snake misses its stroke, it never says anything or gives any sign of what it means to do next. Rikki-tikki did not care to follow them, for he did not feel sure that he could manage two snakes at once. So he trotted off to the gravel path near the house, and sat down to think. It was a serious matter for him. If you read the old books of natural history, you will find they say that when the mongoose fights the snake and happens to get bitten, he runs off and eats some herb that cures him. That is not true. The victory is only a matter of quickness of eye and quickness of foot—snake's blow against the mongoose's jump—and as no eye can follow the motion of a snake's head when it strikes, this makes things much more wonderful than any magic herb. Rikki-tikki knew he was a young mongoose, and it made him all the more pleased to think that he had managed to escape a blow from behind. It gave him confidence in himself, and when Teddy came running down the path, Rikki-tikki was ready to be petted. But just as Teddy was stooping, something wriggled a little in the dust, and a tiny voice said: "Be careful. I am Death!" It was Karait, the dusty brown snakeling that lies for D

3. **Brahm** (bräm): in the Hindu religion, the creator.

choice on the dusty earth; and his bite is as dangerous as the cobra's. But he is so small that nobody thinks of him, and so he does the more harm to people.

Rikki-tikki's eyes grew red again, and he danced up to Karait with the peculiar rocking, swaying motion that he had inherited from his family. It looks very funny, but it is so perfectly balanced a gait that you can fly off from it at any angle you please; and in dealing with snakes this is an advantage. If Rikki-tikki had only known, he was doing a much more dangerous thing than fighting Nag, for Karait is so small, and can turn so quickly, that unless Rikki bit him close to the back of the head, he would get the return-stroke in his eye or his lip. But Rikki did not know: his eyes were all red, and he rocked back and forth, looking for a good place to hold. Karait struck out, Rikki jumped sideways and tried to run in, but the wicked little dusty gray head lashed within a fraction of his shoulder, and he had to jump over the body, and the head followed his heels close.

Teddy shouted to the house: "Oh, look here! Our mongoose is killing a snake"; and Rikki-tikki heard a scream from Teddy's mother. His father ran out with a stick, but by the time he came up, Karait had lunged out once too far, and Rikki-tikki had sprung, jumped on the snake's back, dropped his head far between the forelegs, bitten as high up the back as he could get hold, and rolled away. That bite paralyzed Karait, and Rikki-tikki was just going to eat him up from the tail, after the custom of his family at dinner, when he remembered that a full meal makes a slow mongoose, and if he wanted all his strength and quickness ready, he must keep himself thin. He went away for a dust bath under the castor oil bushes, while Teddy's father beat the dead Karait. "What is the use of that?" thought Rikki-tikki; "I have settled A it all"; and then Teddy's mother picked him up from the dust and hugged him, crying that he had saved Teddy from death, and Teddy's father said that he was a providence, and Teddy looked on with big scared eyes. Rikki-tikki was rather amused at all the fuss, which, of course, he did not understand. Teddy's mother might just as well have petted Teddy for playing in the dust. Rikki was thoroughly enjoying himself.

That night at dinner, walking to and fro among the wine glasses on the table, he might have stuffed himself three times over with nice things; but he remembered Nag and Nagaina, and though it was very pleasant to be patted and petted by Teddy's mother, and to sit on Teddy's shoulder, his eyes would get red from time to time, and he would go off into his long war cry of *Rikk-tikk-tikki-tikki-tchk!*

Teddy carried him off to bed, and insisted on Rikki-tikki's sleeping under his chin. Rikki-tikki was too well bred to bite or scratch, but as soon as Teddy was asleep he went off for his nightly walk round the house, and in the dark he ran up against Chuchundra, the muskrat, creeping round by the wall. Chuchundra is a broken-hearted little beast. He whimpers and cheeps all night, trying to make up his mind to run into the middle of the room; but he never gets there.

"Don't kill me," said Chuchundra, almost weeping. "Rikki-tikki, don't kill me!"

"Do you think a snake-killer kills muskrats?" B said Rikki-tikki scornfully.

"Those who kill snakes get killed by snakes," said Chuchundra, more sorrowfully than ever. "And how am I to be sure that Nag won't mistake me for you some dark night?"

"There's not the least danger," said Rikki-tikki; "but Nag is in the garden, and I know you don't go there."

"My cousin Chua, the rat, told me——" said Chuchundra, and then he stopped.

"Told you what?"

"H'sh! Nag is everywhere, Rikki-tikki. You should have talked to Chua in the garden."

"I didn't—so you must tell me. Quick, Chuchundra, or I'll bite you!"

Chuchundra sat down and cried till the tears rolled off his whiskers. "I am a very poor man," he sobbed. "I never had spirit enough to run out into the middle of the room. H'sh! I mustn't tell you anything. Can't you *hear,* Rikki-tikki?"

Rikki-tikki listened. The house was as still as still, but he thought he could just catch the faintest *scratch-scratch* in the world—a noise as faint as C that of a wasp walking on a windowpane—the dry scratch of a snake's scales on brickwork.

"That's Nag or Nagaina," he said to himself,

A. Foreshadowing

? Find the clue that Kipling planted earlier in the story that foreshadowed Rikki-tikki's rescue of Teddy. (Page 40, right-hand column, lines 18–20, "Teddy's safer with that little beast . . .")

B. Character's Motivation

? Why does Rikki-tikki respond scornfully to Chuchundra? (He is insulted by Chuchundra's belief that a mongoose, who kills vicious snakes, would bother going after a whimpering muskrat.)

C. Vivid Description

? To what does Kipling compare the noise of the snake's scales on the bricks? (He compares it to the faint noise made by a wasp walking on a windowpane.) Suggest another comparison that conveys just how faint this scratching sound is.

A. Responding to the Illustration
Point out to students that this illustration and the one on page 41 were done by the same artist.
? Contrast the illustrations on pages 41 and 44 in terms of the artist's technique and in terms of the overall feeling each illustration conveys. (Students should comment on the difference in the artist's lines. They should notice the sharp contrast between the background in the first illustration—none—and the violent blending of the elements in the second. Students should also comment on the friendly, almost sweet feeling of the first illustration as opposed to the action-packed violent one of the second.)

B. Vocabulary
A *sluice* is an artificial passageway for water.

C. Responding
? How could this line be applied to today's world? What people might say these words today?

A

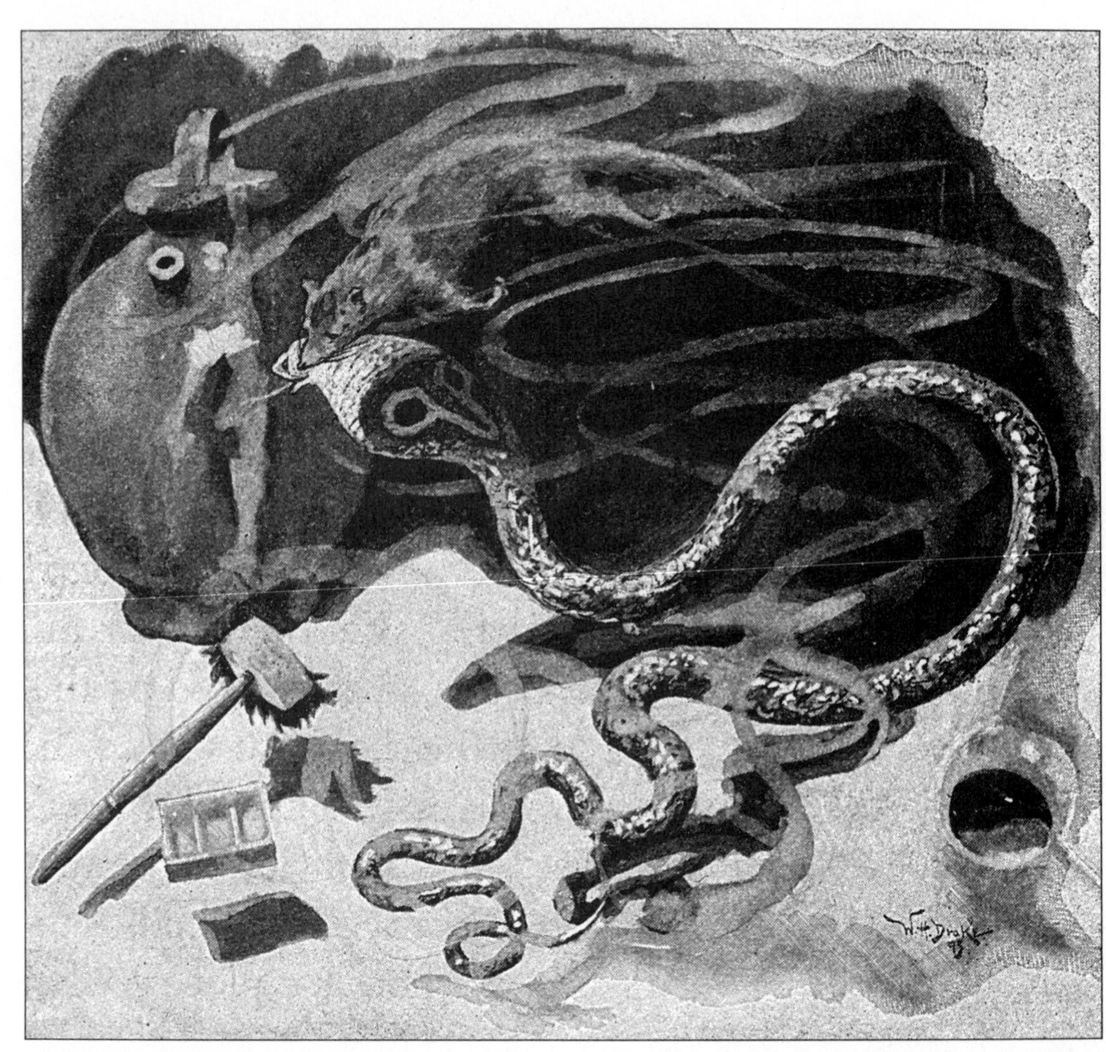

"Then Rikki-tikki was battered to and fro as a rat is shaken by a dog."

Illustration by W. H. Drake.

B "and he is crawling into the bathroom sluice. You're right, Chuchundra; I should have talked to Chua."

He stole off to Teddy's bathroom, but there was nothing there, and then to Teddy's mother's bathroom. At the bottom of the smooth plaster wall there was a brick pulled out to make a sluice for the bath water, and as Rikki-tikki stole in by the masonry curb where the bath is put, he heard Nag and Nagaina whispering together outside in the moonlight.

"When the house is emptied of people," said Nagaina to her husband, "*he* will have to go away, and then the garden will be our own again. Go in quietly, and remember that the big man who killed Karait is the first one to bite. Then come out and tell me, and we will hunt for Rikki-tikki together."

"But are you sure that there is anything to be gained by killing the people?" said Nag. C

"Everything. When there were no people in the bungalow, did we have any mongoose in the garden? So long as the bungalow is empty, we are king and queen of the garden; and remember that as soon as our eggs in the melon bed hatch (as they may tomorrow), our children will need room and quiet."

"I had not thought of that," said Nag. "I will go, but there is no need that we should hunt for Rikki-tikki afterward. I will kill the man and his wife, and the child if I can, and come away quietly. Then the bungalow will be empty, and Rikki-tikki will go."

Rikki-tikki tingled all over with rage and hatred at this, and then Nag's head came through the sluice, and his five feet of cold body followed it. Angry as he was, Rikki-tikki was very frightened as he saw the size of the big cobra. Nag coiled himself up, raised his head, and looked into the bathroom in the dark, and Rikki could see his eyes glitter.

"Now, if I kill him here, Nagaina will know; and if I fight him on the open floor, the odds are in his favor. What am I to do?" said Rikki-tikki-tavi.

Nag waved to and fro, and then Rikki-tikki heard him drinking from the biggest water jar that was used to fill the bath. "That is good," said the snake. "Now, when Karait was killed, the big man had a stick. He may have that stick still, but when he comes in to bathe in the morning he will not have a stick. I shall wait here till he comes. Nagaina—do you hear me?—I shall wait here in the cool till daytime."

A

There was no answer from outside, so Rikki-tikki knew Nagaina had gone away. Nag coiled himself down, coil by coil, round the bulge at the bottom of the water jar, and Rikki-tikki stayed still as death. After an hour he began to move, muscle by muscle, toward the jar. Nag was asleep, and Rikki-tikki looked at his big back, wondering which would be the best place for a good hold. "If I don't break his back at the first jump," said Rikki, "he can still fight; and if he fights—O Rikki!" He looked at the thickness of the neck below the hood, but that was too much for him; and a bite near the tail would only make Nag savage.

"It must be the head," he said at last, "the head above the hood; and, when I am once there, I must not let go."

Then he jumped. The head was lying a little clear of the water jar, under the curve of it; and, as his teeth met, Rikki braced his back against the bulge of the red earthenware to hold down the head. This gave him just one second's purchase,[4] and he made the most of it. Then he was battered to and fro as a rat is shaken by a dog—to and fro on the floor, up and down, and round in great circles, but his eyes were red and he held on as the body cartwhipped over the floor, upsetting the tin dipper and the soap dish and the fleshbrush, B and banged against the tin side of the bath. As he held he closed his jaws tighter and tighter, for he made sure[5] he would be banged to death, and, for the honor of his family, he preferred to be found with his teeth locked. He was dizzy, aching, and felt shaken to pieces when something went off like a thunderclap just behind him; a hot wind knocked him senseless and red fire singed his fur. The big man had been wakened by the noise, and had fired both barrels of a shotgun into Nag just behind the hood.

Rikki-tikki held on with his eyes shut, for now he was quite sure he was dead; but the head did not move, and the big man picked him up and said: "It's the mongoose again, Alice; the little chap has saved *our* lives now." Then Teddy's mother came in with a very white face, and saw what was left of Nag, and Rikki-tikki dragged himself to Teddy's bedroom and spent half the rest of the night shaking himself tenderly to find out whether he really was broken into forty pieces, as he fancied.

When morning came he was very stiff, but well pleased with his doings. "Now I have Nagaina to settle with, and she will be worse than five Nags, and there's no knowing when the eggs she spoke of will hatch. Goodness! I must go and see Darzee," he said. C

Without waiting for breakfast, Rikki-tikki ran to the thornbush where Darzee was singing a song of triumph at the top of his voice. The news of Nag's death was all over the garden, for the sweeper had thrown the body on the rubbish heap.

"Oh, you stupid tuft of feathers!" said Rikki-tikki angrily. "Is this the time to sing?"

"Nag is dead—is dead—is dead!" sang Darzee. "The valiant Rikki-tikki caught him by the head

---

4. **purchase:** here, advantage.
5. **made sure:** here, felt sure.

A. Suspense
? Identify the suspense in this passage. What are you worrying about as you read it? (We know that Rikki-tikki and Nag are about to fight but we don't know exactly when. Kipling creates suspense by depicting Rikki-tikki lying in wait for the proper time to strike and by showing Rikki-tikki's fear of Nag and his need to make the first strike count. We are anxious to discover what the outcome of the battle will be.)

B. Context Clues
? From the words *dipper* and *soap dish,* what do you think a *fleshbrush* is? (A brush to scrub your back with)

C. Foreshadowing
? Can you explain the foreshadowing in this passage? (From Rikki-tikki's words we know that the mongoose will fight a fierce battle with Nagaina and that somehow the cobra's eggs will play an important role in it.)

A. Suspense

How does this paragraph increase our suspense? (We wonder just what Rikki-tikki *does* intend to do with Nagaina's eggs.)

B. Character's Actions

What do you think of Rikki-tikki's killing the baby cobras? At this point in the story, do you or do you not like Rikki-tikki? Explain.

and held fast. The big man brought the bang-stick, and Nag fell in two pieces! He will never eat my babies again."

"All that's true enough, but where's Nagaina?" said Rikki-tikki, looking carefully round him.

"Nagaina came to the bathroom sluice and called for Nag," Darzee went on, "and Nag came out on the end of a stick—the sweeper picked him up on the end of a stick and threw him upon the rubbish heap. Let us sing about the great, the red-eyed Rikki-tikki!" and Darzee filled his throat and sang.

"If I could get up to your nest, I'd roll your babies out!" said Rikki-tikki. "You don't know when to do the right thing at the right time. You're safe enough in your nest there, but it's war for me down here. Stop singing a minute, Darzee."

"For the great, beautiful Rikki-tikki's sake I will stop," said Darzee. "What is it, O Killer of the terrible Nag?"

"Where is Nagaina, for the third time?"

"On the rubbish-heap by the stables, mourning for Nag. Great is Rikki-tikki with the white teeth."

"Bother[6] my white teeth! Have you ever heard where she keeps her eggs?"

"In the melon bed, on the end nearest the wall, where the sun strikes nearly all day. She hid them there weeks ago."

"And you never thought it worthwhile to tell me? The end nearest the wall, you said?"

"Rikki-tikki, you are not going to eat her eggs?"

A "Not eat exactly, no. Darzee, if you have a grain of sense you will fly off to the stables and pretend that your wing is broken, and let Nagaina chase you away to this bush. I must get to the melon bed, and if I went there now she'd see me."

Darzee was a featherbrained little fellow who could never hold more than one idea at a time in his head; and just because he knew that Nagaina's children were born in eggs like his own, he didn't think at first that it was fair to kill them. But his wife was a sensible bird, and she knew that cobra's eggs meant young cobras later on; so she flew off from the nest, and left Darzee to keep the babies warm, and continue his song about the death of Nag. Darzee was very like a man in some ways.

She fluttered in front of Nagaina by the rubbish heap, and cried out, "Oh, my wing is broken! The boy in the house threw a stone at me and broke it." Then she fluttered more desperately than ever.

Nagaina lifted up her head and hissed, "You warned Rikki-tikki when I would have killed him. Indeed and truly, you've chosen a bad place to be lame in." And she moved toward Darzee's wife, slipping along over the dust.

"The boy broke it with a stone!" shrieked Darzee's wife.

"Well! It may be some consolation to you when you're dead to know that I shall settle accounts with the boy. My husband lies on the rubbish heap this morning, but before night the boy in the house will lie very still. What is the use of running away? I am sure to catch you. Little fool, look at me!"

Darzee's wife knew better than to do *that,* for a bird who looks at a snake's eyes gets so frightened that she cannot move. Darzee's wife fluttered on, piping sorrowfully, and never leaving the ground, and Nagaina quickened her pace.

Rikki-tikki heard them going up the path from the stables, and he raced for the end of the melon patch near the wall. There, in the warm litter above the melons, very cunningly hidden, he found twenty-five eggs, about the size of a bantam's eggs,[7] but with whitish skins instead of shells.

"I was not a day too soon," he said; for he could see the baby cobras curled up inside the skin, and he knew that the minute they were hatched they could each kill a man or a mongoose. He bit off the tops of the eggs as fast as he could, taking care to crush the young cobras, and turned over the litter from time to time to see whether he had missed any. At last there were only three eggs left, and Rikki-tikki began to chuckle to himself, when he heard Darzee's wife screaming: B

"Rikki-tikki, I led Nagaina toward the house, and she has gone into the veranda, and—oh, come quickly—she means killing!"

Rikki-tikki smashed two eggs, and tumbled backward down the melon bed with the third egg

6. **Bother:** here, never mind.

7. **bantam's eggs:** small eggs. A bantam is a small chicken.

"It is all over."

Illustration by W. H. Drake.

Responding to the Illustration

? What moment in the story does this picture illustrate? After they've read the story once, students could skim it to find the correlation with the illustration.

Allow students time to study the illustration and to jot down topics for a conversation they think the two animals might be having. (Have them use the caption as a springboard for thinking of ideas.) Then have students work in pairs to write a dialogue that might take place between Rikki-tikki and Darzee as they face each other across the road. Instruct students to decide between themselves who will write Rikki-tikki's words and who will write Darzee's words. Remind students to keep in mind the personalities of the two animals as they write so that their dialogue sounds as though the animals might actually speak it.

Critical Comment
In an essay he wrote about Rudyard Kipling in 1948, writer C. S. Lewis said, "Kipling is intensely loved and hated. Hardly any reader likes him a little. . . . For the moment I will only say that I do not fully belong to either side."

After sharing the quotation with students, ask them to state their opinion of Rudyard Kipling based on their reading of "Rikki-Tikki-Tavi." Encourage students to give honest reasons to support their opinions. Have them tell whether or not they would like to read other works by Kipling.

FURTHER READING FOR STUDENTS
Recommend Rudyard Kipling's *The Jungle Book,* the famous tale of Mowgli, an Indian child who gets lost in the forest and finds shelter with a pack of wolves. Even slower readers can enjoy Kipling's comical *Just So Stories,* which answer such questions as why the leopard got its spots.

A. Character's Reasoning
? To what instinct in Nagaina is Rikki-tikki appealing? (Maternal) Would this appeal be equally valid if it were made to an animal other than a cobra? (Yes. The maternal instinct is universal.)

B. Onomatopoeia
Tell students that onomatopoeia is the use of words with sounds that echo their sense. *Buzz* and *clang* are examples of onomatopoeia. (See page 50 and the detailed discussion of this technique on text page 272.)
? What onomatopoetic words are in this paragraph? *(Whack, rustle)*

C. Character
? What do you think Darzee's wife might say to Darzee when she gets back to the nest? (She will probably yell at him for not being quick-witted and brave enough to do something to stop Nagaina.)

in his mouth, and scuttled to the veranda as hard as he could put foot to the ground. Teddy and his mother and father were there at early breakfast; but Rikki-tikki saw that they were not eating anything. They sat stone-still, and their faces were white. Nagaina was coiled up on the matting by Teddy's chair, within easy striking distance of Teddy's bare leg, and she was swaying to and fro, singing a song of triumph.

"Son of the big man that killed Nag," she hissed, "stay still. I am not ready yet. Wait a little. Keep very still, all you three! If you move I strike, and if you do not move I strike. Oh, foolish people, who killed my Nag!"

Teddy's eyes were fixed on his father, and all his father could do was to whisper, "Sit still, Teddy. You mustn't move. Teddy, keep still."

Then Rikki-tikki came up and cried: "Turn around, Nagaina; turn and fight!"

"All in good time," said she, without moving her eyes. "I will settle my account with *you* presently. Look at your friends, Rikki-tikki. They are still and white. They are afraid. They dare not move, and if you come a step nearer I strike."

"Look at your eggs," said Rikki-tikki, "in the melon bed near the wall. Go and look, Nagaina!"

The big snake turned half round, and saw the egg on the veranda. "Ah-h! Give it to me," she said.

A Rikki-tikki put his paws one on each side of the egg, and his eyes were blood-red. "What price for a snake's egg? For a young cobra? For a young king-cobra? For the last—the very last of the brood? The ants are eating all the others down by the melon bed."

Nagaina spun clear round, forgetting everything for the sake of the one egg; and Rikki-tikki saw Teddy's father shoot out a big hand, catch Teddy by the shoulder, and drag him across the little table with the tea cups, safe and out of reach of Nagaina.

"Tricked! Tricked! Tricked! *Rikk-tck-tck!*" chuckled Rikki-tikki. "The boy is safe, and it was I—I—I that caught Nag by the hood last night in the bathroom." Then he began to jump up and down, all four feet together, his head close to the floor. "He threw me to and fro, but he could not shake me off. He was dead before the big man blew him in two. I did it! *Rikki-tikki-tck-tck!* Come then, Nagaina. Come and fight with me. You shall not be a widow long."

Nagaina saw that she had lost her chance of killing Teddy, and the egg lay between Rikki-tikki's paws. "Give me the egg, Rikki-tikki. Give me the last of my eggs, and I will go away and never come back," she said, lowering her hood.

"Yes, you will go away, and you will never come back; for you will go to the rubbish heap with Nag. Fight, widow! The big man has gone for his gun! Fight!"

Rikki-tikki was bounding all round Nagaina, keeping just out of reach of her stroke, his little eyes like hot coals. Nagaina gathered herself together, and flung out at him. Rikki-tikki jumped up and backward. Again and again and again she struck, and each time her head came with a whack on the matting of the veranda and she gathered herself together like a watch spring. Then Rikki-tikki danced in a circle to get behind her, and Nagaina spun round to keep her head to his head, so that the rustle of her tail on the matting sounded like dry leaves blown along by the wind. B

He had forgotten the egg. It still lay on the veranda, and Nagaina came nearer and nearer to it, till at last, while Rikki-tikki was drawing breath, she caught it in her mouth, turned to the veranda steps, and flew like an arrow down the path, with Rikki-tikki behind her. When the cobra runs for her life, she goes like a whiplash flicked across a horse's neck. Rikki-tikki knew that he must catch her, or all the trouble would begin again. She headed straight for the long grass by the thornbush, and as he was running Rikki-tikki heard Darzee still singing his foolish little song of triumph. But Darzee's wife was wiser. She flew off her nest as Nagaina came along and flapped her wings about Nagaina's head. If Darzee had helped they might have turned on her; but Nagaina only lowered her hood and went on. Still, the instant's delay brought Rikki-tikki up to her, and as she plunged into the rat hole where she and Nag used to live, his little white teeth were clenched on her tail, and he went down with her—and very few mongooses, however wise and old C

Reading Check Test

1. Rikki-tikki-tavi is a cobra. *(False)*
2. The story is set in China. *(False)*
3. Rikki-tikki-tavi discovers a plot to kill Teddy's family. *(True)*
4. Rikki-tikki-tavi's eyes turn blue when he gets angry. *(False)*
5. Rikki-tikki-tavi saves Teddy's life. *(True)*

Closure

Working in small groups, students should list the main events in the fast-moving, action-packed plot of "Rikki-Tikki-Tavi." Have them discuss other stories they have read or TV shows or movies they have seen in which the plot was filled with action.

they may be, care to follow a cobra into its hole. It was dark in the hole; and Rikki-tikki never knew when it might open out and give Nagaina room to turn and strike at him. He held on savagely, and stuck out his feet to act as brakes on the dark slope of the hot, moist earth. Then the grass by the mouth of the hole stopped waving, and Darzee said: "It is all over with Rikki-tikki! We must sing his death song. Valiant Rikki-tikki is dead! For Nagaina will surely kill him underground."

So he sang a very mournful song that he made up on the spur of the minute, and just as he got to the most touching part the grass quivered again, and Rikki-tikki, covered with dirt, dragged himself out of the hole leg by leg, licking his whiskers. Darzee stopped with a little shout. Rikki-tikki shook some of the dust out of his fur and sneezed. "It is all over," he said. "The widow will never come out again." And the red ants that live between the grass stems heard him, and began to troop down one after another to see if he had spoken the truth.

Rikki-tikki curled himself up in the grass and slept where he was—slept and slept till it was late in the afternoon, for he had done a hard day's work.

"Now," he said, when he awoke, "I will go back to the house. Tell the Coppersmith, Darzee, and he will tell the garden that Nagaina is dead."

The Coppersmith is a bird who makes a noise exactly like the beating of a little hammer on a copper pot; and the reason he is always making it is because he is the town crier to every Indian garden, and tells all the news to everybody who cares to listen. As Rikki-tikki went up the path, he heard his "attention" notes like a tiny dinner gong; and then the steady "*Ding-dong-tock!* Nag is dead—*dong!* Nagaina is dead! *Ding-dong-tock!*" That set all the birds in the garden singing, and the frogs croaking; for Nag and Nagaina used to eat frogs as well as little birds.

When Rikki got to the house, Teddy and Teddy's mother (she looked very white still, for she had been fainting) and Teddy's father came out and almost cried over him; and that night he ate all that was given him till he could eat no more, and went to bed on Teddy's shoulder, where Teddy's mother saw him when she came to look late at night.

"He saved our lives and Teddy's life," she said to her husband. "Just think, he saved all our lives."

Rikki-tikki woke up with a jump, for the mongooses are light sleepers.

"Oh, it's you," said he. "What are you bothering for? All the cobras are dead; and if they weren't, I'm here."

Rikki-tikki had a right to be proud of himself; but he did not grow too proud, and he kept that garden as a mongoose should keep it, with tooth and jump and spring and bite, till never a cobra dared show its head inside the walls.

Darzee's Chant

Sung in honor of Rikki-tikki-tavi

Singer and tailor am I—
  Doubled the joys that I know—
Proud of my lilt to the sky,
  Proud of the house that I sew.
Over and under, so weave I my music—so weave
    I the house that I sew.

Sing to your fledglings again,
  Mother, O lift up your head!
Evil that plagued us is slain,
  Death in the garden lies dead.
Terror that hid in the roses is impotent—flung on
    the dung hill and dead!

Who has delivered us, who?
  Tell me his nest and his name.
Rikki, the valiant, the true,
  Tikki, with eyeballs of flame—
Rikk-tikki-tikki, the ivory-fanged, the hunter with
    eyeballs of flame!

Give him the thanks of the birds,
  Bowing with tail-feathers spread,
Praise him with nightingale words—
  Nay, I will praise him instead.
Hear! I will sing you the praise of the bottle-tailed
    Rikki with eyeballs of red!

(*Here Rikki-tikki interrupted, so the rest of the song is lost.*)

A

A. Reading Aloud
You might want to read this passage aloud to students or have one or more volunteers read it aloud to the rest of the class.

ANALYZING THE STORY
Identifying Facts
1. A summer flood washes Rikki out of his burrow and down a ditch. He loses consciousness, later waking up in the garden path. The family revives him and allows him the run of the house and garden.
2. He explores the cotton-wool with which the family dries him, Teddy's shoulder and ear, the bathtubs, the writing table, the big man's cigar, Teddy's nursery, night noises, and the garden.
3. He fights Nag, Nagaina, and Karait.
Rikki-tikki is first attacked from behind by Nagaina, whom he evades, but whom he is too inexperienced to finish off. Then he attacks and kills Karait. This battle prepares him for his fight with Nag and Nagaina.
4. Darzee the tailor-bird warns Rikki when Nagaina tries to catch him from behind, and later Darzee tells Rikki where Nagaina's eggs are hidden. Chuchundra the muskrat alerts Rikki to the cobras' conversation and planned night attack. Darzee's wife lures Nagaina away from her eggs so that Rikki can destroy them, warns Rikki that Nagaina is threatening the human family, and delays the fleeing

Responding to the Story

Analyzing the Story

Identifying Facts

1. Explain how Rikki-tikki comes to live with Teddy and his family.
2. Kipling says the mongoose "is eaten up from nose to tail with curiosity." Describe three incidents that illustrate Rikki-tikki's curiosity.
3. The story's first sentence tells you that Rikki-tikki fights a great war. Whom does he fight? Describe two of the first battles in the war.
4. Although Rikki-tikki does almost all the fighting, he does get help from his friends. Who are Rikki-tikki's friends and how does each one help him?
5. Describe Rikki-tikki's final battle. What is its outcome?

Interpreting Meanings

6. The animals in this story talk and think as if they were humans. Do you think this makes the story better? Or would you have preferred animals without human characteristics? Back up your answer with specific examples from the selection.
7. Where is the story's **climax**—the moment of greatest suspense when the outcome is decided?

Applying Meanings

8. Do you think Kipling is fair to the snakes in this story? How did you feel about them?
9. This story shows that the mongoose and the cobra are natural enemies. Name another pair of animals that seem to be natural enemies. Suggest two or three reasons why the animals fight each other.

Writing About the Story

A Creative Response

1. **Imitating the Writer's Style.** At the end of the story, Rikki-tikki is living with Teddy's family. In a paragraph, describe another adventure the mongoose might have, in the garden or the bungalow. Imitate Kipling's style and use your favorite words and expressions from the story.

"In the dark he ran up against Chuchundra, the muskrat."

Illustration by W. H. Drake.

A Critical Response

2. **Describing a Character.** A personality trait is one aspect of a person's character. Each animal character in this story has distinctive traits. In a paragraph, describe three important personality traits of one of the following characters: Rikki-tikki, Darzee, Darzee's wife, Chuchundra, Nag, Nagaina. Give an example from the story to illustrate each trait.

See Teacher's Manual page 11.

Analyzing Language and Vocabulary

Onomatopoeia

SRW p. 63

Onomatopoeia refers to words that imitate sounds associated with what they mean. Everyday words like *meow, roar,* and *tick-tock* are examples of onomatopoeia. (These words imitate the sounds of a cat, a lion, and a clock.) In literature, such words can make descriptions more vivid by appealing to your sense of hearing.

The following examples of onomatopoeia are from "Rikki-Tikki-Tavi." Explain the meaning of each word and how each imitates sound.

whizz	cheep	ding-dong	hiss
chatter	scratch	whimper	croak

Think of onomatopoeic words you could use to name three animals in your acquaintance.

Nagaina enough for Rikki to catch up with her.

5. When Nagaina is threatening the family, Rikki taunts Nagaina with the last of her eggs, thus distracting her enough for the big man to pull Teddy to safety. Nagaina lashes out at Rikki several times, but then grabs her egg and dashes toward her hole. Thanks to the help of Darzee's wife, Rikki catches up to Nagaina, and latches onto her tail as she disappears down her hole. At first Rikki is feared dead, but he reappears victorious, having destroyed Nagaina and her last egg.

Interpreting Meanings

6. Most students, citing Rikki's feelings and the animals' conversations, will probably prefer the story as written. You could challenge those students who do not like the personification in the story to rewrite a scene in the style they prefer.

7. The climax, or emotional high point, occurs when Rikki-tikki follows Nagaina down her hole. This is where the danger for Rikki is greatest, and the suspense is highest.

Reading About the Writer

Rudyard Kipling (1865–1936) was born in Bombay, India, where his father, a well-educated Englishman, was an illustrator and a professor at the School of Art. When Kipling was nearly six, he and his sister were sent back to England and deposited at a sort of boarding house for several years. Throughout the rest of his life, he was to recall this place as "the house of desolation." Kipling's boarding school days in England were equally lonely. At the age of seventeen, instead of staying in England and going on to college, he returned home to India where he became a journalist.

Kipling was fascinated with the life of British colonials in India and with the vivid contrast they made with the Indian people they ruled. He began to write poems and stories about the life he saw about him. Before he was twenty years old, his stories and poems began appearing in Indian periodicals.

When Kipling returned to London, he was already recognized as an unusually gifted writer. He soon published his first novel and the now famous poems "Mandalay" and "Gunga Din."

In 1892, he married an American, Caroline Balestier, and their globe-trotting honeymoon brought them to her family's place in Brattleboro, Vermont. For a while it seemed as if the Kiplings might settle in America. In fact, they built a grand house with that in mind. Kipling wrote his novel *Captains Courageous,* which he gave a New England setting, and he published *The Jungle Books.*

However, a quarrel with his brother-in-law brought him embarrassing publicity. Not just Brattleboro, but all America was spoiled for him. Kipling gathered his wife and his daughters and returned to England. There, a son, John, was born.

Kipling's novel *Kim* appeared in 1901. Some people think it is his best. *Kim* displays his knowledge and love of India and shows Kipling at the top of his writing form. The novel tells the story of an orphaned Irish boy, Kim, who grows up as a vagabond in India. A series of adventures bring him to his father's old army regiment, to some formal British schooling, and ultimately to employment as an agent of the British secret service.

Kipling won the Nobel Prize for Literature in 1907. He is buried with other famous writers in the Poet's Corner in Westminster Abbey in London.

Applying Meanings

8. Answers will vary. Students may recognize that this story was not written by a conservation-minded individual, and that killing snakes was probably the "right" thing to do at that time. Others will note that the snakes are not just snakes: They represent evil. Thus, it is fair that they are defeated by the good Rikki-tikki.

9. Students will think immediately of dogs and cats. Elicit other pairs, such as bears and mountain lions, or sharks and seals. Students may quickly discern one or two reasons for the enmity. Suggest that they check the library for additional facts about the relationship.

Focusing on Background

"Dear Love . . . from Daddo"

Kipling kept up a constant correspondence with his two children, Elsie and John, while they were away from home. His letters are filled with humor, affection, and even sketches to illustrate his news. The following extract is from a letter written to Elsie when she was twelve years old and on a trip to London. (Mr. Campbell is the name Kipling uses when giving advice or making funny comments.)

"There isn't any other news so I send you a few simple rules for Life in London.

1. Wash early and often with soap and hot water.
2. Do not roll on the grass of the parks. It will come off black on your dress.
3. Never eat penny buns, oysters, periwinkles, or peppermints on the top of a bus. It annoys the passengers.
4. Be kind to policemen. You never know when you may be taken up.
5. Never stop a motor bus with your foot. It is not a croquet ball.
6. Do not attempt to take pictures off the wall of the National Gallery, or to remove cases of butterflies from the Natural History Museum. You will be noticed if you do.
7. Avoid late hours, pickled salmon, public meetings, crowded crossings, gutters, water-carts, and over-eating.

"That is all I can think of at present: but if you ever feel doubtful about your conduct, you have only to write and I myself will instruct you further, said Mr. Campbell.

Dear love from us both.
Ever your
Daddo."

PREREADING

1. **BUILDING ON PRIOR KNOWLEDGE.** Before they read, ask students what they know about the origin of the Christmas tree. The modern Christmas tree originated in western Germany; it evolved from a custom of tree worship that was common among the pre-Christian European tribes. The Christmas tree as we know it resulted from a combination of two elements. One of these elements was a "Paradise Tree," which was a fir tree the German people set up in their homes on December 24, the religious feast day of Adam and Eve. On this tree they hung wafers, representing the host, which is a Christian sign of redemption, and they also hung candles to represent Christ. The other element from which the Christmas tree came was a triangular construction of wood decorated with evergreens, candles, and a star. This triangular construction also had shelves to hold Christmas figurines. By the sixteenth century the Christmas pyramid and the "Paradise Tree" had merged into one symbol, the Christmas tree. German settlers who emigrated to the United States in the seventeenth century brought their holiday custom with them, and by the nineteenth

DEVELOPING VOCABULARY

The following words appear on a test in the Test Book, page 12. (See also the Vocabulary Activity Sheet.)

corded
vendors
fragrance
chuck
forfeited
elect
shut
rationalize
monstrous
inarticulate

★ **Texas Essential Elements/(a) English Language Arts: 1B** Purpose and audience; **3A** Plot/character; **4A** Word meaning; **4F** Generalizations

A CHRISTMAS WISH

Betty Smith

For a detailed lesson plan on this story, see Teacher's Manual pages 12–14. A biography of Betty Smith appears on text page 56.

century the Christmas tree had become an established symbol of the festive season in the United States.

2. ESTABLISHING A PURPOSE. Before students begin reading, you might have them read question 10 on page 55. This will help establish a purpose for their reading.

3. PREREADING JOURNAL. Before they read have students write a brief paragraph in which they tell if they see themselves as the kind of person who is willing to struggle in order to get something they want very much.

SUPPLEMENTARY SUPPORT MATERIAL

1. Vocabulary Activity Sheet
2. Reading Check Test blackline master
3. Selection Test (page 11 of Test Book)
4. Author photograph on *A Gallery of Authors* poster
5. Reader's Response Journal
6. Workbook (page 19)

★ **Texas Essential Elements/(c) Reading: 1C** Dictionaries; **2A** Word meaning; **2B** Multimeaning words; **3A** Main ideas/details; **3D** Generalizations; **3G** Compare/contrast; **3I** Draw conclusions

This is an episode from a famous best-selling novel called *A Tree Grows in Brooklyn*. The story is set in 1912; Brooklyn is a part of New York City. The main character in the story is ten-year-old Francie Nolan; her young brother is called Neeley. The children's father is handsome and loveable, but he drinks too much and does not support the family. Francie's young mother works to keep three slum houses clean.

As this episode opens, Christmas is approaching. Notice how the storyteller helps you feel as if you are seeing everything through Francie's eyes.

Multiple Meanings. At the end of the story's first paragraph, the narrator describes Francie's street as *mean*. The definition of the adjective *mean* in this context is not "stingy" or "nasty" or "cruel," but "poor and shabby." Many English words can have more than one meaning. Usually, the context—the words and sentences surrounding a word—tells you which definition is intended. Sometimes, a word won't make sense to you in a certain context. That could indicate that the word has a meaning that is new to you. In such cases, it's best to check a dictionary to see whether the word has meanings you are not familiar with.

A

The spruce trees began coming into the neighborhood the week before Christmas. Their branches were corded to hold back the glory of their spreading and probably to make shipping easier. Vendors rented space on the curb before a store and stretched a rope from pole to pole and leaned the trees against it. All day they walked up and down this one-sided avenue of aromatic leaning trees, blowing on stiff ungloved fingers and looking with bleak hope at those people who paused. A few ordered a tree set aside for the day; others stopped to price, inspect, and conjecture.[1] But most came just to touch the boughs and surreptitiously[2] pinch a fingerful of spruce needles together to release the fragrance. And the air was cold and still, and full of the pine smell and the smell of tangerines which appeared in the stores only at Christmas time, and the mean street was truly wonderful for a little while.

B

There was a cruel custom in the neighborhood. It was about the trees still unsold when midnight of Christmas Eve approached. There was a saying that if you waited until then, you wouldn't have to buy a tree; that "they'd chuck[3] 'em at you." This was literally true.

At midnight the kids gathered where there were unsold trees. The man threw each tree in turn, starting with the biggest. Kids volunteered to stand up against the throwing. If a boy didn't fall down under the impact, the tree was his. If he fell, he forfeited his chance at winning a tree. Only the roughest boys and some of the young men elected to be hit by the big trees. The others waited shrewdly until a tree came up that they could stand against. The little kids waited for the tiny, foot-high trees and shrieked in delight when they won one.

On the Christmas Eve when Francie was ten and Neeley nine, mama consented to let them go down and have their first try for a tree. Francie had picked out her tree earlier in the day. She had stood near it all afternoon and evening praying that no one would buy it. To her joy, it was still there at midnight. It was the biggest tree in the neighborhood and its price was so high that no one could afford to buy it. It was ten feet high. Its branches were bound with new white rope and it came to a sure pure point at the top.

The man took this tree out first. Before Francie could speak up, a neighborhood bully, a boy of eighteen known as Punky Perkins, stepped forward and ordered the man to chuck the tree at him. The man hated the way Punky was so confident. He looked around and asked;

"Anybody else wanna take a chanct on it?"

Francie stepped forward. "Me, Mister."

A spurt of derisive[4] laughter came from the tree man. The kids snickered. A few adults who had gathered to watch the fun guffawed.

1. **conjecture** (kən·jek'chər): to think of various possibilities.
2. **surreptitiously** (sur'əp·tish'əs·lē): secretly.
3. **chuck:** here, throw.
4. **derisive** (di·rī'siv): ridiculing.

A. Multiple Meanings
To help students better understand the story, you might want them to do the vocabulary exercise on page 55.

B. Responding
? How does this description make you feel?

Critical Comment

Upon its publication, critic Orville Prescott wrote of *A Tree Grows in Brooklyn,* "[It] is a warm, sunny, engaging book as well as a grim one. . . ."

Read the quotation to the students. Ask them to explain what they think the critic meant by his comment and to tell whether or not they agree with it based on the excerpt they have read.

Reading Check Test

1. Francie does not like her neighborhood at Christmas. *(False)*
2. Francie and Neeley try to win a large Christmas tree. *(True)*
3. The tree seller is torn between letting Francie and Neeley compete for the tree and giving it to them. *(True)*
4. Francie and Neeley are knocked down by the Christmas tree. *(False)*
5. Punky Perkins tries to steal the tree from Francie. *(False)*

Closure

Working with a partner, students should define dialect. Have students discuss examples of dialect with which they are familiar from first-hand experience.

A. Vivid Imagery

? What image does Smith use to describe the scene? (She uses the image of a funnel.) Be sure you can visualize the scene.

B. Internal Conflict

Here is the description of the tree seller's internal struggle. (See question 5.)

C. Suspense and Climax

The climax of the story occurs here, when the tree seller throws the tree. Francie and Neeley will either succeed or fail at their goal, and it is here that our suspense is greatest.

? How does the incident make you feel? (It's pathetic and sad.)

D. Expansion

Note the points of ellipsis, which indicate that something has been left out. The omitted word is *bastards,* which would account for the subsequent comment about obscenity and profanity among the people of Francie's neighborhood.

"Aw g'wan. You're too little," the tree man objected.

"Me and my brother—we're not too little together."

She pulled Neeley forward. The man looked at them—a thin girl of ten with starveling hollows in her cheeks but with the chin still baby-round. He looked at the little boy with his fair hair and round blue eyes—Neeley Nolan, all innocence and trust.

"Two ain't fair," yelped Punky.

"Shut your lousy trap," advised the man who held all power in that hour. "These here kids is got nerve. Stand back, the rest of yous. These kids is goin' to have a show at this tree."

The others made a wavering lane. Francie and Neeley stood at one end of it and the big man with the big tree at the other. It was a human funnel with Francie and her brother making the small end of it. The man flexed his great arms to throw the great tree. He noticed how tiny the children looked at the end of the short lane. For the split part of a moment, the tree thrower went through a kind of Gethsemane.[5]

"Oh," his soul agonized, "why don't I just give 'em the tree, say Merry Christmas and let 'em go? What's the tree to me? I can't sell it no more this year and it won't keep till next year." The kids watched him solemnly as he stood there in his moment of thought. "But then," he rationalized, "if I did that, all the others would expect to get 'em handed to 'em. And next year nobody a-tall would buy a tree off of me. They'd all wait to get 'em handed to 'em on a silver plate. I ain't a big enough man to give this tree away for nothin'. No, I ain't big enough. I ain't big enough to do a thing like that. I gotta think of myself and my own kids." He finally came to his conclusion. "Them two kids is gotta live in this world. They *got* to get used to it. They got to learn to give and to take punishment. And it ain't give but *take, take, take* all the time in this world." As he threw the tree with all his strength, his heart wailed out, "It's a rotten, lousy world!"

Francie saw the tree leave his hands. There was a split bit of being when time and space had no meaning. The whole world stood still as something dark and monstrous came through the air. The tree came toward her blotting out all memory of her ever having lived. There was nothing—nothing but pungent darkness and something that grew and grew as it rushed at her. She staggered as the tree hit them. Neeley went to his knees but she pulled him up fiercely before he could go down. There was a mighty swishing sound as the tree settled. Everything was dark, green, and prickly. Then she felt a sharp pain at the side of her head where the trunk of the tree had hit her. She felt Neeley trembling.

When some of the older boys pulled the tree away, they found Francie and her brother standing upright, hand in hand. Blood was coming from scratches on Neeley's face. He looked more like a baby than ever with his bewildered blue eyes and the fairness of his skin made more noticeable because of the clear red blood. But they were smiling. Had they not won the biggest tree in the neighborhood? Some of the boys hollered "Horray!" A few adults clapped. The tree man eulogized[6] them by screaming.

"And now get out of here with your tree, you lousy. . . ."

Francie had heard swearing since she had heard words. Obscenity and profanity had no meaning as such among those people. They were emotional expressions of inarticulate people with small vocabularies; they made a kind of dialect. The phrases could mean many things according to the expression and tone used in saying them. So now, Francie smiled tremulously at the kind man. She knew that he was really saying, "Goodbye—God bless you."

5. **Gethsemane** (geth·sem'ə·nē): here, an occasion of mental anguish. The garden of Gethsemane was the scene of the final agony, betrayal, and arrest of Jesus Christ.

6. **eulogized** (yōō'lə·jīzd'): praised (used sarcastically).

ANALYZING THE STORY

Identifying Facts

1. The trees themselves are interesting, and since the air is cold and still, the smell of the spruce and tangerines is especially sharp and delightful.

2. People can volunteer to have trees thrown at them. If the person is still standing after being hit by the tree, he or she wins that tree. If the person is knocked down, he or she loses the chance at any tree. The biggest trees are thrown first; usually only the older kids volunteer for those. The younger kids wait for a tree they can handle.

3. Francie is very small and frail, and the tree is ten feet tall.

4. She is still standing when the big tree is pulled away from her.

Her nine-year-old brother, Neeley, helps her withstand the blow.

Interpreting Meanings

5. The man would like to give Francie the tree, since he can't sell it anymore and such a gesture would be a symbol of the Christmas spirit. However, he believes that if he does so, next year no one will buy any trees from him, waiting for him to give them all away.

The man finally decides that he has to teach Francie and Neeley how difficult the world is, and throws the tree at them.

6. The opposing force is the huge tree, thrown with all the force that the tree seller can muster.

7. In this neighborhood, people talk like the tree seller all the time. Because of the inflections in the man's voice, Francie can tell he is really being kind and admiring.

8. Examples are: "wanna take a chanct on it"; "Aw, g'wan"; "Shut your lousy trap"; "These here kids is got nerve"; "yous"; "goin' to have a show"; and others.

Applying Meanings

9. Students should recognize that the man is talking from his own bitter experience, and that he does believe this.

10. Answers will vary. The tree seller is probably poor, and needs the money to feed his own children. Students should recognize that he did not have any choice.

Responding to the Story

Analyzing the Story

Identifying Facts

1. This story takes place at Christmas in the Williamsburg section of Brooklyn early in the twentieth century. List three sights or smells that make the mean street "wonderful" at this time of year.
2. Describe the neighborhood custom of giving away unsold Christmas trees at midnight on Christmas Eve.
3. Why do the people standing around the tree lot laugh at Francie when she announces she wants to try for a tree?
4. How does Francie finally obtain a tree? Whose help does she have?

Interpreting Meanings

5. The Christmas tree seller experiences an **internal conflict,** or struggle within his heart and mind, in this story. Describe the opposing thoughts and feelings he struggles with after Francie says she wants to try for a tree. How does the tree seller resolve his conflict?
6. Francie undergoes an **external conflict**—a struggle with an outside force—when she decides to go for a tree. What is that opposing force?
7. The tree seller shouts harsh words at Francie and her brother as they leave the tree lot. Explain why Francie feels the words are really meant to be kind. Do you think she is right?
8. A **dialect** is the special way a language is spoken in a certain region. In this story, the Christmas tree seller uses special language associated with Brooklyn. List five special expressions he uses. SRW p. 31

Applying Meanings

9. The tree seller believes it is important that Francie and her brother learn to take punishment, because "it ain't give but *take, take, take* all the time in this world." Do you agree or disagree with his view of the world?
10. What did you think of the Christmas tree seller? Is he a bad character, or did he not have any choice? Explain.

Writing About the Story

A Creative Response

1. **Describing a Holiday.** The opening of the story tells how Christmas transforms Francie's neighborhood into a wonderful place. Write a paragraph describing what special sights, sounds, smells, and tastes change the neighborhood where you live, or someone you know lives, during your favorite holiday. Does the typical weather affect your feelings for the holiday?

A Critical Response

2. **Analyzing a Character.** A personality trait is a way a character—or a person in real life—thinks, feels, or behaves. There are many such traits. They include being aggressive, being shy, being kind, being quick, and being happy. The way a character deals with a conflict can reveal important personality traits. In a paragraph, describe three important character traits of Francie that are revealed during her struggle to get a Christmas tree. Name these three traits in your first sentence. Then, cite actions and speeches from the selection that reveal those traits.

See Teacher's Manual page 13.

Analyzing Language and Vocabulary

Multiple Meanings

Many English words have more than one meaning. Sometimes all of a word's meanings are similar, and sometimes they are quite different. Explain how the meaning of the italicized word differs in each pair of sentences below. (Many of the sentences are taken from "A Christmas Wish.") Use the **context**—the meaning of the other words in the sentence—to help you. Then look up the italicized word in a dictionary. Can the word have additional meanings? If so, write down at least one of them.

1. **a.** "He looked at the little boy with his *fair* hair and round blue eyes . . ."
   b. " 'Two ain't *fair,*' yelped Punky."
2. **a.** " 'You're too little,' the tree man *objected.*"
   b. A glass Christmas ornament is a fragile *object.*

Additional Speaking Assignment
Working with three other classmates, ask students to tell what they think is the most important word, phrase, passage, or paragraph in the story. Have them explain why it is important.

A. Responding to Focusing on Background
Divide the class into groups of four or five students each. Ask them to discuss how Betty Smith might have felt when the cab driver reminded her that, even though she expressed herself well, she was, after all, only a passenger in his cab. Have them explore how the conversation between Smith and the driver might have continued. Call on one volunteer from each group to summarize the group's discussion for the others.

3. a. "For the split part of a moment, the tree thrower went through a *kind* of Gethsemane."
   b. ". . . Francie smiled tremulously at the *kind* man."
4. a. "There was a mighty swishing sound as the tree *settled.*"
   b. The teacher *settled* the argument between the two girls.
5. a. "The whole world stood still as something dark and monstrous came through the *air.*"
   b. The tree man disliked Punky's confident *air.*

For answers, see Teacher's Manual page 13.

Reading About the Writer

Betty Smith (1904–   ) said about her native Brooklyn, ". . . I am dedicated to publicizing Brooklyn and no other place." After quitting school at the age of fourteen, she worked in odd jobs in New York City. When she was twenty-three, she went to the University of Michigan to finish her education. While she was in Michigan, she wrote for a Detroit newspaper, and she began to have many of her one-act plays published. Her big triumph, however, came in 1943 with her novel *A Tree Grows in Brooklyn,* which she invested with warm, lively recollections of her childhood in Brooklyn. The book found an immediate, enthusiastic audience, selling over four million copies. It was translated into sixteen languages, and popular adaptations were made for both the musical comedy stage and the screen. In an article in which she humorously compares Brooklyn to Manhattan, Betty Smith says, "Most Brooklynites were born in their city, as were there parents and their grandparents. Their roots are deep. . . ."

A

Focusing on Background

A Writer's Fame

As a result of the popularity of *A Tree Grows in Brooklyn,* Betty Smith wrote an article called "Immortal Mortal," in which she describes what it's like to be famous:

"Shortly after my book with attendant publicity came out, I began to feel queer. Riding in the subways I had an idea that all the people were staring at me curiously. Oddly enough, they were staring at me. Yes, they were staring at me because I was staring at them so hard to see if they were staring at me. . . .

"I bought a purse in a Fifth Avenue shop. The salesgirl examined my signature on the check. 'You have the same name,' she decided, 'as the woman who wrote that book.' She sighed. 'What a pity that you have the name and not the fame!' She smiled. I sighed. . . .

"I'll not forget the thrill I had when, for the first time, I actually saw a stranger reading my book in public. It was in a Childs restaurant and the book was propped up on the sugar bowl before her.

" 'Pardon me,' said the author, 'do you like that book?'

" 'I love it,' she replied. I beamed.

" 'I wrote it,' I told her without modesty, 'and I'd like to autograph it for you.' I reached out for the book but she grabbed it and held it to her chest.

" 'Oh, no!' She looked frightened. 'You see, I got it from the library and I have to pay a fine if it's marked up.'

"Well, after that, though I saw many people reading the book in public places, I never again volunteered to autograph a copy.

"I've taken to using taxicabs lately and I discovered a whole new genus of man—the New York hackie. One lowering [overcast] day, I got into a cab. The sociable driver led off with a philosophical discussion on weather vagaries. I made answer in a like vein.

" 'When I was a little girl living in Brooklyn,' I reminisced, 'people used to watch anxiously for snow. My father would say, "Tomorrow it will snow and there will be some work for poor people." . . .'

" 'You ought to read *A Tree Grows in Brooklyn,*' he said. 'There's stuff in there like what you just said. Only it's much better. It stands to reason. The girl who wrote it is a writer and—now I don't mean nothing out of the way—but you're just a passenger.' "

—Betty Smith

PREREADING

1. **BUILDING ON PRIOR KNOWLEDGE.** Before they begin reading, have students discuss the importance of having friends. Ask them to describe the things they enjoy doing with their friends and how they and their friends help each other. Have students speculate on the kind of life a friendless person might lead and on the kinds of things such a person might do to fill the void. Ask students to suggest ways in which lonely people can make friends.

2. **ESTABLISHING A PURPOSE.** Before students begin reading, you might have them read question 9 on page 64. This will help establish a purpose for their reading.

3. **PREREADING JOURNAL.** Before they read, have students write two or three sentences explaining why some people have a hard time making new friends.

★ **Texas Essential Elements/(a) English Language Arts: 1B** Purpose and audience; **3A** Plot/character; **3B** Figurative language; **4F** Generalizations

THE LOST BEACH

Louise Hardeman

Liza and her mother have just moved to a new place. Liza has a puzzling personality, and it is not always easy to understand why she does things. Pause on page 58 after Liza says, "Captain LaBay! Hello!" Write down three adjectives that best describe how Liza behaves. Then, when you finish the story, look at the list and decide whether you still agree with your choices of adjectives. Would you make any substitutions?

For a detailed lesson plan on this story, see Teacher's Manual pages 14–16.
A biography of Louise Hardeman appears on text page 64.

The rays of the sun fell down on the brown water and on the island that clung to the mainland with a long, steel arm. On the side of the island away from the mainland, you could see smaller islands beyond, and after them the sea.

The pot plants that sat on the LaBays' front porch and the vines that twined around its banisters were bent and heavy with dust. They shook a little when the door banged and a small girl ran onto the porch, holding a large, white towel around her head. She went over the banister and with a quick, impatient movement, pulled the towel away. A mass of wet, red hair fell down about her shoulders. She bent backward and jerked suddenly forward again, so that all the red hair hung over the banister. Glancing around to see if anyone were watching, she let her arms hang limp, and began to make hoarse, gagging sounds from her throat.

Similes. Liza has a vivid imagination. She enjoys making up similes, which are comparisons that generally use *like* or *as*. They show how two different things are alike in some way. For instance, Liza says that if she and Captain LaBay fell out of a ship and couldn't swim, they would sink like feathers. She is comparing people and feathers, two very different things. As you read the story, notice the similes that Liza and other characters make up.

Old Mrs. LaBay came to the front door.

"Liza, are you sick?" she asked.

"No. Come and see my hair."

"Well what on earth do you want to make those noises for? You sure you not sick?"

There was a long silence. Mrs. LaBay put down her bowl of half-shelled peas and walked out on the porch.

"Liza?" She tapped the child on her shoulder.

"Look, Mrs. LaBay. Look at my hair."

Mrs. LaBay looked at the thick strands of hair that in one place were dark and wet and in another were bright with the sun. **A**

"It's pretty. It's mighty pretty."

"What does it look like?" the child asked.

Mrs. LaBay searched the sky and the river and her own yard and house.

"It looks like . . . like a pretty red pot plant that has just grown all out of itself."

"And I'm the flowerpot," said Liza, patting herself with both hands.

Mrs. LaBay contorted her face appreciatively and went back into the house.

An upstairs window creaked open and a voice called down, "Liza?"

"Yes, ma'am?"

"When your hair's dry, you come right on back up here and I'll plait it for you."

"Let me wear it down," Liza whined.

"No." The window was closed.

Alone again Liza stood up and felt her hair. It was still damp. She leaned back and cut her eyes around sharply to see it swing near the floor. One

A. Characters' Words

? What does this exchange suggest about the relationship between Mrs. LaBay and Liza? (Mrs. LaBay is concerned for Liza's welfare, and is fond of her. She is willing to play along with Liza's imagination, although the word "contorted " suggests that sometimes it is an effort to do so. From this conversation, you can also tell that Liza likes Mrs. LaBay, likes to play word games with her, and looks up to her.)

SUPPLEMENTARY SUPPORT MATERIAL

1. Vocabulary Activity Sheet
2. Reading Check Test blackline master
3. Selection Test (page 13 of Test Book)
4. Reader's Response Journal
5. Workbook (page 21)

DEVELOPING VOCABULARY

The following words appear on a test in the Test Book, page 14. (See also the Vocabulary Activity Sheet.)

twines	squirm
contorted	huddled
plait	scornfully
amorousness	rigid
scrutinize	horizon

A. Clarification
Later we find that Henrietta is an imaginary pet chicken. See page 60.

B. Active Reading
Tell students to write down any questions they have up to this point. Encourage them to predict answers. Remind students to be alert to information that will enable them to confirm or revise their predictions.

★ **Texas Essential Elements/(c) Reading: 1C** Dictionaries; **3A** Main ideas/details; **3D** Generalizations; **3I** Draw conclusions

of the curved posts that supported the porch roof caught her eye. She looked at it closely, then shook her head from side to side in mock amorousness.

"I love you," she said. "Oh, darling, darling, darling."

She scratched her stomach with all ten fingers and burped. Down near the beach a rowboat was pulling into shore. Liza crowed and pointed a finger at the boat.

A "Look, Henrietta, there's Captain LaBay. Wouldn't you like to see him?" It was more of a confirmation than a question.

Holding her arms in front of her as though she were carrying an object the size of a beach ball, she ran down the steps and across the gravel road and met the boat as it thumped against the sand.

"Captain LaBay! Hello!"

A bearded old man in a shabby uniform stepped out of the boat.

"Hello, Liza. Hello, Henrietta. How're you both?"

Liza grinned at him.

"We're good," she said. "Look at my hair."

The old man pulled his boat well up on the beach and turned back to the child. He took her face in his hand and scrutinized her from different angles.

"Um huh!" He held up long strands of hair. "Liza," he began, "Liza, I have never seen anything to equal the sight of your hair. It is the most beautiful . . ."

"It's long," she interrupted.

"The longest I ever saw," he agreed.

"I'm a flower pot."

"A little, round flower pot," said the Captain.

Liza stuck out her bottom lip and looked down at her short, fat body.

"Round?" she asked.

"Well, not really round," he mused, "sort of round*ed*, nicely rounded."

"Oh," she said. "I wish we could go for a ride."

She spoke shyly, twisting her hair around her finger, and adding, "And then we could ride by the pier and take the twins to ride maybe."

B The Captain frowned out at the sea and patted Liza on the head.

Ebb Tide at Pyla by Albert Marquet (1935). Oil.

Virginia Museum of Fine Arts, Richmond.
Collection of Mr. and Mrs. Paul Mellon.

Humanities Connection: Discussing the Fine Art

Like Kees Van Dongen, whose work appeared in the selection "Princess," French painter Albert Marquet (1875–1947) was a member of the Fauve movement. ? Describe the overall feeling this painting conveys. What aspects of the painting convey this feeling? What do you think the people in the painting are doing on the beach? Having read up to this point, do you think this painting goes with the story? Why or why not?

A. Clarification
Here we learn who Henrietta is. See question 3.

B. Foreshadowing and Suspense
? What does this passage suggest might happen? Cite details to support your answer. Explain the suspense this passage creates. (This passage suggests that Liza might meet the girls and that a conflict might develop between them. Liza's refusal to ask the girls to come for a ride, her change from a laughing voice to a low one as she refuses, the Captain's frown at Liza's refusal, and the silence that ensues are hints that the issue of meeting the girls is an important one, one that will come up again later in the story. Also, the line about the water beginning to get rough foreshadows an incident, a conflict, that will make Liza's life begin to get rough.)

C. Responding
? Look back at the second paragraph of the story. Did you guess what Liza was pretending?

"Haven't you met those little girls yet?" he asked quietly.

Liza twisted away and leaned over the boat.

"I can row."

"I guess we can take a little ride." He held up his large pocket watch. . . . "Mrs. LaBay won't mind and I guess your mama won't either. Well, get in now and let's go."

The Captain yanked his hat down and grunted as he pushed the boat off with one of the oars. When they were well away from the shore, he picked up both oars and the boat moved smoothly over the water. Liza hid her face in her hands.

"You sat on Henrietta!"

The Captain held the oars in mid-air. The boat rocked gently for a while; then the Captain leaned over to one side and reached gingerly underneath himself. He saw laughter behind the hands.

A "She wasn't there, Captain LaBay," Liza said consolingly. "I was just teasing."

She grinned at him, and he smiled back at her pleasure.

"Has Henrietta laid an egg yet?"

"Not a one."

"Well, when she does, you'll tell me about it?"

"I'll give it to you," said Liza and laughed again.

Now they were well away from the island and heading toward a white pier that extended a long way over the water. Liza turned and held her hand to her eyes as a sun shade. She tried to see into the screened pavilion[1] at the end of the walkway.

"Wouldn't you like to ask the girls to come for a ride?" asked the Captain.

"I can't see if they are there."

They rowed in closer to the pavilion. Sounds of talk and laughter could be heard, and then two young girls could be seen, sprawled on the floor. Liza looked up at the Captain and ran her hand through the water.

B "I don't want to," she said in a low voice.

The old man raised his eyebrows and frowned for a minute, then rowed on beyond the pier. They rowed in silence for all the time that it took to get out to the little islands. The water began to get rough.

1. **pavilion** (pə·vil′yən): shelter for resting in the shade.

"And there's the sea," said the Captain.

C "Do you get seasick?"

"You mean did I get seasick?" he informed her with a scowl. She nodded.

"I never got seasick a day in my life, not one out of ten thousand."

"I got seasick."

The Captain was watching the waves.

"I said I got seasick."

"Uh? Oh yes. Is that so? And when was that?"

"Today I was playing like I was aboard a ship and the waves came so high and I was sick over the side."

"And you might be sick over the side now. Look at those waves out there."

She held up her hand to measure them and wrinkled her square nose at him.

"Oh, they're high, all right. They just aren't close to us."

Liza studied the waves.

"If they knocked us over would we sink?"

"No, we'd swim."

"But if we didn't swim, would we sink?"

"I guess we would." The Captain looked thoughtful.

"And would we go down to the bottom of the ocean?"

"I guess we would."

Liza leaned toward the Captain and fixed her eyes on his face.

"Like what? Sink like what?"

"Well now, let me see," said the Captain. "We'd go down like stones."

Liza examined her hands.

"We'd go down like . . . feathers."

Liza scratched her nose.

"We'd go down like . . . like bells."

She smiled up at him and drew her arm through the water like a swinging bell. And he drew out his handkerchief and pretended to mop his brow.

They started rowing back toward the island, and Liza threw her head back and sang one of the ballads she had learned in the second grade.

Oh the days of the Kerry dancing,
Oh the ring of the piper's tune,
Oh for one of those hours of gladness,
Gone, alas, from my life too soon.

She sang in a deep, hoarse voice.

When they came near the island, the Captain stopped rowing and bent over to Liza.

"Don't you think we could take the twins to ride now?"

Liza squirmed around on the seat. "I don't believe they can go. They probably have something else to do."

"We could ask, though. You said you wanted to take them to ride."

Liza began pulling the tangles out of her hair. The Captain watched for a few minutes, then he leaned down until his face was close to hers.

"Liza, look here at me."

She offered him the corners of her eyes.

"Now Liza, you haven't lived here very long and I've been living on this island the good part of my life. And I know that the people here are sometimes slow to take newcomers in. Those Jarvis twins have lived here all their lives and they know everybody on the island. Just because they haven't played with you as much as some of the
A other children doesn't mean they don't like you. They think now they're up in grammar school, they're grown up. When you get to be a little bit older, too, it'll make all the difference in the world. It just takes a while."

Her mouth curved down at the sides like a small, curled seashell.

"They haven't played with me at all."

The Captain cleared his throat with a burst of sound and clamped down on his bottom lip with his teeth.

"Everybody wants to be liked, Liza. It's easier for some than for others."

He picked up the oars again. "Shall we ask them to take a ride?"

"All right," she said and started arranging her hair around her shoulders.

When they came up to the pavilion, the girls stopped talking and peered over the side. Liza was very small in the boat. The Captain waved a hand.

"Hello, there. Come and have a ride with us."

The twins looked at each other.

"We can't," they said. "Mother is punishing us."

"Well, that's too bad," called the Captain. He sat back down in the boat. The twins bent toward each other and whispered.

"Let her come up here."

The Captain looked at Liza closely before he answered. "You mean Liza?" he called up to the twins. "Liza, would you like to go up on the pavilion for a while?"

"All right."

The Captain took her hand and held it while she wobbled over to the ladder. "Have a good time."

She gave him a wide smile and began to climb up to the pavilion.

The twins opened the door for her and she walked over to the board that ran around the inside of it and sat down. Nobody said anything.

"Has the Captain gone?" one of the twins asked her.

She looked out toward the LaBay house but she didn't see the rowboat.

"I guess, so," she said. "What were you playing?"

"We weren't playing; we were talking."

"Oh," said Liza.

The twins were huddled together, and starting at Liza's feet they stared all the way up to her B
head and then all the way down again.

"Who do you play with?" they asked.

"Henrietta," she said, laughing and warming toward them.

The twins shrugged their shoulders at each other.

"Who?"

"Henrietta. She's a chicken."

"A chicken!" The twins cried scornfully.

Liza laughed with deep, catching noises. C

"You can't see her. She's a play chicken."

"How silly," said a twin.

Liza looked startled, but she said nothing.

"Why do you and your mother live at the LaBays' house?" asked one of the twins.

"It's nice."

The twin held her nose tightly between her fingers.

"It is not nice. It's old and ugly. And you live there 'cause it's cheap. And they're poor, too."

"And so are you," added the other twin, her eyes bulging with excitement as she watched Liza.

She looked back toward the house, but still she

A. Making Connections
From the Captain's words, how do you think the twins have treated Liza in the past? (It's obvious that Liza has complained to Captain LaBay about the twins treating her badly or ignoring her.) If Liza and the twins do meet, how do you predict the twins will act toward Liza?

B. Character's Feelings
? How do you think this scrutiny makes Liza feel? (Uncomfortable, odd, hurt)

C. Character's Motivation
? Why do you think Liza has an invisible play chicken? (Liza does not have friends her own age and needs a playmate who is always available to her. Liza's chicken helps her to not feel lonely.)

Two Critical Comments
Jessie Rehder, a teacher of writing, said: " In 'The Lost Beach' the world loses its early morning look when a child comes in contact with the cruelty of other children. We see Liza in the one definitive hour when she realizes that she is not going to be accepted. This is a story in which the character herself carries the idea or theme without thrusting it at the reader."

Educator, author, and scholar John Warriner has noted that "great stories are worth reading because they contain important ideas about life and about people."

Share the quotations with students and have them tell whether or not they agree with them. Then have them discuss how the second quotation pertains to "The Lost Beach."

A. Expanding
You may wish to discuss with students the attraction children have for "dirty" words. Have them elaborate on the attraction people in general have for those things that they should not do or should not have.

B. Responding
? How is this a defeat for Liza? (Notice that a child who has delighted in making up bright similes is forced to use "dirty" words to escape from a bad situation. This climactic moment is a humiliation for Liza.)

C. Character
? How would you characterize the twins? (Cruel, snobbish) Why do you think the twins treat Liza this way? Do you know any children like the twins?

did not see the Captain's boat. She rose and started for the screen door that led to the walkway.

"I have to go," she said.

"No, wait," said a twin, standing in front of her. "Can you swim?"

"No," said Liza quizzically.

"She can't swim," the twin told her sister.

"Oh well," she said, making a face.

Liza looked up at them and hesitated a moment before she spoke.

"But if I sank do you know what it would be like?" she asked.

They waited. She put her hands out, palms up, and leaned her head on her shoulder.

"Like a bell," she said simply.

The twins stood rigid and glass-eyed and then they bent away from each other laughing.

"A bell! A bell! Whoever heard of such a ridiculous thing! A bell!"

Liza darted around the twins and headed for the door, but before she got there, one of them pushed her back and then both of them ran out and locked the door. She put her hands on the screen and stared at them wide-eyed.

"We aren't gonna letcha out," they said. "We're gonna leave you there all night and terrible things will happen to you."

Liza pressed her face against the screen.

"You and your ole ugly clothes and your ole ugly hair. Don't your mama ever comb your hair? And it smells bad too, just like that old house of the LaBays', smells just like fish, and our daddy says . . ."

"Look," said her sister. "Look at the old cry-baby."

"I want to go home," Liza said in a choking voice.

"I wanna go home," the twins mimicked. "What will you give us if we let you go?"

Liza clung to the door handle. Her face was screwed into a confused knot. She waited a long time to answer.

"I'll give you my doll."

"Pooh, who wants a doll!"

"What do you want?" she implored.

"No," they said, "you have to name something and we'll tell you if it's all right."

Liza rubbed her hair against her cheek and wrinkled her forehead in distress. Finally she looked up at the girls with a grave face and in a low, unsteady voice she said, "I'll tell you all the dirty words I know."

The twins' eyes were shining and they moved back and unlocked the door. A

"All right," they warned.

Liza ran onto the walkway. She began to cry then, putting her hands over her ears, and shouting out all the childish words heard in the girls' bathroom at school, and all the words carved furtively on the desks—all the words that had no meaning and couldn't be asked about without a reprimand. She flung away from the twins and ran up the walkway toward the road. B, C

Underneath the pier the captain waited until the twins were talking and laughing again before he started rowing home.

And Liza ran all the way to the house. Mrs. LaBay was waiting on the porch for her with a brush and comb in her hand.

"Liza!" she chided, "where on earth have you been, child? Your mama's gone downtown and she asked me to tell you not to run off like that and to plait your hair for you."

She looked down into the small, unhappy face.

"You been crying?" she asked kindly.

The tears rose up and spilled over again.

"There now, that's all right. You just sit right down here on the floor and we'll have your hair all plaited by the time your mama gets back."

Liza sat down and leaned on Mrs. LaBay's legs. The brush pulled her head back in short jerks.

When they started on the second plait, Captain LaBay came up through the yard. The stairs creaked as he came up on the porch and sat in the rocking chair next to his wife and the child.

"That's done!" said Mrs. LaBay, snapping a rubber band onto the plait. "Would you two like a peach cobbler and a glass of milk?"

"I think we would," said the Captain, and rubbed his hands briskly.

The door clicked shut behind Mrs. LaBay. The Captain leaned over and spoke to Liza.

"Do you know what I wish you would do?"

"What?" she asked in a flat voice.

Reading Check Test

1. The LaBays are Liza's parents. (*False*)
2. Liza has an imaginary play chicken called Henrietta. (*True*)
3. The Captain takes Liza for a ride in his airplane. (*False*)
4. Liza refuses to meet the twins. (*False*)
5. The twins are unkind to Liza. (*True*)

Closure

Working in pairs, students should describe the conflict in this story and tell how it ends. Have them discuss stories they have read or have seen on TV in which the conflict was never resolved.

Still Life with Figure by Walter Williams. Oil and collage.

Courtesy Terry Dintenfass Gallery, New York.

"I wish you'd come up here and sit on my lap."

She rose and climbed obediently onto his lap.

"Woops!" he cried, "you sat on Henrietta!"

She looked around at him with a sober face.

"I was just teasing," he said softly.

They rocked back and forth in the big chair for a time. Now and then the Captain drew in a deep breath and let it out slowly, so that Liza rose and fell like a piece of bright seaweed on a wave.

Mrs. LaBay returned with a tray and put it down in front of them on a low table. The three of them ate cobblers and drank milk in silence. When they had finished, Mrs. LaBay poured them more milk and took the empty dishes back into the house.

The Captain wiped his mouth and hands with his handkerchief and looked at the horizon.

"Liza," he said, "look at that sky!" He slapped her on the hip. She looked up.

"It's blue and silver," the Captain said and waited for the question. It didn't come.

"Like what?" he asked himself aloud. "Blue . . . and silver," he struggled with the words, "blue and silver like . . . the beach in the early morning."

The Captain smiled to himself.

"Like a beach I used to play on when I was a boy."

He looked down at the small head with its carefully plaited hair and placed his hand on top of it.

"Like a lost beach," he said thoughtfully, sadly.

Liza held her glass of milk out in front of them and saw the shadowy reflection of a little girl with a large hand on top of her head. Then something like a smile began at the corners of her mouth and ran upward as she took the last big swallow of milk and looked over the rim of the glass out to sea.

A. Humanities Connection: Responding to the Fine Art

Walter Williams was born in 1920 in New York and now lives in Denmark. Many of his paintings have a mysterious quality to them.

? Describe the little girl in the painting. Could the girl in the painting be Liza? What do you suppose the girl is thinking about? Can you think of a more descriptive title for the painting? (Is there an appropriate line from the story?) Does this painting seem mysterious to you?

B. Theme

? What loss of innocence has Liza experienced—her "lost beach"? (Because of the twins' cruelty, Liza has lost her delight in using her imagination—Henrietta no longer exists for her, and Captain LaBay's talk about the sky goes unheeded. Instead of innocent imaginings, she is forced to shout ugly obscenities. We do get the feeling, however, that her smile at the very end of the story suggests that this loss may not be permanent.)

ANALYZING THE STORY

Identifying Facts

1. Liza and her mother have just moved to an island, and live in the shorefront home of Captain and Mrs. LaBay.

2. She is pretending that she is aboard a ship, with waves so high that she has become seasick.

3. Liza pretends that a post on the porch is someone she loves, and that she has an invisible chicken named Henrietta.

4. Liza tries to be friendly and to start a conversation, but the twins respond unkindly—staring at her rudely and making fun of Henrietta, Liza's home, the LaBays, Liza's similes, and her appearance.

5. Mrs. LaBay brushes her hair and serves her peach cobbler and milk. Captain LaBay comforts her by rocking her on his lap, joking with her, suggesting similes, and telling her about the lost beach.

Interpreting Meanings

6. Liza very much wants to meet the twins, but she is shy and afraid.

Captain LaBay gently encourages her to go over to them, and finally convinces *(Answers continue in left-hand column.)*

(Continued from top.)

her that she shouldn't be afraid. Liza agrees to approach the twins.

7. Though Liza is nervous, she makes a real effort to be friends with the twins. They reject her, and make fun of her.

Answers will vary, depending on students' interpretation of Liza's smile in the last scene. Some may say that the conflict is not resolved, and that Liza will have to deal with the twins at a later time. Others may say that Liza realizes that she doesn't need to play with the twins, and so the conflict with the twins is over for her.

8. Literally, the Captain is referring to a beach he played on as a child; the beach represents any loss or disappointment.

Answers will vary. Liza may be smiling because she is already using her imagination to visit that lost beach.

Applying Meanings

9. See Teacher's Manual page 15.

Responding to the Story

Analyzing the Story

Identifying Facts

1. Where has Liza just moved? With whom do Liza and her mother live?
2. Liza plays pretend games. When you first meet her, she is making gagging noises over the porch rail. It is only later, when she is in the boat with the Captain, that it is clear what she was pretending. Explain what she was pretending on the porch.
3. Describe two other pretend games Liza plays.
4. Liza joins the Jarvis twins in the pavilion. Describe how she gets along with the twins. What must Liza do before the twins let her leave the pavilion?
5. Liza is tearful when she returns to the house. List three things Captain and Mrs. LaBay do to cheer her.

Interpreting Meanings

6. A **conflict** is a struggle between opposing forces. An **internal conflict** occurs in the mind of a character. The character is not sure what to do, and is tugged one way and another. Early in "The Lost Beach," Liza has an inner conflict about whether or not to meet the Jarvis twins. Describe the opposing forces in Liza's mind. How is the conflict resolved?
7. After Liza meets the twins, an **external conflict** erupts. Describe the conflict between Liza and the twins. Is the conflict over by the end of the story?
8. Near the end of the story, the Captain speaks about a "lost beach." Explain what you think he means by this. Why do you think Liza sort of smiles after she hears the Captain speak of the lost beach?

Applying Meanings

9. The Captain says, "Everybody wants to be liked, Liza. It's easier for some than for others." Explain how the Captain's words apply to Liza and to people in real life as well. Do you know people who are more easily liked than others? Why do you think this is so? Is being liked important or unimportant for a person to be happy?

Writing About the Story

A Creative Response

1. **Describing an Experience.** It's not unusual for a family to move from one town to another. Family members must then make new friends. In a paragraph, tell how you, someone you know, or someone you have read about went about making new friends after moving to a new town.

A Critical Response

2. **Analyzing a Relationship.** Although Liza and Captain LaBay are years apart in age, they have established a close friendship. Write a paragraph explaining why you think this friendship works.

See Teacher's Manual page 16.

Analyzing Language and Vocabulary

Similes

SRW p. 81

Liza and the Captain enjoy making up **similes,** or comparisons using words such as *like* or *as*. Similes are used to show that two different things are alike in some way. Similes can be fun to make up. Complete each of the following comparisons to make a simile. Stretch your imagination to create similes you've never heard before.

1. Her complexion was like ______.
2. The hot sand felt like ______ under my feet.
3. The rain sounded like ______ on the tin roof.
4. Her eyes were as bright as ______.
5. The lake was as smooth as ______.
6. The clouds were as fluffy as ______.

Reading About the Writer

Louise Hardeman (1931–) grew up in Louisville, Georgia. She graduated from the University of North Carolina, and since then has held several jobs, including that of an English teacher. She is a member of a poetry workshop, has published several short stories and poems, and is presently writing a novel. About "The Lost Beach," she says that it "began with a simile that was spontaneous and alone until it spun itself a home, a story: 'The sky is blue and silver like the lost beaches of childhood.' "

★ Texas Essential Elements/(a) English Language Arts: 1B Purpose and audience; 3B Figurative language; 4B Main idea; 4E Predict. (c) Reading: 1A Context clues; 3D Generalizations; 3H Predict

Review: Exercises in Reading Fiction

SRW p. 25

CONFLICT

Conflict is important in all literature, whether it's fictional or about actual people. Conflict can be **internal** or **external.** In most stories, the conflict is resolved at the end of the action. In some stories, however, the conflict goes on unresolved forever.
A Read the following excerpt from a short story by Jack London. He has set his story in the Yukon, a vast cold area of Canada that is largely uninhabited. The man in this story—who is never named—has just been abandoned by Bill, his fellow prospector. The man has injured his ankle and can't keep up with the heartless Bill. See if you can identify each conflict as it is introduced in the passage.

Then he turned his gaze and slowly took in the circle of the world that remained to him now that Bill was gone.

Near the horizon the sun was smoldering dimly, almost obscured by formless mists and vapors, which gave an impression of mass and density without outline or tangibility. The man pulled out his watch, the while resting his weight on one leg. It was four o'clock, and as the season was near the last of July or first of August—he did not know the precise date within a week or two—he knew that the sun roughly marked the northwest. He looked to the south and knew that somewhere beyond those bleak hills lay the Great Bear Lake; also, he knew that in that direction the Arctic Circle cut its forbidding way across the

B

A. Expansion
American short-story writer and novelist Jack London (1876–1916) was born in San Francisco. As a boy, London overcame his lack of formal education by reading avidly in the public library. After several years as an adventurer, London left for the Klondike in the Yukon Territory to search for gold. There, he found himself (but no gold), and he soon began writing fiction based on his adventures. At one time London was America's highest paid and most popular writer. Among his famous novels are the critically acclaimed *The Call of the Wild* and *White Fang.* His most famous short story is "To Build a Fire."

B. Responding to the Photograph
? Do you think this photograph is appropriate to illustrate a story whose setting is in the Yukon Territory of Canada? Why or why not?

Answers to Questions

1. The main idea is that the man, left alone, has to struggle across a barren land to save himself.
2. The external conflict involves the man having to travel many miles alone on an injured ankle, through a barren land.
3. These words include *bleak hills, forbidding way, Barrens, tremendous and terrible desolation, vastness, overwhelming force, brutally crushing, complacent awfulness, empty of life.*
4. The man must struggle with his fear of death in the desolate country in order to keep traveling.
5. The last two paragraphs contain details about his internal conflict.
6. The man will go through terrible hardships, but will survive because of his great love of life.
7. Student answers will vary.

Review: Exercises in Reading Fiction/*cont.*

Canadian Barrens. This stream in which he stood was a feeder to the Coppermine River, which in turn flowed north and emptied into Coronation Gulf and the Arctic Ocean. He had never been there, but he had seen it, once, on a Hudson Bay Company chart.

Again his gaze completed the circle of the world about him. It was not a heartening spectacle. Everywhere was soft skyline. The hills were low-lying. There were no trees, no shrubs, no grasses—naught but a tremendous and terrible desolation that sent fear swiftly dawning into his eyes.

"Bill!" he whispered, once and twice; "Bill!"

He cowered in the midst of the milky water, as though the vastness were pressing in upon him with overwhelming force, brutally crushing him with its complacent awfulness. He began to shake as with an ague-fit,[1] till the gun fell from his hand with a splash. This served to rouse him. He fought with his fear and pulled himself together, groping in the water and recovering the weapon. He hitched his pack farther over on his left shoulder, so as to take a portion of its weight from off the injured ankle. Then he proceeded, slowly and carefully, wincing with pain, to the bank.

He did not stop. With a desperation that was madness, unmindful of the pain, he hurried up the slope to the crest of the hill over which his comrade had disappeared—more grotesque and comical by far than that limping, jerking comrade. But at the crest he saw a shallow valley, empty of life. He fought with his fear again, overcame it, hitched the pack still farther over on his left shoulder, and lurched on down the slope.

—from "Love of Life,"
Jack London

1. How would you summarize the **main idea** of this extract?
2. Two conflicts are described in this passage. What is the man's **external conflict**—what specific obstacles is he struggling against?
3. What descriptive words make this man's "enemy" seem very powerful?
4. What is the man's **internal conflict**?
5. Which two passages describe his internal conflict?
6. Considering the story's title, what do you predict is going to happen to this man?
7. Are there any words or phrases in this passage that you did not know? Can you make educated guesses about their meaning?

Writing

1. **Describing an External Force.** Write a paragraph in which you describe a force that might oppose someone in a conflict. Here are some categories of things that often cause conflict, in stories and in real life:

water	animals
air	vegetables
fire	minerals
earth	humans

2. **Describing an Internal Problem.** In a paragraph, describe what is going through the mind of a person as he or she experiences one of these feelings:

shyness	anger
fear	love
dread	jealousy

For evaluation strategies, see Teacher's Manual page 17.

1. **ague (ā'gyo͞o)-fit:** shivering caused by high fever.

★ **Texas Essential Elements/(a) English Language Arts: 1A** Composing process; **1B** Purpose and audience; **1D** Direct quotations; **1E** Formal/informal language; **1H** Proofread; **4I** Follow directions; **2B** Parts of speech

Exercises in Critical Thinking and Writing

For teaching and evaluation strategies, see Teacher's Manual page 17.

A. Conflict
As you go over these different types of conflicts with students, ask them to give an example of each conflict from the stories they've read in this unit.

ORGANIZING INFORMATION

Writing Assignment

Write a dialogue, or a conversation, in which two imaginary characters discuss and resolve (end) a conflict.

Background

In this unit, you have seen characters engaged in the following kinds of conflict:

External Conflicts

1. A person (or animal) vs. another person (or animal)
2. A person vs. a force of nature
3. A person vs. two or more persons, a group, or a whole society

A

Internal Conflicts

4. A person vs. some personal problem (The person struggles to overcome some internal problem, like fear or shyness.)

Prewriting

1. Bring to class two magazine or newspaper photographs (mounted on paper or cardboard) showing close-ups of two different people. Each student should then choose two photographs from the class's "photograph pool."
2. Study your two photographs carefully. Try to interpret what the pictures "say": What is each character like? What can you imagine their relationship would be? Are they friends, relatives, neighbors, enemies, blind dates?
3. Identify a possible conflict the two characters could have. For example, two friends might disagree about something one of them said, or two neighbors might argue about loud music.
4. Once you have identified the source of the conflict, think of two possible outcomes or resolutions. (One should be a happy ending.)
5. Gather your information together in a chart like the following:

Who are my two characters?	
What is their relationship?	
What is the conflict about?	
What are *two* possible outcomes of the conflict? Outcome #1	
Outcome #2	

Writing

Now, write your conversation, or **dialogue** (the actual words the characters say to each other) for one of the outcomes listed in your Prewriting chart. Include details that will tell your reader what your characters do and what they think and feel. To avoid using *said* repeatedly, use verbs like these:

laughed	announced	shouted
murmured	groaned	barked
answered	asked	mumbled
repeated	muttered	whispered

A. Responding

? Is this dialogue realistic to you? What elements make it real? Do you know anybody like Jim? Like Mrs. Silo?

Students might apply the check list at right to the dialogue.

★ **Texas Essential Elements/(a) English Language Arts (continued): 2D** Grammar/punctuation/spelling. **(c) Reading: 3I** Draw conclusions; **4A** Follow directions; **4D** Diagrams/graphs

Exercises in Critical Thinking and Writing/*cont.*

Remember to follow these guidelines for writing dialogue:

1. Enclose each character's exact words in quotation marks. Periods and commas go inside the closing quotation marks.
2. Begin a new paragraph every time the speaker changes.
3. Avoid repeating *said.*
4. Use contractions and informal English to make the dialogue sound natural.
5. Be sure to let the personalities of the characters show through in their speech—a shy person might stammer, an angry person might use short, stern words and exclamation points.

Here is one writer's dialogue based on Outcome #2 in the sample Prewriting chart.

Jim stood in front of the desk, and gulped, "Excuse me, Mrs. Silo. C'n I talk to you for a minute?" Mrs. S. peered over her glasses and nodded, but did not smile (bad sign). "I'd like to talk to you about my grade this quarter," Jim sounded nervous but he plowed on. "I really think I deserve more than a *C.* I turned in all my homework and didn't do any worse than a *B* on my tests."

Mrs. Silo frowned and reached for that old black grade book. "Well," she said, "I don't remember that you did that well. You sit in the back row and never answer in class, and I've had to tell you to be quiet a hundred times."

Mrs. Silo exaggerates.

But Jim remembered that the day before she'd caught him tying Bradley's shoelaces to the desk ahead of him. His timing was all wrong. "Yeh, I know I could be better, but . . . ," Jim's voice trailed off.

"At least you're honest," she grumbled. "Let's see," she muttered, her finger skimming the lines of X's, O's, numbers, and letters. Then she changed. A miracle! "You know, I think you might be right," she said with amazement. She punched numbers quickly into her calculator. "Yes, you *are* right. I'm wrong. I'll change the grade before I leave school today. But I still don't like your conduct, James." She couldn't resist that.

"Thanks, Mrs. Silo," Jim said, very humbly. He heaved a sigh of relief and bounded for the door. A *C* would've meant the end of soccer. Boy, was he lucky! Boy, was Mrs. Silo great. Boy, was he good at math. A

Revising and Proofreading Self-Check (or Partner Check)

1. Does the dialogue show what the conflict is and how it is resolved?
2. Is the dialogue punctuated correctly?
3. Does a new paragraph begin whenever the speaker changes?
4. Have I avoided repeating the verb *said*?
5. Does every sentence start with a capital letter and end with a period or other end punctuation mark?
6. Is the dialogue interesting and natural-sounding? Have I said everything I wanted to say?

CHARACTERS

T. P. and Jake by Thomas Hart Benton (1938). Oil and egg tempera. Collection of Mr. and Mrs. Stephen Sloan.

UNIT TWO **John Leggett**

Humanities Connection: Discussing the Fine Art

Thomas Hart Benton (1889–1975) is best known as an "American scene" painter. During the late 1920's and early 1930's Benton's work illustrated the vulgarity of American urban life. However, during the mid-1930's, the source of Benton's inspiration shifted and he began to paint scenes of Middle Western farmers as they went about their daily life.

? Which character is Jake and which one is T.P.? What could be going on in the painting? From his clothing and setting, what do you know about the boy? Is this a good picture to start off a unit called "Characters"?

Tempera is a painting medium that uses the yolks or whites of eggs, water, and powdered pigments. It is no longer commonly used—for one reason because it dries so rapidly—but some painters like to use it to give them strong colors, exact detail, and an even, flat tone. If you compare this painting to the one, say, on page 76, you'll notice that the one painted in oil and tempera has a flatter quality than the one done just in oil.

Teaching About Character

A study of character enables students to appreciate the subtleties and complexities of what many writers consider the most challenging aspect of the craft of both fiction and nonfiction (biography, autobiography, true narratives). Learning how to get at the root of what makes a character tick makes students more astute readers; it also gives them valuable insights into human nature.

Most of the selections in this unit are short enough to be covered in a single class period. Each, moreover, treats one or more of the elements of character touched upon in the unit introduction: characterization, motivation, suspense, dynamic and static characters, and conflict.

After students have read the unit introduction on pages 71–73 of their text, review characterization. Invite students to volunteer examples of each of the six approaches outlined. Then test their comprehension by writing on the board a list of character clues you have invented about a character and asking students to match each with an approach. (For example, the clue "He carefully placed his fork beside his plate, then lifted his napkin and lightly dabbed the corners of his mouth" is an example of the fourth approach: revealing character by showing the reader how a character acts.)

Although the boldface terms appearing in the post-selection questions are guideposts indicating which skill is covered, you may introduce additional skill coverage as inclination and need dictate. Be careful, however, not to belabor the pedagogical component in any of the selections. All of them have been chosen for their high-interest appeal. The first goal of the student reader, after all, is to enjoy the literature.

Objectives of the Characters Unit

1. To improve reading proficiency and expand vocabulary
2. To gain exposure to notable authors and their works
3. To identify and analyze the approaches to characterization
4. To understand the relationship between character and motivation, suspense and conflict
5. To distinguish between static and dynamic characters
6. To define and identify significant literary techniques: dialogue, exaggeration, dramatic irony, satire, and theme
7. To interpret and respond to literature, orally and in writing, by analyzing character
8. To practice the following critical thinking and writing skills:
   a. Analyzing a motive
   b. Analyzing the writer's craft
   c. Analyzing and describing characters
   d. Analyzing anthropomorphism

Supplementary Support Material: Unit Two

1. Introduction/Understanding the Elements of Character Test (page 23 of Test Book)
2. Word Analogies Test (page 35 of Test Book)
3. Reading Check Test blackline master
4. Unit Review Test (page 37 of Test Book)
5. Critical Thinking and Writing Test (page 41 of Test Book)
6. Instructional Overhead Transparencies

Unit Outline
CHARACTERS

★ Texas Essential Elements/(a) English Language Arts: **3A** Plot/character

Character: writing about the human heart.

—James A. Michener

A

Characters

When storytellers talk about their craft, they are likely to differ on many points. But they probably will agree on one: A key ingredient of a good story is an interesting central character.

We are all fascinated by human nature. We want to know how other people respond to crisis, difficulty, and temptation. To show us this, a good writer must make us believe that a character in a story is a real person who has feelings similar to our own. The character must come alive. He or she must rise up off the page, as real as our next-door neighbor. Really successful characters can seem larger than life. They become the acquaintances of generations of readers, and reveal truths about life and human nature.

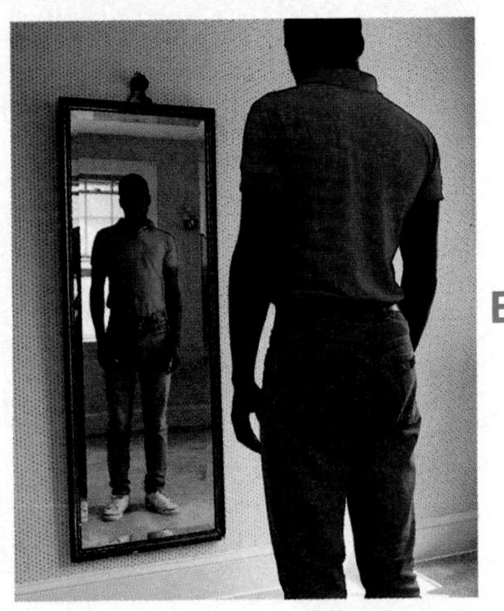

B

Creating Characters

Creating characters is one of the most important and most difficult aspects of the writer's craft. It puts the writer in a godlike role, for he or she is creating human beings to populate the world prepared for them.

How does the writer bring a character to life? First, the writer must be able to imagine the character. The writer might start by imagining the character's appearance, giving color to hair and eyes, and adding a voice and a style of dress. The writer must then invent a whole personality, which may be petty or heroic or happy-go-lucky or something else. The writer must choose from a tremendous number of possibilities while trying to put together a believable character.

Once a character is familiar to the writer, it must then be made familiar to the reader. Revealing what a character is like is called **characterization.** There are six main ways of revealing a character:

SRW p. 21

1. Stating directly what the character is like. "Jim was friendly and open toward most people."

2. Letting the reader enter the head of the character, to become familiar with his or her thoughts and feelings. "Jennifer did not like the looks of the dessert, but decided to eat some to please the cook."

3. Allowing the reader to hear the character speak. The reader can then draw conclusions based on what is said, and how it is said. "Frank said to Mr. Smith, 'I'm not going to be in the play tomorrow, and I don't care whether that puts you in a tight spot.'"

4. Showing the reader how the character acts. Actions can tell a lot about someone. "Janet began to fidget nervously as the teacher started to read aloud the marks."

C

A. Responding to the Quotation

? What kinds of characters do you like to read about most? Based on the selections you've read in Unit 1 (or any other stories you've read), name some characters who seemed the most real to you—who had the most "human heart."

B. Responding to the Photograph

? Do you think the photograph of the man looking at himself in the mirror is a good choice for an introduction to a unit on characters? Explain.

C. Providing Examples

? What examples can you give of each type of characterization?

A. Discussing the Photograph
Tell students that the picture is a still photograph from the TV show *Batman,* which was popular in the 1960's and 1970's. Because comic-book characters such as Batman and Robin usually possess extraordinary qualities that far surpass those of average human beings, it is especially challenging to their writers to make the feelings and motivations of these characters believable. What other characters in TV shows and movies today have superhuman qualities? Are characters on TV today mostly realistic, or mostly superheroic? Which do they prefer?

5. Describing the appearance of a character. "Bill was tall and strong and wore a tee shirt with *Dallas Cowboys* written across the front."

6. Telling the reader what other characters think or say about the character. "Jane said to Carla, 'Michael is a very nice fellow. He always tries to be helpful.'"

A

In the first method of characterization, the writer tells you what the character is like. But with the other methods, you must seek to understand the character yourself. You must be sensitive to just about every detail regarding the character. Each detail can give information on what the character is like. If we read that a girl wants a flamboyant red dress, we suspect that she seeks attention. A If she coaxes her mother into buying it for her, we realize she is clever. If she is rude to the salesclerk, we assume she has a mean streak. If, when looking into the mirror, she remarks "It don't look so good on," we guess that no great care has been taken with her education or that she speaks a dialect. Of course, each detail about the girl must fit with the others. She must seem like a live person with blood in her veins instead of a puppet with different parts sewn together and stuffed with sawdust.

Troubled by Marley's face, Scrooge inspects his house. Illustration by Arthur Rackham for *A Christmas Carol* by Charles Dickens.

B

Why Characters Do What They Do

In order to understand a character's personality, you need to understand *why* a character does the things he or she does. This is called the character's **motivation.** Sometimes the motivation is quickly apparent: Nelson's motivation for taking fifty cents from the kitchen counter is clear when he spends the money on a candy bar. At other times, however, the motivation is not clear. Then **suspense**—anxious curiosity—is created as you look for clues that will help clarify the motivation. Why does Vera get off the bus two stops *after* her house? You keep reading until Vera's motivation is revealed. She might be avoiding the bully who waits at her stop. She might be taking a long look at the house where she used to live, and which she still misses. Or she might be walking by the home of the boy she secretly admires.

Characters Who Change

The central, or main, character in a story almost always changes in some important way in the course of the story. Any character who changes is known as a **dynamic character.** (A character that doesn't change much is called a **static character.**) The character may grow in some way, gain understanding, make an important decision, or take some action that alters his or her life. Perhaps greedy Nelson learns to give to others; or Maria suddenly understands that her grandfather shares many of her own feelings. C

Whatever the change in a character, it usually results from some **conflict,** or struggle between opposing forces. So it is especially important to watch how a character deals with conflict. At the very least, the conflict will probably reveal something about the character's personality.

Some of the characters in the stories that follow are based on real people. Some are totally imaginary. But you will probably find that all of them are interesting. They prove that, of all the wonders of the world, people provide the most interesting show of them all.

A. Vocabulary
Flamboyant (flam·boi′ənt) means strikingly showy or ornate.

B. Responding to the Illustration
Arthur Rackham (1867–1939) first achieved fame for his illustrations of *Grimm's Fairy Tales,* which was published in 1900. Rackham went on to illustrate such classics as *Rip van Winkle* (1905), *Gulliver's Travels* (1909), and *The Wind in the Willows* (1940). Although best known as an illustrator of children's books and fantastic tales, Rackham was also a talented landscape painter in watercolor. Tell students that Scrooge is a character who changes from being unkind and stingy to being kind and generous. ? Do you think this illustration depicts Scrooge before the change in character, or afterward?

C. Dynamic and Static Characters
Scrooge is a good example of a dynamic character. ? Name two characters in stories you have read or TV shows you have seen who changed in an important way. How did those characters change? Now, describe two static characters you have read about or seen in stories or TV shows. Did you find these characters interesting?

Responding to a Story

As an alternative to the instructions suggested in the student text, have student volunteers read the selection aloud as the balance of the class follows along silently. Then instruct students to go back through the excerpt, this time paying attention to the side comments and jotting down on a separate sheet of paper any notes that occur to them. When everyone has finished reading and writing, lead a discussion on the importance of formulating key questions and making predictions while reading. Ask students to write three sentences describing what they *think* this narrator looks like. Share the responses in class: Are there disagreements?

A. Active Reading

Active reading is the process by which a reader combines prior knowledge with information given in the text to question, predict, monitor comprehension, and confirm and revise predictions. Active reading is accomplished by making written and mental notes during reading. As they read this passage and the selections that follow, urge students to try to picture the characters in their minds. Urge them also to write down their thoughts as they read. Tell them to be honest!

B. Characterization

Tell students that this is the mark of good characterization.

★ **Texas Essential Elements/(a) English Language Arts: 3A** Plot/character; **4E** Predict.
(c) Reading: 1A Context clues; **3A** Main ideas/details; **3H** Predict; **3I** Draw conclusions

Responding to a Story

A The following passage is an extract from a longer story. One reader has started reading and has recorded comments on the right-hand side. You might take notes of your own as you read.

"You going to the prom?" asked Schwartz, as we chewed on our salami sandwiches under the stands of the football field, where we preferred for some reason to take lunch at that period of our lives.

"Yep, I guess so," I answered as coolly as I could.

He really doesn't feel very cool about it.

"Who ya takin'?" Flick joined the discussion, sucking at a bottle of Nehi orange.

"I don't know. I was thinking of Daphne Bigelow." I had dropped the name of the most spectacular girl in the entire high school, if not the state of Indiana itself.

Probably he's exaggerating.

"No kidding!" Schwartz reacted in a tone of proper awe and respect, tinged with disbelief.

"Yeh. I figure I'd give her a break."

He must not be very desirable as a date.

Flick snorted, the gassy orange pop going down the wrong pipe. He coughed and wheezed brokenly for several moments. I had once dated Daphne Bigelow and, although the occasion, as faithful readers will recall, was not a riotous success, I felt that I was still in the running. Several occasions in the past month had led me to believe that I was making a comeback with Daphne. Twice she had distinctly acknowledged my presence in the halls between classes, once actually speaking to me.

Flick seems to think it's pretty funny. (Did the writer write another story about this character?)

"Oh, hi there, Fred," she had said in that musical voice.

"Uh . . . hi, Daph," I had replied wittily. The fact that my name is not Fred is neither here nor there; she had *spoken* to me. She had remembered my face from somewhere.

He is really a klutz. This is hardly witty.

And Daphne doesn't even know his name.

"Ya gotta go formal," said Schwartz. "I read on the bulletin board where it said you wear a summer formal to the prom."

"No kidding?" Flick had finished off the orange and was now fully with us. "What's a summer formal?"

I can really hear and see these guys! This is very true to life! B

"That's where you wear one of those white coats," I explained. I was known as the resident expert in our group on all forms of high life. This was because my mother was a fanatical Fred Astaire fan.

"Ya gotta rent 'em," I said with the finality of an expert.

I doubt that he's really an expert. His English is pretty slang-y for a high-life expert.

Two weeks later, each one of us received a prim white envelope containing an engraved invitation.

The Junior Class is proud to invite you to the Junior Prom, to be held at the Cherrywood Country Club beginning eight P.M. *June fifth. Dance to the music of Mickey Eisley and his Magic Music Makers.*

Summer formal required.

The Committee

Reading Check Test

1. Revealing what a character is like is called characterization. *(True)*

2. The reason a character does the things he or she does is called motivation. *(True)*

3. A character who does not change much is a dynamic character. *(False)*

4. A character who makes a life-altering decision is a static character. *(False)*

5. When a character changes, it is usually the result of a conflict. *(True)*

Thinking Over the Story

Begin the discussion by asking students to share with the class their own comments or questions. The following questions, if not touched upon, should be raised: What are the ages of the characters? (Mid to late teens) What evidence suggests this? (Dating, plans to attend a junior prom) What does the narrator's reference to his father as "my old man" suggest about the narrator as a person? (That he uses the slang of the era, that he is slightly lacking in respect, or trying to be a "big deal") What does the conversation between the narrator and his parents reveal about his relationship with them? (That they are interested in the events in his life, that he is willing to discuss his affairs with them)

Finally, encourage students to discuss their predictions about the story. Have them support their predictions with information and possible clues in the passage. (He does *not* end up in love with Wanda Hickey.)

It was the first engraved invitation I had ever received. The puberty rites had begun. That night around the supper table, the talk was of nothing else.

Something's going to happen about this prom. What are "puberty rites," anyway?

"Who ya gonna take?" my old man asked, getting right to the heart of the issue. Who you were taking to the prom was considered a highly significant decision, possibly affecting your whole life, which, in some tragic cases, it did.

Comic! I guess he means that some prom dates end up as your husband or wife and that's not always happy-ever-after.

"Oh, I don't know. I was thinking of a couple of girls." I replied in an offhand manner, as though this slight detail didn't concern me at all. My kid brother, who was taking all this in with sardonic interest, sneered derisively and went back to shoveling in his red cabbage. He had not yet discovered girls. My mother paused while slicing the meat loaf.

No one seems to have much confidence in this guy.
He mentions a lot of details about *food*.

"Why not take that nice Wanda Hickey?"

"Aw, come on, Ma. This is the prom. This is important. You don't take Wanda Hickey to the *prom*."

It sounds pretty believable to me! Maybe Wanda Hickey is someone his parents like.

Wanda Hickey was the only girl who I knew for an absolute fact liked me. Ever since we had been in third grade, Wanda had been hanging around the outskirts of my social circle. She laughed at my jokes and once, when we were twelve, actually sent me a valentine. She was always loitering around the tennis courts, the ball diamonds, the alleys where on long summer nights we played Kick the Can or siphoned gas to keep Flick's Chevy running. In fact, there were times when I couldn't shake her.

She doesn't sound like a winner either. The poor guy—only one girl has ever liked him. Well, given the story's title, I predict he goes with Wanda Hickey. The story will probably be funny and this guy will probably make fun of himself. But I think he will end up falling in love with Wanda Hickey.

—from *Wanda Hickey's Night of Golden Memories,* Jean Shepherd

Thinking Over the Story

This reader had some responses to the narrator. What were they? Did you share them?

Did you respond to any other details as you read? What about the way the characters talk? Do you think it's funny? Is it believable? Does it tell you the kind of people they are?

What kind of character do you think the narrator will turn out to be? What details so far suggest this?

What kinds of characters do his pals seem to be? What about his parents and kid brother?

Did you know the meanings of all the words and expressions? Can you use **context clues** to guess at the meanings? Or do you have to look them up in a dictionary?

This reader also made some **predictions** about what is going to happen next. Perhaps the predictions will turn out to be true, and the reader will feel pleasure, having guessed correctly the story's outcome. But an even greater pleasure might be in a surprise ending, or in a surprising turn of events—something that this reader had not expected. How do you predict this story will end? What do you think the title might mean?

PREREADING

1. **BUILDING ON PRIOR KNOWLEDGE.** Before they read, ask students to reminisce about what they were like when they were five years old. If they don't remember, have them ask a parent or older friend. You might ask students to describe what kinds of parents they think they will be if they decide to have children when they are adults. Be sure students have an appreciation of some of the difficulties involved in dealing with an imaginative five-year-old child.

2. **ESTABLISHING A PURPOSE.** Before students begin reading, you might have them read question 8 on page 80.

3. **PREREADING JOURNAL.** Before they read, have students make a list of at least three things that they remember about their first year in school. Tell them to think of their feelings, friends, activities, lessons, the physical classroom, etc.

Humanities Connection: Discussing the Fine Art
American illustrator Norman Rockwell (1894–1978) is most famous for his depictions of everyday people and scenes from American life, which appeared originally in *The Saturday Evening Post.*

? Describe the facial expression of the boy in the sketch. What do you think the boy is looking at and what thoughts might be going through his mind?

★ **Texas Essential Elements/(a) English Language Arts: 1B** Purpose and audience; **1D** Direct quotations; **1F** Specific words; **2B** Parts of speech; **3A** Plot/character. **(c) Reading: 1C** Dictionaries

CHARLES

For a detailed lesson plan on this story, see Teacher's Manual pages 20–22. A biography of Shirley Jackson appears on text page 80.

Shirley Jackson

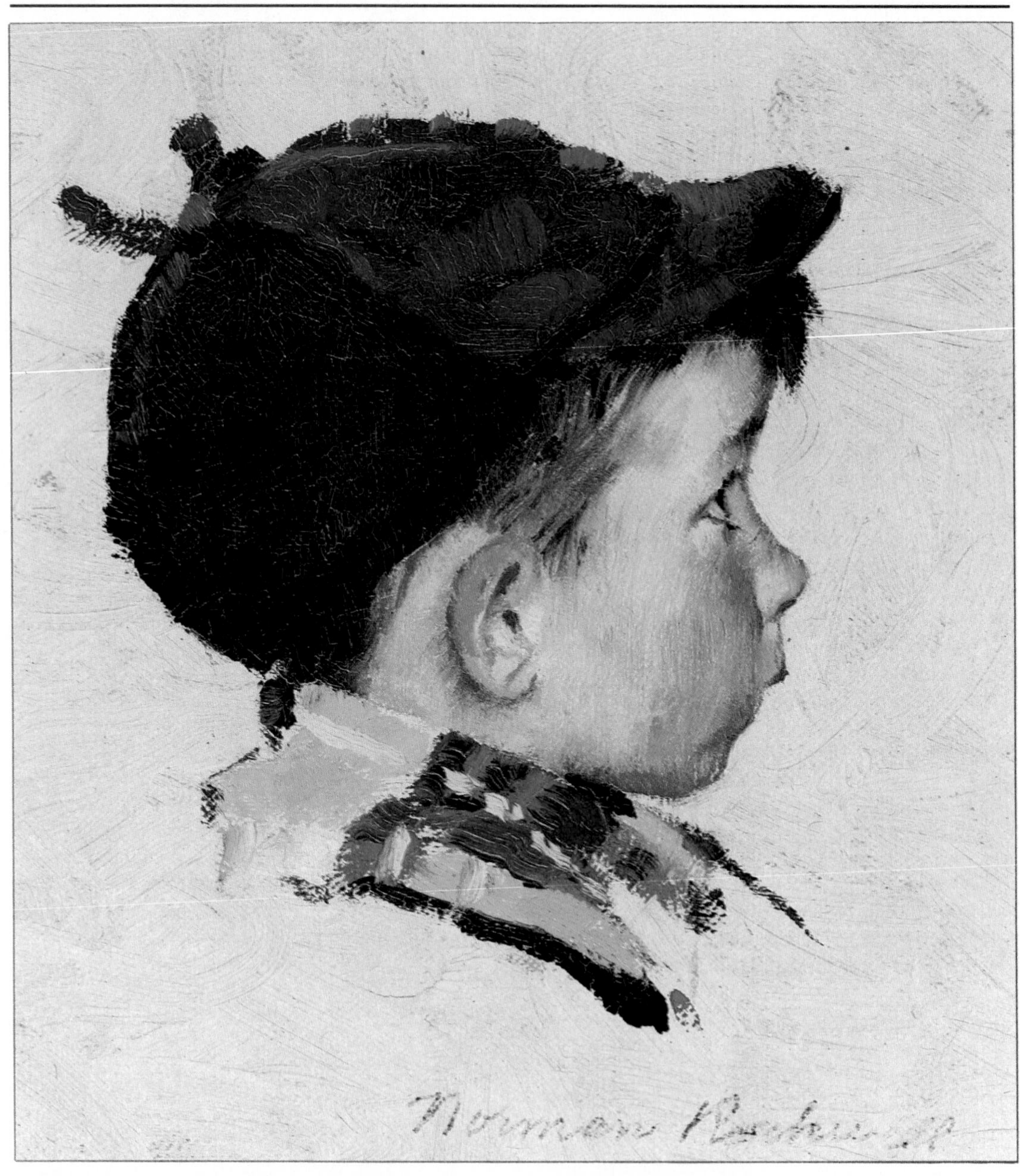

Demonstration sketch for Don Winslow by Norman Rockwell. Oil.

Private collection.

SUPPLEMENTARY SUPPORT MATERIAL

1. Vocabulary Activity Sheet
2. Reading Check Test blackline master
3. Selection Test (page 25 of Test Book)
4. Author photograph on *A Gallery of Authors* poster
5. Connections Between Reading and Writing worksheet
6. Reader's Response Journal
7. Workbook (page 23)

DEVELOPING VOCABULARY

The following words appear on a test in the Test Book, page 26. (See also the Vocabulary Worksheet.)

swagger	simultaneously
raucous	scorn
vain	elaborate
deprive	abandoned
passionately	haggard

★ **Texas Essential Elements/(c) Reading** (continued): **3A** Main ideas/details; **3I** Draw conclusions

This is a story about a mother's concern for her child as he goes off for his first year of school. It is based on the real experiences of the writer's own family—her first child was named Laurence. But it doesn't make any difference whether this story is factually true or not. As you read, see if you get caught up in the sheer fun of it. Who is really the central character—Laurie, the mischievous Charles, or the trusting mother?

The day my son Laurie started kindergarten he renounced[1] corduroy overalls with bibs and began wearing blue jeans with a belt; I watched him go off the first morning with the
A older girl next door, seeing clearly that an era of my life was ended, my sweet-voiced nursery-school tot replaced by a long-trousered, swaggering character who forgot to stop at the corner and wave goodbye to me.

He came home the same way, the front door slamming open, his cap on the floor, and the voice suddenly become raucous shouting, "Isn't anybody *here*?"

At lunch he spoke insolently[2] to his father, spilled his baby sister's milk, and remarked that his teacher said we were not to take the name of the Lord in vain.

"How *was* school today?" I asked, elaborately casual.

"All right," he said.

"Did you learn anything?" his father asked.

Laurie regarded his father coldly. "I didn't learn nothing," he said.

"Anything," I said. "Didn't learn anything."

"The teacher spanked a boy, though," Laurie said, addressing his bread and butter. "For being fresh," he added, with his mouth full.

"What did he do?" I asked. "Who was it?"

Laurie thought. "It was Charles," he said. "He was fresh. The teacher spanked him and made him stand in a corner. He was awfully fresh."

B "What did he do?" I asked again, but Laurie slid off his chair, took a cookie, and left, while his father was still saying, "See here, young man."

The next day Laurie remarked at lunch, as soon as he sat down, "Well, Charles was bad again today." He grinned enormously and said, "Today Charles hit the teacher." C

"Good heavens," I said, mindful of the Lord's name, "I suppose he got spanked again?"

"He sure did," Laurie said. "Look up," he said to his father.

"What?" his father said, looking up.

"Look down," Laurie said. "Look at my thumb. Gee, you're dumb." He began to laugh insanely.

"Why did Charles hit the teacher?" I asked quickly.

"Because she tried to make him color with red crayons," Laurie said. "Charles wanted to color with green crayons so he hit the teacher and she spanked him and said nobody play with Charles but everybody did."

The third day—it was Wednesday of the first week—Charles bounced a seesaw onto the head of a little girl and made her bleed, and the teacher made him stay inside all during recess. Thursday Charles had to stand in a corner during story time because he kept pounding his feet on the floor. Friday Charles was deprived of blackboard privileges because he threw chalk.

On Saturday I remarked to my husband, "Do you think kindergarten is too unsettling for Laurie? All this toughness, and bad grammar, and this Charles boy sounds like such a bad influence."

"It'll be all right," my husband said reassuringly. "Bound to be people like Charles in the world. Might as well meet them now as later."

On Monday Laurie came home late, full of news. "Charles," he shouted as he came up the

Vivid Adverbs. One of Shirley Jackson's trademarks is the use of vivid *adverbs* (words that modify verbs, adjectives, or other adverbs). They help convey with precision her characters' speech, behavior, and feelings. They also add to the story's liveliness and humor. As you read, notice how adverbs help you visualize the characters' actions.

1. **renounced:** gave up.
2. **insolently** (in′sə·lent·lē): with bold disrespect.

A. Character

? How would you describe Laurie's mother's feelings? (Happy but tinged with sadness because her son is growing up) Notice that she tends to exaggerate a bit: *renounced, swaggering.*

B. Characterization

? What method of characterization does Jackson use in this paragraph to reveal Laurie? (She shows how Laurie acts.) What does she reveal about the boy? (His action reveals that he can be disrespectful to adults. Perhaps he is also avoiding his mother's question.)

C. Character

Call students' attention to the dichotomy between Laurie's news and the manner in which he delivers it. Point out that Laurie seems to enjoy relating tales of Charles's bad behavior.

? What does this suggest about Laurie? (That Laurie is enjoying the attention he's getting and the shocked reactions of his parents to his stories.)

A. Character
? What do we learn about Laurie now? (He is being fresh to his father.)

B. Character
? What does this description of Charles tell about Laurie? (He is probably always made to wear a jacket and rubbers—rubber overshoes worn in the rain. There is probably a note of envy in his voice.)

C. Vivid Adverbs
? What vivid adverbs does Jackson use in this passage to help her readers visualize Laurie? (Scornfully, solemnly) What do they tell about Laurie? (*Scornfully* conveys Laurie's tone of voice—as though to say "how could you get so excited about somebody's mother?" *Solemnly* conveys how Laurie moved—he's showing his disapproval of Charles's behavior.)

D. Character
Note again the incongruity between Laurie's news and the way he reports it. This time the news about Charles is good, and Laurie's tone is grim. Things were much more fun when Charles was mischievous.

E. Character
? Why do you think being the teacher's helper improves Charles's behavior? (Perhaps by being singled out to be the teacher's helper, Charles is getting the attention he wants.)

Critical Comment
After Jackson's death in 1965, the *New York Times* wrote: "Shirley Jackson wrote in two styles. She could describe the delights and turmoils of ordinary domestic life with detached hilarity; and she could, with cryptic symbolism, write a tenebrous horror story in the Gothic mold in which abnormal behavior seemed perilously ordinary."

After reading "Charles," ask students if they can imagine this same writer writing a horror story.

hill; I was waiting anxiously on the front steps. "Charles," Laurie yelled all the way up the hill, "Charles was bad again."

"Come right in," I said, as soon as he came close enough. "Lunch is waiting."

"You know what Charles did?" he demanded, following me through the door. "Charles yelled so in school they sent a boy in from first grade to tell the teacher she had to make Charles keep quiet, and so Charles had to stay after school. And so all the children stayed to watch him."

"What did he do?" I asked.

A "He just sat there," Laurie said, climbing into his chair at the table. "Hi, Pop, y'old dust mop."

"Charles had to stay after school today," I told my husband. "Everyone stayed with him."

"What does this Charles look like?" my husband asked Laurie. "What's his other name?"

B "He's bigger than me," Laurie said. "And he doesn't have any rubbers and he doesn't ever wear a jacket."

Monday night was the first Parent-Teachers meeting and only the fact that the baby had a cold kept me from going; I wanted passionately to meet Charles's mother. On Tuesday Laurie remarked suddenly, "Our teacher had a friend come to see her in school today."

"Charles's mother?" my husband and I asked simultaneously.

C "Naaah," Laurie said scornfully. "It was a man who came and made us do exercises, we had to touch our toes. Look." He climbed down from his chair and squatted down and touched his toes. "Like this," he said. He got solemnly back into his chair and said, picking up his fork, "Charles didn't even *do* exercises."

"That's fine," I said heartily. "Didn't Charles want to do exercises?"

"Naaah," Laurie said. "Charles was so fresh to the teacher's friend he wasn't *let* do exercises."

"Fresh again?" I said.

"He kicked the teacher's friend," Laurie said. "The teacher's friend told Charles to touch his toes like I just did and Charles kicked him."

"What are they going to do about Charles, do you suppose?" Laurie's father asked him.

Laurie shrugged elaborately. "Throw him out of school, I guess," he said.

Wednesday and Thursday were routine; Charles yelled during story hour and hit a boy in the stomach and made him cry. On Friday Charles stayed after school again and so did all the other children.

With the third week of kindergarten Charles was an institution in our family; the baby was being a Charles when she cried all afternoon; Laurie did a Charles when he filled his wagon full of mud and pulled it through the kitchen; even my husband, when he caught his elbow in the telephone cord and pulled telephone, ashtray, and a bowl of flowers off the table, said, after the first minute, "Looks like Charles."

During the third and fourth weeks it looked like a reformation in Charles; Laurie reported grimly at lunch on Thursday of the third week, "Charles was so good today the teacher gave him an apple." D

"What?" I said, and my husband added warily,[3] "You mean Charles?"

"Charles," Laurie said. "He gave the crayons around and he picked up the books afterward and the teacher said he was her helper."

"What happened?" I asked incredulously.[4]

"He was her helper, that's all," Laurie said, and shrugged.

"Can this be true, about Charles?" I asked my husband that night. "Can something like this happen?"

"Wait and see," my husband said cynically.[5] "When you've got a Charles to deal with, this may mean he's only plotting."

He seemed to be wrong. For over a week Charles was the teacher's helper; each day he handed things out and he picked things up; no one had to stay after school. E

"The PTA meeting's next week again," I told my husband one evening. "I'm going to find Charles's mother there."

"Ask her what happened to Charles," my husband said. "I'd like to know."

"I'd like to know myself," I said.

On Friday of that week things were back to normal. "You know what Charles did today?"

---

3. **warily:** cautiously.
4. **incredulously** (in·krej′o͞o·ləs·lē): in a manner showing doubt.
5. **cynically** (sin′i·k′lē): doubting the sincerity of another's actions.

READING CHECK TEST

1. Laurie and Charles live next door to each other. *(False)*
2. Laurie tells his parents that Charles hit the teacher. *(True)*
3. Laurie's mother is unable to attend the first Parent-Teacher meeting. *(True)*
4. During the third and fourth week, Charles is better behaved in school. *(True)*
5. Laurie's mother never meets his teacher. *(False)*

CLOSURE

Working with a partner, students should identify the six ways in which writers can reveal character.

A. Character

? What does the adverb *joyfully* reveal about Laurie here? (He relishes telling his father the forbidden word.)

Laurie demanded at the lunch table, in a voice slightly awed. "He told a little girl to say a word and she said it and the teacher washed her mouth out with soap and Charles laughed."

"What word?" his father asked unwisely, and Laurie said, "I'll have to whisper it to you, it's so bad." He got down off his chair and went around to his father. His father bent his head down

A and Laurie whispered joyfully. His father's eyes widened.

"Did Charles tell the little girl to say *that*?" he asked respectfully.

"She said it *twice*," Laurie said. "Charles told her to say it *twice*."

"What happened to Charles?" my husband asked.

"Nothing," Laurie said. "He was passing out the crayons."

Monday morning Charles abandoned the little girl and said the evil word himself three or four times, getting his mouth washed out with soap each time. He also threw chalk.

My husband came to the door with me that evening as I set out for the PTA meeting. "Invite her over for a cup of tea after the meeting," he said. "I want to get a look at her."

B "If only she's there," I said prayerfully.

"She'll be there," my husband said. "I don't see how they could hold a PTA meeting without Charles's mother."

At the meeting I sat restlessly, scanning each comfortable matronly face, trying to determine which one hid the secret of Charles. None of them looked to me haggard[6] enough. No one stood up in the meeting and apologized for the way her son had been acting. No one mentioned Charles.

After the meeting I identified and sought out Laurie's kindergarten teacher. She had a plate with a cup of tea and a piece of chocolate cake; I had a plate with a cup of tea and a piece of marshmallow cake. We maneuvered up to one another cautiously, and smiled.

"I've been so anxious to meet you," I said. "I'm Laurie's mother."

"We're all so interested in Laurie," she said.

"Well, he certainly likes kindergarten," I said. "He talks about it all the time."

"We had a little trouble adjusting, the first week or so," she said primly, "but now he's a fine little helper. With occasional lapses, of course."

"Laurie usually adjusts very quickly," I said. "I suppose this time it's Charles's influence."

"Charles?"

"Yes," I said laughing, "you must have your hands full in that kindergarten, with Charles." C

"Charles?" she said. "We don't have any Charles in the kindergarten."

6. **haggard**: looking worn from worry and exhaustion.

B. Character

? How would this be said "prayerfully"?

C. Surprise Ending and Foreshadowing

? Were you surprised to learn the truth about Laurie and Charles? Can you identify any clues in the story that foreshadowed the outcome? (Page 79, left-hand column, last two paragraphs, "If only she's there, . . . without Charles's mother." Page 79, right-hand column, first paragraph, "None of them looked to me haggard enough. . . . No one mentioned Charles." Same column, sixth paragraph, "We had a little trouble . . . of course.")

ANALYZING THE STORY

Identifying Facts

1. Students may mention some of the following: He wears blue jeans and a belt instead of corduroy overalls, he speaks raucously instead of with a "sweet voice," he speaks insolently to his father, he spills his sister's milk. *(Answers continue on page 80.)*

Responding to the Story

Analyzing the Story

Identifying Facts

1. From the first day Laurie "swaggers" off to school, his mother notices changes in him. List three changes she notices in her son's speech and behavior toward his parents.
2. Laurie's father asks him what Charles looks like. How does Laurie describe him?
3. Every day Laurie brings home another story about Charles, until the third week he is at school. Then Charles's behavior suddenly improves. Explain how the teacher reacts to Charles's improved behavior.
4. Even after Charles's behavior improves, he does not act properly all the time. Explain how he gets the little girl in his class in trouble.
5. How does Laurie's mother learn the truth about Charles?

Interpreting Meanings

6. As they hear more and more from Laurie about Charles, how do Laurie's parents feel about

(Answers begin on page 79.)
2. He describes Charles as bigger than himself, adding that Charles has no rubbers and is not made to wear a jacket.
3. The teacher encourages him by giving him an apple and calling him her helper.
4. He tells her to "say a word" and she does. The teacher washes her mouth out with soap.
5. At a Parent-Teacher meeting, she has a chat with Laurie's teacher in which she mentions the problems the teacher must be having with Charles. The teacher responds that she has no student named Charles in the class.

Interpreting Meanings

6. They become concerned about his influence on Laurie.

Students may say that they are curious about how Charles became what he is.
7. Students will note that, like Charles, Laurie speaks disrespectfully to adults, in this case his parents. Laurie also misbehaves at home, spilling his baby sister's milk and pulling a wagonload of mud through the kitchen. Laurie is unlike Charles, students may note, in his clothes and size. You might want to
(Answers continue in left-hand column.)

(Continued from top.)
follow up by asking how many of Charles's actions were really committed by Laurie, and how many were exaggerations. To what extent are Laurie and Charles one and the same person?
8. Students will note that she believes that Laurie cannot do bad things, and that she misses important evidence when it comes her way.
9. Answers will vary. Students may cite, among other things, the humorous irony in the narrator and her husband's holier-than-thou attitude in their derision of Charles's mother.

Applying Meanings

10. Answers will vary. Some students may suggest that stronger discipline would keep Laurie under control, while others may contend that eventually he'd grow out of his fantasy.

Again, answers will vary. See Teacher's Manual page 21 for suggested possible answers.

Charles? Why do you think they are so eager to meet Charles's mother?

7. In what ways is Charles very similar to Laurie? In what ways are they different? Cite evidence from the story to support your answers.
8. How would you describe the **character** of Laurie's mother?
9. What details in the story become especially funny when you learn the identity of Charles?

Applying Meanings

10. What would you do with Laurie if you were his kindergarten teacher? Do you think this is a believable characterization of a five-year-old and of his doting parents?

Writing About the Story

A Creative Response

1. **Extending the Story.** Write a paragraph telling how Laurie's mother explains to her husband her discovery about Charles at the PTA meeting. Be sure to include a description of the husband's reaction.
2. **Writing a Dialogue.** Write a brief **dialogue,** or conversation, between Laurie and his mother. Start by having the mother tell Laurie what she found out about Charles. Then have Laurie reply, and go on from there.

A Critical Response

3. **Analyzing a Motive.** In a paragraph, explain why you think Laurie makes up the character of Charles. Present your reason, or reasons, for Laurie's behavior in the first, or topic, sentence of the paragraph. Use the rest of the paragraph to explain your interpretation.

See Teacher's Manual page 21.

Reading About the Writer

Shirley Jackson (1919–1965) was born in San Francisco and spent most of her early life in California. She graduated from Syracuse University in 1940. Jackson was a naturally gifted writer with a talent for the comedy to be found in domestic life. But she had an equally arresting talent for gothic horror. Her most famous story, "The Lottery," established her as a literary heir of Edgar Allan Poe. Among her ten books are *Life Among the Savages,* from which "Charles" is taken.

Focusing on Background

A Little Test for Mothers

Jackson writes a humorous questionnaire for fellow suffering mothers (and wives):

"At breakfast I raise a considerable howl about the general sloppy condition of the back porch and the yard. Laurie, Joanne, Sally, and Barry promise that after school there will be a monumental cleaning-up and I will find the yard and porch immaculate. (1) Who has to stay after school to finish his chemistry notebook? (2) Who forgot that today was Girl Scouts? (3) Who calls from the library to say she will be home later? (4) Who stops off at David's house to see David's new steam engine and has to be sent for at five o'clock? (5) Who raises another howl the next morning at breakfast?

"My husband has to catch a train for New York in twenty minutes. (1) Where will his clean shirts be? (2) Who forgot to call the laundry?

"Barry has been waiting all day for two things: the arrival of his grandparents for a visit, and a particular television program on which one of his friends will be visible in the audience. The television program goes on at five-fifteen and lasts till five-thirty. (1) What time will the grandparents arrive? (2) What will be the general tone of the remarks about little children who are so mad for television they can't even say hello properly? (3) Who will eat dinner in dignified silence?"

—Shirley Jackson

Prereading

1. Building on Prior Knowledge. Before they read, have students tell what they know about bird watching. Bird watching, which is the observation of live birds in their natural habitat, developed as a popular pastime and scientific sport almost entirely in the twentieth century. Prior to that time, bird watchers could identify and study species only after they shot them first. Modern bird watching became possible with the development of optical aids, particularly binoculars, that enabled students of birds to see their subjects clearly without harming them. Bird watching, or "birding" as the pros call it, is mostly taken up by adults and avoided by children, since it requires patience and concentration. Students will easily be able to identify with the McKenney sisters' difficulty in becoming sincere bird watchers.

2. Establishing a Purpose. Before students begin reading, you might want them to read question 10 on page 86.

3. Prereading Journal. Before they read, have students write a brief paragraph in which they tell what they think of summer camp (even if they have never been to one). Have them refer back to their responses at the conclusion of the story. See also question 13.

★ **Texas Essential Elements/(a) English Language Arts: 1B** Purpose and audience; **1D** Direct quotations; **2B** Parts of speech; **3A** Plot/character; **4H** Point of view

A LOUD SNEER FOR OUR FEATHERED FRIENDS

For a detailed lesson plan on this selection, see Teacher's Manual pages 22–25. A biography of Ruth McKenney appears on text page 86.

Ruth McKenney

Going off to summer camp is often a child's first experience away from home. Sleeping, eating, and sharing primitive bathrooms with a lot of strange kids can be a painful ordeal at first. In this famous recollection of her own childhood, Ruth McKenney tells how she and her sister Eileen mutiny against camp spirit—that enforced enthusiasm for nature and woodcraft. The story is set several years ago, but you will probably find that many things about children haven't changed. As you read, decide whose side you take: Eileen and Ruth's? Or the Good Sports at Camp Hi-Wah?

A. Conflict ? Predict what you think the conflict of the story will be. Why do you think so? (The conflict will probably be an external one between the Bad Sports and the Good Sports. It will in some way also involve birds.)

B. Visualizing Be sure students talk about what they see the girls doing here.

A From childhood, my sister and I have had a well-grounded dislike for our friends the birds. We came to hate them when she was ten and I was eleven. We had been exiled by what we considered an unfeeling family to one of those loathsome girls' camps where Indian lore is rife[1] and the management puts up neatly lettered signs reminding the clients to be Good Sports. From the moment Eileen and I arrived at dismal old Camp Hi-Wah, we were Bad Sports, and we liked it.

We refused to get out of bed when the bugle blew in the morning, we fought against scrubbing our teeth in public to music, we sneered when the flag was ceremoniously lowered at sunset, we avoided doing a good deed a day, we complained loudly about the food, which was terrible, and we bought some chalk once and wrote all over the Recreation Cabin, "We hate Camp Hi-Wah." It made a wonderful scandal, although unfortunately we were immediately accused of the crime. All the other little campers *loved* dear old Camp Hi-Wah, which shows you what kind of people they were.

B The first two weeks Eileen and I were at Camp Hi-Wah, we sat in our cabin grinding our teeth at our counselor and writing letters to distant relatives. These letters were, if I say so myself, real masterpieces of double dealing and heartless chicanery.[2] In our childish and, we hoped, appealing scrawl, we explained to Great-Aunt Mary Farrel and Second Cousin Joe Murphy that we were having such fun at dear Camp Hi-Wah making Indian pocketbooks.

"We would simply L-O-V-E to make you a pocketbook, dear Aunt Mary," we wrote, "only the leather costs $1 for a small pocketbook or $1.67 for a large size pocketbook, which is much nicer because you can carry more things in it, and the rawhide you sew it up with, just exactly the way the Indians did, costs 40 cents more. We burn pictures on the leather but that doesn't cost anything. If we O-N-L-Y had $1 or $1.67 and 40 cents for the rawhide, we could make you the S-W-E-L-L-E-S-T pocketbook."

As soon as we had enough orders for Indian pocketbooks with pictures burnt on them, we planned to abscond[3] with the funds sent by our trusting relatives and run away to New York City, where, as we used to explain dramatically to our cabin-mates, we intended to live a life of sin. After

1. **rife:** widespread and plentiful.

2. **chicanery** (shi·kān'ər·ē): clever trickiness.
3. **abscond:** run away secretly.

SUPPLEMENTARY SUPPORT MATERIAL

1. Vocabulary Activity Sheet
2. Reading Check Test blackline master
3. Selection Test (page 27 of Test Book)
4. Author photograph on *A Gallery of Authors* poster
5. Reader's Response Journal
6. Workbook (page 25)

DEVELOPING VOCABULARY

The following words appear on a test in the Test Book, page 28. (See also the Vocabulary Activity Sheet.)

exile	solitary
dismal	dolt
sneer	base
reluctant	fraud
loathsome	jaunt

A. Idiom

In the context of the story, what does it mean to "name your own poison"? (It means to choose between two equally boring, or painful, activities—here, bird watching or handicrafts.)

B. Humor

How does McKenney create humor by using exaggeration in this passage? (The McKenney sisters may think of themselves as "big and bad and fierce," but they are just two little girls trying to act tough. It is their own exaggerated perception that we find funny. McKenney also exaggerates when she says the teacher will "mourn" the sisters—she probably feels more relieved as they leave than sad.) This will help students answer question 9.

C. Character

What does it tell you about the narrator—that she prefers vultures to robins or sparrows? (She sees herself as fierce and tough, like a vulture.)

★ **Texas Essential Elements/(c) Reading: 1C** Dictionaries; **2A** Word meaning; **3A** Main ideas/details; **3F** Purpose/point of view/opinion; **3I** Draw conclusions

a few days, our exciting plans for our immediate future were bruited[4] all over the camp, and admirers came from as far away as Cabin Minnehaha, which was way down at the end of Hiawatha Alley, just to hear us tell about New York and sin.

Fame had its price, however. One of the sweet little girls who lived in our cabin turned out to be such a Good Citizen ("Camp Hi-Wah Girls Learn to Be Good Citizens") that she told our dreadful secret to our counselor. Our mail was impounded[5] for weeks, and worst of all, we actually had to make several Indian pocketbooks with pictures burnt on them. My pictures were all supposed to be snakes, although they were pretty blurred. Eileen specialized in what she believed to be the likeness of a werewolf, but Cousin Joe, who had generously ordered three pocketbooks, wrote a nice letter thanking Eileen for his pretty pocketbooks with the pretty pictures of Abraham Lincoln on them. We were terribly disgusted by the whole thing.

It was in this mood that we turned to birds. The handicraft hour at Camp Hi-Wah, heralded by the ten-thirty A.M. bugle, competed for popularity with the bird walks at the same hour. You could, as Eileen had already somewhat precociously[6] learned how to say, name your own poison. After three weeks of burning pictures on leather, we were ready for anything, even our feathered friends. A

So one hot morning in July, the two McKenney sisters, big and bad and fierce for their age, answered the bird walk bugle call, leaving the Indian-pocketbook teacher to mourn her two most backward pupils. We were dressed, somewhat reluctantly, to be sure, in the required heavy stockings for poison ivy and brambles, and carried, each of us, in our dirty hands a copy of a guide to bird lore called *Bird Life for Children*. B

Bird Life for Children was a volume that all the Good Citizens in Camp Hi-Wah pretended to find engrossing.[7] Eileen and I thought it was stupefyingly dull. Our favorite literary character at the time was Dumas' Marguerite de Valois,[8] who took her decapitated lover's head home in a big handkerchief for old times' sake. Eileen, in those days, was always going to name her first girl child Marguerite de Valois.

Bird Life for Children was full of horrid pictures in full color of robins and pigeons and redbirds. Under each picture was a loathsomely whimsical paragraph describing how the bird in question spent his spare time, what he ate, and why children should love him. Eileen and I hated the book so, we were quite prepared to despise birds when we started off that morning on our first bird walk, but we had no idea of what we were going to suffer, that whole awful summer, because of our feathered friends. In the first place, since we had started off making leather pocketbooks, we were three weeks behind the rest of the Hi-Wah bird-lovers. They had been tramping through blackberry bushes for days and days and had already got the hang of the more ordinary bird life around camp, whereas the only bird I could identify at the time was the vulture. Cousin Joe took me to a zoo once, and there was a fine vulture there, a big, fat one. They fed him six live rats every day in lieu[9] of human flesh. I kept a sharp eye out for a vulture all summer, but one never turned up at Camp Hi-Wah. Nothing interesting ever happened around that place. C

On that first bird walk, Eileen and I trotted anxiously along behind the little band of serious-minded bird-lovers, trying desperately to see, or at least hear, even one bird, even one robin. But alas, while other bird-walkers saw, or pretended to see—for Eileen and I never believed them for a moment—all kinds of hummingbirds and hawks and owls and whatnot, we never saw or heard a single, solitary feathered friend, not one.

By the time we staggered into camp for lunch, with stubbed toes, scratched faces, and tangled hair, Eileen and I were soured for life on birds.

4. **bruited** (bro͞ot′ed): spread about, as a report or a rumor.
5. **impounded:** taken away and locked up.
6. **precociously** (prē·kō′shəs·lē): in a manner more developed than normal for the age.
7. **engrossing** (in·grōs′iŋ): extremely interesting.
8. **Dumas' Marguerite de Valois:** The French writer Alexandre Dumas (1802–1870) published the historical novel *Marguerite de Valois* in 1845. The novel is based on the life of a woman who, in the sixteenth century, was married for a time to Henry IV of France. The real Marguerite did not carry out the act described in this story, however.
9. **in lieu** (lo͞o) **of:** instead of.

A

Our bird logs, which we carried strapped to our belts along with the *Guide,* were still chaste[10] and bare, while all the other little bird-lovers had fulsome[11] entries, such as "Saw and heard redbird at 10:37 A.M. Molting."[12]

Still, for the next three days we stayed honest and suffered. For three terrible mornings we endured being dolts among bird-walkers, the laughingstock of Camp Hi-Wah. After six incredibly tiresome hours, our bird logs were still blank. Then we cracked under the strain. The fourth morning we got up feeling grim but determined. We sharpened our pencils before we started off on the now-familiar trail through the second-growth forest.

B

When we got well into the woods and Mary Mahoney, the premier bird-walker of Camp Hi-Wah, had already spotted and logged her first redbird of the morning, Eileen suddenly stopped dead in her tracks. "Hark!" she cried. She had read that somewhere in a book. "Quiet!" I echoed instantly.

10. **chaste** (chāst): here, unused.
11. **fulsome:** full; ample.
12. **molting:** shedding skin or feathers.

The bird-walkers drew to a halt respectfully and stood in silence. They stood and stood. It was not good form even to whisper while fellow bird-walkers were logging a victim, but after quite a long time the Leader, whose feet were flat and often hurt her, whispered impatiently, "Haven't you got him logged yet?"

"You drove him away," Eileen replied sternly. "It was a yellow-billed cuckoo."

"A yellow-billed cuckoo?" cried the Leader incredulously.

"Well," Eileen said modestly, "at least *I* think it was." Then, with many a pretty hesitation and thoughtful pause, she recited the leading features of the yellow-billed cuckoo, as recorded in *Bird Life for Children.*

The Leader was terribly impressed. Later on that morning I logged a kingfisher, a red-headed woodpecker, and a yellow-bellied sapsucker, which was all I could remember at the moment. Each time, I kept the bird-walkers standing around for an interminable period, gaping into blank space and listening desperately to the rustle of the wind in the trees and the creak of their shoes as they went from one foot to another.

C

A. Discussing the Photograph
Tell students that the bird depicted in the photograph is a hummingbird. As you can tell by the relative sizes of the bird and the flower, hummingbirds are very small. Their size ranges from two inches (the size of bumblebees) to nine inches long. The Camp Hi-Wah bird watchers would have had to be experts to spot a hummingbird!

B. Foreshadowing
? What could sharpening their pencils foreshadow? (That they are going to find some way to fill their bird logs)

C. Interpreting
? What are the girls up to? (By the Leader's surprise, we can assume that these birds are not commonly located at Camp Hi-Wah. The girls are faking it.)

Critical Comment

By way of explaining the popularity of McKenney's book *My Sister Eileen,* critic Amy Loveman wrote: ". . . the reminiscences of the sister and herself lie within the experience of every one of us and are the more delightful because they might have been our own."

Write the quotation on the chalkboard and call on a volunteer to read it aloud to the class. Have students discuss the quotation as it pertains to this story. Could, or did, the experiences of the McKenney sisters happen to them? Do they identify with the renegades at all? In what way?

A. Characters' Feelings

? Why do you suppose the sisters are mad? (Because Mary Mahoney and others are capitalizing on the scheme that they devised and that has made them heroines. They don't want to share the limelight with anyone. Also, Mary Mahoney might be trying now to beat the sisters at their own game.)

In a few days Eileen and I were the apple of our Leader's eye, the modest heroes of the Camp Hi-Wah bird walks. Naturally, there were base children around camp, former leading bird-walkers, who spread foul rumors up and down Hiawatha Alley that Eileen and I were frauds. We soon stopped this ugly talk, however. Eileen was the pitcher, and a very good one, too, of the Red Bird ball team and I was the first base. When Elouise Pritchard, the worst gossip in Cabin Sitting Bull, came up to bat, she got a pitched ball right in the stomach. Of course it was only a softball, but Eileen could throw it pretty hard. To vary this routine, I tagged Mary Mahoney, former head bird-walker, out at first base, and Mary had a bruise on her thigh for weeks. The rumors stopped abruptly.

A We had begun to get pretty bored with logging rare birds when the game took on a new angle. Mary Mahoney and several other bird-walkers began to see the same birds we did on our morning jaunts into the forest. This made us pretty mad, but there wasn't much we could do about it. Next, Mary Mahoney began to see birds we weren't logging. The third week after we joined the Camp Hi-Wah Bird Study Circle, everybody except the poor, dumb Leader and a few backward but honest bird-lovers was logging the rarest birds seen around Camp Hi-Wah in twenty years. Bird walks developed into a race to see who could shout

READING CHECK TEST

1. What do the sisters offer to make for relatives back home for a small fee? *Pocketbooks.*
2. What happens to the sisters' mail when their plan to run away is exposed? *It is impounded for weeks.*
3. What camp activity begins at the same time in the morning as the handicraft hour? *The bird walk.*
4. What does Eileen claim to spot on the fourth day of bird watching? *A yellow-billed cuckoo.*
5. What curse do the sisters place on Mary Mahoney for revealing their secret? *The wart curse.*

CLOSURE

Working with a partner, students should define exaggeration and explain how it is used in this story. Have them discuss other stories or books they have read or TV shows or movies they have seen in which exaggeration added to the fun.

"Hark!" first and keep the rest of the little party in fidgety silence for the next five minutes.

A The poor bird walk Leader was in agony. Her reputation as a bird-lover was in shreds. Her talented pupils were seeing rare birds right and left, while the best she could log for herself would be a few crummy old redbirds and a robin or so. At last our Leader's morale collapsed. It was the day when nearly everybody in the study circle swore that she saw and heard a bona fide[13] nightingale.

"Where?" cried our Leader desperately, after the fourth nightingale had been triumphantly logged in the short space of five minutes. Heartless fingers pointed to a vague bush. The Leader strained her honest eyes. No notion of our duplicity[14] crossed her innocent, unwordly mind.

"I can't see any nightingale," our Leader cried, and burst into tears. Then, full of shame, she sped back to camp, leaving the Camp Hi-Wah bird-lovers to their nightingales and guilty thoughts.

Eileen and I ate a hearty lunch that noon because we thought we would need it. Then we strolled down Hiawatha Alley and hunted up Mary Mahoney.

"We will put the Iron Cross on you if you tell," Eileen started off, as soon as we found Mary.

"What's the Iron Cross?" Mary squeaked, startled out of her usual haughty poise.

"Never mind," I growled. "You'll find out if you tell."

13. **bona fide** (bō'nə fīd'): genuine.
14. **duplicity** (do͞o·plis'ə·tē): deception.

We walked past Cabin Sitting Bull, past the flagpole, into the tall grass beyond the ball field.

"She'll tell," Eileen said finally.

"What'll we do?" I replied mournfully. "They'll try us at campfire tonight."

They did, too. It was terrible. We denied everything, but the Head of Camp, a mean old lady who wore middy blouses and pleated serge bloomers,[15] sentenced us to no desserts and eight o'clock bedtime for two weeks. We thought over what to do to Mary Mahoney for four whole days. Nothing seemed sufficiently frightful, but in the end we put the wart curse on her. The wart curse was simple but horrible. We dropped around to Cabin Sitting Bull one evening and in the presence of Mary and her allies we drew ourselves up to our full height and said solemnly in unison, "We put the wart curse on you, Mary Mahoney." Then we stalked away.

We didn't believe for a moment in the wart curse, but we hoped Mary would. At first she was openly contemptuous, but to our delight, on the fourth evening she developed a horrible sty in her eye. We told everybody a sty was a kind of a wart and that we had Mary in our power. The next day Mary broke down and came around to our cabin and apologized in choked accents. She gave Eileen her best hair ribbon and me a little barrel that had a picture of Niagara Falls inside it, if you looked hard enough. We were satisfied.

15. Middy blouses and serge bloomers (pants) are loose old-fashioned women's clothing.

A. Responding

? Do you feel sorry for the Leader? Why or why not? Note: There are no nightingales in North America.

ANALYZING THE STORY

Identifying Facts

1. They refuse to get out of bed when the bugle blows, they fight against brushing their teeth in public, they sneer when the flag is lowered, they avoid doing good deeds, they complain about the food, and they scrawl their feelings over the walls of the Recreation Cabin.
2. The scheme is to offer to make pocketbooks for relatives at home for a small charge, then abscond with the money to New York. They reveal their plan to fellow campers, one of whom reports their intentions to their counselor. As a result, the girls' mail is impounded.
3. The plan is to invent sightings of rare birds. They get away with the ruse briefly, even managing to impress the group leader.
(Answers continue on page 86.)

Responding to the Story

Analyzing the Story

Identifying Facts

1. List three actions the sisters take that show their contempt for camp rules.
2. The sisters devise a money-making scheme to escape camp. Describe that scheme. What is its outcome?
3. Describe the plan the sisters devise to become the best bird watchers. How well does it succeed?
4. How do the sisters stop the rumors going around that they are frauds?
5. How do the sisters retaliate against Mary Mahoney for revealing their bird-watching scheme?

(Answers begin on page 85.)
When the leader is reduced to tears over a particularly impressive sighting, one of the other campers reveals the girls' scheme and they are punished.
4. During a softball game, Eileen pitches the ball into the stomach of one girl, and the narrator tags out another with such force as to leave a bruise.
5. They place the wart curse on her.

Interpreting Meanings
6. Their anger about camp may stem from having been "exiled" by an "unfeeling family." By flouting the camp's authorities, they might, in a way, be getting back at their family who sent them away. Students may say that the girls' resentment may stem from their being spoiled at home. Evidence might include their refusal to get out of bed when told to do so, their sneering at the flag, and their scrawling their dissatisfaction over the walls of the Recreation Cabin.
7. Some students may feel that having an accomplice might have heightened the sense of adventure. Others may argue that mischievous people are usually capable of ill deeds with or without co-conspirators.
(Answers continue in left-hand column.)

(Continued from top.)
8. Most students will appreciate that the escape plan was probably mostly big "talk." The girls, for one thing, would very likely have been too frightened to take the trip. For another, they would probably have been more discreet in their plans if they had really intended to carry them out.
9. See Teacher's Manual page 24 for possible answers.
10. Students will perhaps be familiar with cheers beginning with the words "a loud cheer for . . ." The title is clearly intended as an ironic play on those words. The title captures perfectly the writer's satiric tone.

Applying Meanings
For suggested possible answers to questions 11, 12, and 13, see Teacher's Manual page 24.

Interpreting Meanings

6. Why do the narrator and her sister resent being at camp? Support each reason you give with evidence from the story.
7. Do you think the narrator would have acted differently if her sister had not been at the camp? Why?
8. If the money-making scheme had worked, would the sisters really have escaped from the camp? Or was their fun more in imagining what they might do rather than in actually doing it?
9. Much of the story's humor comes from **exaggeration.** Identify three details or incidents that seem to be exaggerated for humorous effect.
10. What does the story's **title** mean?

Applying Meanings

11. Would you enjoy being friends with the narrator? Why?
12. Would you guess Ruth and Eileen come from a city, country, or suburban home? Why?
13. Does this account of a summer camp experience affect your ideas about camp life? How did you respond to the Bad Sports at Camp Hi-Wah?

Writing About the Story

For evaluation strategies, see Teacher's Manual page 24.

A Creative Response

1. **Writing a Letter.** Imagine you are Mary Mahoney. Write a letter home telling your parents about the narrator and her sister. Include vivid details about the sisters' appearance and behavior. Be sure to have Mary discuss the "wart curse."

A Critical Response

2. **Analyzing the Writer's Craft.** There are six main ways a writer can reveal a character in a story (see page 71). In a paragraph discuss the methods Ruth McKenney uses to reveal what the narrator of the story is like. Quote passages to show how each method is used.

Analyzing Language and Vocabulary

Compound Nouns

Compound nouns are made up of two or more words. They may be written as a single word (*blackberry*), with a hyphen (*hang-up*), or as two separate words (*fire engine*). Check a dictionary for the exact spelling of a compound noun.

1. In the following sentences from the story, find the compound nouns and write them down.
   a. "Our favorite literary character at the time was Dumas' Marguerite de Valois, who took her decapitated lover's head home in a big handkerchief for old times' sake."
   b. "In the first place, since we had started off making leather pocketbooks, we were three weeks behind the rest of the Hi-Wah bird-lovers."
   c. "After six incredibly tiresome hours, our bird logs were still blank."
2. Find ten other compound nouns in the story.

For answers, see Teacher's Manual page 24.

Reading About the Writer

Ruth McKenney (1911–1972) was born in Mishawaka, Indiana. She attended Ohio State University and afterward worked at a variety of "experiential jobs." She sold books, waited on tables, and worked as a printer before she found her true career.

When she was twenty-one, she got her first writing job as a reporter for the *Akron Beacon-Journal* (in Ohio). She then went on to New York where she became a feature writer for a newspaper and a regular contributor to *Harper's* and *The New Yorker.*

McKenney wrote eight books, but she is best remembered for her first one, *My Sister Eileen.* It describes the lighthearted adventures she shared with her attractive sister when they came from the Midwest to live in New York's Greenwich Village. The stories about Ruth and her sister were made into a musical comedy called *Wonderful Town.*

PREREADING

1. BUILDING ON PRIOR KNOWLEDGE. Explain to students that much of what Twain wrote in his first novel *The Adventures of Tom Sawyer* was based on his own experience growing up in a small Missouri town on the Mississippi River during the 1840's and 1850's. Out of this experience sprang the characters Tom and Huck (later to be the main character of Twain's masterpiece *The Adventures of Huckleberry Finn*—see text page 619). One reason Twain's first novel gained vast popularity was that it didn't moralize, a quality that was then common in books about children. The stories about Tom's mischievous pranks continue to be enormously popular today.

Ask students to speculate on how their lives would be different if they lived in a small Missouri town in the nineteenth century. Think about school, housing, clothes, attitudes.

2. ESTABLISHING A PURPOSE. Tell students to think about Tom's character as they read. Would they like to "hang out" with Tom—or does he get into too much trouble? Do they identify with him at all?

3. PREREADING JOURNAL. Before they read, have students write a brief paragraph telling what they predict is going to happen to the people in the illustration on page 90 or 93 or 96. Be sure they describe some conflict they can see in the picture.

Discussing the Illustration

American illustrator Worth Brehm (1883–1928), born in Indianapolis, Indiana, is best known for his illustrations of Twain's *The Adventures of Tom Sawyer* and *The Adventures of Huckleberry Finn.*

? What might the boys in the picture be talking about? Do you think they are supposed to be somewhere else—instead of talking and laughing around a campfire at night?

★ **Texas Essential Elements/(a) English Language Arts: 1B** Purpose and audience; **1E** Formal/informal language; **3A** Plot/character; **4E** Predict; **4F** Generalizations; **4G** Fact/nonfact; **4H** Point of view

FROM THE ADVENTURES OF TOM SAWYER

Mark Twain

Illustration by Worth Brehm.

For a detailed lesson plan on this selection, see Teacher's Manual pages 25–28. A biography of Mark Twain appears on text page 103.

A. Mood

What kind of mood, or feeling, does this paragraph convey? (Virtually all the details indicate a mood of happiness, peace, and contentment. The setting is actually so blissful that readers should be forewarned that something is going to happen which will disrupt that peace.)

SUPPLEMENTARY SUPPORT MATERIAL

1. Reading Check Test blackline master
2. Selection Test (page 29, Test Book)
3. Audiocassette recording (excerpt)
4. Author photograph on *A Gallery of Authors* poster
5. Connections Between Reading and Writing worksheet
6. Reader's Response Journal
7. Workbook (page 27)

B. Vocabulary

Mulatto (mə·lat′ō) derives from the Spanish-Portuguese word *mulato,* meaning "of mixed breed." A mulatto at this time (slavery was not yet abolished in all states) was a person with a black parent and a white parent.

C. Character and Characterization

From this incident in the story, how would you summarize the personality of "Old missis"? (She is tough on the outside but has a soft spot on the inside.) How does Twain reveal her character? (Through the words of Jim and Tom. From their conversation we can infer that "Old missis" is strict about chores, is shrewd about Tom's work habits, and is not above threatening people with physical punishment in order to get them to do their work, although she does not always follow up on her threats.)

★ **Texas Essential Elements/(c) Reading: 1A** Context clues; **1C** Dictionaries; **3A** Main ideas/details; **3D** Generalizations; **3E** Fact/fictional details; **3F** Purpose/point of view/opinion; **3H** Predict; **3I** Draw conclusions

Tom Sawyer may be the most famous American boy of all time. He is the creation of Mark Twain, the great American humorist. In these excerpts from Twain's novel *The Adventures of Tom Sawyer,* we see Tom in three of the memorable experiences in his young, enthusiastic, and often unusual life. Tom lives with his Aunt Polly, and his cousin Mary and half-brother Sid. Not much is known about Tom's parents. Jim works for Aunt Polly.

Dialect. The humor and colorful atmosphere of Mark Twain's stories is due in part to his use of dialect. A *dialect* is a special form of a language used by people in a certain part of the country or in a certain social or economic group. A dialect of English can differ from standard English in its vocabulary, pronunciation, and grammar. There are many dialects in the United States today. There were even more when Twain wrote, in the late nineteenth century. As you read, look for dialect words, such as *skylarking* and *hooked.* In most cases you will be able to figure out their meaning from the context. Some are footnoted. SRW p. 31

Strange Temptations—Strategic Movements—The Innocents Beguiled

A Saturday morning was come, and all the summer world was bright and fresh, and brimming with life. There was a song in every heart; and if the heart was young the music issued at the lips. There was cheer in every face and a spring in every step. The locust trees were in bloom and the fragrance of the blossoms filled the air. Cardiff Hill, beyond the village and above it, was green with vegetation, and it lay just far enough away to seem a Delectable Land, dreamy, reposeful, and inviting.

Tom appeared on the sidewalk with a bucket of whitewash and a long-handled brush. He surveyed the fence, and all gladness left him and a deep melancholy settled down upon his spirit. Thirty yards of board fence nine feet high. Life to him seemed hollow, and existence but a burden. Sighing he dipped his brush and passed it along the topmost plank; repeated the operation; did it again; compared the insignificant whitewashed streak with the far-reaching continent of unwhitewashed fence, and sat down on a tree-box discouraged. Jim came skipping out at the gate with a tin pail, and singing "Buffalo Gals." Bringing water from the town pump had always been hateful work in Tom's eyes, before, but now it did not strike him so. He remembered that there was company at the pump. White, mulatto, and Negro boys and girls were always there waiting their turns, resting, trading playthings, quarreling, fighting, skylarking.[1] And he remembered that although the pump was only a hundred and fifty yards off, Jim never got back with a bucket of water under an hour—and even then somebody generally had to go after him. Tom said: B

"Say, Jim, I'll fetch the water if you'll whitewash some."

Jim shook his head and said:

"Can't, Mars Tom. Old missis, she tole me I got to go an' git dis water an' not stop foolin' roun' wid anybody. She say she spec' Mars Tom gwine to ax me to whitewash, an' so she tole me go 'long an' 'tend to my own business—she 'lowed *she'd* 'tend to de whitewashin'."

"Oh, never mind what she said, Jim. That's the way she always talks. Gimme the bucket—I won't be gone only a minute. *She* won't ever know." C

"Oh, I dasn't, Mars Tom. Old missis she'd take an' tar de head off'n me. 'Deed she would."

"*She!* She never licks anybody—whacks 'em over the head with her thimble—and who cares for that, I'd like to know. She talks awful, but talk don't hurt—anyways it don't if she don't cry. Jim, I'll give you a marvel. I'll give you a white alley!"

Jim began to waver.

"White alley, Jim! And it's a bully taw."[2]

"My! Dat's a mighty gay marvel, *I* tell you!

1. **skylarking:** playing about; frolicking.
2. **marvel . . . taw:** Tom and Jim are discussing a marble. A *taw* is a shooter.

DEVELOPING VOCABULARY

The following words appear on a test in the Test Book, page 30. (See also the Vocabulary Activity Sheet.)

beguile	virtuous
repose	condescend
tranquil	pliant
dilapidate	beseech
muse	felicity

A. Making Inferences

? What happens in this passage? (Aunt Polly catches Jim dawdling with Tom and she throws a slipper at him to get him going. Jim runs off, and Tom immediately starts to paint the fence.)

But, Mars Tom, I's powerful 'fraid ole missis——"

"And besides, if you will I'll show you my sore toe."

A Jim was only human—this attraction was too much for him. He put down his pail, took the white alley, and bent over the toe with absorbing interest while the bandage was being unwound. In another moment he was flying down the street with his pail and a tingling rear, Tom was whitewashing with vigor, and Aunt Polly was retiring from the field with a slipper in her hand and triumph in her eye.

But Tom's energy did not last. He began to think of the fun he had planned for this day, and his sorrows multiplied. Soon the free boys would come tripping along on all sorts of delicious expeditions, and they would make a world of fun of him for having to work—the very thought of it burnt him like fire. He got out his worldly wealth and examined it—bits of toys, marbles, and trash; enough to buy an exchange of *work,* maybe, but not half enough to buy so much as half an hour of pure freedom. **B** So he returned his straitened means to his pocket, and gave up the idea of trying to buy the boys. At this dark and hopeless moment an inspiration burst upon him! Nothing less than a great, magnificent inspiration.

He took up his brush and went tranquilly to work. Ben Rogers hove in sight presently—the very boy, of all boys, whose ridicule he had been dreading. Ben's gait was the hop-skip-and-jump—proof enough that his heart was light and his anticipations high. He was eating an apple, and giving a long, melodious whoop, at intervals, followed by a deep-toned ding-dong-dong, ding-dong-dong, for he was personating a steamboat. As he drew near, he slackened speed, took the middle of the street, leaned far over to starboard and rounded to ponderously and with laborious pomp and circumstance[3]—for he was personating the *Big Missouri,* and considered himself to be drawing nine feet of water. He was boat and captain and engine bells combined, so he had to imagine himself standing on his own hurricane deck giving the orders and executing them:

"Stop her, sir! Ting-a-ling-ling!" The headway ran almost out and he drew up slowly toward the sidewalk.

"Ship up to back! Ting-a-ling-ling!" His arms straightened and stiffened down his sides.

"Set her back on the stabboard! Ting-a-ling-ling! Chow! ch-chow-wow! Chow!" His right hand, meantime, describing stately circles, for it was representing a forty-foot wheel.

"Let her go back on the labboard! Ting-a-ling-ling! Chow-ch-chow-chow!" The left hand began to describe circles.

C "Stop the stabboard! Ting-a-ling-ling! Stop the labboard! Come ahead on the stabboard! Stop her! Let your outside turn over slow! Ting-a-ling-ling! Chow-ow-ow! Get out that head-line! *Lively* now! Come—out with your spring-line—what're you about there! Take a turn round that stump with the bight[4] of it! Stand by that stage, now—let her go! Done with the engines, sir! Ting-a-ling-ling! *Sh't! s'h't! sh't!"* (trying the gauge cocks).

Tom went on whitewashing—paid no attention to the steamboat. Ben stared a moment and then said:

"Hi-*yi! You're* up a stump, ain't you?"

No answer. Tom surveyed his last touch with the eye of an artist, then he gave his brush another gentle sweep and surveyed the result, as before. Ben ranged up alongside of him. Tom's mouth watered for the apple, but he stuck to his work. Ben said:

"Hello, old chap, you got to work, hey?"

Tom wheeled suddenly and said:

"Why, it's you, Ben! I warn't noticing."

"Say—*I'm* going in a-swimming, *I* am. Don't you wish you could? But of course you'd druther *work*—wouldn't you? Course you would!"

Tom contemplated the boy a bit, and said:

"What do you call work?"

"Why, ain't *that* work?"

Tom resumed his whitewashing, and answered carelessly:

"Well, maybe it is, and maybe it ain't. All I know, is, it suits Tom Sawyer."

"Oh, come, now, you don't mean to let on that you *like* it?"

D The brush continued to move.

3. **pomp and circumstance:** stately ceremony.

4. **bight** (bīt): here, a loop or a slack part of a rope.

B. Suspense

? Explain the suspense created by these sentences. (We wonder what Tom's "great, magnificent inspiration" is and how it will get him out of doing his work. The exaggeration of Tom's misery—the "dark and hopeless moment"—places great value on his inspiration.)

C. Ship's Vocabulary

"Stabboard" is slang for "starboard" which is the right side of a ship. "Labboard," slang for "larboard," is the left side. The "gauge cocks" in a steamboat would measure the water or steam needed to propel the boat.

D. Subtitles

? Go back to page 88 and explain what each of Twain's subtitles means. ("Strange Temptations" refers to Tom's temptation to get out of working; "Strategic Movements" refers to Tom's clever whitewashing scheme; and "The Innocents Beguiled" refers to all of Tom's friends whom he tricked into painting for him.)

Responding to the Illustration

? If you had to provide a title for this illustration, what would it be? Why?

"Does a boy get a chance to whitewash a fence every day?"

Illustration by Worth Brehm.

"Like it? Well, I don't see why I oughtn't to like it. Does a boy get a chance to whitewash a fence every day?"

That put the thing in a new light. Ben stopped nibbling his apple. Tom swept his brush daintily back and forth—stepped back to note the effect—added a touch here and there—criticized the effect again—Ben watching every move and getting more and more interested, more and more absorbed. Presently he said:

"Say, Tom, let *me* whitewash a little."

Tom considered, was about to consent; but he altered his mind:

A "No—no—I reckon it wouldn't hardly do, Ben. You see, Aunt Polly's awful particular about this fence—right here on the street, you know—but if it was the back fence I wouldn't mind and *she* wouldn't. Yes, she's awful particular about this fence; it's got to be done very careful; I reckon there ain't one boy in a thousand, maybe two thousand, that can do it the way it's got to be done."

"No—is that so? Oh come, now—lemme just try. Only just a little—I'd let *you,* if you was me, Tom."

"Ben, I'd like to, honest injun: but Aunt Polly—well, Jim wanted to do it, but she wouldn't let him; Sid wanted to do it, and she wouldn't let Sid. Now don't you see how I'm fixed? If you was to tackle this fence and anything was to happen to it——"

"Oh, shucks, I'll be just as careful. Now lemme try. Say—I'll give you the core of my apple."

"Well, here—No, Ben, now don't. I'm afeard ——"

"I'll give you *all* of it!"

Tom gave up the brush with reluctance in his face, but alacrity[5] in his heart. And while the late steamer *Big Missouri* worked and sweated in the sun, the retired artist sat on a barrel in the shade close by, dangled his legs, munched his apple, and planned the slaughter of more innocents. There was no lack of material; boys happened along every little while; they came to jeer, but remained B to whitewash. By the time Ben was fagged out, Tom had traded the next chance to Billy Fisher for a kite, in good repair; and when *he* played out, Johnny Miller bought in for a dead rat and a string to swing it with—and so on, and so on, hour after hour. And when the middle of the afternoon came, from being a poor poverty-stricken boy in the morning, Tom was literally rolling in wealth. He had besides the things before mentioned, twelve marbles, part of a jew's-harp, a piece of blue bottle glass to look through, a spool cannon, a key that wouldn't unlock anything, a fragment of chalk, a glass stopper of a decanter, a tin soldier, a couple of tadpoles, six firecrackers, a kitten with only one eye, a brass doorknob, a dog collar—but no dog—the handle of a knife, four pieces of orange peel, and a dilapidated old window sash.

He had had a nice, good, idle time all the while—plenty of company—and the fence had three coats of whitewash on it! If he hadn't run out of whitewash, he would have bankrupted every boy in the village.

Tom said to himself that it was not such a hollow world, after all. He had discovered a great law of human action, without knowing it—namely, that in order to make a man or a boy covet[6] a thing, it is only necessary to make the thing difficult to attain.[7] If he had been a great and wise philosopher, like the writer of this book, he would now have comprehended that Work consists of whatever a body is *obliged* to do, and that Play consists of whatever a body is not obliged to do. And this would help him to understand why constructing artificial flowers or performing on a treadmill is work, while rolling tenpins or climbing Mont Blanc is only amusement. There are wealthy gentlemen in England who drive four-horse passenger coaches twenty or thirty miles on a daily line, in the summer, because the privilege costs them considerable money; but if they were offered wages for the service, they would turn it into work and then they would resign. C D

The boy mused a while over the substantial change which had taken place in his wordly circumstances, and then wended toward headquarters to report.

5. **alacrity** (ə·lak′rə·tē): eager willingness.

6. **covet:** to want very much.
7. **attain:** to gain or get.

A. Interpretation
? How is Tom going to get Ben to paint the fence—what in Ben is he appealing to? (Tom is appealing to Ben's sense of pride. By saying the fence has "got to be done very careful," Tom is implying that Ben wouldn't be able to do it well enough. He is challenging Ben.)

B. Slang
To be "fagged out" is to be tired out.

C. Theme
In this passage, Twain states his theme.

D. Responding
? Do you agree with this theory? How would you feel if you got paid to do homework?

A. Motivation

? Why do you suppose Aunt Polly feels the need to dilute the compliment she pays to Tom? (She doesn't want Tom to think she is too pleased with him for fear that he will take advantage of her.)

B. Colorful Language

? What does Twain mean when he says that Tom "was too crowded for time." (Tom was in too much of a hurry.)

C. Vocabulary

Pantalettes are long, loose pants frilled at the ankle, And worn to show beneath a skirt.

D. Plot

? What has happened in this passage? (Tom has fallen in love at first sight with the little blue-eyed girl.) What does the sentence "The fresh-crowned hero fell without firing a shot" mean? (The hero, victorious in previous battle, fell in love without any resistance.)

Tom as a General— Triumph and Reward— Dismal Felicity— Commission and Omission

Tom presented himself before Aunt Polly, who was sitting by an open window in a pleasant rearward apartment, which was bedroom, breakfast room, dining room, and library, combined. The balmy summer air, the restful quiet, the odor of the flowers, and the drowsing murmur of the bees had had their effect, and she was nodding over her knitting—for she had no company but the cat, and it was asleep in her lap. Her spectacles were propped up on her gray head for safety. She had thought that of course Tom had deserted long ago, and she wondered at seeing him place himself in her power again in this intrepid way. He said: "Mayn't I go and play now, aunt?"

"What, a'ready? How much have you done?"

"It's all done, aunt."

"Tom, don't lie to me—I can't bear it."

"I ain't, aunt; it *is* all done."

Aunt Polly placed small trust in such evidence. She went out to see for herself; and she would have been content to find twenty percent of Tom's statement true. When she found the entire fence whitewashed, and not only whitewashed but elaborately coated and recoated, and even a streak added to the ground, her astonishment was almost unspeakable. She said:

A "Well, I never! There's no getting round it, you *can* work when you're a mind to, Tom." And then she diluted the compliment by adding, "But it's powerful seldom you're a mind to, I'm bound to say. Well, go 'long and play; but mind you get back some time in a week, or I'll tan you."

She was so overcome by the splendor of his achievement that she took him into the closet and selected a choice apple and delivered it to him, along with an improving lecture upon the added value and flavor a treat took to itself when it came without sin through virtuous effort. And while she closed with a happy Scriptural flourish, he "hooked" a doughnut.

Then he skipped out, and saw Sid just starting up the outside stairway that led to the back rooms on the second floor. Clods were handy and the air was full of them in a twinkling. They raged around Sid like a hailstorm; and before Aunt Polly could collect her surprised faculties and sally to the rescue, six or seven clods had taken personal effect, and Tom was over the fence and gone. There was a gate, but as a general thing he was too crowded B for time to make use of it. His soul was at peace, now that he had settled with Sid for calling attention to his black thread and getting him into trouble.[1]

Tom skirted the block, and came round into a muddy alley that led by the back of his aunt's cow stable. He presently got safely beyond the reach of capture and punishment, and hastened toward the public square of the village, where two "military" companies of boys had met for conflict, according to previous appointment. Tom was General of one of these armies, Joe Harper (a bosom friend) General of the other. These two great commanders did not condescend to fight in person—that being better suited to the still smaller fry—but sat together on an eminence[2] and conducted the field operations by orders delivered through aides-de-camp.[3] Tom's army won a great victory, after a long and hard-fought battle. Then the dead were counted, prisoners exchanged, the terms of the next disagreement agreed upon, and the day for the necessary battle appointed; after which the armies fell into line and marched away, and Tom turned homeward alone.

As he was passing by the house where Jeff Thatcher lived, he saw a new girl in the garden—a lovely little blue-eyed creature with yellow hair plaited into two long tails, white summer frock and embroidered pantalettes. The fresh-crowned hero fell without firing a shot. A certain Amy C, Lawrence vanished out of his heart and left not even a memory of herself behind. He had thought he loved her to distraction,[4] he had regarded his passion as adoration; and behold it was only a poor little evanescent partiality.[5] He had been

1. This refers to an incident in Chapter 1, in which Sid alerted Aunt Polly to a trick Tom had pulled to hide the fact that he had gone swimming.
2. **eminence:** a hill.
3. **aides-de-camp** (ādz'də kamp): French for military assistants.
4. **distraction:** great mental confusion or disturbance.
5. **evanescent partiality** (ev'ə·nes'n't): fleeting affection.

He began to "show off."

Illustration by Worth Brehm.

A. Responding to the Illustration

? What do you think is going through the girl's mind as she watches Tom show off? What does the expression on her face reveal? Do boys do things like this to impress girls today? How about girls: How do they try to get the attention of the boys?

B. Character's Actions

? Do you think this kind of behavior will work? (We have to trust Tom—this must have been the way he won Amy Lawrence.)

A

months winning her; she had confessed hardly a week ago; he had been the happiest and the proudest boy in the world only seven short days, and here in one instant of time she had gone out of his heart like a casual stranger whose visit is done.

B He worshiped this new angel with furtive eye, till he saw that she had discovered him; then he pretended he did not know she was present, and began to "show off" in all sorts of absurd boyish ways, in order to win her admiration. He kept up this grotesque foolishness for some time; but by and by, while he was in the midst of some dangerous gymnastic performances, he glanced aside and saw that the little girl was wending her way toward the house. Tom came up to the fence and leaned on it, grieving, and hoping she would tarry yet a while longer. She halted a moment on the steps and then moved toward the door. Tom heaved a great sigh as she put her foot on the threshold. But his face lit up, right away, for she tossed a pansy over the fence a moment before she disappeared.

The boy ran around and stopped within a foot or two of the flower, and then shaded his eyes

A. Author's Tone
? What does the last sentence tell you about Twain's attitude toward Tom? (Twain is sympathetic. He understands Tom's disappointment and feels sorry for him.)

B. Interpretation
? What does it mean that Aunt Polly was "discharging lightnings of wrath"? (She was glaring angrily—and probably at Tom.)

C. Interpretation
? Aunt Polly dilutes compliments to Tom, punishes him without finding out if he's guilty, and then refuses to make up for it when she's wrong. Why don't we see Aunt Polly as a villainous character? (We know that Aunt Polly has a good heart, but Tom taxes her limits. It's nearly impossible to discipline Tom—he's a parent's nightmare. Although we love Tom for all of his mischief and fun, we feel genuinely sorry for Aunt Polly.)

with his hand and began to look down street as if he had discovered something of interest going on in that direction. Presently he picked up a straw and began trying to balance it on his nose, with his head tilted far back; and as he moved from side to side, in his efforts, he edged nearer and nearer toward the pansy; finally his bare foot rested upon it, his pliant toes closed upon it, and he hopped away with the treasure and disappeared round the corner. But only for a minute—only while he could button the flower inside his jacket, next to his heart—or next his stomach, possibly, for he was not much posted in anatomy, and not hypercritical, anyway.

He returned, now, and hung about the fence till nightfall, "showing off," as before, but the girl never exhibited herself again, though Tom comforted himself a little with the hope that she had been near some window, meantime, and been aware of his attentions. Finally he rode home reluctantly, with his poor head full of visions. A

All through supper his spirits were so high that his aunt wondered "what had got into the child." He took a good scolding about clodding Sid, and did not seem to mind it in the least. He tried to steal sugar under his aunt's very nose, and got his knuckles rapped for it. He said:

"Aunt, you don't whack Sid when he takes it."

"Well, Sid don't torment a body the way you do. You'd be always into that sugar if I warn't watching you."

Presently she stepped into the kitchen, and Sid, happy in his immunity, reached for the sugar bowl—a sort of glorying over Tom which was well-nigh unbearable. But Sid's fingers slipped and the bowl dropped and broke. Tom was in ecstasies. In such ecstasies that he even controlled his tongue and was silent. He said to himself that he would not speak a word, even when his aunt came in, but would sit perfectly still till she asked who did the mischief; and then he would tell, and there would be nothing so good in the world as to see that pet model "catch it." He was so brim full of exultation that he could hardly hold himself when the old lady came back and stood above the wreck discharging lightnings of wrath from over her spectacles. B He said to himself, "Now it's coming!" And the next instant he was sprawling on the floor! The potent palm was uplifted to strike again when Tom cried out:

"Hold on, now, what 'er you belting *me* for? Sid broke it!"

Aunt Polly paused, perplexed, and Tom looked for healing pity. But when she got her tongue again, she only said:

"Umf! Well, you don't get a lick amiss, I reckon. You been into some other audacious[6] mischief when I wasn't around, like enough." C

Then her conscience reproached her, and she yearned to say something kind and loving; but she judged that this would be construed into a confession that she had been in the wrong, and discipline forbade that. So she kept silence, and went about her affairs with a troubled heart. Tom sulked in a corner and exalted his woes. He knew that in her heart his aunt was on her knees to him, and he was morosely[7] gratified by the consciousness of it. He would hang out no signals, he would take notice of none. He knew that a yearning glance fell upon him, now and then, through a film of tears, but he refused recognition of it. He pictured himself lying sick unto death and his aunt, bending over him beseeching one little forgiving word, but he would turn his face to the wall, and die with that word unsaid. Ah, how would she feel then? And he pictured himself brought home from the river, dead, with his curls all wet, and his sore heart at rest. How she would throw herself upon him, and how her tears would fall like rain, and her lips pray God to give her back her boy and she would never, never abuse him anymore! But he would lie there cold and white and make no sign—a poor little sufferer, whose griefs were at an end. He so worked upon his feelings with the pathos[8] of these dreams, that he had to keep swallowing, he was so like to choke; and his eyes swam in a blur of water, which overflowed when he winked, and ran down and trickled from the end of his nose. And such a luxury to him was this petting of his sorrows, that he could not bear to have any worldly cheeriness or any grating de-

6. **audacious** (ô·dā′shəs): rudely bold; daring.
7. **morosely** (mə·rōs′lē): gloomily.
8. **pathos** (pā′thäs): sorrow.

A. Exaggeration

? What exaggeration does Twain use to make Tom's misery humorous? (Examples include "he could not bear any worldly cheeriness," his sorrow was "too sacred for such contact," he "moved in clouds and darkness.")

light intrude upon it; it was too sacred for such contact; and so, presently, when his cousin Mary danced in, all alive with the joy of seeing home again after an agelong visit of one week to the country, he got up and moved in clouds and darkness out at one door as she brought song and sunshine in at the other.

He wandered far from the accustomed haunts of boys, and sought desolate places that were in harmony with his spirit. A log raft in the river invited him, and he seated himself on its outer edge and contemplated the dreary vastness of the stream, wishing, the while, that he could only be drowned, all at once and unconsciously, without undergoing the uncomfortable routine devised by nature. Then he thought of his flower. He got it
A out, rumpled and wilted, and it mightily increased his dismal felicity.[9] He wondered if *she* would pity him if she knew? Would she cry, and wish that she had a right to put her arms around his neck and comfort him? Or would she turn coldly away like all the hollow world? This picture brought such an agony of pleasurable suffering that he worked it over and over again in his mind and set it up in new and varied lights, till he wore it threadbare. At last he rose up sighing and departed in the darkness.

About half past nine or ten o'clock he came along the deserted street to where the Adored Unknown lived; he paused a moment; no sound fell upon his listening ear; a candle was casting a dull glow upon the curtain of a second story window. Was the sacred presence there? He climbed the fence, threaded his stealthy way through the plants, till he stood under that window; he looked up at it long, and with emotion; then he laid him down on the ground under it, disposing himself upon his back, with his hands clasped upon his breast and holding his poor wilted flower. And
B thus he would die—out in the cold world, with no shelter over his homeless head, no friendly hand to wipe the death-damps from his brow, no loving face to bend pityingly over him when the great agony came. And thus *she* would see him when she looked out upon the glad morning, and oh! would she drop one little tear upon his poor, lifeless form, would she heave one little sigh to see a bright young life so rudely blighted, so untimely cut down?

The window went up, a maidservant's discordant voice profaned[10] the holy calm, and a deluge of water drenched the prone martyr's[11] remains!

The strangling hero sprang up with a relieving snort. There was a whiz as of a missile in the air, mingled with the murmur of a curse, a sound as of shivering glass followed, and a small, vague form went over the fence and shot away in the gloom.

Not long after, as Tom, all undressed for bed, was surveying his drenched garments by the light of a tallow dip, Sid woke up; but if he had any dim idea of making any "references to allusions," he thought better of it and held his peace, for there was danger in Tom's eye.

Tom turned in without the added vexation[12] of C
prayers, and Sid made mental note of the omis- D
sion.

Mental Acrobatics—Attending Sunday School—The Superintendent—"Showing Off"—Tom Lionized

The sun rose upon a tranquil world, and beamed down upon the peaceful village like a benediction.[1] Breakfast over, Aunt Polly had family worship: It began with a prayer built from the ground up of solid courses of Scriptural quotations, welded together with a thin mortar of originality; and from the summit of this she delivered a grim chapter of the Mosaic Law, as from Sinai.[2]

9. **felicity:** happiness.

10. **profaned:** treated something sacred with no respect.
11. **prone martyr:** lying-down sufferer.
12. **vexation** (vek·sā'shən): cause of annoyance or distress.
1. **benediction** (ben'ə·dik'shən): blessing.
2. **Sinai:** In the Bible, the mountain where Moses received the law from God. Polly acts as if her rules are ortained by God.

B. Character

? What do Tom's thoughts reveal about him? (They show that he is overly imaginative and given to melodrama and self-pity.)

C. Motivation

? What might motivate Sid to note that Tom did not say his prayers? (It might be a useful weapon against Tom at some future time.)

D. Subtitles

? Go back to page 92 and explain the meanings of each of Twain's subtitles. ("Tom as a General" refers to Tom's playfighting with his "army"; "Triumph and Reward" refers to Tom's impressing the girl he fell in love with who throws him a flower; "Dismal Felicity" refers to Tom's enjoyment of his melancholy; "Commission and Omission" refers to Tom's giving his loved one responsibility for his "dead body" and his later omission to say his prayers.)

A. Discussing the Illustration
? How have classrooms changed since Tom's time? Compare this illustration with the one on page 90. Do you think Brehm should have done all his illustrations in color? Why or why not? When are black-and-white illustrations more effective than color ones? Explain.

B. Character
? What does this passage tell you about Tom? (It indicates that Tom is lazy and tends to look for the easiest way to do something he dislikes. It also indicates that he does not take his religious education as seriously as he might. The Sermon on the Mount, after all, is one of the greatest passages in the New Testament. See Matthew 5:7 and Luke 6:20.)

A

"Let me see it." Illustration by Worth Brehm.

B

Then Tom girded up his loins, so to speak, and went to work to "get his verses." Sid had learned his lesson days before. Tom bent all his energies to the memorizing of five verses, and he chose part of the Sermon on the Mount, because he could find no verses that were shorter. At the end of half an hour Tom had a vague general idea of his lesson, but no more, for his mind was traversing the whole field of human thought, and his hands were busy with distracting recreations. Mary took his book to hear him recite, and he tried to find his way through the fog:

"Blessed are the a—a—"

"Poor—"

"Yes—poor; blessed are the poor—a—a—"

"In spirit—"

"In spirit; blessed are the poor in spirit, for they—they—"

"*Theirs*—"

"For *theirs*. Blessed are the poor in spirit, for *theirs* is the kingdom of heaven. Blessed are they that mourn, for they—they—"

"Sh—"

"For they—a—"

"S, H, A—"

"For they S, H—Oh, I don't know what it is!"

"*Shall!*"

"Oh, *shall*! for they shall—for they shall—a—a—shall mourn—a—a—blessed are they that shall—they that—a—they that shall mourn, for they shall—a—shall *what*? Why don't you tell me, Mary?—what do you want to be so mean for?"

A. Vocabulary
A Barlow knife (named after Englishman Russell Barlow, its maker) is a long, sturdy jackknife. (The one Mary has given Tom is just a toy.)

"Oh, Tom, you poor thickheaded thing, I'm not teasing you. I wouldn't do that. You must go and learn it again. Don't you be discouraged, Tom, you'll manage it—and if you do, I'll give you something ever so nice. There, now, that's a good boy."

"All right! What is it, Mary, tell me what it is."

"Never you mind, Tom. You know if I say it's nice, it *is* nice."

"You bet you that's so, Mary. All right, I'll tackle it again."

And he did "tackle it again"—and under the double pressure of curiosity and prospective gain, he did it with such spirit that he accomplished a shining success. Mary gave him a brand-new "Barlow" knife worth twelve and a half cents; and the convulsion of delight that swept his system shook him to his foundations. True, the knife would not cut anything, but it was a "sure-enough" Barlow, and there was inconceivable grandeur in that—though where the Western boys ever got the idea that such a weapon could possibly be counterfeited to its injury, is an imposing mystery and will always remain so, perhaps. Tom contrived to scarify[3] the cupboard with it, and was arranging to begin on the bureau, when he was called off to dress for Sunday school. A

Mary gave him a tin basin of water and a piece of soap, and he went outside the door and set the basin on a little bench there; then he dipped the soap in the water and laid it down; turned up his sleeves; poured out the water on the ground, gently, and then entered the kitchen and began to wipe his face diligently on the towel behind the door. But Mary removed the towel and said: B

"Now ain't you ashamed, Tom. You musn't be so bad. Water won't hurt you."

Tom was a trifle disconcerted.[4] The basin was refilled, and this time he stood over it a little while, gathering resolution; took in a big breath and began. When he entered the kitchen presently, with both eyes shut and groping for the towel with his hands, an honorable testimony[5] of suds and water was dripping from his face. But when he emerged from the towel, he was not yet satisfactory, for the clean territory stopped short at his chin and his jaws, like a mask; below and beyond this line there was a dark expanse of unirrigated soil that spread downward in front and backward around his neck. C Mary took him in hand, and when she was done with him he was a man and a brother, without distinction of color, and his saturated[6] hair was neatly brushed, and its short curls wrought into a dainty and symmetrical general effect. (He privately smoothed out the curls, with labor and difficulty, and plastered his hair close down to his head; for he held curls to be effeminate, and his own filled his life with bitterness.) Then Mary got out a suit of his clothing that had been used only on Sundays during two years—they were simply called his "other clothes"—and so by that we know the size of his wardrobe. The girl "put him to rights" after he had dressed himself; she buttoned his neat roundabout up to his chin, turned his vast shirt collar down over his shoulders, brushed him off and crowned him with his speckled straw hat. He now looked exceedingly improved and uncomfortable. He was fully as uncomfortable as he looked; for there was a restraint about whole clothes and cleanliness that galled[7] him. He hoped that Mary would forget his shoes, but the hope was blighted; she coated them thoroughly with tallow, as was the custom, and brought them out. He lost his temper and said he was always being made to do everything he didn't want to do. But Mary said, persuasively:

"Please, Tom—that's a good boy."

So he got into the shoes snarling. Mary was soon ready, and the three children set out for Sunday school—a place that Tom hated with his whole heart; but Sid and Mary were fond of it.

Sabbath-school hours were from nine to half past ten; and then church service. Two of the children always remained for the sermon voluntarily, and the other always remained too—for stronger reasons. D The church's high-backed, uncushioned pews would seat about three hundred persons; the edifice was but a small, plain affair, with a sort of pine board tree-box on top of it for a steeple. At the door Tom dropped back a step

3. **scarify:** to nick and cut repeatedly.
4. **disconcerted:** embarrassed.
5. **testimony:** evidence; proof.
6. **saturated:** soaking wet.
7. **galled:** irritated; annoyed.

B. Characterization
? What method of characterization does Twain use in this passage to reveal Tom? (He lets Tom's actions speak for themselves.) What does it tell about Tom? (This is another example of Tom's skirting a hateful chore. He finds no great value in being clean.)

Note the old-fashioned method of washing. This is before modern plumbing.

C. Exaggeration
Here is a good example of Twain's famed use of exaggeration to make us laugh. Another writer might simply have said that Tom's neck was dirty.

D. Clarification
? Who were the two that stayed voluntarily—and who didn't? (Sid and Mary; Tom remained under duress.) What do you think those "stronger reasons" are? (Aunt Polly probably leaves strict instructions with Sid and Mary to make sure that Tom stays.)

A. Exaggeration
Note that Twain vastly overstates the condition of the precocious German boy after his feat. Twain definitely prefers the less intellectual Tom.

B. Foreshadowing
After reading this explanation of the ticket system, what does Tom's ticket-trading foreshadow? (He will probably find some way to win a Bible and achieve glory.) It's ironic that Tom, who shows such little talent for memorizing scriptures, should covet one of these Bibles.

C. Characterization
Identify the two methods of characterization Twain uses in this passage to reveal the superintendent. (Twain describes the superintendent's appearance. He also states directly that the superintendent is earnest, sincere, and honest.) From this description, do you think he is going to be a likable character?

and accosted a Sunday-dressed comrade.

"Say, Billy, got a yaller ticket?"

"Yes."

"What'll you take for her?"

"What'll you give?"

"Piece of lickrish and a fishhook."

"Less see 'em."

Tom exhibited. They were satisfactory, and the property changed hands. Then Tom traded a couple of white alleys for three red tickets, and some small trifle or other for a couple of blue ones. He waylaid other boys as they came, and went on buying tickets of various colors ten or fifteen minutes longer. He entered the church, now, with a swarm of clean and noisy boys and girls, proceeded to his seat and started a quarrel with the first boy that came handy. The teacher, a grave, elderly man, interfered; then turned back a moment and Tom pulled a boy's hair in the next bench, and was absorbed in his book when the boy turned around; stuck a pin in another boy, presently, in order to hear him say "Ouch!" and got a new reprimand[8] from his teacher. Tom's whole class were of a pattern—restless, noisy, and troublesome. When they came to recite their lessons, not one of them knew his verses perfectly, but had to be prompted all along. However, they worried through, and each got his reward—in small blue tickets, each with a passage of Scripture on it; each blue ticket was pay for two verses of the recitation. Ten blue tickets equaled a red one, and could be exchanged for it; ten red tickets equaled a yellow one; for ten yellow tickets the superintendent gave a very plainly bound Bible (worth forty cents in those easy times) to the pupil. How many of my readers would have the industry and application to memorize two thousand verses, even for a Doré Bible?[9] And yet Mary had acquired two Bibles in this way—it was the patient work of two years—and a boy of German parentage had won four or five. He once recited three thousand verses without stopping; but the strain upon his mental faculties was too great, and A he was little better than an idiot from that day forth—a grievous misfortune for the school, for on great occasions, before company, the superintendent (as Tom expressed it) had always made this boy come out and "spread himself." Only the older pupils managed to keep their tickets and stick to their tedious work long enough to get a Bible, and so the delivery of one of these prizes was a rare and noteworthy circumstance; the successful pupil was so great and conspicuous for that day that on the spot every scholar's heart was fired with a fresh ambition that often lasted a couple of weeks. It is possible that Tom's mental stomach had never really hungered for one of those prizes, but unquestionably his entire being B had for many a day longed for the glory and the éclat[10] that came with it.

In due course the superintendent stood up in front of the pulpit, with a closed hymnbook in his hand and his forefinger inserted between its leaves, and commanded attention. When a Sunday-school superintendent makes his customary little speech, a hymnbook in the hand is as necessary as is the inevitable sheet of music in the hand of a singer who stands forward on the platform and sings a solo at a concert—though why, is a mystery: for neither the hymnbook nor the sheet of music is ever referred to by the sufferer. This superintendent was a slim creature of thirty-five with a sandy goatee[11] and short sandy hair; he wore a stiff standing collar whose upper edge almost reached his ears and whose sharp points curved forward abreast the corners of his mouth—a fence that compelled a straight lookout ahead, and turning of the whole body when a side view was required; his chin was propped on a spreading C cravat which was as broad and as long as a banknote, and had fringed ends; his boot toes were turned sharply up, in the fashion of the day, like sleigh runners—an effect patiently and laboriously produced by the young men by sitting with their toes pressed against a wall for hours together. Mr. Walters was very earnest of mien,[12] and very sincere and honest at heart; and he held sacred things and places in such reverence, and so separated

8. **reprimand** (rep′rə·mand′): severe scolding.
9. **Doré** (dô·rā′) **Bible:** French painter and book illustrator (Paul) Gustave Doré (1832?–1883) produced a noted illustrated version of the Bible.
10. **éclat** (ā·klä′): fame.
11. **goatee:** small, pointed beard.
12. **mien** (mēn): manner.

them from worldly matters, that unconsciously to himself his Sunday-school voice had acquired a peculiar intonation which was wholly absent on weekdays. He began after this fashion:

"Now, children, I want you all to sit up just as straight and pretty as you can and give me all your attention for a minute or two. There—that is it. That is the way good little boys and girls should do. I see one little girl who is looking out of the window—I am afraid she thinks I am out there somewhere—perhaps up in one of the trees making a speech to the little birds. (Applausive titter.) I want to tell you how good it makes me feel to see so many bright, clean little faces assembled in a place like this, learning to do right and be good." And so forth and so on. It is not necessary to set down the rest of the oration. It was of a pattern which does not vary, and so it is familiar to us all.

A The latter third of the speech was marred by the resumption of fights and other recreations among certain of the bad boys, and by fidgetings and whisperings that extended far and wide, washing even to the bases of isolated and incorruptible rocks like Sid and Mary. But now every sound ceased suddenly, with the subsidence[13] of Mr. Walters's voice, and the conclusion of the speech was received with a burst of silent gratitude.

A good part of the whispering had been occasioned by an event which was more or less rare—the entrance of visitors: lawyer Thatcher, accompanied by a very feeble and aged man; a fine, portly, middle-aged gentleman with iron-gray hair; and a dignified lady who was doubtless the latter's wife. The lady was leading a child. Tom had been restless and full of chafings and repinings;[14] conscience-smitten, too—he could not meet Amy Lawrence's eye, he could not brook her loving gaze. But when he saw this small newcomer his soul was all ablaze with bliss in a moment. The next moment he was "showing off" with all his might—cuffing boys, pulling hair, making faces—in a word, using every art that seemed likely to fascinate a girl and win her applause. His exaltation had but one alloy—the memory of his humiliation in this angel's garden—and that record in sand was fast washing out, under the waves of happiness that were sweeping over it now.

The visitors were given the highest seat of honor, and as soon as Mr. Walters's speech was finished, he introduced them to the school. The middle-aged man turned out to be a prodigious[15] personage—no less a one than the county judge—altogether the most august[16] creation these children had ever looked upon—and they wondered what kind of material he was made of—and they half wanted to hear him roar, and were half afraid he might, too. He was from Constantinople, twelve miles away—so he had traveled, and seen the world—these very eyes had looked upon the county courthouse—which was said to have a tin roof. B The awe which these reflections inspired was attested by the impressive silence and the ranks of staring eyes. This was the great Judge Thatcher, brother of their own lawyer. Jeff Thatcher immediately went forward, to be familiar with the great man and be envied by the school. It would have been music to his soul to hear the whisperings:

"Look at him, Jim! He's a-going up there. Say—look! he's a-going to shake hands with him—he *is* shaking hands with him! By jings, don't you wish you was Jeff?"

Mr. Walters fell to "showing off," with all sorts of official bustlings and activities, giving orders, delivering judgments, discharging directions here, there, everywhere that he could find a target. The librarian "showed off"—running hither and thither with his arms full of books and making a deal of the splutter and fuss that insect authority delights in. The young lady teachers "showed off"—bending sweetly over pupils that were lately being boxed,[17] lifting pretty warning fingers at bad little boys and patting good ones lovingly. The young gentlemen teachers "showed off" with small scoldings and other little displays of authority and fine attention to discipline—and most of the teachers, of both sexes, found business up at the library, by the pulpit; and it was business that frequently had to be done over again two or three times (with much seeming vexation). The little girls "showed off" in various ways, and the little

13. **subsidence:** quieting or settling down.
14. **repinings** (ri·pīn′iŋs): complaints.
15. **prodigious** (prə·dij′əs): very powerful and great.
16. **august:** majestic and dignified.
17. **boxed:** hit on the head, especially the ears.

A. Figurative Language

To what does Twain compare Sid and Mary? (He compares them to rocks.) In what way are Sid and Mary like rocks? (They are oblivious to distractions and are unchanging, both in their expression and their behavior. You know they are going to be perfect static characters in this novel.)

B. Exaggeration

What is the exaggeration in this passage? (That twelve miles encompasses the world. This exaggeration parallels the townspeople's exaggeration—and his own—of the Judge's stature.)

A. Dramatic Irony
Dramatic irony occurs when we know something that a character in a story or play does not know.

? What dramatic irony do you detect in this passage? (The reader is aware of the deceitful and conniving way in which Tom has won the prize but the Judge is not.) Note that the irony adds to the humor in that, as a prize for his dishonorable behavior, Tom is awarded a Bible.)

Critical Comment
A critic of Twain has noted that "his importance to world literature lies not in the power of his ideas, but in the universality of his characters' dilemmas and his accessibility to readers of all ages."

Discuss the meaning of the quotation with students, making sure they understand the concepts of universality and accessibility. How does the quotation apply to the exerpt they've read from *The Adventures of Tom Sawyer?* Who would enjoy the story more, young people or adults?

B. Making Inferences

? What does Amy discover? (She sees that Tom is avoiding looking at her; and when she turns around to see where his eyes are fixed, she discovers her rival, the Judge's daughter. She realizes that Tom has found a new love.)

C. Responding

? Do you agree with what the Judge says? Why or why not?

boys "showed off" with such diligence that the air was thick with paper wads and the murmur of scufflings. And above it all the great man sat and beamed a majestic judicial smile upon all the house, and warmed himself in the sun of his own grandeur—for he was "showing off," too.

There was only one thing wanting, to make Mr. Walters's ecstasy complete, and that was a chance to deliver a Bible prize and exhibit a prodigy.[18] Several pupils had a few yellow tickets, but none had enough—he had been around among the star pupils inquiring. He would have given worlds, now, to have that German lad back again with a sound mind.

And now at this moment, when hope was dead, Tom Sawyer came forward with nine yellow tickets, nine red tickets, and ten blue ones, and demanded a Bible. This was a thunderbolt out of a clear sky. Walters was not expecting an application from this source for the next ten years. But there was no getting around it—here were the certified checks, and they were good for their face. Tom was therefore elevated to a place with the Judge and the other elect, and the great news was announced from headquarters. It was the most stunning surprise of the decade, and so profound was the sensation that it lifted the new hero up to the judicial one's altitude, and the school had two marvels to gaze upon in place of one. The boys were all eaten up with envy—but those that suffered the bitterest pangs were those who perceived too late that they themselves had contributed to this hated splendor by trading tickets to Tom for the wealth he had amassed in selling whitewashing privileges. These despised themselves, as being the dupes of a wily fraud, a guileful snake in the grass.

A The prize was delivered to Tom with as much effusion as the superintendent could pump up under the circumstances; but it lacked somewhat of the true gush, for the poor fellow's instinct taught him that there was a mystery here that could not well bear the light, perhaps; it was simply preposterous that *this* boy had warehoused two thousand sheaves of Scriptural wisdom on his premises—a dozen would strain his capacity, without a doubt.

Amy Lawrence was proud and glad, and she tried to make Tom see it in her face—but he wouldn't look. She wondered; then she was just a grain troubled; next a dim suspicion came and went—came again; she watched; a furtive glance told her worlds—and then her heart broke, and she was jealous, and angry, and the tears came and she hated everybody. Tom most of all (she thought). B

Tom was introduced to the Judge; but his tongue was tied, his breath would hardly come, his heart quaked—partly because of the awful greatness of the man, but mainly because he was *her* parent. He would have liked to fall down and worship him, if it were in the dark. The Judge put his hand on Tom's head and called him a fine little man, and asked him what his name was. The boy stammered, gasped, and got it out:

"Tom."

"Oh, no, not Tom—it is—"

"Thomas."

"Ah, that's it. I thought there was more to it, maybe. That's very well. But you've another one I daresay, and you'll tell it to me, won't you?"

"Tell the gentleman your other name, Thomas," said Walters, "and say *sir.* You mustn't forget your manners."

"Thomas Sawyer—sir."

"That's it! That's a good boy. Fine boy. Fine, manly little fellow. Two thousand verses is a great many—very, very great many. And you never can be sorry for the trouble you took to learn them; for knowledge is worth more than anything there is in the world; it's what makes great men and good men; you'll be a great man and a good man C yourself, some day, Thomas, and then you'll look back and say, It's all owing to the precious Sunday-school privileges of my boyhood—it's all owing to my dear teachers that taught me to learn—it's all owing to the good superintendent, who encouraged me, and watched over me, and gave me a beautiful Bible—a splendid elegant Bible—to keep and have it all for my own, always—it's all owing to right bringing up! That is what you will say, Thomas—and you wouldn't take any money for those two thousand verses—no indeed you wouldn't. And now you wouldn't mind telling me and this lady some of the things you've

18. **prodigy** (präd'ə·jē): remarkably talented child.

READING CHECK TEST

1. Sid is one of the children Tom talks into whitewashing the fence. *(False)*
2. Tom is punished when Sid breaks the sugar bowl. *(True)*
3. Sid and Mary are fond of Sunday school. *(True)*
4. The new girl Tom sees in Jeff Thatcher's garden turns out to be the daughter of the church superintendent. *(False)*
5. Tom collects enough tickets to earn a Bible. *(True)*

CLOSURE

Working in pairs, students should prepare a description of the kind of boy Tom Sawyer is. Tell them to give examples from the story to support their opinion.

The strain upon pent emotion reached its climax.

Illustration by Worth Brehm.

A. Character's Thoughts

? What do you suppose is going through Tom's mind at this point? (He is surely thinking about how he can get out of his predicament. He may be thinking about what the consequences will be if he *can't* get out of it.)

B. Expansion

? What is wrong with Tom's answer? (Unfortunately, Tom could not have been more off base. David was the second king of Israel and a great warrior. In the famous story, he slays the ten-foot giant Goliath with only five stones. See Samuel 17:4. Tom should have answered "Peter and Andrew.") This will help students answer question 11.

learned—no, I know you wouldn't—for we are proud of little boys that learn. Now, no doubt you know the names of all the twelve disciples. Won't you tell us the names of the first two that were appointed?"

A Tom was tugging at a buttonhole and looking sheepish. He blushed, now, and his eyes fell. Mr. Walters's heart sank within him. He said to himself, it is not possible that the boy can answer the simplest question—why *did* the Judge ask him? Yet he felt obliged to speak up and say:

"Answer the gentleman, Thomas—don't be afraid."

Tom still hung fire.[19]

"Now I know you'll tell *me*," said the lady. "The names of the first two disciples were—"

"DAVID AND GOLIATH!" B

Let us draw the curtain of charity over the rest of the scene.

19. **hung fire:** hesitated.

ANALYZING THE STORY
Identifying Facts

1. He makes the task seem so appealing that his friends are willing to trade prized possessions for the "privilege" of whitewashing.

2. Tom acts respectfully toward his aunt, although he is not above trying to dupe her. She, in return, has her eyes open for mischief, although she seems genuinely to care for him. Tom seems to regard Mary as an older sister, and she, in turn, treats him like a younger brother. Tom and Sid seem to curry Aunt Polly's favor, with Sid sometimes "squealing on" Tom and Tom retaliating.

3. He "shows off" in all sorts of boyish ways, performing feats of derring-do and the like.

4. The children in his Sunday school receive tickets for memorizing verses. Tom trades objects for tickets earned by classmates until he has the requisite total.

The objects he trades for tickets are the selfsame items he collected from his friends in exchange for the privilege of whitewashing.

5. Once he has received his Bible, Judge Thatcher asks him to name the

Responding to the Story

Analyzing the Story

Identifying Facts

1. Tom is not delighted by the idea of whitewashing the fence on Saturday morning. Explain how Tom gets his friends to paint the fence for him.
2. Briefly describe how Tom behaves toward each member of his family, and how each behaves toward him.
3. When Tom sees Judge Thatcher's daughter, he is suddenly smitten by love. Describe how he tries to impress her.
4. Tom knows there is no chance he will ever win a Bible by memorizing verses. Explain how he goes about winning a Bible. How do the things he acquired by his whitewashing scheme help him get the Bible?
5. Tell how Tom's Bible-winning scheme finally backfires, embarrassing him.

Interpreting Meanings

6. Tom, in getting his friends to do the whitewashing, "had discovered a great law of human action." In your own words, explain what Tom learned.
7. **Dramatic irony** occurs in a story when the reader is aware of something that a character in the story is not aware of. Explain how dramatic irony adds to the humor of the story when Tom tells Aunt Polly he has whitewashed the fence.
8. When Sid breaks the sugar bowl, Tom gets blamed for it. Discuss what this incident reveals about the relationship between Aunt Polly and Tom—that is, what feelings regarding one another do Aunt Polly and Tom have?
9. Describe two of the gloomy daydreams Tom has after he is unfairly blamed for breaking the sugar bowl. Why do you think he enjoys the "pleasurable suffering" these imaginings cause him?
10. When Judge Thatcher arrives for a visit to the Sunday school, quite a bit of showing off goes on. What does Tom do to show off, and what do Superintendent Walters and the other Sunday school personnel do? What point is Twain making by describing all this showing off? Is there a message here about the power of authority?
11. Why does Twain say at the end that he will "draw the curtain of charity" over the rest of the scene in church? What is wrong with Tom's answer? How do you imagine the next scene?
12. Do you see any similarity between Tom Sawyer's **character** and the characters of the two McKenney sisters in "A Loud Sneer for Our Feathered Friends"? Explain.

Applying Meanings

13. Twain's novel is set in the nineteenth century. Do you think Tom's behavior in front of Judge Thatcher's daughter is typical of boys and girls even today? Support your answer with real or made-up examples.
14. Although Tom lies and plays tricks, most readers like him. Describe your own reaction to Tom. Explain why you reacted this way. (Have you shared any of his feelings?)

Writing About the Story

A Creative Response

1. **Extending the Story.** Twain mercifully draws the curtain on Tom at the end of the Bible-winning episode. Open the curtain and write a paragraph that explains one of the following:
   a. What happens to Tom, when Aunt Polly finds out what happened at Sunday school?
   b. How do Billy and the other boys, with whom Tom had bartered for tickets, act toward him after the Sunday school incident?

A Critical Response

2. **Analyzing a Character.** You can usually say a lot about an interesting character in a story. In a two- or three-paragraph essay, name and describe Tom's four most important character traits. Include passages from the story in your description. Before you begin to write you should list as many of Tom's character traits as you can. Then go over the list to pick out the four most

See Teacher's Manual page 27.

first two disciples appointed. Tom replies, "David and Goliath." (Simon [Peter] and Andrew were the first disciples.)

Interpreting Meanings

6. Specific wordings will vary. The gist of what students should reply is summed up in the following quotation from the selection: ". . . in order to make a man or boy covet a thing, it is only necessary to make the thing difficult to obtain."

7. Aunt Polly is so pleased with the job Tom has done that she rewards him with an apple. As she is fetching the apple, all the while quoting a passage from the Bible about honesty and good deeds, Tom steals a doughnut from her pantry.

8. Aunt Polly is so accustomed to Tom's misbehaving that she assumes when she sees her broken sugar bowl that he is responsible. Tom, by the same token, is so accustomed to being caught red-handed that on the one occasion when Aunt Polly punishes him unjustly he exaggerates his feelings of righteous indignation for having been wrongly accused.

9. He pictures himself variously dying without forgiving his aunt, and being brought to her dead from drowning. Tom is so rarely falsely accused of wrongdoing that he wants to indulge in his hurt feelings and revenge fantasies.

10. Tom shows off by cuffing boys, pulling hair, and making faces. Walters shows off by giving orders and directions and delivering judgments. Other personnel show off by very conspicuously carrying out their usual chores.

Authority brings self-importance.

11. The following scene would probably show Tom in a state of mortification over his error.

The assembly, with the exception of Walters, is probably doubled over with laughter over Tom's response. Walters probably shares Tom's extreme embarrassment.

12. Answers will vary.

Applying Meanings

13. Student answers will vary.

14. Student responses may be mixed, though most will probably find Tom likable inasmuch as his chicanery has an innocent aspect to it.

important. (You might refer to the lesson on page 125 for guidance.)

Analyzing Language and Vocabulary

Dialect

SRW p. 31

To give an authentic impression of the way their characters talk, writers often use dialects. A **dialect** is a form of speech used by people in a particular region or social group. A dialect can help give a fuller sense of a character's personality, can convey the feeling of a particular place and time, and can also create humor. Mark Twain uses dialects for all these reasons.

Rewrite the sentences below in correct standard English, replacing the italicized words and phrases. Then tell how the changes would affect a reader's impression of Twain's characters.

1. "'She *say* she *spec'* Mars Tom *gwine* to *ax* me to whitewash, *an'* so she *tole* me go *'long an' 'tend* to my own business—she *'lowed* she'd *'tend* to *de whitewashin'.*'"
2. "'You're *up a stump, ain't* you?'"
3. "'I *warn't* noticing.'"
4. "'But of course you'd *druther* work . . .'"
5. "'I *reckon* it wouldn't *hardly do* . . .'"
6. "'But it's *powerful* seldom *you're a mind to,* I'm *bound* to say.'"

With a group, prepare an episode of *Tom Sawyer* for oral reading. Select a section with a lot of dialogue and dialect. Notice that there are several different kinds of dialect in the story. Be sure your readers practice to catch the special flavor of each person's speech.

For answers, see Teacher's Manual page 28.

Reading About the Writer

Mark Twain (1835–1910) is remembered as our greatest comic writer, the man who portrayed for all time the exuberant adventures of American boyhood.

He was born Samuel Langhorne Clemens on the Missouri frontier, and he grew up in Hannibal, a port town on the Mississippi River. As a boy, he watched the teeming traffic of the river and the brawling life of a young nation moving west. He took his famous penname from the cry of the boatman when the water reaches two fathoms; "Mark twain!"

The publication of his first successful book, *The Innocents Abroad,* ushered in over a dozen more works which made Twain rich for a time, and established him as one of the giants of American literature. Among these books are *Roughing It, The Adventures of Tom Sawyer, The Prince and the Pauper, Life on the Mississippi, The Adventures of Huckleberry Finn,* and *A Connecticut Yankee in King Arthur's Court.*

However, Twain's literary career declined. His many enterprises, which included the manufacture of a typesetting machine and a publishing house, lost money. By the mid-1890's he was bankrupt. Then his beloved wife Livvy became chronically ill, and by the time Twain died, Livvy and two of his daughters had also died. His writing vigor had dwindled with his fortunes, and as he grew older, he grew increasingly cynical and sad.

But Twain always believed in the power of laughter. He wrote that we have "unquestionably one really effective weapon—laughter. Power, money, persuasion, supplication—these can lift at a colossal humbug—push it a little—weaken it a little, century by century; but only laughter can blow it to rags and atoms at a blast."

PREREADING

1. BUILDING ON PRIOR KNOWLEDGE. Before they read, ask students to tell what they know about collies. The collie is a working dog that was first bred in Great Britain prior to the eighteenth century. There are two varieties of collie: the rough-coated and the smooth-coated. The rough-coated was originally used to guard and herd sheep; the smooth-coated was used mainly to drive livestock to market. Although their coats differ in appearance, both types of collie are identical in form, each standing from twenty-two to twenty-six inches high and weighing from fifty to seventy pounds. Perhaps the most famed characteristic of the collie is its unswerving loyalty to its owner.

You might also ask students if they ever saw the movie "Lassie" or any of the TV shows.

2. ESTABLISHING A PURPOSE. Before students begin reading, you might have them read question 9 on page 115.

3. PREREADING JOURNAL. Before they read, have students write a brief description of an instance from their own lives (or from the lives of friends or characters in stories) in which adults behaved in ways that seemed cruel or unkind, yet all the while maintaining that the behavior was for the child's own good.

Discussing the Illustration

In addition to her illustrations, British-born Marguerite Kirmse (1885–1954) is known for her sculpture and etchings.

? What is the mood of this illustration? What expression would you say is in the dog's eyes? Imagine that you are the owner of the dog in the illustration. How might you feel on the day on which you must give your dog to another person?

★ **Texas Essential Elements/(a) English Language Arts: 1B** Purpose and audience; **1C** Synthesize information; **1E** Formal/informal language; **3A** Plot/character; **4F** Generalizations

LASSIE COME-HOME

Eric Knight

Illustration by Marguerite Kirmse.

For a detailed lesson plan on this selection, see Teacher's Manual pages 28–31. A biography of Eric Knight appears on text page 116.

SUPPLEMENTARY SUPPORT MATERIAL

1. Reading Check Test blackline master
2. Selection Test (page 31 of Test Book)
3. Reader's Response Journal
4. Workbook (page 29)

DEVELOPING VOCABULARY

The following words appear on a test in the Test Book, page 32. (See also the Vocabulary Activity Sheet.)

guile	pine
coax	plague
allege	gaunt
irascible	ponder
servile	quiver

★ **Texas Essential Elements/(c) Reading: 1C** Dictionaries; **3A** Main ideas/details; **3D** Generalizations; **3G** Compare/contrast; **3I** Draw conclusions; **4D** Diagrams/graphs

You might be familiar with the long-running television serial called "Lassie," which is set in the United States. The TV show is based on this story, which is set many years ago, in a section of England that is known for its sheep farms.

Unless you have a heart of steel, this famous dog story will touch your emotions. Pause on page 107, after Joe leaves Lassie with the Duke, and describe how you think Joe is feeling. How would you feel if you were in the same situation?

Dialect. Like *The Adventures of Tom Sawyer,* this story contains *dialect*—language spoken by people in a certain area or group. The Carraclough family uses the dialect spoken in Yorkshire, England. For example, Mrs. Carraclough says, "Now will ye please tak' that tyke out o' here?" Notice how she uses *ye* for *you, tak'* for *take,* and *o'* for *of.* She also uses the word *tyke* for *dog.* The Yorkshire dialect may look confusing, but if you read this story aloud, you'll find the characters' speech is not difficult to understand. SRW p. 31

The dog had met the boy by the school gate for five years. Now she couldn't understand that times were changed and she wasn't supposed to be there anymore. But the boy knew.

So when he opened the door of the cottage, he spoke before he entered.

"Mother," he said. "Lassie's come home again."

A He waited a moment, as if in hope of something. But the man and woman inside the cottage did not speak.

He held open the door, and the tricolor collie walked in obediently. Going head down, as a collie does when it knows something is wrong, it went to the rug and lay down before the hearth, a black-white-and-gold aristocrat. The man, sitting on a low stool by the fireside, kept his eyes turned away. The woman went to the sink and busied herself there.

"She were waiting at school for me, just like always," the boy went on. He spoke fast, as if racing against time. "She must ha' got away again. I thought, happen this time, we might just—"

"No!" the woman exploded.

The boy's carelessness dropped. His voice rose in pleading.

"But this time, Mother! Just this time. We could hide her. They wouldn't ever know."

"Dogs, dogs, dogs!" the woman cried. The words poured from her as if the boy's pleading had been a signal gun for her own anger. "I'm sick o' hearing about tykes round this house. Well, she's sold and gone and done with, so the quicker she's taken back, the better. Now get her back quick, or first thing ye know we'll have Hynes round here again. Mr. Hynes!"

Her voice sharpened in imitation of the Cockney accent of the south: " 'Hi know you Yorkshiremen and yer come 'ome dogs. Training yer dogs to come 'ome so's yer can see 'em hover and hover again.'

"Well, she's sold, so ye can take her out o' my house and home to them as bought her!"

The boy's bottom lip crept out suddenly, and there was silence in the cottage. Then the dog lifted its head and nudged the man's hand, as a dog will when asking for patting. But the man drew away and stared, silently into the fire.

The boy tried again, with the ceaseless guile of a child, his voice coaxing.

"Look, Feyther, she wants thee to bid her welcome. Aye, she's that glad to be home. Happen they don't tak' good care on her up there? Look, her coat's a bit poorly, don't ye think? A bit o' linseed strained through her drinking water— B that's what I'd gi' her."

Still looking in the fire, the man nodded. But the woman, as if perceiving the boy's new attack, sniffled.

"Aye, tha wouldn't be a Carraclough if tha didn't know more about tykes nor breaking eggs wi' a stick. Nor a Yorkshireman. My goodness, it seems to me sometimes tha chaps in this village thinks more on their tykes nor they do o' their own flesh and blood. They'll sit by their firesides and let their own bairns[1] starve so long as t' dog gets fed."

1. **bairns** (bārnz): children.

A. Mood

? How would you describe the mood the author creates in the first five paragraphs of this story? What clues help you to know this? (The mood is tense. The clues are: The boy feels the need to speak before entering the cottage as if in warning; the man and woman do not speak when the boy comes in; the narrator actually says that something is wrong; the man keeps his eyes turned away; and the woman busies herself at the sink.)

B. Vocabulary

Linseed, or *flaxseed,* is a plant seed that is often used as a soothing ingredient in medicine.

A. Dialect
Summat is dialect for "something."

B. Conflict
? How does this paragraph suggest that the woman has an internal conflict? (By the fact that her words contradict her intended actions. Even though the woman grumbles, says Lassie is going back, and that she will never have another dog, she quickly warms food for Lassie. It is obvious that she cares for Lassie a great deal.)

C. Character and Characterization
? How would you describe Mr. Hynes? How do you learn about him? (He is impolite—a man takes his hat off when he goes indoors as a mark of respect. He is also nosy, rude, and self-important. We learn this through the words of another character.)

D. Context Clues
? From the context, what do you think *irascible* means? (That he uses "unspotted language" and is "vile-tempered" suggests that *irascible* means "prone to anger.")

E. Making Inferences
? What does this really say about the duke? (We can infer that the duke himself is going deaf, and refuses to admit it.)

The man stirred, suddenly, but the boy cut in quickly.

"But she does look thin. Look, truly—they're not feeding her right. Just look!"

"Aye," the woman chattered. "I wouldn't put it past Hynes to steal t' best part o' t' dog meat for himself. And Lassie always was a strong eater."

"She's fair thin now," the boy said.

Almost unwillingly the man and woman looked at the dog for the first time.

"By gum, she is off a bit," the woman said. Then she caught herself. "Ma goodness, I suppose I'll have to fix her a bit o' summat. She can do wi' it. But soon as she's fed, back she goes. And never another dog I'll have in my house. Never another. Cooking and nursing for 'em and as much trouble to bring up as a bairn!" **A** **B**

So, grumbling and chatting as a village woman will, she moved about, warming a pan of food for the dog. The man and boy watched the collie eat. When it was done, the boy took from the mantelpiece a folded cloth and brush, and began prettying the collie's coat. The man watched for several minutes, and then could stand it no longer.

"Here," he said.

He took the cloth and brush from the boy and began working expertly on the dog, rubbing the rich deep coat, then brushing the snowy whiteness of the full ruff and the apron, bringing out the heavy leggings on the forelegs. He lost himself in his work, and the boy sat on the rug, watching contentedly. The woman stood it as long as she could.

"Now will ye please tak' that tyke out o' here?"

The man flared in anger.

"Well, ye wouldn't have me tak' her back looking like a mucky Monday wash, wouldta?"

He bent again, and began fluffing out the collie's petticoats.

"Joe!" the woman pleaded. "Will ye tak' her out o' here? Hynes'll be nosing round afore ye know it. And I won't have that man in my house. Wearing his hat inside, and going on like he's the duke himself—him and his leggings!" **C**

"All right, lass."

"And this time, Joe, tak' young Joe wi' ye."

"What for?"

"Well, let's get the business done and over with. It's him that Lassie runs away for. She comes for young Joe. So if he went wi' thee, and told her to stay, happen she'd be content and not run away no more, and then we'd have a little peace and quiet in the home—though heaven knows there's not much hope o' that these days, things being like they are." The woman's voice trailed away, as if she would soon cry in weariness.

The man rose. "Come Joe," he said. "Get thy cap."

The Duke of Rudling walked along the gravel paths of his place with his granddaughter, Philippa. Philippa was a bright and knowing young woman, allegedly[2] the only member of the duke's family he could address in unspotted language. For it was also alleged that the duke was the most irascible, vile-tempered old man in the three Ridings[3] of Yorkshire. **D**

"Country going to pot!" the duke roared, stabbing at the walk with his great blackthorn stick. "When I was a young man! Hah! Women today not as pretty. Horses today not as fast. As for dogs—ye don't see dogs today like—"

Just then the duke and Philippa came round a clump of rhododendrons[4] and saw a man, a boy, and a dog.

"Ah," said the duke, in admiration. Then his brow knotted. "Carraclough! What are ye doing with my dog?"

He shouted it as if the others were in the next county, for it was also the opinion of the Duke of Rudling that people were not nearly so keen of hearing as they used to be when he was a young man. **E**

"It's Lassie," Carraclough said. "She runned away again, and I brought her back."

Carraclough lifted his cap and poked the boy to do the same, not in any servile gesture, but to

2. **allegedly:** reportedly.
3. **Ridings:** three districts of Yorkshire, England—North Riding, West Riding, and East Riding. (The Ridings no longer exist as administrative districts.)
4. **rhododendrons** (rō'də·den'drənz): trees or shrubs with white, pink, or purple flowers.

A. Character's Feelings and Actions

? Do you think Joe's father is really sorry for stepping on Hynes's foot? Explain. (He is not sorry. He intended to step on Hynes's foot because Hynes threatened and tried to grab Lassie.)

B. Making Inferences

? Why is the path hard to see? (Joe is crying.)

C. Interpreting

? Why is Mr. Carraclough so bad-tempered when he knows Joe is upset? (He is masking his own grief at leaving Lassie and at watching his son force himself to say good-bye to the dog he loves.) This will help students answer question 12.

D. Interpreting

? What do you think is the reason that the Carracloughs stop talking in front of Joe? (It seems apparent from the story that they are having money trouble. The fragmented sentences could refer to Mr. Carraclough's walking around looking for work. They don't want Joe to hear about their problems.)

show that they were as well brought up as the next.

"Ran away again!" the duke roared. "And I told that utter nincompoop Hynes to—where is he? Hynes! Hynes! Hynes, what're ye hiding for?"

"Coming, your lordship!" sounded a voice, far away behind the shrubberies. And soon Hynes appeared, a sharp-faced man in check coat, riding breeches, and the cloth leggings that grooms wear.

"Take this dog," roared the duke, "and pen her up! And, if she breaks out again, I'll—I'll—"

The duke waved his great stick threateningly, and then, without so much as a thank you or kiss the back of my hand to Joe Carraclough, he went stamping and muttering away.

"I'll pen 'er up," Hynes muttered, when the duke was gone. "And if she ever gets awye agyne, I'll—"

He made as if to grab the dog, but Joe Carraclough's hobnailed boot trod heavily on Hynes's foot.

A "I brought my lad wi' me to bid her stay, so we'll pen her up this time. Eigh—sorry! I didn't see I were on thy foot. Come, Joe, lad."

They walked down the crunching gravel path, along by the neat kennel buildings. When Lassie was behind the closed door, she raced into the high wire run where she could see them as they went. She pressed close against the wire, waiting.

The boy stood close, too, his fingers through the meshes touching the dog's nose.

"Go on, lad," his father ordered. "Bid her stay!"

The boy looked around, as if for help that he did not find. He swallowed and then spoke, low and quickly.

"Stay here, Lassie, and don't come home no more," he said. "And don't come to school for me no more. Because I don't want to see ye no more. 'Cause tha's a bad dog, and we don't love thee no more, and we don't want thee. So stay there forever and leave us be, and don't never come home no more."

B Then he turned, and because it was hard to see the path plainly, he stumbled. But his father, who was holding his head very high as they walked away from Hynes, shook him savagely, and snapped roughly: "Look where tha's going!"

Then the boy trotted beside his father. He was thinking that he'd never be able to understand why grown-ups sometimes were so bad-tempered with you, just when you needed them most. C

After that, there were days and days that passed, and the dog did not come to the school gate anymore. So then it was not like old times. There were so many things that were not like old times.

The boy was thinking that as he came wearily up the path and opened the cottage door and heard his father's voice, tense with anger: ". . . walk my feet off. If tha thinks I like—"

Then they heard his opening of the door, and the voice stopped, and the cottage was silent.

That's how it was now, the boy thought. They stopped talking in front of you. And this, somehow, was too much for him to bear. D

He closed the door, ran into the night, and onto the moor, that great flat expanse of land where all the people of that village walked in lonesomeness when life and its troubles seemed past bearing.

A long while later, his father's voice cut through the darkness.

"What's tha doing out here, Joe lad?"

"Walking."

"Aye."

They went on together, aimlessly, each following his own thoughts. And they both thought about the dog that had been sold.

"Tha maun't think we're hard on thee, Joe," the man said at last. "It's just that a chap's for to be honest. There's that to it. Sometimes, when a chap doesn't have much, he clings right hard to what he's got. And honest is honest, and there's no two ways about it.

"Why, look, Joe. Seventeen year I worked in that Clarabelle Pit till she shut down, and a good collier[5] too. Seventeen year! And butties[6] I've had by the dozen, and never one of 'em can ever say that Joe Carraclough kept what wasn't his; nor spoke what wasn't true. Not a man in this Riding can ever call a Carraclough mishonest.

"And when ye've sold a man summat, and

5. **collier:** coal miner.
6. **butties:** buddies.

A. Character's Motivation

? Why do you think Joe's father didn't want to tell Joe that Lassie is in Scotland? (He didn't want to hurt his son any more than Joe had already been hurt by having to give up his dog. He didn't want to shatter the boy's last hopes of ever seeing Lassie again. But, because of Joe's insistence, he knows he must put the subject to rest.)

Illustration by Cyrus LeRoy Baldridge.

ye've taken his brass, and ye've spent it—well, then done's done. That's all. And ye've got to stand by that."

"But Lassie was—"

"Now, Joe! Ye can't alter it, ever. It's done—and happen it's for t' best. No two ways, Joe, she were getting hard to feed. Why, ye wouldn't want Lassie to be going around peaked and pined, like some chaps round here keep their tykes. And if ye're fond of her, then just think on it that now she's got lots to eat, and a private kennel, and a good run to herself, and living like a veritable princess, she is. Ain't that best for her?"

"We wouldn't pine her. We've always got lots to eat."

The man blew his breath, angrily: "Eigh, Joe, nowt pleases thee. Well then, tha might as well have it. Tha'll never see Lassie no more. She run home once too often, so the duke's taken her wi' him to his place in Scotland, and there she'll stay. So it's goodbye and good luck to her, and she'll never come home no more, she won't. Now, I weren't off to tell thee, but there it is, so put it in thy pipe and smoke it, and let's never say a word about it no more—especially in front of thy mother." A

The boy stumbled on in the darkness. Then the man halted.

"We ought to be getting back, lad. We left thy mother alone."

He turned the boy about, and then went on, but as if he were talking to himself.

A "Tha sees, Joe, women's not like men. They have to stay home and manage best they can, and just spend the time in wishing. And when things don't go right, well, they have to take it out in talk. But it don't mean nowt, really, so tha shouldn't mind when thy mother talks hard.

"Ye just got to learn to be patient, and let 'em talk, and just let it go up t' chimney wi' th' smoke."

Then they were quiet, until, over the rise, they saw the lights of the village. Then the boy spoke: "How far away is Scotland, Feyther?"

"Nay, lad, it's a long, long road."

"But how far, Feyther?"

"I don't know—but it's a longer road than thee or me'll ever walk. Now, lad. Don't fret no more, and try to be a man—and don't plague thy mother no more, wilta?" B

Joe Carraclough was right. It is a long road, as they say in the North, from Yorkshire to Scotland. Much too far for a man to walk—or a boy. And though the boy often thought of it, he remembered his father's words on the moor, and he put the thought behind him.

But there is another way of looking at it; and that's the distance from Scotland to Yorkshire. And that is just as far as from Yorkshire to Scotland. A matter of about four hundred miles, it would be, from the Duke of Rudling's place far up in the Highlands to the village of Holdersby.

A. Responding

Comment on Joe's father's words in light of present-day attitudes about women.

B. Character and Characterization

What does the episode on the moor reveal about Joe's father? What method of characterization does the author use? (Joe's father's own words reveal that he is a man of honesty and integrity, that he loves both his son and his wife very much. He refuses to go back on his principles. He tries to protect those that are weaker than he is—by withholding from Joe that Lassie is in Scotland, and by telling Joe not to bug his mother.)

A. Plot and Suspense

? Why is this passage so important to the story? How does it create suspense? (It tells of the near-impossible journey a dog would have to make to get back to the Carracloughs. By describing the journey as being long and arduous, this part not only helps to characterize a dog—Lassie—that would attempt this journey, but it also helps to create suspense—is Lassie going to make it?)

B. Characterization

? How does the author reveal the characters in this passage? (By describing their words and actions upon Lassie's return.)

That would be for a man, who could go fairly straight.

To an animal, how much farther would it be? For a dog can study no maps, read no signposts, ask no directions. It could only go blindly, by instinct, knowing that it must keep on to the south, to the south. It would wander and err, quest and quarter, run into firths and lochs[7] that would send it sidetracking and backtracking before it could go again on its way—south.

A thousand miles, it would be, going that way—a thousand miles over strange terrain.

There would be moors to cross, and burns[8] to swim. And then those great, long lochs that stretch almost from one side of that dour[9] land to another would bar the way and send a dog questing a hundred miles before it could find a crossing that would allow it to go south.

And, too, there would be rivers to cross, wide rivers like the Forth and the Clyde, the Tweed and the Tyne, where one must go miles to find bridges. And the bridges would be in towns. And in the towns there would be officials—like the one in Lanarkshire. In all his life he had never let a captured dog get away—except one. That one was a gaunt, snarling collie that whirled on him right in the pound itself, and fought and twisted loose to race away down the city street—going south.

But there are also kind people, too; ones knowing and understanding in the ways of dogs. There was an old couple in Durham who found a dog lying exhausted in a ditch one night—lying there with its head to the south. They took that dog into their cottage and warmed it and fed it and nursed it. And because it seemed an understanding, wise dog, they kept it in their home, hoping it would learn to be content. But, as it grew stronger, every afternoon toward four o'clock it would go to the door and whine, and then begin pacing back and forth between the door and the window, back and forth as the animals do in their cages at the zoo.

They tried every wile and every kindness to make it bide with them, but finally, when the dog began to refuse food, the old people knew what they must do. Because they understood dogs, they opened the door one afternoon, and they watched a collie go, not down the road to the right, or to the left, but straight across a field toward the south; going steadily at a trot, as if it knew it still had a long, long road to travel.

Ah, a thousand miles of tor and brae,[10] of shire and moor, of path and road and plowland, of river and stream and burn and brook and beck,[11] of snow and rain and fog and sun is a long way, even for a human being. But it would seem too far—much, much too far—for any dog to travel blindly and win through. **A**

And yet—and yet—who shall say why, when so many weeks had passed that hope against hope was dying, a boy coming out of school, out of the cloakroom that always smelled of damp wool drying, across the concrete play yard with the black, waxed slides, should turn his eyes to a spot by the school gate from force of five years of habit, and see there a dog? Not a dog, this one, that lifted glad ears above a proud, slim head with its black-and-gold mask; but a dog that lay weakly, trying to lift a head that would no longer lift, trying to wag a tail that was torn and blotched and matted with dirt and burs, and managing to do nothing much except to whine in a weak, happy, crying way as a boy on his knees threw arms about it, and hands touched it that had not touched it for many a day.

Then who shall picture the urgency of a boy, running awkwardly, with a great dog in his arms, running through the village, past the empty mill, past the Labor Exchange, where the men looked up from their deep ponderings on life and the dole?[12] Or who shall describe the high tone of a voice—a boy's voice calling as he runs up a path: "Mother! Oh, Mother! Lassie's come home! Lassie's come home!" **B**

Nor does anyone who ever owned a dog need to be told the sound a man makes as he bends over a dog that has been his for many years, nor how a woman moves quickly, preparing food—which might be the family's condensed milk stirred into warm water; nor how the jowl of a dog is lifted so that raw egg and brandy, bought

7. **firths and lochs** (läks): inlets and lakes.
8. **burns:** brooks.
9. **dour:** hard; severe.
10. **tor and brae:** hill and slope.
11. **beck:** brooklet.
12. **dole:** government money paid to the unemployed.

with precious pence,[13] should be spooned in; nor how bleeding pads are bandaged, tenderly.

That was one day. There was another day, when the woman in the cottage sighed with pleasure, for a dog lifted itself to its feet for the first time to stand over a bowl of oatmeal, putting its head down and lapping again and again while its pinched flanks quivered.

And there was another day when the boy realized that, even now, the dog was not to be his again. So the cottage rang again with protests and cries, and a woman shrilling: "Is there never to be no more peace in my house and home?" Long after he was in bed that night the boy heard the rise and fall of the woman's voice, and the steady, reiterative[14] tone of the man's. It went on long after he was asleep.

In the morning the man spoke, not looking at the boy, saying the words as if he had long rehearsed them.

"Thy mother and me have decided upon it that Lassie shall stay here till she's better. Anyhow, nobody could nurse her better than us. But the day that t' duke comes back, then back she goes, too. For she belongs to him, and that's honest, too. Now tha has her for a while, so be content."

A In childhood, "for a while" is such a great stretch of days when seen from one end. It is a terribly short time seen from the other.

The boy knew how short it was that morning as he went to school and saw a motorcar driven by a young woman. And in the car was a gray-thatched, terrible old man, who waved a cane and shouted: "Hi! Hi, there! Lad! You there! Hi!"

Then it was no use running, for the car could go faster than you, and soon it was beside you, and the man was saying: "Philippa, will you make this smelly thing stand still a moment? Hi, lad!"

"Yes, sir."

"You're What's-'is-Name's lad, aren't you?"

"Ma feyther's Joe Carraclough."

"I know. I know. Is he home now?"

"No, sir. He's away to Allerby. A mate spoke for him at the pit, and he's gone to see if there's a chance."

"When'll he be back?"

"I don't know. I think about tea."

"Eh, yes. Well, yes. I'll drop round about fivish to see that father of yours. Something important."

It was hard to pretend to listen to lessons. There was only waiting for noon. Then the boy ran home.

"Mother! T' duke is back, and he's coming to take Lassie away."

"Eigh, drat my buttons. Never no peace in this house. Is tha sure?"

"Aye. He stopped me. He said tell Feyther he'll be round at five. Can't we hide her? Oh, Mother."

"Nay, thy feyther—"

"Won't you beg him? Please, please. Beg Feyther to—"

"Young Joe, now it's no use. So stop thy teasing! Thy feyther'll not lie. That much I'll give him. Come good, come bad, he'll not lie."

"But just this once, Mother. Please beg him, just this once. Just one lie wouldn't hurt him. I'll make it up to him. I will. When I'm growed up. I'll get a job. I'll make money. I'll buy him things—and you, too. I'll buy you both anything you want if you'll only—"

For the first time in his trouble, the boy became a child, and the mother, looking over, saw the tears that ran openly down his contorted[15] face. She turned her face to the fire, and there was a pause. Then she spoke.

"Joe, tha mustn't," she said softly. "Tha must learn never to want nothing in life like that. It don't do, lad. Tha mustn't want things bad, like tha wants Lassie."

The boy shook his clenched fists in impatience.

"It ain't that, Mother. Ye don't understand. Don't yer see—it ain't me that wants her. It's her that wants us! Tha's wha made her come all them miles. It's her that wants us, so terrible bad!"

The woman turned and stared. It was as if, in that moment, she were seeing this child, this boy, this son of her own, for the first time in many years. She turned her head down toward the table. It was surrender. **B**

"Come and eat, then," she said. "I'll talk to

13. **pence:** British equivalent of pennies.
14. **reiterative** (rē·it′ər·ə·tiv): repetitive.
15. **contorted:** twisted or distorted out of usual form.

A. Responding
What exactly does this mean? (At the start it seems long if you want the time to fly. At the end, if you don't want it to end, the "while" has been much too brief.) Do you think this is true? Explain.

B. Dynamic Character
? Explain how this passage demonstrates that Joe is a dynamic character. (Joe's ability to step outside himself and view things from another's point of view, in this case Lassie's point of view, is a sign that he is changing from a child to an adult.)

A. Expansion
The Duke, an educated member of the English aristocracy, would speak so called "proper English." By adopting the villagers' way of speaking, he is being condescending to them—as though they wouldn't be able to understand his upper-class diction. (Knight's own description of Yorkshire on page 116 helps to explain this distinction.)

B. Responding
Is withholding information or evading a question just as bad as telling a lie? Explain.

C. Suspense
Do you feel suspense in this passage? Why? (The duke says nothing while scrutinizing the dog in a way that suggests he knows what he is looking for. The staring creates suspense. We are anxious to know if the duke will discern the truth and, if so, what he will do.)

him. I will that, all right. I feel sure he won't lie. But I'll talk to him, all right. I'll talk to Mr. Joe Carraclough. I will indeed."

At five that afternoon, the Duke of Rudling, fuming and muttering, got out of a car at a cottage gate to find a boy barring his way. This was a boy who stood, stubbornly, saying fiercely: "Away wi' thee! Thy tyke's net here!"

"Philippa, th' lad's touched,"[16] the duke said. "He is. He's touched."

Scowling and thumping his stick, the old duke advanced until the boy gave way, backing down the path out of the reach of the waving blackthorn stick.

"The tyke's net here," the boy protested.

"What's he saying?" the girl asked.

"Says my dog isn't here. You going deaf? I'm supposed to be deaf, and I hear him plainly enough. Now, ma lad, what tyke o' mine's net here?"

A As he turned to the boy, the duke spoke in broadest Yorkshire, as he did always to the people of the cottages—a habit which the Duchess of Rudling, and many more members of the duke's family, deplored.[17]

"Coom, coom, ma lad! What tyke's net here?"

"No tyke o' thine. Us hasn't got it." The words began running faster and faster as the boy backed away from the fearful old man who advanced. "No tyke could have done it. No tyke can come all them miles. It isn't Lassie. It's another one that looks like her. It isn't Lassie!"

"Why, bless my heart and sowl," the duke puffed. "Where's thy father, ma lad?"

The door behind the boy opened, and a woman's voice spoke.

"If it's Joe Carraclough ye want, he's out in the shed—and been there shut up half the afternoon."

"What's this lad talking about—a dog of mine being here?"

"Nay," the woman snapped quickly. "He didn't say a tyke o' thine was here. He said it wasn't here."

The woman swallowed and looked about as if for help. The duke stood peering from under his jutting eyebrows. Her answer, truth or lie, was never spoken, for then they heard the rattle of a door opening, and a man making a pursing sound with his lips, as he will when he wants a dog to follow, and then Joe Carraclough's voice said: "This is t' only tyke us has here. Does it look like any dog that belongs to thee?"

With his mouth open to cry one last protest, the boy turned. And his mouth stayed open. For there he saw his father, Joe Carraclough, the collie fancier, standing with a dog at his heels—a dog that sat at his left heel patiently, as any well-trained dog should do—as Lassie used to do. But this dog was not Lassie. In fact, it was ridiculous to think of it at the same moment as you thought of Lassie.

For where Lassie's skull was aristocratic and slim, this dog's head was clumsy and rough. Where Lassie's ears stood in twin-lapped symmetry, this dog had one ear draggling and the other standing up Alsatian[18] fashion in a way to give any collie breeder the cold shivers. Where Lassie's coat was rich tawny gold, this dog's coat had ugly patches of black; and where Lassie's apron was a billowing stretch of snow-white, this dog had puddles of off-color blue-merle mixture. Besides, Lassie had four white paws, and this one had one paw white, two dirty-brown, and one almost black.

That is the dog they all looked at as Joe Carraclough stood there, having told no lie, having only asked a question. They all stood, waiting the duke's verdict. B

But the duke said nothing. He only walked forward, slowly, as if he were seeing a dream. He bent beside the collie, looking with eyes that were as knowing about dogs as any Yorkshireman alive. And those eyes did not waste themselves upon twisted ears, or blotched marking, or rough head. Instead they were looking at a paw that the duke lifted, looking at the underside of the paw, staring intently at five black pads, crossed and recrossed with the scars where thorns had lacerated, and stones had torn. C

For a long time the duke stared, and when he

16. **touched:** here, mentally unbalanced.
17. **deplored:** regretted.

18. **Alsatian** (al·sā'shən): German shepherd dog.

Critical Comment

A magazine advertisement for the movie *Lassie Come-Home* read as follows: "From the pages of Eric Knight's great best-seller . . . comes a great drama. No roar of guns, no bombs, no tanks, no planes here. . . . but emotion deep, human and intense in a story you'll live and love. The kind of story real people like to pass along to their friends."

Tell students to imagine that they got hold of a copy of "Lassie Come-Home" after seeing this ad in their favorite magazine. After reading the story, did the ad give them any false hopes, or did they find the deep, human, and intense emotion?

Illustration by Arthur Fuller.

Reading Check Test

1. Why are Joe's parents upset when he tells them that Lassie has followed him home from school? *They have sold the dog to the Duke of Rudling.*
2. What does Joe's father order the boy to bid Lassie to do before they leave the duke's estate? *To bid Lassie to stay.*
3. Where does Joe's father tell Joe the duke has taken Lassie? *He says the duke has taken the dog to Scotland.*
4. What condition is Lassie in when Joe next sees her in the schoolyard? *Weak and injured.*
5. What offer does the duke make to Joe's father at the end of the story? *The duke offers Joe's father a job as groom.*

Closure

Ask for one volunteer to define dialect. Then ask the class whether the use of it in "Lassie Come-Home" added to their enjoyment of the story. Encourage them to explain their answers.

A. Plot
Who is the dog? (Lassie) When did you first suspect it? What clues did you use?

B. Interpreting
The duke recognizes the disguised dog as Lassie, and Lassie did belong to him. Why is the duke denying it here? (He is admitting that although he penned Lassie up and sent her away to Scotland, Lassie has always "come home" or belonged to the Carracloughs.)

C. True Meanings
What is the duke really saying here? (He is giving Mr. Carraclough grudging respect for his expert work in disguising Lassie—note that he has stopped talking in Yorkshire dialect. He is also showing him that he knows who the dog really is, and wants Lassie back to normal.)

got up, he did not speak in Yorkshire accents anymore. He spoke as a gentleman should, and he said: "Joe Carraclough, I never owned this dog. 'Pon my soul, she's never belonged to me. Never!" **A, B**

Then he turned and went stumping down the path, thumping his cane and saying: "Bless my soul. Four hundred miles! Wouldn't ha' believed it. Five hundred miles!"

He was at the gate where his granddaughter whispered to him fiercely.

"Of course," he cried. "Mind your own business. Exactly what I came for. Talking about dogs made me forget. Carraclough! Carraclough! What're ye hiding for?"

"I'm still here, sir."

"Ah, there you are. You working?"

"Eigh, now. Working," Joe said. That's the best he could manage.

"Yes, working, working!" The duke fumed.

"Well, now—" Joe began.

Then Mrs. Carraclough came to his rescue, as a good housewife in Yorkshire will.

"Why, Joe's got three or four things that he's been considering," she said, with proper display of pride. "But he hasn't quite said yes or no to any of them yet."

"Then say no, quick," the old man puffed. "Had to sack Hynes. Didn't know a dog from a drunken filly. Should ha' known all along no Londoner could handle dogs fit for Yorkshire taste. How much, Carraclough?"

"Well, now," Joe began.

"Seven pounds a week, and worth every penny," Mrs. Carraclough chipped in. "One of them other offers may come up to eight," she lied, expertly. For there's always a certain amount of lying to be done in life, and when a woman's married to a man who has made a lifelong cult of being honest, then she's got to learn to do the lying for two.

"Five," roared the duke—who, after all, was a Yorkshireman, and couldn't help being a bit sharp about things that pertained to money.

"Six," said Mrs. Carraclough.

"Five pound ten," bargained the duke, cannily.

"Done," said Mrs. Carraclough, who would have been willing to settle for three pounds in the first place. "But, o' course, us gets the cottage too."

"All right," puffed the duke. "Five pounds ten and the cottage. Begin Monday. But—on one condition. Carraclough, you can live on my land, but I won't have that thick-skulled, screwlugged, gaytailed eyesore of a misshapen mongrel on my property. Now never let me see her again. You'll get rid of her?" **C**

He waited, and Joe fumbled for words. But it was the boy who answered, happily, gaily: "Oh, no, sir. She'll be waiting at school for me most o' the time. And, anyway, in a day or so we'll have her fixed up and coped[19] up so's ye'd never, never recognize her."

"I don't doubt that," puffed the duke, as he went to the car. "I don't doubt ye could do just exactly that."

It was a long time afterward, in the car, that the girl said: "Don't sit there like a lion on the Nelson column.[20] And I thought you were supposed to be a hard man."

"Fiddlesticks, m'dear. I'm a ruthless realist. For five years I've sworn I'd have the dog by hook or crook, and now, egad, at last I've got her."

"Pooh! You had to buy the man before you could get his dog."

"Well, perhaps that's not the worst part of the bargain."

19. **coped:** shaped.
20. **Nelson column:** monument in London built in honor of Horatio Nelson (1758–1805), a famous British admiral.

ANALYZING THE STORY

Identifying Facts

1. She is waiting for young Joe when he comes out of school and follows the boy home, as she has done for years.

She feels that if young Joe orders Lassie to stay, the dog will obey.

2. The family needed the money, as Mr. Carraclough was out of work. She was hard to maintain and now she is being well cared for.

3. It is about four hundred miles.

The dog travels by instinct, moving in a southerly direction.

4. He dyes the dog's coat in spots and makes it look unkempt in others. He somehow arranges for the dog's ears to appear uneven.

5. He looks at the dog's paws, which are lacerated and scarred from the long trip.

He gets Lassie back by hiring Mr. Carraclough as a groom and arranges for the Carracloughs to live on his estate.

Interpreting Meanings

6. Mrs. Carraclough shows her affection by agreeing to feed the dog after noticing that Lassie looks a bit lean. Mr. Carraclough shows his affection by grooming the dog's fur. Joe displays unbridled love for the dog.

7. First, they are honest people who live by their word. Second, they are selfless people, interested in what is best for the dog.

8. She is telling Joe that he must learn to accept the fact that he won't always be able to get everything he wants, and if he allows himself to love something too much, he will never get over the disappointment of not getting it.

9. Joe wants Lassie but knows the dog belongs to someone else now. Mr. and Mrs. Carraclough want to live up to their agreement but wish they could make their son happy. The duke, despite his crusty exterior, seems to have misgivings about keeping a dog that wants desperately to live with another family. Lassie seems to know that she no longer lives with the Carracloughs but finds it difficult to stay away.

Mr. Carraclough can be an honest man and have Lassie. Joe and his mother are delighted to have Lassie home, and can be proud of Mr. Carraclough.

(Answers continue on page 116.)

Responding to the Story

Analyzing the Story

Identifying Facts

1. As the story opens, how does Lassie show she doesn't understand that she has a new owner? Explain Mrs. Carraclough's reason for insisting that Joe accompany his father to return Lassie to the Duke's house.
2. During their walk together on the moor, Mr. Carraclough reminds his son why they had to sell Lassie. What were the family's reasons?
3. The Duke finally takes Lassie to Scotland in an attempt to keep her from running back home. How far is Scotland from Yorkshire, where the Carracloughs live? Describe how Lassie still manages to get back home.
4. Toward the end of the story, Mr. and Mrs. Carraclough finally decide to try to keep Lassie. Describe what Mr. Carraclough does to Lassie in an attempt to hide her.
5. How does the Duke recognize Lassie, despite Mr. Carraclough's plan? How does he manage to get Lassie back?

Interpreting Meanings

6. Although the Carracloughs had to sell Lassie, it is evident that they care about her very much. Describe how each member of the family shows affection for Lassie when she first comes home with young Joe.
7. Mr. and Mrs. Carraclough return Lassie the first time she runs back home. Name two **character traits,** or qualities, that force them to act this way.
8. Mrs. Carraclough says to Joe, "Tha must learn never to want nothing in life like that. . . . Tha mustn't want things bad, like tha wants Lassie." Explain why this might be good advice.
9. Joe, his father, the Duke, and Lassie all face **conflicts,** or struggles. Each character wants something he or she does not have or cannot keep. Identify each of these characters' conflicts. Then explain how the ending of the story resolves these conflicts.
10. Which **character** do you think is the central figure in the story: Joe, or Lassie? Why?

Applying Meanings

11. Near the end of the story, the narrator says "For there's always a certain amount of lying to be done in life. . . ." What do you think of this statement?
12. After Joe is forced to return Lassie to the Duke, he finds it hard to understand why "grown-ups sometimes were so bad-tempered with you, just when you needed them most." Why would people act like this?
13. "'It's just that a chap's for to be honest. There's that to it. Sometimes, when a chap doesn't have much, he clings right hard to what he's got. And honest is honest, and there's no two ways about it.'" What is Joe's father saying? Do you think people still feel this way today? Explain.

Writing About the Story

A Creative Response

1. **Identifying with a Character.** How would you have felt if you were Lassie, pursuing your goal over miles and miles of hard country? Write a paragraph telling how you feel as you make your perilous journey "home."

A Critical Response

2. **Comparing Lassies.** If you have seen the TV series about Lassie, write a paragraph in which you contrast the character of that Lassie with the original.
3. **Describing Character.** You can learn about a character's personality from several sources—his or her thoughts, physical appearance, actions, and speech; what other characters say about, and how they act toward the character; and direct comments by the writer. See how many of the duke's character traits you can discover in the story. Use a chart like the following to gather your information. Then write a paragraph describing the Duke's character. Open the paragraph with a sentence stating your general impression of the Duke. Use details from the story to support your interpretation. (The lesson on page 125 might help you with this assignment.)

(Answers begin on page 115.)
The Duke is able to retain the dog while not separating her from her loved ones. Lassie, too, is spared disappointment.
10. Some students will feel that Joe is the central character, mainly because they can identify with him as a peer. Others will argue that Lassie is the central figure, the one our interest is focused on, and the one we are "rooting" for.

Applying Meanings
11. Answers will vary. In the case of Mrs. Carraclough, she lies about Joe's wages and opportunities for work in order to get him a better offer. Lying might be excusable here.
12. One reason is that Joe's father is covering up his own discomfort and grief with anger. Another explanation could be that Joe's father is selflessly acting angry in an effort to divert his son's thoughts away from Lassie and toward resentment for his father.
13. The implication seems to be that because he has little in the way of worldly possessions, Mr. Carraclough attaches an especially high value to his self-respect.
Answers will vary.
(Answers continue in left-hand column.)

(Continued from top.)
Students should be encouraged to see that the world still has its share of people who place honesty above material gain.

FURTHER READING FOR STUDENTS
Another moving story about a boy and his pet is "The Gift" (also called "The Red Pony") by John Steinbeck. Students will also enjoy the novel *Old Yeller* by Fred Gipson.

Character Traits	Evidence from the Story

See Teacher's Manual page 30.

Analyzing Language and Vocabulary

Dialect

SRW p. 31

A **dialect** is a version of a language spoken by people in a certain region or group. One of the characteristics of the Yorkshire dialect used in this story is that different words, such as *tha,* are used to indicate *you* or *your.* Read the sentences below aloud to hear how the dialect sounds. Then rewrite them, substituting correct standard English in the appropriate places.

1. "'*Aye, tha* wouldn't be a Carraclough if *tha* didn't know more about *tykes* . . .'"
2. "'Well, *ye* wouldn't have me *tak'* her back looking like a *mucky Monday wash, wouldta?*'"
3. "'*Thy* mother and me have *decided upon it* . . .'"
4. "'. . . I suppose I'll have to fix her a bit *o' summat.*"

Another feature of the Yorkshire dialect is that letters are omitted from some words. Read the following sentences aloud. Then rewrite them, supplying the missing letters for the italicized words.

5. "'I wouldn't put it past Hynes to steal *t'* best part *o' t'* dog meat for himself.'"
6. "'Away wi' *thee.*"
7. "'Now will ye please *tak'* that tyke out *o'* here?'"
8. "'. . . and just let it go up *t'* chimney *wi' th'* smoke.'"

For answers, see Teacher's Manual page 31.

Reading About the Writer

Eric Knight (1897–1943) was born in Yorkshire, England, and by the age of twelve he was working in a textile factory. While still a young man, he emigrated to the United States where he studied art. He gave up the idea of becoming a painter when he found he was color blind.

At the outbreak of World War I, Knight joined the Canadian army. When he was discharged, he turned to journalism and then to writing for films.

He settled on a farm in Pennsylvania and there wrote his successful novels which included *The Flying Yorkshireman* and *Lassie Come-Home.*

During World War II, Knight was commissioned as a major in the U.S. Army. While on his way to an assignment in Africa, he was killed in the crash of a military transport plane.

Focusing on Background

On His Yorkshire Dialect

"Yorkshire dialect itself is a mixture of corrupted English plus the remnants of a language which existed long before the tongue of the middle counties began to grow into the English we have today. The sad thing is that the so-called education of the day frowns on Yorkshire speech as 'low-class' or 'ignorant' or 'uncouth' or many other things. So what with mass education, class-conscious and snobbish parents, sound motion pictures, and radio, what is a fine and honest and most mouth-filling and expressive spoken tongue is dying out in the larger towns. Yet it is strong enough not to die quickly. Old people cannot rid themselves of it, children become bilingual and use one English for teachers and parents and another when beyond their control. Yet the rougher tongue is the stronger of the two. Often, as a child, I was punished because I used a dialectical word and couldn't remember the English word for the same thing."

—Eric Knight

PREREADING

1. BUILDING ON PRIOR KNOWLEDGE. This story is not about an adoring collie, but rather about a bad-tempered Airedale. Present the following information to students as if it were beneath an empty Airedale's cage in a pet shop. Would they choose one to be their pet? (Thurber himself might have benefited from this information.)

Airedales, which are descended from the otterhound and the extinct Old English terrier, are the largest breed of terriers. The Airedale stands approximately twenty-three inches high and weighs from forty to fifty pounds. An intelligent and courageous dog, the Airedale is also powerful and affectionate, although the last quality is not usually apparent to strangers. Because of these traits, the Airedale has been used as a wartime dispatch carrier, police dog, guard, and big-game hunter. It has earned the nickname the "king of the terriers."

2. ESTABLISHING A PURPOSE. Tell students to watch Muggs for evidence of the Airedales' main characteristics, described in Building on Prior Knowledge. How many Airedale characteristics can they check off?

 **Texas Essential Elements/(a) English Language Arts: 1B** Purpose and audience; **3A** Plot/character; **3B** Figurative language; **4B** Main idea; **4I** Follow directions

THE DOG THAT BIT PEOPLE

For a detailed lesson plan on this selection, see Teacher's Manual pages 31–34.
A biography of James Thurber appears on text page 121.

James Thurber

© 1933, 1961 by James Thurber. From *My Life and Hard Times,* Harper & Row.

3. PREREADING JOURNAL. Before they read, have students make a humorous list of things that they have seen dogs or other animals do. Include actions or facial expressions that seem human.

Responding to the Drawing
Thurber was famous for his cartoons, especially his big, wise dogs. It was once said that they looked as if they had been traced from a cookie cutter. Call students' attention to the simplicity with which Thurber captures the essence of the dog. **?** What is the dog's expression? Who do you think is behind him? What do you think he is doing at the table?

SUPPLEMENTARY SUPPORT MATERIAL

1. Reading Check Test blackline master
2. Selection Test (page 33 of Test Book)
3. Author photograph on *A Gallery of Authors* poster
4. Workbook (page 31)

DEVELOPING VOCABULARY

The following words appear on a test in the Test Book, page 34. (See also the Vocabulary Activity Sheet.)

intolerant	grudge
oblivious	vibrations
contain	hoist
persuade	emerge
grate	mortify

A. Plot

For what purpose does Thurber include in his story the incidents about the Scotch terrier and the French poodle? (His purpose is to show with humor just how bad Muggs is by comparing him to some of his most troublesome dogs and then stating that Muggs is worse.) Note that the sentence beginning "But the Airedale . . ." states the main idea of the essay.

B. Conflict

What kind of conflict is at the heart of the story? Who are the parties to the conflict? (External; the dog Muggs is in conflict with the people—everyone—with whom he comes in contact)

C. Exaggeration

How does Thurber use exaggeration in this passage to make us laugh? (Muggs is so useless in frightening the mice that they are actually "friendly" and act like "pet mice," a situation that obviously could never happen.) This will help students answer question 7.

★ **Texas Essential Elements/(c) Reading: 2A** Word meaning; **3A** Main ideas/details; **3I** Draw conclusions

Here is a story that is very different from Eric Knight's treatment of dogdom in "Lassie Come-Home." James Thurber provides us with a comical recollection of a family pet that was no friend to man, woman, or child. Incidentally, if you have a taste for animal stories, you may find it useful to know the imposing word *anthropomorphism*. It means "attributing human emotions and characteristics to animals." This story takes place in Columbus, Ohio, where Thurber grew up.

Probably no one man should have as many dogs in his life as I have had, but there was more pleasure than distress in them for me except in the case of an Airedale named Muggs. He gave me more trouble than all the other fifty-four or -five put together, although my moment of keenest embarrassment was the time a Scotch terrier named Jeannie, who had just had six puppies in the clothes closet of a fourth floor apartment in New York, had the unexpected seventh and last at the corner of Eleventh Street and Fifth Avenue during a walk she had insisted on taking. Then, too, there was the prize winning French poodle, a great big black poodle—none of your little, untroublesome white miniatures—who got sick riding in the rumble seat of a car with me on her way to the Greenwich Dog Show. She had a red rubber bib tucked around her throat and, since a rainstorm came up when we were half way through the Bronx, I had to hold over her a small green umbrella, really more of a parasol. The rain beat down fearfully and suddenly the driver of the car drove into a big garage, filled with mechanics. It happened so quickly that I forgot to put the umbrella down and I will always remember, with sickening distress, the look of incredulity[1] mixed with hatred that came over the face of the particular hardened garage man that came over to see what we wanted, when he took a look at me and the poodle. All garage men, and people of that intolerant stripe, hate poodles with their curious haircut, especially the pom-poms that you got to leave on their hips if you expect the dogs to win a prize.

But the Airedale, as I have said, was the worst of all my dogs. He really wasn't my dog, as a matter of fact: I came home from a vacation one summer to find that my brother Roy had bought him while I was away. A big, burly, choleric[2] dog, he always acted as if he thought I wasn't one of the family. There was a slight advantage in being one of the family, for he didn't bite the family as often as he bit strangers. Still, in the years that we had him he bit everybody but mother, and he made a pass at her once but missed. That was during the month when we suddenly had mice, and Muggs refused to do anything about them. Nobody ever had mice exactly like the mice we had that month. They acted like pet mice, almost like mice somebody had trained. They were so friendly that one night when mother entertained for dinner the Friraliras, a club she and my father had belonged to for twenty years, she put down a lot of little dishes with food in them on the pantry floor so that the mice would be satisfied with that and wouldn't come into the dining room. Muggs stayed out in the pantry with the mice, lying on the floor, growling to himself—not at the mice, but about all the people in the next room that he would have liked to get at. Mother slipped out into the pantry once to see how everything was going. Everything was going fine. It made her so mad to see Muggs lying there, oblivious of the mice—they came running up to her—that she slapped him and he slashed at her, but didn't make it. He was sorry immediately, mother said. He was always sorry, she said, after he bit someone, but we could not understand how she figured this out. He didn't act sorry.

Mother used to send a box of candy every Christmas to the people the Airedale bit. The list finally contained forty or more names. Nobody could understand why we didn't get rid of the dog. I didn't understand it very well myself, but we didn't get rid of him. I think that one or two people tried to poison Muggs—he acted poisoned once in a while—and old Major Moberly fired at him

1. **incredulity** (in'kre·dōō'lə·tē): unwillingness to believe.

2. **choleric** (käl'ər·ik): quick-tempered, mean-tempered.

Comment About the Writer

In a tribute to his long-time friend, E. B. White writes about first sharing an office with Thurber at the *New Yorker Magazine:* "The whole world knows what a funny man he was, but you had to sit next to him day after day to understand the extravagance of his thinking, and the intensity of his interest in others and his sympathy for their dilemmas—dilemmas that he instantly enlarged, put in focus, and made immortal, just as he enlarged and made immortal the strange goings-on in the Ohio home of his boyhood."

once with his service revolver near the Seneca Hotel in East Broad Street—but Muggs lived to be almost eleven years old and even when he could hardly get around he bit a Congressman who had called to see my father on business. My mother had never liked the Congressman—she said the signs of his horoscope showed he couldn't be trusted (he was Saturn with the moon in Virgo)—but she sent him a box of candy that Christmas. He sent it right back, probably because he suspected it was trick candy. Mother persuaded herself it was all for the best that the dog had bitten him, even though father lost an important business association because of it. "I wouldn't be associated with such a man," mother said. "Muggs could read him like a book."

We used to take turns feeding Muggs to be on his good side, but that didn't always work. He was never in a very good humor, even after a meal. Nobody knew exactly what was the matter with him, but whatever it was it made him irascible, especially in the mornings. Roy never felt very well in the morning, either, especially before breakfast, and once when he came downstairs and found that Muggs had moodily chewed up the morning paper he hit him in the face with a grapefruit and then jumped up on the dining room table, scattering dishes and silverware and spilling the coffee. Muggs' first free leap carried him all the way across the table and into a brass fire screen in front of the gas grate but he was back on his feet in a moment and in the end he got Roy and gave him a pretty vicious bite in the leg. Then he was all over it; he never bit anyone more than once at a time. Mother always mentioned that as an argument in his favor; she said he had a quick temper but that he didn't hold a grudge. She was forever defending him. I think she liked him because he wasn't well. "He's not strong," she would say, pityingly, but that was inaccurate; he may not have been well but he was terribly strong.

A

One time my mother went to the Chittenden Hotel to call on a woman mental healer who was lecturing in Columbus on the subject of "Harmonious Vibrations." She wanted to find out if it was possible to get harmonious vibrations into a dog. "He's a large tan-colored Airedale," mother explained. The woman said that she had never treated a dog but she advised my mother to hold the thought that he did not bite and would not bite. Mother was holding the thought the very next morning when Muggs got the iceman but she blamed that slip-up on the iceman. "If you didn't think he would bite you, he wouldn't," mother told him. He stomped out of the house in a terrible jangle of vibrations.

B

One morning when Muggs bit me slightly, more or less in passing, I reached down and grabbed his short stumpy tail and hoisted him into the air. It was a foolhardy thing to do and the last time I saw my mother, about six months ago, she said she didn't know what possessed me. I don't either, except that I was pretty mad. As long as I held the dog off the floor by his tail he couldn't get at me, but he twisted and jerked so, snarling all the time, that I realized I couldn't hold him that way very long. I carried him to the kitchen and flung him onto the floor and shut the door on him just as he crashed against it. But I forgot about the back stairs. Muggs went up the back stairs and down the front stairs and had me cornered in the living room. I managed to get up onto the mantelpiece above the fireplace, but it gave way and came down with a tremendous crash throwing a large marble clock, several vases, and myself heavily to the floor. Muggs was so alarmed by the racket that when I picked myself up he had disappeared. We couldn't find him anywhere, although we whistled and shouted, until old Mrs. Detweiler called after dinner that night. Muggs had bitten her once, in the leg, and she came into the living room only after we assured her that Muggs had run away. She had just seated herself when, with a great growling and scratching of claws, Muggs emerged from under a davenport[3] where he had been quietly hiding all the time, and bit her again. Mother examined the bite and put arnica on it and told Mrs. Detweiler that it was only a bruise. "He just bumped you," she said. But Mrs. Detweiler left the house in a nasty state of mind.

C
D

Lots of people reported our Airedale to the police but my father held a municipal office[4] at the

3. **davenport:** large couch.
4. **municipal office:** job in the city government.

A. Exaggeration
"Quick temper" is quite an exaggeration—the dog is a living terror.

B. Character
? What kind of person is the narrator's mother? (She is good-natured, tolerant, and eccentric—she judges people by their horoscopes, and listens to the advice of mental healers.) She might really be one main character of this narrative.

C. Vocabulary
Arnica (är'ni·k·ə) is an herb used to soothe irritation of bruises and swellings.

D. Humor
Note that here Thurber creates humor not by exaggeration but by understatement. Surely, the narrator's mother is understating the case when she describes Mrs. Detweiler's injury as "only a bruise" occurring when Muggs "bumped" her. Surely also Mrs. Detweiler leaves the house in more than just "a nasty state of mind."

READING CHECK TEST

1. Thurber tells us he has owned only one dog in his lifetime. *(False)*
2. Muggs is an Airedale. *(True)*
3. Thurber's mother hates Muggs because he bites. *(False)*
4. Thurber's mother sends boxes of candy to people Muggs bites. *(True)*
5. As Muggs gets older, he becomes more mellow. *(False)*

CLOSURE

Working in pairs, students should define anthropomorphism. Then have them give examples from the story of Muggs's human-like characteristics.

A. Context Clues
From the context and from footnote 6, what do you think "third man up Missionary Ridge" means? (He was close to the enemy. The first two men up would be the commander and his lieutenant.)

B. Expansion
Uncle Horatio wants to demonstrate his courage and valor.

C. Implication
Thurber, by saying that it was "a roundabout system for running a household" is implying that it was a roundabout system for keeping a dog—why don't they get rid of it?

D. Humor
Why is this vision funny? (All of a sudden, Thurber describes what Muggs sees through Muggs's eyes.) Have you ever seen a dog or cat who was spooked by imaginary "Things"?

E. Responding
Do you think this is an appropriate epitaph for Muggs? Why or why not?

time and was on friendly terms with the police. Even so, the cops had been out a couple times—once when Muggs bit Mrs. Rufus Sturtevant and again when he bit Lieutenant-Governor Malloy—but mother told them that it hadn't been Muggs's fault but the fault of the people who were bitten. "When he starts for them, they scream," she explained, "and that excites him." The cops suggested that it might be a good idea to tie the dog up, but mother said that it mortified[5] him to be tied up and that he wouldn't eat when he was tied up.

Muggs at his meals was an unusual sight. Because of the fact that if you reached toward the floor he would bite you, we usually put his food plate on top of an old kitchen table with a bench alongside the table. Muggs would stand on the bench and eat. I remember that my mother's Uncle Horatio, who boasted that he was the third man up Missionary Ridge,[6] was splutteringly indignant when he found out that we fed the dog on a table because we were afraid to put his plate on the floor. He said he wasn't afraid of any dog that ever lived and that he would put the dog's plate on the floor if we would give it to him. Roy said that if Uncle Horatio had fed Muggs on the ground just before the battle he would have been the first man up Missionary Ridge. Uncle Horatio was furious. "Bring him in! Bring him in now!" he shouted. "I'll feed the——on the floor!" Roy was all for giving him a chance, but my father wouldn't hear of it. He said that Muggs had already been fed. "I'll feed him again!" bawled Uncle Horatio. We had quite a time quieting him.

In his last years Muggs used to spend practically all of his time outdoors. He didn't like to stay in the house for some reason or other—perhaps it held too many unpleasant memories for him. Anyway, it was hard to get him to come in and as a result the garbageman, the iceman, and the laundryman wouldn't come near the house. We had to haul the garbage down to the corner, take the laundry out and bring it back, and meet the iceman a block from home. After this had gone on for some time we hit on an ingenious arrangement for getting the dog in the house so that we could lock him up while the gas meter was read, and so on. Muggs was afraid of only one thing, an electrical storm. Thunder and lightning frightened him out of his senses. (I think he thought a storm had broken the day the mantelpiece fell.) He would rush into the house and hide under a bed or in a clothes closet. So we fixed up a thunder machine out of a long narrow piece of sheet iron with a wooden handle on one end. Mother would shake this vigorously when she wanted to get Muggs into the house. It made an excellent imitation of thunder, but I suppose it was the most roundabout system for running a household that was ever devised. It took a lot out of mother.

A few months before Muggs died, he got to "seeing things." He would rise slowly from the floor, growling low, and stalk stiff-legged and menacing toward nothing at all. Sometimes the Thing would be just a little to the right or left of a visitor. Once a Fuller Brush salesman got hysterics. Muggs came wandering into the room like Hamlet following his father's ghost.[7] His eyes were fixed on a spot just to the left of the Fuller Brush man, who stood it until Muggs was about three slow, creeping paces from him. Then he shouted. Muggs wavered on past him into the hallway grumbling to himself but the Fuller man went on shouting. I think mother had to throw a pan of cold water on him before he stopped. That was the way she used to stop us boys when we got into fights.

Muggs died quite suddenly one night. Mother wanted to bury him in the family lot under a marble stone with such inscription as "Flights of angels sing thee to thy rest" but we persuaded her it was against the law. In the end we just put up a smooth board above his grave along a lonely road. On the board I wrote with an indelible pencil *"Cave Canem."*[8] Mother was quite pleased with the simple classic dignity of the old Latin epitaph.

5. **mortified:** humiliated.
6. **Missionary Ridge:** elevated land in Tennessee and Georgia; site of a Civil War battle.
7. **Hamlet . . . ghost**: In Shakespeare's *Hamlet*, the prince of Denmark (Hamlet) is haunted by his murdered father's ghost, whom nobody else can see.
8. ***"Cave Canem"*** (kä'vā kä'nəm): Latin for "beware of the dog."

Analyzing the Story

Identifying Facts

1. Among the dog's more memorable victims was a Congressman, the narrator himself, a neighbor named Mrs. Detweiler, and Lieutenant-Governor Malloy.

She claims that the Congressman was not a good man and that Muggs knew it, that Muggs "just bumped" Mrs. Detweiler, and that the governor had provoked him by screaming. Thurber ascribes no excuses to her on the occasion when he was bitten.

2. He sits on a bench beside an old kitchen table when he eats.

If anyone stoops to place the dog's food on the floor, he will bite that person.

3. He is afraid of lightning and thunder.

They make a "thunder machine" out of a piece of sheet iron and shake it to bring the dog in.

4. He begins "seeing things," and rushes, snarling, toward nothing.

Interpreting Meanings

5. Student reactions may vary. It might be argued that the dog is the focal point of the action and, hence, is the main character.

6. One theme might be stated thus: "Pet owners are more accepting of their pets' idiosyncrasies than other people tend to be." Another might be stated, "Some dogs are willful, and have a mind of their own."

7. Possibilities include the mother's putting dishes of food down for the mice and the author's picking the dog up by the tail. Each derives its humor from the sheer absurdity of the mental picture it creates for the reader.

8. It is funny first because the words are not usually used as an epitaph and, second, because there is nothing dignified about them.

Students may find humor in the mother's desire to bury Muggs in the family plot and to mark his grave with a marble stone bearing the inscription "Flights of angels sing thee to thy rest."

Applying Meanings

9. Answers will vary.

Responding to the Story

Analyzing the Story

Identifying Facts

1. List three incidents in which Muggs bites people. What excuses does the narrator's mother make for Muggs each time?
2. Describe how Muggs eats his meals. Why does the family feed him this way?
3. What is Muggs's greatest fear? How does the family use this to lure Muggs back into the house?
4. Describe how Muggs behaves shortly before he dies.

Interpreting Meanings

5. Who would you say is the main **character** of the story—the dog, the mother, or the narrator? Why?
6. What is the principal **theme** of the story? What general statement is Thurber making about dogs, about pets and their owners, or about something else? SRW p. 87
7. Like "A Loud Sneer for Our Feathered Friends" (page 81), Thurber's story uses **exaggeration** to make us laugh. Identify two instances of exaggeration in the story, and explain why they are humorous.
8. *Cave canem* means "beware of the dog." Why is it funny that the narrator's mother is "quite pleased with the simple classic dignity of the old Latin epitaph?" What other humorous details in the last paragraph end the story on a funny note?

Applying Meanings

9. Describe how you would treat Muggs if he were your dog.

Writing About the Story

A Creative Response

1. **Writing from Another Point of View.** Write a paragraph from Muggs's point of view. Either describe how the dog feels about one of the characters, or retell one of the incidents in the story from Muggs's perspective. Use the first-person pronoun *I*. SRW p. 69
2. **Writing a Humorous Anecdote.** Write about a funny experience you have had. You may want to write about an incident involving a pet, or one involving one of your family members. Use exaggeration to increase the humorous effect of your anecdote.

A Critical Response

3. **Analyzing Anthropomorphism.** Much of the humor in the story comes from **anthropomorphism**—writing or speaking about animals as if they had human qualities. Write a paragraph in which you cite at least three passages in the story in which the narrator or his mother treats Muggs as if he were a person.

See Teacher's Manual page 33.

Analyzing Language and Vocabulary

The Prefixes *In-* and *Un-*

A **prefix** is a group of letters that can be added to other words to change their meanings. The prefixes *in-* and *un-* can be used as negative prefixes. When added to a word, *in-* or *un-* can reverse the root word's meaning. For example, *inconsiderate* means "not considerate." For each definition on the left, make a word with the same meaning by combining a word from the list on the right with the prefix *in-* or *un-*. Consult a dictionary to check your answers. Then use each new word in a sentence.

1. not ordinary	a. delible
2. not correct	b. usual
3. not respecting the beliefs or practices of others	c. tolerant
4. not erasable	d. accurate

Sometimes the prefix *in-* is used as an intensifier. This means it gives added force to a word. For example, you could get in trouble if you thought that *inflammable* means "not flammable." What does it mean?

For answers, see Teacher's Manual page 34.

Reading About the Writer

James Thurber (1884–1961) was born in Columbus, Ohio. A childhood accident left him blind in one eye and with only partial vision in the other.

A. Responding to Focusing on Background
Ask students to discuss the tone of Thurber's response to the question posed by the students and to tell if they think he was justified in using that tone.

? Do you think he might have answered differently if he had, say, just won a prize for one of his novels? You might lead a class discussion on the subject.

FURTHER READING FOR STUDENTS
James Thurber, *My Life and Hard Times,* his humorous autobiography, from which "The Dog That Bit People" is taken

Despite his troubled vision, Thurber gained a reputation as the greatest humorist of his time. Thurber began his nearly life-long association with *The New Yorker* magazine in 1925. For the rest of his life, he was a staff writer and regular contributor of both prose and cartoons.

During these years, Thurber was a member of the circle of wits who gathered regularly at "the round table" of the Algonquin Hotel, a few doors down the street from the magazine offices. Thurber also emerged as an influential figure in shaping the unique editorial style of *The New Yorker.* He did so in spite of his steadily deteriorating eyesight—during the last part of his life, he was wholly blind.

His many works include that most famous of male fantasies, "The Secret Life of Walter Mitty," *The Male Animal* (a play), and *My Life and Hard Times,* from which this story about Muggs is taken.

A

Focusing on Background

Why Do I Write?

Here is Thurber's answer to a group of students who asked where he gets his ideas for his writings. Do you think Thurber has answered this question once too often?

"You can tell where I get my ideas from the things I write, and then you will know as much about it as I do. To write about people you have to know people, to write about bloodhounds you have to know bloodhounds, to write about the Loch Ness monster you have to find out about it. I write because I have to write and it's a good thing a writer gets paid. If I juggled because I have to juggle I couldn't live. You will have to ask my readers why they read what I write. I hope they read it because it has something to say. You can also say that writers could get more written if they didn't have to answer so many questions about why they write."

—James Thurber

© 1933, 1961 by James Thurber. From *My Life and Hard Times,* Harper & Row.

Answers to Questions

I

A1—B1, B4
A2—B5
A3—B3
A4—B1, B4
A5—B2

★ **Texas Essential Elements/(a) English Language Arts: 1B** Purpose and audience; **3A** Plot/character; **4F** Generalizations. **(c) Reading: 3A** Main ideas/details; **3D** Generalizations

Review: Exercises in Reading Fiction

CHARACTER

I.

One of the famous characters created by Charles Dickens is a man named Mr. Murdstone who is in a novel called *David Copperfield*. All of the following comments refer to Mr. Murdstone. The narrator is David Copperfield.

A

For each passage in column A, tell which method of characterization is used. The methods are cited in column B. SRW p. 21

A. Background
Murdstone is one of Dickens's famous and despicable villains, who beats Davy mercilessly and eventually forces him to leave his mother's home. At the point of the first quoted extract, Mr. Murdstone is wooing Davy's pretty widowed mother.

A

1. "Gradually, I became used to seeing the gentleman with the black whiskers. I liked him no better than at first, and had the same uneasy jealousy of him."
2. "Mr. Murdstone was firm . . ."
3. "He beat me then, as if he would have beaten me to death. . . . Then he was gone, and the door was locked outside . . ."
4. "His hair and whiskers were blacker and thicker, looked at so near, than even I had given them credit for being."
5. " 'I suppose you know, David, that I [Mr. Murdstone is speaking] am not rich. At any rate, you know it now. You have received some considerable education already. Education is costly, and even if it were not, and I could afford it, I am of opinion that it would not be at all advantageous to you to be kept at a school. What is before you is a fight with the world, and the sooner you begin it, the better.' "

B

1. By describing appearance
2. By quoting speech
3. By describing actions
4. By revealing the responses of other characters
5. By stating a character trait directly

II.

Here is a portion of a story set in Jamaica, which is part of the West Indies. The narrator is a young girl named Annie John, who has for a while wanted to play with another girl she calls the Red Girl. Watch how Annie John reveals both her character and the character of the Red Girl.

The Red Girl and I stood under the guava tree looking each other up and down. What a beautiful thing I saw standing before me. Her face was big and round and red, like a moon—a red moon. She had big, broad, flat feet, and they were naked to the bare ground; her dress was dirty, the skirt and blouse tearing away from each other at one side; the red hair that I had first seen standing up on her head was matted and tangled; her hands were big and fat, and her fingernails held at least ten anthills of dirt under them. And on top of that, she had such an unbelievable, wonderful smell, as if she had never taken a bath in her whole life.

I soon learned this about her: She took a bath only once a week, and that was only so that she could be admitted to her grandmother's presence. She didn't like to bathe, and her mother didn't force her. She changed her dress once a week for the same reason. She preferred to wear a dress until it just couldn't be worn anymore. Her mother didn't mind that, either. She didn't like to comb her hair, though on the first day of school she could put herself out for that. She didn't like to go to Sunday school, and her mother didn't force her. She didn't like to brush her teeth, but occasionally her mother said it was necessary. She loved to play marbles, and was so good that only Skerritt boys now played against her. Oh, what an angel she was, and what a heaven she lived in! I, on the other hand, took a full bath every morning and a sponge bath every night. I could hardly go out on my doorstep without putting my shoes on. I was not allowed to play in the sun without a hat on my head. My mother paid a woman who lived five houses away from us sevenpence a week—a penny for each school day and twopence for Sunday—to comb my hair. On Saturday, my mother washed my hair. Before I went to sleep at night I had to make sure

Answers to Questions

II

1. Possible answers include the girl's big round, red face; her big, broad, flat feet; her dirty dress; her matted and tangled hair; her big, fat hands; her dirty fingernails.
2. She takes a bath only once a week; she changes her dress once a week, wearing the same dress until it can no longer be worn; she does not comb her hair; she does not attend Sunday school; she plays marbles and she does so with Skerritt boys.
3. "Oh, what an angel she was, and what a heaven she lived in!"
4. She tells us that she is forced to bathe daily and sponge herself off at night, that she is made to wear shoes at all times, that she must wear a hat in the sun, that her hair is regularly combed, that her uniforms must be clean and creaseless and laid out each night before bed, that her shoes must be shined, that she must attend Sunday school, and that she is forbidden to play marbles or associate with Skerritt boys.
5. The narrator tells us that her clothes were clean and creaseless, her shoes *(Answers continue in left-hand column.)*

(Continued from top.) shined, her hair clean and combed.
6. Students should be able to gather from the information provided that traits b, d, and e are applicable and the other two are not.

Further Reading for Students
Annie John by Jamaica Kincaid, a collection of stories about Annie's growing up in Antigua

my uniform was clean and creaseless and all laid out for the next day. I had to make sure that my shoes were clean and polished to a nice shine. I went to Sunday school every Sunday unless I was sick. I was not allowed to play marbles, and, as for Skerritt boys, that was hardly mentionable.

—from "The Red Girl,"
Jamaica Kincaid

1. Find at least six details that describe the Red Girl's appearance.
2. What do we learn about her actions and the way she behaves?
3. Find the sentence in which the narrator tells us directly how she feels about the Red Girl.
4. In contrast, what does the narrator tell us about her own behavior?
5. What does she tell us about her own appearance?
6. Which of the following character traits would you apply to the narrator?
   a. She is careless of her appearance.
   b. She desires adventure.
   c. She is content with her own life.
   d. She envies the Red Girl's freedom.
   e. She is obedient.

Writing

1. **Contrasting Characters.** Describe two characters who are opposites. Tell specifically how they are different in these ways: (a) in the ways they speak, (b) in the ways they look, and (c) in the ways other people feel about them.
2. **Describing Characters.** Reread the extract from "Wanda Hickey's Night of Golden Memories" on page 74. Then describe a group of people at a family dinner. Try to give your readers a sense of what these people are like by (a) letting us hear them speak, and (b) telling us what they are eating.

For evaluation strategies, see Teacher's Manual page 35.

★ **Texas Essential Elements/(a) English Language Arts: 1A** Composing process; **1B** Purpose and audience; **1H** Proofread; **1I** Spelling generalizations; **2B** Parts of speech; **2D** Grammar/punctuation/spelling; **3A** Plot/character

For teaching and evaluation strategies on this exercise, see Teacher's Manual page 35.

ANALYZING CHARACTER

Writing Assignment

Write a two-paragraph essay about one of the characters in this unit. Identify two of the character's traits, and support what you say with details from the story. (A *trait* is a quality or characteristic, such as kindness, self-confidence, generosity, or cleverness.)

Background

Writers try to create characters that come alive. Instead of just "telling" what a character is like, writers try to "show" us the character's qualities. As readers, we observe what the character *does* and *says,* what *others say about the character,* and even what the character *looks like.* Sometimes a writer tells us directly what a character *thinks* and *feels* and how a character *changes.*

When you **analyze** a character in a story, you look carefully at everything the writer has shown about the character. Based on this evidence, you draw conclusions about the traits that make up the character's personality. You should be able to get a complete picture of what that character is really like.

Prewriting

Choose one of the characters in this unit that you especially like or dislike. Reread the story, and think about what traits the character's actions and words reveal. Write the character's name on a piece of paper, surrounded by all of the traits that occur to you. This type of diagraming is called **clustering.** It can help you to get a complete "picture" of a character and to see his or her outstanding traits.

The following diagram analyzes Ruth McKenney, the narrator of "A Loud Sneer for Our Feathered Friends" (page 81).

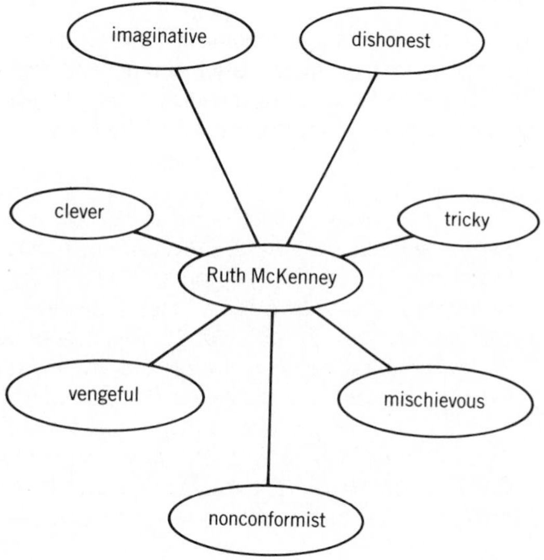

Your next step is to choose two traits to write about. Find details in the story (actions, dialogue, comments by other characters) that illustrate each of the traits, and add these details to your diagram. Here are examples of details that support the trait *tricky*:

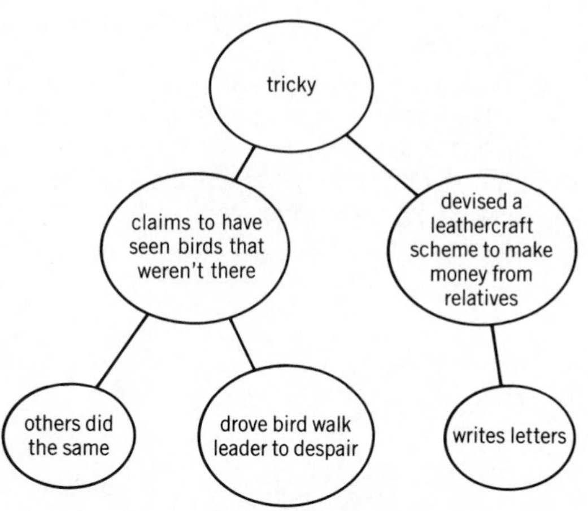

A. Revising
Have students answer the questions in the Revising and Proofreading Self-Check test.

Did the writer of this paragraph leave anything out that you would have included?

★ **Texas Essential Elements/(a) English Language Arts (continued): 4I** Follow directions.
(c) Reading: 1C Dictionaries; **3A** Main ideas/details; **3I** Draw conclusions; **4A** Follow directions; **4D** Diagrams/graphs

Exercises in Critical Thinking and Writing/*cont.*

Writing

In your first paragraph, include a topic sentence that names the character, title, author, and first trait. The rest of this paragraph should cite at least two story details to illustrate the first trait. Follow the same plan (topic sentence + supporting details) for the second paragraph.

The following paragraph is based on the Prewriting diagram:

From what she tells us in "A Loud Sneer for Our Feathered Friends," Ruth McKenney, the writer and narrator, was a tricky child. She and her sister tricked their relatives into sending them money for leather goods they had no intention of making. They wrote letters that were "... real masterpieces of double dealing and heartless chicanery." A second trick involved bird watching. After several "birdless" days, she and her sister began to lie. They claimed they saw and heard birds that they had never laid eyes on. This trick was so successful that the honest bird-walk leader burst into tears and ran away.

Topic sentence names title, author, character, and trait.

Supporting detail #1.

Quotes character's own words.

Supporting detail #2.

A

Revising and Proofreading Self-Check

1. Does the first paragraph include a topic sentence that names the character, story title, and author?
2. Does the first paragraph discuss one character trait and cite details from the story to support it?
3. Does the second paragraph discuss a second trait and cite details from the story to support it?
4. Does every sentence start with a capital letter and end with a period or other end punctuation mark?
5. Are my ideas clearly expressed? Have I said everything I wanted to say?

Partner Check

1. Are there any spelling errors?
2. Are sentences punctuated correctly?
3. Are paragraphs fully developed (at least four sentences long) and indented?
4. Are any sentences unclear? Do I understand what you are trying to say?
5. What do I like best about this paper?
6. What do I think needs improvement?

DISCOVERIES

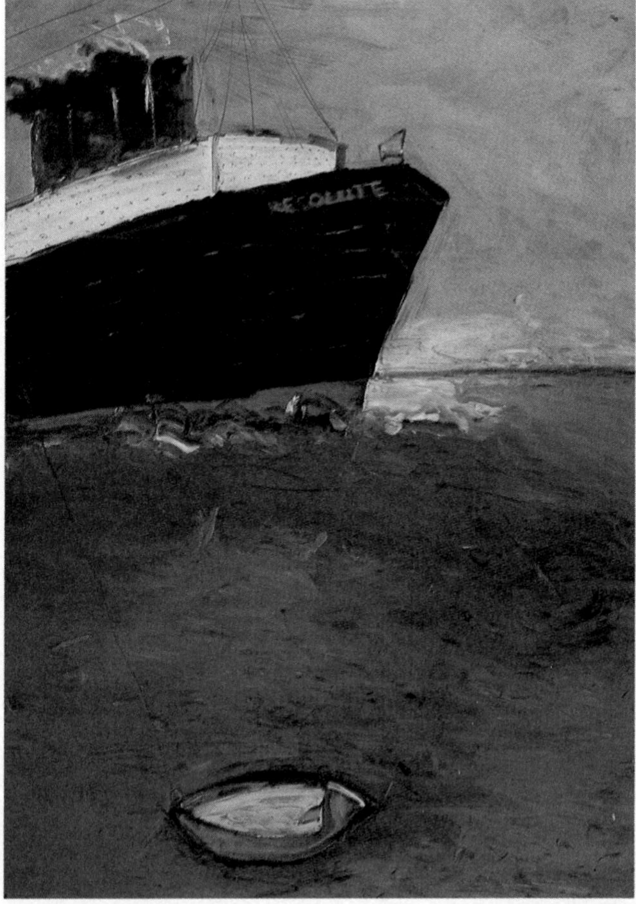

S.S. Resolute with Rescue Craft by Inez Storer (1984). Oil.

Courtesy Rena Bransten Gallery, San Francisco.

UNIT THREE **John Leggett**

Humanities Connection: Discussing the Fine Art

American collage artist and sculptor Inez Storer was born in Santa Monica in 1933. She has had numerous exhibitions of her works.

? How does this painting make the ship look as if it's really moving? (It's cut off by the left border—as though it is moving across a screen; waves are splashing up against the ship.) Where do you think the ship is going? What might it be out to discover?

The rescue craft is in the foreground of the painting—this and its bright yellow color make it stand out and seem important. What do you think the significance of the rescue craft is? Do you think *resolute*—which means "determined"—is a good name for a ship?

Teaching the Short Story

One of the reasons for the continuing popularity of the short story is its flexibility. In this unit, for example, students will find a story in the form of a series of letters ("Southpaw") and excerpts from autobiographies or reminiscences, as well as tales in more traditional fictional forms.

Students should be led to an understanding of common characteristics of all stories: setting, characterization, conflict, and theme (in the form of the discoveries made by characters). It would be helpful to have students work with these characteristics in the rough order listed for two reasons: First, that is generally the order in which these elements are revealed in a story—the reader almost always learns about the setting before encountering characters or a full sense of form and conflict. Second, the order listed is also generally the order of difficulty. It is much more meaningful to discuss the theme, for example, after students have had an opportunity to meet the characters who illustrate that theme.

Although the unit is not formally divided into sections, you should help students recognize the gradual progression of tone in the stories from humorous (the first three selections) to serious (the last five selections). Students may note humor even in some of the serious stories. Since humor can often more easily open the door to good discussion than tragedy, you will want to teach the stories in the order they are presented.

There is enough diversity of character and subject in these stories so that everyone should find something to their particular liking. You are the best judge of which teaching strategy is appropriate to a given group of students. That students enjoy what they are reading should be your paramount goal: The explanation, analysis, and evaluation questions should be framed with that ultimate purpose in mind. With your guidance, the sparks of recognition that can be generated by these stories will kindle an interest in literature leading to a lifetime of pleasure. Your own role as an active reader, and your encouragement of student reading outside the classroom, will also help assure that your students develop good reading habits.

Objectives of the Unit

1. To improve reading proficiency and expand vocabulary
2. To gain exposure to notable authors and their work
3. To define and identify the elements of the short story: setting, character, plot, conflict, point of view, theme
4. To define and identify irony and symbolism
5. To interpret and respond to literature, orally and in writing, through analysis of its elements
6. To practice the following critical thinking and writing skills:
   - **a.** Describing and analyzing a character
   - **b.** Analyzing internal and external conflict
   - **c.** Comparing and contrasting stories
   - **d.** Inferring the theme of a story

SUPPLEMENTARY SUPPORT MATERIAL

1. Introduction/Seeing Ourselves in Literature Test (page 43 of Test Book)
2. Word Analogies Test (page 59 of Test Book)
3. Reading Check Test blackline master
4. Unit Review Test (page 61 of Test Book)
5. Critical Thinking Test (page 65 of Test Book)
6. Instructional Overhead Transparency

Unit Outline

DISCOVERIES

. . . there is in writing the constant joy of sudden discovery, of happy accident.

—Henry Louis Mencken

A

Discoveries

An element of most literature—of fiction, nonfiction, poetry, and drama—is revelation. We might call this the "Ah-hah!" moment. It happens when a character, usually the main one, discovers something important to his or her life.

Such discoveries are likely to be about relationships between people—between members of a family, between schoolmates, between friends or enemies. Even when stories take place in places and times far removed from our own, their revelations are like the ones we experience in our own lives.

B

Suppose we read an account of two friends. Surprisingly, one friend betrays the other. If the story is well-written, we have "lived through" the betrayal ourselves. We believe the tragedy could happen in exactly the way the storyteller relates it. The story has also taught us something. We've learned a lesson about the delicate nature and value of friendship, almost as surely, and far less painfully, as if we had suffered through the experience ourselves.

Literature that endures tends to focus on discoveries about the big events in everyone's life—understanding the nature of love, accepting loss, dealing with ambition, accepting the final loss of death itself.

Coming-of-Age Stories

Many of the stories in this book have to do with the discoveries we all make as we grow up, as we gather the wisdom we need to survive and flourish in adult life. These are often called **rite-of-passage** or **coming-of-age** stories. The discoveries central to these stories are the ones we all make as we pass from childhood into adulthood.

Coming-of-age stories usually deal with the discovery that the world isn't always what we wish it would be. Often these stories are about the acceptance of sound values. They may give us some idea of how to cope with a mother's anxiety, with temptation, with the opposite sex, with a lack of money, with a fear of failure, with the need to be liked.

C

Recognizing Ourselves in Literature

When you find a story that has a character involved in a conflict that seems familiar to you—a situation you can *feel*—you experience the shock of recognition. "Hey! That's me!" you might want to say to yourself. That is the best kind of discovery—and that is what literature is really all about.

A. Discussing the Quotation

Although in the quotation Mencken refers specifically to writing, the quotation can apply to reading as well.

? Name one short story you have read and enjoyed in which a character made a sudden discovery about his or her life or about life in general. What was that discovery? Why did you enjoy reading about it? Explain what you think Mencken means by a "happy accident."

B. Responding

? Name a character in a story you read or in a TV show you saw who experienced a revelation similar to one you experienced in your own life. What was the revelation?

C. Responding

? Suggest other issues that might be central to coming-of-age stories.

Responding to a Story

Students will enjoy this story immensely, for it involves a humorous turn of events. Students may "root" for either Janet or Richard, although at the end of the story, they will realize how human, and likable, both friends are.

Students who follow baseball could explain the jargon to those who do not understand the terms. However, baseball is not the main point of this exchange of letters. The main point is the relationship between the two young people. Elicit from students the character traits in Janet and Richard that they see in themselves or in their friends. Then discuss what each of the friends discovers about the other, and what discoveries they reveal to the reader about themselves.

A. Active Reading

The reading strategy reflected in the sidenotes is an interactive one; it requires the reader to combine his or her existing knowledge with the information presented in the story. By questioning, predicting, monitoring comprehension, and confirming and revising predictions during the reading process, the reader derives maximum understanding and enjoyment from the story.

B. Responding

? Do you agree with this reader's assessment of Richard's reasoning? Explain.

Responding to a Story

A Here is a short story told in an unusual format. In the right-hand margin are one reader's responses to the story. Notice how this reader automatically asks questions and makes predictions about what will happen next. Notice also how the reader looks for the conflict, or struggle, in the story and then, at the end, asks what the characters have learned from the conflict, and whether they have changed.

Southpaw

A southpaw is a left-handed pitcher. Is this a sports story? Who is the southpaw?

The story is told in a series of letters. One person is Richard.

Dear Richard,

Don't invite me to your birthday party because I'm not coming. And give back the Disneyland sweat shirt I said you could wear. If I'm not good enough to play on your team, I'm not good enough to be friends with.

Your former friend,
Janet

P.S. I hope when you go to the dentist he finds twenty cavities.

The other person is Janet. I guess Richard wouldn't let her on his team.

Dear Janet,

Here is your stupid Disneyland sweat shirt, if that's how you're going to be. I want my comic books now—finished or not. No girl has ever played on the Mapes Street baseball team, and as long as I'm captain, no girl ever will.

Your former friend,
Richard

P.S. I hope when you go for your checkup you need a tetanus shot.

They were best friends—maybe Richard was Janet's boyfriend.

Richard doesn't like girls on his team. The conflict in this story is pretty clear. Richard's reasoning is not very smart. B

I like the way they insult each other.

Dear Richard,

I'm changing my goldfish's name from Richard to Stanley. Don't count on my vote for class president next year. Just because I'm a member of the ballet club doesn't mean I'm not a terrific ballplayer.

Your former friend,
Janet

P.S. I see you lost your first game 28–0.

A sign that they were once pretty close.

Janet is rubbing it in.

Dear Janet,

I'm not saving any more seats for you on the bus. For all I care you can stand the whole way to school. Why don't you forget about baseball and learn something nice like knitting?

Your former friend,
Richard

P.S. Wait until Wednesday.

Another sign that they used to be good friends.

This is a low blow. Richard is insulting her.

A. Responding

Do *you* like Janet? Why or why not?

Dear Richard,

My father said I could call someone to go with us for a ride and hot-fudge sundaes. In case you didn't notice, I didn't call you.

Your former friend,
Janet

I like Janet. She's smart and tough.] A

P.S. I see you lost your second game, 34–0.

Richard's team is pretty bad.

Dear Janet,

Remember when I took the laces out of my blue-and-white sneakers and gave them to you? I want them back.

Your former friend,
Richard

P.S. Wait until Friday.

He keeps suggesting that the team will do better. I wonder what's going to happen? I predict Janet will join the team and win every game.

Dear Richard,

Congratulations on your unbroken record. Eight straight losses, wow! I understand you're the laughingstock of New Jersey.

Your former friend,
Janet

P.S. Why don't you and your team forget about baseball and learn something nice like knitting, maybe?

This is a good insult. Richard deserves it.

Dear Janet,

Here's the silver horseback-riding trophy that you gave me. I don't think I want to keep it anymore.

Your former friend,
Richard

P.S. I didn't think you'd be the kind who'd kick a man when he's down.

Now he's feeling sorry for himself. He expects Janet to take his insults, but he doesn't like it when she gives him a taste of his own medicine.

Dear Richard,

I wasn't kicking exactly. I was kicking *back*.

Your former friend,
Janet

P.S. In case you were wondering, my batting average is .345.

Janet is persistent. .345 is a top batting average.

Dear Janet,

Alfie is having his tonsils out tomorrow. We might be able to let you catch next week.

Richard

Richard is beginning to crack. This is the first sign.

A. Responding to the Photograph
In recent years, the issue of whether or not to allow girls to play on boys' sports teams has garnered a fair amount of public attention. This is true not only for low-contact sports such as baseball and softball, but also and especially for high-contact sports such as football and hockey.
? Do you think boys and girls should play on the same sports teams? Why or why not?

Dear Richard,
I pitch.

Janet

Dear Janet,
Joel is moving to Kansas and Danny sprained his wrist. How about a permanent place in the outfield?

Richard

Richard is stubborn. He doesn't want her to pitch.

Dear Richard,
I pitch.

Janet

Dear Janet,
Ronnie caught the chicken pox and Leo broke his toe and Elwood has these stupid violin lessons. I'll give you first base. That's my final offer.

Richard

Already's he's changed his mind about letting her on the team. He's having a lot of bad luck—these letters are funny.

A

READING CHECK TEST

1. Revelation is an element of most literature. *(True)*
2. Such revelations are likely to be about relationships between people. *(True)*
3. Stories that deal with discoveries that children make as they grow to adulthood are called coming-of-age stories. *(True)*
4. Often these stories are about the rejection of sound values. *(False)*
5. Coming-of-age stories usually deal with the discovery that the world is just what people think it should be. *(False)*

Dear Richard,
Susan Reilly plays first base, Marilyn Jackson catches, Ethel Kahn plays centerfield, I pitch. It's a package deal.

Janet

P.S. Sorry about your twelve-game losing streak.

Good for Janet! She drives a hard bargain. She's getting her friends on the team, too.

This detail means that Richard is desperate.

Dear Janet,
Please! Not Marilyn Jackson.

Richard

Dear Richard,
Nobody ever said that I was unreasonable. How about Lizzie Martindale instead?

Janet

Janet is funny. She's been "unreasonable" all the time, in a way.

Dear Janet,
At least could you call your goldfish Richard again?

Your friend,
Richard

Richard is a good sport. I wonder how the team will do now?

What discovery is made in this story? Do the characters change at all? Let's see: Richard discovers that the world is changing and that girls can play baseball well, too. What does Janet discover? A

—Judith Viorst

A. Discovery
? What *does* Janet discover? (That it pays to be tough and stand by your values, even if it can threaten a friendship. She also learns the value of compromise—even if it's only switching teammates, her giving in helps her to make up with Richard.)

Thinking Over the Story

Suppose you were this reader and were using your reading notes to help you write a composition about this story. You would notice several things:

1. You asked a question about the **title** at the opening of the story. Did you ever find the answer?
2. You noticed the unusual **form** of the story.
3. You noticed the **conflict** in the story, between Richard, who doesn't want girls on his team, and Janet, who seems to be a crack ballplayer and is persistent. These two people, you also noted, seemed to have been very good friends before the argument over the team arose.
4. You noticed some **characteristics** of the two people: that Richard uses some pretty dumb reasoning at the start of the story, that Richard can be insulting, that Janet gives it right back to him. You noticed that Janet is smart and tough, that Richard keeps thinking his team will do better, and that Richard finally gives in. You noticed that Janet, once she has won the struggle to get on the team, doesn't stop there; she goes for more (she wants her three girlfriends on the team too).
5. You asked at the end what the characters had **discovered** and if they had changed. You easily realized what Richard had discovered. Do you have any answer to the question about Janet's discovery? Which character changed the most?

You now have six topics you can use in writing about the story:

1. Title
2. Form of story
3. Conflict
4. Characters and what they are like
5. Discoveries made in the story
6. Changes in characters

Suppose you have to limit your topics to three. Which three would you select to write about for this story?

PREREADING

1. BUILDING ON PRIOR KNOWLEDGE. Before they read, have students tell whether they have ever wondered if their parents, or other adult care-givers, ever felt and do still feel the same emotions that they themselves feel. Ask them if they think these adults are really so different from themselves. To help illustrate the point, you might have those students who have seen the movie *Back to the Future* discuss it. The theme of the film that is relevant to the upcoming selection is that although it might be hard for teenagers to imagine it, their parents as young people had—and as adults still do have—feelings similar to those of their children.

2. ESTABLISHING A PURPOSE. Before students begin reading, you might have them read question 6 on page 142.

3. PREREADING JOURNAL. The title is in the narrator, Mike's, voice. As an exercise in first impressions, ask students to describe what they think Mike will be like, judging from the title.

A. Exaggeration No matter when you read this story, you know from the tone that, to Mike, 1999 is an eternity away. He uses this exaggeration to express the common view of most adolescents that youth springs eternal.

B. Tone ? What is Mike's tone? (Informative and a little flip. He writes the way he speaks, which makes it easy for us to identify with him. We can also tell that he has a good sense of humor.)

★ **Texas Essential Elements/(a) English Language Arts: 1B** Purpose and audience; **3A** Plot/character; **4F** Generalizations. **(c) Reading: 3A** Main ideas/details; **3D** Generalizations; **3G** Compare/contrast

GUESS WHAT? I ALMOST KISSED MY FATHER GOOD NIGHT

Robert Cormier

The relationship between children and parents is a strong one, and common to all of us. It is no surprise, then, to find that it is so often explored in fiction. This story by Robert Cormier is modern, but the situation it describes is timeless. Here we see an alert fifteen-year-old boy trying to understand his father. "Voice" is a major element in this story. As you listen to Mike tell his story, think about how he reveals himself through his voice. What does he think of girls? Of school? Of his sisters? What does he prize most? Do you think Mike sounds like a real person?

I've got to get to the bottom of it all somehow and maybe this is the best way. It's about my father. For instance, I found out recently that my father is actually forty-five years old. I knew that he was forty-something but it never meant anything to me. I mean, trying to imagine someone
A over forty and what it's like to be that old is the same as trying to imagine what the world would be like in, say, 1999. Anyway, he's forty-five, and he has the kind of terrible job that fathers have; in his case, he's office manager for a computer equipment concern. Nine-to-five stuff. Four weeks' vacation every year but two weeks must be taken between January and May so he usually ends up painting the house or building a patio or something like that in April, and then we travel the other two weeks in July. See America First. He reads a couple of newspapers every day and never misses the seven o'clock news on television.

Here are some other vital statistics my research turned up: He's five ten, weighs 160 pounds, has a tendency toward high blood pressure, enjoys a glass of beer or two while he's watching the Red Sox on television, sips one martini and never two before dinner, likes his steak medium rare and has a habit of saying that "tonight, by Jove, I'm going to stay up and watch Johnny Carson," but always gropes his way to bed after the eleven o'clock news, which he watches only to learn the next day's weather forecast. He has a pretty good

Puns. Mike says his father has a weakness for "awful puns." A *pun* is a play on the meanings of words. You might have heard this joke: "When is a door not a door?" ("When it's ajar.") This is a pun; to catch the joke, you have to realize that the last word refers at the same time to the word *ajar,* which means "open," and to the phrase "a jar." Sometimes people use puns in naming things or in advertisements to catch our attention. For example, a restaurant uses a pun in calling itself "The Dew Drop Inn." An advertisement against littering uses a pun to make its point. This ad shows a tape measure around the middle of a garbage can; the caption says "New York Has a Waist Problem." A cattle ranch in the West, co-owned by several brothers, also uses a pun in its name: "Where the Sun's Rays Meet." If you've caught all these jokes, you've caught on to puns. Some people think the only way to respond to a pun is to groan. What do you think? B

SRW p. 71

For a detailed lesson plan on this story, see Teacher's Manual pages 38–40. A biography of Robert Cormier appears on text page 143.

SUPPLEMENTARY SUPPORT MATERIAL

1. Vocabulary Activity Sheet
2. Reading Check Test blackline master
3. Selection Test (page 45 of Test Book)
4. Author photograph on *A Gallery of Authors* poster
5. Reader's Response Journal
6. Workbook (page 33)

DEVELOPING VOCABULARY

The following words appear on a test in the Test Book, page 46. (See also the Vocabulary Activity Sheet.)

vital	intimacy
pun	compensation
barreled	engulfed
bedlam	apprehensive
scrutinizing	spiral

Quantrell II by Judy North (1979). Watercolor. Collection of Glenn C. Janss.

Humanities Connection: Discussing the Fine Art

Painter and printmaker Judy North (1937–) studied her craft at the Los Angeles Art Institute and at the San Francisco Art Institute. The accompanying painting, done in North's preferred medium of watercolor, is an excellent example of her creative talent and artistic skill.

? How do you think the artist painted the man's hat? Why do you think she used such dotted and splotchy strokes—what effect do you think she was trying to create? (Perhaps she didn't know the man she was painting very well, and was trying to convey his vagueness through art. Maybe it was raining while she was painting, and she therefore saw the man through a haze of rain.) "Quantrell" is either a made-up word or someone's name. What do you think it is? Why might it be "II"? How well does the picture go with the story?

A. Exaggeration

? Here is more of Mike's funny exaggeration. What can we infer from this statement? (That Mike can never get to use the phone because his sister is always talking on it.)

B. Conflict

This incident establishes the conflict that will drive the plot forward. Note the use of the phrase "for crying out loud." Help students to realize that this phrase indicates shock on Mike's part, shock that develops into a full-blown internal conflict.

C. Interpreting

? Why do you think Mike feels like he's caught his father naked? (For the first time, he is seeing his father stripped of the "father role"—his father is wrapped up in his own thoughts, thoughts which probably don't involve sons, homework, and the seven o'clock news. Watching him sit there in thought, not involved in any "father" activities or behavior, Mike finds him somehow vulnerable.)

D. Figurative Language

? Note the description of Mike's father's shudder. What does this comparison tell about his father's state of mind? (The exaggerated shudder probably reveals a release of built-up tension.)

sense of humor but a weakness for awful puns which he inflicts on us at the dinner table: "Do you carrot all for me? I'm in a stew over you." We humor him. By we, I mean my sisters. Annie, who is nineteen and away at college, and Debbie,
A who is fourteen and spends her life on the telephone. And me: I'm Mike, almost sixteen and a sophomore in high school. My mother's name is Ellen—Dad calls her Ellie—and she's a standard mother: "Clean up your room! Is your homework done?"

Now that you've gotten the basic details, I'll tell you about that day last month when I walked downtown from school to connect with the North Side bus which deposits me in front of my house. It was one of those terrific days in spring and the air smelled like vacation, and it made you ache with all the things you wanted to do and all the places you wanted to see and all the girls you wanted to meet. Like the girl at the bus stop that I've been trying to summon up the nerve to approach for weeks: so beautiful she turns my knees liquid. Anyway, I barreled through Bryant Park, a shortcut, the turf spring-soft and spongy under my feet and the weeping willows hazy with blossom. Suddenly I screeched to a halt, like Bugs Bunny in one of those crazy television cartoons. There's a car parked near the Civil War cannon. Ours. I recognize the dent in the right front fender Annie put there last month when she was home from college. And there are also those decals on the side window that give the geography of our boring vacation trips, *Windy Chasms,* places like that.

The car is unoccupied. Did somebody steal it and abandon it here? Wow, great! I walk past the splashing fountain that displays one of those embarrassing naked cherubs and stop short again. There he is: my father. Sitting on a park bench. Gazing out over a small pond that used to have goldfish swimming around until kids started steal-
B ing them. My father was deep in thought, like a statue in a museum. I looked at my watch. Two-thirty in the afternoon, for crying out loud. What was he doing there at this time of day? I was about to approach him but hesitated, held back for some
C reason—I don't know why. Although he looked perfectly normal, I felt as though I had somehow caught him naked, had trespassed on forbidden territory, the way I'm afraid to have my mother come barging into my bedroom at certain moments. I drew back, studying him as if he were a sudden stranger. I saw the familiar thinning short hair, the white of his scalp showing through. The way the flesh in his neck has begun to pucker like turkey skin. Now he sighed. I saw his shoulders heave, and the rest of his body shudder like the D
chain reaction of freight cars. He lifted his face to the sun, eyes closed. He seemed to be reveling in the moment, all his pores open. I tiptoed away. People talk about tiptoeing but I don't think I ever really tiptoed before in my life. Anyway, I leave him there, still basking on that park bench, because I've got something more important to do at the bus stop. Today, I have vowed to approach the girl, talk to her, say something, *anything*. After all, I'm not exactly Frankenstein and some girls actually think I'm fun to be with. I stall around and miss the two-forty-five deliberately. She never shows up. At three-thirty, I thumb home and pick up a ride in a green MG, which kind of compensates for a rotten afternoon.

At dinner that evening, I'm uncommunicative, thinking of that girl and all the science homework waiting in my room. Dinner at our house is a kind of ritual that alternates between bedlam[1] and boredom with no sense of direction whatever. Actually, I don't enjoy table talk. I have this truly tremendous appetite and I eat too fast, like my mother says. The trouble is that I'm always being asked a question or expected to laugh at some corny joke when my mouth is full, which it usually is. But that evening I stopped eating altogether when my mother asked my father about his day at the office.

"Routine," he said.

I thought of that scene in the park.

"Did you have to wait around all day for that Harper contract?" my mother asked.

"Didn't even have time for a coffee break," he said, reaching for more potatoes.

I almost choked on the roast beef. He lied: My father actually lied. I sat there, terrified, caught in some kind of terrible no-man's-land. It was as if

1. **bedlam:** noise and confusion.

the lie itself had thrust me into panic. Didn't I fake my way through life most of the time—telling half-truths to keep everybody happy, either my parents or my teachers or even my friends? What would happen if everybody started telling the truth all of a sudden? But I was bothered by his motive. I mean—why did he have to pretend that he *wasn't* in the park that afternoon? And that first question came back to haunt me worse than before—what was he doing there, anyway, in the first place? A

I found myself studying him across the table, scrutinizing him with the eyes of a stranger. But it didn't work. He was simply my father. Looked exactly as he always did. He was his usual dull, unruffled self, getting ready to take his evening nap prior to the television news. Stifling a yawn after dessert. Forget it, I told myself. There's a simple explanation for everything.

Let's skip some time now until the night of the telephone call. And let me explain about the telephone setup at our house. First of all, my father never answers the phone. He lets it ring nine or ten or eleven times and merely keeps on reading the paper and watching the television because he claims—and he's right—that most of the calls are for Debbie or me. Anyway a few nights after that happening at the park, the phone rang about ten-thirty and I barreled out of my room because he and my mother get positively explosive about calls after nine on school nights.

When I lifted the receiver, I found that my father had already picked up the downstairs extension. There was a pause and then he said: "I've got it, Mike."

"Yes, sir," I said. And hung up.

I stood there in the upstairs hallway, not breathing. His voice was a murmur and even at that distance I detected some kind of intimacy. Or did the distance itself contribute that hushed, secretive quality? I returned to my room and put a record on the stereo. I remembered that my mother was out for the evening, a meeting of the Ladies' Auxiliary. I got up and looked in the mirror. Another lousy pimple, on the right side of my nose to balance the one on the left. Who had called him on the telephone at that hour of the night? And why had he answered the call in record time? Was it the same person he'd been waiting for in Bryant Park? Don't be ridiculous, Mike, I told myself; think of real stuff, like pimples. Later, I went downstairs and my father was slumped in his chair, newspaper like a fragile tent covering his face. His snores capsized the tent and it slid to the floor. He needed a shave, his beard like small slivers of ice. His feet were fragile, something I had never noticed before; they were mackerel white, half in and half out of his slippers. I went back upstairs without checking the refrigerator, my hunger suddenly annihilated[2] by guilt. He wasn't mysterious: He was my father. And he snored with his mouth open. B C

The next day I learned the identity of the girl at the bus stop: like a bomb detonating. Sally Bettencourt. There's a Sally Bettencourt in every high school in the world—the girlfriend of football heroes, the queen of the prom, Miss Apple Blossom Time. That's Sally Bettencourt of Monument High. And I'm not a football hero, although I scored three points in the intramural basketball tournament last winter. And she *did* smile at me a few weeks ago while waiting for the bus. Just for the record, let me put down here how I found out her name. She was standing a few feet from me, chatting with some girls and fellows, and I drifted toward her and saw her name written on the cover of one of her books. Detective work.

The same kind of detective work sent me investigating my father's desk the next day. He keeps all his private correspondence and office papers in an old battered roll-top my mother found at an auction and sandpapered and refinished. No one was at home. The desk was unlocked. I opened drawers and checked some diary-like type notebooks. Nothing but business stuff. All kinds of receipts. Stubs of canceled checks. Dull. But a bottom drawer revealed the kind of box that contains correspondence paper and envelopes. Inside, I found envelopes of different shapes and sizes and colors. Father's Day cards he had saved through the years. I found one with a scrawled "Mikey" painstakingly written when I was four or five probably. His secret love letters—from Annie and Debbie and me. D

2. **annihilated** (ə·nī′ə·lāt′əd): demolished.

A. Responding
? Why do *you* think Mike's father lied about being in the park?

B. Figurative Language
? Why is his beard like small slivers of ice? (His beard is going gray.)

C. Interpreting
? Why does Mike feel guilty? (When he sees his father in his characteristic doze, he feels guilty that he was actually suspicious of him.)

D. Character
? What do the contents of the desk reveal about Mike's father? (That he is sentimental; that he loves his children very much; that he is a good family man)

A. Humanities Connection: Fine Art and Architecture

Mark Dean (1955–   ) was born in Indianapolis, Indiana, and has studied art in many places, including Rome, Italy. He now lives in Philadelphia with his wife, who is also an artist.

While not strictly Doric or Ionic—two of the five specific styles of classical architecture characterized by the kind of column used—the design of the columns in the painting suggests a classical Greek influence. By placing classical Greek architecture in a modern setting (we know it's modern because of the man's style of dress), Dean conveys the continuing existence of ancient Greek culture in our contemporary society.

? What do you think the title means?

B. Making Inferences

? What can you infer about Mike from this passage? (That he is attuned to the sensitivities of adults, particularly parents; that he is crafty and can get out of tight spots)

A

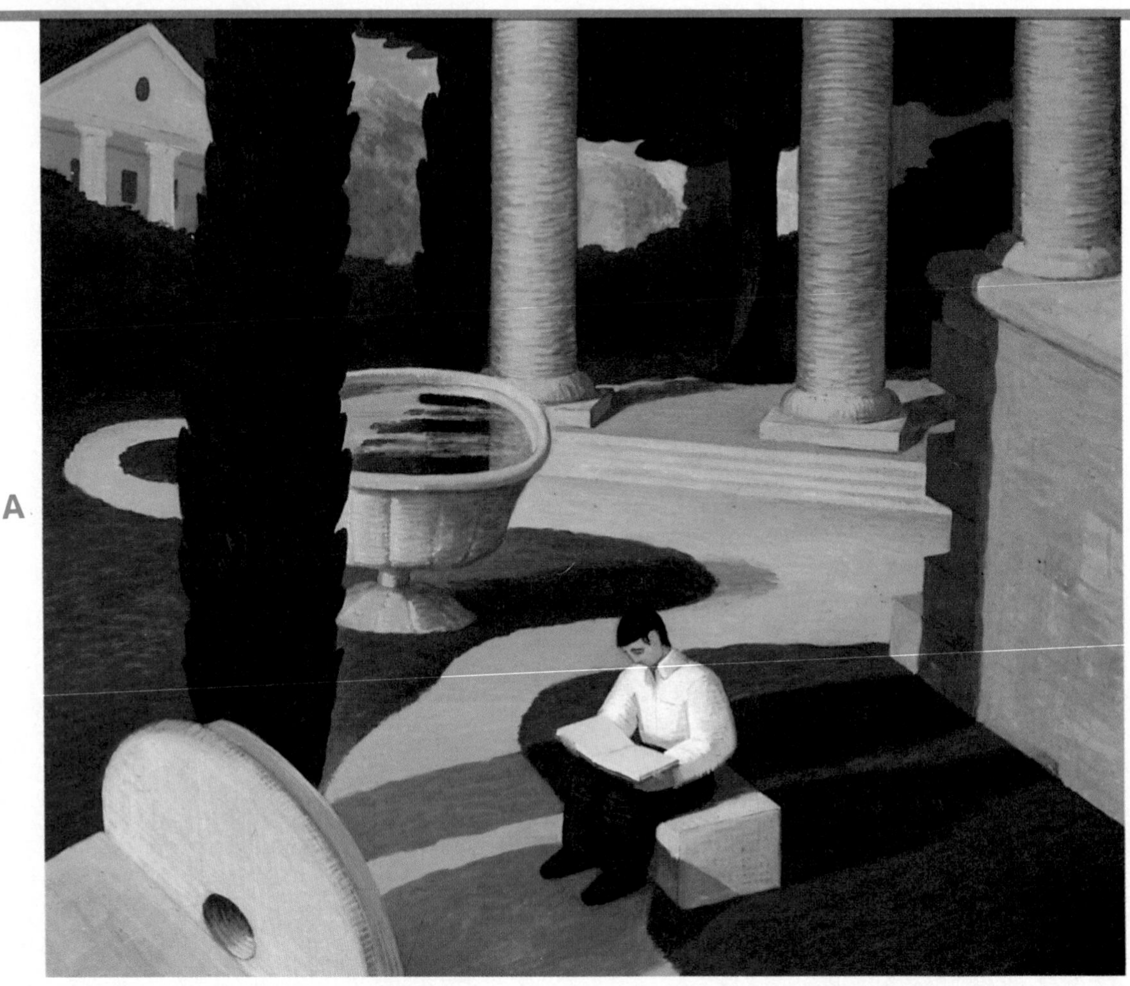

The Sad Story of the Ancient Greeks (detail) by Mark Dean (1983). Casein on panel.

Courtesy Sharpe Gallery, New York, Collection of Stewart Bloom and Carolyn Hunegs.

"Looking for something?"

B His shadow fell across the desk. I mumbled something, letting irritation show in my voice. I have found that you can fake adults out by muttering and grumbling as if you're using some foreign language that they couldn't possibly understand. And they feel intimidated or confused. Anyway they decide not to challenge you or make an issue of it. That's what happened at that moment. There I was snooping in my father's desk and because I muttered unintelligibly when he interrupted me, *he* looked embarrassed while I stalked from the room as if I was the injured party, ready to bring suit in court.

Three things happened in the next week and they had nothing to do with my father: First, I called Sally Bettencourt. The reason why I called her is that I could have sworn she smiled again at me at the bus stop one afternoon. I mean, not a polite smile but a smile for *me,* as if she recognized me as a person, an individual. Actually I called her three times in four days. She was (*a*) not at home and the person on the line (her mother? her sister?) had no idea when she'd arrive; (*b*) she was taking a shower—"Any message?" "No"; (*c*) the line was busy. What would I have said to her, if she'd answered? I've always had the feeling that I'm a real killer on the phone when I don't have to worry about what to do with my hands or how bad my posture is. The second thing that happened was a terrible history test which I almost flunked: a low C that could possibly keep me off the Honor Roll, which would send my mother into hysterics. Number 3: I received my assignment from the Municipal Park Department for my summer job—lifeguard at Pool Number 38. Translation: Pool Number 38 is for children twelve years old and younger, not the most romantic pool in the city.

Bugged by history, I talked Mister Rogers, the teacher, into allowing me some extra work to rescue my mark and I stayed up late one night, my stereo earphones clamped on my head so that I wouldn't disturb anyone as the cool sounds of the Tinted Orange poured into my ears. Suddenly, I
A awoke—shot out of a cannon. My watch said one-twenty. One-twenty in the morning. I yawned. My mouth felt rotten, as if the French Foreign Legion had marched through it barefoot (one of my father's old jokes that I'd heard about a million times). I went downstairs for a glass of orange juice. A light spilled from the den. I sloshed orange juice on my shirt as I stumbled toward the room. He's there: my father. Slumped in his chair. Like death. And I almost drop dead myself. But his lips flutter and he produces an enormous snore. One arm dangles to the floor, limp as a draped towel. His fingers are almost touching a book that had evidently fallen from his hand. I pick it up. Poetry. A poet I never heard of. Kenneth Fearing. Riffling the pages, I find that the poems are mostly about the Depression. In the front of the book there's an inscription. Delicate handwriting, faded lavender ink. "To Jimmy, I'll never forget you, Muriel." Jimmy? My father's name is James and my mother and his friends call him Jim. But Jimmy? I notice a date at the bottom of the page, meticulously recorded in that same fragile handwriting—November 2, 1942—when he was young enough to be called Jimmy. By some girl whose name was Muriel, who gave him a book of poems that he takes out and reads in the dead of night even if they are poems about the Depression. He stirs, grunting, clearing his throat, his hand like a big white spider searching the floor for the book. I replace the book on the floor and glide out of the room and back upstairs.

The next day I began my investigation in earnest and overlooked no details. That's when I found out what size shoes, socks, shirts, etc., that he wears. I looked in closets and bureaus, his workbench in the cellar, not knowing what I was searching for but the search itself important. B
There was one compensation: at least, it kept my mind off Sally Bettencourt. I had finally managed to talk to her on the telephone. We spoke mostly in monosyllables.[3] It took me about ten minutes to identify myself ("The fellow at *what* bus stop?") because apparently all those smiles sent in my direction had been meaningless and my face was as impersonal as a label on a can of soup. The conversation proceeded downward from that point and reached bottom when she said: "Well, thanks for calling, Mark." I didn't bother to correct her. She was so sweet about it all. All the C
Sally Bettencourts of the world are that way: that's why you keep on being in love with them when you know it's entirely useless. Even when you hang up and see your face in the hallway mirror—what a terrible place to hang a mirror—your face all crumpled up like a paper bag. And the following day, she wasn't at the bus stop, of course. But then neither was I.

What I mean about the bus stop is this: I stationed myself across the street to get a glimpse of her, to see if she really was as beautiful as I remembered or if the phone call had diminished her loveliness. When she didn't arrive, I wandered through the business district. Fellows and girls lingered in doorways. Couples held hands crossing the street. A record store blared out "Purple Evenings" by the Tinted Orange. I spotted my father. He was crossing the street, dodging traffic, as if he was dribbling an invisible ball down a basketball court. I checked my watch: two fifty-five. Stepping into a doorway, I observed him hurrying past the Merchants Bank and Appleton's Department Store and the Army-Navy Surplus Supply Agency. He paused in front of the Monument Public Library. And disappeared inside. My father—visiting the library? He didn't even have a library D
card, for crying out loud.

I'm not exactly crazy about libraries, either. Everybody whispers or talks low as if the building has a giant volume knob turned down to practically zero. As I stood there, I saw Laura Kincaid drive up in her new LeMans. A quiet, dark green LeMans. Class. "If I had to describe Laura Kin-

---

3. **monosyllables:** words of one syllable.

A. Figurative Language

? Why is the phrase "shot out of a cannon" effective in visualizing how Mike awakens? (We see Mike suddenly jolted out of his chair. We recognize it as the kind of awakening you have when you fall asleep sitting up.)

B. Interpreting

The search is important in a bigger way than Mike knows—it is a search to get to know his father as a person, and, by extension, a search for his own maturity.

C. Expansion

This situation is similar to the one in the excerpt by Jean Shepherd on page 74. Mike is suffering from a universal dilemma.

D. Characterization

? Why is having Mike repeat the phrase "for crying out loud," which he first uses on page 136, especially effective in making him a believable character? (It makes him real: Just as real people have pet phrases, so too does Mike. We also know from the first time he used it that Mike uses this expression when he's shocked, or dismayed. So here, we know what he's feeling.)

A. Expansion
Canadian-born bandleader Guy Lombardo (1902–1977) attained fame as a result of revolutionizing dance music in the late 1920's and 1930's. He is perhaps most famous for his traditional New Year's Eve performances in New York City, which he gave for approximately forty-eight years. Mike would be speaking scornfully of Guy Lombardo's music since it is of his parents' age, and it's sweet and romantic—Mike would probably call it "sappy."

Critical Comment
Writing about Cormier's novels, one critic has said, "Without moralizing, Cormier's novels stress the importance of self-reliance and self-respect. His combination of realism, sensitivity, and originality has made him popular with both readers and critics."

Write the quotation on the chalkboard and read it aloud to students. Ask for volunteers to list examples from "Guess What? I Almost Kissed My Father Goodnight" that support the quotation. To spur discussion, you might ask: How does Mike take control of a situation? Why does his father's "new" behavior trouble him so much? Would you call Mike self-reliant? Sensitive? Real?

B. Interpreting
? What might this emptiness be? (Emptiness caused by the confusion of growing up. He feels lonely, not only because he feels rejected by Sally, but also because the unconditional security his father has always given him has been shaken.)

C. Character's Motivation
? Why does the narrator not want to look at his father? (By not looking he does not have to think about what's confusing him. Also, perhaps he is afraid of what he might see—maybe some confirmation of his fears. He might also be afraid of blurting out what is bothering him, thereby causing an embarrassing scene at the dinner table.)

caid in one word, it would be 'class,' " I'd heard my father say once. The car drew into a parking space, as if the space had been waiting all day for her arrival. She stepped out of the door. She is blond, her hair the color of lemonade as it's being poured on a hot day. I stood there, paralyzed. A scene leaped in my mind: Laura Kincaid at a New Year's Eve Party at our house, blowing a toy horn just before midnight while I watched in awe from the kitchen, amazed at how a few glasses of booze could convert all these bankers and Rotary Club members and Chamber of Commerce officials into the terrible kind of people you see dancing to Guy Lombardo on television while the camera keeps
A cutting back to Times Square where thousands of other people, most of them closer to my age, were also acting desperately happy. I stood there thinking of that stuff because I was doing some kind of juggling act in my mind—trying to figure out why was she at this moment walking across the street, heading for the library, her hair a lemon halo in the sun, her nylons flashing as she hurried. What was her hurry? There was barely any traffic. Was she on her way to a rendezvous?[4] Stop it, you nut, I told myself, even as I made my way to the side entrance.

The library is three stories high, all the stacks and bookshelves built around an interior courtyard. I halted near the circulation desk with no books in my arms to check out. Feeling ridiculous, I made my way to the bubbler. The spray of water was stronger than I expected: My nostrils were engulfed by water. For some reason, I thought of Sally Bettencourt and how these ridiculous events kept happening to me and I ached with longing for
B her, a terrible emptiness inside of me that needed to be filled. I climbed the stairs to the third floor, my eyes flying all over the place, trying to spot my father. And Laura Kincaid. And knowing all the time that it was merely a game, impossible, ridiculous.

And then I saw them. Together. Standing at the entrance to the alcove that was marked 818 to 897. Two books were cradled in her arms like babies. My father wasn't looking at the books or the shelves or the walls or the ceilings or the floor or anything. He was looking at her. Then, they laughed. It was like a silent movie. I mean—I saw their eyes light up and their lips moving but didn't hear anything. My father shook his head, slowly, a smile lingering tenderly on his face. I drew back into the alcove labeled 453 to 521, across from them, apprehensive, afraid that suddenly they might see me spying on them. His hand reached up and touched her shoulder. They laughed again, still merrily. She indicated the books in her arms. He nodded, an eagerness in his manner. He didn't look as if he had ever snored in his life or taken a nap after dinner. They looked around. She glanced at her watch. He gestured vaguely.

Pressed against the metal bookshelf, I felt conspicuous, vulnerable, as if they would suddenly whirl and see me, and point accusing fingers. But nothing like that happened. She finally left, simply walked away, the books still in her arm. My father watched her go, his face in shadow. She walked along the balcony, then down the spiral stairs, the nylons still flashing, her hair a lemon waterfall. My father watched until she disappeared from view. I squinted, trying to discern his features, to see whether he was still my father, searching for the familiar landmarks of his face and body, needing some kind of verification. I watched him for a minute or two as he stood there looking down, his eyes tracing the path of her departure as if she were still visible. I studied his face: Was this my father? And then this terrible numbness invaded my body, like a Novocaine of the spirit, killing all my emotions. And the numbness even pervaded my mind, slowing down my thoughts. For which I was grateful. All the way home on the bus, I stared out of the window, looking at the landscapes and the buildings and the people but not really seeing them, as if I was storing them in my mind like film to develop them later when they'd have meaning for me.

At dinner, the food lay unappetizingly on my plate. I had to fake my way through the meal, lifting the fork mechanically. I found it difficult not to look at my father. What I mean is—I didn't want to look at him. And because I didn't, I kept C
doing it. Like when they tell you not to think of a certain subject and you can't help thinking of it.

4. **rendezvous** (rän′dā·vo͞o′): prearranged meeting.

Reading Check Test

1. How did Mike feel when he saw his father sitting on a park bench? *He felt surprised, confused, and embarrassed.*
2. Why was Mike surprised when his father answered the phone? *His father seldom got calls at night, but he picked up the phone so quickly.*
3. How did Mike learn Sally Bettencourt's name? *He saw it written on one of her school books.*
4. How did Mike rescue his low mark in history? *He did extra work for the teacher.*
5. How did Mike feel when he saw his father in the library? *He felt apprehensive, then vulnerable, and finally numb.*

Closure

Have students work in pairs and discuss why understanding a character's motivation is important to understanding a story as a whole. Have them tell the reasons behind some of the things that they do.

"Aren't you feeling well, Mike?" my mother asked.

I leaped about five feet off my chair. I hadn't realized how obvious I must have appeared: the human eating machine suddenly toying with his food—steak, at that, which requires special concentration.

"He's probably in love," Debbie said.

And that word *love*. I found it difficult to keep my eyes away from my father.

"I met Laura Kincaid at the library today," I heard my father say.

"Was she able to get a copy of the play?" my mother asked.

"Two of them," he said, munching. "I still think *Streetcar Named Desire* is pretty ambitious for you girls to put on."

"The Women's Auxiliary knows no fear of Tennessee Williams," my mother said in that exaggerated voice she uses when she's kidding around.

A "You know, that's funny, Dad," I heard myself saying. "I saw you in the library this afternoon and was wondering what you were doing there."

"Oh? I didn't see you, Mike."

"He was supposed to pick up the play on my library card. But then Laura Kincaid came by . . ." That was my mother explaining it all, although I barely made out the words.

I won't go into the rest of the scene and I won't say my appetite suddenly came back and that I devoured the steak. Because I didn't. That was two days ago and I still feel funny about it all. Strange I mean. That's why I'm writing this, putting it all down, all the evidence I gathered. That first time in the park when he was sitting there. The telephone call. That book of poetry he reads late at night, "To Jimmy, I'll never forget you. Muriel." Laura Kincaid in the library. Not much evidence, really. Especially when I look at him and see how he's my father all right.

Last night, I came downstairs after finishing my homework and he had just turned off the television set. "Cloudy tomorrow, possible showers," he said, putting out the lights in the den.

We stood there in the half-darkness.

"Homework done, Mike?"

"Yes."

"Hey, Dad."

"Yes, Mike?" Yawning.

I didn't plan to ask him. But it popped out. "I was looking through a book of yours the other day. Poetry by some guy named Fearing or Nearing or something." I couldn't see his face in the half dark. Keeping my voice light, I said: "Who's this Muriel who gave you the book, anyway?" B

His laugh was a playful bark. "Boy, that was a long time ago. Muriel Stanton." He closed the kitchen window. "I asked her to go to the Senior Prom but she went with someone else. We were friends. I mean—I thought we were more than friends until she went to the Prom with someone else. And so she gave me a gift—of friendship—at graduation." We walked into the kitchen together. "That's a lousy swap, Mike. A book instead of a date with a girl you're crazy about." He smiled ruefully. "Hadn't thought of good old Muriel for years."

You see? Simple explanations for everything. And if I exposed myself as a madman and asked him about the other stuff, the park and the telephone call, I knew there would be perfectly logical reasons. And yet. And yet. I remember that day in the library, when Laura Kincaid walked away from him. I said that I couldn't see his face, not clearly anyway, but I could see a bit of his expression. And it looked familiar but I couldn't pin it down. And now I realized why it was familiar: It reminded me of my own face when I looked into the mirror the day I hung up the phone after talking to Sally Bettencourt. All kind of crumpled up. Or was that my imagination? Hadn't my father been all the way across the library courtyard, too far away for me to tell what kind of expression was on his face?

Last night, standing in the kitchen, as I poured a glass of milk and he said: "Doesn't your stomach ever get enough?" I asked him: "Hey, Dad. You get lonesome sometimes? I mean: that's a crazy question, maybe. But I figure grown-ups, like fathers and mothers—you get to feeling *down* sometimes, don't you?"

I could have sworn his eyes narrowed and something leaped in them, some spark, some secret thing that had suddenly come out of hiding.

"Sure, Mike. Everybody gets the blues now and then. Even fathers are people. Sometimes, I C

A. Plot

? Why is this incident important to the plot? (It is important because Mike finally confronts his father with his knowledge of Laura Kincaid, thereby exposing his internal conflict.)

B. Climactic Moment

Mike's confronting his father with the knowledge of Muriel and the book of poetry marks another climactic moment of the story. Telling his father he saw him at the library was the first one. It is as a result of these incidents that Mike is able to better understand his father as well as himself.

C. Theme

Here, Mike's father states so simply the discovery that it has taken Mike this whole story to realize.

Analyzing the Story
Identifying Facts
1. Mike is fifteen—"almost sixteen."
Mike is telling the story to try to make sense out of his father's behavior.
2. One day Mike saw his father sitting on a bench near his parked car during working hours. That night, however, he says his day had been routine, with no time even for a coffee break.
He takes an unusual late-night telephone call after the first ring and talks in a hushed tone. Then, late one evening he finds his father asleep in his chair with a book of poetry inscribed by "Muriel" in his hand. Finally, he spies him talking to a female family friend in the local public library.
3. He observes his father closely at home, especially when he is snoozing in his chair after dinner, listens from a distance when his father is on the phone, and looks through his closet and desk for incriminating evidence. He notes the inscription on the book of poetry his father is reading, and observes his father's expressions carefully when he sees him with Laura Kincaid at the library.
4. The inscription reads, "To Jimmy, I'll never forget you. Muriel." His father ex-

A. Character's Motivation
? Why do you think Mike's father pauses? (Perhaps because there are so many things he thinks of; perhaps because he wants to keep his thoughts to himself. He might also think Mike will not understand what he is about to say—however, we as readers know that Mike probably would understand.)

can't sleep and get up and sit in the dark in the A middle of the night. And it gets lonesome because you think of . . ."

"What do you think of, Dad?"

He yawned. "Oh, a lot of things."

That's all. And here I am sitting up in the middle of the night writing this, feeling lonesome, thinking of Sally Bettencourt, and how I haven't a chance with her and thinking, too, of Muriel Stanton who wouldn't go to the Senior Prom with my father. How he gets lonesome sometimes. And sits up in the night, reading poetry. I think of his anguished face at the library and the afternoon at Bryant Park, and all the mysteries of his life that show he's a person. Human.

Earlier tonight, I saw him in his chair, reading the paper, and I said, "Good night, Dad," and he looked up and smiled, but an absent kind of smile, as if he was thinking of something else, long ago and far away, and, for some ridiculous reason, I felt like kissing him good night. But didn't, of course. Who kisses his father at sixteen?

Responding to the Story

Analyzing the Story

Identifying Facts

1. How old is Mike? Why is he telling this story?
2. Describe the incidents involving the family car and his father's lie that start Mike worrying about his father. What other incidents make Mike certain something is happening to his father?
3. Describe Mike's detective work as he tries to find the answers to his questions about his father.
4. What is the inscription in the book of poetry by Kenneth Fearing? How does Mike's father later explain the inscription?
5. How is Laura Kincaid's presence in the library later explained to Mike?

Interpreting Meanings

6. Find the passage that tells what Mike discovers about his father. How would you state this discovery in your own words?
7. How is the story of Sally Bettencourt related to Mike's discovery about his father?
8. Why did Mike want to kiss his father good night? Do you think he should have?

Applying Meanings

9. What do you think about Mike's worries about his father and about himself? Do you think his feelings are common ones?

Writing About the Story

A Creative Response

1. **Describing a Person.** In the beginning of the story, Mike carefully describes his father. He includes details about his father's physical appearance, his habits, his manner of speaking, and his feelings. In a paragraph, describe a person you know well. In your description, include the types of descriptive details Mike might include.
2. **Using Another Point of View.** We hear only Mike's voice in this story, so we never know what his father—or anyone else—is really thinking. Let the father tell the story (briefly) as he sees it, beginning with the time he is sitting in the park early in the afternoon. End with the incident where Mike almost kisses his father good night. Does the father wonder what Mike is thinking? Does he think his son is acting strangely lately? Does he wish Mike *had* kissed him good night?

SRW p. 69

A Critical Response

3. **Analyzing a Character.** In this story, you get to know how Mike feels about girls, school, his sisters, his parents, and himself. Write a paragraph or two describing Mike's **character,** or personality. Before you write, gather a cluster of traits about Mike, using a diagram like the following. Use as many circles or bubbles as you need. Two are filled in:

plains the inscription by saying that Muriel was a high school classmate with whom he'd wanted to go to the Senior Prom. Muriel gave him the book as a token of friendship after she went to the Senior Prom with someone else.

5. Mike's mother explains that his Dad was supposed to pick up a play when he ran into Laura Kincaid, who was there for the same purpose.

Interpreting Meanings

6. The passage begins on page 141—"You see? Simple explanations for everything"—and continues until the next-to-last paragraph of the story on page 142.

Mike discovers that his father, like him, sometimes gets sad or lonesome.

7. Mike feels sad that he can't make a date with Sally Bettencourt, just as Mike's father felt sad when he was turned down by Muriel Stanton. Mike recognizes the look on his father's face after Laura Kincaid walks away as the same expression that was on his face when he hung up with Sally Bettencourt.

8. Mike feels close to his father after going through a long, and painful, process of finding out that his father can experience the same emotions that he does.

Answers will vary. See Teacher's Manual page 39 for suggested possible answers.

Applying Meanings

9. Answers will vary. See Teacher's Manual page 40.

Additional Writing Assignment

Have students imagine that they are casting directors whose job it is to decide which actors will portray Mike and his father in an upcoming TV special based on "Guess What? I Almost Kissed My Father Goodnight." As such, have students prepare a memo for the show's producer.

FURTHER READING FOR STUDENTS

Students will enjoy other books by Robert Cormier, including *Eight Plus One* and *Beyond the Chocolate War.*

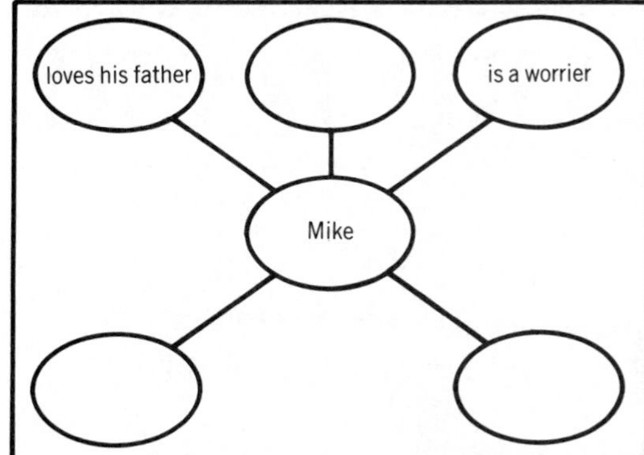

When you finish citing as many characteristics as you can think of, look for details from the story that illustrate each characteristic. Then select one or two characteristics that you think are most important to use in your essay.

See Teacher's Manual page 40.

Analyzing Language and Vocabulary

Puns

SRW p. 71

Many words in English have more than one meaning. Usually a writer or speaker clearly intends only one meaning of a word. But sometimes more than one meaning is purposely intended. A play on the multiple meanings of the same word, or on the meanings of two different words or phrases that sound alike, is called a **pun.**

When a pun is based on a single word that has a double meaning, it is called a **homographic pun.** For example, Mike's father jokes, "I'm in a *stew* over you." The pun is based on two meanings of *stew:* "a cooked mixture of foods" and "a state of worry."

When a pun is based on words that sound alike but are spelled differently, it is a **homophonic pun.** Mike's father makes a homophonic pun when he asks, "Do you *carrot* all for me?" The pun is based on the similar sounds of *carrot* and *care at.*

Make a pun in each sentence below by filling in the blank with a word or phrase from the list. Then tell whether each pun is homographic or homophonic.

deck see food lean buy sales

1. Nobody played cards in Noah's ark because Noah sat on the ______.
2. The blustery winter weather took the wind out of the retailers' ______.
3. I'm on a seafood diet. Every time I ______, I eat it.
4. Telephone advertisement: Make your every *hello* a good ______.
5. What makes the Tower of Pisa ______? It never eats.

For answers, see Teacher's Manual page 40.

Reading About the Writer

Robert Cormier (1925-), a popular "Young Adult" writer, was born in Leominster, Massachusetts. Throughout his early life, he worked as a journalist for newspapers and a radio station in the central part of that state. Although he began writing fiction in the early sixties, it was not until the success of his controversial novel *The Chocolate War* (1974) that he was able to become a full-time novelist and short-story writer. *The Chocolate War* is a best-selling young-adult novel about a boy's rebellion against authority in a New England preparatory school.

Focusing on Background

Reading and Writing

"A man I know who writes and aspires to be a novelist does very little reading, and he's not that successful. But I think it's because he's like the kid who wants to be a ballplayer and never goes to the ballpark or tries to hit a ball. So I'd say reading is the most important thing that I do, besides the actual writing. I'm always asking as I read, 'How did the writer do this? Why do I suddenly have tears in my eyes? Why am I crying?' . . .

"I read a lot of detective stories because they always deliver. They give you a beginning, a middle, and an end—a resolution. The modern novels I read don't always deliver because I'm looking essentially for a story. As in Shakespeare, 'The play's the thing.' "

—Robert Cormier

PREREADING

1. BUILDING ON PRIOR KNOWLEDGE. Before they read, discuss with students the importance of a person's perception of himself or herself and how that perception is shaped and exploited by the media. Some sociologists have suggested that Americans, both young and old, are the most image-conscicus people in the world. Ask students to explain why young people are so concerned about their appearance. Discuss with them the dangers of people evaluating themselves based on their "external" qualities as opposed to their "internal" ones.

2. ESTABLISHING A PURPOSE. Before students begin reading, you might have them read question 10 on page 148.

3. PREREADING JOURNAL. Before they read, have students write about an instance in which they've seen an advertisement in a magazine or on TV that made them want to send away for something. What made the ad so persuasive? Did they go through with it?

Humanities Connection: Responding to the Illustration

American illustrator Norman Rockwell (1894–1978) is best known for his work depicting slices of an idealized American way of life. (See another illustration by Rockwell on page 76.)

? What do you suppose the boy is thinking about as he lifts the dumbbells and looks at the pin-up on his wall?

★ Texas Essential Elements/(a) English Language Arts: 1B Purpose and audience; 1E Formal/informal language; 4B Main idea. (c) Reading: 3A Main ideas/details

THE FIFTY-YARD DASH

William Saroyan

For a detailed lesson plan on this story, see Teacher's Manual pages 40–43. A biography of William Saroyan appears on text page 149.

Printed by permission of the Estate of Norman Rockwell. Copyright © 1922, Estate of Norman Rockwell.

SUPPLEMENTARY SUPPORT MATERIAL

1. Vocabulary Activity Sheet
2. Reading Check Test blackline master
3. Selection Test (page 47 of Test Book)
4. Author photograph on *A Gallery of Authors* poster
5. Reader's Response Journal
6. Workbook (page 35)

DEVELOPING VOCABULARY

The following words appear on a test in the Test Book, page 48. (See also the Vocabulary Activity Sheet.)

potential	impractical
puny	meditating
cordial	fury of anticipation
miscellaneous	impertinent
acrobatic	betrays

Most boys yearn for physical strength, and some of them are particularly gullible when mail-order ads appeal to their ambition for muscles. This idea is central to the humor in William Saroyan's story. As you read the story, you'll probably find other reasons to laugh at twelve-year-old Aram's experience with a mail-order strongman. Watch how the race turns out to be a real learning experience for him.

Phonetic Spellings. Aram's family is Armenian. Uncle Gyko's Armenian accent adds a vivid touch to this story. To help you hear Uncle Gyko's real speech, Saroyan spells his words *phonetically*—that is, according to how they sound. For example, to show how Uncle Gyko says "It is wonderful," he writes "Eat ease wonderful." Reading Uncle Gyko's sentences aloud will help you hear his special ways of pronouncing words.

After a certain letter came to me from New York the year I was twelve, I made up my mind to become the most powerful man in my neighborhood. The letter was from my friend Lionel Strongfort. I had clipped a coupon from *Argosy All-Story Magazine,* signed it, placed it in A an envelope, and mailed it to him. He had written back promptly, with an enthusiasm bordering on pure delight, saying I was undoubtedly a man of uncommon intelligence, potentially a giant, and—unlike the average run-of-the-mill people in the world who were, in a manner of speaking, dreamwalkers and daydreamers—a person who would someday be somebody.

B His opinion of me was very much like my own. It was pleasant, however, to have the opinion so emphatically corroborated,[1] particularly by a man in New York—and a man with the greatest chest expansion in the world. With the letter came several photographic reproductions of Mr. Strongfort wearing nothing but a little bit of leopard skin. He was a tremendous man and claimed that at one time he had been puny. He was loaded all over with muscle and appeared to be somebody who could lift a 1920 Ford roadster and tip it over.

It was an honor to have him for a friend.

The only trouble was—I didn't have the money. I forget how much the exact figure was at the beginning of our acquaintanceship, but I haven't forgotten that it was an amount completely out of the question. While I was eager to be grateful to Mr. Strongfort for his enthusiasm, I didn't seem to be able to find words with which to explain about not having the money, without immediately appearing to be a dreamwalker and a daydreamer myself. So, while waiting from one day to another, looking everywhere for words that would not blight our friendship and degrade me to commonness, I talked the matter over with my uncle C Gyko, who was studying Oriental philosophy at the time. He was amazed at my curious ambition, but quite pleased. He said the secret of greatness, according to Yoga,[2] was the releasing within one's self of those mysterious vital forces which are in all men.

These strength, he said in English which he liked to affect when speaking to me, ease from God. I tell you Aram, eat ease wonderful.

I told him I couldn't begin to become the powerful man I had decided to become until I sent Mr. Strongfort some money.

Mohney! my uncle said with contempt. I tell you, Aram, mohney is nawthing. You cannot bribe God.

Although my uncle Gyko wasn't exactly a puny man, he was certainly not the man Lionel Strongfort was. In a wrestling match I felt certain Mr. Strongfort would get a headlock or a half-nelson or a toehold[3] on my uncle and either make him give up or squeeze him to death. And then again, on the other hand, I wondered. My uncle was nowhere near as big as Mr. Strongfort, but neither was Mr. Strongfort as dynamically furious as my uncle. It seemed to me that, at best, Mr. Strongfort, in a match with my uncle, would have a great

1. **corroborated** (kə·räb′ə·rāt′əd): confirmed.

2. **Yoga:** discipline which helps someone to achieve union with the supreme spirit through meditation and various breathing techniques and postures.

3. **headlock . . . toehold:** wrestling holds.

A. Character
? Based on the language he uses in his letter, how would you characterize Lionel Strongfort? (Persuasive, manipulative, clever)

B. Interpreting
This statement leads us to believe that Mr. Strongfort has found an easy victim.

C. Irony
? Why is this statement ironic, or opposite from what we have been led to believe? (Because Lionel Strongfort is far from being Aram's friend—we can already guess that he only wants to take advantage of him.)

A. Humor

Why is this paragraph funny? (Because Aram's behavior is so excessive and intense) What's the one behavior that we know is an impossible exaggeration? (Trying to tip over roadsters)

B. Interpreting

What do we understand about Aram and his family from this sentence? (Since a twelve-year-old's earned money is used for the family's "bread," or food, we gather that they are probably poor. By Aram's casual manner—"and stuff like that"—we also realize that he is used to not spending money on himself.)

C. Exaggeration

The exaggeration in this paragraph lets us know that the feelings are really Aram's, and are not contained in Mr. Strongfort's letter.

What examples of exaggeration are in this paragraph? ("hymn," "epistle," "legend-quality," "world-feeling," "dignity-of-strength-feeling")

D. Interpreting

Why do you think Aram is susceptible to Mr. Strongfort's persuasiveness? (Even giving plenty of credit to Mr. Strongfort's power of persuasion, Aram is really at fault here because of his over-inflated ego. He wants to believe Mr. Strongfort's compliments.)

Critical Comment

It has been said that "during the Depression, Saroyan's sentimental fiction, with its nostalgia for a former, better time, was received with welcome relief by an American public who sought escape from the bleak reality of their lives."

Ask students to identify several subjects from "The Fifty-Yard Dash" that Saroyan is criticizing about his modern-day life. (Examples include Strongfort's charlatanry and the maltreatment of animals.)

How do Aram and Uncle Gyko devise their own ways of escaping from their lives?

deal of unfamiliar trouble—I mean with the mysterious vital forces that were always getting released in my uncle, so that very often a swift glance from him would make a big man quail and turn away, or, if he had been speaking, stop quickly.

A Long before I had discovered words with which to explain to Mr. Strongfort about the money, another letter came from him. It was as cordial as the first, and as a matter of fact, if anything, a little more cordial. I was delighted and ran about, releasing mysterious vital forces, turning handsprings, scrambling up trees, turning somersaults, trying to tip over 1920 Ford roadsters, challenging all comers to wrestle, and in many other ways alarming my relatives and irritating the neighbors.

Not only was Mr. Strongfort not sore at me, he had reduced the cost of the course. Even so, the money necessary was still more than I could get hold of. B I was selling papers every day, but *that* money was for bread and stuff like that. For a while I got up very early every morning and went around town looking for a small satchel full of money. During six days of this adventuring I found a nickel and two pennies. I found also a woman's purse containing several foul-smelling cosmetic items, no money, and slip of paper on which was written in an ignorant hand: Steve Hertwig, 3764 Ventura Avenue.

Three days after the arrival of Mr. Strongfort's second letter, his third letter came. From this time on our correspondence became one-sided. In fact, I didn't write at all. Mr. Strongfort's communications were overpowering and not at all easy to answer, without money. There was, in fact, almost nothing to say.

It was wintertime when the first letter came, and it was then that I made up my mind to become the most powerful man in my neighborhood and ultimately, for all I knew, one of the most powerful men in the world. I had ideas of my own as to how to go about getting that way, but I had also the warm friendship and high regard of Mr. Strongfort in New York, and the mystical and furious guardianship of my uncle Gyko, at home.

The letters from Mr. Strongfort continued to arrive every two or three days all winter and on into springtime. I remember, the day apricots were ripe enough to steal, the arrival of a most charming letter from my friend in New York. It was a hymn to newness on earth, the arrival of springtime, the time of youth in the heart, of renewal, fresh strength, fresh determination, and many other things. It was truly a beautiful epistle,[4] probably as fine as any to the Romans[5] or anybody else. It C was full of the legend-quality, the world-feeling, and the dignity-of-strength-feeling so characteristic of Biblical days. The last paragraph of the lovely hymn brought up, apologetically, the coarse theme of money. The sum was six or seven times as little as it had been originally, and a new element had come into Mr. Strongfort's program of changing me over from a nobody to a giant of tremendous strength, and extreme attractiveness to women. Mr. Strongfort had decided, he said, to teach me everything in one fell swoop, or one sweep fall, or something of that sort. At any rate, for three dollars, he said, he would send me all his precious secrets in one envelope and the rest would be up to me, and history.

I took the matter up with my uncle Gyko, who by this time had reached the stage of fasting, meditating, walking for hours, and vibrating. We had had discussions two or three times a week all winter and he had told me in his own unique broken-English way all the secrets *he* had been learning from Yoga.

I tell you, Aram, he said, I can do *anything*. Eat ease wonderful.

I believed him, too, even though he had lost a lot of weight, couldn't sleep, and had a strange dynamic blaze in his eyes. He was very scornful of the world that year and was full of pity for the dumb beautiful animals that man was mistreating, killing, eating, domesticating, and teaching to do tricks.

I tell you, Aram, he said, eat ease creaminal to make the horses work. To keal the cows. To teach the dogs to jump, and the monkeys to smoke pipes.

I told him about the letter from Mr. Strongfort.

Mohney! he said. Always he wants mohney. I do not like heem.

---

4. **epistle:** letter.
5. An allusion to the apostle Paul's Epistle to the Romans in the Bible.

READING CHECK TEST

1. How did Aram react when he got Mr. Strongfort's first mailing? *He was delighted to be described as "above average."*

2. How did Uncle Gyko react when he learned of Aram's plan? *He was amazed but pleased.*

3. What were the physical effects of studying Yoga on Uncle Gyko? *He lost weight, couldn't sleep, and had a strange look in his eyes.*

4. How did Aram feel when he finally got Mr. Strongfort's program? *Let down.*

5. How did Aram prepare for the track meet? *He took it easy and meditated, imagining that he won every event.*

CLOSURE

Working in pairs, students should explain to each other the concept of irony. Tell them to cite examples of irony from the story. (Examples include Aram's belief that Mr. Strongfort is his friend; his belief that he will become powerful without any effort; his belief that he will win sports events without training.)

My uncle was getting all his dope free from the theosophy[6]-philosophy-astrology-and-miscellaneous shelf at the public library. He believed, however, that he was getting it straight from God. Before he took up Yoga he had been one of the boys around town and a good drinker of rakhi,[7] but after the light began to come to him he gave up drinking. He said he was drinking liquor finer than rakhi or anything else.

What's that? I asked him.

Aram, he said, eat ease weasdom.

Anyhow, he had little use for Mr. Strongfort and regarded the man as a charlatan.[8]

He's all right, I told my uncle.

But my uncle became furious, releasing mysterious vital forces, and said, I wheel break hease head, fooling all you leatle keads.

A He ain't fooling, I said. He says he'll give me all his secrets for three dollars.

I tell you, Aram, my uncle Gyko said, he does not know any seacrets. He ease a liar.

I don't know, I said. I'd like to try that stuff out.

Eat ease creaminal, my uncle Gyko said, but I wheel geave you tree dollar.

My uncle Gyko gave me the necessary three dollars and I sent them along to Mr. Strongfort. The envelope came from New York, full of Mr. Strongfort's secrets. They were strangely simple. It was all stuff I had known anyhow but had been too lazy to pay any attention to. The idea was to get up early in the morning and for an hour or so to do various kinds of acrobatic exercises, which were illustrated. Also to drink plenty of water, get plenty of fresh air, eat good wholesome food, and keep it up until you were a giant.

I felt a little let down and sent Mr. Strongfort a short polite note saying so. He ignored the note and I never heard from him again. In the meantime, I had been following the rules and growing more powerful every day. When I say *in the meantime,* I mean for four days I followed the rules. On the fifth day I decided to sleep instead of getting up and filling the house with noise and getting my grandmother sore. She used to wake up in the darkness of early morning and shout that I was an impractical fool and would never be rich. She would go back to sleep for five minutes, wake up, and then shout that I would never buy and sell for a profit. She would sleep a little more, waken, and shout that there were once three sons of a king; one was wise like his father; the other was crazy about girls; and the third had less brains than a bird. Then she would get out of bed, and, shouting steadily, tell me the whole story while I did my exercises.

The story would usually warn me to be sensible and not go around waking her up before daybreak all the time. That would always be the moral, more or less, although the story itself would be about three sons of some king, or three brothers, each of them very wealthy and usually very greedy, or three daughters, or three proverbs, or three roads, or something else like that.

She was wasting her breath, though, because I wasn't enjoying the early-morning acrobatics anymore than she was. In fact, I was beginning to feel that it was a lot of nonsense, and that my uncle Gyko had been right about Mr. Strongfort in the first place.

So I gave up Mr. Strongfort's program and returned to my own, which was more or less as follows: to take it easy and grow to be the most powerful man in the neighborhood without any trouble or exercise. Which is what I did.

That spring Longfellow School announced that a track meet was to be held, one school to compete against another; everybody to participate.

Here, I believed, was my chance. In my opinion I would be first in every event. B

Somehow or other, however, continuous meditation on the theme of athletics had the effect of growing into a fury of anticipation that continued all day and all night, so that before the day of the track meet I had run the fifty-yard dash any number of hundreds of times, had jumped the running broad jump, the standing broad jump, and the high jump, and in each event had made my competitors look like weaklings.

This tremendous inner activity, which was strictly Yoga, changed on the day of the track meet into fever.

6. **theosophy:** any philosophy that tries to establish direct mystical contact with divine power.
7. **rakhi:** strong liquor.
8. **charlatan:** pretender or fraud.

A. Conflict
Although Mr. Strongfort is never actually present in the story, his influence over Aram is strong and in conflict with Uncle Gyko's influence. This passage outlines the conflict between Uncle Gyko and Mr. Strongfort that stems from the two men's different characters.
? Why do you think that, despite his feelings, Uncle Gyko gives in to Aram?

B. Interpreting
? Even though Aram learned a valuable lesson from Mr. Strongfort, he is still suffering from some delusions. What are they? (That he is going to become powerful without doing anything; that he will come in first in every event. He probably shouldn't trust his own opinion.)

ANALYZING THE STORY

Identifying Facts

1. Aram wants Lionel Strongfort to make him the strongest man in his neighborhood.

2. Aram's problem is that he doesn't have the money to pay for Mr. Strongfort's program.

3. The "secret of greatness" is the "releasing within one's self of those mysterious vital forces which are in all men."

Uncle Gyko says that strength comes from God.

4. Uncle Gyko knows that Mr. Strongfort is taking advantage of boys' gullibility in order to make money.

5. He borrows three dollars from Uncle Gyko and sends it to Mr. Strongfort.

Aram discovers that Mr. Strongfort's program consists of widely known, common-sense advice about nutrition and exercise.

6. He discovers that he is not as strong or as swift as he thought he was.

7. After he had "exhausted the subject," Uncle Gyko gives up Yoga and goes back to his old ways.

Interpreting Meanings

8. Mr. Strongfort keeps writing to Aram

A. Humor

How does Saroyan achieve humor in this passage? (Again, he uses exaggeration when he has Aram talk about his speed.)

B. Responding

Did you find Aram's overconfidence believable? (It *is* difficult to understand why Aram is so sure of himself. Ask students to suggest reasons for Aram's ignorance—perhaps family members contributed to his attitude. For instance, think of Uncle Gyko's last words: "We can do *anything*.")

C. Discovery

What has Aram discovered? (First, not to be fooled by advertisements full of exaggerated and unrealistic promises; second, he probably learned from the race that he was not as powerful as he once thought and should not have been as confident.)

The time came at last for me and three other athletes, one of them a Greek, to go to our marks, get set, and go; and I did, in a blind rush of speed which I knew had never before occurred in the history of athletics. A

It seemed to me that never before had any living man moved so swiftly. Within myself I ran the fifty yards fifty times before I so much as opened my eyes to find out how far back I had left the other runners. I was very much amazed at what I saw.

Three boys were four yards ahead of me and going away.

It was incredible. It was unbelievable, but it was obviously the truth. There ought to be some mistake, but there wasn't. There they were, ahead of me, going away.

Well, it simply meant that I would have to overtake them, with my eyes open, and win the race. This I proceeded to do. They continued, incredibly, however, to go away, in spite of my intention. I became irritated and decided to put them in their places for the impertinence,[9] and began releasing all the mysterious vital forces within myself that I had. Somehow or other, however, not even this seemed to bring me any closer to them and I felt that in some strange way I was being betrayed. If so, I decided, I would shame my betrayer by winning the race in spite of the betrayal, and once again I threw fresh life and energy into my running. There wasn't a great distance still to go, but I knew I would be able to do it.

Then I knew I wouldn't.

The race was over.

I was last, by ten yards. B

Without the slightest hesitation I protested and challenged the runners to another race, same distance, back. They refused to consider the proposal, which proved, I knew, that they were afraid to race me. I told them they knew very well I could beat them.

It was very much the same in all the other events.

When I got home I was in high fever and very angry. I was delirious all night and sick three days. My grandmother took very good care of me and probably was responsible for my not dying. When my uncle Gyko came to visit me he was no longer hollow-cheeked. It seems he had finished his fast, which had been a long one—forty days or so; and nights too, I believe. He had stopped meditating, too, because he had practically exhausted the subject. He was again one of the boys around town, drinking, staying up all hours, and following the women.

I tell you, Aram, he said, we are a great family. C
We can do *anything*.

9. **impertinence:** shameless disrespect.

Responding to the Story

Analyzing the Story

Identifying Facts

1. What does Aram want Lionel Strongfort to do for him?
2. What is Aram's **problem**—what does he need in order to get what he wants from Mr. Strongfort?
3. According to Uncle Gyko, what is the "secret of greatness"? Where does Uncle Gyko say strength comes from?
4. Why does Uncle Gyko dislike Mr. Strongfort?
5. How does Aram finally manage to obtain Mr. Strongfort's secrets? What does he discover about Mr. Strongfort's program?
6. What does Aram discover about himself as a result of the track meet?
7. What becomes of Uncle Gyko's belief that with Yoga he can do anything?

Interpreting Meanings

8. Why does Mr. Strongfort keep writing to Aram? What does *he* want? Is Uncle Gyko right in saying Mr. Strongfort is a "charlatan"?

because he wants Aram's money.

Uncle Gyko is right, because when Aram gets Mr. Strongfort's "secrets," they turn out to be nothing more than common-sense advice.

9. Aram is probably tense and frustrated over his utter failure, when he thought he would win so easily.

Mr. Strongfort definitely let Aram down by pretending to have more wisdom than he really did. Uncle Gyko let Aram down by leading him to think that meditation alone wins athletic contests.

10. In many ways Aram's character seems to be that of a normal twelve-year-old boy. He aspires to physical strength yet lacks the willpower to stick to a plan in order to achieve his goals.

It is not unusual for children his age either to have exaggerated ambitions or to fall ill in the aftermath of failure. What is perhaps unusual, and therefore slightly unbelievable, is how fervently Aram believes in his powers until the very moment of defeat.

11. The statement "We can do *anything*" is ironic because both Aram and Uncle Gyko have shown that they cannot do "anything"—that is, they cannot achieve the higher goals to which they aspire. That Uncle Gyko nevertheless repeats this tenet at the end of the story is a testament to the fervor of his belief and shows the likelihood that he will continue to be deluded by it.

9. Why do you think Aram is angry and sick when the track meet is over? Do you think that in some ways both Mr. Strongfort *and* Uncle Gyko let Aram down? Explain.

10. What do you think of Aram's **character**? Do you think his ambitions and his reactions to failure are believable?

11. **Irony** is the difference between what someone expects to be true and what actually *is* true. Think about what Uncle Gyko does with his life and about what happens to Aram at the track meet. Then explain the irony in Uncle Gyko's last statement. SRW p. 57

Applying Meanings

12. Both Aram and his uncle become involved in "self-improvement" programs. What similar kinds of programs are offered to people today? Are any of them advertised in magazines, as Lionel Strongfort's was? Do they use his advertising methods?

Writing About the Story

A Creative Response

1. **Writing a Story with a Moral.** Aram's grandmother makes up several stories whose **moral,** or lesson, is "Be sensible." Try writing your own story with a moral. You might want to complete Aram's grandmother's story: "There were once three sons of a king; one was wise like his father; the other was crazy about girls; and the third had less brains than a bird. . . ." The moral of your story could be "Be sensible," or it could be something else.
2. **Making Up Names.** How is Lionel Strongfort's name appropriate to his profession? Make up four names for people in four other lines of work. Make the names suit the work. You might consider these jobs:

   a. Lawyer　**c.** Deep-sea diver
   b. Doctor　**d.** Miner

A Critical Response

3. **Stating a Story's Message.** In a paragraph, state this story's **message,** or its main idea about life and people. Open with a sentence that states this idea; then in the rest of the paragraph, tell how the story illustrates the idea. You might want to choose one of these main ideas:

   a. *Children are often fooled into thinking they can do anything.*
   b. *People don't realize that it takes hard work and discipline to be a powerful person.*
   c. *Promises that life can be easily conquered might be very hurtful to children when they discover that this is not true.*

See Teacher's Manual page 43.

Analyzing Language and Vocabulary

Phonetic Spelling

Uncle Gyko's speech in this story is written using a kind of **phonetic spelling**—spelling based on how words sound. Saroyan does this to help us hear how Uncle Gyko sounds when he speaks English. Listed below are several passages from the story. First read each one aloud to hear Uncle Gyko's accent. Then rewrite them so that the words are spelled correctly instead of phonetically.

1. "Mohney! . . . Mohney is nawthing."
2. ". . . eat ease creaminal to make the horses work. To keal the cows."
3. ". . . eat ease weasdom."
4. "I wheel break hease head, fooling all you leatle keads."
5. "Eat ease creaminal . . . but I wheel geave you tree dollar."

From these quotations, can you tell what English sounds Uncle Gyko has trouble with?

People from different areas in the United States pronounce many words in different ways. Make up a phonetic spelling to show how these words are pronounced where you live. Can you think of another way each word might be pronounced?

1. creek　**4.** water
2. park　**5.** going to
3. car　**6.** sure

For answers, see Teacher's Manual page 43.

Reading About the Writer

William Saroyan (1908–1981) is famous for books and plays about his exuberant Armenian family, who lived in Fresno, California. Two of his best-selling novels are *My Name is Aram* and *The Human Comedy.* His best-known plays are *The Daring Young Man on the Flying Trapeze* and *The Time of Your Life.* You can almost always find an eccentric (or "screwball") character in Saroyan's stories. Often these are the characters who seem, in the end, to be the wisest of all.

Applying Meanings

12. Answers will vary. Most students will be able to point to specific examples of similar types of programs ranging from the physical to the spiritual that use similar advertising methods.

FURTHER READING FOR STUDENTS

Recommend that students read more of *My Name Is Aram;* other Saroyan stories are contained in the collection called *Circus.*

PREREADING

1. BUILDING ON PRIOR KNOWLEDGE. Before they read, have students give their opinions as to if and under what conditions it is permissible for humans to destroy wildlife or plantlife. To help them appreciate the story more fully, ask students to tell whether or not they think they could kill an animal that they believed posed a danger to themselves or to their community. Ask them to describe situations that would justify their actions.

2. ESTABLISHING A PURPOSE. Before students begin reading, you might have them read question 6 on page 152.

3. PREREADING JOURNAL. Before they read, have students write at least two sentences telling what they would do if they suddenly found themselves near a poisonous snake. Can they draw from a real-life experience?

A. Colorful Language

? Why is this expression effective? (Frogs don't have hair—it must have been a pretty close call.) What does it immediately tell you about the narrator? (That he lives in the country; a city-dweller probably wouldn't use such an expression)

B. Responding

? Do you agree with the narrator's statement about the fascination of death? Why or why not?

★ **Texas Essential Elements/(a) English Language Arts: 1B** Purpose and audience; **3B** Figurative language. **(c) Reading: 3A** Main ideas/details

YOU CAN'T JUST WALK ON BY

For a detailed lesson plan on this selection, see Teacher's Manual pages 43–46. A biography of Borden Deal appears on text page 153.

Borden Deal

This short-short piece of Borden Deal's is a recollection of a terrifying encounter with a huge water moccasin (a poisonous snake). The story is riveting. (Could anyone put it aside once the boy raises his hoe?) The story also lets us share the boy's thoughts about the most profound questions a person can try to answer.

A Right in the middle of that wonderful summer, death struck at me and missed by no more than a frog's hair. It came about so unexpected it seemed like an accident. I happened to be messing around, very early one morning, down at the creek. I was all by myself, having risen up and gone out before breakfast, as I liked to do from time to time, to think about the world and other things.

I pushed my way through the fringe growth, hunting a way down to the water, why, I really don't know. The creek was low during this dryness of summer. The water puddled muddily here and there, and the sand of the bottom was dried white. There was a puddle of water, and then the sandbar, and lying on the sandbar was the biggest water moccasin I had ever seen.

I stopped, feeling my breath catch in my throat. He was sound asleep, his massive head laid across the thickest part of his coiled body. He was as big around as the thigh of my leg, though not very long.

B There's something fascinating about seeing death right in front of you. A snake that size can pump enough poison into one bite that a body couldn't get a quarter of a mile before he'd lay down cold on the ground. I stood for as much as two minutes, holding my breath and watching his stillness.

From thinking about death, I started thinking about dealing out death. It's not every morning that you get a chance to kill a snake the size of that one. Besides, if I didn't kill him, I, or somebody else, might be messing around the creek one day and get snakebit. When death lies sleeping in your reach, you can't just walk on by.

I eased back out of the brush, careful not to make a noise for fear I would wake the sleeping snake. I remembered a hoe left hanging on the pasture-lane fence. I ran across the field and got it. It was rusted lightly on the blade, from being left out in the dew and the rain. But when I pressed my thumb along the edge, I could feel that it was still sharp. Sharp enough to kill even a snake of that size.

I sneaked up to where I could see the place where the snake had been, holding my breath, fearing that he had gone. He was coiled the same as before. He wouldn't move before sundown, for sure, unless he was disturbed. I meant to disturb him, though. I meant to kill him.

I worked carefully, getting into position to strike. The snake himself could not have been more quiet. I knew I wouldn't have but the one stroke, so it had better be a good one. I didn't want to get down in the creek bed with him, but

Action Verbs. Borden Deal uses vivid action verbs to help us share this boy's horrifying experience. Good action verbs help us see or hear what is happening. Examples of vivid action would be *gulp* instead of *drink*, *leap* instead of *jump*, and *hissed* instead of *said*.

Supplementary Support Material

1. Vocabulary Activity Sheet
2. Reading Check Test blackline master
3. Selection Test (page 49 of Test Book)
4. Reader's Response Journal
5. Workbook (page 37)

Developing Vocabulary

The following words appear on a test in the Test Book, page 50. (See also the Vocabulary Activity Sheet.)

messing around	instinct
fringe	responsibility
water moccasin	hinged wide
coiled	writhed
a body	spreadeagled

Critical Comment

Writing about Borden Deal, one critic has said, "A universal quality in his writing stems, in part, from his preoccupation with the timeless ritual of self-discovery."

Discuss the notion of self-discovery with students. Why might self-discovery be a recurring event? What is the self-discovery in "You Can't Just Walk On By"?

A

strike safely from above. The bank was steep on this side. I had to be able to reach him, yet be sure the force of my blow wouldn't tumble me down on top of him.

I got my feet set, finally. I was barefooted, and could feel my weight solidly placed on the bank. I had done all so quietly that the snake slept on, even his instinct not warning him. I raised the hoe high over my head in both hands.

There, ready to strike, I hesitated. Even as I held the hoe high, I realized that he was beautiful. He was whole in himself, he was complete, he was beautiful. I wished that we were not enemies, that I did not feel it was my responsibility to kill him. Even as I wished it, I knew that I would have to make the stroke and cut off his evil head.

I made my strike. As I did so, I found myself balancing forward, so that I didn't hit him just behind the head, as I had planned. Instead, I cut him almost exactly in half.

Even as the hoe swished down, he was moving, aroused at last by the threat of danger. He might as well have roared like a lion at the surprise of the attack. The hoe sliced his body in two. The front half struck up toward me, the mouth hinged wide to show the white cotton of its lining. I could even see, as though I had all day to see it in, the great fangs snapping into place.

I dodged back, though he didn't have a chance of reaching me at the far end of the hoe. Him leaping at me like that struck fear deep into my soul.

I struck, he struck, and then his front half slid off into the shallow pool of water alongside the sandbar. The thick-bodied after-half writhed on the sand as though it too were alive with intelligence and evil. B

I had not succeeded in killing him; not immediately, anyway, though he would surely die. Without thinking, I leaped down onto the sandbar where he had been lying and began raking the water of the shallow pool with the blade of the hoe, trying to drag him out so I could finish the job.

A. Responding to the Photograph

? Imagine that you are on a camping vacation. What would you say in a postcard to a friend describing the day on which you saw the snake in the photograph? (Be sure to include descriptive details.)

B. Suspense

? Explain the suspense in this passage. (We feel suspense as the narrator readies himself to strike the snake and we are on edge wondering if the snake will awaken and strike first. Our tension builds as he hesitates, and continues even after he strikes since the snake does not die and is still capable of striking him.

Reading Check Test

1. Why is the boy out by himself so early in the morning? *He likes to use this time to "think about the world and other things."*
2. Why does the boy feel he could kill the snake with the hoe? *The hoe has a razor-sharp edge.*
3. How does the boy propose to kill the snake? *He proposes to chop off the snake's head with the hoe from the safety of the creek bank.*
4. Why does the boy jump down onto the sandbar? *He wants to finish killing the snake.*
5. What does the boy do after he climbs out of the creek? *He sobs.*

Additional Writing Assignment

Tell students to imagine that they are copywriters for a literary magazine that is including the story "You Can't Just Walk On By" in its next issue. As such, have them write a blurb of twenty-five words or less that captures the essence of the narrator's discovery in a way that makes people want to buy the magazine and read the story.

A. Suspense

This paragraph contains more palm-sweating suspense. This time, the suspense comes from the horrifying appearance of the snake. What are some of these details? ("Bloodstained," "hinged open in that horrible gaping," "jaws at right angles," "white cotton of death")

B. Interpreting

What is the effect on the story that the bird is singing after this horrifying event? (It shows that suffering and death are part of everyday life.)

Closure

Have students write two or three sentences explaining the connection between setting and plot in "You Can't Just Walk On By."

It was a very small pool; if it hadn't been muddy, I could have seen the bottom. I didn't see how he could have escaped. But, rake as I might, I couldn't fetch up the bleeding tangle of his living half.

It was my instinct that saved me. I was standing on the sandbar, raking furiously. Suddenly, without knowing why, I turned my head to look down over my shoulder.

A The snake was lying at my naked heel. He had come around in the water to where it curved slightly behind the sandbar. He lay in bloodstained water behind me. Even as I looked, his mouth hinged open in that horrible gaping, the jaws at right angles to each other. I saw the white cotton of death in his jaws and knew he was going to take me with him into his own dying. I'd never make it to the house before I died, too.

Even as I turned my head, and looked, and saw, I dropped the hoe and jumped flat-footed for the opposite bank. He struck, his head hitting the sand where my heel had been an instant before. The bank was high and steep before me, and I spreadeagled myself on it, hands and feet clutching, thinking, hopelessly, that I was falling back on him and he would get me after all.

I don't know to this day how I managed to cling to that steep bank of earth. By sheer will power, nothing else, for there was nothing to hold on to. I clung there and my head was turned still, watching the snake as, leaving a trail of blood, he slid off into the muddy water. Then I managed to climb up the bank until I sat sobbing in safety.

I knew he was dying in the shallow water. The hoe was down there, too, on the sandbar. I couldn't think about getting it back. I sat on the bank, feeling the sweat damp on my shirt, feeling my body shivering in long, cold ripples of death-dread. When I could get my legs under me, I walked beside the pasture-lane fence. I looked about and the world was still with me, the green fields stretching away. Over my head in the sweetgum tree a mockingbird sang as though death had not barely passed me by. B

For the first time in my life, I thought about death, knowing I too could die.

It was a feeling a man could never forget, no matter how long his life. Not ever again would I take life for granted. Every breath I took, every drop of sweat I sweated, every bite of food or sip of good sweet water, would have more meaning.

Responding to the Story

Analyzing the Story

Identifying Facts

SRW p. 79

1. Describe the **setting,** or season and place in which the story begins.
2. What was the boy doing just before he discovered the snake?
3. Explain why he feels he should kill the snake.
4. After cutting the snake in half, the boy searches in the water for its front half. List the two actions he soon takes which save his life.
5. After his narrow escape, what discovery does the boy make about death and living?

Interpreting Meanings

6. What does the **title** of the story mean?
7. The boy hesitates before killing the snake, because he is suddenly aware of its beauty. Why does he think the snake is beautiful? Did you find it surprising and confusing that a snake should be beautiful?
8. Find the passages where the boy calls the snake "evil." Why do you think we so often think of snakes as evil? (If the boy had been threatened by a bear, do you think he'd call it "evil"?)

Applying Meanings

9. Do you think the boy should have "walked on by"? Why or why not? Can you think of other situations in life when "you can't just walk on by"? Explain.
10. What other experiences in life would make a person stop taking life for granted?

ANALYZING THE STORY

Identifying Facts

1. It is summer on a rural Southern creek.
2. He was taking an early morning walk.
3. He sees the snake as evil and dangerous, and wants to rid the creek of a potential safety hazard.
4. First he looks over his shoulder and sees the snake about to strike. Then he jumps to the steep opposite bank and holds on.
5. The boy is reminded that he is mortal, and that life is precious and should not be taken for granted.

Interpreting Meanings

6. People must notice every moment of life, for death may come unexpectedly.
7. The boy admires the snake's wholeness and completeness.

Answers will vary. Students who find it surprising and confusing will note that there is nothing beautiful about a poisonous snake's fangs, however attractive the rest of its body might be. Other students may note that this snake was sleeping peacefully, and that the scales of a water moccasin can be beautiful.
8. Answers will vary. Some students might point to the traditional belief in the snake's evil qualities, which are emphasized in much folk literature and in the Bible.

Applying Meanings

9. Answers will vary. Students who feel he should not have ignored the snake will point to the danger that the snake could later strike someone who was unaware of its presence. Students who feel that he should have walked on by may argue that the snake is part of the balance of nature and that snakes play an important role in, say, helping preserve a farmer's crop by killing rodents and small animals.

Answers will vary. Students may note situations in which a person has been injured or is in danger (for example, trapped in a burning house) when a stranger comes by. The stranger's duty is to help the endangered person, or to go get help.
10. Students should be able to point to a number of such situations a person might have experienced.

Writing About the Story

A Creative Response

SRW p. 69

1. **Writing from Another Point of View.** If snakes could think or talk or write, we'd want to hear the water moccasin's side of the story. Write a paragraph describing the battle from the snake's point of view. Use the first-person pronoun, *I*.

A Critical Response

2. **Responding to the Story.** In a paragraph, describe your response to this story. You might want to fill out a chart like the following before you write:

Elements in Story	My Response to Them
Violence in story	
The boy's decisions	
His attitude toward snakes	
Main idea in story	

See Teacher's Manual page 45.

Analyzing Language and Vocabulary

Action Verbs

Borden Deal uses action verbs to help you experience this episode the way the boy did. Action verbs help you *see* and *hear* the boy's and the snake's movements. For instance, the writer says "the hoe swished down. . . ." Suppose the sentence had read "the hoe came down. . . ." We wouldn't *hear* the sound of the hoe hissing through the air, threatening swift death. Read these passages from the story, and answer the questions that follow.

1. "He might as well have roared like a lion at the surprise of the attack."
   a. What verb helps you *hear* the action?
   b. What tamer phrase could have been used?
2. ". . . the mouth hinged wide to show the white cotton of its lining."
   a. What do you have to know about a snake's mouth to visualize what *hinged* means?
   b. Rephrase this sentence using a less vivid verb.
3. "I could even see . . . the great fangs snapping into place."
   a. What verb helps you *hear* what is happening?
   b. How would you describe this action using a less vivid verb?

For answers, see Teacher's Manual page 45.

Reading About the Writer

Borden Deal (1922–1985), who was born to a family of cotton farmers in Mississippi, traveled around the country for several years looking for work. He finally was able to go to the University of Alabama, where he wrote his first short story. One of Deal's most famous stories is "Antaeus," about a young Southern boy who moves to New York City and teaches a group of city boys to love the land.

Focusing on Background

"Letter to a Son Who Has Declared His Ambition to Become a Writer"

The following is taken from a letter that Borden Deal wrote to his son at college when he decided he wanted to become a writer. Deal gives some valuable advice, and several warnings, to the beginning writer.

". . . Learn to write character. Learn to write dialogue. All beginning writers love description. Why? Because description is easy to write. But beware of description. It is necessary, but it is also a heady wine for a young writer. Use it sparingly. The less description you use, the more effective it is. Remember that. Develop your fiction through character, through scene and action and dialogue. Let your people stand up and walk around; let them carry their own story. Don't impose the heavy burden of description upon them."

—Borden Deal

PREREADING

1. BUILDING ON PRIOR KNOWLEDGE. The boy in this story has never experienced something that he considers important, and he may not have much time. Before they read, ask students: If they were given an opportunity to do or experience anything in the world, what would they choose? Would it be sky-diving? Riding a horse? Traveling? Why would they choose this particular activity?

2. ESTABLISHING A PURPOSE. Tell students to be alert for the narrator's discovery as they read.

3. PREREADING JOURNAL. Before they read, have students pretend that a handicapped friend asked them a favor and have them write a brief journal entry about it. What was the favor? How did they react? Did they grant it?

Texas Essential Elements/(a) English Language Arts: 1B Purpose and audience; **3A** Plot/character; **3B** Figurative language; **4H** Point of view

THE QUIET HEART

Norman Rosten

For a detailed lesson plan on this selection, see Teacher's Manual pages 46–48. A biography of Normal Rosten appears on text page 159.

Supplementary Support Material

1. Vocabulary Activity Sheet
2. Reading Check Test blackline master
3. Selection Test (page 51 of Test Book)
4. Reader's Response Journal
5. Workbook (page 39)

Developing Vocabulary

The following words appear on a test in the Test Book, page 52. (See also the Vocabulary Activity Sheet.)

weird	haughtily
joshing	skeptical
pulsing	wavering
tutor	jaunty
conscious	temper

Texas Essential Elements/(c) Reading: 3A Main ideas/details; **3F** Purpose/point of view/opinion; **3I** Draw conclusions

This story about a fourteen-year-old boy who is very sick and who has never been kissed will almost surely touch you in some way. As you read, try to imagine what each of the three main characters is thinking about that kiss. The story is taken from Rosten's autobiographical account of his own childhood. It is set in the 1920's, in a section of New York City known as Coney Island.

Onomatopoeia. This narrator uses words that imitate the sound he imagines Jumpy's heart makes: *poom-boom, poom-boom.* The use of words whose sound echoes their meaning is called *onomatopoeia* (ăn'ə·mat'ə·pē'ə). Notice how *poom-boom* becomes a threatening sound.

SRW p. 63

Of all the people who moved into our house, I guess I remember Philip the best. He was older than I, about fourteen, sad-eyed, skinny, and had to spend most of the time in a wheelchair. He had something we'd never heard of before on our block: an enlarged heart. Pretty soon we called him Jumpy because his heart could be seen jumping right under his skin when his shirt was open. The spot on his chest would go *poom-boom poom-boom* (without a sound) up and down, no bigger than a dime. It was weird. Yet after a while we got used to it. Watching it was like a game.

When Jumpy was wheeled out in his chair on the sidewalk to sit in the morning sun, he'd wave his arm and call, "It's me, fellas." And we'd crowd around, joshing him, spinning his chair, until someone would say, "Let's see it jump, how about it, Jumpy!" And grinning shyly, he opened his shirt, as we stared at the pulsing circle of flesh—his real alive heart!

Jumpy smiled feebly. "The doctor says I'll get better. I might even go back to school after summer vacation." We said nothing; we didn't know much about hearts, but it didn't look as though he would be in school for a long time.

I would stop into his room almost every day. He sat up in bed, reading or listening to the radio, or just leaning back looking into space. I would sometimes come in and he wouldn't see me, and the room so silent I'd think he was dead. I'd call out, "Jumpy?" And he would turn slowly, his eyes brightening. "Hi, sit down." A

We talked about all kinds of things. Baseball and horses and radios. He had a small crystal set.[1] We wondered how music came from an inch of wire probing a piece of crystal—with no electricity! We talked about school, science, and the tutor who came to the house. That was before he got too sick and stopped studying altogether. We played cards a lot. B

His mother was nice, but sad, as if she knew something was going to happen. She brought us cakes and ice cream while we played our games. They had to be quiet games because he couldn't get excited; that made it worse, his mother explained.

Sometimes my sister would visit. She was shy, and she usually brought him some little gift, like a jelly apple or a small bag of cherries. He loved cherries.

"You look better, Philip," my sister said on these visits. (She never called him Jumpy; she used his real name.)

"Thank you," Jumpy replied.

"You look much better than last week, honest, Philip," she said. And he smiled his thin but intense smile. He never said much to her. She, as well, was embarrassed. She was skinny in her bathing suit and shy all the time. I was conscious of her growing up, and it made me feel a little strange at first. I found myself watching her more after that. Anyway, her growing up and Jumpy's growing up made them shy with each other. I thought he liked her, but I wasn't sure about what she felt.

Once, when we were talking about girls, Jumpy said he thought my sister was a nice kid.

"Did you ever kiss a girl?" I asked him.

"No. Did you?"

"Yes," I said.

"I don't mean sisters," he said.

I had, in fact, earlier that summer, kissed a slender light-haired girl good night. It wasn't much of a kiss, but I recalled the warmth of her lips with a shiver. It was quick; in the movies they

1. **crystal set:** old type of radio.

A. Foreshadowing
This statement shows the gravity of Philip's illness, and foreshadows his eventual death.

B. Character
? Based on the details in this passage starting with "When Jumpy was wheeled . . .," how would you describe Jumpy? (He is friendly, has a good sense of humor, and is a good sport in spite of his handicap. He is optimistic and tries to make his friends comfortable with his disability. Jumpy is intelligent and curious.)

A. Interpreting

? What does the scratching, the word *gulped,* and the pauses in the narrator's speech suggest about his feelings? (He's embarrassed to describe what the kiss was like. Also, since he and the girl "just brushed faces," he probably couldn't go into much detail even if he wanted to.)

B. Conflict

This passage sets the stage for the external conflict that develops between the narrator and his sister. It also establishes the sister's internal and broader conflict regarding her own growing up. (The narrator shows his sensitivity and insight by realizing that not only is he uncomfortable about her maturing, but that she herself is scared.)

C. Foreshadowing

? What does the dream foreshadow? (Philip's death) Why do the boys laugh? (To release tension; somehow, even they know it might foreshadow his death)

were long kisses, but I suppose that was for older people. Anyway, standing on the stoop was bad for your balance, and that slender girl and I just brushed faces, you might say. Still, I wasn't lying when I said I had kissed a girl.

"What was it like?" he wanted to know.

A I scratched my head and gulped one of the cherries. "It was like . . . very different. I wouldn't know how to describe it, Jumpy. All I can say is, I'd do it again if I got the chance."

"I'd sure like to try it," said Jumpy. "But I guess you gotta ask a girl. They just won't come over and kiss you, would they?"

I shook my head. "I don't think so. I never heard of it. Maybe if it was something special they would."

"Well, anyway . . ." Jumpy's voice trailed off. "It ain't going to happen to me, I guess." We continued to play cards.

Later, alone with her, I asked my sister, "What do you think about Jumpy?"

"You mean Philip? I hate that nickname. He's too nice to have such a nickname."

"Do you like him?"

"Oh, he's all right." She looked at me curiously. "Why?"

"Nothing. Only he asks about you a lot. He's goofy about you."

"You know what you are? You're absolutely cuckoo," she said.

I shot back, "He'd love to smooch with you. He keeps saying he'd *love* to kiss you. What about *that*?"

B "I am not interested in kissing Philip," she said imperiously.[2] But underneath I knew the idea scared her. After all, she was just a kid, and she was growing up and thinking about things like kissing. I was. And so was everybody else, I figured.

I kept thinking of Jumpy, in bed most of the time, with a doctor coming by twice a week, and not once being kissed by a girl. When I thought of all the kissing going on on the beach, and under the boardwalk, and practically everywhere—well, it was a shame about Jumpy.

He took a turn for the worse. He wasn't out of the house for days. His mother wouldn't allow any of us to come into his room. Once I peeked in and saw him lying on the bed, his head turned toward the wall. I called out softly, "Hey Jumpy." He moved his head, lifted his arm weakly, but didn't turn. I went away. That night, the doctor arrived on a special visit. My mother met him in the hall and went inside the room with him. I tried to enter, but they wouldn't allow me. I listened at the door. All I could hear were muffled voices and, I thought, a sound of weeping.

The next day, when I asked my mother what happened, she only said, "He's very sick," and went about her work. I waited in the hall until Jumpy's mother came out of a room. When she saw me, she said in a whisper, "My poor little boy." She pressed my hand and went off into the street.

I pushed the door open into Jumpy's room. He was alone. I went up to the bed. I hadn't seen him for over a week, and I was shocked. His face seemed to be stretched thin like paper; the eyes had sunken deep into their sockets; the mouth was thin and blue. His pajama shirt was open, and I could see his heart leaping against his skin; in my ears it suddenly sounded *poom-boom poom-boom* louder and louder. I swallowed and the sound went away.

Jumpy saw me. "Boy, I must be sick with doctors coming around every day."

"You look OK," I lied.

"I don't know, I broke the mirror yesterday lookin'," he said, with that odd persisting smile playing around his mouth. "I must look like some kind of freaky ghost."

I didn't know what to say, because he was right. I pushed his shoulder jokingly. He sighed, leaned back on the pillow, and stared at the ceiling. "Jimmy and the guys send their regards," I said hesitatingly.

He said, "I had a dream about Jimmy. You'll never guess what it was. You won't tell him?" I shook my head. "I mean, he might think I had something against him."

"What'd you dream?" I prodded him.

"You won't laugh? I dreamed he was dead." He started to laugh, and I laughed, and we both laughed so loud I thought we'd both get a stom- C

2. **imperiously:** in a proud, self-important way.

achache. Jumpy started to cough, and I rushed to get him some water. He choked on the water and I had to slap him on the back. Then we got to talking about some other things. Baseball. The law of gravity. And, again, girls. He asked about my sister again; she hadn't been in to say hello for over a week. I mumbled some apology for her and after a while I left.

A I met my sister outside. She was sitting in the sun reading a book. I bought her an ice-cream cone. She looked up, surprised. "Where'd you get the money, Mr. Rockefeller?"

"My allowance, Miss America, ha, ha."

"You always think you're funny when you're not," she said haughtily, licking at the ice cream. We were alone on the bench, and I decided to bring up the subject again.

"I saw Jumpy just now—I mean, Philip. He asked about you." She continued reading. "I was wondering, Sis . . . would you go up and say hello? He's pretty sick."

"I might later on. I'm reading now, can't you see?"

"When you go up, would you do me a favor? Don't get mad. Would you kiss him?" She stopped her reading. Her eyes widened. "Just kiss him. Just once. Would you, please?"

"Why should I?"

"Well, he's awful sick—but it's not catching like a cold or anything. He's so blue. You'd cheer him up. Would you?"

B She snapped her book shut and rose. "Please leave me alone or I'll tell Momma." And she ran into the house.

Not many days later, Jumpy's mother came over to me on the street, her eyes numb. "He's dying. Any day now, the doctor says. We mustn't feel bad. It's best with such a disease."

All that afternoon in my ear, even when I swallowed, was the sound *poom-boom poom-boom,* and any minute that heart might stop!

I spoke to my sister again, as she was leaving the kitchen after dinner. "He asked for you again."

She was skeptical. "You're making that up."

"No," I pleaded. "He's awfully lonely. If you'd see him for a minute, that's all, and just kiss him—"

"If you don't stop that—" She turned to go.

I gripped her arm. "Don't be a stuck-up. If a friend asks you for a kiss, is that a crime?"

"I don't like him."

"Do you have to *like* a fella, I mean a friend, to kiss him, just *one* kiss!"

She broke away and ran to my mother, sobbing. "I won't do it. He wants me to kiss Philip. I won't, I won't!"

My mother, startled, comforted her. "Quiet, you don't have to kiss anyone if you don't want to." She turned to me. "What is it now?"

I kept my eyes lowered. I didn't know how to explain such a thing. "I just asked her to kiss Jumpy. What's so terrible about it?" I was getting sore at my sister. "Anyway, she's a stuck-up!" I ran to the street, sullen, furious, defeated. C

At bedtime, my sister came to my room. I could see she had come to be forgiven. Standing at the door, she said, "I'm sorry I told Momma on you. That was wrong." I didn't answer, I'd gotten too tired thinking of Jumpy and his heart that would stop beating any minute.

She didn't go. "I hope you're not mad," she said. "After all, I don't know Philip, not really, I mean . . ." Her voice trailed off in uncertainty.

"If you do it, I'll give you a dollar. I promise. Gosh, how can you say you don't know him?" She was silent. "It ain't so awful kissing someone. You've kissed me lots of times."

"Kissing you is not the same, and you know it," she replied, wavering.

"It can't be much different with Jumpy. He's my age, about."

"The whole thing is silly, but I'll do it." Her acceptance, finally, was so casual I couldn't understand all the fuss she made earlier. What a screwloose for a sister, I thought! "When do I do it?" she asked.

"Right now," I said. She looked calm, as though she kissed boys every day which I don't think she did, but it crossed my mind. I didn't see her much during the day. "Come on," I said. She followed me down the hallway. We came to his door. I knocked softly. We entered. He was alone, his eyes half-closed. I thought he was asleep until he spoke.

"Hello. I'm glad you came." His eyes, now

A. Expansion
The Rockefellers are an extremely rich family. The patriarch of the family made his fortune in oil during the late 1800's and early 1900's. To be called a Rockefeller is to be called wealthy—usually in a mocking way.

B. Character's Actions
? What does the narrator's sister's behavior reveal about her character? (Even though the narrator is appealing to her reasonably this time, she still avoids the subject of kissing Philip. Her anger reveals that she's not ready to accept her feelings about boys. She may also be annoyed that her brother keeps bugging her to kiss this boy.)

C. Interpreting
? What makes the narrator "sullen, furious, and defeated"? (He's upset that Jumpy is dying and feels helpless; he can't even grant Jumpy a dying wish.)

READING CHECK TEST

1. What did the children in the neighborhood find fascinating about Philip? *His heart pulsated under his skin.*
2. What did the narrator and Philip do together when Philip was really sick? *They talked and played cards.*
3. What dream did Philip have about Jimmy? *He dreamed Jimmy was dead.*
4. Why did the narrator want his sister to kiss Philip? *Philip said he had never been kissed, and the narrator thought it would cheer him up.*
5. How did the narrator react when his sister first refused to kiss Philip? *He was furious and called her stuck-up.*

Additional Speaking Assignment
Divide the class up into groups of three or four students each. Tell students to describe to each other the emotions they felt as they read the story and to cite those portions of the text that made them feel that way. Encourage those students who wish to do so to tell about similar experiences they or people they know have had.

A. Interpreting
By "light" and "jaunty," what do we know about the sister's mood? (She is trying to maintain a confidence and calm that she doesn't feel—she's probably nervous.)

B. Foreshadowing
What does Jumpy's behavior and murmured words foreshadow? (That for Jumpy, there will be no tomorrow.)

CLOSURE
Have students work in groups of three, and summarize the plot of "The Quiet Heart." (They should identify the conflict, the climax, and the resolution.)

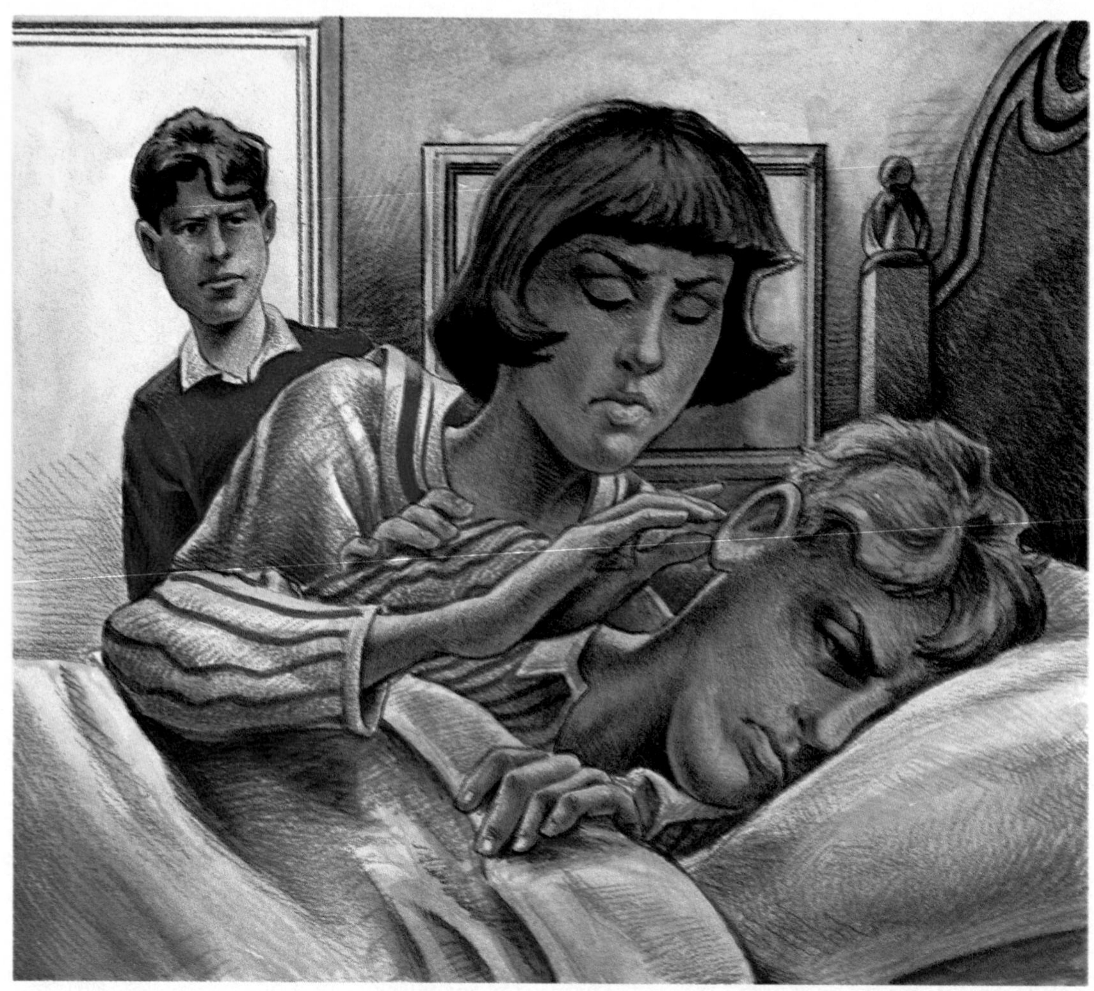

A fully opened, rested on my sister. She walked to the bed, her walk light, almost jaunty. "Hi, Philip. I'm sorry I haven't been up to see you lately. But you look fine."

He smiled weakly. His face was yellowed. He opened his mouth, but his voice was so low I had to lean over to hear him. "Good night," he said.

"Sure, Jumpy, we won't stay," I turned to my sister and nodded to her. "We just dropped in for a quick hello. See you again tomorrow."

B "Tomorrow," he whispered. His fingers reached over but could barely grip my hand.

"See you again," said my sister. She leaned over the bed, her eyes tightly shut, her face moving close to his. With a cry, he turned his head into the pillow. My sister looked at me, her lips trembling, and fled from the room. "Get out," Jumpy shouted. "Leave me alone. I don't want to see anybody!" I backed slowly toward the door, stunned by his anger.

The next afternoon, it was hard for me to imagine it was him in the coffin. I thought of his small heart quiet now under his clean shirt, and the *poom-boom* in my ear was quiet, too.

My sister cried a little. She was mad at me for a long time, for months, and wouldn't talk to me. Sometimes she'd lose her temper and scream at me even when I didn't remember doing anything wrong.

ANALYZING THE STORY
Identifying Facts

1. Philip is called "Jumpy" because his enlarged heart appears to jump beneath his skin.

He is fourteen.

2. Philip wants to know what it feels like to be kissed by a girl.

3. The narrator wants his sister to kiss Philip.

4. Philip turns away angrily and says he wants to be alone.

Interpreting Meanings

5. Answers will vary. Most students will say she did it to please her brother, or at least to get him to stop bothering her about it, or that she did it because he offered her a dollar, or because she felt sorry for Philip.

6. Answers will vary. Some students will say that Philip either sensed that she was doing it mainly to please her brother, not him. Other students may say Philip misinterpreted the kiss as a sign of pity rather than as a genuine token of affection.

7. We know that the narrator's sister likes Philip because she brings him little gifts when he is sick. Also she calls him by his real name, Philip, rather than by his nickname, Jumpy. Her reluctance to kiss him may be attributed primarily to shyness, not lack of feeling.

8. Answers will vary. Most students will say she is angry with her brother both because she had felt "silly" about going through with the gesture in the first place, and because it was her brother who had gotten her into the situation.

9. Answers may vary. Some students will say that the narrator and his sister discovered that it is dangerous to try to manipulate another's feelings, even out of good intentions. Other students will say the boy and girl learned about loss and death, friendship, and growing up.

10. Answers may vary. See Teacher's Manual page 47.

Applying Meanings

11. Answers may vary.

Responding to the Story

Analyzing the Story

Identifying Facts

1. Why is Philip called "Jumpy"? How old is he?
2. At one point, the narrator and Philip discuss kissing. What does Philip want to know?
3. What does the narrator want his sister to do?
4. What happens when his sister tries to kiss Philip?

Interpreting Meanings

5. Why do you think the narrator's sister agreed to kiss Philip?
6. Why do you think Philip responded the way he did when she attempted to kiss him?
7. How do you think the narrator's sister really felt about Philip? Is there any hint in her behavior that she likes him in a special way?
8. After Philip dies, the sister is very angry with the narrator. In your opinion, why is she angry?
9. What do you think the narrator and his sister discovered in this story?
10. Why do you think the writer calls this part of his life story "The Quiet Heart"?

Applying Meanings

11. What did you think of the narrator's plan? What would you have done if you were the narrator, his sister, or Philip?

Writing About the Story

A Creative Response

1. **Having Another Character Tell the Story.** Imagine that the sister is telling this story to a friend. How did she feel about Philip? Why did she at first refuse to kiss him, and why did she change her mind? How did she feel after Philip died? Write a paragraph using the first-person pronoun, *I*.

A Critical Response

2. **Analyzing Conflict.** In this story, there are several **conflicts,** or struggles between opposing forces. Some of these conflicts are **external:** the characters struggle against each other or against other outside forces. Other conflicts are **internal:** these involve opposing desires or emotions within one character's heart and mind. Describe one conflict in the story and tell how it is resolved by the end of the story. You might discuss (a) the sister's internal conflict; (b) the external conflict between the narrator and his sister; or (c) the external conflict Philip is involved in.

See Teacher's Manual page 48.

Analyzing Language and Vocabulary

Onomatopoeia

SRW p. 63

Onomatopoeia is the use of a word whose sound echoes its meaning. We use onomatopoeia every day in words like *buzz, tick-tock,* and *growl.*

Onomatopoeia helps us to hear the sound a word refers to. In this story, the words *poom-boom, poom-boom* help us hear the sound of Philip's heart the way the narrator imagines he hears it.

In each sentence below, fill in the blanks with the word or phrase whose sound best describes its meaning.

1. The bacon ______ in the pan.

   a. cooked **b.** fried **c.** sizzled

2. I heard the ______ of the cable cars.

   a. clatter and clang **b.** noise **c.** sounds

3. The fire ______ in the fireplace.

   a. made noise **b.** crackled **c.** burned

Write three sentences of your own using onomatopoeia. You might describe the sound of a car, of a person eating soup, of a night in the woods, or something else.

For answers, see Teacher's Manual page 48.

Reading About the Writer

Norman Rosten (1914–   ) says that during the Depression in the 1930's he sat in a room for months and months and began to write out of desperation. He went on to write plays, poetry, and an autobiography called *Under the Boardwalk,* from which "The Quiet Heart" is taken. The boardwalk refers to the famous boardwalk on Coney Island, in New York City.

PREREADING

1. **BUILDING ON PRIOR KNOWLEDGE.** Ask students to remember what third grade was like. Who was their teacher, and what was he or she like? What was the atmosphere of the classroom—strict and full of rules? Or was it unrestricted and full of games?

2. **ESTABLISHING A PURPOSE.** Before students begin reading, you might have them read question 11 on page 169.

3. **PREREADING JOURNAL.** Before they read, have students write a brief paragraph in which they pretend they are childless adults spending a week with a group of seven-year-olds. What aspects of young children's behavior would they find unpleasant or annoying? They can make up a short short story with real characters if they like.

A. Making Inferences

? What does Roger's ungrammatical speech tell about him? (Even if the author didn't tell us he was seven, we would know he was a young child because of the way he speaks. His speech makes him real to us—we can really hear him talk.)

B. Responding

? Do you agree with Elizabeth's statement that school isn't supposed to be fun? Why or why not? Do you like Elizabeth so far?

★ **Texas Essential Elements/(a) English Language Arts: 1B** Purpose and audience; **3A** Plot/character; **4H** Point of view. **(c) Reading: 3A** Main ideas/details; **3F** Purpose/point of view/opinion; **3I** Draw conclusions

MISS AWFUL

Arthur Cavanaugh

This story is almost certain to stir strong feelings among young scholars, for it is about a classroom you might recognize. The conflict takes place between two different styles of governing a group of students: the strict and the easy going. You may want to consult your own sentiments about this conflict before reading the story. As you read, see if you agree with the writer, who makes something of a case for law and order.

The whole episode of Miss Awful began for the Clarks at their dinner table one Sunday afternoon. Young Roger Clark was explaining why he could go to Central Park with his father instead of staying home to finish his homework—Miss Wilson, his teacher, wouldn't be at school tomorrow, so who'd know the difference? "She has to take care of a crisis," Roger explained. "It's in Omaha."

"What is?" his older sister, Elizabeth, inquired. "For a kid in third grade, Roger, you talk dopey. You fail to make sense."

Roger ignored the insult. His sister was a condition of life he had learned to live with, like lions. Or snakes. Poisonous ones. Teetering, as always, on the tilted-back chair, feet wrapped around the legs, he continued, "Till Miss Wilson gets back we're having some other teacher. She flew to Omaha yesterday." He pushed some peas around on his plate and was silent a moment. "I hope her plane don't crash," he said.

Roger's mother patted his hand. A lively, outgoing youngster, as noisy and rambunctious as any seven-year-old, he had another side to him, tender and soft, which worried about people. Let the blind man who sold pencils outside the five-and-ten on Broadway be absent from his post, and Roger worried that catastrophe had overtaken him. When Mrs. Loomis, a neighbor of the Clarks in the Greenwich Village brownstone, had entered the hospital, Roger's anxious queries had not ceased until she was discharged. And recently there was the cat which had nested in the downstairs doorway at night. Roger had carried down saucers of milk, clucking with concern. "Is the cat run away? Don't it have a home?" A

Virginia Clark assured her son, "You'll have Miss Wilson safely back before you know it. It's nice that you care so."

Roger beamed with relief. "Well, I like Miss Wilson, she's fun. Last week, for instance, when Tommy Miller got tired of staying in his seat and lay down on the floor—"

"He did what?" Roger's father was roused from his post-dinner torpor.[1]

"Sure. Pretty soon the whole class was lying down. Know what Miss Wilson did?"

"If you'll notice, Mother," Elizabeth interjected, "he hasn't touched a single pea."

"*She* lay down on the floor, too," Roger went on ecstatically. "She said we'd *all* have a rest, it was perfectly normal in the middle of the day. That's what I love about St. Geoff's.[2] It's fun."

"Fun," snorted his sister. "School isn't supposed to be a fun fest. It's supposed to be filling that empty noodle of yours." B

Homonyms. Poor spellers like Roger often have special problems with homonyms. A *homonym* sounds exactly like another word, but it is spelled differently and has a different meaning. For example, *pear* and *pair* are homonyms.

1. **torpor:** sluggishness.
2. **St. Geoff's** (jefs).

For a detailed lesson plan on this story, see Teacher's Manual pages 48–51.

A biography of Arthur Cavanaugh appears on text page 170.

Supplementary Support Material
1. Vocabulary Activity Sheet
2. Reading Check Test blackline master
3. Selection Test (page 53 of Test Book)
4. Reader's Response Journal
5. Workbook (page 41)

Developing Vocabulary
The following words appear on a test in the Test Book, page 54. (See also the Vocabulary Activity Sheet.)

crisis	scathing
homonyms	stiff-backed
capable	martial air
whimsical	evicted
rollicking spirits	

"Miss Wilson got down on the floor?" Mr. Clark repeated. He had met Roger's teacher on occasion; she had struck him as capable but excessively whimsical.[3] She was a large woman to be getting down on floors, Mr. Clark thought. "What did the class do next?" he asked.

"Oh, we lay there a while, then got up and did a Mexican hat dance," Roger answered. "It was swell."

"I'm sure not every day is as frolicsome," Mrs. Clark countered, slightly anxious. She brought in dessert, a chocolate mousse. Roger's story sounded typical of St. Geoffrey's. Not that she was unhappy with his school. A small private institution, while it might be called overly permissive, it projected a warm, homey atmosphere which Mrs. Clark found appealing. It was church-affiliated, which she approved of, and heaven knows its location a few blocks away from the brownstone was convenient. True, Roger's scholastic progress wasn't notable—his spelling, for example, remained atrocious. Friendly as St. Geoffrey's was, Mrs. Clark sometimes *did* wish . . . A

Roger attacked dessert with a lot more zest than he had shown the peas. "So can I go to the park with you, Dad? I've only got spelling left, and who cares about that?" Before his mother could comment, he was up from the table and racing toward the coat closet. "Okay, Dad?"

"I didn't say you could go. I didn't even say I'd take you," Mr. Clark objected. He happened, at that moment, to glance at his waistline and reflect that a brisk hike might do him some good. He pushed back his chair. "All right, but the minute we return, it's straight to your room to finish your spelling."

"Ah, thanks, Dad. Can we go to the boat pond first?"

"We will not," cried Elizabeth, elbowing into the closet. "We'll go to the Sheep Meadow first."

Roger was too happy to argue. Pulling on his jacket, he remarked, "Gee, I wonder what the new teacher will be like. Ready for your coat, Dad?"

B It was just as well that he gave the matter no more thought. In view of events to come, Roger was entitled to a few carefree hours.

3. **whimsical:** full of silly, fanciful ideas.

Monday morning at school started off with perfect normalcy. It began exactly like any other school morning. Elizabeth had long since departed for the girls' school she attended uptown, when Mrs. Clark set out with Roger for the short walk to St. Geoff's. She didn't trust him with the Fifth Avenue traffic yet. They reached the school corner, and Roger skipped away eagerly from her. The sidewalk in front of school already boasted a large, jostling throng of children, and his legs couldn't hurry Roger fast enough to join them. Indeed, it was his reason for getting to school promptly: to have time to play before the 8:45 bell. Roger's school bag was well equipped for play. As usual, he'd packed a supply of baseball cards for trading opportunities; a spool of string, in case anybody brought a kite; a water pistol for possible use in the lavatory; and a police whistle for sheer noise value. Down the Greenwich Village sidewalk he galloped, shouting the names of his third grade friends as he picked out faces from the throng. "Hiya, Tommy. Hey, hiya, Bruce. Hi, Steve, you bring your trading cards?" C

By the time the 8:45 bell rang—St. Geoff's used a cowbell, one of the homey touches—Roger had finished a game of tag, traded several baseball cards, and was launched in an exciting jump-the-hydrant contest. Miss Gillis, the school secretary, was in charge of the bell, and she had to clang it extensively before the student body took notice. Clomping up the front steps, they spilled into the downstairs hall, headed in various directions. Roger's class swarmed up the stairs in rollicking spirits, Tommy Miller, Bruce Reeves, Joey Lambert, the girls forming an untidy rear flank behind them, shrill with laughter.

It wasn't until the front ranks reached the third-grade classroom that the first ominous note was struck.

"Hey, what's going on?" Jimmy Moore demanded, first to observe the changed appearance of the room. The other children crowded behind him in the doorway. Instead of a cozy semicircle—"As though we're seated round a glowing hearth," Miss Wilson had described it—the desks and

A. Making Inferences
? What *does* Mrs. Clark wish? (Probably that Roger was doing a little more learning and a little less playing)

B. Foreshadowing and Suspense
? How does this passage prepare us for what is to come and make us eager to read on? (We gather that things are going to take a turn for the worse, and we wonder what will prevent Roger's future hours from being carefree.)

C. Expansion
The contents of Roger's school bag seem to go along with the permissive attitude at St. Geoff's.

A. Figurative Language

? To what does Cavanaugh compare the new teacher? (He compares her to a ruler and to a witch.) What other details in the paragraph contribute to her severe image? ("Raspish voice," "ancient tweed suit," "bony nose," hair "skewered in a bun," eyes "leering")

B. Vocabulary

Deranged means "insane."

? Why was the giggle deranged? (It was a bit hysterical—this teacher has severely shocked the third-grade class.)

C. Responding

? How do you feel about Miss Orville? What do you feel for her students?

chairs had been rearranged in stiff, rigid rows. "Gee, look, the desks are in rows," commented Midge Fuller, a plump little girl who stood blocking Roger's view. Midge was a child given to unnecessary statements. "It's raining today," she would volunteer to her classmates, all of them shod in slickers and rubbers. Or, "There's the lunchbell, gang." The point to Roger wasn't that the desks had been rearranged. The point was, *why*? As if in answer, he heard two hands clap behind him, as loud and menacing as thunder.

"What's this, what's this?" barked a stern, raspish voice. "You are not cattle milling in a pen. Enough foolish gaping! Come, come, form into lines."

Heads turned in unison, mouths fell agape. The children of St. Geoffrey's third grade had never formed into lines of any sort, but this was not the cause of their shocked inertia.[4] Each was staring, with a sensation similar to that of drowning, at the owner of the raspish voice. She was tall and straight as a ruler, and was garbed in an ancient tweed suit whose skirt dipped nearly to the ankles. She bore a potted plant in one arm and Miss Wilson's roll book in the other. Rimless spectacles glinted on her bony nose. Her hair was gray, like a witch's, skewered in a bun, and there was no question that she had witch's eyes. Roger had seen those same eyes leering from the pages of *Hansel and Gretel*—identical, they were. He gulped at the terrible presence. A

"Are you a class of deaf mutes?" he heard with a start. "Form lines, I said. Girls in one, boys in the other." Poking, prodding, patrolling back and forth, the new teacher kneaded the third grade into position, and ruefully inspected the result. "Sloppiest group I've ever beheld. *March!*" She clapped time with her hands, and the stunned ranks trooped into the classroom. "*One,* two, three, *one,* two—girls on the window side, boys on the wall. Stand at your desks. Remove your outer garments. You, little Miss, with the vacant stare. What's your name?"

"Ja-ja—" a voice squeaked.

"Speak up. I won't have mumblers."

"Jane Douglas."

"Well, Jane Douglas, you will be coat monitor. Collect the garments a row at a time and hang them neatly in the cloakroom. Did you hear me, child? Stop staring." Normally slow-moving, Jane Douglas became a whirl of activity, charging up and down the aisles, piling coats in her arms. The new teacher tugged at her tweed jacket. "Class be seated, hands folded on desks," she barked, and there was immediate compliance. She next paraded to the windows and installed the potted plant on the sill. Her witch's hands fussed with the green leaves, straightening, pruning. "Plants and children belong in classrooms," she declared, spectacles sweeping over the rows. "Can someone suggest why?"

There was total silence, punctured by a deranged giggle, quickly suppressed. B

"Very well, I will tell you. Plants and children are living organisms. Both will grow with proper care. Repeat, *proper.* Not indulgent fawning, or giving in to whims—scrupulosity!"[5] With another tug at the jacket, she strode, ruler straight, to the desk in the front of the room. "I am Miss Orville. *O-r-v-i-l-l-e,*" she spelled. "You are to use my name in replying to all questions."

In the back of the room, Jimmy Moore whispered frantically to Roger. "What did she say her name is?"

Miss Orville rapped her desk. "Attention, please, no muttering in the back." She cleared her voice and resumed. "Prior to my retirement I taught boys and girls for forty-six years," she warned. "I am beyond trickery, so I advise you to try none. You are to be in my charge until the return of Miss Wilson, however long that may be." She clasped her hands in front of her and trained her full scrutiny on the rows. "Since I have no knowledge of your individual abilities, perhaps a look at the weekend homework will shed some light. Miss Wilson left me a copy of the assignment. You have all completed it, I trust? Take out your notebooks, please. At once, at once, I say." C

Roger's head spun dizzily around. He gaped at the monstrous tweed figure in dismay. Book bags were being clicked open, notebooks drawn out—

4. **inertia** (in·ur′shə): an inability to move.

5. **scrupulosity** (skrōō′pyə·läs′ə·tē): preciseness.

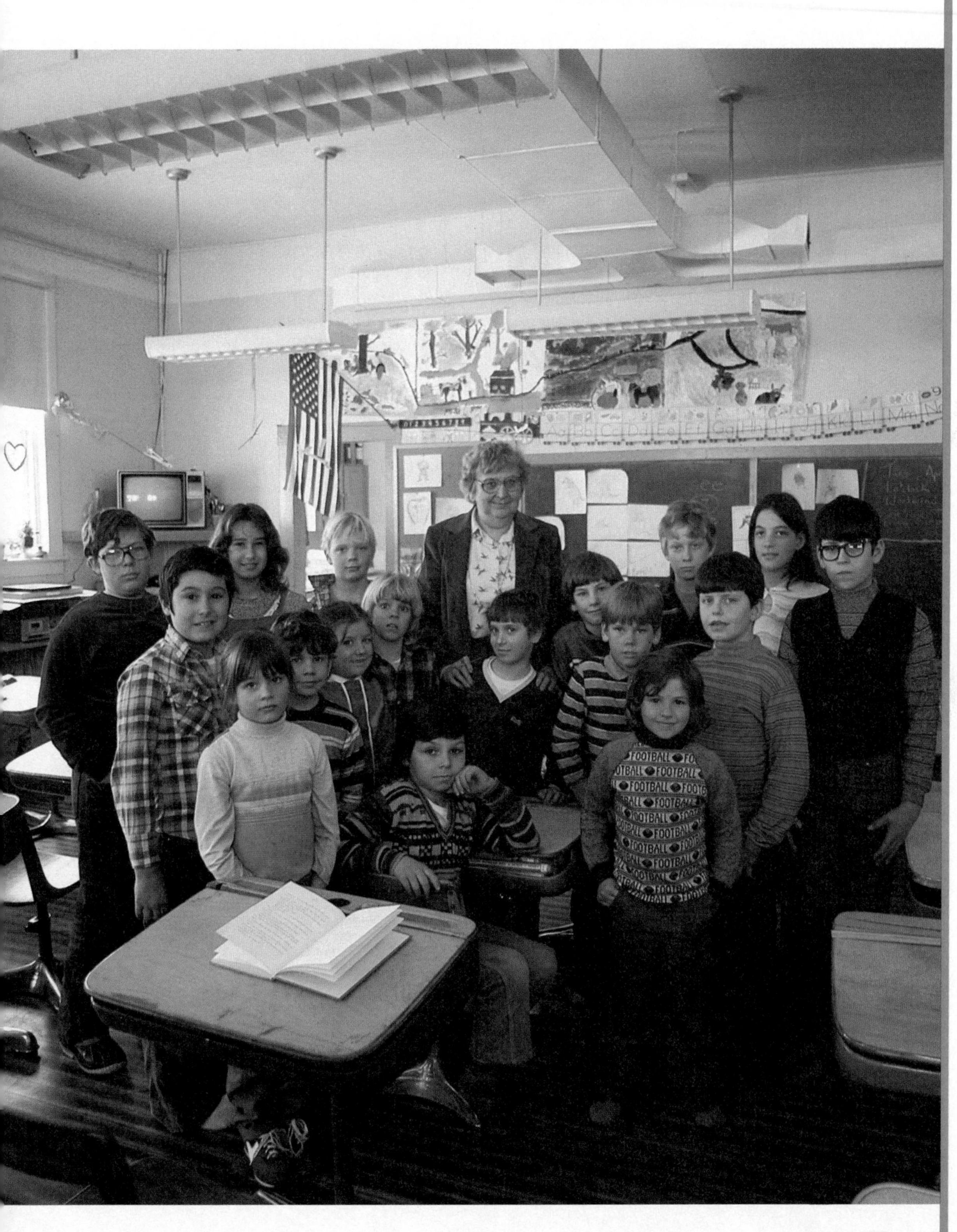

A. Conflict

? What details in this passage indicate that a conflict will develop between Miss Orville and Roger? (Miss Orville's criticism of ill-spelled words in someone's composition in light of the fact that Roger is a notoriously bad speller; Roger's statement that he is "in for it"; Roger's dropping his book bag; Miss Orville's words to Roger and the fixing of her "witch's gaze on him." These details also create suspense—we know Roger is in for a tongue-lashing.)

B. Making Inferences

? Why does Roger not want to speak nor want his mother to speak until they are down the block? (He does not want to be overheard by Miss Orville for fear of punishment.)

C. Vivid Verbs

? Why do you think Cavanaugh chose *bleated* instead of *said?* (*Bleated* creates the image of a crying sheep, goat, or calf. It vividly indicates Roger's misery.)

what was he to do? He had gone to his room after the outing in the park yesterday, but, alas, it had not been to complete his assignment. He watched, horrified, as the tweed figure proceeded among the aisles and inspected notebooks. What had she said her name was? Awful—was that it? Miss Awful! Biting his lip, he listened to her scathing comments.

"You call this chicken scrawl penmanship?" R-r-rip! A page was torn out and thrust at its owner. "Redo it at once, it assaults the intelligence." Then, moving on, "What is this maze of ill-spelled words? Not a composition, I trust."

A Ill-spelled words! He was in for it for sure. The tweed figure was heading down his aisle. She was three desks away, no escaping it. Roger opened his book bag. It slid from his grasp and, with a crash, fell to the floor. Books, pencil case spilled out. Baseball cards scattered, the water pistol, the police whistle, the spool of string . . .

"Ah," crowed Miss Awful, instantly at his desk, scooping up the offending objects. "We have come to play, have we?"

And she fixed her witch's gaze on him.

Long before the week's end, it was apparent to Virginia Clark that something was drastically wrong with her son's behavior. The happy-go-lucky youngster had disappeared, as if down a well. Another creature had replaced him, nervous, harried, continuously glancing over his shoulder, in the manner of one being followed. Mrs. Clark's first inkling of change occurred that same Monday. She had been chatting with the other mothers who congregated outside St. Geoffrey's at three every afternoon to pick up their offspring. A casual assembly, the mothers were as relaxed and informal as the school itself, lounging against the picket fence, exchanging small talk and anecdotes.

"That darling cowbell," laughed one of the group at the familiar clang. "Did I tell you Anne's class is having a taffy pull on Friday? Where else, in the frantic city of New York . . ."

The third grade was the last class to exit from the building on Monday. Not only that, but Mrs. Clark noted that the children appeared strangely subdued. Some of them were actually reeling, all but dazed. As for Roger, eyes taut and pleading, he quickly pulled his mother down the block, signaling for silence. When enough distance had been gained, words erupted from him. B

"No, we don't have a new teacher," he flared wildly. "We got a *witch* for a new teacher. It's the truth. She's from *Hansel and Gretel,* the same horrible eyes—and she steals toys. *Yes,*" he repeated in mixed outrage and hurt. "By accident, you happen to put some toys in your book bag, and she *steals* 'em. I'll fool her! I won't *bring* anymore toys to school," he howled. "Know what children are to her? Plants! She did, she called us plants. Miss Awful, that's her name."

Such was Roger's distress that his mother offered to stop at the Schrafft's on Thirteenth Street and treat him to a soda. "Who's got time for sodas?" he bleated. "I have homework to do. C Punishment homework. Ten words, ten times each. On account of the witch's spelling test."

"Ten words, ten times each?" Mrs. Clark repeated. "How many words were on the test?"

"Ten," moaned Roger. "Every one wrong. Come on, I've got to hurry home. I don't have time to waste." Refusing to be consoled, he headed for the brownstone and the desk in his room.

On Tuesday, together with the other mothers, Mrs. Clark was astonished to see the third grade march down the steps of St. Geoffrey's in military precision. Clop, clop, the children marched, looking neither to the left nor right, while behind them came a stiff-backed, iron-haired woman in a pepper-and-salt suit. "*One*, two, three, *one,* two, three," she counted, then clapped her hands in dismissal. Turning, she surveyed the assemblage of goggle-eyed mothers. "May I inquire if the mother of Joseph Lambert is among you?" she asked.

"I'm Mrs. Lambert," replied a voice meekly, whereupon Miss Orville paraded directly up to her. The rest of the mothers looked on, speechless.

"Mrs. Lambert, your son threatens to grow into a useless member of society," stated Miss Orville in ringing tones that echoed down the street. "That is, unless you term watching television useful. Joseph has confessed that he views three hours per evening."

"Only after his homework's finished," Margery Lambert allowed.

"Madame, he does not finish his homework. He idles through it, scattering mistakes higgledy-piggledy. I suggest you give him closer supervision. Good day." With a brief nod, Miss Orville proceeded down the street, and it was a full minute before the mothers had recovered enough to comment. Some voted in favor of immediate protest to Dr. Jameson, St. Geoffrey's headmaster, on the hiring of such a woman, even on a temporary basis. But since it was temporary, the mothers concluded it would have to be tolerated.

A

Nancy Reeves, Bruce's mother, kept staring at the retreating figure of Miss Orville, by now far down the block. "I know her from somewhere, I'm sure of it," she insisted, shaking her head.

The next morning, Roger refused to leave for school. "My shoes aren't shined," he wailed. "Not what Miss Awful calls shined. Where's the polish? I can't leave till I do 'em over."

"Roger, if only you'd thought of it last night," sighed Mrs. Clark.

"You sound like her," he cried. "That's what *she'd* say," and it gave his mother something to puzzle over for the rest of the day. She was still thinking about it when she joined the group of mothers outside St. Geoffrey's at three. She had to admit it was sort of impressive, the smart, martial[6] air exhibited by the third grade, as they trooped down the steps. There was to be additional ceremony today. The ranks waited on the sidewalk until Miss Orville passed back and forth in inspection. Stationing herself at the head of the columns, she boomed, "Good afternoon, boys and girls. Let us return with perfect papers tomorrow."

"Good aaaaafternoon, Miss Orville," the class sang back in unison, after which the ranks broke. Taking little Amy Lewis in tow, Miss Orville once more nodded at the mothers. "Which is she?" she asked Amy.

Miss Orville approached the trapped Mrs. Lewis. She cleared her throat, thrust back her shoulders. "Amy tells me she is fortunate enough to enjoy the services of a full-time domestic[7] at home," said Miss Orville. "May I question whether she is fortunate—or deprived? I needn't lecture you, I'm sure, Mrs. Lewis, about the wisdom of assigning a child tasks to perform at home. Setting the table, tidying up one's room, are lessons in self-reliance for the future. Surely you agree." There was a nod from Mrs. Lewis. "Excellent," smiled Miss Orville. "Amy will inform me in the morning the tasks you have assigned her. Make them plentiful, I urge you."

B

The lecturing, however, was not ended. Turning from Mrs. Lewis, Miss Orville cast her gaze around and inquired, "Is Roger Clark's mother present?"

"Yes?" spoke Virginia Clark, reaching for Roger's hand. "What is it?"

Miss Orville studied Roger silently for a long moment. "A scallywag, if ever I met one," she pronounced. The rimless spectacles lifted to the scallywag's mother. "You know, of course, that Roger is a prodigy,"[8] said Miss Orville. "A prodigy of misspelling. Roger, spell flower for us," she ordered. "Come, come, speak up."

Roger kept his head lowered. "F," he spelled. "*F-l-o-r.*"

C

"Spell castle."

"K," spelled Roger. "*K-a-z-l.*"

Miss Orville's lips parted grimly. "Those are the results, mind you, of an hour's solid work with your son, Mrs. Clark. He does not apply himself. He wishes to remain a child at play, absorbed in his toys. Is that what you want for him?"

"I—I—" Virginia Clark would have been grateful if the sidewalk had opened up to receive her.

As she reported to her husband that evening, she had never in her life been as mortified. "Spoke to me in front of all the other mothers, in loud, clarion tones," she described the scene. "Do I want Roger to remain a child at play. Imagine."

"By the way, where is Roge?" Mr. Clark asked,

6. **martial:** military.

7. **domestic:** maid.

8. **prodigy:** a highly talented child.

A. Interpreting

? Why do the mothers want to protest? (The mothers are completely intimidated; one of them has been made to feel inadequate as a parent. They can imagine how their children must be suffering.)

B. Reading Aloud

Ask for volunteers to read this passage aloud, imitating the voice of Miss Orville. Tell them to act stern, superior, and intimidating.

C. Character's Feelings

? How do you think Roger feels as he tries to spell *flower* and *castle?* (Humiliated) How do you think Virginia Clark feels? (Embarrassed, guilty—probably as inadequate as Mrs. Lambert and Mrs. Lewis were just made to feel)

A. Character's Behavior and Feelings
Mrs. Clark's gasp and her feeling of urgency regarding Roger's shoes and spelling serve as testimony to the degree to which she too has succumbed to Miss Orville and her tactics.

? Why do you think she has been affected so strongly? (She, like Roger, is submitting to an authority figure, and trying to avoid being humiliated again. Also, probably at the bottom of her heart is the belief that although Miss Orville can be mean, she's got the right values and ideas about discipline.)

B. Character
? What do Miss Orville's actions in the face of her building's demolition reveal about her? (Her actions reveal her to be a person of great conviction and one who is tenacious and stubborn. It makes us feel sorry for this stern woman.)

C. Responding
? What do you think the class is going to do to Miss Awful?

who had come home late from the office. "He's not watching television, or busy with his airplanes—"

"In his room, doing over his homework for the ninety-eighth time. It has to be perfect, he says. But, really, Charles, don't you think it was outrageous?"

Mr. Clark stirred his coffee. "I bet Miss Orville doesn't get down on the floor with the class. Or do Mexican hat dances with them."

"If that's meant to disparage Miss Wilson—" Virginia Clark stacked the dinner dishes irritably. She sometimes found her husband's behavior maddening. Especially when he took to grinning at her, as he was presently doing. She also concluded that she'd had her fill of Elizabeth's attitude on the subject. "At least some teacher's wised up to Roge," had been the Clarks' daughter's comment. "He's cute and all, but I wouldn't want to be in a shipwreck with him." Washing dishes in the kitchen, Mrs. Clark considered that maybe she wouldn't meet Roger in *front* of school tomorrow. Maybe she'd wait at the corner instead. "His shoes," she gasped, and hurried to remind
A her son to get out the polishing kit. The spelling, too, she'd better work on that . . .

It was on Thursday that Nancy Reeves finally remembered where previously she had seen Miss Orville. Perhaps it was from the shock of having received a compliment from the latter.

"Mrs. Reeves, I rejoice to inform you of progress," Miss Orville had addressed her, after the third grade had performed its military display for the afternoon. "On Monday, young Bruce's penmanship was comparable to a chicken's—if a chicken could write. Today, I was pleased to award him an A."

A tug at the tweed jacket, and the stiff-backed figure walked firmly down the street. Nancy Reeves stared after her until Miss Orville had merged into the flow of pedestrians and traffic. "I know who she is," Nancy suddenly remarked,
B turning to the other mothers. "I knew I'd seen her before. Those old ramshackle buildings near us on Hudson Street—remember when they were torn down last year?" The other mothers formed a circle around her. "Miss Orville was one of the tenants," Nancy Reeves went on. "She'd lived there for ages, and refused to budge until the landlord got a court order and deposited her on the sidewalk. I *saw* her there, sitting in a rocker on the sidewalk, surrounded by all this furniture and plants. Her picture was in the papers. Elderly retired schoolteacher . . . they found a furnished room for her on Jane Street, I think. Poor old thing, evicted like that . . . I remember she couldn't keep any of the plants . . ."

On the way home, after supplying a lurid account of the day's tortures—"Miss Awful made Walter Meade stand in the corner for saying a bad word"—Roger asked his mother, "Eviction. What does that mean?"

"It's when somebody is forced by law to vacate an apartment. The landlord gets an eviction notice, and the person has to leave."

"Kicked her out on the street. Is that what they did to the witch?"

"Don't call her that, it's rude and impolite," Mrs. Clark said, as they turned into the brownstone doorway. "I can see your father and I have been too easygoing where you're concerned."

"Huh, we've got worse names for her," Roger retorted. "*Curse* names, you should hear 'em. We're planning how to get even with Miss Awful, just you see." He paused, as his mother opened C
the downstairs door with her key. "That's where the cat used to sleep, remember?" he said, pointing at a corner of the entryway. His face was grave and earnest. "I wonder where that cat went to. Hey, Mom," he hurried to catch up, "Maybe *it* was evicted, too."

Then it was Friday at St. Geoffrey's. Before lunch, Miss Orville told the class, "I am happy to inform you that Miss Wilson will be back on Monday." She held up her hand for quiet. "This afternoon will be my final session with you. Not that discipline will relax, but I might read you a story. Robert Louis Stevenson, perhaps. My boys and girls always enjoyed him so. Forty-six years of them . . . Joseph Lambert, you're not sitting up straight. You know I don't permit slouchers in my class."

It was a mistake to have told the class that Miss Wilson would be back on Monday, that only a few hours of the terrible reign of Miss Awful were left to endure. Even before lunch recess, a certain

READING CHECK TEST

Have students match each quotation with one of these characters: Roger, Miss Orville, Mrs. Clark, Nancy Reeves, Elizabeth, Midge Fuller.

1. "School isn't supposed to be a fun fest. It's supposed to be filling that empty noodle of yours." *Elizabeth*
2. "Can you guess how many thousands of children in the world are denied the gift of schooling?" *Miss Orville*
3. "Spoke to me in front of all the other mothers, in loud, clarion tones. . . . Do I want Roger to remain a child at play. Imagine." *Mrs. Clark*
4. "That dopey old plant she's always fussing over . . . We could rip off all the dopey leaves." *Midge Fuller*
5. "Elderly retired schoolteacher . . . they found a furnished room for her on Jane Street, I think. Poor old thing, evicted like that . . . I remember she couldn't keep any of the plants. . . ." *Nancy Reeves*

spirit of challenge and defiance had infiltrated into the room. Postures were still erect, but not quite as erect. Tommy Miller dropped his pencil case on the floor, and did not request permission to pick it up.

"Ahhh, so what," he mumbled, when Miss Orville remonstrated[9] with him.

"What did you say?" she demanded, drawing herself up.

"I said, so what," Tommy Miller answered, returning her stare without distress.

9. **remonstrated:** reasoned earnestly against something.

Roger thought that was neat of Tommy, talking fresh like that. He was surprised, too, because Miss Awful didn't yell at Tommy or anything. A funny look came into her eyes, he noticed, and she just went on with the geography lesson. And when Tommy dropped his pencil case again, and picked it up without asking, she said nothing. Roger wasn't so certain that Tommy should have dropped the pencil case a second time. The lunchbell rang, then, and he piled out of the classroom with the others, not bothering to wait for permission. A

At lunch in the basement cafeteria, the third B

A. Character's Motivation

Why do you suppose Miss Awful does not yell at Tommy for dropping his pencil case? (She knows that she will be leaving soon and that any further effort to discipline the children would be a waste of time.) What do you think the "funny look" tells about how she feels? (She notes Tommy's insolence and probably feels frustrated and a bit defeated at his, and the other children's, rude behavior.)

B. Bias

By this point, the third-graders are biased against Miss Orville. Except for Roger, the students have formed a prejudice against their substitute teacher, and will not change it, no matter what she does or says. Have students note that even when Miss Orville softens her tone and appeals to the class, the children do not change their rude behavior.

Closure
Working in groups of three, students should state in their own words Miss Orville's attitude toward education. Then ask them to state their own attitude toward education.

A. Irony
? Explain the irony—something that happens contrary to your expectations—of this passage. (The irony is that it is put forth by Roger, who until now has been a strong critic of Miss Orville.)

B. Character's Feelings
? Can *you* explain Roger's feeling? Why do you think *he* can't explain it? (We now remember that Roger worries about people. He probably recognizes in Miss Orville some of the vulnerability present in the blind man and the cat. He can't explain it because his concern conflicts with his previous dislike.)

C. Word Choice
? What do the words "dammed up" suggest? (A *dam* blocks the flow of water; "dammed up" suggests that tears are coming.)

D. Interpreting
? What does this say about Miss Orville's mood? (That the children's cruelty has somehow aged her; that she feels defeated.)

grade talked of nothing except how to get even with Miss Awful. The recommendations showed daring and imagination.

"We could beat her up," Joey Lambert suggested. "We could wait at the corner till she goes by, and throw rocks at her."

"We'd get arrested," Walter Meade pointed out.

"Better idea," said Bruce Reeves. "We could go upstairs to the classroom before she gets back, and tie a string in front of the door. She'd trip, and break her neck."

A "She's old," Roger Clark protested. "We can't hurt her like that. She's too old."

It was one of the girls, actually, who thought of the plant. "That dopey old plant she's always fussing over," piped Midge Fuller. "We could rip off all the dopey leaves. That'd show her."

B Roger pushed back his chair and stood up from the table. "We don't want to do that," he said, not understanding why he objected. It was a feeling inside, he couldn't explain . . . "Aw, let's forget about it," he said. "Let's call it quits."

"The plant, the plant," Midge Fuller squealed, clapping her hands.

Postures were a good deal worse when the third grade reconvened after lunch. "Well, you've put in an industrious week, I daresay . . . ," Miss Orville commented. She opened the frayed volume of *Treasure Island* which she had brought from home and turned the pages carefully to Chapter One. "I assume the class is familiar with the tale of young Jim Hawkins, Long John Silver, and the other wonderful characters."

"No, I ain't," said Tommy Miller.

"Ain't. What word is that?"

"It's the word ain't," answered Tommy.

"Ain't, ain't," somebody jeered.

Miss Orville lowered the frayed volume. "No, children, you mustn't do this," she said with force. "To attend school is a privilege you must not mock. Can you guess how many thousands of children in the world are denied the gift of schooling?" Her lips quavered. "It is a priceless gift. You cannot permit yourselves to squander a moment of it." She rose from her desk and looked down at the rows of boys and girls. "It isn't enough any longer to accept a gift and make no return for it, not with the world in the shape it's in," she said, spectacles trembling on her bony nose. "The world isn't a playbox," she said. "If I have been severe with you this past week, it was for your benefit. The world needs good citizens. If I have helped one of you to grow a fraction of an inch, if just *one* of you—"

She stopped speaking. Her voice faltered, the words dammed up. C She was staring at the plant on the windowsill, which she had not noticed before. The stalks twisted up bare and naked, where the leaves had been torn off. "You see," Miss Orville said after a moment, going slowly to the windowsill. "You *see* what I am talking about? To be truly educated is to be civilized. Here, you may observe the opposite." Her fingers reached out to the bare stalks. "Violence and destruction . . ." She turned and faced the class, and behind the spectacles her eyes were dim and faded. "Whoever is responsible, I beg of you only to be sorry," she said. When she returned to her desk, her back was straighter than ever, but it seemed to take her longer to cover the distance. D

At the close of class that afternoon, there was no forming of lines. Miss Orville merely dismissed the boys and girls and did not leave her desk. The children ran out, some in regret, some silent, others cheerful and scampering. Only Roger Clark stayed behind.

He stood at the windows, plucking at the naked plant on the sill. Miss Orville was emptying the desk of her possessions, books, pads, a folder of maps. "These are yours, I believe," she said to Roger. In her hands were the water pistol, the baseball cards, the spool of string. "Here, take them," she said.

Roger went to the desk. He stuffed the toys in his coat pocket, without paying attention to them. He stood at the desk, rubbing his hand up and down his coat.

"Yes?" Miss Orville asked.

Roger stood back, hands at his side, and lifted his head erectly. "Flower," he spelled, "*F-l-o-w-e-r.*" He squared his shoulders and looked at Miss Orville's brimming eyes. "Castle," Roger spelled. "*C-a-s-t-l-e.*"

Then he walked from the room.

ANALYZING THE STORY

Identifying Facts

1. We learn that Roger is lively, noisy, and outgoing as well as tender and sensitive.

2. The desks have been put into rows and suddenly they hear the loud claps and barking voice of Miss Orville.

Examples include that the children must form lines, and "indulgent fawning or giving in to whims" will not be tolerated.

3. From being a carefree youngster interested mainly in play, Roger becomes a worried slave to his homework.

4. We find that she had been evicted from her apartment and forced to leave her plants behind.

5. Postures begin to droop, things are dropped on the floor and picked up without permission, and during lunch the children discuss ways to get back at Miss Orville.

6. He accepts his confiscated toys from Miss Orville and correctly spells *flower* and *castle,* the two words he has spelled incorrectly in front of his mother earlier in the week.

Responding to the Story

Analyzing the Story

Identifying Facts

1. The story's fourth paragraph describes seven-year-old Roger Clark. According to this paragraph, what **character traits,** or qualities, does Roger have?
2. On Monday morning, what is the third-grade class's first clue that things are going to be different when Miss Wilson is away? List two other things Miss Orville does that Miss Wilson does not do.
3. During the week Miss Orville is in charge, Mrs. Clark notices some drastic changes in her son's behavior. Describe how Roger's behavior has changed.
4. What do you learn about Miss Orville's life?
5. After Miss Orville tells the children their regular teacher is returning, the classroom atmosphere changes. What are three signs that the children now have a different attitude toward Miss Orville?
6. What does Roger do when he stays after class on Miss Orville's last day?

Interpreting Meanings

7. Miss Orville says that children are like plants in some ways. What details in the story indicate that she cares about plants a great deal? What does this suggest about her feelings toward children?
8. Given what you know about Miss Orville's life, can you explain *why* she demands so much of the children? Is she *really* "Miss Awful"?
9. Why do the children destroy the plant? What do you think of what they did?
10. What does Miss Orville discover about the children? What does the phrase "brimming eyes" suggest about her feelings?
11. Roger's actions at the end reveal that he has discovered something. What is this discovery? Why do you think he spells for Miss Orville?

Applying Meanings

12. How would you explain the children's cruelty in this story? How did it affect you? Is it common?
13. How do you feel about these remarks of Miss Orville's?
    a. "To attend school is a privilege you must not mock."
    b. "Can you guess how many thousands of children in the world are denied the gift of schooling?"
    c. "It isn't enough any longer to accept a gift and make no return for it, not with the world in the shape it's in."
    d. "The world isn't a playbox."

Writing About the Story

A Creative Response

1. **Describing a Character.** Write a paragraph describing a teacher, a priest, a rabbi, a Scout leader—anyone who once made an impression on you. Be sure you describe these aspects of the person:
    a. Appearance
    b. Manner of speaking
    c. Actions

A Critical Response

2. **Analyzing a Character.** Write a paragraph in which you describe Miss Orville's character. Before you write, gather data for your composition by filling out a chart like the following:

	Miss Orville
Appearance	
Key actions	
Key speeches	
Responses of other people to her	
Values	

Open your paragraph with a sentence that states your own general response to Miss Orville.

See Teacher's Manual page 51.

Interpreting Meanings

7. She brings a plant to class the first day and fusses over it. Later she makes a comparison between plants and children for the class. When the children destroy her plant, her eyes go dim and her movements falter. Also we learn that she had plants in her old apartment before she was evicted.

It suggests that she also values children highly, and is very concerned that they, too, receive proper care.

8. Answers will vary. We know from the facts behind her eviction that she stands up for what she believes in against all odds, so it is not surprising when she takes the same rigid standard when dealing with children. It appears from what she says about plants and children that she believes the proper care of children demands precision and strict attention to form, and that when these conditions are met, growth *(Answers continue on page 170.)*

(Answers begin on page 169.)
and development comes. Indeed, in the case of Bruce Reeves and Roger Clark, the results are almost immediate, and she recognizes them and appreciates them. She praises Bruce in front of his mother, and she could only be pleased (despite her tears) when Roger correctly spells *castle* and *flower.* So "Miss Awful" may not be so awful after all.

9. The children destroy the plant because they know it will hurt Miss Orville's feelings.

Answers may vary. Most students will say it was wrong to destroy the plant, not only because it hurt Miss Orville's feelings, but also because destruction of property is wrong and shows lack of respect for Miss Orville as a teacher and as a person.

10. Miss Orville discovers that children can be violent and destructive.

The phrase suggests that her feelings have indeed been hurt.

11. Roger has discovered that the part of him that is soft and tender cares a lot about Miss Orville. He probably spells for Miss Orville to try to make her feel better and to show that he respects her. Roger
(Answers continue in left-hand column.)

(Continued from top.)
has also discovered that he can be a good student, and perhaps he wants to show her this.

Applying Meanings

12. Answers will vary. Some students may say that the children were responding defensively because they genuinely feared Miss Orville and felt threatened by her high standards.

Answers will vary.

13. Answers will vary. See Teacher's Manual page 51 for suggested possible answers.

Analyzing Language and Vocabulary

Homonyms

Homonyms are words that sound alike but are spelled differently and have different meanings. For example, *see* and *sea* are homonyms. Homonyms give people difficulty with spelling. For each statement below, choose the correct homonym from the pair in parentheses.

1. (There, Their) books are in the locker.
2. I (new, knew) it was too late to turn back.
3. Nell has a (pane, pain) in her back tooth.
4. The movie (aisle, isle) is full of popcorn.
5. Roger dared not (brake, break) any rules while Miss Orville was his teacher.
6. The (colonel, kernel) had never seen combat.
7. Miss Orville thinks watching television is a (waste, waist) of time.
8. Eldridge's favorite breakfast is (serial, cereal) with milk and fruit.
9. We decided to grill (stakes, steaks) for dinner.
10. The city is putting up a hospital on that (site, sight).

For answers, see Teacher's Manual page 51.

Reading About the Writer

Arthur Cavanaugh (1918–) was born in New York City and has lived there all his life. Many of his short stories are about the members of the Clark family, who bear a strong resemblance to his own family. Cavanaugh has also written several novels, including *The Children Are Gone,* about a babysitter who steals her young charges. His most recent book is a historical novel called *The Faithful,* about the experiences of the Irish immigrants to America.

Focusing on Background

A Real Life Story

" 'Miss Awful' is a story based on the experiences of my son at school. We lived in New York and Frank, who was eight, attended a little school in Greenwich Village. To hear him tell of it, the days at school were a happy mixture of games, crayons, milk and cookies, and outings to the playground across the street. One night when I got home from work, Frank indignantly announced that his teacher was out sick and, worse, replaced by a crabby old lady who did nothing but admonish the class for their lack of discipline and scholarship. 'Honest, you wouldn't believe how awful she is,' Frank assured me. But I noticed a marked change in my son, at night when I came home. Where before he was sprawled in front of the television, I'd find him bent over his homework or actually voluntarily reading a book. The night that I discovered him wrestling with a dictionary, looking up words for a quiz the next day, I knew that 'Miss Awful' had scored a victory on behalf of education. And when the following week I heard from Frank that his regular teacher was back at her desk, the tinge of regret in his voice was unmistakable.

"All of my stories have been drawn from life, usually long after the incident happened, but 'Miss Awful' was the exception, taking shape as the story happened right in front of me."

—Arthur Cavanaugh

PREREADING

1. BUILDING ON PRIOR KNOWLEDGE. Before they read, discuss with students the attachment people have for their pets. To illustrate the point, have students recall the selection "Princess" and ask them to describe the relationship between Doña Nereida and her dog. Have students also recall how Doña Nereida responded to the loss of Princess. Point out that a tragedy such as this often causes people to change their feelings and modify their behavior, as is evidenced by the fact that Doña Nereida invited Judy into her home after Princess's death. Ask students to describe the attachment some pet owners they know have for their pets. Ask those students who are pet owners themselves to describe their own feelings for their pets.

2. ESTABLISHING A PURPOSE. Before students begin reading, you might have them read question 6 on page 177.

3. PREREADING JOURNAL. Before they read, have students write a brief description of what might be their idea of the "saddest day the summer had."

A. Tone

? How would you describe the tone of the story? (Sad, tragic) Why? (Because of the words "saddest day the summer had," "it will be hard to write it," "will break my heart")

B. Expression

This is a common expression used when describing someone who is not very smart. Here, the narrator makes a joke by applying the expression literally to Eleanor.

Texas Essential Elements/(a) English Language Arts: 1B Purpose and audience; **1E** Formal/informal language; **3A** Plot/character; **4F** Generalizations

THE SADDEST DAY THE SUMMER HAD

Dick Perry

Here is a rite-of-passage or coming-of-age story, in which the kids behave in the ways kids often do—they quarrel. They quarrel to pass the time; they quarrel for the sake of quarreling; maybe they quarrel to cover up any affectionate feelings they might have. At any rate, they quarrel until a major event, a loss, causes these same children to reveal entirely different feelings for one another.

A Now I must write about the saddest day the summer had. It will be hard to write it and I may not write it well. It's about Sarah's dog. I haven't told you much about him, hardly mentioned him at all in fact, but I have my reasons. To write about him will break my heart.

But Raymond said this has to do with the summer, too. He said I should tell everything, not just the sunny parts. So I'm going to tell you about Sarah's dog.

As I said, his name was Eleanor Roosevelt, which was a dumb name to give a dog that's a boy. I had nothing against the name itself. Mr. Roosevelt was a nice President. I had nothing against his wife. I'd never met the lady. But I must be honest. I didn't care for Eleanor Roosevelt the dog. B He was dumb. He didn't know enough to come in out of the rain. That's true. He would stand dripping wet in a cloudburst and wonder where the water was coming from. He wouldn't go inside. He figured it was raining everywhere.

Another thing: Sarah kept wanting him to bite us.

"Go bite 'em!" she'd shout at Eleanor. "Sic Raymond! Sic George! Sic, sic, sic!"

But Eleanor was too dumb. He'd look at her, bemused,[1] and wag his tail. Any dog that doesn't know enough to come in out of the rain doesn't know enough to bite people, either. All he knew was that Sarah loved him. That was all he wanted to know. She was his universe. He'd tag after her—or sleep and wait for her return. He wasn't an angry dog. He was a lazy dog.

He was a red-haired dog who stared at other dogs in disbelief; he thought he was people. Once Sarah said he was a River collie but Raymond looked up River collies at the library and said he wasn't. Then Sarah said he was an English springer spaniel, then a Chesapeake Bay retriever, then an Irish setter, then a combination bloodhound, basset, and beagle. Raymond looked these up, too, and said she was nuts. She shouted she had papers to prove it. When Raymond demanded to see the papers she threw a stone and told Eleanor to bite Raymond on the leg, but Eleanor didn't. It was beginning to rain and Eleanor was staring puzzled at the sky, wondering what was making him wet.

Other dogs—and our neighborhood had lots of them—chased streetcars, snarled at the mailman, and pursued bank robbers through the woods, but

Slang. As Raymond and Sarah are teasing each other, Raymond says people think Sarah is "loony." She replies, "A fat lot you know." The word *loony* and the expression "a fat lot" are examples of slang. Some slang words and phrases fall out of use with time. As you read this story, which is set in the 1930's, look for slang expressions that might no longer be fashionable. SRW p. 83

1. **bemused:** stunned and confused.

For a detailed lesson plan on this story, see Teacher's Manual pages 52–54. A biography of Dick Perry appears on text page 178.

SUPPLEMENTARY SUPPORT MATERIAL

1. Vocabulary Activity Sheet
3. Reading Check Test blackline master
3. Selection Test (page 55 of Test Book)
4. Reader's Response Journal
5. Workbook (page 43)

DEVELOPING VOCABULARY

The following words appear on a test in the Test Book, page 56. (See also the Vocabulary Activity Sheet.)

cloudburst	swerve
bemused	complimented
combination	unnerving
distasteful	cringe
touchy	fitfully

Humanities Connection: Responding to the Fine Art

American painter R. A. Parker (1922–   ) was born in South Dakota and educated at the State University of Iowa. Among his distinctions are membership in the National Council on the Arts and a Guggenheim Fellowship.

? What details of the painting stand out more than others? How does the artist accomplish this? What is the first word that comes to your mind when you look at the painting?

★ **Texas Essential Elements/(c) Reading: 3A** Main ideas/details; **3D** Generalizations; **3I** Draw conclusions; **4D** Diagrams/graphs

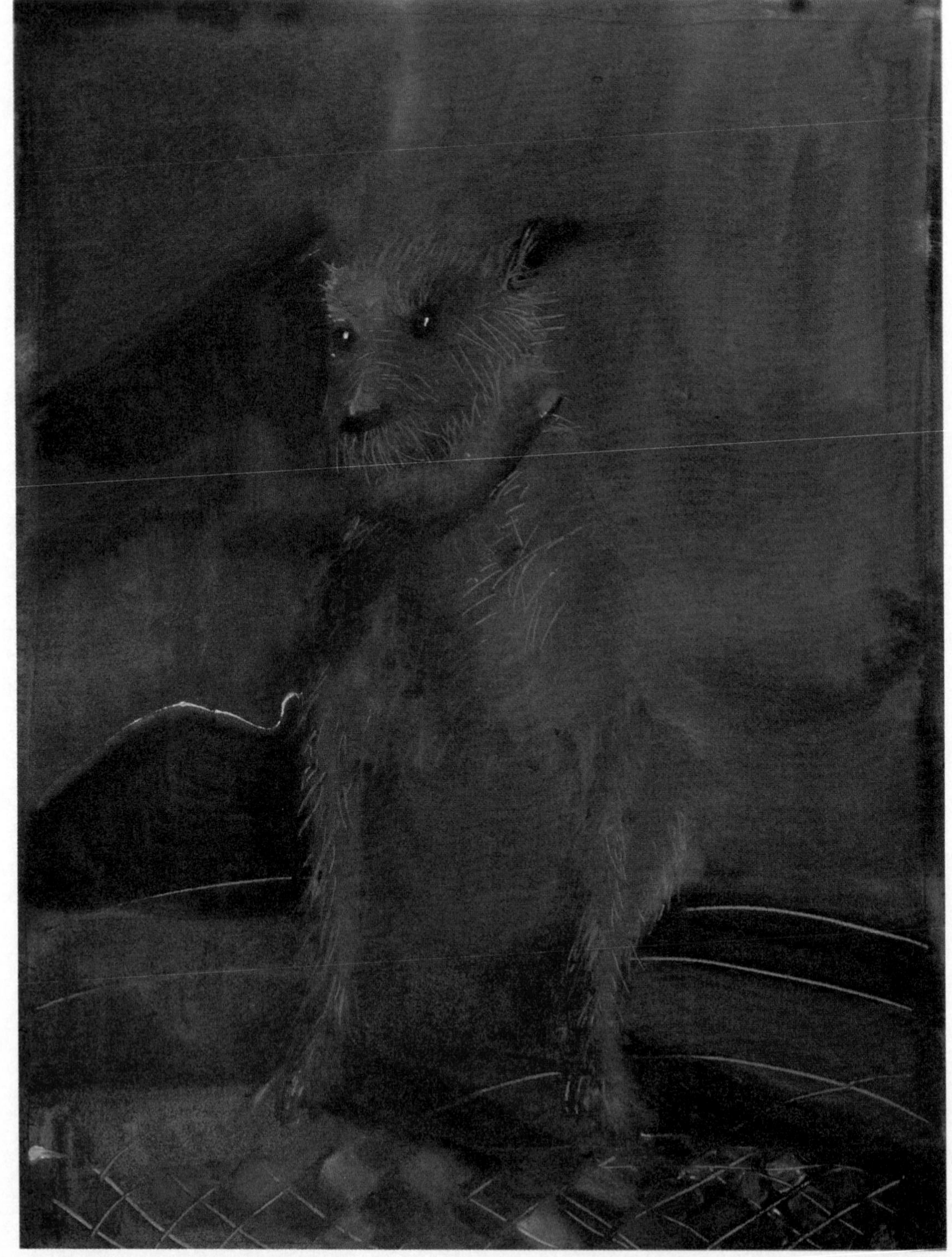

Terry by R. A. Parker (1987). Watercolor. Courtesy Terry Dintenfass Gallery, New York.

not Eleanor. No wood-running for him. He wanted no part of the forest. The idea of walking where there were no sidewalks was distasteful and uncivilized. He didn't know what a tree was. He used a fireplug. Whenever Sarah took him in the woods to play she had to carry him every step of the way. Otherwise Eleanor wouldn't budge. It was dumb. Raymond and I would be horsing in the woods, and along the path would come Sarah, her dog in her arms.

"I'm taking him for a walk," she would say.

"Then why don't you let him walk," I said one time.

She glared at me and stomped away. She was touchy where Eleanor was concerned. But the next time I saw her, she hit me on the jaw. That was three days later, but her memory and her left hook were fierce. A

Raymond, of course, was forever teasing about the dog's name.

"Eleanor Roosevelt is a *girl's* name," he said one day. "You can't give a girl's name to a boy dog."

"A fat lot you know," Sarah said. "I happen to like Eleanor Roosevelt."

She looked for a rock to throw.

"It's not legal," Raymond said. "There's probably something in the Constitution that says you can't name a boy dog after a president's wife."

"The only thing the Constitution doesn't allow," said Sarah, "is drinking beer. And they're even changing *that*!"[2]

"Don't come running to me," said Raymond, "when Secret Service agents come and shoot you."

"My dog will bite them all," Sarah sneered.

"He doesn't know how to bite," Raymond sneered back.

"Someday he's going to bite you something awful," Sarah said, sticking out her tongue.

"You still can't call him Eleanor Roosevelt," Raymond said while her tongue was out. "People think you're loony. What other girl stands around, whistling through her teeth, snapping her fingers, and yelling 'Eleanor Roosevelt'?"

"A fat lot you know," she bellowed. B

Raymond threw up his hands in despair. "They're going to come after you with a net!"

Before she heaved a stone, Raymond ran.

Eleanor Roosevelt—the dog, not the First Lady; see how Sarah confused things—didn't chase Raymond. He had been sleeping throughout their whole argument. When Raymond ran, the dog woke up, stared after Raymond, yawned, checked to see if Sarah was near, and promptly went back to sleep again. He worried about Sarah, but the rest of the world he took as it came. When freight trains rattled by our tenements, he dozed. Unable to solve rain, he didn't try to solve why the ground shook. He worried about Sarah. That was all. He didn't worry about streetcars, dogs, automobiles, rain, where his next meal was coming from, or fleas, which is one reason he had so many.

Sarah was his moon and his sun. When she was away he dozed fitfully, troubled, wondering when she would come back to him. He lay in the sun and dreamed worried dreams of a world without Sarah. But when she called or whistled, his worry vanished. His universe was complete again. He perked up, stretched, shook his head because her whistle hurt, wagged his tail, and ran to her—that is, he ran to her if she was on a sidewalk. If she was in the woods, that was another matter. He couldn't go there. Only animals ran in the woods. There were no sidewalks to run on. If that happened, he would crumble back to sleep and worry some more. C

Oh, he crossed the street, of course. There was a sidewalk on the other side. But beyond the sidewalk was the woods. He would never venture there. To him, crossing the street held no danger. Automobiles slammed on their brakes, honked wildly, and swerved around him. He didn't give them the time of day. Streetcar motormen hated to travel his section of the street. They couldn't make their streetcars swerve and he ignored their clanging bells. So streetcars moved slowly through his domain. He had no time to think of traffic. He spent all his time thinking of Sarah.

But I have been avoiding the day I was supposed to write about. I can't avoid it any longer. It wouldn't be fair.

2. The story takes places in 1933, when Prohibition laws forbidding the sale and manufacture of alcoholic beverages were being struck down.

A. Conflict and Character

What does the fact that Sarah hits the narrator indicate about her? (That she can resort to violence to settle disputes. She finds it difficult to argue the point because she probably realizes the narrator is right—Eleanor should be able to walk in the woods.)

B. Character

What does Sarah's repetition of this phrase tell about her character? (Combined with her use of violence, it shows that she's not a very persuasive arguer—she also resorts to pat insults.)

C. Anthropomorphism

Anthropomorphism is giving human characteristics to an animal. What examples are in this paragraph? (That Eleanor is "troubled" and is "wondering when she will come back to him"; he couldn't go to the woods because "only animals ran in the woods.") This will help students answer question 7.

A. Dialogue, Conflict, and Complications The confrontational nature of this dialogue and of that to follow is symptomatic of and complicates the escalating conflict between Sarah, Raymond, and the narrator.

? How does the tone of the conversation complicate the situation? (The angry tone makes it increasingly difficult for the three to back down and resolve their differences.)

B. Expansion George Herman "Babe" Ruth (1895–1948) is one of professional baseball's legends. A New York Yankee, Ruth was the first great home run hitter. He set numerous major-league records, and was one of the first to be elected to the National Baseball Hall of Fame.

C. Word Choice

? How would the tone of the argument be if the writer had said "cried" instead of "brayed"? (*Braying* is a loud, harsh cry made by a donkey—the tone of the argument is getting more violent.)

Well, nothing much happened that morning. We played baseball in Mount Echo Park and almost won. Sarah, naturally, hit three home runs, whistled through her teeth, and got dirty looks from both teams. That afternoon, after lunch, the three of us—her, Raymond, and me—sat in a tree and discussed the game.

"You freaks," said Sarah, "have got to keep your eye on the ball. That's the only way you'll learn to hit."

"Ha," I said, and meant it.

She looked at me with scorn. "The strikeout king," she snorted, and made a face at me. "You shut your eyes before the pitcher even pitches."

"I don't!"

"You do!"

There was a pause. I had to be honest.

A "Well, not *all* the time," I said.

"See what I mean," Sarah said. "The strikeout king!"

"Quit picking on him," Raymond said. "He's the best outfielder we got."

I felt better.

"He's the only outfielder we got," Sarah said.

I felt bad again.

"Pick on somebody your own size," Raymond said.

That shut her up a minute.

"Anyway," Raymond said, "you got no reason to brag. Your dumb dog is afraid to get his feet dirty. He won't walk in the woods. He's afraid to." Raymond looked at me with pride. "George is braver than *that*."

I didn't know whether to feel complimented or
B not. I'd rather have been compared to Babe Ruth. I was about to tell Raymond this but I didn't get the chance.

"A fat lot you know," Sarah seethed. "Eleanor Roosevelt is afraid of *nothing!*" She glared at me. "You hide from thunder. Eleanor doesn't."

"Yes, but Eleanor is a dog and I'm . . ." I tried to say, wishing they'd leave me out of it. But Sarah didn't let me finish.

C "Scaredy-cat," she brayed. "I'd rather have a dog than a scaredy-cat!"

"You don't have a dog," Raymond said. He was getting angry. "Real dogs go walking in the woods. You have to carry yours!"

"A fat lot you know," Sarah said. She was getting angry, too.

"*I* don't have to carry George," Raymond shouted.

I wished he hadn't shouted that. I wasn't his dog. I was his friend.

"*Eleanor* wouldn't shut his eyes when he's at bat!" Sarah shouted.

"*George* doesn't have fleas!" Raymond shouted back.

They argued like that for a half hour. Sometimes I was ahead, sometimes her dog was. Sometimes Sarah offered to fist fight Raymond. Sometimes he offered to fist fight her. They were careful not to offer to fist fight at the same time.

"I won't fight a girl," Raymond would say.

Another time Sarah would say:

"I won't fight a boy. I hate to see boys cry."

It was an awful afternoon.

"I'll bet," said Raymond, "your dumb dog doesn't know enough to save your life. I'll bet . . ."

"He's fierce as a tiger," Sarah said. "Watch your mouth."

"On *sidewalks,*" Raymond sneered. "He scares people with his snores!"

"A fat lot you know!"

"If you were *really* in trouble," Raymond said, "here in the woods he wouldn't lift a finger. There are no sidewalks here."

Sarah put her hands on her hips. She almost fell out of the tree doing it.

"He'll save my life whenever I want," she said.

Raymond laughed at her.

"Not here," he said. "No sidewalks."

"Up here, too!"

"Prove it!"

She looked at him, furious. But her glance wavered. I saw it and so did Raymond. We knew why. Right then, at that exact moment, her dog was asleep on a sidewalk somewhere, waiting for her to come back to him. Sarah could whistle and he'd cross the street like a blur and zoom to her, unnerving motorists and making streetcar motormen cringe. But would he run into the woods and seek her out? That was the question. He was a sidewalk dog. Would he, perhaps, wait where the sidewalk ended, whining for someone to carry him to the

Critical Comment

In his review of *Raymond and Me That Summer,* the novel from which "The Saddest Day the Summer Had" was taken, writer Kurt Vonnegut said, ". . . It is a book of tears and laughter for people without any sense of humor whatsoever. . . ."

Read the quotation to students and have them discuss it. Then ask students to tell whether they found any humor in the "The Saddest Day the Summer Had" and, if so, to identify it. Have them comment on how the story can evoke tears and laughter from its readers.

A. Responding

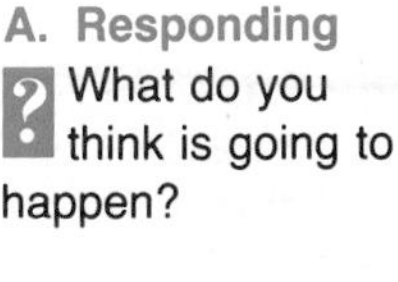
What do you think is going to happen?

rescue in the woods? This was why Sarah's glance wavered. Raymond had backed her into a corner she didn't want to be in.

"Why should I prove it?" she said. "There's nothing but sissy-britches here. There's nothing to be scared of."

"If you call him and he comes," said Raymond, "I'll eat dirt."

That was the supreme challenge. Sarah couldn't refuse. Raymond had put his honor on the line and was waiting for hers.

"Tomorrow," she hedged.

"Now," said Raymond.

He climbed down from the tree.

"Well?" he said.

There was an awful pause.

"I hate you," she said.

She was distressed. But when she looked at Raymond her distress went away. Anger returned. She climbed down from the tree and started along the path.

"Get ready to eat dirt," she said.

We followed her.

Moments later, Sarah, Raymond, and me stood in the shadows at the forest's edge. Our tenements were down the path and across the street. I watched Sarah as she looked from behind a bush and saw, across the street, her dog sleeping fitfully in the sun.

This was her put-up-or-shut-up hour. Would Eleanor Roosevelt come to her—or stop where the sidewalk stopped? A

Reading Check Test

1. Eleanor Roosevelt was a female dog. (*False*)
2. Sarah once hit George on the jaw. (*True*)
3. George was a poor hitter in baseball. (*True*)
4. Raymond bet Sarah that Eleanor Roosevelt wouldn't come to her in the woods. (*True*)
5. The car that hit Eleanor Roosevelt did not stop. (*False*)

Closure

Have students work in pairs and discuss how an author's writing style can affect a story. In this story, the author uses a lot of dialogue. Ask students if this style was effective in telling the story, and why.

A. Suspense

? How does the author prolong suspense in this paragraph? (By portraying Eleanor Roosevelt as doubtful and hesitant, the author prolongs the reader's own doubts about what the dog will do and the suspense of the moment.)

B. Character

? What does Raymond's advice to the narrator indicate about Raymond? (His new-found maturity and sensitivity)

Her eyes narrowed with worry.

"It's your move," said Raymond. "Whistle for Eleanor."

She closed her eyes.

Was she praying?

"I'll show you how wonderful my dog is," she said, putting two fingers to her mouth, and the neighborhood was deafened by the force of her whistle. "Watch," she said. "Now just you watch."

We did.

A Her dog stirred, raised up, cocked his head, and with a look of surprise and doubt searched the hillside for the whistle's source. First his tail thumped with gladness. Sarah had come back. Then it slowed and thumped with hesitation. Sarah had never called him to the woods before, his tail said. He got up, shook himself, and studied the hillside some more. She's never called me to the hill before, his look said.

"Well," said Raymond. "He's not coming."

"He is!" said Sarah—and whistled again.

Her dog couldn't locate Sarah but he knew she was there and she wanted him. Love replaced doubt. Need replaced reason. He was a red smear—tail wagging, body low, feet flying—as he zoomed across the street, ignoring cars, ignoring everything, following his heart to seek his one true north: Sarah behind a tree.

"There!" she shouted gleefully.

But her shout died on her lips.

I can still hear the thud. The car that hit her dog wasn't going fast. The thud was noisier than any noise that ever was. I can still see her dog sailing through the air to crash against a curbstone, dead.

Her shout died when her dog did.

I can still see her running down the path, stumbling, and I can still hear the moan she moaned. I can still see her pick up her lifeless dog, cradle him in her arms, and talk to him words of regret he didn't hear.

As Raymond and I approached, the driver of the car approached. He was a nice man, shaken; he didn't mean harm. I heard him say:

"I'm sorry, I'm sorry. . . ."

Other people came. They always do. They recited where they had been when it happened. They attached great importance to this. They recited what each had seen. They compared notes. They managed to turn the death of Sarah's dog into an event as ordinary as rain. They indexed and catalogued the happening and were done with it. Then they stood and talked of other things.

But Raymond, his face white and his soul in torment, said:

"It was my fault."

Sarah looked at him. The hurt in her eyes showed the hurt in her heart.

She shook her head.

"No," she said. "I called him when I shouldn't have."

She gazed around at neighbors who had ceased to talk of her dog's death.

"I better bury him," she said.

No one moved forward.

They compared the death of this dog with other animal deaths they had witnessed and filed.

"I'll help you," said Raymond.

"No!" she cried, stricken.

Then she looked surprised. She shook her head and tried to smile. It wasn't the day for smiling.

"Please," she said. "But no."

She walked away from the crowd. They hardly noticed her go. She carried her dog across the street into the woods. She walked slowly. There was no need to hurry. It was their last walk in the woods together. Last walks require goodbyes.

I started after her but Raymond touched my arm. B

"Not yet," he said.

She vanished in the shadows of the trees. The driver drove away. The people laughed and talked of other things. A streetcar passed, slowed, then speeded up. Soon motormen would spread the word: No need to slow down there again; the dog is gone.

Raymond and I sat on the curb and watched the hill.

Finally, Raymond sighed a terrible sigh.

"Let's go to her," he said.

We didn't know exactly where she was. We took the main path up the hill. We didn't go too far. Raymond, in front of me, motioned me to stop. He pointed.

But I had seen it, too. It was a fresh-dug grave,

Analyzing the Story
Identifying Facts
1. They are Sarah, Raymond, and George, the narrator.
Sarah criticizes the baseball skills of George and Raymond. Raymond criticizes Sarah's dog. George disagrees with Sarah but does not pursue the argument.
2. He doesn't come inside when it rains. He stares at other dogs as if they are a different species. He is afraid to go in the woods.
3. First they argue about who is the worst baseball player. Then they argue about whether Eleanor Roosevelt is afraid of the woods. George prefers to be left out of the argument, even though he is often the subject.
4. Sarah agrees to call Eleanor from the woods to prove that he is not afraid of going there.
5. He runs out in front of a car and is killed.

Interpreting Meanings
6. The friends learn that a petty argument can have tragic consequences. The friends also learn that tragedy can bring
(Answers continue on page 178.)

Responding
? What do you think is going to have to happen to Sarah before she will be able to think well of the world again?

fresh-covered. It was a little grave but he had been a little dog.

I looked up—and there she was.

Sarah, forlorn, sat in a tree on the highest branch that would hold her. Her hands, black from digging, were in her lap. She didn't swing her feet. She didn't say hello. She stared up to where God was. She didn't look down at us. We were of the world and the world hadn't been too good to her. It had taken her dog away.

Raymond motioned me to follow him. We went along a path. Once out of her sight, he stopped. He looked around. He found some sticks and made them into a cross. He tied the cross together with grass. He worked swiftly and silently. I stood by and said nothing. Then we walked back to where the dog was buried.

Without a word, Raymond forced the cross into the ground to make the grave complete.

Sarah, hearing this, looked down.

"I tried," she said lonesomely. "But I didn't know how to make a cross."

Raymond and Sarah stared at each other the longest time.

Then Raymond said:

"Come on. I'll take you home."

Responding to the Story

Analyzing the Story

Identifying Facts

1. Who are the three main **characters** in this story? How does each one behave toward the others?
2. List three characteristics of Eleanor Roosevelt that make him different from other dogs.
3. After the baseball game, Sarah and Raymond get into an argument. What are they arguing about? What part does George play?
4. What challenge from Raymond does Sarah accept, and why?
5. Describe what happens to Eleanor Roosevelt.

Interpreting Meanings

6. The events of the story bring discovery as well as sadness. Explain what lessons about life and about themselves the friends have learned during the course of this summer day.
7. Find at least three places in the story where the writer tells us what Eleanor is thinking or feeling. Where is Eleanor described as if he is a human being?
8. How did this story make you feel about the dog, the children, and the accident?
9. At the beginning of the story, the writer says he "may not write it well." Do you think he has written it well, or not? Why?
10. Who do you think was responsible for the dog's death—Sarah or Raymond? Or was it no one's direct responsibility?

Applying Meanings

11. After the accident, what do other people say and do? Why do you think they want to turn the tragedy into "an event as ordinary as rain"? Have you seen people respond like this to a tragedy?
12. Explain why people sometimes do not want to talk about a painful event immediately, but instead want to think privately about it.

Writing About the Story

A Creative Response

1. **Writing a Journal Entry.** In a paragraph, write one of the following journal entries. Use the first-person pronoun, *I*.
   a. Sarah describing how she feels about the accident.
   b. Raymond describing his feelings about the part he played in the accident.

A Critical Response

2. **Describing a Character.** In a paragraph, write a character sketch of Eleanor. Before you write, list the ways in which the dog behaves, how he feels about Sarah, and what the narrator says directly about him. Open your paragraph with a statement telling, in general, what kind of a pet Eleanor was. You might organize your details in a chart like the following:

(Answers begin on page 177.) them together after disagreements have driven them apart.
7. Eleanor is described as if he is a human being on page 171 ("All he knew was that Sarah loved him . . ."); page 173, right-hand column ("He worried about Sarah . . ."); and page 176, left-hand column ("Her dog stirred, raised up, cocked his head, and with a look of surprise and doubt searched the hillside . . .").
8. Answers may vary. Most students will feel sorry for the dog, since he was so devoted to his mistress. Students may also pity Raymond and Sarah, for allowing their pride and emotions to get the better of them, as well as admire them for recognizing that their friendship goes deeper than their feelings of anger and pride. The accident itself, though it is discreetly and unsentimentally described, will probably affect some students deeply, especially those who have a pet or who can identify with this situation.
9. Answers may vary. Most students will find the story well written, especially because the descriptions of the action are vivid and the dialogue revealing the char- *(Answers continue in left-hand column.)*

(Continued from top.) acters' motivations and behavior is realistic. Some students may find the beginning of the story, in which the author introduces the dog, sets the scene, and suggests the basis for the conflict, a bit drawn out since it lacks specific action.
10. Answers may vary. (See Teacher's Manual page 53 for suggested possible answers.)

Applying Meanings
11. Other people come to the scene of the accident and tell each other what they saw and where they saw it from, comparing notes with each other.
Answers may vary. (See Teacher's Manual 53.)
12. Answers may vary. (See Teacher's Manual page 53 for suggested possible answers.)

FURTHER READING FOR STUDENTS
Students will enjoy "A Game of Catch" by Richard Wilbur, the touching story of a few kids who play baseball.

	Character Traits
What the narrator says directly about the dog	
How the dog feels about Sarah	
How the dog behaves	

3. **Analyzing Conflict.** Like most literature, this story is about several **conflicts,** or struggles. Some of these conflicts are **external**—they take place between two characters. Some conflicts are **internal**—they take place between opposing desires or feelings within one character's mind and heart. In a paragraph, describe what you believe is this story's most important conflict. Identify this conflict as either external or internal. Then explain why you feel this conflict is very important. Is it ever resolved?

See Teacher's Manual page 54.

Analyzing Language and Vocabulary

Slang

SRW p. 83

Slang is a kind of nonstandard language often used by members of a group. Teen-agers have been especially good at making up new slang words and at adapting existing words for slang use. Most slang words go out of fashion very quickly. Many slang words and expressions that are popular today will require explanations a few years from now.

Below is a group of slang words and expressions, some from today and some from the past. How would each statement be rephrased in standard English? That is, how would you rephrase each statement if you were using it in a formal speech? You may need to ask your parents or older sisters or brothers about some of these.

1. We're going to be late if we don't *skedaddle.*
2. The teachers get together and *rap* about the students.
3. Carmen's dress is *smashing*!
4. I think that album is *groovy.*
5. When it comes to math, James is an *airhead.*
6. Roger has some kind of *hang-up* about tests.
7. That movie is totally *awesome*!
8. Bebe's hairdo is *far out.*
9. Ricardo thinks he's the *cat's pajamas.*
10. Mac's got a *cool* new car.

For answers, see Teacher's Manual page 54.

Reading About the Writer

Dick Perry (1922–) was born in Cincinnati, Ohio. He has always been involved in writing and broadcasting—besides publishing several books and plays, he has worked in advertising, radio, and television. He says humorously of his own life (referring to himself in the third person), "He attended Oberlin College but didn't graduate. He attended University of Chicago but didn't graduate. He attended Western Hills High School and did graduate. In reality, you have to look backward and not forward to show he is any kind of success at all."

PREREADING

1. **BUILDING ON PRIOR KNOWLEDGE.** Before reading this story, ask students whether they have ever found something out gradually through subtle clues and snatches of conversation. What did they find out? (A truth about a relative or neighbor, a family financial problem, something about their parents' past?) What clues led them to this discovery?

2. **ESTABLISHING A PURPOSE.** The headnote sets a good purpose for reading this story.

3. **PREREADING JOURNAL.** Before they read, have students write a brief speech in which they try to persuade their audience of the need to donate food and/or money to the poor.

Texas Essential Elements/(a) English Language Arts: 1B Purpose and audience; **4A** Word meaning; **4E** Predict; **4F** Generalizations

CHRISTMAS

Floyd Dell

This is a true story. It took place in Chicago at the end of the last century, but the story has a very modern flavor. See if you agree that it could take place today, even in your own town. As you read, notice when *you* begin to realize something that the young narrator does not yet know. How does this knowledge make you feel?

A That fall, before it was discovered that the soles of both my shoes were worn clear through, I still went to Sunday school. And one time the Sunday school superintendent made a speech to all the classes. He said that these were hard times and that many poor children weren't getting enough to eat. It was the first time that I had heard about it. He asked everybody to bring some food for the poor children next Sunday. I felt very sorry for the poor children.

Also little envelopes were distributed to all the classes. Each little boy and girl was to bring money for the poor, next Sunday. The pretty Sunday school teacher explained that we were to write our names, or have our parents write them, up in the left-hand corner of the little envelopes. . . . I told my mother all about it when I came home. And my mother gave me, the next Sunday, a small bag of potatoes to carry to Sunday school. I supposed the poor children's mothers would make potato soup out of them. . . . Potato soup was good. My father, who was quite a joker, would always say, as if he were surprised, "Ah! I see we have some nourishing soup today!" It was so good
B that we had it every day. My father was at home all day long and every day, now; and I liked that, even if he was grumpy as he sat reading General Grant's *Memoirs*. I had my parents all to myself, too; the others were away. My oldest brother was in Quincy, and memory does not reveal where the others were: perhaps with relatives in the country.

Taking my small bag of potatoes to Sunday school, I looked around for the poor children; I was disappointed not to see them. I had heard about poor children in stories. But I was told just to put my contribution with the others on the big table in the side room.

I had brought with me the little yellow envelope, with some money in it and sealed up. My mother wouldn't tell me how much money she had put in it, but it felt like several dimes. Only she wouldn't let me write my name on the envelope. I had learned to write my name, and I was proud of being able to do it. But my mother said firmly, *no,* I must *not* write my name on the envelope; she didn't tell me why. On the way to Sunday school I had pressed the envelope against the coins until I could tell what they were; they weren't dimes but pennies.

When I handed in my envelope, my Sunday-school teacher noticed that my name wasn't on it, and she gave me a pencil; I could write my own name, she said. So I did. But I was confused because my mother had said not to; and when I came home, I confessed what I had done. She looked distressed. "I told you not to!" she said. C
But she didn't explain why. . . .

I didn't go back to school that fall. My mother said it was because I was sick. I did have a cold the week that school opened; I had been playing

> **Connotations.** In the first paragraph, the narrator feels pity when he hears about the "poor" children. The word *poor* has many strong connotations. **Connotations** are the emotions and associations that are attached to some words. What feelings do you have about someone called "poor"? Notice how the word *poor* affects the boy's feelings in this true story.

A. Point of View The point of view (discussed in detail on text page 190) is very important to this story, since we only see things through the narrator's eyes.

? From what point of view is the story told? (First-person) How do you know? (The pronoun *I*)

B. Making Inferences

? What two things can we infer from this passage? (Potatoes are a cheap and nourishing staple and often become the mainstay of a diet when times are hard. That they have potato soup every day tells us that they probably can't afford much in the way of food. We can also infer that the father is home every day because he is out of work.)

C. Interpreting

? Why is the mother upset? (Probably because she didn't want the Sunday school to find out that she hardly gave any money—in other words, that she couldn't afford it.)

For a detailed lesson plan on this selection, see Teacher's Manual pages 54–57. A biography of Floyd Dell appears on text page 182.

SRW p. 27

SUPPLEMENTARY SUPPORT MATERIAL

1. Vocabulary Activity Sheet
2. Reading Check Test blackline master
3. Selection Test (page 57 of Test Book)
4. Reader's Response Journal
5. Workbook (page 45)

DEVELOPING VOCABULARY

The following words appear on a test in the Test Book, page 58. (See also the Vocabulary Activity Sheet.)

superintendent	cooped up
distributed	arrogant
nourishing	bewilderment
grumpy	numb
confessed	ebbed

Critical Comment

Writing about Floyd Dell, one critic has said that "his main interest was to show the emotional and intellectual growth of characters."

Discuss the quotation with students and have them tell whether and how successfully Dell achieves his main interest in the story "Christmas."

A. Character's Motivation
The narrator's knowledge of the day on which Christmas fell in 1893 comes as a result of research he did as an adult.
? What motivates the narrator to go through the trouble of researching this information? (He recognizes its importance later on as an event that changed his life.)

B. Conflict
The conflict between the narrator and his parents sets the stage for the revelation to and subsequent transformation of the narrator.
? What is the basis for the conflict between the narrator and his parents? (The narrator expects household gaiety over Christmas but what he experiences instead is household indifference.)

C. Climax
Everything falls into place for the narrator, and he suddenly realizes that he is poor.

★ **Texas Essential Elements/(c) Reading: 2B** Multimeaning words; **3A** Main ideas/details; **3D** Generalizations; **3G** Compare/contrast; **3H** Predict

in the gutters and had got my feet wet because there were holes in my shoes. My father cut insoles out of cardboard, and I wore those in my shoes. As long as I had to stay in the house anyway, they were all right.

I stayed cooped up in the house, without any companionship. We didn't take a Sunday paper anymore, but the *Barry Adage* came every week in the mails; and though I did not read small print, I could see the Santa Clauses and holly wreaths in the advertisements.

A There was a calendar in the kitchen. The red days were Sundays and holidays; and that red 25 was Christmas. (It was on a Monday, and the two red figures would come right together in 1893; but this represents research in the *World Almanac,* not memory.) I knew when Sunday was because I could look out of the window and see the neighbor's children, all dressed up, going to Sunday school. I knew just when Christmas was going to be.

But there was something queer! My father and mother didn't say a word about Christmas. And once, when I spoke of it, there was a strange silence, so I didn't say anything more about it. But I wondered and was troubled. Why didn't they say anything about it? Was what I had said I wanted (memory refuses to supply that detail) too expensive?

I wasn't arrogant[1] and talkative now. I was silent and frightened. What was the matter? Why didn't my father and mother say anything about Christmas? As the day approached, my chest grew tighter with anxiety.

Now it was the day before Christmas. I couldn't be mistaken. But not a word about it from my father and mother. I waited in painful bewilderment all day. I had supper with them, and was allowed to sit up for an hour. I was waiting for them to say something. "It's time for you to go to bed," my mother said gently. I *had* to say something.

"This is Christmas Eve, isn't it?" I asked, as if I didn't know. My father and mother looked at one another. Then my mother looked away. Her face was pale and stony. My father cleared his throat, and his face took on a joking look. He pretended he hadn't known it was Christmas Eve, because he hadn't been reading the papers. He said he would go downtown and find out.

My mother got up and walked out of the room. B I didn't want my father to have to keep on being funny about it, so I got up and went to bed. I went by myself without having a light. I undressed in the dark and crawled into bed.

I was numb. As if I had been hit by something. It was hard to breathe. I ached all through. I was stunned—with finding out the truth.

My body knew before my mind quite did. In a minute, when I could think, my mind would know. And as the pain in my body ebbed, the pain in my mind began. I *knew.* I couldn't put it into words yet. But I knew why I had taken only a little bag of potatoes to Sunday school that fall. I knew why there had been only pennies in my little yellow C envelope. I knew why I hadn't gone to school that fall—why I hadn't any new shoes—why we had been living on potato soup all winter. All these things, and others, many others, fitted themselves together in my mind, and meant something.

Then the words came into my mind and I whispered them into the darkness:

"*We're poor!*"

That was it. I was one of those poor children I had been sorry for, when I heard about them in Sunday school. My mother hadn't told me. My father was out of work, and we hadn't any money. That was why there wasn't going to be any Christmas at our house.

Then I remembered something that made me squirm with shame—a boast. (Memory will not yield this up. Had I said to some nice little boy, "I'm going to be President of the United States"? Or to a nice little girl: "I'll marry you when I grow up"? It was some boast as horribly shameful to remember.)

"*We're poor.*" There in bed in the dark, I whispered it over and over to myself. I was making myself get used to it. (Or—just torturing myself, as one pressed the tongue against a sore tooth? No, memory says not like that—but to keep myself from ever being such a fool again: suffering now, to keep this awful thing from ever happening again. Memory is clear on that; it was more like

1. **arrogant:** extremely proud of oneself and scornful of others.

Reading Check Test

Number the following events in the order in which they happened in the story.

________The boy realizes Christmas is coming. *3*

________The boy is asked to bring in food for poor children. *1*

________The boy decides he doesn't want anything for Christmas. *5*

________The boy doesn't go back to school. *2*

________The boy realizes he is poor. *4*

Closure

Have students work in pairs and have one student tell the other how external conflict differs from internal conflict. Tell students to identify the internal and external conflicts of the narrator in "Christmas."

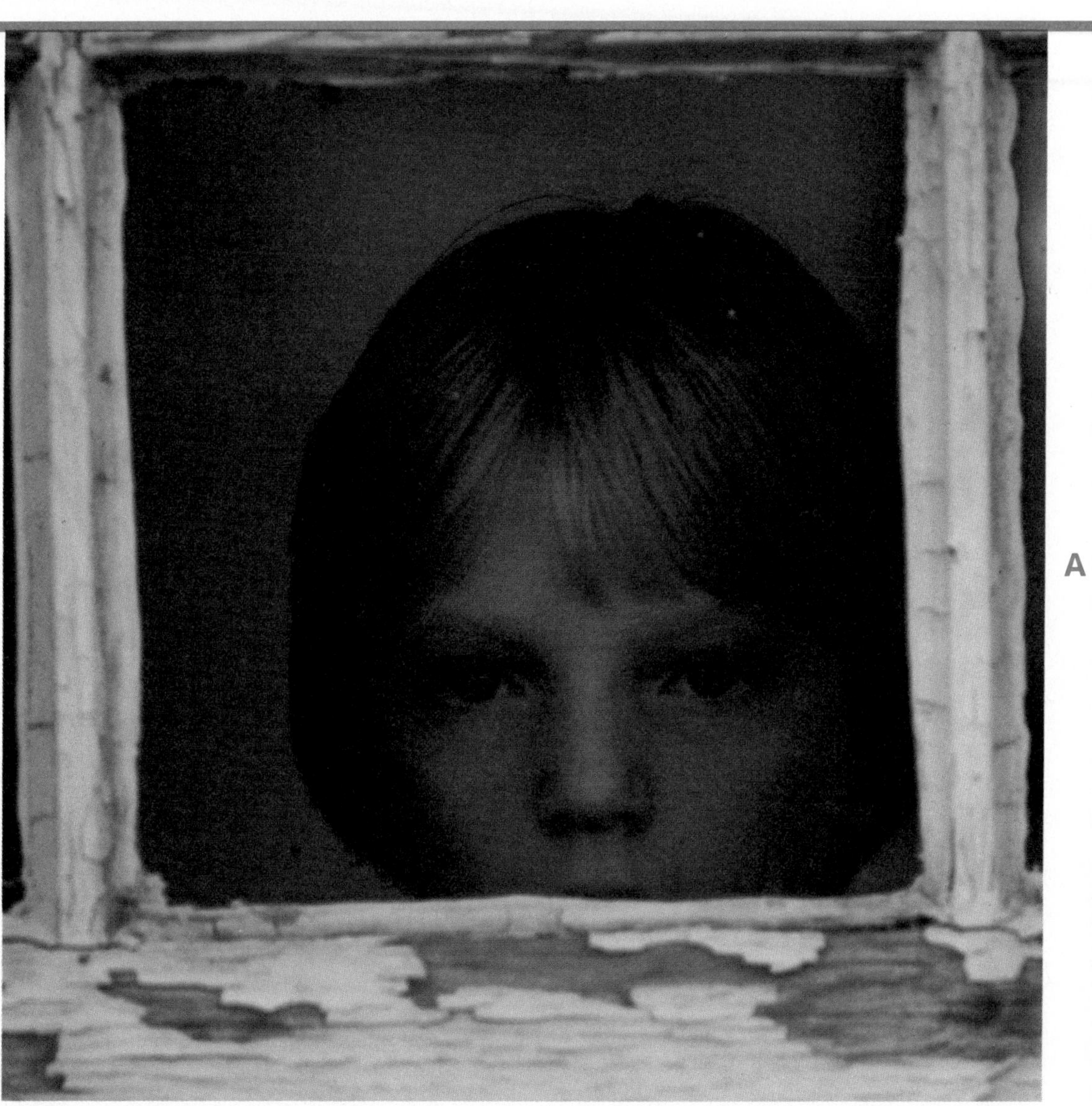

A

A. Responding to the Photograph

? What does the condition of the window paint tell you about the house? About the boy? How would you describe the boy's expression?

B. Interpreting

? Why is repeating "We're poor" like pulling a tooth? (Because it is a painful truth—once "the tooth is pulled," he will have accepted the truth, and there will only be soreness left.)

C. Character's Action

? Why is the narrator's decision to not let anything hurt him again and to never let himself want anything again an important one? (His decision is important because it marks his passage from childhood to adulthood. For better or worse, the narrator will never again be as he was before the Christmas described in the story.)

B pulling the tooth, to get it over with—never mind the pain, this will be the end!)

It wasn't so bad, now that I knew. *I just hadn't known!* I had thought all sorts of foolish things; that I was going to Ann Arbor[2]—going to be a lawyer—going to make speeches in the Square, going to be President! Now I knew better.

I had wanted (something) for Christmas. I didn't want it, now. I didn't want anything.

I lay there in the dark, feeling the cold emotion of renunciation.[3] (The tendrils of desire unfold their clasp on the outer world of objects, withdraw, shrivel up. Wishes shrivel up, turn black, die. It is like that.)

It hurt. But nothing would ever hurt again. I would never let myself want anything again. C

I lay there stretched out straight and stiff in the dark, my fists clenched hard upon Nothing. . . .

In the morning it had been like a nightmare that is not clearly remembered—that one wishes to forget. Though I hadn't hung up any stocking, there was one hanging at the foot of my bed. A bag of popcorn and a lead pencil, for me. They had done the best they could, now they realized that I knew about Christmas. But they needn't have thought they had to. I didn't want anything.

2. **Ann Arbor:** location of the University of Michigan.
3. **renunciation:** giving something up.

ANALYZING THE STORY

Identifying Facts

1. His Sunday school teacher asks his class to write their names on the envelopes, or have their parents write them, and he is very proud to be able to write his name. Later, the narrator says he did not read small print in the newspaper, but he could see Santa Claus in the ads.

2. He brings a small bag of potatoes and an envelope containing three pennies.

3. He discovers that he is poor.

He feels stunned and numb and aches with finding out the truth.

4. He knows that his dreams are going to shrivel up and die.

5. He receives a lead pencil and a bag of popcorn.

He says he didn't want anything.

Interpreting Meanings

6. The narrator has determined that since wanting things had brought him such pain, he can avoid this pain by not wanting anything anymore.

7. Answers will vary. Some students will realize the narrator's poverty at the beginning of the story when he says his shoe soles are worn through. Other *(Answers continue in left-hand column.)*

(Continued from top.) details include his father being at home, his siblings being elsewhere, his being told not to write his name on the envelope, his being kept home from school. The clinching scene occurs when his parents try to pretend that it is not Christmas Eve.

8. They may have thought they could conceal the approach of Christmas from their son. More likely, they themselves were also having difficulty facing up to their poverty.

9. He probably feels shame because he realizes his boast must have appeared vain and unrealistic to the other person.

10. The statement "I felt sorry for the poor children" is ironic because the narrator does not realize that he is one of those poor children.

11. He is giving up the world of desire, whether it be of abstract ideals or material things.

See Teacher's Manual page 56.

Responding to the Story

Analyzing the Story

Identifying Facts

1. Find two details that suggest the narrator is five or six years old when this incident takes place.
2. What does the boy bring to Sunday school?
3. What painful discovery does the boy finally make? How does he first feel?
4. What changes does the boy know are going to take place in his dreams?
5. What does the narrator get in his Christmas stocking? How does he react to the gifts?

Interpreting Meanings

6. Why doesn't the boy want anything anymore?
7. When did you figure out the truth that the narrator discovers toward the end of the story? List three clues earlier in the story that hint at this truth.
8. Why do you think his parents didn't talk about Christmas?
9. Why does the boy feel shame when he remembers a boast he had made?
10. We say that a situation is **ironic** when it turns out to be very different from what we expect it to be. Explain why the last statement at the end of the first paragraph is ironic. SRW p. 57
11. Lying in the dark after his discovery, the boy feels "the cold emotion of renunciation." Explain what he is renouncing, or giving up. Why might giving up something produce an emotion that is *cold?*

Applying Meanings

12. The parents in this story try to protect their young son from knowing the family's troubles. Do you believe they were doing the right thing? Or do you think it would have been better if he had known what problems his family had?

Writing About the Story

A Creative Response

1. **Extending the Story.** After his discovery, the narrator decides "I would never let myself want anything again." Extend the story by writing a paragraph describing how you imagine the boy's life afterward was affected by his experience. (Consider the fact that he became a writer.)

A Critical Response

2. **Comparing Stories.** In "Lassie Come-Home" (page 104), young Joe's mother warns him that he should never want anything in life as badly as he wants Lassie. In this story, the narrator vows, "I would never let myself want anything again." Do Mrs. Carraclough's warning and the narrator's vow stem from the same fear? Discuss your answer in a paragraph.

See Teacher's Manual page 56.

Analyzing Language and Vocabulary

Connotations and Denotations

SRW p. 27

Connotations are all the feelings and associations we attach to certain words. The literal "dictionary" definition of a word is called its **denotation.** For example, the denotation of the word *poor* is simply "having little money." But the word *poor* also has connotations. It makes us feel pity and sympathy. The sentence, "We are poor," has a different effect from the sentence, "We are short of money."

Both words in the pairs below mean more or less the same thing. Which word has positive associations? Which has negative associations? Use each word in a sentence.

1. listen/eavesdrop
2. persuade/brainwash
3. slender/skinny
4. careful/fussy
5. plump/fat

See Teacher's Manual page 57.

Reading About the Writer

Floyd Dell (1886–1969) was a Chicago newspaperman who also wrote plays and novels. He was a member of "the Chicago Group," writers who lived and wrote in the Midwest during the early part of the century. Poets Carl Sandburg, Vachel Lindsay, and Edgar Lee Masters were also members of the Chicago Group.

Answers to Questions

I

1. There are many facts that could be listed. *Basic facts about Johanna:* She is about sixteen and lives alone with her mother in the family compound. Her father disappeared long ago. *Johanna's situation:* Johanna's mother is very ill, and Johanna must fetch a doctor who lives on the other side of the forest. It is a winter night with snow on the ground, and Johanna is walking in the forest.
2. Johanna is facing the forest.
3. She has been forbidden to enter the forest at night, and several members of her family who previously disobeyed this command have never been seen again.
4. Friendly details include "cool, shady copses" and "tall oak trees." Hints of trouble to come include the darkness of the forest, the fact that it was a hard winter, and the note that a hungry wolf or bear might live there.
5. On the one hand, Johanna wants to obey her mother's warning never to go into the forest at night; on the other, she needs someone to treat her mother's serious illness, and the only doctor who can do so lives on the other side of the forest. The desire to treat her mother's illness wins.
6. One might guess that Johanna is going to face a life-threatening problem of her own.
7. Answers will vary, as Johanna could make a number of discoveries. Some examples: She could discover a self-confidence and maturity in herself by making her way safely through the forest. She could discover that her family invented a story to explain some dismaying occurrences.
8. Answers will vary. Perhaps family members died from a contagious disease. Perhaps family members did not like the isolated location and moved to other areas. Perhaps the houses have been emptied because of war or famine or because of a change in the local economy.

★ **Texas Essential Elements/(a) English Language Arts: 1B** Purpose and audience; **3A** Plot/character; **4E** Predict. **(c) Reading: 3A** Main ideas/details; **3H** Predict

Review: Exercises in Reading Fiction

SRW p. 25

CONFLICT

In many stories, one or more characters discover something about themselves or the world they live in. This often happens as the result of overcoming a conflict. Some conflicts are internal, involving a struggle that goes on inside the mind of a character. Other conflicts are external. They involve a character in a struggle with other people or with outside forces.

As you read each of the following excerpts, think about the conflict or conflicts that are taking place in each one.

I.

The forest was dark and the snow-covered path was merely an impression left by Johanna's moccasined feet.

If she had not come this way countless daylit times, Johanna would never have known where to go. But Hartwood was familiar to her, even in the unfamiliar night. She had often picnicked in the cool, shady copses and grubbed around the tall oak trees. In a hard winter like this one, a family could subsist for days on acorn stew.

Still, this was the first night she had ever been out in the forest, though she had lived by it all her life. It was tradition—no, more than that—that members of the Chevril family did not venture into the midnight forest. "Never, never go to the woods at night," her mother said, and it was not a warning so much as a command. "Your father went though he was told not to. He never returned."

And Johanna had obeyed. Her father's disappearance was still in her memory, though she remembered nothing else of him. He was not the first of the Chevrils to go that way. There had been a great-uncle and two girl cousins who had likewise "never returned." At least, that was what Johanna had been told. Whether they had disappeared into the maw[1] of the city that lurked over several mountains to the west, or into the hungry jaws of a wolf or bear, was never made clear. But Johanna, being an obedient girl, always came into the house with the setting sun.

For sixteen years she had listened to that warning. But tonight, with her mother pale and sightless, breathing brokenly in the bed they shared, Johanna had no choice. The doctor, who lived on the other side of the wood, must be fetched. He lived in the cluster of houses that rimmed the far side of Hartwood, a cluster that was known as the "Village," though it was really much too small for such a name. The five houses of the Chevril family that clung together, now empty except for Johanna and her mother, were not called a village, though they squatted on as much land.

—from "Johanna," Jane Yolen

1. List all the facts you know about Johanna and her situation.
2. What dangerous external element is Johanna facing?
3. What reason, or reasons, does Johanna have to believe she may be in danger?
4. What details of description **foreshadow,** or hint at, trouble to come?
5. What **internal conflict** does Johanna have? What are the two opposing desires in this conflict? Which desire has won the struggle?
6. What might you imagine is going to happen to Johanna?
7. Suppose you were asked to finish Johanna's story. Name at least three discoveries she might make as a result of her perilous journey.
8. What possible explanations can you propose for the fact that the houses of the Chevrils are empty—except for Johanna's?

1. **maw:** mouth.

Answers to Questions

II

1. Mike's mother doesn't like his moustache; Mike does.
2. Mike feels he is entitled to half-price admission at the local movie theater because he is seventeen; the woman in the box office disagrees. Also, Mike doesn't own his own car, must study to win a college scholarship, and likes his moustache; his girlfriend Cindy doesn't especially like any of these facts.
3. Mike seems most concerned about the conflict with Cindy.

She plays a part in two of Mike's three conflicts, and Mike refers to her several times.

4. The conflict with his mother could become internal if Mike begins to have doubts about his moustache.

Mike would probably have to shave off the moustache, since that would solve several of his problems.

Review: Exercises in Reading Fiction/*cont.*

II.

[My mother] frowned and started the routine.

"That hair," she said. Then admitted: "Well, at least you combed it."

I sighed. I have discovered that it's better to sigh than argue.

"And that moustache." She shook her head. "I still say a seventeen-year-old has no business wearing a moustache."

"It's an experiment," I said. "I just wanted to see if I could grow one." To tell the truth, I had proved my point about being able to grow a decent moustache, but I also had learned to like it.

"It's costing you money, Mike," she said.

"I know, I know."

The money was a reference to the movies. The Downtown Cinema has a special Friday night offer—half-price admission for high-school couples, seventeen or younger. But the woman in the box office took one look at my moustache and charged me full price. Even when I showed her my driver's license. She charged full admission for Cindy's ticket, too, which left me practically broke and unable to take Cindy out for a hamburger with the crowd afterward. That didn't help matters, because Cindy has been getting impatient recently about things, like the fact that I don't own my own car and have to concentrate on my studies if I want to win that college scholarship, for instance. Cindy wasn't exactly crazy about the moustache, either.

—from "The Moustache,"
Robert Cormier

1. What **external conflict** is Mike involved in with his mother?
2. What are two other **external conflicts** mentioned in the excerpt?
3. Which of these three conflicts seems to concern Mike most? How do you know?
4. Which conflict threatens to turn itself into an **internal conflict**? If that were to happen, what decision might Mike have to make?

Writing

1. **Inventing an External Conflict.** Write two or three paragraphs about a character involved in an external conflict. The conflict might be with another person or with an outside force. Try to make your reader share the character's feelings about the conflict.
2. **Inventing an Internal Conflict.** Invent a character who is dealing with an internal conflict. Write two or three paragraphs about the conflict. Use the first-person pronoun *I*.

For evaluation strategies,
see Teacher's Manual page 58.

★ Texas Essential Elements/(a) English Language Arts: 1A Composing process; 1B Purpose and audience; 1H Proofread; 1I Spelling Generalizations; 2B Parts of speech; 2D Grammar/punctuation/spelling

Exercises in Critical Thinking and Writing

For teaching and evaluation strategies, see Teacher's Manual page 58.

SRW p. 53

MAKING INFERENCES AND JUDGMENTS

Writing Assignment

Write an essay in which you discuss one inference and one judgment that you made about the characters in "Christmas" (page 179). Write two paragraphs.

Background

Making Inferences

A A writer doesn't tell you *everything* about the characters in a story. You are often required to make **inferences**—educated guesses based on facts or evidence. You make inferences about a character's motivation (reasons for behavior), thoughts, and feelings. Your inferences are based on everything the writer tells you about the character, what the character does and says, as well as your own understanding about the way people behave.

For example, in "The Quiet Heart" (page 154), the writer does not answer any of the following questions directly. To answer each of these questions, you have to make inferences.

1. Why is the narrator so friendly to Philip?
2. How does Philip feel about his illness?
3. Why does the sister stop visiting Philip?
4. Why does she finally agree to kiss Philip?
5. Why does Philip refuse the kiss?

Making Judgments

You also make judgments as you read stories. **Judgments** are opinions or critical evaluations. Here are three questions about "The Quiet Heart" that involve making judgments.

1. What do you think of the narrator's behavior toward Philip?
2. Do you think the narrator was right or wrong to try to arrange a kiss for Philip?
3. What do you think of the sister's behavior?

There are no right or wrong answers to these questions. Judgments are always personal, even though intelligent judgments should be based on certain agreed-upon standards of what is good or bad. When you write about a character in a story, you should try to give reasons or examples to support your judgments.

Prewriting

Reread "Christmas" (page 179) carefully, and jot down your answers to the following questions. None of these questions are answered directly in the story; you will have to make inferences based on the information the writer gives. For each answer, find details in the story to support your inference.

Making Inferences

1. Why is the mother so insistent about *not* writing the narrator's name on the envelope?
2. Why does the narrator stop going to school?
3. How do the parents feel when the child asks, "This is Christmas Eve, isn't it?"
4. How do you think the narrator will act on Christmas Day?

The following questions involve making judgments about the characters in "Christmas." Give evidence to explain each answer.

Making Judgments

1. Do you think the parents were right or wrong in keeping their problems secret from the narrator?
2. Do you think they were right or wrong in keeping the narrator home from school?
3. What do you think of the narrator's reaction to his discovery that his family is poor? Does he overreact? Or is his reaction natural?

A. Making Inferences
You can point out to students the points in the stories in the previous unit where they should have made inferences as they read. (The annotations will make these passages easily identifiable.) Did students make them automatically, or did the inferences have to be pointed out?

Texas Essential Elements/(c) Reading: 3H Predict; 3I Draw conclusions; 4A Follow directions
(a) English Language Arts: 4I Follow directions

Exercises in Critical Thinking and Writing/*cont.*

Writing

Choose one of the questions listed in the chart on Making Inferences and one from the chart on Making Judgments. Follow this plan for your essay:

Paragraph 1: Cite the title and writer of the story. Discuss one of the inferences you made, and give details from the story to support your inference.
Paragraph 2: State your judgment, and give a reason or example to explain why you feel the way you do.

The following model paragraph discusses one question from the list on page 185, and makes several inferences.

In "The Quiet Heart" by Norman Rosten, the narrator tells us what Philip looks like and what he says, but we have to guess what Philip thinks and feels about his illness. At the beginning of the story, Philip is hopeful as he jokes with the boys: "The doctor says I'll get better. I might even go back to school after summer vacation." Philip doesn't seem to feel sorry for himself and is always cheerful when the narrator visits. He must be very lonely confined to bed, unable to study, in a silent room. As he gets weaker and the doctor comes more frequently and visitors are kept away, Philip must realize how sick he is. When the boys laugh so hard about Philip's dream that Jimmy is dead, I think they're both really thinking about Philip's death—but aren't able to talk about it. At the very end of the story, Philip gets angry when the sister tries to kiss him. He's probably exhausted and weak and feeling how unfair it is that he is dying. I also think he doesn't want people to feel sorry for him.

Topic sentence cites title and author and identifies subject of inference: How Philip feels about his illness.

Feeling #1: hopeful.

Quotes directly from story.

Feeling #2: cheerful.

Feeling #3: lonely.

Feeling #4: realizes he is dying.

Cites detail from story.

Feeling #5: angry at unfairness.

Feeling #6: doesn't want pity.

Revising and Proofreading Self-Check

1. Does the first paragraph contain a topic sentence that names the story title and author and identifies the inference question to be discussed?
2. Does the first paragraph contain details from the story to support the inference?
3. Does the second paragraph contain a topic sentence that states the judgment? Does the paragraph contain details from the story to support the judgment?
4. Does every sentence start with a capital letter and end with a period or other end punctuation mark?
5. Are my ideas clearly expressed? Have I said everything I wanted to say?

Partner Check

1. Are there any spelling errors?
2. Are sentences punctuated correctly?
3. Are paragraphs fully developed (at least four sentences long) and indented?
4. Are there any sentences or ideas that are unclear? Do I understand what you are trying to say?
5. What do I like best about this paper?
6. What do I think needs improvement?

THE ELEMENTS OF A SHORT STORY

Ten Cents a Ride by Louis Bouché (1942). Oil. The Metropolitan Museum of Art, New York. George A. Hearn Fund, 1942.

UNIT FOUR **John Leggett**

HUMANITIES CONNECTION: DISCUSSING THE FINE ART

American painter Louis Bouché (1896–1969) was born and raised in New York City. During the 1930's, Bouché painted a number of murals in public buildings, including Radio City Music Hall in New York City. His easel paintings most often depict scenes from everyday life.

? What is the setting of the painting, and how do you know? (A boat, most likely a ferry, mid-1900's. We can guess this from the depiction of a corridor with a bench, the water outside, and the title of the painting.) Who do you think the men are? What story could you tell about what might be happening in the painting?

TEACHING THE SHORT STORY

Since the beginning of time, storytelling has had several functions in society: to teach, to amuse or entertain, to arouse emotional response, and to challenge the mind of the listener or reader. Ask students to relate the last time they told a story, and to tell why, where, when, for whom, and for what purpose they told the story. If they can understand that the stories they are reading in their textbooks were written for basically the same purposes, they will be well on their way to understanding the unit.

In this unit, students will be led to recognize the components that make up a short story: characterization, plot (basic situation, internal and external conflict, complications, climax, resolution), setting, suspense, point of view, and theme. In addition, they will investigate the use of language techniques such as jargon, descriptive detail, voice, similes, and phonetic spelling.

You can either have students read each story in order or choose the ones that seem best for your students. Each story includes the basic narrative elements. (Of course, the first-person, third-person limited, and omniscient points of view will appear in different stories.)

OBJECTIVES OF THE SHORT STORY UNIT

1. To improve reading proficiency and expand vocabulary
2. To gain exposure to notable authors and their work
3. To define and identify the elements of a short story
4. To respond to fiction through oral and written expression
5. To practice the following critical thinking and writing skills:
   a. Summarizing a plot
   b. Analyzing character
   c. Identifying and explaining the function of setting
   d. Determining point of view
   e. Comparing and contrasting stories
   f. Associating personal experiences with a short story
   g. Identifying the theme of a story

SUPPLEMENTARY SUPPORT MATERIAL: UNIT FOUR

1. Introduction/Understanding the Elements of a Short Story Test (page 67 of Test Book)
2. Word Analogies Test (page 83 of Test Book)
3. Reading Check Test blackline master
4. Unit Review Test (page 85 of Test Book)
5. Critical Thinking and Writing Test (page 89 of Test Book)
6. Understanding a Short Story (Study and Reinforcement Worksheet, page 1)
7. Instructional Overhead Transparencies

Unit Outline

THE ELEMENTS OF A SHORT STORY

★ Texas Essential Elements/(a) English Language Arts: 3A Plot/character; 4B Main idea; 4H Point of view. (c) Reading: 3A Main ideas/details; 3F Purpose/point of view/opinion

> *. . . the short story consists of one single flight of the imagination, complete: up and down.*
>
> —William Carlos Williams

SRW p. 49

A

A Story's Building Blocks

B

Why do we read stories? Some people say there are two reasons: One is to enjoy ourselves, and the other is to learn something. Whatever your reason for reading, you will find that a well-made short story contains several important elements. Knowing something about these elements of storytelling will help you understand why a story interests you, makes you laugh, or makes you sad.

Characters and Plot

SRW p. 67

A story has at least one **character,** who may be a person, an animal, or even a machine. A story also has a plot, which tells us "what happens" to that character or characters. An interesting character helps draw us into a story and *feel* the effects of the plot.

The plot is the story's skeleton. **Plot** is a series of related episodes, one growing out of another. The episodes in a plot often create **suspense,** or anxious curiosity. Suspense is what keeps us reading: It keeps us glued to the story because we are curious to find out "What happens next?" In fact, the real power of a story lies in its ability to create suspense. A good storyteller makes us worry about the campers cooking their trout over the campfire by showing us the bear watching from the trees.

What is a plot made up of? A plot consists of four parts, or building blocks:

1. The first part of a plot is the introduction. This is like an entryway to the story. It tells us the **basic situation:** who the characters are and what they want. Usually this is where we find out about the conflict in the story. **Conflict** is a struggle. It gives the story its principal energy. An **external conflict** involves a character's struggle with another person, or with a force of nature (a tornado, a bear, an icy mountain path). An **internal conflict** takes place in a character's mind. Here is the introduction to a fairy tale you know well. The conflict is provided by a hungry wolf.

> There was once a sweet, trusting girl called Little Red Riding Hood because she wore a cap of red velvet. One day Little Red set off for her grandmother's house in the woods with a basket of food. When she entered the woods, she met a wolf. She didn't think the wolf was bad, so she wasn't frightened. The wolf greeted Little Red and found out where she was going. The wolf thought to himself: "That girl and her grandmother will make a tasty meal."

A. Responding to the Quotation
The quotation is from William Carlos Williams's book *A Beginning on the Short Story.*

Discuss Williams's comparison of a short story to a flight—perhaps of stairs, or maybe a flight in air. Point out that a story does just that—it builds up the suspense until the climax is reached, and descends into a resolution. (See the diagram on page 253 which illustrates the essence of Williams's quote.)

B. Responding to the Illustration
What do you think the person depicted in this illustration is like? (Mean, cranky, demanding) What details suggest this? (Posture, evil expression, that the person is in bed and perhaps being waited on)

A. A Different Version of the Story
Ask students to point out the elements of plot in James Thurber's satire—or ridicule—of "Little Red Riding Hood":

"One afternoon a big wolf waited in a dark forest for a little girl to come along carrying a basket of food to her grandmother. Finally a little girl did come along and she was carrying a basket of food. 'Are you carrying that basket to your grandmother?' asked the wolf. The little girl said yes, she was. So the wolf asked her where her grandmother lived and the little girl told him and he disappeared into the woods.

"When the little girl opened the door of her grandmother's house she saw that there was somebody in bed with a nightcap and nightgown on. She had approached no nearer than twenty-five feet from the bed when she saw that it was not her grandmother but the wolf, for even in a nightcap a wolf does not look any more like your grandmother than the Metro-Goldwyn lion looks like Calvin Coolidge. So the little girl took an automatic out of her basket and shot the wolf dead.

"Moral: It is not so easy to fool little girls nowadays as it used to be."

B. Responding to the Illustration
? What does the illustration show? (A knight killing a dragon) Is it illustrating the basic situation, the conflict, the climax, or the resolution of a plot? (The climax)

2. In the second part of a plot, one or more of the characters acts to resolve the conflict. We start to see **complications** develop, leading to the story's climax. Now serious complications develop in Red's conflict with the wolf:

A

> The wolf zoomed ahead to the grandmother's house. It got into the house by trickery and then ate up the grandmother. Afterward, the wolf put on grandma's clothes and got into her bed. Little Red arrived soon after. She thought something was fishy about the character in the bed, but she didn't run away. The wolf ate her too. It then fell asleep and began snoring loudly.

3. The **climax** is the story's most emotional or suspenseful moment. This is when the situation is altered and the conflict is decided one way or another.

> A hunter passing by the grandmother's house heard the snoring. Thinking something was the matter with grandma, he went inside and saw the sleeping wolf. He figured the wolf had swallowed the grandmother whole. He didn't shoot the wolf, but slit it open with a knife. Out popped Little Red, still alive. And then out came the grandmother, also still living and breathing. They were saved!

4. The fourth and last part of a story is its **resolution.** This is when the loose ends of the story are tied up. The story is closed.

> All three people were happy. The hunter carried home the wolf's fur to make a hat. The grandmother devoured the basket of food. And Little Red Riding Hood resolved never to stop to talk to strangers again.

SRW p. 69

Point of View: The Voice Telling the Story

When a good reader starts a story, he or she will automatically ask, "Who is telling this story?" When you do this, you are asking about point of view. **Point of view** is the vantage point from which a story is told. In some stories, the narrator—or storyteller—is **omniscient** ("all knowing"). This narrator is "above the action," looking down on it like a god. This narrator can tell you everything about all the characters, even their most private thoughts.

> Ted courageously strutted down the mountain, ready to slay the vicious dragon and save his lady, the fair Rosalie. The dragon watched the boy, licking his lips in anticipation of dinner. Rosalie watched too, wondering how this boy planned to rescue her—he was so skinny.

B

A story can also be told by one of the characters. In this viewpoint, the character speaks as "I." We call this **first-person point of view.** ("I" is the first-person pronoun.) In this point of view, we know only what this one character can tell us. Sometimes that isn't very reliable.

As I walked toward the dragon's cave, I was feeling quite brave. I was thinking of Rosalie with her long black hair and sweet voice. I was sure I could lick the dragon because of the huge muscles on my arms and legs.

Often, a story is seen through the eyes of one character, but the character is not telling the story. This is called the **limited third-person point of view.** In this point of view, an omniscient narrator zooms in on one character and tells the story from his or her vantage point. Our knowledge is limited to what the character sees, thinks, and feels.

SRW p. 69

Ted neared the dragon's cave, beginning to wonder whether Rosalie was really worth the risk. He noticed the beast's red rolling eyes and scaly skin, and heard Rosalie's screams. The truth is that he was beginning to wish he'd stayed at home.

A

Theme: The Story's Main Idea

SRW p. 87

A good story also has a **theme.** This is the main idea the story expresses about life and people. Theme is what the writer intends to say to us by writing the story. It is the message that we take away from the story. The discovery of theme gives it lasting meaning for us.

B

How do you find the story's theme? If you finish a story and aren't sure what its point is, you should go back over the story. Sometimes the theme is stated directly in a key sentence or paragraph. ("Real friends respect each other's feelings.") Mostly, however, you'll have to think about the story to figure out its theme. Here are some steps to take in discovering a theme:

1. Identify some important passages or individual sentences in the story and think about what they add up to.

2. Think about how the main character has changed in the story, and what the character has learned. Sometimes what the character learned can be stated as the theme. ("If you are self-centered, you can hurt yourself as well as others.")

3. Think about the title of the story and what it means.

4. Test your statement of theme against the story. Does anything in the story contradict it? If so, you'll have to change your statement of theme somewhat.

Stories and Feelings

Many people might read a story about a teen-age romance, or about revenge among criminals, or about a dog who acts like a person. Each of these readers will respond to the story in a somewhat different way. As human beings, we bring our own complex individuality to our reading experience. The differences among us account for one of the joys of reading stories and of sharing our responses to them.

A. Complications

? What are the complications that are developing in this short sketch? (The dragon's fierceness, Rosalie's screams, his wanting to be safe at home)

B. Theme

You might ask students what they think the themes are of some of the stories they have read in the previous units.

Responding to a Story

The short works in this section should pique students' interest in the unit. The setting and characterization are vivid, the conflict is clear, the suspense builds quickly, and the theme shows the triumph of cleverness over might. The sidenotes track the development of the story so even your slower readers should be able to follow the story without help.

See if you can elicit from students answers to the questions in the sidenotes. Also, ask students to evaluate the sidenotes. Do they agree with them? Would they have asked other questions? Have the notes touched on the most important elements of the story?

Stress the constant act of predicting and testing predictions that goes on during reading. You may wish to have a different student read each section of the story. When each student stops, ask the class to predict what the story will involve, what the conflict will be, who will be involved in the conflict, and how the conflict will be resolved.

Finally, talk with your students about the importance of setting in "Rolls for the *(Discussion continues in left-hand column.)*

(Continued from top.) Czar." Discuss how a different setting would change the impact of the story. (You may have to explain the czar's life-and-death power over his subjects in pre-Revolutionary Russia.) Compare "Rolls for the Czar" to other stories in which setting has a strong effect on the conflict or the theme.

A. Analyzing

? How *is* the writer doing this? (By including the word *rolls* in the title, by describing the baker Markov and how delicious his rolls are, and by indicating that the rolls often occupy the czar's thoughts)

★ **Texas Essential Elements/(c) Reading: 1A** Context clues

Responding to a Story

Rolls for the Czar

This is a tale of the days of the Czars, of ermine and gold and pure white bread.

What's a Czar? What's ermine?

In Saint Petersburg the Czar held court with pomp and ceremony that dazzled peasants and ambassadors alike. His Winter Palace covered acres by the side of the frozen Neva. It had pillars of lapis lazuli and of rare stone from the Urals. Its halls held treasures from all the world.

Palace: Czar must be like a king. Neva? Must be a body of water since it's frozen.

Lapis lazuli? Urals? Lapis must be something like marble. I've never heard of the Urals.

Once a year the Czar paid a visit of state to Moscow, the trade center of the Imperial Domain where the rich merchants lived. Here he would sit in the throne room of the Kremlin, where his ancestors once ruled warring Muscovy.

The story is set in Russia, long ago.

There was another great man in Moscow—a baker, Markov by name. The master bakers of the city were famous, and Markov was prince among them. His cakes and pastry were renowned throughout all the Russias, but his rolls were the best of all: pure white, like the driven snow of the steppes, a crust just hard enough to crunch, the bread not too soft, but soft enough to hold the melted butter.

Sounds good! Rolls are in the title.

Merchant princes from the gold rivers of Siberia, chieftains from the Caucasus in high fur hats, nobles from their feudal estates in the country, all came to Moscow to eat Markov's rolls.

Something's going to happen with these rolls.

The Czar himself was a mighty eater and especially fond of Markov's delicacies. So one day in February, when it came time for a visit to Moscow, he was thinking of Markov and his art, anticipating the rolls. His private car bore the imperial coat of arms. The rest of the train was filled with grand dukes, princes of the blood, and noble ladies. The railroad track ran straight as an arrow five hundred miles through the snow, the white birch forests, and the pines.

The narrator tells us the Czar's thoughts.

Relatives?

The train chuffed into the Moscow station, into a morning of sun and frost. The sun sparkled on the gold domes of churches, it glittered on the cuirasses of a regiment of guards, all men of noble birth. Smoke rose straight up from chimneys. Twin jets of steam snorted from the nostrils of the three horses of the Czar's troika. The Czar had a fine appetite.

Neat description.

Cuirasses: must be some sort of metal weapon since they belong to guards.

The horses' hoofs kicked up gouts of snow as they galloped over the moat and through the gate in the Kremlin wall. The Czar walked up the royal staircase, carpeted in red and lined with bowing servants. He was thinking of the rolls.

Troika: must be a horsedrawn carriage.
I predict he doesn't get his rolls.
Gouts? Must be clumps but I've never heard of the word.

The writer is making me think these rolls are pretty important.] A

He went through the formal greetings with a distracted look, then sat down eagerly at the breakfast table. Not a glance did he give the caviar, the smoked sterlets, the pheasant in aspic. He watched the door. When a royal footman came through carrying a silver platter loaded with rolls, the Czar smiled. All was well.

Ordinary rolls are better than fancy food. (What are sterlets? Fish? Ham? Sausage? Oysters?)

READING CHECK TEST

1. The plot of a story is a series of related episodes. *(True)*
2. The climax is a story's most emotional or suspenseful moment. *(True)*
3. The part of the story that ties up loose ends is called the external conflict. *(False)*
4. In the omniscient point of view, the story is told by one of the characters in the story. *(False)*
5. The theme is the message that the writer of a story wants the reader to take away from it. *(True)*

A. Expansion
Siberia is a very cold region in northern Russia where, for centuries, rulers have sent prisoners.

B. Responding
? What do you think Markov *is* thinking?

The Czar rubbed his hands and took a steaming roll. He broke it open and the smile vanished from his face. A dead fly lay embedded in the bread. Courtiers crowded around to look.

Here's the problem!

"Bring Markov here!" said the Czar, with one of his terrible glances.

He's going to kill the baker.

The banquet room was silent in tense horror. Markov came in puffing slightly but bearing himself with the pride of a master artist.

"Look at this, Markov," said the Czar, pointing at the fly, "and tell me what it is."

Markov looked and stood frozen for a moment. Princes, nobles, and servants all leaned forward waiting for doom to strike him. The Czar could bend horseshoes in his bare hands. A word from him and the bleak wastes of Siberia lay waiting. [A]

The writer is telling me how powerful and angry the Czar is.

No man could tell what Markov thought, but they knew that a fly had endangered his life. He reached to the platter and picked up the fly. He put it in his mouth and ate it. Every eye watched him swallow.

I wonder what he *is* thinking? [B]

Disgusting.

"It is a raisin, Sire," he said.

Clever!

Wrath faded from the Czar's face. He broke out laughing and the nobles relaxed.

The problem's solved.

"Markov," he said, "we grant you a coat of arms with a fly as a motif. A fly imperiled your life and a fly saved your life."

Why does he let the guy go?

And the Czar went on with his rolls.

Now, what's the moral of this story? I'm sure it has one. The story's comical, but it has serious moments.

—Robin Kinkead

Thinking Over the Story

The story takes place before the Russian Revolution, when the Czar was the supreme ruler of Russia. To get a sense of the setting, you might look at a map of Russia and find the Neva River, Leningrad (formerly called Saint Petersburg), and the Ural Mountains. There are several Russian-English words in the story that add to the sense of place. This reader has figured out most of them from the **context,** or words and phrases surrounding the unfamiliar word. You might want to look up the others in a dictionary.

The story's **conflict** is not evident until more than halfway through the story. As you are reading the beginning, you might be thinking, "But, what's the conflict going to be? What's this story *about*?" This reader made a guess about the conflict; another reader might have made a different prediction: "I bet, since the rolls are so famous, that the baker will be asked to bake special rolls for the Czar and will get a reward for them." This is a good guess, but not right either.

This reader would now go back and think about the story and try to answer his or her own unanswered questions, especially the one about the story's **moral**.

When you write about the story, use your response notes to guide you. In this case, you would think about the following points: (1) the power of the Czar and the fear he instills in everybody; (2) the conflict between absolute power and simple cleverness; (3) finally, the Czar's recognition of the baker's cunning and the reward for his clever solution.

You might, after reading the story, think about other questions that did not come up in your notes: (1) What qualities of Markov should have led you to predict that he would find a way out of his danger? (2) How many people may have suffered after displeasing the Czar who were *not* as clever as the baker?

PREREADING

1. BUILDING ON PRIOR KNOWLEDGE. Before reading the story, explore with students the ways people can change over time. You can spur the discussion with such questions as: What problems might occur if the person changed too much? In what areas would a person have to change for the worse in order to damage a friendship?

2. ESTABLISHING A PURPOSE. Before students begin reading, you might have them read question 7 on page 197.

3. PREREADING JOURNAL. Have students create an imaginary character and write one description of the character after the first meeting and one description of the person after twenty years had passed. What were the changes in appearance? In personality? Urge them to use vivid details. (If they have trouble thinking up a character, tell them to flip through the textbook and choose a person in one of the paintings or illustrations, and write a description of that person as they appear twenty years later.)

A. Setting and Plot

Make sure students note the details of setting. The time of day (nighttime and its attendant darkness) and the weather (cold, rainy, and so windy that people are concealed by their outer garments) are integral to the plot because they enable both the uniformed policeman and later the plain-clothes man to hide their identities.)

? What mood does the setting create? (Cold, lonely, and somewhat portentous) This will help students answer question 5.

B. Character

? From his appearance, what do you think this man is like? (The words *pale, square-jawed, keen,* and *white scar* all suggest a sense of evil. The fact that he is wearing a diamond pin is odd—the neighborhood described in the first three paragraphs does not seem to be a wealthy one. Although students may not recognize it as such, this is the typical gangster image.)

★ **Texas Essential Elements/(a) English Language Arts: 1B** Purpose and audience; **1D** Direct quotations; **3A** Plot/character; **3C** Literary traditions; **4B** Main idea

AFTER TWENTY YEARS

O. Henry

A lot can happen in twenty years. When two friends meet after twenty years have gone by, you expect to see some changes. Still, you may not expect all the changes that the two friends in this story experience. Pause after paragraph 6, after the face of the man in the doorway is revealed. From the description of his appearance, try to guess what the man is like. Then read on to see if you are correct. What surprises might this famous O. Henry story hold in store for you?

A The policeman on the beat moved up the avenue impressively. The impressiveness was habitual and not for show, for spectators were few. The time was barely ten o'clock at night, but chilly gusts of wind with a taste of rain in them had well nigh depeopled the streets.

Trying doors as he went, twirling his club with many intricate and artful movements, turning now and then to cast his watchful eye down the pacific thoroughfare, the officer, with his stalwart form and slight swagger, made a fine picture of a guardian of the peace. The vicinity was one that kept early hours. Now and then you might see the lights of a cigar store or of an all-night lunch counter, but the majority of the doors belonged to business places that had long since been closed.

Unfamiliar Words. O. Henry loved long words and fancy words. (He read dictionaries for pleasure!) Although this story is written in a plainer style than most of his stories, you will come across some typical O. Henry word choices. For example, in paragraph 2 he says "pacific thoroughfare." Most people would just say "peaceful street." Some of O. Henry's difficult words can be figured out by examining their structure, or by looking at context clues, or by thinking of words that the unfamiliar word resembles. *Pacific,* for example, resembles *pacifist,* "a person who loves peace." It also resembles *pacifier,* the device you give babies to keep them peaceful.

When about midway of a certain block, the policeman suddenly slowed his walk. In the doorway of a darkened hardware store a man leaned with an unlighted cigar in his mouth. As the policeman walked up to him, the man spoke up quickly.

"It's all right, officer," he said reassuringly. "I'm just waiting for a friend. It's an appointment made twenty years ago. Sounds a little funny to you, doesn't it? Well, I'll explain if you'd like to make certain it's all straight. About that long ago there used to be a restaurant where this store stands—'Big Joe' Brady's restaurant."

"Until five years ago," said the policeman. "It was torn down then."

The man in the doorway struck a match and lit his cigar. The light showed a pale, square-jawed face with keen eyes, and a little white scar near his right eyebrow. His scarfpin was a large diamond, oddly set. B

"Twenty years ago tonight," said the man, "I dined here at 'Big Joe' Brady's with Jimmy Wells, my best chum and the finest chap in the world. He and I were raised here in New York, just like two brothers, together. I was eighteen and Jimmy was twenty. The next morning I was to start for the West to make my fortune. You couldn't have dragged Jimmy out of New York; he thought it was the only place on earth. Well, we agreed that night that we would meet here again exactly twenty years from that date and time, no matter what our conditions might be or from what distance we might have to come. We figured that in twenty years each of us ought to have our destiny

For a detailed lesson plan on this story, see Teacher's Manual pages 59–62. A biography of O. Henry appears on text page 198.

SUPPLEMENTARY SUPPORT MATERIAL
1. Vocabulary Activity Sheet
2. Reading Check Test blackline master
3. Selection Test (page 69 of Test Book)
4. Author photograph on *A Gallery of Authors* poster
5. Workbook (page 47)
6. Audiocassette recording
7. Connections Between Reading and Writing worksheet
8. Reader's Response Journal

Developing Vocabulary

The following words appear on a test in the Test Book, page 70. (See also the Vocabulary Activity Sheet.)

beat, destiny
habitual, corresponded
intricate, dismally
stalwart, absurdity
keen, egotism

★ **Texas Essential Elements/(c) Reading: 1A** Context clues; **1B** Structural analysis; **3A** Main ideas/details; **3I** Draw conclusions; **4D** Diagrams/graphs

Rainy Night by Charles Burchfield (1930). Watercolor.

San Diego Museum of Art. Gift of Anne R. and Amy Putman.

worked out and our fortunes made, whatever they were going to be."

"It sounds pretty interesting," said the policeman. "Rather a long time between meetings, though, it seems to me. Haven't you heard from your friend since you left?"

"Well, yes, for a time we corresponded," said the other. "But after a year or two we lost track of each other. You see, the West is a pretty big proposition, and I kept hustling around over it pretty lively. But I know Jimmy will meet me here if he's alive, for he always was the truest, stanchest old chap in the world. He'll never forget. I came a thousand miles to stand in this door tonight, and it's worth it if my old partner turns up."

The waiting man pulled out a handsome pocket watch, the lids of it set with small diamonds. A

"Three minutes to ten," he announced. "It was exactly ten o'clock when we parted here at the restaurant door."

"Did pretty well out West, didn't you?" asked the policeman. B

"You bet! I hope Jimmy has done half as well. He was a kind of plodder, though, good fellow as

Humanities Connection: Discussing the Fine Art

American painter Charles Burchfield (1893–1967) is known for his realistic watercolors of the American scene. Burchfield's work during the 1920's and 1930's is characterized by the loneliness and harshness of American small towns and cities. (Another painting by Burchfield appears on text page 274.)

? How does this painting contribute to the effect of the story so far? What details match the story? (The weather, the emptiness, the man in a doorway)

A. Making Inferences

What does this detail tell you about the man's character? (The man's display of diamonds shows not only his wealth, but also the ostentation of his wealth.)

B. Understatement

In view of the man's obvious wealth, the policeman's comment is quite an understatement.

A. Expression
From the context, what do you think this expression means? (The policeman is asking if the man will leave at exactly ten if his friend doesn't show up, or if he will wait a while for him to come.)

B. Interpreting
This is the first clue that things are not as they appear.

C. Climax
The turning point of the story occurs when Bob realizes that his companion is not his friend Jimmy Wells.

D. Humanities Connection: Discussing the Fine Art
Charles Roth, an American artist, was primarily interested in the human figure, and his technique reflects a disciplined use of black ink to the exclusion of all other colors.
As you can see by the date, the etching depicts a policeman from many decades ago. What differences are there between his appearance and that of policemen today?

he was. I've had to compete with some of the sharpest wits going, to get my pile. A man gets in a groove in New York. It takes the West to put a razor edge on him."

The policeman twirled his club and took a step or two.

"I'll be on my way. Hope your friend comes
A around all right. Going to call time on him sharp?"

"I should say not!" said the other. "I'll give him half an hour at least. If Jimmy is alive on earth, he'll be here by that time. So long, officer."

"Good night, sir," said the policeman, passing on along his beat, trying doors as he went.

There was now a fine, cold drizzle falling, and the wind had risen from its uncertain puffs into a steady blow. The few foot passengers astir in that quarter hurried dismally and silently along, with coat collars turned high and pocketed hands. And in the door of the hardware store, the man who had come a thousand miles to fill an appointment, uncertain almost to absurdity, with the friend of his youth, smoked his cigar and waited.

About twenty minutes he waited, and then a tall man in a long overcoat, with collar turned up to his ears, hurried across from the opposite side of the street. He went directly to the waiting man.

"Is that you, Bob?" he asked, doubtfully.

"Is that you, Jimmy Wells?" cried the man in the door.

"Bless my heart!" exclaimed the new arrival, grasping both the other's hands with his own. "It's Bob, sure as fate. I was certain I'd find you here if you were still in existence. Well, well, well! Twenty years is a long time. The old restaurant's gone, Bob; I wish it had lasted, so we could have had another dinner there. How has the West treated you, old man?"

"Bully; it has given me everything I asked for. You've changed lots, Jimmy. I never thought you B
were so tall by two or three inches."

"Oh, I grew a bit after I was twenty."

"Doing well in New York, Jimmy?"

"Moderately. I have a position in one of the city departments. Come on, Bob; we'll go around to a place I know of and have a good long talk about old times."

The two started up the street, arm in arm. The man from the West, his egotism[1] enlarged by success, was beginning to outline the history of his career. The other, submerged in his overcoat, listened with interest.

At the corner stood a drugstore, brilliant with electric lights. When they came into this glare, each of them turned simultaneously to gaze upon the other's face.

The man from the West stopped suddenly and released his arm.

"You're not Jimmy Wells," he snapped. C

D
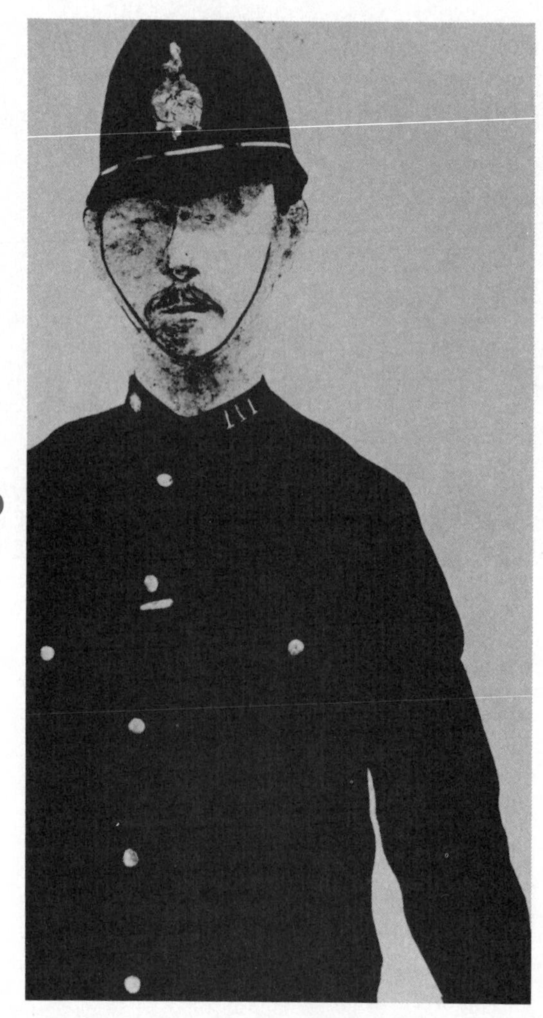
An Arm of the Law by Charles Roth (1920). Etching.

1. **egotism** (ē'gə·tiz'm): conceit.

Reading Check Test

1. The man in the doorway is waiting for his friend Jimmy Wells. *(True)*
2. The man last saw Jimmy ten years before. *(False)*
3. The man recognizes Jimmy as soon as he sees him. *(False)*
4. The second man is a plain-clothes police officer. *(True)*
5. He was told about "Silky" Bob by Jimmy Wells, the police officer who first approached Bob. *(True)*

Closure

Working with a partner, students should explain how the setting of a story creates mood. Have them give details of setting from "After Twenty Years" that help create the story's mood.

"Twenty years is a long time, but not long enough to change a man's nose from a Roman to a pug."

"It sometimes changes a good man into a bad one," said the tall man. "You've been under arrest for ten minutes, 'Silky' Bob. Chicago thinks you may have dropped over our way and wires us she wants to have a chat with you. Going quietly, are you? That's sensible. Now, before we go to the station, here's a note I was asked to hand you. You may read it here at the window. It's from Patrolman Wells."

The man from the West unfolded the little piece of paper handed him. His hand was steady when he began to read, but it trembled a little by the time he had finished. The note was rather short.

Bob: I was at the appointed place on time. When you struck the match to light your cigar, I saw it was the face of the man wanted in Chicago. Somehow I couldn't do it myself, so I went around and got a plain-clothes man to do the job. A

Jimmy

A. Irony

What is the irony in the surprise ending of the story? (That Bob gets arrested by the old friend with whom he had planned on having a pleasant reunion.)

Responding to the Story

Analyzing the Story

Identifying Facts

1. Where and when was the last meeting of Jimmy Wells and Bob?
2. On the evening the story takes place, do Bob and Jimmy Wells recognize each other? Explain.
3. Describe what Jimmy Wells does after speaking with Bob.
4. What happens to Bob at the end of the story?

Interpreting Meanings

SRW p. 79

5. Describe the **setting** of the story—the place, the time of day, and the weather. What emotions does the setting help arouse in you? (Would you feel differently if the setting were noontime in a park on a sunny day?)
6. Several details about Bob's appearance and behavior warn us that he might not be honest, or that he is hiding from someone. For instance, we first see him in a *dark* doorway with an *unlighted* cigar. List and discuss three other clues that pointed to Bob's shady past.
7. A **conflict** in literature is a struggle between opposing forces. What is the **external conflict** in "After Twenty Years"? What is Jimmy's **internal conflict**? Explain.
8. What is the resolution of the external conflict? The internal conflict?
9. How would you state the **theme** of this story? What truth about friendship and honor does it reveal to you?

SRW p. 87

Applying Meanings

10. How would you feel if you met a good friend from the past and found out he or she was doing something against the law? Discuss the **internal conflict** that might arise in such circumstances.

Writing About the Story

A Creative Response

1. **Inventing a Conversation.** Make up a conversation between Bob and Jimmy Wells during their last get-together before the evening the story takes place. The conversation should include information on the following topics: (a) their activities together over the past few years; (b) their thoughts about each other; (c) their plans for the future. Both characters should say something about each topic.

A Critical Response

2. **Analyzing a Character.** In the note to Bob at the end of the story, Jimmy says, "Somehow I couldn't do it myself, so I went around and got a plain-clothes man to do the job." In a paragraph, explain why you think Jimmy couldn't do it himself. What's the difference in Jimmy's mind between doing it himself and having someone else do it? End your paragraph with a statement telling how you felt about Jimmy's decision.

See Teacher's Manual page 61.

Analyzing the Story

Identifying Facts

1. The two met exactly twenty years before, at the restaurant that used to be where Bob is standing.
2. Jimmy recognizes Bob, but Bob does not recognize Jimmy. Jimmy recognized Bob from the picture that the Chicago police had sent. Bob probably was not expecting Jimmy to be a police officer.
3. Jimmy moves off, and probably goes to his precinct house. There, he talks to a plain-clothes officer, plans the arrest, and writes the note to Bob.
4. Bob is arrested, reads the note from Jimmy, and is clearly affected by the note's significance.

(Answers continue on page 198.)

(Answers begin on page 197.)

Interpreting Meanings

5. The story takes place on a cold, windy, deserted New York City street. It is ten o'clock at night.

Answers will vary. Students should note moods such as eeriness, spookiness, loneliness. They might think of a place like "The Twilight Zone." Students should be able to distinguish the different moods associated with a sunny scene.

6. Details include Bob's hurry to explain his presence, the little scar near his eyebrow, and the odd emphasis on his rich attire. (Since students are so far removed from the original setting of this story, they may not realize how out-of-place the diamonds are, and that they could indicate ill-gained riches.)

7. The external conflict is between "Silky" Bob and the plain-clothes police officer who is arresting him.

Jimmy's conflict is between his duty to arrest Bob, and his loyalty to Bob as a cherished friend from his youth.

8. The resolution is that the plain-clothes officer arrests Bob, and Bob goes quietly.

Jimmy finally decides to arrest Bob, but has another officer do it.

(Answers continue in left-hand column.)

(Continued from top.)

9. The theme is probably best stated as the law must always win out over friendship.

Applying Meanings

10. If students answer too quickly about how they would resolve their internal conflicts, remind them that putting a friend behind bars (or, conversely, letting a person go free whom you know should be arrested) is not something that is done lightly. Have students brainstorm reasons for both sides of the argument, and then decide which side is best.

Additional Writing Assignment

Have students work in pairs and write the lead paragraphs of a newspaper article that describes the arrest of "Silky" Bob.

Further Reading for Students

Two famous O. Henry stories that students will enjoy are "The Gift of the Magi" and "The Ransom of Red Chief."

Analyzing Language and Vocabulary

Prefixes Derived from Latin

O. Henry describes the plain-clothes policeman as being "submerged in his overcoat." Even if you didn't know what *submerged* meant, you could make a good guess if you knew that the prefix *sub-* means "under or below." Prefixes are word parts added before a word or a root to form a new word. Many common prefixes are derived from Latin, the language of the ancient Romans.

Here is a short list of Latin prefixes and their commonly used meanings:

Prefix	Meaning	Example
bi-	two	bicycle
de-	away from, undo	derail, defrost
pre-	before	prearrange
re-	again	reread
semi-	half	semicircle
sub-	under, below	submarine

1. What does O. Henry mean when he says the streets are "depeopled"?
2. For each prefix above, give two additional examples of words in which they are used.
3. Use each of these additional examples in a separate sentence.

For answers, see Teacher's Manual page 61.

Reading About the Writer

O. Henry is the penname of William Sydney Porter (1862–1910). Porter was born in North Carolina. He left home when he was twenty to seek his fortune in Texas. There he edited a humor magazine called *The Rolling Stone,* but he also took an ill-fated job as a bank teller. He was accused of embezzling funds from the bank, and instead of staying for the trial, he fled to Honduras. No one knows if he was guilty or innocent but skipping town didn't help his case. He later returned to Texas because his wife was ill, and he was arrested at once and jailed. In jail he was said to have met a prison guard named Orrin Henry who gave him the idea for his penname. After jail, Porter went to New York and lived there for the last eight years of his life. He wrote about his experiences in Texas and in Honduras, but many of his best known stories are set in New York City's streets and tenements and cheap hotels. O. Henry is known for his snappy surprise endings. Some of his most popular stories are "The Gift of the Magi," "The Ransom of Red Chief," and "The Furnished Room."

Focusing on Background

O. Henry's New Yorkers

"Whatever O. Henry permitted his characters to do, he made them do it in an utterly authentic milieu. The city [New York] in the summer was 'the smells of hot asphalt, underground caverns, gasoline, patchouli [perfume made from a mint plant], orange peel, sewer gas, Egyptian cigarettes, mortar, and the undried ink on newspapers.' A day began with 'the early morning people passing through the square to their work—sullen people, with sidelong glances and glum faces, hurrying, hurrying, hurrying.' By nightfall, the '3,126 lights on the Rialto were alight . . . Diners, heimgangers [loafers], shopgirls, confidence men, panhandlers, actors, highwaymen, millionaires, and bystanders hurried, skipped, strolled, sneaked, swaggered and scurried. . . .' "

—Gilbert Millstein,
The New York Times

PREREADING

1. BUILDING ON PRIOR KNOWLEDGE. To give students a historical perspective, you might want to briefly discuss World War II with them and Britain's role in the war. On September 3, 1939, two days after Germany attacked Poland, Great Britain and France declared war on Germany and World War II began. France surrendered to Germany in 1940, leaving Great Britain without allies in western Europe. During the Battle of Britain (1940–1941), Germany tried to conquer Britain. Britain's Royal Air Force, to which the pilot in this story belonged, had such good planes and pilots, however, that the Germans were forced to give up their daylight air attacks (this fact is alluded to on page 202, right-hand column, end of the second paragraph). By 1941, Germany gave up its attempts to invade Britain, although it continued its raids into 1945. On Dec. 8, 1941, a day after Japan attacked Pearl Harbor, Hawaii, the United States entered the war. World War II finally ended on Sept. 12, 1945.

2. ESTABLISHING A PURPOSE. The headnote sets a good purpose for reading the story.

3. PREREADING JOURNAL. Ask students to write a brief paragraph about what it's like to wake up in a strange place. They can use a real experience, or they can invent one.

★ **Texas Essential Elements/(a) English Language Arts: 1B** Purpose and audience; **1E** Formal/informal language; **3A** Plot/character; **4E** Predict; **4F** Generalizations; **4H** Point of view

BEWARE OF THE DOG

Roald Dahl

Roald Dahl is an expert storyteller and a master at the art of surprise. This story is guaranteed to put you in the sky. When you come down, you will almost surely have some doubts, as the pilot does, about where you are. It is well to remember that the story takes place during World War II. At this time, a great part of European territory—including France—was occupied by the German army. The story is told from the vantage point of a British fighter pilot. As the story opens, he is trying to get back home to England after a bombing mission against German targets somewhere in Europe. This story requires some detective work. As you read, pay close attention to details.

For a detailed lesson plan on this story, see Teacher's Manual pages 62–64.
A biography of Roald Dahl appears on text page 208.

Down below there was only a vast white undulating sea of cloud. Above there was the sun, and the sun was white like the clouds, because it is never yellow when one looks at it from high in the air.

He was flying the Spitfire.[1] His right hand was on the stick and he was working the rudder-bar with his left leg alone. It was quite easy. The machine was flying well. He knew what he was doing.

Everything is fine, he thought. I'm doing all right. I'm doing nicely. I know my way home. I'll be there in half an hour. When I land I shall taxi in and switch off my engine and I shall say, help me to get out, will you. I shall make my voice sound ordinary and natural and none of them will take any notice. Then I shall say, someone help me to get out. I can't do it alone because I've lost one of my legs. They'll all laugh and think that I'm joking and I shall say, all right, come and have a look. . . . Then Yorky will climb up on to the wing and look inside. He'll probably be sick because of all the blood and the mess. I shall laugh and say, for God's sake, help me get out.

He glanced down again at his right leg. There was not much of it left. The cannon shell had taken him on the thigh, just above the knee, and now there was nothing but a great mess and a lot of blood. But there was no pain. When he looked down, he felt as though he were seeing something that did not belong to him. It had nothing to do with him. It was just a mess which happened to be there in the cockpit; something strange and unusual and rather interesting. It was like finding a dead cat on the sofa.

He really felt fine, and because he still felt fine, he felt excited and unafraid. A

A. Point of View ? The point of view in this story is crucial. From what point of view is this story told? (Third-person limited)

I won't even bother to call up on the radio for the bloodwagon, he thought. It isn't necessary. And when I land I'll sit there quite normally and say, some of you fellows come and help me out, will you, because I've lost one of my legs. That will be funny. I'll laugh a little while I'm saying it; I'll say it calmly and slowly, and they'll think I'm joking. When Yorky comes up on to the wing and gets sick, I'll say, Yorky . . . have you fixed my car yet. Then when I get out I'll make my report. Later I'll go up to London and see Bluey. I'll say, Bluey I've got a surprise for you. I lost a B

B. Basic Situation ? What have you learned so far about the basic situation of the story? (The setting of the story is Europe during World War II. The pilot flying the plane is severely wounded, but a very skilled flier. He thinks to himself rationally because he knows that he must stay calm and not panic; he has a sense of humor. The pilot wants to reach his home base in England, where he will receive medical attention.)

Jargon. To make his story as realistic as possible, Dahl uses specialized language, or *jargon*, related to airplanes. You will understand the meaning of some of the jargon from your own experience or from the context of the story. Other specialized words, especially the names of World War II airplanes, will probably require explanation. Some have been explained in footnotes. SRW p. 59

1. **Spitfire**: British fighter plane used in World War II.

SUPPLEMENTARY SUPPORT MATERIAL

1. Vocabulary Activity Sheet
2. Reading Check Test blackline master
3. Selection Test (page 71 of Test Book)
4. Author photograph on *A Gallery of Authors* poster
5. Reader's Response Journal
6. Workbook (page 49)

DEVELOPING VOCABULARY

The following words appear on a test in the Test Book, page 72. (See also the Vocabulary Activity Sheet.)

cowling	squadron
giddy	duet
bail out	lather
unconscious	delirious
throttled back	hoisted

A. Interpreting
You can tell by the way the pilot's thoughts are wandering farther and farther away from the situation at hand that he is becoming delirious.

B. Suspense
? How does Dahl heighten suspense in this passage? (By having the pilot express his predictions with rational certainty. We already trust the pilot's skill and so we believe these predictions. Also, the amount of detail Dahl provides prolongs the suspense because it makes it seem as though the pilot has more time than he really does.)

C. Expression
"To fall in the drink" is a British expression meaning "to fall in the ocean."

★ **Texas Essential Elements/(c) Reading: 1C** Dictionaries; **3A** Main ideas/details; **3D** Generalizations; **3F** Purpose/point of view/opinion; **3H** Predict; **3I** Draw conclusions

leg today. But I don't mind so long as you don't. It doesn't even hurt. We'll go everywhere in cars. I always hated walking except when I walked down the street of the coppersmiths in Baghdad, but I could go in a rickshaw. I could go home and chop wood, but the head always flies off the ax. A Hot water, that's what it needs; put it in the bath and make the handle swell. I chopped lots of wood last time I went home and I put the ax in the bath . . .

Then he saw the sun shining on the engine cowling[2] of his machine. He saw the sun shining on the rivets in the metal, and he remembered the airplane and he remembered where he was. He realized that he was no longer feeling good; that he was sick and giddy. His head kept falling forward on to his chest because his neck seemed no longer to have any strength. But he knew that he was flying the Spitfire. He could feel the handle of the stick between the fingers of his right hand.

B I'm going to pass out, he thought. Any moment now I'm going to pass out.

He looked at his altimeter.[3] Twenty-one thousand. To test himself he tried to read the hundreds as well as the thousands. Twenty-one thousand and what? As he looked the dial became blurred and he could not even see the needle. He knew then that he must bail out; that there was not a second to lose, otherwise he would become unconscious. Quickly, frantically, he tried to slide back the hood with his left hand, but he had not the strength. For a second he took his right hand off the stick and with both hands he managed to push the hood back. The rush of cold air on his face seemed to help. He had a moment of great clearness. His actions became orderly and precise. That is what happens with a good pilot. He took some quick deep breaths from his oxygen mask, and as he did so, he looked out over the side of the cockpit. Down below there was only a vast white sea of cloud and he realized that he did not know where he was.

C It'll be the Channel,[4] he thought. I'm sure to fall in the drink.

He throttled back, pulled off his helmet, undid his straps and pushed the stick hard over to the left. The Spitfire dipped its port wing and turned smoothly over on to its back. The pilot fell out.

As he fell, he opened his eyes, because he knew that he must not pass out before he had pulled the cord. On one side he saw the sun; on the other he saw the whiteness of the clouds, and as he fell, as he somersaulted in the air, the white clouds chased the sun and the sun chased the clouds. They chased each other in a small circle; they ran faster and faster and there was the sun and the clouds and the clouds and the sun, and the clouds came nearer until suddenly there was no longer any sun but only a great whiteness. The whole world was white and there was nothing in it. It was so white that sometimes it looked black, and after a time it was either white or black, but mostly it was white. He watched it as it turned from white to black, then back to white again, and the white stayed for a long time, but the black lasted only for a few seconds. He got into the habit of going to sleep during the white periods, of waking up just in time to see the world when it was black. The black was very quick. Sometimes it was only a flash, a flash of black lightning. The white was slow and in the slowness of it, he always dozed off.

One day, when it was white, he put out a hand and he touched something. He took it between his fingers and crumpled it. For a time he lay there, idly letting the tips of his fingers play with the thing which they had touched. Then slowly he opened his eyes, looked down at his hand and saw that he was holding something which was white. It was the edge of a sheet. He knew it was a sheet because he could see the texture of the material and the stitchings on the hem. He screwed up his eyes and opened them again quickly. This time he saw the room. He saw the bed in which he was lying: He saw the gray walls and the door and the green curtains over the window. There were some roses on the table by his bed.

Then he saw the basin on the table near the roses. It was a white enamel basin and beside it there was a small medicine glass.

This is a hospital, he thought. I am in a hospital. But he could remember nothing. He lay back on his pillow, looking at the ceiling and wondering

2. **cowling** (kou'ling): metal covering of an airplane engine.
3. **altimeter** (al·tim'ə·tər): instrument measuring altitude.
4. **Channel**: English Channel; the body of water that separates Great Britain from France.

Spitfires at Duxford, England.

A. Making Inferences
? What happened? (His leg was amputated.)

what had happened. He was gazing at the smooth grayness of the ceiling which was so clean and gray, and then suddenly he saw a fly walking upon it. The sight of this fly, the suddenness of seeing this small black speck on a sea of gray, brushed the surface of his brain, and quickly, in that second, he remembered everything. He remembered the Spitfire and he remembered the altimeter showing twenty-one thousand feet. He remembered the pushing back of the hood with both hands and he remembered the bailing out. He remembered his leg.

It seemed all right now. He looked down at the end of the bed, but he could not tell. He put one hand underneath the bedclothes and felt for his knees. He found one of them, but when he felt for the other, his hand touched something which was soft and covered in bandages. A

Just then the door opened and a nurse came in.

''Hello,'' she said. ''So you've waked up at last.''

She was not good-looking, but she was large and clean. She was between thirty and forty and she had fair hair. More than that he did not notice.

''Where am I?''

''You're a lucky fellow. You landed in a wood near the beach. You're in Brighton.[5] They brought you in two days ago, and now you're all fixed up. You look fine.''

''I've lost a leg,'' he said.

---

5. **Brighton** (brīt′'n): town in southern England.

A. Expansion "Ringing up" is the British expression for calling on the telephone.

B. Complication and Foreshadowing The noise of the German plane is the first complication to confront the pilot since he's been in the hospital. It is also the first clue that he may not be where he was told he is.

"That's nothing. We'll get you another one. Now you must go to sleep. The doctor will be coming to see you in about an hour." She picked up the basin and the medicine glass and went out.

But he did not sleep. He wanted to keep his eyes open because he was frightened that if he shut them again everything would go away. He lay looking at the ceiling. The fly was still there. It was very energetic. It would run forward very fast for a few inches, then it would stop. Then it would run forward again, stop, run forward, and every now and then it would take off and buzz around viciously in small circles. It always landed back in the same place on the ceiling and started running and stopping all over again. He watched it for so long that after a while it was no longer a fly, but only a black speck upon a sea of gray, and he was still watching it when the nurse opened the door, and stood aside while the doctor came in. He was an Army doctor, a major, and he had some last war ribbons on his chest. He was bald and small, but he had a cheerful face and kind eyes.

"Well, well," he said. "So you've decided to wake up at last. How are you feeling?"

"I feel all right."

"That's the stuff. You'll be up and about in no time."

The doctor took his wrist to feel his pulse.

"By the way," he said, "some of the lads from A your squadron[6] were ringing up and asking about you. They wanted to come along and see you, but I said that they'd better wait a day or two. Told them you were all right and that they could come and see you a little later on. Just lie quiet and take it easy for a bit. Got something to read?" He glanced at the table with the roses. "No. Well, nurse will look after you. She'll get you anything you want." With that he waved his hands and went out, followed by the large clean nurse.

When they had gone, he lay back and looked at the ceiling again. The fly was still there and as he lay watching it he heard the noise of an airplane in the distance. He lay listening to the sound of its engines. It was a long way away. I wonder what it is, he thought. Let me see if I can place it. Suddenly he jerked his head sharply to one side. Anyone who has been bombed can tell the noise of a Junkers 88. They can tell most other German bombers for that matter, but especially a Junkers 88. The engines seem to sing a duet. There is a deep vibrating bass voice and with it there is a high pitched tenor. It is the singing of the tenor B which makes the sound of a Ju-88 something which one cannot mistake.

He lay listening to the noise and felt quite certain about what it was. But where were the sirens and where the guns? That German pilot certainly had a nerve coming near Brighton alone in daylight.

The aircraft was always far away and soon the noise faded away into the distance. Later on there was another. This one, too, was far away, but there was the same deep undulating bass and the high swinging tenor and there was no mistaking it. He had heard that noise every day during the Battle.[7]

He was puzzled. There was a bell on the table by the bed. He reached out his hand and rang it. He heard the noise of footsteps down the corridor. The nurse came in.

"Nurse, what were those airplanes?"

"I'm sure I don't know. I didn't hear them. Probably fighters or bombers. I expect they were returning from France. Why, what's the matter?"

"They were Ju-88s. I'm sure they were Ju-88s. I know the sound of the engines. There were two of them. What were they doing over here?"

The nurse came up to the side of his bed and began to straighten out the sheets and tuck them in under the mattress.

"Gracious me, what things you imagine. You mustn't worry about a thing like that. Would you like me to get you something to read?"

"No, thank you."

She patted his pillow and brushed back the hair from his forehead with her hand.

---

6. **squadron** (skwäd'rən): group of military pilots.

7. **Battle**: Battle of Britain (1940–1941). Soon after gaining control of France in mid-1940, the Germans tried to conquer Great Britain. They attacked by air almost daily, but the British held on. The Germans suffered heavy losses and gave up the attempt at conquest by the middle of 1941.

"They never come over in daylight any longer. You know that. They were probably Lancasters or Flying Fortresses."[8]

"Nurse."

"Yes."

"Could I have a cigarette?"

"Why certainly you can."

She went out and came back almost at once with a packet of Players and some matches. She handed one to him and when he had put it in his mouth, she struck a match and lit it.

"If you want me again," she said, "just ring the bell," and she went out.

Once toward evening he heard the noise of another aircraft. It was far away, but even so he knew that it was a single-engined machine. It was going fast; he could tell that. He could not place it. It wasn't a Spit, and it wasn't a Hurricane. It did not sound like an American engine either. They make more noise. He did not know what it was, and it worried him greatly. Perhaps I am very ill, he thought. Perhaps I am imagining things. Perhaps I am a little delirious. I simply do not know what to think.

That evening the nurse came in with a basin of hot water and began to wash him.

"Well," she said, "I hope you don't think that we're being bombed."

A She had taken off his pajama top and was soaping his right arm with a flannel.[9] He did not answer.

She rinsed the flannel in the water, rubbed more soap on it, and began to wash his chest.

"You're looking fine this evening," she said. "They operated on you as soon as you came in. They did a marvelous job. You'll be all right. I've got a brother in the RAF,"[10] she added. "Flying bombers."

He said, "I went to school in Brighton."

She looked up quickly. "Well, that's fine," she said. "I expect you'll know some people in the town."

"Yes," he said, "I know quite a few."

She had finished washing his chest and arms. Now she turned back the bedclothes so that his left leg was uncovered. She did it in such a way that his bandaged stump remained under the sheets. She undid the cord of his pajama trousers and took them off. There was no trouble because they had cut off the right trouser leg so that it could not interfere with the bandages. She began to wash his left leg and the rest of his body. This was the first time he had had a bed bath and he was embarrassed. She laid a towel under his leg and began washing his foot with the flannel. She said, "This wretched soap won't lather at all. It's the water. It's as hard as nails."

He said, "None of the soap is very good now and, of course, with hard water[11] it's hopeless." As he said it he remembered something. He remembered the baths which he used to take at school in Brighton, in the long stone-floored bathroom which had four baths in a row. He remembered how the water was so soft that you had to take a shower afterward to get all the soap off your body, and he remembered how the foam used to float on the surface of the water, so that you could not see your legs underneath. He remembered that sometimes they were given calcium tablets because the school doctor used to say that soft water was bad for the teeth. B

"In Brighton," he said, "the water isn't . . . "

He did not finish the sentence. Something had occurred to him; something so fantastic and absurd that for a moment he felt like telling the nurse about it and having a good laugh. C

She looked up. "The water isn't what?" she said.

"Nothing," he answered. "I was dreaming."

She rinsed the flannel in the basin, wiped the soap off his leg and dried him with a towel.

"It's nice to be washed," he said. "I feel better." He was feeling his face with his hand. "I need a shave."

"We'll do that tomorrow," she said. "Perhaps you can do it yourself then."

---

8. **Lancasters**: British heavy bombers. **Flying Fortresses**: American heavy bombers.
9. **flannel**: washcloth.
10. **RAF**: abbreviation for Royal Air Force, Great Britain's air force.
11. **hard water**: water that contains mineral salts that keep soap from making a good lather.

A. Interpreting

? Why doesn't the pilot answer? (He is confused; he is probably suspicious of her because she so casually dismissed his concern over the German planes. For all he knows, perhaps they *are* being bombed.)

B. Complication

? How does this incident further complicate the pilot's predicament? (This is another piece of contradictory information that adds to his confusion.)

C. Responding

? What do you think has occurred to the pilot? (Probably that he has been taken prisoner of war.)

Humanities Connection: Discussing the Fine Art
Henri Matisse (1869–1954) is regarded by some as the most important French painter of the twentieth century. His paintings, whose subjects are often still lifes and interiors, are characterized by a bold use of color and pattern (note the floor and the suggestion of wallpaper in this painting). Another painting by Matisse appears on page 255.

? What time of day would you say it is in the painting? (The purplish shade of the sky suggests that it is dusk.) What kind of room do you think this is? What is outside? How far away would you say the figures are from the window?

Interior (The Closed Window) by Henri Matisse (1918–1919). Oil.

Virginia Museum of Fine Arts, Collection of Mr. and Mrs. Paul Mellon.

That night he could not sleep. He lay awake thinking of the Junkers 88s and of the hardness of the water. He could think of nothing else. They were Ju-88s, he said to himself. I know they were. And yet it is not possible, because they would not be flying around so low over here in broad daylight. I know that it is true and yet I know that it is impossible. Perhaps I am ill. Perhaps I am behaving like a fool and do not know what I am doing or saying. Perhaps I am delirious. For a long time he lay awake thinking these things, and once he sat up in bed and said aloud, "I will prove that I am not crazy. I will make a little speech about something complicated and intellectual. I will talk about what to do with Germany after the war." But before he had time to begin, he was asleep.

A

He woke just as the first light of day was showing through the slit in the curtains over the window. The room was still dark, but he could tell that it was already beginning to get light outside. He lay looking at the gray light which was showing through the slit in the curtain and as he lay there he remembered the day before. He remembered the Junkers 88s and the hardness of the water; he remembered the large pleasant nurse and the kind doctor, and now a small grain of doubt took root in his mind and it began to grow.

He looked around the room. The nurse had taken the roses out the night before. There was nothing except the table with a packet of cigarettes, a box of matches, and an ashtray. The room was bare. It was no longer warm or friendly. It was not even comfortable. It was cold and empty and very quiet.

B

Slowly the grain of doubt grew, and with it came fear, a light, dancing fear that warned but did not frighten; the kind of fear that one gets not because one is afraid, but because one feels that there is something wrong. Quickly the doubt and the fear grew so that he became restless and angry, and when he touched his forehead with his hand, he found that it was damp with sweat. He knew then that he must do something; that he must find some way of proving to himself that he was either right or wrong, and he looked up and saw again the window and the green curtains. From where he lay, that window was right in front of him, but it was fully ten yards away. Somehow he must reach it and look out. The idea became an obsession with him and soon he could think of nothing except the window. But what about his leg? He put his hand underneath the bedclothes and felt the thick bandaged stump which was all that was left on the right-hand side. It seemed all right. It didn't hurt. But it would not be easy.

He sat up. Then he pushed the bedclothes aside and put his left leg on the floor. Slowly, carefully, he swung his body over until he had both hands on the floor as well; then he was out of bed, kneeling on the carpet. He looked at the stump. It was very short and thick, covered with bandages. It was beginning to hurt and he could feel it throbbing. He wanted to collapse, lie down on the carpet and do nothing, but he knew that he must go on.

With two arms and one leg, he crawled over toward the window. He would reach forward as far as he could with his arms, then he would give a little jump and slide his left leg along after them. Each time he did it, it jarred his wound so that he gave a soft grunt of pain, but he continued to crawl across the floor on two hands and one knee. When he got to the window he reached up, and one at a time he placed both hands on the sill. Slowly he raised himself up until he was standing on his left leg. Then quickly he pushed aside the curtains and looked out.

C

He saw a small house with a gray tiled roof standing alone beside a narrow lane, and immediately behind it there was a plowed field. In front of the house there was an untidy garden, and there was a green hedge separating the garden from the lane. He was looking at the hedge when he saw the sign. It was just a piece of board nailed to the top of a short pole, and because the hedge had not been trimmed for a long time, the branches had grown out around the sign so that it seemed almost as though it had been placed in the middle of the hedge. There was something written on the board with white paint. He pressed his head against the glass of the window, trying to read what it said. The first letter was a G, he could see that. The second was an A, and the third was an R. One after another he managed to see what the

A. Character's Motivation

? Why does the pilot say he will make a speech about Germany? (He is exhibiting the same behavior that he did in the plane: He is trying to keep calm by thinking rationally. By making up a complicated and rational speech in his head about what to do with Germany after the war, he will prove to himself that he is not crazy and imagining things.)

B. Setting

? What does the change in the way the pilot perceives the setting tell about his frame of mind? (Like the room, the pilot is feeling "cold" and "empty." He no longer feels secure in his surroundings.)

C. Suspense

Dahl creates suspense by describing in detail the pilot's trip to the window. We wonder what he thinks he might see to resolve his dilemma, and we feel the pain in his leg as he moves.

Critical Comment
Author Joyce Carol Oates has said ". . . Dahl writes stories that are almost frightening and almost amusing, crafted along old-fashioned lines of 'suspense'. . ."

Lead a discussion about how Dahl creates suspense in "Beware of the Dog." How does he keep us on the edge of our chair as we read the story? Have students give examples from the story.

A. Climax
This is the turning point of the story. The pilot sees the French sign and his suspicions are confirmed. He is not in a hospital in England, but rather in German-occupied France.

B. Character's Motivation
? Why does the pilot look more carefully at the nurse now? (He now sees her as the enemy, and is looking for qualities that betray her as such. He is perhaps wondering what clues he first missed when looking at her.) What do her mannerisms suggest? (That she is nervous and afraid to meet the pilot's eyes. Not only is he suspicious of her, but she is suspicious of him: He knows the sound of German planes, and he used to live in Brighton—the place where she and the doctor are pretending he is.)

letters were. There were three words, and slowly he spelled the letters out aloud to himself as he managed to read them. G-A-R-D-E A-U C-H-I-E-N, *Garde au chien.*[12] That is what it said.

A He stood there balancing on one leg and holding tightly to the edges of the window sill with his hands, staring at the sign and at the whitewashed lettering of the words. For a moment he could think of nothing at all. He stood there looking at the sign, repeating the words over and over to himself. Slowly he began to realize the full meaning of the thing. He looked up at the cottage and at the plowed field. He looked at the small orchard on the left of the cottage and he looked at the green countryside beyond. "So this is France," he said. "I am in France."

Now the throbbing in his right thigh was very great. It felt as though someone was pounding the end of his stump with a hammer and suddenly the pain became so intense that it affected his head. For a moment he thought he was going to fall. Quickly he knelt down again, crawled back to the bed and hoisted himself in. He pulled the bedclothes over himself and lay back on the pillow, exhausted. He could still think of nothing at all except the small sign by the hedge and the plowed field and the orchard. It was the words on the sign that he could not forget.

It was some time before the nurse came in. She came carrying a basin of hot water and she said, "Good morning, how are you today?"

He said, "Good morning, nurse."

The pain was still great under the bandages, but he did not wish to tell this woman anything. He looked at her as she busied herself with getting the washing things ready. B He looked at her more carefully now. Her hair was very fair. She was tall and big-boned and her face seemed pleasant. But there was something a little uneasy about her eyes. They were never still. They never looked at anything for more than a moment and they moved too quickly from one place to another in the room. There was something about her movements also. They were too sharp and nervous to go well with the casual manner in which she spoke.

She set down the basin, took off his pajama top and began to wash him.

"Did you sleep well?"

"Yes."

"Good," she said. She was washing his arms and his chest.

"I believe there's someone coming down to see you from the Air Ministry after breakfast," she went on. "They want a report or something. I expect you know all about it. How you got shot down and all that. I won't let him stay long, so don't worry."

He did not answer. She finished washing him and gave him a toothbrush and some tooth powder. He brushed his teeth, rinsed his mouth, and spat the water out into the basin.

Later she brought him his breakfast on a tray, but he did not want to eat. He was still feeling weak and sick and he wished only to lie still and think about what had happened. And there was a sentence running through his head. It was a sentence which Johnny, the Intelligence Officer of his squadron, always repeated to the pilots every day before they went out. He could see Johnny now, leaning against the wall of the dispersal hut with his pipe in his hand, saying, "And if they get you, don't forget, just your name, rank, and number. Nothing else. For God's sake, say nothing else."

"There you are," she said as she put the tray on his lap. "I've got you an egg. Can you manage all right?"

"Yes."

She stood beside the bed. "Are you feeling all right?"

"Yes."

"Good. If you want another egg I might be able to get you one."

"This is all right."

"Well, just ring the bell if you want any more." And she went out.

He had just finished eating, when the nurse came in again.

She said, "Wing Commander Roberts is here. I've told him that he can only stay for a few minutes."

She beckoned with her hand and the Wing Commander came in.

"Sorry to bother you like this," he said.

12. ***Garde au chien*** (gärd ō shyen): French, "beware of the dog."

Reading Check Test

1. Who is Peter Williamson? *A British fighter pilot.*

2. Why does he turn his airplane upside down? *So that he can bail out.*

3. When does Williamson remember what happened to him? *When he watches the fly on the ceiling of his room.*

4. What language do the nurse and doctor speak? *English.*

5. What does Williamson reveal to the Wing Commander? *Only his name, rank, and number.*

Closure

Working in pairs, students should explain to each other how jargon adds to the realism of this story. Have them quote examples of the airplane jargon, and explain how it helps bring them into the story.

He was an ordinary RAF officer, dressed in a uniform which was a little shabby. He wore wings and a DFC.[13] He was fairly tall and thin with plenty of black hair. His teeth, which were irregular and widely spaced, stuck out a little even when he closed his mouth. As he spoke he took a printed form and a pencil from his pocket and he pulled up a chair and sat down.

"How are you feeling?"

There was no answer.

"Tough luck about your leg. I know how you feel. I hear you put up a fine show before they got you."

The man in the bed was lying quite still, watching the man in the chair.

The man in the chair said, "Well, let's get this stuff over. I'm afraid you'll have to answer a few questions so that I can fill in this combat report. Let me see now, first of all, what was your squadron?"

The man in the bed did not move. He looked straight at the Wing Commander and he said, "My name is Peter Williamson. My rank is Squadron Leader and my number is nine seven two four five seven." **A**

13. **DFC**: abbreviation for Distinguished Flying Cross, a medal awarded to members of the RAF for special achievement.

A. Expansion

To give out his squadron number would help the enemy identify the location and the strength of the pilot's RAF unit.

Analyzing the Story

Identifying Facts

1. The main character is Peter Williamson, a fighter pilot in the Royal Air Force. He is trying to fly back to England after a mission over France. He has just been hit by cannonfire on his right leg.

2. Answers will vary, but most students should say the white sheet. They will connect that with Williamson's injury, and assume that he is in a hospital.

3. The noise is the engine sound of a Junkers 88, a German bomber, flying at a low altitude during the daytime.

4. The pilot remembers that, when he was in school at Brighton, the water was so soft that he had to take a shower to get the soap lather off. Because he still thinks he is in England, this conflicting information is confusing.

(Answers continue on page 208.)

Responding to the Story

Analyzing the Story

Identifying Facts

1. Describe the situation as the story opens. Who is the main **character,** what is he doing, and what has just happened to him?
2. When the pilot wakes up, what detail first tells you (and him) that he is in a hospital?
3. What noise does the pilot hear from his hospital bed that suggests the hospital may not be what it seems?
4. When the nurse complains about the hardness of the water, what does the pilot remember about his own experience in Brighton? Explain how this adds to his confusion.

Interpreting Meanings

5. What does the pilot realize when he sees the sign reading "Garde au chien"? Where is he? Into whose hands has he fallen?
6. To what lengths had the pilot's captors gone to persuade him he was in England? How many of the details can you identify?
7. The pilot thinks of Johnny's words, "And if they get you, don't forget, just your name, rank, and number. Nothing else." Who are "they"? Why didn't Johnny want the pilots to say anything else? Explain whether the pilot follows Johnny's instructions.
8. The point of view throughout the story is **limited third-person.** We are so close to the pilot that we see the world as he does. Find the passages in the beginning which describe the sun, clouds, and sky, and the change from light to darkness. What is happening to the pilot in these passages? Do you think this is a believable way of describing what the pilot is thinking and feeling? SRW p. 69
9. What can you tell about the **character** of the pilot, Peter Williamson, from the way he is thinking about his badly wounded leg and how he plans to deal with it?
10. After the pilot finds himself in the hospital, his main **conflict,** or struggle, involves trying to discover exactly where he is. By the end of the story he has a new conflict. What is this new problem? How do you think it is going to be resolved?

Applying Meanings

11. Think of the events beginning with the blurring of the figures on the altimeter and ending with the pilot's awareness of the fly on the ceiling. What do you guess from this episode about the writer's familiarity with flying? Even if you have never fallen from an airplane, do the details in this description help you feel what it would be like? How?

(Answers begin on page 207.)

Interpreting Meanings

5. He realizes that the people in the hospital have been tricking him. He is in occupied France, and has been captured by the Germans.

6. His captors had recreated a British hospital scene, even bringing in people who could speak flawless English. Details include the decor of the room, the actions and speech of the nurse and the doctor, the medals worn by the doctor and Wing Commander, the British cigarettes (Players).

7. "They" are the Germans—the enemy.

Giving additional information could endanger the rest of the squadron, or give the Germans knowledge of troop strength.

The pilot does follow Johnny's instructions after he realizes that he is in occupied France. The other information he gives before then seems inconsequential.

8. The pilot is going through periods of consciousness and unconsciousness. He can't tell which way is up or down.

9. Williamson obviously has a great will to live. In addition, he seems to have a high threshold of pain, and is very brave

(Answers continue in left-hand column.)

(Continued from top.)

when faced with terrible circumstances.

10. The new conflict is how to keep from giving information to the Wing Commander, or whoever will be interrogating him. Since Williamson seems to have a very strong character, he may not give in to his captors, or at least not for a long while.

Applying Meanings

11. The writer is probably very familiar with flying.

The details do give a good idea of what it is like turning head over heels in the air, falling through clouds, and looking up at the brilliant sun. Students should comment on the sensory details included in the description.

FURTHER READING FOR STUDENTS

Roald Dahl, *The Best of Roald Dahl*

———, *Charlie and the Chocolate Factory*

———, *James and the Giant Peach.*

Writing About the Story

A Creative Response

1. **Continuing a Story.** Write a paragraph describing what you think would happen to Peter Williamson if the story continued. Before you start, you might want to think about these questions: Does he escape? Is he rescued? Does the nurse help?

A Critical Response

2. **Summarizing a Story.** Write a paragraph summarizing the story. Briefly mention each main event of the story, and tell how one event leads to another. (For help in this assignment, see page 253.) Begin by completing this topic sentence: *"Beware of the Dog" tells the story of how a World War II pilot comes to realize. . . .*
3. **Explaining a Title.** The title of the story refers to a sign that is posted, in different languages, all over the world. Write a paragraph explaining what other possible meaning the title could have, as it relates to the story. (Hint: Who is the dog? Who must beware, and why?)

See Teacher's Manual page 64.

Analyzing Language and Vocabulary

Jargon

SRW p. 59

The term **jargon** refers to the specialized vocabulary of a particular group. In this story, the author uses the jargon of airplanes and flight to make the story as specific and realistic as possible. Match each word on the left with the appropriate definition. Which words can be used outside the context of flight?

1. stick	a. to drive a plane on the runway
2. cowling	b. group of military pilots
3. cockpit	c. pilot compartment
4. squadron	d. metal covering of an airplane engine
5. port	e. lever that controls the altitude and movement of a plane
6. taxi	f. left-hand side

For answers, see Teacher's Manual page 64.

Reading About the Writer

Roald Dahl (1916–   ) is an English writer well known for his short stories and children's books, including *Charlie and the Chocolate Factory* and *James and the Giant Peach.* When World War II broke out in 1939, Dahl joined the Royal Air Force of Britain as a fighter pilot. He was seriously wounded when his fighter plane was shot down and was hospitalized for four months. His writing career began after he was sent to Washington as an assistant to the British ambassador (see Focusing on Background). Dahl often ends his stories on surprising notes, sometimes they are even shockers. In his story "Lamb to the Slaughter," he has two policemen eat a leg of lamb without knowing they are eating the murder weapon.

Focusing on Background

A Surprising Start

Roald Dahl, before he went to Washington D.C., had never thought of publishing a word. One day he was approached by the English writer C. S. Forester for an interview about his flying experiences for *The Saturday Evening Post.* Dahl tells about the experience:

"Forester was a very distinguished old boy. . . . He reckoned he could get a good piece out of me. We had lunch, and he started taking notes, but it became so bothersome that we weren't in fact eating any lunch, so I said: 'Why don't you let me scribble some notes later. I'll send them round to you; meanwhile we'll have lunch.'

"Well, when I got down to these notes I got a bit carried away, to tell you the truth, and they turned out to be more like a story. Forester or somebody detected a kind of quality in it—anyway an acceptable style. Anyhow that was the piece the *Post* used, more or less. It was called 'A Piece of Cake.' They paid me a thousand dollars for it. . . .

"As I got into the way of it they [the following stories] became less and less realistic and more fictional. I began to see I could handle fiction. . . . Anyhow, it made me realize that this was what I'd have to do in future; since I could write, that's what I'd do."

—Roald Dahl

PREREADING

1. **BUILDING ON PRIOR KNOWLEDGE.** Before they read, have students tell what they think it might be like to be an orphan and to live in an orphanage. Do they have personal experience? Or do they know someone who is an orphan? Have they read any stories about orphans? You might bring up how easy it might be for an orphan to become attached to an adult who is kind and caring. Why might it be easy for an adult to become attached to an orphan? What needs might each of them have that the other might be able to fill?

2. **ESTABLISHING A PURPOSE.** The headnote sets a good purpose for reading this story.

3. **PREREADING JOURNAL.** Before they read, have students make a list of qualities an adult might have that would make an orphan want to be with him or her.

★ **Texas Essential Elements/(a) English Language Arts: 1B** Purpose and audience; **3B** Figurative language; **4E** Predict; **4F** Generalizations

A MOTHER IN MANNVILLE

For a detailed lesson plan on this story, see Teacher's Manual pages 65–67. A biography of Marjorie Kinnan Rawlings appears on text page 215.

Marjorie Kinnan Rawlings

We usually like stories when we have an emotional response to them. When this happens, it generally means that the writer has tapped into something that is important to us. In this story, the writer touches the need for love that is common to everyone. As you read, be aware of how the story is making you feel. What details in the story strike the right chords?

A The orphanage is high in the Carolina mountains. Sometimes in winter the snowdrifts are so deep that the institution is cut off from the village below, from all the world. Fog hides the mountain peaks, the snow swirls down the valleys, and a wind blows so bitterly that the orphanage boys who take the milk twice daily to the baby cottage reach the door with fingers stiff in an agony of numbness.

"Or when we carry trays from the cookhouse for the ones that are sick," Jerry said, "we get our faces frostbit, because we can't put our hands over them. I have gloves," he added. "Some of the boys don't have any."

He liked the late spring, he said. The rhododendron was in bloom, a carpet of color, across the mountainsides, soft as the May winds that stirred the hemlocks. He called it laurel.

"It's pretty when the laurel blooms," he said. "Some of it's pink and some of it's white."

I was there in autumn. I wanted quiet, isolation, to do some troublesome writing. I wanted mountain air to blow out the malaria[1] from too long a time in the subtropics. I was homesick, too, for the flaming of maples in October, and for corn shocks and pumpkins and black-walnut trees and the lift of hills. I found them all, living in a cabin that belonged to the orphanage, half a mile beyond the orphanage farm. When I took the cabin, I asked for a boy or man to come and chop wood for the fireplace. The first few days were warm, I found what wood I needed about the cabin, no one came, and I forgot the order. B

I looked up from my typewriter one late afternoon, a little startled. A boy stood at the door, and my pointer dog, my companion, was at his side and had not barked to warn me. The boy was probably twelve years old, but undersized. He wore overalls and a torn shirt, and was barefooted. C

He said, "I can chop some wood today."

I said, "But I have a boy coming from the orphanage."

"I'm the boy."

"You? But you're small."

"Size don't matter, chopping wood," he said. "Some of the big boys don't chop good. I've been chopping wood at the orphanage a long time."

I visualized mangled and inadequate branches for my fires. I was well into my work and not inclined to conversation. I was a little blunt.

"Very well. There's the ax. Go ahead and see what you can do."

I went back to work, closing the door. At first

1. **malaria** (mə·ler′ē·ə): disease characterized by chills and fever, transmitted by certain mosquitoes.

Description. The writer of this story uses description to help you "see" the action, the characters, and the setting more vividly. Be alert for her imaginative descriptions of everyday objects. SRW p. 29

A. Setting
? Rawlings gives vivid details of the setting in these first paragraphs. What words make you "see" and "feel" her surroundings? ("Snowdrifts," "fog hides the mountain peaks," "snow swirls," "wind blows so bitterly," "carpet of color," "soft as the May winds that stirred the hemlocks") Tell students to note these vivid details throughout the story. This will help them answer the Analyzing Language and Vocabulary exercises.

B. Point of View
? From what point of view is the story told? (First person) How do you know? (The pronoun *I*)

C. Making Inferences
? What does the boy's appearance tell about his style of living? (He is probably poor since he wears a torn shirt and no shoes.)

SUPPLEMENTARY SUPPORT MATERIAL

1. Vocabulary Activity Sheet
2. Reading Check Test blackline master
3. Selection Test (page 73 of Test Book)
4. Author photograph on *A Gallery of Authors* poster
5. Audiocassette recording
6. Connections Between Reading and Writing worksheet
7. Reader's Reponse Journal
8. Workbook (page 51)

DEVELOPING VOCABULARY

The following words appear on a test in the Test Book, page 74. (See also the Vocabulary Activity Sheet.)

orphanage	mangled
frostbit	astonishing
flaming of maples	integrity
companion	courtesy
visualized	duplicate

A. Descriptive Details

? What color is the boy's hair? (Pale yellow—probably with a silken quality) What does she mean when she says "a light sun had touched him with the same suffused glory . . ."? (Her praise of his chopped wood probably made him glow with pleasure.)

Texas Essential Elements/(c) Reading: 1C Dictionaries; **3A** Main ideas/details; **3D** Generalizations; **3H** Predict; **3I** Draw conclusions

the sound of the boy dragging brush annoyed me. Then he began to chop. The blows were rhythmic and steady, and shortly I had forgotten him, the sound no more of an interruption than a consistent rain. I suppose an hour and a half passed, for when I stopped and stretched, and heard the boy's steps on the cabin stoop, the sun was dropping behind the farthest mountain, and the valleys were purple with something deeper than the asters.

The boy said, "I have to go to supper now. I can come again tomorrow evening."

I said, "I'll pay you now for what you've done," thinking I should probably have to insist on an older boy. "Ten cents an hour?"

"Anything is all right."

We went together back of the cabin. An astonishing amount of solid wood had been cut. There were cherry logs and heavy roots of rhododendron, and blocks from the waste pine and oak left from the building of the cabin.

"But you've done as much as a man," I said. "This is a splendid pile."

I looked at him, actually, for the first time. His hair was the color of the corn shocks, and his eyes, very direct, were like the mountain sky when rain is pending—gray, with a showing of that miraculous blue. As I spoke a light sun had touched him with the same suffused glory with A which it touched the mountains. I gave him a quarter.

"You may come tomorrow," I said, "and thank you very much."

He looked at me, and at the coin, and seemed to want to speak, but could not, and turned away.

"I'll split the kindling tomorrow," he said over his thin ragged shoulder. "You'll need kindling and medium wood and logs and backlogs."

At daylight I was half awakened by the sound of chopping. Again it was so even in texture that I went back to sleep. When I left my bed in the cool morning, the boy had come and gone, and a stack of kindling was neat against the cabin wall. He came again after school in the afternoon and worked until time to return to the orphanage. His name was Jerry; he was twelve years old, and he had been at the orphanage since he was four. I could picture him at four, with the same gray-blue eyes and the same—independence? No, the word that comes to me is "integrity."

The word means something very special to me, and the quality for which I use it is a rare one. My father had it—there is another of whom I am almost sure—but almost no man of my acquaintance possesses it with the clarity, the purity, the simplicity of a mountain stream. But the boy Jerry had it. It is bedded on courage, but it is more than brave. It is honest, but it is more than honesty. The ax handle broke one day. Jerry said the woodshop at the orphanage would repair it. I brought money to pay for the job and he refused it.

"I'll pay for it," he said. "I broke it. I brought the ax down careless."

"But no one hits accurately every time," I told him. "The fault was in the wood of the handle. I'll see the man from whom I bought it."

It was only then that he would take the money. He was standing back of his own carelessness. He was a free-will agent and he chose to do careful work, and if he failed, he took the responsibility without subterfuge.[2]

And he did for me the unnecessary thing, the gracious thing, that we find done only by the great of heart. Things no training can teach, for they are done on the instant, with no predicated experience. He found a cubbyhole beside the fireplace that I had not noticed. There, of his own accord, he put kindling and "medium" wood, so that I might always have dry fire material ready in case of sudden wet weather. A stone was loose in the rough walk to the cabin. He dug a deeper hole and steadied it, although he came, himself, by a short cut over the bank. I found that when I tried to return his thoughtfulness with such things as candy and apples, he was wordless. "Thank you" was, perhaps, an expression for which he had had no use, for his courtesy was instinctive. He only looked at the gift and at me, and a curtain lifted, so that I saw deep into the clear well of his eyes, and gratitude was there, and affection, soft over the firm granite of his character. **A**

He made simple excuses to come and sit with me. I could no more have turned him away than if he had been physically hungry. I suggested once that the best time for us to visit was just before supper, when I left off my writing. After that, he waited always until my typewriter had been some time quiet. One day I worked until nearly dark. I went outside the cabin, having forgotten him. I saw him going up over the hill in the twilight toward the orphanage. When I sat down on my stoop, a place was warm from his body where he had been sitting.

He became intimate, of course, with my pointer, Pat. There is a strange communion between a boy and a dog. Perhaps they possess the same singleness of spirit, the same kind of wisdom. It is difficult to explain, but it exists. When **B** I went across the state for a weekend I left the dog in Jerry's charge. I gave him the dog whistle and the key to the cabin, and left sufficient food. He was to come two or three times a day and let out the dog, and feed and exercise him. I should return Sunday night, and Jerry would take out the dog for the last time Sunday afternoon and then leave the key under an agreed hiding place.

My return was belated[3] and fog filled the mountain passes so treacherously that I dared not drive at night. The fog held the next morning, and it

2. **subterfuge** (sub'tər·fyo͞oj'): deception.

3. **belated** (bi·lāt'id): later than intended or expected.

A. Figurative Language

? How does this phrase reveal Jerry's character? (Granite is a very hard rock made of many minerals: Rawlings, by comparing Jerry's character to granite, is describing him as a mixture of very strong qualities. They are softened by the emotions of affection and gratitude.)

B. Comparing and Contrasting Stories

? What do you think Rawlings means by a "strange communion"? (A close, communicative bond) Recall the story "Lassie Come-Home" in Unit Two. Describe the relationship between Joe and Lassie and tell whether it supports the statements Rawlings makes in this passage about a boy and a dog. Do you agree with what she says?

Comment from the Author
Rawlings set this story in North Carolina where she did actually spend time to do some writing. She describes it in one of her letters to her publisher: "After a search, found simply an ideal cabin and location. A new, attractive cabin of undressed white oak, hand made furniture, big fireplace, electric lights, bathroom, electric stove and water heater, and a gorgeous mountain view. A village within walking distance. Just enough isolation. Brought my Proust [French author] and my pointer [Pat]—perfect company for work!" Rawlings wrote "Mother in Mannville" during her stay in this mountain cabin.

A. Complication
The intimacy that has developed between Jerry and the narrator is a complication, since we know that it is a temporary friendship. We know that Jerry is naturally attached to this older woman who is kind and listens to him—perhaps as an unconscious substitute for a real mother. We feel a bit apprehensive that something might happen to disrupt this closeness, especially as the narrator will leave the area soon.

B. Complication
What does her reaction tell about the narrator? (Her anger and resentment show that she feels strongly about abandoning children; and that perhaps she has gotten too close to Jerry.)

C. Interpreting
Why is the narrator unable to say anything more than she does? (She does not want to reveal her anger against Jerry's mother and risk prejudicing him against his own mother.)

was Monday noon before I reached the cabin. The dog had been fed and cared for that morning. Jerry came early in the afternoon, anxious.

"The superintendent said nobody would drive in the fog," he said. "I came just before bedtime last night and you hadn't come. So I brought Pat some of my breakfast this morning. I wouldn't have let anything happen to him."

"I was sure of that. I didn't worry."

"When I heard about the fog, I thought you'd know."

He was needed for work at the orphanage and he had to return at once. I gave him a dollar in payment, and he looked at it and went away. But that night he came in darkness and knocked at the door.

"Come in, Jerry," I said, "if you're allowed to be away this late."

"I told maybe a story," he said. "I told them I thought you would want to see me."

"That's true," I assured him, and I saw his relief. "I want to hear about how you managed with the dog."

He sat by the fire with me, with no other light, and told me of their two days together. The dog lay close to him, and found a comfort there that I did not have for him. And it seemed to me that being with my dog, and caring for him, had brought the boy and me, too, together, so that he felt that he belonged to me as well as to the animal.

"He stayed right with me," he told me, "except when he ran in the laurel. He likes the laurel. I took him up over the hill and we both ran fast. There was a place where the grass was high and I lay down in it and hid. I could hear Pat hunting for me. He found my trail and he barked. When he found me, he acted crazy, and he ran around and around me, in circles."

We watched the flames.

"That's an apple log," he said. "It burns the prettiest of any wood."

We were very close.

A He was suddenly impelled to speak of things he had not spoken of before, nor had I cared to ask him.

"You look a little bit like my mother," he said. "Especially in the dark, by the fire."

"But you were only four, Jerry, when you came here. You have remembered how she looked, all these years?"

"My mother lives in Mannville," he said.

For a moment, finding that he had a mother shocked me as greatly as anything in my life has ever done, and I did not know why it disturbed me. Then I understood my distress. I was filled with a passionate resentment that any woman should go away and leave her son. A fresh anger added itself. A son like this one——The orphanage was a wholesome place, the executives were kind, good people, the food was more than adequate, the boys were healthy, a ragged shirt was no hardship, nor the doing of clean labor. Granted, perhaps, that the boy felt no lack, what about the mother? At four he would have looked the same as now. Nothing, I thought, nothing in life could change those eyes. His quality must be apparent to an idiot, a fool. I burned with questions I could not ask. In any, I was afraid, there would be pain. B

"Have you seen her, Jerry—lately?"

"I see her every summer. She sends for me."

I wanted to cry out. "Why are you not with her? How can she let you go away again?"

He said, "She comes up here from Mannville whenever she can. She doesn't have a job now."

His face shone in the firelight.

"She wanted to give me a puppy, but they can't let any one boy keep a puppy. You remember the suit I had on last Sunday?" He was plainly proud. "She sent me that for Christmas. The Christmas before that"—he drew a long breath, savoring the memory—"she sent me a pair of skates."

"Roller skates?"

My mind was busy, making pictures of her, trying to understand her. She had not, then, entirely deserted or forgotten him. But why, then ——I thought, "But I must not condemn her without knowing."

"Roller skates. I let the other boys use them. They're always borrowing them. But they're careful of them."

What circumstance other than poverty——

"I'm going to take the dollar you gave me for taking care of Pat," he said, "and buy her a pair of gloves."

I could only say, "That will be nice. Do you know her size?" C

READING CHECK TEST

1. The writer is staying in a cabin near an orphanage. (*True*)
2. Jerry is a boy who lives nearby in Mannville. (*False*)
3. Jerry's mother visits him once a year and sends him gifts. (*False*)
4. The narrator can understand why Jerry has been left in the orphanage. (*False*)
5. At the end of the story, the narrator gets Jerry's mother's name and plans to write to her. (*False*)

CLOSURE

Have students work in groups of three to discuss the importance of including sensory details in descriptions. Have them describe their rooms at home using sensory details.

"I think it's eight and a half," he said.

He looked at my hands.

"Do you wear eight and a half?" he asked.

"No. I wear a smaller size, a six."

"Oh! Then I guess her hands are bigger than yours."

I hated her. Poverty or no, there was other food than bread, and the soul could starve as quickly
A as the body. He was taking his dollar to buy gloves for her big stupid hands, and she lived away from him, in Mannville, and contented herself with sending him skates.

"She likes white gloves," he said. "Do you think I can get them for a dollar?"

"I think so," I said.

I decided that I should not leave the mountains without seeing her and knowing for myself why she had done this thing.

The human mind scatters its interests as though made of thistledown,[4] and every wind stirs and moves it. I finished my work. It did not please me, and I gave my thoughts to another field. I should need some Mexican material.

I made arrangements to close my Florida place. Mexico immediately, and doing the writing there, if conditions were favorable. Then, Alaska with my brother. After that, heaven knew what or where.

I did not take time to go to Mannville to see Jerry's mother, nor even to talk with the orphanage officials about her. I was a trifle abstracted about the boy, because of my work and plans. And after my first fury at her—we did not speak of her again—his having a mother, any sort at all,
B not far away, in Mannville, relieved me of the ache I had had about him. He did not question the anomalous[5] relation. He was not lonely. It was none of my concern.

He came every day and cut my wood and did small helpful favors and stayed to talk. The days had become cold, and often I let him come inside the cabin. He would lie on the floor in front of the fire, with one arm across the pointer, and they would both doze and wait quietly for me. Other days they ran with a common ecstasy through the laurel, and since the asters were now gone, he brought me back vermilion maple leaves, and chestnut boughs dripping with imperial yellow. I was ready to go.

I said to him, "You have been my good friend, Jerry. I shall often think of you and miss you. Pat will miss you too. I am leaving tomorrow."

He did not answer. When he went away, I remember that a new moon hung over the mountains, and I watched him go in silence up the hill. I expected him the next day, but he did not come. The details of packing my personal belongings, loading my car, arranging the bed over the seat, where the dog would ride, occupied me until late in the day. I closed the cabin and started the car, noticing that the sun was in the west and I should do well to be out of the mountains by nightfall. I stopped by the orphanage and left the cabin key C
and money for my light bill with Miss Clark.

"And will you call Jerry for me to say goodbye to him?"

"I don't know where he is," she said. "I'm afraid he's not well. He didn't eat his dinner this noon. One of the boys saw him going over the hill into the laurel. He was supposed to fire the boiler this afternoon. It's not like him, he's unusually reliable."

I was almost relieved, for I knew I should never see him again, and it would be easier not to say goodbye to him.

I said, "I wanted to talk with you about his mother—why he's here—but I'm in more of a hurry than I expected to be. It's out of the question for me to see her now. But here's some money I'd like to leave with you to buy things for him at Christmas and on his birthday. It will be better than for me to try to send him things. I could so easily duplicate—skates, for instance."

She blinked her honest spinster's eyes.

"There's not much use for skates here," she said.

Her stupidity annoyed me.

"What I mean," I said, "is that I don't want to duplicate things his mother sends him. I might have chosen skates if I didn't know she had already given them to him."

"I don't understand," she said. "He has no D
mother. He has no skates."

4. **thistledown** (this′'l·doun′): soft fluff attached to the flower head of the thistle.
5. **anomalous** (ə·näm′ə·ləs): unusual, out of the ordinary.

A. Interpreting
? What does the narrator mean when she says "the soul could starve as quickly as the body"? (That people need love as well as food for nourishment)

B. Interpreting
? What ache did she have about him? (She cared about and admired him so much that she probably felt he deserved a mother and she might have been feeling responsible for filling this role.)

C. Character's Actions and Feelings
? What do Jerry's silence and his neglect of his duties indicate about his feelings? (Because this behavior is uncharacteristic of Jerry, we know that he is very upset. He will miss the narrator very much.)

D. Resolution
This surprise ending is the resolution of the story; it makes us sit back and think about Jerry's motivation for lying about having a mother in Mannville.

ANALYZING THE STORY
Identifying Facts

1. She is there to do some difficult writing; she also hopes the mountain air will make her feel better, and she wants to see the fall colors.
2. Jerry is twelve years old, and has been at the orphanage for eight years.
3. Jerry does kind, considerate things for the narrator, like fixing a stone in the walk and placing dry wood inside the cabin. He also befriends and cares for the narrator's dog, and gives the narrator companionship.
4. He tells the narrator that his mother is alive and living in Mannville. He claims that she buys him gifts—including a new suit and roller skates. Supposedly, he sees her every summer, but she can't keep him with her because she doesn't have a job.
5. Miss Clark tells the narrator that Jerry does not have a mother; he has been lying about her to the narrator all along.

Interpreting Meanings

6. These details include Jerry coming to sit by the narrator; his intimate relationship with the dog; the narrator's statement that "We were very close"; Jerry's

Responding to the Story

Analyzing the Story

Identifying Facts

1. Explain why the **narrator,** or person telling the story, is in the mountains.
2. How long has Jerry lived at the orphange? How old is he?
3. Jerry becomes more than just a chore-boy for the narrator. What else does he do at the cabin?
4. What does Jerry tell the narrator about his mother?
5. What does the narrator's conversation with Miss Clark at the end of the story reveal?

Interpreting Meanings

6. As the story progresses, the narrator and Jerry become more and more like a family. What details suggest this?
7. Many of Marjorie Kinnan Rawlings's stories include animals. Explain how the narrator's dog Pat is important to this story. (How do Jerry and Pat get along, and what does this tell you about Jerry?)
8. Explain why the narrator becomes angry when Jerry tells her that he has a mother who lives nearby.
9. This story also contains conflicts, or struggles, though they are not discussed directly. Describe the narrator's **internal conflict,** or struggle between conflicting inner desires and emotions. What internal conflict of Jerry's might have led him to make up the story about his mother?
10. The narrator admired Jerry for his honesty. Do you think she changes her mind? Do you think Jerry has proved he is not honest at all? Explain.

Applying Meanings

11. Do you think this story has a message for people in general? Explain what it reveals about our need for love. (Think about both the narrator's affection for Jerry, and Jerry's made-up story about his mother. What do you think Jerry's deep affection for Pat says, about this theme?)

Writing About the Story

A Creative Response

1. **Writing from Another Point of View.** Imagine you are Jerry, and write a paragraph describing the narrator from Jerry's **point of view.** What does she look like to you? What kind of personality does she have? How do you view her job, her background? What is her dog like? SRW p. 69
2. **Extending the Story.** What happens next to Jerry? In a paragraph, write a conclusion to the story.

A Critical Response

3. **Responding to an Ending.** Some readers feel "cheated" that the final events of this story do not resolve either character's problem, or **conflict.** Explain your reaction to the "surprise ending." Did you feel cheated? Did you expect it? Was it believable? Write a paragraph explaining your opinion.

See Teacher's Manual page 66.

Analyzing Language and Vocabulary

Description

SRW p. 29

Description is a kind of writing that helps us see something, or smell it, taste it, hear it, feel its textures and temperatures. Description often is intended to create a mood or emotion. When the narrator describes the mountains in the spring as "a carpet of color," we can imagine that the hills look as if they are covered with a colorful rug. Because carpets are soft and pleasant to walk on, the description creates a pleasant feeling about the mountains.

Here are some other descriptive passages from the story:

1. "Fog hides the mountain peaks. . . ."
   a. How would you picture the mountains from this description?
   b. Can you think of another way of describing the fog on the mountains that would create a different feeling?
2. " . . . his eyes, very direct, were like the mountain sky when rain is pending—gray, with a showing of that miraculous blue."

belief that the narrator looks something like his mother; the relaxed way that Jerry stays in the cabin with her and the dog; Jerry's hurt when the narrator tells him she is leaving.

7. The fact that Pat doesn't bark to warn the narrator that Jerry has arrived marks Jerry as a special person. Pat seems to be the narrator's closest (and only) friend; since Pat so quickly warms to Jerry, it indicates that the narrator will too. Jerry is sensitive, loves animals, and enjoys the companionship of the dog.

8. She becomes angry because she cannot understand how any mother could leave a child in an orphanage. Some students may realize that she is angry because she has grown to love Jerry.

9. The narrator's conflict is between her desire to act like a mother to Jerry, and her lifestyle that takes her all over the world. In addition, she is angry at Jerry's mother, but can't do anything about the relationship.

Jerry is lonely, and misses having a mother. Thus, he may have made up a mother to make himself feel less lonely.

10. Most students will see that she probably wouldn't change her mind. Jerry's honesty is unaffected by his need to have a mother. The story is not so much a lie as an attempt to deal with a very hard reality.

a. What exactly is the color of Jerry's eyes?
b. According to this description, how does the narrator feel about Jerry?
c. Can you think of another way of describing the color of his eyes to suggest a feeling of uneasiness or fear about Jerry?

3. The narrator, when speaking of Jerry's special quality of integrity, says "almost no man of my acquaintance possesses it with the clarity, the purity, the simplicity of a mountain stream."

a. What do you feel when you think of a mountain stream?
b. The narrator herself defines integrity as honesty based on courage. According to the description above, how is integrity like a mountain stream?
c. How would the effect of the description be different if she had compared Jerry's integrity to, say, a block of granite?

4. ". . . he brought me back vermilion maple leaves, and chestnut boughs dripping with imperial yellow."

a. What does the word *vermilion* mean?
b. Boughs, or branches, don't really "drip" with color. By using this verb, what comparison is the writer suggesting?
c. What does the word *imperial* mean? What shade of yellow do you think "imperial yellow" would be? How would your feelings about the boughs be different if she had described them as "watery yellow"?

For answers, see Teacher's Manual page 66.

Reading About the Writer

"Writing is agony," says **Marjorie Kinnan Rawlings** (1896–1953). Rawlings grew up in the state of Washington and went to the University of Michigan where she graduated with honors. For ten years after she left college, she did a lot of moving and traveling, working as a newspaper reporter and writing stories. Frustrated at her difficulty in getting these stories published, she impulsively bought an orange grove in Cross Creek, Florida. Delighted with the people and scenery she found in these Florida backwoods, she made them the main subjects of her writings.

Today, Rawlings is remembered for her picture of Southern rural poverty, painted with affection and humor. She won her greatest fame with a best-selling novel called *The Yearling,* about a boy in Florida and his love for his pet fawn. The novel won the Pulitzer Prize, was translated into thirteen languages, and was made into a successful movie. It is still a favorite among young adults.

Applying Meanings

11. Answers will vary. Students should see that the story shows that we need to love as well as be loved.

Further Reading for Students

Students might enjoy Marjorie Kinnan Rawlings's award-winning novel *The Yearling,* about a boy and his pet fawn.

Focusing on Background

Marjorie's Stories

After Rawlings's first novel was published, her editor suggested that she write a book for young readers. This suggestion eventually led to her great novel *The Yearling.* Rawlings's first reaction, however, was described in her response to the editor's letter:

"Your suggestion has brought back a whole train of memories of my Washington childhood, that I hadn't thought of in years and years. They are memories of spring and summer evenings and nights when I sat on the cool stone steps of a Baptist church and told stories to the other children. We'd usually play our strenuous running games in the long twilight, and then when Tony the Italian lamplighter lit the red-glass lamps all along our street, we'd gather deliciously close together on the church steps and I'd 'cut loose.' I can remember very distinctly the feeling of smugness that came over me when one of the youngsters would run up the street calling to any stragglers, 'Marjorie's going to tell stories!' and the hauteur[1] with which I refused to begin until everyone was there. There was a tumultuous Irish child that shrieked and screamed if any of the details depressed him—particularly what I realize now must have been my very celebrated imitation of a wolf howl. He got to be such a nuisance that I recall saying sternly, 'You'll have to take Jimmy home now—there's going to be a wolf in the next one.' "

—Marjorie Kinnan Rawlings

1. **hauteur** (hō·tur′): haughtiness.

PREREADING

1. BUILDING ON PRIOR KNOWLEDGE. Before they read, ask students to think back to when they were eleven years old. Did they ever have anything embarrassing or humiliating happen to them (or see it happen to someone else)? What was the experience? Discuss with them whether they think there is any connection between one's age and one's susceptibility to embarrassment or humiliation.

2. ESTABLISHING A PURPOSE. The headnote sets a good purpose for reading this story.

3. PREREADING JOURNAL. Have students write a brief paragraph about what they think is the best way to deal with embarrassment or humiliation. Would it be walking away? Yelling or crying? Keeping quiet?

A. Tone

How would you describe the tone of the story? (Conversational, informal—see the vocabulary tint block "Recreating Thoughts" at the bottom of the text page.)

B. Responding

Do you agree with the narrator here?

C. Colorful Language

What does this image suggest? (The sound of pennies rattling inside a tin box is jarring—the emptiness, or lack of experience, she feels is equally uncomfortable.)

D. Conflict

How does the narrator's external conflict lead to her internal one? (The narrator's inability to respond to Mrs. Price makes her feel inadequate and makes her wish she were older.)

★ Texas Essential Elements/(a) English Language Arts: 1B Purpose and audience; 4G Fact/nonfact. (c) Reading: 3A Main ideas/details; 3E Fact/fictional details; 3I Draw conclusions

ELEVEN

For a detailed lesson plan on this story, see Teacher's Manual pages 67–69. A biography of Sandra Cisneros appears on text page 219.

Sandra Cisneros

Most of this story takes place in the mind of Rachel, the narrator. It is her eleventh birthday, and she thinks about how hard it can be to act older than you feel. As you read the story, see if you think Rachel is "acting her age." Can you identify with some of Rachel's feelings?

What they don't understand about birthdays and what they never tell you is that when you're eleven, you're also ten, and nine, and eight, and seven, and six, and five, and four, and three, and two, and one. And A when you wake up on your eleventh birthday you expect to feel eleven, but you don't. You open your eyes and everything's just like yesterday, only it's today. And you don't feel eleven at all. You feel like you're still ten. And you are—underneath the year that makes you eleven.

Like some days you might say something stupid, and that's the part of you that's still ten. Or maybe some days you might need to sit on your mama's lap because you're scared, and that's the part of you that's five. And one day when you're all grown up maybe you will need to cry like if you're three, and that's okay. That's what I tell Mama when she's sad and needs to cry. Maybe she's feeling three.

Because the way you grow old is kind of like an onion or like the rings inside a tree trunk or B like my little wooden dolls that fit one inside the other, each year inside the next one. That's how being eleven years old is.

Recreating Thoughts. Thoughts in your head are almost never as orderly or as clearly formed as the sentences you say and write. The writer of this story tries to recreate the thoughts of the narrator. In doing so, she has written long sentences that often contain several main ideas. See if you think these sentences sound like a person's thoughts.

You don't feel eleven. Not right away. It takes a few days, weeks even, sometimes even months before you say eleven when they ask you. And you don't feel smart eleven, not until you're almost twelve. That's the way it is.

Only today I wish I didn't have just eleven years rattling inside me like pennies in a tin Band-Aid box. Today I wish I was one-hundred-and-two C instead of eleven because if I was one-hundred-and-two I'd have known what to say when Mrs. Price put the red sweater on my desk. I would've known how to tell her it wasn't mine instead of just sitting there with that look on my face and D nothing coming out of my mouth.

"Whose is this?" Mrs. Price says, and she holds the red sweater up in the air for all the class to see. "Whose? It's been sitting in the coatroom for a month."

"Not mine," says everybody. "Not me."

"It has to belong to somebody," Mrs. Price keeps saying, but nobody can remember. It's an ugly sweater with red plastic buttons and a collar and sleeves all stretched out like you could use it for a jump rope. It's maybe a thousand years old and even if it belonged to me I wouldn't say so.

Maybe because I'm skinny, maybe because she doesn't like me, that stupid Felice Garcia says, "I think it belongs to Rachel." An ugly sweater like that, all raggedy and old, but Mrs. Price believes her. Mrs. Price takes the sweater and puts it right on my desk, but when I open my mouth nothing comes out.

"That's not, I don't, you're not . . . not mine," I finally say in a little voice that was maybe me when I was four.

Supplementary Support Material

1. Vocabulary Activity Sheet
2. Reading Check Test blackline master
3. Selection Test (page 75 of Test Book)
4. Reader's Response Journal
5. Workbook (page 53)

Critical Comment

About her writing, Cisneros said once, "If I were asked about what it is I write about, I would have to say I write about those ghosts inside that haunt me, that will not let me sleep, of that which even memory does not like to mention. . . . Aren't we constantly attempting to give up the ghost, to put it to sleep once and for all each time we pick up the pen?"

Ask students whether they think that it was Cisneros's "ghosts" that prompted her to write "Eleven." Why might an incident like this one become a "ghost" that must be put to sleep?

A. Making Inferences

? What is "the part of [her] that's three"? (Tears)

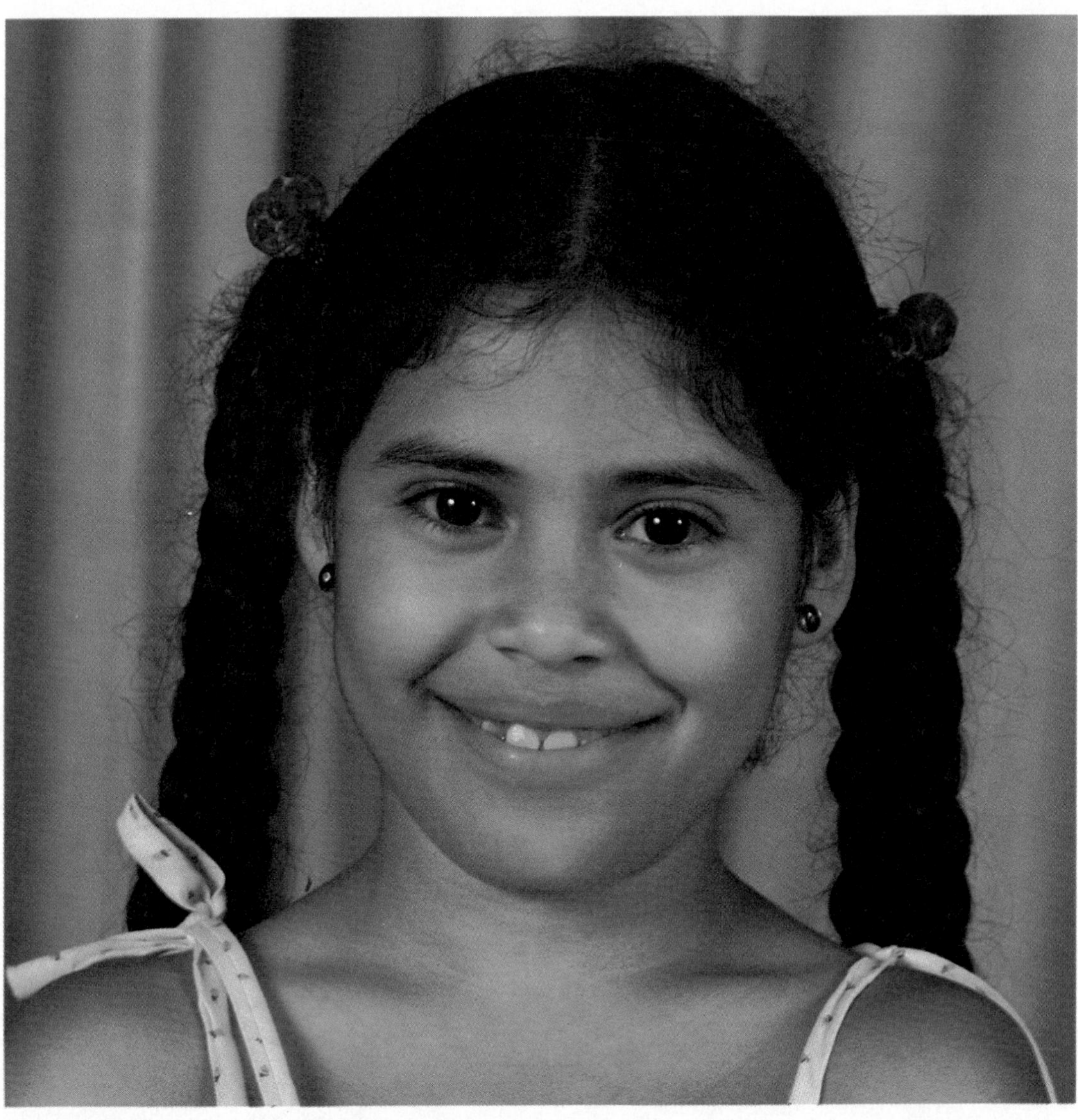

"Of course it's yours," Mrs. Price says, "I remember you wearing it once." Because she's older and the teacher, she's right and I'm not.

Not mine, not mine, not mine, but Mrs. Price is already turning to page 32, and math problem number four. I don't know why but all of a sudden
A I'm feeling sick inside, like the part of me that's three wants to come out of my eyes, only I squeeze them shut tight and bite down on my teeth real hard and try to remember today I am eleven, eleven. Mama is making a cake for me for tonight, and when Papa comes home everybody will sing happy birthday, happy birthday to you.

But when the sick feeling goes away and I open my eyes, the red sweater's still sitting there like a big red mountain. I move the red sweater to the corner of my desk with my ruler. I move my pencil and books and eraser as far from it as possible. I even move my chair a little to the right. Not mine, not mine, not mine.

In my head I'm thinking how long till lunch time, how long till I can take the red sweater and

Reading Check Test

1. Rachel feels that she is completely grown up. (*False*)
2. In school that day, there is a conflict between Rachel and Mrs. Price over an umbrella. (*False*)
3. Rachel feels that if she were older, she would have known what to say to Mrs. Price. (*True*)
4. Rachel loves Mrs. Price. (*False*)
5. Rachel decides not to let what happened in school ruin her birthday. (*False*)

Closure

Ask students to work in pairs and discuss what they think the theme of "Eleven" is.

A. Descriptive Details

How does the writer make us feel as uncomfortable as Rachel is when she puts on the sweater? (The words "smells like cottage cheese," "stand there with my arms apart," "sweater hurts me," "itchy and full of germs")

B. Interpreting

Why do you think Mrs. Price pretends that everything's alright? (She probably feels guilty and regretful that because of her hasty assumption that the sweater was Rachel's she caused Rachel to be so upset. She probably pretends that nothing happened because she does not want to admit her mistake in front of the class.)

C. Figurative Language

The image of the kite reveals that Rachel really is growing up—she realizes that time heals wounds, and that as she gets older this painful incident will hurt less and less.

throw it over the schoolyard fence, or leave it hanging on a parking meter, or bunch it up into a little ball and toss it in the alley. Except when math period ends Mrs. Price says loud and in front of everybody, "Now, Rachel, that's enough," because she sees I've shoved the red sweater to the tippy-tip corner of my desk and it's hanging all over the edge like a waterfall, but I don't care.

"Rachel," Mrs. Price says. She says it like she's getting mad. "You put that sweater on right now and no more nonsense."

"But it's not . . ."

"Now!" Mrs. Price says.

This is when I wish I wasn't eleven, because all the years inside of me—ten, nine, eight, seven, six, five, four, three, two, and one—are all pushing at the back of my eyes when I put one arm through one sleeve of the sweater that smells like cottage cheese, and then the other arm through the other and stand there with my arms apart as if the sweater hurts me and it does, all itchy and full of germs that aren't even mine. A

That's when everything I've been holding in since this morning, since when Mrs. Price put the sweater on my desk, finally lets go, and all of a sudden I'm crying in front of everybody. I wish I was invisible but I'm not. I'm eleven and it's my birthday today and I'm crying like I'm three in front of everybody. I put my head down on the desk and bury my face in my stupid clown sweater arms. My face all hot and spit coming out of my mouth because I can't stop the little animal noises from coming out of me, until there aren't any more tears left in my eyes, and it's just my body shaking like when you have the hiccups, and my whole head hurts like when you drink milk too fast.

But the worst part is right before the bell rings for lunch. That stupid Phyllis Lopez, who is even dumber than Felice Garcia, says she remembers the red sweater is hers! I take it off right away and give it to her, only Mrs. Price pretends like everything's okay. B

Today I'm eleven. There's a cake Mama's making for tonight, and when Papa comes home from work we'll eat it. There'll be candles and presents and everybody will sing happy birthday, happy birthday to you, Rachel, only it's too late.

I'm eleven today. I'm eleven, ten, nine, eight, seven, six, five, four, three, two, and one, but I wish I was one-hundred-and-two. I wish I was anything but eleven, because I want today to be far away already, far away like a tiny kite in the sky, so tiny-tiny you have to close your eyes to see it. C

Responding to the Story

Analyzing the Story

Identifying Facts

1. What examples does Rachel give to show how she sometimes feels and behaves younger than she is?
2. Why does Mrs. Price think the old sweater belongs to Rachel?
3. What does Rachel do with the sweater? What does she make herself think about to comfort herself?
4. How does Mrs. Price react when she learns that she has been mistaken about the sweater?
5. How does the incident with the sweater make Rachel feel younger than she is?

Interpreting Meanings

6. What does Rachel mean when she says, "when you're eleven, you're also ten, and nine" and so on?
7. What assumption does Mrs. Price seem to make about Rachel?
8. What does Rachel mean when she says "everybody will sing happy birthday . . . only it's too late"?

Applying Meanings

9. What incidents can you think of—either from real life or from fiction—in which adults have acted much younger than you might have expected them to?

Analyzing The Story

Identifying Facts

1. Examples include feeling like ten when she wakes up on her eleventh birthday; saying something stupid (ten); being scared (five); feeling a need to cry (three).

2. Felice Garcia says she thinks it belongs to Rachel. Mrs. Price may think more of Felice Garcia than of Rachel, and so believes Felice. Or Mrs. Price may look at skinny Rachel and decide that the ugly sweater is hers.

3. Rachel pushes the sweater to the corner of her desk.

She thinks about the birthday party she will have later to comfort herself.

4. Mrs. Price seems unconcerned—she "pretends like everything's okay."

5. Because she is humiliated, she can't think of anything to say. She answers in a little voice that sounds to her like the one she had when she was four years old, and begins crying as when she was three.

Interpreting Meanings

6. Rachel means that there are certain situations in which you will always act younger than you are.

7. Answers will vary. Mrs. Price assumes that Rachel is wrong about the sweater. She may also be assuming that Rachel should be grateful for the sweater, or that Rachel is just the sort of person to have a sweater like the red one.

8. She probably means that it is too late for her to have a "happy" birthday, since it has already been ruined. She has been made to feel so young that she feels she cannot enjoy a celebration of her growing up.

Applying Meanings

9. Answers will vary. Students should define what "acted much younger" means when applied to adults.

Further Reading for Students

Students will enjoy Sandra Cisneros's short book *The House on Mango Street,* about the experiences of a young Mexican girl growing up in an American city.

Writing About the Story

A Creative Response

SRW p. 69

Changing the Point of View. How do you think Mrs. Price felt about the incident with the sweater? Write a conversation in which she tells her husband or some other adult about the incident.

See Teacher's Manual page 68.

Analyzing Language and Vocabulary

Recreating Thoughts

Reread the paragraph beginning "Only today I wish I didn't have just eleven years rattling inside me. . . ." The sentences in this paragraph are good examples of the style of writing Cisneros chose for telling her story. For example, she purposely repeats phrases, such as "one-hundred-and-two." She does this because she is trying to capture the way thoughts form in someone's head and the way a young person might talk. The second sentence might have begun, "Today I wish I was one-hundred-and-two because then I'd have known. . . ." That would have sounded more like normal writing. But it would also have sounded less like the way Rachel's mind works and the way she speaks.

Write a short paragraph in which a very young child tells about something that happened in school. Try to imitate the way children speak when they are about seven years old.

For answers, see Teacher's Manual page 69.

Reading About the Writer

Sandra Cisneros (1954–   ) was born in Chicago. Her parents are Mexican Americans, and she grew up speaking both Spanish and English. She has written two books of poetry, *Bad Boys* and *My Wicked, Wicked Ways,* and a novel called *The House on Mango Street.* Cisneros teaches writing at California State University at Chico.

Focusing on Background

Crossing the Threshold

"I've managed to do a lot of things in my life I didn't think I was capable of and which many others didn't think me capable of either. Especially because I am a woman, a Latina, an only daughter in a family of six men. My father would've liked to have seen me married long ago. In our culture men and women don't leave their father's house except by way of marriage. I crossed my father's threshold with nothing carrying me but my own two feet. . . ."

—Sandra Cisneros

PREREADING

1. BUILDING ON PRIOR KNOWLEDGE. Before they read, ask students what they know about the American West of the late 1800's. In this exciting era of gold-hungry prospectors, cowboys, outlaws, and farmers who did back-breaking labor to tame the West, crime was not uncommon. The law was also hard to enforce, for one reason because of the great distances between settlements. Many citizens took the law into their own hands.

2. ESTABLISHING A PURPOSE. Before students begin reading, have them read question 11 on page 226.

3. PREREADING JOURNAL. Before they read, have students write two or three sentences telling whether or not they enjoy Western movies or books and why.

Humanities Connection: Discussing the Fine Art
American artist Victor Higgins (1884–1949) specialized in impressionist paintings of Indian subjects and landscapes such as this one. ? Judging from this painting, what would you say the climate is in Taos Valley? (Probably hot and dry. The orange, yellow, and brown rocks in the foreground, and the reflections of these colors in the clouds convey heat. The mountains in the distance, however, look cooler—they are purple, pink, and beige, which are cooler colors.) Do you think you would want to travel through this valley?

Texas Essential Elements/(a) English Language Arts: 1B Purpose and audience; **3B** Figurative language; **4B** Main idea; **4F** Generalizations

WINE ON THE DESERT

Max Brand

Taos Valley by Victor Higgins (1935). Oil.

The Snite Museum of Art, University of Notre Dame, Indiana. Gift of Mr. and Mrs. John T. Higgins.

For a detailed lesson plan on this story, see Teacher's Manual pages 69–71. A biography of Max Brand appears on page 227.

Supplementary Support Material

1. Vocabulary Activity Sheet
2. Reading Check Test blackline master
3. Selection Test (page 77 of Test Book).
4. Reader's Response Journal
5. Workbook (page 55)

Developing Vocabulary

The following words appear on a test in the Test Book, page 78. (See also the Vocabulary Activity Sheet.)

posse	brim
emblem	peg leg
hollow	earnestly
hammock	resolution
gingerly	seized

Texas Essential Elements/(c) Reading: 1C Dictionaries; **2A** Word meaning; **3A** Main ideas/details; **3D** Generalizations; **3I** Draw conclusions; **4D** Diagrams/graphs

In fiction, villains are nearly as common as heroes. The central figure in this story is one such villain, and his heart is as evil as they come. After the first paragraph, note what you've already learned about (1) the setting, (2) what Durante has done, and (3) where Durante is going.

Similes. This writer has chosen his words carefully to help us experience the heat and dryness of the desert. One way he creates this experience is by using similes. A *simile* is a comparison between two unlike things, using a specific word of comparison such as *like, as, than,* or *resembles*. You will find a simile in the first sentence to help you feel the discomfort, even agony, of extreme thirst. SRW p. 81

There was no hurry, except for the thirst, like clotted salt, in the back of his throat, and Durante rode on slowly, rather enjoying the last moments of dryness before he reached the cold water in Tony's house. There was really no hurry at all. He had almost twenty-four hours' head start, for they would not find his dead man until this morning. After that, there would be perhaps several hours of delay before the sheriff gathered a sufficient posse[1] and started on his trail. Or perhaps the sheriff would be fool enough to come alone.

Durante had been able to see the wheel and fan of Tony's windmill for more than an hour, but he could not make out the ten acres of the vineyard until he had topped the last rise, for the vines had been planted in a hollow. The lowness of the ground, Tony used to say, accounted for the water that gathered in the well during the wet season. The rains sank through the desert sand, through the gravels beneath, and gathered in a bowl of clay hardpan[2] far below.

A In the middle of the rainless season the well ran dry but, long before that, Tony had every drop of the water pumped up into a score of tanks made of cheap corrugated iron. Slender pipelines carried the water from the tanks to the vines and from time to time let them sip enough life to keep them until the winter darkened overhead suddenly, one November day, and the rain came down, and all the earth made a great hushing sound as it drank. Durante had heard that whisper of drinking when he was here before; but he never had seen the place in the middle of the long drought.

The windmill looked like a sacred emblem to Durante, and the twenty stodgy, tar-painted tanks blessed his eyes; but a heavy sweat broke out at once from his body. For the air of the hollow, unstirred by wind, was hot and still as a bowl of soup. A reddish soup. The vines were powdered with thin red dust, also. They were wretched, dying things to look at, for the grapes had been gathered, the new wine had been made, and now the leaves hung in ragged tatters. B

Durante rode up to the squat adobe house and right through the entrance into the patio. A flowering vine clothed three sides of the little court. Durante did not know the name of the plant, but it had large white blossoms with golden hearts that poured sweetness on the air. Durante hated the sweetness. It made him more thirsty. C

He threw the reins of his mule and strode into the house. The water cooler stood in the hall outside the kitchen. There were two jars made of a porous stone, very ancient things, and the liquid which distilled through the pores kept the contents cool. The jar on the left held water; that on the right contained wine. There was a big tin dipper hanging on a peg beside each jar. Durante tossed off the cover of the vase on the left and plunged it in until the delicious coolness closed well above his wrist. D

"Hey, Tony," he called. Out of his dusty throat the cry was a mere groaning. He drank and called again, clearly, "Tony!"

A voice pealed from the distance.

Durante, pouring down the second dipper of water, smelled the alkali dust which had shaken off his own clothes. It seemed to him that heat was radiating like light from his clothes, from his body, and the cool dimness of the house was soaking it up. He heard the wooden leg of Tony bumping on the ground, and Durante grinned; then

1. **posse** (päs′ē): group of men gathered by a sheriff to assist in arresting a criminal.
2. **hardpan:** layer of hard soil that blocks the flow of water.

A. Basic Situation

What is the basic situation of the story? (Durante, who has just killed a man, is escaping from the sheriff by going to his friend Tony's house, which is in the desert.)

B. Colorful Language

Why does Durante describe the windmill as a sacred emblem? (To Durante, because he is so thirsty, it is an emblem of life because it pumps water from the well into the tanks.)

C. Expansion

Adobe (ə·dō′bē) bricks, which are dried in the sun, are a common building material in the American Southwest because they make cooler houses than wood or stone do.

D. Interpreting

What does this gesture tell us about Durante? (That he can be inconsiderate and selfish; he just put his dusty, dirty hand in the water cooler, from which people drink, so he could cool off.)

A. Expansion
Nogalez is just inside the Mexican border, south of Arizona. This sentence gives us the setting of the story—southern Arizona.

B. Making Inferences
? What do we know about Tony from the dialogue so far? (We know that he is probably Mexican since he speaks broken English, he sent Julia—probably his wife—to a town in Mexico, and he cooks tortillas, a traditional Mexican dish.)

C. Interpreting
? Why does Durante seem uncomfortable when he hears how Tony shot the rabbit? (He's probably thinking about the crime he just committed and the danger he is in.)

D. Vocabulary
A *buzzard* is a large, heavy, slow-moving bird of prey.

E. Foreshadowing
Tony's tale about his father and how someone dies in the desert foreshadows Durante's death. This will help students answer question 9.

Tony came in with that hitch and sideswing with which he accommodated the stiffness of his artificial leg. His brown face shone with sweat as though a special ray of light were focused on it.

"Ah, Dick!" he said. "Good old Dick! . . . How long since you came last! . . . Wouldn't Julia be glad! Wouldn't she be glad!"

"Ain't she here?" asked Durante, jerking his head suddenly away from the dripping dipper.

A "She's away at Nogalez," said Tony. "It gets so hot. I said, 'You go up to Nogalez, Julia, where the wind don't forget to blow.' She cried, but I made her go."

"Did she cry?" asked Durante.

"Julia . . . that's a good girl," said Tony.

"Yeah . . . ," said Durante. He put the dipper quickly to his lips. . . . Afterward he said: "You wouldn't throw some water into that mule of mine, would you, Tony?"

Tony went out with his wooden leg clumping loud on the wooden floor, softly in the patio dust. Durante found the hammock in the corner of the patio. He lay down in it and watched the color of sunset flush the mists of desert dust that rose to the zenith.[3] The water was soaking through his body; hunger began, and then the rattling of pans in the kitchen and the cheerful cry of Tony's voice:

"What you want, Dick? I got some pork. You don't want pork. I'll make you some good Mexican beans. Hot, Ah ha, I know that old Dick. I have plenty of good wine for you, Dick. Tortillas. Even Julia can't make tortillas like me. . . . And what about a nice young rabbit?"

B "All blowed full of buckshot?" growled Durante.

"No, no. I kill them with the rifle."

"You kill rabbits with a rifle?" repeated Durante, with a quick interest.

"It's the only gun I have," said Tony. "If I catch them in the sights, they are dead. . . . A wooden leg cannot walk very far. . . . I must kill them quick. You see? They come close to the house about sunrise and flop their ears. I shoot through the head."

"Yeah? Yeah?" muttered Durante. "Through the head?" He relaxed, scowling. He passed his hand over his face, over his head. C

Then Tony began to bring the food out into the patio and lay it on a small wooden table; a lantern hanging against the wall of the house included the table in a dim half circle of light. They sat there and ate. Tony had scrubbed himself for the meal. His hair was soaked in water and sleeked back over his round skull. A man in the desert might be willing to pay five dollars for as much water as went to the soaking of that hair.

Everything was good. Tony knew how to cook, and he knew how to keep the glasses filled with his wine.

"This is old wine. This is my father's wine. Eleven years old," said Tony. "You look at the light through it. You see that brown in the red? That's the soft that time puts in good wine, my father always said."

"What killed your father?" asked Durante.

Tony lifted his hand as though he were listening or as though he were pointing out a thought.

"The desert killed him. I found his mule. It was dead, too. There was a leak in the canteen. My father was only five miles away when the buzzards showed him to me." D

"Five miles? Just an hour. . . . Good Lord!" said Durante. He stared with big eyes. "Just dropped down and died?" he asked.

"No," said Tony. "When you die of thirst, you always die just one way. . . . First you tear off your shirt, then your undershirt. That's to be cooler. . . . And the sun comes and cooks your bare skin. . . . And then you think . . . there is water everywhere, if you dig down far enough. E You begin to dig. The dust comes up your nose. You start screaming. You break your nails in the sand. You wear the flesh off the tips of your fingers, to the bone." He took a quick swallow of wine.

"Without you seen a man die of thirst, how d'you know they start to screaming?" asked Durante.

"They got a screaming look when you find them," said Tony. "Take some more wine. The desert never can get to you here. My father showed me the way to keep the desert away from the hollow. We live pretty good here? No?"

3. **zenith** (zē'nith): point in the sky directly overhead.

The Marin House, John's Horse Jack, Mabel Luhan Estate by John Marin (c. 1929). Watercolor and pencil.

Courtesy Kennedy Galleries, New York City.

A

"Yeah," said Durante, loosening his shirt collar. "Yeah, pretty good."

Afterward he slept well in the hammock until the report of a rifle waked him and he saw the color of dawn in the sky. It was such a great, round bowl that for a moment he felt as though he were above, looking down into it.

He got up and saw Tony coming in holding a rabbit by the ears, the rifle in his other hand.

"You see?" said Tony. "Breakfast came and called on us!" He laughed.

Durante examined the rabbit with care. It was nice and fat and it had been shot through the head. Through the middle of the head. Such a shudder went down the back of Durante that he washed gingerly before breakfast; he felt that his blood was cooled for the entire day.

It was a good breakfast, too, with flapjacks and stewed rabbit with green peppers, and a quart of strong coffee. Before they had finished, the sun struck through the east window and started them sweating.

"Gimme a look at that rifle of yours, Tony, will you?" Durante asked.

"You take a look at my rifle, but don't you steal the luck that's in it," laughed Tony. He brought the fifteen-shot Winchester. B

"Loaded right to the brim?" asked Durante.

"I always load it full the minute I get back home," said Tony.

"Tony, come outside with me," commanded Durante.

They went out from the house. The sun turned the sweat of Durante to hot water and then dried his skin so that his clothes felt transparent.

"Tony, I gotta be mean," said Durante. "Stand right there where I can see you. Don't try to get

A. Humanities Connection: Discussing the Fine Art
Although in his earliest watercolors John Marin (1870–1953) focused primarily on urban subjects, in his later work he abandoned the city to express the vitality of nature. ? What do you think the climate is in this picture? (Probably hot since the house is open, and the grass and ground are brownish-green and brown, which suggests that the land is dry and parched.)

B. Irony
Tony's comment implies that his rifle is lucky. In fact, it turns out to be just the opposite for Durante. Durante's taking the rifle causes Tony to retaliate, and this retaliation leads to Durante's death.

A. Character
? Now, how do you feel about Durante? (We despise him for his cruelty to Tony, who is a hard-working, well-meaning, and generous character.)

B. Making Inferences
? What does the rabbit have to do with Durante returning to the desert? (He saw an example of Tony's skill with the rifle; he knows that if he ever returned after killing off Tony's prize vineyard, that Tony would kill him as easily as he killed the rabbit.)

C. Irony and Foreshadowing
This passage is ironic and foreshadows Durante's predicament. Contrary to what Durante thinks, it is he and not the sheriff who has plenty of wine but no water.

close. . . . Now listen. . . . The sheriff's gonna be along this trail sometime today, looking for me. He'll load up himself and all his gang with water out of your tanks. Then he'll follow my sign across the desert. Get me? He'll follow if he finds water on the place. But he's not gonna find water."

"What you done, poor Dick?" said Tony. "Now look. . . . I could hide you in the old wine cellar where nobody . . ."

"The sheriff's not gonna find any water," said Durante. "It's gonna be like this."

He put the rifle to his shoulder, aimed, fired. The shot struck the base of the nearest tank, ranging down through the bottom. A semicircle of darkness began to stain the soil near the edge of the iron wall.

Tony fell to his knees. "No, no, Dick! Good Dick!" he said. "Look! All the vineyard. It will die. It will turn into old, dead wood. Dick . . ."

A "Shut your face," said Durante. "Now I've started, I kinda like the job."

Tony fell on his face and put his hands over his ears. Durante drilled a bullet hole through the tanks, one after another. Afterward, he leaned on the rifle.

"Take my canteen and go in and fill it with water out of the cooling jar," he said. "Snap into it, Tony!"

Tony got up. He raised the canteen and looked around him, not at the tanks from which the water was pouring so that the noise of the earth drinking was audible, but at the rows of his vineyard. Then he went into the house.

Durante mounted his mule. He shifted the rifle to his left hand and drew out the heavy Colt from its holster. Tony came dragging back to him, his head down. Durante watched Tony with a careful revolver but he gave up the canteen without lifting his eyes.

"The trouble with you, Tony," said Durante, "is you're yellow. I'd of fought a tribe of wildcats with my bare hands before I'd let 'em do what I'm doing to you. But you sit back and take it."

Tony did not seem to hear. He stretched out his hands to the vines.

"Ah, my God," said Tony. "Will you let them all die?"

Durante shrugged his shoulders. He shook the canteen to make sure that it was full. It was so brimming that there was hardly room for the liquid to make a sloshing sound. Then he turned the mule and kicked it into a dogtrot.

Half a mile from the house of Tony, he threw the empty rifle to the ground. There was no sense packing that useless weight, and Tony with his peg leg would hardly come this far.

Durante looked back, a mile or so later, and saw the little image of Tony picking up the rifle from the dust, then staring earnestly after his guest. Durante remembered the neat little hole clipped through the head of the rabbit. Wherever he went, his trail never could return again to the vineyard in the desert. But then, commencing to picture to himself the arrival of the sweating sheriff and his posse at the house of Tony, Durante laughed heartily. B

The sheriff's posse could get plenty of wine, of course, but without water a man could not hope to make the desert voyage, even with a mule or a horse to help him on the way. Durante patted the full, rounding side of his canteen. He might even now begin with the first sip but it was a luxury to postpone pleasure until desire became greater. C

He raised his eyes along the trail. Close by, it was merely dotted with occasional bones, but distance joined the dots into an unbroken chalk line which wavered with a strange leisure across the Apache Desert, pointing toward the cool blue promise of the mountains. The next morning he would be among them.

A coyote whisked out of a gully and ran like a gray puff of dust on the wind. His tongue hung out like a little red rag from the side of his mouth; and suddenly Durante was dry to the marrow. He uncorked and lifted his canteen. It had a slightly sour smell; perhaps the sacking which covered it had grown a trifle old. And then he poured a great mouthful of lukewarm liquid. He had swallowed it before his senses could give him warning.

It was wine.

He looked first of all toward the mountains. They were as calmly blue, as distant as when he had started that morning. Twenty-four hours not on water, but on wine.

READING CHECK TEST

1. Why is Durante on the run? *He has killed a man.*

2. Who is Durante running from: *The sheriff*

3. Who does Durante get food, water, and shelter from? *Tony*

4. How does Durante intend to escape the sheriff? *By draining all the water from Tony's water tanks*

5. What proves to be Durante's downfall? *The canteen of wine that Tony gives him*

CLOSURE

Have each student explain to a partner the technique of foreshadowing and how it adds to the enjoyment of a story. Tell students to give examples of foreshadowing from "Wine on the Desert."

A. Foreshadowing

? Find the clue in the story that foreshadowed Tony's filling the canteen with wine. (Page 224, left-hand column: "Tony got up. He raised the canteen and looked around him, not at the tanks from which the water was pouring . . . but at the rows of his vineyard.")

B. Making Inferences

We know that Durante is becoming delirious with thirst since his mind starts to wander and he dreams of water.

C. Plot and Character

? Why in addition to having Tony put wine in the canteen do you think Brand had him poison Durante? (To show that Durante was a fool for believing that Tony would not retaliate against his cruelty. Tony's physical blinding of Durante reflects Durante's blind selfishness and insensitivity.)

D. Interpreting

? What passage does this recall? (The one on page 222, right-hand column, where Tony describes how someone dies in the desert)

A "I deserve it," said Durante. "I trusted him to fill the canteen. . . . I deserve it. Curse him!" With a mighty resolution, he quieted the panic in his soul. He would not touch the stuff until noon. Then he would take one discreet sip. He would win through.

Hours went by. He looked at his watch and found it was only ten o'clock. And he had thought that it was on the verge of noon! He uncorked the wine and drank freely and, corking the canteen, felt almost as though he needed a drink of water more than before. He sloshed the contents of the canteen. Already it was horribly light.

Once, he turned the mule and considered the return trip; but he could remember the head of the rabbit too clearly, drilled right through the center. The vineyard, the rows of old twisted, gnarled little trunks with the bark peeling off . . . every vine was to Tony like a human life. And Durante had condemned them all to death.

He faced the blue of the mountains again. His heart raced in his breast with terror. Perhaps it was fear and not the suction of that dry and deadly air that made his tongue cleave to the roof of his mouth.

The day grew old. Nausea began to work in his stomach, nausea alternating with sharp pains. When he looked down, he saw that there was blood on his boots. He had been spurring the mule until the red ran down from its flanks. It went with a curious stagger, like a rocking horse with a broken rocker; and Durante grew aware that he had been keeping the mule at a gallop for a long time. He pulled it to a halt. It stood with wide-braced legs. Its head was down. When he leaned from the saddle, he saw that its mouth was open.

"It's gonna die," said Durante. "It's gonna die . . . what a fool I been . . ."

The mule did not die until after sunset. Durante left everything except his revolver. He packed the weight of that for an hour and discarded it, in turn. His knees were growing weak. When he looked up at the stars, they shone white and clear for a moment only, and then whirled into little racing circles and scrawls of red.

He lay down. He kept his eyes closed and waited for the shaking to go out of his body, but it would not stop. And every breath of darkness was like an inhalation of black dust.

He got up and went on, staggering. Sometimes he found himself running.

Before you die of thirst, you go mad. He kept remembering that. His tongue had swollen big. Before it choked him, if he lanced it with his knife the blood would help him; he would be able to swallow. Then he remembered that the taste of blood is salty.

Once, in his boyhood, he had ridden through a pass with his father and they had looked down on the sapphire of a mountain lake, a hundred thousand million tons of water as cold as snow . . . B

When he looked up, now, there were no stars; and this frightened him terribly. He never had seen a desert night so dark. His eyes were failing, he was being blinded. When the morning came, he would not be able to see the mountains, and he would walk around and around in a circle until he dropped and died.

No stars, no wind; the air as still as the waters of a stale pool, and he in the dregs at the bottom . . .

He seized his shirt at the throat and tore it away so that it hung in two rags from his hips.

He could see the earth only well enough to stumble on the rocks. But there were no stars in the heavens. He was blind: He had no more hope than a rat in a well. Ah, but Italian devils know how to put poison in wine that steal all the senses or any one of them: and Tony had chosen to blind Durante. C

He heard a sound like water. It was the swishing of the soft deep sand through which he was treading; sand so soft that a man could dig it away with his bare hands. . . . D

Afterward, after many hours, out of the blind face of that sky the rain began to fall. It made first a whispering and then a delicate murmur like voices conversing, but after that, just at the dawn, it roared like the hoofs of ten thousand charging horses. Even through that thundering confusion the big birds with naked heads and red, raw necks found their way down to one place in the Apache Desert.

ANALYZING THE STORY
Identifying Facts
1. The story takes place in the Apache Desert. Details include Durante's thirst; "the last moments of dryness"; the well running dry in the middle of the dry season; the grapevines sipping "enough life"; the heavy sweat that breaks out on Durante when he enters the hollow; the hot, still air of the hollow; the wretched, dying grapevines.
2. He is fleeing because he has killed a man.
3. Durante destroys the water system so that the sheriff, who is sure to be following Durante, will not be able to cross the desert in pursuit. The sheriff will need water, and the only place to find it is at Tony's house.
4. Tony secretly fills Durante's canteen with wine instead of water. He knows that Durante will not be able to cross the desert on wine, and that he will die of thirst. He also puts poison in the wine.
5. If Durante returns to Tony's ranch, Tony will kill him with his rifle.

Interpreting Meanings
6. He dies of thirst.
The birds are buzzards, which are

Responding to the Story

Analyzing the Story

Identifying Facts
SRW p. 79

1. The **setting** is an important element in this story. Where does the story take place? List four details in the first four paragraphs that describe the intense heat and dryness.
2. Why is Durante fleeing from the sheriff?
3. Explain why he destroys Tony's water system.
4. What does Tony secretly do to defeat Durante?
5. Why won't Durante return to Tony's ranch after he discovers he does not have the proper supplies for a full day's trip across the desert?

Interpreting Meanings

6. What finally happens to Durante? What do you infer, or guess, about those big birds at the story's end?
7. Durante is not a nice fellow. We would not want him along on our vacation trip. What do we know about him that makes us dislike him? Which of his several offenses struck you as most unforgivable?
8. Tony is smart enough to run a very fancy irrigation system for his vineyard and to contrive a thirsty end for Durante. But he is not nearly so clever in his choice of friends. How do you suppose he came to be so chummy with Durante? What did you think of Tony?
9. How does the story of Tony's father **foreshadow,** or hint at, the end of this story? SRW p. 43
10. Why doesn't Durante like to think of the rabbit?
11. We get a sense of **irony** when something happens that is the opposite of what a character had planned or expected. How is it ironic that the rain comes when it does? SRW p. 57
12. Do you think the **theme** of the story is revealed in the final scene, where Durante's villainy is punished by those agonies in the desert? How would you state the story's theme?

Applying Meanings

13. In real life, have you found people who are one hundred percent villain like Durante? Or is villainy more a matter of the way we perceive people? Explain.

Writing About the Story

A Creative Response

1. **Presenting an Argument.** Imagine that the sheriff arrives and Tony is charged with murder. Write a paragraph telling whether you think Tony should be found guilty or not guilty of murder. Support your opinion with details from the story.

A Critical Response
SRW p. 67

2. **Summarizing a Story's Plot.** To *summarize* means "to state the main points in brief form" (see page 253). Write a paragraph summarizing the main events of this story. Be sure to tell how one event is related to another event. Before you write, fill out a chart like the following one to be sure you've covered all parts of the plot:

Elements of Plot	"Wine on the Desert"
Introduction to the story (Who are the characters? What are their conflicts?)	
Complications (What happens to make the conflict more complex and create suspense?)	
Climax (What event is the high point—that emotional peak which makes us realize how the story will end?)	
Resolution (How is the story completed?)	

See Teacher's Manual page 71.

Analyzing Language and Vocabulary

Similes
SRW p. 81

A **simile** states a comparison between two unlike things, using a specific word of comparison such as *like, as, than,* or *resembles.* Similes are common in everyday speech as well as in literature. When we say "Mary is as quiet as a mouse," or "Larry walks like an elephant," we are using similes.

birds of prey that often feed on dead meat. The spot they have found is Durante's final resting place.
7. He has killed a man, and feels no guilt. He is concerned only with himself. He accepts Tony's hospitality; then, to save himself, he threatens Tony's existence by shooting holes in the water tanks. This also will kill Tony's grapevines.

Answers will vary. Killing the man may be the highest crime, but treating Tony as he does may be the most unforgivable offense.
8. Answers will vary. Perhaps Durante and Tony became friends before Durante turned to crime. Tony is a good-hearted, honest, and generous man.
9. It foreshadows the end of the story because Durante dies in exactly the same way that Tony's father died.
10. It may be that Durante has already hatched his plan by the time Tony shoots the rabbit. Thus, he knows what his end will be if Tony catches him after he destroys the water tanks.
11. It is ironic because it comes too late to help Durante. Also, the fact that it is raining so soon after Durante leaves Tony means that the sheriff and the posse would be able to follow Durante anyhow, and shooting Tony's water tanks has less meaning. Rain also signifies rebirth; the rain is cleaning the earth after the evil presence of Durante is gone.
12. Answers will vary. Students may view Durante's suffering and death as indicating an obvious theme—"good triumphs over evil." See Teacher's Manual page 71.

Applying Meanings
13. Answers will vary. See Teacher's Manual page 71.

FURTHER READING FOR STUDENTS
You can recommend to students who liked this story to read *Max Brand's Best Western Stories.* They might also like to read some of his numerous Western adventure novels, such as *Dan Barry's Daughter* (1976), and *Storm on the Range* (1980).

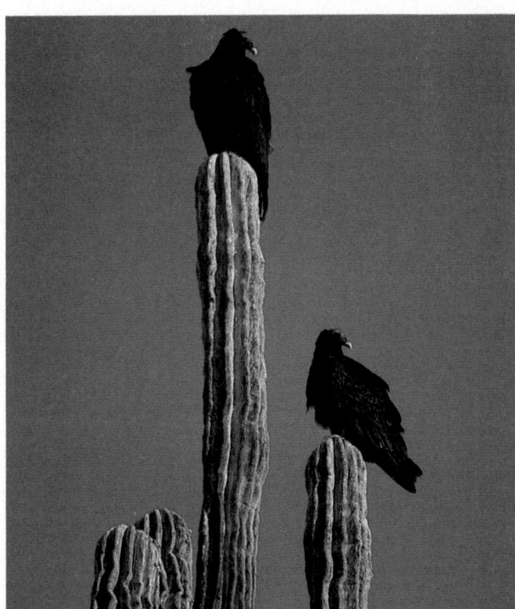

Max Brand uses similes in his story to describe the desert setting and the characters. For example, the narrator uses a simile when he says that the air "was hot and still as a bowl of soup." It's hard to think of the air we breathe as soup, but if you use your imagination, you can feel how the heat, thickness, and stillness of the windless desert air is like a hot, thick, still bowl of soup.

Here are some other similes from the story. Answer the questions to show that you understand the comparisons they are based on.

1. "There was no hurry, except for the thirst, like clotted salt, in the back of his throat."
   a. What is Durante's thirst compared to?
   b. As you read this, how does it make you feel? (How would it feel to have salt stuck in your throat?)
2. "A coyote whisked out of a gully and ran like a gray puff of dust on the wind."
   a. What is the simile?
   b. In what ways could a running animal be like a puff of dust?
3. "[The mule] went with a curious stagger, like a rocking horse with a broken rocker. . . ."
   a. What is the mule compared to?
   b. How would you picture the mule walking?
4. " . . . the air is still as the waters of a stale pool. . . . "
   a. What is the simile?
   b. Brand uses this simile as another way of describing the dryness. Does the simile work? Would you want to drink, or even swim, in a "stale pool"?
5. "He had no more hope than a rat in a well."
   a. What is Durante compared to in this simile?
   b. How does the comparison show Durante's helplessness?
6. " . . . it [the rain] roared like the hoofs of ten thousand charging horses."
   a. What is the rain compared to?
   b. Is it a heavy rain, a drizzle, or a shower? How do you know?
   c. How could rain "roar"?

For answers, see Teacher's Manual page 71.

Reading About the Writer

Max Brand (1892–1944?) was only one of Frederick Faust's many pen names. Faust was born in Seattle, Washington. Because of his father's career, the family was forced to move frequently. Faust once wrote, ". . . as the 'new kid' in each of the nineteen schools I attended there were always the bruising fistfights. I went for years with a swollen, scarred face . . . losing the few friends I found when my father changed jobs and I moved to a new school. In defense, I withdrew utterly into a world of books and daydreams. I . . . *lived* in the printed lives of others."

Faust was left an orphan when he was only thirteen and he was forced to make his own living. He managed to save up enough money to get himself through high school, and eventually he was able to attend—and to graduate with honors from—the University of California at Berkeley. As "Max Brand" he is well-known for his fast-paced adventure stories set in the American West. According to his biographer, "in his work, king-sized heroes ride in pursuit of queen-sized heroines on a landscape of mythological dimensions . . . ." Faust wrote more than one hundred novels, as well as many short stories and poems. He was killed during World War II while working as a war correspondent.

PREREADING

1. **BUILDING ON PRIOR KNOWLEDGE.** Before they begin reading, ask students to discuss the ways in which technological advances in medicine have made it possible for people to live longer, better, and happier lives. Ask them whether they think it is right to use humans as subjects in medical experiments in order to advance this technology.

2. **ESTABLISHING A PURPOSE.** Before students begin reading, you might have them read question 16 on page 29.

3. **PREREADING JOURNAL.** Before students read, have them write two or three sentences telling what they would do if they were asked to participate in an experiment that might make them the smartest person in the world.

SUPPLEMENTARY SUPPORT MATERIAL

1. Reading Check Test blackline master
2. Author photograph on *A Gallery of Authors* poster
3. Connections Between Reading and Writing worksheet
4. Reader's Response Journal

A. Responding to the Photograph

? Based on the sentences written on the chalkboard, what might you guess about Charlie, the main character of this story? (That he has a learning disability, or that he is mentally handicapped)

★ **Texas Essential Elements/(a) English Language Arts: 1B** Purpose and audience; **1E** Formal/informal language; **1H** Proofread; **1I** Spelling generalizations; **3A** Plot/character; **4B** Main idea; **4E** Predict; **4F** Generalizations

FLOWERS FOR ALGERNON

For a detailed lesson plan on this story, see Teacher's Manual pages 72–75. A biography of Daniel Keyes appears on text page 250.

Daniel Keyes

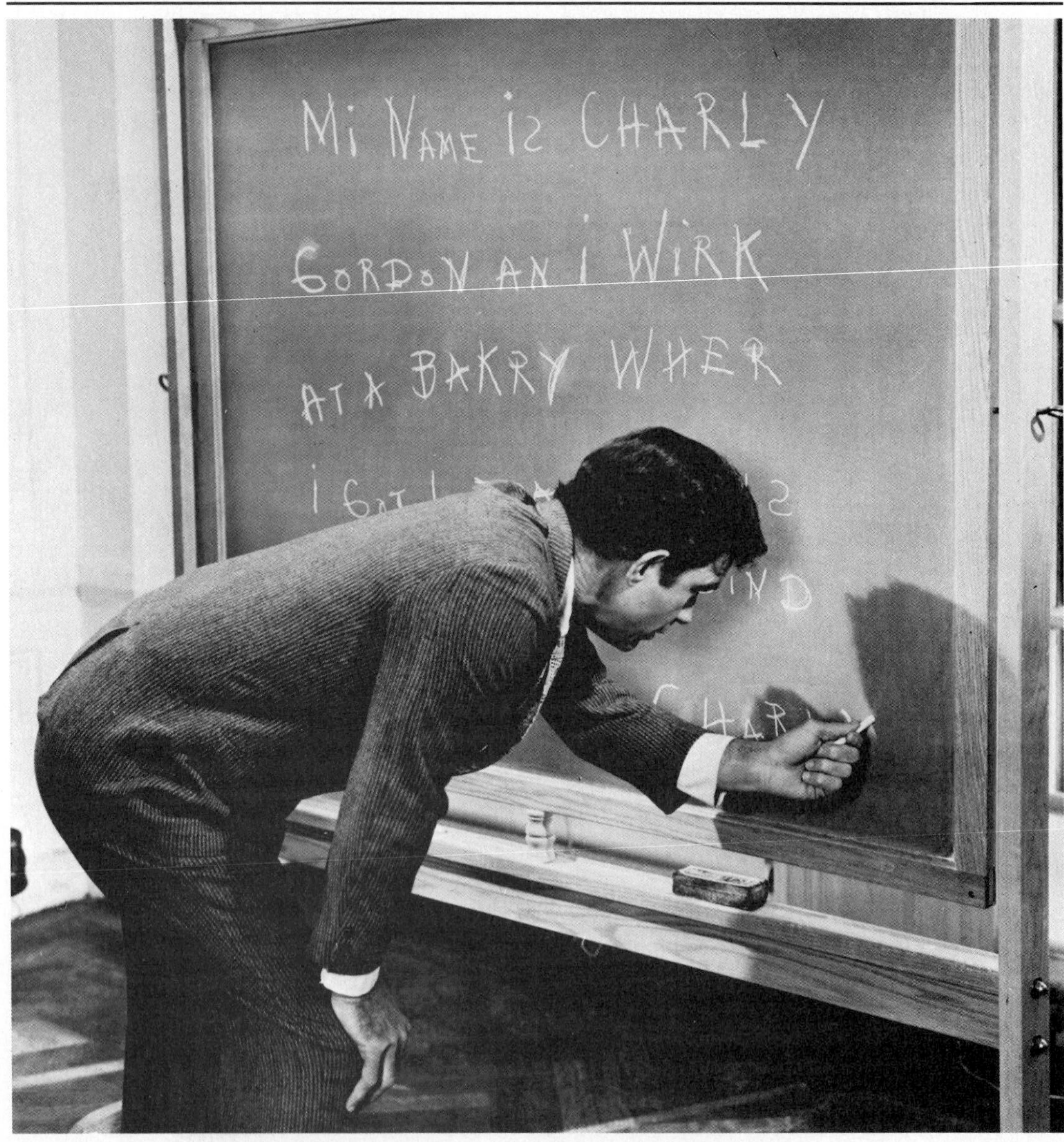

All photographs accompanying the story are taken from the movie *Charly,* starring Cliff Robertson as Charly and Claire Bloom as Miss Kinnian. The scenes from the movie do not always exactly match the events in the story.

SUPPLEMENTARY SUPPORT MATERIAL: PART ONE

1. Vocabulary Activity Sheet
2. Selection Test (page 79 of Test Book)
3. Workbook (page 57)

DEVELOPING VOCABULARY

The following words appear on a test in the Test Book, page 80. (See also the Vocabulary Activity Sheet.)

laboratory	accomplishing
marooned	advise
unconscious	petition
contributed	acquire
shrew	ignorance

Texas Essential Elements/(a) English Language Arts (continued): 4H Point of view. **(c) Reading: 1A** Context clues; **1B** Structural analysis; **1C** Dictionaries; **3A** Main ideas/details; **3D** Generalizations; **3F** Purpose/point of view/opinion;

Have you ever thought about how intelligence is distributed among us? Everyone knows what an advantage it is to have a few more "smarts" than the next person. Did it ever occur to you that in our day of scientific and technological breakthroughs there might be some way of making people smarter?

That notion must have occurred to Daniel Keyes and prompted him to write "Flowers for Algernon." Charlie Gordon is the hero of this unusual story. As you read about Charlie's experience, notice how his changing intelligence is signalled by changes in his ability to read and write.

Before you read, think about whether you believe people would be happier if they could be made smarter.

Phonetic Spelling. Charlie's diary entries provide many reminders that English words aren't always spelled the way they sound. Charlie often misspells words. Often he spells them *phonetically*—based on the way they sound. By using the context clues in the surrounding words and sentences and by "sounding out" Charlie's words, you will easily understand his meaning.

I

progris riport 1—martch 5 1965

Dr Strauss says I shud rite down what I think and evrey thing that happins to me from now on. I dont know why but he says its importint so they will see if they will use me. I hope they use me. Miss Kinnian says maybe they can make me smart. I want to be smart. My name is Charlie Gordon. I am 37 years old and 2 weeks ago was my birthday. I have nothing more to write now so I will close for today.

progris riport 2—martch 6

I had a test today. I think I faled it. and I think that maybe now they wont use me. What happind is a nice young man was in the room and he had some white cards with ink spilled all over them. He sed Charlie what do you see on this card. I was very skared even tho I had my rabits foot in my pockit because when I was a kid I always faled tests in scool and I spilled ink to. A

I told him I saw a inkblot. He said yes and it made me feel good. I thot that was all but when I got up to go he stopped me. He said now sit down Charlie we are not thru yet. Then I dont remember so good but he wantid me to say what was in the ink. I dint see nuthing in the ink but he said there was picturs there other pepul saw some picturs. I cudnt see any picturs. I reely tryed to see. I held the card close up and then far away. Then I said if I had my glases I could see better I usally only ware my glases in the movies or TV but I said they are in the closit in the hall. I got them. Then I said let me see that card agen I bet Ill find it now.

I tryed hard but I still couldnt find the picturs I only saw the ink. I told him maybe I need new glases. He rote something down on a paper and I got skared of faling the test. I told him it was a very nice inkblot with littel points all around the eges. He looked very sad so that wasnt it. I said please let me try agen. Ill get it in a few minits becaus Im not so fast sometimes. Im a slow reeder too in Miss Kinnians class for slow adults but Im trying very hard. B

He gave me a chance with another card that had 2 kinds of ink spilled on it red and blue.

He was very nice and talked slow like Miss Kinnian does and he explaned it to me that it was a *raw shok*.[1] He said pepul see things in the ink. I said show me where. He said think. I told him I think a inkblot but that wasnt rite eather. He said what does it remind you—pretend something. I closd my eyes for a long time to pretend. I told him I pretend a fowntan pen with ink leeking all over a table cloth. Then he got up and went out.

I dont think I passed the *raw shok* test.

progris riport 3—martch 7

Dr Strauss and Dr Nemur say it dont matter about the inkblots. I told them I dint spill the ink on the

1. **raw shok**: Rorschach (rôr′shäk) test, a psychological test in which the person being tested tells what a series of inkblots suggests to him or her.

A. Making Inferences

? What might have happened to Charlie when he failed tests in school that would make him so afraid of failing this test? (He was probably made fun of.)

B. Interpreting

? Why do you think Charlie thinks pictures are hidden in the inkblots? (Probably because when he was in school, the answers always seemed "hidden" from Charlie since other people could get them and he couldn't. He is generalizing this experience to all tests.)

A. Stating a Message

Through Charlie's words, what is Keyes saying here? (He is ridiculing the effectiveness of these psychological tests in determining personality.)

B. Foreshadowing

Tell students to pay attention as they read for instances in which Charlie compares himself to Algernon. This will help them to better understand the significance of Algernon's behavior to Charlie's future when Part II of the story unfolds.

C. Expansion

The "eye-q" or IQ (intelligence quotient) for average adults is 100. Someone who has an IQ of 70 or lower is legally considered mentally retarded. An IQ of 140 or over signifies a genius.

D. Interpreting

What is the word that Charlie cannot understand? (Motivation) Why is Algernon's, but not Charlie's, "motor-vation" his cheese? (The cheese at the end of the maze is what makes Algernon run through it. In psychological experiments on animals, food is used to condition them into performing a certain behavior. Human beings, however, often require psychological motivation to perform tasks—in this case, Charlie's motivation is his competitive desire to beat Algernon at the maze.)

★ **Texas Essential Elements/(c) Reading** (continued): **3G** Compare/contrast; **3H** Predict; **3I** Draw conclusions

cards and I couldn't see anything in the ink. They said that maybe they will still use me. I said Miss Kinnian never gave me tests like that one only spelling and reading. They said Miss Kinnian told that I was her bestist pupil in the adult nite scool becaus I tryed the hardist and reely wantid to lern. They said how come you went to the adult nite scool all by yourself Charlie. How did you find it. I said I askd pepul and sumbody tole me where I shud go to lern to read and spell good. They said why did you want to. I told them becaus all my life I wantid to be smart and not dumb. But its very hard to be smart. They said you know it will probly be tempirery. I said yes. Miss Kinnian told me. I dont care if it herts.

Later I had more crazy tests today. The nice lady who gave it me told me the name and I asked her how do you spell it so I can rite it in my progris riport. THEMATIC APPERCEPTION TEST. I dont know the first 2 words but I know what *test* means. You got to pass it or you get bad marks. This test looked easy becaus I could see the picturs. Only this time she dint want me to tell her the picturs. That mixd me up. I said the man yesterday said I shoud tell him what I saw in the ink she said that dont make no difrence. She said make up storys about the pepul in the picturs.

I told her how can you tell storys about pepul you never met. I said why shud I make up lies. I never tell lies any more becaus I always get caut.

She told me this test and the other one that raw shok was for getting personalty. I laffed so hard. I said how can you get that thing from inkblots (A) and fotos. She got sore and put her picturs away. I dont care. It was sily. I gess I faled that test too.

Later some men in white coats took me to a difernt part of the hospitil and gave me a game to play. It was like a race with a white mouse. They called the mouse Algernon. Algernon was in a box with a lot of twists and turns like all kinds of walls and they gave me a pencil and a paper with lines and lots of boxes. On one side it said START and on the other end it said FINISH. They said it was *amazed* and that Algernon and me had the same *amazed* to do. I dint see how we could have the same *amazed* if Algernon had a box and I had a paper but I dint say nothing. Anyway there wasnt time becaus the race started.

One of the men had a watch he was trying to hide so I wouldnt see it so I tryed not to look and that made me nervus.

Anyway that test made me feel worser than all the others because they did it over 10 times with difernt *amazeds* and Algernon won every time. I dint know that mice were so smart. Maybe thats because Algernon is a white mouse. Maybe white mice are smarter than other mice. (B)

progris riport 4—Mar 8

Their going to use me! Im so excited I can hardly write. Dr Nemur and Dr Strauss had a argament about it first. Dr Nemur was in the office when Dr Strauss brot me in. Dr Nemur was worryed about using me but Dr Strauss told him Miss Kinnian rekemmended me the best from all the people who she was teaching. I like Miss Kinnian becaus shes a very smart teacher. And she said Charlie your going to have a second chance. If you volenteer for this experament you mite get smart. They dont know if it will be perminint but theirs a chance. Thats why I said ok even when I was scared because she said it was an operashun. She said dont be scared Charlie you done so much with so little I think you deserv it most of all.

So I got scaird when Dr Nemur and Dr Strauss argud about it. Dr Strauss said I had something that was very good. He said I had a good *motor-vation.* I never even knew I had that. I felt proud when he said that not every body with an eye-q (C) of 68 had that thing. I dont know what it is or where I got it but he said Algernon had it too. Algernons *motor-vation* is the cheese they put in his box. But it cant be that because I didnt eat (D) any cheese this week.

Then he told Dr Nemur something I didnt understand so while they were talking I wrote down some of the words.

He said Dr Nemur I know Charlie is not what you had in mind as the first of your new brede of intelek** (coudnt get the word) superman. But most people of his low ment** are host** and uncoop** they are usualy dull apath** and hard to reach. He has a good natcher hes intristed and eager to please.

Dr Nemur said remember he will be the first human beeng ever to have his inteligence trippled by surgicle meens.

Dr Strauss said exakly. Look at how well hes lerned to read and write for his low mentel age its as grate an acheve** as you and I lerning einstines therey of **vity without help. That shows the intenss motor-vation. It comparat** a tremen** achev** I say we use Charlie.

I dint get all the words and they were talking to fast but it sounded like Dr Strauss was on my side and like the other one wasnt.

Then Dr Nemur nodded he said all right maybe your right. We will use Charlie. When he said that I got so exited I jumped up and shook his hand for being so good to me. I told him thank you doc you wont be sorry for giving me a second chance. And I mean it like I told him. After the operashun Im gonna try to be smart. Im gonna try awful hard.

progris ript 5—Mar 10

Im skared. Lots of people who work here and the nurses and the people who gave me the tests came to bring me candy and wish me luck. I hope I have luck. I got my rabits foot and my lucky penny and my horse shoe. Only a black cat crossed me when I was comming to the hospitil. Dr Strauss says dont be supersitis Charlie this is sience. Anyway Im keeping my rabits foot with me.

I asked Dr Strauss if Ill beat Algernon in the race after the operashun and he said maybe. If the operashun works Ill show that mouse I can be as smart as he is. Maybe smarter. Then Ill be abel to read better and spell the words good and know lots of things and be like other people. I want to be smart like other people. If it works perminint they will make everybody smart all over the world. **A**

A. Character
What does this passage reveal about Charlie? (That he is competitive; that he equates being smart with being "like other people." It also reveals his innocence: he believes that "they" can make everybody smart all over the world; he assumes that people all over the world share his desire to be smart.)

A. Character's Feelings
? How is Charlie feeling? (Impatient, frustrated, angry, abandoned, hurt)

B. Irony
This statement proves ironic in that exactly the opposite happens: Algernon's increased intelligence is only temporary.

C. Interpreting
? What do we know from this incident at the factory? (Even though Charlie says that the workers at the factory are his friends, we know the painful truth is that they make fun of him all the time, and he takes their mocking as friendship. Here, the phrase "ignorance is bliss" truly applies.)

They dint give me anything to eat this morning. I dont know what that eating has to do with getting smart. Im very hungry and Dr Nemur took away my box of candy. That Dr Nemur is a grouch. Dr Strauss says I can have it back after the operashun. You cant eat befor a operashun. . . .

Progress Report 6—Mar 15

The operashun dint hurt. He did it while I was sleeping. They took off the bandijis from my eyes and my head today so I can make a PROGRESS REPORT. Dr Nemur who looked at some of my other ones says I spell PROGRESS wrong and he told me how to spell it and REPORT too. I got to try and remember that.

I have a very bad memary for spelling. Dr Strauss says its ok to tell about all the things that happin to me but he says I shoud tell more about what I feel and what I think. When I told him I dont know how to think he said try. All the time when the bandijis were on my eyes I tryed to think. Nothing happened. I dont know what to think about. Maybe if I ask him he will tell me how I can think now that Im suppose to get smart. What do smart people think about. Fancy things I suppose. I wish I knew some fancy things already.

Progress Report 7—Mar 19

Nothing is happining. I had lots of tests and different kinds of races with Algernon. I hate that mouse. He always beats me. Dr Strauss said I got to play those games. And he said some time I got to take those tests over again. Those inkblots are stupid. And those pictures are stupid too. I like to draw a picture of a man and a woman but I wont make up lies about people. A

I got a headache from trying to think so much. I thot Dr Strauss was my frend but he dont help me. He dont tell me what to think or when Ill get smart. Miss Kinnian dint come to see me. I think writing these progress reports are stupid too.

Progress Report 8—Mar 23

I'm going back to work at the factery. They said it was better I shud go back to work but I cant tell anyone what the operashun was for and I have to come to the hospitil for an hour every night after work. They are gonna pay me money every month for lerning to be smart.

Im glad Im going back to work because I miss my job and all my frends and all the fun we have there.

Dr Strauss says I shud keep writing things down but I dont have to do it every day just when I think of something or something speshul happins. He says dont get discoridged because it takes time and it happins slow. He says it took a long time with Algernon before he got 3 times smarter than he was before. Thats why Algernon beats me all the time because he had that operashun too. That makes me feel better. I coud probly do that *amazed* faster than a reglar mouse. Maybe some day Ill beat Algernon. Boy that would be something. So far Algernon looks like he mite be smart perminent. B

Mar 25 (I dont have to write PROGRESS REPORT on top any more just when I hand it in once a week for Dr Nemur to read. I just have to put the date on. That saves time.)

We had a lot of fun at the factery today. Joe Carp said hey look where Charlie had his operashun what did they do Charlie put some brains in. I was going to tell him but I remembered Dr Strauss said no. Then Frank Reilly said what did you do Charlie forget your key and open your door the hard way. That made me laff. Their really my friends and they like me. C

Sometimes somebody will say hey look at Joe or Frank or George he really pulled a Charlie Gordon. I dont know why they say that but they always laff. This morning Amos Borg who is the 4 man at Donnegans used my name when he shouted at Ernie the office boy. Ernie lost a packige. He said Ernie for godsake what are you trying to be a Charlie Gordon. I dont understand why he said that. I never lost any packiges.

Mar 28 Dr Strauss came to my room tonight to see why I dint come in like I was suppose to. I told him I dont like to race with Algernon any more. He said I dont have to for a while but I shud come in. He had a present for me only it wasnt a present but just for lend. I thot it was a little television but it wasnt. He said I got to turn it on when I go to sleep. I said your kidding why shud I turn it on when Im going to sleep. Who ever herd of a thing like that. But he said if I want to get smart I got to do what he says. I told him I dint think I was going to get smart and he put his hand on my sholder and said Charlie you dont know it yet but your getting smarter all the time. You wont notice for a while. I think he was just being nice to make me feel good because I dont look any smarter.

Oh yes I almost forgot. I asked him when I can go back to the class at Miss Kinnians school. He said I wont go their. He said that soon Miss Kinnian will come to the hospital to start and teach me speshul. I was mad at her for not comming to see me when I got the operashun but I like her so maybe we will be frends again.

Mar 29 That crazy TV kept me up all night. How can I sleep with something yelling crazy things all night in my ears. And the nutty pictures. Wow. I dont know what it says when Im up so how am I going to know when Im sleeping.

Dr Strauss says its ok. He says my brains are lerning when I sleep and that will help me when Miss Kinnian starts my lessons in the hospitil (only I found out it isnt a hospitil its a labatory). I think its all crazy. If you can get smart when your sleeping why do people go to school. That thing I dont think will work. I use to watch the late show and the later show on TV all the time and it never made me smart. Maybe you have to sleep while you watch it.

PROGRESS REPORT 9–April 3

Dr Strauss showed me how to keep the TV tuned low so now I can sleep. I dont hear a thing. And I still dont understand what it says. A few times I play it over in the morning to find out what I lerned when I was sleeping and I dont think so.
A Miss Kinnian says maybe its another langwidge or something. But most times it sounds american. It talks so fast faster than even Miss Gold who was my teacher in 6 grade and I remember she talked so fast I couldnt understand her.

I told Dr Strauss what good is it to get smart in my sleep. I want to be smart when Im awake. He says its the same thing and I have two minds. Theres the *subconscious* and the *conscious* (thats how you spell it.) And one dont tell the other one what its doing. They dont even talk to each other. Thats why I dream. And boy have I been having crazy dreams. Wow. Ever since that night TV. The late late late late late show.

I forgot to ask him if it was only me or if everybody had those two minds.

(I just looked up the word in the dictionary Dr Strauss gave me. The word is *subconscious. adj. Of the nature of mental operations yet not present in consciousness; as, subconscious conflict of desires.*) There's more but I still dont know what it means. This isnt a very good dictionary for dumb people like me. B

Anyway the headache is from the party. My friends from the factery Joe Carp and Frank Reilly invited me to go with them to Muggsys Saloon for some drinks. I dont like to drink but they said we will have lots of fun. I had a good time.

Joe Carp said I shoud show the girls how I mop out the toilet in the factery and he got me a mop. I showed them and everyone laffed when I told that Mr Donnegan said I was the best janiter he ever had because I like my job and do it good and never come late or miss a day except for my operashun.

I said Miss Kinnian always said Charlie be proud of your job because you do it good.

Everybody laffed and we had a good time and they gave me lots of drinks and Joe said Charlie is a card when hes potted. I dont know what that means but everybody likes me and we have fun. I cant wait to be smart like my best friends Joe Carp and Frank Reilly. C

I dont remember how the party was over but I think I went out to buy a newspaper and coffee for Joe and Frank and when I come back there was no one their. I looked for them all over till late. Then I dont remember so good but I think I got sleepy or sick. A nice cop brot me back home. Thats what my landlady Mrs Flynn says.

But I got a headache and a big lump on my head and black and blue all over. I think maybe I fell but Joe Carp says it was the cop they beat up drunks some times. I dont think so. Miss Kinnian says cops are to help people. Anyway I got a bad D

A. Interpreting
Note that here Charlie's spelling and sentence structure begin to improve.

B. Plot
? Why is the incident with the dictionary important here? (Because it shows how much progress Charlie has made: now, he is smart enough to know when to use the dictionary and how to use it.)

C. Character
? How would you characterize Joe Carp and Frank Reilly? (Insensitive, unintelligent, unkind) What did they do to Charlie? (They got him drunk, made him go out on an errand, and ran off before he got back.)

D. Interpreting
? Do you think the cops beat up Charlie? (Probably not. Joe Carp told him this because Charlie most likely got the lump on his head from falling when he was drunk. Joe doesn't want anybody to know what happened or discover his own part in it.)

A. Stating a Message
Here, Keyes is criticizing the use of animals for experiments.

headache and Im sick and hurt all over. I dont think Ill drink anymore.

April 6 I beat Algernon! I dint even know I beat him until Burt the tester told me. Then the second time I lost because I got so exited I fell off the chair before I finished. But after that I beat him 8 more times. I must be getting smarter to beat a smart mouse like Algernon. But I dont *feel* smarter.

I wanted to race Algernon some more but Burt said thats enough for one day. They let me hold him for a minut. Hes not so bad. Hes soft like a ball of cotton. He blinks and when he opens his eyes their black and pink on the eges.

I said can I feed him because I felt bad to beat him and I wanted to be nice and make frends. Burt said no Algernon is a very specshul mouse with an operashun like mine, and he was the first of all the animals to stay smart so long. He told me Algernon is so smart that every day he has to solve a test to get his food. Its a thing like a lock on a door that changes every time Algernon goes in to eat so he has to lern something new to get his food. That made me sad because if he couldnt lern he would be hungry.

I dont think its right to make you pass a test to eat. How woud Dr Nemur like it to have to pass a test every time he wants to eat. I think Ill be frends with Algernon. A

April 9 Tonight after work Miss Kinnian was at the laboratory. She looked like she was glad to see me but scared. I told her dont worry Miss Kinnian Im not smart yet and she laffed. She said I have confidence in you Charlie the way you

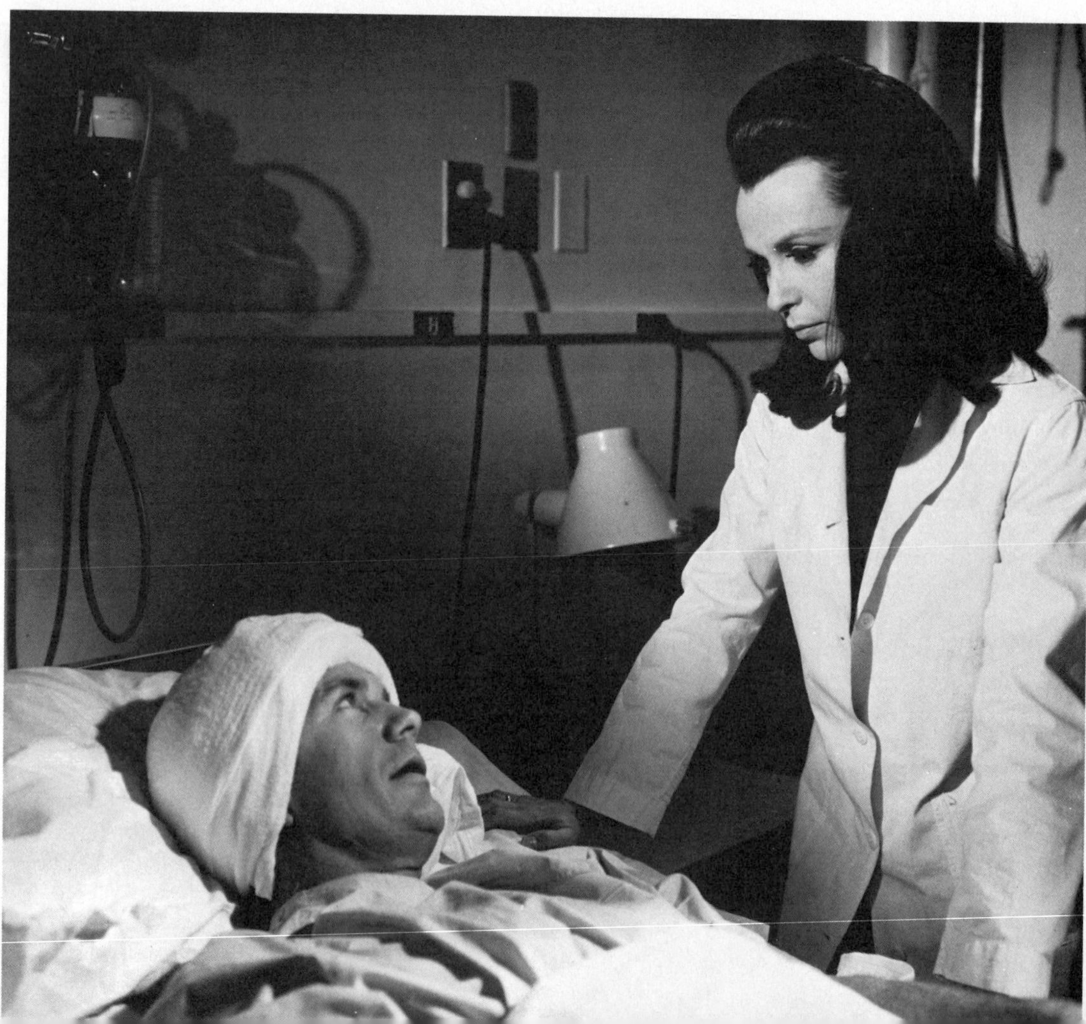

struggled so hard to read and right better than all the others. At werst you will have it for a littel wile and your doing somthing for sience.

We are reading a very hard book. I never read such a hard book before. Its called *Robinson Crusoe* about a man who gets merooned on a dessert Iland. Hes smart and figers out all kinds of things so he can have a house and food and hes a good swimmer. Only I feel sorry because hes all alone and has no frends. But I think their must be somebody else on the iland because theres a picture with his funny umbrella looking at footprints. I hope he gets a frend and not be lonly.

April 10 Miss Kinnian teaches me to spell better. She says look at a word and close your eyes and say it over and over until you remember. I have lots of truble with *through* that you say *threw* and *enough* and *tough* that you don't say *enew* and *tew*. You got to say *enuff* and *tuff*. Thats how I use to write it before I started to get smart. Im confused but Miss Kinnian says theres no reason in spelling.

Apr 14 Finished *Robinson Crusoe*. I want to find out more about what happens to him but Miss Kinnian says thats all there is. *Why.*

Apr 15 Miss Kinnian says Im lerning fast. She read some of the Progress Reports and she looked at me kind of funny. She says Im a fine person and Ill show them all. I asked her why. She said
A never mind but I shouldnt feel bad if I find out that everybody isnt nice like I think. She said for a person who god gave so little to you done more than a lot of people with brains they never even used. I said all my frends are smart people but there good. They like me and they never did anything that wasn't nice. Then she got something in
B her eye and she had to run out to the ladys room.

Apr 16 Today, I learned, the *comma,* this is a comma (,) a period, with a tail, Miss Kinnian, says its importent, because, it makes writing, better, she said, somebody, could lose, a lot of money, if a comma, isnt, in the, right place, I dont have, any money, and I dont see, how a comma, keeps you, from losing it.

But she says, everybody, uses commas, so Ill use, them too.

Apr 17 I used the comma wrong. Its punctuation. Miss Kinnian told me to look up long words in the dictionary to lern to spell them. I said whats the difference if you can read it anyway. She said its part of your education so from now on Ill look up all the words Im not sure how to spell. It takes a long time to write that way but I think Im remembering. I only have to look up once and after that I get it right. Anyway thats how come I got the word *punctuation* right. (Its that way in the dictionary.) Miss Kinnian says a period is punctuation too, and there are lots of other marks to lern. I told her I thot all the periods had to have tails but she said no.

You got to mix them up, she showed? me'' how. to mix! them) up,. and now; I can! mix up all kinds'' of punctuation, in! my writing? There, are lots! of rules? to lern; but Im gettin'g them in my head.

One thing I? like about, Dear Miss Kinnian: (thats the way it goes in a business letter if I ever go into business) is she, always gives me' a reason'' when—I ask. She's a gen'ius! I wish I cou'd be smart'' like, her;

(Punctuation, is; fun!)

April 18 What a dope I am! I didn't even understand what she was talking about. I read the grammar book last night and it explanes the whole thing. Then I saw it was the same way as Miss Kinnian was trying to tell me, but I didn't get it. I got up in the middle of the night, and the whole thing straightened out in my mind.

Miss Kinnian said that the TV working in my sleep helped out. She said I reached a plateau. That's like the flat top of a hill.

After I figgered out how punctuation worked, I read over all my old Progress Reports from the beginning. Boy, did I have crazy spelling and punctuation! I told Miss Kinnian I ought to go over the pages and fix all the mistakes but she said, ''No, Charlie, Dr. Nemur wants them just as they are. That's why he let you keep them after they were photostated, to see your own progress. You're coming along fast, Charlie.''

A. Character's Motivation

? Why do you think Miss Kinnian says this? What does it reveal about her feelings for Charlie? (She wants to prepare Charlie for a harsh reality of life so that he will not be shocked and hurt when he finds it out for himself. It shows that she cares a great deal for Charlie.)

B. Making Inferences

? What is really happening here? (Miss Kinnian gets tears in her eyes and wants to hide it from Charlie.)

A. Interpreting
Why don't they race anymore? (Because Charlie's intelligence has surpassed Algernon's; now Charlie will always win the maze.)

B. Plot and Character
Why is this incident important? (Because it shows that Charlie has reached the stage of self-awareness: He discovers the true character of those he called friends.)

C. Making Inferences
Why would Mrs. Flynn be afraid of Charlie? (Probably because he is changing in front of her eyes, and she is frightened of a change that doesn't seem to have a cause.)

D. Expansion
Charlie has now achieved a talent that most people do not have—that of a photographic memory.

A That made me feel good. After the lesson I went down and played with Algernon. We don't race anymore.

April 20 I feel sick inside. Not sick like for a doctor, but inside my chest it feels empty like getting punched and a heartburn at the same time.

I wasn't going to write about it, but I guess I got to, because its important. Today was the first time I ever stayed home from work.

Last night Joe Carp and Frank Reilly invited me to a party. There were lots of girls and some men from the factory. I remembered how sick I got last time I drank too much, so I told Joe I didn't want anything to drink. He gave me a plain coke instead. It tasted funny, but I thought it was just a bad taste in my mouth.

We had a lot of fun for a while. Joe said I should dance with Ellen and she would teach me the steps. I fell a few times and I couldn't understand why because no one else was dancing besides Ellen and me. And all the time I was tripping because somebody's foot was always sticking out.

Then when I got up I saw the look on Joe's face and it gave me a funny feeling in my stomack. "He's a scream," one of the girls said. Everybody was laughing.

Frank said, "I ain't laughed so much since we sent him off for the newspaper that night at Muggsy's and ditched him."

"Look at him. His face is red."

"He's blushing. Charlie is blushing."

"Hey, Ellen, what'd you do to Charlie? I never saw him act like that before."

I didn't know what to do or where to turn. Everyone was looking at me and laughing and I felt naked. I wanted to hide myself. I ran out into the street and I threw up. Then I walked home. It's a funny thing I never knew that Joe and Frank and the others liked to have me around all the time to make fun of me.

B Now I know what it means when they say "to pull a Charlie Gordon."

I'm ashamed.

PROGRESS REPORT 10

April 21 Still didn't go into the factory. I told Mrs. Flynn my landlady to call and tell Mr. Donnegan I was sick. Mrs. Flynn looks at me very funny lately like she's scared of me. C

I think it's a good thing about finding out how everybody laughs at me. I thought about it a lot. It's because I'm so dumb and I don't even know when I'm doing something dumb. People think it's funny when a dumb person can't do things the same way they can.

Anyway, now I know I'm getting smarter every day. I know punctuation and I can spell good. I like to look up all the hard words in the dictionary and I remember them. I'm reading a lot now, and Miss Kinnian says I read very fast. Sometimes I even understand what I'm reading about, and it stays in my mind. There are times when I can close my eyes and think of a page and it all comes back like a picture. D

Besides history, geography, and arithmetic, Miss Kinnian said I should start to learn a few foreign languages. Dr. Strauss gave me some more tapes to play while I sleep. I still don't understand how that conscious and unconscious mind works, but Dr. Strauss says not to worry yet. He asked me to promise that when I start learning college subjects next week I wouldn't read any books on psychology—that is, until he gives me permission.

I feel a lot better today, but I guess I'm still a little angry that all the time people were laughing and making fun of me because I wasn't so smart. When I become intelligent like Dr. Strauss says, with three times my I.Q. of 68, then maybe I'll be like everybody else and people will like me and be friendly.

I'm not sure what an I.Q. is. Dr. Nemur said it was something that measured how intelligent you were—like a scale in the drugstore weighs pounds. But Dr. Strauss had a big argument with him and said an I.Q. didn't weigh intelligence at all. He said an I.Q. showed how much intelligence you could get, like the numbers on the outside of a measuring cup. You still have to fill the cup up with stuff.

Then when I asked Burt, who gives me my intelligence tests and works with Algernon, he said that both of them were wrong (only I had to promise not to tell them he said so). Burt says that the I.Q. measures a lot of different things including some of the things you learned already, and it really isn't any good at all.

So I still don't know what I.Q. is except that mine is going to be over 200 soon. I didn't want to say anything, but I don't see how if they don't know *what* it is, or *where* it is—I don't see how they know *how much* of it you've got.

Dr. Nemur says I have to take a *Rorshach Test* tomorrow. I wonder what *that is*.

April 22 I found out what a *Rorshach* is. It's the test I took before the operation—the one with the inkblots on the pieces of cardboard. The man who gave me the test was the same one.

I was scared to death of those inkblots. I knew he was going to ask me to find the pictures and I knew I wouldn't be able to. I was thinking to myself, if only there was some way of knowing what kind of pictures were hidden there. Maybe there weren't any pictures at all. Maybe it was just a trick to see if I was dumb enough to look for something that wasn't there. Just thinking about that made me sore at him.

"All right, Charlie," he said, "you've seen these cards before, remember?"

"Of course I remember."

The way I said it, he knew I was angry, and he looked surprised. "Yes, of course. Now I want you to look at this one. What might this be? What do you see on this card? People see all sorts of things in these inkblots. Tell me what it might be for you—what it makes you think of."

I was shocked. That wasn't what I had expected him to say at all. "You mean there are no pictures hidden in those inkblots?"

He frowned and took off his glasses. "What?"

"Pictures. Hidden in the inkblots. Last time you told me that everyone could see them and you wanted me to find them too."

He explained to me that the last time he had used almost the exact same words he was using now. I didn't believe it, and I still have the suspicion that he misled me at the time just for the fun of it. Unless—I don't know any more—could I have been *that* feebleminded?

We went through the cards slowly. One of them looked like a pair of bats tugging at something. Another one looked like two men fencing with swords. I imagined all sorts of things. I guess I got carried away. But I didn't trust him any more, and I kept turning them around and even looking on the back to see if there was anything there I was supposed to catch. While he was making his notes, I peeked out of the corner of my eye to read it. But it was all in code that looked like this:

WF+A DdF− Ad orig. WF−A SF+obj

The test still doesn't make sense to me. It seems to me that anyone could make up lies about things that they didn't really see. How could he know I wasn't making a fool of him by mentioning things that I didn't really imagine? Maybe I'll understand it when Dr. Strauss lets me read up on psychology.

April 25 I figured out a new way to line up the machines in the factory, and Mr. Donnegan says it will save him $10,000 a year in labor and increased production. He gave me a $25 bonus.

I wanted to take Joe Carp and Frank Reilly out to lunch to celebrate, but Joe said he had to buy some things for his wife, and Frank said he was meeting his cousin for lunch. I guess it'll take a little time for them to get used to the changes in me. Everybody seems to be frightened of me. When I went over to Amos Borg and tapped him on the shoulder he jumped up in the air.

People don't talk to me much anymore or kid around the way they used to. It makes the job kind of lonely.

April 27 I got up the nerve today to ask Miss Kinnian to have dinner with me tomorrow night to celebrate my bonus.

At first she wasn't sure it was right, but I asked Dr. Strauss and he said it was okay. Dr. Strauss and Dr. Nemur don't seem to be getting along so well. They're arguing all the time. This evening when I came in to ask Dr. Strauss about having dinner with Miss Kinnian, I heard them shouting. Dr. Nemur was saying that it was *his* experiment and *his* research, and Dr. Strauss was shouting back that he contributed just as much, because he found me through Miss Kinnian and he performed the operation. Dr. Strauss said that someday thousands of neurosurgeons might be using his technique all over the world.

A. Stating a Message
Keyes is criticizing yet another aspect of the science of psychology—that of trying to measure intelligence.

B. Character
? What do Charlie's words and angry tone of voice reveal about him? (That he is more sensitive to how he is viewed by others, and he is no longer willing to be spoken to as though he were a child.)

A. Expression

What does "riding to glory on someone's coattails" mean? (Associating with someone who is on his or her way to achieving fame, and trying to benefit personally from that association)

B. Figurative Language

How is Charlie like a sponge? (Just as a sponge soaks up liquid, Charlie is soaking up knowledge.)

C. Making Inferences

What is Miss Kinnian afraid of? (That Charlie's intelligence will decrease) Why does Charlie compare this to the elderly people thinking of death? (Because if his new-found intelligence were taken away, it would be a kind of death for him. Gaining intelligence has opened the world up to him—losing it would put him back in darkness.)

Dr. Nemur wanted to publish the results of the experiment at the end of this month. Dr. Strauss wanted to wait a while longer to be sure. Dr. Strauss said that Dr. Nemur was more interested in the Chair of Psychology at Princeton than he was in the experiment. Dr. Nemur said that Dr.
A Strauss was nothing but an opportunist[2] who was trying to ride to glory on *his* coattails.

When I left afterward, I found myself trembling. I don't know why for sure, but it was as if I'd seen both men clearly for the first time. I remember hearing Burt say that Dr. Nemur had a shrew of a wife who was pushing him all the time to get things published so that he could become famous. Burt said that the dream of her life was to have a bigshot husband.

Was Dr. Strauss really trying to ride on his coattails?

April 28 I don't understand why I never noticed how beautiful Miss Kinnian really is. She has brown eyes and feathery brown hair that comes to the top of her neck. She's only thirty-four! I think from the beginning I had the feeling that she was an unreachable genius—and very, very, old. Now, every time I see her she grows younger and more lovely.

We had dinner and a long talk. When she said that I was coming along so fast that soon I'd be leaving her behind, I laughed.

"It's true, Charlie. You're already a better reader than I am. You can read a whole page at a glance while I can take in only a few lines at a time. And you remember every single thing you read. I'm lucky if I can recall the main thoughts and the general meaning."

"I don't feel intelligent. There are so many things I don't understand."

She took out a cigarette and I lit it for her. "You've got to be a *little* patient. You're accomplishing in days and weeks what it takes normal people half a lifetime to do. That's what makes it
B so amazing. You're like a giant sponge now, soaking things in. Facts, figures, general knowledge. And soon you'll begin to connect them, too. You'll see how the different branches of learning are related. There are many levels, Charlie, like steps on a giant ladder that take you up higher and higher to see more and more of the world around you.

"I can see only a little bit of that, Charlie, and I won't go much higher than I am now, but you'll keep climbing up and up, and see more and more, and each step will open new worlds that you never even knew existed." She frowned. "I hope . . . I just hope to God——"

"What?"

"Never mind, Charles. I just hope I wasn't wrong to advise you to go into this in the first place." C

I laughed. "How could that be? It worked, didn't it? Even Algernon is still smart."

We sat there silently for awhile and I knew what she was thinking about as she watched me toying with the chain of my rabbit's foot and my keys. I didn't want to think of that possibility any more than elderly people want to think of death. I *knew* that this was only the beginning. I knew what she meant about levels because I'd seen some of them already. The thought of leaving her behind made me sad.

I'm in love with Miss Kinnian.

PROGRESS REPORT 11

April 30 I've quit my job with Donnegan's Plastic Box Company. Mr. Donnegan insisted that it would be better for all concerned if I left. What did I do to make them hate me so?

The first I knew of it was when Mr. Donnegan showed me that petition. Eight hundred and forty names, everyone connected with the factory, except Fanny Girden. Scanning the list quickly, I saw at once that hers was the only missing name. All the rest demanded that I be fired.

Joe Carp and Frank Reilly wouldn't talk to me about it. No one else would either, except Fanny. She was one of the few people I'd known who set her mind to something and believed it no matter what the rest of the world proved, said or did—and Fanny did not believe that I should have been fired. She had been against the petition on principle and despite the pressure and threats she'd held out.

2. **opportunist** (äp′ər·to͞on′ist): someone who acts only to further his or her own interests.

ANALYZING PART I

Identifying Facts

1. Charlie's full name is Charlie Gordon. He has just turned 37. He is not smart, but he wants to be. He keeps a rabbit's foot for luck. He wears glasses on certain occasions.

2. Algernon is a laboratory rat whose intelligence has been surgically increased. The first time Charlie races Algernon, Algernon wins ten straight times.

3. The operation is supposed to increase his intelligence.

4. His writing becomes better.

Charlie begins to read more difficult books, like *Robinson Crusoe.* Miss Kinnian continues to tutor him, but she begins to look scared. When he takes the Rorschach test again, he realizes how feeble-minded he was. Charlie begins to recognize other people's characters. He thinks up a money-saving strategy for his boss; and he begins to understand the doctors' motivations for this experiment.

Interpreting Meanings

5. The story is told from the first-person point of view—Charlie's diary.

The technique allows readers to get very close to Charlie, and to feel what he is feeling.

6. They don't understand what has happened to Charlie and they feel threatened by him.

This suggests that people are not really interested in how other people improve themselves, especially if that improvement threatens their positions. It implies that people are selfish.

7. Charlie probably means that the relationships between himself and others were based on his feeble-mindedness. Now that he is intelligent, neither he nor the others know how to deal with it.

Answers will vary.

Applying Meanings

8. In the Biblical story of Genesis, Adam and Eve ate the forbidden fruit from the tree of knowledge. They, and the rest of humankind, were punished for this transgression. Fanny is making the point that Charlie, like Adam and Eve, is acquiring knowledge that he was not meant to acquire.

9. They think Charlie is just someone to have fun with.

"Which don't mean to say," she remarked, "that I don't think there's something mighty strange about you, Charlie. Them changes. I don't know. You used to be a good, dependable, ordinary man—not too bright maybe, but honest. Who knows what you done to yourself to get so smart all of a sudden. Like everybody around here's been saying, Charlie, it's not right."

"But how can you say that, Fanny? What's wrong with a man becoming intelligent and wanting to acquire knowledge and understanding of the world around him?"

She stared down at her work and I turned to leave. Without looking at me, she said: "It was evil when Eve listened to the snake and ate from the tree of knowledge. It was evil when she saw that she was naked. If not for that none of us would ever have to grow old and sick, and die."

Once again now I have the feeling of shame burning inside me. This intelligence has driven a wedge between me and all the people I once knew and loved. Before, they laughed at me and despised me for my ignorance and dullness; now, they hate me for my knowledge and understanding. What in God's name do they want of me?

They've driven me out of the factory. Now I'm more alone than ever before. . . .

Responding to the Story

Analyzing Part I

Identifying Facts

1. List three or four facts that Charlie reveals about himself in his first two progress reports.
2. Who is Algernon? What happens when Charlie first races Algernon?
3. What is the operation supposed to do for Charlie?
4. After the operation, what is the first sign that Charlie is changing? What other changes in his studies, in his activities at the laboratory, and in his relationships with people indicate that he is becoming an intellectual superman?

Interpreting Meanings

5. From what **point of view,** or vantage point, is the story told? How does this technique contribute to the way the story makes you feel?
6. Why do you think that nearly everyone in the factory signed the petition to have Charlie fired? What does this suggest about people? Do you think their behavior is believable?

SRW p. 69

7. After the operation proves successful, Charlie says, "This intelligence has driven a wedge between me and all the people I once knew and loved." What do you think he means by this? Do you think intelligence can actually do this to people?

Applying Meanings

8. Reread Fanny Girden's reaction to the change in Charlie (above). How does the account of Adam and Eve and the forbidden fruit relate to what happened to Charlie? How do *you* feel about using science and technology to change a person's intelligence or personality?
9. Why do Charlie's fellow workers tease him so? What is the usual human response toward "the fool," or, as we are more likely to say, "the dummy"? Why do you suppose this is so? How do you feel about it?

SUPPLEMENTARY SUPPORT MATERIAL: PART TWO

1. Vocabulary Activity Sheet
2. Selection Test (page 81 of Test Book)
3. Workbook (page 59)

DEVELOPING VOCABULARY

The following words appear on a test in the Test Book, page 82. (See also the Vocabulary Activity Sheet.)

justified	artificial
sensation	amnesia
oversensitive	predictions
equivalent	introspective
technique	impaired

A. Making Inferences

? From Dr. Strauss's reminder, what do we know about Charlie's progress? (That he is gradually surpassing the average intelligence level.) Tell students to watch for details of Charlie's approach to the genius level.

II

May 15 Dr. Strauss is very angry at me for not having written my progress reports in two weeks. He's justified because the lab is now paying me a regular salary. I told him I was too busy thinking and reading. When I pointed out that writing was such a slow process that it made me impatient with my poor handwriting, he suggested that I learn to type. It's much easier to write now because I can type nearly seventy-five words a minute. Dr. Strauss continually reminds me of the
A need to speak and write simply so that people will be able to understand me.

I'll try to review all the things that happened to me during the last two weeks. Algernon and I were presented to the American Psychological Association sitting in convention with the World Psychological Association last Tuesday. We created quite a sensation. Dr. Nemur and Dr. Strauss were proud of us.

I suspect that Dr. Nemur, who is sixty—ten years older than Dr. Strauss—finds it necessary to see tangible[1] results of his work. Undoubtedly the result of pressure by Mrs. Nemur.

Contrary to my earlier impressions of him, I realize that Dr. Nemur is not at all a genius. He has a very good mind, but it struggles under the

1. **tangible** (tan′jə·b′l): real; definite.

specter of self-doubt. He wants people to take him for a genius. Therefore, it is important for him to feel that his work is accepted by the world. I believe that Dr. Nemur was afraid of further delay because he worried that someone else might make a discovery along these lines and take the credit from him.

Dr. Strauss, on the other hand, might be called a genius, although I feel that his areas of knowledge are too limited. He was educated in the tradition of narrow specialization; the broader aspects of background were neglected far more than necessary—even for a neurosurgeon.

A I was shocked to learn that the only ancient languages he could read were Latin, Greek, and Hebrew, and that he knows almost nothing of mathematics beyond the elementary levels of the calculus of variations. When he admitted this to me, I found myself almost annoyed. It was as if he'd hidden this part of himself in order to deceive me, pretending—as do many people, I've discovered—to be what he is not. No one I've ever known is what he appears to be on the surface.

Dr. Nemur appears to be uncomfortable around me. Sometimes when I try to talk to him, he just looks at me strangely and turns away. I was angry B at first when Dr. Strauss told me I was giving Dr. Nemur an inferiority complex. I thought he was mocking me and I'm oversensitive at being made fun of.

How was I to know that a highly respected psychoexperimentalist like Nemur was unacquainted with Hindustani and Chinese? It's absurd when you consider the work that is being done in India and China today in the very field of his study.

I asked Dr. Strauss how Nemur could refute Rahajamati's attack on his method and results if Nemur couldn't even read them in the first place. C That strange look on Dr. Strauss's face can mean only one of two things. Either he doesn't want to tell Nemur what they're saying in India, or else—and this worries me—Dr. Strauss doesn't know either. I must be careful to speak and write clearly and simply so that people won't laugh.

May 18 I am very disturbed. I saw Miss Kinnian last night for the first time in over a week. I tried to avoid all discussions of intellectual concepts and to keep the conversation on a simple, everyday level, but she just stared at me blankly and asked me what I meant about the mathematical variance equivalent in Dorberman's Fifth Concerto.

When I tried to explain, she stopped me and laughed. I guess I got angry, but I suspect I'm approaching her on the wrong level. No matter what I try to discuss with her, I am unable to communicate. I must review Vrostadt's equations in *Levels of Semantic Progression.* I find that I don't communicate with people much anymore. Thank God for books and music and things I can think about. I am alone in my apartment at Mrs. Flynn's boarding house most of the time and seldom speak to anyone.

May 20 I would not have noticed the new dishwasher, a boy of about sixteen, at the corner diner where I take my evening meals if not for the incident of broken dishes.

They crashed to the floor, shattering and sending bits of white china under the tables. The boy stood there, dazed and frightened, holding the empty tray in his hand. The whistles and catcalls from the customers (the cries of "hey, there go the profits!" . . . *"Mazel tov!"* . . . and "well, *he* didn't work here very long . . ." which invariably seem to follow the breaking of glass or dishware in a public restaurant) all seemed to confuse him.

When the owner came to see what the excitement was about, the boy cowered as if he expected to be struck and threw up his arms as if to ward off the blow.

"All right! All right, you dope," shouted the owner, "don't just stand there! Get the broom and sweep that mess up. A broom . . . a broom, you idiot! It's in the kitchen. Sweep up all the pieces."

The boy saw that he was not going to be punished. His frightened expression disappeared and he smiled and hummed as he came back with the broom to sweep the floor. A few of the rowdier customers kept up the remarks, amusing themselves at his expense.

"Here, sonny, over here there's a nice piece behind you . . ."

A. Humor

? What is humorous about this statement? (That Charlie is shocked at what he believes are Dr. Strauss's limitations. To be able to read Latin, Greek, and Hebrew is quite a sophisticated accomplishment. Calculus of variations is a high level math—even being familiar with the "elementary levels" indicates a high intellect.)

B. Interpreting

? Why is Charlie giving Dr. Nemur an inferiority complex? (Because Charlie is now more intelligent than Dr. Nemur. The doctors have created an intellectual monster.)

C. Interpreting

? Which do you think it is? (That Dr. Strauss doesn't know either. Dr. Nemur and Dr. Strauss are doctors, not scholars, and even if they knew the theories, they most likely would not know the languages of Hindustani and Chinese.)

Class Discussion: Bias
You might want to lead a discussion on the bias, or prejudice, that exists against the mentally retarded. Ask students if they think that the customers in the restaurant would have made such a commotion over the incident of dropped dishes if the boy hadn't been mentally retarded. It is this bias that is present in the restaurant, and the world, that causes Charlie's explosive loss of temper. Ask students what other examples of bias against the mentally retarded they see in the story, or in their own lives.

A. Interpreting
? How is the hungry child like a feeble-minded person? (The child is hungry for food; the feeble-minded person, although he or she doesn't know how to acquire it, is hungry for intelligence.)

B. Suspense
? How do the progress reports of May 23 and 24 create suspense? (They imply that Algernon may be in the first stages of regression. We anxiously wonder whether Charlie, having undergone the same operation, will also begin to regress.)

"C'mon, do it again . . ."

"He's not so dumb. It's easier to break 'em than to wash 'em . . ."

As his vacant eyes moved across the crowd of amused onlookers, he slowly mirrored their smiles and finally broke into an uncertain grin at the joke which he obviously did not understand.

I felt sick inside as I looked at his dull, vacuous[2] smile, the wide, bright eyes of a child, uncertain but eager to please. They were laughing at him because he was mentally retarded.

And I had been laughing at him, too.

Suddenly I was furious at myself and all those who were smirking at him. I jumped up and shouted, "Shut up! Leave him alone! It's not his fault he can't understand! He can't help what he is! But for God's sake . . . he's still a human being!"

The room grew silent. I cursed myself for losing control and creating a scene. I tried not to look at the boy as I paid my bill and walked out without touching my food. I felt ashamed for both of us.

How strange it is that people of honest feelings and sensibility, who would not take advantage of a man born without arms or legs or eyes—how such people think nothing of abusing a man born with low intelligence. It infuriated me to think that not too long ago I, like this boy, had foolishly played the clown.

And I had almost forgotten.

I'd hidden the picture of the old Charlie Gordon from myself because now that I was intelligent it was something that had to be pushed out of my mind. But today in looking at that boy, for the first time I saw what I had been. *I was just like him!*

Only a short time ago, I learned that people laughed at me. Now I can see that unknowingly I joined with them in laughing at myself. That hurts most of all.

I have often reread my progress reports and seen the illiteracy, the childish naiveté, the mind of low intelligence peering from a dark room, through the keyhole, at the dazzling light outside. I see that even in my dullness I knew that I was inferior, and that other people had something I lacked—something denied me. In my mental blindness, I thought that it was somehow connected with the ability to read and write, and I was sure that if I could get those skills I would automatically have intelligence, too.

Even a feeble-minded man wants to be like other men.

A child may not know how to feed itself, or what to eat, yet it knows of hunger. A

This then is what I was like. I never knew. Even with my gift of intellectual awareness, I never really knew.

This day was good for me. Seeing the past more clearly, I have decided to use my knowledge and skills to work in the field of increasing human intelligence levels. Who is better equipped for this work? Who else has lived in both worlds? These are my people. Let me use my gift to do something for them.

Tomorrow, I will discuss with Dr. Strauss the manner in which I can work in this area; I may be able to help him work out the problems of widespread use of the technique which was used on me. I have several good ideas of my own.

There is so much that might be done with this technique. If I could be made into a genius, what about thousands of others like myself? What fantastic levels might be achieved by using this technique on normal people? On *geniuses?*

There are so many doors to open. I am impatient to begin.

PROGRESS REPORT 12

May 23 It happened today. Algernon bit me. I visited the lab to see him as I do occasionally, and when I took him out of his cage, he snapped at my hand. I put him back and watched him for a while. He was unusually disturbed and vicious.

May 24 Burt, who is in charge of the experimental animals, tells me that Algernon is changing. He is less cooperative; he refuses to run the maze any more; general motivation has decreased. And he hasn't been eating. Everyone is upset about what this may mean. B

May 25 They've been feeding Algernon, who now refuses to work the shifting-lock problem. Every-

2. **vacuous** (vak'yo͞o·wəs): stupid.

one identifies me with Algernon. In a way we're both the first of our kind. They're all pretending that Algernon's behavior is not necessarily significant for me. But it's hard to hide the fact that some of the other animals who were used in this experiment are showing strange behavior.

A Dr. Strauss and Dr. Nemur have asked me not to come to the lab anymore. I know what they're thinking but I can't accept it. I am going ahead with my plans to carry their research forward. With all due respect to both of these fine scientists, I am well aware of their limitations. If there is an answer, I'll have to find it out for myself.
B Suddenly, time has become very important to me.

May 29 I have been given a lab of my own and permission to go ahead with the research. I'm on to something. Working day and night, I've had a cot moved into the lab. Most of my writing time is spent on the notes which I keep in a separate folder, but from time to time I feel it necessary to put down my moods and my thoughts out of sheer habit.

I find the *calculus of intelligence* to be a fascinating study. Here is the place for the application of all the knowledge I have acquired. In a sense it's the problem I've been concerned with all my life.

May 31 Dr. Strauss thinks I'm working too hard. Dr. Nemur says I'm trying to cram a lifetime of research and thought into a few weeks. I know I should rest, but I'm driven on by something inside that won't let me stop. I've got to find the reason

A. Making Inferences

? Why don't Drs. Strauss and Nemur want Charlie to come to the lab anymore? (They don't want Charlie to witness Algernon's deterioration. They know it will upset and perhaps depress Charlie.)

B. Interpreting

? Why is time all of a sudden important to Charlie? (Although the doctors are trying to deny the facts, Charlie knows that he will probably go through the same deterioration as Algernon, and very soon.)

A. Interpreting
? Why does Charlie call the work of the two doctors "ashes"? (Because the increase of intelligence is not permanent, and Charlie's mind will eventually deteriorate, like fire into ashes.)

B. Expansion
This formula means that the greater the increase of intelligence, the faster the deterioration will take place.

for the sharp regression[3] in Algernon, I've got to know *if* and *when* it will happen to me.

June 4

LETTER TO DR. STRAUSS *(copy)*

Dear Dr. Strauss:

Under separate cover I am sending you a copy of my report entitled "The Algernon–Gordon Effect: A Study of Structure and Function of Increased Intelligence," which I would like to have you read and have published.

As you see, my experiments are completed. I have included in my report all of my formulas, as well as mathematical analysis in the appendix. Of course, these should be verified.

Because of its importance to both you and Dr. Nemur (and need I say to myself, too?) I have checked and rechecked my results a dozen times in the hope of finding an error. I am sorry to say the results must stand. Yet for the sake of science, I am grateful for the little bit that I here add to the knowledge of the function of the human mind and of the laws governing the artificial increase of human intelligence.

I recall your once saying to me that an experimental *failure* or the *disproving* of a theory was as important to the advancement of learning as a success would be. I know now that this is true. I am sorry, however, that my own contribution to the field must rest upon the ashes of the work of two men I regard so highly. A

Yours truly,
CHARLES GORDON

encl.: rept.

June 5 I must not become emotional. The facts and the results of my experiments are clear, and the more sensational aspects of my own rapid climb cannot obscure the fact that the tripling of intelligence by the surgical technique developed by Drs. Strauss and Nemur must be viewed as having little or no practical applicability (at the present time) to the increase of human intelligence.

As I review the records and data on Algernon, I see that although he is still in his physical infancy, he has regressed mentally. Motor activity is impaired; there is a general reduction of glandular activity; there is an accelerated loss of coordination.

There are also strong indications of progressive amnesia.[4]

As will be seen by my report, these and other physical and mental deterioration syndromes can be predicted with statistically significant results by the application of my formula.

The surgical stimulus to which we were both subjected has resulted in an intensification and acceleration of all mental processes. The unforeseen development, which I have taken the liberty of calling the *Algernon–Gordon Effect,* is the logical extension of the entire intelligence speedup. The hypothesis[5] here proven may be described simply in the following terms: Artificially increased intelligence deteriorates at a rate of time directly proportional to the quantity of the increase. B

I feel that this, in itself, is an important discovery.

As long as I am able to write, I will continue to record my thoughts in these progress reports. It is one of my few pleasures. However, by all indications, my own mental deterioration will be very rapid.

I have already begun to notice signs of emotional instability and forgetfulness, the first symptoms of the burnout.

June 10 Deterioration progressing. I have become absent-minded. Algernon died two days ago. Dissection shows my predictions were right. His brain had decreased in weight and there was a general smoothing out of cerebral convolutions as well as a deepening and broadening of brain fissures.

I guess the same thing is or will soon be happening to me. Now that it's definite, I don't want it to happen.

I put Algernon's body in a cheese box and buried him in the backyard. I cried.

3. **regression** (ri·gresh′ən): return to an earlier state.

4. **amnesia** (am·nē′zhə): loss of memory.
5. **hypothesis** (hī·päth′ə·sis): theory.

June 15 Dr. Strauss came to see me again. I wouldn't open the door and I told him to go away. I want to be left to myself. I have become touchy and irritable. I feel the darkness closing in. It's hard to throw off thoughts of suicide. I keep telling myself how important this introspective journal will be.

A

It's a strange sensation to pick up a book that you've read and enjoyed just a few months ago and discover that you don't remember it. I remembered how great I thought John Milton was, but when I picked up *Paradise Lost* I couldn't understand it at all. I got so angry I threw the book across the room.

I've got to try to hold on to some of it. Some of the things I've learned. Oh, God, please don't take it all away.

June 19 Sometimes, at night, I go out for a walk. Last night I couldn't remember where I lived. A policeman took me home. I have the strange feeling that this has all happened to me before—a long time ago. I keep telling myself I'm the only person in the world who can describe what's happening to me.

B

June 21 Why can't I remember? I've got to fight. I lie in bed for days and I don't know who or where I am. Then it comes back to me in a flash. Fugues of amnesia. Symptoms of senility[6]—second childhood. I can watch them coming on. It's so cruelly logical. I learned so much and so fast. Now my mind is deteriorating rapidly. I won't let it happen. I'll fight it. I can't help thinking of the boy in the restaurant, the blank expression, the silly smile, the people laughing at him. No—please—not that again . . .

C

June 22 I'm forgetting things that I learned recently. It seems to be following the classic pattern—the last things learned are the first things forgotten. Or is that the pattern? I'd better look it up again. . . .

I reread my paper on the *Algernon–Gordon Effect* and I get the strange feeling that it was written by someone else. There are parts I don't even understand.

Motor activity impaired. I keep tripping over things, and it becomes increasingly difficult to type.

June 23 I've given up using the typewriter completely. My coordination is bad. I feel that I'm moving slower and slower. Had a terrible shock today. I picked up a copy of an article I used in my research, Krueger's "Über Psychische Ganzheit," to see if it would help me understand what I had done. First I thought there was something wrong with my eyes. Then I realized I could no longer read German. I tested myself in other languages. All gone.

June 30 A week since I dared to write again. It's slipping away like sand through my fingers. Most of the books I have are too hard for me now. I get angry with them because I know that I read and understood them just a few weeks ago.

I keep telling myself I must keep writing these reports so that somebody will know what is happening to me. But it gets harder to form the words and remember spellings. I have to look up even simple words in the dictionary now and it makes me impatient with myself.

Dr. Strauss comes around almost every day, but I told him I wouldn't see or speak to anybody. He feels guilty. They all do. But I don't blame anyone. I knew what might happen. But how it hurts. D

July 7 I don't know where the week went. Todays Sunday I know because I can see through my window people going to church. I think I stayed in bed all week but I remember Mrs. Flynn bringing food to me a few times. I keep saying over and over Ive got to do something but then I forget or maybe its just easier not to do what I say Im going to do.

I think of my mother and father a lot these days. I found a picture of them with me taken at a beach. My father has a big ball under his arm and my mother is holding me by the hand. I don't remember them the way they are in the picture. All I E

6. **senility** (si·nil′ə·tē): memory loss typical of old age.

A. Interpreting
? Why do you think Charlie is contemplating suicide? (Because for Charlie, losing his intelligence is almost like a death; however, its progress is torturous. He is tempted to escape the painful mental decline he is experiencing.)

B. Making Connections
? Why does he feel this has happened to him before? (He is probably reminded of the time he was brought home by a policeman after Frank and Joe got him drunk at a party.)

C. Conflict
? What is Charlie struggling with here? (With helplessness and fear in the face of the inevitable)

D. Responding
? Do you think Dr. Strauss, or anyone else, should feel guilty?

E. Interpreting
Here we can see signs of the old Charlie Gordon returning: he no longer is using punctuation when he writes, and his speech is more childlike.

A. Conflict
? Charlie has almost regressed to the point at which we first met him. Then, however, he was content in his ignorance. What is his conflict now? (Although he has lost his intelligence, he has kept some intellectual awareness, which makes him realize when people are mocking him. His decline, therefore, is a double-edged sword.) This will help students answer question 12.

B. Responding
? Do you agree with Mr. Donnegan that Charlie "has guts"?

remember is my father drunk most of the time and arguing with mom about money.

He never shaved much and he used to scratch my face when he hugged me. My mother said he died but Cousin Miltie said he heard his mom and dad say that my father ran away with another woman. When I asked my mother she slapped my face and said my father was dead. I don't think I ever found out which was true but I dont care much. (He said he was going to take me to see cows on a farm once but he never did. He never kept his promises. . . .)

July 10 My landlady Mrs Flynn is worried about me. She says the way I lay around all day and dont do anything I remind her of her son before she threw him out of the house. She said she doesnt like loafers. If Im sick its one thing, but if Im a loafer thats another thing and she wont have it. I told her I think Im sick.

I try to read a little bit every day, mostly stories, but sometimes I have to read the same thing over and over again because I dont know what it means. And its hard to write. I know I should look up all the words in the dictionary but its so hard and Im so tired all the time.

Then I got the idea that I would only use the easy words instead of the long hard ones. That saves time. I put flowers on Algernons grave about once a week. Mrs Flynn thinks Im crazy to put flowers on a mouses grave but I told her that Algernon was special.

July 14 Its sunday again. I dont have anything to do to keep me busy now because my television set is broke and I dont have any money to get it fixed. (I think I lost this months check from the lab. I dont remember.)

I get awful headaches and asperin doesnt help me much. Mrs Flynn knows Im really sick and she feels very sorry for me. Shes a wonderful woman whenever someone is sick.

July 22 Mrs Flynn called a strange doctor to see me. She was afraid I was going to die. I told the doctor I wasnt too sick and that I only forgot sometimes. He asked me did I have any friends or relatives and I said no I dont have any. I told him I had a friend called Algernon once but he was a mouse and we used to run races together. He looked at me kind of funny like he thought I was crazy.

He smiled when I told him I used to be a genius. He talked to me like I was a baby and he winked at Mrs Flynn. I got mad and chased him out because he was making fun of me the way they all used to. A

July 24 I have no more money and Mrs Flynn says I got to go to work somewhere and pay the rent because I havent paid for over two months. I dont know any work but the job I used to have at Donnegans Plastic Box Company. I dont want to go back there because theyll laugh at me. But I dont know what else to do to get money.

July 25 I was looking at some of my old progress reports and its very funny but I can't read what I wrote. I can make out some of the words but they dont make sense.

Miss Kinnian came to the door but I said go away I dont want to see you. She cried and I cried too but I wouldnt let her in because I didnt want her to laugh at me. I told her I didnt like her any more. I told her I didnt want to be smart any more. Thats not true. I still love her and I still want to be smart but I had to say that so shed go away. She gave Mrs Flynn money to pay the rent. I dont want that. I got to get a job.

Please . . . please let me not forget how to read and write . . .

July 27 Mr Donnegan was very nice when I came back and asked him for my old job as janitor. First he was very suspicious but I told him what happened to me then he looked very sad and put his hand on my shoulder and said Charlie Gordon you got guts. B

Everybody looked at me when I came downstairs and started working in the toilet sweeping it out like I used to I told myself Charlie if they make fun of you dont get sore because you remember their not so smart as you once thot they were. And besides they were once your friends and if they laughed at you that doesnt mean anything because they liked you too.

READING CHECK TEST

1. Charlie is picked for the project because he fails the Rorschach test. *(False)*
2. His teacher, Miss Kinnian, encourages Charlie to learn. *(True)*
3. His friends at work are happy to see Charlie become smart. *(False)*
4. Algernon is the name of a rat that has undergone the same operation as Charlie has. *(True)*
5. Even though Charlie becomes very smart, he never defeats Algernon in the race through the maze. *(False)*
6. Charlie realizes that the people who he thought were his friends were really making fun of him. *(True)*
7. Charlie goes from being mentally retarded to being a genius. *(True)*
8. The increased intelligence is permanent for Algernon, but temporary for Charlie. *(False)*
9. At the story's end, Charlie is still smarter than he was at the story's beginning. *(False)*
10. Charlie wants everybody's sympathy after his mental deterioration. *(False)*

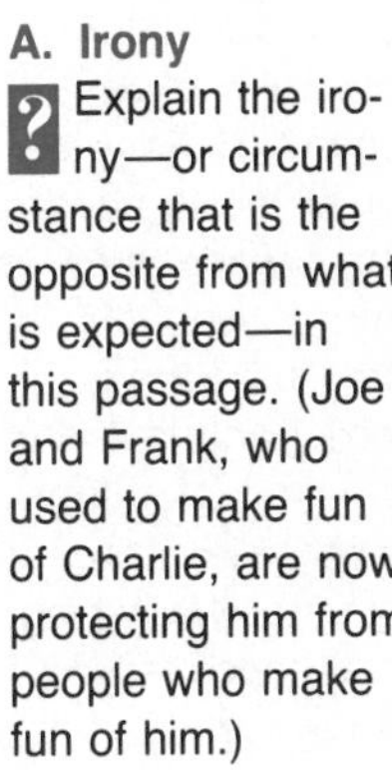

A. Irony

? Explain the irony—or circumstance that is the opposite from what is expected—in this passage. (Joe and Frank, who used to make fun of Charlie, are now protecting him from people who make fun of him.)

One of the new men who came to work there after I went away made a nasty crack he said hey Charlie I hear your a very smart fella a real quiz kid. Say something intelligent. I felt bad but Joe Carp came over and grabbed him by the shirt and said leave him alone you lousy cracker or Ill break your neck. I didnt expect Joe to take my part so I guess hes really my friend.

Later Frank Reilly came over and said Charlie if anybody bothers you or trys to take advantage you call me or Joe and we will set em straight. I said thanks Frank and I got choked up so I had to turn around and go into the supply room so he wouldnt see me cry. Its good to have friends. **A**

July 28 I did a dumb thing today I forgot I wasnt in Miss Kinnians class at the adult center anymore like I used to be. I went in and sat down in my old seat in the back of the room and she looked at me funny and she said Charles. I dint remember she ever called me that before only Charlie so I said hello Miss Kinnian Im redy for my lesin today

CLOSURE

Have students work in groups of four, and tell each other what they believe is the most important phrase, passage, or paragraph in the story. Have them explain their choice.

ANALYZING PART II
Identifying Facts

1. Charlie is now more intelligent than Dr. Nemur, Dr. Strauss, and Miss Kinnian. The same problems he had with his friends at work he is now having with these three people.
2. Charlie first laughs at the boy's misfortune, but then sees the vacant look in his eyes and realizes that the boy is as he used to be. He is ashamed of himself and the other people who were laughing, and gets angry.

He vows to help others who are as he was by working to make the technique that made him smarter available to a wide range of people.
3. Charlie's experiments show that the surgical increase in intelligence is not permanent, and in fact, may make the

A. Character's Attitude

? How would you summarize Charlie's attitude about his experience? (He is grateful for having had the chance to be smart, even if it was just for a little while, and to make a contribution to science. He does not regret anything that happened. He is also proud of his accomplishments while he was smart.)

only I lost my reader that we was using. She startid to cry and run out of the room and everybody looked at me and I saw they wasnt the same pepul who use to be in my class.

Then all of a suddin I remembered some things about the operashun and me getting smart and I said holy smoke I reely pulled a Charlie Gordon that time. I went away before she come back to the room.

Thats why Im going away from New York for good. I dont want to do nothing like that agen. I dont want Miss Kinnian to feel sorry for me. Evry body feels sorry at the factery and I dont want that eather so Im going someplace where nobody knows that Charlie Gordon was once a genus and now he cant even reed a book or rite good.

Im taking a cuple of books along and even if I cant reed them Ill practise hard and maybe I wont forget every thing I lerned. If I try reel hard maybe Ill be a littel bit smarter than I was before the operashun. I got my rabits foot and my luky penny and maybe they will help me.

If you ever reed this Miss Kinnian dont be sorry for me Im glad I got a second chanse to be smart becaus I lerned a lot of things that I never even new were in this world and Im grateful that I saw it all for a littel bit. I dont know why Im dumb agen or what I did wrong maybe its becaus I dint try hard enuff. But if I try and practis very hard maybe Ill get a littel smarter and know what all the words are. I remember a littel bit how I had a nice feeling with the blue book that has the torn cover when I red it. Thats why Im gonna keep trying to get smart so I can have the feeling agen. Its a good feeling to know things and be smart. I wish I had it rite now if I did I would sit down and reed all the time. Anyway I bet Im the first dumb person in the world who ever found out something importent for sience. I remember I did something but I dont remember what. So I gues its like I did it for all the dumb pepul like me. A

Good-by Miss Kinnian and Dr Strauss and everybody. And P.S. please tell Dr Nemur not be such grouch when pepul laff at him and he would have more frends. Its easy to make frends if you let pepul laff at you. Im going to have lots of frends where I go. P.P.S. Please if you get a chanse put some flowers on Algernons grave in the bakyard. . . .

Responding to the Story

Analyzing Part II

Identifying Facts

1. At the beginning of Part II, what difficulties is Charlie having in his relationships with Dr. Nemur, Dr. Strauss, and Miss Kinnian?
2. How does Charlie react when the dishwasher drops the dishes? Why does he react this way? What does the incident make him decide to do in the future?
3. Charlie writes a report called "The Algernon–Gordon Effect." What does his research reveal about the result of the experiment?
4. List several changes which indicate Charlie's mental deterioration.
5. At the end of the story, why does Charlie decide to leave New York? What consolations for the loss of his intelligence does he mention?

Interpreting Meanings

6. What do you think is going to become of Charlie after the story is over? How do you know?
7. **Foreshadowing** is the use of hints or clues about what will happen next. What does Miss Kinnian say during their dinner date in Part I that **foreshadows** Charlie's eventual deterioration?
8. Contrast the abilities, desires, and personality traits of Dr. Nemur and Dr. Strauss. Do you think they were working for Charlie's benefit, to further their own careers, or both? Explain.

SRW p. 43

subject worse off than before the operation.

4. Changes include that he has instances of emotional instability and forgetfulness; that he forgets where he lives and has difficulty typing; that he forgets the languages he has learned; that he can no longer read the books he used to be able to; that his writing becomes worse.

5. He is leaving New York because he doesn't want people to feel sorry for him.

"Anyway I bet Im the first dumb person in the world who ever found out something importent for sience . . . So I gues its like I did it for all the dumb pepul like me."

Interpreting Meanings

6. Charlie will go to another city, and his life will be much the same as it was before the operation. As he notes, "Its easy to make friends if you let pepul laff at you. Im going to have lots of frends where I go."

7. "I just hope I wasn't wrong to advise you to go into this in the first place."

8. Dr. Nemur seems to be more interested in advancing his career. He wants to publish the report on Charlie and Algernon soon, and seems eager to move ahead quickly. Dr. Strauss seems more interested in Charlie. However, when Charlie starts to decline, they are both interested in his welfare, although Dr. Strauss is the only one who visits him.

9. Frank and Joe are now true friends and defend Charlie when people bother him. They realize that Charlie has done a very brave thing. They may also be ashamed of how they treated him before.

10. He wants to be smart.

He wants to help others who are like what he was.

At first, he wants to hold onto some of his intelligence. At the end, he wants to be treated like a regular person, not pitied for his experiences.

11. Before he becomes intelligent, Charlie knows he is not smart, but it doesn't upset him. When he becomes smart, he is embarrassed and ashamed to realize how feeble-minded

(Answers continue on page 250.)

9. Frank and Joe change their attitude toward Charlie several times throughout the story. When his intelligence first increases, they are uncomfortable and perplexed, and vote to have him fired. How does their behavior change after Charlie returns to his low IQ? Why do you think they react this way?
10. Charlie's **conflicts,** or struggles, and his goals change throughout the course of the story. What does he want most of all when we first meet him? What does he want after he becomes smart? What does he want after his intelligence deteriorates?
11. Charlie undergoes two major changes in the story—the huge increase in intelligence, and the swift deterioration. How are his feelings about himself affected by these changes?
12. At the end of the story, we see Charlie in the same mental state that he was in when we met him. Can you find any evidence, however, that he kept some of what he learned while he was so smart? (What has he learned about other people and about how they viewed him?) In your opinion, would Charlie have been better off, or worse off, if he had never undergone the experiment?
13. What emotions did you feel as you read Charlie's story?

Applying Meanings

14. Look back at your answer to the second part of question 8 at the end of Part I (page 239). Explain whether your answer would be the same now that you have read Charlie's whole story.
15. At the end, Charlie says, "Its easy to make frends if you let pepul laff at you." How does this statement make you feel? Do you think Charlie is speaking the truth? Explain.
16. Do you think this story has a message that is important today? Explain your answer.

Writing About the Story

A Creative Response

1. **Writing a Diary Entry.** This story's structure is built on Charlie's progress reports, which are like a diary. Pick another character from the story and write a diary entry corresponding to one of Charlie's reports. For example, what might Miss Kinnian have written the night she and Charlie had dinner? What might Frank have written after Charlie returned to work at the factory? Use the first-person pronoun *I*.
2. **Presenting an Argument.** Imagine that people could choose between a long life of average quality and a shorter life of higher quality. Write a paragraph explaining which life you think most people would choose. Provide reasons for your answer.

A Critical Response

3. **Analyzing a Story's Title.** Although the main character of this story is Charlie Gordon, the title is "Flowers for Algernon." In a paragraph, explain the significance of the title. Could the title have any special meaning?
4. **Analyzing a Story's Theme.** Write a paragraph explaining the **theme,** or main idea, revealed by the events of this story. Before you write, answer the questions that follow. Then think what central idea your answers add up to.
   a. Does the main character change in the course of the story?
   b. What does he learn?
   c. Does the narrator make any key statements about life or people?
   d. Does the title signify anything special about the story?

SRW p. 87

(Answers begin on page 249.)
he was. He is also pleased and proud of his new accomplishments. The swift deterioration makes him worried, angry, and afraid. When he is back to his original self, he is glad he underwent the experiment, and although he is sad, he is more comfortable with himself.
12. He knows that he did something to advance science, and to help people like him. He understands that people laugh at him, and he knows that his friends in New York all pity him.
Answers will vary. Some students may say that Charlie could have been spared needless pain. Others may say that Charlie learned from the experience, and suffered no lasting harm.
13. Answers will vary, and may include pity, sadness, happiness, and so on.

Applying Meanings
14. Answers will vary.
15. Answers will vary. Students may feel sad, because the statement, when applied to Charlie's situation, shows how insensitive humans can be. The statement's real meaning is that a sense of humor and the ability to laugh and let others laugh at your mistakes to a certain
(Answers continue in left-hand column.)

(Continued from top.)
extent is healthy and necessary.
16. The story has several important messages. First, it raises doubts about the ability of science and technology to improve people's lives. Second, it reveals that human beings can be cruel and uncaring toward people who are less fortunate than they. Third, it teaches that humans should be more considerate of those who have handicaps. Students may find other major themes.

e. Does the story end happily or sadly? What does this suggest about the author's purpose in writing?

See Teacher's Manual page 75.

Analyzing Language and Vocabulary

Phonetic Spelling

As you know, many English words are spelled very differently from the way they are pronounced. Charlie's spelling at the beginning and ending of the story is **phonetic**—it is based on how words actually sound to his ear. We can understand his meaning from the sounds he writes and from context clues. For example, Charlie writes *pepul* for *people, laff* for *laugh,* and *luky* for *lucky.*

1. Write a correct spelling for each of the following phonetically spelled words from Charlie's first two progress reports.

   a. shud
   b. rite
   c. faled
   d. skared
   e. pockit
   f. happind

2. In Progress Report 4 (page 230), Charlie uses asterisks to represent the missing letters in the words he overhears, but does not understand. Can you figure out the complete words from Charlie's fragments?

   a. intelek**
   b. ment**
   c. host**
   d. uncoop**
   e. apath**
   f. acheve**
   g. **vity
   h. comparat**
   i. a tremen**

   Did you guess with the help of the sentence's context? Or by guessing from the part of the word cited?

3. Rewrite the first two paragraphs of Charlie's July 28 entry. Use proper spelling, capitalization, and punctuation. Be sure to pay close attention to context clues and to the phonetic clues in Charlie's words. When you have rewritten the entries, see if your picture of Charlie has changed when you've changed his language.

For answers, see Teacher's Manual page 75.

Reading About the Writer

Daniel Keyes (1927–   ) won the Hugo Award in 1959, given by the Science Fiction Writers of America, for "Flowers for Algernon." The story has been widely translated, and Keyes even expanded it into a novel, which won another science fiction prize, the Nebula Award, in 1966. The story was made into a successful movie called *Charly,* starring Cliff Robertson, and a television play called *The Two Worlds of Charlie Gordon.* Daniel Keyes was born in Brooklyn, New York. He has been an English teacher as well as a merchant seaman and a photographer.

★ Texas Essential Elements/(a) English Language Arts: 1B Purpose and audience; 4B Main idea. (c) Reading: 1A Context clues; 2A Word meaning; 3A Main ideas/details

Review: Exercises in Reading Fiction

SRW p. 35

FABLES

A Centuries ago in ancient Greece, a slave named Aesop told very short stories with practical moral lessons. Many of his tales used animal characters. Aesop often used his tales to make fun of his political enemies.

Fables like Aesop's have been told in nearly every culture on earth. One of the best-known "fabulists" in America is James Thurber, who wrote two books of fables, *Fables for Our Time* and *Further Fables for Our Time.*

Read this fable and answer the questions that follow.

The Scotty Who Knew Too Much

Several summers ago there was a Scotty who went to the country for a visit. He decided that all the farm dogs were cowards, because they were afraid of a certain animal that had a white stripe down its back. "You are a pussy-cat and I can lick you," the Scotty said to the farm dog who lived in the house where the Scotty was visiting. "I can lick the little animal with the white stripe, too. Show him to me." "Don't you want to ask any questions about him?" said the farm dog. "Naw," said the Scotty. "*You* ask the questions."

So the farm dog took the Scotty into the woods and showed him the white-striped animal and the Scotty closed in on him, growling and slashing. It was all over in a moment and the Scotty lay on his back. When he came to, the farm dog said, "What happened?" "He threw vitriol," said the Scotty, "but he never laid a glove on me."

A few days later the farm dog told the Scotty there was another animal all the farm dogs were afraid of. "Lead me to him," said the Scotty. "I can lick anything that doesn't wear horseshoes." "Don't you want to ask any questions about him?" said the farm dog. "Naw," said the Scotty. "Just show me where he hangs out." So the farm dog led him to a place in the woods and pointed out the little animal when he came along. "A clown," said the Scotty, "a pushover," and he closed in, leading with his left and exhibiting some might fancy footwork. In less than a second the Scotty was flat on his back, and when he woke up the farm dog was pulling quills out of him. "What happened?" said the farm dog. "He pulled a knife on me," said the Scotty, "but at least I have learned how you fight out here in the country, and now I am going to beat *you* up." So he closed in on the farm dog, holding his nose with one front paw to ward off the vitriol and covering his eyes with the other front paw to keep out the knives. The Scotty couldn't see his opponent and he couldn't smell his opponent and he was so badly beaten that he had to be taken back to the city and put in a nursing home.

Moral: It is better to ask some of the questions than to know all the answers.

—James Thurber

© 1940 by James Thurber. © 1968 by Helen Thurber. Reprinted from *Fables for Our Time,* published by Harper & Row.

A. Fables
Have students discuss fables with which they are familiar. They may know some of Aesop's famous fables such as "The Fox and the Crow," "The Town Mouse and the Country Mouse," and "The Ant and the Grasshopper."

Answers to Questions

1. He comes in conflict with the farm dogs, a skunk, and a porcupine.
2. The Scotty thinks he is better than the other dogs, and he thinks he knows everything.
3. This animal is a skunk.
4. He thought it was a cat.
5. He means "a stinging, burning substance."
6. This animal is a porcupine.
7. He infers that the porcupine pulled a knife on him.
8. The Scotty had one paw in front of his nose and one paw in front of his eyes to protect against the vitriol and the knives. Thus, he could neither see nor smell the other dog.
9. Answers will vary. Students should recognize the pompous know-it-all, one who listens only to himself or herself, and never learns anything.
10. The Scotty is totally ignorant of country animals, and he interprets everything that happens to him in terms of the city.
11. The moral states the meaning of the story. If the Scotty had asked the farm dog what his opponents were like, he
(Answers continue in left-hand column.)

(Continued from top.)
would have been able to prepare himself to fight them.
12. Answers will vary. Thurber is saying that we would all be much better off if we listened to others and found the information we needed before making decisions or taking action.

Review: Exercises in Reading Fiction / *cont.*

1. Who or what does the Scotty come in **conflict** with when he visits the country?
2. How would you describe the Scotty's real problem?
3. What do you infer is the "certain animal that had a white stripe down its back"?
4. What mistaken inference did the Scotty make about the animal?
5. From the **context,** what would you guess the Scotty is using the word *vitriol* to mean? Check your answer in a dictionary.
6. What animal do you infer the Scotty met the second time—the one with the quills?
7. What erroneous inference did the Scotty make about the reason the animal defeated him?
8. Why was the farm dog able to beat the Scotty?
9. Do you recognize a familiar **character type** in the Scotty? How would you describe that type?
10. How does the Scotty show that his knowledge is limited to his city experiences?
11. What does the **moral** have to do with the story?
12. What is the **theme** of this fable—what **main idea** would you say Thurber is expressing about some people in the world?

Writing

Creating a Fable. Here are some famous moral lessons. See if you can write a story that illustrates one of them. The second list below cites some animal characters that are often used in fables; you might use some of them too.

1. Out of sight, out of mind.
2. Absence makes the heart grow fonder.
3. Too many cooks spoil the soup.
4. Many hands make light work.

a. ravens
b. crows
c. foxes
d. chickens
e. wolves
f. donkeys

For evaluation strategies, see Teacher's Manual page 76.

★ **Texas Essential Elements/(a) English Language Arts: 1A** Composing process; **1B** Purpose and audience; **1H** Proofread; **2B** Parts of speech; **4C** Sequential order; **4D** Cause/effect; **4F** Generalizations; **4I** Follow directions

Exercises in Critical Thinking and Writing

For teaching and evaluation strategies, see Teacher's Manual page 76.

SRW p. 67

SUMMARIZING A PLOT

Writing Assignment

Write a plot summary of "Flowers for Algernon" (page 228). In your summary, identify the story's basic situation, conflict, complications, and resolution. Write two paragraphs.

Background

Plot is the sequence of events in a story. When you **summarize** a plot, you mention the story's most important events in the order in which they occur. The diagram below shows the key elements of a story's plot:

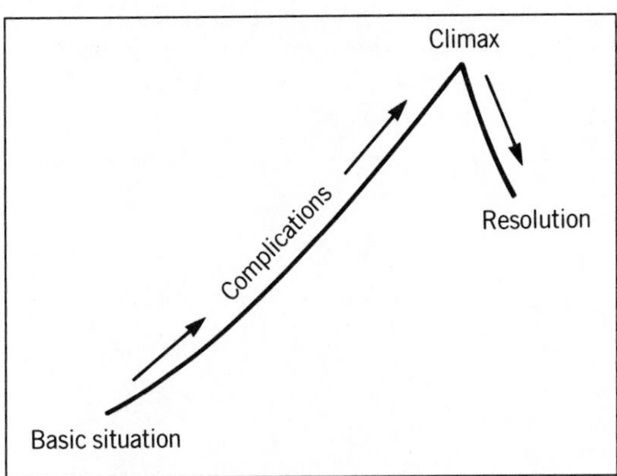

1. The beginning of a story introduces the **basic situation.** (This part of a story, novel, or play is sometimes called the **exposition.**) Here we are introduced to the main **characters** and the **conflict,** the main character's struggle against an opposing force.
2. In the diagram, the next events in the plot are shown on a slanted line that moves uphill. These **complications** are new problems that arise as the main character tries to solve his or her conflict.
3. The highest point on the action line is the **climax,** which occurs near the story's end. This is when your interest and suspense are most intense. At this point, it becomes clear to you how the conflict must end.
4. The **resolution** is the final tying up of the story's details. This part of the story is often very brief. The resolution brings the story's plot to an end.

Recognizing Cause and Effect. In a well-written story, events don't just happen by chance. Some events **cause** other events to happen. The result, or consequence, of a cause is called an **effect.** To understand a story, you should be able to recognize causes and their effects. For example, in "Beware of the Dog" (page 199), two seemingly unimportant events actually *cause* the man's actions at the story's end.

Cause 1: The narrator hears airplanes he recognizes as German bombers.
Cause 2: The narrator remembers that the water in Brighton is not hard, but very soft.

Effect 1: He becomes suspicious.
Effect 2: He drags himself to the window.
Effect 3: He sees a sign written in French and realizes where he is.
Effect 4: He realizes that he is really a prisoner of war.
Effect 5: The narrator gives only his name, rank, and number.

An effect can also be the cause of a succeeding action or event. Notice that Effect 1 causes Effect 2; Effect 3 causes Effect 4; and so on. SRW p. 19

Prewriting

1. Reread the first few pages of "Flowers for Algernon," and try to state the basic situation in one or two sentences. Describe Charlie, his goal, and the tests he is involved in.
2. Now skim (read very quickly) the rest of the story, and take notes. List the story's most important events in *chronological order,* the order in which they occur.

★ **Texas Essential Elements/(c) Reading: 3B** Sequential order; **3C** Cause/effect; **3D** Generalizations; **4A** Follow directions

Exercises in Critical Thinking and Writing/*cont.*

3. You don't have room in a paragraph to tell everything that happens, so go back over your list and cross out the less important events. You should end up with 8-10 of the *most important* events.
4. Look back at your list to identify cause-effect relationships. Which event causes—sets in motion—the rest of the action? What other events cause later events?
5. Finally, look over your list to identify the basic plot elements of conflict, major complications, climax, and resolution.

Writing

Paragraph 1: Write a topic sentence that mentions the title, author, and what the story is about. You may use the following topic sentence for Paragraph 1, or write your own.

> "Flowers for Algernon," by Daniel Keyes, is a story about a thirty-seven-year-old retarded man named Charlie Gordon, who is temporarily changed into a genius. At the beginning of the story, . . .

The rest of Paragraph 1 should summarize the story's most important events in chronological order. Point out cause-effect relationships by using expressions such as *because, thus, therefore, consequently,* and *as a result.*

Paragraph 2: Identify the basic plot elements. Tell what the conflict is, and mention some of the major complications (such as the brief romance between Charlie and Miss Kinnian). Identify the climax, and tell how the conflict is resolved.

Revising and Proofreading

1. In Paragraph 1, have I included a topic sentence? Have I then summarized the story's most important events in the order in which they occurred?
2. In Paragraph 2, have I identified the basic plot elements?
3. Are my ideas clearly expressed? Have I said everything I wanted to say?
4. Does every sentence start with a capital letter and end with a period or other end punctuation mark?

THE ELEMENTS OF POETRY

Open Window, Collioure by Henri Matisse (1905). Oil.

From the Collection of Mrs. John Hay Whitney.

UNIT FIVE **John Malcolm Brinnin**

Humanities Connection: Responding to the Fine Art

Henri Matisse (1869–1954) was one of the most influential artists of the twentieth century. His paintings are distinguished by vivid patterns and intense colors in unusual combinations.

Matisse made no attempt to paint realistically. This painting is a good example of his impressionistic style. You might have students note the details that make the objects distinguishable, even though they lack clear-cut forms. Begin with the view of the boats out of the window.

? What kind of boats could they be? How do you know? How far is the sea from the window? What kinds of plants are in the open window? What season is it? Is this scene pleasant to look at, or threatening? Why?

Be sure they are given an opportunity to share their responses in class.

Teaching Poetry

Poetry is often difficult for students to grasp, and thus they may turn away from it, calling it "boring" or "irrelevant." What students need to know is that poetry requires them to think in a different way. With many poems they will have to think in pictures; they will have to let the words of the poems produce images in their minds. Since poetry involves compact language, they will have to be alert to words with two or three meanings or with strong connotations. If one meaning doesn't fit the meaning of the poem, they must move on to the next.

This is why it is important to have students read each poem several times, both to themselves and aloud. Impress upon them that they should not skim a poem, for they will miss the meaning. Indeed, there is no need for skimming, since the poems in this unit are, in general, relatively short.

For each poem that you teach, you may want to introduce the major literary element before students read, and then have students read the poem looking for that element. Discuss how the element affects the meaning or sound of the poem, and then have students read the poem again, or listen to someone read with expression, and see what else they can get out of the poem.

The literary elements dealt with in this unit include rhyme, rhythm, refrain, meter, free verse, alliteration, onomatopoeia, images, similes, metaphors, personification, and figures of speech. In addition, this unit teaches about narrative and lyric poems, ballads and songs, and theme.

Objectives of the Poetry Unit

1. To improve reading proficiency and expand language knowledge
2. To read aloud with expression
3. To gain exposure to notable authors and their work
4. To respond to poetry through oral and written expression
5. To identify and define the elements of poetry
6. To use the following critical thinking and writing skills:
   a. Analyzing poetry
   b. Comparing and contrasting poems
   c. Analyzing a poet's style
   d. Using vivid language
   e. Understanding and using figurative language
   f. Identifying the theme of a poem
   g. Recognizing how sound effects are used in poetry

SUPPLEMENTARY SUPPORT MATERIAL: UNIT FIVE

1. Word Analogies Test (page 125 of Test Book)
2. Unit Review Test (page 127 of Test Book)
3. Critical Thinking and Writing Test (page 131 of Test Book)
4. Understanding a Poem (Study and Reinforcement Worksheet, page 3)
5. Instructional Overhead Transparencies

Unit Outline

THE ELEMENTS OF POETRY

SUPPLEMENTARY SUPPORT MATERIAL

1. Selection Test (page 95 of Test Book)
2. Reader's Response Journal
3. Workbook (page 61)

PREREADING

1. **BUILDING ON PRIOR KNOWLEDGE.** You might see if any students can tell their classmates what they know about the Great Depression of the 1930's, when many unemployed and homeless people became hobos and "rode the rails" to look for work. The illustration on page 263 will help students picture the typical "hobo" with his belongings in a kerchief carried at the end of a stick.

2. **ESTABLISHING A PURPOSE.** Before students read, tell them to be aware of the imaginative details in the poem. For each detail of hobo paradise, have students guess which problem or condition of the hobos' real life the singer is addressing.

3. **PREREADING JOURNAL.** Before they read, have students write two sentences describing their own imaginary paradise. After they have read the poem, they can use writing exercise 1 on text page 263 to fill in the details.

★ **Texas Essential Elements/(a) English Language Arts: 1B** Purpose and audience; **1E** Formal/informal language; **3B** Figurative language. **(c) Reading: 3I** Draw conclusions

Hobos, or tramps, often used to travel the country by sneaking onto trains. They might hide inside boxcars or "ride the rods," the dangerous practice of lying on the draw rods under the cars and directly over the wheels. Sometimes hobos gathered in camps close to the railroad. The hobo's life was hard. The following song describes an imaginary hobo paradise. It contains much *imagery,* language that appeals to our senses, particularly our sense of sight. As you read, watch for "word pictures" that help you actually see the hobos' imaginary world. SRW p. 51

For a detailed lesson plan on this poem, see Teacher's Manual page 78.

The Big Rock Candy Mountains

Anonymous

One evening when the sun was low
And the jungle° fires were burning,
Down the track came a hobo hamming°
And he said, Boys, I'm not turning;
I'm headed for a land that's far away
Beside the crystal fountains.
So come with me, we'll go and see
The Big Rock Candy Mountains.

In the Big Rock Candy Mountains
There's a land that's fair and bright,
Where the handouts grow on bushes
And you sleep out every night.
Where the box-cars all are empty
And the sun shines every day
On the birds and the bees
And the peppermint trees
The lemonade springs
Where the whangdoodle° sings,
In the Big Rock Candy Mountains.

In the Big Rock Candy Mountains
All the cops have wooden legs
And the bulldogs all have rubber teeth
And the hens lay hard-boiled eggs;
The farmers' trees are full of fruit
And the barns are full of hay:
O I'm bound to go
Where there ain't no snow,
A And the rain don't fall,
The wind don't blow,
In the Big Rock Candy Mountains.

2. **jungle:** hobo camp.
3. **hamming:** showing off.
18. **whangdoodle:** imaginary bird.

A. Interpreting

? Why would hobos be concerned about the weather? (Their real-life homelessness leaves them vulnerable to snow, rain, and wind.) This passage may help students answer question 6, text page 262.

Closure

Working in pairs, one student should define refrain and the other one should identify the refrain of this poem.

Analyzing the Poem

Identifying Details

1. Line 3 identifies the speaker. He has joined a group of hobos gathered around a fire near a railroad track.

2. Shelter is unnecessary, since "the sun shines every day," and you can "sleep out every night." If you prefer, the "barns are full of hay." Food comes freely, with handouts growing on bushes, apples on trees, hens laying hard-boiled eggs, and lakes of stew and dumplings.

3. The sun shines every day, with no snow, rain, or wind to worry about.

4. Overall, the perfection of the world is fantastic. Specific details include the bushes that yield handouts, the lemonade springs, the rubber-toothed bulldogs, the hens that lay hard-boiled eggs, the stream of soda water, the lakes of stew and dumplings, and the tin jails.

5. The refrain "In the Big Rock Candy Mountains" reinforces the desirability of this land, and keeps attention focused on it.

A. Interpreting

? What do these and other references to law enforcement suggest about the hobos' real world? (They frequently clash with police.) This passage can help students answer question 6.

B. Making Comparisons

Have students compare line 49 with line 12 of the poem. They will note that the hobos' paradise becomes even more exaggerated. Now the hobos not only sleep out every night, but they also sleep all day.

C. Refrain

? What is the refrain of this poem? (The refrain appears in the last line of every stanza.)

In the Big Rock Candy Mountains
You never change your socks
And the little streams of sodywater
Come a-trickling down the rocks;
The shacks° all have to tip their hats
And the railroad bulls° are blind;
There's a lake of stew,
And of dumplings too,
You can paddle all around
In a big canoe,
In the Big Rock Candy Mountains.

In the Big Rock Candy Mountains
A The jails are made of tin
And you can bust right out again
As soon as they put you in;
There ain't no short-handled shovels,
No axes, saw, or picks:
O I'm going to stay
B Where you sleep all day,
Where they hung the jerk
That invented work,
In the Big Rock Candy Mountains.
I'll see you all
This coming fall
C In the Big Rock Candy Mountains.

35. **shacks:** tramps.

36. **bulls:** policemen.

Responding to the Poem

Analyzing the Poem

Identifying Details

1. List lines and details in the song that tell you the main speaker is a hobo. Where is he when he describes the world of the Big Rock Candy Mountains?
2. The poem describes the hobo's ideal world. How are food and shelter provided in this world?
3. Explain what the weather is like in the hobo's dream world.
4. What details in the poem tell you that this desired world is pure fantasy?
5. A **refrain** is a word, phrase, line, or group of lines that is repeated in a song or poem. Identify the refrain in this song.

Interpreting Meanings

6. "The Big Rock Candy Mountains" describes the hobo's dream world. Describe what you think the real world is like for a hobo.
7. Song lyrics often contain language that appeals to our senses. Find two **images** for each of the following senses: sight (something that creates a word picture), taste, and touch.

Applying Meanings

8. How is the song from *The Wizard of Oz,* "Somewhere Over the Rainbow," like this song? How is it different? List two or three reasons people often believe life would be better in another place.

Interpreting Meanings

6. Answers will vary, but students should understand that life is hard for such a person.

7. Suggestions will vary. Some images may be classed in more than one category; for example, "lemonade springs" appeals to both sight and taste.

Applying Meanings

8. Students may suggest that we know the flaws in what we have, but not in what we don't have; that what we have never seems as desirable as what we don't have; that we are constantly imagining an ideal world.

Additional Writing Assignment

From their reading of the poem and the discussions in class, have students write about a typical day in a hobo's life. Where might he wake up? What might he eat for breakfast? What would be the day's activity? Urge them to include some dialogue, using hobo slang words.

Writing About the Poem

A Creative Response

1. **Describing an Imaginary Place.** This song creates a detailed picture of one person's idea of a perfect world. Describe your own version of a dream world. Be sure to supply specific details to help your reader clearly imagine this place. Details might include things to eat, places to live or visit, ways to entertain yourself, and activities you will or won't perform. You may write in poetry or prose.

A Critical Response

2. **Analyzing the Speaker's Feelings.** Write a paragraph explaining what the song reveals about how the hobo feels about work and the law. First describe the hobo's attitude toward work and the law. Then list the details from the song that reveal his opinions.

See Teacher's Manual page 79.

Analyzing Language and Vocabulary

Slang

SRW p. 83

People in almost every age group, occupation, and area use **slang**—informal language that includes invented words and familiar words that have been given new meaning. Slang words are often colorful and are sometimes humorous as well.

Many hobo slang words began partly as a sort of secret code that outsiders could not understand. Some hobo slang words originated simply to name things that were important or unique to hobo life.

Answer the following questions about the hobo slang words below.

jungle bulls handouts

1. These three hobo slang words are used in the song. Explain what each word means.
2. Discuss how you think each of these three slang terms was invented. That is, how does each term make a comparison or give a description that illustrates its meaning?
3. Read over the poem again and find other slang words that are used. What do they mean?
4. Why do you think hobos needed special words for these particular things? Name three or four other things you would expect hobos to invent slang terms for.

For answers, see Teacher's Manual page 79.

Responding to the Photograph

? What mood does this photo create—lonely, peaceful, sad? Considering the title and the photo accompanying it, what do you think the tone of the poem will be?

If any students in the class have been in such a setting, ask them to describe what it was like to their classmates.

Bury Me Not on the Lone Prairie

Anonymous

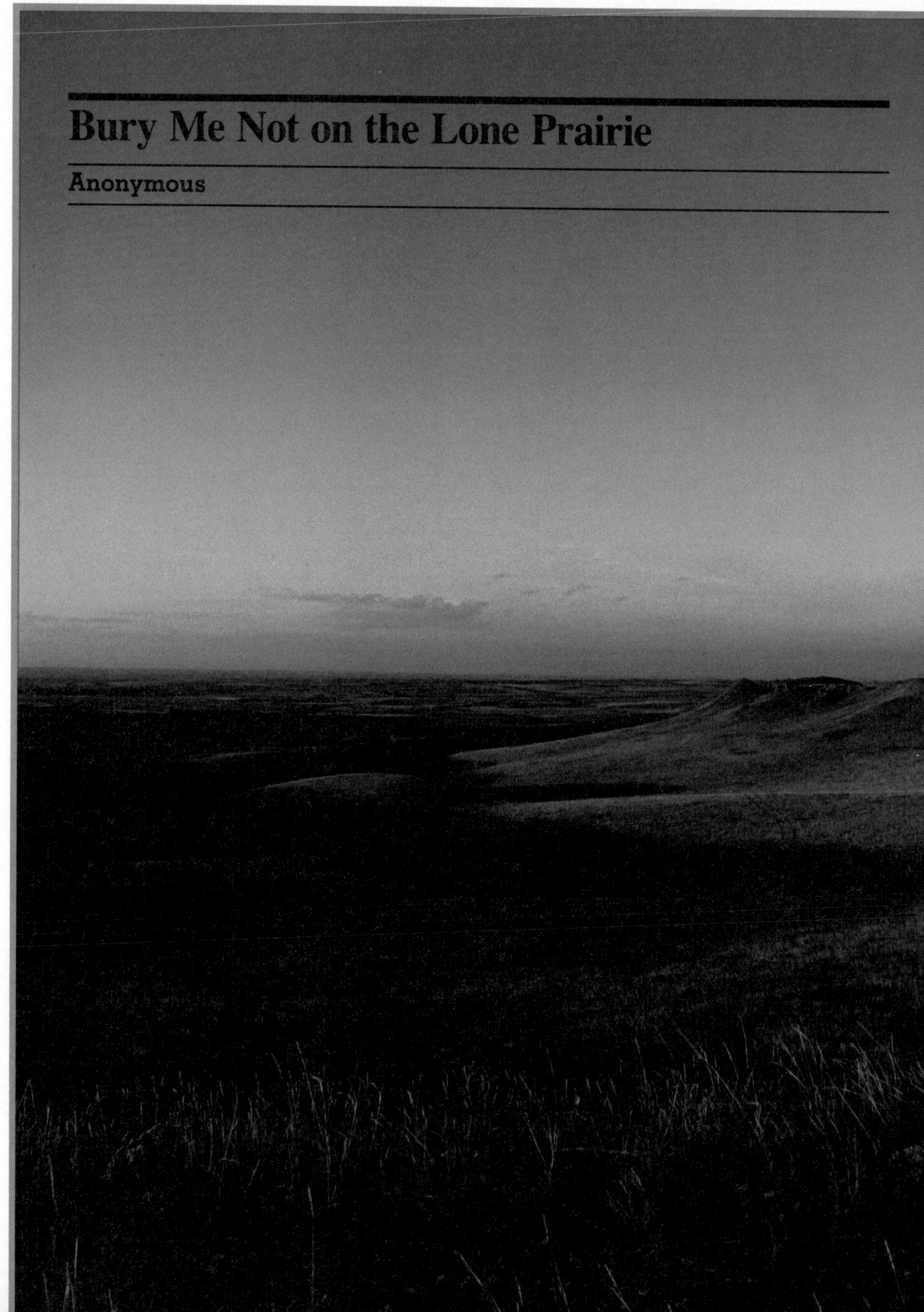

SUPPLEMENTARY SUPPORT MATERIAL

1. Selection Test (page 95 of Test Book)
2. Audiocassette recording
3. Reader's Response Journal
4. Workbook (page 63)
5. Instructional Overhead Transparency

PREREADING

1. **BUILDING ON PRIOR KNOWLEDGE.** Ask students what they know about the American frontier. (Their perceptions are probably drawn from Western movies and television shows.) How does the familiar image of tough cowboys carousing in saloons contrast with this photograph and the title of the poem?

2. **ESTABLISHING A PURPOSE.** To guide students' reading of the poem, ask them to think about the question at the end of the headnote. You might also want to use the vocabulary exercise to get the students thinking about mood and feeling.

3. **PREREADING JOURNAL.** Before they read, have students name three places that would make people feel lonely.

For a detailed lesson plan on this poem, see Teacher's Manual page 79.

The people who went to the American West and Midwest in the nineteenth century were frequently in search of freedom and adventure as well as better living conditions. These people gave us some of our most enduring folk songs. Some of the songs are happy, but others reflect the danger and the hardship of life in a new land. What details in the following stanzas help create the feeling or mood of the song?

A "O bury me not on the lone prairie,"
These words came low and mournfully
From the pallid° lips of a youth who lay
On his dying bed at the close of day . . .

"O bury me not on the lone prairie
Where the wild coyote will howl o'er me.
In a narrow grave just six by three
O bury me not on the lone prairie . . .

"O bury me not on the lone prairie
Where the buffalo paws o'er the prairie sea,
Where the buzzard sails and the wind goes free—
O bury me not on the lone prairie . . ."

But we buried him there on the lone prairie,
Where the owl all night hoots mournfully,
B And the blizzard beats and the wind blows free
O'er his lonely grave on the lone prairie.

3. **pallid:** pale.

A. Mood

? In two lines the poem has already established a strong mood or feeling. What is the mood, and what words help to create it? (The words *bury, lone, low,* and *mournfully* help establish a gloomy mood.)

B. Responding

? Why do you think the youth's friends do not honor his dying request?

CLOSURE

Have one student define connotation to the class. Ask the class to supply three words to describe the picture on page 264 that have unfavorable connotations. (Perhaps bleak, empty, lonely) Then supply three that are favorable. (Peaceful, sunny, unpolluted, etc.)

ANALYZING THE POEM

Identifying Details

1. Line 1 in stanza 1, stanzas 2 and 3. Lines 2–4 in stanza 1, and stanza 4 (lines 13–16).

2. He is dying.

3. The coyote howls, the buffalo paws, the buzzard sails, the owl hoots.

The wind goes free, and the blizzard beats.

4. No.

5. Prairie (accent on last syllable), coyote (with two syllables).

Interpreting Meanings

6. Perhaps he has led a lonely life. Or perhaps he is new to the prairie and is overwhelmed by its loneliness.

7. Responses will vary.

8. Responses will vary.

Applying Meanings

9. Encourage students to be specific about their reasons, and to explore the specific features of the setting that spark a reaction and what that reaction is.

FURTHER READING FOR STUDENTS

Students might enjoy other cowboy or Western songs such as "Red River Valley," "As I Walked Out in the Streets of Laredo," "The Lone Star Trail," and "I Ride an Old Paint."

★ **Texas Essential Elements/(a) English Language Arts: 1B** Purpose and audience; **3C** Literary traditions. **(c) Reading: 3I** Draw conclusions

Responding to the Poem

Analyzing the Poem

Identifying Details

1. Which lines and stanzas of the song are spoken by the youth? Which lines and stanzas are spoken by his companions?
2. Describe what is happening to the youth.
3. The poem describes the wild nature of the prairie. List details that it gives about prairie animals. List details that it gives about the prairie's weather.
4. Do the youth's companions honor his request?
5. Songwriters often alter the pronunciation of certain words to make them fit the **rhythm pattern.** Read this song aloud. What words must you pronounce in nonstandard ways to create a regular rhythm? SRW p. 77

Interpreting Meanings

6. Why do you think the youth doesn't want to be buried on the prairie?
7. Describe how the last stanza made you feel. Were you surprised at the way the youth's companions reacted to his request?
8. You may have sung this folk song. Sometimes song lyrics are effective without music; sometimes they are not. One poet has said that taking music from song lyrics is like "tearing the wings from a bird." Do you agree or disagree? Explain the reasons for your opinion.

Applying Meanings

9. Most people feel happier in some settings than in others. Thousands of people love the prairie and find it beautiful, yet the youth of the poem does not. Name an area or setting that you instinctively like and one that you instinctively dislike. Explain the reasons for your feelings about these places.

Writing About the Poem

A Creative Response

Extending the Story. Although this song or poem seems simple, it has an element of mystery. Write a paragraph in which you fill in the story's gaps. Be sure to answer the following questions: Who is the young man? Where did he come from? What has happened to him? To whom does he speak, and why do they not grant his last wish? Make sure your story fits in with the details in the poem.

See Teacher's Manual page 80.

Analyzing Language and Vocabulary

Connotations

SRW p. 27

A word's literal definition, sometimes called its dictionary meaning, is its **denotation.** But the emotional effect of a word depends largely on its **connotations**—the feelings and ideas associated with the word. The prairie portrayed in this song is lonely and hostile. Make a list of the words and phrases in the song that suggest feelings of loneliness and danger. Then think of several words that would create the opposite feelings—of companionship and safety.

For answers, see Teacher's Manual page 80.

Supplementary Support Material

1. Selection Test (page 95 of Test Book)
2. Audiocassette recording
3. Reader's Response Journal
4. Workbook (page 65)

Prereading

1. **Building on Prior Knowledge.** You may want to tell students briefly about courtly love, the late medieval convention that prescribed the conduct and even the emotions of ladies and the knights who were their adoring but chaste lovers. According to this convention, the knight would worship his lady as though she were on a pedestal and perform deeds of valor to impress her. He might wear the lady's colors in battle, compose verses for her, and be inspired by her, but she was in every way "above him." The lady in the poem thinks according to these codes of behavior, while the Count first follows them, then flouts them. King Francis might be Francis I of France (reigned 1515–1547).

2. **Establishing a Purpose.** Although this is a short poem, we get a good idea of what each of the three characters is like. Ask students to think about the traits of each character the poem introduces. Given these descriptions, is the ending expected or is it a surprise?

Texas Essential Elements/(a) English Language Arts: 1B Purpose and audience; 2C Oral language; 4A Word meaning. (c) Reading: 1A Context clues; 2A Word meaning; 2B Multimeaning words

This poem has several elements of an exciting story—unusual setting, romantic characters, and dramatic action—packed into just a few lines. The poem's resolution offers another element, a clear moral, or lesson. Before you read the poem, think about what you think the title means. After you finish the poem, see whether your guess was on target.

For a detailed lesson plan on this poem, see Teacher's Manual pages 80–81.

The Glove and the Lions

A **Leigh Hunt**

King Francis was a hearty king, and loved a royal sport,
And one day, as his lions fought, sat looking on the court.
The nobles filled the benches, and the ladies in their pride,
B And 'mongst them sat the Count de Lorge, with one for whom
he sighed:
And truly 'twas a gallant thing to see the crowning show,
Valor and love, and a king above, and the royal beasts below.

Ramped° and roared the lions, with horrid laughing jaws;
They bit, they glared, gave blows like beams, a wind went with
their paws;
With wallowing might and stifled roar they rolled on one another,
Till all the pit with sand and mane was in a thunderous smother;
The bloody foam above the bars came whisking through the air;
Said Francis then, "Faith, gentlemen, we're better here than there."

De Lorge's love o'erheard the King, a beauteous lively dame,
With smiling lips and sharp bright eyes, which always seemed
the same;
She thought, "The Count, my lover, is brave as brave can be;
He surely would do wondrous things to show his love of me;
C King, ladies, lovers, all look on; the occasion is divine;
I'll drop my glove to prove his love; great glory will be mine."

She dropped her glove, to prove his love, then looked at him
and smiled;
He bowed, and in a moment leaped among the lions wild;
The leap was quick, return was quick, he had regained his place,
Then threw the glove, but not with love, right in the lady's face.
"By Heaven," said Francis, "rightly done!" and he rose from
where he sat;
"No love," quoth he, "but vanity, sets love a task like that."

7. **ramped:** rushed violently.

A. Biography
A biography of Leigh Hunt appears on text page 269. Before students read the poem, you might want to note that Hunt's own outspokenness might be related to the defiant and outspoken note on which the poem ends.

B. Choral Reading
You might have a group of students prepare the poem for a choral reading. Be sure they assign specific lines to (1) a chorus, (2) a female voice, (3) a male voice (Francis). See suggestions on student page for assigning parts.

C. Responding
? Do you think this is an unreasonable demand? What other unreasonable demands might people make of their friends to "prove" their friendship or love?

CLOSURE
Ask students to briefly define rhythm. Then have them read the poem out loud, maybe one student for each stanza. Have them identify the rhythm as regular (songlike) or irregular.

Humanities Connection: Responding to the Fine Art
William Merritt Chase (1849–1916), an American portrait and still-life painter and teacher of painting, helped establish the fresh, spontaneous color and technique that became typical of early twentieth-century American art. But his earlier work, like this portrait, still used the darker colors characteristic of the German artists under whom he studied.

? Is this how you pictured the Count de Lorge's lady? If not, how did you picture her?

★ **Texas Essential Elements/(c) Reading** (continued): **3I** Draw conclusions; **4E** Rate of reading

Ready for the Ride by William Merritt Chase (1877). Oil.

The Union League Club, New York.

ANALYZING THE POEM

Identifying Details

1. The setting is daytime at a stadium where a lion fight is taking place.

2. King Francis loves a good contest, but also loves fairness. He judges wisely in this case. De Lorge is a gallant knight who accepts the lady's challenge, but whose love-struck eyes are opened by it. The lady is a vain, selfish woman who is willing to endanger de Lorge for the attention it will bring her.

3. Every phrase in the first five lines confirms their violence.

The king says he is glad he and the others are not down in the arena.

4. She decides to test de Lorge's love in order to gain the attention and admiration of the court.

5. The lady drops her glove and smiles at de Lorge. He bows, leaps among the lions, retrieves the glove, leaps out of the arena, and throws the glove in her face. The king commends de Lorge.

Interpreting Meanings

6. She is beautiful, but her "smiling lips and sharp bright eyes" always seem the same.

Her thoughts show concern not for de Lorge, but only for what glory will accrue to her.

7. Up until now, he has loved the lady; any gallant knight accepts a challenge. With the whole court watching, he felt he could hardly do otherwise.

8. Her challenge opens his eyes about her true nature, and kills his love and respect for her.

Most students will applaud his behavior.

Evaluating the Poem

9. Answers will vary.

Responding to the Poem

Analyzing the Poem

Identifying Details

SRW p. 79

1. Describe the poem's **setting**—the place and time of the action.
2. List the poem's major **characters.** Describe each in a sentence or two.
3. What details in the second stanza show that the lions are battling violently? How does the king show his respect for the lions' strength and fury?
4. What does the count's lady decide to do? Why does she do it?
5. The last stanza is packed with action. In your own words, summarize the main events of this stanza.

Interpreting Meanings

SRW p. 21

6. The poet **characterizes** the lady, or reveals her personality, by describing her appearance and her thoughts. How do her looks reveal her character? How much concern do her thoughts show for the count, in comparison with herself?
7. Why do you think the count takes the risk of leaping into the midst of the lions? What does that say about his character? Include two or more specific reasons in your answer.
8. Discuss why the count throws the glove at his lady. Do you feel he was right in throwing it?

Evaluating the Poem

9. In your opinion, which would have been the smarter thing for the count to do: jump into the arena for the glove or refuse to do so? What would you have done in his place? Explain the reasons for your answer.

Writing About the Poem

A Creative Response

1. **Imagining a Reaction.** Pretend you are the count's lady. Write a paragraph in which the lady gives her reaction to having the glove thrown in her face. Is she angry at Count de Lorge? Or is she angry with herself? What does she think about the king's comment? Use the first-person pronoun, *I*.

A Critical Response

2. **Explaining an Opinion.** Normally, if a nobleman insulted a lady of the court, we would expect him to be punished. The count certainly insults the lady by flinging her glove into her face. Yet the king says the action was "rightly done." What does the king mean by this? Do you agree with him? Explain your response in a paragraph. The first sentence of your paragraph should state whether the king was right or wrong. You should then explain what the king meant. The paragraph should conclude with your reasons why the king was right or wrong.

See Teacher's Manual page 81.

Analyzing Language and Vocabulary

Multiple Meanings

Many words have more than one meaning. When you read, you must use **context**—the words, phrases, and sentences surrounding a word—to understand which meaning the writer intends the word to have. Sometimes, however, more than one of a word's meanings could fit a situation.

1. The poet calls the count's lady "a beauteous lively dame." Look up the word *dame* in a good dictionary. List the meaning or meanings of this word that you think might be appropriate in the poem. Then list the meaning or meanings you think are *not* appropriate for the word as used in the poem.
2. Look up the word *lady* in the dictionary. How many meanings are listed? Write down which meaning or meanings you think the poet had in mind when he described the woman as a *lady.*

For answers, see Teacher's Manual page 82.

Reading About the Writer

Leigh Hunt (1784–1859) was born in England. Hunt was only thirteen years old when he began writing poetry. He was frail, however, and could not attend a university because of his health. Later, he was a magazine editor who was outspoken about his political views. Once, after insulting the Regent, Hunt and his brother ended up in jail for three years. During and after these years, Hunt often kept company with such famous poets as Lord Byron, Percy Bysshe Shelley, and John Keats.

FURTHER READING FOR STUDENTS

Students will enjoy other story-poems such as "The Charge of the Light Brigade" and "The Revenge: A Ballad of the Fleet" by Alfred Lord Tennyson; "The Skeleton in Armor" and "The Wreck of the *Hesperus*" by Henry Wadsworth Longfellow; and "Lochinvar" by Sir Walter Scott.

SUPPLEMENTARY SUPPORT MATERIAL
1. Reading Check Test blackline master
2. Introduction/Sounds of Poetry Test (page 97 of Test Book)

A. Responding to the Quotation
The quotation is by English-born American poet W. H. Auden. You might ask students if any of them are musicians, or if any of them like to sing. Does this interest in music help them understand what Auden says here?
? Auden says he doesn't quite know how listening to music helps to create poetry. If you were having a conversation with him, what ideas might you give him after he said this?
Now might be a good time to play, or replay, the recordings of "Bury Me Not on the Lone Prairie" and "The Glove and the Lions."
? Do you think the music for "Bury Me Not on the Lone Prairie" goes well with the poem? What kind of music do you think would fit the poem "The Glove and the Lions"?

For teaching suggestions on this section, see Teacher's Manual page 82.

A

Through listening to music I have learned much about how to organize a poem, how to obtain variety and contrast through changes of tone, tempo, and rhythm, though I could not say just how.

—W. H. Auden

SRW p. 49

The Sounds of Poetry

Poets use the sounds of words to help them express their feelings and ideas. When you read a poem aloud, you usually can hear whether its sounds are harsh or musical, nervous or lulling, fast or slow, lighthearted or somber. For example, listen to the sounds in the following lines from an old fifteenth-century poem. (Blacksmiths in the old days worked at open furnaces and hammered iron into various useful objects, such as horseshoes.)

Sootty, swart smiths,
smattered with smoke,
Drive me to death,
with the din of their dents.
Such noise at night
no man hear, never:
With knavish cries
and clattering of knocks!

—from "The Blacksmiths,"
retold by Wesli Court

You are probably unsure of the exact meaning of some of these words. But the sounds of words like *din, clattering,* and *knocks* should suggest the terrible noise blacksmiths make with their hammers. If you are paying close attention, you might even notice all the hissing *s* sounds in the first lines. If you know anything about a blacksmith's work, you'll know that the hot iron hisses when it's put in cold water.

Poets use various techniques to make words ring in our ears and echo their meaning. The most common sound devices in poetry are rhythm, rhyme, alliteration, and onomatopoeia.

SRW p. 77

Rhythm: The Rise and Fall of Our Voices

Rhythm refers to the rise and fall of our voices as we use language. As in music, a poem's rhythm can be fast or slow, light or solemn. It might also sound just like everyday speech.

SRW p. 45

Poetry that is written in **meter** has a regular pattern of stressed and unstressed syllables. Poetry that is written in **free verse** does not have a regular pattern of stressed and unstressed syllables. Free verse sounds like ordinary speech.

When poets write in meter, they count out the number of stressed syllables (or strong beats) and unstressed syllables (or

A. Rhythm

Many childhood poems, such as Mother Goose rhymes and jumping-rope songs, have sing-song rhythms which make them easy and fun to remember. Ask students if they can recall some of these poems. (Some of the many examples might be: "Ring around the rosie"; "Hickory dickory dock/The mouse ran up the clock")

weaker beats) in each line. Then they repeat the pattern throughout the poem. To avoid sounding sing-song, poets usually vary the basic pattern from time to time. Try reading aloud the following lines from this famous poem. Can you hear that each line has four stressed syllables alternating with four unstressed syllables?

A

Day after day, day after day,
We stuck, nor breath nor motion;
As idle as a painted ship
Upon a painted ocean.
—from *The Rime of the Ancient Mariner,*
Samuel Taylor Coleridge

A poem's rhythm can be shown by using accent marks (′) for stressed syllables and cups (˘) for unstressed syllables. This marking is called **scanning:**

B

Dáy ăftĕr dáy, dáy ăftĕr dáy
da DUM da DUM da DUM da DUM

B. Scanning

Have students scan a few lines from the poems they came up with above.

Rhyme: Chiming Sounds

SRW p. 73

Rhyme is the repetition of the sound of a stressed syllable and any unstressed syllables that follow: *sport* and *court; smother* and *another; sputtering* and *muttering.* The echoing effect of rhyme gives us pleasure. It makes us look forward to hearing certain chiming sounds throughout the poem. In the verse from *The Rime of the Ancient Mariner,* the rhyming words are *motion* and *ocean.*

Rhymes like *motion/ocean* in Coleridge's verse are called **end rhymes** because they occur at the ends of lines. **Internal rhymes** occur within lines, as in this line from Leigh Hunt's poem:

Then threw the *glove,* but not with *love,* right in the lady's face.

SRW p. 75

C

Poets will often use a pattern of rhymes, called a **rhyme scheme.** To describe a rhyme scheme, assign a new letter of the alphabet to each new rhyme. The rhyme scheme of Coleridge's verse is *abcb.*

C. Rhyme Scheme

What is the rhyme scheme of "The Glove and the Lions"? *(aabbcc)*

Alliteration: Repeating Consonants

D, E

Another way poets create sound effects is through the use of alliteration. **Alliteration** is the repetition of consonant sounds in words that are close together. In this verse from Coleridge's poem, the sounds of *f, b,* and *s* are repeated:

The fair breeze blew, the white foam flew,
The furrow followed free;
We were the first that ever burst
Into that silent sea.
—from *The Rime of the Ancient Mariner,*
Samuel Taylor Coleridge

D. Alliteration

What examples of alliteration are in the poem on page 270? (*S*ooty, *sw*art, *sm*iths, *sm*attered, *sm*oke; *d*rive, *d*eath, *d*in, *d*ents; *n*oise, *n*ight, *n*o, ma*n*, *n*ever, *kn*avish, *kn*ocks; *c*ries, *c*lattering)

E. Expansion

It may help students to understand alliteration by using its most exaggerated form—tongue twisters. For instance: "Peter Piper picked a peck of pickled peppers. If Peter Piper picked a peck of pickled peppers, how many pecks of pickled peppers did Peter Piper pick?"

Ask students to think of some of their own favorite tongue twisters.

Reading Check Test

1. Free verse has a regular pattern of stressed and unstressed syllables, while poems written in meter do not. *(False)*
2. Rhyme is the repetition of the sound of a stressed syllable and any unstressed syllables that follow. *(True)*
3. Internal rhymes occur at the ends of lines, while end rhymes occur within lines. *(False)*
4. Alliteration is the repetition of consonant sounds in words that are close together. *(True)*
5. Onomatopoeia is the use of words whose sounds echo their sense. *(True)*

A. Onomatopoeia
? What other examples of onomatopoeia can you think of?

B. Responding
You might ask students to act out or explain the nonsense words in this excerpt. Ask them to strike an uffish pose, to whiffle, burble, and galumph.

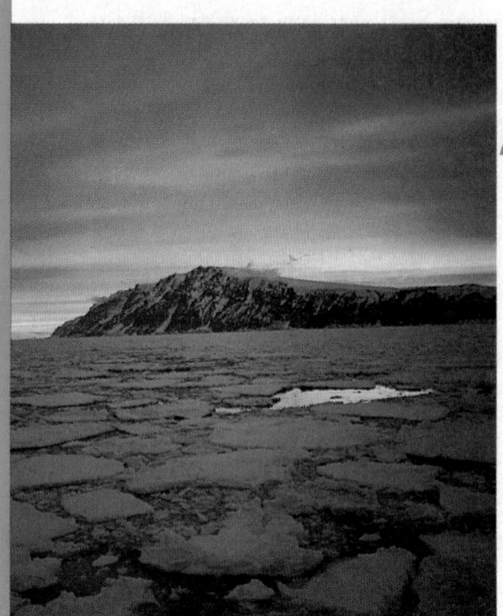

Onomatopoeia: Sound Echoes Sense

A **Onomatopoeia** (än'ə·mat'ə·pē'ə) is the use of words with sounds that echo their sense. *Crash, bang, boom, hiss* are all commonly used examples of onomatopoeia. Here is another verse from Coleridge's poem that uses onomatopoeia to help us hear the sounds of ice (a *swound* is a faint).

The ice was here, the ice was there,
The ice was all around:
It cracked and growled, and roared and howled,
Like noises in a swound!

—from *The Rime of the Ancient Mariner,*
Samuel Taylor Coleridge

Sometimes alliteration is used for the purpose of onomatopoeia. For example, the repeated *s* sounds in this line by Robert Bridges helps us hear the hushed sounds of snow:

Silently sifting and veiling road, roof, and railing

(Note the internal rhyme in that line too.)

To see how sounds alone can sometimes suggest sense, read these lines of a famous nonsense poem. You will not find all the words in a dictionary, but you can make a good guess as to what kinds of sounds are being described.

B

And, as in uffish thought he stood,
The Jabberwock, with eyes of flame,
Came whiffling through the tulgey wood,
And burbled as it came!

One, two! One, two! And through and through
The vorpal blade went snicker-snack!
He left it dead, and with its head
He went galumphing back.

—from "Jabberwocky,"
Lewis Carroll

SRW pp. 11, 63

PREREADING

1. **BUILDING ON PRIOR KNOWLEDGE.** Before students read the poem, it might interest them to know a little about the Klondike region, which is in northwestern Canada. In 1896, a miner, George Carmack, and his Indian friends made a gold strike on Bonanza Creek and began the Klondike Gold Rush of 1897–1898. By 1900, more than two million dollars worth of gold was produced by simple hand methods of mining. Many people braved the freezing temperatures of the region—an average of 16°F during the seven-month winter—to find their fortune. Ask students to imagine what it must have been like for Sam McGee, going from the mild temperatures of his native Tennessee to the bitter cold of the Klondike winter. Would the lure of gold attract them in spite of the Arctic climate?

2. **ESTABLISHING A PURPOSE.** This is a very "cold" poem. Tell students to watch for all the details that describe the cold as they read. Can they picture the setting and feel the cold?

★ **Texas Essential Elements/(a) English Language Arts: 1B** Purpose and audience; **3C** Literary traditions

In the 1890's, the Klondike gold rush drew thousands of fortune-seekers to northwestern Canada. The following poem tells the story of an unfortunate gold-seeker named Sam McGee. A *cremation* is the burning of a dead body. Before reading the poem, think about the *mood* you would expect to find in a poem about a cremation. Then see whether the poem meets your expectations.

The Cremation of Sam McGee

Robert W. Service

There are strange things done in the midnight sun
By the men who moil° for gold;
The Arctic trails have their secret tales
That would make your blood run cold;
The Northern Lights° have seen queer sights,
But the queerest they ever did see
Was that night on the marge° of Lake Lebarge
I cremated Sam McGee. A

Now Sam McGee was from Tennessee, where the cotton blooms and blows,
Why he left his home in the South to roam 'round the Pole, God only knows.
He was always cold, but the land of gold seemed to hold him like a spell;
Though he'd often say in his homely way that "he'd sooner live in hell."

On a Christmas Day we were mushing our way over the Dawson Trail.
Talk of your cold! through the parka's fold it stabbed like a driven nail.
If our eyes we'd close, then the lashes froze till sometimes we couldn't see;
It wasn't much fun, but the only one to whimper was Sam McGee.

And that very night, as we lay packed tight in our robes beneath the snow,
And the dogs were fed, and the stars o'erhead were dancing heel and toe,
He turned to me, and "Cap," says he, "I'll cash in this trip, I guess;
And if I do, I'm asking that you won't refuse my last request."

Well, he seemed so low that I couldn't say no; then he says with a sort of moan:
"It's the cursed cold and it's got right hold till I'm chilled clean through to the bone. B
Yet 'tain't being dead—it's my awful dread of the icy grave that pains;
So I want you to swear that, foul or fair, you'll cremate my last remains."

A pal's last need is a thing to heed, so I swore I would not fail;
And we started on at the streak of dawn; but ah! he looked ghastly pale.
He crouched on the sleigh, and he raved all day of his home in Tennessee;
And before nightfall a corpse was all that was left of Sam McGee.

A. Rhyme Scheme

? What is the rhyme scheme of the poem? (The first stanza is *abcbdefe;* the other stanzas are *aabb.*)

B. Internal Rhyme

Have the students identify the internal rhymes in this stanza. (Line 1: low, no; line 2: cold, hold, bone; line 3: dead, dread; line 4: swear, fair)

As an extended exercise, you can ask them to find all the internal rhymes in the poem—there is an example in almost every line. This will help them answer question 6.

---

2. **moil:** toil. 5. **Northern Lights:** bands of light sometimes appearing in the night sky of the Northern hemisphere.
7. **marge:** edge.

For a detailed lesson plan on this poem, see Teacher's Manual page 83. A biography of Robert W. Service appears on text page 277.

Supplementary Support Material

1. Selection Test (page 99 of Test Book)
2. Author photograph on *A Gallery of Authors* poster
3. Audiocassette recording
4. Reader's Response Journal
5. Workbook (page 67)

Humanities Connection: Responding to the Fine Art

Charles Burchfield (1893–1967) was an American painter whose post-1940 watercolors expressed his love for nature. "I'm going to give you more sounds and dreams," he wrote of his decision to stop painting towns and to emphasize instead nature and the changing seasons. "And—yes, I'm going to make people smell what I want them to, and with visual means."

? Do you think Burchfield achieves his purpose in this painting? What do you hear and smell when you look at this picture? Is it dreamlike? How would Sam McGee like this scene?

Winter Moonlight by Charles Burchfield (1951). Watercolor.

Courtesy Wichita Art Museum, Wichita, Kansas. The Roland P. Murdock Collection.

CLOSURE

Have one student define conflict. Then have students note all the conflicts within the poem (Sam McGee versus the cold; the narrator versus the physical hardship of the trail; the narrator versus the unpleasant task before him).

A. Responding

? Do you feel that all promises must be kept? Would you have kept this one?

B. Alliteration and Onomatopoeia

? Find the alliteration in these two lines of description. (*F*lames, *f*urnace; just *s*oared, *s*eldom *s*ee; fu*r*nace *r*oared; *h*eavens, *h*uskies *h*owled; *b*egan to *b*low) How does the alliteration make the furnace's heat and the bad weather outside more vivid? Find the onomatopoeia in these two lines. ("Roared"; "howled") Do you think onomatopoeia makes the description more vivid? Why?

C. Comparing to Other Media

In line 53, the poet refers to his "grisly fear." Much of this poem's mood, setting, and even story are similar to those of a horror movie. As in this poem, the corpse in a typical horror movie often returns to life.

? Despite these similarities, how is the mood of the poem different from that of a horror movie? For instance, what examples of humor in the poem keep it from being as horrifying as it could be?

There wasn't a breath in that land of death, and I hurried, horror-driven,
With a corpse half hid that I couldn't get rid, because of a promise given;
It was lashed to the sleigh, and it seemed to say: "You may tax your brawn and brains,
But you promised true, and it's up to you to cremate those last remains." A

Now a promise made is a debt unpaid, and the trail has its own stern code.
In the days to come, though my lips were dumb, in my heart how I cursed that load.
In the long, long night, by the lone firelight, while the huskies, round in a ring,
Howled out their woes to the homeless snows—O man! how I loathed the thing.

And every day that quiet clay seemed to heavy and heavier grow;
And on I went, though the dogs were spent and the grub was getting low;
The trail was bad, and I felt half mad, but I swore I would not give in;
And I'd often sing to the hateful thing, and it hearkened° with a grin.

Till I came to the marge of Lake Lebarge, and a derelict° there lay;
It was jammed in the ice, but I saw in a trice it was called the "Alice May."
And I looked at it, and I thought a bit, and I looked at my frozen chum;
Then "Here," said I, with a sudden cry, "is my cre-ma-tor-e-um."

Some planks I tore from the cabin floor, and I lit the boiler° fire;
Some coal I found that was lying around, and I heaped the fuel higher;
The flames just soared, and the furnace roared—such a blaze you seldom see;
And I burrowed a hole in the glowing coal, and I stuffed in Sam McGee. B

Then I made a hike, for I didn't like to hear him sizzle so;
And the heavens scowled, and the huskies howled, and the wind began to blow.
It was icy cold, but the hot sweat rolled down my cheeks, and I don't know why;
And the greasy smoke in an inky cloak went streaking down the sky.

I do not know how long in the snow I wrestled with grisly fear;
But the stars came out and they danced about ere° again I ventured near;
I was sick with dread, but I bravely said: "I'll just take a peep inside.
I guess he's cooked, and it's time I looked;" . . . then the door I opened wide. C

And there sat Sam, looking cold and calm, in the heart of the furnace roar;
And he wore a smile you could see a mile, and he said: "Please close that door!
It's fine in here, but I greatly fear you'll let in the cold and storm—
Since I left Plumtree, down in Tennessee, it's the first time I've been warm."

40. **hearkened** (här′kənd): listened carefully. 41. **derelict:** an abandoned ship. 45. **boiler:** the steam engine of the ship. 54. **ere** (er): before.

ANALYZING THE POEM
Identifying Details
1. The strangest occurred the night he cremated Sam McGee.
2. He fears being forever trapped in the cold and ice.
3. He asks that he be cremated.
He now has a much heavier load on the sleigh. The dogs become worn out, his food runs low, and the trail is bad.
4. He sets fire to an abandoned boat he finds on the shore of Lake Lebarge, and stuffs Sam's body in the coals.
5. He finds Sam sitting there, smiling and reveling in the delightful warmth.
6. Every line has an internal rhyme.

Interpreting Meanings
7. He was lured there for some reason, perhaps by the promise of gold, but he hates the cold.
8. The narrator wants to fulfill his promise, but his task is a terribly difficult one.
9. It changes in the last stanza.
Among obvious choices are "crema-tor-e-um," "I stuffed in Sam McGee," and "to hear him sizzle so." More perceptive readers will point out that the wording in the first half of the poem, as well as the overall rhythm and the discovery of a

Responding to the Poem

Analyzing the Poem

Identifying Details

1. In the first stanza, the speaker claims that strange things have happened in the Arctic region. What does he claim is the strangest of all?
2. Sam says he doesn't fear death, but something else. Describe what he fears.
3. What does Sam ask the speaker to do with his corpse? List some of the difficulties the speaker faces in accomplishing the task.
4. Explain how the speaker finally manages to keep his promise.
5. What surprise greets the speaker when he returns to check on the cremation?
6. This poem has a very strong **rhyme.** You are probably used to poems that have **end rhymes,** or rhymes at the ends of lines. This poem uses end rhymes, but it uses internal rhymes as well. **Internal rhymes** are rhymes contained within one line. For example, *done* and *sun* in the poem's first line are internal rhymes. Read the poem aloud, listening carefully. List three examples of internal rhyme. SRW p. 73

Interpreting Meanings

7. Whether in prose or poetry, a good story needs a **conflict**—a struggle between opposing forces. A conflict may occur between characters, between a character and nature, or between opposing thoughts and feelings within one character. Describe the opposing forces in the conflict Sam feels about being in the Klondike territory.
8. Describe the conflict that Sam's last request creates for the narrator. Is it an external or an internal conflict, or both?
9. The middle part of the poem has many frightening details that create a grim, dark **mood.** At what point in the poem does this mood change? What words and details before this point hint that the mood might change?

Evaluating the Poem

10. Why do you think this poem has been so popular for so many years? What did you like best about it?

Writing About the Poem

A Creative Response

1. **Extending the Story.** The narrator says he does not know why Sam left Tennessee. Write a paragraph explaining why you think Sam decided to leave his home and travel to the Klondike. Discuss what lures might tempt Sam to stay in a place he so obviously dislikes.
2. **Illustrating the Poem.** Draw a picture of the final scene when the narrator opens the door of the furnace and sees, to his shock, Sam alive and well (and warm). Before you begin drawing, make a list of all the details of the scene.

A Critical Response

3. **Comparing and Contrasting Two Poems.** This poem's situation resembles that of "Bury Me Not on the Lone Prairie" (page 264). In both, a character tries to make arrangements for what will happen after his death. In one or two paragraphs **compare** and **contrast** the two poems. That is, show how they are similar and different. Concentrate on the meanings of the poems, not on their form. Be sure to answer the following questions: What feelings toward the setting does the dying character of each poem have? What request does each dying character make? Are the requests granted?

See Teacher's Manual page 84.

Analyzing Language and Vocabulary

Alliteration

SRW p. 11

Alliteration is the repetition of consonant sounds in words that are close together in a poem. Alliteration often involves sounds at the beginning of words, but it can also involve sounds within or at the end of words. This example from "The Cremation of Sam McGee" contains both kinds of alliteration: "In the *l*ong, *l*ong night, by the *l*one fire*l*ight. . . ."

Alliteration creates sound echoes in a poem. These echoes can make a poem more musical, make it livelier, make it more memorable, or create emphasis.

Find five other examples of alliteration in the poem. Describe what you think each example adds to the poem.

For answers, see Teacher's Manual page 84.

derelict ship, also suggest something other than tragedy.

Applying Meanings

10. Answers will vary. Students might cite the rhyme and rhythm, the gruesome topic, and the surprise ending as reasons for the poem's popularity.

Reading About the Writer

Born in England, **Robert W. Service** (1874–1958) arrived in Canada in 1894. He lived in Vancouver for a while and traveled along the Canadian Pacific Coast. In 1902 he took a job with the Canadian Bank of Commerce and was transferred to Yukon Territory, which includes the Klondike. Two of Service's most popular poems are "The Cremation of Sam McGee" and "The Shooting of Dan McGrew," poems that many people can recite from memory.

Focusing on Background

A ***"I'll Tell You a Story Jack London Never Got"***

Robert W. Service talks about the origin of "The Cremation of Sam McGee":

". . . My second ballad was the result of an accident. One evening I was at loose ends, so I thought I would call on a girl friend. When I arrived at the house, I found a party in progress. I would have backed out, but was pressed to join the festive band. As an uninvited guest I consented to nibble a nut. Peeved at my position, I was staring gloomily at a fat fellow across the table. He was a big mining man from Dawson [in the Klondike], and he scarcely acknowledged his introduction to a little bank clerk. Portly and important, he was smoking a big cigar with a gilt band. Suddenly he said: 'I'll tell you a story Jack London never got.' Then he spun a yarn of a man who cremated his pal. It had a surprise climax which occasioned much laughter. I did not join, for I had a feeling that here was a decisive moment of destiny. I still remember how a great excitement usurped me. Here was a perfect ballad subject. The fat man who ignored me went his way to bankruptcy, but he had pointed me the road to fortune.

"A prey to feverish impatience, I excused myself and took my leave. It was one of those nights of brilliant moonlight that almost goad me to madness. I took the woodland trail, my mind seething with excitement and a strange ecstasy. As I started in: *There are strange things done in the midnight sun,* verse after verse developed with scarce a check. As I clinched my rhymes I tucked the finished stanza away in my head and tackled the next. For six hours I tramped those silver glades, and when I rolled happily into bed, my ballad was cinched. Next day, with scarcely any effort of memory I put it on paper. Word and rhyme came eagerly to heel. My moonlight improvisation was secure and, though I did not know it, 'McGee' was to be the keystone of my success."

—Robert W. Service

A. Responding to Focusing on Background

? What might be *your* "decisive moment of destiny"—or incident that might change your life? (For instance, meeting the person you want to spend the rest of your life with, winning the lottery, seeing a moving play and deciding to be an actor or actress)

FURTHER READING FOR STUDENTS

Robert Service, "The Shooting of Dan McGrew." Another chilling tale is Jack London's "To Build a Fire," about a man battling excruciating cold as he travels across the Yukon. (This story is included in *Elements of Literature: Second Course.*)

Supplementary Support Material

1. Selection Test (page 101, Test Book)
2. Author photograph on *A Gallery of Authors* poster
3. Audiocassette recording
4. Connections Between Reading and Writing worksheet
5. Reader's Response Journal
6. Workbook (page 69)

Prereading

1. **Establishing a Purpose.** Tell students to be listening for the use of sound effects in the poem. Ask them what mood these sounds create. This will help them answer questions 8 and 9.

2. **Prereading Journal.** To prepare students for the use of sound effects in the poem, and for the Analyzing Language and Vocabulary exercise, have them brainstorm ten onomatopoetic words.

Texas Essential Elements/(a) English Language Arts: 1B Purpose and audience; **2C** Oral language; **3C** Literary traditions; **4F** Generalizations. **(c) Reading: 1C** Dictionaries; **3D** Generalizations; **4E** Rate of reading

The highwayman in this famous poem is a robber who lived in eighteenth-century England. Highwaymen used to stop stagecoaches as they drove over the lonely moorlands of northern England and Scotland. They would then rob the rich passengers of their money and jewels. Some highwaymen were considered heroes by the Scots because they shared the money with the poor. Highwaymen were often romantic figures who dressed in expensive clothes. The story told in this poem is based on a true story that the poet heard while he was on vacation in that part of England where highwaymen used to lie in wait for the stagecoaches. Read the poem aloud to hear the galloping hooves of the highwayman's spirited horse. How does the poet create this impression?

The Highwayman

For a detailed lesson plan on this poem, see Teacher's Manual pages 84–85. A biography of Alfred Noyes appears on text page 283.

Alfred Noyes

Part 1

The wind was a torrent of darkness among the gusty trees,
The moon was a ghostly galleon° tossed upon cloudy seas,
The road was a ribbon of moonlight over the purple moor,
And the highwayman came riding—
  Riding—riding—
The highwayman came riding, up to the old inn door.

He'd a French cocked hat on his forehead, a bunch of lace at his chin,
A coat of the claret° velvet, and breeches of brown doeskin;
They fitted with never a wrinkle; his boots were up to the thigh!
And he rode with a jeweled twinkle,
  His pistol butts a-twinkle,
His rapier hilt° a-twinkle, under the jeweled sky.

Over the cobbles he clattered and clashed in the dark innyard
And he tapped with his whip on the shutters, but all was locked and barred;
He whistled a tune to the window, and who should be waiting there
But the landlord's black-eyed daughter, A
  Bess, the landlord's daughter,
Plaiting° a dark red love knot into her long black hair.

And dark in the dark old innyard a stable wicket° creaked
Where Tim the ostler° listened; his face was white and peaked;
His eyes were hollows of madness, his hair like moldy hay,
But he loved the landlord's daughter,
  The landlord's red-lipped daughter,
Dumb as a dog he listened, and he heard the robber say—

"One kiss, my bonny sweetheart, I'm after a prize tonight,
But I shall be back with the yellow gold before the morning light;
Yet, if they press me sharply, and harry° me through the day,
Then look for me by moonlight,
  Watch for me by moonlight, B
I'll come to thee by moonlight, though hell should bar the way."

He rose upright in the stirrups; he scarce could reach her hand,
But she loosened her hair i' the casement!° His face burned like a brand
As the black cascade of perfume came tumbling over his breast;
And he kissed its waves in the moonlight,
  (Oh, sweet black waves in the moonlight!)
Then he tugged at his rein in the moonlight, and galloped away to the west.

2. **galleon** (gal'ē·ən): large sailing ship. 8. **claret** (klar'it): deep red, like claret wine. 12. **rapier** (rā'pē·ər) **hilt:** sword handle. 18. **plaiting:** braiding. 19. **wicket:** small door or gate. 20. **ostler** (äs'lər): stableman. 27. **harry:** to trouble by attacking repeatedly. 32. **casement:** window that opens outward on hinges.

A. Onomatopoeia

? Which words in these seven lines exemplify onomatopoeia? ("Clattered," "clashed," "tapped," "whistled," "creaked")

B. Repetition

? What word is repeated most often here? ("Moonlight") Where was it used previously in the poem? (In line 3) Why do you think Noyes repeats "moonlight" so often? (Moonlight will be important later in the narrative—see lines 52–55) How does the repetition affect the mood of the poem? (It keeps reminding us of the romantic but dangerous setting—the moonlit moor and innyard.)

A. Repetition Have students note that the repetition of the word *marching* echoes the repetition of the word *riding* in stanza 1.

? In what other ways do these three lines resemble the last three lines in the first stanza? (The same rhythm, the same punctuation, repetition of the word *came*, the same last phrase) How are these repetitions ironic? (As Part 2 begins, the reader is waiting for the highwayman's return, as in stanza 1. But, those who arrive are the highwayman's enemies.)

B. Vocabulary *Priming* means that they are getting their guns ready to fire.

Part 2

He did not come in the dawning; he did not come at noon;
And out o' the tawny sunset, before the rise o' the moon,
When the road was a gypsy's ribbon, looping the purple moor,
A redcoat troop came marching—
A Marching—marching—
King George's men came marching, up to the old inn door.

They said no word to the landlord, they drank his ale instead,
But they gagged his daughter and bound her to the foot of her narrow bed;
Two of them knelt at her casement, with muskets at their side!
There was death at every window;
And hell at one dark window;
For Bess could see, through her casement, the road that *he* would ride.

They had tied her up to attention, with many a sniggering jest;
They had bound a musket beside her, with the barrel beneath her breast!
"Now keep good watch!" and they kissed her. She heard the dead man say—
Look for me by moonlight;
Watch for me by moonlight;
I'll come to thee by moonlight, though hell should bar the way!

She twisted her hands behind her; but all the knots held good!
She writhed her hands till her fingers were wet with sweat or blood!
They stretched and strained in the darkness, and the hours crawled by like years,
Till, now, on the stroke of midnight,
Cold, on the stroke of midnight,
The tip of one finger touched it! The trigger at least was hers!

The tip of one finger touched it; she strove no more for the rest!
Up, she stood to attention, with the barrel beneath her breast,
She would not risk their hearing: she would not strive again;
For the road lay bare in the moonlight;
Blank and bare in the moonlight;
And the blood in her veins in the moonlight throbbed to her love's refrain.

Tlot-tlot; tlot-tlot! Had they heard it? The horse hoofs ringing clear;
Tlot-tlot; tlot-tlot, in the distance? Were they deaf that they did not hear?
Down the ribbon of moonlight, over the brow of the hill,
The highwayman came riding,
Riding, riding!
B The redcoats looked to their priming! She stood up, straight and still!

Tlot-tlot, in the frosty silence! *Tlot-tlot,* in the echoing night!
Nearer he came and nearer! Her face was like a light!
Her eyes grew wide for a moment; she drew one last deep breath,
Then her finger moved in the moonlight,
Her musket shattered the moonlight,
Shattered her breast in the moonlight and warned him—with her death.

Responding to the Illustration

? What stanzas in the poem does this illustration portray? (The second two stanzas of Part 2) Is this the way you picture Bess?

CLOSURE

Have students memorize the first stanza and at least one other stanza which includes sounds that appeal to them. Then have them identify the sound effects (rhythm, rhyme, alliteration, or onomatopoeia) that they especially like in that stanza.

FURTHER READING FOR STUDENTS

Alfred Noyes, *Drake.* An epic poem about the sixteenth-century English navigator and admiral.

Howard Pyle, *The Adventures of Robin Hood.* Legends about another romantic outlaw.

Other rousing narrative poems include Joaquin Miller's "Columbus"; Robert Browning's "The Pied Piper of Hamlin" and "How They Brought the Good News from Ghent to Aix"; and Rudyard Kipling's "Danny Deever."

A. Alliteration

? Find all the alliteration in this line. (*He*, *h*is, *h*ighway; *l*ay, *l*ace; *b*lood, *b*unch; *th*e wi*th*, *th*roat)

B. Responding

? How do you find this ending? Sad? Happy? Ghostly? Why?

He turned; he spurred to the westward; he did not know who stood
Bowed, with her head o'er the musket, drenched with her own red blood!
Not till the dawn he heard it, his face grew gray to hear
How Bess, the landlord's daughter,
  The landlord's black-eyed daughter,
Had watched for her love in the moonlight, and died in the darkness there.

Back, he spurred like a madman, shrieking a curse to the sky,
With the white road smoking behind him, and his rapier brandished high!
Blood-red were his spurs i' the golden noon; wine-red his velvet coat,
When they shot him down on the highway,
  Down like a dog on the highway,
A And he lay in his blood on the highway, with a bunch of lace at his throat.

And still of a winter's night, they say, when the wind is in the trees,
When the moon is a ghostly galleon tossed upon cloudy seas,
When the road is a ribbon of moonlight over the purple moor,
A highwayman comes riding—
  Riding—riding—
A highwayman comes riding, up to the old inn door.

B
Over the cobbles he clatters and clangs in the dark innyard;
And he taps with his whip on the shutters, but all is locked and barred;
He whistles a tune to the window, and who should be waiting there
But the landlord's black-eyed daughter,
  Bess, the landlord's daughter,
Plaiting a dark red love knot into her long black hair.

Responding to the Poem

Analyzing the Poem

Identifying Details

1. On what kind of night does the story begin? List three details that help make the description of this night vivid in your mind.
2. What details describe the highwayman and Bess as a handsome couple?
3. What is the highwayman planning to do after leaving Bess? What does he promise her?
4. What part does Tim the ostler play in the story? What is his motive?
5. Describe what the redcoats do to Bess. What is the only way Bess is able to warn the highwayman of the waiting danger?
6. What finally happens to the highwayman?

Interpreting Meanings

7. The final two stanzas of "The Highwayman" are similar to the poem's first and third stanzas. What are the differences? Explain what the differences indicate about the meaning of the last stanzas.
8. Powerful **rhythm** adds to the drama of this poem. Read aloud the tenth through thirteenth stanzas. Would you describe their rhythm as fast or slow? Does the rhythm of these stanzas help you imagine the poem's action?
9. **Alliteration** is the repetition of a consonant sound in words near one another. An example in the poem is "The moon was a ghostly galleon." List at least five other examples of alliteration in the poem.

SRW pp. 11, 77

ANALYZING THE POEM

Identifying Details

1. It is a winter night, clear and windy.

The wind is described as "a torrent of darkness," the moon as "a ghostly galleon," the road as "a ribbon of moonlight."

2. He wears elegant clothes, including a red jacket and lace at his throat, and she has lustrous black hair and eyes and red lips.

3. He is planning a raid, but will return to her before daylight, or at the latest by moonlight the next night.

4. He tells the soldiers about the highwayman's planned return.

Jealousy—he too loves Bess.

5. They tie her up to the foot of her bed, a musket leaning on her chest.

She maneuvers her finger onto the trigger of the musket, and when she hears the highwayman coming, she pulls the trigger.

6. When he learns of Bess's death, he rides back, mad with rage, and is shot down on the highway.

Interpreting Meanings

7. The stanzas at the beginning recount the events of a specific night. Those at the end describe a pattern of nights.

A legend has arisen that the highwayman and Bess still meet on such nights.

8. Fast.

The drive of the rhythm suggests fast-paced action, high emotion, and intense excitement.

9. Many examples are possible. You might have the class make a master list of alliterative phrases.

Evaluating the Poem

10. If most students believe she is noble, you might want to play devil's advocate and insist her sacrifice is pointless.

A. Responding to Focusing on Background

? What kinds of stories most excite you? What places have you been to that would be suitable settings for an exciting story?

Evaluating the Poem

10. Bess makes a great sacrifice because of her love for the highwayman. In your opinion, is her sacrifice noble or pointless? Explain the reasons for your answer.

Writing About the Poem

A Creative Response

1. **Writing From Another Point of View.** The poem concerns itself mainly with the highwayman and Bess. We never learn much about the other characters. Pretend you are either Tim the ostler or one of the soldiers who come to the inn. Write a paragraph explaining how the character reacts to the death of Bess. SRW p. 69

A Critical Response

2. **Summarizing the Story.** In one paragraph, summarize the plot of "The Highwayman." Include in your summary the words **conflict, climax,** and **resolution.** In a second paragraph, tell what you think of the characters in the poem: the highwayman, Bess, Tim, and the redcoats. Is there a hero in the poem? Who is the villain?

See Teacher's Manual page 86.

Analyzing Language and Vocabulary

Onomatopoeia

SRW pp. 63, 73, 77

Noyes uses many sound devices, such as **rhythm, repetition,** and **rhyme,** to make the poem fun to listen to. Another sound device he uses is onomatopoeia. **Onomatopoeia** is the use of words that echo the sounds they refer to. *Screech, buzz,* and *splash* are all examples of onomatopoeia. This device can add to a poem's effect by filling it with the actual sounds it describes.

Read the poem aloud, listening closely to the sound of the words. Point out examples of onomatopoeia in the poem that describe the following sounds:

1. The sound of the highwayman's horse in the stone courtyard of the inn (stanza 3)
2. The sound of the highwayman's whiphandle against the window (stanza 3)
3. The sound of the horse's hooves (stanzas 12 and 13)
4. The sound of the highwayman's voice as he curses his enemies (stanza 15)

For answers, see Teacher's Manual page 86.

Reading About the Writer

British poet, novelist, biographer, and essayist, **Alfred Noyes** (1880–1958) was often called the most popular poet of his time. People enjoyed reading his verse because of its thumping rhythms and its technical simplicity. Noyes considered himself a traditionalist, and he frowned upon the experimental styles of his famous contemporaries James Joyce and T. S. Eliot. His favorite topics were the sea and fantasy lands. Some of his other well-known poems are *Drake,* an epic about the voyager Sir Francis Drake, his favorite hero, and "The Barrel Organ," with its famous refrain "Come down to Kew in lilac time . . . (it isn't far from London)."

A

Focusing on Background

"One Blustery Night . . ."

"In the little cottage on the edge of Bagshot Heath where I had taken rooms shortly after I left Oxford I wrote 'The Highwayman' and hoped to complete my poem on Drake. Bagshot Heath in those days was a wild bit of country, all heather and pinewoods. 'The Highwayman' suggested itself to me one blustery night when the sound of the wind in the pines gave me the first line:

The wind was a torrent of darkness among the gusty trees.

"It took me about two days to complete the poem. Shortly afterward it appeared in *Blackwood's Magazine.* It illustrates the unpredictable chances of authorship, that this poem, written in so short a time, when I was twenty-four, should have been read so widely. . . .

"I think the success of the poem in all these ways was due to the fact that it was not an artificial composition, but was written at an age when I was genuinely excited by that kind of romantic story."

—Alfred Noyes

SUPPLEMENTARY SUPPORT MATERIAL

1. Selection Test (page 103 of Test Book)
2. Reader's Response Journal
3. Workbook (page 71)

PREREADING

PREREADING JOURNAL. Before students read this poem, have them write down a list of their own real (or imaginary) collections.

CLOSURE

Ask students to define alliteration. Then ask them to make up another item of Hector's collection using alliteration.

A. Rhyme
The first line, also the title of the poem, contains good examples of the repetitions that characterize the poem as a whole. **?** What internal rhyme can you find in the first line? (*Hector* the *Collector*) Can you find at least four more examples of internal rhyme? (See lines 7, 9, 11, 15, 19)

B. Alliteration
Have students list all the alliteration in the first 11 lines. What sounds are alliterated in lines 13 and 14? This will help them answer question 3. The alliteration makes the poem fun to read out loud.

C. Responding
? Do you think this ending is sad or funny? Is it both? Explain. What would *you* call Hector's treasure?

D. Responding to the Illustration
Look closely at Silverstein's illustration of his poem. How many items of Hector's collection can you find?

★ **Texas Essential Elements/(a) English Language Arts: 1B** Purpose and audience; **2C** Oral language. **(c) Reading: 4E** Rate of reading

Poetry can use several kinds of repetition. *Rhyme* repeats vowel sounds, such as in the words *moon* and *June* or *befriend* and *attend*. Rhythm repeats a pattern of stressed and unstressed syllables. *Alliteration* repeats consonant sounds, as in the expressions *French fries* and *dead duck*. Shel Silverstein uses all three kinds of repetition in the following poem. Watch for them.

SRW p. 11, 73, 77

Hector the Collector

For a detailed lesson plan on this poem, see Teacher's Manual pages 86–87. A biography of Shel Silverstein appears on text page 285.

Shel Silverstein

A Hector the Collector
Collected bits of string,
Collected dolls with broken heads
And rusty bells that would not ring.
Pieces out of picture puzzles,
Bent-up nails and ice-cream sticks,
B Twists of wires, worn-out tires,
Paper bags and broken bricks.
Old chipped vases, half shoelaces,
Gatlin' guns° that wouldn't shoot,
Leaky boats that wouldn't float
And stopped-up horns that wouldn't toot.
Butter knives that had no handles,
Copper keys that fit no locks,
Rings that were too small for fingers,
Dried-up leaves and patched-up socks.
Worn-out belts that had no buckles.
'Lectric trains that had no tracks.
Airplane models, broken bottles,
Three-legged chairs and cups with cracks.
Hector the Collector
Loved these things with all his soul—
Loved them more than shining diamonds,
Loved them more than glistenin' gold.
Hector called to all the people,
"Come and share my treasure trunk!"
And all the silly sightless people
C Came and looked . . . and called it junk.

10. **Gatlin' guns:** Gatling guns, a type of early machine gun.

D

"Hector the Collector" from *Where the Sidewalk Ends: The Poems and Drawings of Shel Silverstein.*

Copyright © 1974 by Evil Eye Music, Inc. Reprinted by permission of Harper & Row, Publishers, Inc.

ANALYZING THE POEM

Identifying Details

1. Almost every line yields an example. All are broken or worn with age.
2. He considers them treasures. They call them junk.
3. There are many examples; for instance, the *t* sound in "Collected bits of string."
4. Four. Lines 1, 2, and 21 each has two stressed beats.

Interpreting Meanings

5. Among the possibilities: They have caught his eye; they may be useful someday; they spark his memory of the past; they spark his imagination about their history.
6. If students think Hector is the silly one, move the discussion into question 7.

Applying Meanings

7. If students say they own no such objects, ask them about old toys or sporting equipment, blankets, or pictures. With more mature classes, you can go further: How much of everything they and their families own might someone with a different political, religious, or social perspective consider junk?

Responding to the Poem

Analyzing the Poem

Identifying Details

1. Hector collects many kinds of things. List five of these things. What do these items have in common?
2. Explain what Hector thinks of the things in his collection. What do other people think of them?
3. The poem contains many examples of **alliteration,** the repetition of a consonant sound in words that are close together. Identify four examples. SRW p. 11
4. The poem's **rhythm**—its pattern of stressed and unstressed beats—adds to its comical effect. Read the poem out loud. How many stressed beats do most lines have? Point out three lines in the poem that have a different number of stressed beats. SRW p. 77

Interpreting Meanings

5. Why do you think Hector places so much value on the things he collects?
6. Reread the last two lines of the poem. Do you agree that the people are "silly" and "sightless"? Explain why or why not.

Applying Meanings

7. Do you have something you treasure that other people might call junk? If so, first tell what it is and why you value it. Then explain why other people might not understand its value.

Writing About the Poem

A Creative Response

Imitating the Poem. Write a poem of five to ten lines listing the collection of someone else, perhaps someone who is the opposite of Hector. This character might, for example, collect only valuable items, or perhaps clothing or souvenirs or jewelry. Briefly introduce this collector, then list the items in his or her precious collection in careful detail. Try to make your poem look and sound like "Hector the Collector."

See Teacher's Manual page 87.

Reading About the Writer

Shel Silverstein (1923–) has made a name for himself as a poet and a writer of children's books. He says he "also writes songs, draws cartoons, sings, plays guitar, and has a good time." Silverstein grew up in Chicago and now lives on a houseboat off Sausalito, California, when he is not traveling around the world. "What I do is good," says Silverstein. "I wouldn't let it out if I didn't think it was." His works include *The Giving Tree* (a children's story) and *A Light in the Attic* (a collection of poems). "Hector the Collector" is from another collection called *Where the Sidewalk Ends.*

FURTHER READING FOR STUDENTS

Shel Silverstein, *The Giving Tree.* A fable about the fruits of generosity.

———, *A Light in the Attic.* A collection of poems.

SUPPLEMENTARY SUPPORT MATERIAL

1. Selection Test (page 103 of Test Book)
2. Audiocassette recording
3. Reader's Response Journal
4. Workbook (page 73)
5. Instructional Overhead Transparency

PREREADING

1. **BUILDING ON PRIOR KNOWLEDGE** Ask students what they know about tom-cats. Have they ever heard tom-cats screeching or wailing at night? If so, ask them to describe the sounds. (It is a blood-curdling noise.) This is probably what prompted the poet to describe the true nature of a tom-cat as demonic.

2. **ESTABLISHING A PURPOSE** Have students read Analyzing Language and Vocabulary, text page 287. Then suggest that they think about rhythm and its effect on the poem's mood. Does the steady rhythm help them feel the motion of a cat stalking the night? Be sure to have the poem read aloud.

A. Alliteration
? Trace the repetition of the consonant sound "c" as in *c*at throughout the poem. (Stanza 1: *C*at, *c*omes; stanza 2: *c*oal; stanza 3: *c*rouches, *c*apers, *c*urved, *c*laws; stanza 4: *c*lan, s*c*orn; stanza 5: li*ck*, sil*k*y; stanza 6: *c*rouch) This will help them answer question 3.

B. Rhythm
Note how Marquis uses a series of accented one-syllable words with many hard consonants to create his portrait of the hard-hearted animal.

CLOSURE
Ask students to define rhythm. Then, using the first line of the poem, ask students to compose their own second line, imitating Marquis's steady rhythm.

★ **Texas Essential Elements/(a) English Language Arts: 2C** Oral language. **(c) Reading: 1C** Dictionaries; **4E** Rate of reading

Before reading this poem, think of three words that describe your own attitude, or feelings, about cats. Then see whether or not the poem expresses similar feelings.

The Tom-Cat

Don Marquis

For a detailed lesson plan on this poem, see Teacher's Manual pages 87–88. A biography of Don Marquis appears on text page 287.

At midnight in the alley
A A Tom-Cat comes to wail,
And he chants the hate of a million years
As he swings his snaky tail.

Malevolent, bony, brindled,°
Tiger and devil and bard,°
His eyes are coals from the middle of Hell
B And his heart is black and hard.

He twists and crouches and capers
And bares his curved sharp claws,
And he sings to the stars of the jungle nights
Ere° cities were, or laws.

Beast from a world primeval,°
He and his leaping clan,
When the blotched red moon leers° over the roofs,
Gives voice to their scorn of man.

He will lie on a rug tomorrow
And lick his silky fur,
And veil the brute in his yellow eyes
And play he's tame, and purr.

But at midnight in the alley
He will crouch again and wail,
And beat the time for his demon's song
With the swing of his demon's tail.

5. **brindled:** gray or tawny and streaked or spotted with a darker color. 6. **bard:** poet. 12. **ere** (er): before. 13. **primeval** (prī-mē'v'l): of the earliest times. 15. **leers:** looks slyly or with evil intent.

ANALYZING THE POEM
Identifying Details

1. He goes to an alley. He wails, twists, crouches, capers, bares his claws, and sings to the stars.
2. He lies on the rug, licks his fur, pretends he is tame, and purrs.
3. Many examples are possible. See note A on page 286.

Interpreting Meanings

4. Examples include *hate, snaky tail, malevolent, devil, coals, Hell, black* and *hard heart, beast, brute, demon.*
5. They hate humanity because people have tried to tame them and put them on rugs and put collars around their necks. People have limited their territory and do not understand their wild nature.
6. They suggest the cat's wild, primitive jungle origins.

The jungle refers to the cat's original home, which perhaps he misses in the city. The jungle is still in his blood. It seems that the tom-cat retains part of his original heritage. He has never been quite domesticated (as the dog has been).
7. He might like the comfort, but he's faking at being tame (line 20). It sounds as if he'd prefer his old jungle life (lines 11–12). He certainly dislikes his "owners" (line 16). (He'd probably call them his captors. They've changed his jungle habitat into cities.)

Applying Meanings

8. The nature of cats is evil, thinly veiled by civilization.

Responses will vary.

Responding to the Poem

Analyzing the Poem

Identifying Details

1. Where does the tom-cat go at midnight? List the things he does then.
2. List the things the tom-cat does in the daytime.
3. Like "Hector the Collector," this poem is rich in **alliteration,** the repetition of a consonant sound in words that are close together. Find at least five examples of alliteration in "The Tom-Cat."
SRW p. 11

Interpreting Meanings

4. What words and phrases in the poem make the tom-cat seem evil?
5. Discuss who or what you think cats have hated for "a million years."
6. Reread lines 11–13. What idea about the cat's nature do these lines suggest? Can you explain why the lines refer to a jungle, though the rest of the poem seems to be set in a city?
7. Discuss whether you think the tom-cat in the poem really likes being a pet. Quote passages from the poem to support your answer.

Applying Meanings

8. Describe the overall impression of cats created by this poem. Do you think this is an accurate picture of cats? Or do you feel the poet is all wrong? Explain your opinion.

Writing About the Poem

A Creative Response

Writing a List. Read Marquis's list describing his appearance and his likes and dislikes (see "Focusing on Background"). Imitate his style and write a list of your own, listing your, or an imaginary person's, likes and dislikes. Add a few details every once in a while describing your speaker's appearance.

See Teacher's Manual page 88.

Analyzing Language and Vocabulary

Scanning a Poem

SRW p. 77

Rhythm—a pattern of stressed and unstressed beats or syllables—can make a powerful contribution to a poem's overall effect. The rhythm can help make a poem funny or dramatic, joyous or mournful. To analyze a poem's rhythm, you should **scan** it, or mark its pattern of stressed and unstressed beats. A stressed beat is marked with the symbol ʹ. An unstressed beat is marked with the symbol ˘.

Here is how you would scan this verse from Emily Dickinson's poem "I Started Early, Took My Dog":

> I started early, took my dog,
> And visited the sea.
> The mermaids in the basement
> Came out to look at me

The rhythm of "The Tom-Cat" is very regular. Read one stanza of the poem aloud to help you feel the stressed and unstressed beats. Then scan this stanza. Then read the whole poem aloud. Can you make it sound like a primitive chant or a magic spell?

For answers, see Teacher's Manual page 89.

Reading About the Writer

Don Marquis (1878–1937) is primarily known as the columnist for the *New York Evening Sun* who created the characters of archy and mehitabel. Archy is a cockroach who types notes to his boss in the newsroom, but he can't manage to type capital letters. Mehitabel is an alley cat. Marquis preferred to be remembered for his more serious works. "It would be one on me," he once said, "if I should be remembered for creating a cockroach character."

Additional Writing Assignment
Have students write their own original description of a cat they know or have seen. Is this cat similar to or different from Marquis's tom-cat? Tell them to include details about its appearance, its actions, its voice, and the way it moves.

FURTHER READING FOR STUDENTS
T. S. Eliot, *Old Possum's Book of Practical Cats.* A collection of poems about cats; the famous Broadway musical was based on these poems.

A. Responding to the Art
Compare this cat to the one pictured on text page 286. Which cat is more like the cat in Marquis's poem? Why?

Focusing on Background
Marquis Outlines His Life

"This is the outline of my life in its relation to the times in which I live. . . .

"It seems more modest, somehow, to put it in the third person:

". . . Has assured carriage, walking boldly into good hotels and mixing with patrons on terms of equality; weight, two hundred pounds; face slightly asymmetrical but not definitely criminal in type; . . . likes beefsteak and onions; wears No. 8 shoe; fond of Francis Thompson's poems; . . . imitates cats, dogs, and barnyard animals for the amusement of young children; . . . has always been careful to keep thumbprints from possession of police; . . . sometimes wears glasses, but usually operates undisguised; . . . superstitious, especially with regard to psychic phenomena; eyes blue; does not use drugs nor read his verses to women's clubs; ruddy complexion; no photograph in possession of police; . . . prominent cheekbones; avoids Bohemian society, so called, and has never been in a thieves' kitchen, a broker's office, nor a class of short-story writing; . . . dislikes Roquefort cheese, *Tom Jones,* Wordsworth's poetry, absinthe cocktails, most musical comedy, public banquets, physical exercise, . . . steam heat, toy dogs, poets who wear their souls outside, organized charity, magazine covers, and the gas company; dislikes prunes, tramp poets, and imitations of Kipling; . . . would likely come along quietly if arrested."

—Don Marquis

A

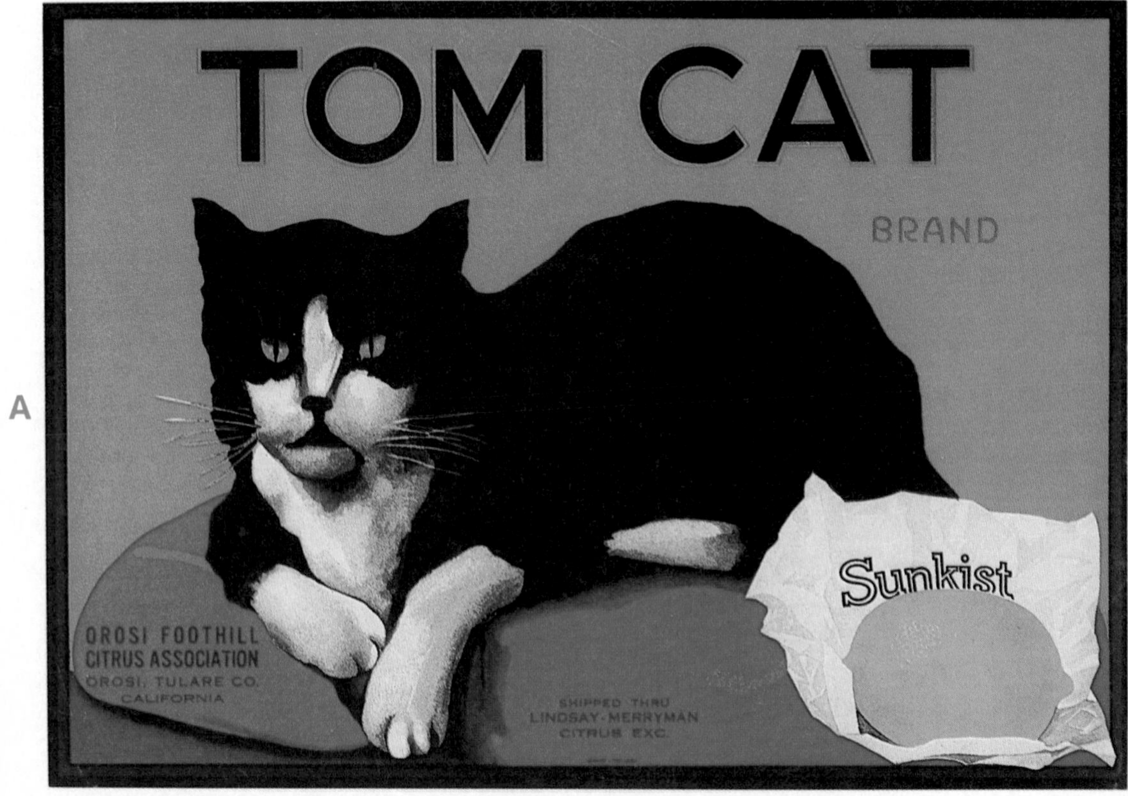

Supplementary Support Material

1. Selection Test (page 105 of Test Book)
2. Author photograph on *A Gallery of Authors* poster
3. Audiocassette recording
4. Reader's Response Journal
5. Workbook (page 75)

Prereading

1. **Building on Prior Knowledge.** Ask students to list all the characteristics they associate with dragons. Then ask them to think about the name Custard. Does it seem like an appropriate name for a dragon? (Be sure they know that custard is a pudding.)

2. **Establishing a Purpose.** Remind students that a poet is free to break ordinary rules of grammar, vocabulary, and spelling (a poet's "poetic license"). Ask students: Does Nash use this freedom well, or do you think he should have refrained from inventing words and changing spellings? Did you like the effect? (See questions 7 and 8.)

3. **Prereading Journal.** Tell students to invent four new words of their own that rhyme with dragon, and write down their definitions.

For a detailed lesson plan on this poem, see Teacher's Manual page 89.
A biography of Ogden Nash appears on text page 293.

Ogden Nash twists rhyme, rhythm, and other elements of poetry to create a very unusual poem. Like most poets, he even invents words. Look for three words that Nash has made up.

The Tale of Custard the Dragon

Ogden Nash

A
Belinda lived in a little white house,
With a little black kitten and a little gray mouse,
And a little yellow dog and a little red wagon,
And a realio, trulio, little pet dragon.

Now the name of the little black kitten was Ink,
And the little gray mouse, she called her Blink,
And the little yellow dog was sharp as Mustard,
But the dragon was a coward, and she called him Custard.

Custard the dragon had big sharp teeth,
And spikes on top of him and scales underneath,
B Mouth like a fireplace, chimney for a nose,
And realio, trulio daggers on his toes.

C Belinda was as brave as a barrel full of bears,
And Ink and Blink chased lions down the stairs,
Mustard was as brave as a tiger in a rage,
But Custard cried for a nice safe cage.

Belinda tickled him, she tickled him unmerciful,
Ink, Blink and Mustard, they rudely called him Percival,
They all sat laughing in the little red wagon
At the realio, trulio, cowardly dragon.

Belinda giggled till she shook the house,
And Blink said Weeck! which is giggling for a mouse,
Ink and Mustard rudely asked his age,
When Custard cried for a nice safe cage.

Suddenly, suddenly they heard a nasty sound,
And Mustard growled, and they all looked around.
Meowch! cried Ink, and Ooh! cried Belinda,
For there was a pirate, climbing in the winda.

Pistol in his left hand, pistol in his right,
And he held in his teeth a cutlass bright,
D His beard was black, one leg was wood;
It was clear that the pirate meant no good.

A. Rhyme and Rhythm
Note this poem's regular rhyme scheme: *abab.* Note also the singsong quality of the rhythm.

B. Similes
Although a detailed explanation of simile is given on page 309 of the text book, you might want to introduce students to the technique while they study this poem. Tell them that a simile is an imaginative comparison between two very different things using the words "like" or "as." Then, ask them to pick out the similes in the poem. (Lines 11, 15, 37, 38, 40, 53, and 55)

C. Alliteration
? What two consonants are used alliteratively in this line? (*b* and *l*)

D. Responding
? What do you predict will happen?

A. Onomatopoeia
? How many examples of onomatopoeia can you find in this line? ("Clatter," "clank," "jangling")

Belinda paled, and she cried Help! Help!
But Mustard fled with a terrified yelp,
Ink trickled down to the bottom of the household,
And little mouse Blink strategically mouseholed.

But up jumped Custard, snorting like an engine,
Clashed his tail like irons in a dungeon,
A With a clatter and a clank and a jangling squirm
He went at the pirate like a robin at a worm.

The pirate gaped at Belinda's dragon,
And gulped some grog from his pocket flagon,
He fired two bullets, but they didn't hit,
And Custard gobbled him, every bit.

CLOSURE

Have students memorize one stanza that contains rhymes they especially like. Then have them identify those rhymes in class.

FURTHER READING

Students will have fun reading other poems by Ogden Nash:

Ogden Nash, *I Wouldn't Have Missed It: Selected Poems*

———, *Parents Keep Out: Elderly Poems for Youngerly Readers*

———, *Pocket Book of Ogden Nash*

A. Repetition

? Where have you seen these stanzas before? (They are nearly complete repetitions of stanzas 1 and 4.) What different meaning do you get from the last line now? (Now the last line can be taken seriously. Custard, still cowardly, longs still for a safe cage. His brave response to a sudden threat did not change his nature.)

Belinda embraced him, Mustard licked him,
No one mourned for his pirate victim.
Ink and Blink in glee did gyrate
Around the dragon that ate the pyrate.

Belinda still lives in her little white house,
With her little black kitten and and her little gray mouse,
And her little yellow dog and her little red wagon,
And her realio, trulio, little pet dragon.

A

Belinda is as brave as a barrel full of bears,
And Ink and Blink chase lions down the stairs.
Mustard is as brave as a tiger in a rage,
But Custard keeps crying for a nice safe cage.

Responding to the Poem

Analyzing the Poem

Identifying Details

1. List the inhabitants of the little white house. Describe each in a sentence.
2. How does Custard differ from the house's other inhabitants? What does Custard cry for?
3. Describe how others in the house treat Custard.
4. How does everyone except Custard act when the pirate appears? Describe how Custard reacts to the pirate.
5. How do the others treat Custard after he faces the pirate?
6. In the first stanza Nash uses **repetition** to create a bouncy, fairy-tale-like mood. Point out the repetition in the first stanza. Then list three other examples of repetition in the poem.

Interpreting Meanings

7. What made-up words does Ogden Nash use in the first stanza? How do these words indicate the **tone,** or attitude, of the poet toward his subject matter? For example, do these words make the poem seem more serious? More frightening? Sillier? Funnier? SRW p. 89
8. Nash is famous for his unusual **rhymes;** he will even change a spelling or invent a word if it suits his purpose. For instance, he changes the spelling of *window* to *winda* to make it rhyme with *Belinda.* Point out two other examples of unusual rhymes. Then explain what makes them unusual. SRW p. 73

Evaluating the Poem

9. Did you enjoy the poem's story and its unexpected rhymes and made-up words? Quote passages from the poem in explaining your response to it.

Writing About the Poem

A Creative Response

1. **Imitating the Writer's Technique.** Write a paragraph in which you describe a monster that is very different from what monsters are usually like. Give your monster an appropriate name.

A Critical Response

2. **Explaining Irony. Irony** occurs when there is a difference between what we expect to happen and what actually happens. In a paragraph, describe the irony in the actions of the characters of the house when the pirate appears. That is, explain what we expect these characters to do, and how they act instead. SRW p. 57

See Teacher's Manual page 90.

ANALYZING THE POEM

Identifying Details

1. Belinda, Ink, Blink, Mustard, and Custard. See Teacher's Manual page 89 for descriptions.
2. He is not brave. He wants "a nice safe cage."
3. They tease and mock him. Belinda tickles him, the others call him Percival, all four laugh at him, and Ink and Mustard insult him.
4. Belinda turns pale and screams for help, and everyone except Custard flees. Custard becomes a true dragon and attacks the pirate.
5. They thank and praise him.
6. The word *little* is repeated six times. Stanzas 4 and 11 are basically the same, as are lines 16 and 24. "Realio, trulio" is repeated four times.

Interpreting Meanings

7. *Realio, trulio.* They establish a silly, humorous tone.
8. *Unmerciful/Percival, household/mouseholed, gyrate/pyrate.*

Supplementary Support Material

1. Selection Test (page 105 of Test Book)
2. Author photograph on *A Gallery of Authors* poster
3. Reader's Response Journal
4. Workbook (page 77)

Prereading

Establishing a Purpose. You can use the headnote to guide students' reading. Ask them to look for unusual word usage and to decide if such unusual usage contributes to the poems' comical effect.

Closure

Have students memorize one stanza that they particularly like, and be ready to explain their choice.

A. Grammar

? What violations of the usual rules of grammar can you find here? ("I begs," "Is those things," "is they")

B. Responding

? Do you agree? What would Don Marquis (page 286) think?

★ Texas Essential Elements/(c) Reading: 1B Structural analysis; 2A Word meaning

These short poems show Ogden Nash up to the tricks he is famous for. Read them for enjoyment. Notice how he plays with rhythm, rhyme, words, and even grammar for comic effect.

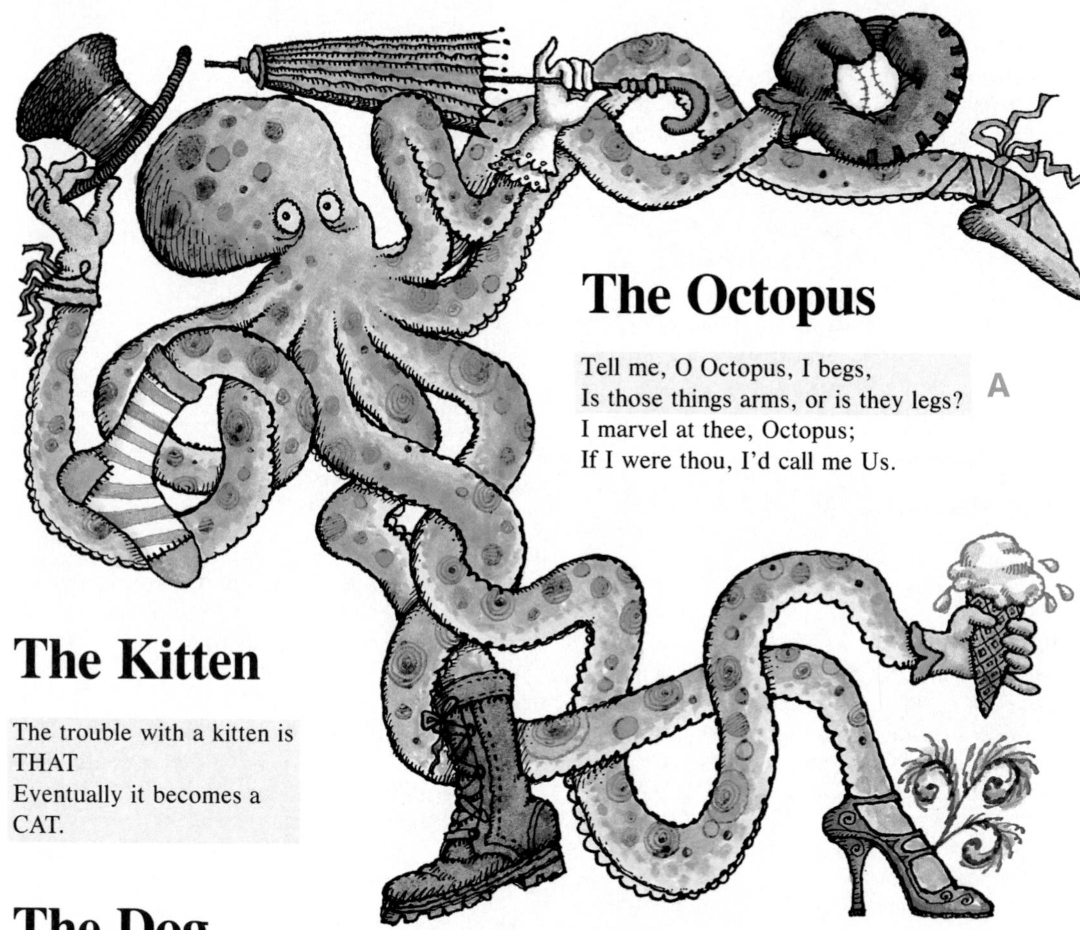

The Octopus

Tell me, O Octopus, I begs,
Is those things arms, or is they legs? A
I marvel at thee, Octopus;
If I were thou, I'd call me Us.

The Kitten

B The trouble with a kitten is
THAT
Eventually it becomes a
CAT.

The Dog

The truth I do not stretch or shove
When I state the dog is full of love.
I've also proved, by actual test,
A wet dog is the lovingest.

The Porcupine

Any hound a porcupine nudges
Can't be blamed for harboring grudges,
I know one hound that laughed all winter
At a porcupine that sat on a splinter.

The Germ

A mighty creature is the germ,
Though smaller than the pachyderm.°
His customary dwelling place
Is deep within the human race.
His childish pride he often pleases
By giving people strange diseases.
Do you, my poppet,° feel infirm?
You probably contain a germ.

2. **pachyderm** (pak'ə·durm'): any thick-skinned, hoofed animal like the elephant or the rhinocerous.
7. **poppet:** child.

For a detailed lesson plan on these poems, see Teacher's Manual pages 90–91.

A biography of Ogden Nash appears on text page 293.

ANALYZING THE POEM
Interpreting Meanings
1. His multiple arms suggest multiple creatures.
2. Kittens are very nice animals.
He is suggesting that cats are not nice creatures.
3. Wet dogs have come up to him, full of affection, begging to be patted and hugged.
4. He remembers his own misery when a porcupine got him.
5. By carrying diseases, they can harm much larger creatures.
6. Responses will vary.

A. Responding to the Biography
? Considering the tone of the poems you have just read, are you surprised that the author of these poems held the jobs Nash did?

Responding to the Poems

Analyzing the Poems

Interpreting Meanings

1. If the speaker of the first poem were an octopus, why would he call himself "Us"?
2. In "The Kitten," the speaker says the problem with kittens is that they become cats. What point is he making about kittens? About cats?
3. What kind of "test" do you think led the speaker in "The Dog" to say a wet dog is "the lovingest"?
4. In "The Porcupine," why do you think the hound enjoys remembering the porcupine's misfortune?
5. Why does the speaker call germs mighty even though they are very small?
6. What did you think of these short poems? Did some affect you differently than others? Quote passages from the poems in explaining your reaction.

Writing About the Poems

A Creative Response

Describing an Animal. A *bestiary* is a collection of animal descriptions, either real or imaginary. The five short poems by Ogden Nash could be described as a small comic bestiary. Writing in either prose or poetry, add at least one description to this comic collection of creatures. Describe any animal that strikes your fancy: a duck or a dinosaur, a monkey or a monster. If you like, you may write several short pieces.

See Teacher's Manual page 91.

Analyzing Language and Vocabulary

Prefixes

The prefixes *octa-, octo-,* and *oct-* mean "eight." Thus, an octopus has eight arms or legs—or feet (*-pus* comes from a root meaning "foot").

1. The following words begin with a prefix meaning "eight." Write down the meaning of each word. You'll probably have to use a dictionary.

   a. octagon **b.** octet **c.** octogenarian

2. The words below begin with the prefix *tri-,* which means "three." Define each word in a sentence or two. Check a dictionary where necessary.

   a. triangle **c.** tricycle **e.** tripod
   b. triathlon **d.** tripartite

For answers, see Teacher's Manual page 91.

Reading About the Writer

For many years, **Ogden Nash** (1902–1971) has been enjoyed for his comical poetry and his clever, funny rhymes. Nash held many serious jobs before he turned to writing "silly" verse. He taught school, worked on Wall Street, wrote for an advertising agency, and labored on the editorial staff of a publishing company. Nash's first attempt at light verse was something of a doodle that ended up in the garbage can; but he fished it out and sent it to a magazine that bought it. Nash admitted having "intentionally maltreated and man-handled every known rule of grammar, prosody, and spelling." A

SUPPLEMENTARY SUPPORT MATERIAL
1. Selection Test (page 105 of Test Book)
2. Reader's Response Journal
3. Workbook (page 79)

PREREADING
ESTABLISHING A PURPOSE. Use the headnote to establish a purpose to the students' reading. Tell them also to think about what elements of their own lives might help a stranger to understand them.

CLOSURE
Have one student explain to the class the concept of free verse. Then, have each student compose two lines in free verse to follow the line "I have a craving for."

A. Expansion
It might interest students to know that the cat is not one of the twelve animal signs in Chinese astrology. In the Chinese custom, each animal is associated with certain personality traits, and a person's year of birth identifies him or her with that animal. (For instance, if someone was born in the year of the ox, he or she is likely to be hardworking.)
? What do you think the traits of a cat might be? What might Badikian be telling about herself by saying she was born in the year of the cat? (Her attitude toward cats is probably not shared by Marquis, page 286.)

B. Responding
? From these two lines, what do you think her mother was like?

C. Responding
? How does the poet visually show her "craving for wide open spaces"? (The line "wide open spaces" is placed on the second half of the line, leaving an open space.)

★ **Texas Essential Elements/(a) English Language Arts: 3B** Figurative language.
(c) Reading: 1B Structural analysis; **2A** Word meaning

This poem is just what its title says it is: It is a list of "elements" that the writer might use to write a longer poem. "The year of the cat" refers to the Chinese custom of identifying certain years with certain animals: ox, rat, etc. Even from this short list, what can you tell about the poet's life?

elements for an autobiographical poem:

Beatriz Badikian

A — i was born in
the year of the cat

— my parents are immigrants
a life made of beginnings

— Dante gave me my name°
by way of my father

— my father told me all about
ancient lands and lost civilizations

B — my mother dressed me in red
my hair was too straight for her

— my father told me
i would be a speaker
a leader
a fighter

— i left my parents' home
by way of marriage and divorce

— i am an island
a collector of postcards
matchboxes
people

— Sandra says i have
metamorphosized from seagulls

— i have a craving for C
wide open spaces
and poems that don't rhyme

5. Dante is an Italian poet who wrote *The Divine Comedy* in which a beautiful young woman named Beatrice leads the hero to Heaven.

Responding to the Poem

Analyzing the Poem

Identifying Details

1. According to the poem, what facts do you know about the speaker's life?
2. What does she like and dislike?
3. Is this poem written in **free verse** or in **meter**?

SRW p. 45

Interpreting Meanings

4. What do you think the speaker means when she says her life is "made of beginnings"?
5. Do you think her father helped her become a poet? Explain.
6. What do you think she means when she says she is an island? Do you think Sandra is being complimentary when she says she metamorphosized (or magically changed her form) from seagulls?

Writing About the Poem

A Creative Response

Imitating the Writer's Technique. Imitating this poet, list the elements you might use for an autobiographical poem, either about yourself or someone else. Consider these elements:

For a detailed lesson plan on this poem, see Teacher's Manual pages 91–92. A biography of Beatriz Badikian appears on text page 295.

Analyzing the Poem

Identifying Details

1. She was born in the year of the cat, her parents are immigrants, her name came from a literary reference, she learned about ancient civilizations from her father, her hair is straight, her father thought she would be a strong person, she has been married and divorced, she collects things and people, she is close to someone named Sandra.

2. She likes wide open spaces, poems that don't rhyme, postcards, matchboxes, and people.

3. It is in free verse.

Interpreting Meanings

4. Immigrants have to begin their lives over again in their new country. The poet may be referring to starting a new life after each new move.

5. Probably, her father was interested in literature (Dante) and in history.

6. Answers will vary. Some students may think she is saying that she is basically alone. Others may say that she is surrounded by other people and things, but that she is different. Most will see it as complimentary, as seagulls fly far out to sea and ride the wind.

Gregorita (detail) by Robert Henri. Oil.

The Thomas Gilcrease Institute of American History and Art, Tulsa, Oklahoma.

1. Parents
2. Name
3. What the speaker identifies with
4. What other people tell the speaker
5. Likes and dislikes

See Teacher's Manual page 92.

Analyzing Language and Vocabulary

Related Words

The word *metamorphosis* means a "marvelous transformation." In the unit on Greek and Roman mythology in this book, you will read many stories of metamorphoses, in which humans turn into flowers, trees, and animals.

1. What kinds of metamorphoses occur in the world of nature?
2. In what other words is the prefix *meta-* used?

For answers, see Teacher's Manual page 92.

Reading About the Writer

Beatriz Badikian (1951–) was born of Greek parents in Buenos Aires, Argentina. In 1970, she moved to the United States and she now lives in Chicago. Her collection of poetry *Akewa is a Woman* was published in 1983 and her works have appeared in *The Third Woman, Imagine,* and other literary journals. She currently writes a regular column called "Straight Lines and Circles" for the newsletter of The Feminist Writer's Guild.

Comment About the Writer

You can tell students that "Sandra" in the ninth stanza of the poem is writer Sandra Cisneros (see page 216 of the text book), with whom Badikian has been good friends for many years. Badikian says that the lines refer to a comment Cisneros once made about her. She said she was convinced that Badikian had been a seagull in another life since her voice was so sweet and high, "like seagulls' cries as they break over the waves."

Humanities Connection: Responding to the Fine Art

Robert Henri (1865–1929) was an influential American portrait painter and art teacher. He became a leader of a group of painters that specialized in painting realistic scenes of everyday life. Henri's work has a dark sparkling quality.

? Does this picture fit your image of the poet? Why or why not?

Supplementary Support Material
1. Reading Check Test blackline master
2. Introduction/Images: Appealing to Our Senses Test (page 107 of Test Book)

A. Discussing the Quotation
The American poet John Ciardi suggests that visual images are fundamental not only to poetry but to the very way we think. To help them understand the quotation better, have one student describe in class something that happened to him or her last week. While the student is speaking, have the other students jot down all the visual images the speaker uses. Tell students that poets often do much the same thing the speaker just did—they record their experiences by using pictures, or images.

B. Responding
 Which images in the previous poems worked that way for you?

C. Responding to the Photograph
Like poetry, pictures can also evoke strong feelings. Describe in words the images you see in this photograph. How do they make you feel? Happy? Lonely? Cozy? Curious?

296

★ **Texas Essential Elements/(a) English Language Arts: 3B** Figurative language

For teaching suggestions on this section, see Teacher's Manual page 92. A

SRW p. 49

Images: Appealing to Our Senses B

SRW p. 51

Thoughts are made of pictures.

—John Ciardi

To help you share their experiences of the world, poets will create images. Most **images** are words that help us see pictures, but images can also appeal to our senses of hearing, taste, smell, and touch. Poets hope that their images will unlock our storehouse of memories and stir our imaginations. They hope their images will make us say, "Oh yes, I see what you mean."

C

READING CHECK TEST

1. Images only appeal to the sense of sight. (*False*)
2. Most of the images poets create are visual. (*True*)
3. Poets also create images that appeal to our sense of hearing. (*True*)
4. Poets even occasionally create images that appeal to our senses of taste, smell, and touch. (*True*)
5. Images do not help the poet convey feelings. (*False*)

Word Pictures and More

SRW p. 51

Most of the images poets create are visual. That is, they help you picture people, places, and things in your "mind's eye." In "The Highwayman," for example, the poet creates a vivid word picture of his main character:

A

He'd a French cocked hat on his forehead, a bunch of lace
 at his chin,
A coat of the claret velvet, and breeches of brown doeskin;
They fitted with never a wrinkle: his boots were up to the
 thigh!
And he rode with a jeweled twinkle,
 His pistol butts a-twinkle,
His rapier hilt a-twinkle, under the jeweled sky.

—from "The Highwayman,"
Alfred Noyes

Poets also create images that appeal to our sense of hearing. In the following lines, for example, you can not only see the highwayman enter the innyard, but you can also hear his horse's hoofbeats, the tap of his whip, and his whistle:

B

Over the cobbles he clattered and clashed in the dark
 innyard
And he tapped with his whip on the shutters, but all was
 locked and barred;
He whistled a tune to the window, and who should be
 waiting there . . .

—from "The Highwayman,"
Alfred Noyes

Poets even occasionally create images that appeal to our senses of taste, smell, and touch. In the next lines, the poet creates images that help you imagine the heat of the highwayman's flushed face and the smell of Bess's perfumed hair:

. . . His face burned like a brand
As the black cascade of perfume came tumbling over his
 breast;
And he kissed its waves in the moonlight.

—from "The Highwayman,"
Alfred Noyes

Images and Feelings

Images help the poet convey feelings. Noyes's highwayman is an outlaw, but the way he is described makes us feel that he is a dashing, romantic character, and we suspect Noyes thinks so too.

A. Responding

? On the chalkboard, list with the class all the visual images Noyes uses in this stanza. What additional colors do you see—colors omitted by the poet? How about his eyes, his hair? How would it change your perception of the highwayman if, say, his velvet jacket were shocking pink instead of claret?

B. Responding

? List all the sounds you hear in this stanza. Then list at least three sounds you hear which the poet omits.

SUPPLEMENTARY SUPPORT MATERIAL

1. Selection Test (page 109 of Test Book)
2. Audiocassette recording
3. Reader's Response Journal
4. Workbook (page 81)
5. Instructional Overhead Transparency

PREREADING

ESTABLISHING A PURPOSE. Have students read question 4 on this page before they read the poem. The search for visual imagery can help establish a purpose to their reading.

A. Responding
? Do you think the poet will really take this journey? Why or why not?

B. Imagery
Some of these images picture Daisy; some picture the Pacific Northwest. ? Give two examples of each. (Daisy: "velvet mouth," "big brown horsy eye"; Pacific Northwest: "windbreak of pines," "a leaning rock") This will help students answer questions 4 and 5.

CLOSURE
Working with a partner, one student should list the senses that images can appeal to. The other student should think of an example of an image for each sense. (You might offer them examples of subjects they could use, such as pets, thunderstorms, empty houses.) Let them share their work in class.

★ **Texas Essential Elements/(a) English Language Arts: 3B** Figurative language. **(c) Reading: 3I** Draw conclusions

The following poem uses language that appeals to your senses. Notice how the poet helps you to share his dream of a cross-country horseback ride into a snowy wilderness.

Daisy

For a detailed lesson plan on this poem, see Teacher's Manual page 93.
A biography of Edward Field appears on text page 299.

Edward Field

Daisy is my horse's name.
She's small for a horse and piebald°
like those the Indians ride bareback in the movies.

A
We'll set out overland, she and I,
for the great Pacific Northwest,
a wild land of lakes and forests to wander in.

Come blizzard in the high meadows,
I'll get off and lead her,
our heads low in the driving snow, looking for shelter,

a windbreak of pines or maybe a leaning rock.
And as Daisy dozes steamily overhead,
I'll sleep, rolled up in a blanket at her feet

B
until a velvet mouth wakes me
to a big brown horsey eye
and a clear morning in the snowfields.

2. **piebald** (pī′bôld′): covered with patches or spots of two colors.

Responding to the Poem

Analyzing the Poem

Identifying Details

1. Describe Daisy's appearance.
2. Where does the speaker hope to travel with Daisy? What does he imagine this new landscape will be like?
3. List the things the speaker imagines he and Daisy will do to cope with heavy snows.
4. **Imagery** is language that appeals to the senses (sight, hearing, touch, taste, smell). A **visual image** helps you to see a picture in your mind. List five images in "Daisy" that help you see the weather and landscape of the journey.
SRW p. 51
5. There are three images in the last stanza of the poem. Identify the two images that refer to the horse. Which sense does each one appeal to.

Interpreting Meanings

6. Daisy does not sound like a large, powerful horse. Why do you think the speaker feels she is the right kind of horse to take on the journey?
7. Most people today live in cities. They try to be as comfortable as they can, and they travel as swiftly as possible. Why do you think the speaker wants to go on this slow journey? What might he be trying to leave behind? What might he be hoping to find?

Analyzing the Poem

Identifying Details

1. She is a small, piebald horse with brown eyes and a "velvet mouth."
2. He wants to go to the Pacific Northwest, with its lakes, forests, and high meadows.
3. He will lead her, looking for a windbreak in the pines or under a leaning rock.
4. See note B page 298.
5. "A velvet mouth" appeals to touch; "a big brown horsy eye" appeals to sight.

Interpreting Meanings

6. She seems friendly, companionable, and experienced.
7. Among the possibilities: He wants to enjoy nature, to explore a new territory, to test his own endurance, to have fun with his horse, to relax, to experience a journey that offers adventure and harmony with the natural world.

Evaluating the Poem

8. The poem is written in free verse. Student preferences will vary.

Evaluating the Poem

8. Is this poem written in **meter** or in **free verse**? Do you like the poem as much as some of the other poems you have read? Explain why or why not. SRW p. 45

Writing About the Poem

A Creative Response

1. **Describing an Imaginary Journey.** If you could take a trip anywhere, by horse, car, plane, or any other means, where would you go? What would your journey be like? Write a **free verse** poem (a poem without regular patterns of rhyme or rhythm) about this imaginary trip. Try to use vivid imagery, or language appealing to the five senses, so your reader can share the experience.

A Critical Response

2. **Analyzing a Title.** In a paragraph, explain whether you think "Daisy" is the best title for this poem. What would you think of a title such as "A Journey"? Discuss the reasons for your opinion.

See Teacher's Manual page 93.

Reading About the Writer

Like many poets, **Edward Field** (1924–   ) held several jobs before he turned his full attention to writing. To support himself, he was a warehouse worker, a machinist, a clerk, and an actor. Besides writing poetry, he has also translated foreign works, and written several narrations for documentary movies. Field currently lives in New York City. His books of poetry include *Stand Up, Friend, with Me* and *Variety Photoplays,* from which the poem "Daisy" was taken.

Comment from the Writer

When asked why Field wrote his poem "Daisy," he responded: "The books we read as children can fix in our hearts symbols and dreams we carry the rest of our lives. I devoured all the western novels on the library shelves, especially Max Brand [see text page 220] and Zane Grey, where I learned to love the relationship of a man and his horse—and even now sometimes dream a horse is my friend."

Further Reading for Students

Other horse poems that students might enjoy are Vachel Lindsay's "The Bronco That Would Not Be Broken," Robert Frost's "The Runaway" (included in *Elements of Literature: Second Course*), and James Wright's "A Blessing."

Supplementary Support Material

1. Selection Test (page 109 of Test Book)
2. Reader's Response Journal
3. Workbook (page 83)

Prereading

Establishing a Purpose. Ask students what they first picture when they think of a shepherd's hut. Tell them to watch for details that differ from their own pictures as they read the poem.

Closure

Have students work in pairs and list at least five images describing the picture on page 195, 210, 264, or 274. Reword them to use images of sight, sound, taste, smell, and touch (including temperature).

A. Responding

? How might smoke stagger?

B. Rhyme Scheme

? What is the rhyme scheme of this poem? (The closest rhyme scheme is *aabb;* however, note that lines 5 and 6 do not rhyme exactly.)

C. Personification

This is a good poem to use to introduce students to personification (discussed in depth on text page 310). Tell them that personification is when a nonhuman thing or quality is talked about as if it were human or alive. Ask them which objects in the poem are made to seem human or alive. (The smoke staggers, the clothes become inhabited by ghosts and take on active "life.")

D. Responding to the Photograph

? Name one important image from the poem that is present in this picture of an Irish peasant's cottage, and one that is absent. (Smoke is present; flapping clothes are absent.)

★ **Texas Essential Elements/(a) English Language Arts: 1B** Purpose and audience; **1F** Specific words; **2B** Parts of speech; **3B** Figurative language. **(c) Reading: 3I** Draw conclusions

This poem shows how a poet's imagination can turn an everyday sight into a magical picture.

Watch for striking visual images at the beginning and end of the poem.

The Shepherd's Hut

For a detailed lesson plan on this poem, see Teacher's Manual page 94. A biography of Andrew Young appears on text page 301.

Andrew Young

A The smear of blue peat° smoke
That staggered on the wind and broke,
The only sign of life,
Where was the shepherd's wife,
Who left those flapping clothes to dry,
Taking no thought for her family?
For, as they bellied out
And limbs took shape and waved about,
I thought, She little knows
That ghosts are trying on her children's clothes.

B,C

1. **peat:** decayed plant matter from a bog, used as a fuel in places like Scotland and Ireland.

D

ANALYZING THE POEM

Identifying Details

1. The peat smoke.
2. The shepherd's wife.
She has left the clothes on the line to dry.
3. The clothes are billowing out.
He imagines that ghosts are trying them on.
4. Color: *blue;* shape: *smear, staggered.*
5. Sketches will vary.

Interpreting Meanings

6. He is pleased and warmed; it probably makes him smile. (However, students might see something ominous in the picture of ghosts trying on children's clothes—there is a sense that the place has been abandoned or is haunted.)

Responses will vary. Perhaps he comes upon the scene from over a hill or around a curve in the road. Maybe he is a traveler.

Responding to the Poem

Analyzing the Poem

Identifying Details

1. What does the speaker say is the only sign of life around the hut?
2. The speaker wonders where one particular person is. Who is this person? What has this person done?
3. In lines 7 and 8, what is happening to the family clothes? What does the speaker imagine is the reason for this?
4. The first two lines of the poem form an **image** of the smoke rising from the hut's chimney. Which words in these lines let you see the color and shape of the smoke?
5. This poem probably created a clear picture in your mind even though very little of the scene is described. Can you transfer the picture in your mind to paper? Sketch the scene in the poem as you see it. If possible, use colors in the picture.

Interpreting Meanings

6. How do you think the poet feels about this scene? Where do you imagine the speaker is, and what might he have been doing before he saw the hut?

Writing About the Poem

A Creative Response

1. **Explaining an Occurrence.** This poet takes a common sight—clothes waving as they dry on a line—and creates an imaginative explanation for it. Write a poem or short essay in which you invent a new, imaginative explanation for one of the following occurrences:

   a. A tea kettle whistling
   b. Birds sitting on telephone wires
   c. Moths being attracted to light
   d. A clock ticking
   e. Stars twinkling

See Teacher's Manual page 95.

Analyzing Language and Vocabulary

Vivid Nouns and Verbs

SRW p. 51

"The Shepherd's Hut" uses precise, striking nouns and verbs to create vivid visual images. What if some of the key words were different? For example, imagine that the poem's first line read, "The *column* of blue peat smoke" instead of "The *smear* of blue peat smoke." How is the image altered by changing one word? How would the image be different again if the poet had written, "The *cloud* of blue peat smoke"?

Replace the following words in the poem with other words that have similar meanings. Explain how the images in the poem are changed when the words are changed.

1. smear (line 1)
2. staggered (line 2)
3. broke (line 2)
4. flapping (line 5)
5. bellied (line 7)
6. limbs (line 8)
7. waved (line 8)

For answers, see Teacher's Manual page 95.

Reading About the Writer

A clergyman, a botanist, and a poet, **Andrew Young** (1885–1971) was born in Elgin, Scotland. He attended theological school in Edinburgh, and in 1920 he became a Presbyterian minister. He later became a vicar of the Anglican church. Many of Young's poems are about nature, although he also wrote religious poems about a vision of life after death, which are collected in a volume called *Out of the World and Back.*

Supplementary Support Material
1. Selection Test (page 109 of the Test Book)
2. Reader's Response Journal
3. Workbook (page 85)

Prereading

1. **Establishing a Purpose.** Have students read writing exercise 2 on text page 303 before they read the poem. Then, have them read the poem's first four lines, and ask them what they think the tone of this poem will be. As they read, do they find their predictions are correct?

2. **Prereading Journal.** Before students read the poem, ask them to write a short list of things *they* would like to talk to a giraffe about if they were given the chance.

A. Imagery
? What images does Livingstone use to portray the giraffe's height? (He calls the giraffe "lofty." The trees, which he's gazing through, are compared to ships's masts. He'd like to "toboggan down" its neck, and "swing on" its tail.)

B. Imagery
? What do you have to know about giraffes to understand this image? (When they bend down to drink, their long spindly legs span out and the animal does look like a collapsible toy—like one of those toys that has a button you push from underneath and the whole thing collapses.)

C. Responding
? Why do you think the speaker feels ugly here?

Closure
Have students describe the tone of the poem, now that they have finished reading it. Have them pick out the details that make the poem funny. This can be an oral or written exercise.

 **Texas Essential Elements/(a) English Language Arts: 1B** Purpose and audience; **3B** Figurative language

Have you ever wondered what an animal is thinking as you stare at it in a zoo? The speaker of this poem worries about what a giraffe is thinking as he observes him.

Conversation with a Giraffe at Dusk in the Zoo

Douglas Livingstone

Hail, lofty,
necking quizzically
through the topgallant° leaves
with your lady.

A

No good making eyelashes at
the distance from me to you
though I confess I should like
to caress your tender horns
and toboggan down your neck,
perhaps swing on your tail.

Your dignity fools no one,
you get engagingly awkward
B
when you separate and collapse
yourself to drink;
and have you seen
yourself cantering?

Alright, alright, I know
C
I'm ugly standing still,
squat-necked, so high.

Just remember there's one or two
things about you too, hey,
like, like, birds now;
they fly much higher.

3. **topgallant:** nautical term used to describe a high rail or mast.

For a detailed lesson plan on this poem, see Teacher's Manual pages 95–96.
A biography of Douglas Livingstone appears on text page 303.

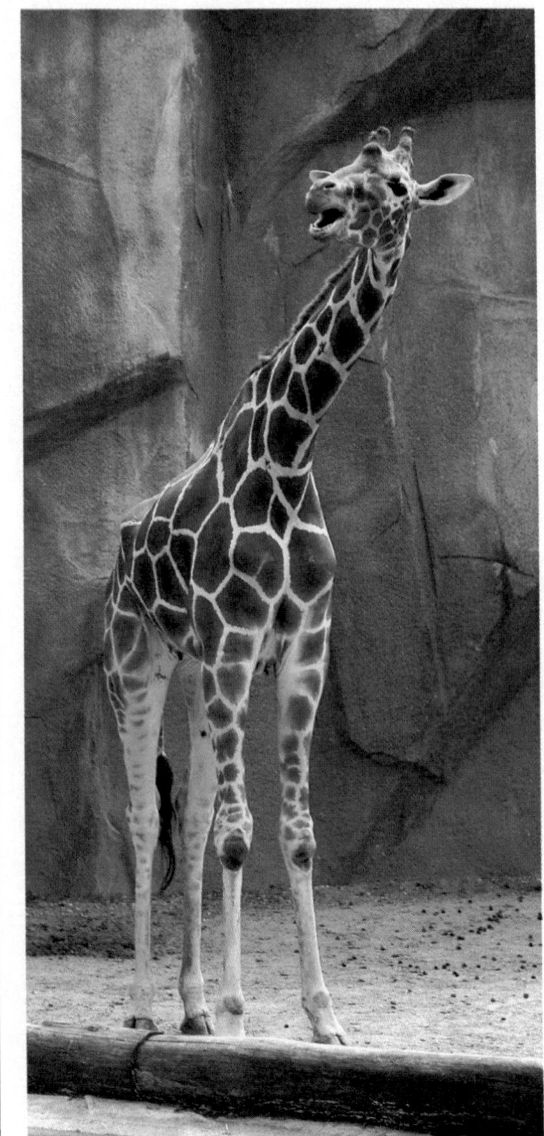

ANALYZING THE POEM

Identifying Details

1. They are at the zoo. It is dusk.

2. He would like to stroke the giraffe's horns, slide down its neck, and swing on its tail.

3. He imagines he looks ugly, "squat-necked," and short.

4. The surface message is that birds fly higher than the giraffe can reach, but in effect the speaker is enviously trying to "cut down" the "lofty" giraffe.

Interpreting Meanings

5. See notes A and B on page 302.

6. "I should like to caress your horns." This image of "tender" horns suggests that the giraffe is not at all threatening.

7. Stateliness: proper pride and self-respect; a bearing that seems to deserve honor.

When the giraffe drinks or runs, it is awkward.

Applying Meanings

8. Encourage students to be specific in the responses, rather than relying on labels like *cute, funny,* or *wild.* If students have difficulty being specific, you might suggest library research.

Additional Writing Assignment

In a paragraph, have students describe how they probably look to their pets or, if they have none, to some other animal of their choice.

FURTHER READING FOR STUDENTS

E. B. White, *Stuart Little* (1945) and *Charlotte's Web* (1952). Two famous stories told from an animal's point of view.

Responding to the Poem

Analyzing the Poem

Identifying Details

1. According to the title, where are the speaker and the giraffe he is talking to? What time of day is it?
2. List the activities from the second stanza that the speaker would like to do.
3. In the fourth stanza, how does the speaker imagine he looks to the giraffe?
4. In the last stanza, what does the speaker tell the giraffe?

Interpreting Meanings

5. List three **visual images**—words that create pictures in your mind. Which do you think is the most striking? Why? SRW p. 51
6. Find an image appealing to your sense of touch. Is it important to the poem?
7. The speaker says the giraffe's "dignity fools no one." What is *dignity?* In your own words, explain what the giraffe does that isn't dignified.

Applying Meanings

8. Think of an unusual animal you have seen in nature, in a zoo, or on television. Describe this animal and explain what made it interesting to you. If the animal could speak, what questions would you ask it?

Writing About the Poem

A Creative Response

1. **Writing from Another Point of View.** The poem presents the speaker's feelings about the giraffe. Turn the tables, and have the giraffe give its opinion about a human being. Remember that the giraffe probably thinks its shape is best, and that people have weird shapes. Write a poem or a paragraph including specific points the giraffe makes about the human.

SRW p. 69

A Critical Response

2. **Analyzing Tone. Tone** is the attitude, or feeling, a writer takes toward his or her subject. Write a paragraph in which you discuss how you think the poet feels about giraffes. Do you think the animal arouses more than one emotion in the speaker? If so, explain what you think these mixed feelings are. Support your opinion with evidence from the poem.

See Teacher's Manual page 96.

Reading About the Writer

Douglas Livingstone (1932–) was born of Scottish parents in Kuala Lumpur, Malaya. Although he currently resides in South Africa, he has also lived in Australia, Sri Lanka, Zimbabwe, Scotland, and Zambia. According to Livingstone himself, "I have been to more schools than I care to remember, in several continents. . ." Livingstone is a bacteriologist who does research on sea microorganisms. (He also used to be a professional scuba diver.) Some of his works are *The Scull in the Mud,* and *Sjambok and Other Poems from Africa.* "Conversation with a Giraffe at Dusk in the Zoo" is from a book of poems called *Eyes Closed Against the Sun.*

A. Humanities Connection: Responding to the Fine Art
George Catlin (1796–1872) was a self-taught American artist who specialized in paintings and sketches of American Plains Indians. He gained real-life experience from traveling with different Indian tribes for six years.

? What feelings does this painting evoke? What kind of mood does it set for the poem? Do you see scenes like this in America today?

B. Alliteration
Have students watch for the alliteration used in the poem.

? What alliteration is there in the title?

C. Responding to Imagery

? How would this line feel different if the poet had said "screech" instead of "sing"?

D. Responding to Imagery

? What do the words *gore* and *bellow* mean? What images would you associate with these words—pleasant or unpleasant ones? When you read them in the context of this poem, do they make you feel differently?

CLOSURE
Ask students to describe two contrasting sights they see when they read this poem.

SUPPLEMENTARY SUPPORT MATERIAL

1. Selection Test (page 111 of Test Book)
2. Audiocassette recording
3. Reader's Response Journal
4. Workbook (page 87)

PREREADING

ESTABLISHING A PURPOSE. Use the headnote as a purpose-setting exercise.

Elk and Buffalo Grazing Among the Prairie Flowers by George Catlin (1830–1840). Oil.

The buffalo, or American bison, once roamed the prairies of the United States in large numbers. But reckless hunting nearly made the animals extinct. At the time when this poem was written, in the early twentieth century, the buffalo was a seriously endangered species. The number of buffalo has increased somewhat since then. Before reading the poem, think about its title. What do you imagine it means?

For a detailed lesson plan on this poem, see Teacher's Manual page 97.
A biography of Vachel Lindsay appears on text page 305.

The Flower-Fed Buffaloes

Vachel Lindsay

The flower-fed buffaloes of the spring
In the days of long ago,
Ranged where the locomotives sing
And the prairie flowers lie low;
The tossing, blooming, perfumed grass
Is swept away by wheat,
Wheels and wheels and wheels spin by
In the spring that still is sweet.
But the flower-fed buffaloes of the spring
Left us long ago.
They gore no more, they bellow no more,
They trundle around the hills no more:
With the Blackfeet° lying low,
With the Pawnees° lying low.

13. **Blackfeet:** Indians of the West and Canada; also called Blackfoot.
14. **Pawnees:** Indians of the Midwest.

ANALYZING THE STORY
Identifying Details

1. Trains and wheat farms. They lie low.
2. They have been replaced by wheat. (The land has been cultivated.)

Interpreting Meanings

3. They too ranged the prairie, hunting the buffalo.
It could mean lying close to the earth, low growing; hiding to avoid detection; or being dead and buried.
4. Yes, the poem is also about the Blackfeet and Pawnee, for their survival depended on the buffalo herds. Thus, when the flowers were destroyed, the buffalo were also destroyed. And when the buffalo were destroyed, so were the Indian civilizations.
5. "Locomotives sing" (sound); "prairie flowers lie low" (sight); "Wheels and wheels and wheels spin by" (sight and sound); "spring that still is sweet" (smell); "they bellow no more" (sound).

Applying Meanings

6. You could use this project for work in interviewing techniques and oral history.
You might want to explore with students both the good and the bad that change generates.

FURTHER READING FOR STUDENTS

You might suggest some readings by and about Native Americans: Margot Astrov, *American Indian Prose and Poetry* (1962). George Grinnell, *Blackfoot Lodge Tales: The Story of a Prairie People* (1962). ———, *Pawnee Hero Stories and Folk Tales* (1961). N. Scott Momaday, *The Names* (1976).

Texas Essential Elements/(a) English Language Arts: 1B Purpose and audience; **3B** Figurative language. **(c) Reading: 2A** Word meaning

Responding to the Poem

Analyzing the Poem

Identifying Details

1. In the early nineteenth century buffalo ranged the prairie and ate spring flowers. According to the poem, what dominates the prairie now? What do the flowers do now?
2. Discuss what has become of the prairie grasses.

Interpreting Meanings

3. What did the Indians once do? Do you think "lying low" can have more than one meaning?
4. Is the poem about the Blackfeet and Pawnee, as well as the buffalo? Explain.
5. "The Flower-Fed Buffaloes" contains **images** that appeal to your senses. For instance, the line "The tossing, blooming, perfumed grass" appeals to the senses of smell and sight. List other images in the poem that help you see, hear, and smell the scene. SRW p. 51

Applying Meanings

6. This poem is about change in the prairie region of the United States. What changes have occurred in your own community over the past ten or so years? (You may want to talk to some adults.) What has disappeared? What has been built? How do you feel about the changes?

Writing About the Poem

A Creative Response

1. **Imitating the Writer's Technique.** Write a paragraph or two that presents a picture of a place that is changing and will soon disappear. You might write about a beach, a field, or a prairie that is about to become a housing development or shopping mall. Use images to help your readers visualize the place as it is now.

A Critical Response

2. **Analyzing Tone.** Vachel Lindsay's poem presents a picture of the changed world of the American West. How would you describe the speaker's **tone,** or attitude toward this subject? In a paragraph, discuss how you think the speaker feels about the changes that have occurred on the prairie. Quote passages from the poem to support your analysis of the speaker's feelings.

See Teacher's Manual page 98.

Analyzing Language and Vocabulary

Native American Names

A great many rivers, mountains, and other landmarks in the United States were given English versions of Indian names, from the Appalachian Mountains in the East to the Willamette River in the West. Use a good dictionary to answer these questions.

1. Which of our fifty states have names from the Native American languages?
2. Is there an American city named for the buffalo?
3. Sometimes English speakers did not always know the meanings of the names the Indians provided. What is the real meaning of the name *Chicago*? What Native American language is it from?
4. The Native American tribal groups themselves had names that had distinctive meanings. What do the names Tlingit, Pawnee, and Navaho mean?

For answers, see Teacher's Manual page 98.

Reading About the Writer

Vachel Lindsay (1879–1931) was from Springfield, Illinois, and he became a self-appointed booster of the old values of middle America. Lindsay made long walking tours around the country, arriving in towns and villages like a revivalist preacher, seeking any audience who would listen to his poems in exchange for food and lodging. Many of his poems were on popular American subjects—Abraham Lincoln, pioneering, the Salvation Army. Lindsay won a wide following among people who had never before paid any attention to poetry. Some of his most popular poems are "Abraham Lincoln Walks at Midnight," "The Ghosts of the Buffaloes," and "In Praise of Johnny Appleseed."

Supplementary Support Material

1. Selection Test (page 111 of Test Book)
2. Audiocassette recording
3. Author photograph on *A Gallery of Authors* poster
4. Reader's Response Journal
5. Workbook (page 89)

Prereading

Establishing a Purpose. Before students read the poem, have them read the language and vocabulary exercise on text page 308. This discussion of free verse will help establish a purpose to their reading.

Closure

Discuss with students the three words they used to describe bats, as instructed in the headnote. Would they revise their lists now? Why?

A. Imagery

? How many images of motion can you find in these two lines? (Dances, doubling, looping, soaring, somersaulting)

B. Responding

? Why might Jarrell think that the bats are happy?

C. Alliteration

? Find the alliteration here. (*H*appiness, *h*unts, *h*er, *h*igh; *n*ight, i*n*, hu*n*ts, a*n*d, shi*n*ing, *N*eedlepoi*n*ts, sou*n*d; a*ll*, f*l*ies, *l*ike, need*l*epoints; *sh*e, *sh*arp, *sh*ining)

D. Imagery

Note the use of a visual image for a sound.

E. Personification

A detailed discussion of personification appears on page 310, but you can use this poem to introduce the concept to the students. Ask them to go through the poem and find details that portray the mother bat and young bat as if they were a human mother and child.

★ **Texas Essential Elements/(a) English Language Arts: 1B** Purpose and audience; **2C** Oral language; **3B** Figurative language. **(c) Reading: 4E** Rate of reading

This poem uses imagery to give a fresh, unexpected view of bats. Before reading the poem, think of three words that come to mind when you think of these animals. After you finish the poem, decide whether you still make the same associations with bats.

Bats

For a detailed lesson plan on this poem, see Teacher's Manual pages 98–99. A biography of Randall Jarrell appears on text page 308.

Randall Jarrell

A bat is born
Naked and blind and pale.
His mother makes a pocket of her tail
And catches him. He clings to her long fur
By his thumbs and toes and teeth.
A And then the mother dances through the night
Doubling and looping, soaring, somersaulting—
Her baby hangs on underneath.
B All night, in happiness, she hunts and flies.
Her high sharp cries C
D Like shining needlepoints of sound
Go out in the night and, echoing back,
Tell her what they have touched.
She hears how far it is, how big it is,
Which way it's going:
She lives by hearing.
The mother eats the moths and gnats she catches
In full flight; in full flight
The mother drinks the water of the pond
She skims across. Her baby hangs on tight.
Her baby drinks the milk she makes him
In moonlight or starlight, in mid-air.
Their single shadow, printed on the moon
Or fluttering across the stars,
Whirls on all night; at daybreak
The tired mother flaps home to her rafter.
The others all are there.
They hang themselves up by their toes,
They wrap themselves in their brown wings.
Bunched upside-down, they sleep in air.
Their sharp ears, their sharp teeth, their quick sharp faces
Are dull and slow and mild.
E All the bright day, as the mother sleeps,
She folds her wings about her sleeping child.

ANALYZING THE POEM

Identifying Details

1. It is naked, blind, and pale.
2. He uses thumbs, toes, and teeth to cling to her fur.
3. He says they are high and sharp, "like shining needlepoints of sound."
4. She eats moths and gnats, and drinks pond water.
   It nurses in mid-air.
5. She flies all night.
   She goes to her rafter.
6. They were sharp; now they become dull, slow, and mild.
   It is wrapped in its mother's wings.
7. Many examples are possible.

Interpreting Meanings

8. Lines 10-16 give an accurate, though poetic, description.

Applying Meanings

9. Discuss with students the words and images that make the bat appealing. (See Closure.)

A. Responding to the Photograph
Use the picture to help students understand how the bats can fold up their wings to wrap themselves as they sleep. (See lines 29–30.)
? Do these bats look like any bats, or pictures of bats, that you have seen? How does this photograph make you feel?

A

Responding to the Poem

Analyzing the Poem

Identifying Details

1. What does the newborn bat look like?
2. Where does the young bat stay when his mother hunts at night? How does he manage to stay there?
3. How does the poet describe the cries of the bat?
4. List the things the mother eats and drinks. How is the baby nourished?
5. How long does the mother fly? Where does she go when her hunt is over?
6. How do the bats' faces change in sleep? How is the young bat protected while it sleeps?
7. "Bats" is rich in **imagery,** or language that appeals to the senses. Read through the poem and list all the images you can find that appeal to your senses of sight, hearing, taste, and touch.

SRW p. 51

Interpreting Meanings

8. Look in an encyclopedia or other reference work to learn how a bat uses echo-location to guide its flight. Does the poem accurately describe how bats navigate? Explain.

FURTHER READING FOR STUDENTS
Theodore Roethke's poem "The Bat" provides a different point of view. It's included in *Elements of Literature: Third Course.*
Josephine Johnson, "Tenants of the House." A gripping story about a couple who battles an invasion of bats into their attic.

A. Using Focusing on Background
You could use this comment as an occasion to ask students to evaluate the poems they have read so far in this unit.

? Which poems did you think were the "good" ones? Do you agree with Jarrell that a good poem is rare?

Applying Meanings

9. Many people hate and fear bats. This poem, however, offers a different opinion. Did the poem change the way you view bats? Explain the reasons for your reaction.

Writing About the Poem

A Creative Response

1. **Writing a Description.** In "Bats," Randall Jarrell presents a sympathetic portrait of an animal that usually gets little sympathy from humans. Perhaps you admire or appreciate something that most people don't care for. This could be a tattered shirt, a broken toy, or a pet snake. Write a one-paragraph description of this item. Include details that will help your audience see the item as you see it. SRW p. 29

A Critical Response

2. **Analyzing a Poem.** In a paragraph, tell how the poet makes the bat mother and child seem like humans. What does the mother do to take care of her child? How does she feel about him? How does she feel during her hunts? Quote passages from the poem to support your analysis.

See Teacher's Manual page 99.

Analyzing Language and Vocabulary

Reading Aloud

SRW p. 45

Poems written in **free verse** do not rely on a regular pattern of stressed and unstressed syllables for their rhythm. Instead, they use the natural rhythms of ordinary speech.

In reading a free-verse poem aloud, you should speak naturally and let the poet's use of normal speech rhythms come through. Pause slightly at the ends of lines without end punctuation, and longer at the ends of lines with commas. Pause even longer at the ends of sentences or at dashes.

In free verse, if a line is very short, the poet often wants it to receive special emphasis because it is important. Longer lines should be read in one breath, if possible.

Make sure the meaning of the poem is clear to you. Thinking about the meaning of each line, and the emotions it arouses in you, will help you give the poem expression.

First read "Bats" silently to yourself. Think about how it makes you feel. Then read the poem aloud two or three times. Can you make it sound like natural speech, and yet like poetry?

Reading About the Writer

Randall Jarrell (1914–1965) believed passionately in the value of poetry. As a critic, Jarrell could be quite harsh, sometimes overly so, in his reviews. But his supporters have said that Jarrell despised bad poetry because he loved literature. Many of his own poems were influenced by his experiences in World War II. He also wrote about childhood, and about the children's world of fairy tales and animals. His principal books include *Little Friend, Little Friend* and *Losses.* "Bats" is taken from another book called *The Lost World.*

A Focusing on Background

Writing Poetry

"How hard it is to write a good poem! How few good poems there are! What strange things you and I are, if we are. When we are! To have written one good poem—*good* used seriously—is an unlikely and marvelous thing that only a couple of hundred writers of English, at the most, have done—it's like sitting out in the yard in the evening and having a meteorite fall in one's lap . . ."

—Randall Jarrell

Supplementary Support Material
1. Reading Check Test blackline master
2. Introduction/Figures of Speech: Making Connections Test (page 113 of Test Book)

 **Texas Essential Elements/(a) English Language Arts: 3B** Figurative language

What can be explained is not poetry.
—Jack Yeats

A For teaching suggestions on this section, see Teacher's Manual page 100.

Figures of Speech: Making Connections

SRW p. 49

In our everyday language, we use many expressions that are not literally true: "Charlie's bragging gets under my skin." "Gilda's money is burning a hole in her pocket." When we use expressions like these, we do not mean them literally; we are speaking **figuratively.** That is, our listeners know the words do not carry their ordinary meaning. Bragging, after all, does not really pierce skin, and money cannot cause a pocket to catch fire.

The meaning of such figurative expressions depends on comparisons. Bragging is *compared* to something that causes pain or annoyance, such as a thorn. Money is *compared* to something so hot that it cannot be held and must be gotten rid of. Expressions like these that are not literally true are called **figures of speech.** Because they can express so much meaning in interesting and surprising ways, figures of speech are an important element in poetry. B

There are many kinds of figures of speech; some people say there are about 300 different types. But the most common are similes, metaphors, and personification.

Similes: Using "Like" or "As"

SRW p. 81

A **simile** is a comparison of two unlike things using the words *like, as, than,* or *resembles.* In "The Tale of Custard the Dragon" (page 289), for example, the poet uses a simile when he tells us that Custard has a "mouth like a fireplace."

Here are three famous similes:

I wandered lonely as a cloud (William Wordsworth)
My love is like a red, red rose (Robert Burns)
There is no frigate like a book (Emily Dickinson) C

Metaphors: Identifying Two Different Things

SRW p. 61

Like a simile, a **metaphor** also makes a comparison between two unlike things, but a metaphor makes the comparison without using *like, as, than,* or *resembles.* For example, in "The Highwayman," Alfred Noyes does not use a simile and say the moon was *like* a ghostly galleon. He uses a metaphor and says "The moon *was* a ghostly galleon tossed upon cloudy seas." Try this experiment: The next time you see the full moon among the clouds, think of Noyes's metaphor. See if it helps you think of the night sky as a vast ocean, with the clouds as whitecaps and the moon sailing steadily through the turbulence. If you see the moon in this new way, you have discovered the power of metaphors.

A. Discussing the Quotation
Discuss with students the meaning of Yeats's quotation and help them to understand his implication. The essence and beauty of poetry stems in part from two things: its ability to defy one pat explanation and its ability to speak in different ways to different people. If poetry loses this ability, then it loses its essence and is no longer poetry. It is prose.
? Suggest other art forms to which this quotation might apply. (Paintings, sculpture, music, dance) What do all these things have in common? (They are all imaginative attempts to create something new and to explain the world in human terms.)

B. Expanding
You might want to discuss and give examples showing the difference between imaginative figures of speech, such as those used in poetry, and a cliché.

C. Responding
? Suggest other similes to express loneliness, love, and the pleasures of reading.

Reading Check Test

1. A figure of speech is literally true. *(False)*
2. The meaning of a figurative expression depends on the comparison it makes. *(True)*
3. A simile uses the words *like, as, than,* or *resembles* to compare two unlike things. *(True)*
4. A metaphor also uses *like, as, than,* or *resembles* to compare two unlike things. *(False)*
5. Personification gives nonhuman qualities to human beings. *(False)*

A. Responding

? Suggest other metaphors for the sun and for hope.

B. Responding

? How would you personify the house in which you live, a neighbor's pet, and the sky?

C. Responding to the Photograph

? What similes and metaphors would you use to convey your feelings about the flowers in the photograph?

Here are two other famous metaphors:

The glorious lamp of heaven, the sun (Robert Herrick)
Hope is the thing with feathers (Emily Dickinson)

A

Personification: Making the World Human

SRW p. 65

Personification is giving human qualities to nonhuman things. For instance, when Robert Service writes in "The Cremation of Sam McGee" that "the heavens scowled," he is personifying the heavens. The heavens, or skies, do not scowl, or frown and look angry; only people scowl. By making us think about things as if they were human, poets help us see the whole world as human.

B

Here is a famous example of personification. This poet is describing a meadow full of daffodils. He personifies the daffodils by describing them as dancing; only people dance.

Ten thousand saw I at a glance,
Tossing their heads in sprightly dance.

—from "Daffodils,"
William Wordsworth

C

Here is Wordsworth's complete poem, which often goes under the title "I Wandered Lonely as a Cloud":

I wandered lonely as a cloud
That floats on high o'er vales and hills,
When all at once I saw a crowd,
A host of golden daffodils,
Beside the lake, beneath the trees,
Fluttering and dancing in the breeze.

Continuous as the stars that shine
And twinkle on the milky way,
They stretched in never-ending line
Along the margin of a bay;
Ten thousand saw I at a glance,
Tossing their heads in sprightly dance.

The waves beside them danced, but they
Outdid the sparkling waves in glee;
A poet could not but be gay,
In such a jocund company;
I gazed—and gazed—but little thought
What wealth the show to me had brought:

For oft, when on my couch I lie
In vacant or in pensive mood,
They flash upon that inward eye
Which is the bliss of solitude;
And then my heart with pleasure fills,
And dances with the daffodils.

Supplementary Support Material

1. Selection Test (page 115 of Test Book)
2. Audiocassette recording
3. Reader's Response Journal
4. Workbook (page 91)

Prereading

Establishing a Purpose. The headnote sets a purpose for reading.

Closure

Working in pairs, students should define simile and metaphor. Then ask them to choose three other natural phenomena, such as fire, wind, and rain, and provide one simile and one metaphor for each.

Students might enjoy puzzling over these riddles:

Black within, and
red without,
Four corners round
about. (Chimney)

In Spring I look gay,
Decked in comely array,
In Summer more clothing I wear;
When colder it grows,
I fling off my clothes,
And in Winter quite naked appear.
(Tree)

Texas Essential Elements/(a) English Language Arts: 1B Purpose and audience.
(c) Reading: 3G Compare/contrast; **3I** Draw conclusions

A poem's speaker is not always a person. An animal, or even an object, may be the voice in a poem. A person is not the speaker of this poem. As you read it, try to identify the speaker.

Rhyming Riddle

For a detailed lesson plan on this poem, see Teacher's Manual page 100. A biography of Mary Austin appears on text page 311.

Mary Austin

A I come more softly than a bird,
And lovely as a flower;
I sometimes last from year to year
And sometimes but an hour.

I stop the swiftest railroad train
Or break the stoutest tree.
And yet I am afraid of fire
And children play with me.

The answer is snow.

A. Similes

? What kind of figure of speech is in these lines? (Similes) Identify the similes. ("More softly than a bird," "lovely as a flower") What makes these similes rather than metaphors? (They contain the words "than" and "as.")

Responding to the Poem

Analyzing the Poem

Identifying Details

1. How does the poem's speaker arrive? How long does the speaker last?
2. In the first two lines of the poem, the speaker is compared to gentle things. What are they? In lines 5 and 6, the speaker says it can do things that demand great strength. What are they?
3. What does this speaker fear?
4. What do children do with the speaker?

Interpreting Meanings

5. Have you figured out the answer to the riddle? Who or what is the speaker of the poem? How do all the clues in the poem work, once you identify the speaker?
6. "Rhyming Riddle" presents several **contrasts.** For instance, the speaker says it can last a long time or a very short time. Find two other contrasts in the poem and explain how they are true.

Applying Meanings

7. The riddle is an ancient form of puzzle, and remains very popular today. What riddles do you know? Why do you think people like riddles? Do you like them? Why or why not?

Writing About the Poem

A Creative Response

Writing a Riddle. In many riddles, an object speaks and presents clues to its identity. Pick an object and let it describe itself using the first-person pronoun *I*. Give clues to its identity that are helpful but not too easy. (After all, a riddle should be puzzling.) Exchange your riddles in class to see if your speaker can be identified.

See Teacher's Manual page 101.

Reading About the Writer

Mary Austin (1868–1934) was attracted to the Southwest and fascinated by the people who lived there. Her best writings are about the Native Americans of the Southwest and their folklore, although she also wrote about mysticism, religion, American politics, World War I, and world hunger. Austin was born in Illinois and migrated West with her mother and her brother by train in 1888. She later settled in Carmel, California, where she formed friendships with many writers, including Jack London.

Analyzing the Poem

Identifying Details

1. Softly. Sometimes "from year to year / And sometimes but an hour."
2. A bird and a flower.
   It can stop trains and topple trees.
3. Fire.
4. They play with the speaker.

Interpreting Meanings

5. Snow.
   Once they have solved the riddle, students will enjoy explaining each clue.
6. It is very strong and yet it fears fire and children play with it.

Applying Meanings

7. See Teacher's Manual page 101 for suggestions.

SUPPLEMENTARY SUPPORT MATERIAL

1. Selection Test (page 115 of Test Book)
2. Audiocassette recording
3. Reader's Response Journal
4. Workbook (page 93)

PREREADING

1. **ESTABLISHING A PURPOSE.** Before students begin reading the poem, talk about thunderstorms and how they sound and the effects they have on nature. The headnote of the poem will supply a purpose for their reading.

2. **PREREADING JOURNAL.** Ask the students to write three sentences describing their own picture of what "thunder" would look like. Tell them to use their imagination freely.

CLOSURE

Working with a partner, have students define onomatopoeia. Then ask them to choose three natural phenomena other than thunder and to suggest onomatopoetic words for them.

A. Expansion
Notice that, like many giants in folk literature, this one feeds on bones.

B. Personification
? What is personified in this line? (The moon) What is the moon doing? (Hiding in fear behind a cloud)

C. Responding
? What would you say to the bad-tempered Giant?

D. Responding to the Illustration
? What is happening in this picture? How would you draw a picture of thunder?

★ **Texas Essential Elements/(a) English Language Arts: 1B** Purpose and audience; **3B** Figurative language. **(c) Reading: 3G** Compare/contrast

What causes thunder and lightning? Here's one poet's nonscientific explanation. To get the full effect of the poem, read it out loud. What words and sounds suggest the noise of thunder?

Giant Thunder

For a detailed lesson plan on this poem, see Teacher's Manual page 101.

James Reeves

Giant Thunder, striding home,
Wonders if his supper's done.

A "Hag wife, hag wife, bring me bones!"
"They are not done," the old hag moans.

"Not done? Not done?" the giant roars,
And heaves the old wife out of doors.

Cries he, "I'll have them, cooked or not!"
And overturns the cooking pot.

He flings the burning coals about;
See how the lightning flashes out!

Upon the gale the old hag rides,
B The clouded moon for terror hides.

All the world with thunder quakes;
Forest shudders, mountain shakes;

From the cloud the rainstorm breaks;
Village ponds are turned to lakes;
Every living creature wakes.

Hungry giant, lie you still!
C Stamp no more from hill to hill—
Tomorrow you shall have your fill.

D

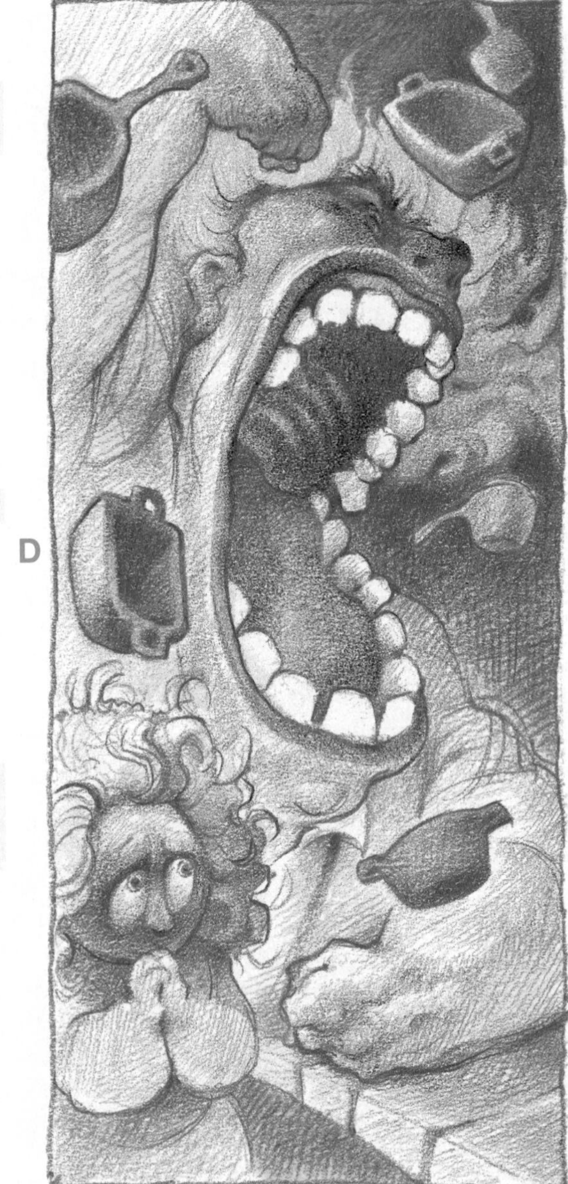

Analyzing the Poem
Identifying Details
1. His supper is not done.
2. He throws her outside. He overturns it.
3. His rage becomes a storm, and nature reacts in terror.
Ponds become lakes, and living creatures awaken.
4. He begs him to stop stamping about and to be still.
He says that tomorrow the giant will have enough to eat.

Interpreting Meanings
5. It is created by a giant stamping over the hills.
It is created when the giant flings burning coals about.
6. Most students will say that he is not. Of course, this poem is like a fairy tale, and exists under a different set of rules than does our society.
Answers will vary.
7. He strides, asks for supper, has a wife, and so on.

Responding to the Poem

Analyzing the Poem

Identifying Details

1. Why does Giant Thunder become angry with his wife when he gets home?
2. What does the giant do to his wife? What does he do with the cooking pot?
3. Describe how nature reacts to the actions of the giant and his wife. What happens to the ponds and the living creatures?
4. What does the speaker ask the giant to do in the poem's last lines? What promise does the speaker make to the giant?

Interpreting Meanings

5. What explanation does this poem suggest for the noise of thunder? What explanation does it give for lightning?
6. Do you think Giant Thunder is justified in his anger? If you were his wife, would you have reacted differently from the wife in the poem?
7. Find all the details in the poem that **personify** thunder. Are the details appropriate?

Applying Meanings

8. People often personify forces of weather and nature. We say "Old Man Winter," for example. We often illustrate the March wind as a cloud shaped like a head, puffing cold air. Can you list two or three other such personifications of weather or nature? Why do you think people personify natural forces?

Writing About the Poem

A Creative Response

SRW p. 65

1. **Personifying Something in Nature.** "Giant Thunder" uses personification to describe a powerful force of nature. Pick a natural force or thing that interests you: It may be gentle, like a rainbow, or powerful, like an earthquake. In a prose paragraph or a poem, describe your subject as if it were a person. You might want to tell what your subject looks like, how it acts and speaks, and with whom it associates.

A Critical Response

SRW p. 21

2. **Analyzing a Character Type.** Giants are popular characters in fairy tales. List three other stories, poems, or movies that have giants as characters. Then, in a paragraph, compare the giant in this poem to these other giant characters. What qualities do some or all of the giants seem to share? You might want to think about how the giants look, how they behave, and what they eat.

See Teacher's Manual page 102.

Analyzing Language and Vocabulary

Onomatopoeia

SRW p. 63

One way poets create images of sound is through **onomatopoeia,** or words that echo the sounds they refer to. The word *moans* in line 4 is an example of onomatopoeia. *Moan* sounds like a moan. If you read it aloud, you can hear the actual moaning sound of the old hag's voice.

Find an example of onomatopoeia in the third stanza. Then think of one or more onomatopoeic words to describe each of the following sounds.

1. Pots and pans falling
2. Birds singing
3. Someone falling into a pool
4. A train moving along its track
5. Someone walking in heavy boots

For answers, see Teacher's Manual page 102.

Reading About the Writer

James Reeves (1909–) is a poet and also an anthologist, a broadcaster, a critic, an editor, and a lecturer. Reeves was born in London and began writing poetry at the age of 11. He has won great acclaim for his collections of children's poems, *The Wandering Moon, The Blackbird in the Lilac, Prefabulous Animiles,* and *The Ragged Robin.*

Applying Meanings
8. Among the possibilities: Mother Nature, Old Sol (the sun), the lion as the king of the jungle, Jack Frost, the man in the Moon, the old man who snores and causes thunder (in the nursery rhyme).
People use personification (or metaphor) to explain mysterious events; by personifying nonhuman nature, we personalize it and make it seem more familiar and less threatening. Metaphors exercise the human ability to see similarities in the world, rather than distinctions. Seeing something like human rage in a volcanic eruption makes the terrifying eruption manageable. In ancient times, people appeased these spirits in nature by gifts and sacrifices.

Additional Writing Assignment
Tell students to imagine that Giant Thunder's neighbor is Giant Lightning. Have them re-create the situation in the poem, only now Giant Lightning comes home to *his* wife.

SUPPLEMENTARY SUPPORT MATERIAL

1. Selection Test (page 117 of Test Book)
2. Audiocassette recording
3. Reader's Response Journal
4. Workbook (page 95)

PREREADING

1. **ESTABLISHING A PURPOSE.** The headnote provides a purpose-setting activity for the poem.

2. **PREREADING JOURNAL.** Before students read the poem, have them write a short description of what they would imagine a "strange tree" looks like. Where might they see this strange tree?

CLOSURE

Working in groups of three, students should discuss how the atmosphere of "Strange Tree" could be changed by using different words, details, and images. Encourage them to be specific in their suggestions.

A. Rhyme

? Identify the rhyme scheme of this stanza. *(abcb)*

B. Personification

? How does the personification in the poem make you feel? Is this a "good" tree or a "sinister" one?

Texas Essential Elements/(a) English Language Arts: 3B Figurative language; **4A** Word meaning. **(c) Reading: 2A** Word meaning; **2B** Multimeaning words

Have you ever seen something in nature that seemed to resemble a person? The speaker in this poem sees some very people-like qualities in a large, old tree. How do you think the speaker feels about the tree?

Strange Tree

For a detailed lesson plan on this poem, see Teacher's Manual page 103.

Elizabeth Madox Roberts

A
Away beyond the Jarboe house
 I saw a different kind of tree.
Its trunk was old and large and bent,
 And I could feel it look at me.

The road was going on and on
 Beyond, to reach some other place.
I saw a tree that looked at me,
 And yet it did not have a face.

It looked at me with all its limbs;
 It looked at me with all its bark.
The yellow wrinkles on its sides
 Were bent and dark.

And then I ran to get away,
 But when I stopped and turned to see,
The tree was bending to the side
 And leaning out to look at me. B

Responding to the Poem

Analyzing the Poem

Identifying Details

1. Where does the narrator find the strange tree? Draw a sketch showing the location of the tree, based on details in the poem.
2. What detail in the last line of the second stanza makes it seem strange that the tree can "look" at the narrator?
3. What does the narrator do in the final stanza? What is the tree doing now?

Interpreting Meanings

4. Explain how the last line of stanza 1 suddenly **personifies,** or gives human qualities to, the tree. That is, what human quality or ability does the tree suddenly have?
5. The tree is indeed "strange." Do you think the speaker finds the tree interesting and friendly, or do you think she finds it disturbing and frightening? Quote passages from the poem to support your opinion.
6. Describe the poem's **rhythm**—its pattern of stressed and unstressed syllables. Remember that you mark a stressed syllable with a ´ and an unstressed syllable with a ˘. For example,

 Ĭts trúnk wăs óld ănd lárge ănd bént.

 You'll notice that most lines have a very similar rhythmic pattern. One line, however, is quite different. Identify this line and suggest a reason why the poet altered the pattern. SRW p. 77

Applying Meanings

7. Have you ever encountered anything that was *not* alive but which, on a dark night or on a lonely road, seemed to be alive?

Writing About the Poem

A Creative Response

SRW p. 65

1. **Analyzing Personification.** People seem to enjoy personifying things in nature. For years, for ex-

Analyzing the Poem

Identifying Details

1. Beyond the Jarboe house.
The sketch should place the tree near a road, which continues on beyond it. A house should appear in the foreground.
2. It has no face and looks at the narrator with limbs, bark, and wrinkles (not eyes).
3. She runs away but stops to look back. It is bending sideways and leaning out to look at the speaker.

Interpreting Meanings

4. It has the ability to look at the world.
5. Disturbing and frightening.
Several details confirm this, including the fact that even the road seems to want to get away ("reach some other place").
6. Line 12 has only two stresses, a variation which emphasizes the line and makes the image more threatening.

Applying Meanings

7. Responses will vary. Think of houses, trees, bushes, lamppost, billboard, telephone pole. See Teacher's Manual page 103.

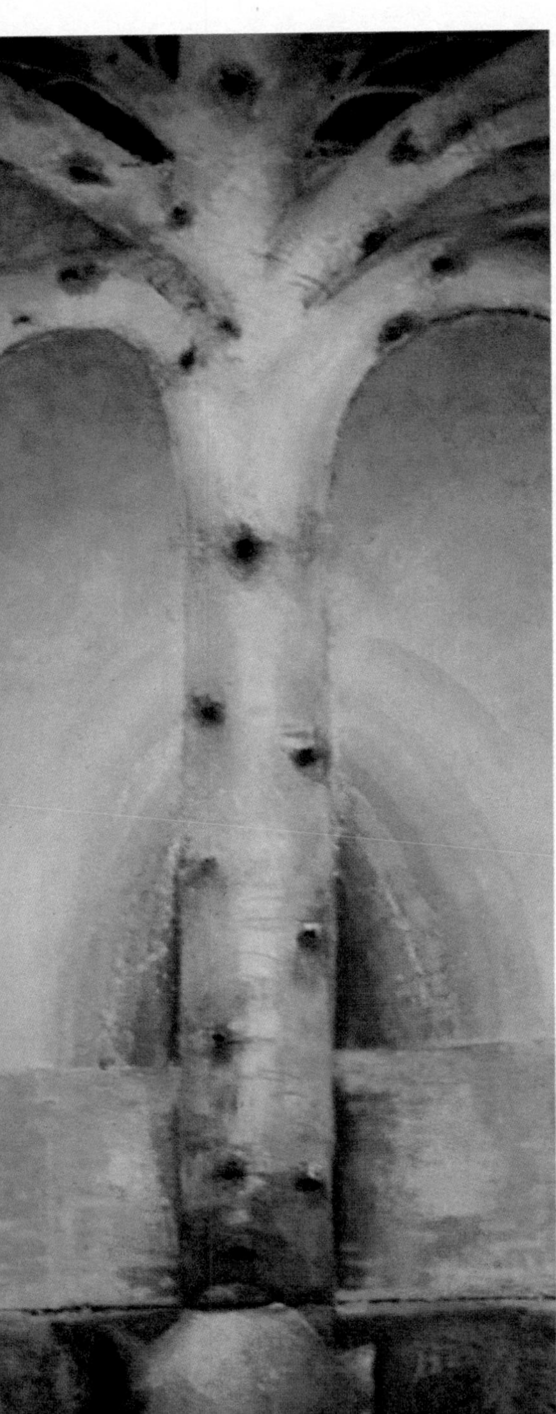

Solitary Tree by Mary A. Armstrong (1984). Oil.

Courtesy Victoria Munroe Gallery, New York.

ample, people have spoken of the "man in the moon." They have seen features on the surface of the moon that give it the appearance of a man's face. Choose something in nature that looks to you like a person. Then explain in a paragraph how it resembles a person. Include precise details of the natural object in your explanation.

A Critical Response

SRW p. 15

2. **Analyzing Atmosphere. Atmosphere** is the mood or overall feeling of a work of literature. A poem's atmosphere could be peaceful, tense, spooky, or dreamy. In a paragraph, describe the atmosphere of this poem. Then list the words, details, and images in the poem that create this atmosphere.

See Teacher's Manual page 104.

Analyzing Language and Vocabulary

Multiple Meanings

Many common words have several meanings. All the words listed below are connected with trees; A explain what part of a tree each word refers to. Then list at least one other meaning for each word. (You may want to consult a dictionary.) Tell whether the various meanings of each word seem to be related in any way.

1. trunk
2. bark
3. limb
4. root
5. leaf
6. branch

Reading About the Writer

Elizabeth Madox Roberts (1881–1941) was born in Kentucky, and except for some years at the University of Chicago, she spent the rest of her life there. As a child she was frail, and health problems haunted her entire life. But she loved to listen to pioneer tales and to observe rural life, landscape, and folklore.

For answers, see Teacher's Manual page 104.

A. Humanities Connection: Responding to the Fine Art

? If you were to personify this tree, what would you say it is doing? What is it feeling? What feelings does it evoke in you? Do you think the atmosphere of this painting is similar to or different from the atmosphere of the poem? Explain.

Further Reading for Students

Even though it's an old chestnut, most students will enjoy reading Joyce Kilmer's "Trees."

SUPPLEMENTARY SUPPORT MATERIAL

1. Selection Test (page 117 of Test Book)
2. Audiocassette recording
3. Author photograph on *A Gallery of Authors* poster
4. Workbook (page 97)
5. Instructional Overhead Transparency

PREREADING

ESTABLISHING A PURPOSE. Before students begin reading the poem, have them look at the picture and predict what this cat will do next about the snow. See if May Swenson's cat behaves the way they predict this one will.

CLOSURE

Working in pairs, students should list one simile and one metaphor from this poem. Have them share their lists in class.

A. Alliteration
These two lines provide excellent examples of alliteration. Be sure to have students read aloud.

B. Onomatopoeia
? What poetic technique is used in this line? (Onomatopoeia) How do you know? (The word *buzz* echoes the very sound it names.)

C. Responding
? Compare this cat to the one in the poem on page 286. Which cat seems more real to you? Which do you like better? Why?

D. Responding to the Photograph
? What is this cat thinking? Whom or what is it looking at? How would this cat get along with the one pictured on page 286? With the one pictured on page 288?

★ **Texas Essential Elements/(a) English Language Arts: 1B** Purpose and audience

In this poem we get a fresh look, through the eyes of a cat, at a familiar aspect of nature. Before reading the poem, think about how cats you know respond to rain, snow, ice, heat.

Cat & the Weather

For a detailed lesson plan on this poem, see Teacher's Manual page 104.

May Swenson

Cat takes a look at the weather:
snow;
A puts a paw on the sill;
his perch is piled, is a pillow.

Shape of his pad appears:
will it dig? No,
not like sand,
like his fur almost.

But licked, not liked:
too cold.
Insects are flying, fainting down.
He'll try

to bat one against the pane.
B They have no body and no buzz,
and now his feet are wet;
it's a puzzle. D

Shakes each leg,
then shakes his skin
to get the white flies off;
looks for his tail,

tells it to come on in
by the radiator.
World's turned queer
somehow: all white,

no smell. Well, here
inside it's still familiar.
C He'll go to sleep until
it puts itself right.

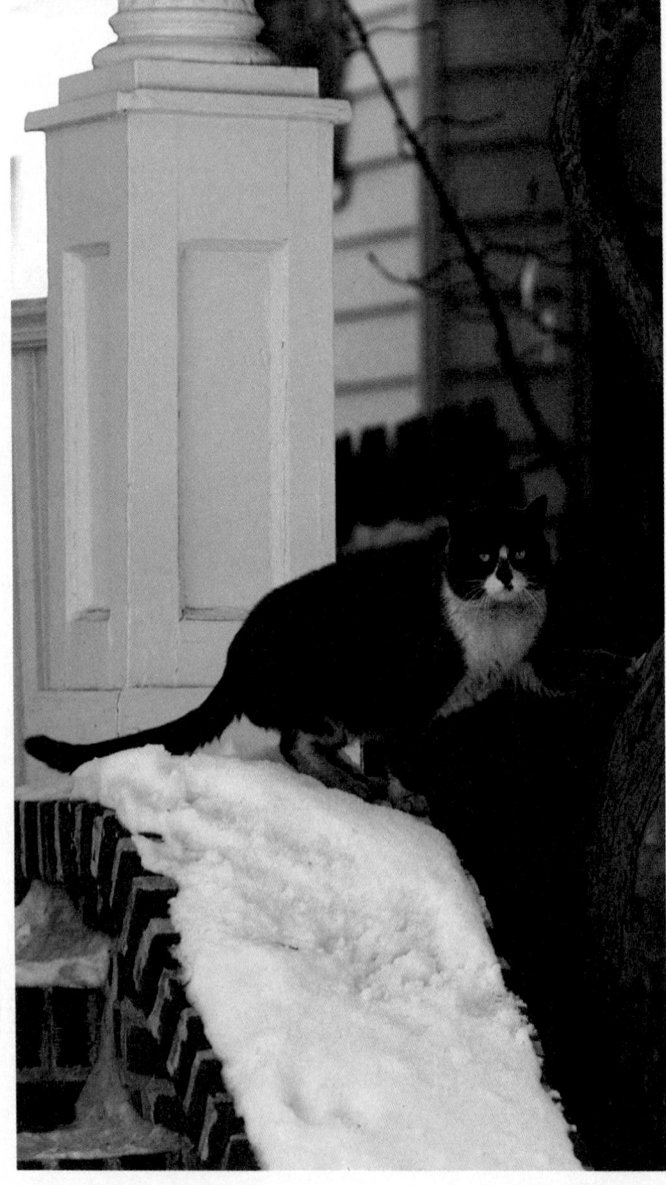

A biography of May Swenson appears on page 317.

ANALYZING THE POEM

Identifying Details

1. The snow has piled up on it. A pillow.
2. He puts a paw on it and licks it. It is too cold.
3. They have "no body and no buzz," and his paws are wet after he hits them.
4. Inside near the radiator. It's queer and unfamiliar.

Interpreting Meanings

5. It collects but can be tamped down, has a soft texture, is cold, comes silently from the sky, is white, has no smell, and is wet.
6. A pillow.
The mound of snow is round and white and soft.
7. The snow is "not like sand" but "like his fur almost."
Its soft texture.
8. Its tail presented as if it can hear and respond and as if it has a will of its own.

Applying Meanings

9. Remind students about the familiar advice: "Go to bed. Things'll look better in the morning."

Responding to the Poem

Analyzing the Poem

Identifying Details

1. When the cat sees the snow, he tests a favorite resting place, the windowsill. What has happened to the sill? What does the cat think is on the windowsill?
2. What does the cat do to test the snow? What doesn't he like about the snow?
3. The cat apparently thinks the snowflakes are insects. But what still puzzles the cat about these "bugs"?
4. Where does the cat finally decide to go? Why does he prefer to leave the snow?
5. List five facts about snow the cat discovers.

Interpreting Meanings

6. A **metaphor** is a comparison between two dissimilar things. The opening stanza contains a metaphor describing the snow on the windowsill. What does this metaphor compare the snow to? What does this comparison tell you about how the snow looks?
7. A **simile** compares one thing to another, dissimilar thing by using a word such as *like* or *as*. Identify two similes in the second stanza. What information about snow do these similes convey?
8. In the sixth stanza, what part of the cat is **personified?** In what ways is this part treated as if it had human qualities?

SRW pp. 61, 65, 81

Applying Meanings

9. Do you think people, like this cat, tend to prefer the familiar to the new? Can you think of times that we too might "go to sleep" till things are put "right"?

Writing About the Poem

A Creative Response

Describing an Impression. Imagine you are an animal or a small child seeing something common—a thunderstorm, a rainbow, a car, an airplane—for the first time. Write a poem or a paragraph describing your impressions. Use similes and metaphors to describe the new thing.

See Teacher's Manual page 105.

Analyzing Language and Vocabulary

Homonyms

Homonyms are words that sound alike but have different meanings and, usually, different spellings.

1. What homonym can you name for the word weather? What does the homonym mean?
2. Is it a *pain* or a *pane* to wash the window *pain* or *pane?*
3. When you tell someone a story, are you telling a *tale* or a *tail?*
4. Would you talk about the *tail end* of a story or the *tale end* of a story?

For answers, see Teacher's Manual page 105.

Reading About the Writer

May Swenson (1919–   ) was born in Logan, Utah, and has spent most of her adult life in or around New York City. "The poet works (and plays) with the elements of language," Swenson says, "forming and transforming his material to the point where a new perception emerges. . . ." Swenson's books of poetry include: *Another Animal, Iconographs: Poems,* and *New and Selected Things Taking Place.* "Cat & the Weather" is from a collection called *To Mix with Time.*

Comment from the Writer

May Swenson talks about poetry as an exploration of the unknown: "I confess to being envious, in a way, of the astronaut; though only in my imagination, where I can make him hero and lone adventurer. What an array of absolutely new sensations is handed him, like a Christmas paintbox, what an incomparable toy, his capsule with its console of magic dials, gauges, buttons, and signal lights, and what a knight in shining plastic he is in his silver suit. To escape the earthball, its tug, and one's own heaviness!"

Additional Writing Assignment

Have students pretend they are a cat, and have them write a short paragraph about something else they find strange and new. They should use the first-person pronoun, *I.* Spur their imaginations by asking them questions such as: Will the puzzling thing be inside or outside? Why have they not encountered it before?

Supplementary Support Material
Introduction/A Poem's Message Test (page 119 of Test Book)

Further Reading for Students
You might have students read Dickinson's comment on poetry on text page 634. Here is another poem on poetry:

There is no Frigate like a Book
To take us Lands away
Nor any Coursers like a Page
Of prancing Poetry—
This Travel may the poorest take
Without offense of Toll–
How frugal is the Chariot
That bears the Human soul.
—Emily Dickinson

A. Discussing the Quotation
The quotation is from the noted American journalist and writer E. B. White. (Students might know him as the author of *Stuart Little* and *Charlotte's Web.*) Discuss with students how mystification can intensify our enjoyment of all sorts of things. You might suggest how a dark setting, a suspicious-looking character, and a multitude of conflicting clues about a recently committed crime can intensify the suspense of a mystery movie. This suspense prompts us to predict what will happen next and makes us interact with the story. Help students to see that part of the enjoyment of reading any text comes from this kind of interaction. If a poet were to reveal meaning outright, the reader would lose the pleasure of personalizing the poem and of discovering its meaning for himself or herself. (The poem would become a sermon.)

Texas Essential Elements/(a) English Language Arts: 3B Figurative language

SRW p. 49

A

A poet's pleasure is to withhold a little of his meaning, to intensify by mystification. He unzips the veil from beauty, but does not remove it. A poet utterly clear is a trifle glaring.

—E. B. White

For teaching suggestions on this section, see page 105 of Teacher's Manual.

A Poem's Message

A poet's message can be open, but most poems have hidden "messages." In "The Glove and the Lions," for example, Leigh Hunt's message is not hard to find. He states it clearly in the last line: "No love, . . . but vanity, sets love a task like that."

In contrast, Randall Jarrell's message in "Bats" is not obvious. On the surface, the poem seems to be merely a description of a bat and how she carries and feeds her young. But you notice that the mother bat "dances" through the night. She hunts "in happiness." She "folds her wings about her sleeping child." Once you realize that Jarrell has deliberately chosen images that would wipe away any negative feelings you might have toward bats, you are close to discovering his message. You move another step closer when you realize that by personifying the bats, he makes you think of them as capable of human emotions, such as joy, tenderness, and love. Jarrell's message emerges from all the elements of the poem. It might be stated in a single sentence: "The special bond between a mother and her newborn child can be found even among creatures we consider ugly."

In trying to find a poet's hidden message, think about all the elements of the poem: its sounds, images, and figures of speech. Then depend on your instincts. In the long run, they will probably tell you, as well as anything else can, what the poet is communicating to you.

You will find that your statement of a poem's meaning will differ from everyone else's statement. You will also find that you can never completely summarize what the poem means or suggests to you. At the end, a poem always remains in part a mystery.

SUPPLEMENTARY SUPPORT MATERIAL
1. Selection Test (page 121 of Test Book)
2. Reader's Response Journal
3. Workbook (page 99)

PREREADING
ESTABLISHING A PURPOSE. The headnote will help establish a purpose for reading.

CLOSURE
Ask students to summarize the message that Dickinson conveys in this poem and to tell what they think of it.

A. Rhyme
Notice that one rhymed sound links the two stanzas (say/day).

B. Interpreting
? What experiences could you have with words that are positive and life-giving? What experiences would be destructive? Do you think Dickinson is talking about destructive words, or positive ones? (It could be both.) Try reading the poem as if someone just said "I love you." Then try reading it as if someone had just been cruel to you.

★ **Texas Essential Elements/(a) English Language Arts: 1B** Purpose and audience. **(c) Reading: 3F** Purpose/point of view/opinion; **3G** Compare/contrast

Few writers have been able to pack as many ideas into as few words as Emily Dickinson could. In this poem she is saying something about words themselves. Do you agree with her opinion?

A Word

For a detailed lesson plan on this poem, see Teacher's Manual page 106.

Emily Dickinson

A word is dead
When it is said,
A Some say.

I say it just
Begins to live
B That day.

Responding to the Poem

Analyzing the Poem

Interpreting Meanings

1. How might a word or statement be "dead," or lifeless and unchanging, once it is said?
2. How might a word or statement just begin to "live," or become full of life and meaning, once it is said?

Evaluating the Poem

3. Do you think this could be a poem about poetry, as well as about the power of language?
4. What do you think of the speaker's opinion?

Writing About the Poem

A Critical Response

Expressing a View. The first stanza of the poem presents one view of words. The second stanza presents a contrasting view. In a paragraph, first state which of the two opinions you agree with. Then support your view by explaining the reasons for your choice. You may want to give examples from your own experience.

See Teacher's Manual page 106.

Reading About the Writer

Not until years after her death did **Emily Dickinson** (1830–1886) become one of the most highly regarded of all American poets. Dickinson led an unusually private life, which has since caused much curiosity and speculation. She was born, lived, and died in Amherst, Massachusetts. After a normal, sociable childhood and adolescence, Dickinson became a recluse at the age of twenty-six. She dressed only in white, stayed in her house or garden, and saw only her family and a few close friends. All this time she was also privately perfecting her art—she was writing her poetry. She once described her feelings about poetry: "If I read a book and it makes my body so cold no fire can ever warm me, I know that is poetry." Upon Dickinson's death, her sister Lavinia was shocked to discover almost 1700 poems written on envelopes, paper bags, and scraps of papers, all neatly tied up into little packets. It looked as if the poet was hoping someone would find the poems and publish them. While she lived, only seven of her poems appeared in print.

ANALYZING THE POEM
Interpreting Meanings
1. Once spoken, a word is gone; though one might take it back, amend it, or apologize for it, still it is gone.
2. A word is a stimulus; anything can happen because of it: Love may grow, people may die, anything. Words have an ongoing effect. They are remembered, sometimes forever.

Evaluating the Poem
3. Remind students of how poetry stays alive in our minds and of how poems written two thousand years ago are still read (still live) today.
4. Answers will vary.

SUPPLEMENTARY SUPPORT MATERIAL

1. Selection Test (page 121 of Test Book)
2. Author photograph on *A Gallery of Authors* poster
3. Reader's Response Journal
4. Workbook (page 99)

PREREADING

ESTABLISHING A PURPOSE. The headnote will help establish a purpose for their reading. Have students look for the "weapons" in the poem.

CLOSURE

Have students tell how McGinley's and Dickinson's poems make them feel. Use their responses to stimulate class discussion.

A. Rhythm and Rhyme

Notice that in four short lines the poet uses internal rhyme (stones/bones, sting/thing) and alliteration (lines 1 and 2).

? What other children's chants are you familiar with? How does their rhythm compare with the rhythm of "A Choice of Weapons"?

ANALYZING THE POEM

Interpreting Meanings

1. It disagrees that words are harmless, it also adds another source of pain.
2. There are physical weapons (sticks and stones), verbal weapons (words), and a purely psychological weapon (silence).
   She believes silence is the worst.
   Responses will vary, but ask students to give examples that illustrate their opinions.
3. The speaker is referring to words hurled in anger, words used deliberately to hurt, words chosen skillfully or cunningly to do damage.

★ **Texas Essential Elements/(a) English Language Arts: 1B** Purpose and audience

This poem reinterprets a well-known chant:

> **Sticks and stones may break my bones,**
> **But words will never hurt me.**

As you read the poem, notice how the poet has changed the chant. What weapon does the poet choose?

A Choice of Weapons

For a detailed lesson plan on this poem, see Teacher's Manual page 107.

Phyllis McGinley

Sticks and stones are hard on bones.
A Aimed with angry art,
Words can sting like anything.
But silence breaks the heart.

Responding to the Poem

Analyzing the Poem

Interpreting Meanings

1. Explain how the poem changes the childhood chant quoted in the headnote.
2. Notice the title of the poem—"A Choice of Weapons." The poem speaks of three types of weapons that can hurt another person. Describe each weapon. Then explain which weapon the speaker feels is most hurtful. Do you agree with the speaker?
3. The poem speaks of words "Aimed with angry art." Explain what kinds of words are meant. Include examples of such words in your explanation.

Writing About the Poem

A Critical Response

Comparing Two Poems. The speakers of both "A Choice of Weapons" and "A Word" (page 319) offer an opinion on the power of language. In a paragraph, first state whether both speakers have the same opinion. Then present evidence from the poems to support your statement.

See Teacher's Manual page 107.

Reading About the Writer

Known for her "light poetry," **Phyllis McGinley** (1905–1978) also wrote books for children, essays, movie scripts, and serious poetry. Many of her poems are written on domestic subjects: suburbia, women, daughters, child-raising, the school system, and husbands. McGinley lived for many years in Larchmont, New York, a suburb of New York City. "I remind myself of a robin when I'm working," McGinley said. "You know how a robin goes about pulling a worm out of the ground, hanging on to it for dear life. That's how I worry about a poem." She was awarded the Pulitzer Prize in 1961 for her collection of poems *Times Three,* in which "A Choice of Weapons" appears.

Further Reading for Students

Carl Sandburg wrote this poem about words:

Little girl, be careful what you say
when you make talk with words, words—
for words are made of syllables
and syllables, child are made of air—
and air is so thin—air is the breath of
God—
air is finer than fire or mist,
finer than water or moonlight,
finer than spider-webs in the moon,
finer than water-flowers in the morning:
and words are strong, too,
stronger than rocks or steel
stronger than potatoes, corn, fish, cattle,
and soft, too, soft as little pigeon-eggs,
soft as the music of hummingbird wings.
So, little girl, when you speak greetings,
when you tell jokes, make wishes or
prayers,
be careful, be careless, be careful,
be what you wish to be.

A

L'il Sis by William H. Johnson (c. 1944). Oil.

The National Museum of American Art, Smithsonian Institution, Washington D.C. Gift of the Harmon Foundation.

A. Humanities Connection: Responding to the Fine Art

William H. Johnson (1901–) was born in South Carolina and studied art in Paris and in the south of France. He has an extensive exhibition record and has won several art prizes, including one from the National Academy of Design.

? Do you think the subject of this painting has been the victim of "sticks and stones," "words," "silence," or perhaps all three? Contrast this painting with the one on page 268. How are they different with respect to color? Which one is more realistic? Which style of painting do you like better? Why?

Supplementary Support Material

1. Selection Test (page 121 of Test Book)
2. Audiocassette recording
3. Reader's Response Journal
4. Workbook (page 101)

Prereading

Establishing a Purpose. Ask students if they've ever heard this story (they probably have). Tell them to look for details in this poem that are different from the version they know.

Closure

Call on a volunteer to explain what we mean when we say that someone "cried wolf." Have another volunteer give an example of someone who cried wolf too many times.

A. Alliteration
Notice the alliteration created by the initial consonant sound in "neighbors," "noon," and "nine."

B. Responding
? How do you feel about this outcome and the neighbors' attitude?

Humanities Connection: Responding to Music
Sergei Prokofiev (1891–1953) is considered to be the leading Soviet composer of his time. His symphonic fairy tale *Peter and the Wolf* (1936) is based on the same fable on which Untermeyer based his poem. His work, in which each animal in the meadow is portrayed by a different musical instrument, ranks among one of the most popular orchestral compositions of our time. If you play this recording, see if students can see any parallels between it and "The Boy and the Wolf."

★ **Texas Essential Elements/(a) English Language Arts: 1B** Purpose and audience

A fable is a brief story, in poetry or prose, that teaches a practical lesson about life. The lesson usually is spelled out in a moral at the end of the story. You're probably familiar with Aesop's fables. This poem retells one of his famous stories. Read it out loud to enjoy the rhyme and rhythm.

The Boy and the Wolf

SRW p. 35

Louis Untermeyer

A boy employed to guard the sheep
Despised his work. He liked to sleep.
And when a lamb was lost, he'd shout,
"Wolf! Wolf! The wolves are all about!"

A The neighbors searched from noon till nine,
But of the beast there was no sign,
Yet "Wolf!" he cried next morning when
The villagers came out again.

One evening around six o'clock
A real wolf fell upon the flock.
"Wolf!" yelled the boy. "A wolf indeed!"
But no one paid him any heed.

Although he screamed to wake the dead,
B "He's fooled us every time," they said,
And let the hungry wolf enjoy
His feast of mutton, lamb—and boy.

The moral's this: The man who's wise
Does not defend himself with lies.
Liars are not believed, forsooth,°
Even when liars tell the truth.

19. **forsooth:** an old-fashioned word meaning "truly."

The Shepherd's Boy and the Wolf by Antonio Frasconi (1958). Woodcut. From *Some Well-Known Fables*. Permission granted by the artist.

For a detailed lesson plan on this poem, see Teacher's Manual page 108. A biography of Louis Untermeyer appears on text page 323.

ANALYZING THE POEM
Identifying Details
1. He guards the sheep. Sleep.
2. He shouts "Wolf! Wolf!" They search the area all afternoon and evening.
3. A wolf actually attacks the flock. They ignore the boy's shouts.
4. The scansion should indicate iambic tetrameter.

There are small variations in lines 4, 11, and 20.

Interpreting Meanings
5. If we are wise, we will not lie to cover our mistakes, because once we get a reputation for lying, others will never believe us.
6. If the class does not raise the issue of "little white lies," you might want to do so. (Is there any such thing?)

Comment from the Writer
Louis Untermeyer tells about his beginnings as a writer: "At ten I fancied myself a storyteller; my brother was a rewarding listener. Our beds were in the front room on the third floor—the cook and upstairs maid had two rooms in the back—and every night I would tell Martin another episode in the saga which was not so much an invention as a plagiarized improvisation. Growing in action and complexity as I went along, it was a hodgepodge of everything I could lay my mind on—the Arabian Nights, the Rover Boys, Jason and the Golden Fleece, Oliver Optic's Onward and Upward series, King Arthur and Lancelot, the Three Musketeers, the historical juveniles of G. A. Henty—a violently romantic serial in which I was the invincible adventurer, the long-awaited lover, the full-blooded but unblemished boy-knight who rose from rags to riches. I talked Martin to sleep and myself into dreams that were extensions of my fantasies. . . ."

FURTHER READING FOR STUDENTS
Another good poem that is based on one of Aesop's fables is "The Fox and the Crow" by Marianne Moore.

Responding to the Poem

Analyzing the Poem

Identifying Details

1. What is the boy's job? What does the boy prefer to do instead?
2. What does the boy do if a lamb is lost? Describe how the neighbors usually respond.
3. What finally happens one evening? Tell how the neighbors react.
4. **Scan** one stanza of the poem—that is, mark its pattern of stressed and unstressed syllables. Is the rhythm the same in each stanza? (To *hear* the rhythm of the poem, read it out loud.)

Interpreting Meanings

5. Summarize the moral of this fable in your own words.

Applying Meanings

6. Do you agree with the moral of the story? Can you think of real-life examples of people who have tried to defend themselves with lies?

Writing About the Poem

A Creative Response

1. **Writing a Fable.** Fables can be fun to write. Try your hand at writing a fable set in your own community, with a moral similar to the one in the poem. Your fable should be short and told very directly. Don't describe the setting or characters in detail. Underline the moral at the end of the story. Since many fables involve animals that speak and behave like humans, you may want to write your fable with animal characters.

SRW p. 35

A Critical Response

SRW p. 89

2. **Analyzing Tone.** In a paragraph, describe the poem's **tone,** or the poet's attitude toward his subject. Is it comical, serious, or sarcastic? Tell what details in the poem support your opinion—including the way the story *sounds.*

See Teacher's Manual page 108.

Analyzing Language and Vocabulary

Rhymes and Eye-Rhymes

SRW p. 73

The words *dead* and *said* rhyme, even though they don't look as if they should. But the words *bead* and *dead* do not rhyme, even though they look as if they should. Words that are spelled similarly and look as if they should rhyme but don't are called eye-rhymes.

1. Find two other examples of rhyming words in the poem that do not look as if they should rhyme but do.
2. Think of at least one eye-rhyme for each of these words:

   a. meat **b.** dough **c.** two

3. Think of words that rhyme with these words but do not look as if they should:

   a. do **b.** go **c.** die **d.** bird

For answers, see Teacher's Manual page 109.

Reading About the Writer

For more than twenty years, **Louis Untermeyer** (1885–1977) worked for his father in the jewelry business in New York. Then after studying in Europe for two years, Untermeyer began to write for a living. Despite being denied a high school diploma because he failed geometry, Untermeyer became a respected poet, essayist, lecturer, translator, and anthologist. "The Boy and the Wolf" is included in *The Magic Circle,* one of Untermeyer's many collections of poetry for young people.

Supplementary Support Material
1. Selection Test (page 123 of Test Book)
2. Audiocassette recording
3. Reader's Response Journal
4. Workbook (page 103)

Prereading

Establishing a Purpose. Before students begin reading the poem, have them read question 4. Together with a review of the subunit introduction on text page 318, this question will help establish a purpose for their reading.

Closure

Working in small groups, students should discuss the various ways they have stated the theme of "The Pasture." Have them give reasons to support their interpretations.

A. Repetition and Theme
The repetition of this line suggests that it is particularly important to the message the poet wants to impart to his readers.

Analyzing the Poem

Identifying Details
1. He wants to rake the leaves away from the pasture spring.
   He may stay to watch the water clear.
2. He will fetch the calf that's in the pasture with its mother.

Interpreting Meanings
3. Spring
4. The small pleasures of life don't take long; we are wise to indulge in them when the opportunity arises.
   Each poem will be a small pleasure; he would like readers to "come along" and linger a bit with each.
5. If the "you" and "I" were anyone definite, the theme would become more specific, more tied to the particular relationship. See Teacher's Manual page 109.

★ **Texas Essential Elements/(a) English Language Arts: 3C** Literary traditions; **4B** Main idea. **(c) Reading: 3A** Main ideas/details; **3I** Draw conclusions

Robert Frost spent much of his life as a New England farmer. Many of his most famous poems are about nature and rural life. Frost asked that this poem be printed at the front of all collections of his poetry. Why do you think it would make a good starting point for a book of poems?

The Pasture

For a detailed lesson plan on this poem, see Teacher's Manual page 109. A biography of Robert Frost appears on text page 325.

Robert Frost

I'm going out to clean the pasture spring;
I'll only stop to rake the leaves away
(And wait to watch the water clear, I may):
I shan't be gone long.—You come too.

I'm going out to fetch the little calf
That's standing by the mother. It's so young
It totters when she licks it with her tongue.
 I shan't be gone long.—You come too.

Responding to the Poem

Analyzing the Poem

Identifying Details

1. In the first stanza, what does the speaker say he is going out to do? What may he wait to watch?
2. In the second stanza, what else does the speaker say he is going to do?

Interpreting Meanings

3. What season of the year do you think this poem takes place in?
4. Summarize in your own words the **theme,** or message, of "The Pasture." Why do you think Robert Frost wanted the poem printed at the front of all collections of his poetry? SRW p. 87
5. The "you" and "I" of the poem are never really identified. Would it make a difference if you knew who they were? Would the poem have a different meaning if you knew the speaker was a grandfather talking to his grandchild? Or a girl talking to her boyfriend? What if the speaker was the writer talking to *you?* Explain your answer.

Writing About the Poem

A Creative Response

Imitating the Poem. Write a one-stanza poem of your own that keeps the last line of Frost's poem. In your first three lines, tell about something you are about to do. Start the poem with the words "I'm going out to. . . ." Try to create one striking visual image. See Teacher's Manual page 110.

Comment from the Writer

Frost was asked if his poetry contained a message for his readers: " 'Message?' he repeats thoughtfully. 'No, No, I have no message, for I have set it down already in my works. But now I do remember a story. Years ago—many years ago—someone asked me what my definition of poetry was. And I replied poetry is something 'necessary.' . . .

" 'Yes,' he goes on, while we shake his distinguished hand, 'tell your readers that without poetry it is impossible to live, and counter to all that there is ugly and unpleasant on the earth, there still remains for us this hope and this incentive: that poetry is unavoidable in the contemporary world!' "

A

Two Cows by Frances Hynes (1982). Watercolor. Courtesy Terry Dintenfass Gallery, New York.

A. Humanities Connection: Responding to the Fine Art

? In what part of the country is this picture set? In what season? Is the atmosphere of this painting similar to or different from the atmosphere of Robert Frost's poem?

Further Reading for Students

Other poems that Robert Frost has written about love and communication include "Mending Wall," "Death of the Hired Man" (both included in *Elements of Literature: Fifth Course*), and "Dust of Snow" (included in *Elements of Literature: Second Course*).

Reading About the Writer

Winner of four Pulitzer Prizes for poetry, **Robert Frost** (1874–1963) was for years the best-known poet in America. Frost was born in California, but he was raised in New England, which became the setting for almost all his poetry. As a young man, Frost had tried raising chickens on a farm that his grandfather had given him, but he was unsuccessful. He also had a difficult time trying to sell his poems. Discouraged, he moved to England, where he found a publisher for his first two collections of poems (*A Boy's Will* and *North of Boston*). The books were an immediate success, and by the time Frost returned to the United States, publishers were interested in his work. The United States Government, which honored Frost many times, issued one citation which declared his poems to "have helped guide American thought with humor, and wisdom, setting forth to our minds a reliable representation of ourselves and of all men. . ." Frost had the rare pleasure of seeing his poems become classics during his lifetime.

SUPPLEMENTARY SUPPORT MATERIAL

1. Selection Test (page 123 of Test Book)
2. Audiocassette recording
3. Author photograph on *A Gallery of Authors* poster
4. Connections Between Reading and Writing worksheet
5. Reader's Response Journal
6. Workbook (page 105)
7. Instructional Overhead Transparency

PREREADING

1. **ESTABLISHING A PURPOSE.** Before students begin reading the poem, review with them the definition of dialect. Then tell them to read this poem aloud to hear how the poet has imitated the woman's own dialect. This will help establish a purpose for their reading.

2. **PREREADING JOURNAL.** Before students read this poem, have them briefly write down what they think the poem might be about. What might happen in a situation that involved a woman and a "rent man"?

Humanities Connection: Responding to the Fine Art

Laura Wheeler Waring (1877–1948) was known for her paintings of distinguished blacks. She was also a teacher of art.

? What do you think the woman in this painting could be thinking about? What do you think she was doing immediately before the moment captured in this painting? If you could speak to this woman, what would you say? How do you think she might reply?

CLOSURE

Call on a volunteer to define dialect. Then have three students tell the class whether or not dialect adds to their enjoyment of poems, short stories, plays, novels, TV shows, and movies.

Anna Washington Derry by Laura Wheeler Waring (1972). Oil.

National Museum of American Art, Smithsonian Institution, Washington D.C. Gift of the Harmon Foundation.

ANALYZING THE POEM

Identifying Details

1. He comes to collect the rent.
2. The sink is broken, the water doesn't run, the back window is cracked, the kitchen floor squeaks, the cellar has rats, and the attic leaks.
3. He says that making repairs is not his responsibility.
4. Neither is pleased.

Interpreting Meanings

5. It means to pass the responsibility onto someone else.

He says he is not responsible for solving the problems.

6. Most students will believe it is. Among possible reasons: The problems are serious ones; she apparently has reported them before; she deserves a decent place to live.

7. In the first five stanzas, even-numbered lines rhyme (lines 2, 4, and 6 in stanza 1; lines 2 and 4 in stanzas 2–5). Line 29 almost rhymes with line 27.

They make the poem seem lighthearted. (More mature students may recognize the irony in using a light tone to convey a serious message.)

8. Answers will vary. One possible message is that, no matter what the result, people should always fight for their rights. Another is that people should not be allowed to evade their responsibilities.

★ **Texas Essential Elements/(a) English Language Arts: 1E** Formal/informal language; **2C** Oral language; **3C** Literary traditions. **(c) Reading: 4E** Rate of reading

This poem is set in Harlem, a section of New York City where most people live in rented apartments. The speaker of the poem is a woman who has reason to be angry at her landlord. Read the poem aloud to hear echoes of the woman's own speech.

Madam and the Rent Man

For a detailed lesson plan on this poem, see Teacher's Manual page 110. A biography of Langston Hughes appears on text page 328.

Langston Hughes

A

The rent man knocked.
He said, Howdy-do?
I said, What
Can I do for you?
He said, You know
Your rent is due.

I said, Listen
Before I'd pay
I'd go to Hades°
And rot away.

The sink is broke,
The water don't run,
And you ain't done a thing
You promised to've done.

B

Back window's cracked,
Kitchen floor squeaks,
There's rats in the cellar,
And the attic leaks.

C

He said, Madam
It's not up to me.
I'm just the agent,
Don't you see?

I said, Naturally
You pass the buck.
If it's money you want,
You're out of luck.

He said, Madam, I ain't pleased.
I said, Neither am I

D

So we agrees.

9. **Hades** (hā'dēz): the underworld in Greek mythology.

A. Speakers

? Who are the two speakers in the poem? (The rent man and an "I" who we presume is "madam.") Be sure students know which lines are spoken by which character.

B. Inference

? What is the condition of the building? (Pretty bad: a broken sink, creaky window and floor, rats, leaks)

C. Interpreting

? Does the rent man own the building? (No. He's the agent—the rent-collector.)

D. Responding

? With whom do you sympathize, Madam or the rent man? Why?

Responding to the Poem

Analyzing the Poem

Identifying Details

1. Why does the rent man come to the speaker's door?
2. In stanzas 3 and 4, the speaker gives reasons for refusing to do as the rent man wants. List her reasons.
3. How does the rent man respond?
4. What do the speaker and the rent man agree about?

Interpreting Meanings

5. What does "pass the buck" mean? How has the rent collector "passed the buck"?
6. The woman in the poem doesn't speak politely to the rent collector. Do you think her bluntness is justified?
7. Read "Madam and the Rent Man" out loud. Then describe its **rhyme scheme**—its pattern of rhyming sounds. Discuss whether the rhymes make the poem seem serious or light-hearted.
8. Do you think this poem has a message? Explain.

SRW p. 75

327

A. Responding

? Have you ever done this with something you wrote? With what aspect of your work were you dissatisfied? Instead of throwing your work away, what might you have done to improve it?

FURTHER READING FOR TEACHERS

Hughes has a series of poems spoken by this hard-working, plain-talking strong woman: "My name is Johnson—Madam Alberta K. The Madam stands for business. I'm smart that way." Other poems spoken by this woman include "Madam and the Phone Bill," "Madam and the Minister," "Madam's Calling Cards." See the section called "Madam to You" in *Selected Poems of Langston Hughes* (1974, paperback).

Writing About the Poem

A Creative Response

Creating a Dialogue. The rent collector and the woman have a dialogue—a conversation between two people. Notice that the poet uses the characters' ordinary speech patterns and vocabulary to make their dialogue sound authentic. Write a dialogue of your own between two people who disagree over something: perhaps over something like money, children, noise, food. Use the characters' own speech patterns and their own special vocabulary to make the dialogue sound authentic. Before you write, decide whether you will make your dialogue funny or serious.

See Teacher's Manual page 111.

Analyzing Language and Vocabulary

Dialect

SRW p. 31

A **dialect** is a form of a language that is spoken in a certain area or by a particular group of people. A dialect differs from the standard language in vocabulary, pronunciation, and grammar. "Madam and the Rent Man" uses a dialect spoken by blacks living in New York City. For example, the speaker of the poem says "The sink is broke" (dialect) instead of "The sink is broken" (standard English). Writers use dialect to give you a sense of a character's personality and background. Dialect can also be fun to read. Find five other examples of dialect in this poem. Then rewrite each example in standard English. Would the poem's effect be different if standard English were used throughout?

For answers, see Teacher's Manual page 111.

Reading About the Writer

Langston Hughes (1902–1967) always had a wide following among the people he wrote about. Hughes once said, "I knew only the people I had grown up with, and they weren't people whose shoes were always shined, who had been to Harvard, or who had heard of Bach. But they seemed to me good people, too." Hughes, who was born in Joplin, Missouri, traveled widely and held many jobs before settling in Harlem, where he earned his living from writing and lecturing. He was a busboy in Washington, D.C., when the famous poet Vachel Lindsay (see page 304), on a poetry-reading tour, visited the hotel where he worked. One night, Hughes left three poems at Lindsay's place at the table; the next morning Lindsay read Hughes's poems at the poetry reading, and the new poet's career was begun. Hughes became a major literary figure in what is now known as the Harlem Renaissance of the 1920's. His poems often imitate the rhythms of blues and of jazz. "Madam and the Rent Man" is from a collection called *One-Way Ticket.*

Focusing on Background

Singing the Blues

"My two years in Washington were unhappy years, except for poetry and the friends I made through poetry. I wrote many poems. I always put them away new for several weeks in a bottom drawer. Then I would take them out and reread them. If they
A seemed bad, I would throw them away. They would all seem good when I wrote them and, usually, bad when I would look at them again. So most of them were thrown away.

"The blues poems I would often make up in my head and sing on the way to work. (Except that I could never carry a tune. But when I sing to myself, I think I am singing.) One evening, I was crossing Rock Creek Bridge, singing a blues I was trying to get right before I put it down on paper. A man passing on the opposite side of the bridge stopped, looked at me, then turned around and cut across the roadway.

"He said: 'Son, what's the matter? Are you ill?'

" 'No,' I said. 'Just singing.'

" 'I thought you were groaning,' he commented. 'Sorry!' And went his way.

"So after that I never sang my verses aloud in the street any more."

—Langston Hughes

SUPPLEMENTARY SUPPORT MATERIAL

1. Selection Test (page 123 of Test Book)
2. Audiocassette recording
3. Workbook (page 107)

PREREADING

ESTABLISHING A PURPOSE. Before students begin reading the poem, have them read the headnote. This will quickly establish a purpose for their reading.

CLOSURE

Ask for three volunteers to summarize what they think this poem is really about: Is it about a trip to an ancestral home? Or is it about growing up and making a journey to a place where one's parents can't follow?

Texas Essential Elements/(a) English Language Arts: 1B Purpose and audience; **3B** Figurative language; **4B** Main idea. **(c) Reading: 3A** Main ideas/details

Have you ever wondered about your family roots—what your ancestors were like and where they came from? The speaker in this poem wonders about his roots. Are his feelings like yours?

Going to Norway

For a detailed lesson plan on this poem, see Teacher's Manual page 111. A biography of Jack Anderson appears on text page 330.

Jack Anderson

I asked my parents,
"Have you ever thought
of going to Norway?
You are Andersons
and deserve to know
Norway, where we all began.
Do you not wonder
how things are in Norway?
I know that I wonder."
And my parents said,
"Yes,
we shall go to Norway,
we are Andersons
and want to see where
our people began.
We are growing old:
we must go now."
Yet they stayed
on the dock, staring
at the water
as ship after ship
sailed toward the north,
toward Norway.
So I said
to my parents, "Now,
you must leave now.
These are the boats
that are leaving for Norway.
A It is not long
or far."
Then my parents said,
"Yes, we want to see
Norway: we are Andersons.
But it is far."
They stayed
where they were, watching
the boats leave for Norway
and trying to picture it,
even testing a few words
of that dear language
on their tongues
—but standing
still, never moving, B
never climbing aboard,
though I kept pleading,
"Please, now, you must leave now
if you want to see Norway."
"Norway?" they murmured,
"Norway? Ah, where is that?" C
They stood very still,
grayness crept through their hair; D
it frightened me to see them
growing so old,
for I had not thought
such a thing possible.
At last I said,
"I must go
to Norway. I am
an Anderson E
and want to know
where all of us began.
I must go now."
They stood
on the dock, waving
out at the water and I
waved back over the water F
which darkened between us
with distance and tears.

A. Expansion
Note the feeling of urgency in the narrator's words as compared to the almost mechanical response of the parents. Note also that the narrator maintains that Norway is not far, while the parents insist that it is.

B. Interpreting
? What broader meaning might be coming through here? In what ways do people "stand still," "never move," "never climb aboard"?

C. Interpreting
? What seems to have happened now? (The parents seem to have forgotten where they came from and who they are.)

D. Responding
? How do you feel about the speaker's parents? Do they remind you of anyone?

E. Responding
? Do you think the speaker does the right thing by going to Norway on his own?

F. Personification
? What figure of speech do you spot in these lines? (Personification) How do you know? (The water is weeping.)

ANALYZING THE POEM
Identifying Details
1. First they say they will go immediately; then they say they want to go, but it is too far; finally they deny knowing even where Norway is.
2. He realizes that they are growing old. He feels afraid.
3. He decides to go to Norway. They stay behind, waving good-bye.

Interpreting Meanings
4. The subject is a voyage.
Possible answer: If we do not develop a sense of wonder and discovery when we are young, we may stay in one spot forever and never experience the world.
5. Among the possibilities: fear—of what they'll discover, or of the unfamiliar; inertia—too much comfort where they are, too much trouble to move.
6. Literally, distance makes water look darker, but the speaker is also referring to the psychological distance between him and his parents: He is doing what they did not dare to do. See Teacher's Manual page 112.
(Answers continue in left-hand column.)

(Continued from top.)
Applying Meanings
7. Answers will vary. See Teacher's Manual page 112 for suggested possible answers.

Additional Writing Assignment
Have students write a paragraph explaining what "Norway" might symbolize in this poem. (Experience? Maturity? Knowledge? Change?)

FURTHER READING FOR STUDENTS
Advanced students might enjoy Alex Haley's book *Roots*. Carl Sandburg's poem "The Red Son" could be compared with "Going to Norway." Judith Wright's poem "Legend" is also on the theme of growing up and setting forth on a voyage into the unknown. (Wright's poem is in *A Flock of Words: An Anthology of Poetry for Children and Others* [1969].)

Responding to the Poem

Analyzing the Poem

Identifying Details

1. Three times in the poem, the speaker asks his parents to go to Norway. Summarize the answer his parents give to each request.
2. In lines 44–49, what does the narrator suddenly realize about his parents? How does this realization make him feel?
3. Explain what the narrator finally decides he must do. What do his parents do?

Interpreting Meanings

SRW p. 87

4. The **subject** of a poem, story, or play is what it is about. The subject can be childhood, happiness, love, or anything else. The **theme,** or message, is the idea the writer expresses about the subject. A theme always must be stated in a full sentence. A theme could be, "Childhood is a time of innocence." Identify the subject of "Going to Norway." Then explain what you think is the theme of the poem.
5. Although the parents say they want to go to Norway, they never actually go. Why do you suppose they keep putting off the trip?
6. The poem ends with the speaker parting from his parents. Explain what you think the last three lines mean. That is, in what ways could distance darken the water? How could the water be darkened by tears?

Applying Meanings

7. Have you ever thought about where your ancestors came from? List three reasons why some people would want to know their family background. What reasons might other people have for not wanting to make that backward "journey" to the past?

Writing About the Poem

A Creative Response

1. **Extending the Poem.** Imagine that the speaker has reached Norway. Write a letter he might send back to his parents describing what he sees and feels there.

A Critical Response

2. **Explaining a Discovery.** Write a paragraph in which you discuss what the speaker has discovered in the course of the poem. Why do you think he wanted his parents to take the journey? Why do you think he finally decides to make the trip himself? In what new way does he see his parents and himself at the end of the poem?

See Teacher's Manual page 112.

Reading About the Writer

Jack Anderson (1935–) was born in Milwaukee and attended Northwestern University and Indiana University. He has since been a dance critic for the magazine *Dance* and *The New York Times.* Anderson's books include *The Hurricane Lamp, City Joys,* and *The Dust Dancers.*

Answers to Questions

I.

1. a. It is compared with a win in a card game.
b. Cards are dealt, and the Cards dealt a loss to the Dodgers.
c. The St. Louis Cardinals.
2. a. The writer is comparing the team to an airplane that has been grounded and can't fly.
b. *Jets* are high-pressured streams of air. *Rams* are male sheep, very aggressive. (Note that no sports team would call itself the Ewes or Lambs.)
3. a. It is saying the Giants have lost.
b. Since the team is named the Giants, it means that they have been reduced to human size. Actually, it means they have been shown to be only ordinary.
4. a. It is saying that the Saints do not have a chance of winning.
b. Saints are religious people who pray.
5. a. It means to be weaponless or weak.
b. Answers will vary. "Weak (Pathetic, Pitiful, Awful) Tigers Lose Again."

II.

1. It can be eaten or used to wash hair; it can be boiled, poached, fried, or scrambled; it can thicken a sauce; it is the only way to produce a chicken.
2. "The Pullet Surprise" is a pun on the Pulitzer Prize.
3. Eggomania would be an abnormal interest in eggs.
4. The rhyme scheme is *ababcdcdcece.*
5. Answers will vary. (Try comestible/digestible, fryable/reliable.)

★ **Texas Essential Elements/(a) English Language Arts: 3B** Figurative language

Review: Exercises in Reading Poetry

FIGURES OF SPEECH AND SOUNDS

I.

The kind of language we normally associate with poetry is also found in other kinds of writing and in everyday speech. Here are some sports headlines that use words in surprising and playful ways.

1. Cards Deal a Loss to Dodgers

- **a.** What is the Cards' win compared with?
- **b.** Why is the comparison especially appropriate for a team nicknamed the "Cards"?
- **c.** What is the real name of the "Cards"?

2. Jets Grounded by Rams

- **a.** By using the verb *grounded,* what is the writer comparing the Jets' loss to? Why is this verb appropriate for a team named the "Jets"?
- **b.** What comparisons are implied in the names *Jets* and *Rams*?

3. Giants Are Cut Down to Size

- **a.** What is this headline saying in plain, literal language?
- **b.** What play on words is used in this headline—that is, what double meaning does "cut down to size" take on?

4. Saints Haven't Got a Prayer

- **a.** What is this headline saying in plain, literal language?
- **b.** Why is the expression "haven't got a prayer" especially appropriate here?

5. Toothless Tigers Lose Again

- **a.** What does it mean, figuratively, to be "toothless"?
- **b.** How would you state this headline in plain, literal language?

II.

The writer of the following poem plays with language in the way the writers of the headlines do. (In order to understand one joke in the poem, you should know these two facts: The Pulitzer Prize is an award given to various writers each year; and a *pullet* is a kind of chicken.)

Eggomania

Consider the egg. It's a miracle,
  A thing so diverse for its size
That we hardly can help growing lyrical
  When given the Pullet Surprise.

The scope of this peerless comestible°
  Must drive other foods to despair,
Since it's not only fully digestible
  But great for shampooing the hair;

It's boilable, poachable, fryable;
  it scrambles, it makes a sauce
    thicken;
It's also the only reliable
  Device for producing a chicken.

—Felicia Lamport

1. In your own words, list the details that support the statement made in the first two lines.
2. A *pun* is a play on words that sound the same. What is the pun in line 4?
3. Egomania (ē'gō·mā'nē·ə) is a psychological term meaning an abnormal sense of one's own importance. The word *ego* in psychology means "self" or "I." What is "eggomania"? How would you pronounce it?
4. Use letters to describe the rhyme scheme of the poem.
5. Which rhymes seem especially clever to you?

III.

Here is a humorous poem by Robert Frost, who also wrote "The Pasture" (page 324). This poem in-

5. **comestible** (kə·mes'tə·b'l): food.

III.

1. It is set in a garden.
2. When the speaker stepped on its blade, the handle rose up and hit him in the head.
3. He asks whether there was a rule that the *weapon* should be turned into a tool. (See the quotation from the Bible above.)
4. Lines 3, 6, 8–10, and 12.
   Lines 4, 5, 7, 11, and 13–16. (Note that these are also the only lines that do not end with an accented syllable.)
5. *aaababccddbeefefgg*
6. Answers will vary. (Try sense/prepense, step on/weapon.)
7. A hoe that is lying on the ground, that is not being used.
8. It refers to the head or face.
   The seat of my pants. The seat also gives it the humorous meaning of having one's brains in one's buttocks.
9. Personifying the hoe.
10. The hoe shows its objection to being stepped on by hitting the speaker in the head. However, the speaker also objects, and could be said to have been stepped on by the "rulemakers."

★ **Texas Essential Elements/(a) English Language Arts: 1B** Purpose and audience; **3B** Figurative language

Review: Exercises in Reading Poetry/*cont.*

cludes an allusion to a famous quotation from the Bible: "They shall beat their swords into plowshares." The Biblical passage refers to a time of world peace, when people will turn their weapons into tools, such as plows for farming.

The Objection to Being Stepped On

At the end of the row
I stepped on the toe
Of an unemployed hoe.
It rose in offense
And struck me a blow
In the seat of my sense.
It wasn't to blame
But I called it a name.
And I must say it dealt
Me a blow that I felt
Like malice prepense.°
You may call me a fool,
but *was* there a rule
The weapon should be
Turned into a tool?
And what do we see?
The first tool I step on
Turned into a weapon.

—Robert Frost

1. Where is the poem set?
2. What did the hoe do to the speaker?
3. What question does the speaker ask as a result of the hoe's action?
4. The **rhythm** of the poem is regular, but it may not be as regular as it seems at first. Here are the first two lines, with accent marks to show their stressed and unstressed syllables:

   At the end of the row
   I stepped on the toe

   Copy the poem on paper. Write accent marks to show the rhythm of each line. (See page 271

SRW p. 77

   for help with scanning a poem.) Which lines in the poem have the same rhythm as the first line? Which lines have the same rhythm as the second line? Which line has a rhythm that is different from both these patterns?
5. Use the letters *a, b, c,* etc., to show the rhyme scheme of the poem. (The first five lines, for example, are rhymed *a a a b a.*)
6. What rhymes strike you as especially clever or surprising?
7. What is an "unemployed hoe"?
8. Line 6 includes the unusual phrase "the seat of my sense." What does this mean? What other expression do you hear echoed in this line:

   a. The seat of government?
   b. The seat of my pants?
   c. The seat of power?

9. The hoe has a toe, is unemployed, and struck the speaker. What can you say the poet is doing here?

   a. Personifying the hoe
   b. Using a simile
   c. Using imagery

10. What meaning do you find in the poem's title? (Who was stepped on?)

Writing

1. **Writing Headlines.** Write three humorous headlines, like the ones about the sports teams. Your headlines might be about sports, national or local events, show business celebrities, or any other topic you are interested in. Be sure each headline you write uses at least one word in a surprising, playful way.
2. **Writing Rhyming Lines.** Write a pair of rhyming lines about an animal. First pick an animal. Then list as many words as you can think of that rhyme with the name of the animal. Finally, write two lines that rhyme and say something (serious or silly) about the animal you've chosen.

For evaluation strategies, see Teacher's Manual page 114.
SRW p. 73

11. **malice prepense:** injury or harm (malice) that was planned in advance.

★ Texas Essential Elements/(a) English Language Arts: **1A** Composing process; **1C** Synthesize information; **1H** Proofread; **1I** Spelling generalizations; **2B** Parts of speech; **2D** Grammar/punctuation/spelling; **4I** Follow directions

Exercises in Critical Thinking and Writing

For teaching and evaluation strategies, see Teacher's Manual page 114.

SRW pp. 87, 89

COMPARING AND CONTRASTING POEMS

Writing Assignment

Write a brief essay in which you compare and contrast "A Word" (page 319) and "A Choice of Weapons" (page 320). Write at least two paragraphs.

Background

When you **compare** two poems (or stories or plays), you tell how they are alike. When you **contrast** two works, you point out the ways in which they are different. Poems can be compared and contrasted if they have at least one thing in common—a similar subject, perhaps, or similar images or figures of speech or ideas. You can recognize similarities and differences by focusing on the **elements** in each poem.

Prewriting

Reread both poems, and fill in a chart such as the one that follows. The first section is filled in.

When you've completed your chart, indicate in some way the similarities and differences. You can put a + sign next to things the poems have in common, and a 0 next to the things that are different. (See the model chart.) Or you can use highlight pens to color code similarities and differences. You could mark the similarities with pink, for example, and the differences with yellow.

Elements of Poetry	Dickinson poem	McGinley poem
Subject (What is the poem about?)	words +	words +
Theme (What does the poem say about the subject?)		
Figures of speech (Does the poet use similes, metaphors, or personification?)		
Sound (Does the poet use rhyme, meter, alliteration?)		
Tone (Is the poem serious, humorous, mocking, mournful?)		

Your last Prewriting step is to make two lists summarizing the similarities and differences:

Similarities
1. Both poems are about words.
2.
3. etc.

Differences
1.
2.
3. etc.

Writing

Follow this plan in organizing your essay:

Paragraph 1: Mention the titles and authors of the poems. Tell about at least two similarities. Cite lines from the poems.
Paragraph 2: Tell about at least two differences.

Listed below are some words and phrases that are often found in comparison/contrast essays:

For instance	On the other hand
For example	In contrast
Similarly	Besides
Both	In spite of
At the same time	In conclusion
As a result	Therefore
Consequently	However

★ Texas Essential Elements/(c) Reading: 4A Follow directions; 4D Diagrams/graphs

Exercises in Critical Thinking and Writing/*cont.*

Revising and Proofreading Self-Check

1. Does the first paragraph mention both poems' titles and authors?
2. Have I discussed two or three similarities in the first paragraph and two or three differences in the second paragraph?
3. Have I used examples from both poems to get my ideas across?
4. Does every sentence start with a capital letter and end with a period or other end punctuation mark?
5. Are my ideas clearly expressed? Have I said everything I want to say?

Partner Check

1. Are there any spelling errors?
2. Are sentences punctuated correctly?
3. Are paragraphs fully developed (at least four sentences long) and indented?
4. Are any sentences unclear? Do I understand what you are trying to say?
5. What do I like best about this paper?
6. What do I think needs improvement?

Alternative poems for this assignment are cited below. Have students compare and contrast (1) speakers, (2) use of figures of speech, and (3) messages.

Mama Is a Sunrise

When she comes slip-footing through the door,
she kindles us
like lump coal lighted,
and we wake up glowing.
She puts a spark even in Papa's eyes
and turns out all our darkness.

When she comes sweet-talking in the room,
she warms us
like grits and gravy,
and we rise up shining.
Even at night-time Mama is a sunrise
that promises tomorrow and tomorrow.

—Evelyn Tooley Hunt

Because

i wrote a poem
for you because
you are
my little boy

i wrote a poem
for you because
you are
my darling daughter

and in this poem
i sang a song
that says
as time goes on
i am you
and you are me
and that's how life
goes on

—Nikki Giovanni

(See the Instructional Overhead Transparencies)

THE ELEMENTS OF DRAMA

UNIT SIX — Robert Anderson

Discussing the Photograph

To introduce the teleplay that students will read in this unit, you might discuss with them how complicated a process television production is. As this photograph shows, the off-camera crew works as hard as the people on camera do—there are many technical jobs to be done that work to achieve the relaxed effect we eventually see on screen. Ask students to see if they can identify the specifics in the photograph: the prop men in the background; the actors waiting for a cue from an unseen director; the overhead lights and microphones; and the stage manager in the foreground, who communicates with the director by a headset and microphone.

? Who do you think is the host of the show? Who do you think the guests might be? Does the set of the show give you any hints about the topic they might discuss?

Teaching About Drama

The concept of a play should seem natural enough to your students, who have seen many dramatic productions on television and who may have acted in school plays. The actual study of drama does, of course, add new terminology and concepts that must be mastered. You should have little trouble keeping interest level high, as students will find it easy to relate to the characters in the teleplay in this unit. Therefore, students will have little trouble coping with the demands of the unit.

The major part of the unit is a full-length teleplay, *Brian's Song.* The introductory material gives an overview of drama in general and the teleplay in particular. In order to reinforce what is taught about plot, conflict, and characters, mention stories that students have read and ask volunteers to tell about those elements in short stories. Help students understand that these elements are just as important to holding one's interest in a drama.

After you have introduced the unit, you might have students watch an assigned teleplay at home. Ask them to note examples of lighting, scenery, props, and pacing of lines and to summarize the plot of the drama. Discuss the play in class, and have students make up stage and camera directions for the various scenes they saw.

Objectives of the Drama Unit

1. To improve reading proficiency and expand vocabulary
2. To identify and analyze the elements of drama
3. To understand the relationships among story, plot, conflict, and character
4. To distinguish between internal and external conflict
5. To distinguish between the protagonist and the antagonist
6. To define and identify significant literary techniques: dialogue, foreshadowing, and character
7. To interpret and respond to drama, orally and in writing, through analysis of elements
8. To practice the following critical thinking and writing skills:
   a. Analyzing a character's thoughts and feelings
   b. Preparing a eulogy
   c. Analyzing change in character
   d. Recognizing personality traits
   e. Summarizing a plot
   f. Recognizing cause and effect

SUPPLEMENTARY SUPPORT MATERIAL: UNIT SIX

1. Introduction/Understanding the Elements of Drama Test (page 133 of Test Book)
2. Word Analogies Test (page 139 of Test Book)
3. Reading Check Test blackline master
4. Unit Review Test (page 141 of Test Book)
5. Critical Thinking and Writing Test (page 145 of Test Book)
6. Understanding a Drama (Study and Reinforcement Worksheet, page 5)
7. Instructional Overhead Transparencies

Unit Outline

THE ELEMENTS OF DRAMA

A. Discussing the Quotation
Lillian Hellman (1907–1984) was a playwright and a motion picture screenwriter whose dramas bitterly attacked injustice and selfishness. Two of her well-known plays are *The Little Foxes* (1939) and *Toys in the Attic* (1960). In this quotation, she echoes a sentiment that has guided modern playwrights since Henrik Ibsen (1828–1906) popularized the "well-made play," in which every detail leads toward the climax of the story.

B. Acting Out
? How would you say this line to convey Mary's true feelings?

C. Expansion
This strict theater rule does not apply to all dramatizations. For instance, situation comedies use the "step on" approach to get a laugh. Very often, one character's speech will be disrupted, usually by a laugh track—a sound track of recorded laughter—because of another character's comic behavior. Ask students if they can think of an example of a show they've seen in which one character was deliberately "stepping on" another character to get a laugh.

SRW p. 49

A

Drama: Speech and Movement

In a good play, each detail falls into useful place. And you know that the shortest line, the smallest stage movement, has an end in view, and is not being used to trick us . . .

—Lillian Hellman

A play is not written to be read. It is written to be acted out on a stage, using speech and movements. You shouldn't have to read a program before you see a play. A good playwright will tell you everything you need to know, right on the stage.

In a short story, a writer might write this:

Mary said, "Yes, I agree with you." But she really didn't.

In a playscript, this might be written:

Mary. Yes, I agree with you. (*She really doesn't.*)

B

It is up to the actress to think of a way of speaking this line to convey the fact that Mary doesn't mean what she says. A play has no all-knowing storyteller who can take us inside Mary's mind and tell us what she is thinking.

In a movie or television show, the director might come in for a close-up of Mary's face as she says the line, so that we can see the contradiction in her eyes. In the theater, the director might have the actress pause a moment, or make some significant movement to indicate that she doesn't mean what she says, before saying the line.

C

On the stage, a pause or a movement always draws the audience's attention. When we watch a play, we tend to *watch* first, and *listen* second. One of the crimes of the theater is to "step on" another actor's line—that is, to move while he or she is speaking.

A true story about the theater can illustrate the importance of movement. Once, in a college production of a play, a boy playing a clown got his finger stuck in the neck of a bottle during another actor's big scene. The audience watched the clown's efforts to get his finger out of the bottle and didn't hear a word the other actor said. The stage manager finally had to bring down the curtain because the audience was in hysterics.

The Elements of Drama

Story and Plot

SRW p. 67

Technically, **story** is the relationship between characters, and **plot** is the sequence of incidents which develop or change this relationship. Generally, however, when someone asks what the plot of the play is, he or she is asking about "what happens" in the play, which includes both story and plot.

In drama, as in fiction, a plot consists of five basic parts, which are sometimes called its "bare bones."

A. Identifying
All these elements appear not only in drama but in most works of fiction. ? Which stories that you read earlier in this book include some of the elements listed here? (Possible responses: "Three Skeleton Key" opens with a good deal of exposition; "A Mother in Mannville" includes a lot of detail about setting; the plot of "Christmas" depends on the use of foreshadowing; all the stories in the first four units of the book deal with conflict, complications, and climax; and every story in the book has a resolution.)

B. Expansion
Hamlet, the prince of Denmark, has good reason to believe that his uncle murdered his father, then married his mother and took over the throne. Since he lacks real proof, however, he keeps talking himself out of taking action. *The Glass Menagerie* appears in *Elements of Literature: Fifth Course.*

SRW pp. 43, 79

A

1. In the **exposition,** the playwright introduces us to the **characters** and their environment (the **setting**) and perhaps sneaks in a little **foreshadowing** of the dramatic problem which is to follow.

2. Once we know something about the characters, a dramatic problem or **conflict** develops: A group of people is trapped in an elevator; a detective is looking for a murderer; a girl is trying to win a boy; a boy is fighting for self-respect. Someone wants something. Something is at stake. The character meets with problems or obstacles.

3. As the character tries to achieve something despite the obstacles, more problems and **complications** arise. (It has been said that in a play, you get a character up a tree, then you throw stones at him, and then you get him down.)

4. We reach the most exciting part of the play when we come to the **climax.** This is the moment when we know that the problem will soon be resolved one way or another. In a crime story, for example, this might be the moment when the detective finally traps the murderer on the rooftop and the shooting begins.

5. Finally, in the **resolution** of the play, all the problems are resolved either happily or unhappily, and the story is ended.

SRW p. 25

Conflict: The Key Element

The key word in drama is **conflict.** You've seen from the discussion of the "bare bones" that all plays involve people in a conflict, or struggle, of some kind.

We usually find that a conflict starts when a character wants something important, but has to overcome an obstacle to get it. The obstacle might be something outside the character, something causing an **external conflict:** the girl's parents who do not care for the boy, or the murderer who is eluding the detective. Or the character's goal may be hard to reach because of an **internal conflict** or problem that exists within the character's mind or heart.

B

Hamlet, in Shakespeare's play, can't avenge his father's murder because he is too indecisive. Laura, in Tennessee Williams's *The Glass Menagerie,* can't get what she wants because she is too shy. Whatever the obstacle, the person who has something important at stake will take measures to resolve the conflict and get what he or she wants.

Characters: The Protagonist

The person who wants something is generally called the **protagonist.** If there is a person opposing this character, that person is called the **antagonist.**

As the conflict or struggle is worked out, the protagonist usually changes. He or she may develop new strengths. In addition, we may learn complex psychological truths about the person. A play can keep us interested for only a short time in how the people are going to get out of that stalled elevator. In a good play, we come

Responding to a Teleplay
If you have access to a videotape recorder and a television, you might demonstrate the camera directions on text page 339 using the tape of a movie or TV show.

Ask students if they have ever seen reruns of the television show *Little House on the Prairie* or read any of the books that make up the nine-book series. The series was written by Laura Ingalls Wilder (1867–1957), who tells the story of her pioneer family's experiences during the late 1800's. They traveled in a covered wagon, moving from place to place in the northwest of the United States. During their travels, they braved many hardships, including fierce blizzards and an invasion of grasshoppers that ruined their crops. The TV show takes place in a town in which they lived for quite a while.

★ **Texas Essential Elements/(a) English Language Arts: 3A** Plot/character; **4E** Predict. **(c) Reading: 1A** Context clues; **3H** Predict

to understand the psychology of the characters. We want to discover their hidden fears and struggles.

These elements of plot, conflict, and characters, of course, are only the basics of drama. They are like the frame that a sculptor uses to hold the clay. What makes the play great are the talents of the writer. These include the gift of telling a good story and of telling it truly.

Responding to a Teleplay

Reading a screenplay or teleplay is different from reading the script of a play written for the stage. In a screenplay (a play for the movies) or a teleplay (a script for TV), you also have to read camera directions. You have to use these directions to imagine what you would see on the movie or TV screen.

B

Here are some useful terms for reading teleplays:

Fade-in: the picture appears on the screen.
Fade-out: the picture goes away.
Ext.: exterior (outdoors).
Int.: interior (inside).
Long shot: a camera shot from far off.
Close shot: a close-up camera shot.
Pan: a swiveling movement of the camera, from one side to the other.
O.S.: off screen.
P.O.V.: point of view (of some character).
Montage: several images appear on the screen at once.
Beat: pause.
Hold: the camera remains focused on one image for a few seconds.
Day: daytime scene.
Night: night scene.

Here is the opening of a teleplay for an episode of the long-running series *Little House on the Prairie*. One reader's responses are on the right.

Fade-in:
1. Ext. Walnut Grove Schoolhouse—Day

A Monday morning, the children arriving for school, some playing in the yard before the bell summons them inside. LAURA INGALLS *is playing "Run-Sheep-Run" with* WILLIE OLESON *and some other boys.* BANDIT *is gamboling along with them.* NELLIE OLESON *is watching* LAURA*'s unlady-like conduct with proper disapproval.* C[CARRIE *is playing "Ring-around-Rosie" with the girls.*

The games sound old-fashioned. If I were watching this, I'd know what they're wearing.
Who is Bandit? A dog?

Camera picks up outsized ADAM SIMMS *and his son,* LUKE, *as they drive up in their battered old wagon.* ADAM *is a simple, self-effacing farmer, honest-eyed, salt-of-the-earth, about 40.* LUKE D[*is 15, a young L'il Abner-type, very big for his age, with muscles to match, wears only bib overalls—no shirt, no shoes. A nice, natural, unassuming kid. As* ADAM *pulls up, and he and* LUKE *dismount,* LUKE *taking his lunch bucket, the other children stop their activity, naturally curious about the newcomer.*

If Adam is honest-eyed, he must be a "good guy." I wonder what a L'il Abner-type is.

OK. I've got a picture of these two.

2. Favoring NELLIE

Staring at LUKE *with big eyes—a case of love at first sight.*

"Favoring" isn't on the list of terms. What could it mean? (Focusing on?)

A. Identifying
? Can you name some productions in which character development is kept to a minimum in favor of plot? (Action movies would be good examples.) What plays or movies can you think of that emphasize the psychology of the characters more than the action?

B. Camera Directions
Although camera directions can make a teleplay somewhat difficult to read, they also give an interesting glimpse of what goes into making a TV movie work.

C. Expansion
Carrie is Laura's younger sister.

D. Expansion
L'il Abner was the naive, likable title character of a newspaper comic strip (begun in 1934) set in the Ozark Mountains in the Midwest.

Thinking Over the Teleplay

1. Answers will vary. Luke is a likable person, as is Laura. Nellie seems to be a little stern.

Luke is dressed very simply, indicating that his family probably does not have much money. He is a "nice, natural, unassuming kid." Adam, Luke's father, is down-to-earth and serious. Laura is a fun-loving, straightforward child who doesn't always follow the rules of etiquette. Nellie seems too proper for her age.

2. Answers will vary. Students may say that Nellie will try to make friends with Luke.

3. Answers will vary. Students may say that Laura and Nellie will compete for Luke's friendship.

A. Definition
Another Angle indicates that the action is continuing from the previous shot but is photographed by a different camera.

A *3. Another Angle*

As ADAM *hitches up the horse, straight-forward* LAURA *walks over to* LUKE, NELLIE *nudging nearer.*

I can picture Nellie hanging back.

Laura. Hi. You comin' to school here?
Luke. That's what my pa says.
Laura. My name's Laura Ingalls. What's yours?
Luke. Luke Simms.
Nellie. I'm Nellie Oleson. We own the Mercantile.

Nellie sounds like a pain. I can picture her.

LUKE *doesn't know what to say to that, but he apparently likes what he sees. He smiles:*

Does Luke like Nellie?

Luke. That's nice.
Adam (*calls*). Come on, son.

As LUKE *follows his father into the schoolhouse, Hold* LAURA *and* NELLIE*—the latter watching* LUKE *go with shining eyes. Then* NELLIE *scowls, turns to* LAURA.

Nellie likes Luke.

Nellie. Don't you have any manners?
Laura. Sure. I got plenty of manners.
Nellie. All bad! It isn't proper for a girl to speak to a boy first.
Laura. Aw . . . that's old-fashioned.

As NELLIE *tosses her curls and minces away,* LAURA *calls after:*

How does someone "mince"?

Laura. And dumb!

—from "Here Come the Brides"

Thinking Over the Teleplay

Did you have any additional questions as you read this script?

1. How do you picture the **characters** you've met so far? What do you know about them?
2. What do you **predict** is going to happen next?
3. Can you predict what the **conflict** or problem in the teleplay will be?

READING CHECK TEST

1. A play is written to be acted out, not to be ________. (*read*)

2. The ________ is the sequence of events that changes the relationships among characters. (*plot*)

3. In the ________, the audience is introduced to the characters and the setting. (*exposition*)

4. The most exciting part of a play is the ________. (*climax*)

5. The script of a television drama is called a ________. (*teleplay*)

★ **Texas Essential Elements/(a) English Language Arts: 1B** Purpose and audience; **3A** Plot/character.
(c) Reading: 1A Context clues; **1C** Dictionaries; **2A** Word meaning; **3A** Main ideas/details; **3I** Draw conclusions

Brian's Song

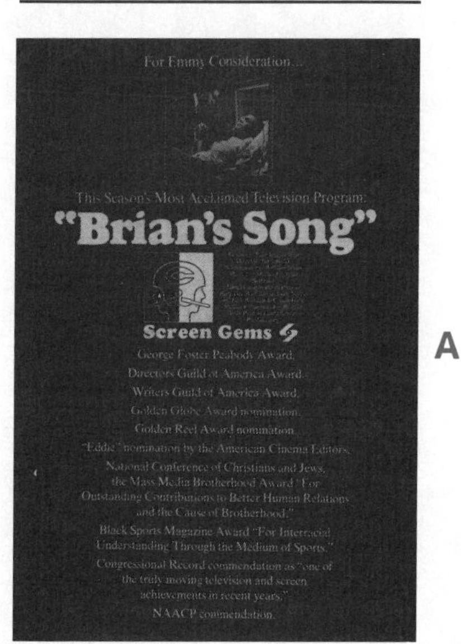

Brian's Song, by William Blinn, is an award-winning television drama that is based on a true story about two members of the Chicago Bears professional football team. Television dramas share many characteristics with plays and movies, but they also have some special characteristics.

Television: A Special Type of Drama

Television may be the most intimate form of drama. It can make you feel very close to characters, because it brings them right into your own home.

A television drama is much more likely than a play to have a **narrator**—a voice that comments on the action. The narrator of a television drama may create **suspense,** or a feeling of anxious curiosity. For example, the narrator might begin the drama with, "If I had known then what I know now, I never would have entered the dark house."

A television drama can also switch scenes more often and more quickly than a play. Many kinds of action that might be hard to portray realistically in a play—a car chase, an underwater scene—can easily be filmed for television.

The written form of any drama is called a **script.** The script of a movie is called a **screenplay.** The script of a television drama is called a **teleplay.** Like all drama scripts, a teleplay includes directions about props, setting, and how the actors should move and speak. But a teleplay also contains instructions for camera and sound effects. These instructions will help you visualize the drama as you read it.

The Story

Brian's Song is the story of two men who compete with each other, joke with each other, like each other, get angry at each other, and finally love each other. As soon as we meet the two men, it is clear that they differ in some important ways—one is quiet and shy, one noisy and kidding; one is black, one white. We immediately sense the possibility of dramatic conflict of many kinds. How and under what circumstances will these men clash? Who will win? Will their struggle change them in some way? We sit back to enjoy the unfolding story, satisfied that we have been presented with the material for an absorbing drama.

The story is filled with additional conflicts besides the conflicts between Brian Piccolo and Gale Sayers. Other struggles small and large take place, with everything from a place on the team to a human life at stake. As soon as one problem is resolved, another takes its place. We are constantly wondering, "What will happen next?"

Often a writer will defend a poorly written story by saying, "But it's all true. It really happened." However it's not enough that a story is true. It must be believable as well. In a drama, the audience's belief is more important than the actual truth.

A. Discussing the Photograph
This ad, paid for by the production company responsible for *Brian's Song,* appeared in magazines and newspapers (such as *Variety*) that are read by people in the television business. The top line of copy indicates that it was intended to win votes from the members of the Television Academy of Arts and Sciences, in the hope of garnering an Emmy Award.

B. Definition
The word *prop* is a short form of *property* and designates any moveable object, other than costumes and scenery, used in the staging of a play, movie, or television production.

PREREADING

1. **BUILDING ON PRIOR KNOWLEDGE.** Plays are a special kind of fiction because a playwright does not give extensive descriptions or tell an audience what to think of a character. In a play, other techniques like dialogue and stage directions have to replace the narrator's voice. We can learn a great deal from a character's lines and expressions. The abilities of the actors and actresses play an important role in plays, for it is they who portray the characters the writer has created—Hollywood has made an institution out of favorite actors and actresses. In a teleplay, we learn a lot about plot from camera shots. For instance, if we are shown a young woman and then a succession of shots, supposedly through her eyes, of couples in love, we can assume that she is lonely and wishes she had a boyfriend.

Tell students to notice how quickly and easily they get to know Brian and Gale, just by reading the lines the playwright has given them to speak and by absorbing the information about setting and conflict provided by the cameras. Tell them to think of how the actors who play the roles of Brian and Gale would say their lines.

Responding to the Photograph

This is a publicity photograph of Brian Piccolo, released by the Chicago Bears while he was a member of their team. Like most publicity photos, this one is intended to show its subject in a certain light. Brian Piccolo was not an extremely fast runner; this photograph emphasizes his agility rather than his speed as a running back.

? Looking at this photograph, what do you think Brian Piccolo is like as a person? What sort of expression is on Piccolo's face? (Note: Some of the photographs used in this selection are from the 1970 television movie. These pictures show James Caan as Brian Piccolo and Billy Dee Williams as Gale Sayers.)

Note on Vocabulary

A running section called "Football Vocabulary" explains the football terms that appear in the text.

BRIAN'S SONG

For a detailed lesson plan on this teleplay, see Teacher's Manual pages 116–121. For information on William Blinn, see page 378.

William Blinn

2. ESTABLISHING A PURPOSE. This play startles you from the outset because it tells you how it's going to end. However, it's a play you cannot put down: Something keeps you reading. Tell students to be aware as they read of the elements that keep them reading, even though they know how the story ends.

3. PREREADING JOURNAL. Before they read, have students write a brief paragraph telling what they think, judging from the title, the play might be about. Why did the playwright call it Brian's "Song" and not "Story" or "Life"?

Football Vocabulary

defensive linemen: players who hold the line against the advancing offense, which has the ball

blocking sled: To increase blocking strength, players hurl themselves against the padded metal arm of the sled.

rope framework: players run through this grid made of rope to increase agility

Like many teleplays, *Brian's Song* occasionally uses a narrator, or unseen voice, to comment on or explain the action. After you read the narrator's introduction, think about what emotions and expectations the narrator asks you to feel as the drama opens.

Characters

Narrator, voice that comments on the action
Brian Piccolo, **Gale Sayers** — running backs for the Chicago Bears
George Halas, coach of the Bears
J. C. Caroline, **Abe Gibron**, **Ed McCaskey** — assistant coaches of the Bears
Atkins, **Evey**, **O'Bradovich** — players for the Bears
Reporters
Linda Sayers, Gale's wife
Joy Piccolo, Brian's wife
Speaker, at an awards ceremony
Jack Concannon, quarterback of the Bears
Announcer, radio sportscaster
Doctor Fox, who treats Gale Sayers
Nurses
Hotel Official
Player, Gale's new roommate
Mr. Eberle, hospital official
Doctor, who gives Brian anesthesia
M.C., master of ceremonies

Camera Directions and Audio Instructions. This teleplay includes camera directions (directions for filming or videotaping the action) as well as audio instructions (directions for sound effects). You should be able to understand most of the terms. If you are unsure of the meaning of a term, look for clues in the words and phrases around it. Check a dictionary if the meaning is still unclear. Use the camera directions and audio instructions to help you picture the story.

Part One

Fade-in: Exterior—Rolling Countryside—Day (Helicopter Shot)—The terrain is farmland, flat, tranquil, soothing in its simplicity. As our view gets closer to the ground, we start to hear the Narrator's voice.

Narrator (*Voice Over*). This is a story about two men, one named Gale Sayers, the other Brian Piccolo. They came from different parts of the country. They competed for the same job. One was white; the other black. One liked to talk; the other was as shy as a three-year-old. Our story's about how they came to know each other, fight each other, and help each other. . . . (*Beat*) Ernest Hemingway said that every true story ends in death. Well, this *is* a true story. A

[*As the helicopter continues its descent, we follow a cab down a two-lane asphalt road. We follow the cab as we roll opening credits.*]

[*Direct Cut to: Exterior—Campus-type area—Day—On sign reading: "Training Camp of the Chicago Bears," an NFL insignia beneath the lettering. We pan off the sign, moving by a number of red brick buildings, the kind of ivied architecture seen at any number of small universities in the Middle West. Coming up the curving blacktopped drive is the cab.*] B

[*Exterior—Practice Field—Series of cuts—The Bears are going through the various routines and exercises. Defensive linemen scuttling crablike back and forth as a coach switches a ball from hand to hand. Men working on the blocking shed, throwing their bulk against the padded metal arm. Players negotiating the rope framework, some alternating, crossing over, others hopping from square to square. Throughout these cuts, the sounds of men under strain, struggling for breath, grunting with effort as they bear down.*] C

[*As we zoom toward the far end of the field, we see* GALE SAYERS *standing by the driver's side of the cab, his suitcase next to him.* SAYERS *is in his early twenties, his handsome face normally enigmatic,*[1] *guarded. He's dressed in slacks and sport*

1. **enigmatic** (en′ig·mat′ik): perplexing; hard to understand.

A. Foreshadowing
Ernest Hemingway (1899–1961) is a widely respected American writer who won the Nobel Prize in literature.
? How does it affect your response to the teleplay to know that it is a "true story" and that it "ends in death"? (The statement makes us sad, but it sparks our interest. It must be a good story if the writer can give away the ending at the beginning.)

B. Expansion
NFL stands for National Football League, the organization of professional competitive football teams in the United States.

C. Figurative Language
? What image does this description provoke? (The defensive linemen are, like crabs, moving sideways back and forth. Because they usually move crouching down, they are described as "scuttling.")

Football Vocabulary
rookie: first-year player

A. Character
What contrast between Gale and Brian do we notice immediately? (Gale is "enigmatic, guarded," and stiff in his manner; Brian has an easy smile, good sense of humor, and he enjoys people.)

B. Interpreting
What causes the awkwardness in this scene? (Gale doesn't realize that Brian wants to shake hands. Then Brian thinks Gale doesn't want to.) How do you think the actors would have portrayed "stuttering reactions"?

C. Interpreting
Is Brian being funny and teasing here or mean and jeering? How do you know? (Funny; we know that his "smile is a nice one" and that he is just trying to break the ice with Gale—not an easy task.)

D. Responding
Why doesn't Gale smile or respond to Brian? (He doesn't know how to take Brian's joking; he is afraid that Brian is making fun of him.)

E. Character
What do these directions tell us about Gale? (He is very nervous about meeting Halas.) Why might he be feeling this way? (Perhaps he is afraid of authority; he is new and wants to make a good impression; he is shy about meeting people.)

Supplementary Support Material: Part One

1. Vocabulary Activity Sheet
2. Reading Check Test blackline master
3. Selection Test (page 135 of Test Book)
4. Connections Between Reading and Writing worksheet (complete play)
5. Reader's Response Journal (complete play)
6. Workbook (page 109)

coat, but even in this kind of "civilian" garb, it doesn't take a practiced eye to note the lean, hard compactness of a born athlete.]

Brian *(Voice Over)*. Heads up! Look out!

[GALE *looks toward the sound of the voice just in time to react to the football* hurtling *down toward him. He gets a hand up and slaps it away, over the cab.* GALE *walks across to the other side of the road to get the football and throws it to the young man now approaching him. He's wearing a Bears sweat shirt, workout shorts, football cleats. This is* BRIAN PICCOLO*—early twenties, with a smile that comes easily and nicely. He takes life and people as he finds them, and he generally finds them worthwhile, enjoyable, and a little funny. The face is strong and handsome.* GALE *throws the ball back across the road to him.*] A

Gale. Here you go.
Brian. Thanks.

[BRIAN *heaves the ball back to the practice area offstage, though he makes no move to return there himself.* GALE *is a little ill at ease as* BRIAN *just stands there looking at him with a half smile.*]

Brian. You're Gale Sayers.
Gale. Yeah.
Brian. I'm Brian Piccolo. We met at the All-America game last June in Buffalo.

B [BRIAN *has extended his hand, but* GALE *is holding his suitcase. A short beat as* GALE *switches hands, but by the time it's done,* BRIAN *has taken back his hand, and there's a moment of stuttering reactions. Finally, they shake hands.* GALE'*s head is down, face guarded.*]

Gale. Sorry I didn't remember. But I'm not very good at that kind of stuff.

[PICCOLO'*s smile is a nice one.*]

Brian *(a quiet put-on)*. Golly, that's okay. I can see why you might forget, but I sure couldn't. No way. That was a heckuva talk we had, man. I mean, I walked up and said: "I'm Brian Piccolo. I hear we'll both be playing for the Bears." And you said—I'll never forget it—you said: "Uh-huh." Just like that. "Uh-huh." And whenever I'm feeling depressed or low, why, I think about that advice. Lot of guys wouldn't have taken the time to talk to me like that, but not you. "Uh-huh," you said. Just like that. Right out. C

[BRIAN *grins.* GALE *does not. His expression is neutral. A short beat.*]

Gale. Where do I go to check in?

[PICCOLO'*s smile goes. The total lack of reaction from* GALE *is puzzling. He nods toward one of the buildings offstage.*] D

Brian. That building over there. That's where Halas is.
Gale. Thanks.

[*The word comes in a characteristic flat tone.* GALE *moves off for the building.* BRIAN *stands there a moment, looking after him thoughtfully.*]

Brian. Hey . . .

[GALE *stops, looking back.*]

Gale. What?
Brian. You ever met Halas before?
Gale. Talked to him on the phone a couple times. That's all.
Brian. Well, look, let me give you a little hint. He's a good guy and all, but he's deaf in his left ear and he's too vain to admit it. So stay on his right-hand side, or he won't hear a word you say.
Gale. Uh–okay. Thanks.
Brian. Rookies have to stick together, man.

[*With a wave of his hand,* BRIAN *starts off, moving at an easy lope back onto the practice field.* SAYERS *stands there, watching* BRIAN, *not knowing precisely what to make of him. After a moment, he turns and starts for the building pointed out by* PICCOLO.]

[*Direct Cut to: Interior—Bears' Main Office Corridor—Full Shot—*GALE *comes in looking about uneasily, then heads for the end of the corridor. He stops in front of a door with a nameplate reading "Coach George Halas," wipes his sweating palms on his trouser legs, then knocks on the door.*]

Halas *(impatiently, offstage)*. Yeah, come in. E

[GALE *stands motionless for a second, gathering his forces, then opens the door and steps inside.*]

Developing Vocabulary

The following words appear on a test in the Test Book, page 136. (See also the Vocabulary Activity Sheet.)

pan	perusal
enigmatic	cadence
hurtling	conglomeration
vain	hazing
relishing	residual

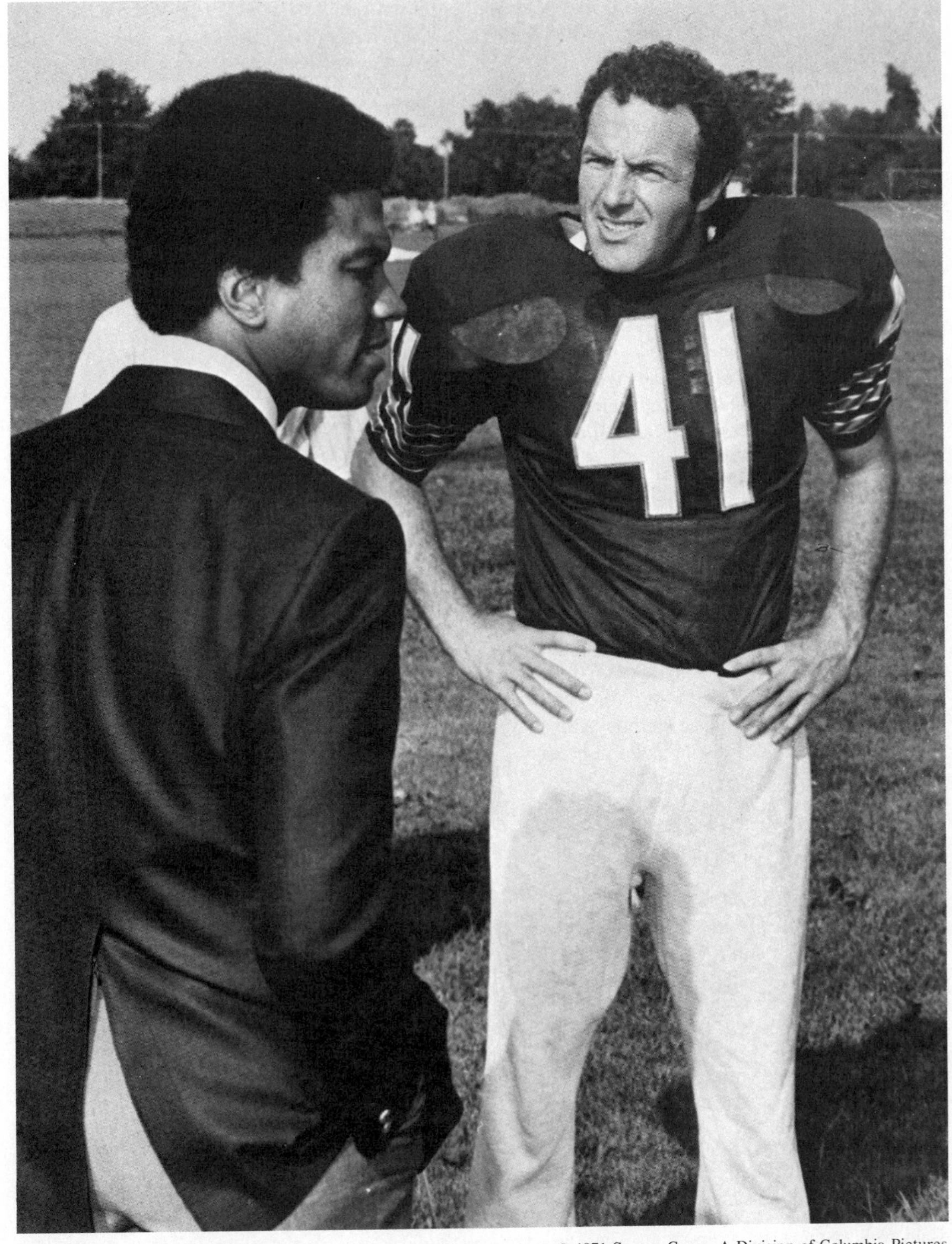

"Rookies have to stick together, man."

© 1971 Screen Gems, A Division of Columbia Pictures Industries, Inc. All rights reserved.

Responding to the Photograph

? In your opinion, are these two actors portraying Brian and Gale successfully? How? (It would seem they are. Brian's relaxed hands-on-hips stance shows his easygoing nature. His expression shows puzzlement at Gale's seeming indifference. Gale is looking away from Brian; his hands in his pockets reflect his discomfort.)

Football Vocabulary
running back: an offensive player who handles the ball
blitz: a strategy whereby almost all the defensive players charge the quarterback while he is trying to pass
screen: to protect another player, for whom a short pass is intended, with a wall of blockers

A. Interpreting
? From this line, and from what we have seen so far, what is Gale's relationship to the Bears? (His selection to play on the team represents his entrance into professional football.)

B. Plot
Here Gale, along with the audience, finds out that he and Brian are going to come into direct conflict—they will be competing for the same position.

C. Making Inferences
? What is the realization? (That Brian has played a practical joke on Gale: Brian knew Gale would follow his advice and make a fool of himself during his first meeting with Halas. This incident sets up an immediate conflict—how will Gale retaliate?)

[*Interior—*HALAS*'s Office—As* GALE *comes into the office, he starts to speak, but his voice is only a dry croak.*]

[*The office is in a state of organized chaos. Cardboard filing boxes, cartons of books and papers. Reels of film and, standing behind an ancient desk, a large man of some years, some strength, and much power:* HALAS. *He holds a framed picture, hammer, and nails. He looks at the young man standing in the doorway.*]

Halas. I'm George Halas.
Gale. I know. *(Quickly)* I mean, everyone knows who you are. I'm Gale Sayers.
Halas. Come on in, Gale. You can give me a hand hanging this thing. My good luck picture. First professional team I ever played on. The Decatur Staleys in 1920.

[GALE *steps in, closing the door, still awed and afraid.* HALAS *moves to an empty place on the wall, his back to* GALE.]

Halas. How's your leg? I read where it was hurt.
Gale. It's fine. Hundred percent.
Halas. How about your head?
Gale. My head? Nothin' wrong with my head.
Halas. Good. Because being in the All-Star game puts you three weeks behind everybody else. New terminology, new plays to learn. Won't be easy.
A **Gale** *(beat).* NFL ain't supposed to be easy.

[*A smile and look from* HALAS. *He nods.*]

Halas. Right. Give me a hand.

[GALE *moves behind the desk, where* HALAS *is holding the picture up against the wall.* HALAS *starts hammering a nail.*]

Halas. About all I can promise you is a fair shot at running back. But you're going to have a lot of
B company. Jon Arnett, Ralph Kurek, Brian Piccolo . . . going to be very crowded out there.

[GALE *looks at* HALAS *for a second, realizing he's on the man's left side, recalling the advice given him by* BRIAN *earlier. He rumbas around behind and then to the other side of the Coach.*]

Gale. Well, a fair shot is all I want. Can't ask for more than that.

[HALAS *notes* GALE*'s shift with a puzzled look, then drives the nail home. He turns back to the desk, once more placing* GALE *on his left side.*]

Halas. We plan to use our backs a good deal as receivers this year. You do much pass catching when you were in college?

[*He looks back to where* GALE *was, only to find that* GALE *has crossed behind him.*]

Gale. Well, yes sir, I did, but it was usually safety-valve stuff. Once in awhile we'd screen.

[HALAS *moves to one of the filing cabinets nearby.*]

Halas. Well, I generally prefer to get a back into the pattern, unless the other team has a tendency to blitz. That's another thing you'll have to get used to, checking out the linebackers, make sure they aren't coming.

[HALAS *looks back to* GALE, *but once again, he's the man who isn't there.* GALE *has managed to cross behind him again, squeezing in between* HALAS *and the wall, struggling to make the move seem casual.*]

Gale. Yes sir, I know . . . (HALAS *starts back to the desk, once again forcing* GALE *to do an end around.*) . . . and especially on teams like the Cardinals, I guess . . .
Halas *(exasperated).* Sayers—what's the matter with you?
Gale. I-I don't know what you mean . . .
Halas. I know you've got moves, but you don't have to show them to me now! You're hopping around here like a pauper in a pay toilet!
Gale *(sputtering).* Well, I-I was just trying to stay on the side with your good ear . . .
Halas. Good ear? What are you talking about, good ear?
Gale. Well, Brian Piccolo told me that—he said—uh—he—uh . . .

[HALAS *waits for the sentence to end, but it's not going to. For the realization is slowly dawning on* GALE *that he has been had.* GALE *struggles to manufacture a smile as* HALAS *stares at him.*] C

[*Direct Cut to: Interior—Dining Hall—Night—The table is piled with food being assaulted by a num-*

A *ber of large men, who ladle on portions that would choke a garbage disposal. At a centrally placed table, we can see* HALAS, *his coaches, and key players. Seated on one side of* HALAS *is* ED MCCASKEY, *a handsome man in his early fifties. On the other side is* ABE GIBRON, *a man who is all football. One man at the table is standing. This is* J. C. CAROLINE, *a man in his late twenties, tall and lean, built for speed. He has a packet of three-by-five index cards he consults as he speaks.*]

Caroline. Some of you guys who pulled in today haven't had a chance to hear what's going to be expected of you, so pipe down for a little bit, let me talk.

[GALE *is seated at one of the rear tables, exchanging "pass-the-salt" conversations with the other men nearby, all of whom are black. The man next to* GALE *finishes his plate and vacates the chair as* CAROLINE *continues to speak offstage.* BRIAN PICCOLO *approaches and starts to unload his tray in the place next to* GALE. GALE *tries to hide his displeasure.*]

Caroline *(droning offstage).* You new guys are going to be given a playbook tomorrow. It's like
B the Bible, except the Gideons don't replace it for free. Neither do the Bears. Lose the playbook and the fine is five hundred dollars. No exceptions, no appeal. Five–double–o. Second thing is curfew. You don't like it; I don't like it. Well, that's just tough sleddin', because that fine is ten bucks for every fifteen minutes and there's no appeal from that either. Now—for talking in team meeting . . .

[CAROLINE *becomes aware of* GALE *and* BRIAN *speaking offstage.*]

Brian. Sayers, we can't go on meeting like this—my wife's getting suspicious.
Gale. Buzz off. I'm trying to listen to the Man.
Brian. No need, no need. I've been through this lecture twice already. If you lose the playbook, a fine of five big ones. Lose the playbook a second time, and they cut off your foot and feed it to the defensive platoon.
Gale. Just cool it, would you please?
Brian. Just trying to be helpful.
Gale. Yes—like you "helped" me with Halas. Well, I don't need your kind of . . .
Caroline *(loudly offstage). Mister* Sayers!

[J. C. CAROLINE *fixes* GALE *with the look that's chilled any number of feckless flankers. Every eye in the room is on* GALE, *and most are relishing his pained reaction.*]

Caroline *(continuing).* I was mentioning the fine for talking in a team meeting. Did you happen to hear me?
Gale. No, I did not.
Caroline. The fine is twenty-five dollars, Mister Sayers. And it's just been levied on you, *dig?*
Gale *(seething).* Yeah.

[PICCOLO *stares straight ahead, lips trembling as he tries to mask the laughter building up within him.*]

Brian *(softly).* Sorry, man. . . .

[GALE *glares at him, homicide in mind. Slow homicide.*]

[*Full Shot*—CAROLINE *gets to his feet, tapping the water glass for attention.*]

Caroline. It's been brought to my attention that unless Sayers was saying his beads[2] it might be fair if Mr. Piccolo was to give us a little song.
Say—a fight song. Wake Forest, wasn't it, Mr. C
Piccolo?

[*Angle to* BRIAN *and* GALE—GALE'*s look acknowledges that there may be some justice in this old world after all. To his surprise, however, the singing troubles* BRIAN *not at all. He smiles, rising, and when he sees the surprise on* GALE'*s face, leans over to whisper.*]

Brian. Can't let it get to you, man—it's all a question of *style*. Style, I say . . . D

[*He is up on the chair, launching into the Wake Forest fight song, giving it a rousing tempo, and booming volume.* BRIAN *thrives on this kind of thing.* GALE'*s eye falls on something offstage in the direction of* BRIAN'*s plate.*]

---

2. **beads:** rosary, a string of beads used for keeping count in saying prayers.

A. Humor
? How does the writer create humor here? (Exaggeration; he is making the point that the men are huge and so are their appetites. This is an example of why this teleplay, although meant to be acted, is also fun to read. The writer, less humorously, could have just said, "The men ladle out huge portions.")

B. Expansion
The Gideon Society leaves Bibles in hotel rooms, in the hope that people will take them away when they leave.

C. Expansion
Wake Forest is the college that Brian attended.

D. Character
? What have we learned about the differences between Gale and Brian so far? (Gale tends to take things seriously—he doesn't have much of a sense of humor. To Brian, on the other hand, everything is one big joke.)

Football Vocabulary
offensive back: also called a running back (see definition on page 346)
"fake draw, screen right": Brian was supposed to fake a hand-off to the left in order to draw the defense to the left, so that he would be free to throw to the right.

A. Character
? What does Gale's revenge on Brian show about Gale's character? (Gale is stronger than we thought, and he *does* have a sense of humor. This scene heightens our interest in the play since we know it's going to be a humorous battle from here on in.)

B. Technique
? What is the effect of the succession of camera shots? (These scenes reveal the following things: the Bears are worked very hard; Gale and Brian have to work side by side as teammates; Brian and Gale are both fast runners—Gale is faster; both men are very competitive; Halas is impressed with Gale's running speed.)

C. Humor
? What is Brian's joke here? (That he is deliberately letting Gale win in order to build up Gale's confidence)

[GALE's *Point of View—The Plate—Shot is centered on two mammoth dollops of mashed potatoes swimming in rich brown gravy.*]

[*Angle on* GALE*—He takes a spoon and fork, glancing up to make sure* BRIAN *is still concentrating on the song, then moves to transfer the potatoes to the seat of* BRIAN*'s chair.*]

[*Angle on* BRIAN*—As he finishes the song,* BRIAN *waves a cordial hand to those clapping, then hops down lightly and sits—without looking.* GALE *just sits there, looking at* BRIAN*, enjoying the rush of expressions that go rolling across his face. Disbelief. Dread. Realization. A look to the absent mashed potatoes on his plate. Acceptance. By the time he slowly swings to look over to* GALE, GALE *is just getting to his feet, face composed. Before he goes, however, he reminds* BRIAN.]

A **Gale.** It's all a question of style—style, I say. . . .

[*He moves off, camera closing on* PICCOLO. *He turns squishily, watching* GALE *saunter off. He can't quite work up a smile, but neither can he get to a point of being very angry about it. He can take it as well as hand it out, it seems.*]

[*Direct Cut to: Exterior—Practice Field—Day—Tight on* GIBRON—ABE GIBRON *is an assistant coach possessed of a strong voice. When we pull back, we will see that* GIBRON *is presently riding herd on a number of offensive backs,* SAYERS *and* PICCOLO *in the forefront, as they lower their heads and dig against the resistance of the harness looped about their shoulders and fastened to a stone wall.* GIBRON *will not be happy until one of the men pulls down the wall.*]

Gibron. Dig! Dig! Dig! Come on! What's wrong with you? You're not trying! You're not trying! You make me sick! Dig—dig—dig!

[*Hard Cut to: Exterior—Practice Field—Day—Full Shot—Fifty men hit the dirt then are up on their feet, running in place.*]

Gibron. Mark! Set! Go!

[SAYERS *and* PICCOLO *come out of a sprinter's crouch, taking each other on in wind sprints, their faces locked with drive and desire.*]

[*Angle to the Forty-Yard Line—*HALAS *and a number of other coaches are standing.* GALE *tears across the line a full stride ahead of the others. Stopwatches are held out for* HALAS*'s* *perusal. He notes the results and is pleased.*]

[*Angle on* GALE *and* BRIAN*—They draw up, both sagging, leaning forward, hands on knees as they try to pull more air in. This may be the tenth wind sprint they've run today. Between gasps of breath:*] B

Brian. Well—I think it's working.
Gale. What's working?
Brian. I'm getting you overconfident. C

[*Hard Cut to: Interior—Team Meeting Room—Day—On Blackboard—A play is diagrammed on the blackboard, the area covered with circles and X's, dotted lines and arrows.* HALAS *is the man with the chalk. No need to hear what he's saying—his look and the manner in which he raps the chalk against the slate gets the message across.*]

[*Angle on* SAYERS *and* PICCOLO*—They are seated near the front with the rest of the players, all of whom are studying the board as if their lives depended on it. Which, in one sense, it does. The look of exhaustion is shared by all as they listen and frantically scribble notes.*]

[*Direct Cut to: Exterior—Practice Field—Day—Full Shot—The offense and defense take measure of one another. They line up, the ball is snapped. There is a brief flurry of motion, then the quarterback is downed by a large man from the defensive unit. As they all untangle themselves to the accompaniment of whistles,* BRIAN *gets up and finds himself being glared at by* ABE GIBRON.]

Gibron. Pic! You bonehead! That was a fake draw, screen right! What's your assignment on a fake draw, screen right?
Brian. My assignment on a fake draw, screen right, is to pick up the linebacker, if he's coming, unless the linebacker is Dick Butkus. Then I simply notify the quarterback and send for a priest.

[*Laughter from the others on this, which only enrages* GIBRON.]

Brian Piccolo at a gathering with other Chicago athletes. Ice-hockey star Stan Mikita is to Piccolo's immediate left; football great Dick Butkus is behind his left shoulder.

[*Angle on* GALE—*He is smiling broadly at* PICCOLO*'s reply—smiling, perhaps, in spite of himself.*]

Gibron *(offstage)*. Come on, you guys, don't! You just encourage him, that's all! Knock it off!

A

[*Direct Cut to: Exterior—Practice Field—Night—Full Shot*—GALE *moves along the walk bordering the practice area dressed in casual sports clothes, an after-dinner stroll. He nears us, then stops, looking offstage, expression puzzled.*]

[*His Point of View—On* BRIAN—*In the middle of the empty practice field,* BRIAN *falls into a three-point stance, counts off a whispered* cadence *of signals, then breaks to his right. Just as he's about to turn upfield, he brakes sharply and cocks his arm, letting an imaginary pass go. Apparently, the imaginary receiver caught the ball, because* PICCOLO*'s expression is pleased as he turns back—and sees* GALE *watching his pantomime. He shrugs.*]

Brian. I'm dynamite until there's someone playing against me.

[*Another Angle*—GALE *moves to him, still a little puzzled.*]

Brian. Practicing the halfback option. I'm not too good at it, and it looks as if they want to use it a lot. B

Gale *(politely)*. Oh, you'll get the hang of it.

Brian *(smiles)*. Wish I was as sure of that as you are. Tell you the truth, Sayers—I envy you.

Gale. How come?

Brian. Because they've got a lot of money tied up in you. They can't cut you.

Football Vocabulary

three-point stance: crouched down with one hand touching the ground

halfback option: the choice of the halfback to run or to throw the ball when he gets the ball from the quarterback

cut: to be dropped from the team

A. Interpreting

? What does this exchange show about Brian's relationship with the team he has just joined? (He is obviously the team comedian.)

B. Character

? What new quality in Brian is revealed here? (Vulnerability, insecurity. His behavior and speech here seem out of character for the self-confident, practical joker we met before.)

Football Vocabulary
flanker: wide receiver who catches passes and is a fast runner

A. Identifying
The "Old Man" is Coach Halas.

B. Figurative Language
? Why is "turtle shell" a good term for Gale's reserve? (Turtles traditionally represent the quality of timidity; their shells are thick, tough, and hard to crack.)

C. Atmosphere
? What is the atmosphere of the room? Why does Gale think they've asked him to come? (The atmosphere is tense and uncomfortable. Halas is beating around the bush, and Gale is expecting bad news.)

D. Expansion
A flanker has less responsibility than a running back.

E. Allusion
The title character of Harriet Beecher Stowe's novel *Uncle Tom's Cabin* was a lovable old black slave who wanted to please people—especially his white owners. Some blacks use "Uncle Tom" to refer to blacks who try to make too favorable an impression on whites.

[GALE *looks at him for a second, then turns abruptly and starts off.*]

Brian *(simply).* And you're too good to get cut, bonus or no bonus.

[GALE *stops, turns back slowly.*]

Brian *(beat).* And I'm too good, too, but I'm not sure I've proved that to the Old Man yet. A

[GALE *is thrown off stride mentally.* PICCOLO'S *easy directness takes some getting used to.* BRIAN *views him with a small smile.*]

B **Brian.** Sayers—I am bending over backward to get through that turtle shell of yours. Can't you at least say thank you or something?

Gale. Well—I don't do things like you do—telling jokes and all that kind of—you know—I—I'm more of a . . . *(considers)* Thanks.

[*A quick nod, then* GALE *turns and heads back in the direction of the dormitory.* PICCOLO *smiles, taking even this small breakthrough as some kind of progress. He gets to his feet and is about to go through the halfback option once more.*]

Gale. Hey, Piccolo?

Brian. Yeah?

Gale. Try it going to your left. They don't look for a right-handed guy to throw going to his left.

[BRIAN *nods, smiling as their eyes meet;* GALE'S *look still a guarded one.*]

Brian *(beat).* Thanks.

Gale *(he shrugs, glances down).* Well, like you said—we rookies got to stick together.

[*Hard Cut to: Interior—Hallway Outside* HALAS'S *Office—Day—On Door—*GALE *raps on the door several times.*]

Halas *(offstage).* Come on in, Gale.

[GALE *opens the door and steps in, camera following to reveal* HALAS *behind the desk,* ED MCCASKEY *seated nearby, and* J. C. CAROLINE *drawing on the blackboard.* GALE *views the three with a mixture of fear and curiosity.*]

Halas. You know Ed McCaskey, don't you, Gale? And J. C.?

[*Affirmative ad-libs*[3] *come from* GALE *and the other two men.* HALAS *nods toward a pitcher of iced tea.*]

Halas. Want some iced tea?

Gale. Uh, yeah. Please.

[HALAS *pours him a glass, the cubes tinkling.* GALE *fidgets.* HALAS *hands him the glass.*]

Halas. Tell you what we wanted to talk to you about, Gale. . . . See, I'm an old-timer in a lot of ways . . . *(A look to* CAROLINE *and* MCCASKEY*)* At least that's what people keep telling me—but I don't think it's all that uncommon for a man my age to get used to the way things are—to be comfortable with things. You understand what I'm saying. C

Gale *(baffled).* I guess so . . .

Halas. Well, what it comes down to is that J. C. here had a notion and he talked to Ed about it, and Ed thinks it's a good idea—and I guess maybe it's time for some changes around here. You follow me?

Gale. You want me to play flanker, not running back. D

[*The other three exchange a smile at this.*]

McCaskey. Not that simple, Gale. J. C.'s point—and one I agree with—is that it's time the Bears roomed together by position—without any regard to race.

Caroline. We'd like you and Brian Piccolo to room together.

Gale *(smiles with relief).* Is that all? Is that what this is about?

Caroline. Is that *all*?

Gale. Yeah. You had me worried. I thought it was something really . . .

[*Tight on* CAROLINE.]

Caroline *(pointing, pinning* GALE *to the chair).* Sayers—this *is* something, really. This is a white man and a black man rooming together on a team where that's never been done before. You're going to be called Uncle Tom by some blacks and uppity by some whites. *(Beat)* You're going to rock the E

3. **affirmative ad-libs:** improvised remarks meaning "yes."

A boat, Sayers—and there's plenty of people around who are already seasick.

[*A beat, as* CAROLINE *holds* GALE'*s gaze, then straightens up.* HALAS *has a small smile on his face.*]

Halas. Have a glass of iced tea, J. C. *(Leans forward)* What J. C. is saying is that there may be pressures, Gale. Severe ones. *(Simply)* Now! What do *you* say?

[GALE *takes a breath, looking beyond the three men, giving the question the introspection it deserves.*]

[*Direct Cut to: Interior—Dormitory Hallway—Night—*BRIAN *comes down the hallway, wearing a windbreaker and casual slacks. Offstage we can hear the sound of muted rock music.* BRIAN'*s face is set, dour, and depressed. He stops in front of one of the doors, pulls a key out of his pocket, then registers: That music is coming from his room. He looks down at the space between the door and floor. There's light peeping out from within the room. Puzzled, he puts the key in the lock and opens the door cautiously.*]

[*Interior—The Room—A picture is thumbtacked to a bulletin board, of* JOY PICCOLO *and a baby girl. We pan over to reveal another picture tacked up on the bulletin board next to* JOY'*s. The second*
B *picture is of* LINDA SAYERS. *We pan down from this picture to find* GALE *sprawled out on the bed, the radio blaring by his side. He reaches out and turns off the radio.*]

Gale. Hi. We're rooming together.
Brian. Says who?
Gale. Who else?
Brian *(sourly).* Terrific. Sort of a shame he couldn't ask me how I felt about it, isn't it?
Gale *(warily).* Look, if you want me out . . .
Brian. No, stay, I don't want you out. I'm just steamed at the Old Man for not putting me in the scrimmage this afternoon. *(Beat)* Is that your wife?
Gale. Yeah.
Brian. She's pretty.
Gale. So's yours. And the little girl.

Brian *(still down).* Thanks. I'm supposed to call her tonight—tell her how I'm doing. Be the shortest phone call in history.
Gale. Maybe not.

[*When* PICCOLO *looks over at him,* GALE *smiles.*]

Gale. Pic—they wouldn't assign us to room together unless we *both* made the team.

[BRIAN *looks over at* GALE *and it hits him. He moves to* GALE, *pulling him off the bed and shoving him toward the door.*]

Brian. Come on! We've got to call our wives!
Gale. I already called Linda, right after . . .
Brian. That was just for practice! This is for real! Come on!

[*And the two of them go tumbling out into the corridor.*]

[*Full Shot—The Corridor—*ATKINS, O'BRADOVICH, *and* EVEY *are standing a few feet away—huge men, arms like hams, necks like tree stumps.* C
Their expressions are insolent, challenging, but not cruel. Each of them has a coffee can in hand. Each container holds a sticky-looking, evil-smelling conglomeration of honey, cereal, sand, catsup, and whatever they could lay their hands on. They move in unison toward BRIAN *and* GALE.]

Atkins. Congratulations on making the team, gentlemen. Well done.
Evey. As you know, Coach Halas frowns on the hazing[4] of new men.
O'Bradovich. But now that you've made the team—it's really like—you're one of us.

[*All three have wooden spoons in the ooze, lifting the dripping brown gunk for all to see. In a second, they're tearing down the hall.* GALE *and* BRIAN *are bent low, the three pursuers bellowing with the thrill of the hunt. The last words echo in the corridor as doors are opened and men stick their heads out to see which rookies are getting it now.*]

Atkins *(yelling).* Welcome to the Chicago Bears!

4. **hazing:** initiating new members by bullying them or making them do ridiculous things.

Football Vocabulary
scrimmage: here, a practice game

A. Interpreting
What does Caroline mean here? (That there are racial tensions in the air)

B. Character
What *did* Gale say to Halas? (Obviously that he *would* take the risk and room with Brian) What does this decision show about Gale? (Strength of character—he doesn't let what other people say bother him. Also, it shows that he must like Brian more than he has let on.)

C. Exaggeration
Try to picture—or draw—men with "arms like hams, and necks like tree stumps." The writer creates humor here with his use of exaggeration.

A. Making Inferences
? Judging from the picture of the two men, what have they just been doing? (Gale has been playing; Brian has been watching from the sidelines.)

B. Interpreting
? Why does Brian spell out his name? (He wants to get his name in the papers—unlike Gale, Brian loves publicity.)

C. Drawing Conclusions
? There have been several clues about how Brian is doing on the team as compared to Gale. What are those hints, and what conclusion can you draw from them? (Brian's statement that Gale is too good to be cut; his anger at not being put in the scrimmage one day; his watching from the sidelines while Gale plays; and his comment "I want to play too." These clues suggest that Gale is a better player than Brian. Brian, however, takes it in stride and maintains his good nature.)

[*Cut to: Interior—Bears' Locker Room—Day—* GALE *is in front of his locker, pulling off his jersey, which is muddy and torn. Two reporters are on each side of him.* PICCOLO, *whose uniform looks as if he stepped out of a catalog, is seated in front of his locker, taking it all in with a certain objective humor.* GALE *is ill at ease in this kind of situation.*] A

Reporter #1. Is playing in the NFL easier than you thought it would be?

Gale. Only played one game. Not exactly an expert.

Reporter #2. But you didn't look as if you were having too much trouble out there.

Gale. The blocks were there.

Brian. Sure is different from the way you were talking last night, Gale. *(To reporters)* He calls the offensive line the "seven blocks of silly-putty."

Gale. Pic—

Reporter #1. You're Brian Piccolo?

Brian. P—I—C—C—O—L—O, yes. B

[*Direct Cut to: Game Footage—A long run from scrimmage by* SAYERS.]

Brian *(Voice Over).* Gale, when you run, do you think about what you're doing, or do you just do it?

Gale *(Voice Over).* I just do it.

Brian *(Voice Over).* Well, start thinking about it, will you? I want to play, too. C

[*Interior—Pizza Parlor—Night—Full Shot—Grouped about one of the tables are* GALE, BRIAN, *and their wives,* JOY PICCOLO *and* LINDA SAYERS. *They're at ease with one another, just now finishing off a casual, enjoyable evening on the town. They are listening to one of* BRIAN*'s stories. He's*

Gale, Brian, and Joy at the banquet where Gale is named Rookie of the Year.

© 1971 Screen Gems, A Division of Columbia Pictures Industries, Inc. All rights reserved.

telling it well, laughing as he does so, and it's a catching kind of thing for the women. GALE, *being* GALE, *allows himself a small smile, but little beyond that.*]

Brian. Now—picture this—Quarterback Jack Concannon calls a trap, see . . . *(To* LINDA *and* JOY*)* You know what a trap is?

Linda *(unsure).* I think so, but—maybe . . .

Brian. Well—uh—all the linemen go one way and hopefully the defense guys go that way, too. If they do, there's a big hole, see? If they don't—bad news. Anyway—Concannon calls a trap up the middle, Gale carrying the ball. It works like they draw it on the blackboard. Forty-three yards. Beautiful. So, Halas sees Gale's winded; he tells me to go in. So, I go in; Gale comes out. We get in the huddle—Concannon decides he's going to get foxy. He calls the *same* play. The very same play. Last thing they'll be looking for, he says. Now—the trap play is also called the "sucker play" because the defense really looks bad when it works—and defenses don't like to look bad—makes 'em surly.[5]

[JOY, *who's heard this story a hundred times already, has started to laugh, anticipating* BRIAN*'s big finish.*]

A **Brian.** So—we come out of the huddle—ball's snapped—all our linemen go one way—and it's like I'm looking at a team portrait of the Los Angeles Rams—Hello, Deacon Jones . . . Merlin Olsen, how's the family . . . Rosey Grier. . . .

[*Laughter from them all.* GALE*'s smile has broadened now and* BRIAN*'s having a fine old time.*]

Brian. I mean—I was afraid to get up. I figured not everything was going to come with me. . . .

Joy *(nicely).* You never saw anyone so black and blue.

Gale. Yeah—it was like rooming with a black player again.

[GALE *grins—and the other three gape, looking at him with expressions of shock. His smile turns uneasy, bewildered. He checks to make sure there's no anchovy hanging off his chin.*]

5. **surly:** bad-tempered.

Linda. Gale—you told a *joke.*

Brian. Joy—did you hear it? The great Stone Face from Kansas told a joke!

[BRIAN *turns to the other patrons, cupping his hands about his mouth.*]

Brian *(yelling).* Chicago! There's hope for us all! Sayers *speaks*!

Gale. Aw, come *on,* Pic . . .

[*But* GALE*'s smiling, pleased with himself if the truth were known, as is* LINDA SAYERS. *The camera holds on them.*] B

[*Direct Cut to: Footage of a* SAYERS *Run—Slow Motion—This footage should be the most impressive of all, selling the power and grace of* SAYERS*'s ability.*]

Brian *(Voice Over).* Magic—I think I'm going to write you a speech.

Gale *(Voice Over).* What kind of speech?

Brian *(Voice Over).* Acceptance speech for "Rookie of the Year." You can't miss.

Gale *(Voice Over).* And I got to give a *speech*? You're putting me on!

[*Direct Cut to: Interior—Banquet Dais—Night—Offstage the sound of a speaker drones on.* GALE, LINDA, BRIAN, *and* JOY *are on the dais—the men in tuxedos, the women in formal gowns.* BRIAN *has a crumpled piece of paper in his hand. He leans into* GALE, *speaking in an urgent whisper.*]

Brian. From the top. One more time.

Gale *(harried, by rote).* I'd like to thank you all for this honor, though it's really not right to give it to one man. Football is a—team sport, and I . . .

Speaker *(Offstage).* Gale Sayers!

[*A spotlight floods the area and we hear offstage applause.* GALE *is urged to his feet by* BRIAN *and* LINDA. *He moves toward the speaker's platform, petrified. All we can see is* GALE*; the harsh pinpoint of the carbon arc*[6] *is centered on him with no residual spillage. He looks at the trophy for a second.*]

Gale *(trembling).* I'd—I'd like to thank you all for this honor, though it's really not right . . . C

6. **carbon arc:** spotlight.

A. Expansion Defensive linemen, on an average, weigh about 250 pounds.

B. Interpreting What is the effect of this scene at the pizza parlor? (It shows the close friendship that is developing between Brian and Gale. Gale's joke shows that Brian's easy good nature is rubbing off on Gale. He also doesn't mind being teased as much as he used to.)

C. Foreshadowing From Gale's behavior before the speech, how well do you think he will do? (He's obviously been practicing, over and over, a speech Brian helped him with; he is "harried," "petrified," and "trembling"—he probably won't do very well at all.)

Football Vocabulary
second string: alternate players
fullback: bigger, stronger running back who leads interference and blocks for the ball carrier
"break away for sixty . . . ten sixes": "If I can't get sixty yards in one run, I can get ten yards six times."

A. Expansion Death Valley is a hot, dry desert area in California and Nevada.

B. Interpreting The "other spot" is the halfback position—that is, the ball carrier.

C. Conflict How does this conversation reveal both an external and an internal conflict for Brian? (His external conflict is making halfback on the team; his internal conflict is competing with a good friend.)

D. Allusion *The Maltese Falcon,* a 1941 film starring Humphrey Bogart, was about the smuggling of a rare and valuable statue of a falcon.

E. Interpreting What does this shot tell the audience? (That another season is about to begin)

[*He stops. He stops because he can't think of the next word.* JOY *and* LINDA *agonize in the silence, trying to pray more words out of* GALE. BRIAN *can't believe it. He starts to slowly tear the speech up, shaking his head, grinning.* GALE*'s mouth is* A *like Death Valley.*]

Gale. Thank you.

[BRIAN *tosses the pieces of paper in the air.*]

Brian. Who'd believe it—who'd ever believe it . . .

[*Direct Cut to: Exterior—*SAYERS*'s House—Night.*]

Brian. Hey, Gale?

[GALE *holds on the porch.* LINDA *waves a hand toward the car.*]

Linda (*to* GALE). Too cold out here. I'll warm your side of the bed.

[*She moves into the house as* BRIAN *gets out of the car and trots to* GALE.]

Gale. What do you want, man? It's freezing out here!
Brian. Something I've got to tell you.
Gale. What is it?

[GALE *notes an edge to* BRIAN*'s voice, an undercurrent of reluctance, shyness.* BRIAN *looks him directly in the eye.*]

Brian. Joy and I had a long talk last night—about whether or not I should ask to be traded. We decided that I wouldn't ask. I like the guys on the team; I like the town. *(Beat)* What I *don't* like is playing second string.
Gale *(quietly)*. I don't blame you.
Brian. Now—*maybe* I've got a shot at fullback. But I don't think Halas thinks I'm big enough. He'll probably go with Ralph Kurek. The other B spot is yours—and that's the job I'm gunning for, Gale.

[GALE *starts to reply, but* BRIAN *silences him with a gesture.*]

Brian. Let me get it said. *(Beat)* I'm a better blocker than you are and I'm as good a receiver. And if I can't break away for sixty, I can still get ten sixes, and it adds up the same way. I'm going to come into camp next year in the best shape ever, and I think I've got a realistic chance to blow you out of the lineup. . . . And that's just what I'm going to try to do.
Gale. I understand, man—that's your job.
Brian. Yeah—but I don't like to do "a job" on a friend. C
Gale *(small smile)*. Don't worry; you won't.

[*There's no anger between them, just resolve. After a beat, there is a light tap on the car horn.* BRIAN *looks at the trophy; he touches it lightly.*]

Brian *(imitating the movie actor Humphrey Bogart)*. It's a Maltese Falcon, kid—get this inside—and the free world is safe. D

[*With that* BRIAN *moves back to the car, camera holding on* GALE *as he looks after his friend, then down to the trophy.*]

[*Direct Cut to: Interior—*HALAS*'s Office—Day—On Picture—Another team picture is being tacked on the wall, the printing identifying it as last year's Bear team.*] E

[*Direct Cut to: Exterior—Practice Field Area—Day—*GALE *and* BRIAN *take positions in a line for wind sprints. Their look to each other is friendly, but neither has precisely a fix on what attitude is the working one. They speak as the line moves forward. There are sounds of the other men yelling offstage.*]

Brian. Hi. You just pull in?
Gale. Yeah. Would have been here this morning, but the flight was delayed by fog in Detroit. You look in good shape.
Brian. I am. Worked hard this winter.
Gibron *(yelling offstage)*. Go!

[BRIAN *takes off, arms pumping.* GALE *is laughing at a joke* BRIAN *has just told, so that* BRIAN *passes the forty at least three seconds before* GALE.]

[GALE *draws up from his leisurely sprint. They haven't even kept the clock on his effort.*]

Gale. Mind if I try it again?
Halas. Might be a good idea.

[GALE *starts to retrace his steps to the goal line, then looks back to* GIBRON *and* HALAS.]

Football Vocabulary
Concannon's earphones: The coaches above the field talk to the coaches on the field about game strategies; Concannon, the quarterback, has just received his instructions.

A. Acting Out
There is little dialogue in these three scenes; the actors' expressions govern the action and advance the plot. Ask students to imitate the instructions the writer gives the actors: Gale, "not frightened, but properly impressed"; both men, "there's very little 'give' in either man's expression"; Gale, "impassive outwardly, but fully aware of what is going on."

B. Expansion
Jim Brown and Lennie Moore were famous running backs. Brian attaches a common Italian ending to their names.

C. Conflict
? What is Gale's internal conflict here? (He is glad that he made the position he wanted; yet, he is disappointed that his victory has to mean his friend's defeat.)

D. Making Inferences
? What do the conditions of the men's uniforms signify? (That Brian has been playing very little as compared to Gale)

Gale. What was Pic's time like?
Gibron *(consults his clipboard).* Must be out to get you. . . . He's about half a second faster this year than last.

[GALE *is not frightened, but properly impressed. He nods, taking it in. His expression denies his statement.*]

Gale. That's really terrific . . .

[*Direct Cut to: Exterior—Practice Field—Day—Full Shot—A number of men dot the area going through calisthenics. We find* GALE *and* BRIAN *doing sit-ups, each being helped by another player who anchors their feet. They're facing in opposite directions so that, as they come up, they're looking at each other. The looks are not hostile, but there's very little "give" in either man's expression.*]

[*Direct Cut to: Exterior—Practice Field—Day—Full Shot—The offense and defense are performing the one-on-one drill. This time, it's* BRIAN *who's the offensive back and the move he puts on the defensive man is a beauty. As* BRIAN *tears out of the frame, we zoom in on* GALE, *impassive*[7] *outwardly, but fully aware of what's going on.*]

A [*Direct Cut to: Interior—Dormitory Hallway—Night—Full Shot—*GALE *and* BRIAN *come in from the outside, both wearing light jackets,* BRIAN *carrying a pizza box.*]

Brian. That's why you'll never cut it, Sayers—pizza has magical properties that give Italian guys strength and speed.
Gale. Yeah—a lot of great Italian running backs, all right.
B **Brian.** Yeah. Jim Brownanelli. Lennie Moorelli. All those guys.

[*Angle to Stairway—*J. C. CAROLINE *is putting up a large sheet of paper on a bulletin board.* BRIAN *moves by him, taking the stairs two at a time, and ad-libs a greeting which is returned by* J. C. GALE *comes by.*]

Gale. What's that, J. C.?
Caroline. Starting lineups for the first exhibition.

7. **impassive:** not showing emotion.

[GALE'S *eyes move toward the landing of the second floor. The shadow of* BRIAN PICCOLO *can be seen. His head turns slowly, listening.*]

Gale. What's the backfield?
Caroline *(as he goes).* Concannon, Ralph Kurek, and you.

[*If ever there were mixed emotions in a man, now is that time.* GALE *looks up.*]

[*His Point of View—*BRIAN'S *Shadow—Sagging, head lowered. A long beat, then* BRIAN *takes a breath, straightens his shoulders and moves off, the shadow disappearing.*]

Brian *(offstage).* Come on, Magic . . . pizza's getting cold.

[*Tight on* GALE*—He leans against the wall, disappointed and yet relieved at the same time. He looks toward the second-story landing once more, as we start to hear the growing roar of a large crowd, the unwavering roar of the hero seekers.*] C

[*Direct Cut to: Exterior—Wrigley Field—Day—Game Footage—The stands are crowded with spectators. The day is damp and gray. The Chicago Bears are playing the San Francisco 49ers.*]

[*Angle to Bears' Bench—*GALE'S *uniform, muddy and begrimed;* PICCOLO'S *with only a smudge or two.* HALAS *and* GIBRON *pace restlessly up and down the sidelines, yelling to the defensive unit, as are all the other players. Quarterback* CONCANNON *is on the phones, listening intently.*] D

[*Angle to Field—The ball is snapped to 49er quarterback* JOHN BRODIE *who backpedals looking for a receiver going deep.* BRODIE *gets the pass off, but it falls into the hands of a defensive back from the Chicago Bears.*]

[*Angle to Bench—Every man is on his feet yelling. There is a flurry of activity—*GALE *is pulling on his helmet, receiving a pat from* BRIAN. CONCANNON *takes off the earphones and moves with the rest of the offensive team onto the field.*]

[*Angle to Stands.*]

Linda. Go get 'em, Gale!! You can do it, honey!

Football Vocabulary
pitch out: when the quarterback tosses the ball behind him to the running back instead of handing it off

A. Interpreting
What do you think Joy is disturbed about? (Probably that Brian hasn't been playing much, and that Gale is always chosen to go out on the field. She is probably worried about his state of mind.)

B. Technique
The writer uses a technique here that could never be used on stage. What effect is the camera achieving? (In a freeze frame, the action stops and a still picture fills the frame. The effect of these freeze frames is to prolong the agonizing moment of Gale's injury. The camera's focus on each character increases the tension as we see their reactions.)

C. Interpreting
What is Gale's mood here? (He is furious about his knee. The anger is probably covering up his fear about the gravity of the injury, since he knows he may not be able to play football again.)

A [*Tight on* JOY PICCOLO—*Happy at this turn of events, but also painfully aware of something else, her eyes move from the field to the bench.*]

[*Her Point of View—On* BRIAN—*With his back to the stands, helmet off, Number 41 paces restlessly back and forth along the sidelines. His attention is on the game, but the gaze drops a few times as inward moments take over.*]

[*Angle to Bears' Huddle.*]

Concannon. Yours, Gale. Twenty-eight toss. South. Line. On three. *Break!*

[*Full Shot—The team comes out of the huddle, moving with precision into formation.* CONCANNON *looks over the defense and calls out the signals in a rhythmic cadence. The ball is snapped and* CONCANNON *pivots, the move coordinated with the pulling of the guards and* GALE*'s instantaneous break to his left. The ball is tossed back to* GALE. *He takes the pitch-out and has the ball well in hand as he starts to look for an opening in the upfield area.*]

[*On* BRIAN—*He is at the water bucket, dipper poised as he stops to watch the play develop.*]

[*Back on* GALE—*Seemingly from nowhere, a San Francisco 49er uniform comes hurtling into frame and we freeze frame just before the shoulder of the player tears into* GALE*'s knee. All crowd noises are killed. Only silence. The frame moves again now and we can see the awful impact. Freeze frame on this instant. The picture comes to life in short bursts as* GALE *crumples, knee landing at an angle to set one's teeth on edge, in jerky, grainy images.*]

[*On* BRIAN—*A freeze frame slowly moves forward half a step; he realizes what he's witnessing.*]

[*On* LINDA *and* JOY—*They are very much afraid of what they're seeing.* LINDA*'s hand flies to her mouth.*]

[*Back on* GALE—*He hits the ground, one hand already going to the knee, the ball forgotten about. He tries to get to his feet and the instant he puts any pressure on the knee, his head snaps back in reaction to the agony that assualts him. We freeze frame on* GALE, *every muscle contorted, and we hear the sound of a siren wailing, wailing, wailing.*] B

[*Hard Cut to: Exterior—*SAYERS*'s Home—Day—Full Shot—The car, driven by* LINDA, *pulls to a halt in the driveway.* GALE *opens the door and starts to get out. He's using two metal canes, the right leg swung out before him, stiff and unbending. His face is chiseled with tension and anger—cold, acid anger.*]

Linda. Can I help?
Gale. No.

[*He makes his way slowly toward the front door, still not accustomed to the canes, not yet using his body weight to help himself. Instead, it's a halting, unnatural motion—painful to execute, more painful for* LINDA *to watch. She hurries past him to open the front door.*]

[*Interior—The Living Room—Day—Full Shot—* GALE *comes in, no reaction to being home in his eyes. He moves to the first chair and sits.*]

Linda. It's good to have you home, Gale.
Gale. Yeah. Good to be home.

[*But his eyes admit it was a reply made because it was the reply expected.*]

Linda. Can I get you anything?
Gale. No. I'm fine.
Linda. It's about lunch time. You want a sandwich or anything?
Gale. Not hungry; you go ahead, though.
Linda. Are you sure?
Gale *(with an edge)*. Yes, I'm sure.

[*The emotional moat he's built is too wide to be crossed at this point.* LINDA *kisses him lightly on the cheek, then rises and moves to the kitchen. She pauses at the door looking back at him, a tentative smile on her face, but* GALE*'s expression doesn't match or encourage the smile. Disheartened,* LINDA *leaves the room.*] C

[*Tight on* GALE—*His hand moves toward the injured knee, the cast large beneath the trouser leg.*

Alone, the mask falters slightly and the fear is unmistakable. Then, after a moment or two, we, and GALE, *start to hear the sound of a man singing. We've heard the song before. It's* BRIAN *singing the Wake Forest fight song.* GALE *looks with disbelief toward another door off the living room. Using the canes,* GALE *pulls himself to an upright position and makes his way slowly across the room to the door. He pulls it open.*]

[*Angle Down Basement Stairway—The singing is louder now. A beat, then* BRIAN*'s smiling face appears at the bottom. He's wearing old clothes, carries a crescent wrench in one hand.*]

Brian. Hey, Magic . . . thought you'd never get here.

[*He moves back out of sight and we hear the sound of something metal being tapped upon.* GALE *enters frame and starts the steps carefully.*]

Gale. Pic—what are you doing down there?

[*Interior—Basement—Full Shot—This is not a recreation room. A washer and dryer are in a corner. Opposite them,* BRIAN PICCOLO *is tightening bolts on a metal framework that will eventually be used as a leg-lift machine.* GALE *negotiates the last few steps.*]

Brian. It's not a bad act, Gale, but a peg-legged pirate does it better.
Gale *(indicating machine)*. What's that supposed to be?
Brian. It's not "supposed" to be anything but what it is—a leg-lift machine.
Gale. What for?
Brian. What *for?* Gale—getting that knee back into shape is not going to be a take-it-easy number. If you're afraid, that's understandable, but . . .
A **Gale** *(hard)*. I am *not* afraid!
Brian *(quietly)*. You ought to be, Gale.
Gale. Pic, maybe you think this is a real friendly thing you're doing, but . . .
Brian. And you can put that in your ditty bag, too, you stupid jackass—friendship hasn't got one thing to do with this . . .

[PICCOLO *is halfway up the steps now. He stops, looking back at* GALE, *weighing whether or not to go on.* SAYERS*'s expression is stubborn and angry, but no more so than* BRIAN*'s. A beat, then* BRIAN *sits on one of the steps.*]

Brian. Gale—when I was in high school—I was one of the best backs in the state. Unfortunately for me, *the* best back in the state, Tucker Fredrickson, went to the same school. And the colleges would come down to watch us and Tuck ended up at Auburn—and I ended up at Wake Forest. Good school, nice place, but not exactly center ring, you follow? *(Beat)* So—I work my butt off at Forest. And my senior year—I led the nation in rushing and scoring . . . *(Softly)* I mean—I led the *entire* nation. *(Beat)* So, I look around for a pro team, and I pick the Bears. Then, who else comes to the Bears—Sayers. Big gun from a big school, and I'm number two all over again. *(Beat)* B Well, Gale—I'm number one guy now, but for all the wrong reasons. And if you don't come back one hundred percent, people are always going to say that I got in on a pass, a lucky break, and I won't take it that way. *(Rises)* I am going to beat you, Magic, but it won't mean a thing unless you're at your best, not one second slower, one degree weaker. I'm going to work your tail off getting you into shape again—for *my* sake. *(As he goes)* I won't take the job from a cripple.

[BRIAN *turns and goes up the stairs.* GALE *stands there, rage stilled, cooled, then turns, looking steadily at the leg-lift machine. He moves to it, running his fingertips over it lightly, seeking reassurance from the chilled metal.*]

[*Direct Cut to: Exterior—City Park—Day—On* GALE*—It's a blustery, cold day. The wind drives ribbons of dry snow along the walk.* GALE *moves toward us, using a wooden cane, the limp noticeable, but not as bad as previously seen. He wears an overcoat, the collar turned up, and a grim expression. In his free hand he carries a small radio. A sportscaster is heard over the sound of the wind.*]

Announcer *(Voice Over)*. And in Los Angeles, the Chicago Bears trimmed the Rams by a score of seventeen to sixteen. Quarterback Jack Concannon was eight for fourteen passing, and the run-

Football Vocabulary
"eight for fourteen passing": He threw fourteen passes and eight were caught.

A. Making Inferences
? How do we know Gale is lying? (He interrupts Brian too quickly; his tone and his emphasis on "not." We, as well as Brian, know that he is terrified.)

B. Conflict
? This is an emotionally charged speech from Brian. What conflicts are emphasized in this speech—both for Brian and for Gale? (Brian's internal conflict regarding his own ability; Gale's fear regarding his injury and therefore his future; the conflict between Brian and Gale as competitors)

Football Vocabulary
carry: to hold the ball and run with it
game ball: a ball that's used in the game is often awarded to the most effective player in that game.

A. Interpreting
What does this action suggest, even without dialogue? (Gale is determined to meet Brian's challenge.)

B. Foreshadowing
What does this conversation foreshadow, considering our knowledge of Brian? (He's probably going to help Gale work out—he has a stake in Gale's recovery and cannot let him give up.)

ning game was ably manned by Brian Piccolo, who gained 105 yards in fourteen carries. Piccolo was awarded the game ball.

A [GALE *is adjacent to a litter basket. He stops for a beat, his back to us, then deposits the cane into the basket. His step seems to have more drive to it when he moves on.*]

[*Direct Cut to: Exterior—Park Area—Day—On* GALE—*It's early morning as* GALE, *dressed in a sweatsuit, comes jogging toward us. His expression is stoic,*[8] *the pace quite slow, the sort of speed one recommends to those just discharged from the hospital after hernial surgery. But the pace is steady and dogged.*]

Doctor Fox *(Voice Over; filter).* Hello?
Brian *(Voice Over; filter).* Doctor Fox? This is Brian Piccolo. How's he doing?
Doctor Fox *(Voice Over; filter).* Very well, I think. Though it's boring going through those exercises all by yourself. It's drudgery and it's painful, and a lot of people just give up when they're alone in
B that situation.

[*Direct Cut to: Interior—*SAYERS'*s Basement—Night—*GALE *is lying on his back, feet in the air, as he strains to lift the platform bearing a sizable portion of weights. He's drenched with sweat, puffing. We pan up from his face to the knee, seeing the wicked-looking scar that creases the flesh. As he starts to lift the platform, we pull back to reveal* PICCOLO *seated nearby. He has a small kitchen egg timer in his hand.*]

Brian. And—ten. *(Setting timer)* Minute rest, then one more set.
Gale. *Another* one?
Brian. Last one tonight. Hang in there.

[GALE *remains on the floor under the weight machine. He sighs, getting his breath back.*]

Brian. How's the knee feel?
Gale *(dispirited).* Oh, one day it feels strong as ever; the next day it's like I got spaghetti for ligaments.

---

8. **stoic** (stō′ik): showing no emotion.

Football Trivia: Brian Piccolo

William Blinn, to consolidate events and action, changed some facts in his play. According to the following media guide put out by the Chicago Bears, which facts did he stick to, and which ones did he change?

"Piccolo, who has been Gale Sayers' alternate since 1966, had never carried the ball more than nine times in an NFL game until Nov. 10, 1968. When Sayers suffered his knee injury in the second period that day, Piccolo, who hadn't been called to run up to that time in the game, wound up with eighteen rushes for 67 yards and caught four passes for 54. Those were his heaviest chores since 1964 at Wake Forest when he led the nation on offense with 1,044 yards on 252 carries."

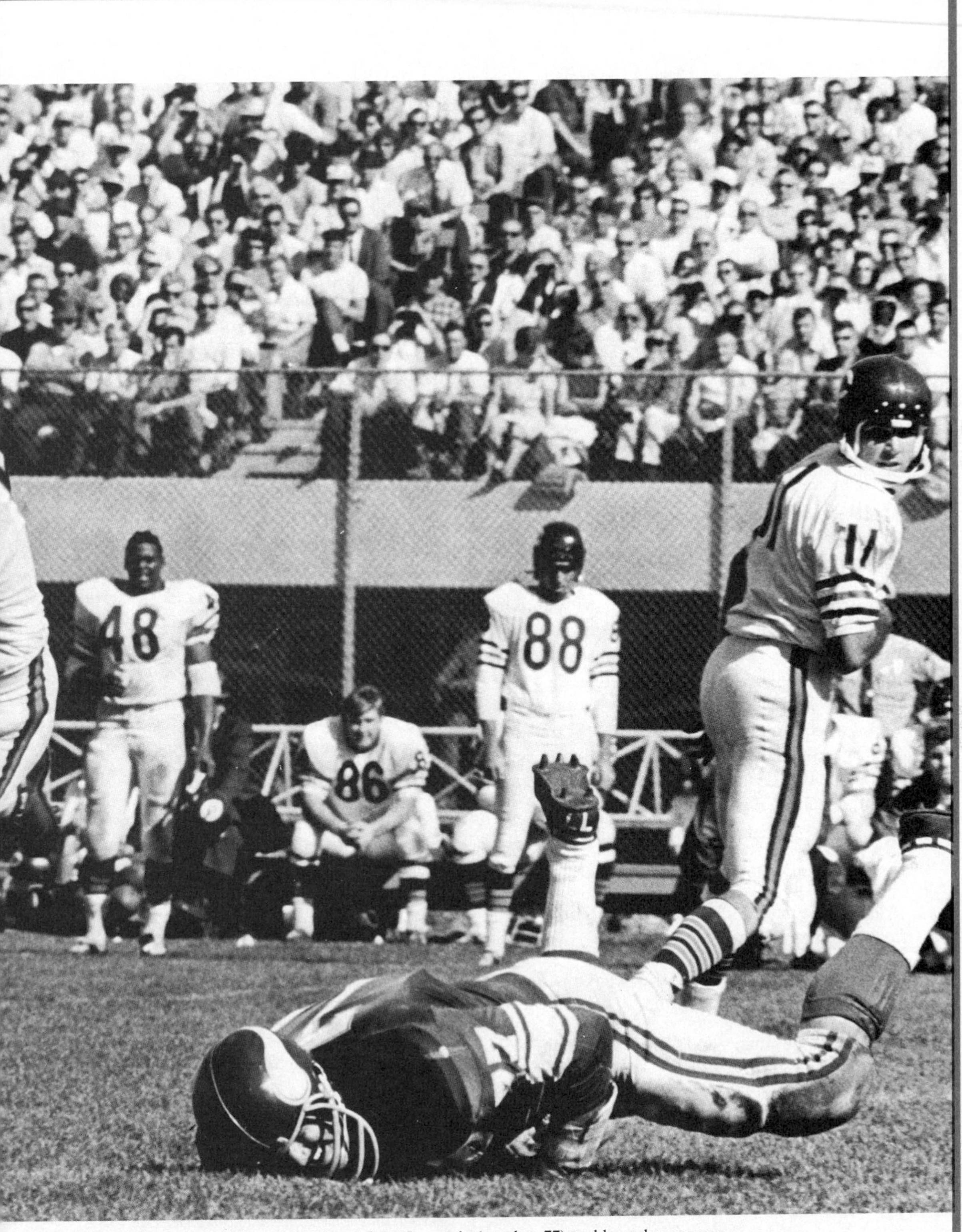

Brian Piccolo (number 41) breaks Vikings' Gary Larsen's (number 77) tackle and scampers for nine yards during the second quarter of the Minnesota-Chicago game on October 1, 1967.

359

READING CHECK TEST
PART ONE

1. Brian and Gale are fast friends from the very start of the teleplay. (*False*)
2. Because of Brian, Gale is fined twenty-five dollars during a team meeting. (*True*)
3. The coaches tell Gale that he and Brian will be roommates. (*True*)
4. It is common for black and white players on the Bears to room together. (*False*)
5. Brian injures his knee during a game. (*False*)

A. Foreshadowing
This remark of Brian's foreshadows an event that will actually prompt Gale to speak. Little does Brian know now that it will be his own illness.

B. Expression
In a poker game, "to up the ante" is to raise the amount each player must bet in order to stay in the game.

C. Responding
? What emotions are involved as Gale falls? (Gale's and Brian's fear that Gale has reinjured his knee; Brian's guilt for leading Gale on a path that he was perhaps not ready for; anxious suspense on the part of Brian, Gale, and the audience to see the extent of the damage)

Brian *(beat)*. You know—if it doesn't come all the way back—it won't be the end of the world, Gale.
Gale. That so?
Brian. Football's terrific, man, but it's still just a job.
Gale. It's the only job I know how to do. *(Beat)* I'm not like you—I can't talk and all that stuff.
Brian. Talking now . . .
Gale. It's different.
A **Brian** *(beat)*. You'll learn how to talk, once you find something that's got to be said.

[*The egg timer chirps once and* GALE *lifts his legs to the underside of the platform bearing the weights.*]

Brian. Third set. Ten reps. *Go.*

[GALE *starts to lift. The first three or four times go smoothly enough, but about halfway through the fifth one . . .*]

Gale *(straining)*. I'll never make ten, man—no juice left . . .
Brian. Come on, Magic! Hang tough! Five. Way to go—six—lookin' good, Magic, Come on . . .
Gale. No—way . . .
Brian. You aren't getting out that easy! Come on! You can do it! Seven! Fantastic! Three more, man! Work on it! Are these the legs of a murderer? Come on, Gale! Eight! Got it! Two more!
Gale. No—way. . . .

[BRIAN *is leaning over* GALE, *mind seeking a ploy.*]

Brian. Can't make it, huh? Weakling's giving up, is that it? Is that what you're doing?

[GALE *looks up at* BRIAN *expressionlessly—then a stifled laugh breaks from his lips. He smiles.*]

Gale. Come on, man—don't make me laugh.

[GALE *starts to laugh and lets the weights come to rest on the stops.* BRIAN *just stands there without any comprehension of how his maneuver could have backfired so badly.*]

[*Direct Cut to: Exterior Wooded Area—Day—Long Shot—*BRIAN *and* GALE *move along a narrow dirt road that winds through the trees. Their pace is no longer that of a jog, but one more suited to a brisk 880.*[9]]

[*Closer—Trucking—We move back in front of the two of them as they run, both in control, arms pumping smoothly, the motion fluid and easy. After a few seconds,* BRIAN *looks over briefly at* GALE, *then he picks up the pace a little, opening a few yards between them.* GALE *takes this with some surprise, but matches* BRIAN *and closes the gap. But it's only temporary, for* BRIAN *ups the ante once more, the pace now at 440*[10] *clip.* B GALE'*s eyes flash as* BRIAN *moves away, but he picks it up again. He's shoulder to shoulder with* PIC.]

Brian. A beer for the first man to the bridge!
Gale. You're on!

[*Different Angle—*BRIAN *peels off from the road and crashes into the trees flanking the road.* GALE *is a little surprised at this cross-country route, but he's right after* BRIAN, *though he's got about five or six yards to make up due to the momentary hesitation. There are no paths here, no easy routes. The trees and shrubs make it necessary to dart this way and that, hurdle logs, scramble up steep slopes and gullies.* BRIAN *is in the lead, but* GALE'*s responding to the challenge, charging after him at full bore. They come to a creek bed five or six inches deep, and as they go splashing through it, we go to slow motion—droplets exploding into the sunlight, the two men calling on reserves from deep within. The small stream dwindles to loose shale.*]

[*The Fall—A scant step behind* PICCOLO, GALE *loses his footing on the stones and takes a head-over-heels tumble, a really bad one, pinwheeling over and over violently.* PICCOLO *halts immediately, looking back at* GALE *with concern.*] C

[*On* BRIAN*—He is gasping for breath, looking to* GALE.]

[*On* GALE*—He meets* BRIAN'*s look. Every breath hurts, sears. He glances down at the knee, then*

9. **880:** race of 880 yards, or half a mile. The pace is slower than a dash, but faster than a long-distance race.
10. **440:** race of 440 yards, or a quarter mile. The pace is much faster than for an 880-yard race.

ANALYZING PART ONE
Identifying Facts

1. The directions include mention of farmland, rolling countryside, flat and simple land, and a campus-type area bearing a sign that identifies it as an NFL training camp.
2. In the directions, Brian is described as wearing a Bears sweat shirt, and Gale as wearing street clothes. This shows that Brian is already a part of what is going on, whereas Gale is still an outsider. From the first lines of dialogue, we learn that Brian and Gale have met before; that Gale is shy and uneasy and Brian is good-natured and easygoing.
3. Gale is black and Brian is white, and up to this point in the Bears' organization, black players roomed with black players, and white players roomed with white players.
4. The normally retiring Gale cracks a joke.
5. Gale becomes very discouraged after his injury, and he must conquer his self-pity to rehabilitate himself.
6. Brian assembles a leg-lift machine in Gale's basement and offers to help Gale regain his strength.

Because of Gale's injury, Brian is able to become starting halfback. He wants to retain that position, but not because Gale is injured. He wants to beat Gale out for the position fairly.

Interpreting Meanings

7. At the beginning of the drama, the two are rivals for one position on the team. Gradually they become fellow players, then friends, and then best friends.
8. Only one of the players can be the starting halfback—the star. The other must sit on the bench. Gale and Brian are both proud, competitive players. Although they are friends, their paramount interest is the starting job.

Brian could probably be a starting halfback on another team. However, he wants to prove himself on the Bears.
9. Gale's comment shows his awareness of his debt to Brian for helping him recover from his injury and self-doubt.

Applying Meanings

10. Answers will vary.

stands slowly, brushing the stones from the palms of his hands. He nods.]

[*Full Shot—Like catapults,*[11] *they both turn and take off.*]

[*They burst out of the trees,* GALE *a step behind. This is the final all-out sprint for the tape. Nothing held in reserve at this point, they pull great gulps of air in, straining. And with each step,* GALE *moves up. An inch, no more, but that inch is repeated with each step, every stride bringing him closer to* BRIAN*'s shoulder.*]

[*Long Shot—As they near a small wooden footbridge, moving, it seems, as one, mirror images of black and white. They both literally hurl themselves at the imaginary tape and tumble across the bridge with their momentum, sprawling in the soft grass on the other side. After a long moment, they both sit up, shaky smiles on their faces, though they're still puffing like a Saint Bernard in Palm Springs.*]

Brian. I—think—I—owe—you—a—beer.
Gale (*shakes head*). I—think—I—owe—you—a—lot—more—than—that.
Brian. Yeah—you're—healthy.
Gale. Yeah.

[*And they look at each other, the expressions of both growing a little serious, aware that, as friends, they are still competitors; there's only one brass ring on this merry-go-round.*]

11. **catapults:** slingshots or other devices for throwing objects.

Responding to the Play

Analyzing Part One

Identifying Facts

1. A play usually opens with an introductory scene that gives you some information about its **setting,** or the place and time in which it occurs. As *Brian's Song* begins, what details in the **stage directions** and **camera directions,** or instructions for actors and cameras, tell you *where* the characters are?
2. The first scene of a play also gives you information about the characters. What details in the opening scene's stage directions and in its **dialogue**—the lines spoken by the characters—give you some information about *who* Gale and Brian are?
3. Explain why it is a potential problem for Gale and Brian to be roommates.
4. Soon after Gale and Brian make the team, they and their wives go out to dinner together. What does Gale do during this meal that shows the effect of Brian's easy-going friendship?
5. The injury to Gale's knee is a serious physical obstacle to his return to playing football. But this is not the only obstacle to Gale's recovery. What other obstacle must Gale overcome?
6. Describe what Brian does to help Gale recover from his injury. What reasons does Brian give for helping?

Interpreting Meanings

7. Change is important in most dramas. Describe how the relationship between Gale and Brian changes during the first part of the drama. How do they feel about one another as the drama begins, and how do these feelings change?
8. Explain how Brian's decision to stay with the Bears and try to win the position of halfback creates a **conflict,** or struggle, between him and Gale. Identify the **internal conflict** between desires or emotions that this decision also creates for Brian.
9. After Brian and Gale race each other, Gale says, "I think I owe you a lot more than that." What do you think he means by this comment?

Applying Meanings

10. In what other situations in life could friends also be competitors? Do you think Brian and Gale deal with their problems in a believable way?

SUPPLEMENTARY SUPPORT MATERIAL: PART TWO

1. Vocabulary Activity Sheet
2. Reading Check Test blackline master
3. Selection Test (page 137 of Test Book)
4. Workbook (page 111)

DEVELOPING VOCABULARY

The following words appear on a test in the Test Book, page 138. (See also the Vocabulary Activity Sheet.)

calisthenics, gait, beaming, festooned, footage, remnants, exuberantly, intertwined, somber, craving

Football! Vocabulary

number two halfback: a substitute for the halfback

"four point three rushing average": Brian averages 4.3 yards for each time he runs (rushes) with the ball.

A. Making Inferences

? Why is Coach Halas smiling here? (Because Gale is back in the line-up; probably also because Halas knows that Brian was instrumental in getting Gale there)

B. Humor

? What is Brian's joke here? (He is pretending Gale is asking him if he knows the song by the title "You got a four point three . . ." A "bar" here means a measure of music.)

Part Two

Gibron *(Voice Over).* What do you think training camp is? You think training camp is some kind of picnic? Is that what you think? Because there's no man assured of a job around here, let me tell you, and if you think you are, then you got one more think comin', gentlemen!

[*As* GIBRON*'s voice started to come over, we also started to hear the sounds of the Chicago Bears calling out a cadence as they go through their calisthenics.*]

[*Hard Cut to: Exterior—Practice Area—Day—Full Shot—The backs step through the ropes, knees high. We pick up* GALE *going through the obstacle course, with* BRIAN *right behind him, both handling it with relative ease. We pan them, then all of them leave the frame to hold on the grizzled features of* COACH HALAS. *His eyes are masked by dark glasses, but there's a smile tugging on the corners of his mouth.*] A

[*Direct Cut to: Interior—Dormitory Room—Night—On* GALE*—The playbook is in front of him. We pan across the room to find* BRIAN*, same look, same activity. A beat, then there is a knock on the door.* BRIAN *opens the door and reacts with some surprise on seeing* COACH HALAS *standing in the hallway. He nods pleasantly.* GALE*, too, is surprised and sits up.*]

Halas. Hello, Brian. Mind if I come in for a moment?

Brian. No, no. Of course not. Come on in, Coach.

[*And* HALAS *comes in, moving by* BRIAN*. The two young men look to each other, neither having any notion that might explain this unprecedented visit.*]

Halas. How's the knee, Gale?

Gale. Fine, Coach. Feels strong.

Brian. Look, if you want to talk to Gale, I can just walk on down to . . .

Halas. No, actually, I'd like to talk to both of you.

[*Chilling portent.*[1] *They both smile, as does* HALAS, *but only the Old Man's has any relaxation in it. Long Beat. Throat clearings from* GALE *and* BRIAN.]

Brian. Well—uh—how do things look this year, Coach?

Halas. Fine. Just fine. Matter of fact, there's one boy I'm very impressed with. Brian, I wouldn't be surprised to see him replace you as number two halfback.

[HALAS *lets the moment run on for a second.*]

Halas. Because I'm making you number one fullback.

[*Tight on* BRIAN*—He sits there looking at* HALAS *much as Papa Dionne*[2] *must have looked at the doctor.*]

[*On* GALE*—Beaming, really and deeply pleased for his friend.*]

Gale. Hey, Pic—you and me the starting backfield—what do you say?

[*Full Shot—*BRIAN *just shakes his head back and forth, an empty smile flopping about on his face.*]

Gale. Coach—I didn't think it was possible—but I think you finally found a way to shut him up!

[*Hard Cut to: Game Footage—Alternating Between Runs of* PICCOLO *and* SAYERS.]

Gale *(Voice Over).* Hey, Pic?

Brian *(Voice Over).* Yeah?

Gale *(Voice Over).* You know you got a four point three rushing average?

Brian *(Voice Over).* No, man, but hum a few bars and I'll see if I can fake it. B

Gale *(Voice Over; overlapping).* Aw, Pic. . . .

[*Exterior—Angle to Football Field—End Zone—*BRIAN *breaks through a hole in the center of the line, keeping his feet as he gets to the end zone, flipping the ball high into the air. The first person to him is* GALE, *slapping him exuberantly on the back as they move with their teammates toward the bench.*]

[*Direct Cut to: Interior—Locker Room—Day—*

1. **portent:** something foreshadowing an event about to occur.

2. **Papa Dionne:** father of quintuplets born in Canada in 1934.

Football Trivia: Gale Sayers

NFL Records

Most touchdowns, rookie season: 22 (14 run, 6 receiving, 2 returns), 1965

Highest kickoff return average, career: 30.56, 1965–71

Most kickoff returns for TD [touchdown], career: 6, 1965–71 (tied with Ollie Matson and Travis Williams)

Most combined kick returns for TD, season: 4, 1967 (tied with 6 others)

Most combined kick returns for TD, game: 2, vs. San Francisco, 12/3/67 (tied with 11 others)

Brian Piccolo and Gale Sayers take a break during a preseason game against the Cleveland Browns.

A. Interpreting
? Why is this exchange unsettling? (Professional football players often deliberately change their weight. They will either gain weight to be better blockers, or lose weight to be faster runners. Brian is losing bulk *and* he's slower—something is wrong.)

B. Responding
? What do you think the writer means by "lies and prayers"? (That Brian and Gale are at the same time trying to kid themselves and hope that nothing is wrong with Brian's health)

Full Shot—The team is being weighed in, GIBRON *by the scales, sliding the weights up and down the bar and calling out the result for each man. There is some good-natured catcalling as some of the larger linemen are weighed, most of it coming from* BRIAN, *who is next in line with* GALE *close behind him.* BRIAN *takes his place.* GIBRON *starts to readjust the weights.*]

Brian. Scrimmage tomorrow, Abe. Going to give us any trick plays?
Gibron. Only trick I'd like to give you is how to keep some meat on you. You're down another pound.
Brian. But what's there is choice; admit it.
Gibron. Two-o-six and a quarter. Skinniest fullback in the league.
Brian. Gibron, you run the fat off us, then complain that we're too thin. You're a hard man to please.

[BRIAN *grins, used to* GIBRON'*s grumbles, and moves off.* GALE *is next in line.*]

Gibron *(to* GALE*)*. Ought to tell your Italian friend to load up on the pasta.
Gale. Probably just wants to be quicker, Gibron.
Gibron. Well, it ain't workin'. He lost ten pounds and he's half a second slower over a forty-yard sprint. Lighter *and* slower don't total out to much of a threat, you know. *(Checks the weight)* One ninety-nine. Next.

A [*We move with* GALE *as he steps off the scale, camera closing on him. He glances off at* GIBRON, *then in the direction taken by* BRIAN. *His eyes are puzzled; it's a weird combination* GIBRON *pointed out. Strange. Unsettling.* GALE *lets it sink in.*]

[*Direct Cut to: Game Footage of* GALE *and* BRIAN*—Running the ball, alternating. Two cuts, the first being the best footage of* PICCOLO *as either runner or receiver, the last being a punt return by* SAYERS *that goes all the way. This final cut, the punt return, is to lead directly into the following staged sequence.*]

[*Angle to Bears' Sideline—*GALE *comes off the field with the rest of the punt-return unit, among whom is* BRIAN. *Typically,* GALE *barely smiles at the congratulations he gets. He moves to the bench and sits,* BRIAN *by his side. They pull off their helmets, eyes on the game. Both are winded, but with one difference.* GALE *is clearly buoyed, exhilarated.* BRIAN *simply seems tired.*]

Gale. Nice block.
Brian. Thanks. *(Beat)* Must be ninety million pounds of pollen in the air.

[GALE *glances over at* BRIAN *casually and might see what we are now noting.* GALE'*s respiration is swiftly slowing down, approaching normal.* BRIAN'*s is not, he's still winded and badly so.* BRIAN *rises, moving for the water bucket near the phone desk.* GALE *watches him, then rises, moving for the sidelines to view the upcoming kickoff, camera moving with him. He finds an opening in the men standing there, then, in the hush just prior to the kicker's runup—the sound of* BRIAN *coughing.* GALE *turns back.*]

[*His Point of View—On* BRIAN*—The roar of the crowd overwhelms the sound of* PICCOLO'*s coughing. He takes down a fair amount of water, but that doesn't help.* BRIAN *coughs once more, though it's more evident in the motion of his shoulders and chest than in a sound; he's making an effort to stifle his cough.*]

Gale. You ought to get Fox to give you something for that hay fever.
Brian. He did. Doesn't help. The only thing I'm allergic to is Ray Nitschke.[3] *(Yelling)* All right, Butkus! Stick it in their ear, babe!

[BRIAN *moves off, back toward the bench.* GALE *looks to the playing field, but his thoughts are elsewhere. He glances back.*]

[*His Point of View—Angle to* PICCOLO*—Seated once more on the bench, his helmet off, still using more effort than one would expect to get his wind back. He sees* GALE *looking at him and smiles, giving a thumbs-up sign.*]

[*On* GALE*—Nodding, returning both the smile and the sign, and both are, at one and the same time, lies and prayers.*] B

3. **Ray Nitschke** (nitch'kē): all-star linebacker for the Green Bay Packers.

[Direct Cut to: Interior—Bears' Locker Room—Day—Full Shot—Most players are dressed now or seated in front of their lockers tying their shoes. We find HALAS *as he comes out of his office, his expression somber. He pulls up a stool beside* GALE *and sits, drained, enervated.]*

Gale. Lookin' at you, I'd never know we won the game.
Halas *(small smile).* I don't feel very much like a winner at the moment.
Gale. Why not?
Halas *(a deep breath).* Gale, I'm sending Brian Piccolo back to Chicago. He won't make the rest of the road trip with us. Ralph Kurek's going to start next week.
Gale *(beat).* Why?
Halas. Because I've had a policy on this team from the very start—the best player plays, no exceptions. And right now—Kurek is the best player.
Gale. Look, a lot of guys take a while to get on track for a season, slow starters, and . . .
Halas *(finishing for him).* And Brian Piccolo has never been one of those guys, Gale. He's always been in shape, able to give one hundred percent. But he isn't doing that anymore, and that worries me. *(With regret)* I don't know why—something physical—or whether he's got personal problems, something with his wife or children—but the truth is that something is taking the edge off of him—and I want to find out what that something is. For his sake and the team's. Can't afford to lose a back that good.
Gale *(resigned).* When's he going to find out?
Halas. Abe's telling him now. That's why I didn't want you to go right back to the hotel.
Gale. I wouldn't want to be in *your* shoes about ten minutes from now.

A

[Direct Cut to: Interior—Hotel Room—Night—On Suitcase—A bundle of wadded-up clothes is thrown into the suitcase. We pull back to reveal PICCOLO *in the act of packing, moving from closet and dresser to the suitcase on the bed.* GALE *maintains a low profile, not wanting to draw any fire from* BRIAN.]

Brian. Who'd believe it? I mean, really, who'd believe it!
Gale. Halas just wants you to see the doctor, and . . .
Brian. Halas doesn't know what he wants! Gibron's his boy and you should have heard *that* lecture! Kept telling me to patch things up with me and Joy. And he just smiles that Father Flanagan smile of his and says I shouldn't be afraid to level with him. B
Gale. Pic, be fair, now. Doctor Fox says that . . .
Brian. Oh, spare me any crud about your great team doctor. Wants me to get a physical for the cough, right? No allergy. Then what is it, I say! Want to hear what he says? *Could* be a virus. *Could* be a staph infection. *Could* be any one of a thousand things. It's like being treated in a Chinese restaurant—two from column A, three from column B! C
Gale. He's just trying to help, Pic . . .

[A beat, then BRIAN *sits on the bed, calming somewhat, but still angry and frustrated.]*

Brian. Yeah—I suppose you're right—but it's all so pointless, Gale. I know perfectly well what's wrong with me.

[He looks over at GALE, *eyes radiating sincerity.]*

Brian. Gale—I think I'm pregnant. D

[Direct Cut to: Interior—Visiting Team Locker Room—Day—Full Shot—The Chicago Bears suit up. Linemen pound each other's shoulder pads to a tighter fit. Some of the players sit in front of their lockers, wide-eyed, seeing nothing. Others move about nervously, bouncing on the balls of their feet, trembling with caged energy.]

*[Angle to Training Table—*GALE*'s ankle is wrapped tightly with adhesive tape. His face has the look of a carving, somber, dark, guarded. The trainer finishes the job and* GALE *nods his thanks, moving off the table, another man following behind him at once. We move with him as he strides toward a door at the other end of the locker room. He passes by* GIBRON *who is going over the attack plan with* CONCANNON *and the second-string quarterback, past linemen who are simply yelling at each other, wordless growls and bellows.* GALE *stops in front of the door bearing the word:* Coach. *He knocks on the door.]*

A. Interpreting
? What does Halas's conversation with Gale indicate—about both Brian and pro football? (It is an ominous sign about Brian's health. Pro football is a tough field with no room for sentiment.)

B. Expansion
"Father Flanagan smile" is a reference to the kind of ever-cheerful priests who appeared as characters in movies years ago.

C. Making Inferences
? What else is Brian feeling besides anger? (Fear—which the anger is covering up) What does his reaction remind you of? (Gale's reaction when he injured his knee)

D. Responding
? Throughout his ordeal, Brian maintains his sense of humor. Watch for examples of it and ask yourself whether you would be able to keep cracking jokes if you were in Brian's situation.

A. Atmosphere
What is the atmosphere of the room? What details evoke it? (Somber, grim, tense; Halas's dark glasses, McCaskey's pill taking, their looks to each other; their delay in answering Gale) How, as a director, would you have them stand and move to show their mood?

B. Technique
As with Gale's knee injury, what effect does this succession of freeze frames have? (It prolongs the agony of the moment.)

C. Responding
Why is this an unusual offer from Gale? (Everyone knows how shy he is and how terrified he gets when speaking in front of a group.) Why do you think Gale wants to tell the team himself? (Gale's telling the team will personalize the tragedy for him; it will help him accept it. The playwright may also be referring to Brian's statement on page 360: "You'll learn how to talk, once you find something that's got to be said.")

Halas. Come in.

[*Interior—The Coach's Office—Day—Full Shot—* HALAS *is seated behind the desk, hat and dark glasses on.* ED MCCASKEY *is at a water cooler in the corner, drawing a paper cup out of the container, using the water to wash down a pill. At first, both men seem quite normal, but it's a facade and one that's being eroded with each passing second.*]

Gale. Which end of the field you want me to take if we lose the toss?

[MCCASKEY *and* HALAS *stare at him for a second, then look to each other.* GALE *is a little baffled by the delay; the question is a standard one. Some kind of communication is going on between the two older men. They nod.*]

A **Halas.** Come on in, Gale. Close the door.

[*There is something in that tone, something vulnerable and sad, out of key.* GALE *steps into the room and closes the door as requested. There is a short silence, each of the other men hoping they'll not have to take the lead.*]

Halas. Gale—we've just had a phone call from Memorial Hospital . . .

[HALAS *removes the glasses. His eyes are red. He takes a breath.*]

Halas. Brian Piccolo has cancer.

[*Awe has within it an element of fear, of facing something so basic, so large, that one cannot ever truly cope with it.* GALE *reacts with prayerful disbelief and awe.*]

Gale. Oh, God . . .

[*Full Shot—*HALAS *kneads the bridge of his nose, the eyes closed as if hoping the curtain of his eyelids will allow time for a scene change.*]

Halas. They've scheduled an operation for tomorrow morning.
Gale *(feeling)*. An operation to do what?
McCaskey *(evenly, calmly)*. Gale, they've got to remove part of Brian's right lung.

[*This strikes* GALE *like whiplash. He starts to sink weakly into a nearby chair, and as he does so the frame freezes several times, giving the same look associated with the knee injury. As he sinks into the chair, the image moves with stuttering, uneven speed.*] B

Halas *(offstage)*. The doctors don't have any explanation, Gale. It must be something Brian has carried around inside him all his life. What set it off, they don't know. As to whether or not they found it in time—well, they don't know that either, I'm afraid.

[GALE*'s eyes are glazed. His spirit has been blindsided.*[4] HALAS *and* MCCASKEY *are no less affected.*]

McCaskey *(to* HALAS*)*. Who tells them?
Halas *(sighs, nodding)*. I know. It's my responsibility and I'll . . .
Gale *(interrupting)*. I'll tell them. C
Halas *(surprised)*. You, Gale?
Gale *(rising)*. That's right, me. I'll tell them. Let's go. *(To* MCCASKEY*)* Does Linda know?
McCaskey. I don't think so . . .
Gale. Call her and tell her.

[*He pulls open the door, looking to* HALAS. *The Coach and* MCCASKEY *trade a swift look, then* HALAS *gets to his feet. As he moves to the door,* MCCASKEY *picks up the phone on the desk and starts to dial.*]

[*Interior—The Locker Room—Day—Full Shot—* HALAS *and* GALE *come out of the Coach's room.* HALAS*'s presence is noted quickly and the players gather around in a loose semicircle.* GALE *appears very much in control of himself, in command of the situation.*]

Halas *(to players)*. Gale has something he'd like to say to you all. Gale . . .

[GALE *attempts to sustain eye contact with the other members of the team, but it swiftly becomes clear to him that he can't make it. Initially, his voice is strong and clear, but he can't hold it for long.*]

Gale. You—you all know that we hand out a game ball to the outstanding player. Well, I'd like to

4. **blindsided:** hit on the side opposite to the direction in which one is looking.

change that a little. We just got word that Brian Piccolo—that he's sick. Very sick. It looks like—uh—that he might not ever play football again—or—for a long time . . . *(Beat)* And—I think we should all dedicate ourselves to—give our maximum effort to win this ballgame, and give the game ball to Pic. We can all sign it and take it up to him at the hosp . . .

[*His voice tightens with abrupt anguish. He turns away, hiding his tears.*]

Gale *(continuing, softly).* Oh, my *God* . . .

[*Direct Cut to: Interior—*BRIAN*'s Hospital Room—Day—Tight on* BRIAN*—Garbed in a hospital gown, looking strangely out of place, a young man of two hundred pounds is in something approximating a doll's wardrobe. He's grinning from ear to ear, holding up the front page of the sports section, the headline of which reads:* COLTS DUMP BEARS 24–21.]

Brian *(Voice Over).* Fantastic! Who'd believe it! Sayers, you've got great moves on the field, but in the locker room, I've got to tell you, you're a klutz!

[*It is important to stress that the humor is* not *role playing; the fun has no element of stiff upper lip in it.*]

Brian. When you dedicate a game to someone, you are supposed to go out and *win* the game,
A idiot! Pat O'Brien[5] never said "Blow one for the Gipper," you know.

[*Full Shot—*GALE *and* JACK CONCANNON *stand at the end of the bed. At a small table near the window, the flowers and cards have been cleared away by* J. C. CAROLINE *and a few other players. In place of these niceties, they are opening up two cartons of pizza and two six-packs of beer.* JOY PICCOLO *stands next to her husband.*]

Gale. Bad—you are so bad.

Caroline. We probably would have won if Concannon had called the trap play more, but he hates to use it unless you're there for the repeat.

[*The men at the table have started putting pieces of pizza on paper napkins and begin to distribute them.*]

Joy. Brian, do you think this is such a good idea? I mean, pepperoni pizza and beer *isn't* on your diet.

Brian. Joy—are you telling me as I lie on this bed of pain, my body whittled away at by a ruthless band of strangers with Exacto knives—are you telling me I can't have any *pizza?*

[JOY *studies* BRIAN*, then looks to the other men. She shakes her head, exasperated*[6] *and loving them all very much.*]

Joy. Pass the pizza, please . . .

[*With smiles, the others crowd around the bed as* JOY *moves to the table. After a second or two to get the first bite down:*]

Brian. Hey—who wants to see my scar?

[*Instant negative replies from all. As these trail off, the door is opened offstage and they all look around. A nurse enters. She gazes at her patient, who has just had a lung removed, as he visits with his wife and friends, all of whom have pizza in hand.*]

Nurse #1. *Out! Now! No* discussion! *Out!*

[*Full Shot—*GALE, BUTKUS, CONCANNON, CAROLINE, *and* MAYES *quickly gather the pizza cartons and head for the door, ad-libbing farewells, ducking their heads like schoolboys as they pass the nurse.* GALE *is the last in line.* JOY *straightens up from kissing* BRIAN *goodbye.*]

Brian. Hey, take Gale down and have him give that little girl his autograph, will you? *(To* GALE*)* Little girl I met the day I came in here. We had our operations on the same day. Told her I'd get your autograph. You don't mind, do you?

---

5. **Pat O'Brien:** actor who played the title role in a film biography of football coach Knute Rockne. In the film, Rockne asks his Notre Dame players to "Win one for the Gipper," George Gipp, a star player who had died.

6. **exasperated** (ig·zas′pə·rā′tid): very annoyed.

Football Vocabulary

trap play: see Brian's own explanation on page 353.

A. Drawing Conclusions

? What is Brian referring to? (Gale publicly dedicated the game ball to Brian, and the Bears then lost the game.)

Responding to the Photograph

? What do you think is happening in this scene? What is making Joy smile? Did Brian just crack a joke? What is the expression on Brian's face?

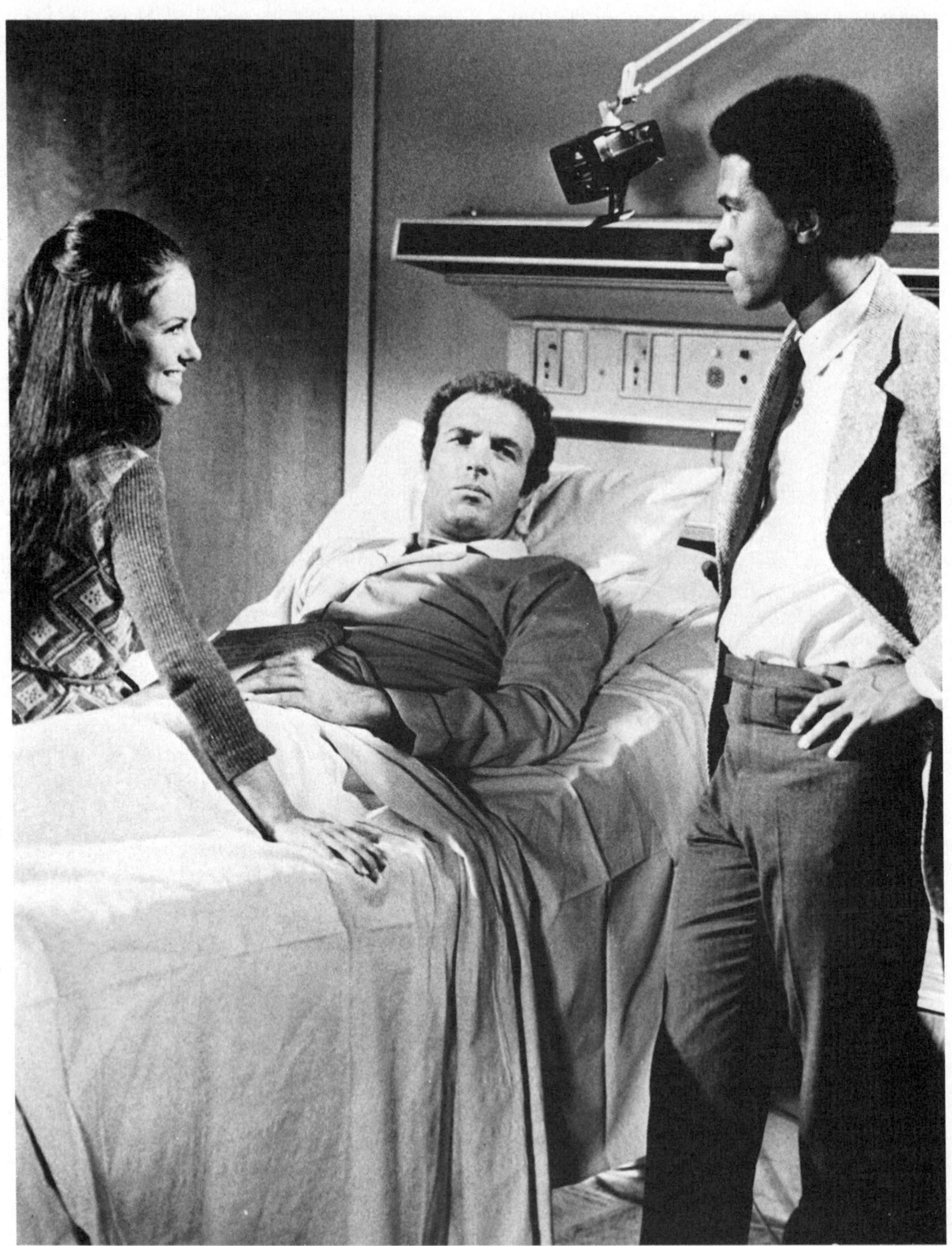

Joy and Gale with Brian, in his hospital room.

© 1971 Screen Gems, A Division of Columbia Industries, Inc. All rights reserved.

Football Vocabulary
kicker: player who kicks off to start the play, or kicks field goals. Kickers don't have to be strong or quick since they usually don't have to block or run.

A. Foreshadowing
This incident foreshadows Brian's death. Remember that Patti and Brian had their operations on the same day, which somehow links them. Joy may be facing Brian's possible death for the first time.

B. Contrast
? Why do you think the playwright inserts footage of Gale at this point in the teleplay? (To set Gale's health, energy, and success as a contrast to Brian's illness)

C. Expansion
Red Grange, a famous football player of the 1920's, was known for his ability to avoid tacklers.

D. Characters
? What new qualities do we learn abut Brian? (In addition to an enduring sense of humor, Brian's strength, determination, and confidence keep him going and hoping through his illness. Notice that it is Brian who is comforting Joy, instead of the other way around.)

Gale. No problem. Be glad to.
Joy. I'll see you tonight.

[*He blows a kiss at her and they all leave. The* NURSE *holds for a second in the door, reinforcing her disapproval. She sighs and steps out of the door. Once it's closed,* BRIAN *throws back the covers and puts his feet over the side. There's a good deal of strain and discomfort involved, but it's well within* BRIAN'*s tolerance. He stands with his back to the window, then starts for the door, his gait a shuffle.*]

Brian. There he goes sports fans—can you believe it—power, speed, grace, and agility all wrapped up in . . .

[BRIAN *halts as the door is opened once again by the* NURSE. *Their eyes fight to a draw.*]

Brian. Don't come any closer, Miss Furman. White lisle stockings turn me on!

[*Direct Cut to: Children's Ward—Angle to Nurses' Station—The walls here are festooned with crayon drawings made by the patients. The nurses' station has a number of stuffed animals on the counter. As* JOY *and* GALE *approach, one of the nurses hangs up the phone and turns to them with a pleasant smile.*]

Nurse #2. May I help you?
Joy. My name is Mrs. Piccolo. My husband's a patient on the third floor and he told me about a little girl—Patti Lucas—who wanted this gentleman's autograph.

[*The* NURSE *nods nicely, holding up a finger as she flips swiftly through the Rolodex in front of her.*]

Nurse #2. I'm sorry, Mrs. Piccolo—Patti isn't with us anymore.
Joy. Well, do you have a home address? My husband wanted her to have the autograph very much.
Nurse #2 (*beat*). Mrs. Piccolo—Patti's dead. She passed away early this morning. A

[GALE *places his hand gently on* JOY'*s shoulder.* JOY *nods, forcing a smile mouthing the "thank you," though her voice is absent.* GALE *is a few feet behind her as they start for the elevator bank.*]

[*Direct Cut to: Game Footage of* GALE *in an End Run, Preferably Slow Motion—The crowd noise is at a frenzied peak, then the frame freezes.*] B

Brian (*Voice Over*). Look at that knee, will you? That thing is really beautiful!

[*Exterior—Hospital Grounds—Day—Full Shot—* BRIAN *is wheeled onto the hospital lawn. He's looking at a sports magazine which he holds up so* JOY *can see the picture. They stop beneath a large tree bordering the walk.*]

Brian. Nothing wrong with that knee; I'll tell you that.
Joy. Congratulations, Doctor Piccolo.
Brian. Yeah—but you know what—I've been thinking. With Gale healthy, and Ralph Kurek healthy—I'm going to have a rough time getting back into the lineup next year. And I was thinking—what's so difficult about being a kicker? I mean, I wonder if it's something you can teach yourself. 'Cause you don't need a lot of wind or stamina or size . . .

[*He looks down at* JOY *and the look on her face is weakening, hopeful still, but with more effort required on her part with each day that goes by.* BRIAN *reads that look like a compass.*]

Brian. All right, Gloomy Gus—what do you think of my brainstorm?
Joy (*floundering*). Well—I don't know, Brian—I'm no expert on kickers and things . . .
Brian. You just did an end run that Red Grange would be proud to call his own. C
Joy. Don't make fun of me, Brian. I'm scared.
Brian (*evenly*). What of?
Joy (*sputtering with disbelief*). What *of*? What *of*? You can't be serious! You know perfectly well what of!
Brian (*absolutely sincere*). No, I don't, Joy. I swear to God I don't. (*Taking her hands*) Look—I'm not an idiot. This thing is bad—I know that—but it's a detour, Joy—that's all. It's not going to stop me because I'm not going to *let* it stop me. No way . . . (*Quietly*) I've got too much to do yet, Joy.

[*Her face in his hands,* BRIAN *bends to kiss* JOY. *As their lips meet, we start to boom up and back.* D

A. **Interpreting**

? With this knowledge, what connection can we make about the scene between Joy and Brian that same afternoon? (Joy must have known that Brian's health was getting worse, which is why she broke down even in the face of Brian's courage and optimism.)

B. **Character**

? What does it mean that Gale wishes he were "strong enough to cry"? (Gale is very self-controlled when it comes to his emotions; he wishes he could let go and vent his grief.)

JOY leans her head against BRIAN's knee, his hand stroking her hair.]

[*Direct Cut to: Game Footage of SAYERS—Fielding a punt, signaling for a fair catch, then deciding to let it roll. And roll it does, further and further back toward his own goal. By the time he realizes he should have caught it, there are a number of defensive men all around the ball, making any return impossible. From the time the ball struck earth and took off, we have heard:*]

Brian *(Voice Over).* Pick it up! Pick it up, dummy! Gale! Joy, look at him!
Nurse *(Voice Over).* Now, Mister Piccolo, calm down.
Brian *(Voice Over).* Calm down! How can I calm down? You'd think the ball was wearing a white sheet.

[*Direct Cut to: Interior—Hotel Room—Night—Full Shot—GALE is on the bed, shoes off, talking on the phone with BRIAN, the mood one of good-natured give-and-take. Seated on the other bed is a football player, GALE's new roommate. There is a room-service cart in evidence, remnants there of sandwiches and glasses of milk. We intercut this with BRIAN in his hospital room. There is no one else present with BRIAN.*]

Gale. Well, I was going to catch it, but when it started coming down, I said I wonder what Pic would do in a situation like this, and ducking seemed to be the answer.
Brian. Well, at least you won the game.
Gale. That's right.
Brian. Didn't dedicate this one to me, though, did you?

[*In the hotel room, there is a knock on the door. The player goes to answer it. He opens the door to reveal a hotel official, who exchanges a few words with the football player, then is allowed into the room.*]

Gale. Nope. Dedicated this one to Butkus.
Brian. Why?
Gale. He threatened us. *(Beat)* How you doin'? Pic? Really?
Brian. Hanging in there, Magic. Doing what they tell me to do. You could do me a favor, though.
Gale. You got it. Name it.
Brian. Call Joy, will you? When she left tonight, she was really down. I never saw her that down.
Gale. I'll call her as soon as I get back.
Brian. Thanks, I appreciate it.
Gale. Okay. Good night.
Brian. Good night.

[*GALE hangs up, then looks a question to the hotel clerk.*]

Hotel Official. Mister Sayers, while you were on the phone, there was a lady who called. She seemed very upset.

[*He hands GALE a piece of folded paper. GALE unfolds it.*]

Hotel Official. I hope I've not overstepped my authority.
Player. I'm sure you did the right thing. Thank you very much.

[*The PLAYER ushers the hotel official out the door, closes it, then glances back at GALE, who sags, drained.*]

Gale. It's Joy Piccolo. She says it's urgent.

[*Direct Cut to: Interior—PICCOLO Living Room—Night—On Clock—The time is 3:30. We pull back to reveal JOY, in robe and slippers, pouring coffee for GALE and LINDA. The SAYERSES have dumped their coats on the couch.*]

Joy. I know it's an awful thing, to make you fly all the way back here in the middle of the night, but . . .
Gale. It doesn't bother me, so don't let it bother you.

[*JOY smiles feebly and sits, her hands tightly intertwined, struggling to maintain her composure. A long beat.*]

Linda. Just say it, Joy . . .
Joy *(nods, a childlike move).* They found more of the tumor . . . A

[*The tears come. Her face twists, crumpling under the terror and the fear. LINDA moves to her, holding her, both women rocking back and forth. GALE swallows bitterly, probably wishing he was strong enough to cry. He pulls a handkerchief out of his* B *pocket and places it on the coffee table within* JOY*'s reach. She nods her appreciation, dabbing her eyes.*]

Joy. They told me today—they want to operate again—and I was going to tell Brian—but I—couldn't, Gale. I don't know whether or not he can take the disappointment. And if he can't—I know *I* can't. *(Beat)* The doctor is going to tell him tomorrow morning. If you could be there when he finds out—it might help.
Gale. I'll be there, Joy.

[*Direct Cut to: Interior of* BRIAN*'s Room—Day—On Football Game—This is a board game with charts and dice and miniature scoreboard. As we pull back, we find* BRIAN *and* GALE *seated on opposite sides of the small table near the window. They both roll their dice.*]

Gale. What'd you try?
Brian. End run.
Gale. Oh, Lordy—I was in a blitz.

[BRIAN *starts to consult the complicated chart that will give him the results of the play.*]

Gale *(indicating game chart).* Well—did you gain or what?

A [*The door is opened by* MR. EBERLE, *a nervous, uncertain sort, more at home with facts and figures than with flesh and blood. A name tag hangs from the lapel of his coat.* BRIAN *looks up with a smile.*]

Brian. Hi. Can I help you?
Eberle. Well, I'm sorry if I'm disturbing anything . . .
Brian. Don't worry—I can beat him later. What can I do for you?
Eberle *(rummaging through papers).* I know this is a bother at a time like this, Mr. Piccolo, but hospitals have their rules and regulations, you see, and I'll need your signature on this surgical consent for the operation.

[*He hands* BRIAN *the piece of paper, but* BRIAN *is scarcely aware of it. He looks at* EBERLE *uncomprehendingly, stunned.* GALE *is searching for a way to ease this, but before he can locate his voice,* EBERLE *notes the bewilderment on* BRIAN*'s face.*]

Eberle. The doctor *has* been here, hasn't he? He's talked with you, I mean?
Brian. No . . .
Eberle *(looking to watch).* Oh—well, I suppose I might be running a little ahead of my schedule today. Perhaps I better come back after the doctor has . . .
Brian. What would the doctor have to say to me? Man, I've *had* my operation, *right?*

[*Silence, and that's the worst answer there can be. After a beat,* BRIAN *looks over slowly to* GALE.] B

Brian. Talk to me, Magic . . .

[GALE *discovers his voice after a second, but it emerges with anguish.*]

Gale. The tests show—there's more of the tumor than they thought, Pic. They have to operate again . . .

[*Once more,* EBERLE, *seeking nothing more than escape, steps forward, holding out the surgical consent and a fountain pen.*]

Eberle. So, if you'll just sign the consent, Mr. . . .
Brian *(turning away).* No!
Eberle. But putting this off won't be—
Brian. Are you deaf? I said *no!*
Eberle. Mr. Sayers—can't you talk to your friend?

[BRIAN *has moved to the window, shoulders hunched as if gathering himself for a blow of enormous force.* GALE *looks at him, then turns to* EBERLE.]

Gale. No, Mr. Eberle, I think I'd rather talk to *you.*
Eberle. But . . .
Gale. Brian is a professional athlete, Mr. Eberle. And a professional gets into a habit after awhile. He gets himself ready for a game mentally as well as physically. Because he knows those two things are all tied up together. And there's a clock going inside him, so that when the game starts, he's one hundred percent mentally and physically. And what Pic is saying to you now, is that you're

Football Vocabulary
end run: a strategy whereby the quarterback hands the ball back to the running back, who runs around the line to score a touchdown
blitz (see definition on page 346)

A. Suspense
The entrance of Mr. Eberle creates suspense because we, like Gale, are waiting for the arrival of the doctor to tell Brian the bad news. We are also not comforted by the fact that Mr. Eberle is "more at home with facts and figures than with flesh and blood."

B. Making Inferences
? Why is silence the worst answer? (It confirms Brian's fears that he has not had his last operation.)

Here is some more of Gale Sayers's acceptance speech:

". . . But to return to my part in all of this tonight, something very personal is represented in this award.

"There were skeptics—and there probably still are some—who wrote or said what they must have believed firmly—that Gale Sayers would never bring back the full 100 percent of his ability to football, especially a certain expert who spent a lot of time at our training camp. . . .

"He didn't know that inside of me there was a fierce determination to prove my worth, to prove my mettle. . . .

"It is something special to do a job that few people say can be done. Maybe that's how courage is spelled out—at least in my case. Although there were detractors, there were also a few people who never stopped believing in me and encouraging me to keep driving. I'd like to acknowledge their support, here and now—especially our team physician, Dr. Ted Fox, Coach Halas, and Buddy Young, to Commissioner Pete Rozelle, and my teammate, roommate, and friend, Brian Piccolo. Brian Piccolo, who in a humorous, kindly, and sometimes unkindly

A. Recalling
This is one of the longest speeches Gale has made so far in the play. What does Brian's statement remind us of? (Again, that he himself said that Gale would talk when he had something important to say.)

B. Character
Once more we have to be astounded at Brian's ability to bounce back and make jokes. If you were Brian, how would you react to the news Brian has just been given?

C. Foreshadowing
"Putting to sleep" is an expression often used when animals, usually pets, are mercifully killed because of illness or pain. Here, it foreshadows Brian's death.

scheduling this game before he can get ready. Couldn't it wait until over the weekend?
Eberle. Well, yes, it *could,* but . . .
Gale. Then *let* it.
Eberle *(a beat, looks to* BRIAN*).* First thing Monday morning, Mr. Piccolo.
Brian. Okay.
Eberle. I'll see you then.

[GALE *looks back to* BRIAN, *who continues to gaze out the window. A beat, as* BRIAN *strains to salvage some control.*]

Brian. Thanks, Gale . . .
Gale. No sweat.
A **Brian.** Thought you were the guy who didn't talk very well.
Gale. Well—I roomed with an Italian, you know how they are.

[BRIAN *turns away from the window. He moves back to the game board, idly scanning the setup. A beat, then a small smile appears on his face.*]

B **Brian.** Guess what? I scored a touchdown.

[*We hold on* BRIAN.]

[*Cut to Black over Following:*]

Nurse #1's Voice. Good morning, Mr. Piccolo. Time to wake up now.

[*Fade in—Medium Shot—Nurse #1—She is looking into lens, smiling Cheshirely,*[7] *a hypodermic needle in hand.*]

Nurse # 1. I'm going to give you a little shot to help you relax, Mr. Piccolo. You'll be going up to the operating room in about an hour.
Brian *(offstage).* My wife here?
Nurse #1. You'll see her when you come down, Mr. Piccolo. Now, this won't hurt a bit.
Brian *(offstage).* Yes—you're being very brave about it all.

[*Direct Cut to: Interior—Operating Room—Up Angle—A doctor, masked and gowned, leans into the lens, arms held up away from his body.*]

C **Doctor.** Mr. Piccolo—we're going to put you to sleep now . . .
Brian *(offstage).* That's the—worst—choice of words—I ever heard in my life . . .

[*As we start a slow fade to black, we begin to hear the sound of applause, growing louder and louder with each second. Then, in utter darkness:*]

M.C. *(offstage). Gale Sayers!!!*

[*Cut to: Interior—Banquet Hall—Night—Dressed in a tuxedo,* GALE *starts as he becomes aware of the explosion of sounds being directed at him. Other men at his table poke* GALE, *all laughing as they urge him to his feet. Startled, he rises and the camera pans him as he is almost passed along from table to table.*]

[*The Dais—*GALE *smiles, still at a loss, and moves toward the toastmaster, who is holding out a large trophy to him. As* GALE *accepts the trophy with a muttered thank you, the applause builds once more.* GALE *looks down at the inscription on the trophy.*]

[*Insert—The Inscription—It reads:* George S. Halas Award—Most Courageous Player—to Gale Sayers.]

[*Tight on* GALE*—He looks out, nodding acknowledgment to the applause. Slowly it starts to trail off, then dies. A moment of throat clearings, chairs shifting into better position. When it is absolutely still,* GALE *begins to speak.*]

Gale. I'd like to say a few words about a guy I know—a friend of mine. His name is Brian Piccolo and he has the heart of a giant—and that rare form of courage that allows him to kid himself and his opponent—cancer. He has the mental attitude that makes me proud to have a friend who spells out courage twenty-four hours a day, every day of his life.

[GALE *takes a sip of water.*]

Gale. You flatter me by giving me this award—but I tell you here and now I accept it for Brian Piccolo. Brian Piccolo is the man of courage who should receive the George S. Halas Award. It is mine tonight; it is Brian Piccolo's tomorrow.

7. **Cheshirely** (chesh'ir·lē): like the grinning Cheshire cat in Lewis Carroll's *Alice's Adventures in Wonderland.*

way, urged me day after day to fight my way back. Brian Piccolo, who has the sheer, solid raw courage, which entitles him to win over a sickness that makes my knee injury seem unimportant.

"In the middle of last season Brian was struck down by the deadliest, most shocking enemy any of us can ever face—cancer. Compare his courage with that which I am supposed to possess, as symbolized by this award. There was never any doubt in my mind that I'd run again, knee injury or no. But think of Brian and his courage and fortitude shown in the months since last November; in and out of hospitals; hoping to play football again, but not too sure at any time what the score was or might be. . . ." —Gale Sayers

Football Vocabulary

"fourth and eight . . . punt": Fourth down and eight yards to go is a desperate situation in football. The team can either punt—kick the ball to the other team—or go for a new set of downs, which there is little chance of getting. Brian is admitting to Gale that "they," or the doctors, won't let him give up, although he wants to. Gale's next line, "Go for it, then" (which is said when the decision is to go for the downs) gives Brian the encouragement he needed to keep fighting.

A [*Not a sound out there.* GALE *clutches the award tightly and his eyes sparkle with tears. No attempt is made to hide those tears.*]

B **Gale.** I love Brian Piccolo—and I'd like all of you to love him, too. And, tonight—when you hit your knees . . . *(Beat)* Please ask God to love him . . .

[GALE *steps quickly out of the spotlight. We hold on the empty circle for several seconds before the sound comes. First, one or two people, then more, and swiftly an avalanche of thunder.*]

[*Direct Cut to: Interior—*BRIAN'*s Hospital Room—Day—On* BRIAN*—*JOY *places the phone on the pillow next to him. When the angle widens, we see* LINDA *is also present. There is an IV stand*[8] *next to the bed, a tank of oxygen in the corner.* BRIAN'*s face is drawn, the flesh pallid*[9] *and shiny. We intercut the conversation with* GALE *in his hotel room.*]

Brian. Hi, Magic . . .
Gale. How are you, Pic?
Brian. Oh, hangin' in there. . . . *(Beat)* Heard what you did at the banquet. If you were here, I'd kiss you . . .
Gale. Glad I'm not there, then.
Brian. Hey, Gale? They said you gave me a pint of blood. Is that true?
Gale. Yeah.
Brian. That explains it, then.
Gale. Explains what?
C **Brian.** I've had this craving for chitlins all day.

[GALE *smiles on the other end.*]

Gale. I'll be in tomorrow morning, man. I'll see you then.
Brian. Yeah—I ain't going nowhere. . . .

[JOY *takes the phone and hands it to* LINDA, *who takes the receiver to the window where the cradle is located. Camera closes on* LINDA, *who raises the phone to her ear.*]

Linda. Gale?
Gale. How is he, Linda? *Really?*
Linda *(softly, yet urgently). Hurry.* Gale—please hurry.

D [*Direct Cut to: Interior—*BRIAN'*s Room—On* ED MCCASKEY*—He is seated in a chair by the door, rosary beads sliding through his fingers. The room is striped with sunlight from the partially closed venetian blinds. The door is opened and* GALE *and* LINDA *come in.* BRIAN'*s eyes are closed, and his frame seems small beneath the blankets.* JOY *bends to him as* GALE *moves quietly to the other side of the bed.*]

Joy. Brian—Gale's here.

[BRIAN'*s hand comes up from the sheet in greeting.* GALE *takes the hand in his.* BRIAN'*s words come slowly, breath on a ration.*]

Brian. Hello, Magic.
Gale *(after a beat).* How's it going, Pic?
Brian. It's fourth and eight, man—but they won't let me punt.
Gale. Go for it, then.
Brian. I'm trying, Gale—Dear God, how I'm trying . . .

[*Suddenly* BRIAN'*s head snaps back, his hand convulsing on* GALE'*s.* JOY *leans close to her husband.*]

[*Seconds go by. Then, slowly,* BRIAN'*s body relaxes and his head touches the pillow.* JOY *blots the perspiration from his brow. His eye goes to* GALE.]

Brian. Remember that first year . . . couldn't get a word out of you. . . .
Gale. Couldn't get you to shut up. . . .
Brian. Remember how you got me with those mashed potatoes. . . .
Gale. You deserved it—the way you sang that dumb fight song—twice, you did it—at camp, and that time down in my basement. . . . *(Beat)* And that 32 trap play—remember that?
Brian. Yeah. How could I forget?

[*There is a pause.* BRIAN'*s look turns reflective. He smiles.*]

Brian. You taught me a lot about running, Gale, I appreciate it.

8. **IV stand:** short for intravenous (in′trə·vē′nəs) stand which holds liquid medication injected directly into the veins.
9. **pallid:** pale.

A. Character
That Gale does not try to hide his tears this time shows that he is now "strong enough to cry."

B. Expression
"Hit your knees": Gale is referring to saying your prayers before bed.

C. Vocabulary
"Chitlins" or chitterlings are a popular food of blacks in the South.

D. Expansion
Rosary beads are a string of prayer beads that Catholics use when praying.

373

A. Mood
? This is a heartbreaking thing for Brian to say. What does it imply? (That Brian, the ever-confident and unbeatable optimist, has lost hope that he will live)

B. Symbol
McCaskey's closing the blinds visually symbolizes Brian's life coming to a close.

Gale. I wouldn't be running if I hadn't had you pushin' me—helping me. . . .
Brian. I'll get you next training camp. . . .
Gale. I'll be waiting. . . .
Brian. Yeah. . . . *(sigh)* Gale, I'm feeling kind of punk. . . . I think I'll sack out for a while, okay?
Gale. Sure thing.

[*Angle to their hands—*GALE *gently lets go of* BRIAN*'s hand, which falls limply back onto the sheet.* GALE*'s hand rests on the other for a beat, then he moves away.*]

[*Full Shot—The nun opens the door for* GALE *and* LINDA. GALE *stops, looking back, his voice choked.*]

Gale. See you tomorrow, Pic. . . .

[*Tight on* BRIAN*—He turns his head toward* GALE. *He lifts the hand closest to the door and gives a thumbs-up.*]

A **Brian.** If you say so. . . .

[*Offstage, the sound of the door closing.* BRIAN *pulls* JOY *close to him, his arms about her. His eyes close, his breathing slackens.* JOY*'s lips are close to* BRIAN*'s ear.*]

Joy. I love you, Brian—I love you. . . .

[BRIAN *forces his eyes open and looks at her for a long beat. He finds a smile.*]

Brian. Who'd believe it, Joy—who'd ever believe it. . . .

[*And they close for the last time. This stillness will endure.*]

[*Dissolve to: Exterior—Hospital Parking Lot—Night—On* GALE *and* LINDA*—Arm in arm they move slowly along the line of cars in the parking lot until they come to their own.* GALE *opens the door on* LINDA*'s side and helps her in. As he closes the door, he looks to the hospital.*]

[*His Point of View—Hospital Window—Zooming in on* MCCASKEY *in* BRIAN*'s room. He slowly* B *closes the blinds.*]

[*Tight on* GALE*—He gazes at the hospital.*]

Comment from a Producer

When asked what was an indispensable requirement for a good picture, Samuel Goldwyn, one of Hollywood's greatest producers of the 1930's, replied: "The author. A great picture has to start with a great story. Just as water can't rise higher than its source, so a picture can't rise higher than its source."

You might discuss this quotation with the class. Do they think that *Brian's Song* started with a great story? Do they agree that a picture can't rise above the story?

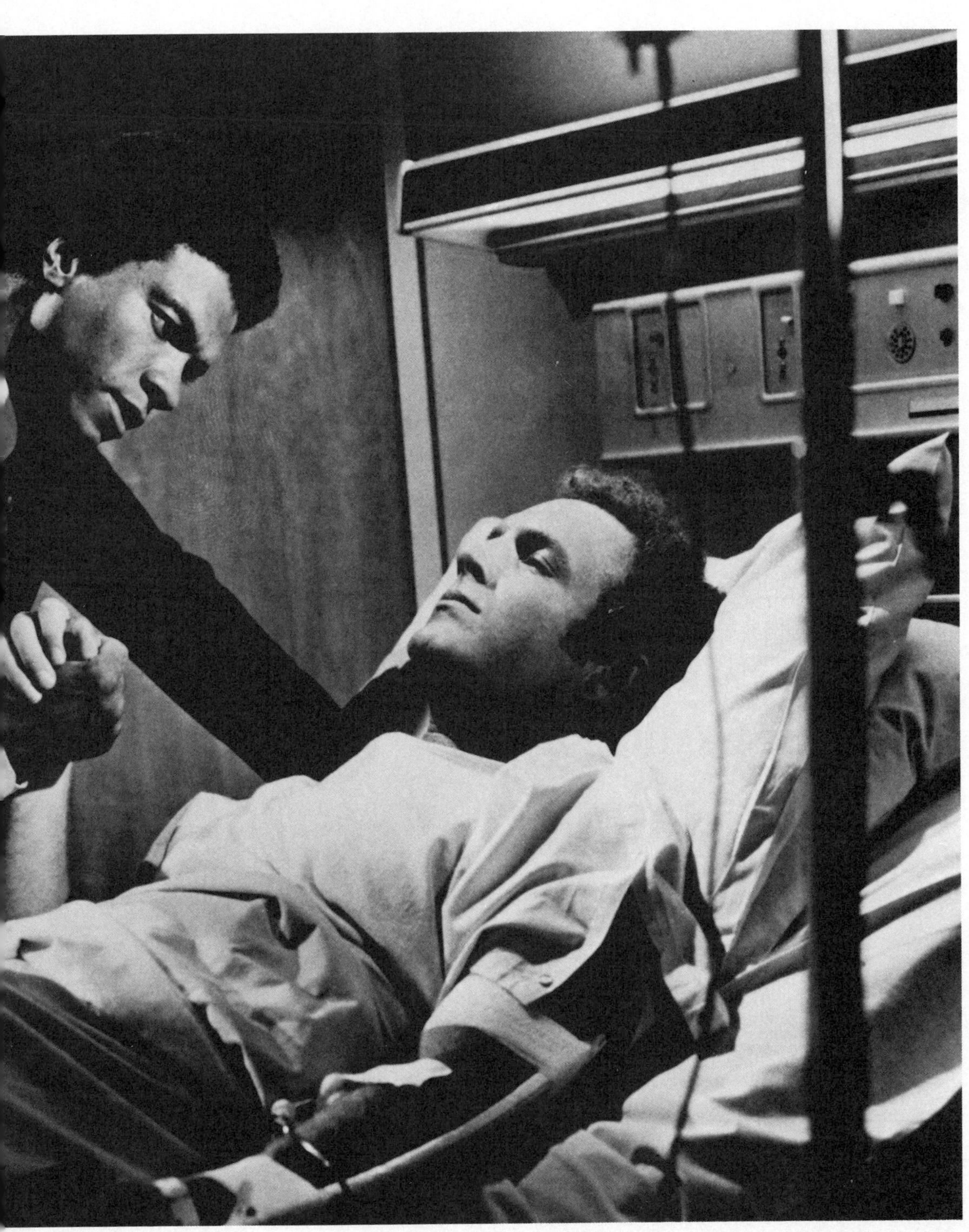

"I wouldn't be running if I hadn't had you pushin' me—helping me."

© 1971 Screen Gems, A Division of Columbia Industries, Inc. All rights reserved.

Analyzing Part Two
Identifying Facts

1. He promotes Brian to starting fullback, meaning that Brian and Gale will be starting together.
2. Brian is losing weight and running slower.
3. Brian learns he needs a second operation when a hospital administrator comes in to have him sign a consent form. He is shocked and scared and refuses to sign the form.
4. He announces that the award really should be given to Brian.
5. Brian grows weaker and weaker, and finally dies of cancer.

Interpreting Meanings

6. Brian is Gale's closest friend. Gale's acceptance of this task is a way of expressing his feelings about Brian.
7. Joy shows great courage in dealing with Brian's illness, and great caring. She keeps up Brian's spirits even when she knows he is getting worse.
8. Patti is a little girl whom Brian met in the hospital, where she too was a patient. He promised to get her Gale's autograph.

When Gale and Joy go to look for Pat-

A. Ending

? How does this ending shot of Gale and Brian's race affect you? (Answers will vary; but the idea is that this play is really about a beautiful and close friendship—and it is that idea, not the tragedy of Brian's death, that viewers should come away with.)

Brian Piccolo (1943–1970).

Narrator *(Voice Over)*. Brian Piccolo died of cancer at the age of twenty-six. He left a wife and three daughters.

[*Superimpose over the close shot of* GALE SAYERS *in the parking lot, footage from the footrace between* GALE *and* BRIAN, *ending with slow motion of their contest that freezes on a tight shot of* BRIAN.] **A**

Narrator *(Voice Over)*. He also left a great many loving friends who miss him and think of him often. But, when they think of him, it's not how he died that they remember but, rather, how he lived. . . . *(Beat)* How he *did* live. . . .

[*And as* GALE *moves around to his side of the car and starts to get in, the image of* BRIAN *takes precedence, smiling and full of life. A good face to study for a moment or two.*]

[*Fade-out.*]

Responding to the Play

Analyzing Part Two

Identifying Facts

1. What change in the team does Coach Halas make at the start of the new season?
2. What are the first signs of Brian's illness?
3. Who tells Brian that he needs a second operation? Describe how Brian reacts to the news.
4. Describe what Gale does when he is given the Most Courageous Player award.
5. What finally happens to Brian?

Interpreting Meanings

6. Explain why Gale wants to tell the team about Brian's illness, instead of having Coach Halas tell them.
7. Brian's illness is a painful time for his wife, Joy. Discuss what qualities of **character,** or personality traits, Joy reveals during this time.
8. Who is Patti Lucas? How does the incident in which Gale and Joy look for her **foreshadow,** or hint at, the ending of the drama? SRW p. 43
9. What do you think the play's title means? Explain how it relates to the play.
10. How did you feel after reading the end of *Brian's Song?* Can you explain why?

Applying Meanings

11. At the end of the play, the narrator says about Brian, "It's not how he died that they remember but, rather, how he lived." What do you think the narrator means by this? What other people that you have known or heard about could you apply this statement to?
12. Brian Piccolo faces his illness with courage and good humor. Do you think this alone would make him a hero? Explain why or why not.

ti, they find out that she has died. Since Patti and Brian had their operations on the same day, it suggests that Brian will share Patti's fate.

9. Students might note several possible associations. The title suggests a song of praise, showing Brian's good qualities. It also suggests that the play is depicting the essence of Brian—what he was like and his effect on others. It also echoes the final speech by the narrator, since a song is something that is easily remembered.

10. Most students will find the story sad and moving, but uplifting.

Applying Meanings

11. The suggestion here is that Brian lived life to the fullest, and that it is his positive attitude toward life, his decency, and his love for others that people will remember.

12. Students' answers will depend on their definition of *hero.* It would be helpful to let students discuss what the word means. They might ponder whether a hero needs to be well-known, or whether anyone can be a hero.

Writing About the Whole Play

A Creative Response

1. **Writing a Diary Entry.** Write a diary entry that expresses the thoughts and feelings of one of the following characters. Use the first person pronoun "I."
   - **a.** *Brian Piccolo* the day he first meets Gale Sayers at training camp
   - **b.** *Gale* or *Linda Sayers* immediately after Gale's knee injury
   - **c.** *Joy Piccolo* when she finds out that Brian has cancer

A Critical Response

2. **Analyzing Change in Character.** Part of the enjoyment of reading or seeing a good drama is observing how a character changes and grows. Write a paragraph in which you trace the stages of Gale's growth in *Brian's Song.* Begin when he is a shy person at his first training camp. Continue your analysis until he has become the self-assured man at the end of the drama. You might note the changes in how Gale feels about public speaking and in the way he delivers speeches.
3. **Writing About an Outstanding Personality Trait.** Brian Piccolo is a study in good humor. Write two paragraphs discussing this personality trait. In the first paragraph, cite examples of Brian's sense of humor. In the second paragraph, discuss how Brian's good humor affects him and his relationships with others. That is, what is its effect on Gale and the development of Gale's personality? What do Brian's teammates think of him? How does his humor help him handle his illness?

See Teacher's Manual page 119.

Analyzing Language and Vocabulary

Camera Directions and Audio Instructions

A teleplay or screenplay contains **stage directions,** which are directions for props and for how the characters should speak and move. It also includes **camera directions,** which are directions for filming each scene, and **audio instructions,** which are directions for sound effects. Many of the terms used in *Brian's Song* may be new to you. However, you probably learned the meaning of these terms as you read the teleplay. In some cases the **context,** or words and phrases surrounding a term, probably helped you understand the meaning. In other cases the term itself described its meaning. For example, the context probably allowed you to guess that a *shot* is the picture on the screen. And the word *close-up* suggests its meaning—"a view that gives a close look at a face or at some detail."

From your reading of the teleplay, match each term below with its definition. If you're unsure of a term's meaning, look it up in a dictionary.

1. fade-in
2. voice over
3. cut
4. beat
5. pan
6. zoom
7. slow motion
8. intercut
9. freeze frame
10. long shot

- **a.** view from a distance
- **b.** cut back and forth between two shots
- **c.** to appear gradually out of a darkened screen
- **d.** to make a sudden change from one scene or shot to another
- **e.** to stop the film to focus on one frame, like a photograph
- **f.** comments or narration by the voice of an unseen person
- **g.** pause in dialogue
- **h.** the action on the screen moves slowly
- **i.** to quickly move in for a close view, or away for a distant view
- **j.** to swivel a camera from one side to the other

For answers, see Teacher's Manual page 119.
SRW p. 33

Research Assignment: Distinguishing Fact from Nonfact

Have students research the life of Brian Piccolo. (A good book about his life is *Brian Piccolo: A Short Season* by Jeannie Morris.) Have them write an essay in which they compare Brian Piccolo's real life with the way he is portrayed in William Blinn's play.

About the Playwright

William Blinn was born in Ohio, and graduated from The American Academy of Dramatic Arts in New York City. He formed an independent organization called Echo Grove Productions, which creates videos and performs stage productions. His theatrical achievements include writing for and producing "The Wonder Years" and "Our House," two syndicated television series about families; co-authorship of the movie *Purple Rain* (1985); and producer of a successful one-woman show that premiered in New York City. For his teleplay of *Brian's Song,* he received an Emmy Award, the George Foster Peabody Award, the Writers Guild of America Award, and the Black Sports Magazine Award.

Focusing on Background

"The Short Courageous Life of Brian Piccolo"

"Brian Piccolo and I began rooming together in 1967, and we became close friends. It's easy to make a big deal out of the fact that he was white and I'm black and to wonder how we got along. But there was nothing to it, although I admit at first we did feel each other out. I had never had a close relationship with a white person before, except maybe George Halas (the owner of the Chicago Bears), and Piccolo had never really known a black person before. I remember that he wondered at first, 'Are they really different? Do they sleep in chandeliers, or what?'

"The best thing about our relationship as it developed was that we could kid each other all the time about race. It was a way, I guess, of easing into each other's world. . . .

"I was in the room when Pic came in. 'What are you doing here?' he said.

"I said, 'We're in together.'

"He was surprised, but I had known about it. They had asked me if I had any objections to rooming with Brian. I said no. I'd been rooming with a fellow who got cut and I think Pic was rooming with a quarterback, and they decided maybe they ought to room guys together by position. Also, I think Bennie McRae, one of our co-captains, suggested that they start some integrated rooming.

"It really didn't make any difference. I think they tend to make too much of it. Friends like to room with friends, and it has nothing to do with segregation.

"You can bet we didn't eat dinner together in Birmingham that weekend. We joked about it, but we went our separate ways. I don't know if we ate dinner with one another more than a couple of times that first year. But by the end of that first year, we had both loosened up quite a bit.

"I think Pic helped open me up because he was such a happy-go-lucky guy. . . . He was really a comfort to me during the 1969 exhibition season and into the regular season, especially those early games when the writers had written me off because of my torn-up knee. He would read what they were saying about me, and he'd say, 'Don't worry about them. You're running fine. The holes aren't there, you know. Just keep your chin up.' . . .

"Because of my injury and my mental state afterward, I got to know Pic even better and became closer to him than almost anybody else on the team. And then when he became ill, it seemed that our friendship deepened and we got to understand each other even better. And that's when I found out what a beautiful person he really was. . . . He was loose about it [his illness] because that was his way. His attitude was, what's the use of getting solemn and serious? It doesn't change things. His only concern, he said, was for his wife and his three small daughters. . . .

"The funeral was held that Friday [June 19, 1970], a clean lovely morning, and I went through it like a sleepwalker. The only thing I remember about the service was one line: 'The virtuous man, though he dies before his time, will find rest.'

"It was at the cemetery, as the priest was delivering his final words, that I broke down. He referred to the trophy and to our friendship, and it was too much for me. I cried.

"As soon as the service was ended, Joy came over and put her arms around me and I told her how sorry I was. 'Don't be sorry, Gale,' she said. 'I'm happy now because I know Brian is happy and I don't have to watch him suffer any more. He's through suffering now.'

"She comforted me, and I thought to myself, if she can be that composed, Brian must have really given her something. And I thought, well, he gave us all something, all of us who knew him. . . ."

—Gale Sayers

★ **Texas Essential Elements/(a) English Language Arts: 1B** Purpose and audience; **1E** Formal/informal language. **(c) Reading: 3I** Draw conclusions

Review: Exercises in Reading Drama

A. About the Author
The play *The Marriage Proposal* was written by the Russian playwright and short story writer Anton Chekhov (1860–1904). He once said that the aim of serious literature "is truth, unconditional and honest."

SRW p. 33

DIALOGUE

In one important way, drama is different from all other forms of story-telling. In a novel, a short story, or even a narrative poem, the writer can speak directly to the reader. A novel or a short story, for example, can include a paragraph like this:

> When Tom got out of bed, he was as hungry as a bear. But he knew he'd have to skip breakfast. The copy for the school newspaper was due at the printer's before 8:00, and he had to meet Laura before his first class.

A writer of fiction can give a reader all sorts of important information this way. But a playwright can't. The audience at a play learns everything through what they can see and hear. So playwrights have to depend on physical action and on their most important tool—dialogue.

Dialogue is important in all forms of storytelling. But nowhere is it more important than in drama. In a play, dialogue has to tell us what the characters are thinking, what happened before the story began, and what is happening offstage. And while it does all these things, it has to sound like normal conversation.

A Here is an excerpt from a humorous play that takes place in Russia during the nineteenth century. The characters are two men who own neighboring pieces of property. Choobookov is middle-aged, and the father of an unmarried daughter; Lomov, who has come to visit him, is young and unmarried.

Choobookov. Why, of all people! My old friend, Ivan Vassilevich! How nice to see you. This really is a surprise, old boy. How *are* you?

Lomov. Very well, thank you. And may I ask how *you* are?

Choobookov. Not bad at all, old friend, with the help of your prayers and so on. Please have a seat. Now, really, it's not very nice of you to neglect your neighbors, my dear boy. And what are you all dressed up for? Morning coat, gloves, and so on! Are you off on a visit, old boy?

Lomov. No, I'm just calling on you, Stepan Stepanovich, my esteemed neighbor.

Choobookov. But why the morning coat, old friend? This isn't New Year's Day!

Lomov. Well, you see, the fact of the matter is . . . *(Takes his arm)* I've burst in on you like this . . . my esteemed neighbor, in order to ask a favor of you. I've already had the honor more than once of turning to you for help and you've always, so to speak, uh! . . . But forgive me, my nerves . . . I must have a sip of water, dear Stepan Stepanovich. *(Drinks some water.)*

Choobookov *(aside).* He's after my money. Fat chance! *(To* LOMOV*)* What is it, my dear fellow?

Lomov. Well, you see, my Stepan dearovich, uh! I mean dear Stepanovich . . . uh! I mean, my nerves are in a terrible condition, which you yourself are so kind as to see. In short, you're the only one who can help me, although, of course I've done nothing to deserve it and . . . and I don't even have the right to count on your help. . . .

Choobookov. Now, now; don't beat about the bush, old friend. Out with it! Well?

Lomov. All right, here you are. The fact of the matter is, I've come to ask for your daughter Natalia's hand in marriage.

Choobookov *(overjoyed).* My *dearest* friend! Ivan Vassilevich. Could you repeat that—I'm not sure I heard right!

Lomov. I have the honor of asking—

Choobookov *(breaking in).* My oldest and dearest friend. I'm *so* delighted and so on. Yes really, and all that sort of thing. *(Hugging and kissing him)* I've been yearning for this for ages. It's been my constant desire. *(Sheds a tear)* And I've always loved you like a son, you wonderful person, you. May God grant you love and guidance and so on, it's been my most fervent wish. . . .

Answers to Review Questions

1. In Choobookov's first speech, he says that Lomov's visit "really is a surprise."
2. Lomov speaks haltingly and says "forgive me, my nerves"; he stops to take a drink of water at one point; at another point misorders his speech, referring to the other man as "my Stepan dearovich."
3. It is clear that he thinks Lomov is after his money, and equally clear that he does not like Lomov very much.
4. He seems relieved and elated.
It's funny that Choobookov, who doesn't really think highly of Lomov, so hastily—and with such effusive language—approves Lomov's proposal to marry his daughter.
5. These phrases show that Choobookov thinks so little of Lomov that he cannot even be bothered to hold a proper conversation with him.
6. When he learns of Lomov's intentions, he hugs and kisses him, whereas a minute before he hardly even wanted to speak to him.

Review: Exercises in Reading Drama/*cont.*

> **Lomov** *(deeply moved).* Stepan Stepanovich, my esteemed friend, do you think I may count on her accepting me?
> **Choobookov.** A handsome devil like you? How could she possibly resist?
>
> —from *A Marriage Proposal,* Anton Chekhov

1. Which line of dialogue tells the audience that it is unusual for Lomov to visit Choobookov?
2. Lomov's halting speech shows that he is very nervous and insecure in this scene. What other examples in Chekhov's dialogue show Lomov's uncertainty?
3. In a play, an **aside** is when a character says something that the other characters on stage are not supposed to hear. What does Choobookov's aside tell the audience about his real feelings for Lomov?
4. What is Choobookov's reaction when Lomov says he wants to marry the older man's daughter? Given what we already know about Choobookov's feelings toward Lomov, why is his reaction funny?
5. It is important to the play that the audience know that Choobookov is not very sincere about his feelings toward Lomov. How does Choobookov's use of such phrases "and so on" show his insincerity?
6. How do we know from Chekhov's dialogue that Choobookov is desperate to have his daughter married?

Writing

1. **Creating Setting Through Dialogue.** Suppose you were writing a play in which the first scene takes place in a totally dark location. Write a dialogue between two or more characters establishing the setting for the audience. Before you write, decide where the characters are. Try to make the dialogue sound as much like real conversation as possible.
2. **Using Dialogue for Characterization.** Invent a scene in which two characters have a conversation. Use the dialogue to get your audience to understand how these two characters are very different from each other. If you think it is necessary, introduce the dialogue with a paragraph describing the scene where it is taking place.
3. **Using Dialogue for Plot.** Suppose you were planning a play in which some very important event had taken place before the action on stage begins. One of your first jobs would be to tell the audience about this event through dialogue. Invent a scene in which two characters have a conversation about something that has already happened. In writing your dialogue, keep two goals in mind. First, you have to reveal all the facts that you want your audience to have. Second, you have to write the spoken lines so that they sound like things the characters would actually say to each other.

For evaluation strategies, see Teacher's Manual page 120.

★ Texas Essential Elements/(a) English Language Arts: 1A Composing process; 1B Purpose and audience; 1H Proofread; 1I Spelling generalizations; 2B Parts of speech; 2D Grammar/punctuation/spelling; 4B Main idea

For teaching and evaluation strategies, see Teacher's Manual page 121.

EVALUATING AND RESPONDING TO A PLAY

Writing Assignment

Write a paragraph in which you **evaluate** *Brian's Song,* giving reasons to support your opinion of the play. Write a second paragraph in which you discuss your **responses** to the play.

Background

Evaluations are judgments based on standards, or rules. You make evaluations all the time. When you decide that a movie is excellent or terrible, you are evaluating it.

Here are some standards against which you might evaluate a serious play or movie:

1. The characters are believable.
2. The play arouses your emotions.
3. There are no "wasted" scenes. Every scene contributes to the total effect.
4. The play makes an important statement about life or people.
5. The play keeps your interest throughout.

A **response** is a less formal kind of judgment. Your responses are based on your own personal experiences and ideas. Your answers to the following questions are responses:

1. Did you like or dislike the play? Why?
2. What experiences have you had or heard about that remind you of *Brian's Song*?
3. What lesson do you think *Brian's Song* teaches?
4. How did reading *Brian's Song* make you feel? Why do you think it made you feel this way?

Prewriting

Fill out a chart such as the following. Use VERY MUCH, AVERAGE, NOT MUCH, or NOT AT ALL for each evaluation in the Rating column.

Evaluation	Rating	Examples
How believable were the characters?		
How emotionally involved were you?		
How well constructed was the play?		
Did the play say something important?		
Did the plot keep you interested?		

Response	Reasons/Examples
Did you like the play?	
Did the play remind you of similar experiences?	
What feelings did you have as you read the play?	

Use your chart as an outline for your essay.

Writing

Paragraph 1: Write a topic sentence that names the work and summarizes your evaluation. Here is one possible topic sentence for the first paragraph.

> *Brian's Song* is an emotional and powerful movie about the tragic death of a young football player.

For the rest of paragraph 1, give reasons for your evaluation. Use two or three details from your prewriting chart. (In one paragraph you won't be able to use all of the information in the chart.)

Paragraph 2: Begin with a topic sentence that tells how you responded to the movie. Use your prewriting chart for details to support your response. As an example, here is one writer's second paragraph about her responses to *Brian's Song*:

Exercises in Critical Thinking and Writing/*cont.*

I especially liked *Brian's Song* for the message that it gives about friendship. I have always believed that friends are important. But sometimes we take our friends for granted. Brian Piccolo and Gale Sayers had a really strong friendship. Each helped the other, even though they were in fierce competition for the same spot on the team. Brian spent a lot of time and energy helping Gale get back the use of his injured knee. In a sense, Brian saved Gale's life then. When Brian was ill and dying, Gale was always there for him and for Brian's wife Joy. I enjoyed the play because it makes a statement about something I think is important—friendship.

Topic sentence states response and gives a reason.

Discusses friendship in general.

Discusses friendship in the play.

Revising and Proofreading Self-Check

1. Does each paragraph have a good strong topic sentence?
2. In Paragraph 1, have I supported my evaluation with reasons and examples?
3. In Paragraph 2, have I explained my responses?
4. Are my ideas clearly expressed? Have I said everything I wanted to say?
5. Does every sentence start with a capital letter and end with a period or other end punctuation mark?

Partner Check

1. Are there any spelling errors?
2. Are sentences punctuated correctly?
3. Are the paragraphs indented?
4. Is each paragraph fully developed (topic sentence with supporting statements)?
5. Are there any sentences or ideas that are unclear or confusing?
6. What do I like best about this paper? What needs improvement?

FANTASY AND SCIENCE FICTION

The Blank Signature by René Magritte (c. 1956). Oil.

National Gallery of Art, Washington. Collection of Mr. and Mrs. Paul Mellon.

UNIT SEVEN **John Leggett**

HUMANITITES CONNECTION: DISCUSSING THE FINE ART

René Magritte (1898–1967) was born in Belgium and was part of the Surrealist movement, a major art movement between 1920 and 1940. Surrealistic, or "super-realistic," painting combines outer reality (the world as we see it) with inner reality, the supernatural world of fantasy and dreams. Magritte is best known for presenting impossible images in a realistic style. The effect is usually that of a visual pun or riddle. (Another painting by Magritte appears on page 9.)

? What is unusual about this painting? (Part of the horse's front end and the rider's hand disappear into a strip of misty space; the rest of the horse reappears as if it has passed through the mist. The horse's back legs seem to step through an impossible space between the trees.) Why do you think Magritte named his painting *The Blank Signature?*

TEACHING FANTASY AND SCIENCE FICTION

Students should enjoy these selections, which combine mystery, fantasy, and science fiction. This blend of literary ingredients should captivate and amuse the students—and, in some cases, will challenge them by presenting visions of the future.

"The Listeners" is a famous narrative poem with a ghostly theme. "The Water of Life" and "Young Ladies Don't Slay Dragons" are good examples of fairy tales, the latter a playful variation on the form. "The Monkey's Paw" is a classic tale of horror, suspenseful to the very end. "The Story of the Fisherman" is a familiar and delightful fantasy from *The Arabian Nights.* And, the unit concludes with three typical science fiction stories: "The Fun They Had," "The Naming of Names," and "Collecting Team." You may wish to omit one or several of these stories, or concentrate on one type of story—say the three science fiction tales at the end of the unit. Or, you may prefer to give the students a more balanced selection; if so, the instructional material in the unit covers basic elements of fantasy and horror stories, fairy tales and science fiction.

The variety of the unit's stories and of the suggested teaching strategies will allow you to modify your presentation to the students. Choose the stories you think your class will enjoy best, and choose the teaching methods that will best suit their collective abilities. Encourage your students to read with concentration and care, with open-mindedness and imagination. Above all, try to instill in them the habit of reading with a sense of fun.

OBJECTIVES OF THE UNIT

1. To improve reading proficiency and expand vocabulary
2. To gain exposure to notable authors of fantasy and science fiction
3. To define and identify the main elements of fantasy and science fiction
4. To define and identify significant literary techniques: imagery, satire, use of details, delineation of theme, irony, metaphor, foreshadowing
5. To interpret and respond to fantasy and science fiction, orally and in writing, through analysis of their elements
6. To practice the following critical thinking and writing skills:
   - a. Analyzing a poem
   - b. Analyzing a fairy tale
   - c. Writing about fantasy
   - d. Writing about theme
   - e. Comparing two fairy tales
   - f. Analyzing a fantasy
   - g. Supporting a main idea
   - h. Summarizing a plot
   - i. Predicting a story's outcome

SUPPLEMENTARY SUPPORT MATERIAL: UNIT SEVEN

1. Introduction/Understanding the Elements of Fantasy and Science Fiction Test (page 147 of Test Book)
2. Word Analogies Test (page 165 of Test Book)
3. Reading Check Test blackline master
4. Unit Review Test (page 167 of Test Book)
5. Critical Thinking and Writing Test (page 171 of Test Book)
6. Instructional Overhead Transparency

Unit Outline

FANTASY AND SCIENCE FICTION

A. Discussing the Quotation
The quotation is from *Aspects of the Novel* (1927), an important work of literary criticism by English writer E. M. Forster. Reacting against the Victorian emphasis on "serious" literature, Forster said that imagination must be cultivated if one is to have a happy life. He compares fantasy to a "bar of light." Like light, he said, the power of the imagination transforms literature and life. Ask students to write either Forster's quotation or the word "fantasy" in a circle on their papers. Then have them cluster related words and phrases around the center as they think of them. To get them thinking, ask them to think of their favorite books or movies that are fantasies, and what qualities they had.

B. Expansion
Mary Shelley (1797–1851), a novelist and the second wife of the famous poet Percy Bysshe Shelley, is considered the "Mother of Science Fiction." *Frankenstein* (see the movie still on text page) was based on the idea that scientific knowledge can be dangerous.

SRW p. 39

A

Fantasy and Science Fiction

The power of fantasy penetrates into every corner of the universe. . .

—E. M. Forster

Fantasy: Creating New Worlds

Fantasy escapes from the real world we know and creates a new world altered by the writer's imagination. We all know fantasy from the fairy tales we read as children.

Fantasy is the kind of writing that carries us from the here and now into another time or place, where unfamiliar forces, perhaps supernatural ones, are at play. To enter this world, the writer uses a device, some sort of "magic carpet."

To travel with Lewis Carroll's Alice, for example, we must go down a rabbit hole and through a looking glass, or mirror. When we go with L. Frank Baum's Dorothy into Oz, we travel astride a Kansas twister.

Fantasy can also take us on journeys in time. It can take us back into the past, to King Arthur's Camelot or J.R.R. Tolkien's Middle Earth, or it can take us into the future to view H. G. Wells's war of the worlds. To accomplish this, the fantasy writer can simply pull this year's calendar off the wall and replace it with one reading A.D. 526 or 3000.

We are all aware of our dependency on the rational part of our mind. This is the part of the mind that thinks and reasons, that gets us dressed and fed, to school or work, through games and social obligations. However marvelous this rational mind is, it has its limitations. Think of the ant's mind. The ant's mind tells it to carry grains of sand this way and that, without (as far as we know) giving the ant a grasp of the spaces that exist beyond its anthill.

Unlike the ant, we have imaginations. They tell us that beyond our workaday lives lie worlds we cannot conceive. Nor is the astronomer with her big lens, nor the microbiologist with his small one, a great deal better off. No one really knows what these worlds are like, because no one's ever experienced them.

That unknown territory is fantasy's realm. It is a place and time where things are different from what we know. That difference entertains us. It also satisfies our need to speculate on what lies out there in the inscrutable beyond.

inscrutable (in·skro͞ot′ə·b'l): mysterious

Science Fiction: Fiction of the Future

B

Science fiction is at least as old as the nineteenth century. In 1818 the British writer Mary Shelley wrote a science-fiction novel called *Frankenstein.* It is about a scientist who tried to create new life by assembling a lot of body parts from different people. In 1864, Jules Verne wrote his *Journey to the Center of the Earth.*

Additional Writing Assignment
Imagine that you are a teen-ager living either in A.D. 526 or 3000. Suppose that you keep a diary and that this has been your birthday. Write five sentences telling what you did. Include activities that will show the year you are in.

Responding to a Story
In addition to using the side notes and the comments in "Thinking Over the Story" on text page 387, you might ask the class questions such as the following: (1) As you read the beginning of *The Hobbit,* what was your first reaction to the story? (2) What emotions did you feel? (3) Which word, phrase, or image (or word picture) made the greatest impact on you? (4) Do you think that this will be an interesting story? Why or why not? (5) Does this story remind you of any other story, film, or poem? (6) What connections do you see between this story and anything else in your life, either now or in your past? (Based on "Dialogue with a Text" by Robert E. Probst, *English Journal,* 1/88.)

A. Technology
? What are some examples of physical laws? (Examples include the law of gravity and the fact that nothing travels faster than light.) You may want to explain that science fiction authors often create inventions that extend physical laws as we know them.
? In science fiction, how do space ships travel faster than the speed of light to other galaxies? (Usually by passing through openings in space, or "space warps." Think of "hyperspace" in the *Star Wars* movies.)

B. Expansion
J. R. R. Tolkien's fantasies grew out of his interest in Norse mythology, his love for inventing language, and the stories he made up and read to his son. *The Hobbit* is the story of Bilbo Baggins's quest to recover a treasure that had been stolen by a dragon. One critic states that "Tolkien's work has become the standard by which all other fantasies are judged: It is a cornerstone in a literary education."

Verne admitted that he felt restricted by known fact, and so he decided to move beyond fact into possibility.

Science fiction—often called fiction of the future—is a separate category of fantasy. Science fiction, like fantasy, is set in a world different from our own, but it is not a kind of writing in which "anything goes." Its rules can be as strict as those of physics. Science fiction seems to lie in an area between realistic fiction A and total fantasy. It must conform to physical laws as we know them (or we don't believe it). Science fiction must also be based on scientific knowledge, especially on the latest developments of technology.

The best of science fiction appeals to our intelligence, as it searches the mysteries of human existence—the "galaxies" within ourselves as well as those beyond. It also appeals to our imagination, to our sense of awe and wonder at being a part of a mysterious and unknown universe.

Galaxies: groups of millions of stars. The word is also used metaphorically here to mean the vast realms of our imagination.

Science fiction is an expression of our wonder about how and why the world works and what its future can be.

Responding to a Story

B The following is taken from the beginning of a novel by J. R. R. Tolkien called *The Hobbit.* The notes in the right hand margin are the thoughts of one reader who was reading the novel for the first time. Notice how the reader figures out that he or she is reading a fantasy. Notice how the reader uses context clues to understand unfamiliar words. Note the reader's response to the details.

In a hole in the ground there lived a hobbit. Not a nasty, dirty, wet hole, filled with the ends of worms and an oozy smell, not yet a dry, bare, sandy hole with nothing in it to sit down on or to eat: it was a hobbit-hole, and that means comfort.

What's a hobbit? Sounds like a made-up word.

It had a perfectly round door like a porthole, painted green, with a shiny yellow brass knob in the exact middle. The door opened on to a tube-shaped hall like a tunnel: a very comfortable tunnel without smoke, with panelled walls, and floors tiled and carpeted, provided with polished chairs, and lots and lots of pegs for hats and coats—the hobbit was fond of visitors. The tunnel wound on and on, going fairly but not quite straight into the side of the hill—The Hill, as all the people for many miles round called it—and many little round doors opened out of it, first on one side and then on another. No going upstairs for the hobbit: bedrooms, bathrooms, cellars, pantries (lots of these), wardrobes (he had whole rooms devoted to clothes), kitchens, dining-rooms, all were on the same floor, and indeed on the same passage. The best rooms were all on the left hand side (going in), for these were the only ones to have windows, deep-

How can a hole in the ground be comfortable? Eating must be important to hobbits. This is set in an imaginary world—holes in the ground don't have doors. Hobbits must be pretty small.

They sure live in luxury! I can really picture this setting.

"People"—must mean the other hobbits in the neighborhood.

I'm pretty sure pantries are small rooms where food is stored—so I was right, hobbits must like to eat a lot.

These best rooms must be for the visitors he likes so much.

Reading Check Test

1. Fantasy is the most realistic kind of fiction. *(False)*
2. Authors of fantasy often create a world that is different from this one. *(True)*
3. All science fiction stories are fantasies. *(True)*
4. It was not until the twentieth century that people began writing science fiction. *(False)*
5. Science fiction appeals to both imagination and intelligence. *(True)*

A. Responding to the Illustration This illustration shows Gandalf the Wizard visiting Bilbo Baggins. **?** How do you think Baggins feels about his visitor? (Great respect, even awe) Since you can't see Baggins's face, what clues lead you to this conclusion? (Dropped mail; Baggins's head tilted back; Baggins looking up) How does the artist emphasize Gandalf's mystery and power? (Gandalf is much larger than Baggins. The use of dark blue and black, night colors, convey a feeling of mystery and the supernatural.)

set round windows looking over his garden and meadows beyond, sloping down to the river.

This hobbit was a very well-to-do hobbit, and his name was Baggins. . . . The mother of our particular hobbit—what is a hobbit? I suppose hobbits need some description nowadays, since they have become rare and shy of the Big People, as they call us. They are (or were) a little people, about half our height, and smaller than the bearded Dwarves. Hobbits have no beards. There is little or no magic about them, except the ordinary everyday sort which helps them to disappear quietly and quickly when large stupid folk like you and me come blundering along, making a noise like elephants which they can hear a mile off. They are inclined to be fat in the stomach; they dress in bright colors (chiefly green and yellow); wear no shoes, because their feet grow natural leathery soles and thick warm brown hair like the stuff on their heads (which is curly); have long clever brown fingers, good-natured faces, and laugh deep fruity laughs (especially after dinner, which they have twice a day when they can get it). Now you know enough to go on with.

—from *The Hobbit,*
J. R. R. Tolkien

Finally—we're going to find out!

This is definitely a fantasy—I know dwarves don't exist.

How nice even to have everyday magic!

The writer likes the hobbits so I guess they're going to be the story's heroes.

Oh yes—the hobbit's door is painted green.

They must be funny looking creatures.

They are good—nothing evil about them.

This beginning makes me want to read the whole book.

A

Thinking Over the Story

Every reader who reads the beginning of this novel will have a different response. Some will become so gripped that they will go out and get themselves a copy of the novel and continue reading. Some might find the descriptions unappealing and uninteresting. Suppose you wanted to write about this beginning, and discuss how you knew that this novel was a fantasy. By looking at your response notes, you would see right away that: (1) The characters are imaginary—they are not normal everyday people. They will have magical and strange qualities. (2) The author creates a world which is completely alien to you, yet one that has recognizable elements (such as the rich furniture, desire for comfort, plenty of food). After reading this excerpt, you might ask whether the hobbit is going to have an adventure (he seems so lazy). What other questions might you ask?

PREREADING

1. **BUILDING ON PRIOR KNOWLEDGE.** Tell students that the poem they are about to read has some of the elements of a ghost story, perhaps the most popular kind of fantasy. You might want to lead a discussion on ghost stories. Ask how many in the class enjoy reading ghost stories and why. What are some of the elements that you would expect to find in a ghost story? (Scary setting, ghostly characters, mysterious plot)

2. **ESTABLISHING A PURPOSE.** Tell students to notice how the poem makes them feel as they read. Tell them to watch for the details that give them this feeling.

3. **PREREADING JOURNAL.** Ask students to briefly describe a setting that gives them either a scary feeling or a happy feeling. They can describe a real setting or make one up. Tell them to use descriptive details that will help readers picture this place.

A. Short Story Elements

? Judging from the first four lines, what elements of a short story does this poem contain? (Setting, characters, dialogue, conflict, plot)

B. Fantasy

? What is the supernatural element in the poem? (Phantoms in the house listen to the Traveler's calls.)

C. Vocabulary

Turf is surface soil that contains roots and grass.

D. Imagery

? Images, or word pictures, appeal to your senses and make you see and hear what is happening in the poem. Find two images that help you visualize the scene and two images that help you hear the sounds that seem so loud in the silence. (There are many examples.)

E. Atmosphere

? What mood or atmosphere does the setting and the situation evoke? (Mystery) Notice the poet's repeated use of the "s" sound throughout the poem.

★ **Texas Essential Elements/(a) English Language Arts: 1B** Purpose and audience; **3B** Figurative language; **4E** Predict. **(c) Reading: 3A** Main ideas/details; **3H** Predict; **3I** Draw conclusions

No one has ever figured out exactly who the listeners are in this famous poem, but many people have theories about them. As you read, try to visualize this scene. Try also to hear the sounds that break the forest's silence. At the end of the poem, you'll have many questions, but you'll probably never get all the answers.

The Listeners

For a detailed lesson plan on this poem, see Teacher's Manual pages 123–125. A biography of Walter de la Mare appears on text page 390.

Walter de la Mare

"Is there anybody there?" said the Traveler,
Knocking on the moonlit door;
A And his horse in the silence champed the grasses
Of the forest's ferny floor:
And a bird flew up out of the turret,°
Above the Traveler's head:
And he smote° upon the door again a second time;
"Is there anybody there?" he said.
But no one descended to the Traveler;
No head from the leaf-fringed sill
Leaned over and looked into his gray eyes,
Where he stood perplexed and still.
But only a host of phantom listeners
That dwelt in the lone house then
Stood listening in the quiet of the moonlight
To that voice from the world of men:
B Stood thronging the faint moonbeams on the dark stair,
That goes down to the empty hall,
Hearkening° in an air stirred and shaken
By the lonely Traveler's call.
And he felt in his heart their strangeness,
Their stillness answering his cry,
C While his horse moved, cropping the dark turf,
'Neath the starred and leafy sky;
For he suddenly smote on the door, even
Louder, and lifted his head:
"Tell them I came, and no one answered,
That I kept my word," he said.
Never the least stir made the listeners,
Though every word he spake°
Fell echoing through the shadowiness of the still house
From the one man left awake:
Ay, they heard his foot upon the stirrup,
D And the sound of iron on stone,
And how the silence surged softly backward,
E When the plunging hoofs were gone.

5. **turret:** small tower on top of a house.

7. **smote:** pounded.

19. **Hearkening:** listening carefully.

30. **spake:** spoke.

SUPPLEMENTARY SUPPORT MATERIAL

1. Vocabulary Activity Sheet
2. Reading Check Test blackline master
3. Selection Test (page 149, Test Book)
4. Audiocassette recording
5. Connections Between Reading and Writing worksheet
6. Reader's Response Journal
7. Workbook (page 113)

DEVELOPING VOCABULARY

The following words appear on a test in the Test Book, page 150. (See also the Vocabulary Activity Sheet.)

champed	dwelt
turret	thronging
smote	hearkening
perplexed	spake
phantom	awake

CLOSURE

Divide students into pairs. Have each pair come up with a visual image and a sound image that develops a mood. (It might be fun to write the name of different moods—joy, sadness, fear, anger—on paper strips. Have each pair take one strip from a hat. Give students two minutes to make up their images.)

Choral Reading

After students have read the poem silently, have volunteers prepare to read the poem aloud. Reader 1: lines 1, 8, 27–28; Reader 2: lines 2–7; Reader 3: lines 9–20; Reader 4: lines 21–26, 29–32; Together: lines 33–36. Tell them to read with expression and a sense of mystery.

Responding to the Photograph

Have students give one detail that supports their answer to each of the following questions.

? What kind of building stands near the middle of the photograph? (Old castle or fort; small windows, brick walls) In what condition is the building? (Poor; bricks on the right have fallen) What kind of weather is suggested? (Stormy; dark clouds) What season do you think is shown? (Winter; barren fields) What feeling does the photo give you? (Gloom, mystery)

ANALYZING THE POEM

Identifying Details

1. The first two times, the Traveler asks, "Is there anybody there?" After knocking a third time, he says, "Tell them I came, and no one answered,/That I kept my word."

2. They are "phantom listeners"; they dwell in the house; they are silent, strange, and still.

They are said to be "phantom listeners"; they congregate in silence and darkness; the Traveler feels their "strangeness" and "stillness."

3. He felt the listeners' "strangeness" and "stillness."

4. The sound of the words spoken by the Traveler.

Interpreting Meanings

5. The Traveler is "the one man left awake." No one else is "awake" because everyone has either left or died; all who remain are phantoms.

6. It is the sound of a horse's hooves striking stone pavement or cobblestone, as the Traveler rides away.

7. Answers may vary. Students will *(Answers continue in left-hand column.)*

(Continued from top.) probably say that the Traveler came because he had promised to come, or felt some responsibility to come.

Again, students' answers may vary. Most will say that the former inhabitants of the house died. (This in turn suggests that the Traveler was away a very long time.)

8. Answers will vary. See Teacher's Manual page 124.

9. Words that begin with the letter *s* include *said, silence, smote, second, still, stood, stair, stirred, shaken, strangeness, stillness, starred, sky, suddenly, stir, spake, shadowiness, stirrup, sound, stone, surged,* and *softly.*

The repeated "s" sounds give the poem a hushed, whispered quality, which contributes to the mood of mystery.

Evaluating the Poem

10. Most students will agree that the strangeness and mystery would be lost.

Responding to the Poem

Analyzing the Poem

Identifying Details

1. The Traveler knocks on the door and calls out three times. What does he say the first two times? What does he tell the listeners the third time?
2. Tell what you know about the listeners. What details suggest that they are not human?
3. What did the Traveler feel "in his heart"?
4. What sound echoes through the stillness of the house?

Interpreting Meanings

5. In line 32, who do you think is "the one man left awake"? Why do you think no one else is "awake"?
6. What is the sound of "iron on stone" (line 34)?
7. Why do you think the Traveler came to the house in the forest? What might have happened before he got there?
8. Who do you think the listeners are?
9. Find and list ten words in the poem that begin with the letter *s*. Say these words to yourself. Why do you think the poet repeats this sound throughout the poem?

Evaluating the Poem

10. Do you think the poem would have been more effective if the poet had told you who the Traveler was, who was listening, and what the Traveler wanted? Explain your opinion.

Writing About the Poem

A Creative Response

1. **Writing a Journal Entry.** Suppose the Traveler keeps a journal. Every night he writes down what happened to him that day. He also tells how he feels about what happened. Write the Traveler's journal entry on the night he visited the house in the forest. Tell what promise he had made to the inhabitants of the house.
2. **Extending the Poem.** What happened inside the house after the Traveler galloped away? In a paragraph, describe what you think happened.

A Critical Response

3. **Analyzing the Poem.** In a chart, write out all the questions you still have about this poem. Put them in one column. In a second column, write out some possible answers. Do you think the poem leaves too many unanswered questions?

See Teacher's Manual page 125.

Analyzing Language and Vocabulary

Images

SRW p. 51

Poets use words to create pictures, or images, in your mind. Images can also help you hear sounds, or taste something, smell it, or feel its temperature or texture. Many images in "The Listeners" contrast moonlight and darkness, loud sounds and silence. One of each type of image is listed in the following chart. Complete the chart by listing one more image for each type.

Moonlight	Darkness
1. "the moonlit door" 2.	1. "on the dark stair" 2.
Loud Sounds	**Silence**
1. "And he smote upon the door again" 2.	1. "Stood listening in the quiet" 2.

For answers, see Teacher's Manual page 125.

Reading About the Writer

Walter de la Mare (1873–1956) was born in England and spent twenty years working in the London office of an oil company. Eventually, he received a grant which allowed him to write full time. De la Mare is known for his enchanting poems and tales that take place in the region that hovers between the real and the unreal. Some people believe that he wrote "The Listeners" after he had gone to a school reunion and found he was the only one who came. Others think this ruins the poem's mystery. In any case, no one really knows what de la Mare meant by his haunting poem.

PREREADING

1. **BUILDING ON PRIOR KNOWLEDGE.** Before students read the story, you might want to discuss fairy tales and their recurring elements. Ask students to list some fairy tales they have read. (For suggestions, some familiar tales by the Grimm brothers are listed at the end of the information about the Grimms on page 393.) Then, have students make up a chart with two or three fairy tale titles at the left and a list of headings like these at the top: Hero (Good Character); Hero's Supernatural Powers; Goal of Quest; Tests or Difficulties; Strange Helpers; Winning Qualities (such as honesty). Have students complete the chart to familiarize them with what makes a fantasy story a fairy tale.

2. **ESTABLISHING A PURPOSE.** The headnote sets a good purpose for reading the story.

3. **PREREADING JOURNAL.** Before they read, ask students to write three sentences which begin their own fairy tale. They should introduce the characters, their conflict, and the quest they will have to go on to resolve this conflict.

Texas Essential Elements/(a) English Language Arts: 1B Purpose and audience; **1E** Formal/informal language; **4B** Main idea. **(c) Reading: 2A** Word meaning; **3A** Main ideas/details; **3I** Draw conclusions; **4D** Diagrams/graphs

THE WATER OF LIFE

Jakob and Wilhelm Grimm

"The Water of Life" is a folk tale. It is one of the many fairy tales collected by the Grimm brothers—Jakob and Wilhelm. They did not make up these stories themselves; they wrote them down after interviewing peasants who knew the tales by heart. It is difficult to know how old the stories are or where they originated. All of the tales had been handed down orally from generation to generation long before the brothers Grimm began their research.

One element that often occurs in folk tales is the *quest*, a dangerous, difficult journey taken in search of something of value. As you read, think about the quest in this story. Judging by what you are told about the characters, whose quest do you think will be successful? SRW p. 41

For a detailed lesson plan on this story, see Teacher's Manual pages 125–128. For information on the Grimm brothers, see the annotation entitled "The Grimm Brothers" on page 393.

A There was once a king who had an illness, and no one believed that he would come out of it with his life. He had three sons who were much distressed about it, and went down into the palace garden and wept. There they met an old man who inquired as to the cause of their grief. They told him that their father was so ill that he would most certainly die, for nothing seemed to cure him. Then the old man said: "I know of one more remedy, and that is the water of life; if he drinks of it he will become well again; but it is hard to find."

The eldest said: "I will manage to find it," and went to the sick king, and begged to be allowed to go forth in search of the water of life, for that alone could save him. "No," said the king, "the danger of it is too great. I would rather die."

B But he begged so long that the king consented. The prince thought in his heart: "If I bring the water, then I shall be best beloved of my father, and shall inherit the kingdom." So he set out, and when he had ridden forth a little distance, a dwarf stood there in the road who called to him and said: "Whither away so fast?" "Silly shrimp," said the prince, very haughtily, "it is nothing to do with you," and rode on. But the little dwarf had grown angry, and had wished an evil wish. Soon after this the prince entered a ravine, and the further he rode the closer the mountains drew together, and at last the road became so narrow that he could not advance a step further; it was impossible either to turn his horse or to dismount from the saddle, and he was shut in there as if in prison.

The sick king waited long for him, but he came not. Then the second son said: "Father, let me go forth to seek the water," and thought to himself: "If my brother is dead, then the kingdom will fall to me." At first the king would not allow him to go either, but at last he yielded, so the prince set out on the same road that his brother had taken, and he too met the dwarf, who stopped him to ask whither he was going in such haste. "Little shrimp," said the prince, "that is nothing to do with you," and rode on without giving him another look. But the dwarf bewitched him, and he, like the other, rode into a ravine, and could neither go forward nor backward. So fare haughty people. C

Archaic Words. In this story, you will come across some *archaic* words—old-fashioned words that are rarely used today. Some of these archaic words will be strange to you. You will be able to figure out the meaning of most of them from their *context*—the other words and sentences surrounding each unfamiliar word. For example, on page 391, a character says, "Whither away so fast?" Although we no longer use *whither*, we can tell that the character is asking, "Where are you hurrying to?"

A. Conflict

? What problem or conflict sets the plot in motion? (The king vs. his illness)

B. Folk Tale

The Grimms' fairy tales were folk tales—or stories that originate among the folk or common people and are handed down orally from generation to generation. Folk tales are usually about common people, or common subjects.

? In the first two paragraphs, what feelings would seem most true-to-life to the peasants who told the story? (The sons' sadness; the love between the king and his sons)

C. Character

? What qualities in the two older brothers does their conflict with the dwarf reveal? (Pride; lack of respect)

SUPPLEMENTARY SUPPORT MATERIAL

1. Vocabulary Activity Sheet
2. Reading Check Test blackline master
3. Selection Test (page 151 of Test Book)
4. Reader's Response Journal
5. Workbook (page 115)

DEVELOPING VOCABULARY

The following words appear on a test in the Test Book, page 152. (See also the Vocabulary Activity Sheet.)

whither	appease
haughty	lament
ravine	proclaim
seemly	expire
enchanted	incessant

A. Responding to the Illustration

? Which incident in the story is illustrated here? (The door springs open.) What will happen next? (The prince will give the lions bread.)

A

The Grimm Brothers
Jakob Grimm (1785–1863) and Wilhelm Grimm (1786–1859) were German scholars who were best known for their collections of folk tales and their comparisons of the folk literature of European countries. The Grimms spent more than twelve years transcribing—without the benefit of tape recorders—about two hundred tales. Their goal was to reflect the values, dreams, and wishes of the German peasants who had been passing down these tales orally for centuries. The Grimms made as few changes as possible, trying to keep the plot, language, rhythm, and repetition of the oral tales. The first volume was published in 1812. Some famous tales that they collected are: "The Frog Prince," "Briar Rose" ("Sleeping Beauty"), "Rumpelstiltskin," "Rapunzel," "Cinderella," "Snow White and the Seven Dwarfs," "Red Riding Hood," "Hansel and Gretel."

As the second son also remained away, the youngest begged to be allowed to go forth to fetch the water, and at last the king was obliged to let him go. When he met the dwarf and the latter asked him whither he was going in such haste, he stopped, gave him an explanation, and said: "I am seeking the water of life, for my father is sick unto death." "Do you know, then, where that is to be found?" "No," said the prince. "As you
A have borne yourself as is seemly, and not haughtily like your false brothers, I will give you the information and tell you how you may obtain the water of life. It springs from a fountain in the courtyard of an enchanted castle, but you will not be able to make your way to it if I do not give you an iron wand and two small loaves of bread. Strike thrice with the wand on the iron door of the castle, and it will spring open: Inside lie two lions with gaping jaws, but if you throw a loaf to each of them, they will be quieted. Then hasten to fetch some of the water of life before the clock strikes twelve, else the door will shut again, and you will be imprisoned."

The prince thanked him, took the wand and the bread, and set out on his way. When he arrived, everything was as the dwarf had said. The door sprang open at the third stroke of the wand, and when he had appeased the lions with the bread, he entered the castle, and came to a large and splendid hall, wherein sat some enchanted princes whose rings he drew off their fingers. A sword and a loaf of bread were lying there, which he carried away. After this, he entered a chamber, in which was a beautiful maiden who rejoiced when she saw him, kissed him, and told him that he had set her free, and should have the whole of her kingdom, and that if he would return in a year their wedding should be celebrated; likewise she told
B him where the spring of the water of life was, and that he was to hasten and draw some of it before the clock struck twelve. Then he went onward, and at last entered a room where there was a beautiful newly made bed, and as he was very weary, he felt inclined to rest a little. So he lay down and fell asleep. When he awoke, it was striking a quarter to twelve. He sprang up in a fright, ran to the spring, drew some water in a cup which stood near, and hastened away. But just as he was passing through the iron door, the clock struck twelve, and the door fell to with such violence that it carried away a piece of his heel.

He, however, rejoicing at having obtained the water of life, went homeward, and again passed the dwarf. When the latter saw the sword and the loaf, he said: "With these you have won great wealth; with the sword you can slay whole armies, and the bread will never come to an end."

But the prince would not go home to his father without his brothers, and said: "Dear dwarf, can you not tell me where my two brothers are? They C went out before I did in search of the water of life, and have not returned."

"They are imprisoned between two mountains," said the dwarf. "I have condemned them to stay there, because they were so haughty." Then the prince begged until the dwarf released them, but he warned him and said: "Beware of them, for they have bad hearts."

When his brothers came, he rejoiced, and told them how things had gone with him, that he had found the water of life, and had brought a cupful away with him, and had rescued a beautiful princess, who was willing to wait a year for him, and then their wedding was to be celebrated, and he would obtain a great kingdom. After that they rode on together, and chanced upon a land where war and famine reigned, and the king already thought he must perish, for the scarcity was so great. Then the prince went to him and gave him the loaf, wherewith he fed and satisfied the whole of his kingdom, and then the prince gave him the sword also, wherewith he slew the hosts of his enemies, and could now live in rest and peace. The prince then took back his loaf and his sword, and the three brothers rode on. But after this they entered two more countries where war and famine reigned and each time the prince gave his loaf and his sword to the kings, and had now delivered three kingdoms, and after that they went on board a ship and sailed over the sea.

During the passage, the two eldest conversed apart and said: "The youngest has found the water of life and not we, for that our father will give him the kingdom—the kingdom which belongs to us, and he will rob us of all our fortune." They then began to seek revenge, and plotted with each other

A. Archaic Language
? How would you say this in modern English? ("Because you have behaved properly . . .")

B. Eventful Plot
Notice that the plot is packed with action. It might be fun to have students draw the sequence of events. Have them draw a maze or castle that has at least three rooms, and number the rooms in order, 1, 2, 3. In each room they should draw the prince and show something that happened to him there. Under each room write a caption that tells what happened in that room. They should also draw and write what happened at 11:45 and 12.

C. Moral Lesson
? What qualities are admired in this tale? (Love, forgiveness, courage)

A. Conflict
? What is the second battle in the conflict between the youngest prince and his two brothers? (They steal the magic water and substitute salt water.)

Comment from a Critic
Bruno Bettelheim, author of *The Uses of Enchantment: The Meaning and Importance of Fairy Tales,* believes that "folk fairy tales" enrich the inner lives of children by addressing directly their "anxieties and dilemmas." For example, in many fairy tales, including "The Water of Life" and "Cinderella," the youngest of three children is often "simple" or innocent. Children identify with this child who goes out into the world, finds a way out of extremely difficult situations, and becomes a great success. "Only exaggerated hopes and fantasies of future achievements can balance the scales so that the child can go on living and striving."

B. Vocabulary
aught: anything

C. Fairy Tales
Point out that a similar scene is in "Snow White and the Seven Dwarfs," when the stepmother orders the hunter to kill Snow White and bring back her heart as proof. Ask a volunteer to tell how the hunter tricks Snow White's stepmother. (He takes her the heart of a deer and tells her it is Snow White's heart.)

D. Figurative Language
? What is this figure of speech called? (Metaphor) What does it mean? (He was happy; his heart was no longer heavy.)

E. The Quest
? What is the goal of the princes's second journey? (The princess) When the two princes ride beside the road, what quality do they reveal? (Greed; lack of single-minded love)

A to destroy him. They waited until they found him fast asleep, then they poured the water of life out of the cup, and took it for themselves, but into the cup they poured salt seawater.

Now therefore, when they arrived home, the youngest took his cup to the sick king in order that he might drink out of it, and be cured. But scarcely had he drunk a very little of the salt seawater than he became still worse than before. And as he was lamenting over this, the two eldest brothers came, and accused the youngest of having intended to poison him, and said that they had brought him the true water of life, and handed it to him. He had scarcely tasted it, when he felt his sickness departing, and became strong and healthy as in the days of his youth. After that they both went to the youngest, mocked him, and said: "You certainly found the water of life, but you have had the pain, and we the gain; you should have been cleverer, and should have kept your eyes open. We took it from you whilst you were asleep at sea, and when a year is over, one of us will go and fetch the beautiful princess. But beware that you do not disclose aught of this to our father; indeed he does not trust you, and if you say a single word, you shall lose your life into the bargain, but if you keep silent, you shall have it as a gift." B

The old king was angry with his youngest son, and thought he had plotted against his life. So he summoned the court together, and had sentence pronounced upon his son, that he should be secretly shot. And once when the prince was riding forth to the chase, suspecting no evil, the king's huntsman was told to go with him, and when they were quite alone in the forest, the huntsman looked so sorrowful that the prince said to him: "Dear huntsman, what ails you?" The huntsman said: "I cannot tell you, and yet I ought." Then the prince said: "Say openly what it is, I will pardon you." "Alas!" said the huntsman, "I am to shoot you dead, the king has ordered me to do it." Then the prince was shocked, and said: "Dear huntsman, let me live; there, I give you my royal garments; give me your common ones in their stead." The huntsman said: "I will willingly do that, indeed I would not have been able to shoot you." Then they exchanged clothes, and the C huntsman returned home, while the prince went further into the forest.

After a time three wagons of gold and precious stones came to the king for his youngest son, which were sent by the three kings who had slain their enemies with the prince's sword, and maintained their people with his bread, and who wished to show their gratitude for it. The old king then thought: "Can my son have been innocent?" and said to his people: "Would that he were still alive, how it grieves me that I have suffered him to be killed!" "He still lives," said the huntsman, "I could not find it in my heart to carry out your command," and told the king how it had happened. Then a stone fell from the king's heart, and D he had it proclaimed in every country that his son might return and be taken into favor again.

The princess, however, had a road made up to her palace which was quite bright and golden, and told her people that whosoever came riding straight along it to her, would be the right one and was to be admitted, and whoever rode by the side of it, was not the right one, and was not to be admitted. As the time was now close at hand, the eldest thought he would hasten to go to the king's daughter, and give himself out as her rescuer, and thus win her for his bride, and the kingdom to boot. Therefore he rode forth, and when he arrived in front of the palace, and saw the splendid golden road, he thought: "It would be a sin and a shame if I were to ride over that," and turned aside, and rode on the right side of it. But when he came to the door, the servants told him that he was not the right one, and was to go away again.

Soon after this the second prince set out, and when he came to the golden road, and his horse had put one foot on it, he thought: "It would be a sin and a shame, a piece might be trodden off," E and he turned aside and rode on the left side of it, and when he reached the door, the attendants told him he was not the right one, and he was to go away again.

When at last the year had entirely expired, the third son likewise wished to ride out of the forest to his beloved, and with her forget his sorrows. So he set out and thought of her so incessantly, and wished to be with her so much, that he never noticed the golden road at all. So his horse rode

Reading Check Test

1. The dwarf brings trouble upon the two older brothers because they are haughty. *(True)*
2. On his way to finding the water of life, the youngest brother meets a beautiful maiden who deceives him. *(False)*
3. Passing through three countries, each torn by war and famine, the youngest brother forgets to use his magic sword and loaf of bread. *(False)*
4. The king, believing the youngest son to be treacherous, orders him secretly shot. *(True)*
5. The youngest brother proves himself worthy of the princess when he rides along the golden road. *(True)*

Closure

Ask each student to tell the class the name of the most interesting fairy tale he or she has ever read or heard. The students should then tell one way in which their favorite tale is like "The Water of Life."

A onward up the middle of it, and when he came to the door, it was opened and the princess received him with joy, and said he was her savior, the lord of the kingdom, and their wedding was celebrated with great rejoicing. When it was over she told him that his father invited him to come to him, and had forgiven him. So he rode thither, and told him everything; how his brothers had betrayed him, and how he had nevertheless kept silence. The old king wished to punish them, but they had put to sea, and never came back as long as they lived. B

A. Quest

? Why did the princess build the golden road up to her palace? (It was a test that whoever wanted to marry her had to pass. Since she didn't know the young prince well, perhaps she wanted to make sure he loved her more than gold.)

B. Theme

? What do you think is the theme or moral lesson of this tale? (Good triumphs over evil.)

Additional Writing Assignment

You don't usually find out much about the characters in a fairy tale or their motivation (why they do what they do). Choose one of the brothers, the princess, the king, or the dwarf. Write a paragraph in which you tell more about the character you have chosen. Describe the character's looks; give him or her a name. Tell enough about the character's past to explain why he or she is a good or evil person.

ANALYZING THE STORY
Identifying Facts
1. They seek the water of life.
2. Though somewhat naive, he is honest, modest, generous, and faithful.
3. Passing through three countries ravaged by war and famine, he offers the kings his magic sword and loaf of bread; with these, each king is able to feed his people and fend off his enemies.
4. They wait until he is asleep, take the water of life for themselves, and replace it with seawater.
5. The king condemns the son to death. The son is able to escape because the huntsman who is to execute him cannot bring himself to do so. They exchange clothes, and the prince escapes into the forest.
6. The princess orders that any man who approaches by the side of her golden road is not to be admitted. The two older brothers ride along the side; the youngest brother rides right up the middle of it, and so is received by the princess with joy and love.
7. Three brothers, three separate quests for the water of life, youngest brother has to strike "thrice with the wand" upon the *(Answers continue in left-hand column.)*

(Continued from top.)
castle door. (See Teacher's Manual page 127 for complete list.)

Interpreting Meanings
8. The two older haughty brothers are thwarted in their search for the water of life, and are later banished for their trickery. They also prove themselves unworthy of the princess because their motivations are dishonorable. The youngest son prevails in the end because he is motivated entirely by love and loyalty.
9. See Teacher's Manual page 127.
10. It is true. See Teacher's Manual page 127.

Applying Meanings
11. Answers will vary.

FURTHER READING FOR TEACHERS
Elizabeth Cook, *The Ordinary and the Fabulous* (1976).

Responding to the Story

Analyzing the Story

Identifying Facts

1. Each of the three brothers sets out on a **quest.** What are they searching for?
2. How is the youngest son different from his older brothers?
3. After finding the water of life for his father, what deeds does the youngest son accomplish on his return home?
4. On the way home, how do his brothers trick the youngest son?
5. What **conflict** threatens the youngest son after he returns home? How does he escape?
6. When the three brothers go to seek the beautiful princess, the youngest son passes yet another test. What is the test, and what does he do to pass it?
7. Things and events often come in three's in fairy tales—three characters, three tests, three journeys. Go back through this story. Make a list of all the uses of "three" that you find. What other "three's" can you think of in other fairy tales?

Interpreting Meanings

8. Fairy tales often point out a **moral lesson,** an instructive message about how we should lead our lives. How do the events of the story support a moral lesson about pride versus love?
9. Fairy tales almost always include elements of the supernatural—spirits, fairies, or magic. In this story, the water of life is supernatural because it has magical powers to cure any illness. List three other supernatural elements in this story.
10. Good usually triumphs over evil in fairy tales. Explain whether or not this is true in "The Water of Life."

Applying Meanings

11. Fairy tales take place in a make-believe world that could never exist. Why, then, do you think they are so popular? Do you think the characters and their conflicts in the fairy tale are similar in some way to the problems we face in real life?

Writing About the Story

A Creative Response

1. **Writing an Original Fairy Tale.** Write a fairy tale that teaches a lesson about human behavior. Have the hero or heroine of your tale undergo a trial. If you wish, set the tale in modern times. In your story, use at least one element from each column of the following chart.

Characters	Events	Objects
Three sisters	Contest	Magic ring
Toad	Test	Treasure chest
Beast or dragon	Rescue	Wand
Wicked king or queen	Threatened kingdom	Magic potion
		Shield or sword
Fairy godmother	Famine	Magic carpet
Witch	Disguise	Book of magic

A Critical Response

2. **Analyzing the Fairy Tale.** Some critics say that fairy tales reflect our deepest fears and our strongest wishes. Write two paragraphs explaining whether or not you think this is true about "The Water of Life." Before you begin writing, make a list of all the evil things in the story that you might fear, and all the good things in the story that you might wish for.

See Teacher's Manual page 127.

Analyzing Language and Vocabulary

Archaic Words

In "The Water of Life" the characters use several old-fashioned English words and expressions. Rewrite each of the following sentences so that the italicized word or phrase is recast into modern English. Use a dictionary if necessary.

1. " 'I am seeking the water of life, for my father is *sick unto death.*' "
2. " 'Then *hasten to fetch* some of the water of life before the clock strikes twelve. . . .' "
3. "Then the prince went to him and gave him the loaf, *wherewith* he fed and satisfied the whole of his kingdom. . . ."
4. " 'But beware that you do not disclose *aught* of this to our father. . . .' "

For answers, see Teacher's Manual page 128.

PREREADING

1. BUILDING ON PRIOR KNOWLEDGE. Ask students to answer the questions in the headnote. Discuss gender stereotypes in fairy tales. (A stereotype is a printing plate cast from a mold; it has come to mean a "fixed mental pattern with no individual differences, as if cast from a mold.") Women in fairy tales are usually passive, submissive, and decorative. Discuss how this stereotype differs from the nontraditional "modern" woman of today.

2. ESTABLISHING A PURPOSE. After you read the opening conversation between the king and queen, write down how you think this story may be different from other fairy tales you have read. After you read the story, see if you still agree with what you wrote.

3. PREREADING JOURNAL. Ask students to briefly describe how they would go about slaying a vicious, fire-breathing dragon. Urge them to use their imaginations—will they use a magical weapon or sheer brute strength?

★ **Texas Essential Elements/(a) English Language Arts: 1B** Purpose and audience; **2C** Oral language; **3A** Plot/character; **4B** Main idea; **4G** Fact/nonfact. **(c) Reading: 3A** Main ideas/details; **3E** Fact/fictional details

YOUNG LADIES DON'T SLAY DRAGONS

For a detailed lesson plan on this story, see Teacher's Manual pages 128–130.

Joyce Hovelsrud

At first glance, the following story may seem very much like a traditional fairy tale. But you will soon find it taking some unusual twists and turns. Before you read, think about the kinds of heroes and heroines you usually find in fairy tales. Who usually slays the dragon? What does the heroine usually do? When does the prince usually show up?

A A dragon with exceedingly evil intentions was plaguing the Palace of Hexagon. Night and day he lurked about the courtyard walls, belching fire and smoke, and roaring in a most terrible fashion. Things looked bad for the royal household.

"Mercy," said the queen.

"Dear me," said the king. "One of these days he'll get a royal blaze going, and when he does—poof! That'll be it."

"Well, what are you going to do about it?" asked the queen sharply. "I mean, you can't just sit there counting out your money and ignoring the problem." B

"I have asked every brave man in the kingdom to slay the dragon," said the king. "They all said they had more important things to do."

"Nonsense," said the queen with a breathy sigh. "What could be more important than saving the palace from a monstrous dragon? Perhaps you should offer a reward."

"I *have* offered a reward," said the king. "No one seems interested."

"Well, then, offer something of value to go with it," said the queen. And with that, she slammed the honey jar on the table and stomped out of the room. C

"I'll slay the dragon," said the Princess Penelope, jumping from behind an antique suit of armor. There, she had just happened to be listening to the conversation while oiling a rusty joint.

The king blinked his eyes twice—once with shock because he was taken by surprise, and once with pride because he was taken by his daughter's dazzling beauty. "You can't slay a dragon," he said. "Why don't you go knit a vest for the palace poodle or something?"

The princess flexed the arm of the ancient armor. "See? No more clink." She smiled.

"No more clink," said the king vacantly.

"And I just fixed the drawbridge, too," said the princess. "You won't have to worry about the clank anymore."

"Clink, clank, clunk," said the king. "I have more important worries anyway."

"I know," said Penelope. "The dragon. I *said* I'd slay him for you."

"Nonsense," said the king. "Young ladies don't slay dragons."

"They don't oil armor or fix drawbridges, either," said the princess matter-of-factly.

The king scratched his head and thought about that for a while. Princess Penelope was always giving him something to think about. For one thing, he thought her beauty was unsurpassed by

Dialogue. This story contains a great deal of dialogue, or conversation between characters. Some of it is funny. As you read this dialogue, think about the kind of voice each character has and how he or she might speak.

A. Ironic Contrast

? What details in the first paragraph make the dragon almost too terrible to be believed? ("Exceedingly evil," "plaguing," "belching fire and smoke," "roaring in a most terrible fashion") Notice how the author surprises you and creates humor by following these exaggerated details with understated, or weakly inappropriate, reactions from the king and queen.

B. Allusion

Allusions are references to other works of literature.

? To what nursery rhyme does the queen allude here? ("Sing a Song of Sixpence." The second stanza goes: "The king was in his counting house,/Counting all his money;/The queen was in the parlor,/Eating bread and honey.") Tell students to watch for the second allusion to this rhyme (in the eighth paragraph).

C. Responding

? Can you imagine a queen "stomping" in a typical fairy tale?

SUPPLEMENTARY SUPPORT MATERIAL

1. Vocabulary Activity Sheet
2. Reading Check Test blackline master
3. Selection Test (page 153 of Test Book)
4. Audiocassette recording
5. Reader's Response Journal
6. Workbook (page 117)

DEVELOPING VOCABULARY

The following words appear on a test in the Test Book, page 154. (See also the Vocabulary Activity Sheet.)

plague	squint
stomp	conjures
dazzling	ignited
flex	charred
unsurpassed	winsome

A. Point of View
What is the point of view of this story? (Third-person omniscient) How do you know? (We have found out both the king's thoughts and Penelope's thoughts.)

B. Alliteration
What is the alliteration in this sentence? ("Whittled," "whistle," "willow"; "supposed," "sewing," "seam")

C. Responding
From what you have learned about Penelope so far, do you have confidence in her as a dragon-slayer?

D. Irony
The author of this tale uses primarily irony of situation; the contrast is between what you expect will happen in fairy tales, and what happens in this one. You expect the king to be powerful; he turns out to be henpecked. The princess turns out to be gifted not only with beauty but with mechanical ability and courage.

that of any princess on earth. For another, it seemed she never behaved as beautiful princesses should.

"Slaying dragons is men's work," he said finally, "and that's that."

The princess didn't really think that was that. But she knew her father did. So she said no more about it—to him, anyway.

It seemed to her that a young lady could do anything she wanted, if she set her mind to it. And (A) in her tender years she had set her mind to many things the king and queen had said only men could do.

(B) She once whittled a whistle from a green willow stick when she was supposed to be sewing a fine seam.

She once built a birdhouse for the palace puffin when she was supposed to be practicing her lute lesson.

And once she even killed a mouse. She had come into the bedchamber to find her mother standing on a chair and screaming—as queens do in the presence of mice. "Don't worry, Mother, I'll get him," Penelope said.

"Young ladies don't kill mice," the queen said. "For heaven's sake, stand on a chair and scream along with me."

But Penelope didn't stand on a chair and scream. She caught the mouse and disposed of it tidily.

Well, she would dispose of the dragon, too. And she would get some ideas on how to go about it. (C)

(D)

A. Allusion

? To what nursery song does the cook refer? ("Three Blind Mice") How does this allusion and those on page 398 add to the humor of this tale? (The stock, or stereotypical, responses from nursery rhyme characters contrast with Penelope's modern language and actions.)

She went to speak to the royal cook. "How would you slay a dragon?" she asked.

A "I would cut off his head with a carving knife," said the cook. "But of course you couldn't do that."

"Why not?" asked the princess.

"Young ladies don't slay dragons," the cook said.

"My father said that, too," said Penelope, and she went to speak to the royal tailor. "How would you slay a dragon?" she asked.

"I would stab him through the heart with a long needle," the tailor said.

"Would you lend me a long needle?" asked the princess.

"Young ladies don't slay dragons," the tailor said. "Besides, I don't have a needle long enough or strong enough."

So Princess Penelope went to the royal court jester. "How would you slay a dragon?" she asked.

"I would tell him such a funny story he would die laughing," said the jester.

"Do you have such a funny story?" asked Penelope.

B "There aren't any stories *that* funny," said the jester. "Besides, young ladies don't slay dragons."

"You may be in for a surprise," said the princess, and she went to speak to the royal wizard. "How would you slay a dragon?" she asked.

The royal wizard thought a long time. Then he said, "Why do you want to know?"

"Because I want to slay the dragon," Penelope said matter-of-factly.

"Well, if you really want the truth," the wizard said, "the fact is, young ladies don't slay dragons."

"How do you know they don't?" Penelope asked.

C "Everybody knows that," the wizard said. "Don't ask me how I know—it's just a fact."

"Well, then," the princess said, "if a brave young man wanted to save the palace from a smoke-blowing, flame-throwing, fierce, and wicked dragon, what advice would you give him?" The royal wizard wrinkled his forehead, squinted his eyes, and made arches with his fingers while he thought. Then he said, "I would advise him to fight fire with fire."

"I see," said Penelope.

"My feet are cold," said the wizard. "Do me a favor and slide that hot bucket over here. I want to warm my toes on it."

Penelope did as he bade. "How does the bucket stay hot?" she asked.

"It's filled with a magic liquid that burns without fire," said the wizard. "I conjured it up myself."

"A good bit of magic," said Penelope admiringly. "Can you get the liquid to flame up?"

"If I want flames, I just drop a hot coal into the bucket," said the wizard. And then he fell asleep. He always fell asleep after talking three minutes, and now his three minutes were up. Besides, it was nap time for everybody in the palace.

But how anybody could sleep through the dragon's terrible roaring was a mystery to Penelope. And how anybody could sleep while evil threatened the palace was another mystery to her.

The wizard had given the princess an idea, though, and she tiptoed out of the room.

She found a pipe in her collection of iron and sealed it at one end. She tiptoed back to the wizard's room and filled the pipe with liquid from the magic bucket. With a pair of tongs, she took a hot coal from the fire and tiptoed away. She paused in the great hall long enough to don a suit of armor—minus the helmet that hurt her ears and hung low over her eyes. Finally she found a shield she could lift.

Then, clanking, she made her way through the courtyard to the gates. Though she was not strong enough to open them, she managed to push herself sideways through the iron bars. And she wasn't the least bit afraid. D

Now, the dragon was the biggest, the most ferocious dragon that ever lived. Princess Penelope didn't know that, but she rather suspected it, for why else wouldn't the brave men in the kingdom come to slay him?

And the dragon, who was also the wisest dragon that ever lived, had a hunch someone was after him. So he crept slowly around the walls to see who it was—roaring terrible roars and belching the sky full of fire and smoke as he went.

B. Creating Humor

? Why does the author repeat "Young ladies don't slay dragons" so many times? (Each time the writer repeats this ridiculous line, she increases the comic effect. Note that the writer is imitating the use of repetition in fairy tales to make us laugh.)

C. Tone

The tone of this parody or spoof of a traditional fairy tale is light and ironic. Although it pokes fun at the conventions of fairy tales, its underlying, more serious purpose is to mock the idea that women are the weaker sex. Because the author believes that most people today agree with her, her satire is more entertaining than serious.

D. Humor

? What details exaggerate the apparent inequality of the conflict between Penelope and the dragon?

A. Humorous Dialogue

What is funny about Penelope's muttered comment here? (It is understated and thus inappropriate for the situation. It also makes her sound like a modern young woman complaining about her date.)

B. Conflict

How does Penelope succeed in confronting the dragon? (She turns and faces him as he pursues her.) What does this maneuver tell you about her character? (She is brave and clever. She also has a sense of humor.)

A "I wish he wouldn't smoke so much," Penelope muttered as she crept after him. Rounding the corner, she could just make out the monstrous tip of the dragon's tail disappearing around the corner ahead.

"This will never do," she said after the third corner. Turning, she crept the other way—and she met the dragon face to face! B

Now, it isn't easy to describe the ferocious battle that ensued, but it went something like this.

READING CHECK TEST

1. The dragon is mainly interested in Princess Penelope. *(False)*
2. Penelope believes she can defeat the dragon. *(True)*
3. She is, in all things, confident and unafraid. *(True)*
4. She fashions a weapon out of an iron pipe and a magic liquid that she takes from the royal wizard. *(True)*
5. The dragon dies and metamorphoses into a frog. *(False)*

CLOSURE

Divide the class into groups. Have each group, without consulting the dictionary, define irony. Ask each group also to list examples of irony in "Young Ladies Don't Slay Dragons." (Make sure they mention the irony in the title.)

"Stop or I'll shoot," said Penelope calmly.

"What's a nice girl like you doing out slaying dragons?" sneered the dragon as he crept toward her, blinking several times because of her dazzling beauty.

"I said, stop or I'll shoot."

"You don't *shoot* dragons," the dragon said, coming closer. "Everybody I ever heard of slays them with swords."

"I'm not like everybody you ever heard of," Penelope said.

"I wonder why that is," the dragon said. And though he didn't know it at the time, the dragon had spoken his last words. B

Princess Penelope raised her lead pipe, ignited the liquid with her hot coal, and dealt the deadly dragon a deadly blow.

Now, nobody would believe the terrible fire that followed, so it isn't necessary to describe it. But it was like the end of the world.

At last the smoke cleared away. And there, standing among the charred remains of the world's most ferocious dragon was—the world's most handsome prince. Penelope couldn't believe her eyes.

"I've been waiting for something like that to happen," said the prince, smiling a handsome smile and blinking a winsome blink. "You'll marry me, of course." C

But—Penelope was the world's most beautiful princess. Having her for a wife was more than the prince had dared dream, especially while bouncing about in the body of a dragon.

"I have a kingdom ten times the size of this pea patch," he added, "and it's all yours if you'll say yes."

Penelope gazed into his eyes a long time. Thoughtfully, she said, "I've been waiting for someone like you to ask me something like that. But there's something you should know about me first. I wouldn't be happy just being a queen and doing queen-things. I like to fix drawbridges, build birdhouses, slay dragons—that sort of thing."

"It so happens I have bridges, birds, and dragons to spare," said the prince hopefully.

"Then my answer is yes," said Penelope.

And with that they saddled up a white horse and rode off into the sunset.

Now, even though this is the end of the story, you realize, of course, they are still living happily ever after.

A. Humor

? What is funny about this dialogue? (It is incongruous—not only does the dragon talk, but instead of attacking Penelope, he is asking her curious questions.)

B. Character's Actions

? How does the dragon's insistence on playing the role of a fairy tale dragon cause his downfall? (Insisting that no one shoots dragons, he moves too close, and Penelope is able to get him with her pipe.)

C. Responding to a Thematic Twist

? Does the prince's proposal surprise you? Why does he want to marry Penelope? Does Penelope's acceptance of his proposal surprise you, or did you expect it? Why do you think she agrees to marry the prince?

Additional Writing Assignment

Write the letter that Penelope might have sent to her parents after three months of marriage.

ANALYZING THE STORY

Identifying Facts

1. She especially likes to do things that conventional princesses don't do, such as oil armor, fix drawbridges, build birdhouses—and slay dragons.

2. The wizard will only tell her that "young ladies don't slay dragons." So she asks him to imagine that "a brave young man" wants to battle the dragon; this draws the looked-for answer from the wizard.

3. The dragon turns into a handsome prince, and Penelope accepts his offer of marriage on the condition that she can continue to do the things she likes to do—including slaying dragons.

Interpreting Meanings

4. She wields an iron (or lead) pipe full of magic liquid that burns without fire. Fighting the dragon, she turns this device into a kind of flame-thrower by igniting the liquid with a hot coal.

5. Penelope is forthright, bold, courageous, clever, resourceful, persistent, self-assured, and open-minded. Most students will find her like a typical modern girl, unbound by traditional attitudes *(Answers continue in left-hand column.)*

(Continued from top.) about the role of women in society.

6. See Teacher's Manual page 129.

7. The theme is given on page 398: "It seemed to her that a young lady could do anything she wanted, if she set her mind to it." This might be restated as follows: You can accomplish anything if you try hard enough, regardless of your sex.

Applying Meanings

8. However, the relationship is a broad one; in life, as in this story, there are those who blindly adhere to convention, and those who naturally resist, challenge, and sometimes even overcome conventional attitudes.

FURTHER READING FOR TEACHERS

C. S. Lewis, *The Screwtape Dunces.*

FOR STUDENTS

Florence Heide, *The Shrinking of Treehorn.*

402

Responding to the Story

Analyzing the Story

Identifying Facts

1. How is Penelope an unusual fairy tale princess? What things has Penelope done that "only men should do"?
2. How does Penelope trick the wizard into helping her?
3. What two surprises take place toward the end of the story?

Interpreting Meanings

4. In some fantasies, one or more characters may have magic powers. Often, a character's source of power is some supernatural object, such as a wand. What is the source of Penelope's magic power?
5. Describe Penelope's **character,** or personality. Is she like a typical modern girl? List a few of her qualities.
6. The writer of "Young Ladies Don't Slay Dragons" **satirizes,** or pokes fun at, fairy tales by presenting characters and situations that are just the reverse of those found in traditional tales. For example, in most fairy tales, brave men are eager to pursue dragons for a reward. In this tale, all the brave men have "more important things to do." Give three other examples of reversed characters or reversed situations in the story.
7. How would you state the **theme,** or main idea, of this story?

SRW p. 87

Applying Meanings

8. Do you think this fairy tale has any relationship to life as you know it? Do you think the characters in the fairy tale are like real people in the world as you know it? Explain.

Writing About the Story

A Creative Response

1. **Designing a Poster.** Design a reward poster that the king might have printed. Describe the job to be done and offer a reward to the future dragon-killer.

A Critical Response

2. **Distinguishing Reality from Fantasy.** The realistic elements in "Young Ladies Don't Slay Dragons" help us believe in the fantasy world that the author has created. In a paragraph, explain how the author has combined the real with the supernatural. Before you write, you might want to make two lists—one of the realistic elements in the story, and one of the fantastic elements.

See Teacher's Manual page 130.

Analyzing Language and Vocabulary

Reading the Story Aloud

Read the story aloud to a group of younger children. You might want to find some friends who would be willing to prepare a reading together, and act out the story. Each of you could read the lines of a different character. A narrator could read the descriptive and explanatory material in the story. Rehearse your reading at least twice before presenting it. Try to speak as you think your character might have spoken. You can change the tone, speed, and loudness of your voice as you show different feelings. (For instance, does the king act with usual kingly authority? Or is he afraid of his feisty daughter? How will you portray the wizard—full of magic and wisdom, or lazy and tired?)

PREREADING

1. BUILDING ON PRIOR KNOWLEDGE. Before students begin reading, ask them if they like to watch scary movies or read scary stories. Ask them to name some of the elements that these stories share (mysterious settings, ghostly characters, exciting plot, characters in danger, vivid descriptions). Tell students that details of setting are usually very important when writers want to build a mood of supernatural horror.

2. ESTABLISHING A PURPOSE. The headnote sets a good purpose for reading the story.

3. PREREADING JOURNAL. If someone offered to sell you a magic object for a small sum of money—say twenty dollars—and told you that with this object you could obtain three wishes, what would you do? Write five sentences telling what you would do and why.

★ Texas Essential Elements/(a) English Language Arts: 4B Main idea; 4E Predict. (c) Reading: 1A Context clues; 1C Dictionaries; 2A Word meaning; 3A Main ideas/details; 3H Predict

THE MONKEY'S PAW

W. W. Jacobs

"The Monkey's Paw" is a masterpiece of horror which has been popular for almost ninety years, both as a one-act play and as a short story. Read up until just before the visitor is walking through the door. Think of what you have found out about the setting and about the lives of Mr. White, Mrs. White, and their son Herbert. What mood does this opening passage create?

A

I

Without, the night was cold and wet, but in the small parlor of Lakesnam Villa the blinds were drawn and the fire burned brightly. Father and son were at chess, the
B former, who possessed ideas about the game involving radical changes, putting his king into such sharp and unnecessary perils that it even provoked comment from the white-haired old lady knitting placidly by the fire.

"Hark at the wind," said Mr. White, who, having seen a fatal mistake after it was too late, was amiably desirous of preventing his son from seeing it.

"I'm listening," said the latter, grimly surveying the board as he stretched out his hand. "Check."[1]

C "I should hardly think that he'd come tonight," said his father, with his hand poised over the
D board.

"Mate," replied the son.

"That's the worst of living so far out," bawled Mr. White, with sudden and unlooked-for violence; "of all the beastly, slushy, out-of-the-way places to live in, this is the worst. Pathway's a bog, and the road's a torrent. I don't know what people are thinking about. I suppose because only two houses on the road are let,[2] they think it doesn't matter."

"Never mind, dear," said his wife soothingly; "perhaps you'll win the next one."

Mr. White looked up sharply, just in time to intercept a knowing glance between mother and son. The words died away on his lips, and he hid a guilty grin in his thin gray beard.

"There he is," said Herbert White, as the gate banged to loudly and heavy footsteps came toward the door.

The old man rose with hospitable haste, and, opening the door, was heard condoling[3] with the new arrival. The new arrival also condoled with himself, so that Mrs. White said, "Tut, tut!" and coughed gently as her husband entered the room,

Context Clues. This story was written by an English writer, and it takes place in England. Some of the words and expressions in the story will be strange to you, but the **context**—the words and sentences surrounding the word—should help you figure out most of them. For example, the first word of the story, if it were written by an American, would probably be *outside* rather than *without*. And the family would probably be in a *living room* or a *family room*, rather than a *parlor*. But you can easily figure out what these words mean by thinking about the passage as a whole and by using clues to help you guess at their meanings.

1. **check:** in the game of chess, a move that directly attacks the king. **Checkmate** is a move that makes the king unable to move and means the end of the game.
2. **let:** rented.

3. **condoling:** expressing sympathy (for the bad weather).

A. Reading Aloud
For a second reading of the story, you may want to assign parts for each page and have students prepare to read aloud in class.

B. Setting
Point out that this story is set in winter, a season that in literature is associated with sad endings. The outside world of nature with its uncaring cold, rain, and wind is contrasted with the human world inside the warm parlor where father, son, and mother care about each other.

C. Conflict
? What minor conflict adds interest to the beginning of the story? (Mr. White vs. his son in chess) What does this conflict reveal about the Whites? (They know each other well; they enjoy being together.)

D. Suspense
? What comment creates suspense on this page? ("I should hardly think that he'd come tonight . . .") What questions do you have as a result of this comment? (Who is coming? Why? Will he get here?)

For a detailed lesson plan on this story, see Teacher's Manual pages 130–133. A biography of William W. Jacobs appears on text page 412.

SUPPLEMENTARY SUPPORT MATERIAL

1. Vocabulary Activity Sheet
2. Reading Check Test blackline master
3. Selection Test (page 155, Test Book)
4. Audiocassette recording
5. Connections Between Reading and Writing worksheet
6. Reader's Response Journal
7. Workbook (page 119)

DEVELOPING VOCABULARY

The following words appear on a test in the Test Book, page 156. (See also the Vocabulary Activity Sheet.)

fancy	resolution
enthralled	furtive
dubious	broach
marred	sinister
prosaic	averted

A. Suspense
? What details about the paw build an atmosphere of suspense and mystery? (It had a spell put on it by a holy man; he wanted to show that fate rules people's lives; three men can have three wishes from it.)

B. Interpreting
? Notice that the first man's last wish was for death. Explain what this wish implies about the first two wishes. (They must have driven him to despair.)

C. Foreshadowing
? What clues indicate that the paw brought unhappiness to the sergeant and bodes ill for any wisher? (His face whitens; his glass taps against his teeth; he doesn't know if he would take three more wishes; he throws the paw into the fire.)

followed by a tall burly man, beady of eye and rubicund of visage.[4]

"Sergeant Major Morris," he said, introducing him.

The sergeant major shook hands, and, taking the proffered seat by the fire, watched contentedly while his host got out whiskey and tumblers and stood a small copper kettle on the fire.

At the third glass his eyes got brighter, and he began to talk, the little family circle regarding with eager interest this visitor from distant parts, as he squared his broad shoulders in the chair and spoke of strange scenes and doughty deeds, of wars and plagues and strange peoples.

"Twenty-one years of it," said Mr. White, nodding at his wife and son. "When he went away he was a slip of a youth in the warehouse. Now look at him."

"He don't look to have taken much harm," said Mrs. White politely.

"I'd like to go to India myself," said the old man, "just to look around a bit, you know."

"Better where you are," said the sergeant major, shaking his head. He put down the empty glass and, sighing softly, shook it again.

"I should like to see those old temples and fakirs[5] and jugglers," said the old man. "What was that you started telling me the other day about a monkey's paw or something, Morris?"

"Nothing," said the soldier hastily. "Leastways, nothing worth hearing."

"Monkey's paw?" said Mrs. White curiously.

"Well, it's just a bit of what you might call magic, perhaps," said the sergeant major offhandedly.

A His three listeners leaned forward eagerly. The visitor absent-mindedly put his empty glass to his lips and then set it down again. His host filled it for him.

"To look at," said the sergeant major, fumbling in his pocket, "it's just an ordinary little paw, dried to a mummy."

He took something out of his pocket and proffered it. Mrs. White drew back with a grimace, but her son, taking it, examined it curiously.

"And what is there special about it?" inquired Mr. White as he took it from his son and, having examined it, placed it upon the table.

"It had a spell put on it by an old fakir," said the sergeant major, "a very holy man. He wanted to show that fate ruled people's lives, and that those who interfered with it did so to their sorrow. He put a spell on it so that three separate men could each have three wishes from it."

His manner was so impressive that his hearers were conscious that their light laughter jarred somewhat.

"Well, why don't you have three, sir?" said Herbert White cleverly.

The soldier regarded him in the way that middle age is wont to regard presumptuous youth. "I have," he said quietly, and his blotchy face whitened.

"And did you really have the three wishes granted?" asked Mrs. White.

"I did," said the sergeant major, and his glass tapped against his strong teeth.

"And has anybody else wished?" inquired the old lady.

"The first man had his three wishes, yes," was the reply. "I don't know what the first two were, but the third was for death. That's how I got the paw." B

His tones were so grave that a hush fell upon the group.

"If you've had your three wishes, it's no good to you now, then Morris," said the old man at last. "What do you keep it for?"

The soldier shook his head. "Fancy, I suppose," he said slowly. "I did have some idea of selling it, but I don't think I will. It has caused enough mischief already. Besides, people won't buy. They think it's a fairy tale, some of them, and those who do think anything of it want to try it first and pay me afterward."

"If you could have another three wishes," said the old man, eyeing him keenly, "would you have them?"

"I don't know," said the other. "I don't know."

He took the paw, and dangling it between his front finger and thumb, suddenly threw it upon the fire. White, with a slight cry, stooped down and snatched it off. C

4. **rubicund** (ro͞o'bi·kund') **of visage** (viz'ij): red-faced.
5. **fakirs** (fə·kîrs'): Muslim or Hindu holy men, some of whom claim to be able to perform miracles.

Historical Background

Elicit what students know about the history of British colonial rule in India. (Some of them may have seen films about India.) Britain maintained control over India from 1747 until 1947. The wars to which the author refers were probably the popular rebellions of 1857 when Muslims and Hindus united against British rule. During this time, British officers and enlisted men grew increasingly distant from Indian society, and the little understanding they had of Indian culture was replaced by suspicion, hostility, and fear. Since he "wanted to show that fate rules men's lives," the fakir that cast the spell on the monkey's paw was most likely a Muslim holy man. According to the doctrine of Mohammed, God is all powerful and decrees everything that happens. We might assume that the fakir was using the monkey's paw to "teach" the occupying enemy that humans must submit to the will of God (which Sgt. Morris understands as "fate"), and that one population was not meant to rule another.

Responding to the Illustration

The illustrator has used an original technique to create dramatic light and shadow. The background of the illustration is dark; the three members of the White family are brightly colored figures in the darkness. Sgt. Morris's face seems to glow in the firelight as he holds the grotesque monkey's paw in front of him. He is the focus of the illustration, and looms like Fate over the others. The Whites hover behind him, their faces reflecting varying degrees of curiosity, fear, doubt, and interest.

A. Suspense
How does the sergeant's comment heighten suspense? (You wonder if foolish wishes will be granted, or have been granted in the past. And if they were, what were the consequences?

B. Vocabulary
cleared: bought

C. Interpreting
What does Herbert's suggesting a wish, his wink, and his playing dramatic chords suggest about him? (That he believes least in the power of the paw. Because we have been led to believe the paw is dangerous, we worry that Herbert is being so careless.)

D. Foreshadowing
After you've read the story, what meaning does this comment take on? (The wish does come true and the couple does get the money. But Herbert is right—he never does see it.)

E. Setting and Mood
What details of setting in this paragraph create a mood of suspense and fear? ("Outside, the wind was higher than ever . . ."; ". . . the old man started nervously at the sound of a door banging . . ."; "A silence unusual and depressing . . .")

"Better let it burn," said the soldier solemnly.

"If you don't want it, Morris," said the old man, "give it to me."

"I won't," said his friend doggedly. "I threw it on the fire. If you keep it, don't blame me for what happens. Pitch it on the fire again, like a sensible man."

The other shook his head and examined his new possession closely. "How do you do it?" he inquired.

"Hold it up in your right hand and wish aloud," said the sergeant major, "but I warn you of the consequences."

"Sounds like *The Arabian Nights,*"[6] said Mrs. White, as she rose and began to set the supper. "Don't you think you might wish for four pairs of hands for me?"

A Her husband drew the talisman[7] from his pocket and then all three burst into laughter as the sergeant major, with a look of alarm on his face, caught him by the arm. "If you must wish," he said gruffly, "wish for something sensible."

Mr. White dropped it back into his pocket, and placing chairs, motioned his friend to the table. In the business of supper, the talisman was partly forgotten, and afterward the three sat listening in an enthralled fashion to a second installment of the soldier's adventures in India.

"If the tale about the monkey paw is not more truthful than those he has been telling us," said Herbert, as the door closed behind their guest, just in time for him to catch the last train, "we shan't make much out of it."

"Did you give him anything for it, Father?" inquired Mrs. White, regarding her husband closely.

"A trifle," said he, coloring slightly. "He didn't want it, but I made him take it. And he pressed me again to throw it away."

"Likely," said Herbert, with pretended horror. "Why, we're going to be rich, and famous, and happy. Wish to be an emperor, Father, to begin with: then you can't be bossed around."

He darted round the table, pursued by the maligned Mrs. White armed with an antimacassar.[8]

Mr. White took the paw from his pocket and eyed it dubiously. "I don't know what to wish for, and that's a fact," he said slowly. "It seems to me I've got all I want."

"If you only cleared the house, you'd be quite B happy, wouldn't you?" said Herbert, with his hand on his shoulder. "Well, wish for two hundred pounds,[9] then; that'll just do it."

His father, smiling shamefacedly at his own credulity,[10] held up the talisman, as his son, with a solemn face somewhat marred by a wink at his mother, sat down at the piano and struck a few impressive chords.

"I wish for two hundred pounds," said the old man distinctly.

A fine crash from the piano greeted the words, C interrupted by a shuddering cry from the old man. His wife and son ran toward him.

"It moved," he cried, with a glance of disgust at the object as it lay on the floor. "As I wished it twisted in my hands like a snake."

"Well, I don't see the money," said his son, as he picked it up and placed it on the table, "and I D bet I never shall."

"It must have been your fancy, Father," said his wife, regarding him anxiously.

He shook his head. "Never mind, though; there's no harm done, but it gave me a shock all the same."

They sat down by the fire again while the two men finished their pipes. Outside, the wind was higher than ever, and the old man started nervously at the sound of a door banging upstairs. A E silence unusual and depressing settled upon all three, which lasted until the old couple rose to retire for the night.

"I expect you'll find the cash tied up in a big bag in the middle of your bed," said Herbert, as he bade them good night, "and something horrible squatting up on top of the wardrobe watching you as you pocket your ill-gotten gains."

6. ***The Arabian Nights:*** collection of tales from ancient Arabia, Persia, and India (see page 413).
7. **talisman** (tal'is·mən): object that has magic powers, supposed to bring good luck.
8. **antimacassar** (an'ti·mə·kas'ər): small cover placed on the back or arms of a chair to prevent soiling.
9. **two hundred pounds:** English money equal to about one thousand dollars at the time of this story.
10. **credulity:** tendency to believe anything one hears.

A. Interpreting

? What does this tell us about how Herbert felt about the paw? (That he was more worried about the paw than he let on the night before)

B. Context Clues

? If you don't know the meaning of "frivolous," its meaning becomes clear when you look at the rest of the sentence. Does Herbert expect his remark to be taken seriously? What does "frivolous" mean? (Silly)

C. Making Inferences

? What is Mrs. White grumbling about? (The sergeant drank quite a lot of the Whites' whiskey; Mrs. White is reminded of this when she thinks about paying the tailor's bill.)

D. Irony

? When Mrs. White first sees the stranger, why does she think he has come? (To tell them how they will get the money) How is his news ironic? (His news is tragic—the Whites were expecting the good news that they were rich.)

E. Suspense

? How does the author keep you guessing about what will happen next in this passage? (The stranger reveals the information to you and to the Whites a little at a time. You feel the anxiety in their questions.)

II

A In the brightness of the wintry sun next morning as it streamed over the breakfast table Herbert laughed at his fears. There was an air of prosaic wholesomeness about the room which it had lacked on the previous night, and the dirty, shriveled little paw was pitched on the sideboard with a carelessness which betokened no great belief in its virtues.

"I suppose all old soldiers are the same," said Mrs. White. "The idea of our listening to such nonsense! How could wishes be granted in these days? And if they could, how could two hundred pounds hurt you, Father?"

B "Might drop on his head from the sky," said the frivolous Herbert.

"Morris said the things happened so naturally," said his father, "that you might if you so wished attribute it to coincidence."

"Well, don't break into the money before I come back," said Herbert, as he rose from the table. "I'm afraid it'll turn you into a mean, avaricious[11] man, and we shall have to disown you."

His mother laughed, and followed him to the door, watched him down the road, and returning to the breakfast table, was very happy at the expense of her husband's credulity. All of which did not prevent her from scurrying to the door at the postman's knock, nor prevent her from referring somewhat shortly to retired sergeant majors of C bibulous[12] habits when she found that the post brought a tailor's bill.

"Herbert will have some more of his funny remarks, I expect, when he comes home," she said, as they sat at dinner.

"I dare say," said Mr. White, pouring himself out some beer; "but for all that, the thing moved in my hand; that I'll swear to."

"You thought it did," said the old lady soothingly.

"I say it did," replied the other. "There was no thought about it. I had just—— What's the matter?"

11. **avaricious** (av'ə·rish'əs): greedy for money.
12. **bibulous** (bib'yoo·ləs): drinking.

His wife made no reply. She was watching the mysterious movements of a man outside, who, peering in an undecided fashion at the house, appeared to be trying to make up his mind to enter. In mental connection with the two hundred pounds, she noticed that the stranger was well dressed and wore a silk hat of glossy newness. Three times he paused at the gate, and then D walked on again. The fourth time he stood with his hand upon it, and then with sudden resolution flung it open and walked up the path. Mrs. White at the same moment placed her hands behind her, and hurriedly unfastening the strings of her apron, put that useful article of apparel beneath the cushion of her chair.

She brought the stranger, who seemed ill at ease, into the room. He gazed furtively at Mrs. White, and listened in a preoccupied fashion as the old lady apologized for the appearance of the room, and her husband's coat, a garment which he usually reserved for the garden. She then waited patiently for him to broach[13] his business, but he was at first strangely silent.

"I—was asked to call," he said at last, and stooped and picked a piece of cotton from his trousers. "I came from Maw and Meggins."

The old lady started. "Is anything the matter?" she asked breathlessly. "Has anything happened to Herbert? What is it? What is it?"

Her husband interposed. "There, there, Mother," he said hastily. "Sit down and don't jump to conclusions. You've not brought bad news, I'm sure, sir," and he eyed the other wistfully. E

"I'm sorry——" began the visitor.

"Is he hurt?" demanded the mother.

The visitor bowed in assent. "Badly hurt," he said quietly, "but he is not in any pain."

"Oh, thank God!" said the old woman, clasping her hands. "Thank God for that! Thank——"

She broke off suddenly as the sinister meaning of the assurance dawned upon her and she saw the awful confirmation of her fears in the other's averted face. She caught her breath, and turning to her husband, laid her trembling old hand upon

13. **broach:** introduce; bring up.

Literary Background

One of the earliest masters of the short story was Edgar Allan Poe (1809–1849). (See text page 633 for excerpt of a poem by Poe.) As both critic and writer he established standards for the detective story and the horror tale which are still being followed today. In a well-written short story, he wrote, every detail should contribute toward making a single effect on the reader. Poe also wrote that every event in a well-built plot should be important to the development of the story. Discuss some of the events, descriptive details, and lines of dialogue in Jacobs's story. Consider what each one adds to the development of the plot and the single effect—a growing sense of horror—on the reader.

A. Recalling a Clue

What does the visitor's announcement remind us of? (That the sergeant said the wishes often came true so naturally that one could attribute it to coincidence.)

B. Motivation

Why does Mr. White collapse? (He believes that his wish brought the money, thereby causing his son's death.)

C. Understanding Plot

What is the most important conflict in this story? (The Whites vs. their fate, or the monkey's paw)

D. Mood

What specific details show that the mood inside the house has changed? ("House steeped in shadow and silence"; "nothing to talk about"; "their days were long to weariness")

his. There was a long silence.

A "He was caught in the machinery," said the visitor at length, in a low voice.

"Caught in the machinery," repeated Mr. White, in a dazed fashion, "yes."

He sat staring blankly out at the window, and taking his wife's hand between his own, pressed it as he had been wont to do in their old courting days nearly forty years before.

"He was the only one left to us," he said, turning gently to the visitor. "It is hard."

The other coughed, and, rising, walked slowly to the window. "The firm wished me to convey their sincere sympathy with you in your great loss," he said, without looking around. "I beg that you will understand I am only their servant and merely obeying orders."

There was no reply; the old woman's face was white, her eyes staring, and her breath inaudible; on the husband's face was a look such as his friend the sergeant might have carried into his first action.

"I was to say that Maw and Meggins disclaim all responsibility," continued the other. "They admit no liability at all, but in consideration of your son's services they wish to present you with a certain sum as compensation."

Mr. White dropped his wife's hand, and rising to his feet, gazed with a look of horror at his visitor. His dry lips shaped the words, "How much?"

"Two hundred pounds," was the answer.

B Unconscious of his wife's shriek, the old man smiled faintly, put out his hands like a sightless man, and dropped, a senseless heap, to the floor.

C

III

In the huge new cemetery, some two miles distant, the old people buried their dead, and came back to a house steeped in shadow and silence. It was all over so quickly that at first they could hardly realize it, and remained in a state of expectation as though of something else to happen—something else which was to lighten this load, too heavy for old hearts to bear. But the days passed, and expectations gave place to resignation—the hopeless resignation of the old, sometimes miscalled apathy.[14] Sometimes they hardly exchanged a word, for now they had nothing to talk about, and their days were long to weariness. D

It was about a week after that that the old man, waking suddenly in the night, stretched out his hand and found himself alone. The room was in darkness, and the sound of subdued weeping came from the window. He raised himself in bed and listened.

"Come back," he said tenderly. "You will be cold."

"It is colder for my son," said the old woman, and wept afresh.

The sound of her sobs died away on his ears. The bed was warm, and his eyes heavy with sleep. He dozed fitfully, and then slept until a sudden wild cry from his wife awoke him with a start.

"The monkey's paw!" she cried wildly. "The monkey's paw!"

He started up in alarm. "Where? Where is it? What's the matter?"

She came stumbling across the room toward him. "I want it," she said quietly. "You've not destroyed it?"

"It's in the parlor, on the bracket,"[15] he replied, marveling. "Why?"

She cried and laughed together, and bending over, kissed his cheek.

"I only just thought of it," she said hysterically. "Why didn't I think of it before? Why didn't you think of it?"

"Think of what?" he questioned.

"The other two wishes," she replied rapidly. "We've only had one."

"Was not that enough?" he demanded fiercely.

"No," she cried triumphantly; "we'll have one more. Go down and get it quickly, and wish our boy alive again."

The man sat up in bed and flung the bedclothes from his quaking limbs. "You are mad!" he cried, aghast.

"Get it," she panted; "get it quickly, and wish—Oh, my boy, my boy!"

---

14. **apathy** (ap′ə·thē): indifference; unconcern.
15. **bracket:** shelf.

Comment from a Critic
Children's author Catherine Storr in *The Cool Webb: The Pattern of Children's Reading* states that ". . . children should be allowed to feel fear and I believe that they must also be allowed to meet terror and pity and evil." She mentions that Walter de la Mare (author of the poem "The Listeners," page 388) once said that children were "impoverished if they were protected from everything that might frighten them . . . the child who hadn't known fear could never be a poet." In another discussion in *The Cool Webb,* children's book editor Julia McCrae comments that "resolution, the sense of an ending" to the horror is all-important.

You may want to discuss the resolution of "The Monkey's Paw." To spur discussion, you can ask the following questions: In the last paragraph of the story, how are the conflicts resolved? (The "ghost" disappears.) Does the horror continue or has it ended? (It has ended.) How might the Whites feel about this experience when they look back at it?

A. Conflict
Notice how this violent conflict contrasts with the tender relationship between Mr. and Mrs. White in Part I. She is almost insane with her desire to have her son back. He is afraid of her. Why does Mr. White resist his wife's command? (The monkey's paw has already brought such tragedy into their lives, and he cannot imagine any good coming from such an evil object. He probably also remembers that the last wish of a previous owner was for death, indicating that the luck only gets worse.)

B. Mood
? What details heighten the mood of mystery and terror? ("Chilled with the cold"; "pulsating shadows")

C. Interpreting
? Why does the author mention that "a stair creaked . . ."? (Stairs creak when people walk on them. The author shocks us, and Mr. White, by saying the stair creaked, then relieves us as he attributes the creak to a mouse.)

Her husband struck a match and lit the candle. "Get back to bed," he said unsteadily. "You don't know what you are saying."

"We had the first wish granted," said the old woman feverishly; "why not the second?"

"A coincidence," stammered the old man.

"Go and get it and wish," cried his wife, quivering with excitement.

The old man turned and regarded her, and his voice shook. "He has been dead ten days, and besides he—I would not tell you else, but—I could only recognize him by his clothing. If he was too terrible for you to see then, how now?"

"Bring him back," cried the old woman, and dragged him toward the door. "Do you think I fear the child I have nursed?"

He went down in the darkness, and felt his way to the parlor, and then to the mantelpiece. The talisman was in its place, and a horrible fear that the unspoken wish might bring his mutilated son before him ere he could escape from the room seized upon him, and he caught his breath as he found that he had lost the direction of the door. His brow cold with sweat, he felt his way round the table, and groped along the wall until he found himself in the small passage with the unwholesome thing in his hand.

A Even his wife's face seemed changed as he entered the room. It was white and expectant, and to his fears seemed to have an unnatural look upon it. He was afraid of her.

"Wish!" she cried, in a strong voice.

"It is foolish and wicked," he faltered.

"Wish!" repeated his wife.

He raised his hand. "I wish my son alive again."

The talisman fell to the floor, and he regarded it shudderingly. Then he sank trembling into a chair as the old woman, with burning eyes, walked to the window and raised the blind.

B He sat until he was chilled with the cold, glancing occasionally at the figure of the old woman peering through the window. The candle end, which had burned below the rim of the china candlestick, was throwing pulsating shadows on the ceiling and walls, until, with a flicker larger than the rest, it expired. The old man, with an unspeakable sense of relief at the failure of the talisman, crept back to his bed, and a minute or two afterward the old woman came silently and apathetically beside him.

Neither spoke, but both lay silently listening to the ticking of the clock. A stair creaked, and a C squeaky mouse scurried noisily through the wall. The darkness was oppressive, and after lying for some time screwing up his courage, the husband took the box of matches, and striking one, went downstairs for a candle.

At the foot of the stairs the match went out, and he paused to strike another, and at the same moment a knock, so quiet and stealthy as to be scarcely audible, sounded on the front door.

The matches fell from his hand. He stood motionless, his breath suspended until the knock was repeated. Then he turned and fled swiftly back to his room, and closed the door behind him. A third knock sounded through the house.

"*What's that?*" cried the old woman, starting up.

"A rat," said the old man, in shaking tones—"a rat. It passed me on the stairs."

His wife sat up in bed listening. A loud knock resounded through the house.

"It's Herbert!" she screamed. "It's Herbert!"

She ran to the door, but her husband was before her, and catching her by the arm, held her tightly.

"What are you going to do?" he whispered hoarsely.

"It's my boy; it's Herbert!" she cried, struggling mechanically. "I forgot it was two miles away. What are you holding me for? Let go. I must open the door."

"Don't let it in," cried the old man, trembling.

"You're afraid of your own son," she cried, struggling. "Let me go. I'm coming, Herbert; I'm coming."

There was another knock, and another. The old woman with a sudden wrench broke free and ran from the room. Her husband followed to the landing, and called after her appealingly as she hurried downstairs. He heard the chain rattle back and the bottom bolt drawn slowly and stiffly from the socket. Then the old woman's voice, strained and panting.

Reading Check Test

1. Sergeant Major Morris encourages Mr. White to accept the monkey's paw. *(False)*
2. A holy man put a spell on the paw to show that people's lives are governed by fate. (*True*)
3. Mr. White's first wish was to be given a promotion at his office. (*False*)
4. Mrs. White decides to wish for her own death, so she can join her son Herbert. (*False*)
5. Mr. White uses his third wish to undo his second wish. *(True)*

Closure

Ask a volunteer to tell the class why "The Monkey's Paw" is considered a fantasy. Then have each student give an example of a supernatural or magic character or event that would make any story a fantasy.

"The bolt," she cried loudly. "Come down. I can't reach it."

A But her husband was on his hands and knees groping wildly on the floor in search of the paw. If he could only find it before the thing outside got in. A perfect fusillade[16] of knocks reverberated through the house, and he heard the scraping of a chair as his wife put it down in the passage against the door. He heard the creaking of the bolt as it came slowly back, and at the same moment he found the monkey's paw, and frantically breathed his third and last wish. B

The knocking ceased suddenly, although the echoes of it were still in the house. He heard the chair drawn back and the door opened. A cold wind rushed up the staircase, and a long loud wail of disappointment and misery from his wife gave him courage to run down to her side, and then to the gate beyond. The street lamp flickering opposite shone on a quiet and deserted road. C

16. **fusillade** (fyo͞o′sə·lād): rapid and continuous discharge (as of bullets).

A. Interpreting

? What detail tells you that Mr. White's expectation of what is outside is quite different from Mrs. White's? ("If he could only find it before the thing outside . . ." as compared to Mrs. White's "It's my boy; it's Herbert!")

B. Plot

? What do you think is Mr. White's final wish? ("I wish him dead again.") Why doesn't the author tell you what it is? (It is more interesting to leave it to your imagination.)

C. Mood or Atmosphere

? Although Mr. White saves himself and his wife from something horrible, the mood at the end of the story is far from triumphant. What *is* the mood at the end of the story? (Sad, lonely) What details convey this mood? ("A cold wind," "wail of disappointment and misery," "quiet and deserted road.")

ANALYZING THE STORY
Identifying Facts
1. Three different men would be granted three wishes from it. An old holy man put the spell on the monkey's paw to show that people's lives are ruled by fate, and that those who interfered with it would be sorry.
2. Mr. White is more inclined to believe the power of the monkey's paw; Herbert finds the idea interesting but is more amused than taken in by it.
3. He wishes for two hundred pounds. Herbert is killed at work; and the wished-for two hundred pounds arrive as compensation for his death.
4. He wishes that Herbert return to life. He makes the wish upon the urging of his wife. It is implied that Herbert returns from the grave—a living corpse. Given what happens at the very end, it is clear that Mr. White's final wish is that Herbert be dead again.

Interpreting Meanings
5. Details are drawn curtains, fire burning brightly, father and son playing chess, mother knitting, whiskey and tumblers and a copper kettle for the guest. *(Answers continue in left-hand column.)*

(Continued from top.)
Details are the cold wet night; the wind; the isolation; the muddy, slushy road.
6. Details are the darkness and cold of the parlor, the unwholesomeness of the paw, the flickering candle, the loud knock at the door, the cold wind rushing in.
7. Answers may vary. Most students will agree that Herbert was chosen as the victim because he had the least faith in the paw. Mr. and Mrs. White also held him dearest, and his death was a suitable punishment for their interference in fate.
He should have said, "I wish for such-and-such but on the condition that nothing else be changed or affected in any way whatsoever."

FURTHER ACTIVITY
The Horror of It All (58-min. film); clips of horror films made for English classes by Wombat Productions.

Responding to the Story

Analyzing the Story

Identifying Facts

1. According to the visitor, what spell was put on the monkey's paw? Why was the spell laid?
2. How is Mr. White's attitude toward the paw different from Herbert's?
3. What is the first wish Mr. White makes? What two things happen after the wish is made?
4. What is Mr. White's second wish? Who suggests it? What happens after the wish is made? What do you guess is Mr. White's third wish?

Interpreting Meanings

SRW p. 79

5. At the beginning of "The Monkey's Paw," Jacobs contrasts the comfortable, secure **setting** inside the White's house with the stormy setting outdoors. List three specific **details** that reflect warmth, light, and happiness at the beginning of the story. List three details that describe the weather outside.
6. List three specific **details** that suggest cold, darkness, and horror at the story's end.
7. In most stories that involve the granting of three wishes, the wishes are foolishly wasted. In a tragic story like "The Monkey's Paw," the wishes bring disaster. Why do you think Herbert White was chosen to be the victim of the first wish? To avoid disaster, how should Mr. White have worded each wish?

Applying Meanings

8. Many people enjoy stories and movies about creatures such as vampires, ghosts, zombies, and ghouls. Tell why you do or don't like such stories. How did you feel about this one?

Writing About the Story

A Creative Response

1. **Extending the Story.** Sergeant Major Morris only hints at what happened when his three wishes were granted. Of the first owner, we hear only that his final wish was for death. In a paragraph, tell what Morris's three wishes might have been and what the previous owner's wishes were.

A Critical Response

SRW p. 87

2. **Writing About the Theme.** Like most stories, horror stories usually reveal a **theme,** or basic idea about people and life. From the following list, choose the theme you think is most important in this story. In a paragraph, tell how the story reveals this theme. Be sure to use details and events from the story to support your opinion.
   a. People should not use supernatural means to interfere with the normal course of their lives.
   b. The love of money is the root of all evil.
   c. We never know how happy we really are until disaster happens.

See Teacher's Manual page 132.

Analyzing Language and Vocabulary

Context Clues

The **context** of a word, or the words and sentences that surround it, can often help you figure out its meaning. Read the following passages from "The Monkey's Paw." Using the context, make an educated guess about the meaning of each italicized word. What more common word might a modern writer have used? Check your guesses in a dictionary.

1. "'. . . of all the beastly, slushy, out-of-the-way places to live in, this is the worst. Pathway's a *bog,* and the road's a torrent.'" (Page 403)
2. ". . . his host got out whiskey and *tumblers.* . . ." (Page 404)
3. "The soldier regarded him in the way that middle age is *wont* to regard presumptuous youth." (Page 404)
4. "'It moved,' he cried. . . . 'It must have been your *fancy,* Father. . . .'" (Page 406)

For answers, see Teacher's Manual page 132.

Reading About the Writer

William Wymark Jacobs (1863–1943) grew up in London, near the Thames River where his father worked on the docks. His first job was at a bank; later he worked for the post office. But Jacobs was a storyteller at heart, and he soon began writing. His early experiences on the docks and the tales he heard from the seamen are reflected in his novels. "The Monkey's Paw" is his most famous short story. It has been made into a one-act play.

PREREADING

1. **BUILDING ON PRIOR KNOWLEDGE.** Ask students what they know about *The Thousand and One Nights (The Arabian Nights).* They may recall hearing or reading some of the tales, or even seeing some of them dramatized on TV. The most familiar characters are Aladdin, Sindbad, and Ali Baba. Ask them what they know about genies.

Approximately six hundred stories make up *The Thousand and One Nights;* they range in length from one-page anecdotes to narratives of more than two hundred pages. The collection includes fairy tales, myths, legends, farces, and romances.

2. **ESTABLISHING A PURPOSE.** Tell students that this is one of the oldest stories they have ever read. Tell them to see if they can think of at least one reason why people liked this story and told it over and over for more than a thousand years.

3. **PREREADING JOURNAL.** Ask students to write three sentences about whether they would choose to be big and strong or small and clever (bright, quick-witted) and why.

Texas Essential Elements/(a) English Language Arts: 1B Purpose and audience; **1C** Synthesize information; **1E** Formal/informal language; **2B** Parts of speech; **3B** Figurative language; **3C** Literary traditions; **4B** Main idea

THE STORY OF THE FISHERMAN

For a detailed lesson plan on this story, see Teacher's Manual, pages 133–135.

from *The Thousand and One Nights*

The following tale is taken from a collection of Indian, Persian, and Arabian folk tales called *The Thousand and One Nights* (also known as *The Arabian Nights*). The collection was first published in 1548. The oldest tales date from the tenth century.

The frame story for this collection is a tale in itself. There was once a king of India who became disillusioned with women because he believed they were all unfaithful. His dislike of women was so intense he would marry a new girl each day and then kill her the next morning. Finally, there were no more unmarried girls left in the land except his
A **advisor's daughter, Scheherazade. The advisor gave his beautiful daughter up to the king reluctantly. But Scheherazade thought up a scheme that would spare her the awful fate of the king's other wives. Her clever strategy was to begin a new tale every night, but to leave off at the most exciting part. The king would then have to wait until the next night to find out what happened. In this way, she passed a thousand and one nights—by which time the king no longer wanted to kill her.**

"The Story of the Fisherman" is one of the oldest and simplest tales in the collection. As you read the tale, think of where Scheherazade would have stopped for the night.

SRW p. 41

There was an aged fisherman who was so poor that he could scarcely earn as much as would maintain himself, his wife, and three children. He went every day to fish betimes[1] in the morning; and imposed it as a law upon himself not to cast his nets above four times a day. He went one morning by moonlight, and, coming to the seaside, undressed himself. Three several times did he cast his net, and have a heavy haul. Yet, to his indescribable disappointment and de-
B spair, the first proved to be an ass, the second a basket full of stones, and the third a mass of mud and shells.

As day now began to appear he said his prayers, for he was a good Mussulman,[2] and commended himself and his needs to his Creator. Having done this, he cast his nets the fourth time, and drew them as formerly, with great difficulty; but, instead of fish, found nothing in them but a vessel of yellow copper, having the impression of a seal upon it. This turn of fortune rejoiced him: "I will sell it," said he, "to the founder, and with the C
money buy a measure of corn." He examined the vessel on all sides, and shook it, to try if its con-

D

Archaic Pronouns. As you read the story, you will notice the use of the personal pronouns *thee* and *thou.* These are called *archaic* words, meaning that they are no longer in common use. This translation kept the pronouns because they add a mythical flavor to the story. A few centuries ago, these pronouns were used when talking to someone very close to the speaker (such as a husband to a wife, or wife to a husband). Or, they were used to talk to someone who was inferior to the speaker, or in a lower social position. Note which character uses these pronouns in "The Story of the Fisherman."

1. **betimes:** early.
2. **Mussulman:** Muslim.

A. Scheherazade (shə·her′ə·zä′d). An illustration of Scheherazade appears on text page 533.

B. Vocabulary
ass: a donkey (probably the carcass of a donkey)

C. Vocabulary
founder: metalworker

D. Character
? What have you learned about the character of the fisherman so far? (He is a poor man who reacts quickly and with great feeling to every situation. He is religious and cares about his family.)

Folk Tale
Like "The Water of Life," this story is a folk tale. It is an ancient tale, originally handed down orally, and it is about a simple fisherman trying to eke out a living.

SUPPLEMENTARY SUPPORT MATERIAL
1. Vocabulary Activity Sheet
2. Reading Check Test blackline master
3. Selection Test (page 157 of Test Book)
4. Reader's Response Journal
5. Workbook (page 121)

DEVELOPING VOCABULARY
The following words appear on a test in the Test Book, page 158. (See also the Vocabulary Activity Sheet.)

despair	potent
founder	appease
ascend	stratagem
hearken	conjure
rebellious	adjuration

A. Reading Aloud Ask three of your best readers to prepare to read this scene aloud in class. You will need a narrator, a fisherman, and a genie. The student who reads the fisherman's words should practice conveying terror, humility, and cunning. The student who reads the genie's words should practice expressing ferocity, arrogance, and finally, desperation.

B. Expansion Traditionally, when a character frees a genie from a bottle, or whatever vessel he has been imprisoned in, the genie, in return for the favor, offers to grant that person a wish, or wishes.

C. Understanding Theme ? Explain in your own words what this sentence means. (Answers will vary but should include the idea that inspiration comes when the need for it is greatest.)

★ **Texas Essential Elements/(c) Reading: 1C** Dictionaries; **3A** Main ideas/details; **3I** Draw conclusions; **4D** Diagrams/graphs

tents made any noise, but heard nothing. This circumstance, with the impression of the seal upon the leaden cover, made him think it enclosed something precious. To try this, he took a knife and opened it. He turned the mouth downward, but nothing came out; which surprised him extremely. He placed it before him, but while he viewed it attentively, there came out a very thick smoke, which obliged him to retire two or three paces back.

The smoke ascended to the clouds, and extending itself along the sea and upon the shore, formed a great mist, which we may well imagine filled the fisherman with astonishment. When the smoke was all out of the vessel, it reunited and became a solid body, of which was formed a genie twice as high as the greatest of giants. At the sight of such a monster, the fisherman would fain[3] have fled, but was so frightened that he could not move.

A The genie regarded the fisherman with a fierce look, and exclaimed in a terrible voice, "Prepare to die, for I will surely kill thee." "Ah!" replied the fisherman, "Why would you kill me? Did I

B not just now set you at liberty, and have you already forgotten my kindness?" "Yes, I remember it," said the genie, "but that shall not save thy life: I have only one favor to grant thee." "And what is that?" asked the fisherman. "It is," answered the genie, "to give thee thy choice, in what manner thou wouldst have me put thee to death." "But wherein have I offended you?" demanded the fisherman. "Is that your reward for the service I have rendered you?" "I cannot treat thee otherwise," said the genie: "and that thou mayest know the reason, hearken to my story."

"I am one of those rebellious spirits that opposed the will of Heaven.

"Solomon, the son of David, commanded me to acknowledge his power, and to submit to his commands: I refused, and told him I would rather expose myself to his resentment than swear fealty[4] as he required. To punish me, he shut me up in this copper vessel; and that I might not break my prison, he himself stamped upon this leaden cover his seal with the great name of God engraven upon it. He then gave the vessel to a genie, with orders to throw me into the sea.

"During the first hundred years of my imprisonment, I swore that if anyone should deliver me before the expiration of that period, I would make him rich. During the second, I made an oath, that I would open all the treasures of the earth to anyone that might set me at liberty. In the third, I promised to make my deliverer a potent monarch, to be always near him in spirit, and to grant him every day three requests, of whatsoever nature they might be. At last, being angry, or rather mad, to find myself a prisoner so long, I swore, that if anyone should deliver me, I would kill him without mercy, and grant him no other favor but to choose the manner of his death; and therefore, since thou hast delivered me today, I give thee that choice."

The fisherman was extremely grieved, not so much for himself, as on account of his three children; and bewailed the misery they must be reduced to by his death. He endeavored to appease[5] the genie, and said, "Alas! Be pleased to take pity on me, in consideration of the service I have done you." "I have told thee already," replied the genie, "it is for that very reason I must kill thee. Do not lose time," interrupted the genie; "all thy reasonings shall not divert me from my purpose: make haste, and tell me what kind of death thou preferest?"

Necessity is the mother of invention. The fisherman bethought himself of a stratagem.[6] "Since C
I must die then," said he to the genie, "I submit to the will of Heaven; but before I choose the manner of my death, I conjure you by the great name which was engraven upon the seal of the prophet Solomon, the son of David, to answer me truly the question I am going to ask you."

The genie, finding himself obliged to a positive answer by this adjuration,[7] trembled; and replied to the fisherman, "Ask what thou wilt, but make haste."

"I wish to know," asked the fisherman, "if you

3. **fain:** gladly.
4. **fealty** (fē′əl·tē): loyalty.

5. **endeavor** (in·dev′ər) **to appease:** to try to calm, pacify.
6. **stratagem** (strat′ə·jem): trick or scheme.
7. **adjuration** (aj′o͞o·rā′shən): command.

READING CHECK TEST

1. The fisherman's first thought is to sell the copper vessel for a measure of corn. *(True)*
2. The genie first appeared in a cloud of smoke, which then forms itself into something recognizable. *(True)*
3. From the first days of his imprisonment, the genie swore to kill whoever freed him. *(False)*
4. The fisherman intimidates the genie by referring to the prophet Solomon, son of David. *(True)*
5. The fisherman at last takes pity on the genie and releases him a second time. *(False)*

CLOSURE

Divide the class into small groups. Ask each group to come up with a definition of "theme" as an element in literature. Also have each group tell about an incident (either true or made up) that would teach the same moral lesson as "The Story of the Fisherman."

Illustration by Edmund Dulac from *The Thousand and One Nights*.

Humanities Connection: Responding to the Fine Art

Edmund Dulac (1882–1953) was a French painter. His watercolors for *The Thousand and One Nights* made him famous. Dulac's genie is a giant, winged half-man, half-monster. His elongated arms, huge hands, and towering legs are a fearsome contrast to the little fisherman, who covers his eyes and falls back in horror.

? How are the fisherman's clothes a contrast to the genie's? (The fisherman's outfit is simple and functional while the genie wears a richly decorated garment and barbaric jewelry.)

Language Connection

The word "genie" comes from the Arabic "jinni," a supernatural being. Many words came into English from Persian or Arabic. You may want to have students look up the derivation of the following English words:
Persian: check, caravan, khaki
Arabic: algebra, coffee, cotton.

ANALYZING THE STORY

Identifying Facts

1. It is made of yellow copper and has the impression of a seal on it.
2. Very thick smoke comes out of the vessel, spreads into a great mist along the shore, and forms itself into a gigantic genie.
3. He will allow him to choose the manner of his own death.
4. First he swears to make his deliverer rich; then he swears to "open all the treasures of the earth" to anyone who sets him free; then he swears to make his deliverer a great monarch, to stay with him, and to grant him three wishes daily, and, finally, he swears to kill whoever frees him, and only to allow him to choose the manner of his own death.
5. He claims not to believe that the genie was actually in the vessel; whereupon the genie gets back in, and the fisherman reseals the vessel.

Interpreting Meanings

6. The genie is gigantic in size; can dissolve himself into a cloud of smoke; can live forever; and has the power to make someone fabulously rich or powerful, and to kill someone in any way whatsoever.

A. Moral Lesson
What do you think the theme of the story is? (Good wins out over evil; cleverness is more powerful than size and strength.) Why do you think so many people enjoyed hearing and telling this story? (They identified with the fisherman; the genie might represent authority or the wealthy.)

B. Humor
What comic device creates humor here? (The fisherman and the genie reverse roles. Now the fisherman has the power, and the genie begs for mercy.)

C. Frame Story
Notice that here the fisherman begins telling the genie a story. In *The Thousand and One Nights* "The Story of the Fisherman" is a frame story inside a frame story. Scheherazade tells the story about the fisherman; the fisherman, in turn, tells several other stories. Eventually the fisherman does release the genie, becomes wealthy, and lives "happily ever after."

were actually in this vessel. Dare you swear it by the name of the great God?" "Yes," replied the genie, "I do swear, by that great name, that I was." "In good faith," answered the fisherman, "I cannot believe you; the vessel is not capable of holding one of your feet, and how should it be possible that your whole body could lie in it?" "Is it possible," replied the genie, "that thou dost not believe me after the solemn oath I have taken?" "Truly not I," said the fisherman; "nor will I believe you, unless you go into the vessel again."

Upon which the body of the genie dissolved and changed itself into smoke, extending as before upon the seashore; and at last, being collected, it began to reenter the vessel, which it continued to do till no part remained out; when immediately the fisherman took the cover of lead, and having speedily replaced it on the vessel, "Genie," cried he, "now it is your turn to beg my favor; but I shall throw you into the sea, whence I took you: A and then I will build a house upon the shore, where I will reside and give notice to all fishermen who come to throw in their nets, to beware of such a wicked genie as thou art, who hast made an oath to kill him that shalt set thee at liberty."

B The genie omitted nothing that he thought likely to prevail with the fisherman: "Open the vessel," said he, "give me my liberty, and I promise to satisfy thee to thy own content." "Thou art a traitor," replied the fisherman; "I should deserve to lose my life, if I were such a fool as to trust thee: Thou wilt not fail to treat me in the same C manner as a certain Grecian king treated the physician Douban. It is a story I have a mind to tell thee, therefore listen to it."

Responding to the Story

Analyzing the Story

Identifying Facts

1. Describe the vessel that the fisherman draws from the sea with the fourth casting of his nets.
2. What happens when he breaks the seal and opens the vessel?
3. What is the one "favor" the genie promises to grant the fisherman?
4. List the different oaths the genie makes during the centuries of his imprisonment.
5. How does the fisherman manage to trick the genie?

Interpreting Meanings

6. The presence of the genie is the supernatural element that makes this story a fairy tale. Describe the genie's supernatural qualities.
7. Why is the genie's last oath to kill whoever rescues him?
8. Do you think this tale has a **moral lesson**? If so, what is it? (Think of the fact that a simple fisherman managed to defeat a powerful genie.)

Applying Meanings

9. After the fisherman recaptures the genie, the genie begs to be released and promises to grant the fisherman his wishes. The fisherman refuses, however, saying he would be a fool to set the genie free again. What would you have done? Would you have stood your ground as the fisherman did? Or would you have been tempted to let him out and perhaps be granted a wish? What other stories do you know of in which wishes are a part of the plot? Do they turn out happily or tragically?

Writing About the Story

A Creative Response

1. **Describing a Character.** As you were reading the story, how did you picture the genie? Was he ugly? Attractive? Wearing jewels? Wearing rags? Write a paragraph describing the genie's appearance.

7. He makes this final oath out of anger; no one has freed him for three hundred years, despite his initially generous vows.
8. The lessons are that size and strength often are no match for wit, that might is not necessarily right, and that it is better to be meek and right than to be strong and wrong.

Applying Meanings
9. Answers will vary, depending on how widely students have read. One story that all the students should mention is "The Monkey's Paw," which ends quite tragically.

Humanities Connection: Book Illustration
A frontispiece is an illustration facing the first page of a book. This frontispiece from the Lane editions of *The Thousand and One Nights* imitates Islamic design elements and reflects Arabic interest in book illumination (decoration with color and design) and handwriting (calligraphy) as art forms. Notice that the natural shapes of leaves, stems, and plants have been stylized to create an elaborate over-all pattern of decorative arabesques. Because the Koran (the Moslem's sacred book) bans the worship of idols, Arab artists did not paint figures on large canvases or sculpt in the round, but wealthy Moslems loved and collected fine books. The Persians developed the art of book illumination to a high level. Persian shahs, or rulers, employed hundreds of court artists to create miniature paintings for manuscripts that became royal treasures.

FURTHER READING FOR TEACHERS
Indris Shah, ed., *World Tales.*
FOR STUDENTS
George Selden, *The Genie of Sutton Place.*
Jean Russell Larson, ed., *Palace in Bagdad: Seven Tales from Arabia.*

A Critical Response

2. **Analyzing Two Fairy Tales.** Although "The Story of the Fisherman" and "The Water of Life" are very different stories, they have similarities. Write two paragraphs in which you show how, despite their plot and character differences, they are both genuine fairy tales. Before you begin writing, it might help to fill out the following chart.

Fairy Tale Elements	"The Water of Life"	"The Story of the Fisherman"
The supernatural		
Good triumphing over evil		
Tricks played on a character		
Moral lesson		
Happy ending		

See Teacher's Manual page 134.

Analyzing Language and Vocabulary

Archaic Pronouns

The archaic, or old-fashioned, personal pronouns *thee, thou, thy,* and *thine* fell out of use in the eighteenth century. But they were used commonly when these tales were written. These pronouns were used in two ways: (1) when speaking to someone familiar or intimate with the speaker, or (2) when addressing an inferior, or someone in a lower position than the speaker. In Shakespeare's time, these pronouns could be used to insult. People would deliberately use *thee* and *thou* to show their superiority to others.

In "The Story of the Fisherman," it is the genie who addresses the fisherman as *thee* and *thou.* The fisherman, being a simple mortal, is obviously the genie's inferior.

The two archaic forms of *you* (*thou* and *thee*) are used in the same way as we use *I* and *me. Thou* is the subject of the verb, and *thee* is the object of the verb. The possessive form *thy* is used as we use *your,* and the form *thine* is used the way we use *yours.*

Fill in the blanks in the following sentences using *thee, thou, thy,* or *thine.* Notice the archaic verb forms that are used with these pronouns.

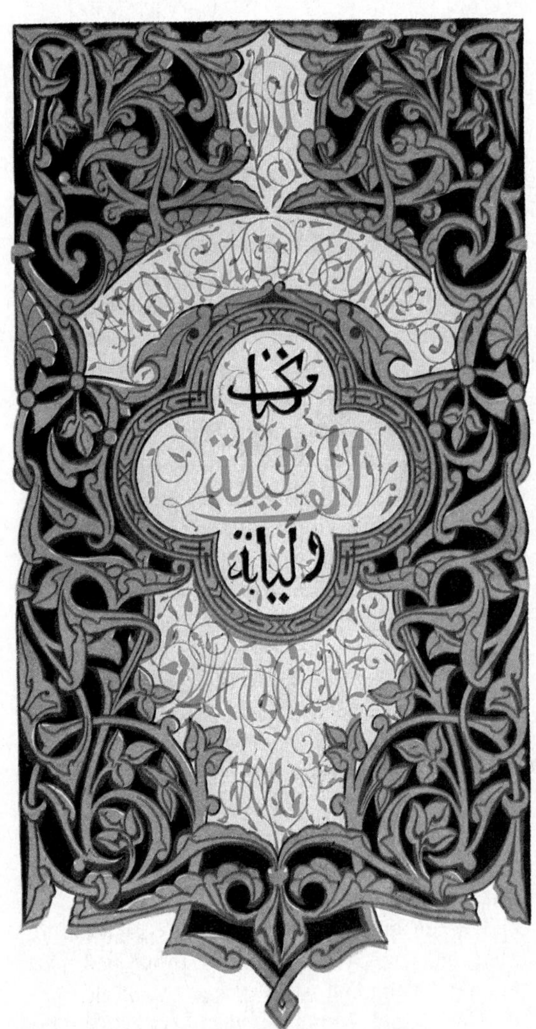

Frontispiece for *The Thousand and One Nights.*

1. _______ hast heard one of the stories from *The Thousand and One Nights.*
2. The genie would like to grant _______ one wish.
3. _______ hast given the book to _______ friend.
4. How many fairy tales hast _______ heard when _______ wast young?
5. I will tell _______ a story if _______ homework is done.

Rewrite the sentences using the pronoun *you* and modern verb forms. Does *you* have a different form when it is used as a subject or an object (like *thou* and *thee*)?

For answers, see Teacher's Manual page 135.

PREREADING

1. **BUILDING ON PRIOR KNOWLEDGE.** Before students read, find out how much experience they've had with computers. If your school has computers, review the educational purposes for which they are used. In this 1951 story, Asimov was quite daring to suggest that by 2155 every home would own a teaching machine. In 1951 few families even owned a TV. Computers were huge pieces of equipment housed in refrigerated laboratories. It was not until the early 1970s, with the development of the silicon chip, that the computer industry began to expand at a tremendous rate. Each tiny chip could be etched with thousands of electronic circuits, so computers could be made much smaller and produced less expensively than ever before. Today computers have become so common that we take them for granted in homes, schools, cars, stores, offices—even in games and toys.

2. **ESTABLISHING A PURPOSE.** The headnote sets a good purpose for reading the story.

3. **PREREADING JOURNAL.** Tell students that in the late 1970's, some people predicted that computers would soon replace textbooks, pencils, paper, perhaps even teachers. Have students write five sentences telling whether they think this will ever come to pass and why.

A. Irony
There are ironic contrasts throughout the story between the way the children imagine the past to have been—and the way it was (or is). **?** What is ironic about Tommy's comment that people must have thrown books away when they were through with them? (People today keep favorite books to reread. Tommy would have been astounded at the idea of libraries.) What is ironic about his idea that a TV screen is better than a book because it lasts longer? (The words on a TV screen go by in a flash, while a book can last for many years.)

★ **Texas Essential Elements/(a) English Language Arts: 1B** Purpose and audience; **4B** Main idea; **4G** Fact/nonfact. **(c) Reading: 1A** Context clues; **1B** Structural analysis; **3A** Main ideas/details

THE FUN THEY HAD

Isaac Asimov

Science fiction is a kind of fantasy that usually concerns changes that science may bring about in the future. Many science fiction stories take you to an imaginary world, such as another planet, the future on Earth, or the distant past. But some SF stories take place in such present settings as the subway system in New York City.

This story was written in 1951, many years before computers became common teaching instruments in schools and at home. As you read, think about how the writer feels about these "mechanical teachers." Have any of his predictions come true?

For a detailed lesson plan on this story, see Teacher's Manual, pages 135–137. A biography of Isaac Asimov appears on text page 422.

Margie even wrote about it that night in her diary. On the page headed May 17, 2155, she wrote, "Today Tommy found a real book!"

It was a very old book. Margie's grandfather once said that when he was a little boy *his* grandfather told him that there was a time when all stories were printed on paper.

They turned the pages, which were yellow and crinkly, and it was awfully funny to read words that stood still instead of moving the way they were supposed to—on a screen, you know. And then, when they turned back to the page before, it had the same words on it that it had had when they read it the first time.

A "Gee," said Tommy, "what a waste. When you're through with the book, you just throw it away, I guess. Our television screen must have had a million books on it and it's good for plenty more. I wouldn't throw *it* away."

"Same with mine," said Margie. She was eleven and hadn't seen as many telebooks as Tommy had. He was thirteen.

She said, "Where did you find it?"

"In my house." He pointed without looking, because he was busy reading. "In the attic."

"What's it about?"

"School."

Margie was scornful. "School? What's there to write about school? I hate school." Margie always hated school, but now she hated it more than ever. The mechanical teacher had been giving her test after test in geography and she had been doing worse and worse until her mother had shaken her head sorrowfully and sent for the County Inspector.

He was a round little man with a red face and a whole box of tools with dials and wires. He smiled at her and gave her an apple, then took the teacher apart. Margie had hoped he wouldn't know how to put it together again, but he knew how all right and, after an hour or so, there it was again, large and ugly with a big screen on which all the lessons were shown and the questions were asked. That wasn't so bad. The part she hated most was the slot where she had to put homework and test papers. She always had to write them out in a punch code they made her learn when she was six years old, and the mechanical teacher calculated the mark in no time.

The inspector had smiled after he was finished and patted her head. He said to her mother, "It's not the little girl's fault, Mrs. Jones. I think the

Words from Greek. The root *tele-* comes from a Greek word meaning "far off" or "far away." *Telebook* is a word that Asimov made up for a book shown on television. In what way is a book shown on television a "faraway" book? Do we have another name for such "books" today?

Supplementary Support Material

1. Vocabulary Activity Sheet
2. Reading Check Test blackline master
3. Selection Test (page 159 of Test Book)
4. Author photograph on *A Gallery of Authors* poster
5. Reader's Response Journal
6. Workbook (page 123)

Developing Vocabulary

The following words appear on a test in the Test Book, page 160. (See also the Vocabulary Activity Sheet.)

crinkly	geared
county	progress
code	loftily
calculate	dispute
sector	nonchalantly

Technological Background

The artist has drawn a teaching machine that reflects Asimov's 1951 idea of what a computer might become by the year 2155. Like other computers in 1951, this one is a mainframe; that is, the parts—wire, gears, dials, and a circuit board—are mounted on frames in a cabinet. Asimov could not have imagined that circuits eventually would be reduced 250 times to fit on a chip so tiny that it could pass through the eye of a needle. Information used to be stored as patterns of holes on cards or tape. (That is why Margie had to write out her papers in punch code.) Now computers store information on magnetic tape, floppy discs, and hard discs. Asimov may have been one of the first to suggest that information could be displayed on a video screen. (Science fiction writers come up with ideas for some inventions long before they can be produced commercially.)

Drawing a Futuristic Setting

Tell students that a person's ideas about the future often reflect how they feel about present-day life. For example, Asimov's story might reflect his concern over the growing dependence on machines. Have students draw a room in their futuristic house that reflects how they feel about a certain modern-day subject—for example, fast food, video games, cars.

Texas Essential Elements/(c) Reading (continued): 3E Fact/fictional details; **3G** Compare/contrast; **3I** Draw conclusions

Reading Check Test

1. Margie and Tommy are sister and brother. *(False)*
2. Margie's teacher is a kind of robot, with a big screen and a slot in which to insert homework. *(True)*
3. Tommy's book is a collection of sonnets by Shakespeare. *(False)*
4. At first Margie doesn't believe that an ordinary man can be a teacher. *(True)*
5. In the end, she thinks longingly about the fun children once had going to school. *(True)*

Closure

Divide the class into pairs of students. Ask each pair to find one element of fantasy in "The Fun They Had." Then have each pair give a specific example of something—real or fantastic—that would create a better life in the future than people have today. Each pair should identify its example as real or fantastic.

A. Character

How does Tommy relate to Margie? (Patronizing; he calls her "stupid" and pretends to know much more than she.) Why do you think he behaves this way? (He is showing off, as most children do, since he knows more about these old schools than Margie does.)

B. Theme

What do you think Asimov values most highly about today's schools? (Teachers and students relating to one another; human interaction and cooperation) What problems does he foresee in machine-taught learning? (Isolation; boredom; valuing information more than people)

C. Responding

Did this story make you value school more than you did before you read it?

geography sector was geared a little too quick. Those things happen sometimes. I've slowed it up to an average ten-year level. Actually, the overall pattern of her progress is quite satisfactory." And he patted Margie's head again.

Margie was disappointed. She had been hoping they would take the teacher away altogether. They had once taken Tommy's teacher away for nearly a month because the history sector had blanked out completely.

So she said to Tommy, "Why would anyone write about school?"

A Tommy looked at her with very superior eyes. "Because it's not our kind of school, stupid. This is the old kind of school that they had hundreds and hundreds of years ago." He added loftily, pronouncing the word carefully, "*Centuries* ago."

Margie was hurt. "Well, I don't know what kind of school they had all that time ago." She read the book over his shoulder for a while, then said, "Anyway, they had a teacher."

"Sure they had a teacher, but it wasn't a *regular* teacher. It was a man."

"A man? How could a man be a teacher?"

"Well, he just told the boys and girls things and gave them homework and asked them questions."

"A man isn't smart enough."

"Sure he is. My father knows as much as my teacher."

"He can't. A man can't know as much as a teacher."

"He knows almost as much I betcha."

Margie wasn't prepared to dispute that. She said, "I wouldn't want a strange man in my house to teach me."

Tommy screamed with laughter. "You don't know much, Margie. The teachers didn't live in the house. They had a special building and all the kids went there."

"And all the kids learned the same thing?"

"Sure, if they were the same age."

"But my mother says a teacher has to be adjusted to fit the mind of each boy and girl it teaches and that each kid has to be taught differently."

"Just the same, they didn't do it that way then. If you don't like it, you don't have to read the book."

"I didn't say I didn't like it," Margie said quickly. She wanted to read about those funny schools.

They weren't even half finished when Margie's mother called, "Margie! School!"

Margie looked up. "Not yet, mamma."

"Now," said Mrs. Jones. "And it's probably time for Tommy, too."

Margie said to Tommy, "Can I read the book some more with you after school?"

"Maybe," he said, nonchalantly. He walked away whistling, the dusty old book tucked beneath his arm.

Margie went into the schoolroom. It was right next to her bedroom, and the mechanical teacher was on and waiting for her. It was always on at the same time every day except Saturday and Sunday, because her mother said little girls learned better if they learned at regular hours.

The screen was lit up, and it said: "Today's arithmetic lesson is on the addition of proper fractions. Please insert yesterday's homework in the proper slot."

Margie did so with a sigh. She was thinking about the old schools they had when her grandfather's grandfather was a little boy. All the kids from the whole neighborhood came, laughing and shouting in the schoolyard, sitting together in the schoolroom, going home together at the end of the day. They learned the same things so they could help one another on the homework and talk about it. B

And the teachers were people. . . .

The mechanical teacher was flashing on the screen: "When we add the fractions 1/2 and 1/4 . . ."

Margie was thinking about how the kids must have loved it in the old days. She was thinking about the fun they had. C

ANALYZING THE STORY

Identifying Facts

1. He considers individual volumes to be "a waste"; he points out that his television screen can produce "a million books." Yet he reads the old book with great interest, and later carries it away tucked under his arm.

2. Margie's teacher is a "mechanical teacher," a kind of robot. She goes to school in her own house.

3. She hates school—the big screen with questions and lessons flashing across it, the punch code she must use, the slot in which she must place her homework, the coldness and isolation of the whole experience.

4. The title comes at the very end, and refers to the fun that children once had attending school together

Interpreting Meanings

5. Asimov implies that education is becoming cold and mechanistic (especially with its emphasis on computers), that it happens too quickly and lacks the joy of interaction with peers and caring adults. Children, he fears, no longer *enjoy* learning and reading.

6. Answers will vary slightly, but students should understand that the message has to do with the pleasures of learning; reading should be appreciated as a joyful experience, and students should recognize the fun of school.

7. Most students will feel some irony by the end of the story, either because they don't consider school to be very much fun or because they acknowledge that for a child like Margie, today's educational system *would* seem like a lot of fun.

8. Time and science will not change how children and parents relate to one another; how reluctant children are to attend school; and how problematic technology, however advanced, can be.

Applying Meanings

9. Most students will say that they prefer attending their own school, because they are with friends, teachers are people, and learning involves interaction with others.

10. Answers may vary. Some students will agree that *(Answers continue on page 422.)*

Responding to the Story

Analyzing the Story

Identifying Facts

1. Why does Tommy say he prefers telebooks to the old book he has found? List two actions that show that he actually likes the old book a great deal.
2. What kind of teacher does Margie have? Where does Margie go to school?
3. How does Margie feel about the way she is taught?
4. Where do you learn what the title of the story means?

Interpreting Meanings

5. Although Asimov's story is humorous, he does make some important points about education. Judging from this story, how do you think Asimov feels about education today? Is there any aspect of modern-day teaching that seems to worry him? Explain.
6. How would you state the **message** or main idea in this story? What do you think of the message?
7. When a situation turns out to be different from what a character thinks it should be, we get a sense of **irony.** If someone in a book written a hundred years ago says, "People will never set foot on the moon because it would take too long to get there," that is ironic. We know that people have gotten to the moon, and probably will go even farther. Do you feel any irony when you read the last paragraph of "The Fun They Had"? SRW p. 57
8. In Asimov's future world, certain things have changed. Other things seem to be exactly the same as they are today. List three things that, according to Asimov, time and science will not change.

Applying Meanings

9. Would you rather go to Margie's school or to your own school? Give at least three reasons for your answer.
10. Do you agree that books as you know them may become rare in the distant future? Tell why you agree or disagree. Would you like to live in a world without books?

Writing About the Story

A Creative Response

1. **Writing About the Future.** What do *you* think life will be like in the year 2155? Imagine that you are a child living in that year. Write a journal entry that describes a normal day in your life—your school, your friends, your after-school activities. Will your school be like Margie's and Tommy's, or will it be different?

A Critical Response

2. **Analyzing the Fantasy.** All the characters and objects in "The Fun They Had" are realistic. Why, then, is this story still considered a fantasy? In two paragraphs, point out the fantastic and realistic elements in the story. Be sure to develop your ideas with examples from the story.

See Teacher's Manual page 137.

Analyzing Language and Vocabulary

A Greek Root

Look at the list of words below. Since they all begin with the Greek root *tele,* you know that the meaning of each of them involves something far away. In the sentences that follow, use context clues to help you fill in the blank with the correct word from the list.

telegram telecast telescope
telephone telephoto

1. A photographer who wants to take a picture of faraway scenes uses a ______ lens.
2. If you use a ______, you may be able to see stars that are far off.
3. We made a long-distance ______ call to my grandfather last night.
4. Even though it's late to send Kathleen a gift, you could send her a ______ wishing her "Happy Birthday."
5. Did you stay up to watch the ______ of the President's speech?

Now make up your own word using the root *tele-*. Write a sentence using your new word. Provide context clues in the sentence to help your readers understand the meaning of your word.

For answers, see Teacher's Manual page 137.

(Answers begin on page 421.)
books will be phased out, because people don't seem to enjoy reading any more; others will disagree, arguing that there will always be those who prefer reading a book to staring at a television screen.

Additional Writing Assignment
Imagine that you have traveled by time machine to the place and time of your choice, either in the past or in the future. Write a postcard from that place telling relatives where you are and why you chose to go there for a week.

A. Vocabulary
conventions: rules; ways of doing things

B. Irony
? What does Asimov mean when he says "Writing . . . does have one or two insignificant flaws"? How "insignificant" is "the fact that a writer almost never can make a living at it"? (It is very significant.) Why is this statement ironic? (He means the opposite.)

FURTHER READING FOR TEACHERS
Reginald Bretnor, ed., *Modern Science Fiction: Its Meaning and Its Future.*
FOR STUDENTS
Stephen Manes, *The Boy Who Turned Into a TV Set.*

Reading About the Writer

Isaac Asimov (1920–) was born in Russia and came to the United States with his parents when he was three years old. He earned a Ph.D from Columbia University and has taught at the Boston University School of Medicine. He has published over two hundred books, as well as many short stories and scholarly articles—*The New York Times* called him "a writing machine." He submitted his first story to a science fiction magazine when he was only fourteen. The story was rejected, but the editor encouraged Asimov and helped him improve his writing. This pattern was to continue for several years, with the editor guiding the young writer throughout his early career. In addition to his novels and stories, Asimov has written a two-volumes autobiography. His nonfiction titles include *Words from the Myths* and *Words of Science.*

Asimov talks about "The Fun They Had" in the first volume of his autobiography. A friend of his asked him to write a short story for young readers for a newspaper. Asimov says: "I thought about it and decided to write a little story about school. What could interest children more? It would be about a school of the future, by way of teaching machines, with children longing for the good old days when there were old-fashioned schools that children loved. I thought the kids would get a bang out of the irony." He wrote the story at one sitting and earned ten dollars for it.

Focusing on Background

A Writer's Hints

Asimov wrote these suggestions for future writers:

"Every once in a short while I get a letter from some eager young would-be writer asking me for some 'hints' on the art of writing science fiction.

"The feeling I have is that my correspondents think there is some magic formula jealously guarded by the professionals, but that since I'm such a nice guy I will spill the beans if properly approached.

"Alas, there's no such thing, no magic formula, no secret tricks, no hidden short-cuts.

"I'm sorry to have to tell you that it's a matter of hard work over a long period of time. If you know of any exceptions to this, that's exactly what they are—exceptions.

"There are, however, some general principles that could be useful, to my way of thinking, and here they are:

"(1) *You have to prepare for a career as a successful science fiction writer—as you would for any other highly specialized calling.* . . . The basic tool for any writer is the English language . . . Take it from an old war-horse, if your spelling and grammar are rotten, you won't be writing a great and gorgeous story. . . . For a science fiction writing career, it is not enough to know the English language; you also have to know science. . . . You will have to be a diligent reader of science fiction itself to learn the conventions and the tricks of the trade . . . A

"(2) *You have to work at the job.* The final bit of schooling is writing itself. . . . Write from the very beginning, then, and keep on writing.

"(3) *You have to be patient.* Since writing is itself a schooling, you can't very well expect to sell the first story you write (Yes, I know Bob Heinlein[1] did it, but he was Bob Heinlein. You are only you.) . . . If each story you write is one more step in your literary education, a rejection shouldn't matter. . . . But what if you write and write and write and you don't seem to be getting any better and all you collect are printed rejection slips? Once again, it may be that you are not a writer and will have to settle for a lesser post such as that of Chief Justice of the Supreme Court.

"(4) *You have to be reasonable.* Writing is the most wonderful and satisfying task in the world, but it does have one or two insignificant flaws. Among those flaws is the fact that a writer can almost never make a living at it. . . . So while you're trying to be B a writer, make sure you find another way of making a decent living—and don't quit your job after you make your first sale."

—Isaac Asimov

1. **Bob Heinlein:** Robert Heinlein is a noted SF writer.

PREREADING

1. **BUILDING ON PRIOR KNOWLEDGE.** Before students read, you might want to present the following information as though it appeared under a satellite picture of Mars in a science museum. How many facts does Bradbury stick to? Does he contradict any?

Mars is the fourth planet in distance from the sun. Mars is a little more than half the size of Earth; its gravity is weaker than Earth's. There is so little oxygen on Mars that humans and animals could not survive there without special equipment. Mars is called the red planet because red dust covers its surface. Martian sky ranges from pink tones to purple depending on how much dust is in the air. Scientists believe that rain fell on Mars long ago. There may be small amounts of water but none of it flows over the ground; there is little water in its atmosphere. Huge dust storms develop because of the extremely strong Martian winds. The wind has eroded valleys and ridges; one great valley is four times deeper than the Grand Canyon.

2. **ESTABLISHING A PURPOSE.** As you read, look for details that help you see and feel the setting of the story. What mood does the setting create?

★ **Texas Essential Elements/(a) English Language Arts: 1B** Purpose and audience; **3A** Plot/character; **3B** Figurative language; **4B** Main idea; **4D** Cause/effect. **(c) Reading: 1C** Dictionaries

THE NAMING OF NAMES

Ray Bradbury

Long before the first space probes, Ray Bradbury began to weave fantasies about the planet Mars. "The Naming of Names," like all of his fiction, is not concerned with technology. Bradbury's Martian tales are really fantasies. They seem real to you because they are about real human beings and their problems—even though they take place in fantastic settings.

You won't recognize Mars in this story. The setting has been imagined by Bradbury. But if you're like many readers, you'll find that this Mars stays in your memory. It will become even more real than the actual "red planet" that has been probed and photographed. Read the first paragraph and stop. How do you know right away that this story will be a fantasy?

For a detailed lesson plan on this story, see Teacher's Manual pages 138–140. A biography of Ray Bradbury appears on text page 435.

A The rocket metal cooled in the meadow winds. Its lid gave a bulging *pop*. From its clock interior stepped a man, a woman, and three children. The other passengers whispered away across the Martian meadow, leaving the man alone among his family.

The man felt his hair flutter and the tissues of his body draw tight as if he were standing at the center of a vacuum. His wife, before him, seemed almost to whirl away in smoke. The children, small seeds, might at any instant be sown to all the Martian climes.[1]

B The children looked up at him, as people look to the sun, to tell what time of their life it is. His face was cold.

"What's wrong?" asked his wife.

"Let's get back on the rocket."

"Go back to Earth?"

"Yes! Listen!"

The wind blew as if to flake away their identities. At any moment that Martian air might draw his soul from him, as marrow comes from a white bone. He felt submerged in a chemical that could C dissolve his intellect and burn away his past.

They looked at Martian hills that time had worn with a crushing pressure of years. They saw the old cities, lost like thin children in their meadows, lying like children's delicate bones among the blowing lakes of grass.

"Chin up, Harry," said his wife. "It's too late. We've come at least thirty-five million miles or more." D

The children with their dandelion hair hollered at the deep dome of Martian sky. There was no answer but the racing hiss of wind through the stiff grass.

He picked up the luggage in his cold hands. "Here we go," he said—a man standing on the edge of a sea, ready to wade in and be drowned.

They walked into town.

Their name was Bittering. Harry and his wife Cora, Tom, Laura, and David. They built a small

Metamorphosis. When you talk about this story, you'll have to use the word metamorphosis. *Metamorphosis* means a "transformation—a marvelous change in appearance or form." In ancient myths and fairy tales, you might already have read about such metamorphoses. A toad changes into a prince, for example, or a girl changes into a tree. Like those old stories, this story is about marvelous transformations which change people from one form to another. Not only people change—in this fantasy setting, *everything* is subject to a kind of magic.

1. **climes:** regions.

A. Science Fiction
? How do you know this story is science fiction? (Future setting; Mars; interplanetary travel by rocket)

B. Interpreting
? What does this statement mean? (Children often look to adults to find out how they should react in an unknown situation.)

C. Point of View
? What is the point of view of this story—whose thoughts and feelings does the author emphasize? (Third person; Mr. Bittering's)

D. Mood
? What details establish a mood of mystery? ("Whispered away"; "almost to whirl away in smoke"; "that Martian air might draw his soul from him"; "lost like thin children"; "lying like children's delicate bones"; "a man standing on the edge of a sea")

Supplementary Support Material

1. Vocabulary Activity Sheet
2. Reading Check Test blackline master
3. Selection Test (page 161 of Test Book)
4. Author photograph on *A Gallery of Authors* poster
5. Reader's Response Journal
6. Workbook (page 125)

Developing Vocabulary

The following words appear on a test in the Test Book, page 162. (See also the Vocabulary Activity Sheet.)

vacuum	archeology
amiss	reluctant
convivial	indifferent
anachronism	villa
subtle	dwindled

A. Conflict

? Why does Mr. Bittering want to return to Earth? (He fears Mars; he fears that Mars may change him.) What conflict involving Mr. Bittering is basic to the story? (Mr. Bittering vs. Mars, or his need to stay vs. his desire to go home)

B. Stating a Message

? From Mrs. Bittering's statement, what is Bradbury criticizing about present-day life? (Nuclear war)

C. Foreshadowing

? What details in David's answer give clues about what happens later? ("Maybe there're Martians around we don't see"; ". . . I think I see things moving around those towns"; "I wonder if . . . Martians mind us living here . . . if they won't do something to us.")

white cottage and ate good breakfasts there, but the fear was never gone. It lay with Mr. Bittering and Mrs. Bittering, a third unbidden partner at every midnight talk, at every dawn awakening.

A "I feel like a salt crystal," he often said, "in a mountain stream, being washed away. We don't belong here. We're Earth people. This is Mars. It was meant for Martians. For heaven's sake, Cora, let's buy tickets for home!"

B But she only shook her head. "One day the atom bomb will fix Earth. Then we'll be safe here."

"Safe and insane!"

Tick-tock, seven o'clock sang the voice-clock; *time to get up*. And they did.

Something made him check everything each morning—warm hearth, potted blood-geraniums—precisely as if he expected something to be amiss. The morning paper was toast-warm from the 6:00 A.M. Earth rocket. He broke its seal and tilted it at his breakfast place. He forced himself to be convivial.

"Colonial days all over again," he declared. "Why, in another year there'll be a million Earthmen on Mars. Big cities, everything! They said we'd fail. Said the Martians would resent our invasion. But did we find any Martians? Not a living soul! Oh, we found their empty cities, but no one in them. Right?"

A river of wind submerged the house. When the windows ceased rattling, Mr. Bittering swallowed and looked at the children.

C "I don't know," said David. "Maybe there're Martians around we don't see. Sometimes nights I think I hear 'em. I hear the wind. The sand hits my window. I get scared. And I see those towns way up in the mountains where the Martians lived a long time ago. And I think I see things moving around those towns, Papa. And I wonder if those Martians *mind* us living here. I wonder if they won't do something to us for coming here."

"Nonsense!" Mr. Bittering looked out the windows. "We're clean, decent people." He looked at his children. "All dead cities have some kind of ghosts in them. Memories, I mean." He stared at the hills. "You see a staircase and you wonder what Martians looked like climbing it. You see Martian paintings and you wonder what the

Discussing the Illustration

The illustrator has used a watercolor technique and soft colors to relate the art to an important idea in the story: that Mars is changing the Earth people into Martians. Notice that the Bitterings seem to be merging with the background. There is no definite line between the children's faces, for instance, and the surrounding walls. To discuss the illustration, you may want to ask some of the following questions:

? What is happening in this illustration? How would you describe the expression on each of the faces that you can see? What do you think Laura might be thinking about? Suppose that you didn't know that this illustration was for a story about Mars; what might make you realize that the setting is somehow alien and mysterious? What mood or feeling does the illustration give you?

A. Reading Aloud
You may want to ask six students to prepare to read this scene aloud (down to " 'We know,' they said.") You will need a narrator, Laura, Mrs. Bittering, Mr. Bittering, and the two boys.

B. Plot
? How does the war on Earth suddenly affect Mars? (The rockets have been blown up so Mars will be cut off from Earth for at least five years.)

C. Metaphor
A metaphor compares two different things without using words such as "like" or "as"; for example, in the metaphor "the rockets had spun a silver web across space" the author compares metal rockets to spiders, and the rockets' frequent trips back and forth between Earth and Mars to the spiders' silver web.
? What metaphors does Bradbury use in this paragraph? ("Jigsaw heaps"; "unsnaked wire"; "cinnamon dust"; "wine airs"; "harvested storage")

D. Simile
? What is the one simile (a direct comparison that does use "as" or "like") in this paragraph? ("Baked like gingerbread shapes")

★ **Texas Essential Elements/(c) Reading** (continued): **3A** Main ideas/details; **3C** Cause/effect; **3I** Draw conclusions

painter was like. You make a little ghost in your mind, a memory. It's quite natural. Imagination." He stopped. "You haven't been prowling up in those ruins, have you?"

"No, Papa." David looked at his shoes.

"See that you stay away from them. Pass the jam."

"Just the same," said little David. "I bet something happens."

A Something happened that afternoon.

Laura stumbled through the settlement, crying. She dashed blindly onto the porch.

"Mother, Father—the war, Earth!" she sobbed. "A radio flash just came. Atom bombs B hit New York! All the space rockets blown up! No more rockets to Mars, ever!"

"Oh, Harry!" The mother held onto her husband and daughter.

"Are you sure, Laura?" asked the father quietly.

Laura wept. "We're stranded on Mars, forever and ever!"

For a long time there was only the sound of the wind in the late afternoon.

Alone, thought Bittering. *Only a thousand of us here. No way back. No way. No way.* Sweat poured from his face and his hands and his body; he was drenched in the hotness of his fear. He wanted to strike Laura, cry, "No, you're lying! The rockets will come back!" Instead, he stroked Laura's head against him and said, "The rockets will get through, someday."

"In five years maybe. It takes that long to build one. Father, Father, what will we do!"

"Go about our business, of course. Raise crops and children. Wait. Keep things going until the war ends and the rockets come again."

The two boys stepped out onto the porch.

"Children," he said, sitting there, looking beyond them, "I've something to tell you."

"We know," they said.

Bittering wandered into the garden to stand alone in his fear. C As long as the rockets had spun a silver web across space, he had been able to accept Mars. For he had always told himself: *Tomorrow, if I want, I can buy a ticket and go back to Earth.*

But now: The web gone, the rockets lying in jigsaw heaps of molten girder[2] and unsnaked wire. Earth people left to the strangeness of Mars, the cinnamon dusts and wine airs, to be baked like gingerbread shapes in Martian summers, put into harvested storage by Martian winters. D What would happen to him, the others? This was the moment Mars had waited for. Now it would eat them.

He got down on his knees in the flower bed, a spade in his nervous hands. *Work,* he thought, *work and forget.*

He glanced up from the garden to the Martian mountains. He thought of the proud old Martian names that had once been on those peaks. Earthmen, dropping from the sky, had gazed upon hills, rivers, Martian seas left nameless in spite of names. Once Martians had built cities, named cities; climbed mountains, named mountains; sailed seas, named seas. Mountains melted, seas drained, cities tumbled. In spite of this, the Earthmen had felt a silent guilt at putting new names to these ancient hills and valleys.

Nevertheless, man lives by symbol and label. The names were given.

Mr. Bittering felt very alone in his garden under the Martian sun, an anachronism[3] bent here, planting Earth flowers in a wild soil.

Think. Keep thinking. Different things. Keep your mind free of Earth, the atom war, the lost rockets.

He perspired. He glanced about. No one watching. He removed his tie. *Pretty bold,* he thought. *First your coat off, now your tie.* He hung it neatly on a peach tree he had imported as a sapling from Massachusetts.

He returned to his philosophy of names and mountains. The Earthmen had changed names. Now there were Hormel Valleys, Roosevelt Seas, Ford Hills, Vanderbilt Plateaus, Rockefeller Rivers, on Mars. It wasn't right. The American settlers had shown wisdom, using old Indian prairie names: Wisconsin, Minnesota, Idaho, Ohio, Utah,

2. **molten girder:** *girders* are large metal beams that, here, support the framework of the rockets. *Molten* means that they've melted.
3. **anachronism** (ə·nak'rə·niz'm): something that is out of its proper time in history.

The Naming of a Planet
The earliest astronomers, who wrote about the fourth planet three thousand years ago, were the Babylonians. Noting its red color, they called the planet "Nergal" for their god of death. The Greeks called the planet "Ares" and the Romans changed the name to "Mars." Both Ares and Mars are essentially the same god, the god of war. (See pages 475–476 for a description of Ares.) The two small moons of Mars are Deimon (terror) and Phobos (fear), the horses that pulled Mars's chariot.

A. Theme
? To what group does Mr. Bittering compare the Martians? (The Indians) In what ways does he think that the Martians were like the Indians? (Both had "named" their hills, valleys, and mountains; settlers came uninvited into their lands; the Indians tried to push back the invaders. Mr. Bittering worries that a similar situation may happen on Mars.)

A
B
Milwaukee, Waukegan, Osseo. The old names, the old meanings.

Staring at the mountains wildly, he thought: *Are you up there? All the dead ones, you Martians? Well, here we are, alone, cut off! Come down, move us out! We're helpless!*

The wind blew a shower of peach blossoms.

He put out his sun-browned hand, gave a small cry. He touched the blossoms, picked them up. He turned them; he touched them again and again. Then he shouted for his wife.

"Cora!"

She appeared at a window. He ran to her.

"Cora, these blossoms!"

She handled them.

"Do you see? They're different, they've changed! They're not peach blossoms anymore!"

"Look all right to me," she said.

"They're not. They're *wrong!* I can't tell how. An extra petal, a leaf, something; the color, the smell!"

The children ran out in time to see their father hurrying about the garden, pulling up radishes, onions, and carrots from their beds.

"Cora, come look!"

They handled the onions, the radishes, the carrots among them.

"Do these look like carrots?"

"Yes. . . . No." She hesitated. "I don't know."

"They've changed."

"Perhaps."

"You know they have! Onions but not onions, carrots but not carrots. Taste: the same but different. Smell: not like it used to be." He felt his heart pounding, and he was afraid. He dug his fingers into the earth. "Cora, what's happening? What is it? We've got to get away from this." He ran across the garden. Each tree felt his touch. "The roses. The roses. They're turning green."

C

And they stood looking at the green roses.

And two days later. Tom came running. "Come see the cow. I was milking her and I saw it. Come on!"

They stood in the shed and looked at their one cow.

It was growing a third horn.

And the lawn in front of their house very quietly and slowly was coloring itself like spring violets. Seed from Earth, but growing up a soft purple.

"We must get away," said Bittering. "We'll eat this stuff and then we'll change—who knows to what. I can't let it happen. There's only one thing to do. Burn this food."

"It's not poisoned."

"But it is. Subtly, very subtly. A little bit. A very little bit. We mustn't touch it."

He looked with dismay at their house. "Even the house. The wind's done something to it. The air's burned it. The fog at night. The boards, all warped out of shape. It's not an Earthman's house anymore."

"Oh, your imagination!"

He put on his coat and tie. "I'm going into town. We've got to do something now. I'll be back."

"Wait, Harry!" his wife cried.

But he was gone.

In town, on the shadowy steps of the grocery store, the men sat with their hands on their knees, conversing with great leisure and ease.

Mr. Bittering wanted to fire a pistol in the air.

D

What are you doing, you fools! he thought. *Sitting here! You've heard the news—we're stranded on this planet. Well, move! Aren't you frightened? Aren't you afraid? What are you going to do?*

"Hello, Harry," said everyone.

"Look," he said to them. "You did hear the news, the other day, didn't you?"

They nodded and laughed. "Sure. Sure, Harry."

"What are you going to do about it?"

"Do, Harry, do? What *can* we do?"

"Build a rocket! That's what!"

"A rocket, Harry? To go back to all that trouble? Oh, Harry!"

"But you *must* want to go back. Have you noticed the peach blossoms, the onions, the grass?"

"Why, yes, Harry, seems we did," said one of the men.

"Doesn't it scare you?"

"Can't recall that it did, much, Harry."

"Idiots!"

B. Making Inferences
? Why does Mr. Bittering think that the Martian names should have been kept? (He thinks that Earthmen really don't belong on Mars; the Martians resent their coming and will destroy them.)

C. Suspense
? Through whose eyes do we see the changes? (Mr. Bittering's) How does this build suspense? (We share his excitement and wonder and even his fear.) What does he fear will happen next? (That he and his family will change)

D. Character
? How is Harry different from the other men? How does he feel? What does he want to do? (He is scared and wants to return to Earth. The others seem to be content.)

A. Reading Aloud
? You might have students prepare to read this scene (to the space on page 429) aloud. You will need a narrator, Sam, and Harry. Tell them to omit dialogue tags that just identify the speaker. Ask them to try to portray the dramatic contrast between Sam's "quiet good humor" and Harry's desperation.

B. Interpreting
Sam and the others are curiously detached and uncaring while Harry is frantic and worried. The fact that Sam has old blueprints and rocket materials suggests that at one time he too was eager to build a rocket and get back to Earth. His present detachment might foreshadow that Harry also will eventually accept life on Mars, just as these men have accepted it.

C. Irony
? How is Sam's reaction to Harry ironic? (Harry expects Sam to be worried, but Sam is quite unconcerned.)

A "Now, Harry."

Bittering wanted to cry. "You've got to work with me. If we stay here, we'll all change. The air. Don't you smell it? Something in the air. A Martian virus, maybe. Some seed, or a pollen. Listen to me!"

They stared at him.

"Sam," he said to one of them.

"Yes, Harry?"

"Will you help me build a rocket?"

B "Harry, I got a whole load of metal and some old blueprints.[4] You want to work in my metal shop, on a rocket, you're welcome. I'll sell you that metal for five hundred dollars. You should be able to construct a right pretty rocket, if you work alone, in about thirty years."

Everyone laughed.

"Don't laugh!"

Sam looked at him with quiet good humor.

"Sam," Bittering said. "Your eyes——"

"What about them, Harry?"

"Didn't they used to be gray?"

"Well, now, I don't remember."

"They were, weren't they?"

"Why do you ask, Harry?"

"Because now they're kind of yellow-colored."

"Is that so, Harry?" Sam said casually. C

4. **blueprints:** detailed plans for building something, with white lines on a blue background.

A. Motivation

? Why does Harry ask Sam about the changes in Sam's appearance? (He wants to make Sam realize that Mars is changing him.)

B. Interpreting

? How did Harry break Sam's mirror? (He dropped it in shock when he realized that he is also changing.)

C. Metamorphosis

Metamorphosis means a magical change in form.

? Why does Harry want only food that came from Earth? (He thinks that food grown on Mars will change him.) What do you think might be changing the Earth people? Are these natural or supernatural changes? (Supernatural)

"And you're taller and thinner——"

"You might be right, Harry."

A "Sam, you shouldn't have yellow eyes."

"Harry, what color eyes have *you* got?" Sam said.

"My eyes? They're blue, of course."

"Here you are, Harry." Sam handed him a pocket mirror. "Take a look at yourself."

Mr. Bittering hesitated, and then raised the mirror to his face.

There were little, very dim flecks of new gold captured in the blue of his eyes.

"Now look what you've done," said Sam, a

B moment later. "You've broken my mirror."

Harry Bittering moved into the metal shop and began to build the rocket. Men stood in the open door and talked and joked without raising their voices. Once in a while they gave him a hand on lifting something. But mostly they just idled and watched him with their yellowing eyes.

"It's suppertime, Harry," they said.

His wife appeared with his supper in a wicker basket.

"I won't touch it," he said. "I'll eat only food from our deep freeze. Food that came from Earth. Nothing from our garden."

His wife stood watching him. "You can't build a rocket."

"I worked in a shop once, when I was twenty. I know metal. Once I get it started, the others will help," he said, not looking at her, laying out the blueprints.

"Harry, Harry," she said, helplessly.

"We've got to get away, Cora. We've *got* to!"

The nights were full of wind that blew down the empty moonlit sea meadows past the little white chess cities lying for their twelve-thousandth year in the shallows. In the Earthmen's settlement, the Bittering house shook with a feeling of change.

Lying abed, Mr. Bittering felt his bones shifted, shaped, melted like gold. His wife, lying beside him, was dark from many sunny afternoons. Dark she was, and golden, burnt almost black by the sun, sleeping, and the children metallic in their beds, and the wind roaring forlorn and changing through the old peach trees, the violet grass, shaking out green rose petals.

The fear would not be stopped. It had his throat and heart. It dripped in a wetness of the arm and the temple and the trembling palm.

A green star rose in the east.

A strange word emerged from Mr. Bittering's lips.

"*Iorrt. Iorrt.*" He repeated it.

It was a Martian word. He knew no Martian.

In the middle of the night, he arose and dialed a call through to Simpson, the archeologist.

"Simpson, what does the word *Iorrt* mean?"

"Why, that's the old Martian word for our planet Earth. Why?"

"No special reason."

The telephone slipped from his hand.

"Hello, hello, hello, hello," it kept saying while he sat gazing out at the green star. "Bittering? Harry, are you there?"

The days were full of metal sound. He laid the frame of the rocket with the reluctant help of three indifferent men. He grew very tired in an hour or so and had to sit down.

"The altitude," laughed a man.

"Are you *eating,* Harry?" asked another.

"I'm eating," he said angrily. C

"From your deep freeze?"

"Yes!"

"You're getting thinner, Harry."

"I'm not!"

"And taller."

"Liar!"

His wife took him aside a few days later. "Harry, I've used up all the food in the deep freeze. There's nothing left. I'll have to make sandwiches using food grown on Mars."

He sat down heavily.

"You must eat," she said. "You're weak."

"Yes," he said.

He took a sandwich, opened it, looked at it, and began to nibble at it.

"And take the rest of the day off," she said. "It's hot. The children want to swim in the canals and hike. Please come along."

A. Character

What do Cora's words and actions reveal about her personality? (She is kind and loving; she is tranquil and more accepting about changes in herself and the children than Harry is.)

B. Setting and Mood

How does this setting affect Harry? (The quiet, deep water calms him and makes him more willing to accept change.) What kind of mood or feeling do these details of setting evoke? (Peaceful; lazy; content)

C. Conflict

What internal conflict is suggested here? (Harry vs. himself) Why does he agree to let his son use the Martian name? (He is tired of fighting everyone; he is tired of being the only one who is afraid.)

D. Imagery

What sense, in addition to the visual, does Bradbury emphasize on this page? (Sense of touch) Find at least one detail that appeals to that sense. ("A few tremblings shook him . . ."; "waves of pleasant heat"; "He felt the steady, slow current drift him"; ". . . his body cold and his heart pounding . . ."; "You kept your bare feet cool all day . . .")

"I can't waste time. This is a crisis!"

"Just for an hour," she urged. "A swim'll do you good."

He rose, sweating. "All right, all right. Leave me alone. I'll come."

"Good for you, Harry."

The sun was hot, the day quiet. There was only an immense staring burn upon the land. They moved along the canal, the father, the mother, the racing children, in their swimsuits. They stopped and ate meat sandwiches. He saw their skin baking brown. And he saw the yellow eyes of his wife and his children, their eyes that were never yellow before. A few tremblings shook him but were carried off in waves of pleasant heat as he lay in the sun. He was too tired to be afraid.

"Cora, how long have your eyes been yellow?"

A She was bewildered. "Always, I guess."

"They didn't change from brown in the last three months?"

She bit her lips. "No. Why do you ask?"

"Never mind."

They sat there.

"The children's eyes," he said. "They're yellow, too."

"Sometimes growing children's eyes change color."

"Maybe *we're* children, too. At least to Mars. That's a thought." He laughed. "Think I'll swim."

They leaped into the canal water, and he let himself sink down and down to the bottom like a golden statue and lie there in green silence. All was water, quiet and deep, all was peace. He felt the steady, slow current drift him easily.

If I lie here long enough, he thought, *the water will work and eat away my flesh until the bones show like coral. Just my skeleton left. And then the water can build on that skeleton—green things, deep water things, red things, yellow things. Change. Change. Slow, deep, silent change. And isn't that what it is up there?*

He saw the sky submerged above him, the sun made Martian by atmosphere and time and space.

B *Up there, a big river,* he thought, *a Martian river, all of us lying deep in it, in our pebble houses, in our sunken boulder houses, like crayfish hidden, and the water washing away our old bodies and lengthening the bones and——*

He let himself drift up through the soft light.

Tom sat on the edge of the canal, regarding his father seriously.

"*Utha,*" he said.

"What?" asked his father.

The boy smiled. "You know. *Utha*'s the Martian word for 'father'."

"Where did you learn it?"

"I don't know. Around. *Utha!*"

"What do you want?"

The boy hesitated. "I—I want to change my name."

"Change it?"

"Yes."

His mother swam over. "What's wrong with Tom for a name?"

Tom fidgeted. "The other day you called Tom, Tom, Tom. I didn't even hear. I said to myself, that's not my name. I've a new name I want to use."

Mr. Bittering held to the side of the canal, his body cold and his heart pounding slowly. "What is this new name?"

"Linnl. Isn't that a good name? Can I use it? Can I, please?"

Mr. Bittering put his hand to his head. He thought of the rocket, himself working alone, himself alone even among his family, so alone. C

He heard his wife say, "Why not?"

He heard himself say, "Yes, you can use it."

"Yaaa!" screamed the boy. "I'm Linnl, Linnl!"

Racing down the meadowlands, he danced and shouted.

Mr. Bittering looked at his wife. "Why did we do that?"

"I don't know," she said. "It just seemed like a good idea."

They walked into the hills. They strolled on old mosaic paths, beside still-pumping fountains. The paths were covered with a thin film of cool water all summer long. You kept your bare feet cool all the day, splashing as in a creek, wading. D

They came to a small deserted Martian villa with a good view of the valley. It was on top of a hill. Blue marble halls, large murals, a swimming pool. It was refreshing in this hot summertime. The Martians hadn't believed in large cities.

"How nice," said Mrs. Bittering, "if we could move up here to this villa for the summer."

"Come on," he said. "We're going back to town. There's work to be done on the rocket."

A But as he worked that night, the thought of the cool blue-marble villa entered his mind. As the hours passed, the rocket seemed less important.

In the flow of days and weeks, the rocket receded and dwindled. The old fever was gone. It frightened him to think he had let it slip this way. But somehow, the heat, the air, the working conditions——

He heard the men murmuring on the porch of his metal shop.

"Everyone's going. You heard?"

"All going. That's right."

Bittering came out. "Going where?" He saw a couple of trucks, loaded with children and furniture, drive down the dusty street.

"Up to the villa," said the men.

"Yeah, Harry. I'm going. So is Sam. Aren't you Sam?"

"That's right, Harry. What about you?"

"I've got work to do here."

"Work! You can finish the rocket in the autumn, when it's cooler."

He took a breath. "I got the frame all set up."

"In the autumn is better." Their voices were lazy in the heat.

"Got to work," he said.

"Autumn," they reasoned. And they sounded so sensible, so right.

Autumn would be best, he thought. *Plenty of time then.*

No! cried part of himself, deep down, put away, locked tight, suffocating. *No! No!*

"In the autumn," he said.

"Come on, Harry," they all said.

B "Yes," he said, feeling his flesh melt in the hot liquid air. "Yes, in the autumn. I'll begin work again then."

"I got a villa near the Tirra Canal," said someone.

"You mean the Roosevelt Canal, don't you?"

"Tirra. The old Martian name."

"But on the map——"

"Forget the map. It's Tirra now. Now, *I* found a place in the Pillan Mountains——"

"You mean the Rockefeller Range," said Bittering.

"I meant the Pillan Mountains," said Sam.

"Yes," said Bittering, buried in the hot swarming air. "The Pillan Mountains."

Everyone worked at loading the truck in the hot still afternoon of the next day.

Laura, Tom, and David carried packages. Or, as they preferred to be known, Ttil, Linnl, and Werr carried packages.

The furniture was abandoned in the little white cottage.

"It looked just fine in Boston," said the mother. "And here in the cottage. But up in the villa? No. We'll get it when we come back in the autumn."

Bittering himself was quiet.

"I've some ideas on furniture for the villa," he said after a time. "Big, lazy furniture."

"What about your *Encyclopedia*? You're taking it along, surely?"

Mr. Bittering glanced away. "I'll come and get it next week."

They turned to their daughter. "What about your New York dresses?"

The bewildered girl stared. "Why, I don't want them anymore."

They shut off the gas, the water, they locked the doors, and walked away. Father peered into the truck.

"Gosh, we're not taking much," he said. "Considering all we brought to Mars, this is only a handful!" C

He started the truck.

Looking at the small white cottage for a long moment, he was filled with a desire to rush to it, touch it, say goodbye to it, for he felt as if he were going away on a long journey, leaving something to which he could never quite return, never understand again.

Just then, Sam and his family drove by in another truck.

"Hi, Bittering! Here we go!"

The trucks swung down the ancient highway out of town. There were sixty others traveling the same direction. The town filled with a silent, heavy dust from their passage. The canal waters lay blue in the sun, and a quiet wind moved in the strange trees.

A. Plot
It becomes clear that the hiking and swimming trip is a kind of turning point in Harry's conflict and in the plot.

? How is Harry different after he returns? (The rocket seems less important; he keeps thinking about the Martian villa.)

B. Symbol

? Explain the significance of Harry's giving up work on the rocket. What does the rocket symbolize or represent? (The rocket represents his hope of returning to Earth; it also stands for the technological civilization that Bradbury contrasts with the natural, peaceful Martian life. When Harry gives up work on the rocket, he is giving up his denial and resistance to living on Mars.)

C. Metamorphosis

? In addition to their appearance, in what other ways have the Bitterings changed? (They no longer value the furniture, clothes, and books they brought from Earth. They need fewer material possessions.)

Drawing a Martian

Bradbury tells us little about how the original Martians looked. Students who are interested in art might want to try sketching Martians in a way that reveals their character traits and life style as well as their physical appearance. Try to obtain *Guide to Extra-Terrestrials* by Wayne Barlowe and Ian Summers, a wonderful sketchbook of aliens based on "their biological conditions." It is available in paperback from Workman Publishing Company, New York.

Comment from the Writer

Ray Bradbury has written, ". . . with energy and enthusiasm, and what wit I could summon, I charted my own Mars and went through a naming-of-names, building cities and towns, and creating a wild and special new world. . . ."

Discuss with students whether they like Bradbury's special world on Mars, and whether they would like to live in it. You might want to assign them to read *The Martian Chronicles,* from which "The Naming of Names" was taken, in which Bradbury "charts Mars."

A. Important Detail

? Explain the significance of "They did not look back again." (The family leaves their Earth life with little regret. They are looking forward to their new lives.)

B. Simile

? Find two examples of similes in this paragraph. For each simile, tell what the two things being compared have in common. ("Summer moved like flame upon the meadows." Both summer and flame are hot. "Rubber tires . . . hung suspended like stopped clock pendulums . . ." Both hang from supports and swing back and forth in a mechanical way. By comparing an image of the deserted town to a stopped clock, Bradbury may be inferring that the lives of the converted Earth people are no longer ruled by time.)

"Goodbye, town!" said Mr. Bittering.

"Goodbye, goodbye!" said the family, waving to it.

A They did not look back again.

Summer burned the canals dry. Summer moved like flame upon the meadows. In the empty Earth settlement, the painted houses flaked and peeled. Rubber tires upon which children had swung in backyards hung suspended like stopped clock pendulums[5] in the blazing air. B

5. **pendulums** (pen′joo·ləms): weights, hung from supports, that swing back and forth and regulate the movement of clocks.

Reading Check Test

1. The Bitterings have come to Mars to escape the threat of nuclear war on Earth. *(True)*
2. Harry Bittering senses from the start that something in the Martian environment threatens him. *(True)*
3. The first change they notice is that their hair is slowly turning violet. *(False)*
4. Harry never gives up his dream of building a rocket in which to return to Earth. *(False)*
5. When Earth explorers arrive five years later, they find a thriving suburban community in the valley. *(False)*

Closure

Suppose that you could send a "rocket-gram" of not more than ten words to the men who have just arrived on Mars. What would you tell them? (Ask students to exchange their messages.) Now have them pretend that they have received the rocketgram on Mars. Ask them to tell what they would do in response to it.

At the metal shop, the rocket frame began to rust.

In the quiet autumn, Mr. Bittering stood, very dark now, very golden-eyed, upon the slope above his villa, looking at the valley.

"It's time to go back," said Cora.

"Yes, but we're not going," he said quietly. "There's nothing there anymore."

"Your books," she said. "Your fine clothes."

"Your *Illes* and your fine *ior uele rre,*" she said.

"The town's empty. No one's going back," he said. "There's no reason to, none at all."

The daughter wove tapestries and the sons played songs on ancient flutes and pipes, their laughter echoing in the marble villa.

Mr. Bittering gazed at the Earth settlement far away in the low valley. "Such odd, such ridiculous houses the Earth people built."

"They didn't know any better," his wife mused. "Such ugly people. I'm glad they've gone."

They both looked at each other, startled by all they had just finished saying. They laughed.

Where did they go? he wondered. He glanced at his wife. She was golden and slender as his daughter. She looked at him, and he seemed almost as young as their eldest son.

"I don't know," she said.

"We'll go back to town maybe next year, or the year after, or the year after that," he said, calmly. "Now—I'm warm. How about taking a swim?"

They turned their backs to the valley. Arm in arm they walked silently down a path of clear running spring water. . . . **A**

B Five years later a rocket fell out of the sky. It lay steaming in the valley. Men leaped out of it, shouting: "We won the war on Earth! We're here to rescue you! Hey!"

But the American-built town of cottages, peach trees, and theaters was silent. They found a half-finished rocket frame, rusting in an empty shop.

The rocket men searched the hills. The captain established headquarters in an abandoned bar. His lieutenant came back to report.

"The town's empty, but we found native life in the hills, sir. Dark people. Yellow eyes. Martians. Very friendly. We talked a bit, not much. They learn English fast. I'm sure our relations will be most friendly with them, sir."

"Dark, eh?" mused the captain. "How many?"

"Six, eight hundred, I'd say, living in those marble ruins in the hills, sir. Tall, healthy. Beautiful women."

"Did they tell you what became of the men and women who built this Earth settlement, Lieutenant?"

"They hadn't the foggiest notion of what happened to this town or its people."

"Strange. You think those Martians killed them?"

"They look surprisingly peaceful. Chances are a plague[6] did this town in, sir."

"Perhaps. I suppose this is one of those mysteries we'll never solve. One of those mysteries you read about."

The captain looked at the room, the dusty windows, the blue mountains rising beyond, the canals moving in the light, and he heard the soft wind in the air. He shivered. Then, recovering, he tapped a large fresh map he had thumbtacked to the top of an empty table.

"Lots to be done, Lieutenant." His voice droned on and quietly on as the sun sank behind the blue hills. "New settlements. Mining sites, minerals to be looked for. Bacteriological specimens taken. The work, all the work. And the old records were lost. We'll have a job of remapping to do, renaming the mountains and rivers and such. Calls for a little imagination.

"What do you think of naming those mountains the Lincoln Mountains, this canal the Washington Canal, those hills—we can name those hills for you, Lieutenant. Diplomacy. And you, for a favor, might name a town for me. Polishing the apple. And why not make this the Einstein Valley, and further over. . . . Are you *listening,* Lieutenant?"

The lieutenant snapped his gaze from the blue color and the quiet mist of the hills far beyond the town.

"What? Oh, *yes,* sir!"

6. **plague** (plāg): a deadly disease that spreads rapidly.

A. Metamorphoses

? How does Harry Bittering now feel about the physical changes that have happened to him and his wife? (He likes the changes; he and his wife seem young and healthy; they care for each other more.) What do the Bitterings now seem to value most? (Their children, each other, other people, happiness, health, creating beauty in music and weaving, enjoying nature, enjoying their environment)

B. Irony

In dramatic irony readers know something that a character does not know. Irony comes from the difference between what the character thinks is true and what the reader knows to be true.

? What is ironic about the comments that the rocket men make? What do you know that they don't know? (The people that were left on Mars don't want to be rescued.)

ANALYZING THE STORY
Identifying Facts
1. The threat of nuclear annihilation on Earth made them feel that Mars would be a safe place.
2. He feels the alienness of the environment acutely; he feels that they are somehow being sucked into it and changed by it.
3. They lived in the mountains a long time ago but now seem to have vanished.
4. A nuclear war on Earth ends all transportation to and from Mars. Now knowing that he must remain there, Harry is deeply troubled and frightened.
5. Peach blossoms seem differently shaped; roses have turned green; a cow grows a third horn; grass turns purple; people seem taller and thinner; and eyes begin to change color. Harry fears that he will be changed.
6. They change physically; they become lethargic and lazy; they find themselves speaking a strange, new language; they adopt new names; they feel themselves settling in, becoming more and more comfortable, forgetting their past.
7. He decides he would like to swim in the canal, and feels quite at peace in the

Responding to the Story

Analyzing the Story

Identifying Facts

1. Why did the Bitterings come to Mars?
2. Even though the family has all the comforts of Earth life in their Martian home, why is Harry uncomfortable and anxious?
3. What do you learn about the old inhabitants of Mars? What seems to have happened to them?
4. What event on Earth changes Harry's outlook on Martian living?
5. Describe the changes Harry notices taking place all around him. What does he fear?
6. Describe the various things that happen to the Bitterings as they adapt to life on Mars. What **metamorphoses** do they undergo?
7. The picnic along the canal marks a turning point in the story. What details indicate that Harry is changing his mind about leaving? What other **metamorphoses** are noted on this picnic?
8. Once they move to the Martian villa, how does the family regard the old Earth settlements? What indicates that they have become healthier and more beautiful?
9. When a rocket finally comes again to Mars, what has happened to the Earth settlement? What "native life" does the Lieutenant find?

Interpreting Meanings

10. What does the story suggest happened to the original Martians who used to live in the Martian towns? Who or what do you think causes the **metamorphoses** of the people who come to Mars? Can you find any clues suggesting that the wind has something to do with it?
11. What in the Lieutenant's behavior suggests that his future may be similar to that of the Bitterings?
12. Explain what the story's title means.
13. Not only does the Bittering family change physically, but they also change mentally. What changes do you notice in their attitudes? How do the Martians seem to be different from the Earth people—in attitudes as well as in appearance? Which people do you think Bradbury likes better, and why?

Applying Meanings

14. What **main idea** do you think this story expresses about the way "advanced civilizations" take over a country? Have conquerors throughout history put their own names and imprints on the countries they've settled? Have they been changed by these countries?
15. Do you think you would react to the Martian environment as Harry does at first, or as his wife and children did? Does the life appeal to you? Scare you? Would you want to get back to Earth? Support your opinions with reasons.

Writing About the Story

A Creative Response

1. **Writing an Advertisement.** Write a television ad selling the idea of going to Bradbury's Mars either to live or to vacation. Describe what you would show in photographs, what you would say, and the kind of music or sounds you would use.
2. **Creating a Language.** Make up five Martian words. For each word, write a sentence that will show what the word means.

A Critical Response

SRW p. 79

3. **Supporting a Main Idea.** In one paragraph, explain how **setting** is all-important to "The Naming of Names." How does the setting affect the characters? How does it change their ideas about life? Use this statement as your main idea: *This story could not have happened in any other setting.* Include details from the story.

See Teacher's Manual page 140.

Analyzing Language and Vocabulary

Metaphors and Metamorphoses

SRW p. 61

A **metamorphosis** is a marvelous transformation from one shape or form to another one. A **metaphor** is a verbal comparison between two very different things. In a metaphor, as in a metamorphosis, one thing *becomes* another, different thing. In the second paragraph of this story, Bradbury calls the children "small seeds, [which] might at any instant be sown to all the Martian climes." If we use our imagination we can see how this metaphor is true: The water; his wife's eyes have changed color; his son is overjoyed when he is allowed to change his name; his wife talks of moving to a villa in the hills.

8. They find them odd and ridiculous.

They have become younger and stronger, golden-eyed, tanned, and slender. They laugh and play and seem to enjoy the natural environment.

9. The settlement is silent and deserted. The Lieutenant finds what he believes to be Martians—dark, yellow-eyed, friendly beings.

Interpreting Meanings

10. It is suggested that somehow the original Martians have vaporized, become part of the planet's very atmosphere. It is this atmosphere, manifested in the ever-present wind, that seems to cause the various metamorphoses. The wind is referred to throughout the story, as at the beginning: "The wind blew as if to flake away their identities."

11. The Lieutenant gazes off dreamily into the distance, and has to be "snapped" back to attention by the Captain.

12. The title refers to the naming of places on Mars. In a larger sense, it refers to the relationship between name and identity: What we call ourselves and others signifies a great deal about who we are and who we think we are. At first, Harry thinks of Martian places as having Earth names; later he forgets the Earth names; in the end, it is implied that even he and his family have assumed Martian names.

13. Gradually they begin to accept their situation and even to enjoy it. As they become Martians, they become more friendly, casual, and peaceful. Physically, they become dark, yellow-eyed, tall, and slender.

He seems to admire the Martians' beauty, casualness, and love of pleasure and peace.

Applying Meanings

14. The story suggests that "advanced civilizations" can never completely take over another civilization, that indeed, it is more likely that it will itself be transformed. (See Teacher's Manual page 139.)

15. Answers will vary.

children will remain on Mars and their children will produce more children, just as seeds produce more generations of flowers.

Here are some other metaphors from "The Naming of Names." Answer the questions that follow each one.

1. The other passengers whispered away across the Martian meadow . . . ?
   a. What does the word *whisper* suggest about the rocket's motion?
   b. How would the metaphor change if the verb *slithered* were used instead?
2. "A river of wind submerged the house."
   a. What is the wind compared to?
   b. How could wind "submerge" a house?
   c. How would your image of what is happening to the house be different if the sentence had read: "The wind howled around the house"?
3. "As long as the rockets had spun a silver web across space, he had been able to accept Mars."
   a. What words reveal that the rockets are compared to spiders?
   b. What is the spider's web compared to?

For answers, see Teacher's Manual page 140.

Reading About the Writer

Ray Bradbury (1920–   ) was born in Waukegan, Illinois, and has been a full-time writer all his adult life. He first began writing when he was twelve. He says that he was inspired to write by a circus performer called Mr. Electrico, with whom he developed a brief friendship. Mr. Electrico told the young Bradbury that they had met before in another life—that he had died in Mr. Electrico's arms during World War I in France. Bradbury stated that, as a result of that encounter, he had been uplifted by two gifts: "the gift of having lived once before (and of being told about it) . . . and the gift of trying somehow to live forever."

Although Bradbury has been called "the world's greatest living science-fiction writer," he prefers to be called an "idea writer." Among his most famous novels are *The Martian Chronicles, Fahrenheit 451* (the temperature at which book paper catches fire and burns), *Dandelion Wine,* and *Something Wicked This Way Comes* (in which the main character is based on his childhood friend Mr. Electrico). Bradbury once said: "My stories have led me through my life. They shout, I follow. They run up and bite me on the leg—I respond by writing down everything that goes on during the bite. When I finish, the idea lets go, and runs off."

Focusing on Background

A Comment from the Writer

Ray Bradbury writes about his interest in Mars:

"I have always looked on myself as some sort of Martian. My affinity for the planet is immense and prolonged and most affectionate-fine. . . .

"And even if we never were Martians in our deep, dark root years of prehistory, the day is fast coming when we shall name ourselves so.

"I foresaw this (not smugly, I hope) when, some twenty-three years ago, I wrote a strange tale entitled 'Dark They Were, and Golden-Eyed' [another title for 'The Naming of Names'].

"In that Martian story, I told of a man and his family who helped colonize Mars, who eat of its foods and live in its strange seasons, and stay on when everyone else goes back to Earth, until the day finally comes when they find that the odd weathers and peculiar temperatures of the Red Planet have melted their flesh into new shapes, tinted their skin, and put flecks of gold into their now most fantastic eyes, and they move up into the hills to live in old ruins and become—Martians.

"Which is the history I predict for us on that far world. The ruins may not be there. But if necessary we will *build* the ruins, and live in them and name ourselves as my transplanted Earthmen did. And will not be of Earth any more but will truly be Martians . . .

"We are, then—at this moment, because we dream it so—Martians. We wish to be that thing and so will be it."

—Ray Bradbury

PREREADING

1. BUILDING ON PRIOR KNOWLEDGE. Ask students what they know about space travel. Some of them may have seen the Star Trek films or the film *2001: A Space Odyssey.* Interplanetary travel in science fiction is far ahead of actual space travel. In stories and films, giant space ships explore planets throughout our galaxy and even beyond it. Ask students why they think space scientists are so interested in exploring beyond our solar system. (It is not likely that any other planet in our system can support life.) For more on space travel, see page 438.

2. ESTABLISHING A PURPOSE. Tell students to look at the illustration on page 439. Ask them what question immediately comes to their minds. Have them write down the question. As they read, ask them to look for the answer.

3. PREREADING JOURNAL. Tell students to suppose that it is the far future and they have been assigned to a space ship that is collecting extraterrestrial animals for zoos on Earth. In three sentences have them tell what they would like best and least about this assignment.

A. Language

? So far what technical words tell you that the setting is a space ship? Define each word in the context of the rest of the sentence or paragraph. (Thermocouple: something that indicates temperature; deceleration; slowing down speed; coordinates: system used to indicate location; survey ship: exploration ship; viewport: window; orbit: path in space around a planet)

B. Point of View

? What is the point of view of this story? (First person) What do you find out about the narrator? (He is the pilot. He feels "gloomy" whenever he has to land on an unexplored planet.)

★ **Texas Essential Elements/(a) English Language Arts: 1B** Purpose and audience; **1F** Specific words; **4E** Predict; **4F** Generalizations

COLLECTING TEAM

Robert Silverberg

The oldest and probably still the most fascinating science fiction stories deal with space travel. In the seventeenth century, writers dared to imagine fantastic empires on the moon. Now that scientists know more about the moon and the nearby planets in our solar system, space-travel fantasies are set on the planets of other solar systems. The vast distances between stars make such travel impossible in the real world (or so we think today). But in the world of fantasy, this kind of imaginary voyage goes on all the time. In the following story, a spaceship makes a routine landing on an unexplored planet. As you read, be aware of clues that show that this expedition of the "collecting team" is *not* routine.

For a detailed lesson plan on this story, see Teacher's Manual pages 141–143.
A biography of Robert Silverberg appears on text page 446.

From fifty thousand miles up, the situation looked promising. It was a middle-sized, brown-and-green, inviting-looking planet, with no sign of cities or any other such complications. Just a pleasant sort of place, the very sort we were looking for to redeem what had been a pretty futile expedition.

I turned to Clyde Holdreth, who was staring reflectively at the thermocouple.

"Well? What do you think?"

"Looks fine to me. Temperature's about seventy down there—nice and warm, and plenty of air. I think its worth a try."

Lee Davison came strolling out from the storage hold, smelling of animals, as usual. He was holding one of the blue monkeys we picked up on Alpheraz, and the little beast was crawling up his arm. "Have we found something, gentlemen?"

"We've found a planet," I said. "How's the storage space in the hold?"

"Don't worry about that. We've got room for a whole zoofull more, before we get filled up. It hasn't been a very fruitful trip."

"No," I agreed. "It hasn't. Well? Shall we go down and see what's to be seen?"

"Might as well," Holdreth said. "We can't go back to Earth with just a couple of blue monkeys and some anteaters, you know."

"I'm in favor of a landing too," said Davison. "You?"

I nodded. "I'll set up the charts, and you get your animals comfortable for deceleration."

Davison disappeared back into the storage hold, while Holdreth scribbled furiously in the logbook, writing down the coordinates of the planet below, its general description, and so forth. Aside from being a collecting team for the zoological department of the Bureau of Interstellar Affairs, we also double as a survey ship, and the planet down below was listed as *unexplored* on our charts.

I glanced out at the mottled brown-and-green ball spinning slowly in the viewport, and felt the A
warning twinge of gloom that came to me every time we made a landing on a new and strange
world. Repressing it, I started to figure out a land- B
ing orbit. From behind me came the furious chatter of the blue monkeys as Davison strapped them

Specialized Vocabulary. The author of "Collecting Team" bases his fantasy on two fields of science: space travel and zoology, which is the study of animals and animal life. To make his story sound scientific and therefore "real," he uses specialized vocabulary from both sciences. Use a good dictionary to find the meanings of important words in the story that you don't know. You'll be able to make intelligent guesses about some words from context clues.

SUPPLEMENTARY SUPPORT MATERIAL

1. Vocabulary Activity Sheet
2. Reading Check Test blackline master
3. Selection Test (page 163 of Test Book)
4. Reader's Response Journal
5. Workbook (page 127)

DEVELOPING VOCABULARY

The following words appear on a test in the Test Book, page 164. (See also the Vocabulary Activity Sheet.)

acceleration	nebulous
bizarre	sabotage
preposterous	jettison
bonanza	clamber
habitat	meander

A. Making Inferences

? Why do you think Davison is nervous? (He is probably feeling nervous excitement, since they have come across a zoological gold mine and their trip has so far been unsuccessful.)

B. Vocabulary

You can tell students that a "species" is a group of animals that have related characteristics and can mate to reproduce their own kind.

C. Important Detail

? What effect does the narrator's impression that the giraffelike creature is trying to communicate have on the reader? (It creates suspense—this is the first clue of something sinister existing on the planet.)

D. Theme

Zoologists have given each species a Latin name. In this case, "Davison" is "changed" to Latin.

? Why would the extraterrestrial animals have Davison's name as part of their species name? (He found them so they would be named in his honor.) How might Davison be like the Earthmen in "The Naming of Names"?

★ **Texas Essential Elements/(c) Reading: 1C** Dictionaries; **2A** Word meaning; **3A** Main ideas/details; **3D** Generalizations; **3H** Predict; **3I** Draw conclusions; **4D** Diagrams/graphs

into their acceleration cradles, and under that the deep, unmusical honking of the Rigelian anteaters, noisily bleating their displeasure.

The planet was inhabited, all right. We hadn't had the ship on the ground more than a minute before the local fauna[1] began to congregate. We stood at the viewport and looked out in wonder.

A "This is one of those things you dream about," Davison said, stroking his little beard nervously. "Look at them! There must be a thousand different species out there." B

"I've never seen anything like it," said Holdreth.

I computed how much storage space we had left and how many of the thronging creatures outside we would be able to bring back with us. "How are we going to decide what to take and what to leave behind?"

"Does it matter?" Holdreth said gaily. "This is what you call an embarrassment of riches, I guess. We just grab the dozen most bizarre creatures and blast off—and save the rest for another trip. It's too bad we wasted all that time wandering around near Rigel."

"We *did* get the anteaters," Davison pointed out. They were his finds, and he was proud of them.

I smiled sourly. "Yeah. We got the anteaters there." The anteaters honked at that moment, loud and clear. "You know, that's one set of beasts I think I could do without."

"Bad attitude," Holdreth said. "Unprofessional."

"Whoever said I was a zoologist, anyway? I'm just a spaceship pilot, remember. And if I don't like the way those anteaters talk—and smell—I see no reason why I——"

"Say, look at that one," Davison said suddenly.

I glanced out the viewport and saw a new beast emerging from the thick-packed vegetation in the background. I've seen some fairly strange creatures since I was assigned to the zoological department, but this one took the grand prize.

It was about the size of a giraffe, moving on long, wobbly legs and with a tiny head up at the end of a preposterous neck. Only it had six legs and a bunch of writhing snakelike tentacles as well, and its eyes, great violet globes, stood out nakedly on the ends of two thick stalks. It must have been twenty feet high. It moved with exaggerated grace through the swarm of beasts surrounding our ship, pushed its way smoothly toward the vessels, and peered gravely in at the viewport. One purple eye stared directly at me, the other at Davison. Oddly, it seemed to me as if it were trying to tell us something. C

"Big one, isn't it?" Davison said finally.

"I'll bet you'd like to bring one back, too."

"Maybe we can fit a young one aboard," Davison said. "If we can find a young one." He turned to Holdreth. "How's that air analysis coming? I'd like to get out there and start collecting. Gosh, that's a crazy-looking beast!"

The animal outside had apparently finished its inspection of us, for it pulled its head away and, gathering its legs under itself, squatted near the ship. A small doglike creature with stiff spines running along its back began to bark at the big creature, which took no notice. The other animals, which came in all shapes and sizes, continued to mill around the ship, evidently very curious about the newcomer to their world. I could see Davison's eyes thirsty with the desire to take the whole kit and caboodle back to Earth with him. I knew what was running through his mind. He was dreaming of the umpteen thousand species of extraterrestrial wildlife roaming around out there, and to each one he was attaching a neat little tag: *Something-or-other davisoni.* D

"The air's fine," Holdreth announced abruptly, looking up from his test-tubes. "Get your butterfly nets and let's see what we can catch."

There was something I didn't like about the place. It was just too good to be true, and I learned long ago that nothing ever is. There's always a catch someplace.

Only this seemed to be on the level. The planet was a bonanza for zoologists, and Davison and Holdreth were having the time of their lives, hip-deep in obliging specimens.

"I've never seen anything like it," Davison said for at least the fiftieth time, as he scooped up a

1. **fauna** (fô′nə): animals of a specific region.

Scientific Background
Dr. Isaac Asimov (see page 418) estimates that as many as 600 million planets in our Milky Way galaxy may be able to support higher life forms. A major problem that stands in the way of interplanetary travel is that stars in our galaxy are about five light-years apart, and scientists say that a space ship can never go as fast as the speed of light. S-F writers "solve" this problem in several ways. In *Star Trek,* the *Enterprise* space ship is powered by "anti-matter" to travel at "warp" speed. Usually the *Enterprise* cruises at warp 6, which is supposedly 216 times the speed of light! When some writers talk about warp speed, they mean that the ship goes through a hole in space where it can magically go faster than light. This imaginary invention may be called "hyperspace" (*Star Wars* movies) or "stargate," but the general concept is the same. In "Collecting Team" the crew is stranded when the "drive mechanism" is destroyed. This mechanism is undoubtedly the device that enables the ship to travel between stars at faster than light speed.

A. Vocabulary
insect-faceted: Most insects have eyes that are made up of many parts or "facets." Each facet can see.

B. Suspense
The author builds suspense by telling you why the narrator feels uneasy about the planet. ? What doesn't make sense to the narrator about the way the animals behave? (They don't mind being caught; they live together happily; there are just a few of each kind; they all seem to be herbivores.)

C. Setting
? Why does the terrain seem strange to the narrator? (It has great contrasts next to each other, quite unlike Earth where wind, water, glaciers, and changes within the Earth create extensive land forms. You would never see a tropical rain forest adjacent to a dry desert on Earth.)

small purplish squirrel-like creature and examined it curiously. The squirrel stared back, examining Davison just as curiously.

"Let's take some of these," Davison said. "I like them."

"Carry 'em on in, then," I said, shrugging. I didn't care which specimens they chose, as long as they filled up the storage hold quickly and let me blast off on schedule. I watched as Davison grabbed a pair of the squirrels and brought them into the ship.

Holdreth came over to me. He was carrying a
A sort of a dog with insect-faceted eyes and gleaming furless skin. "How's this one, Gus?"

"Fine," I said bleakly. "Wonderful."

He put the animal down—it didn't scamper away, just sat there smiling at us—and looked at me. He ran a hand through his fast-vanishing hair. "Listen, Gus, you've been gloomy all day. What's eating you?"

"I don't like this place," I said.

"Why? Just on general principles?"

"It's too *easy,* Clyde. Much too easy. These animals just flock around here waiting to be picked up."

Holdreth chuckled. "And you're used to a struggle, aren't you? You're just angry at us because we have it so simple here!"

"When I think of the trouble we went through just to get a pair of miserable vile-smelling anteaters, and——"

"Come off it, Gus. We'll load up in a hurry, if you like. But this place is a zoological gold mine!"

I shook my head. "I don't like it, Clyde. Not at all."

Holdreth laughed again and picked up his faceted-eyed dog. "Say, know where I can find another of these, Gus?"

"Right over there," I said, pointing. "By that tree. With its tongue hanging out. It's just waiting to be carried away."

Holdreth looked and smiled. "What do you know about that!" He snared his specimen and carried both of them inside.

I walked away to survey the grounds. The planet was too flatly incredible for me to accept on face value, without at least a look-see, despite the blithe way my two companions were snapping up specimens.

For one thing, animals just don't exist this way—in big miscellaneous quantities, living all together happily. I hadn't noticed more than a few of each kind, and there must have been five hundred different species, each one stranger-looking than the next. Nature doesn't work that way.

For another, they all seemed to be on friendly terms with one another, though they acknowledged the unofficial leadership of the giraffe-like creature. Nature doesn't work *that* way, either. I hadn't seen one quarrel between the animals yet. That argued that they were all herbivores,[2] which didn't make sense ecologically. B

I shrugged my shoulders and walked on.

Half an hour later, I knew a little more about the geography of our bonanza. We were on either an immense island or a peninsula of some sort, because I could see a huge body of water bordering the land some ten miles off. Our vicinity was fairly flat, except for a good-sized hill from which I could see the terrain.

There was a thick, heavily-wooded jungle not too far from the ship. The forest spread out all the way toward the water in one direction, but ended abruptly in the other. We had brought the ship down right at the edge of the clearing. Apparently most of the animals we saw lived in the jungle.

On the other side of our clearing was a low, broad plain that seemed to trail away into a desert in the distance; I could see an uninviting stretch of barren sand that contrasted strangely with the fertile jungle to my left. There was a small lake to the side. It was, I saw, the sort of country likely to attract a varied fauna, since there seemed to be every sort of habitat within a small area. C

And the fauna! Although I'm a zoologist only by osmosis,[3] picking up both my interest and my knowledge secondhand from Holdreth and Davison, I couldn't help but be astonished by the wealth of strange animals. They came in all dif-

2. **herbivores** (hur'bə·vôrz'): animals that feed chiefly on grass or other plants.
3. **osmosis** (äs·mō'sis): here, absorption (he's picked it up from his companions).

A. Foreshadowing

? Why does this comment create foreshadowing? (We felt uneasy when the narrator first expressed his misgivings about the planet—now we really believe the narrator's opinion. He has found facts to support his uncertainty: The terrain and the animals are too varied, and the giraffe still seems to be trying to communicate.)

B. Character

The narrator is the pilot and the other men are zoologists.

? In what more important ways does the narrator differ from the other two men? (He is more suspicious and objective. He is "cooler," less emotional than the others. His career doesn't depend on these expeditions.)

C. Conflict

? What is the unstated conflict between the narrator and the others? (The narrator dislikes the planet; he thinks there's something wrong. He may want to leave as soon as possible. The others are overwhelmed by the wealth of extraterrestrials, and so have no suspicions about the planet.)

ferent shapes and sizes, colors and odors, and the only thing they all had in common was their friendliness. During the course of my afternoon's wanderings a hundred animals must have come marching boldly right up to me, given me the once-over, and walked away. This included half a dozen kinds that I hadn't seen before, plus one of the eye-stalked, intelligent-looking giraffes and a furless dog. Again, I had the feeling that the giraffe seemed to be trying to communicate.

A I didn't like it. I didn't like it at all.

I returned to our clearing, and saw Holdreth and Davison still buzzing around, trying to cram as many animals as they could into our hold.

"How's it going?" I asked.

"Hold's all full," Davison said. "We're busy making our alternate selections now." I saw him carrying out Holdreth's two furless dogs and picking up instead a pair of eight-legged penguinish things that uncomplainingly allowed themselves to be carried in. Holdreth was frowning unhappily.

"What do you want *those* for, Lee? Those dog-like ones seem much more interesting, don't you think?"

"No," Davison said. "I'd rather bring along these two. They're curious beasts, aren't they? Look at the muscular network that connects the ——"

"Hold it, fellows," I said. I peered at the animal in Davison's hands and glanced up. "This *is* a curious beast," I said. "It's got eight legs." B

"You becoming a zoologist?" Holdreth asked, amused.

"No—but I am getting puzzled. Why should this one have eight legs, some of the others here six, and some of the others only four?"

C

A. Paraphrasing ? State the narrator's argument here in your own words. (Answers will differ, but should include these ideas: "There must be something wrong here. Animals on any planet have the same number of legs. On this planet they have different numbers of legs. How could they have developed that way?")

B. Making Inferences ? Why do you think Gus is afraid to stay longer? (He may suspect that the animals are not what they seem, or that something will attack them. His intuition tells him they should leave right away.)

C. Interpreting ? Why is Davison's look so accusatory? (In Davison's opinion, the narrator's insistence that they leave *is* criminal—he thinks the narrator is jeopardizing his reputation.)

D. Vocabulary **solderbeam** (sod·er·bēm): tool for melting and fusing metal.

They looked at me blankly, with the scorn of professionals.

A "I mean, there ought to be some sort of logic to evolution here, shouldn't there? On Earth we've developed a four-legged pattern of animal life; on Venus, they usually run to six legs. But have you ever seen an evolutionary hodgepodge like this place before?"

"There are stranger setups," Holdreth said. "The symbiotes[4] on Sirius Three, the burrowers of Mizar—but you're right, Gus. This *is* a peculiar evolutionary dispersal. I think we ought to stay and investigate it fully."

Instantly I knew from the bright expression on Davison's face that I had blundered, had made things worse than ever. I decided to take a new tack.

B "I don't agree," I said. "I think we ought to leave with what we've got, and come back with a larger expedition later."

Davison chuckled. "Come on, Gus, don't be silly! This is a chance of a lifetime for us—why should we call in the whole zoological department on it?"

I didn't want to tell them I was afraid of staying longer. I crossed my arms. "Lee, I'm the pilot of this ship, and you'll have to listen to me. The schedule calls for a brief stopover here, and we have to leave. Don't tell me I'm being silly."

"But you are, man! You're standing blindly in the path of scientific investigation, of——"

"Listen to me, Lee. Our food is calculated on a pretty narrow margin, to allow you fellows more room for storage. And this is strictly a collecting team. There's no provision for extended stays on any one planet. Unless you want to wind up eating your own specimens, I suggest you allow us to get out of here."

They were silent for a moment. Then Holdreth said, "I guess we can't argue with that, Lee. Let's listen to Gus and go back now. There's plenty of time to investigate this place later when we can take longer."

"But—oh, all right," Davison said reluctantly. He picked up the eight-legged penguins. "Let me stash these things in the hold, and we can leave." He looked strangely at me, as if I had done something criminal. C

As he started into the ship, I called to him.

"What is it, Gus?"

"Look here, Lee. I don't *want* to pull you away from here. It's simply a matter of food," I lied, masking my nebulous suspicions.

"I know how it is, Gus." He turned and entered the ship.

I stood there thinking about nothing at all for a moment, then went inside myself to begin setting up the blastoff orbit.

I got as far as calculating the fuel expenditure when I noticed something. Feedwires were dangling crazily down from the control cabinet. Somebody had wrecked our drive mechanism, but thoroughly.

For a long moment, I stared stiffly at the sabotaged drive. Then I turned and headed into the storage hold.

"Davison?"

"What is it, Gus?"

"Come out here a second, will you?"

I waited, and a few minutes later he appeared, frowning impatiently. "What do you want, Gus? I'm busy and I——" His mouth dropped open. "*Look at the drive!*"

"You look at it," I snapped. "I'm sick. Go get Holdreth, on the double."

While he was gone I tinkered with the shattered mechanism. Once I had the cabinet panel off and could see inside, I felt a little better; the drive wasn't damaged beyond repair, though it had been pretty well scrambled. Three or four days of hard work with a screwdriver and solderbeam might D get the ship back into functioning order.

But that didn't make me any less angry. I heard Holdreth and Davison entering behind me, and I whirled to face them.

"All right, you idiots. Which one of you did this?"

They opened their mouths in protesting squawks at the same instant. I listened to them for a while, then said, "One at a time!"

"If you're implying that one of us deliberately sabotaged the ship," Holdreth said, "I want you to know——"

4. **symbiotes** (sim'bī·ōtz'): animals living in a close, interdependent state.

"I'm not implying anything. But the way it looks to me, you two decided you'd like to stay here a while longer to continue your investigations, and figured the easiest way of getting me to agree was to wreck the drive." I glared hotly at them. "Well, I've got news for you. I can fix this, and I can fix it in a couple of days. So go on—get
A about your business! Get all the zoologizing you can in, while you still have time. I——"

Davison laid a hand gently on my arm. "Gus," he said quietly, "*We didn't do it*. Neither of us."

Suddenly all the anger drained out of me and was replaced by raw fear. I could see that Davison meant it.

"If you didn't do it, and Holdreth didn't do it, and *I* didn't do it—then who did?"

Davison shrugged.

"Maybe it's one of us who doesn't know he's
B doing it," I suggested. "Maybe——" I stopped. "Oh, that's nonsense. Hand me that tool kit, will you, Lee?"

They left to tend to the animals, and I set to work on the repair job, dismissing all further speculations and suspicions from my mind, concentrating solely on joining Lead A to Input A and Transistor F to Potentiometer K, as indicated. It was slow, nerve-harrowing work, and by mealtime I had accomplished only the barest preliminaries. My fingers were starting to quiver from the strain of small-scale work, and I decided to give up the job for the day and get back to it tomorrow.

I slept uneasily, my nightmares punctuated by the moaning of the accursed anteaters and the occasional squeals, chuckles, bleats, and hisses of the various other creatures in the hold. It must have been four in the morning before I dropped off into a really sound sleep, and what was left of the night passed swiftly. The next thing I knew, hands were shaking me, and I was looking up into the pale, tense faces of Holdreth and Davison.

I pushed my sleep-stuck eyes open and blinked. "Huh? What's going on?"

Holdreth leaned down and shook me savagely. "Get up, Gus!"

I struggled to my feet slowly. "Heck of a thing to do, wake a fellow up in the middle of the ——"

I found myself being propelled from my cabin and led down the corridor to the control room. Blearily, I followed where Holdreth pointed, and then I woke up in a hurry.

The drive was battered again. Someone—or *something*—had completely undone my repair job of the night before.

If there had been bickering among us, it stopped. This was past the category of a joke now; it couldn't be laughed off, and we found ourselves working together as a tight unit again, trying desperately to solve the puzzle before it was too late.

"Let's review the situation," Holdreth said, pacing nervously up and down the control cabin. "The drive has been sabotaged twice. None of us knows who did it, and on a conscious level each of us is convinced *he* didn't do it."

He paused. "That leaves us with two possibilities. Either, as Gus suggested, one of us is doing it unaware of it even himself, or someone else is doing it while we're not looking. Neither possibility is a very cheerful one."

"We can stay on guard, though," I said. "Here's what I propose: First, have one of us awake at all times—sleep in shifts, that is, with
somebody guarding the drive until I get it fixed. C
Two—jettison[5] all the animals aboard ship."

"*What?*"

"He's right," Davison said. "We don't know what we may have brought aboard. They don't seem to be intelligent, but we can't be sure. That purple-eyed baby giraffe, for instance—suppose he's been hypnotizing us into damaging the drive ourselves? How can we tell?"

"Oh, but——" Holdreth started to protest, then stopped and frowned soberly. "I suppose we'll have to admit the possibility," he said, obviously unhappy about the prospect of freeing our captives. "We'll empty out the hold, and you see if you can get the drive fixed. Maybe later we'll recapture them all, if nothing further develops."

We agreed to that, and Holdreth and Davison cleared the ship of its animal cargo while I set to work determinedly at the drive mechanism. By nightfall, I had managed to accomplish as much as I had the day before. D

5. **jettison** (jet'ə·s'n): throw overboard.

A. Conflict
? What conflict on this page adds to the suspense? (The crew vs. the unknown creature who is damaging the drive)

B. Interpreting
? What do you think Gus's interrupted thought is? (Perhaps that someone or something on the planet is wrecking the drive without them being aware of it.)

C. Character
? Compared to the other two men, what qualities seem to be the narrator's strengths? (Answers will vary but might include some of these ideas: Gus seems to think more quickly than the others and is more objective; he weighs alternatives and is decisive; he is a good leader and has practical, technical knowledge.)

D. Predicting Plot
? What do you think will happen next?

A. Suspense

What new problem increases the suspense? (They are running out of food.)

B. Mood

Compare the mood of the animals outside the ship with the mood of the men inside. (The animals are friendly and relaxed. Some of them are even interested in the ship. The men inside are tense and scared.)

C. Expression

To "knock off" is to go to bed.

D. Suspense

The precipitation of manna every night adds to the suspense. What questions does it make you think of? (Where does the manna come from? Will the crew eat it? Will it change them somehow?)

I sat up as watch the first shift, aboard the strangely quiet ship. I paced around the drive cabin, fighting the great temptation to doze off, and managed to last through until the time Holdreth arrived to relieve me.

Only—when he showed up, he gasped and pointed at the drive. It had been ripped apart a third time.

Now we had no excuse, no explanation. The expedition had turned into a nightmare.

I could only protest that I had remained awake my entire spell on duty, and that I had seen no one and no thing approach the drive panel. But that was hardly a satisfactory explanation, since it either cast guilt on me as the saboteur or implied that some unseen external power was repeatedly wrecking the drive. Neither hypothesis made sense, at least to me.

A By now we had spent four days on the planet, and food was getting to be a major problem. My carefully budgeted flight schedule called for us to be two days out on our return journey to Earth by now. But we still were no closer to departure than we had been four days ago.

The animals continued to wander around outside, nosing up against the ship, examining it, almost fondling it, with those pseudo-giraffes staring soulfully at us always. The beasts were as friendly as ever, little knowing how the tension was growing within the hull. The three of us walked around like zombies, eyes bright and lips clamped. We were scared—all of us. B

Something was keeping us from fixing the drive.

Something didn't want us to leave this planet.

I looked at the bland face of the purple-eyed giraffe staring through the viewport, and it stared mildly back at me. Around it was grouped the rest of the local fauna, the same incredible hodgepodge of improbable genera and species.

That night, the three of us stood guard in the control-room together. The drive was smashed anyway. The wires were soldered[6] in so many places by now that the control panel was a mass of shining alloy, and I knew that a few more such sabotagings and it would be impossible to patch it together anymore—if it wasn't so already.

The next night, I just didn't knock off. I continued soldering right on after dinner (and a pretty skimpy dinner it was, now that we were on close rations) and far on into the night. C

By morning, it was as if I hadn't done a thing.

"I give up," I announced, surveying the damage. "I don't see any sense in ruining my nerves trying to fix a thing that won't stay fixed."

Holdreth nodded. He looked terribly pale. "We'll have to find some new approach."

"Yeah. Some new approach."

I yanked open the food closet and examined our stock. Even figuring in the synthetics we would have fed to the animals if we hadn't released them, we were low on food. We had overstayed even the safety margin. It would be a hungry trip back—if we ever did get back.

I clambered through the hatch and sprawled down on a big rock near the ship. One of the furless dogs came over and nuzzled in my shirt. Davison stepped to the hatch and called down to me.

"What are you doing out there, Gus?"

"Just getting a little fresh air. I'm sick of living aboard that ship." I scratched the dog behind his pointed ears, and looked around.

The animals had lost most of their curiosity about us, and didn't congregate the way they used to. They were meandering all over the plain, nibbling at little deposits of a white doughy substance. It precipitated every night. "Manna,"[7] we called it. All the animals seemed to live on it. D

I folded my arms and leaned back.

We were getting to look awfully lean by the eighth day. I wasn't even trying to fix the ship anymore; the hunger was starting to get me. But I saw Davison puttering around with my solderbeam.

"What are you doing?"

"I'm going to repair the drive," he said. "You don't want to, but we can't just sit around, you

6. **soldered** (säd'ərd): patched together with a metal alloy.

7. **manna:** in the Bible, manna is the food miraculously given to the Israelites during their forty years of wandering in the wilderness.

know." His nose was deep in my repair guide, and he was fumbling with the release on the solder-beam.

I shrugged. "Go ahead, if you want to." I didn't care what he did. All I cared about was the gaping emptiness in my stomach, and about the dimly
A grasped fact that somehow we were stuck here for good.

"Gus?"

"Yeah?"

"I think it's time I told you something. I've been eating the manna for four days. It's good. It's nourishing stuff."

"You've been eating—the manna? Something that grows on an alien world? You crazy?"

"What else can we do? Starve?"

I smiled feebly, admitting that he was right. From somewhere in the back of the ship came the sounds of Holdreth moving around. Holdreth had taken this thing worse than any of us. He had a
B family back on Earth, and he was beginning to realize that he wasn't ever going to see them again.

"Why don't you get Holdreth?" Davison suggested. "Go out there and stuff yourselves with the manna. You've got to eat something."

"Yeah. What can I lose?" Moving like a mechanical man, I headed toward Holdreth's cabin.
C We would go out and eat the manna and cease being hungry, one way or another.

"Clyde?" I called. "Clyde?"

I entered his cabin. He was sitting at his desk, shaking convulsively, staring at the two streams of blood that trickled in red spurts from his slashed wrists.

"*Clyde!*"

He made no protest as I dragged him toward the infirmary cabin and got tourniquets around his arms, cutting off the bleeding. He just stared dully ahead, sobbing.

I slapped him and he came around. He shook his head dizzily, as if he didn't know where he was.

"I—I——"

"Easy, Clyde. Everything's all right."

"It's *not* all right," he said hollowly. "I'm still alive. Why didn't you let me die? Why didn't you——"

Davison entered the cabin. "What's been happening, Gus?"

"It's Clyde. The pressure's getting him. He tried to kill himself, but I think he's all right now. Get him something to eat, will you?"

We had Holdreth straightened around by evening. Davison gathered as much of the manna as he could find, and we held a feast.

"I wish we had nerve enough to kill some of the local fauna," Davison said. "Then we'd have a feast—steaks and everything!"

"The bacteria," Holdreth pointed out quietly. "We don't dare."

"I know. But it's a thought."

"No more thoughts," I said sharply. "Tomorrow morning we start work on the drive panel again. Maybe with some food in our bellies we'll be able to keep awake and see what's happening here."

Holdreth smiled. "Good. I can't wait to get out of this ship and back to a normal existence. I just can't wait!"

"Let's get some sleep," I said. "Tomorrow we'll give it another try. We'll get back," I said with a confidence I didn't feel.

The following morning I rose early and got my tool kit. My head was clear, and I was trying to put the pieces together without much luck. I started toward the control cabin.

And stopped.

And looked out the viewport.

I went back and awoke Holdreth and Davison. "Take a look out the port," I said hoarsely.

They looked. They gaped.

"It looks just like my house," Holdreth said. "My house on Earth."

"With all the comforts of home inside, I'll bet." I walked forward uneasily and lowered myself through the hatch. "Let's go look at it."

We approached it, while the animals frolicked around us. The big giraffe came near and shook its head gravely. The house stood in the middle of D
the clearing, small and neat and freshly painted.

I saw it now. During the night, invisible hands had put it there. Had assembled and built a cozy little Earth-type house and dropped it next to our ship for us to live in.

A. Character

What does Davison's decision to fix the drive reveal about his state of mind? (He is desperate and frustrated.)

B. Character

How is Holdreth's situation different from the others? (He has a family on Earth.) Review the comments made by Davison and Holdreth in the story. How is Davison different from Holdreth? (Davison is more ambitious, more interested in fame. Holdreth is more interested in zoology.)

C. Making Inferences

What does Gus mean when he says "cease being hungry, one way or another"? (Either the manna will satisfy their hunger, or it will kill them.)

D. Climax

What is the point of highest interest, or the climax of the story? (The men look out the viewport and see a house outside.)

Reading Check Test

1. Gus is the leader of the team and the most experienced zoologist. *(False)*
2. The species that the men encounter are highly varied and almost all hostile. *(False)*
3. The planet's landscape is like a vast, unending tropical rain forest. *(False)*
4. In the end, the men realize that they themselves are responsible for the repeated sabotage of the ship's drive mechanism. *(False)*
5. They come to understand that now they are themselves creatures kept in a "zoo." *(True)*

Closure

Ask students to list five ways in which we use animals for our benefit today. Have the students exchange their lists with partners. On the partners' lists, have them number each use from 1 for the most essential to humanity to 5 for the least essential to humanity. When the lists are returned, see if the students agree with their partners.

ANALYZING THE STORY
Identifying Facts
1. Their task is to collect living specimens for the zoological department of the Bureau of Interstellar Affairs.
2. The planet seems too hospitable; there are too many different species and only a few of each kind; all the species are friendly, both toward each other and toward the men; and the life there does not reflect any kind of normal evolutionary pattern.
3. They discover that wires connecting the control panel of the ship to the drive mechanism have been cut. They decide to get rid of the animals because they suspect that one of them has been the saboteur.
4. They eat the manna because they have run out of ordinary food, and all the other animals eat it. They will not eat any of the animals because they fear bacteria.
5. They realize the superbeings on the planet have deliberately kept them there; these superbeings are the real "collecting team"; and now the men have themselves become specimens in a larger "zoo."
(Answers continue on page 446.)

"Just like my house," Holdreth repeated in wonderment.

"It should be," I said. "They grabbed the model from your mind, as soon as they found out we couldn't live on the ship indefinitely."

Holdreth and Davison asked as one, "What do you mean?"

"You mean you haven't figured this place out yet?" I licked my lips, getting myself used to the fact that I was going to spend the rest of my life here. "You mean you don't realize what this house is intended to be?"

They shook their heads, baffled. I glanced around, from the house to the useless ship to the jungle to the plain to the little pond. It all made sense now.

"They want to keep us happy," I said. "They knew we weren't thriving aboard the ship, so they—they built us something a little more like home."

"*They*? The giraffes?"

"Forget the giraffes. They tried to warn us, but it's too late. They're intelligent beings, but they're prisoners just like us. I'm talking about the ones who run this place. The super-aliens who make us sabotage our own ship and not even know we're doing it, who stand someplace up there and gape at us. The ones who dredged together this motley assortment of beasts from all over the galaxy. Now we've been collected too. This whole place is just a zoo—a zoo for aliens so far ahead of us we don't dare dream what they're like."

I looked up at the shimmering blue-green sky, where invisible bars seemed to restrain us, and sank down dismally on the porch of our new home. I was resigned. There wasn't any sense in struggling against *them*.

I could see the neat little placard now: A

EARTHMEN. Native Habitat, Sol III. B

A. Irony
? What is ironic about the conclusion of the story? How is what happens on this planet just the reverse of what the men expected to happen? (The Earthmen had expected to capture extraterrestrials for Earth's zoos. Instead, aliens have trapped the Earthmen and put them in their own zoo.)

B. Theme
In their stories about the future, writers show how they feel about things that are going on today.
? What do you think Silverberg might be saying about the ways people relate to animals today? What is the main idea of the story? (He probably thinks that people are often thoughtless or even cruel in their capturing of and experimentation on animals. The main idea is that we may perhaps be too proud of our advanced civilization and intelligence. Silverberg may be warning us that advanced beings may someday treat us as we now treat animals.)

Responding to the Story

Analyzing the Story

Identifying Facts

1. Why is the collecting team traveling from planet to planet?
2. List three things that cause the narrator to mistrust the planet.
3. What delays the team's departure from the planet? Why do they decide to get rid of all of the animals on the spaceship?
4. Why do the men finally decide to eat the "manna"? What prevents them from killing and eating one of the animals?
5. What is the surprise at the end of the story? Who is really the "collecting team"?

Interpreting Meanings

6. Does the story suggest what is going to happen next? How do you feel about the way it ends?
7. What is unusual about the geography of the planet? At the end of the story, what explanation for the unusual geography is suggested?

SRW p. 43

8. **Foreshadowing** is the use of clues that hint at the way the story will end. List three details that foreshadow the end of this story. When did you guess what its ending would be?
9. In science fiction, the characters are usually not very well developed. Often they stand for different types of people. For instance, in this story, Davison might represent people who ignore danger in their greed for success and fame. What type of person or what point of view do you think Gus and Holdreth represent?

Applying Meanings

10. This story tells what happens to a group of humans who capture different animal species for study and experimentation. What do you think of the practice of capturing animals for study and for viewing in zoos? Do you look at it as taking away their freedom, or as contributing to human knowledge? Does this story give you a new way of looking at zoos? Explain.

(Answers begin on page 445.)

Interpreting Meanings

6. Through foreshadowing (for instance, the references to the apparent efforts of the giraffelike creature to communicate), and through the narrator's dawning awareness of what is really occurring, the story does suggest what will happen. Most students will enjoy the story's end.

7. The geography is almost ideally varied: "every sort of habitat" is there in a very small area—ocean, lake, forest, and plain. The explanation is that the whole planet is designed to serve as a habitat or zoo, so that all specimens will feel "at home."

8. Details are: the narrator's immediate "warning twinge of gloom"; the giraffe-like creature that seems to want to communicate; all of the narrator's sensible misgivings; the particular landscape and lack of evolutionary design; and the mysterious recurrent sabotage of the ship's drive mechanism.

9. Gus represents the rational, perceptive, balanced, and impartial, though nevertheless fallible, leader. Holdreth represents the "weak link," the good man with somewhat less courage and will.

(Answers continue in left-hand column.)

(Continued from top.)

Applying Meanings

10. Answers will vary. Some students will argue against the idea of zoos, seeing them as oppressive and inhumane. But most others will contend that *humane* zoos are possible, and that the need to understand all forms of life is imperative. However, students will probably agree that this story makes them think again about what it might actually be like to be kept *in* a zoo.

FURTHER READING FOR STUDENTS

Robert Silverberg, *Night Wings: Lost Race of Mars.*
Keith Deutsch, *Space Travel in Fact and Fiction.*
Pierre Boulle, *Planet of the Apes.*
Madeline L'Engle, *A Wrinkle in Time.*

Writing About the Story

A Creative Response

1. **Extending the Story.** What do you think might happen next if the story were to continue? Will the Earthmen meet the super-aliens? Will they find a way to repair the spaceship? Make up the next episode of "Collecting Team."
2. **Writing a Description.** Imagine another animal that the collecting team hasn't seen yet. Describe the creature in a paragraph. Use specific details, as Silverberg does. SRW p. 29

A Critical Response

SRW p. 67

3. **Summarizing a Plot.** In a brief essay, write a summary of the plot of "Collecting Team." Before you write, fill out a chart like the following to be sure you've covered all the major elements of a plot:

Basic situation	"Collecting Team"
Conflict	
Complications	
Climax	
Resolution	

For help in writing a summary, see page 253.

See Teacher's Manual page 142.

Analyzing Language and Vocabulary

Specialized Vocabulary

Every science has its own special vocabulary of technical terms. The writer of "Collecting Team" uses words from the vocabularies of space travel and zoology, the science that studies animals. Using a dictionary, tell which of the following words come from space travel and which come from zoology. Then choose three words from each science and use each of these words in a sentence.

1. blast off
2. deceleration
3. drive mechanism
4. ecologically
5. fauna
6. galaxy
7. genera
8. habitat
9. herbivores
10. jettison

Which words are also part of general usage—that is, not limited to space travel or zoology?

For answers, see Teacher's Manual page 143.

Reading About the Writer

Robert Silverberg (1935–) was born in New York City and graduated from Columbia University. His career has always been as a full-time writer. He has published an astonishing number of short stories, novels, and nonfiction works. He won the World Science Fiction Society Hugo Award in 1969 for *Nightwings: Lost Race of Mars.* According to Silverberg, the purpose of science fiction is "to show the reader something he has never been able to see with his own eyes, something strange and unique, beautiful and troubling . . ."

Focusing on Background

The Origin of the Story

Robert Silverberg was asked what gave him the idea to write the story "Collecting Team." This is his answer:

"One thing that appeals to me about science fiction—the main thing, perhaps—is the sense of the richness and diversity of the universe that it gives me. That was what led me to begin reading it when I was very young, and that was what led me to write it too. Through science fiction, I can experience the extraordinary range of *possibility* that the world has to offer.

"Going to the zoo does something of the same thing for me. Looking at the platypus, the aardvark, the tapir, even the familiar old pelican, I realize again and again what a wondrous and varied place our planet is, and how many strange and splendid creatures inhabit it.

"So it seemed logical to me, one day when I was looking about for a new story idea, to combine the two experiences, the one that science fiction offers and the one of visiting the zoo . . ."

—Robert Silverberg

Answers to Questions

1. Details are psychiatrist, train station, unhappiness, marriage, and work.
2. Most students will say they would trust the narrator; he sounds honest and sane, and his tone is intelligent, serene, and confident.
3. The first clue is the narrator's reference to his psychiatrist. Other clues are the imagery of a growing Grand Central Station and his mention of a tunnel he "got into."
4. Answers will vary. Some students will say it is a case of wish fulfillment, and that the narrator is wishing for escape or for an adventure.
5. Answers will vary.

Texas Essential Elements/(a) English Language Arts: 4G Fact/nonfact; **4H** Point of view. **(c) Reading: 3E** Fact/fictional details; **3F** Purpose/point of view/opinion

Review: Exercises in Reading Fiction

FANTASY

A writer of fantasy wants to transport us to another world. Some might do this with a simple announcement of the setting, such as, "Once upon a time, in a land far away." Other writers prefer to mix the real with the fantastic, as in the following excerpt. The story is about Grand Central Station, a large railroad terminal in New York City.

The presidents of the New York Central and the New York, New Haven, and Hartford railroads will swear on a stack of timetables that there are only two. But I say there are three, because I've *been* on the third level at Grand Central Station. Yes, I've taken the obvious step: I talked to a psychiatrist friend of mine, among others. I told him about the third level at Grand Central Station, and he said it was a waking-dream wish fulfillment. He said I was unhappy. That made my wife kind of mad, but he explained that he meant the modern world is full of insecurity, fear, war, worry, and all the rest of it, and that I just want to escape. Well, who doesn't? Everybody I know wants to escape, but they don't wander down into any third level at Grand Central Station.

. . . Sometimes I think Grand Central is growing like a tree, pushing out new corridors and staircases like roots. There's probably a long tunnel that nobody knows about feeling its way under the city right now, on its way to Times Square, and maybe another to Central Park. And maybe—because for so many people through the years Grand Central *has* been an exit, a way of escape—maybe that's how the tunnel I got into . . . . But I never told my psychiatrist friend about that idea.

—from "The Third Level,"
Jack Finney

A

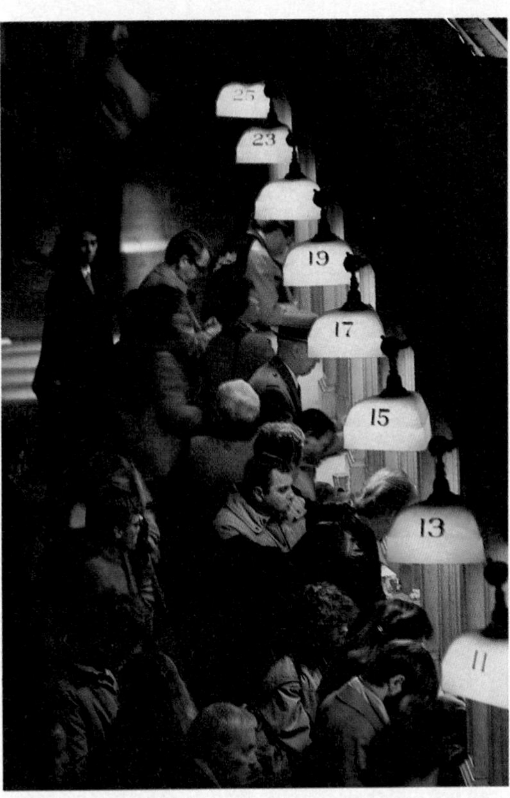

1. What realistic details make you think this will be a commonplace story about ordinary people?
2. Do you trust the narrator? Find some examples in the way he speaks that support your answer.
3. What is the first clue that the story might deal with something out of the ordinary? What other clues are there?
4. "Wish fulfillment" is a term from psychology used when a person says or believes something that he or she wishes were true. Do you think the narrator's belief about Grand Central is a case of wish fulfillment? If so, what do you think he's wishing for?
5. This excerpt is from the beginning of "The Third Level." What do you think will happen next in the story? How will it end? Try to obtain a copy of the story so you can see whether your prediction is similar to what Finney wrote.

A. About the Writer
Jack Finney (b. 1911) writes primarily short stories. His best known work is his science fiction novel *The Body Snatchers* (1955), which was made into a film.

Answers to Questions

1. Details are the bright cold April day, the hard wind, the glass doors of the mansion, the odors in the hallway, the broken lift. These details are for the most part unpleasant.

2. It is Hate Week.

Given this context, the reader is uncertain as to what Hate Week is; immediately the world of this passage is unfamiliar.

3. In our system, it is one o'clock. The use of the military system suggests that Winston's world is an oppressive and dictatorial one.

4. The poster clearly implies an authoritarian presence, a "Big Brother" who watches over all. The depressing day, the drab interior, the random cutting off of a basic service, and the reference to Hate Week—all these details suggest an oppressed and unhappy society.

A. About the Author
George Orwell (1903–1950), an English writer, also wrote *Animal Farm.* The novel *1984* has been made into a film.

Texas Essential Elements/(a) English Language Arts: 1B Purpose and audience; **4G** Fact/nonfact.
(c) Reading: 3A Main ideas/details; **3E** Fact/fictional details

Review: Exercises in Reading Fiction/*cont.*

SCIENCE FICTION

Works of science fiction can be divided in many different ways. One way of classifying them is according to the kind of world they picture for the future. Some science fiction stories show us a frightening future, one ruled by hostile alien beings or all-powerful machines. Other stories depict the future as a time when most problems will have been solved and people will be comfortable and happy.

The science fiction excerpt that follows was published in 1949. It is set in England and it includes some British terms, such as *lift* for elevator and *flat* for apartment. Read the excerpt and decide which kind of future world the story describes.

It was a bright cold day in April, and the clocks were striking thirteen. Winston Smith, his chin nuzzled into his breast in an effort to escape the vile wind, slipped quickly through the glass doors of Victory Mansion. . . .

The hallway smelt of boiled cabbage and old rag mats. At one end of it a colored poster, too large for indoor display, had been tacked to the wall. It depicted simply an enormous face, more than a meter wide: the face of a man of about forty-five, with a heavy black mustache and ruggedly handsome features. Winston made for the stairs. It was no use trying the lift. Even at the best of times it was seldom working, and at present the electric current was cut off during working hours. It was part of the economy drive for Hate Week. The flat was seven flights up, and Winston . . . went slowly, resting several times on the way. On each landing, opposite the lift shaft, the poster with the enormous face gazed from the wall. It was one of those pictures which are so contrived that the eyes follow you about when you move. BIG BROTHER IS WATCHING YOU, the caption beneath it ran.

—from *1984*,
by George Orwell

A

1. Which details of the setting in this story could describe almost any city in the world today? Do those details present a pleasant or an unpleasant setting?
2. Winston Smith and his fellow citizens are facing an economy drive. What is the reason for it? How is this a hint that Winston's world is not as familiar to us as we might have thought when we began reading?
3. The twenty-four hour system of telling time (continuing to count after twelve o'clock noon, instead of starting again from "1") is used in the military. In the first sentence, the clock is striking thirteen—what time is it in our system? Does the use of this military system give you a hint about Winston's world?
4. What does the poster tell you about Winston's world? What does it and the other details in the excerpt suggest about the kind of society this science fiction story depicts?

Writing

1. **Mixing Fantasy and Reality.** Write a beginning for a fantasy about someone like you. Describe your character and setting as realistically as possible. Include at least one hint that something fantastic is about to happen. Try to make your hint sound casual and matter-of-fact, the way Jack Finney does in "The Third Level."
2. **Creating a Science Fiction Setting.** Assume you are going to write a story set at least 100 years in the future. How do you imagine the world will be at that time? Write a list of details that would describe the world in your story. Then write at least two paragraphs to begin your story. The paragraph should describe what this future world will be like. Include several of the details from your list. Also, try to create a positive or negative feeling about the world of your story.

For evaluation strategies, see Teacher's Manual page 144.

★ Texas Essential Elements/(a) English Language Arts: **1A** Composing process; **1B** Purpose and audience; **1H** Proofread; **1I** Spelling generalizations; **2B** Parts of speech; **2D** Grammar/punctuation/spelling

Exercises in Critical Thinking and Writing

For teaching and evaluation strategies on this exercise, see Teacher's Manual page 144.

PREDICTING OUTCOMES

Writing Assignment

Each of the following statements changes one fact from a story in this unit. What do you think would happen if:

1. In "The Monkey's Paw" (page 403), the paw comes with *four* wishes.
2. In "Collecting Team" (page 436), Gus (the pilot and narrator) has a chance to talk with the Alien in charge of the planet's "zoo."
3. In "The Naming of Names" (page 423), Mr. Bittering finishes his rocket before the supply of "earth" food in his freezer runs out.

Choose one of these stories, and write at least one paragraph telling what you think would happen if the changed fact were true.

Background

As you read a story, you ask yourself many questions that you are probably not even aware of: "What does this mean? Why is she doing that? What will happen next? How will the story end?" It is human nature to try to **predict outcomes**—to guess what will happen next. For example, when did you first guess that the fisherman would save his own life by tricking the genie in "The Story of the Fisherman" (page 413)?

When did you guess the outcome of "Collecting Team" (page 436)?

In order to predict an outcome, you must make a logical guess based on what you already know. Then you must judge whether the outcome you predict is probable, possible, or impossible.

Probable: Something is likely to happen.
Possible: Something could happen but isn't very likely to.
Impossible: Something could not happen.

Prewriting

Try out all three of the assignments; think about what would happen if the one fact changed. Then choose the one you find most interesting to think about. You might make a diagram to brainstorm about possible outcomes. As an example, here is a diagram that predicts outcomes for the following assignment: *What if the fisherman in "The Story of the Fisherman" (page 413) is unable to trick the genie into returning to his jar?*

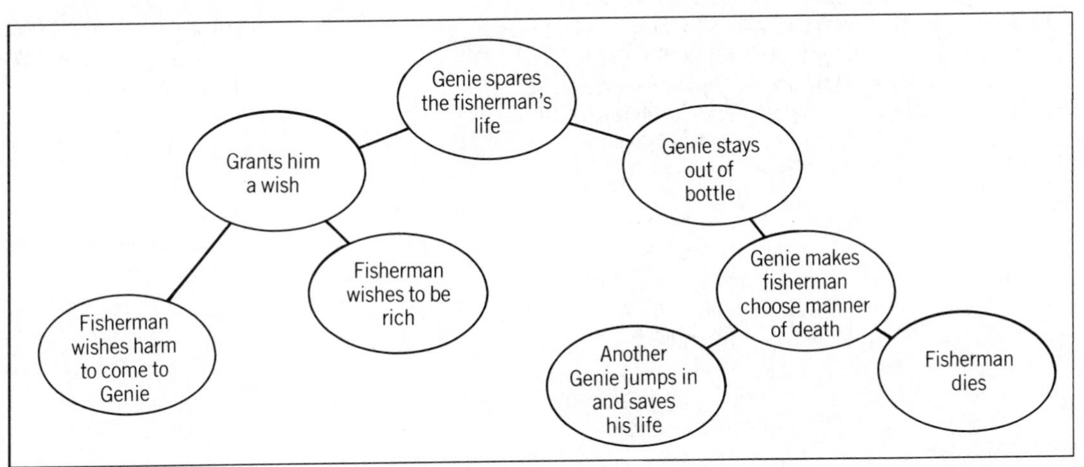

★ Texas Essential Elements/(a) English Language Arts (continued): **4E** Predict; **4I** Follow directions.
(c) Reading: **3H** Predict; **4A** Follow directions

Exercises in Critical Thinking and Writing/*cont.*

If you were writing (or reading) a realistic story, at this point you'd have to decide which of the outcomes you've predicted is most probable (most likely to happen). But since you're in a fantasy and science-fiction unit, almost anything is possible. You can decide which outcome most interests you—which one you'd like to pursue. Once you've chosen an outcome, add to your diagram some specific details about setting, a new character's appearance, events, etc.

Writing

Write a paragraph describing the outcome you predict for either 1, 2, or 3 in the Writing Assignment. (If you wish, you may also try writing the actual story ending based on your prediction.) Include specific details from your Prewriting diagram.

As a guide, here is the beginning of a paragraph summarizing one of the outcomes in the Prewriting chart.

The fisherman, seeing no way out of his predicament, finally chose the sea as his manner of death. After all, it had governed his joys and woes for as long as he could remember. Just as he was about to inform the genie of his decision, the earth began to rumble, and thick smoke began to billow from the ground. Even the genie looked nervous. A great growling voice said "You cannot take petty revenge on this poor soul! I hereby banish you forever!!" The fisherman looked up, terrified, to see who his rescuer was . . .

Revising and Proofreading Self-Check

1. Have I included enough specific details to make the ending interesting?
2. Does the outcome seem to "fit" the rest of the story?
3. Does every sentence start with a capital letter and end with a period or other end punctuation mark?
4. Are my ideas clearly expressed? Have I said everything I wanted to say?

Partner Check

1. Are there any spelling errors?
2. Are sentences punctuated correctly?
3. Are all the sentences and ideas clearly stated?
4. Does the predicted outcome seem logical? Is it interesting? Satisfying?
5. What do I like best about this paper? What needs improvement?

THE MYTHS OF GREECE AND ROME

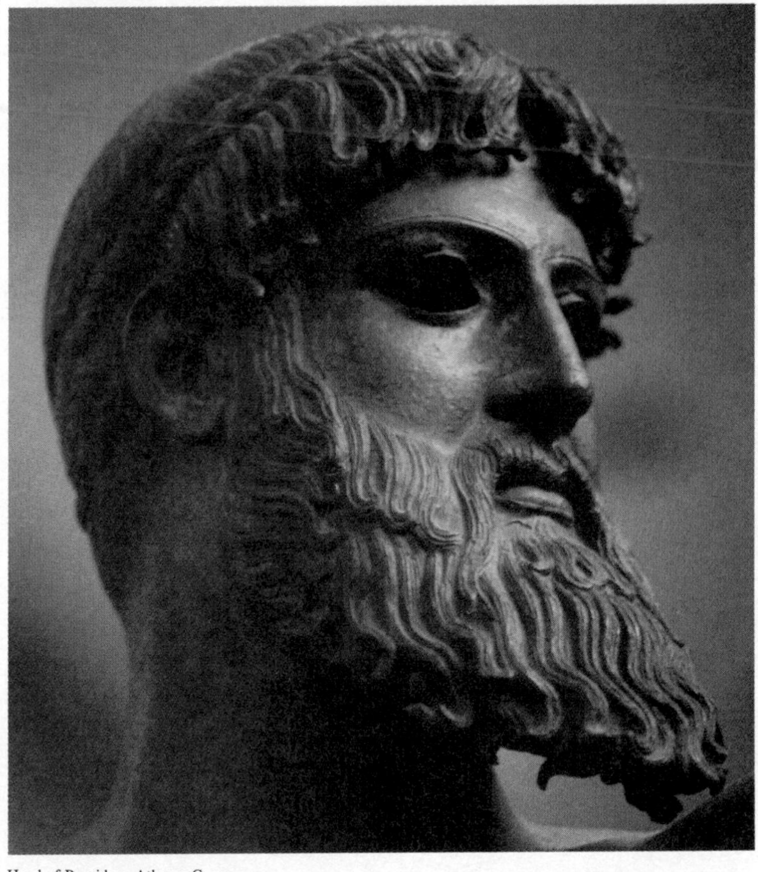

Head of Poseidon. Athens, Greece.

UNIT EIGHT

David Adams Leeming

Humanities Connection: Discussing the Fine Art

The sculpture is of Poseidon, god of the seas and rivers. As students will learn in "The Palace of Olympus" (page 473), he was one of Zeus's older brothers and the second most powerful god. Notice the waves in his beard, which are like the waves of the sea. When the statue was first sculpted it had eyelashes, and beautiful gems filled the eye sockets, but the stones and lashes have been lost over time.

Teaching the Myths of Greece and Rome

This unit will introduce students to classical mythology through lively, readable modern retellings. Explain that a culture's myths reveal that culture's system of beliefs. The Greek and Roman myths are an expression of how people in those societies viewed the universe and their places in it. Although these myths hold no religious truths for us anymore, their themes and symbols continue to reverberate through our culture. Their language also continues to echo through our own: Some sixty percent of the English vocabulary comes from Latin, for example.

Tell your class that myths are not only enlightening but exciting to read. These stories are full of love, adventure, and violence. They are also often very humorous.

Have students read the unit introduction on text pages 453–454, which lists some of the visible reflections of classical mythology in our culture. Some of your students will know enough about classical myths to think of still other familiar images, words, or ideas from Greek and Roman mythology; the many examples include the signs of the Zodiac and the figure of Cupid on Valentine's Day cards. Students may also have heard some mythical stories.

Discuss with your class the passages "What Is a Myth?" and "Collectors of Myths" on pages 454–456. To check students' grasp of the term *myth,* name several short stories from the textbook students have already read, and have the class explain why these are not myths.

Finally, have students read "The Uses of Mythology" on page 456. Stress that myths were not mere entertainment but provided answers to important questions people had about themselves and their world.

Objectives of the Unit

1. To improve reading proficiency and expand vocabulary
2. To identify the purposes of mythology
3. To gain exposure to the classical heritage of Western culture
4. To identify principal deities and heroes of classical mythology
5. To gain exposure to the work of noted mythologists
6. To define and identify the terms *metamorphosis, hubris,* and *pietas*
7. To define and identify the following literary elements: *theme, moral, motive, tone,* and *character*
8. To interpret and respond to myths orally and in writing through an analysis of their elements
9. To practice the following critical thinking and writing skills:
   a. Analyzing theme
   b. Analyzing a character's motives
   c. Comparing characters
   d. Supporting a topic sentence
   e. Writing a research report
   f. Comparing myths
   g. Comparing a myth and a contemporary poem
   h. Analyzing details

SUPPLEMENTARY SUPPORT MATERIAL: UNIT EIGHT

1. Word Analogies Test (page 203 of Test Book)
2. Unit Review Test (page 205 of Test Book)
3. Critical Thinking and Writing Test (page 209 of Test Book)
4. Understanding a Myth (Study and Reinforcement Worksheet, page 7)
5. Instructional Overhead Transparencies

Unit Outline

THE MYTHS OF GREECE AND ROME

A. **Humanities Connection: Discussing Architecture**
There are three classic styles of Greek columns: Doric, Ionic, and Corinthian. They range from simple and plain (the Doric) to very ornamental (the Corinthian). The columns that mark the entrances of the houses along this street are Ionic.

★ **Texas Essential Elements/(a) English Language Arts: 3C** Literary traditions; **3D** Folklore/legends/myths. **(c) Reading: 1B** Structural analysis

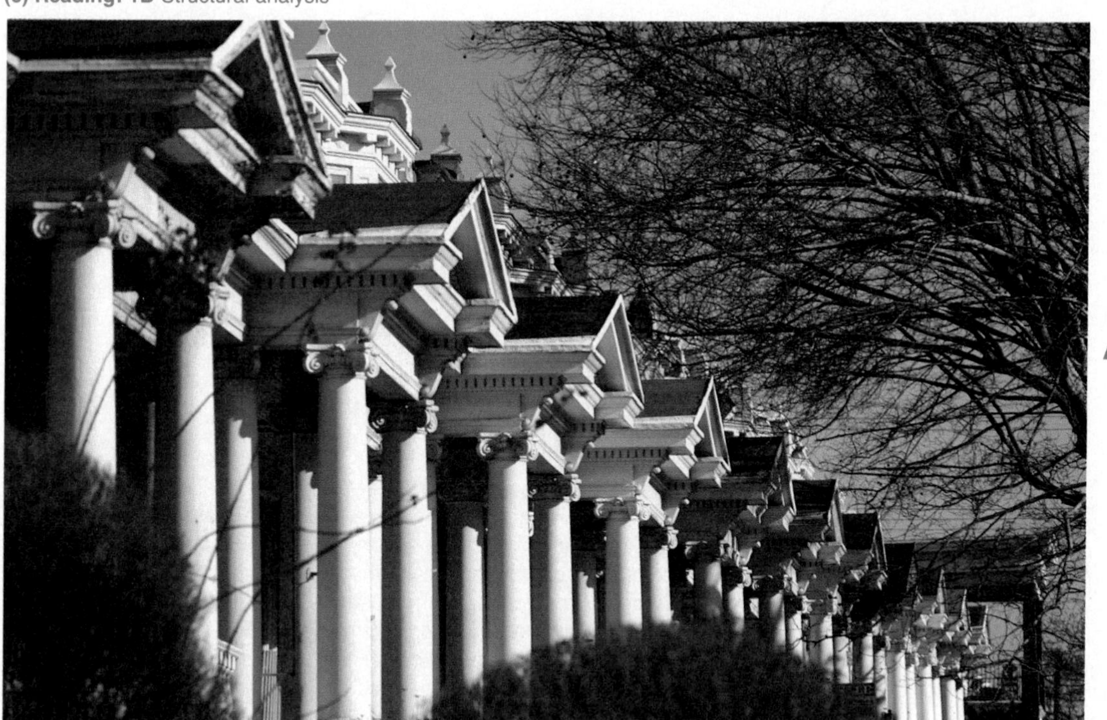

A

I made my song a coat
Covered with embroideries
Out of old mythologies . . .

—from "A Coat,"
William Butler Yeats

B

Myths All Around Us

It is difficult to imagine what our civilization would be like without the mythology of ancient Greece and Rome. The ancient immortals are still around us in spirit. For instance, you might pass imitations of their "houses" almost every day. Whenever you see a large building with many columns holding up a roof, you are looking at an imitation of a Greek temple. If you have visited one of the great national capitals of the world—Washington, D.C., Paris, Rome, or London—you have seen many copies of "classical" temples. The Capitol building in Washington is built on the style of a classical temple, the White House resembles a classical temple, and so do the New York Public Library, Saint Paul's Cathedral in London, Saint Peter's in Rome, and—probably—your own state capitol building. Even a walk down most of our local main streets will take us past post offices, town halls, banks, and churches with tall columns that make them look something like the structures that were once built in Greece and Rome to honor the gods.

B. **Responding to the Quotation**
William Butler Yeats (1865–1939) was an Irish poet and dramatist who won the Nobel Prize for literature in 1923. The coat of "old mythologies" represents the personal, cultural, and political history that surrounds each of our lives. Mythology is a body of stories—new and ancient—that affects our lives now just as it affected the lives of the ancient Greeks and Romans. Yeats's "song" may be his life, his poem, or the story within his poem. The "old mythologies" he embroiders are probably made up of ancient Irish myths, Greek myths, stories he has heard throughout his lifetime, and even stories he himself created.

A. Themes
Many poets and artists refer to the places and characters of ancient mythology because these stories are filled with timeless themes. The situations in which the characters find themselves and the behavior of the mythological figures reflect events and human behavior of every age.

Introductory Supplementary Support Material

1. Introduction/Understanding the Elements of Myth Test (page 173 of Test Book)
2. Reading Check Test blackline master

B. Responding
? Ask students what mythological stories, if any, they have read. Have they heard about any mythological characters even if they haven't read any myths? (e.g., Zeus, Venus, Mars, Athena)

C. Humanities Connection: Discussing the Fine Art
The disk (or discus) throw is one of the oldest individual sports. The Greeks considered the disk-throwing champion their greatest athlete. The "perfect" human form was very important to the Greeks and Romans. Note the musculature on the man's body and the beauty of his face.
? Compare this disk thrower with the contemporary disk thrower in the photograph on text page 455. Name two similarities and two differences between them.

And if you go to any one of the great museums of Europe or America, you will find statues and paintings of classical gods and heroes—as many as you will find of characters and events from American history.

If you read poetry in English classes, you will come across references to such ancient places as Troy and Carthage. You will read references to such monsters as the Sirens and the Cyclops, to such gods and heroes as Poseidon, Odysseus (whose Roman name is Ulysses), Athena, and Prometheus. These are all names
A from mythology—names that poets and artists expect us to recognize.

Why Are the Myths Important?

There is good reason for the continued presence of these strange beings and places in our lives. They are all related to those great classical civilizations of Greece and Rome that were so important to our development as a society. These civilizations gave us much of our astronomy, our mathematics, our philosophy, our architecture, our medicine, our monetary system, and our systems of government and law. We should remember, for instance, that the word *democracy* comes from the Greek word *demokratia,* meaning "rule of the people." This was a kind of government that first flourished in the ancient Greek city-state of Athens.

It is true, of course, that people no longer believe in the Greek and Roman gods and goddesses. But the stories still fascinate us as literature, and they still reveal "truths" about who we are and why we behave as we do. These stories have been a basic part of the education of young people from the time of the ancient Greeks down to the present day. Such stories as the kidnapping of Persephone, the quest for the Golden Fleece, and the wanderings of
B Odysseus, are an important part of Western culture.

C 

Disk thrower.

Museo Nazionale, Rome, Italy.

What Is a Myth?

The word *mythology* means the study of myths. The word *myth* itself comes from the Latin word *mythos* and from the Greek word *muthos,* meaning "story." *Muthos,* in turn, comes from *mu,* meaning "to make a sound with the mouth." Perhaps we could say, then, that myths are as basic to us as language itself.

But when we say a story is a "myth" what do we really mean? How is a myth different from a folktale, a legend, or a fairy tale? We do not call the story of Tom Sawyer a myth, even though we know that no Tom Sawyer ever existed. We do not even call the stories of Paul Bunyan or Daniel Boone myths, even though these heroes have supernatural powers and so seem, like Hercules, to be "bigger than life."

Myths are stories that are always in some sense religious. Myths represent the deepest wishes and fears of "primitive" human beings. They helped these people to understand the mysterious

A and sometimes frightening forces of the universe—forces such as seasonal changes, fire, lightning, drought, floods, and death. Myths probably originated when people began to ask questions about the creation of the world and about their role in it. The first "myth-makers" might have been wise old men and women who had a magical talent for telling stories to "explain" the natural world. These strange, dream-like stories of the extraordinary deeds of beings we call gods and heroes are what we now call "myths."

The birth of Athena from the head of Zeus (c. 560–550 B.C.). Athenian cup.

British Museum.

B

Collectors of Myths

Of course, the early myth-makers would not have known how to write. Most of the myths we will read here originated in the area around the Mediterranean Sea. These old myths were passed on from generation to generation by word of mouth by the many tribes who passed through or who lived in the part of the world we now call Greece and western Turkey.

Many years later, the myths were written down. The first famous collectors of the Greek myths were the poets Homer and Hesiod (he'sē·əd). Both of these poets probably lived about eight hundred years before the birth of Christ. The myths told by Homer are found in his two great epic poems, the *Iliad* and the *Odyssey.* Hesiod's stories are collected in his books called *Theogony* (which means "the origin of the gods") and *Works and Days.*

By the second century B.C., the Romans had conquered the Greeks and had adopted the Greek myths as their own. But the Romans added a new tone to the old stories. This tone reflected

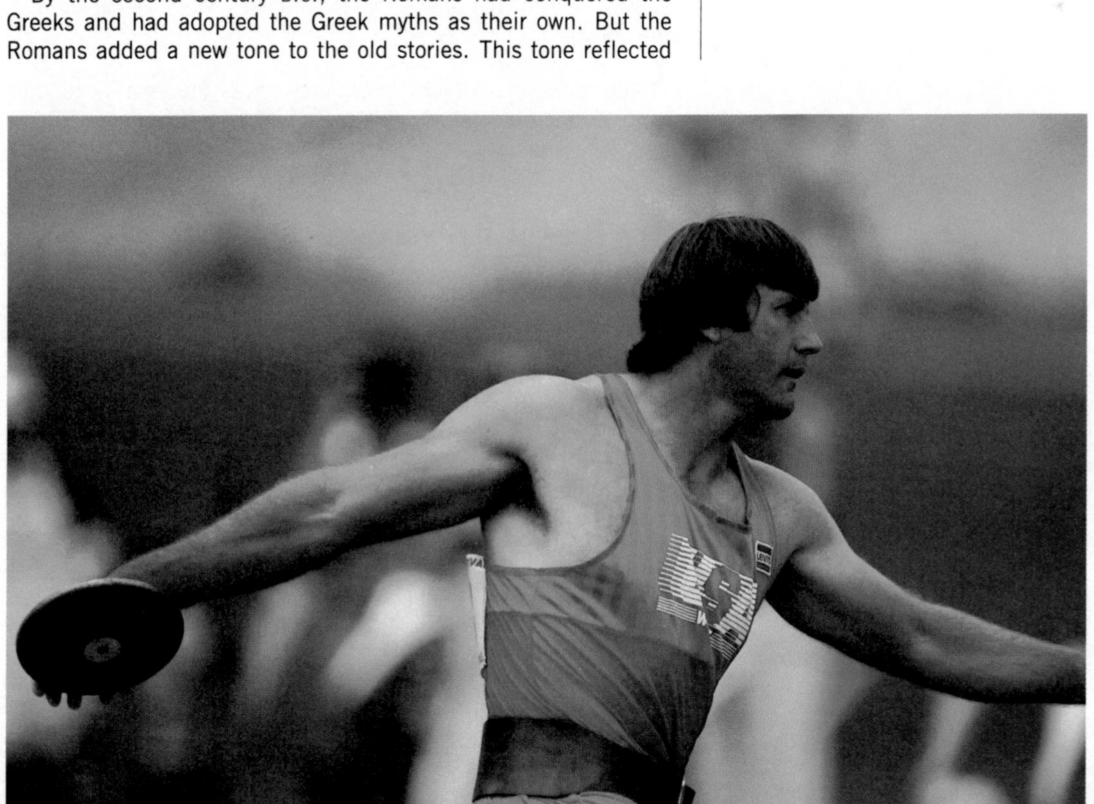

A. Themes
Nearly all cultures have myths that explain natural phenomena. These myths often contain similar elements, even though the cultures themselves are far apart. For example, accounts of a great flood can be found in the Mexican and Central American story of the destruction of the Men of Wood, the Greek story of Deucalion and Pyrrha, the Sumerian story of Uta-Naphishtim in the *Epic of Gilgamesh,* and the biblical account of Noah's Ark.

B. Humanities Connection: Responding to the Fine Art
This Athenian cup shows Athena being born out of Zeus's head. As one story recounts, Zeus was complaining of an awful headache one day, so Hephaestus, the craftsman of the gods, kindly split open Zeus's head to find the source of the pain. Out sprung Zeus's daughter Athena, goddess of war, clad in full armor.

A. Responding to the Photograph
When we look at this photograph of the stars, we can easily understand why the sky has always filled people with wonder and awe. There are more than fifty different versions of a North American Indian myth called Star Husband. In this myth, a girl who wishes for a star is lifted up into the sky, where she marries a star. Later, she tries to escape back to earth by a rope that drops through a hole in the sky.

B. Expansion
Ovid (43 B.C.–A.D. 17 or 18) was best known for his witty, sophisticated love poems. Ovid's *Metamorphoses* was the first work that successfully linked all the Greek myths to the Roman myths. Many of the stories involve a metamorphosis, or a change in physical form, appearance, or character.

C. Responding
? What might three of the "deepest fears and hopes" be? (Examples include fears about death, war, illness; hopes for love, health, prosperity, peace)

READING CHECK TEST

1. Modern architecture shows the influence of the ancient civilizations of ________. *Greece and Rome*
2. The study of myths is called________. *mythology*
3. Myths represent the deepest wishes and________of human beings. *fears*
4. The myths told by Homer are contained in his two great epic poems,________and________. *the* Iliad, *the* Odyssey
5. The two great Roman myth writers were________and________. *Ovid, Virgil*

A

the fact that the Romans were less serious about religion than the Greeks were. Much of what we think of as funny and even disrespectful toward the gods in Greco-Roman mythology comes from the collection of myths retold by the Roman poet Ovid in his great work called *Metamorphoses.* B

The other great Roman myth-maker was the poet Virgil, who wrote a long epic called the *Aeneid* about the founding of Rome by the hero Aeneas.

The Uses of Mythology

The Greek and Roman myth-makers were different from one another, but they all could tell stories well. They all could speak to the real concerns of ordinary people about the mysteries of life. Great myths are never merely silly or superstitious tales. Like all true art, the great myths give us insights into the nature of our world.

The rest of this unit will be based on the "uses" of Greek and Roman mythology. We will see that the classical myths were used for these purposes:

1. To explain the creation of the world
2. To explain natural phenomena
3. To give story form to ancient religious practices
4. To teach moral lessons
5. To explain history
6. To express, as dreams do, the deepest fears and hopes of the human race C

Supplementary Support Material
Introduction/Myths of Creation Test (page 175 of Test Book)

★ **Texas Essential Elements/(a) English Language Arts: 3D** Folklore/legends/myths

Myths of Creation

For teaching suggestions on this section, see Teacher's Manual page 147.

There are many Greek creation stories. One story became the official version in Athens in the fifth century B.C. This was the story told by the poet Hesiod. Hesiod's creation story is male-dominated, or patriarchal (from the word *patriarch,* meaning "father"). The main figure in this creation story is the cruel father-god called Uranus. Earlier versions of the creation story had emphasized the creative powers of the kind earth-mother, Gaia (gā′ə).

Parts of Hesiod's story are retold here by Jay Macpherson, one of our most important modern "mythologists," or students of mythology.
A The story begins with Chaos, or nothingness, and the birth of Earth and Sky—the earth-mother and the sky-father. Then a tremendous struggle for power in the universe takes place. The Golden Age (or Paradise) follows, and we come finally to the rise of the god Zeus. We learn of the creation of humans and we are told how a god called Prometheus brought fire to Earth and was cruelly punished for it. We hear the famous story of the woman Pandora who disobeyed the gods and released evil into the world. There, in the Pandora story, we find a reason for the pain and trouble that are mixed with the joys of life.

B

Head of Zeus, a copy of a lost Greek original of the 4th century B.C.

A. Expansion
The word *chaos* also means "confusion" and "disorder." As the great English poet John Milton writes: "First there was chaos, the vast immeasurable abyss, outrageous as a sea, dark, wasteful, wild."

B. Humanities Connection: Responding to the Fine Art
? Look closely at Zeus's features here. Write four sentences describing what you think the god's character might be like: wise, gentle, loving, arrogant, tyrranical. Zeus appears to be fairly young in this statue. Tell students that gods are usually portrayed as young, and good-looking because one of their outstanding, and most enviable, traits was their immortality.

A. Expansion
When the goddesses and gods traveled down to Earth, they often disguised themselves. It was believed that Zeus could not show himself in his godly form to mortals because the brilliance of his appearance would kill them. When Athena wanted to help Odysseus in the *Odyssey,* she disguised herself as a wise old man; when she wanted to test the boastful Arachne, she came as a ragged old lady.

B. Humanities Connection: Discussing the Fine Art
Dionysus was the god of wine, fertility, and music. Nayos is a large Greek island in the southern Aegean Sea.

C. Humanities Connection: Discussing the Fine Art
This marble bust of Athena shows the goddess with her characteristic helmet of war. The Greeks were known for their remarkable ability to carve marble. Although marble is an extremely hard substance, the sculptor has made it appear soft and flowing.

The Gods and Goddesses of Ancient Greece and Rome

B

Head of Dionysus (460 B.C.). Greek silver coin of Naxos.

A

The myths of ancient Greece and Rome are stories about gods and goddesses. According to the stories, the divinities lived on Mount Olympus, and many of them often traveled down to spend time with ordinary people.

To the ancients, a god or goddess was a powerful being, often identified with a natural force. They were also capable of cruelty, jealousy, lying, and even murder. In fact, they represent everything—both good and bad—that people are capable of.

The Romans so admired the Greek culture that they absorbed the Greek myths into their own religion. For that reason, many of the Roman gods are the same as those of the Greeks, with different names. The following chart will help you identify some of the characters in the myths in this unit.

C

Bust of Athena (c. 430–420 B.C.). Marble. After the Greek original by Cresilas.

Apollo by Dosso Dossi (c. 1530–1540). Oil.

A

Greek Name	Roman Name	Area of Power
Cronus (krō′nəs)	Saturn	ruler of the Titans
Zeus (zo͞os)	Jupiter (Jove)	the sky; the weather; the chief god
Hera (hēr′ə)	Juno	queen of the gods; protector of women and marriage
Ares (âr′ēz)	Mars	war
Poseidon (pō·sī′dən)	Neptune	the seas; horses
Apollo (ə·pol′ō) (also Phoebus Apollo)	Apollo	the sun; youth; music; archery; healing; prophecy
Artemis (är′tə·mis)	Diana	the moon; hunting; wild animals; childbirth
Hades (hā′dēz)	Pluto	the underworld
Eros (er′os)	Cupid	love
Aphrodite (af′rə·dī′tē)	Venus	love; beauty; pleasure
Hephaestus (hi·fes′təs)	Vulcan	fire; craftsman for the gods
Hermes (hur′mēz)	Mercury	messenger of the gods; god of secrets, tricks, and the thieves
Athena (ə·thē′nə)	Minerva	wisdom; war; crafts
Demeter (di·mē′tər)	Ceres	corn and agriculture; an earth goddess
Dionysus (dī′ə·nī′səs)	Bacchus	wine; fertility; music

B

A. Humanities Connection: Discussing the Fine Art
Dosso Dossi (1479?–1542) was an Italian painter best known for his portraits and paintings of historical subjects. Notice how human Apollo appears in the painting.
? Refer to Apollo's "Area of Power" in the chart below. What two characteristics of Apollo are shown in the painting? (Youth and music)

B. Responding
? Some of the Greek and Roman names of the goddesses and gods may be familiar to you. List two or three places or products that use or make reference to the names listed in this chart. (Some examples are the Apollo performance hall, the Cupid gift shop, the Mercury automobile, the restaurant Poseidon, the Bacchus wine store)

PREREADING

1. BUILDING ON PRIOR KNOWLEDGE. As the myth about Pandora suggests (see text page 468) suggests, human beings are basically very curious creatures. We like to know how things are made and where things come from. Nearly every culture has its own set of myths or folklore to explain natural phenomena. Ask students whether they remember asking adults such questions as those listed in the headnote. What other questions did they ask? What answers were they given? As they read these origin myths, you might ask them to think of other stories they may know that explain how the world began.

2. ESTABLISHING A PURPOSE. As students read the following myths, have them list the most powerful god or goddess of each generation from Chaos to Zeus. (Chaos, Night and Depth, Eros, Gaia and Uranus, Cronus, Zeus)

3. PREREADING JOURNAL. Have students write on a piece of paper the name of their favorite animal in the zoo and place the paper in a hat. Pass the hat around, and have each student pick a name from it. Then have them write a short myth about how they imagine this animal came into existence. (Remind students that their answers can be made up or based on scientific information. They should use as many details as possible.)

A. Character
? What is the Roman name for Eros? (Cupid) According to later myth writers, Eros was the son of Venus, or Greek Aphrodite.

B. Expansion
Students might enjoy drawing a picture of one of Gaia's offspring, using their imagination to fill in details.

★ **Texas Essential Elements/(a) English Language Arts: 3D** Folklore/legends/myths. **(c) Reading: 1C** Dictionaries

IN THE BEGINNING

Retold by Jay Macpherson

"In the Beginning" and "After the Earth Appeared" contain *origin* myths. They explained to the ancient Greeks how certain things in the world came to be. Here are some of the questions they answer. As you read, watch for their imaginative answers:

1. **Why do we have to suffer and die?**
2. **Why do people have to work so hard for a living?**
3. **Who or what determines how long we will live?**
4. **What makes the wind blow?**
5. **Who holds up the sky?**
6. **Why does the volcano erupt with fire and terrible noises?**

For a detailed lesson plan on this myth, see Teacher's Manual pages 148–149.

A biography of Jay Macpherson appears on text page 471.

The Creation

In the beginning, before the heavens and the earth, all there was was Chaos, the dark and formless void. And after ages of time had passed, there appeared two tremendous beings, the most ancient goddess Night and her brother Erebus, the Depth. And from these two was born A Eros, who is Love, the most powerful of all the gods. After him arose Gaia, the great Earth-Mother, who brought forth from herself first the world we live on and then Uranus,[1] the starry sky, that lies above and around her and is the eternal home of the blessed gods. Then subtle Eros brought the Earth-Mother and the Sky-Father together in love, and from them in the course of time were born a series of strange and monstrous creatures, the early births of time. First came the three brothers Gyges,[2] Cottus, and Briareos,[3] huger than mountains, fifty-headed and hundred-handed, terrifying to look upon. So at least thought their father Uranus, and he took them from their mother and shut them up in the dark places under the earth. Gaia next bore the three Cyclops,[4] the Wheel-Eyed ones, smaller than the Hundred-Handed but still giants, and each having a single round eye in the center of his forehead. These too their father shut away in the earth, afraid less of their size and strength than of their skill at forging metal weapons, for they were the first smiths.

The last children of Gaia were the twelve Titans, six sons and six daughters, larger than mortal men but not monstrous, endowed with beauty and majesty. Then Gaia, weary of Uranus's cruel treatment of her other children, appealed to her Titan sons to avenge their sufferings. She offered them B a sharp sickle of adamant, the hardest of stones, with which to wound their father and drive him away. Only Cronus, the youngest and bravest, dared attempt such a deed. He waited until night fell and Uranus came down to embrace Gaia; then he took the sickle and maimed his father, severing the embrace of Earth and Sky. Then Cronus ruled in his father's place over the whole world; but he would not release his monstrous elder brothers from their captivity under the earth.

1. **Uranus** (yoor′ə·nəs).
2. **Gyges** (gī′gēs).
3. **Briareos** (brī·ar·ē′əs).
4. **Cyclops** (sī′kläps).

Words from Mythology. Many English words have a connection with Greek and Roman mythology. For example, the prefix *geo-*, as in *geography,* comes from the Greek word *gaia,* meaning "the earth." In Greek mythology Gaia is the goddess of the earth. Remembering names from mythology can often help you understand the meaning of some words in English. What other names resemble modern English words?

Supplementary Support Material
1. Vocabulary Activity Sheet
2. Reading Check Test blackline master
3. Selection Test (page 177 of Test Book)
4. Reader's Response Journal
5. Workbook (page 129)

Developing Vocabulary
The following words appear on a test in the Test Book, page 178. (See also the Vocabulary Activity Sheet.)

smith	cornucopia
adamant	oracle
girdles	battlements
paradise	routed
impious	verge

A

The six Titan brothers took their six sisters for wives, and their progeny[5] were the gods that fill the land and sea and air. To his oldest brother Oceanus, Cronus gave the stream that girdles the earth, and his children were the deities of the water. His innumerable sons were the Rivers of the earth, and his daughters were the nymphs[6] of fountain, lake, and stream, as well as of the sea. The nymphs are a gentle and kindly race, beloved by gods and men; but one of them, whose name is Styx, the Hateful, is unlike the others. Her stream rises in a sunless underground cavern and her waters are chill and numbing to the heart. Even the gods if they swear by Styx fear to break their oath. B

The most beautiful of Uranus's Titan children were the light-god Hyperion and his sister-wife Thea, who lived in a palace of clouds in the eastern sky and whose children were Helios the Sun, Selene the Moon, and Eos the Dawn. Eos became the mother of Phosphorus the Morning Star, Hesperus the Evening Star, and the Planets, the wandering stars. C Her other children are Eurus, Zephyrus, Notus, and Boreas, the Four Winds that blow from east, west, south, and north.

5. **progeny** (präj′ə·nē): children, or descendants.
6. **nymphs:** minor nature goddesses.

A. Responding to the Photograph
? From your reading of the myth so far, what event might this photograph illustrate? Uranus's disgust at his sons? Cronus's severing the earth and sky?

B. Expansion
The river Styx is one of the rivers that separates Hades, or the underworld, from the world above. It was believed that when a person died, he or she was ferried across the river Styx to Hades by the boatman Charon.

C. Scientific Connection
The Morning Star and Evening Star are not stars but planets. The planets, usually Venus or Mercury, can be seen either after sunset or before sunrise. Because they move in a smaller orbit than the earth, they appear to move from one side of the sun to another. The ancient Greeks did not realize that the Morning Star and the Evening Star were one and the same celestial body.

A. Vocabulary
plowshares: the cutting blades of a plow

B. Interpreting
? Why would the absence of metals and precious stones on earth be included in a list of peaceful elements? (It indicates that there was no monetary system and therefore there was no greed.)

C. Making Inferences
? What aspect of human behavior is important to Zeus? (That mortals respect, obey, and honor the gods)

D. Vocabulary
swaddling bands: the bands of cloth that were wrapped around infants in former times (also called swaddling clothes)

E. Expansion
The Horn of Plenty has come to be a symbol of nature's productivity.
? Is the Horn of Plenty a part of an American tradition? (Thanksgiving festivities)

★ **Texas Essential Elements/(a) English Language Arts: 3D** Folklore/legends/myths. **(c) Reading: 1C** Dictionaries

The Golden Age

The long reign of Cronus, whom the Romans called Saturn, was the happy time that the poets call the Golden Age. It was then that men came into being, formed from earth mixed with rainwater by Prometheus, the wise son of the Titan Iapetus.[7] He made them in the image of the gods, unlike the animals, standing erect and looking up to heaven. In those days the whole earth was a paradise, a land of eternal spring like the dwellings of the gods. The earth brought forth its produce without man's labor and unwounded by A his sharp plowshares; the rivers ran with milk and nectar, and honeydew dripped from the bitter oak. The animals lived at peace with one another and with man, and man was at peace with his neighbor. B Metals and precious stones slept undisturbed in the ground; there was no war, no commerce, and no need for courts of law.

The men of the Golden Age lived innocently, honoring the gods, and they died peacefully without sickness or creeping age. There was as yet no women on the earth, and so the good race passed away without leaving children; but their spirits inhabit the middle air between earth and heaven and watch in love and benevolence over the righteous, blessing their flocks and fields. After they had gone, loss and change began to enter the world, which now endured progressively worse ages, the Silver, the Brazen, and the harsh Age of Iron. In the Silver Age began the four seasons as we know them, with their succession of heat and cold. In those days men began to build shelters and to sow corn in the ground, harnessing bullocks[8] to the yoke. The men of the Silver Age were foolish and impious,[9] and Zeus, Cronus's successor, destroyed them because they would not honor the gods. Then he created a third race, the men of bronze, who cared for nothing but warfare and died by their own violence. Last came C the present race, the men of iron; these too in their turn shall Zeus destroy, say the poets.

7. **Iapetus** (ē·a′pə·təs).
8. **bullocks:** bulls.
9. **impious** (im′pē·əs): here, lacking respect and dutifulness for the gods.

The War in Heaven

When Cronus drove away his father, Uranus had cursed him, saying that he should in turn be overthrown by his own children. Through all the long years of his happy reign, this remembrance troubled Cronus and disturbed his peace. Every time his wife Rhea bore him a child, he took it from her and swallowed it, in order to defeat the prophecy. After he had swallowed in this way her first five children, Hestia, Demeter, Hera, Hades, and Poseidon, Rhea resolved that the sixth child should escape the fate of the others, and she went for counsel to her mother Earth. On Earth's advice, she hid herself from Cronus in a cave of Mount Ida on the island of Crete, where she was delivered of a male child, whom she called Zeus. She left him with the nymphs of the mountains to be nursed, and returned to Cronus. With her she brought a large smooth stone from the mountainside, and this she wrapped in swaddling-bands and gave to Cronus, D telling him that this was the latest-born of her sons. Cronus, suspecting nothing, swallowed the stone as he had done his children.

Meanwhile the infant Zeus grew and flourished, nursed by the good nymphs and by a stranger foster mother, the silky-white she-goat Amalthea who gave him milk and played with him. There is a story that one day the little god grasped her horn too roughly and broke it off. He immediately made a new one grow in its place, and the old horn he gave to the nymphs in thanks for their care, promising that they should always find it full of whatever foods they most wished for, fruit and grain and honey and every other good thing. The nymphs treasured the gift of Zeus, which was called the Horn of Plenty (Latin, *cornucopia*). E

The other friends of Zeus in the Cretan cave were a band of armed youths called the Curetes,[10] warriors born from the earth, who entertained him with leaping dances, clashing their spears against their shields when necessary to drown the noise

10. **Curetes** (kyə′rēts).

A. Recalling

Who did Cronus keep imprisoned in the earth? (See text page 460: the Cyclops and the Hundred-Handed—Gyges, Cottus, and Briareos) Who originally placed them there? (Uranus)

Texas Essential Elements/(a) English Language Arts: 1B Purpose and audience; 3D Folklore/legends/myths; 4B Main idea. (c) Reading: 3A Main ideas/details; 3I Draw conclusions

of his crying, for fear Cronus should hear it from his high palace.

When Zeus had come to manhood, Gaia sent to him Metis, ("Counsel"), one of the daughters of Oceanus, who told him the time had come for him to avenge the wrongs done by his father. Acting on her instructions, he came to Cronus's golden palace, where he introduced himself as a stranger. When Cronus was far gone in wine, Zeus slipped into his cup a powerful herb that Metis had given him from Earth. No sooner had Cronus swallowed it than he vomited up first Rhea's stone, then his five elder children, all now full-grown. His brothers Hades and Poseidon joined to help Zeus bind their father in chains; but Cronus called aloud for his Titan brothers, who came running to attack the young intruders. The younger gods, seeing the Titans advancing on them, fled out of heaven to the top of Mount Olympus above the clouds, where they gathered their forces for the war that must follow.

For ten years war was waged between the younger gods and the Titans, and still the issue hung undecided. Finally Zeus, weary of the useless struggle, set out to consult the wisdom of Mother Earth at her mysterious oracle[11] in the Pythonian cave. The words that came to him were clear, but their meaning was obscure: "Let him who would conquer in the war first set free those imprisoned in Tartarus." Zeus knew nothing of A the events that had taken place in heaven before he was born, nor did he know that Gaia still hated Cronus for leaving her elder children in captivity, so he was puzzled by her message.

It happened that among the Titans there was one, the wise Prometheus, who would not fight on the side of the elder gods. He of all the living saw deepest into the secrets of time, and he knew that the reign of Cronus was running out and would soon give place to that of the Olympians. First he tried unsuccessfully to persuade his father and brothers to lay down their arms. Then, rather than fight against them himself, he came to Zeus and offered to interpret to him the oracle of Earth.

The Cyclops (detail) by Odilon Redon (1898–1900). Oil on wood.

Collection of the State Museum Kröller-Müller, Otterlo, Netherlands.

B

When Zeus understood all that had gone before, he descended with Prometheus to the underworld, soon reaching the gate of brass-walled Tartarus, the dreadful place where Gaia's monstrous children lay imprisoned. The entrance was guarded by a she-serpent, which Zeus killed. He brought the Cyclops back to the upper world to help him against the Titans, and the Hundred-Handed with them, but only after he had made them swear to go and live beyond the farthest bounds of the ocean, so terrifying was their destructive power.

The Cyclops immediately set up a smithy in the depths of Etna the Sicilian volcano; and the sky above soon flared red as they hammered out gifts for their friend Zeus and his brothers. To the eldest, Poseidon, they gave a trident[12] with three sharp prongs of adamant; to the second, Hades, a helmet of invisibility; and to Zeus himself, the thunderbolts that tear through all resistance and

11. **oracle** (ôr'ə·k'l): place where mortals consulted a priestess for advice. The priestess was inspired by the gods.

12. **trident:** three-pronged spear.

B. Humanities Connection: Discussing the Fine Art

Odilon Redon (1840–1916) was the foremost painter of the symbolist movement. This movement of the late nineteenth century included artists and writers who rejected realism and tried to express their ideas and emotions through the use of symbolic figures and objects. The symbolist paintings often had a mysterious or dreamlike quality. In this painting, Redon depicts the Cyclops Polyphemus, who fell in love with the nymph Galatea. Although it is difficult to see in this detail, the nymph is depicted as sleeping below the giant. Redon paints the giant, not as fierce and ugly as the Cyclops were described to be, but more as though he were a figment of the imagination, perhaps invented in the dreams of the sleeping nymph.

READING CHECK TEST

1. The first two gods to appear out of Chaos were Night and Erebus. *(True)*
2. When Cronus overthrew Uranus, Cronus released his brothers from their captivity under the earth. *(False)*
3. The reign of Cronus was a violent, war-torn era. *(False)*
4. Zeus was the son of Prometheus. *(False)*
5. The Cyclops made thunderbolts for Zeus that helped him defeat the Titans. *(True)*

CLOSURE

Break students into groups of threes and have them briefly answer the questions posed in the headnote.

A. Humanities Connection: Discussing the Fine Art
Peter Paul Rubens (1577–1640) is considered the greatest Flemish painter of the 1600's. His paintings are known for their vast scale, brilliant colors, and emotional intensity. He used the Greek myths as the subject matter for many of his paintings.
? What does the red in this painting remind you of? (Most students will say blood and fire.) Notice how the positions of the bodies, the facial expressions, and the feeling of great movement contribute to the sense of confusion and violence in this painting.

B. Etymology
A picture of Atlas supporting the world was often used as the frontispiece for early collections of maps. Gradually, people began to use the word *atlas* to refer to a book of maps, and this has become the common meaning of the word today.

A

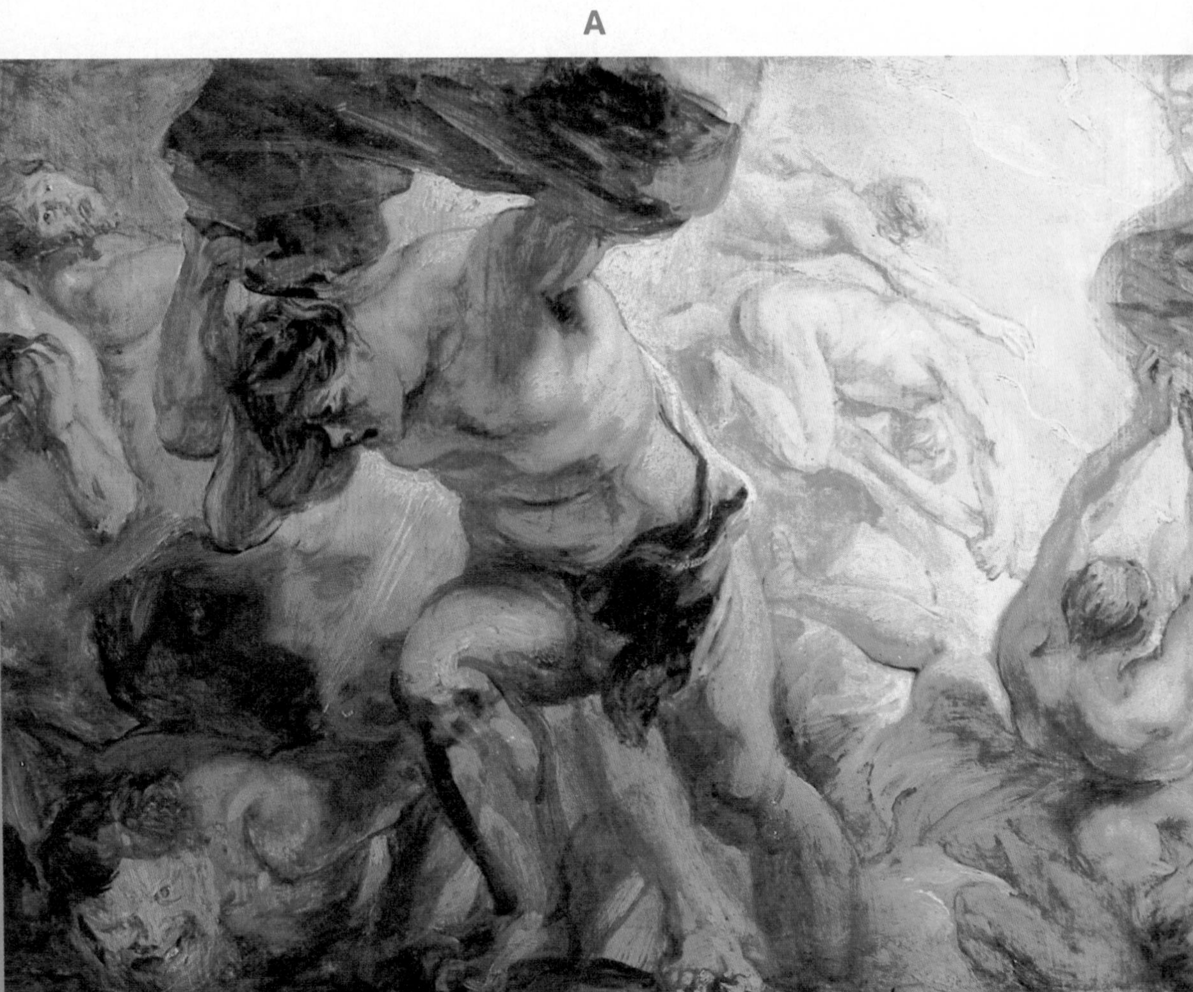

The Fall of the Titans by Peter Paul Rubens (c. 1637). Oil.

make him dreaded by gods and men. It is on this tremendous weapon that his power mainly rests, and he alone has the secret and the use of it.

Armed with their three gifts, the Olympians once more advanced to the assault on heaven. This time they were crushingly successful: The Titans could not stand against the new weapons, but fled thunder-scarred out over the battlements and plunged into the depths below. The Olympians pursued them, giving all they captured into the charge of the Hundred-Handed, who stowed them away in those very underworld caverns from which they themselves had just been released. A remnant of the Titanic forces, Cronus and a few followers, got away to a high mountain in Northern Greece, where they held out for a time, sheltering in caves from the dreaded thunderbolts; but at last they were routed out of this stronghold and fled away over the sea, finding a haven, some say, in sunny Italy before the Romans were ever thought of. Others say that the hunted king came to rest only among the mists and glooms of Britain, far on the ocean's remotest verge. No stories tell his end.

In the last flight one prisoner was taken: Atlas, a brother of Prometheus, a giant of great strength. Zeus ordained as his punishment that he should stand at the western edge of the world bearing on his shoulders the weight of the sky. No wonder B his name is thought to mean "he who suffers."

ANALYZING THE MYTHS
Identifying Facts
1. Chaos was the only thing that existed.
2. Eros, the god of Love, was the most powerful of the gods.

Together they created a series of monstrous creatures, including the brothers Gyges, Cottus, and Briareos and the three Cyclops.
3. Uranus shut his children away in the earth, believing that Gyges, Cottus, and Briareos were too terrifying to look at and that the Cyclops were too skilled at forging metal weapons.
4. The twelve Titans were Gaia's last children, six sons and six daughters, who were bigger than ordinary human beings and endowed with grace and beauty.

Gaia asked her sons to avenge Uranus's mistreatment of her children.
5. Cronus used an adamant sickle to maim his father and drive him away. Afterward he ruled in Uranus's place.
6. The Golden Age was a happy time when there was paradise on earth, a land of perpetual spring, where the rivers ran with milk and nectar, sweetened dew dripped from the bitter oak, and animals lived in peace with one another and with humans. In the Silver Age the four seasons began, with their periods of heat and cold, and for the first time people had to plant crops and harness animals for work. The Brazen Age was a period of violence and warfare between men. The Age of Iron is the harsh period in which people now live.

During the Golden Age there were no women, only men who lived innocently and honored the gods. In the Silver Age, people were foolish and impious and would not honor the gods. In the Brazen Age, people only liked to fight wars. The people of the Age of Iron are the present race of humans.
7. Uranus's curse was that Cronus would one day be overthrown by his own children.

He swallowed every child borne by his wife, Rhea.
8. She gave birth to Zeus in a cave so that Cronus would not see, and left him with mountain nymphs to nurse. She then wrapped a stone in swaddling clothes *(Answers continue on page 466.)*

Responding to the Myths

Analyzing the Myths

Identifying Facts

1. According to the first creation myth, what existed in the universe in the beginning of all time?
2. Who was the most powerful of all the gods? What happened when this god brought together the Earth-Mother and the Sky-Father?
3. What did Uranus do to his children, and why?
4. Who were the Titans? What did Gaia ask them to do?
5. How did Cronus come to rule the world?
6. Describe the Golden Age and the three ages that came after it—the Silver Age, the Brazen Age, and the Age of Iron. What kind of people lived in each age?
7. What curse did Uranus place on Cronus? How did Cronus try to avoid the curse?
8. How did Rhea help Zeus escape the fate of his brothers and sisters? How did Zeus rescue his five brothers and sisters—the other children of Cronus and Rhea?
9. For ten years, war raged in heaven between the Titans and the younger gods led by Zeus. Explain how Mother Earth helped Zeus gain new allies in this war. Who were these new allies? Who helped Zeus understand Mother Earth's puzzling message?
10. What gifts did the Cyclops make for Poseidon, Hades, and Zeus? Describe how these gifts helped the Olympians defeat the Titans.
11. According to the myth "The Golden Age," how were people created?

Interpreting Meanings

12. How do the gods seem more human than divine?
13. Although the gods are all-powerful, they often have to obey higher rules. In the myths you have just read, what are some of these rules?

Writing About the Myths

A Creative Response

1. **Writing a Newspaper Article.** Write a news article of one or two paragraphs describing the war between the Olympians and the Titans. Be sure to answer "the five W's" of journalism: **Who? What? Where? When? Why?**
2. **Extending a Myth.** Write a story or description based on one of these mythic events. You might want to tell your story as if you are the main character involved. In this case, you would use the pronoun *I*.
   a. Life in the Golden Age
   b. Zeus growing up in the Cretan cave ("The War in Heaven")
   c. Cronus hiding out in the mists and gloom of Britain ("The War in Heaven")

A Critical Response

SRW p. 87

3. **Identifying Theme.** A story's theme is the main idea that the author is trying to reveal to the reader. Choose one of the myths from this section, and write a paragraph in which you identify its theme. Tell what details in the myth helped you uncover this theme.

See Teacher's Manual page 150.

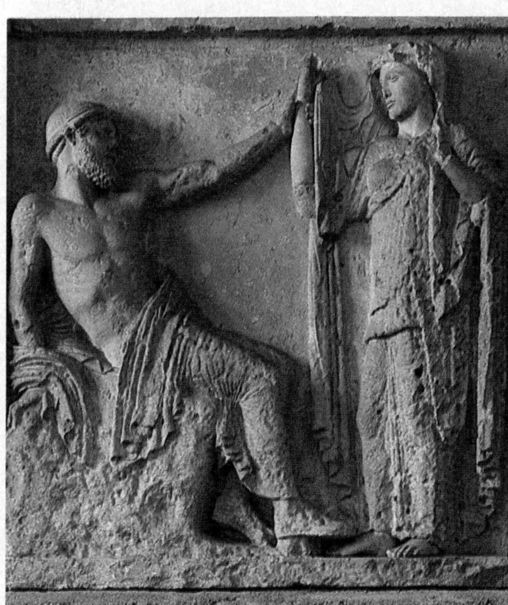

The First Meeting of Zeus and Hera. A metope from the Greek temple at Selinus, Sicily (c. 470–460 B.C.).

(Answers begin on page 465.)
and gave it to Cronus to swallow.

Zeus gave his father an herbal potion that caused him to vomit them up.

9. Earth told Zeus that the war would be won by the person who freed those imprisoned in Tartarus.

The new allies were the imprisoned children of Gaia, the Cyclops and the brothers Gyges, Cottus, and Briareos.

10. The Cyclops made a trident with prongs of adamant for Poseidon, a helmet of invisibility for Hades, and thunderbolts for Zeus.

Prometheus interpreted the message for Zeus.

The Titans could not withstand the new weapons and fled. Those that were not imprisoned by the Hundred-Handed were routed again by Zeus's thunderbolts on a mountain in northern Greece, and finally fled across the sea.

11. Prometheus used earth mixed with rainwater to create people in the image of the gods.

12. Answers will vary, but students might note two aspects in particular: The gods are motivated by the same emotions as humans are, including selfishness,
(Answers continue in left-hand column.)

(Continued from top.)
hatred, and greed; the gods also have human form, must grow to adulthood, and are susceptible to wounds or imprisonment.

13. The gods are bound to obey the laws of destiny and fate.

A. Humanities Connection: Discussing the Fine Art
Dirck Van Baburen (1590–1624) was a Dutch painter who closely followed the style of Caravaggio, the famous Italian painter known for his dramatic and realistic paintings of religious subjects. Baburen's figures tend to have squared-off skulls, awkward facial features, and red noses. Notice that the bodies in this painting appear very realistic. The veins are sticking out in Prometheus's arm, his face is red with pain, and his hands are red from the shackles that are binding him. You can see Hermes's winged hat in the upper right-hand corner.

A

Chaining of Prometheus by Baburen. Oil. Rijksmuseum, Amsterdam, Holland.

PREREADING

1. **BUILDING ON PRIOR KNOWLEDGE.** Names were very important to the ancient Greeks and Romans. They were usually derived from words that identified a dominant characteristic of the person or being. For example, in the myths included in "In the Beginning," Phosphorous's name comes from the Greek word *phosphoros,* which means "bringer of light"; Atlas's name comes from the Greek *tlan,* which means "bearing" or "base"; and, as we learn in the next myth, Prometheus's name means "forethought" from the Greek *pro-,* "before," and *mathein,* "to learn." Tell students they can find out something about the character they are reading about just by knowing that character's name. What does *Pandora* mean?

2. **ESTABLISHING A PURPOSE.** As they read, have students list the questions these origin myths answered for the Greeks.

3. **PREREADING JOURNAL.** If you were the god or goddess in charge of giving out traits (such as speed, cleverness, the ability to fly) to human beings, what traits would you give them?

 **Texas Essential Elements/(a) English Language Arts: 3D** Folklore/legends/myths

AFTER THE EARTH APPEARED

Retold by **Jay Macpherson**

For a detailed lesson plan on this myth, see Teacher's Manual pages 150–152. A biography of Jay Macpherson appears on text page 471.

Prometheus

For a long time after the earth appeared, its hills and valleys and broad meadows lay untenanted, except for the nymphs and the satyrs, godlings of the countryside, who danced and played and chased one another in forest and field. A We have seen already how Prometheus at last created man. A different story tells how the gods charged with the task not only Prometheus but also his brother Epimetheus. Since the name of Prometheus means "he who thinks before" and that of his brother, "he who thinks afterward," it seems that Epimetheus did not have all his brother's wisdom. He began with the creation of the animals; and he was so lavish with the gifts he gave them—gifts of strength and speed and cunning, strong claws and sharp teeth, warm coverings of feathers and fur—that there was nothing left over for man, his poor shivering last creation. So Epimetheus called upon his wise brother to repair the mistake. Prometheus not only made man upright and beautiful, but he decided to use his craft to win extra advantages for man from Zeus, the king of the gods. Once when gods and men had met together, Prometheus cut up a great ox for them all to feast on. Dividing the body into two portions, he wrapped all the good meat up in the skin so that it looked very unappetizing, but the bones he set apart, covering them over with fat. Then he asked Zeus which portion he would take for himself and his fellow-gods. Zeus, deceived by the rich look of the glistening fat, chose with it the heap of bones that it concealed; and from then on when men killed cattle to eat, it was the bones that they sacrificed to the gods, keeping the meat for themselves. B

When Zeus saw that he had been outwitted, he was angry, and in revenge he refused to give mankind the gift Prometheus wanted for them, the precious blessing of fire, but jealously guarded it in his heavenly halls. The friend of man, undaunted, went up to Olympus and stole away a flickering flame in a hollow stalk of fennel[1] to give to the helpless race of mortals in place of the animals' strength and speed, sharp teeth, and warm skins.

Then Zeus looked down from Olympus and saw everywhere on the broad earth the far-shining fires, and his anger against Prometheus knew no bounds. He sent two of his strong servants to bind him to a rock in the Caucasus Mountains, where he lay for long ages stretched out, held down by C his chains, exposed alike to hot sun and fierce winds and piercing cold. To increase his torments, Zeus sent an eagle to tear continually at his liver; and because the Titan was immortal like Zeus himself, his sufferings were to be without end.

There was still a third reason for Zeus's cruelty, besides Prometheus's two victories over him. When Prometheus had helped Zeus against Cronus and the other Titans, it was not because he thought Zeus's reign would be any more just than the reigns of Cronus and Uranus before him, but because he alone of all the dwellers in heaven knew the secrets of Fate, and he saw that it was of no use to struggle against what was to come. The Fates are three sisters, Clotho, Lachesis, and

1. **fennel** (fen''l): herb used in cooking and in medicine.

For a detailed lesson plan on this myth, see Teacher's Manual pages 150–152. A biography of Jay Macpherson appears on text page 471.

A. Recalling
How did Prometheus create man? (By mixing earth with rainwater)

B. Expansion
Sacrifice is a religious ceremony in which something is given to the gods. People make sacrifices in order to receive physical or spiritual benefits. The ancient Greeks sacrificed animals, roasting the flesh on an altar. They probably wanted to give this gift of food to their gods, without going hungry themselves. This myth of Prometheus offered them the perfect solution.

C. Character
What kind of god does Zeus appear to be? (Most will say he is an angry and vengeful god.) At what other time have we been told about Zeus's angry behavior? (See text page 462, "when the men of the Silver Age were foolish and impious . . .")

A. Hercules
Hercules was believed to be the greatest hero of Greece and the stongest man on earth. Hera, Zeus's jealous wife, hated Hercules because he was Zeus's son by another woman. One day she threw Hercules into a fit of madness, during which he killed his wife and children without knowing it. As penance, he had to complete twelve nearly impossible tasks, called the twelve labors of Hercules. Rescuing Prometheus was one of the twelve.

B. Making Connections
You might want to ask the students to compare the Greek account of Pandora to the biblical account of the first woman. (Similarities include the fact that both were created after man; both were told not to do something and their curiosity led them to disobey the order; both indirectly caused humankind to suffer because of their disobedience. Some of the differences are that in the Pandora myth, Zeus is an arbitrary, vindictive god, while in the biblical account, God is just and fair; in the Pandora myth women are created as a punishment for men, whereas in the biblical account, women are created as company for men.)

SUPPLEMENTARY SUPPORT MATERIAL
1. Vocabulary Activity Sheet
2. Reading Check Test blackline master
3. Selection Test (page 179 of Test Book)
4. Audiocassette recording of "Prometheus"
5. Reader's Response Journal
6. Workbook (page 131)

DEVELOPING VOCABULARY
The following words appear on a test in the Test Book, page 180. (See also the Vocabulary Activity Sheet.)

untenanted	treacherous
lavish	wrest
undaunted	bloody-natured
dread	corrupt
irresistible	prophecy

★ **Texas Essential Elements/(a) English Language Arts: 3D** Folklore/legends/myths

Atropos, the daughters of Night, who sit in a cave spinning the thread of man's life. The first sister spins the thread, the second draws it out, and the third, the most dreaded, is she who cuts it off. Prometheus, who was admitted to their counsels, knew not only that Zeus was destined to hold the supreme power, but also that another was to come after him and seize the power in his turn. This successor was to be one of Zeus's many sons—Zeus himself knew that much: It was Prometheus who kept the crucial secret of who would be the child's mother—her name, and whether she was goddess, nymph, or mortal woman. Like his father and his grandfather, Zeus lived in fear of his eventual overthrow and would have given anything to prevent it or put it off. Underestimating his old friend as he had done before, and forgetting that without Prometheus's help it would have taken him much longer to become lord of Olympus, he thought he could torture Prometheus into telling what he knew. But Prometheus with his superhuman endurance remained steadfast.

Most stories agree that at last Prometheus was released from his mountaintop. The deed is ascribed to the greatest of the heroes, Zeus's son Heracles, who sailed to his rescue in a golden cup lent to him by the Sun. Prometheus never told Zeus who was to be the mother of his destroyer, but he did warn him not to marry the sea nymph Thetis, as his heart was set on doing, because she was destined to bear a son who would be greater than his father. Zeus prudently changed his mind and bestowed the lady on a minor hero named Peleus. A

Thetis, however, had all the tricky character of her native element, and Peleus did not win her easily. He seized her one day as she slept on the seashore, whereupon she awoke in a fright and changed herself into all kinds of creatures—a bird, a tree, a tigress, a raging fire—in her struggle to escape him. But the hero held her fast, and at length she returned to her proper form and agreed to become his wife. Zeus gave the couple a famous wedding which was attended by a great throng of gods and men. Their son was Achilles, the hero of the Trojan war, a greater man than his father Peleus but a mortal like other men, not a contender for the throne of heaven.

Pandora's Box

Zeus's revenge did not stop with the punishment of Prometheus. Though he could not take the gift of fire away from men once it had been kindled in a thousand places on the earth, he was determined they should suffer for their possession of it.

This story agrees with the story of the Golden Age: At first the life of man on earth was happier than it is now, and then miseries and discontents gradually crept in. It seems that Prometheus and Epimetheus created men only, not women. When Zeus was angry with mankind, he devised the worst punishment he could think of, and invented woman. Hephaestus,[2] the smith of the gods, was instructed to form her from the earth and make her irresistibly beautiful. Each of the gods gave her his own special gift or skill, and from this she was called Pandora, "all-gifted." When she was perfected with every gift and arrayed in all her loveliness, this treacherous treasure was taken down to earth by Hermes, the messenger-god who wears winged helmet and sandals to speed his flight, and given to Prometheus's foolish brother Epimetheus. Now Prometheus had warned his brother not to accept anything from Zeus, even if it looked like a gift sent in friendship; but Epimetheus as usual acted first and thought afterward. He accepted the maiden from Hermes and led her into his house, and with her a great jar—some say a box or chest—which the gods had sent with her, telling her to keep it safely but never never think of opening it. This was too much for a lively girl like Pandora, who among her gifts was endowed with the first feminine curiosity. After restraining it for a little while, she at last gave in and lifted the lid from the jar, and from that moment began the sorrows of mankind. For each of the gods had stored in it the worst thing he was able to give, and wonderful as had been the gifts with which they endowed her, just as dreadful were the evils that rushed eagerly from the jar in a black stinking cloud like pestilent insects—sickness and suffering, hatred and jealousy and greed, B
and all the other cruel things that freeze the heart

2. **Hephaestus** (hi·fes'təs).

A. **Responding to the Illustration**
This drawing shows Pandora opening the box of "gifts."

? What is expressed by the position of Epimetheus's raised arms? (He looks as though he is trying to shield himself. He appears to be in great despair, and perhaps also in pain.) Notice that the swirling lines of the drawing create the feeling of madness and doom. The lines rising out of the box may appear as gushing water, smoke, or fire.

★ **Texas Essential Elements/(a) English Language Arts: 1B** Purpose and audience; **3D** Folklore/legends/myths. **(c) Reading: 3A** Main ideas/details; **3I** Draw conclusions; **4D** Diagrams/graphs

A

Pandora's Box. Drawing by Walter Crane.

and bring on old age. Pandora tried to clap the lid on the jar again, but it was too late. The happy childhood of mankind had gone forever, and with it the Golden Age when life was easy. From then on man had to wrest a hard living by his own labor from the unfriendly ground. Only one good thing came to man in the jar and remains to comfort him in his distress, and that is the spirit of Hope.

Deucalion's Flood

One more story is told of the early ages of the world. As time went on mankind became less and less noble, and evil and crime walked in open daylight on the face of the earth. When Cronus wounded his father Uranus, two new kinds of creature sprang from the blood where it had dripped down on the earth. One group was the three sisters called Erinyes[3] or Furies, terrible to look at, who track down and punish the wicked, especially those who murder their own kin. The other was the race of Giants, cruel and bloody-natured, who at last grew so arrogant that they resolved to conquer the stronghold of the gods. To do this they piled Mount Pelion on top of Mount Ossa as a base from which to reach Olympus; but when they had got that far, Zeus hurled at them one of his thunderbolts, so that the mountains came crashing down, overwhelming the Giants in their fall, and the Earth received the blood of her sons in torrents. So that they should not be forgotten, she breathed life into the blood where it had mixed with the ground, and formed a new race of men, violent and cruel in their turn. B These intermarried with the race already on the earth and further corrupted their nature; and so it was that evil and crime walked abroad, while Shame and the maiden Justice departed from mankind.

The gods seeing this became greatly perturbed, and Zeus resolved to visit the earth in disguise and take a closer look. Asking here and there for hospitality as a weary traveler, he was so unkindly received that he lost patience, and hastening back to Olympus he called a council of the gods. Before all the assembled divinities of earth and sky and sea, he announced his decision to destroy mankind and replace them with a better race who would honor the gods. At first his intention was to launch a flight of thunderbolts against the earth; but remembering an old prophecy that the whole universe would eventually be consumed by fire, he laid his thunderbolts aside and chose instead to let the heavens open and destroy man with a flood. C Accordingly he sent forth Notus the south wind to drive the rain out of the clouds onto the earth. At Zeus's request Poseidon called together the rivers and sent them out to break down their banks and spread themselves as far as possible over the land; then he struck the earth with his trident, and torrents of water gushed up from under the ground. The floods rushed triumphantly toward the sea, carrying before them crops and

3. **Erinyes** (i·rin′ē·ez).

B. **Interpreting**
Remind students that myths often represent human fears.

? What kind of society is described here? (A society without justice and shame, and one filled with violence, cruelty, evil and crime. Because society has sunk so low, Zeus is somehow justified in destroying it.)

C. **Making Connections**

? What other famous account of a flood does this remind you of? (Most students will be reminded of the account of Noah's ark.) Tell students to watch for similarities and differences between the accounts.

Reading Check Test

1. Epimetheus gave all the best gifts to the ________, leaving none for humans. *(animals)*
2. Zeus was angry at Prometheus for stealing ________ for humankind. *(fire)*
3. The only good thing to escape from Pandora's box was ________. *(hope)*
4. All human beings except Deucalion and Pyrrha died in a great ________. *(flood)*
5. The stones Pyrrha threw behind her as she left the temple became ________. *(women)*

Closure

Divide students into groups of four. On the basis of "After the Earth Appeared," have them list all the things, good and bad, that were given to humans by the gods.

A. Responding

? Why do you think they were instructed to veil their heads? (Probably out of respect for the gods)

B. Expansion

One interpretation of the myth suggests that the stones thrown by Pyrrha and Deucalion were made of marble, and that the veins running through our bodies originated from these marble stones.

orchards, cattle and men, houses and temples, even the sacred images of the gods. Those buildings that did not collapse under the fury of the waters were overwhelmed by the high waves, and fish swam through their doorways and gazed at the rooms with their cold eyes. Soon the waters had covered everything: The whole world was sea, and sea without a shore.

At first some tried to escape by climbing the tops of hills, but the floods soon swept them away. Others took to boats, the curved keels gliding for a time above what had been homesteads and plowed land. Beside them, for as long as they could keep up, swam all kinds of animals, wolves and sheep jostling together in their desperate efforts to escape. Birds took to the air, and wandered long in search of somewhere to rest; at last their wings grew weary and they dropped into the sea. Most of mankind was swallowed up by the waves. Even those in the boats soon died, succumbing to famine and to the sicknesses brought on by the universal stench of corruption.

In the whole world, only one spot of land still showed above the waves: the double peak of cloud-piercing Parnassus in the north of Greece. To this place after many days came floating a huge wooden chest, from which there stepped out on the dry land one man and one woman, Deucalion and his wife Pyrrha, the children respectively of Prometheus and of Epimetheus. The wisdom of Prometheus was responsible for their preservation. Knowing of Zeus's intention to destroy mankind before even Zeus himself knew it, he instructed his son and his niece and daughter-in-law to build the chest and stock it with all the provisions they would need.

Being pious people, Deucalion and Pyrrha made it their first action to give thanks to the gods for their escape. When he saw this, Zeus in pity drove back the waters with the help of Boreas the north wind, whom all this time he had kept imprisoned, and Poseidon called in all the floods he had sent out before. It was fitting that mankind should be restored from this pair, now sitting discouraged on the mountaintop; for they had kept their hands clean from the general guilt, and besides being gentle and upright they honored the gods. Coming down from the mountain as the floods ebbed, they could see no signs of life, and felt all the horror of being the only living creatures on an empty and desolated earth. As they wandered along, they came to a temple of the goddess Themis, one of Uranus's Titan daughters who now had a place on Olympus and was worshiped beside the younger gods. Disregarding the waterweeds that slimed the steps and hung in festoons from the discolored roof, Deucalion and Pyrrha entered the temple and implored the goddess's help and advice. After they had stood praying for a while, the voice of the goddess came to them, as if from a great distance but clearly. "Depart from my temple," it said, "veil your heads, loosen the girdles[4] of your garments, and cast behind you the bones of your greater mother." This command greatly terrified the man and his wife. Even if both their mothers were not buried far away, how could they do anything so inhuman and disrespectful? Deucalion first understood what the goddess meant. "It is Earth that is the great mother of us all, and her bones are these stones that lie on the ground." They walked away from the temple, veiled their heads, loosened their garments, and began to throw stones behind them as they walked. The stones falling to the ground lost their stiffness and hardness and began to take the form of human beings. Those Deucalion threw became men, and those Pyrrha threw became women. Ovid, the Roman poet who tells the story, explains, "So it comes about that we are a hard race, accustomed to labor, still bearing the mark of our stony origin."

4. **girdles:** belts or sashes.

ANALYZING THE MYTHS
Identifying Facts
1. At a feast of the gods and men, Zeus was tricked by Prometheus into choosing the bones of an ox for himself and the gods, leaving the meat to men.
2. Prometheus used a hollow stalk of fennel to steal fire for humanity from heaven, where it was closely guarded.
3. Zeus's anger against Prometheus knew no bounds.

For ages Prometheus was chained to a rock, where he was exposed to extremes of heat and cold, and an eagle continually tore at his liver.

Hercules, the son of Zeus, rescued him.
4. Prometheus knew the identity of the mother of the man who would overthrow Zeus.

Zeus did not marry Thetis, who was destined to have a son who would be greater than his father.
5. The three Fates are Clotho, Lachesis, and Atropos.

Clotho spins the thread of each person's life, Lachesis draws it out, and Atropos cuts it off.
6. Women were created as a punishment for men. The first woman was Pandora.
7. Pandora released evil into the world when she opened the jar into which each god and goddess had placed the worst thing he or she could give.

Hope was the only good thing in the jar of evils that Pandora opened.
8. See Teacher's Manual, page 152 for detailed answer.

Interpreting Meanings
9. From these myths, people would learn to respect and honor the gods. The gods' punishment can often be unjust, but people should not underestimate or test their power and anger.

FURTHER READING FOR STUDENTS
Myths from other cultures are included in the anthology *Man the Myth-Maker,* edited by W. T. Jewkes.

Responding to the Myths

Analyzing the Myths

Identifying Facts

1. How does the myth "Prometheus" explain why people sacrificed only the bones of cattle to the gods?
2. How does this myth explain the origin of fire?
3. What was Zeus's response to the fires he saw on earth? How did Prometheus suffer for what he gave to humanity? Who finally rescues Prometheus?
4. What secret did Prometheus know about Zeus? How did Zeus avoid having his son depose him, just as he had deposed Cronus?
5. Name the three Fates. Explain the role that each one has in every person's life.
6. According to the myth "Pandora's Box," why were women created? Who was the first woman?
7. How does the myth explain the existence of evil in the world? How does it explain the existence of hope?
8. What was Zeus's reason for destroying the earth and its inhabitants? Why were Deucalion and Pyrrha spared? Describe how a new human race was created.

Interpreting Meanings

9. Myths often teach moral lessons. What would the myths about Prometheus's punishment, Pandora, and the flood teach people about their responsibilities to the gods?

Applying Meanings

10. What objections might some people have to the Pandora myth and to the way it depicts women?

Writing About the Myths

A Creative Response

1. **Describing an Object.** Use your imagination to write a description of Pandora's jar or box. How large was it? What was it made of? How was it decorated? What did Pandora see when she opened the lid? Use as many vivid, precise details as you can.

A Critical Response

2. **Analyzing a Character's Motives.** A **motive** is any desire, feeling, or idea that makes a character act in a certain way. Think about the role of Prometheus in these myths. What motivates him to abandon the other Titans and to ally himself first with Zeus and later with humans? Write two paragraphs in which you analyze Prometheus's motives.

See Teacher's Manual page 152.

Analyzing Language and Vocabulary

Words from Mythology

SRW p. 91

1. Copy the following chart on your paper. Fill in the boxes to show the relationship between the modern words and the names from mythology.

Modern Word	Meaning of Word	Name from Mythology	Who Had the Name
geology	study of the earth	Gaia	Earth-Mother
gigantic	very big		
chaotic	in total disorder		
oceanic	vast		
helium	a gas used to inflate balloons		
zephyr	a gentle breeze		

2. Choose three of the modern words from the chart. Write an original sentence for each. For example: "To the small child, the empty stage seemed *oceanic.*"

For answers, see Teacher's Manual page 153.

Reading About the Writer

Jay Macpherson (1931–) was born in England and was sent to Canada as a little girl to escape the bombing in London during World War II. For many years she has taught English at the University of Toronto. Her retelling of the classical myths, *The Four Ages of Man,* is used as a textbook in Canadian schools. Her poetry collection called *The Boatman* won the Governor General's Award for Poetry.

PREREADING

1. BUILDING ON PRIOR KNOWLEDGE. It might interest students to know that mythical beings fall into three groups. One group includes gods and goddesses who resemble animals, called *theriomorphic,* from two Greek words meaning "the shape of an animal." Many theriomorphic beings appear in Egyptian mythology. For example, their god Anubis is often represented as a dog. A second group is called *anthropomorphic,* from two Greek words meaning "in the shape of man." The Greek gods and goddesses belong in this category. They were physically born, they fell in love and fought with one another, and they basically behaved as human beings do. A third group has no specific name; these beings are part human, part animal.

2. ESTABLISHING A PURPOSE. The headnote sets a good purpose for reading this myth.

3. PREREADING JOURNAL. Have students write a brief description of their idea of a palace. What kind of furniture does it have? Who lives there? Where is it? They can compare their imagined palace with the Olympian palace after they read the myth.

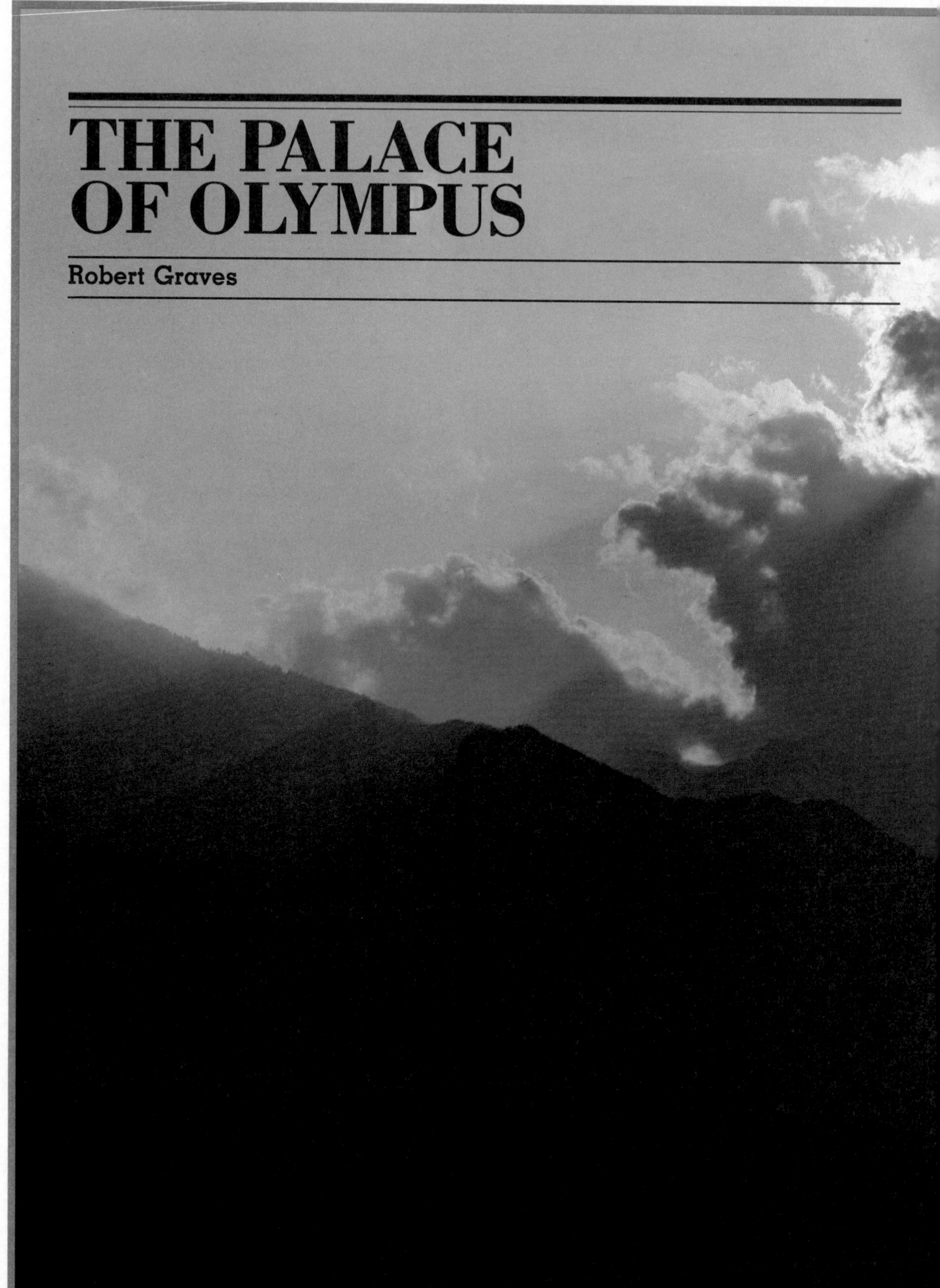

THE PALACE OF OLYMPUS

Robert Graves

Supplementary Support Material

1. Vocabulary Activity Sheet
2. Reading Check Test blackline master
3. Selection Test (page 181 of Test Book)
4. Author photograph on *A Gallery of Authors* poster
5. Reader's Response Journal
6. Workbook (page 133)

Developing Vocabulary

The following words appear on a test in the Test Book, page 182. (See also the Vocabulary Activity Sheet.)

quarrelsome	emblem
armory	herald
conceited	hearth
banished	souvenirs
ornamented	immortal

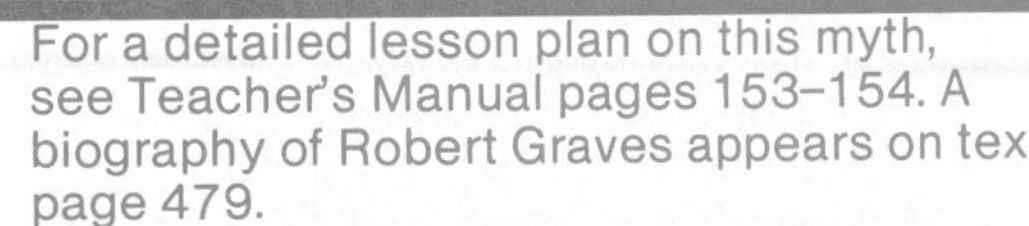
For a detailed lesson plan on this myth, see Teacher's Manual pages 153–154. A biography of Robert Graves appears on text page 479.

The Greeks imagined their major gods as belonging to one large family. Life in their palace on Mount Olympus, however, was far from perfect. The family members quarreled, misbehaved, and were often petty and cruel. Look for examples of the gods' human behavior as you read.

Word Origins and Histories. Many interesting words have their origins in mythology. For example, the word *titanic* comes from the name of the Titans—the race of gigantic gods who were overthrown by the Olympians. In the following selection, try to find other mythological names that are at the root of modern English words.

The twelve most important gods and goddesses of ancient Greece, called the Olympians, belonged to the same large quarrelsome family. Though thinking little of the smaller, old-fashioned gods over whom they ruled, they thought even less of mortals. All the Olympians lived together in an enormous palace, set well above the usual level of clouds at the top of Mount Olympus, the highest mountain in Greece. Great walls, too steep for climbing, protected the palace. The Olympians' masons, gigantic one-eyed Cyclops, had built them on much the same plan as royal palaces on earth. A

At the southern end, just behind the Council Hall, and looking toward the famous Greek cities of Athens, Thebes, Sparta, Corinth, Argos, and Mycenae,[1] were the private apartments of King Zeus, the Father-god, and Queen Hera, the Mother-goddess. The northern end of the palace, looking across the valley of Tempe toward the wild hills of Macedonia, consisted of the kitchen, banqueting hall, armory, workshops, and servants' quarters. In between came a square court, open to the sky, with covered cloisters and private rooms on each side, belonging to the other five Olympian gods and the other five Olympian goddesses. Beyond the kitchen and servants' quarters B

1. **Mycenae** (mī·sē′nē).

A. Recalling
What did the myth "The War in Heaven" tell us was the Cyclops's specialty when Zeus freed them from the underworld? (They were the first smiths.)

B. Responding
? Why might Zeus want his quarters to overlook the Greek cities instead of facing the more scenic view of valley and hills? (From what we have learned about Zeus so far, we can assume that it probably boosts his pride to look down on his "creations." He might also want to be able to watch mortals in case any mischief should occur.)

A. Interpreting
Note that this story differs slightly from the account of Cronus's departure in "The War in Heaven." Tell students that the information in many of the myths varies somewhat, and that no one story is the "correct" account.

B. Character
Hades's name probably meant "the unseen one." Because the Greeks were afraid to attract his attention by mentioning his name, they usually referred to him as "Pluto" (which is also the god's Roman name). The name *Pluto* derives from the Greek word meaning "wealth," and it suggests the wealth of the earth beneath the crops.

C. Expansion
In ancient Greece, men were legally permitted to have several wives.

D. Descriptive Details
? Note the description of each god's or goddess's throne and how it reflects their area of power and their individual qualities. For instance, why are the decorations on Poseidon's throne appropriate? (The "gray-green, white-streaked marble" is like the sea with its white-capped waves. Both coral and mother-of-pearl are semiprecious stones found in the sea.)

★ **Texas Essential Elements/(a) English Language Arts: 1B** Purpose and audience; **3A** Plot/character; **3C** Literary traditions; **3D** Folklore/legends/myths

stood cottages for smaller gods, sheds for chariots, stables for horses, kennels for hounds, and a sort of zoo where the Olympians kept their sacred animals. These included a bear, a lion, a peacock, an eagle, tigers, stags, a cow, a crane, snakes, a wild boar, white bulls, a wild cat, mice, swans, herons, an owl, a tortoise, and a tank full of fish.

In the Council Hall the Olympians met at times to discuss mortal affairs—such as which army on earth should be allowed to win a war, and whether they ought to punish some king or queen who had been behaving proudly or disgustingly. But for the most part they were too busy with their own quarrels and lawsuits to take much notice of mortal affairs. King Zeus had an enormous throne of polished black Egyptian marble, decorated in gold. Seven steps led up to it, each of them enameled with one of the seven colors of the rainbow. A bright blue covering above showed that the whole sky belonged to Zeus alone; and on the right arm of his throne perched a ruby-eyed golden eagle clutching jagged strips of pure tin, which meant that Zeus could kill whatever enemies he pleased by throwing a thunderbolt of forked lightning at them. A purple ram's fleece covered the cold seat. Zeus used it for magical rainmaking in times of drought. He was a strong, brave, stupid, noisy, violent, conceited god, and always on the watch lest his family should try to get rid of him; having once himself got rid of his wicked, idle, cannibalistic father, Cronus, King of the Titans and Titanesses. The Olympians could not die, but Zeus, with the help of his two elder brothers, Hades and Poseidon, had banished Cronus to a distant island in the Atlantic—perhaps the Azores, perhaps Torrey Island, off the coast of Ireland. **A** Zeus, Hades, and Poseidon then drew lots for the three parts of Cronus's kingdom. Zeus won the sky; Poseidon, the sea; Hades, the underworld; **B** they shared the earth between them. One of Zeus's emblems was the eagle, another was the woodpecker.

Cronus managed at last to escape from the island in a small boat and, changing his name to Saturn, settled quietly among the Italians, and behaved very well. In fact, until Zeus discovered his escape and banished him again, Saturn's reign was known as the Golden Age. Mortals in Italy lived without work or trouble, eating only acorns, wild fruit, honey, and pig-nuts, and drinking only milk or water. They never fought wars, and spent their days dancing and singing.

Queen Hera had an ivory throne, with three crystal steps leading up to it. Golden cuckoos and willow leaves decorated the back, and a full moon hung above it. Hera sat on a white cowskin, which she sometimes used for rainmaking magic if Zeus could not be bothered to stop a drought. She disliked being Zeus's wife, because he was frequently marrying mortal women and saying, with a sneer, **C** that these marriages did not count—his brides would soon grow ugly and die; but she was his Queen, and perpetually young and beautiful.

When first asked to marry him, Hera had refused; and had gone on refusing every year for three hundred years. But one springtime Zeus disguised himself as a poor cuckoo caught in a thunderstorm, and tapped at her window. Hera, not seeing through his disguise, let the cuckoo in, stroked his wet feathers, and whispered: "Poor bird, I love you." At once, Zeus changed back again into his true shape, and said: "Now you must marry me!" After this, however badly Zeus behaved, Hera felt obliged to set a good example to gods and goddesses and mortals, as the mother of heaven. Her emblem was the cow, the most motherly of animals; but, not wishing to be thought as plain-looking and placid as a cow, she also used the peacock and the lion.

These two thrones faced down the Council Hall toward the door leading into the open courtyard. Along the sides of the hall stood ten other thrones—for five goddesses on Hera's side, for five gods on Zeus's.

Poseidon, god of the seas and rivers, had the second-largest throne. It was of gray-green, white-streaked marble, ornamented with coral, gold, and mother-of-pearl. **D** The arms were carved in the shape of sea beasts, and Poseidon sat on sealskin. For his help in banishing Cronus and the Titans, Zeus had married him to Amphitrite, the former sea-goddess, and allowed him to take over all her titles. Though Poseidon hated to be less important than his younger brother, and always went about scowling, he feared Zeus's thunderbolt. His only weapon was a trident, with which he could stir up

A. Character

Note that Hephaestus is the only god who is not physically ideal.

B. Expansion

The Gorgons were three female monsters who had snakes for hair. Their faces were so hideous that one glimpse of them would turn a human or beast to stone. The hero Perseus was set the task of killing the Gorgon Medusa and bringing back her head. Athena had her own reasons for hating Medusa, so she helped Perseus complete his task. The Gorgons' heads on her throne probably represent her victory over Medusa.

C. Expansion

Athens, named for Athena, is the capital of Greece. As the story goes, Athena and Poseidon were both vying for the title of patron of Athens. Poseidon, to prove his power, gave a blow of his trident and produced a sea in the city. Athena, in turn, gave Athens the gift of the olive tree. Either the king of Athens or the gods ruled that Athena had made a more useful gift. In a rage, Poseidon flooded Athens.

D. Ares

Ares is known as the god of war.

★ **Texas Essential Elements/(c) Reading: 1B** Structural analysis; **1C** Dictionaries; **2A** Word meaning; **3A** Main ideas/details; **3I** Draw conclusions

the sea and so wreck ships; but Zeus never traveled by ship. When Poseidon felt even crosser than usual, he would drive away in his chariot to a palace under the waves, near the island of Euboea, and there let his rage cool. As his emblem Poseidon chose the horse, an animal which he pretended to have created. Large waves are still called "white horses" because of this.

Opposite Poseidon sat his sister Demeter, goddess of all useful fruits, grasses, and grains. Her throne of bright green malachite[2] was ornamented with ears of barley in gold, and little golden pigs for luck. Demeter seldom smiled, except when her daughter Persephone—unhappily married to the hateful Hades, god of the dead—came to visit her once a year. Demeter had been rather wild as a girl, and nobody could remember the name of Persephone's father: probably some country god married for a drunken joke at a harvest festival. Demeter's emblem was the poppy, which grows red as blood among the barley.

Next to Poseidon sat Hephaestus, a son of Zeus and Hera. Being the god of goldsmiths, jewelers, blacksmiths, masons, and carpenters, he had built all these thrones himself, and made his own a masterpiece of every different metal and precious stone to be found. The seat could swivel about, the arms could move up and down, and the whole throne rolled along automatically wherever he wished, like the three-legged golden tables in his workshop. Hephaestus had hobbled ever since birth, when Zeus roared at Hera: "A brat as weak as this is unworthy of me!"—and threw him far
A
out over the walls of Olympus. In his fall Hephaestus broke a leg so badly that he had to wear a golden leg-iron. He kept a country house on Lemnos, the island where he had struck earth; and his emblem was the quail, a bird that does a hobbling dance in springtime.

Opposite Hephaestus sat Athene, goddess of wisdom, who first taught him how to handle tools, and knew more than anyone else about pottery, weaving, and all useful arts. Her silver throne had golden basketwork at the back and sides, and a crown of violets, made from blue lapis lazuli[3], set above it. Its arms ended in grinning Gorgons' B
heads. Athene, wise though she was, did not know the names of her parents. Poseidon claimed her as his daughter by a marriage with an African goddess called Libya. It is true that, as a child, she had been found wandering in a goatskin by the shores of a Libyan lake; but rather than admit herself the daughter of Poseidon, whom she thought very stupid, she allowed Zeus to pretend she was his. Zeus announced that one day, overcome by a fearful headache, he had howled aloud like a thousand wolves hunting in a pack. Hephaestus, he said, then ran up with an axe and kindly split open his skull, and out sprang Athene, dressed in full armor. Athene was also a battle-goddess, yet never went to war unless forced—being too sensible to pick quarrels—and when she fought, always won. She chose the wise owl as C
her emblem; and had a town house at Athens.

Next to Athene sat Aphrodite, goddess of love and beauty. Nobody knew who her parents were, either. The South Wind said that he had once seen her floating in a scallop shell off the island of Cythera, and steered her gently ashore. She may have been a daughter of Amphitrite by a smaller god named Triton, who used to blow roaring blasts on a conch, or perhaps by old Cronus. Amphitrite refused to say a word on the subject. Aphrodite's throne was silver, inlaid with beryls and aquamarines, the back shaped like a scallop shell, the seat made of swan's down, and under her feet lay a golden mat—an embroidery of golden bees, apples, and sparrows. Aphrodite had a magic girdle, which she would wear whenever she wanted to make anyone love her madly. To keep Aphrodite out of mischief, Zeus decided that she needed a hard-working, decent husband; and naturally chose his son Hephaestus. Hephaestus exclaimed: "Now I am the happiest god alive!" But she thought it disgraceful to be the wife of a sooty-faced, horny-handed, crippled smith and insisted on having a bedroom of her own. Aphrodite's emblem was the dove, and she would visit Paphos, in Cyprus, once a year to swim in the sea, for good luck.

Opposite Aphrodite sat Ares, Hephaestus's
tall, handsome, boastful, cruel brother, who loved D
fighting for its own sake. Ares and Aphrodite were

2. **malachite** (mal'ə·kīt'): green mineral.
3. **lapis lazuli** (lap'is laz'yoo·lī): a blue semiprecious stone.

A. Vocabulary
A python is a large snake. In Greek mythology, the Python was a monstrous snake or dragon that lived at Delphi. When Apollo came to establish his oracle at Delphi, he killed the Python, which was ravaging the land. His seat of python skin probably represents his victory over the monster.

B. Humanities Connection: Discussing Architecture
The famous temple dedicated to Artemis was built in Ephesus, on the west coast of what is now Turkey. Built in about 550 B.C. and considered one of the seven wonders of the world, the temple was famous for its decoration and its extensive use of marble. Only the foundation and parts of the temple remain today.

The twelve Olympians: Hestia, Hephaestus, Aphrodite, Ares, Demeter, Hermes, Hera, Poseidon, Athene, Zeus, Artemis, and Apollo. Relief from Tarentum, Italy.

continually holding hands and giggling in corners, which made Hephaestus jealous. Yet if he ever complained to the Council, Zeus would laugh at him, saying: "Fool, why did you give your wife that magic girdle? Can you blame your brother if he falls in love with her when she wears it?" Ares's throne was built of brass, strong and ugly—those huge brass knobs in the shape of skulls, and that cushion-cover of human skin! Ares had no manners, no learning, and the worst of taste; yet Aphrodite thought him wonderful. His emblems were a wild boar and a bloodstained spear. He kept a country house among the rough woods of Thrace.

Next to Ares sat Apollo, the god of music, poetry, medicine, archery, and young unmarried men—Zeus's son by Leto, one of the smaller goddesses, whom he married to annoy Hera. Apollo rebelled against his father once or twice, but got well punished each time, and learned to behave more sensibly. His highly polished golden throne had magical inscriptions carved all over it, a back
A shaped like a lyre, and a python skin to sit on. Above hung a golden sun-disk with twenty-one rays shaped like arrows, because he pretended to manage the Sun. Apollo's emblem was a mouse; mice were supposed to know the secrets of earth, and tell them to him. (He preferred white mice to ordinary ones; most boys still do.) Apollo owned a splendid house at Delphi on the top of Mount Parnassus, built around the famous oracle which he stole from Mother Earth, Zeus's grandmother.

Opposite Apollo sat his twin-sister Artemis,
goddess of hunting and of unmarried girls, from B
whom he had learned medicine and archery. Her throne was of pure silver, with a wolfskin to sit on, and the back shaped like two date palms, one on each side of a new-moon boat. Apollo married several mortal wives at different times. Once he chased a girl named Daphne, who cried out for help to Mother Earth and got turned into a laurel tree before he could catch and kiss her. Artemis, however, hated the idea of marriage, although she kindly took care of mothers when their babies were born. She much preferred hunting, fishing, and swimming in moonlit mountain pools. If any mortal happened to see her without clothes, she used to change him into a stag and hunt him to death. She chose as her emblem the she-bear, the most dangerous of all wild animals in Greece.

Last in the row of gods sat Hermes, Zeus's son by a smaller goddess named Maia, after whom the

READING CHECK TEST

1. Poseidon ruled over the ________. (*sea*)
2. Hera was the wife of ________. (*Zeus*)
3. The emblem of Athena, the goddess of wisdom, is the ________. (*owl*)
4. The god of music and poetry was named ________. (*Apollo*)
5. The ________ decided the life span of each human being. (*Fates*)

CLOSURE

In groups of four, students should list all the major Olympic gods and goddesses and write a one-sentence description about each.

A month of May is called: Hermes, the god of merchants, bankers, thieves, fortune-tellers, and heralds, born in Arcadia. His throne was cut out of a single piece of solid gray rock, the arms shaped like rams' heads, and a goatskin for the seat. On its back he had carved a swastika,[4] this being the shape of a fire-making machine invented by him—the fire-drill. Until then, housewives used to borrow glowing pieces of charcoal from their neighbors. Hermes also invented the alphabet; and one of his emblems was the crane, because cranes fly in a V—the first letter he wrote. Another of Hermes's emblems was a peeled hazel stick, which he carried as the messenger of the Olympians: White ribbons dangled from it, which foolish people often mistook for snakes.

Last in the row of goddesses sat Zeus's eldest sister, Hestia, goddess of the home: on a plain, uncarved, wooden throne, and a plain cushion woven of undyed wool. Hestia, the kindest and most peaceable of all the Olympians, hated the continual family quarrels, and never troubled to choose any particular emblem of her own. She used to tend the charcoal hearth in the middle of the Council Hall. B

That made six gods and six goddesses. But one day Zeus announced that Dionysus, his son by a mortal woman named Semele,[5] had invented wine, and must be given a seat in the Council. Thirteen Olympians would have been an unlucky number; so Hestia offered him her seat, just to keep the peace. Now there were seven gods and five goddesses; an unjust state of affairs because, when questions about women had to be discussed, the gods outvoted the goddesses. C Dionysus's throne was gold-plated fir wood, ornamented with bunches of grapes carved in amethyst (a violet-colored stone), snakes carved in serpentine (a stone with many markings), and various horned animals besides, carved in onyx (a black and white stone), sard (a dark red stone), jade (a dark green stone), and carnelian (a pink stone). He took the

4. **swastika:** a very old symbol in the form of a cross with each arm bent at a right angle. A swastika is found in the art of many cultures. Today, in the twentieth century, it is associated with the Nazis, who used the twisted cross as their emblem.

5. **Semele** (sem'ə·lē).

A. Character

? What do these three kinds of people have in common? (Money) Hermes was also considered the god of travelers. He marks their paths with heaps of stones (which is probably the reason his throne is solid stone). It is said that when he was only a day old, he invented the lyre out of a tortoise shell, using sheep gut for the strings. He later traded the lyre for Apollo's cows and the position of keeper of the herds.

B. Interpreting

Some say that Hestia is not found in many myths because she was quiet and did not like to get involved with the arguments and intrigues of the other Olympians.

C. Expansion

This fact would provide the Greeks with a reason for any unfairness to women in their daily life.

ANALYZING THE MYTH
Identifying Facts

1. The Palace of Olympus was an enormous version of the kind of royal castles found on earth. It was situated high above the clouds and surrounded by great walls too steep to climb.

It was located on top of Mount Olympus, the highest mountain in Greece.

The twelve most important gods and goddesses of ancient Greece lived there.

Behind the Council Hall at the southern end of the palace were the private apartments of Zeus and Hera. The northern part of the palace contained the kitchen, banquet hall, armory, workshops, and servants' quarters. In between was an open courtyard with the rooms of the other Olympians on each side. Beyond the servants' quarters were cottages for minor gods, the stables, the kennels, and a zoo.

2. The Olympians liked to decide which army should be allowed to win a war and how they should punish kings and queens who behaved proudly or disgustingly.

The gods were too busy with their own quarrels and lawsuits.

3. They drew lots.

A. Etymology The word *nemesis* comes from the Greek *nemein,* which means "to distribute" or "deal out." Today, the word has come to mean "anyone or anything by which one must inevitably be defeated or frustrated; downfall."

B. Character ? What does this suggest about Zeus's character? (This is another example of the god's ungrateful and self-important behavior.)

tiger for his emblem, having once visited India at the head of a drunken army and brought tigers back as souvenirs.

Of the other gods and goddesses living on Olympus, Heracles the porter slept in the gatehouse; and Poseidon's wife Amphitrite has already been mentioned. There were also Dionysus's mother Semele, whom he persuaded Zeus to turn into a goddess; Ares's hateful sister Eris, goddess of quarrels; Iris, Hera's messenger, who used to run along the rainbow; the Goddess Nem-
A esis, who kept a list for the Olympians of proud mortals due to be punished; Aphrodite's wicked little son Eros, god of love, who enjoyed shooting arrows at people to make them fall ridiculously in love; Hebe, goddess of youth, who married Heracles; Ganymede, Zeus's handsome young cupbearer; the nine Muses, who sang in the Banqueting Hall; and Zeus's ancient mother,
B Rhea, whom he treated very shabbily, though she had once saved his life by a trick when Cronus wanted to eat him.

In a room behind the kitchen sat the three Fates, named Clotho, Lachesis, and Atropos. They were the oldest goddesses in existence, too old for anybody to remember where they came from. The Fates decided how long each mortal should live: spinning a linen thread, to measure exactly so many inches and feet for months and years, and then snipping it off with a pair of shears. They also knew, but seldom revealed, what would be the fate of each Olympian god. Even Zeus feared them for that reason.

The Olympians drank nectar, a sweet drink made from fermented honey; and ate ambrosia, said to be an uncooked mixture of honey, water, fruit, olive oil, cheese, and barley—though this may be doubted. Some claim that certain speckled mushrooms were the true food of the Olympians, created whenever Zeus's thunderbolt struck the earth; and that this kept them immortal. Because the Olympians also loved the smell, though not the taste, of roast beef and mutton, mortals used to sacrifice sheep and cattle to them, afterward eating the meat themselves.

Responding to the Myth

Analyzing the Myth

Identifying Facts

1. Briefly describe the Palace of Olympus. Where was it? Who lived there? How was it laid out? Draw a floor plan to show the various parts of the palace.
2. What kinds of mortal affairs interested the Olympians? What prevented the gods from becoming too involved?
3. How did Zeus, Hades, and Poseidon divide Cronus's kingdom? Tell which part each received, and which part they shared. Who, of the three, was considered the winner?
4. What happened to Cronus? Describe his new reign.
5. Copy the following chart on your paper. Complete the boxes for each of the gods listed in the chart.

Name of God	Areas of Control	Emblems
Zeus	sky	eagle, woodpecker
Hades	the underworld	none
Hera	mother of heaven	
Poseidon		
Demeter		
Hephaestus		
Athene		
Aphrodite		
Ares		
Artemis		
Hermes		

Zeus ruled the sky, Poseidon commanded the sea, and Hades controlled the underworld. They shared the earth between them.

Zeus was considered the winner.

4. Cronus was banished to a distant island in the Atlantic, but he escaped and settled in Italy.

Mortals lived without trouble or work, and they never fought wars. Instead they danced and sang all day, eating acorns, fruit, honey, and pig-nuts and drinking milk and water.

5. See Teacher's Manual, page 154.

6. The writer says Zeus was a strong, brave, stupid, noisy, violent god who was always suspicious of his family.

Hera disliked Zeus because he often married mortal women.

7. Poseidon hated to be less important than his brother.

Poseidon had a trident he used to stir up the sea and wreck ships. Zeus never traveled by ship.

8. Zeus hurled Hephaestus over the wall of Olympus. He fell on the island of Lemnos.

9. The Fates—Clotho, Lachesis, and Atropos—were the oldest.

They knew the fate of each of the gods, including Zeus.

6. How does the writer describe Zeus's personality? Why did Hera dislike being Zeus's wife?
7. Why did Poseidon dislike Zeus? What was Poseidon's main weapon, and how did Zeus avoid it?
8. Describe how Hephaestus broke his leg.
9. Which three goddesses were the oldest? Why did Zeus fear them?

Interpreting Meanings

10. In your opinion, which god or goddess seems the most likable? The least likable?
11. **Tone** is the attitude or feeling that the writer has toward a subject. What tone does Robert Graves take toward the gods and goddesses? What do you think of his tone? SRW p. 89
12. Choose two or three of the emblems that you listed in the chart above. Explain why each emblem suits the personality of that particular god.

Applying Meanings

13. How are some of the gods' emblems still used today? Think of the owl, eagle, peacock, dove, and trident.

Writing About the Myth

A Creative Response

1. **Keeping an Imaginary Journal.** Pretend that you are one of the Olympian gods or goddesses. Write a journal for one week in which you tell all the important events that happen to you. Be sure to mention any quarrels you might have with other gods or goddesses.

A Critical Response

2. **Comparing Characters.** After reading about Olympus, do you think the male and female gods are treated equally? Are power and responsibilities distributed fairly among them? Write a paragraph using details from the myths to support your opinion.

See Teacher's Manual page 155.

Analyzing Language and Vocabulary

Word Origins and Histories

Did you notice that Hades does not have a throne in the Palace of Olympus, even though he is one of the three lords of the universe? The original meaning of Hades's name helps explain his absence from Olympus. In ancient Greek *Hades* meant "the Unseen." When the Greeks said that their dead "went to Hades," they were not referring to a place, but to the god himself. Since only the gods lived in the Palace of Olympus, Hades's throne and the spirits of the dead that he ruled had to be somewhere else.

Dictionaries are an ideal place to start learning about such word origins and their histories as well as the modern meanings of old words. Use a good dictionary to help you answer the following questions about words from mythology.

1. In today's usage, what does *Hades* usually refer to—to a person or to a place?
2. According to the selection, the goddess Iris was "Hera's messenger, who used to run along the rainbow." What did this goddess's name originally mean? What are two modern meanings of *iris*?
3. The goddess Nemesis kept a list of "proud mortals due to be punished." According to the dictionary, what did her name originally mean? What does it mean today when we say someone or something is a *nemesis*?
4. What do we mean by the adjective *titanic* today? Why was it appropriate that the largest ocean liner of its day was called the *Titanic*? What is the origin of the word in mythology?
5. Look up the origin of the word *Olympics*. Does it have anything to do with the home of the gods?

For answers, see Teacher's Manual page 155.

Reading About the Writer

Robert Graves (1895–1985) was an English poet, novelist, critic, mythographer, translator, and editor. He taught English literature at Oxford University and at the Egyptian University in Cairo. He has published many volumes of poetry, several novels, and many nonfiction works. His novel *I, Claudius,* about the Emperor of ancient Rome, is often rerun as a TV serial. Graves once told his students that "the poet's chief loyalty is to the goddess Calliope [the muse of poetry], not to his publisher."

Interpreting Meanings

10. Answers will vary.

11. Robert Graves's tone is very familliar and indulgent. At times, Graves also mocks the deities.

12. A variety of answers can be expected.

Applying Meanings

13. A host of answers can be expected, although students might refer to the United States (the eagle), the NBC-TV network (the peacock), peace (the dove), and wisdom (the owl).

Further Reading for Teachers

A good reference book on Greek and Roman mythology is *The Meridian Handbook of Classical Mythology,* by Edward Tripp.

SUPPLEMENTARY SUPPORT MATERIAL

1. Reading Check Test blackline master
2. Introduction/Myths of Nature Test (page 183 of Test Book)

A. Expansion The *Homeric Hymns* were written to honor various gods, and many of the myths today come from these hymns. They are believed to belong to the end of the 8th century or beginning of the 7th century B.C. There are thirty-three hymns altogether. These hymns were first believed to be written by Homer but are now attributed to his followers.

B. Reading Aloud Ask for a volunteer to read this hymn aloud. Suggest that the student pause slightly at the end of each line. Tell students to remember that this is a hymn of praise and invocation and should be read with expression.

★ **Texas Essential Elements/(a) English Language Arts: 3D** Folklore/legends/myths

Myths of Nature

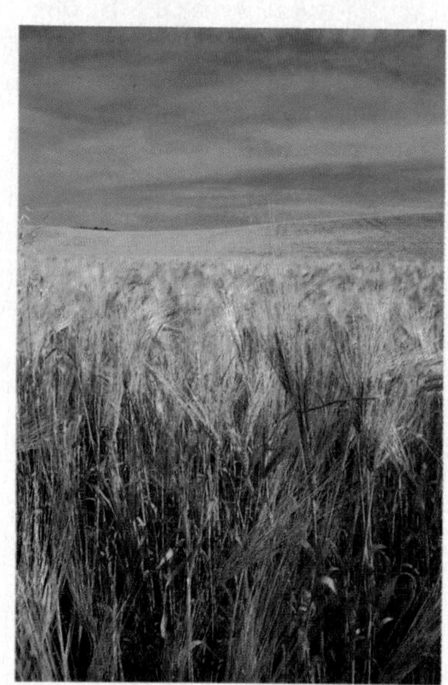

For teaching suggestions on this section, see Teacher's Manual page 155.

The ancient Greeks—especially in the early days before the development of the great Athenian civilization—did not possess anything like the scientific knowledge we have today. Yet, they were just as curious about their natural surroundings as we are. They longed for explanations. Why did the anemone flower grow, why was there night and day, why did the seasons change? For answers to these and other questions, the ancient people had to turn to their myth-makers. These strange men and women were believed to be directly in touch with the source of all knowledge—with the gods themselves. The myth-makers were the guardians of a "primitive" science that provided necessary explanations. The anemone grew because of the spilling of the blood of the boy Adonis. Night and day were the results of the movements of the Sun god Helius. The seasons changed because of something terrible that happened to a girl named Persephone (pər·sef′ə·nē).

The story of Persephone is best told in the *Homeric Hymns.* It is also told by the Roman poet Ovid in the fifth book of his *Metamorphoses.* Demeter, as we will remember, was the goddess of agriculture. It was she who was responsible for the earth's fruitfulness, in a continual sequence of spring and summer before fall or winter ever existed. Demeter had a beautiful daughter named Persephone. Here is a Homeric hymn to Demeter. The city is Athens. A

I begin
by singing
Demeter
in her beautiful hair,
majestic,
goddess,
Demeter,
her and her
very beautiful daughter,
Persephone.

Greetings,
goddess!
Preserve
this city and
direct
this song. B

—Translated by Charles Boer

The story itself is told here by the English translator and mythologist Rex Warner. Because he primarily uses Ovid's version of the myth, he uses the Roman rather than the Greek names for the gods and goddesses. Our main characters are Ceres (Demeter), Proserpine (Persephone), and Pluto (Hades). We also find other important figures who play roles: Jupiter (Zeus), Venus (Aphrodite), and Cupid (Eros), all of them troublemakers.

PREREADING

1. BUILDING ON PRIOR KNOWLEDGE. Because we are used to the comforts of indoor heating and because many foods and materials are imported from warm climates during the winter, we are not affected by the change of seasons the way Greeks and Romans were. Dependent on crops for food and clothing, the Greeks and Romans considered Ceres one of their most important deities, and they developed elaborate rituals to worship the goddess. A famous but mysterious celebration was started in the town of Eleusis, one of the places Ceres visited when searching for her daughter, Proserpine. This ritual, called the Eleusian Mysteries, was celebrated every five years at harvest time and lasted nine days—the number of days Ceres was said to have searched for her daughter. The chief part of the ceremony took place within the temple, but what was done there is a mystery, for those who beheld it were bound by vows of silence.

2. ESTABLISHING A PURPOSE. The headnote sets a good purpose for reading this myth.

3. PREREADING JOURNAL. Have students make a list of three things they associate with each season. Then, have them list what they think a child living in ancient Greece would associate with each season.

Texas Essential Elements/(a) English Language Arts: 1B Purpose and audience; **3A** Plot/character; **3D** Folklore/legends/myths; **4B** Main idea. **(c) Reading: 1B** Structural analysis

CERES AND PROSERPINE

For a detailed lesson plan on this myth, see Teacher's Manual page 156.
A biography of Rex Warner appears on page 485.

Retold by **Rex Warner**

Ancient people looked to myths for answers to questions that they had about nature, just as we turn to science today. They wondered, for example, why the growth of crops was linked to the seasons. Like us, they even wondered why there were seasons at all. As you read the myth of Ceres and Proserpine (the Roman names for Demeter and Persephone), note how squabbling among the gods affects life on earth. Pause at the point after Ceres begs Jupiter for help, and think about what you would do next if you were Jupiter. Then finish reading the myth, and compare your ideas to his.

A The huge three-cornered island of Sicily is piled upon the body of the rebellious giant Typhoeus, who once dared to attack the gods in heaven. Often he struggles to free himself, but his hands and arms are pinned down by mountains and over his head is the weight of Etna, through which he spouts out ashes and flames in his fierce insatiable rage. But his efforts to push off him and roll away the cities and mountains that cover his body often cause earthquakes, and then Pluto, the king of the underworld, fears lest the earth should split open and light be let in to terrify the thin and trembling ghosts of the dead.

It was in fear of such an event that, on one occasion, Pluto left his shadowy kingdom and, in a chariot drawn by black horses, came to the land of Sicily to inspect its foundations and see that all was well. He examined everything and, finding that there were no signs of weakness anywhere, he laid aside his fears.

But Venus, the goddess of love, who is worshiped in the Sicilian city of Eryx, saw him as he wandered through the land. She put her arms round her winged son, Cupid, and said to him: "My dear son, you who bring me all my power and my success, take your arrows, with which you conquer everything, and shoot one into the heart of that god who rules the world below. The heaven and the sea already own the power of love. Why should the underworld be exempt? Besides it is time that something was done to show our power, because in heaven I am not given the same honor that I used to have. Two goddesses, Minerva and the huntress Diana, will have nothing to do with me, and Ceres's daughter Proserpine, if I allow it, will choose to remain unmarried. So, if you want to increase my power and yours, make Pluto fall in love with Proserpine." B

Cupid, at his mother's bidding, took his quiver and chose from his thousand arrows the one that

English Prefixes Derived from Greek. "Ceres and Proserpine" uses Roman rather than Greek names for the gods because it is based on the Roman poet Ovid's version of the myth. Roman names often are similar to Greek names. Ovid's famous book of myths is called *Metamorphoses*. This word means "transformations" or "magical changes in form." It comes from the Greek prefix *meta-* meaning "over," and the noun *morphē* meaning "shape" or "form." As you read, look for the many magical changes that occur in the myth.

A. Recalling

? What other explanation for the eruptions of the same volcano was given in this unit? (On text page 463, the noise and fire of Etna is attributed to the Cyclops's smithy.)

B. Character

? List four adjectives that describe Venus's character during this scene. (Adjectives might include vain, manipulative, tricky, greedy, jealous.)

SUPPLEMENTARY SUPPORT MATERIAL

1. Vocabulary Activity Sheet
2. Reading Check Test blackline master
3. Selection Test (page 185 of Test Book)
4. Reader's Response Journal
5. Workbook (page 135)

DEVELOPING VOCABULARY

The following words appear on a test in the Test Book, page 186. (See also the Vocabulary Activity Sheet.)

insatiable	famine
foundations	plagues
exempt	indignation
bidding	realm
guardian	arbitration

Humanities Connection: Discussing the Fine Art

This terracotta, or brownish-red earthenware, relief was done around 470–450 B.C. It shows Pluto, god of the underworld, and his wife, Proserpine, seated on their thrones. Pluto is holding a cypress branch and a stalk of narcissus blossoms, both of which are associated with him.

 **Texas Essential Elements/(c) Reading** (continued): **3A** Main ideas/details; **3I** Draw conclusions

Persephone and Hades Enthroned.

Museo Nationale, Reggio Calabria, Italy.

READING CHECK TEST

1. Cupid made Pluto fall in love with Proserpine. (*True*)
2. Proserpine was happy to go along with Pluto to the underworld. (*False*)
3. A nymph told Ceres what happened to Proserpine. (*True*)
4. In anger at the loss of her daughter, Ceres made plants and crops stop growing. (*True*)
5. Because Proserpine had eaten seven pomegranate seeds in the underworld, she had to spend part of every year there. (*True*)

CLOSURE

Have students work in groups of three and discuss how they think Ceres and Hades felt about each other. To spark discussion, you might ask the following questions: How do you think Hades felt when Proserpine left the underworld to return to Ceres? Do you think he was jealous? Lonely? Do you think that Ceres was jealous and lonely?

seemed to him sharpest and most sure in flight.
A He bent the bow across his knee and with the barbed arrow of love he struck Pluto to the heart.

Not far from the city of Etna there is a lake of deep water and here, even more than in the smooth gliding rivers of Asia, one may hear the songs of swans. Woods lie like a crown around the waters and keep off the rays of the sun. In the shade of the branches grow flowers of every color. Here it is perpetual spring, and here Proserpine, with her companions, was playing and gathering
B violets or white lilies. In her girlish excitement she filled her basket and heaped the flowers in her arms, trying to pick more than any of the others, and suddenly, all in the same moment, Pluto saw her, fell in love with her and carried her off, so violent were the feelings that he had.

Terrified, the girl kept on calling out for her friends and for her mother, especially for her mother. She had, in her struggles, torn her dress at the top and all the flowers began to fall out of it. The loss of her flowers made her cry even more.

Meanwhile Pluto urged on his chariot, calling to his horses by name and shaking the black reins on their strong necks and streaming manes. They galloped through deep lakes, over mountains and past pools steaming with sulphur. Proserpine still cried for help, but only in one case did anyone try to help her. This was the nymph Cyane, who rose waist-high out of the water called after her name, recognized Proserpine and called to Pluto: "You shall go no further! You cannot marry Ceres's daughter against her mother's will, and, as for the daughter, you ought to have wooed her, not seized upon her by force."

As she spoke she stretched out her hands in Pluto's way to prevent him passing, but he, furious with her for obstructing him, urged on his terrible horses and, seizing his royal scepter in his strong arm, struck the pool to its depths. As he
C struck it, the earth gaped open and down into the earth plunged the black chariot and horses.

Cyane, however, in grief for the fate of the goddess and at the way in which the rights of her own fountain had been set aside, began to melt away in tears and to dissolve into the very waters of which she was the guardian nymph. You might have seen her limbs becoming soft, her bones beginning to bend and her nails losing their brittleness. First the most slender parts melted away; her dark hair, fingers, legs, and feet turned into cold water. Then shoulders, back, and breast flowed into the stream. Water instead of blood ran through her vanishing veins, and in the end there was nothing left that you could touch.

Meanwhile, Proserpine's terrified mother was searching for her, but searching in vain, through every land and every sea. All day she looked for her daughter and at night she lit two torches from the fire of Etna and continued the search in the cold darkness. It would take too long to tell the names of all the lands and seas where she wandered; but, when she had been everywhere in the world, she came back again to Sicily and passed by Cyane. If Cyane had still been a nymph and had not turned into water, she would have told the mother where her daughter was. Now she had no means of speaking, but she did succeed in making some sign, for, floating on her waters, she carried Proserpine's belt, which had fallen there as she was carried down into the lower world.

When Ceres recognized the belt, she tore her hair and beat her breast, as if this was the first news she had had of her daughter being stolen away. She still did not know where she was, but she cursed every land in the world and especially Sicily, saying that they were ungrateful to her and did not deserve to have the fruits of the earth. She broke in pieces the plows that turn over the soil; she brought death upon the farmers and upon their animals; she made the harvests fail and put blights and diseases among the young plants. Nothing grew but weeds and thorns and thistles. Throughout the world people were dying of famine or of plagues; and still Ceres was unable to find out where her daughter was.

There is a river called Arethusa, which rises in Greece, then descends into the earth and, after diving below the sea, comes into the light again in Sicily. Now this river Arethusa raised her head from her Sicilian stream, and brushing back her wet hair to the sides of her head, she spoke to Ceres. "O mother of fruit," she said, "and mother of the girl so sought for throughout the world, cease your long labor, and do not be angry with this land which does not deserve your anger, since

A. A Different Version
Another popular version of this myth has it that Pluto fell in love with Proserpine of his own accord. When he asked Jupiter's permission to marry her, Jupiter, not wanting to offend Ceres by letting her daughter be taken away to the underworld, told Pluto he would have to carry her off.

B. Expansion
It is clear that Proserpine is fairly young. Girls in ancient Greece were generally married at the age of fourteen.

C. Setting
? Compare the setting of the flower gatherers to the setting of Pluto's chariot ride. What details vividly contrast the two settings? (Spring setting: "smooth gliding rivers," "woods lie like a crown around the waters," "flowers of every color," "perpetual spring." Setting of ride: "black reins," "streaming manes," "pools steaming with sulfur," "earth gaped open.")

ANALYZING THE MYTH
Identifying Facts
1. Venus, noting that Minerva and Diana will have nothing to do with her and that Proserpine will remain unmarried if she does not intervene, wants to make him fall in love as a way of reasserting her power.
2. Against her will, Proserpine is carried off by Pluto in his chariot to the underworld.
3. Ceres believes that they were ungrateful to her and did not deserve to have the fruits of the earth.

Nothing would grow but weeds and thorns and thistles; animals perished, and throughout the world people died of famine and plague.
4. Jupiter says Proserpine can return only if she has not eaten any food while she was in the underworld.
5. Ascalaphus testifies that Proserpine ate seven grains of a pomegranate while she was in the underworld.

He divides the year into two parts so that Proserpine can live half the year with Pluto and half with her mother.

Interpreting Meanings
6. Cyane melts away in tears and dis-

A. Expression
It was said that anybody who ate food in the underworld would have to remain there for at least four months of the year. In some accounts, Proserpine is tricked or forced by Pluto into eating the pomegranate seeds just before she leaves the underworld to return to her mother. This assures Pluto that Proserpine will return to him.

B. Allegory
This myth is considered an allegory—a story in which the characters and setting and events stand for certain other people or events or concepts. The annual return to earth of Proserpine is an allegory of the sprouting of the seed in spring after staying underground during the winter.

it did not aid the theft of your daughter. I can give you certain news of her. While I was gliding on my path below the earth, down in the depths of the lower world, I saw Proserpine there with my own eyes. She looked sad certainly, and her face showed that she had not yet recovered from her fear, but she reigns there as the great queen of the dark world, the all-powerful wife of the ruler of the dead."

When Ceres heard these words, she stood still as if she had been turned to stone, and was for long like one out of her mind. Finally grief and pain took the place of horror. She mounted her chariot and went up to the bright shores of heaven. There, with cloudy face and hair all loose, she stood in indignation before Jupiter, and said: "Jupiter, I have come to beg your aid for the child who is yours and mine. If you have no respect for the mother, at least the daughter should touch a father's heart. At last I have found her—if you can call it finding her, when she is still lost to me, and when all I know is where she has been carried away. Let Pluto give her back. Your daughter does not deserve to have a robber for her husband."

Jupiter replied: "It is true that she is our daughter and I can understand your feelings. Yet, if we call things by their right names, we shall find that no great harm has been done. It was love that caused the theft. Then, if only you will approve the match, Pluto would be no unworthy son-in-law for us. To be the brother of Jupiter and to have in his own realm power as great as mine is a big thing. Nevertheless, if you are resolved on separating them, Proserpine shall return to heaven—but only on one condition, only if she has touched no food with her lips while she has been in the world below. This is the decision of the Fates."

So he spoke, but Ceres was still determined to have her daughter back. This, however, was what the Fates would not allow, because the girl had already tasted food. While she wandered thoughtlessly in Pluto's gardens, she had picked a red pomegranate from a swaying bough, had cut into the yellow rind and eaten seven grains of the fruit. The only one who saw her do this was a boy called Ascalaphus, the child of one of the nymphs of the underground lakes of Avernus. This boy bore witness against her and prevented her return. Then Proserpine in anger dashed water in his face and turned him into a bird, giving him a beak and feathers, big round eyes and long hooked claws. He became that unpleasant and ill-omened bird, the sluggish screech owl. A

And now Jupiter in arbitration between his brother Pluto and his sad sister Ceres, divided the year into two parts. Now Proserpine is goddess of both worlds and spends half the year with her mother and half with her husband. Her face became bright again at once, and so did her heart. Before, even Pluto had thought that she looked sad, but now she was like the sun which, after being hidden behind a rain cloud, comes out again into the open air. B

Responding to the Myth

Analyzing the Myth

Identifying Facts

1. What two reasons does Venus give for wanting Pluto to fall in love with Proserpine?
2. Describe what happens to Proserpine after Cupid shoots Pluto with his arrow.
3. Why does Ceres curse "every land in the world"? Explain what results from the curse.
4. What one condition does Jupiter set for Proserpine's return to her mother?
5. Tell what prevents Proserpine from returning to her mother. Explain what Jupiter does to resolve the dispute between Pluto and Ceres.

solves into the waters of a lake. Ceres, the goddess of agriculture, cursed every land in the world. The earth would grow nothing but weeds, thorns, and thistles, and famine and pestilence were everywhere. Ascalaphus is turned into a bird by Proserpine.
7. The half-year when Proserpine is with her mother is spring and summer.

When she returns to her husband, Pluto, the seasons change to fall and winter.
8. Venus makes Pluto fall in love with Proserpine to assert her own power; Ceres makes people on earth suffer when she loses her daughter; Proserpine turns Ascalaphus into a bird after he testifies against her.

Jupiter's decision to divide the year into two parts is fair and just.

Ceres's feelings for her daughter, Proserpine, and Pluto's love for Proserpine show the gods to be loving.

Applying Meanings
9. Student answers will vary.
10. Despite what Ceres did on earth in her anger, she was the goddess of agriculture.

Interpreting Meanings

6. What **metamorphosis,** or marvelous change, takes place for Cyane, Ceres, the earth, and Ascalaphus?
7. What do you suppose happens to the earth during the half-year when Proserpine is with her mother? What happens when Proserpine returns to her husband Pluto?
8. What incidents in the myth reveal the gods as petty and spiteful? As fair and just? As loving?

Applying Meanings

9. Describe a moment when a person today might like to be able to change form magically.
10. Given what happened when Ceres was on earth, why is it appropriate that oat or bran or wheat flakes are called *cereals* today?

Writing About the Myth

A Creative Response

1. **Keeping an Imaginary Diary.** Imagine you are Proserpine. Write diary entries in which you describe your thoughts and feelings about each of the following: playing with your companions by the lake near Etna; being the wife of Pluto and queen of the underworld; turning Ascalaphus into a screech owl; returning to your mother.

A Critical Response

SRW p. 87

2. **Writing About Theme.** A story's **theme** is the main idea that the author wants to reveal to the reader. Choose one of the statements below, and explain in a paragraph why you think it best expresses the theme of "Ceres and Proserpine." Support your argument with evidence from the myth.
   a. The relations among the gods are responsible for the natural order on earth.
   b. The seasons are the result of Ceres's anger and spite.
   c. The harmony of nature is a compromise between opposing forces.

See Teacher's Manual page 157.

Analyzing Language and Vocabulary

English Prefixes Derived from Greek

A **prefix** is a word part that is added to the beginning of a word to change the word's meaning. Many prefixes that we use today come from ancient Greek. Here are some common ones:

Prefix	Meaning	Example
anti-	against	*antidote:* something that acts against a poison
auto-	of oneself	*autobiography:* the life story of oneself
hydro-	water	*hydroelectricity:* electricity produced by water power
meta-	over	*metamorphosis:* a changing from one form to another
sym- or *syn-*	together, same	*synonym:* a word having almost the same meaning as another

Match the word in the left-hand column with its meaning in the right-hand column. Then use each word in a sentence.

1. antibiotic
2. autograph
3. hydroplane
4. metabolism
5. synchronize

a. process of changing food into energy
b. aircraft that can land on water
c. one's own signature
d. to move or happen at the same time
e. drug used against bacteria

For answers, see Teacher's Manual page 157.

Reading About the Writer

Rex Warner (1905–1986) was an English novelist and a famous translator of the Greek classics. He taught in England and Egypt, and moved to the United States in 1961, where he settled and taught in Connecticut. Some of his well-known translated works include *Prometheus Bound* by the Greek playwright Aeschylus. He also wrote several collections of myths for young people.

SUPPLEMENTARY SUPPORT MATERIAL

1. Reading Check Test blackline master
2. Introduction/Myth and Ritual Test (page 187 of Test Book)

A. Discussing the Photograph This is a contemporary photograph of the ruins of a temple in Corinth, Greece. Poseidon was considered to be the patron of the isthmus of Corinth. Helios, the sun god, was the patron of the mountain above the city.

B. Expansion This celebration, Lesser Eleusinia, was held in honor of Persephone's return to Demeter.

A

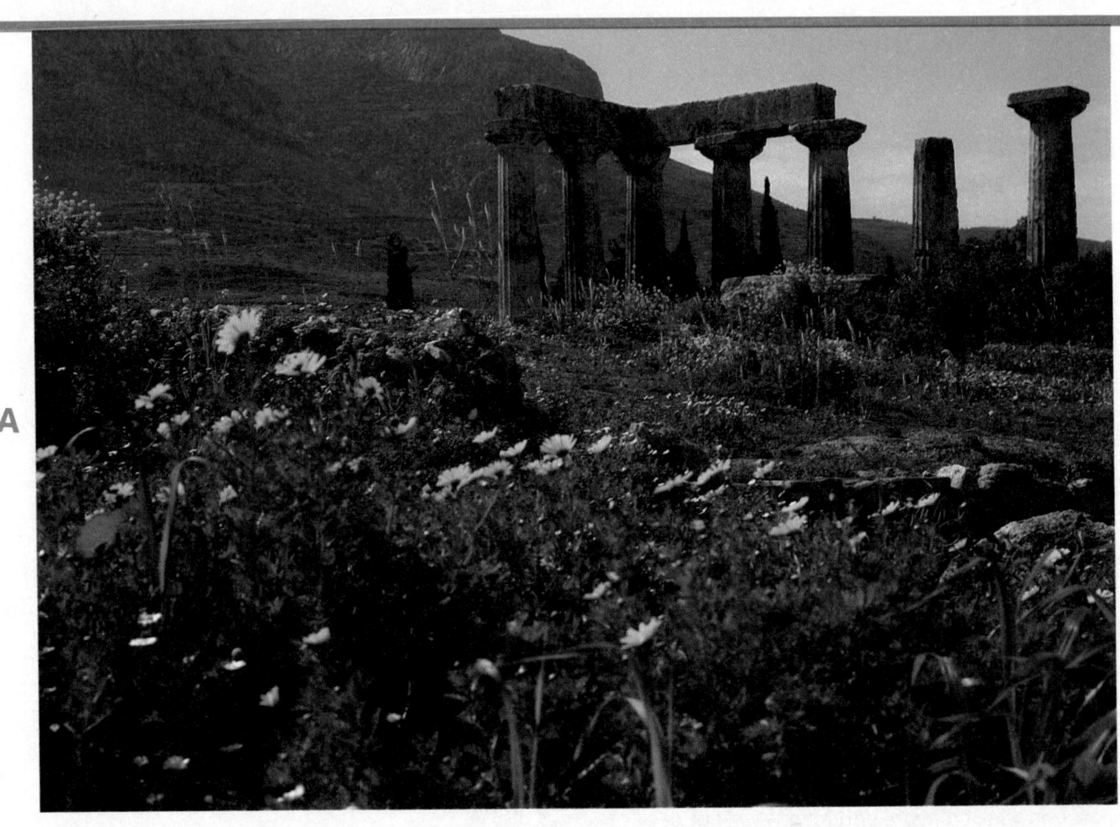

Myth and Ritual

For teaching suggestions on this section, see Teacher's Manual page 158.

Religious rituals were important to the ancient Greeks, just as they are to us today. The Greeks had rituals to celebrate the great moments of change in life—birth, marriage, and death—just as we do. Greek rituals often were connected with changes in the seasons as well. One important ritual (or "mystery") that marked the coming of spring was based on the myth of Demeter and Persephone This ritual was performed at a sacred place near Athens called Eleusis (e·lo͞o'sis). B

Each spring in Athens there were other rituals performed to honor the god of wine, Dionysus. It was thought that these festivals would ensure prosperity and fertility for the coming year.

In very ancient times, seasonal rituals were probably much more barbaric than they were in Athens in the civilized fifth century B.C. There are indications that in certain early rituals, humans—usually children—were sacrificed to the gods to ensure fertility. The dead victim was literally planted in Mother Earth as a seed from which crops would grow.

The Flower Myths

The flower stories that we will read here—those of Narcissus and Adonis—are, of course, stories that explain natural phenomena. But it is also possible that the myths have their original roots in this strange practice of human sacrifice. The myths of the flowers are told by Ovid in his *Metamorphoses.*

Reading Check Test

1. The Greeks had religious rituals to celebrate important events in their lives. *(True)*
2. The ritual that marked the coming of spring was based on the myth of Dionysus. *(False)*
3. Dionysus was the god of wine. *(True)*
4. The origins of the flower myths might lie in the practice of human sacrifice. *(True)*
5. Dionysus spent all his time on Mount Olympus. *(False)*

 **Texas Essential Elements/(a) English Language Arts: 3D** Folklore/legends/myths

The Myths of Dionysus

The story of Dionysus is an extremely old one. The mythologist Robert Graves suggests that the story of Dionysus developed from the old tradition of a sacred king who was annually sacrificed to the Great Earth Mother. Wherever Dionysus came from, he became one of the most important of the gods to the Greeks, especially to the common people. He was a god who was, it is true, dangerous, but he was a god who chose to spend more time down on the earth than up on Mount Olympus. And, as you will see, Dionysus was a god who could experience death. Dionysus traveled from place to place converting people to his worship. His story was told by many myth-makers. 

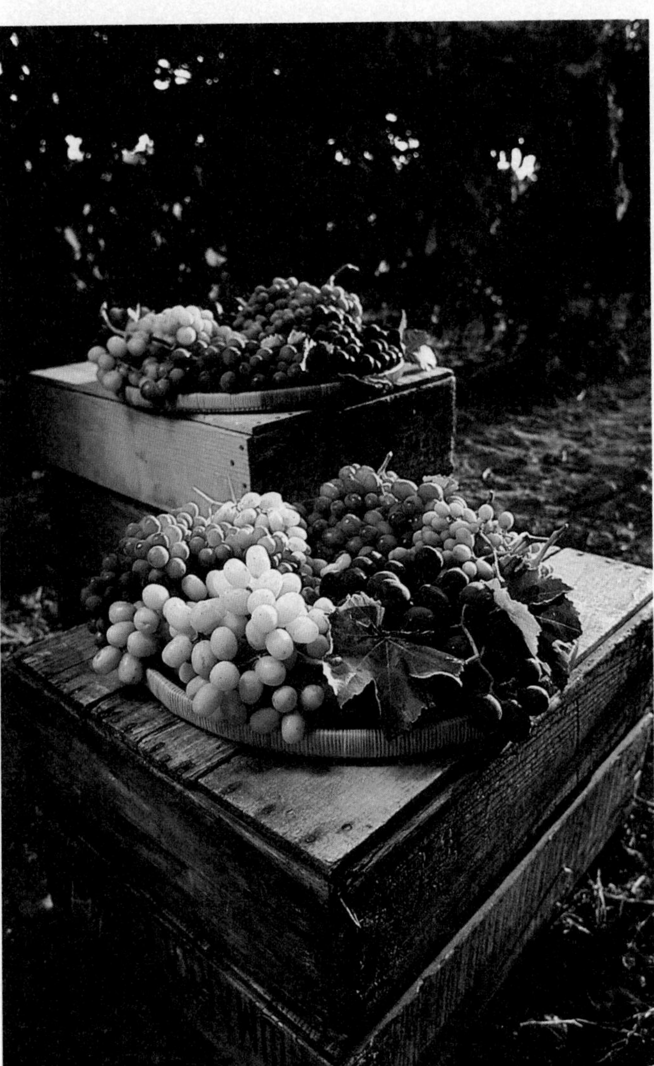

B

A. Character
Dionysus was known for his severe punishments.

B. Responding to the Photograph
The followers of Dionysus were often described as holding poles wrapped with grapevines and ivy. When he came across people he liked, he offered them knowledge about growing grapes and making wine.

? What is wine made from? (Crushed and fermented grapes)

PREREADING

1. **BUILDING ON PRIOR KNOWLEDGE.** We are all familiar with busybodies and people who are completely self-absorbed. These kinds of characters appear in books, in movies, and on television and often resemble friends, relatives, and classmates. The following myth attempts to discourage this behavior by telling a moralistic story. At the same time, the myth explains the creation of a flower, Narcissus, and the origin of echoes.

2. **ESTABLISHING A PURPOSE.** While you read this myth, look for instances when the characters act kindly and cruelly. Think about whether the characters seem appealing, or petty and self-centered.

3. **PREREADING JOURNAL.** This myth involves love, jealousy, and punishment. Ask students, from what they know of the gods and goddesses so far, to write briefly about who they think will be involved in this struggle. What roles might they play, and what actions might they take?

Humanities Connection: Responding to the Fine Art
Giovanni Antonio Boltraffio (1467–1516) was born in Milan and studied art under Leonardo da Vinci. Throughout the history of art, there have been many artists, called followers, who imitated the styles of other well-known artists that they admired. The practice was a respected craft in itself.

Notice that, aside from the garland around his head, Narcissus is not shown wearing typical clothes from the early Greek period. Many painters choose mythical or historical themes for their work and then incorporate clothing, surroundings, and other details from their own times.

? Write five adjectives to describe Narcissus in this painting. How would you describe the expression on Narcissus's face?

★ **Texas Essential Elements/(a) English Language Arts: 1B** Purpose and audience; **3A** Plot/character; **3D** Folklore/legends/myths. **(c) Reading: 1A** Context clues; **1B** Structural analysis; **2A** Word meaning

NARCISSUS

For a detailed lesson plan on this myth, see Teacher's Manual pages 158–159. A biography of Roger Lancelyn Green appears on text page 491.

Retold by **Roger Lancelyn Green**

The myth of Narcissus includes two instances of characters magically changing form. Like "Ceres and Proserpine" this myth also explains natural phenomena—the origin of echoes and of a delicate, fragrant spring flower.

Narcissus by a follower of G. A. Boltraffio.

Supplementary Support Material

1. Vocabulary Activity Sheet
2. Reading Check Test blackline master
3. Selection Test (page 189 of Test Book)
4. Connections Between Reading and Writing worksheet
5. Reader's Response Journal
6. Workbook (page 137)

Developing Vocabulary

The following words appear on a test in the Test Book, page 190. (See also the Vocabulary Activity Sheet.)

detained
scornful
pines away

Texas Essential Elements/(c) Reading (continued): 3A Main ideas/details; **3I** Draw conclusions

Up on the wild, lonely mountains of Greece lived the Oreades,[1] the nymphs of the hills, and among them one of the most beautiful was called Echo. She was one of the most talkative, too, and once she talked too much and angered Hera, wife of Zeus, king of the gods.

When Zeus grew tired of the golden halls of Mount Olympus, the home of the immortal gods, he would come down to earth and wander with the nymphs on the mountains. Hera, however, was jealous and often came to see what he was doing. It seemed strange at first that she always met Echo, and that Echo kept her listening for hours on end to her stories and her gossip.

A But at last Hera realized that Echo was doing this on purpose to detain her while Zeus went quietly back to Olympus as if he had never really been away.

"So nothing can stop you talking?" exclaimed Hera. "Well, Echo, I do not intend to spoil your pleasure. But from this day on, you shall be able B only to repeat what other people say—and never speak unless someone else speaks first."

Hera returned to Olympus, well pleased with the punishment she had made for Echo, leaving the poor nymph to weep sadly among the rocks on the mountainside and speak only the words which her sisters and their friends shouted happily to one another.

She grew used to her strange fate after a while, but then a new misfortune befell her.

There was a beautiful youth called Narcissus who was the son of a nymph and the god of a nearby river. He grew up on the plain of Thebes until he was sixteen years old, and then began to hunt on the mountains toward the north where Echo and her sister Oreades lived.

As he wandered through the woods and valleys, many a nymph looked upon him and loved him. But Narcissus laughed at them scornfully, for he loved only himself.

Farther up the mountains Echo saw him. And at once her lonely heart was filled with love for the beautiful youth, so that nothing else in the world mattered but to win him.

1. **Oreades** (ôr′ē·adz′).

Now she wished indeed that she could speak to him words of love. But the curse which Hera had placed upon her tied her tongue, and she could only follow wherever he went, hiding behind trees and rocks, and feasting her eyes vainly upon him.

One day Narcissus wandered farther up the mountain than usual, and all his friends, the other Theban youths, were left far behind. Only Echo followed him, still hiding among the rocks, her heart heavy with unspoken love.

Presently Narcissus realized that he was lost, and hoping to be heard by his companions, or perhaps by some mountain shepherd, he called out loudly:

"Is there anybody here?"

"Here!" cried Echo.

Narcissus stood still in amazement, looking all round in vain. Then he shouted, even more loudly:

"Whoever you are, come to me!"

"Come to me!" cried Echo eagerly.

Still no one was visible, so Narcissus called again:

"Why are you avoiding me?"

Echo repeated his words, but with a sob in her breath, and Narcissus called once more:

"Come here, I say, and let us meet!"

"Let us meet!" cried Echo, her heart leaping C with joy as she spoke the happiest words that had left her lips since the curse of Hera had fallen on her. And to make good her words, she came running out from behind the rocks and tried to clasp her arms about him.

But Narcissus flung the beautiful nymph away from him in scorn.

"Away with these embraces!" he cried angrily, his voice full of cruel contempt. "I would die before I would have you touch me!"

"I would have you touch me!" repeated poor Echo.

"Never will I let you kiss me!"

Words from Mythology. The English word *narcissistic* comes from the myth of Narcissus. As you read, look for the major flaw in Narcissus's personality. It will help you determine the meaning of this word.

A. Character

? How does Zeus's behavior strike you here? (Most students will think he acts childishly and sneakily. Some may think he is plainly dishonest. The ancient Greeks who were listening to or reading this myth for the first time would already know the characters of Zeus and Hera; they would not be surprised at the behavior of either one.)

B. Climax

This myth contains two connected stories. The climax of the first story—Hera's punishment of Echo—leads to the second half of the myth.

C. Suspense

By repeating only the last words of Narcissus's lines, Echo is able to say what she would like to say to him. Note how different the meaning of his words become. This contrast helps to create a feeling of suspense: What will happen when they do meet?

READING CHECK TEST

(This test covers "Narcissus" and "The First Anemones.")

1. Hera decides to punish Echo for telling lies. *(False)*

2. When Echo dies, her voice dies with her. *(False)*

3. Aphrodite causes Narcissus to fall in love with his own reflection. *(True)*

4. A tree grows in the spot where Smyrna dies. *(True)*

5. Adonis's blood turns into white narcissus flowers. *(False)*

CLOSURE

Break the class up into groups of three and have them define *metamorphosis.* Then, have them identify the metamorphosis in this myth.

A. Interpreting
Keep in mind that this is only one version of this story, and it presents one opinion about what it means to be in love.
? What do you think the storyteller means here by saying "she had been a true lover"? (That she gave herself over completely to one she loved)

B. Expansion
? What other phenomenon does this myth explain? (The quality of water that lets it reflect images)

C. Moral Lesson
? What do you think the morals of the myth are? (Don't gossip and meddle in other people's business; too much vanity is ugly and dangerous.)

"Kiss me! Kiss me!" murmured Echo, sinking down among the rocks, as Narcissus cast her violently from him and sped down the hillside.

"One touch of those lips would kill me!" he called back furiously over his shoulder.

"Kill me!" begged Echo.

A And Aphrodite, the goddess of love, heard her and was kind to her, for she had been a true lover. Quietly and painlessly, Echo pined away and died. But her voice lived on, lingering among the rocks and answering faintly whenever Narcissus or another called.

"He shall not go unpunished for this cruelty," said Aphrodite. "By scorning poor Echo like this he scorns love itself. And scorning love, he insults me. He is altogether eaten up with self-love. . . . Well, he shall love himself and no one else, and yet shall die of unrequited[2] love!"

It was not long before Aphrodite made good her threat, and in a very strange way. One day, tired after hunting, Narcissus came to a still, clear pool of water away up the mountainside not far from where he had scorned Echo and left her to die of a broken heart.

With a cry of satisfaction, for the day was hot and cloudless, and he was parched with thirst, Narcissus flung himself down beside the pool and leaned forward to dip his face in the cool water.

What was his surprise to see a beautiful face looking up at him through the still waters of the pool. The moment he saw, he loved—and love was a madness upon him so that he could think of nothing else.

"Beautiful water nymph!" he cried. "I love you! Be mine!"

Desperately he plunged his arms into the water—but the face vanished and he touched only the pebbles at the bottom of the pool. Drawing out his arms, he gazed intently down, and as the water grew still again, saw once more the face of his beloved.

B Poor Narcissus did not know that he was seeing his own reflection: for Aphrodite hid this knowledge from him—and perhaps this was the first time that a pool of water had reflected the face of anyone gazing into it.

2. **unrequited** (un·ri·kwīt′əd): unreturned.

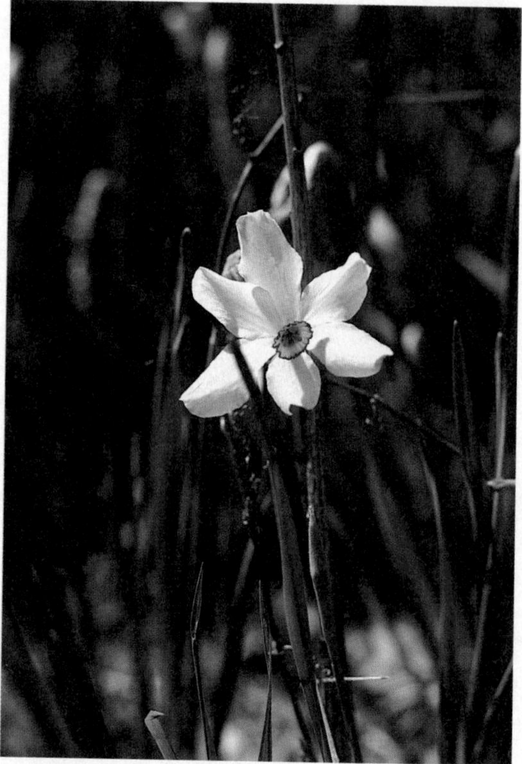

Narcissus seemed enchanted by what he saw. He could not leave the pool, but lay by its side day after day looking at the only face in the world which he loved—and could not win; and pining just as Echo had pined.

Slowly Narcissus faded away, and at last his heart broke.

"Woe is me for I loved in vain!" he cried.

"I loved in vain!" sobbed the voice of Echo among the rocks.

"Farewell, my love, farewell," were his last words, and Echo's voice broke and its whisper shivered into silence: "My love . . . farewell!"

So Narcissus died, and the earth covered his bones. But with the spring, a plant pushed its green leaves through the earth where he lay. As the sun shone on it a bud opened and a new flower blossomed for the first time—a white circle of petals round a yellow center. The flowers grew and spread, waving in the gentle breeze which whispered among them like Echo herself come to kiss the blossoms of the first narcissus flowers. C

ANALYZING THE MYTH

Identifying Facts

1. Hera is jealous and wants to see what Jupiter is doing.

2. Echo is one of the Oreades, a beautiful nymph of the hills who annoys Hera by talking too much while Zeus is sneaking back to Mount Olympus.

Hera allows Echo only to repeat what other people say.

3. Narcissus is vain.

He loves only himself.

4. Narcissus becomes lost while he is hunting, but Echo has followed him and they meet when he calls for help.

She pines away and dies. Only her voice remains.

5. She curses Narcissus to love only himself and to die of unrequited love.

Narcissus falls in love with his reflection and tries to touch it, but it disappears every time he disturbs the water.

6. Lying by the pool, Narcissus fades away and dies of a broken heart.

He is "reborn" as a flower.

Interpreting Meanings

7. She is too talkative.

Echo can only speak when someone else speaks first, and then she can only say a few words.

8. He loves only himself.

Aphrodite's curse is appropriate because even Narcissus's love of himself must go unrequited.

9. Answers will vary depending on students' definition of lovers.

It can be said that they finally become lovers because Echo is seen kissing the blossoms of the first narcissus flowers. On the other hand, Aphrodite's curse says that Narcissus will love no one but himself.

Applying Meanings

10. The gods often act like humans, which means they are not always fair.

Answers will vary, although students might note that while the punishments meted out by the gods may seem appropriate, they are extremely harsh.

Responding to the Myth

Analyzing the Myth

Identifying Facts

1. Tell why Hera decides to visit the earth.
2. Who is Echo, and what does she do that annoys Hera? How does Hera punish Echo?
3. What is Narcissus's problem? Why does he scorn the nymphs?
4. Describe how Echo and Narcissus meet. What happens to Echo after Narcissus runs away from her?
5. What curse does Aphrodite place on Narcissus? Tell what happens when he sees the beautiful face in the water.
6. Describe how Narcissus dies. How is he "reborn"?

Interpreting Meanings

7. What is the major flaw in Echo's character? Explain why Hera's curse is an appropriate punishment for this flaw.
8. What is the major flaw in Narcissus's character? Explain why Aphrodite's curse is an appropriate punishment for this flaw.
9. Is it possible that Aphrodite finally succeeds in joining Echo and Narcissus together as true lovers? Cite evidence from the myth to support your opinion.

Applying Meanings

10. Are the gods fair? What do you think of their actions in this myth?

Writing About the Myth

A Creative Response

1. **Expressing an Opinion.** Each of the main characters in this myth has a strong opinion about one or more of the other characters. Imagine that you are either Hera, Aphrodite, Echo, or Narcissus. In a paragraph write about one of the following:
   a. What Hera thinks of Echo
   b. What Aphrodite thinks of either Echo or Narcissus
   c. What Echo thinks of either Hera or Narcissus
   d. What Narcissus thinks of Echo
2. **Updating the Myth.** In a paragraph, explain how this myth might be modernized to take place today. Consider the names you'd give the characters, the conflict you would place them in, and the way you'd resolve their conflict. Where would you set your story of a modern-day Narcissus and Echo?

See Teacher's Manual page 159.

Analyzing Language and Vocabulary

Words from Mythology

SRW p. 91

The names of characters from mythology are at the core of quite a few modern English words. For example, our word *echo* is derived from the name of the nymph. Answer the following questions about words related to mythological characters. Use a dictionary if you need help.

1. What kind of personality flaw does a *narcissistic* person have?
2. What name of a common breakfast food is derived from Ceres, the name of the goddess of agriculture?
3. Jove is another name for Jupiter. What kind of person is *jovial*?
4. Pluto's name in ancient Greek meant "the rich one." What kind of person do you suppose a *plutocrat* is?

For answers, see Teacher's Manual page 160.

Reading About the Writer

Roger Lancelyn Green (1918–   ) began his career as an actor in London theaters. He began writing in 1945 and published several volumes of poetry, as well as biographies of such writers as Andrew Lang, C. S. Lewis, and Lewis Carroll. He has adapted fairy tales, the legends of King Arthur, and Norse myths, as well as the myths and legends of ancient Greece. He has visited Greece over twenty times to study its history, literature, mythology, and archaeological remains.

PREREADING

1. **BUILDING ON PRIOR KNOWLEDGE.** Keep in mind the symbols of change in the earlier myths. In the myth of Proserpine, Ceres's love for her daughter and her sense of peace is symbolized by year-round spring. When Ceres loses her daughter to Pluto, her despair and anger is symbolized by winter. When Jupiter arranges for Proserpine to spend six months with Pluto and six months with Ceres, Ceres divides the year in accordance with her joyous months spent with her daughter, making one half fruitful and the other barren. The story of Adonis is also symbolic of life, death, and rebirth and the changing of the seasons.

2. **ESTABLISHING A PURPOSE.** Tell students to watch for the metamorphoses, or changes in form, that take place in this myth.

A. Metamorphosis
Note the first metamorphosis in this myth.
? If you were Smyrna, would you now regret your prayer to be turned into another form?

B. Etymology
It might interest students to know that the name *Adonis* comes from the Greek *adon,* which means "lord." During the festivals that honored Adonis, the women would mournfully repeat "Adoni, Adoni"—"My lord, my master."

★ **Texas Essential Elements/(a) English Language Arts: 1B** Purpose and audience; **3D** Folklore/legends/myths; **4B** Main idea. **(c) Reading: 2A** Word meaning; **3A** Main ideas/details

THE FIRST ANEMONES

Retold by **Roger Lancelyn Green**

Each April in ancient Athens, women used to force seeds to grow in very small pots on the rooftops of their houses. These "Adonis gardens," as they were called, would flourish briefly, then die. This springtime custom is still practiced today in Cyprus, a Greek island in the Mediterranean sea. How do you think the myth of Adonis made people feel?

For a detailed lesson plan on this myth, see Teacher's Manual pages 158–159. A biography of Roger Lancelyn Green appears on text page 491.

There was once a princess called Smyrna who dwelt in the island of Cyprus. At first she lived happily in that beautiful island, which was under the special care of Aphrodite, the goddess of love and beauty. But Smyrna was wicked at heart. She turned away from the true worship of Aphrodite, and soon became so wicked that there was nothing for her father the king to do but order his people to kill her.

Smyrna, however, escaped in a ship which was sailing to that part of Asia Minor which we now call Turkey. Even there she was not safe, but was forced to flee farther and farther north until at last she sank exhausted to the ground near the seashore in the country of Lydia.

"I know that I deserve the cruelest punishment possible," she sobbed. "I know that I am too evil to live—perhaps I am too evil to die also. Forgive me, Aphrodite, and you other goddesses. Spare me the pain of being burnt to death. Spare me also whatever punishment may wait me in the land of the dead: I know that dark Hades is king there—but his wife, Persephone, is kind and merciful. Gods and goddesses, if you indeed have such powers as we believe you have, let me neither live nor die. Change me, instead, into some other form so that I may be a woman no longer."

Aphrodite heard her prayer, and so did Persephone. Together they whispered a request to kindly Mother Earth, and at once a change began to come over Smyrna. The soil seemed to catch and hold her: she was rooted to the ground by her toes, while her legs and body grew bark over them and turned into the trunk of a tree. Soon her arms became branches and her fingers twigs, while her hair turned into leaves. A

Smyrna was no longer a woman but had become the tree which bore her name in ancient Greece, though the Romans changed it a little into Myrrh. Now she wept tears not of salt water but of sweet-smelling gum, which oozed out of the bark and was soon sought for eagerly as a rare and wonderful perfume.

But an even stranger thing was to happen. Hardly had Smyrna turned into the first myrrh tree when the bark opened suddenly and a baby boy tumbled out.

He was such a beautiful child that Aphrodite decided to bring him up in secret, make him immortal, and marry him. She gave him the name of Adonis, and hid him away in a magic chest which she asked Persephone to guard for her in her kingdom under the earth. B

Changes in Meaning over Time. The meanings and spellings of words often change over time. For example, in "The First Anemones" you will learn how the name of a princess, *Smyrna,* changed to *myrrh,* the name of a tree. As you read, look for these other words that have changed similarly over the centuries: *Adonis, Muse, Calliope,* and *Parnassus.* Can you think of any modern meanings of these words?

Supplementary Support Material

1. Vocabulary Activity Sheet
2. Reading Check Test blackline master
3. Selection Test (page 189 of Test Book)
4. Reader's Response Journal
5. Workbook (page 137)

Developing Vocabulary

The following words appear on a test in the Test Book, page 190. (See also the Vocabulary Activity Sheet.)
merciful
companion
anxious
memorial

Traditional Belief

It was believed that every year, Adonis returned to certain places near rivers to be mortally wounded. The waters would then turn to blood. The phenomenon of water turning red was actually caused by reddish particles that washed from the rocks during such natural occurrences as high tides.

A. Vocabulary
An epic poem is a very long poem that tells a story.

READING CHECK TEST
See the test on page 490, which covers "Narcissus" and "The First Anemones."

CLOSURE
Divide students into groups of three, and have them first define *conflict,* and then make a list of all the conflicts in this myth. How was each one resolved?

B. Interpreting
? Why do you think Adonis chooses to spend his free time with Aphrodite instead of with Persephone? (Although we might first take his decision as proof of his affection for Aphrodite, we soon realize that it is probably due to his love of hunting, which he can only do on earth. Also, it is probably not very pleasant spending time in the underworld.)

C. Theme
This myth of rebirth is similar to the myth of Persephone, which explains the changes of the seasons. The theme of rebirth is common in myths and folklore in nearly every culture. In this account, the blooming of the anemones marks the time of year when Adonis would leave Persephone and the underworld and return to the love of Aphrodite, just as the growth of plantlife marks the coming of spring.

Adonis grew fast, and when Aphrodite came to claim him back he was already grown to be a handsome boy—and Persephone had fallen in love with him herself, and refused to restore him to Aphrodite.

The goddess of love complained to Zeus, the king of the gods, in his high palace on Mount Olympus in northern Greece.

Zeus decided not to judge the case himself. Aphrodite and Persephone were both his daughters, and he did not wish to make an enemy of either of them. So he chose Calliope,[1] one of the nine Muses, to be the judge. The Muses were lesser goddesses who ruled over the arts, Calliope
A being the Muse of epic poetry. Their home was on Mount Helicon by the magic fountain of Hippocrene which caught the first blush of the morning: but sometimes they wandered on Mount Parnassus not far away, which was sacred to Apollo, the bright god of light and music and prophecy, who was their leader.

Calliope did her best to be fair. She told Adonis that he must spend a third of every year with Persephone, a third with Aphrodite, and a third wherever he chose.

B Adonis soon chose to spend the four months which were his own with Aphrodite as well as the four when he was hers by right.

As Adonis grew from a boy into a man, his one love was for hunting. All day he would cheer on his hounds, chasing with them through the woods and thickets, up hill and down dale, in pursuit of hares, deer, and even wild boars.

Aphrodite grew more and more in love with him; but he cared nothing for her, nor for any mortal woman either, except as a companion in the chase. Indeed it seemed as if love had been left out of him altogether; and not even the goddess of love herself could wake the slightest passion in him.

Aphrodite did everything she could think of. She even joined him in the chase, wearing short skirts and carrying a bow and arrows like her half-sister Artemis, the goddess of hunting. Adonis found her a wonderful companion; but he did not learn to love her except as a friend.

"I'll go away and leave you!" exclaimed Aphrodite at last. "When I have gone, you'll realize that you can't do without me, and that you really love me all the time."

"Then I'll go hunting all by myself!" cried the selfish Adonis.

"Be very careful," said Aphrodite anxiously. "Keep away from lions and bears and wolves. Even wild boars can be dangerous."

But Adonis paid little attention, and at last Aphrodite flew away in her airy chariot drawn by birds, to see whether absence might make him learn to love her.

Adonis, however, had not a thought for her. He set out hunting at once, and wandered for a long time through the forests which grew where the city of Smyrna, named after his mother, was later to stand.

But suddenly, instead of being the hunter, he became the hunted. A huge wild boar came rushing at him, snorting wildly and clashing its sharp tusks. Adonis fled, and hid in a field of wild lettuces. But the boar soon found him, and in a moment had given him a deadly wound in the thigh.

Then at last Adonis cried out to Aphrodite for help, and she came speeding to his side, the mountains echoing to her cries of grief.

"Persephone has won," she sobbed. "Now you will have to dwell in her dark land forever: for you are still but mortal, and all who die become her subjects. But every year the women of Asia shall mourn you as I mourn now. And see! A memorial of you shall spring from the earth forever!"

Adonis could see nothing, for his eyes had closed in death. But the blood which dripped from his wound and sank into the ground was already sending up a new flower. All round him grew the delicate, short-lived blossoms of the anemone—the flower that blooms only to fall at the soft breath of the wind wailing for lost Adonis. And every year, just as Adonis himself once returned from the land of the dead to wander the woods with shining Aphrodite, so his blood rises through the earth and lives for a while in the sunshine in the anemone blossoms. C

1. **Calliope** (kə·lī′ə·pē′).

ANALYZING THE MYTH
Identifying Facts
1. Smyrna becomes so wicked that her father orders that she be killed.

She becomes a tree. Her toes turn into roots, her legs and body turn into a tree trunk, her arms and fingers become branches and twigs, and her hair turns into leaves.

2. Adonis tumbled out of a split in the bark of the myrrh tree. He grows up inside a magic chest guarded by Persephone in the underworld.

Persephone and Aphrodite fall in love with him.

They argue over who should have Adonis for themselves. The dispute is settled by the muse Calliope, who orders that Adonis spend a third of every year with Aphrodite, a third with Persephone, and a third wherever he chose.

3. Hunting becomes Adonis's real love. Adonis treats Aphrodite as a friend; he does not love her.

4. Adonis is mortally wounded by a wild boar.

His blood, which sinks into the ground, turns into anemone flowers.

Responding to the Myth

Analyzing the Myth

Identifying Facts

1. Why must Smyrna leave Cyprus? Describe the **metamorphosis** that takes place when she prays to Aphrodite.
2. Describe Adonis's miraculous birth and his childhood. Which two goddesses fall in love with him? What argument do they have over the boy, and how is it settled?
3. What becomes Adonis's "one love"? How does Adonis treat Aphrodite?
4. Tell how Adonis dies. What **metamorphosis** takes place when he dies?

Interpreting Meanings

5. Do you think Adonis's death was or was not an accident? Give evidence from the myth to support your answer.
6. Anemones have strong roots but delicate flowers. Their name comes from the Greek word for wind, because when the wind blows, anemones lose their leaves very quickly. Why is it appropriate that Adonis turned into such a plant? Can you think of another flower that Adonis might have turned into?

Applying Meanings

7. Do you think people could find a lesson in this love story? Explain your answer.
8. Do you think there are "Adonis"-type characters around today?

Writing About the Myth

A Creative Response

1. **Writing a Myth.** Both "Narcissus" and "The First Anemones" tell how a certain flower came to be. Choose a flower that you particularly like, and write a brief myth explaining its origin. You might try one of these:
   - **a.** Cactus
   - **b.** Dogwood
   - **c.** Sunflower
   - **d.** Venus fly-trap
   - **e.** Black-eyed Susan
2. **Writing a Letter.** When Adonis is killed, Aphrodite says that Persephone has won. Imagine you are Persephone. Write a letter to Aphrodite in which you express your feelings about Adonis and his fate.

A Critical Response

SRW p. 87

3. **Writing About Theme.** A story's **theme** is the main idea that the author is trying to reveal to the reader. Choose one of the statements below, and explain in a paragraph why you think it best expresses the theme of "The First Anemones." Support your opinion with details from the myth.
   - **a.** The love of a god for a mortal can prove fatal.
   - **b.** Beauty fades, but love endures.
   - **c.** The gods are only partially responsible for a person's fate.

See Teacher's Manual page 160.

Analyzing Language and Vocabulary

Changes in Meaning Over Time

Many words from mythology have a modern meaning in addition to their mythological one. For example, *nectar* in mythology was the drink that made the gods immortal. Today *nectar* refers to the liquid in flowers that bees gather to make honey. Use your knowledge of mythology plus a good dictionary to help you complete the following chart of words from mythology that have modern meanings.

Word	Mythological Meaning	Modern Meaning
myrrh	Roman name for Princess Smyrna	tree used in making perfume
adonis		
calliope		
muse		
parnassus		

For answers, see Teacher's Manual page 161.

Interpreting Meanings
5. An argument can be made for either case.

As Aphrodite notes, Persephone stood to gain from Adonis's death since his ghost would then descend to the underworld where she reigns. On the other hand, Aphrodite did warn Adonis that wild boars were dangerous, implying that his death might have been an accident.

6. Although Adonis was very strong and athletic, he flourished only for a short time before he died.

Answers will vary.

Applying Meanings
7. The lesson might be that there can be no happiness when a person's love is not returned. Another lesson might be that there can only be trouble when two people love the same person.

8. Answers will vary, but students might consider people who put sport above everything and everyone else.

PREREADING

1. BUILDING ON PRIOR KNOWLEDGE. Dionysus was a god who could be kind and helpful to humans, but he could also be cruel and drive them to commit horrifying deeds. The dual view of this god, who is at the same time joyful and heartless, seems contradictory at first. But the truth is, both ideas arose from the fact that he is the god of wine. Wine is good as well as bad—it cheers the heart, but it also gets people drunk and makes them lose their senses. The Greeks saw facts very clearly—they could see the ugly side of wine drinking as well as the delightful side.

2. ESTABLISHING A PURPOSE. The headnote sets a good purpose for reading the myth.

3. PREREADING JOURNAL. You might have students go back to page 497 and read the description of Dionysus's throne. On the basis of this description and what they know so far about the god, have them write a brief paragraph or so on the way they picture the god. Is he neat and richly dressed? Or does he wear wild colorful clothing? What might he wear as a crown?

A. A Different Version
In some accounts, Zeus is said to have rescued the unborn child (which was his) and placed him in his thigh, so the child would escape the notice of jealous Hera. He kept the infant there until he was ready to be born.

B. Expansion
Pan was Hermes's son. He had goat's horns and goat's hoofs instead of feet. He was the god of goatherds and shepherds. A wonderful musician, he often played on his reeds at night. It was believed that the sounds lone travelers heard at night were made by Pan, and so the word *panic* evolved.

C. Expansion
The rites of Dionysus developed into an annual festival that took place in the spring, when the vines began to grow their branches. It lasted for five days, and was filled with peace and enjoyment. No one worked, and even the prisoners were released to join in the revelry.

★ **Texas Essential Elements/(a) English Language Arts: 1B** Purpose and audience; **1C** Synthesize information; **3D** Folklore/legends/myths. **(c) Reading: 2A** Word meaning

THE MYSTERIES OF DIONYSUS

For a detailed lesson plan on this myth, see Teacher's Manual pages 161–162. A biography of Olivia Coolidge appears on page 499.

Retold by **Olivia Coolidge**

In ancient times, as today, many people in Greece grew grapes for wine-making. Like the drink that he represents, Dionysus, the god of wine, can be both good and dangerous. As you read, notice all the things about Dionysus that seem good and all the things about him that seem frightening. Why do you suppose the Greeks had mixed feelings about this god?

Dionysus, or Bacchus, god of wine, was one of the gods most important to daily life in Greece. Wine mixed with water was the common drink of both rich and poor. The cultivation of the vine was the common care of every farmer, so that the harvesting and the treading of the grapes in the wine press were almost as important events as the reaping which was sacred to Demeter. Then too Dionysus was a particularly human god. Wine made the tongue loosen and the heart be at ease. It was associated with gaiety and feasting. It brought refreshment after a day of toil, and sound sleep to the weary or sorrowful. For all these reasons the Greeks thought of Dionysus as a god who was in his way very close to them. He dwelt on earth more than on Olympus. He was born late, in the age of mortal heroes rather than the age of gods, and he was born of a mortal woman. Semele, a princess of the royal house of Thebes, was his mother. Zeus loved her, and she implored him to appear to her in his divine glory, but when she had persuaded him to do so, she was burned to ashes by the fire of his heavenly presence. Zeus saved the infant and sent him to (A) Asia to be brought up. There he lived in the woodland glades with the nymphs and satyrs, who were little, goat-legged gods with pointed ears and (B) shaggy hair, followers of Pan, the great god of the woodlands. These played with Dionysus, while old, fat Silenus[1] was tutor to the child. At least it was so at first, but as the boy grew older, it was he who led and the others who followed him.

Dionysus became a beautiful young god with long, curling locks and the pink-and-white complexion of one who feasts in shady halls rather than running, wrestling, or working in the open air. Yet he was in a way an outdoor god, and those who followed him were woodland creatures. When he was grown and the time was come, he gave to man the vine and traveled with it through all the eastern lands across to India. He returned thence across Asia and came finally to Greece. With him came all the nymphs and satyrs, laughing and dancing about the car in which he rode, while behind him followed old Silenus, rolling from side to side on the back of an ass. He himself stood in his car wreathed with ivy, and all the noisy crowd about him had ivy and vine leaves in their hair. They stripped rods from the trees, twining them with ivy and vine, and since men love music with feasting, they had pipes to entertain them and the rhythmic beat of clashing cymbals to which they danced. All sorts of wild beasts joined Dionysus's train, their savagery forgotten under the influence of wine. Leopards drew his ivy car. Spotted lynxes and lions followed him. The whole group, dancing, reveling, and making wild music, poured through the land, leaving the vine wherever they went and instituting the rites of Dionysus. (C)

The ceremonies of Dionysus were mysteries. That is to say, they were secret from all but those

1. **Silenus** (sī·lē′nəs).

SUPPLEMENTARY SUPPORT MATERIAL

1. Vocabulary Activity Sheet
2. Reading Check Test blackline master
3. Selection Test (page 189 of Test Book)
4. Reader's Response Journal
5. Workbook (page 139)

DEVELOPING VOCABULARY

The following words appear on a test in the Test Book, page 190. (See also the Vocabulary Activity Sheet.)
implore
reveling
frenzy

A. Humanities Connection: Responding to the Fine Art

An amphora is an ancient Greek jar with two handles that was used to hold beverages. Notice the grapevines that seem to sprout from the figure of Dionysus. He appears to be holding a large cup of wine. The woman on his right is probably one of the Bacchantes, his followers. A satyr is a horned, woodland creature who has a man's body, a goat's legs, and a horse's tail.

B. Character

The word *maddened* is often used to describe the effect that Dionysus had on people. The power to inflict madness was said to be one of his fiercest weapons.

C. Expansion

The worship of the Bacchantes is also described as being lovely, pure, and freeing. The women would leave the cities and go to the wilderness where Dionysus would give them berries, herbs, and milk, and they would sleep on the soft grass. They would worship under the open sky and feel the ecstasy and wild beauty of the world.

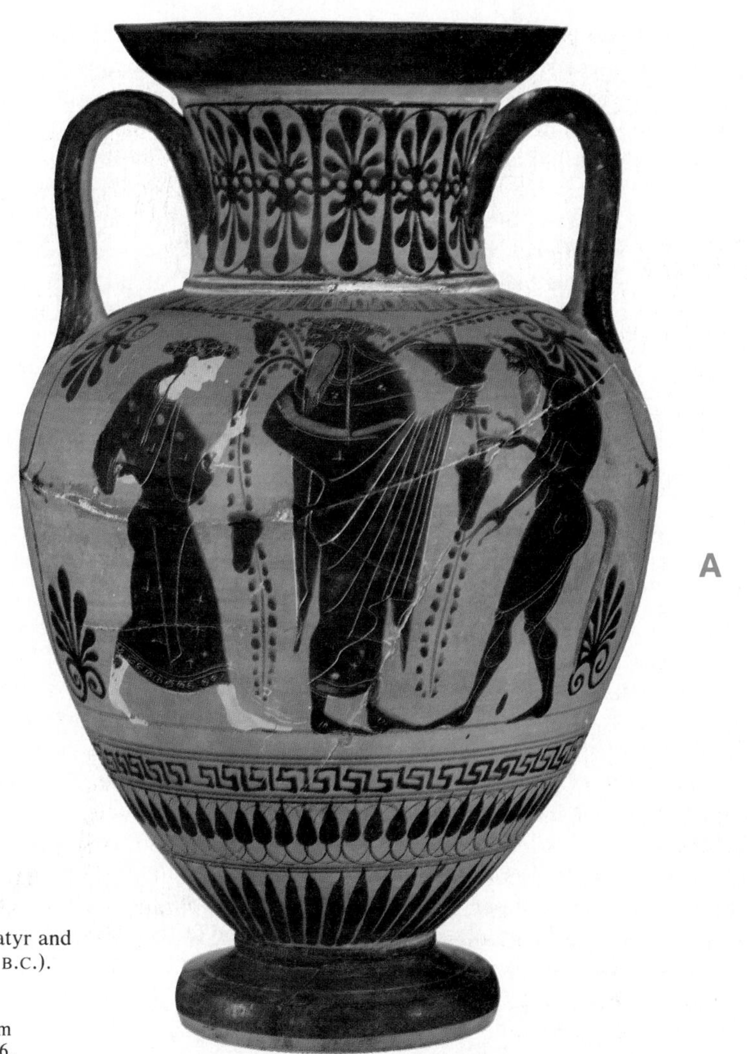

Dionysus between a satyr and a woman (6th century B.C.). Greek amphora.

The Metropolitan Museum of Art, Rogers Fund, 1906.

A

who had been initiated. They were held outside the cities on the mountains or in the woodland and were open to anyone, though they concerned chiefly women. The women worshipers were called Bacchantes after the other name of Dionysus, and they were smitten by the god with a mad frenzy. When, for instance, he came to Thebes, his mother's home, the people would not receive him, and in revenge he maddened the women. They left their homes, their husbands, and their young children, and poured out of the city one and all, from fair-haired girl to toothless grandmother, to revel with Dionysus on the mountains. B

There, clothed in skins of leopard or of fawn, they wreathed their streaming hair with ivy, split wands from trees, and ran laughing and shrieking through the woods. Nothing could hurt them in their ecstasy. In sudden frenzy they would hunt savage beasts and tear them limb from limb. Even Pentheus, king of Thebes and Dionysus's greatest enemy, was slain in this way as he went out to spy on the mysterious revels. His own mother and her followers fell on him and, taking him for a mountain lion in their madness, killed him. C

Such were the Bacchic revels, for if Dionysus was often kindly, he could be fierce and terrible.

Reading Check Test

1. Dionysus was also known as Bacchus. *(True)*
2. Dionysus spent all his time on Mount Olympus, never visiting earth. *(False)*
3. Dionysus's followers were quiet and peaceful. *(False)*
4. The pirates who tried to capture Dionysus were changed into dolphins. *(True)*
5. Dionysus was both god of wine and god of tragedy. *(False)*

Closure

In groups of four, students should scan the myth and make two brief lists: one of the good qualities and deeds of Dionysus and one of the bad.

A. Interpreting
Note the similarity between Dionysus's flashy clothing and his elaborate throne described on text page 477. (Students might compare this description of the god to their own in the Prereading Journal.)

B. Interpreting
? Why do you think that Dionysus waited until he was captured and the pirates were heading out to sea before revealing himself? (He probably wanted to test them.)

C. Responding
? Do you think that Dionysus acted fiercely and terribly or do you think that he acted fairly?

D. Origin
Here we find out the origin of dolphins. What do they have in common with the pirates? (Their home is at sea; the dolphins are black, as was the clothing of the pirates; dolphins' calls might be similar to screams of the pirates.)

A One story says that as he stood alone on a headland that overlooked the sea, some pirates saw him and, noting his rich garments of scarlet and gold, determined to capture him. They made for shore, seized him, and thrust him into their ship. Then the rest of them took up the oars and put their backs into the work, lest in a moment the alarm be sounded and the friends of this rich young prince come out to rescue him. The helmsman, however, kept watch on the prisoner and saw a smile in his dark eyes, while the bonds fell off his hands and feet as though they had never been tied. At that he guessed the truth and called out in terror to his companions, "This is no prince that we have in our boat, but a god. Bonds cannot hold him. Let us set him on shore at once, lest he loose a tempest on us and destroy us."

The captain, however, had no glance to spare for the prisoner. His mind was already dwelling on the rich ransom he would get. Without taking any notice of the helmsman, he ordered his men to hoist the sail. Even as they seized the sheets,[2] a strange scent of wine filled the air, and the rowers bending forward saw a dark trickle flowing past their feet. Then a vine spread suddenly along the top of the square sail. It put out flowers while they gaped at it. Tendrils wriggled down the mast, and dark purple clusters hung down across the canvas. Up the mast from the deck coiled an ivy stalk to meet the vine. Berries and blossoms grew out upon it as it mounted. Even the oars grew garlands until the rowers could move no more. They called out in panic to the helmsman to see if he could put them in to land, but it was too late B to get rid of their dangerous passenger. Amidships a black, shaggy bear stood up from nowhere with a growl and lurched toward them. As they recoiled, from behind them came a far louder roar, and there in the bows beside the god, a lion crouched ready to spring. Before anyone had time to make a movement, the lion had the captain in his jaws. At that the pirates jumped overboard with screams of fright and were changed there into C black dolphins. Only the helmsman was left on D the deserted ship, for Dionysus saved him because he had urged the others to release the god. As he guided the helm, the ship of itself sailed the god across to Greece.

Dionysus is also important because he was god of tragedy. Every year at his festival there was a dramatic contest in the outdoor theater at Athens. Three playwrights were chosen, each of whom wrote three tragedies, presenting some one of the legends of ancient Greece. All the citizens of Athens went to listen, and a prize was given to the man whose plays were judged the best. Plays were written in honor of Dionysus by some of the greatest dramatists of all time. These have made the name and festival of Dionysus famous even today.

2. **sheets:** here, ropes used to operate sails.

Responding to the Myth

Analyzing the Myth

Identifying Facts

1. According to the first paragraph, in what ways was Dionysus "a particularly human god"?
2. Describe Dionysus's miraculous birth. What happened to his mother?
3. What was the god Dionysus's gift to the human race?
4. Describe the kinds of gods, creatures, and people that traveled with Dionysus.
5. What did Dionysus do to the people of Thebes when they refused to receive him? Describe how the Theban king Pentheus died.
6. Describe how Dionysus transformed the ship of the pirates who kidnaped him. What happened to the pirates who jumped overboard? Why did Dionysus spare the helmsman?

ANALYZING THE STORY

Identifying Facts

1. Dionysus, the god of wine, was associated with gaiety and feasting. Wine made the tongue loosen, put the heart at ease, and provided a refreshing drink after a day of work.

2. Dionysus was saved by Zeus after his mother was consumed by fire.

His mother was burned to ashes by the fire of Zeus's presence.

3. He gave the wine to the human race.

4. Dionysus was accompanied by Selenus, nymphs, satyrs, and wild beasts including leopards, lions, and spotted lynxes.

5. Dionysus made the women maddened. They then left their homes to join him in revelry.

Pentheus was torn limb from limb by his mother and her followers.

6. Flowering vine tendrils spread along the sail and the mast; clusters of grapes hung across the sails; an ivy stalk rose from the deck to meet the vine, and garlands grew on the oars. He turned the pirates into black dolphins.

He spared the helmsman because he had urged the others to release Dionysus.

7. Every year, the Athenians held a festival in honor of Dionysus at which a dramatic contest was held.

Interpreting Meanings

8. Wine puts the heart at ease, provides refreshment, and helps bring sleep.

9. He can drive them mad or he can change them into other forms.

Wine can have both good and bad effects on people.

7. Explain how Athens honored Dionysus each year.

Interpreting Meanings

8. According to the myth, in what ways is Dionysus's gift beneficial to mortals?

9. In what ways is Dionysus dangerous to mortals? Why is this characteristic of his personality appropriate for a god of wine?

Applying Meanings

10. Wine can be destructive if it is misused. What other things in life are both destructive and helpful, depending on how they are used? Is Prometheus's gift of fire (page 467) also both good and bad?

Writing About the Myth

A Critical Response

1. **Doing Research.** The Theater of Dionysus sits at the base of the Acropolis in Athens. It is still used today for performances of the plays that were first produced there in honor of Dionysus 2500 years ago. Use your library to gather information about the Theater of Dionysus. In two paragraphs write a description of the theater as it appeared in ancient times and of the dramatic festivals that were held there.
2. **Analyzing the Myths.** In a brief essay, develop the following topic sentence. Use specific examples from the myths to support what you say.

Metamorphosis is a key element in Greek mythology.

See Teacher's Manual page 163.

Analyzing Language and Vocabulary

Precise Meanings

This myth offers many clues to how worshipers probably behaved at the mysteries of Dionysus. Use a dictionary to find a definition for each of the following words. Write down the precise meaning of each word. Then use these words in a short description of what you imagine the mysteries of Dionysus must have been like.

1. ecstasy
2. frenzy
3. panic
4. revel
5. shriek

For answers, see Teacher's Manual page 163.

Reading About the Writer

Olivia Coolidge (1908–) was born in England and graduated from Oxford University. She taught Latin, Greek, and English in England and in the United States. As well as retelling the Greek and Norse myths, she also wrote about such famous people as Edith Wharton and Abraham Lincoln. Her books include *Greek Myths, The Maid of Artemis,* and *The Apprenticeship of Abraham Lincoln.*

A

A. Humanities Connection: Studying Architecture

This theater is located in Dodona, Greece. Dodona is a city known for its many oracles, which were interpreted from the sounds of oak trees. Zeus was worshiped in this city.

FURTHER READING FOR STUDENTS

Students might enjoy reading some native Indian myths. One good collection is *American Indian Myths and Legends,* edited by Richard Edoes and Alfonso Ortiz.

Supplementary Support Material
Introduction/Myths and Morality Test
(page 191 of Test Book)

A. Responding to the Illustration Gustave Doré (1832–1883) was a French painter and illustrator. This illustration is made from a wood engraving. Instead of using a pencil or pen to draw the lines, an engraver carves them into a piece of wood, which is then covered in ink and printed on paper. This process was popular because it allowed artists to reproduce their work. In the familiar fairy tale, Bluebeard gives his young wife the keys to his castle because he is going on a trip. He tells her that she may go anywhere in the castle except one room, which is locked. Intensely curious, she disobeys his orders. (Who have you just read about who is known for her curiosity?) Some versions of this story end happily for the young wife and some do not.

 **Texas Essential Elements/(a) English Language Arts: 3C** Literary traditions; **3D** Folklore/legends/myths

Myths and Morality

For teaching suggestions on this section, see Teacher's Manual page 163.

Human beings have always used stories to teach lessons. The Greeks and the Romans were especially fond of using myths to teach morality and good sense. We have already read several myths that could be considered as moral lessons. The myth about Pandora's box tells us something about the dangers of curiosity. The Narcissus story is at least partly about the rewards of vanity.

If the goal of these stories was to teach a moral lesson to Greek and Roman students, they still have a certain power for us today. The myths of Phaethon and of Daedalus and Icarus seem a bit far-fetched until we hear a father warn his teen-aged child about driving too fast or too recklessly. And these myths are by no means intended only for children. The Phaethon story certainly should make a parent wary of making rash promises. The well-known story of King Midas's gold is perhaps directed primarily at the adult tendency to put too much value on money. These stories were told by Ovid in his *Metamorphoses* as well as by earlier writers.

A

Bluebeard giving his wife the keys to the castle (1867). Wood engraving after Gustave Doré.

PREREADING

1. **BUILDING ON PRIOR KNOWLEDGE.** Because Helius, the god of the sun, drove his chariot above the world, he was considered to be the "all-seeing" god. For this reason, the gods and goddesses often invoked him as a witness to their oaths.

2. **ESTABLISHING A PURPOSE.** Judging from this myth, Helius himself should have taken an oath. As they read, have students think about what oath he should have taken to prevent this catastrophe.

SUPPLEMENTARY SUPPORT MATERIAL

1. Vocabulary Activity sheet
2. Reading Check Test blackline master
3. Selection Test (page 193, Test Book)
4. Author photograph on *A Gallery of Authors* poster
5. Audiocassette recording
6. Reader's Response Journal
7. Workbook (page 141)

Texas Essential Elements/(a) English Language Arts: 1B Purpose and audience; **3C** Literary traditions; **3D** Folklore/legends/myths. **(c) Reading: 3I** Draw conclusions

PHAETHON

Retold by **Robert Graves**

The myth of Phaethon (fā′ə·thän′)—about a boy in a hurry to be like his father—may have been a story that Greek parents told children when they asked, "Why does the sun rise in the east and set in the west?" Like many stories for children, this myth also contains a moral lesson.

A The Sun, whose name was Helius, owned a palace near Colchis in the Far East beyond the Black Sea. He counted among the smaller gods, because his father had been a Titan. At cockcrow every morning, Helius harnessed four white horses to a fiery chariot—so bright that nobody could look at it without hurting his eyes— B which he drove across the sky to another palace in the Far West, near the Elysian Fields.[1] There he unharnessed his team, and when they had grazed, loaded them and the chariot on a golden C ferryboat, in which he sailed, fast asleep, round the world by way of the Ocean Stream until he reached Colchis again. Helius enjoyed watching what went on in the world below, but he could never take a holiday from work.

Phaethon, his eldest son, was constantly asking permission to drive the chariot. "Why not have a day in bed for a change, Father?" Helius always answered, "I must wait until you are a little older." Phaëthon grew so impatient and bad-tempered—throwing stones at the palace windows, and pulling up the flowers in the garden—that at last Helius said, "Very well, then, you may drive it tomorrow. But keep a firm hold of the reins. The horses are very spirited." Phaethon tried to show off before his younger sisters, and the horses, realizing that he did not know how to manage the reins, starting plunging up and down. D The Olympians felt icy cold one minute, and the next saw trees and grasses scorching from the heat. "Stop those stupid tricks, boy!" shouted Zeus.

"My team is out of control, Your Majesty," E gasped Phaethon.

Zeus, in disgust, threw a thunderbolt at Phaethon, and killed him. His body fell into the River Po. The little girls wept and wept. Zeus changed them to poplar trees.

1. **Elysian** (i·lizh′ən) **Fields:** area of complete bliss; paradise.

Allusions. If someone were to say to you, "You're opening a Pandora's box," that speaker would expect you to recognize the allusion to mythology and to understand the message. Such allusions occur often in speech and literature. Can you think of any allusions to mythology that are used by people in the United States space program?

SRW p. 13

A. Recalling
? Why would being a son of a Titan make him a "smaller god"? (Because in their long war, the Olympians were victorious over the Titans and therefore more powerful)

B. Interpreting
? What does this act of the sun god represent? (The sunrise)

C. Making Inferences
? Why do you think Helius sailed around the world to get back to Colchis instead of driving across the sky? (This was the ancient Greek's way of explaining the advent of nightfall.)

D. Interpreting
? What caused the drastic change in temperature? (The fire of the sun, which is symbolized by the chariot, was drawn close to the earth and then far from the earth by the spirited horses.)

E. Vocabulary
Ironically, the word *phaeton* today means a light open carriage drawn by two horses.

For a detailed lesson plan on this myth, see Teacher's Manual pages 163–164. A biography of Robert Graves appears on page 479.

Developing Vocabulary

The following words appear on a test in the Test Book, page 194. (See also the Vocabulary Activity Sheet.)

grazed
spirited
scorching

Reading Check Test

(This test covers "Phaethon" and "Daedalus and Icarus.")

1. Phaethon was the god of the sun. *(False)*
2. Because Phaethon could not control his father's chariot, Zeus killed him. *(True)*
3. Daedalus's son Icarus died because he flew too close to the sun. *(True)*
4. Cocalus's daughters figured out the solution to Minos's problem. *(False)*
5. Minos finally recaptured Daedalus. *(False)*

Closure

Break the class up into groups of four and have students discuss whether they think Zeus acted fairly in killing Phaethon. What else could Zeus have done to save the world?

Responding to the Myth

Analyzing the Myth

Identifying Facts

1. According to this myth, why does the sun rise and set every day?
2. What happens on earth when Phaethon takes over his father's job?
3. What does Zeus do when Phaethon admits that he has lost control?
4. According to this myth, what is the origin of the poplar tree? (Can you imagine what part of the tree their tears became?)

Interpreting Meanings

5. Considering the description of Helius's daily journey, how do you suppose the Greeks pictured the world? For example, did they imagine the world as round or flat? How far did their knowledge of other lands extend? What was the Ocean Stream? You might try drawing a map of the world as the Greeks imagined it.
6. In ancient Greece, people who were overly impatient, arrogant, or proud were said to have *hubris*. Such persons were thought to step outside the bounds of acceptable behavior. As a result, they invited the punishment of the gods. According to this myth, in what ways does Phaethon display hubris?
7. Do you think that Helius is partially responsible for his son's death? What moral lesson for parents might this myth contain?

Writing About the Myth

A Creative Response

Updating the Myth. Read the following poem. Then write a brief essay in which you tell how the poet has updated the Phaethon myth. Consider these points in your essay:

a. How is the father like Apollo (or Helius)?
b. How is the boy like Phaethon?
c. What is the equivalent of the sun's chariot?
d. In modern terms, what could the fire-breathing horses be? What could the Crab, the Bear, the Serpent, the Archer, and the Bull be? What could the purple doors of dawn be?
e. Why doesn't the modern father want his son to have the car?

Phaethon

Apollo through the heavens rode
  In glinting gold attire;
His car was bright with chrysolite,°
  His horses snorted fire.
He held them to their frantic course
  Across the blazing sky.
His darling son was Phaethon,
  Who begged to have a try.

"The chargers are ambrosia-fed
  They barely brook control;
On high beware the Crab, the Bear,
  The Serpent round the Pole;
Against the Archer and the Bull°
  Thy form is all unsteeled!"
But Phaethon could lay it on;
  Apollo had to yield.

Out of the purple doors of dawn
  Phaethon drove the horses;
They felt his hand could not command.
  They left their wonted courses.
And from the chariot Phaethon
  Plunged like a falling star—
And so, my boy, no, no, my boy,
  You cannot take the car.

—Morris Bishop

See Teacher's Manual page 165.

Analyzing Language and Vocabulary

Allusions

SRW p. 13

An **allusion** is a reference to a work of literature or to an actual event, person, or place. When a speaker or writer makes an allusion, he or she expects the audience to recognize the reference and understand its meaning. For example, if someone

3. **chrysolite:** a transparent mineral, usually green.
13. **Crab . . . Bull:** constellations of stars, named for animals and people.

ANALYZING THE MYTH

Identifying Facts

1. Helius drives a fiery chariot, which represents the sun, from his palace in the Far East to another palace in the Far West.

2. First it becomes very cold and then the trees and grasses get scorched from the heat.

3. He kills him with a thunderbolt.

4. Zeus turned Phaethon's sisters into poplar trees when they were weeping over Phaethon's death.

The leaves probably represent their tears.

5. They thought it was round.

Their knowledge of other lands extended to the Atlantic Ocean in the west to the land east of the Black Sea.

The Ocean Stream was the Atlantic Ocean.

Students might draw a map showing southern Europe, North Africa, the Middle East, and western Asia. The rest of the world might be depicted as ocean or unknown lands.

6. Phaethon showed hubris by demanding to drive the chariot before he was ready and by showing off in front of his sisters.

7. Yes. Helius is partly to blame.

The moral lesson is that parents should only allow a child to do something when the parents feel the child is ready, not when the child feels ready.

A. Humanities Connections: Responding to the Fine Art

Peter Paul Rubens (1577–1640) was a renowned Flemish painter. (For information on Rubens, see page 464, on which another painting by Rubens appears.) This painting shows Phaethon falling out of the chariot as he plunges through the sky. The horses are wildly out of control. The red in the painting creates a feeling of heat and chaos, while the brushstrokes indicate swirling confusion. We can see the panic and terror in the expressions of Phaethon and the two horses.

A

The Fall of Phaethon by Peter Paul Rubens (c. 1637). Oil.

were to refer to "the golden touch," the person would be alluding to the Midas myth (page 507). If someone described a place as an "Olympian paradise," you would picture it as being very grand and luxurious. As you can see, a simple allusion can say a lot.

The following sentences contain allusions to mythology. For each sentence, identify the allusion, and explain its meaning.

1. By raising the subject of taxes, the mayor opened a Pandora's box of angry comments from the audience.
2. We need leaders who can offer Promethean solutions to the nation's problems.
3. The criminal was as crooked as Cronus.
4. The years that Alice spent in San Francisco were a golden age for her.
5. The cave was as dismal as Hades's underworld.

For answers, see Teacher's Manual page 165.

PREREADING

1. BUILDING ON PRIOR KNOWLEDGE. Daedalus was believed to have been an ingenious and cunning Athenian. However, it is difficult to know whether Daedalus really existed since he is credited with completing both mythical and mortal tasks. For instance, he was said to have constructed the Labyrinth, a prison for the monster Minotaur, but he was also supposed to have invented the ax and the saw—quite mortal achievements. He is credited, too, with fixing arms and legs on the primitive statues of the gods and goddesses.

2. ESTABLISHING A PURPOSE. Tell students to be aware of the mythical elements in the story and the elements that connect Daedalus to the mortal world.

SUPPLEMENTARY SUPPORT MATERIAL

1. Vocabulary Activity Sheet
2. Reading Check Test blackline master
3. Selection Test (page 193, Test Book)
4. Author photograph on *A Gallery of Authors* poster
5. Audiocassette recording
6. Reader's Response Journal
7. Workbook (page 143)

DEVELOPING VOCABULARY
The following words appear on a test in the Test Book, page 194. (See also the Vocabulary Activity Sheet.)
clever
whorls
scalded

A. Humanities Connection: Responding to the Fine Art
Albrecht Dürer (1471–1528) was a German painter, engraver, and designer, and one of the foremost artists of Germany during the Renaissance. His woodcuts have been called inventive and exuberant, although some were grim and grotesque. This woodcut shows Icarus falling toward the water after his wings melted. Have the students note the expression on Daedalus's face and on Icarus's face. Note that some of the geese are flying with Daedalus while another is plunging into the sea.

★ **Texas Essential Elements/(a) English Language Arts: 1B** Purpose and audience; **1C** Synthesize information; **3D** Folklore/legends/myths. **(c) Reading: 1C** Dictionaries; **3A** Main ideas/details; **3I** Draw conclusions

DAEDALUS

For a detailed lesson plan on this myth, see Teacher's Manual pages 163–164. A biography of Robert Graves appears on page 479.

Retold by **Robert Graves**

In this story about Daedalus (ded''l·əs) and his enemy, King Minos, the gods are barely mentioned. It is a story mainly of human adventures and intrigue. In fact, some scholars suspect that Daedalus and Minos may have actually lived and that their stories became exaggerated over the centuries. Do you think Daedalus and Minos may have actually lived? As you read, keep track of the details that seem true to life and of those that the myth-maker might have made up.

A

Daedalus and Icarus by Albrecht Dürer (1493). Woodcut.

READING CHECK TEST
See the test on page 502, which includes "Phaethon" and "Daedalus and Icarus."

CLOSURE
Have students work in pairs and devise a way of making the wings so they wouldn't melt.

A Daedalus, the Athenian, a wonderfully skillful smith taught by Athene and Hephaestus, grew jealous of his nephew Talus and killed him. Talus, though only twelve years old, had invented the saw, which he copied in brass from the teeth of a snake. To avoid being hanged, Daedalus fled to Crete,[1] where King Minos, Europa's son, welcomed him. Minos was short of good workmen. Daedalus married a Cretan girl, by whom he had a son named Icarus;[2] and made Minos all sorts of statues, furniture, machines, weapons, armor, and toys for the palace children. After some years he asked for a month's holiday, and when Minos said: "Certainly not!" decided to escape.

He knew it would be useless to steal a boat and sail away, because Minos's fast ships would soon overtake him. So he made himself and Icarus a pair of wings each, to strap on their arms. The big
B quills he threaded to a frame; but the smaller feathers were held together by beeswax. Having helped Icarus with his pair of wings, Daedalus warned him: "Be careful not to fly too low, my
C boy, for fear of the sea spray; or too high, for fear of the sun."

Daedalus flew off, Icarus followed; but presently soared so near the sun that the wax melted and the feathers came unstuck. Icarus lost height, fell into the sea and drowned.
D

Place Names Borrowed from the Ancient World. Many modern place names have links to mythology or to classical history. For example, the Greek island of Icaria was named after Daedalus's son, Icarus. What places in the United States have names borrowed from the Greeks and Romans?

Daedalus buried his son's body on a small island, later called Icaria, where the sea had washed it up; then sadly flew on to the court of King Cocalus in Sicily. Minos pursued him by ship, but Daedalus begged the Sicilians not to reveal his hiding place. However, the clever Minos took a large triton[3] shell, and offered a bag of gold to anyone who could pass a linen thread through all the shell's whorls,[4] and out through a tiny hole at the very top. When he came to Cocalus's palace, Cocalus, anxious to win the reward, took the shell indoors and asked Daedalus to solve the problem for him. "That is easy," said Daedalus. "Tie the gossamer from a spider's web to the hind leg of an ant, put the ant into the shell, and then smear honey around the hole at the top. The ant will smell the honey and go circling up all the whorls in search of it. As soon as the ant reappears, catch it, tie a woman's hair to the other end of the gossamer, and pull it carefully through. Then tie a linen thread to the end of the hair, and pull that through as well."

Cocalus followed his advice. Minos, seeing the threaded shell, paid him the gold, but said sternly: "Only Daedalus could have thought of this! I shall burn your palace to the ground, unless you give him up."

Cocalus promised to do so, and invited Minos to take a warm bath in the new bathroom built by Daedalus. But Cocalus's daughters, to save their friend—who had given them a set of beautiful dolls, with movable arms and legs—poured boiling E
water down the bathroom pipe instead of warm, and scalded Minos to death. Cocalus pretended that Minos had died by accident: tripping over the bathmat and falling into the tub before cold water could be added. Fortunately the Cretans believed this story.

1. **Crete:** Greek island in the Mediterranean.
2. **Icarus** (ik'ər·əs).
3. **triton** (trīt''n): any of several large sea snails with a long spiral shell.
4. **whorls** (wôrlz): turns in a spiral shell.

A. Recalling
? What special skills were Athena and Hephaestus known for? (Their skill at crafts)

B. Vocabulary
Quills are feathers.

C. Suspense
Daedalus's words of advice create suspense. They inform us of the danger involved in the flight and of the skill needed to fly safely.

D. Comparing
? How are Phaethon and Icarus alike? (Both are impetuous, and neither heeds the knowledgeable advice of his father.)

E. Interpreting
Not only is Daedalus clever at performing tasks, but he is also clever enough to make allies in a place where he knows he might run into trouble.

ANALYZING THE MYTH
Identifying Facts
1. Daedalus is a smith.
2. He builds wings using feathers and beeswax.
3. He tells Icarus to fly neither too low for fear of the sea spray, nor too high for fear of the sun.

Icarus flies too close to the sun and his wings melt. He falls into the sea and drowns.
4. He tells Cocalus to tie the gossamer from a spider's web to the hind leg of an ant and to place the ant in the shell. He tells him next to place honey around the hole at the top of the shell to which the ant will then make its way. Once the ant appears with the gossamer, Cocalus is to tie a woman's hair to the gossamer and thread that through. Finally Cocalus is to attach a linen thread to the hair and pull it through too.

He threatens to burn down the palace of Cocalus unless he gives up Daedalus.
5. While Minos is taking a bath, they pour boiling water down the bathroom pipe and scald him to death.
(Answers continue in left-hand column.)

(Continued from top.)

Interpreting Meanings
6. Daedalus is artful because he can build any manner of things, from wings to furniture to statues. He is also crafty because he knows how to solve the problem set by Minos and how to escape from Crete.
7. There are a variety of answers. For example: Daedalus is jealous of Talus for inventing the saw; Cocalus is greedy for Minos's gold; Cocalus is deceitful when he pretends that Minos died when he slipped on a bathmat; Cocalus's daughters are guilty of murder.

Daedalus is guilty of jealousy, deceit, and murder.
8. It can be said that Minos should not have denied Daedalus's request for a vacation, and that he should not have tricked Cocalus, nor should he have threatened to burn down Cocalus's palace. At the same time, it is debatable whether he should have been killed for it.
9. Answers will vary but it does seem strange.

Responding to the Myth

Analyzing the Myth

Identifying Facts

1. What is Daedalus's occupation? Why does he flee to Crete?
2. How does Daedalus escape from Crete?
3. What warning does Daedalus give Icarus? What happens to Icarus?
4. What solution to Minos's puzzle does Daedalus give King Cocalus? What does Minos do once the puzzle is solved?
5. Explain how Cocalus's daughters murder King Minos.

Interpreting Meanings

6. Daedalus's name in ancient Greek means "the artful crafter." In what ways is Daedalus not only artful but also crafty?
7. Find examples of each of the following in the myth: jealousy, greed, deceit, murder. Is Daedalus guilty of any of these things?
8. Do you think Minos deserves his fate? Give reasons for your opinion.
9. The great Greek historian Herodotus tells that the Cretans, on hearing of Minos's death, attacked Sicily. However, they failed to avenge their king's murder and sailed home. Based on what you know about justice in mythology, do you think it strange that Cocalus and his daughters go unpunished for Minos's murder? Why or why not?

Applying Meanings

10. Can you think of any incidents in real life that might resemble incidents or characters in this famous myth?

Writing About the Myth

A Critical Response

1. **Writing a Research Report.** King Minos is murdered in a bath that Daedalus designed. Use your library to research some of the ingenious methods that ancient people, especially the Romans, used in designing their baths. Write a short report describing how they were built and used.
2. **Comparing Myths.** In a paragraph, tell how this myth is like, and unlike, the myth about Phaethon (page 501). In your essay, first tell how the stories are alike; then tell how they differ. Consider these elements of the myths:
   a. The role of the fathers in the myths
   b. The role of the sons
   c. The flaws in the sons' characters
   d. The tragic endings
   e. The morals

See Teacher's Manual page 166.

Analyzing Language and Vocabulary

Place Names Borrowed from the Ancient World

When the first Europeans settled the land that became the United States, they needed names for their towns and cities. Some names, such as Milwaukee, they borrowed from the Native Americans. Others, such as New London, they took from their own homelands. For other names, they often looked to ancient Greece and Rome for ideas.

Use the index in an atlas or other geographical reference book to identify (a) the state or states in which the following American cities are located and (b) the location of the original Greek or Roman city.

1. Ithaca
2. Athens
3. Rome
4. Alexandria
5. Syracuse
6. Olympia
7. Thebes
8. Etna
9. Naples
10. Troy

For answers, see Teacher's Manual page 166.

PREREADING

1. **BUILDING ON PRIOR KNOWLEDGE.** The myth students are about to read also involves a moral lesson. Aristotle, a master of reason, said, "The friend of wisdom is also a friend of myth." Stories involving the making of wishes are used in many cultures to present moral lessons. In the Western world, the popular version is the fairy tale in which someone is granted "three wishes." ("The Monkey's Paw" on text page 403 is a good example.)

2. **ESTABLISHING A PURPOSE.** Before students read the myth, have them read question 8.

SUPPLEMENTARY SUPPORT MATERIAL

1. Vocabulary Activity Sheet
2. Reading Check Test blackline master
3. Selection Test (page 193 of Test Book)
4. Author photograph on *A Gallery of Authors* poster
5. Reader's Response Journal
6. Workbook (page 145)

Texas Essential Elements/(a) English Language Arts: 1B Purpose and audience; **3D** Folklore/legends/myths. **(c) Reading: 3A** Main ideas/details

KING MIDAS'S EARS

Retold by **Robert Graves**

People who are said to have "a golden touch" are usually considered gifted at whatever they do. The myth of King Midas, whose touch actually turned things to gold, shows us someone unable to control this miraculous gift. After reading the first four paragraphs, try to think of one word to describe the flaw in Midas's character. Is your opinion the same after you have read about Midas's other misfortunes?

For a detailed lesson plan on this myth, see Teacher's Manual pages 167–168.

A biography of Robert Graves appears on text page 479.

Midas, a pleasure-loving King of Macedonia, planted the first rose garden in the world, and spent all his days feasting and listening to music. One morning his gardeners complained: "A drunken old satyr[1] is entangled in your best rosebush."

"Bring the wretch here," said Midas.

The satyr proved to be Silenus, who had gone to India and back as Dionysus's tutor. He told Midas exciting stories about India, and about a new continent lying across the Atlantic, where tall, happy, long-lived mortals inhabited wonderful
A cities; and how these giants had once sailed to Europe in hundreds of ships, but thought everything there so dull and ugly that they soon sailed home again.

Midas entertained Silenus for five days and nights, listening to these stories, and then sent him safe to Dionysus. Dionysus gratefully promised to grant Midas any wish he pleased; and Midas chose
B the magic power of transforming into gold whatever he touched. It was great fun at first: making gold roses and golden nightingales out of the ordinary ones. Then, by mistake, he turned his own daughter into a statue, and also found that the food he ate and the wine he drank were turning to gold in his mouth; so that he nearly died of hunger and thirst. Dionysus laughed loudly at Midas, but let him wash off the "golden touch" in the Phrygian river Pactolus—the sands of which are still bright with gold—and restore his daughter, too. He also helped him to become King of Phrygia.

One day Apollo asked Midas to judge a musical competition between himself and a Phrygian shepherd named Marsyas. This is how it came about. The goddess Athene had invented the double flute, made from stags' bones, and played enchanting tunes on it at a banquet of the Olympians. But Hera and Aphrodite began to giggle, and Athene could not guess why. So she went to Phrygia and played the flute all by herself, watching her reflection in a woodland stream. When she saw how silly her puffed cheeks and red face made her look, she threw away the flute, with a curse on anyone who picked it up. Marsyas happened to find the flute, and when he put it to his lips, such wonderful tunes flowed out that he challenged Apollo to C
this competition.

Apollo ordered the Muses and Midas to act as judges. When Marsyas played the flute, and Apollo the lyre, the judges could not at first agree which had given the best performance. Apollo then told Marsyas: "In that case, I challenge you to play your instrument upside down, as I do mine." So saying, he turned the lyre upside down, and played almost as well as before. Since Marsyas could not, of course, do the same with his D
flute, the Muses announced: "Apollo wins."

"No, that was an unfair test," said Midas.

However, the Muses were against him, nine to

1. **satyr** (sāt′ər): mythical creature with the head and body of a man, and the legs of a goat.

A. Interpreting
The myths were one way the ancient Greeks learned about geography and people in other lands. ? What does this description of Europe suggest about the land and people of India? (That it is exotic, colorful, and pretty)

B. Character
? What does Midas's wish say about his character? (That he is greedy)

C. Foreshadowing
Marsyas's challenge foreshadows danger. We know that the gods and goddesses do not like to be challenged, and anyone foolish enough to do so is quickly punished.

D. Making Inferences
? Why can Apollo play his instrument upside down but Marsyas cannot? (Because the lyre is a stringed instrument, like a harp, it can be played in any position. On a flute, however, the finger holes and keys are only on one side.)

READING CHECK TEST

1. Dionysus gave Midas the golden touch as a reward for (a) growing beautiful roses, (b) judging a contest, or (c) being kind to Silenus. *c*

2. Midas's golden touch prevented him from (a) eating, (b) sleeping, or (c) playing the flute. *a*

3. Apollo decided to hold a musical contest between himself and (a) Athene, (b) Midas, or (c) Marsyas. *c*

4. Midas thought Apollo's trick for winning the contest was (a) clever, (b) unfair, or (c) funny. *b*

CLOSURE

Working in pairs, students should briefly write whether or not Midas should have told Apollo that he won the competition fairly.

DEVELOPING VOCABULARY

The following words appear on a test in the Test Book, page 194. (See also the Vocabulary Activity Sheet.)
entangled
inhabited
transforming
sprouted

A. Humanities Connection: Responding to the Fine Art

Theodore Grosse (1839–1891) was a German painter known for his portraits and his paintings of historical subjects. He painted many mythological scenes and figures.

In this painting, Midas is shown judging the music contest. Marsyas is playing his flute. Note that the painter has already given Midas his ears. ? Why do you think Apollo is not portrayed in this painting?

B. Interpreting

? An ass is a donkey. Why was Midas so ashamed of his ass's ears? (Because donkeys had the reputation of being stupid; they are ugly.)

A

The Judgment of Midas (detail) by Theodore Grosse.

B

one, and Apollo told Marsyas: "You must die, miserable mortal, for daring to challenge the god of music himself!" He shot Marsyas through the heart, flayed[2] him, and gave his skin to the satyrs for making drums.

Then he called Midas an ass, and touched his ears, which sprouted up, long and hairy, like an ass's. Midas blushed, covered them with a tall Phrygian cap, and begged the Muses not to talk about the matter. Unfortunately Midas's barber had to know, because Phrygians cut their hair very short; but Midas threatened to kill him if he told a living creature. The barber, bursting with the secret, dug a hole in the bank of the Pactolus river, looked carefully around, for fear anyone might be listening, and then whispered into the hole: "King Midas has ass's ears." He filled up the hole at once to bury the secret, and went away happy. But a reed sprouted from the hole and whispered to the other reeds: "King Midas has ass's ears; King Midas has ass's ears!" Soon the birds got hold of the news and brought it to a man named Melampus, who understood their language. Melampus told his friends, and at last Midas, driving out in his chariot, heard all his people shouting in chorus: "Remove that cap, King Midas! We want to see your ears!" Midas first cut off the barber's head, and then killed himself for shame.

2. **flayed:** stripped off the skin.

ANALYZING THE MYTH
Identifying Facts
1. He is described as a pleasure-loving king of Macedonia.
We know that he spends all his days feasting and listening to music.
2. Midas asks that whatever he touches turn to gold.
He turns his daughter into gold, as well as his food and wine.
Dionysus lets Midas wash off the "golden touch" in the river Pactolus.
3. Athene's flute produced such beautiful tunes that Marsyas decided to challenge Apollo.
Apollo challenges Marsyas to play his flute upside down.
4. Apollo calls Midas an ass for choosing Marsyas's playing above his own.
5. Midas's barber, who knew about his ears, couldn't keep the secret to himself any longer, so he dug a hole in the river bank into which he whispered the secret. A reed grew in that spot and began to whisper the secret to the other reeds. Birds picked up the secret and conveyed it to Melampus, who told his friends.

Responding to the Myth

Analyzing the Myth

Identifying Facts

1. How is King Midas described in the first sentence? What do we know about his **character**?
2. What wish does Midas ask of Dionysus? What goes wrong when the wish is granted? How is Midas saved?
3. Why does Marsyas challenge the god to a musical competition? What does Midas object to in the contest?
4. Why is Midas given asses' ears?
5. Explain how the secret of Midas's ears becomes general knowledge.

Interpreting Meanings

6. How would you have worded the wish for the golden touch in order to avoid the problems that Midas had?
7. Explain how Apollo makes sure that he will win the contest.
8. In what ways is Midas greedy? Foolish? Vain? Which of these traits do you think is Midas's main flaw? Give reasons for your opinion.
9. How many metamorphoses are contained in this myth? What origins do they explain? (Think of the river sands and the flute.)

Applying Meanings

10. What would we mean if we said someone had a "Midas touch"? Would it be a compliment?

Writing About the Myth

A Creative Response

1. **Writing a Description.** Imagine how Midas's rose garden looked after he began turning everything into gold. Write a paragraph describing the garden. Use vivid details to help your readers picture the scene clearly. SRW p. 29

A Critical Response

2. **Updating the Myth.** Read the following poem. Then write a brief essay in which you explain the ways in which this "modern Croesus" (krē'səs) is like King Midas. (Note: Croesus was a king of an ancient country called Lydia and was supposed to be fabulously wealthy. A *requiem* is a lament for the dead. The last two lines refer to an old custom of putting pennies on the lids of a dead person's eyes, to keep them shut.)

The Minotaur. Illustration by Steele Savage.

Requiem for a Modern Croesus

To him the moon was a silver dollar, spun
Into the sky by some mysterious hand; the sun
Was a gleaming golden coin—
His to purloin;°
The freshly minted stars were dimes of delight
Flung out upon the counter of the night.

In yonder room he lies,
With pennies on his eyes.

—Lew Sarett

4. **purloin:** steal.

See Teacher's Manual page 168.

Interpreting Meanings
6. Midas might have wished that anything he touched would turn to gold if he wanted it to.
7. He challenges Marsyas to play his flute upside down, as Apollo does with his lyre.
8. Greedy because he wants to turn things into gold; foolish in his phrasing of the wish; vain because he tries to conceal the ass's ears.
Many of Midas's mistakes can be seen to result from all these flaws combined.
9. There are five: the daughter turns to gold, then back again; the flute begins to play wonderful tunes; Midas's ears turn into ass's ears; and the reed grows from the river sands.
It explains why reeds whisper and why flutists look the way they do when they play.
10. It would mean that the person could make money out of anything he or she attempted.

SUPPLEMENTARY SUPPORT MATERIAL

1. Reading Check Test blackline master
2. Introduction/Myths and History Test (page 195 of Test Book)

A. Humanities Connection: Responding to the Fine Art
It is interesting to note that this medieval illumination changes the historical period of the Trojan War by showing the warriors dressed in clothing characteristic of the Middle Ages. Similarly, the painting "Narcissus" (text page 488) shows the subject clothed in Renaissance dress. In this way, some artists depict the contemporary importance of well-known mythic and historical subjects. ? Choose a Greek god or goddess and describe what clothing they might wear today. (Artemis might wear jeans, hiking boots, and a flannel shirt, for example; Poseidon might wear a snazzy wet suit and matching flippers.)

 **Texas Essential Elements/(a) English Language Arts: 3C** Literary traditions; **3D** Folklore/legends/myths

Myths and History

For teaching suggestions on this section, see page 169.

In ancient times, before the Athenian civilization, the Greeks did not have historians like the ones that we have now. But they did have epic poets, such as Homer, who wandered from village to village spreading "news." Poets like Homer were not just entertainers who composed and sang stories to make people feel good. People depended on these poets to inform them about important events of the recent and distant past. Homer's epic poem called the *Iliad* and other stories that grew out of it were exciting tales about such well-known "stars" as Agamemnon, Achilles, Hector, Paris, and Helen. But they were also a kind of fictional record of a real war that was probably fought over the control of an important waterway perhaps as early as 1200 B.C.

A

A medieval illumination showing the entrance of the Trojan horse into Troy. Troy is depicted as a walled fortress and the people as medieval knights.

Bibliothèque Nationale, Paris.

Reading Check Test

1. The historians of the ancient Greeks were epic poets like Homer. *(True)*
2. The *Iliad* describes the events of a long war in about 1200 B.C. *(True)*
3. There are no remains of the city of Troy today. *(False)*
4. Homer's *Odyssey* is about the wanderings of a soldier after the Trojan War has ended. *(True)*
5. Virgil's *Aeneid* describes how the epic hero Aeneas founded France. *(False)*

The Trojan War

We know there is real history behind the Trojan myths because the
A ruins of a real city called Troy have been discovered near the straits called the Dardanelles or the Hellespont in Western Turkey. It is interesting to note that this waterway has been fought over many times since the days of Helen and Paris—most recently during World War I. The ruins of the ancient Troy show clear signs of a terrible war and much destruction at about the time when the events of Homer's epic might have taken place. The war might not have been caused by the elopement of Helen and Paris as the myths tells us. It might not have ended when the Wooden Horse containing soldiers was taken into Troy. But there really was a long
B and difficult war, and the *Iliad* and stories related to it allowed people of the eighth century B.C.—Homer's time—to share in its excitement and horror.

Homer's next epic, the *Odyssey,* is also a real record of the pain and the let-down feeling that often follows a great war. On his wanderings after the Trojan War, Odysseus is the lost, aging soldier with no way of getting home to his family. There must have been many soldiers in this situation after the real Trojan War, just as there are after all wars today.

Although the Romans did have historians, they too used epic poetry to "explain" things that might have happened in the days before recorded history. Where Homer told about the Trojan War from the point of view of the victorious Greeks, the Romans were on the Trojans' side. The poet Virgil in his epic the *Aeneid* tells how Rome was founded by the refugee Trojan hero Aeneas, who was forced to flee the burning city of Troy. The *Aeneid* gives us an interesting "explanation" for the very real Punic Wars between Carthage and Rome. In the *Aeneid,* the wars are caused when Aeneas, founder and hero of Rome, loved and then deserted Dido, queen of Carthage.

In the following story, Robert Graves retells the imaginary account of how the Trojan War began. Priam was King of Troy. Priam's son Paris eloped with the beautiful Helen, even though she was married to King Menelaus of Sparta.

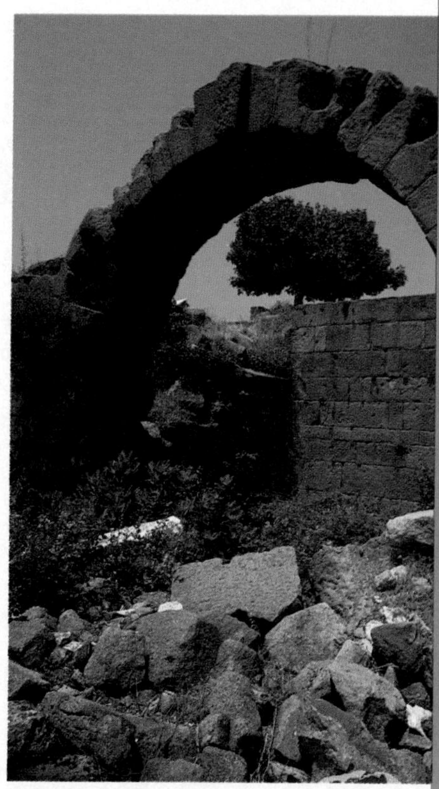

The ruins of Troy.

A. Expansion
? Look at the map on text page 520 and locate the Dardanelles.

B. Expansion
The Homeric epics do not only reflect information about events, such as the Trojan War. The poems also tell us about the life styles and beliefs of the people to whom the stories were first told, just as stories that students write will tell something about their lives and the world around them.

LEGEND A story of extraordinary deeds that is handed down from one generation to the next. Legends are based to some extent on fact. The myths about the Trojan War are legends.

PREREADING

1. **BUILDING ON PRIOR KNOWLEDGE.** The Homeric tradition is known as an oral tradition. During this time, most people could not read and write, and stories such as the *Iliad* were sung aloud to gatherings of people. Bards traveled from place to place recounting the tales of Paris, Helen, and the Trojan War. Because the stories were passed from generation to generation, and place to place, by word of mouth, slightly different versions of the stories emerged.

2. **ESTABLISHING A PURPOSE.** Before they read the myth, have students read question 8 on page 515.

A. Interpreting Dreams are very important throughout the Homeric tales, as well as throughout myths and folklore in general. Dreams were thought to offer signs that would reveal events in the future.

B. Foreshadowing ? Do you think it will be possible to avoid Troy's ruin if it has already been determined by the Fates and prophesied by the dream? (We have already been shown that no one can alter a decision made by the Fates.) Calchas's words foreshadow Paris's involvement in the destruction of Troy.

C. Character In some versions of the myth, Paris is known to be the most handsome man in the world.

★ **Texas Essential Elements/(a) English Language Arts: 1B** Purpose and audience; **3D** Folklore/legends/myths; **4D** Cause/effect. **(c) Reading: 1A** Context clues; **3A** Main ideas/details; **3C** Cause/effect; **3I** Draw conclusions

PARIS AND QUEEN HELEN

For a detailed lesson plan on this myth, see Teacher's Manual pages 169–170. A biography of Robert Graves appears on page 479.

Retold by **Robert Graves**

As you read this account of the cause of the Trojan War, think about how wars begin today. Are the human passions that caused this ancient conflict still responsible for bloodshed today?

Priam had sent his envoys to Salamis to demand the release of his sister Hesione, who had been taken from Troy by Hercules. Those at Salamis, however, sent word that they would not let her go (she was actually now married and did not want to return).

King Priam sulked on hearing the envoys' account of their visit to Salamis, and when his own son Paris ran away with Queen Helen of Sparta and brought her to Troy, the king refused to send her back. It was this decision that provoked the long, calamitous Trojan War, which benefited nobody, not even the conquerors.

Here is the story of Paris and Helen. Paris was Priam's son by Queen Hecuba who, just before his birth, dreamed that instead of a child she bore
A a blazing faggot,[1] from which wriggled countless fiery serpents. Priam asked Apollo's prophet Calchas what the dream meant. Calchas answered: "This child will be Troy's ruin. Cut his throat as soon as he is born!" Priam could not bring himself to kill any baby, especially his own son, but the warning frightened him; so he gave the child to his chief cattleman, saying: "Leave him behind a bush somewhere in the woods on Mount Ida, and
B don't go there again for nine days."

The cattleman obeyed. But on the ninth day, passing through the busy valley in which Paris had been left, he found a she-bear suckling him. Amazed at this sight, the cattleman brought Paris up with his own children.

1. **faggot:** bundle of sticks.

Paris grew to be tall, handsome, strong, and C
clever. He was always invited by the other cattlemen to judge bullfights. Almighty Zeus, watching from his palace on far-off Olympus, noticed how honestly he gave his verdict on such occasions; and one day chose him to preside over a beauty contest at which he did not care to appear himself. This is what had happened. The goddess of quarrels, Eris by name, was not invited to a famous wedding (that of the sea-goddess Thetis and King Peleus of Phthia[2]), attended by all the other gods and goddesses. Eris spitefully threw a golden apple among the guests, after scratching on the peel:

Context Clues. You will often encounter unfamiliar words when you read. A sure way to learn an unfamiliar word's meaning is to look it up in a dictionary. Another method is to examine the context—the surrounding words, phrases, and sentences—for clues. For example, in the first paragraph of "Paris and Queen Helen," you will find the word *calamitous*. What other words in the sentence offer hints that the word refers to something "bad" or "disastrous"?

2. **Phthia** (thē′ə).

Supplementary Support Material

1. Vocabulary Activity Sheet
2. Reading Check Test blackline master
3. Selection Test (page 197 of Test Book)
4. Author photograph on *A Gallery of Authors* poster
5. Workbook (page 147)

Developing Vocabulary

The following words appear on a test in the Test Book, page 198. (See also the Vocabulary Activity Sheet.)

sulked	summoned
provoked	eloped
prophet	vast
verdict	rapturously
spitefully	gloomy

Helen and Priam. Detail of vase. Museum, Tarquinia.

Humanities Connection: Responding to the Fine Art

This vase shows Queen Helen pouring wine into a bowl for Paris's father, King Priam.

? What do you think the presence of the Greek column, the sword, and the shield means? (Perhaps that Priam has returned home—the column—from a long day of war—the shield and sword)

Reading Check Test

1. According to a prophecy, Paris would grow up to curse the destruction of Sparta. *(False)*
2. Paris had to judge which of three goddesses was the best musician. *(False).*
3. Paris awarded the golden apple to the goddess of love. *(True)*
4. Paris's skill as a fighter caused Helen to fall in love with him. *(False)*
5. Menelaus prevented Paris from taking Helen to Troy. *(False)*

Closure

To help students understand how stories changed over time, divide the class into groups of six or eight. One person in each group should think of a very short story, about one or two paragraphs long. Play Whisper down the Lane with the story. See how the story changes by the time it reaches the last person in the group.

A. Plot
Here is another example of how the gods and goddesses took their anger and revenge out on the human race.

B. Character
? List three adjectives to describe Paris. (Excited, proud, adventurous, self-confident) He is actually very similar to Phaethon (text page 501). In what ways are the two young men alike?

C. Recalling
? Why does Paris want to go to Sparta? (To find Queen Helen, who Aphrodite promised will fall in love with Paris)

"For the Most Beautiful!" They would have handed the apple to Thetis, as the bride; but were afraid of offending the three far more important goddesses present: Hera, almighty Zeus's wife; Athene, his unmarried daughter, who was goddess not only of wisdom but of battle; and his daughter-in-law Aphrodite, goddess of love. Each of them thought herself the most beautiful, and they began quarreling about the apple, as Eris had intended. Zeus's one hope of domestic peace lay in ordering a beauty contest and choosing an honest judge.

So Hermes, herald of the gods, flew down with the golden apple and a message for Paris from Zeus. "Three goddesses," he announced, "will visit you here on Mount Ida, and almighty Zeus's orders are that you shall award this apple to the most beautiful. They will all, of course, abide by your decision." Paris disliked the task, but could not avoid it.

The goddesses arrived together, each in turn unveiling her beauty; and each in turn offering a bribe. Hera undertook to make Paris Emperor of Asia. Athene undertook to make him the wisest man alive and victorious in all his battles. But Aphrodite sidled up, saying: "Darling Paris, I declare that you're the handsomest fellow I've seen for years! Why waste your time here among bulls and cows and stupid cattlemen? Why not move to some rich city and lead a more interesting life? You deserve to marry a woman almost as beautiful as myself—let me suggest Queen Helen of Sparta. One look at you, and I'll make her fall so deep in love that she won't mind leaving her husband, her palace, her family—everything, for your sake!" Excited by Aphrodite's account of Helen's beauty, Paris handed her the apple; whereupon Hera and Athene went off angrily, arm in arm, to plot the destruction of the whole Trojan race. A

Next day, Paris paid his first visit to Troy, and found an athletic festival in progress. His foster-father, the cattleman, who had come too, advised him against entering the boxing contest which was staged in front of Priam's throne; but Paris stepped forward and won the crown of victory by sheer courage rather than skill. He put his name down for the foot race, too, and ran first. When Priam's sons challenged him to a longer race, he beat them again. They grew so annoyed, to think that a mere peasant had carried off three crowns of victory in a row, that they drew their swords. Paris ran for protection to the altar of Zeus, while his foster-father fell on his knees before Priam, crying: "Your Majesty, pardon me! This is your lost son."

The king summoned Hecuba, and Paris's foster-father showed her a rattle left in his hands when he was a baby. She knew it at once; so they took Paris with them to the palace, and there celebrated a huge banquet in honor of his return. Nevertheless, Calchas and the other priests of Apollo warned Priam that unless Paris were immediately put to death, Troy would go up in smoke. He answered: "Better that Troy should burn, than that my wonderful son should die!"

Priam made ready a fleet to sail for Salamis and rescue Queen Hesione by force of arms. Paris offered to take command, adding: "And if we can't bring my aunt home, perhaps I may capture some Greek princess whom we can hold as a hostage." He was of course already planning to carry off Helen, and had no intention of fetching his old aunt, in whom no Trojan but Priam took the least interest, and who felt perfectly happy at Salamis. B

While Priam was deciding whether he should give Paris the command, Menelaus,[3] king of Sparta, happened to visit Troy on some business matter. He made friends with Paris and invited him to Sparta; which enabled Paris to carry out his plan easily, using no more than a single fast ship. He and Menelaus sailed as soon as the wind blew favorably and, on arrival at Sparta, feasted together nine days running. C Under Aphrodite's spell, Helen loved Paris at first sight, but was greatly embarrassed by his bold behavior. He even dared to write "I love Helen!" in wine spilt on the top of the banqueting table. Yet Menelaus, grieved by news of his father's death in Crete, noticed nothing; and when the nine days ended, he set sail for the funeral, leaving Helen to rule in his absence. This was no more than Helen's due, since he had become king of Sparta by marrying her.

That same night Helen and Paris eloped in his fast ship, putting aboard most of the palace trea-

3. **Menelaus** (men′ə·lā′əs).

ANALYZING THE MYTH
Identifying Facts
1. Priam couldn't bear to kill his son himself, but he was frightened by a prophecy that his son would be Troy's ruin.

Priam tells him to leave the boy behind a bush on Mount Ida for nine days.

Priam expects that the child will die.

A she-bear suckles Paris, and the cattleman finds him alive after nine days and raises him with his own family.

2. Paris is tall, handsome, strong, clever, honest, courageous, and bold.

Paris judges the bullfights because he is so honest.

3. Eris, the goddess of quarrels, throws the apple.

She feels spiteful because she was not invited to a famous wedding attended by all the other gods and goddesses.

"For the Most Beautiful" is written on the apple.

4. Hera offers to make Paris Emperor of Asia. Athene promises to make him the wisest man alive and victorious in all his battles. Aphrodite promises to make Helen of Sparta fall in love with him.

Paris gives the apple to Aphrodite.

5. After an athletic festival at which Paris *(Answers continue on page 516.)*

A sures that she had inherited from her foster-father. And Paris stole a great mass of gold out of Apollo's temple, in revenge for the prophecy made by his priests that he should be killed at birth. Hera spitefully raised a heavy storm, which blew their ship to Cyprus; and Paris decided to stay there some months before he went home—Menelaus might be anchored off Troy, waiting to catch him. In Cyprus, where he had friends, he collected a fleet to raid Sidon, a rich city on the coast of Palestine. The raid was a great success: Paris killed the Sidonian king, and captured vast quantities of treasure.

When at last he returned to Troy, his ship loaded with silver, gold, and precious stones, the Trojans welcomed him rapturously. Everyone thought Helen so beautiful, beyond all comparison, that King Priam himself swore never to give her up, even in exchange for his sister Hesione. Paris quieted his enemies, the Trojan priests of Apollo, by handing them the gold robbed from the god's treasury at Sparta; and almost the only two people who took a gloomy view of what would now happen were Paris's sister Cassandra, and her twin brother Helenus, both of whom possessed the gift of prophecy. This they had won accidentally, while still children, by falling asleep in Apollo's temple. The sacred serpents had come up and licked their ears, which enabled them to hear the god's secret voice. Yet it did them no good: because Apollo arranged that no one would believe their prophecies. Time after time Cassandra and Helenus had warned Priam never to let Paris visit Greece. Now they warned him to send Helen and her treasure back at once if he wanted to avoid a long and terrible war. Priam paid not the least attention. B

A. Character
? What kind of person is Helen? (Disloyal, adventurous, romantic, greedy)

B. Suspense and Foreshadowing
Priam's lack of interest creates suspense regarding the events that will follow, and it foreshadows the fall of Troy.

Responding to the Legend

Analyzing the Legend

Identifying Facts

1. Why does King Priam give his baby son to the chief cattleman? What does Priam instruct the cattleman to do with the boy? What does Priam expect to happen to the child? Explain what actually happens.
2. Find words or phrases in the story that describe Paris. Why is he always asked to judge the bullfights?
3. Who throws the golden apple among the wedding guests? Why does she do it? What is written on the apple?
4. Tell what each of the three goddesses offers Paris as a bribe. To whom does Paris give the apple?
5. Tell how Paris becomes reunited with his real parents. What does Priam say when the priests of Apollo advise that Paris be killed?
6. What does Paris take from Sparta in addition to Helen? How does Paris quiet the priests of Apollo after his return to Troy?
7. Who are Cassandra and Helenus? What gift do they possess? Why does the gift do them no good?

Interpreting Meanings

8. What qualities does Paris possess that make him seem heroic?
9. In your opinion, is Priam better as a king or as a father? Consider Priam's reactions to the prophecies about Paris in your answer.
10. The story states that Paris disliked the task of judging the beauty contest, but could not avoid it. Why do you suppose Paris felt this way?
11. Considering what Paris brings back to Troy, what do you suppose was the real cause of the historical Trojan War?

(Answers begin on page 515.)
beats Priam's sons in the competition, the sons pursue him with their swords to the altar of Zeus, at which time Paris's foster-father tells him the truth.

Priam says that it is better that Troy should burn than that his son should die.

6. Paris takes most of the treasures that Helen had inherited, as well as a mass of gold from Apollo's temple.

He gives them the gold robbed from the treasury of Apollo in Sparta.

7. They are twins, the sister and brother of Paris.

They possess the gift of prophecy.

Apollo arranged that no one would believe their prophecies.

8. Paris is handsome, strong, courageous, and clever.

9. Priam is better as a father. He says, "Better that Troy should burn than my wonderful son should die." He cares more for his son than for his kingdom.

10. Paris felt that he could not avoid judging the contest because he was ordered to do it by Zeus himself.

11. The war may have been caused by the treasure looted by Paris from Menelaus's palace and from the temple of

(Answers continue in left-hand column.)

(Continued from top.)
Apollo in Sparta.

Applying Meanings

12. Marlowe knew the story of how the Greeks sailed their ships to Troy in order to rescue the beautiful Helen.

FURTHER READING FOR STUDENTS

For the whole story, you might refer students to Robert Graves's *The Siege and Fall of Troy.*

Applying Meanings

12. Christopher Marlowe, a sixteenth-century English poet, wrote a line that has become a famous reference to Helen of Troy. He says she had "the face that launched a thousand ships." After reading the story of how the Trojan War began, tell how you think Marlowe came up with this line.

Writing About the Legend

A Creative Response

1. **Writing a Diary Entry.** The story states that Helen loved Paris at first sight but was greatly embarrassed by his bold behavior. Imagine you are Helen. Write a diary entry describing your first meeting with Paris at the Spartan banquet.

A Critical Response

2. **Analyzing Details.** "Paris and Queen Helen" contains many details that can be considered historical, such as Paris's attack on Sidon. Other details, such as the beauty contest, seem purely mythological. Analyze the story, listing details according to whether they seem historical or legendary. Then, in two paragraphs, explain what this story suggests caused the Trojan War.

See Teacher's Manual page 171.

Judgment of Paris (15th century). Florence, Italy.

Analyzing Language and Vocabulary

Context Clues

A word's **context** consists of the words, phrases, and sentences surrounding it. Examining an unfamiliar word's context can often help you make an "educated guess" about the meaning of the difficult word. For example, in the first paragraph of "Paris and Queen Helen," the phrases "which benefited nobody, not even the conquerors" offer a good clue to the meaning of *calamitous:* A war that benefits nobody is a disaster. If you guessed that *calamitous* means "disastrous" or "causing great loss and sorrow," you were correct.

For each of the following excerpts from "Paris and Queen Helen," examine the context of the italicized word. Then select the best meaning from among the choices in the list.

1. "He [Paris] was always invited by the other cattlemen to judge bullfights. Almighty Zeus . . . noticed how honestly he gave his *verdict* on such occasions."

   a. approval　　**c.** criticism
   b. decision　　**d.** truth

2. "[Zeus] one day chose him to *preside* over a beauty contest at which he did not care to appear himself."

   a. compete　　**c.** avoid completely
   b. witness　　**d.** have authority

3. "[They] were afraid of offending . . . Hera, almighty Zeus's wife; Athene, his unmarried daughter . . . ; and his daughter-in-law Aphrodite. . . . Zeus's one hope of *domestic* peace lay in ordering a beauty contest. . . ."

   a. heavenly　　**c.** having to do with home
   b. doomed　　**d.** having to do with war

4. "[Menelaus] set sail for the funeral, leaving Helen to rule in his absence. This was no more than Helen's *due,* since he had become king of Sparta by marrying her."

   a. payment　　**c.** moisture
   b. right　　**d.** debt

5. "When at last he returned to Troy, his ship loaded with silver, gold, and precious stones, the Trojans welcomed him *rapturously.*

   a. noisily　　**c.** joyfully
   b. suspiciously　　**d.** enviously

For answers, see Teacher's Manual page 171.

PREREADING

1. **BUILDING ON PRIOR KNOWLEDGE.** As we have seen in the myths up to this point, the gods and goddesses wield a great deal of power over the lives of mortals. It was believed that they had almost as large a part in the Trojan War as did the Trojans and the Greeks. After all, it was Athena and Hera who began it.

2. **ESTABLISHING A PURPOSE.** The headnote sets a good purpose for reading the myth.

3. **PREREADING JOURNAL.** Have students choose one of the following writing activities: Write a letter *to* Priam trying to convince him that he must send Helen back to Greece in order to save his city. Or, write a letter *from* Priam explaining why he refuses to send Helen back.

Texas Essential Elements/(a) English Language Arts: 1B Purpose and audience; **3C** Literary traditions; **3D** Folklore/legends/myths; **4D** Cause/effect. **(c) Reading: 3A** Main ideas/details; **3C** Cause/effect

THE WOODEN HORSE

Retold by **Edith Hamilton**

The ruins of Troy reveal that it was a city with massive walls. Homer says that the Greeks fought the Trojans outside those walls for ten years. Many terrible things happened and much heroic blood was shed all around. Weary of fighting, the Greeks resorted to trickery. As you read, make note of all the tricks that the Greeks—and the Trojans—use during their last great battle.

For a detailed lesson plan on this myth, see Teacher's Manual pages 171–172.

A biography of Edith Hamilton appears on page 521.

A Troy did not fall because Paris was dead. He was, indeed, no great loss. At last the Greeks learned that there was a most sacred image of Pallas Athene in the city, called the Palladium, and that as long as the Trojans had it Troy could not be taken. Accordingly, the two greatest of the chieftains left alive by then, Odysseus[1] and Diomedes,[2] determined to try to steal it. Diomedes was the one who bore the image off. In a dark night he climbed the wall with Odysseus's help, found the Palladium, and took it to the camp. With this great encouragement the Greeks determined to wait no longer, but devise some way to put an end to the endless war.

They saw clearly by now that unless they could get their army into the city and take the Trojans by surprise, they would never conquer. Almost ten years had passed since they had first laid siege to the town, and it seemed as strong as ever. The
B walls stood uninjured. They had never suffered a real attack. The fighting had taken place, for the most part, at a distance from them. The Greeks must find a secret way of entering the city, or accept defeat. The result of this new determination and new vision was the stratagem of the wooden horse. It was, as anyone would guess, the
C creation of Odysseus's wily mind.

He had a skillful worker in wood make a huge wooden horse which was hollow and so big that it could hold a number of men. Then he persuaded—and had a great deal of difficulty in doing so—certain of the chieftains to hide inside it, along with himself, of course. They were all terror-stricken except Achilles's son Neoptolemus, and indeed what they faced was no slight danger. The idea was that all the other Greeks should strike camp, and apparently put out to sea, but they would really hide beyond the nearest island where they could not be seen by the Trojans. Whatever happened they would be safe; they could sail home if anything went wrong. But in that case the men inside the wooden horse would surely die.

Odysseus, as can be readily believed, had not overlooked this fact. His plan was to leave a single Greek behind in the deserted camp, primed with a tale calculated to make the Trojans draw the horse into the city—and without investigating it. Then, when night was darkest, the Greeks inside were to leave their wooden prison and open the city gates to the army, which by that time would have sailed back, and be waiting before the wall.

A night came when the plan was carried out. Then the last day of Troy dawned. On the wall the Trojan watchers saw with astonishment two D
sights, each as startling as the other. In front of the Scaean[3] gates stood an enormous figure of a horse, such a thing as no one had ever seen, an apparition so strange that it was vaguely terrifying, even though there was no sound or movement coming from it. No sound or movement anywhere,

1. **Odysseus** (ō·dis′yo͞os).
2. **Diomedes** (dī′ə·mē′dēz).
3. **Scaean** (sē′ən).

A. Interpreting
Paris was mortally wounded by an arrow toward the end of the Trojan War. He was not known as a great warrior during the war.

B. Expansion
Troy, like other cities of the time, was surrounded by a wall for protection.

C. Expansion
Odysseus was the king of Ithaca. He was known for his shrewdness during the Trojan War. He is the protagonist of Homer's epic poem the *Odyssey,* which tells of Odysseus's long journey home from Troy.

D. Making Inferences
? Who are the "Trojan watchers"? (Guards positioned on the top of the city's walls in order to watch for signs of the enemy)

Legend
The myths about the Trojan War are called legends. Legends are stories that are handed down in the oral tradition, and may contain a great deal of myth and fantasy, but are based on fact.

SUPPLEMENTARY SUPPORT MATERIAL

1. Vocabulary Activity Sheet
2. Reading Check Test blackline master
3. Selection Test (page 199 of Test Book)
4. Reader's Response Journal
5. Workbook (page 149)

DEVELOPING VOCABULARY

The following words appear on a test in the Test Book, page 200. (See also the Vocabulary Activity Sheet.)

determined	monstrosity
devising	appease
slight	foundations
prime	respite
terrifying	debris

A. Humanities Connection: Responding to the Fine Art Giovanni Battista Tiepolo (1696–1770) was an Italian painter who developed a grand, colorful mural style of painting. His murals usually show active figures painted in pastel shades and spaced in vast settings. Notice the fear, or awe, expressed by many of the Trojan men and women.

B. Suspense Notice that the description of the Trojans' conclusion builds the tension here and creates suspense. After ten long years of embittered fighting, it would seem unlikely that the Greeks had given up so easily, and with such a great gift!

C. Character Note the way that Odysseus is described here. His reputation leads us to believe that the scheme of the wooden horse will bring victory for the Greeks.

A

The Procession of the Trojan Horse into Troy by G. D. Tiepolo.

indeed. The noisy Greek camp was hushed; nothing was stirring there. And the ships were gone. Only one conclusion seemed possible: The Greeks had given up. They had sailed for Greece; they
B had accepted defeat. All Troy exulted. Her long warfare was over; her sufferings lay behind her.

The people flocked to the abandoned Greek camp to see the sights: Here Achilles had sulked so long; there Agamemnon's tent had stood; this was the quarters of the trickster, Odysseus. What rapture to see the places empty, nothing in them now to fear. At last they drifted back to where that monstrosity, the wooden horse, stood, and they gathered around it, puzzled as to what to do with it. Then the Greek who had been left behind in the camp discovered himself to them. His name was Sinon, and he was a most plausible speaker. He was seized and dragged to Priam, weeping and protesting that he no longer wished to be a Greek. The story he told was one of Odysseus's master-pieces. Pallas Athene had been exceedingly angry, C
Sinon said, at the theft of the Palladium, and the Greeks in terror had sent to the oracle to ask how they could appease her. The oracle answered:

A. Vocabulary
"To make expiation" means "to make amends." Sinon is saying that he was going to be sacrificed so that the Greeks could make amends for robbing the temple and return home safely to Troy.

B. Modern Meanings
Today, *sinon* means "one who deceives and betrays by false tales."

"With blood and with a maiden slain you calmed the winds when first you came to Troy. With blood must your return be sought. With a Greek life make expiation." He himself, Sinon told Priam, was the wretched victim chosen to be sacrificed. All was ready for the awful rite, which was to be carried out just before the Greeks' departure, but in the night he had managed to escape and hidden in a swamp had watched the ships sail away. A

It was a good tale and the Trojans never questioned it. They pitied Sinon and assured him that he should henceforth live as one of themselves. B

So it befell that by false cunning and pretended tears those were conquered whom great Diomedes had never overcome, nor savage Achilles, nor ten years of warfare, nor a thousand ships. For Sinon did not forget the second part of his story. The wooden horse had been made, he said, as a votive[4] offering to Athene, and the reason for its immense size was to discourage the Trojans from taking it into the city. What the Greeks hoped for was that the Trojans would destroy it and so draw down upon them Athene's anger. Placed in the city, it would turn her favor to them and away from the Greeks. The story was clever enough to have had by itself, in all probability, the desired effect; but Poseidon, the most bitter of all the gods against Troy, contrived an addition which made the issue certain. The priest Laocoön,[5] when the horse was first discovered, had been urgent with the Trojans to destroy it. "I fear the Greeks even when they bear gifts," he said. Cassandra, Priam's daughter, had echoed his warning, but no one ever listened to her and she had gone back to the palace before Sinon appeared. Laocoön and his two sons heard his story with suspicion, the only doubters there. As Sinon finished, suddenly over the sea came two fearful serpents swimming to the land. Once there, they glided straight to Laocoön. They wrapped their huge coils around him and the two lads and they crushed the life out of them. Then they disappeared within Athene's temple. C D

There could be no further hesitation. To the horrified spectators Laocoön had been punished for opposing the entry of the horse which most certainly no one else would now do. All the people cried,

"Bring the carven image in.
Bear it to Athene,
Fit gift for the child of Zeus."
Who of the young but hurried forth?
Who of the old would stay at home?
With song and rejoicing they brought death in,
  Treachery and destruction. E

They dragged the horse through the gate and up to the temple of Athene. Then, rejoicing in their

---

4. **votive:** given in an act of devotion.
5. **Laocoön** (lā·äk′ə·wän′).

C. Interpretation
? What do these lines suggest caused the fall of Troy? (Trickery) What surprisingly was not responsible for the end of the war? (The physical power of the great warriors)

D. Interpreting
? According to the logic of this story, why would Athena have become angry at the Trojans' destruction of the horse? (Because according to this made-up story, the horse was a special gift to the goddess from the Greeks. If it were destroyed, she would clearly get mad at the responsible parties.

E. Interpretating
? Where was death, treachery, and destruction hiding? (Inside the wooden horse)

READING CHECK TEST

1. Odysseus and some other warriors hid underneath the wooden horse. *(False)*
2. Sinon told the Trojans that Athena would be pleased if they took the horse. *(True)*
3. Cassandra and Laocoön thought the Trojans should leave the horse alone. *(True)*
4. To the Trojans, Laocoön's death was a sign that it would be dangerous to bring the horse inside. *(False)*
5. After the Greeks got inside Troy, the Trojans defeated them. *(False)*

CLOSURE

Divide students into groups of four and have them name all the conflicts in this story.

Additional Writing Assignment

Write a newspaper article describing the departure of the Greeks and the presence of a huge wooden horse outside the city gates.

A. Recalling

? Where was the Greek army? (They had sailed away *temporarily.* They returned in time to enter the city and come to the aid of their men in the horse.)

B. Interpreting

? What does the writer mean by saying that "this spirit often turned the victors into the vanquished"? (The "victors" are the Greeks; the "vanquished" are the Trojans. Some Trojans, disguised in Greek armor, killed Greek soldiers who didn't recognize them for who they really were.)

C. Expansion

Aeneas (see text page 522) is the protagonist of Virgil's epic poem the *Aeneid.*

D. Interpreting

? Why do you think Menelaus accepted Helen back? (She was his queen; the war was supposedly started in order to get her back. Menelaus probably blamed Paris more for kidnapping her than Helen for leaving.)

good fortune, believing the war ended and Athene's favor restored to them, they went to their houses in peace as they had not for ten years.

In the middle of the night the door in the horse opened. One by one the chieftains let themselves down. They stole to the gates and threw them wide, and into the sleeping town marched the Greek army. What they had first to do could be carried out silently. Fires were started in buildings throughout the city. By the time the Trojans were awake, before they realized what had happened, while they were struggling into their armor, Troy was burning. They rushed out to the street one by one in confusion. Bands of soldiers were waiting there to strike each man down before he could join himself to others. It was not fighting, it was butchery. Very many died without ever a chance of dealing a blow in return. In the more distant parts of the town the Trojans were able to gather together here and there and then it was the Greeks who suffered. They were borne down by desperate men who wanted only to kill before they were killed. They knew that the one safety for the conquered was to hope for no safety. This spirit often turned the victors into the vanquished. The quickest-witted Trojans tore off their own armor and put on that of the dead Greeks, and many and many a Greek thinking he was joining friends discovered too late that they were enemies and paid for his error with his life.

On top of the houses they tore up the roofs and hurled the beams down upon the Greeks. An entire tower standing on the roof of Priam's palace was lifted from its foundations and toppled over. Exulting, the defenders saw it fall and annihilate a great band who were forcing the palace doors. But the success brought only a short respite. Others rushed up carrying a huge beam. Over the debris of the tower and the crushed bodies they battered the doors with it. It crashed through and the Greeks were in the palace before the Trojans could leave the roof. In the inner courtyard around the altar were the women and children and one man, the old king. Achilles had spared Priam, but Achilles's son struck him down before the eyes of his wife and daughters.

By now the end was near. The contest from the first had been unequal. Too many Trojans had

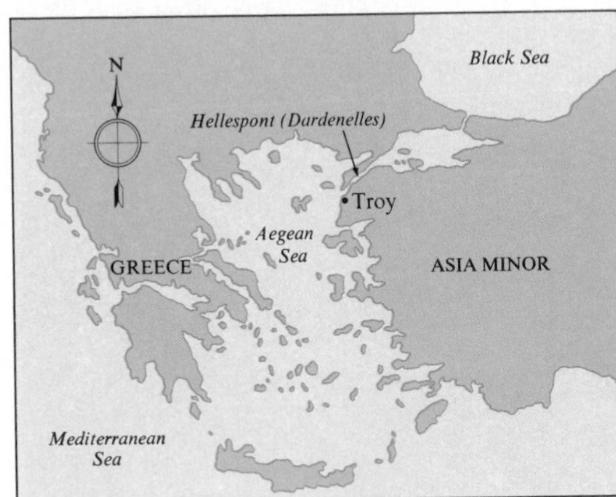

been slaughtered in the first surprise. The Greeks could not be beaten back anywhere. Slowly the defense ceased. Before morning all the leaders were dead, except one. Aphrodite's son Aeneas alone among the Trojan chiefs escaped. He fought the Greeks as long as he could find a living Trojan to stand with him, but as the slaughter spread and death came near he thought of his home, the helpless people he had left there. He could do nothing more for Troy, but perhaps something could be done for them. He hurried to them, his old father, his little son, his wife, and as he went his mother Aphrodite appeared to him, urging him on and keeping him safe from the flames and from the Greeks. Even with the goddess's help he could not save his wife. When they left the house she got separated from him and was killed. But the other two he brought away, through the enemy, past the city gates, out into the country, his father on his shoulders, his son clinging to his hand. No one but a divinity could have saved them, and Aphrodite was the only one of the gods that day who helped a Trojan.

She helped Helen too. She got her out of the city and took her to Menelaus. He received her gladly, and as he sailed for Greece she was with him.

When morning came what had been the proudest city in Asia was a fiery ruin. All that was left of Troy was a band of helpless captive women, whose husbands were dead, whose children had been taken from them. They were waiting for their masters to carry them overseas to slavery. . . .

ANALYZING THE MYTH

Identifying Facts

1. The ten-year siege has had no effect on Troy.

The Greeks realize that they must find a secret way of entering the city.

2. The wooden horse was hollow and so big that it could hold a number of men inside.

His plan is to trick the Trojans into drawing the horse into the city. Then, at night, the men in the horse will come out and open the gates to the rest of the Greek army.

3. Sinon is the Greek who is left behind to trick the Trojans into taking the wooden horse into the city.

First he tells them that he was supposed to be sacrificed as an offering to Pallas Athene but that he escaped. Then he tells them that the wooden horse is a votive offering to Athene and that the reason it is so big is that the Greeks did not want the Trojans to be able to bring the horse into the city.

4. In the middle of the night, the Greeks come out of the horse and open the gates for the rest of the Greek army. Troy is destroyed along with most of its people.

5. Aeneas is the only one to escape.

Aphrodite helps him escape.

Interpreting Meanings

6. He is brave, a good leader, and extremely clever.

He resorts to trickery and deception to obtain his objectives.

7. The Trojans feel sorry for Sinon when he tells them he was supposed to be sacrificed. They do not destroy the wooden horse because Sinon tells them that it is an offering to Athena and that to destroy it would invoke her wrath.

Poseidon sends two serpents to attack Laocoön and his sons, who had voiced suspicions about the wooden horse.

8. Yes, even after ten years of war, Troy was unharmed and the Greeks were on the point of giving up.

The Trojans were too hasty in believing that the Greeks had left.

Applying Meanings

9. A variety of responses are possible here.

Responding to the Legend

Analyzing the Legend

Identifying Facts

1. What effect, according to the second paragraph, has the Greeks' ten-year siege had on Troy? What do the Greeks realize they must do to avoid defeat?
2. Describe the wooden horse that Odysseus orders made. What is his plan involving this horse?
3. Who is Sinon? What two tales does he tell in order to trick the Trojans?
4. What happens after the Trojans drag the horse into the city?
5. Who is the only Trojan chieftain to survive? Who helps him escape?

Interpreting Meanings

6. The ancient Greeks considered Odysseus one of their great national heroes. What characteristics does Odysseus possess that you would normally associate with a hero? Which of his characteristics might you think unworthy of a hero?
7. Why don't the Trojans kill Sinon and destroy the wooden horse? What role do the gods play in their decision?
8. Considering that all but one of the gods desert the Trojans, do you think the Trojans had a chance of defeating the Greeks? In what ways might the Trojans have been responsible for their own downfall?

Applying Meanings

9. Have any people in recent history been fooled as the Trojans were—by trickery or false promises?

Writing About the Legend

A Creative Response

Writing an Introduction. Imagine that you are the general of the victorious Greek army and that Odysseus is to be honored at an award ceremony. In one paragraph write your introduction of Odysseus. Be sure to praise Odysseus's character and to mention what he did to deserve the honor.

See Teacher's Manual page 173.

Analyzing Language and Vocabulary

Antonyms

An **antonym** is a word whose meaning is opposite or nearly opposite to the meaning of another word. For example, *wily* means "deceitful" and "sly." Possible antonyms for *wily* are *honest, open,* and *forthright.* Knowing antonyms for words can help you gain a new perspective and deepen your understanding of what you read.

For each of the following excerpts from "The Wooden Horse," choose the word from among the choices that is most nearly opposite in meaning to the italicized word.

1. "The Greeks had given up. They had sailed for Greece; they had accepted defeat. All Troy *exulted.*"

   a. rejoiced **c.** wept
   b. praised **d.** pursued

2. "His name was Sinon, and he was a most *plausible* speaker. . . . The story he told was one of Odysseus's masterpieces."

   a. praiseworthy **c.** seemingly honest
   b. eloquent **d.** genuinely honest

3. "An entire tower . . . toppled over. Exulting, the defenders saw it fall and *annihilate* a great band who were forcing the palace doors."

   a. preserve **c.** frighten
   b. encourage **d.** destroy

For answers, see Teacher's Manual page 173.

Reading About the Writer

Edith Hamilton (1867–1963) graduated from Bryn Mawr College where she majored in Latin and Greek. She remained as a teacher at Bryn Mawr until she was 63 years old. The classics had been a part of Hamilton's life from the time she was seven years old and read *Six Weeks' Preparation for Caesar* in Latin. She became so identified with Greece that in 1957 she was named an honorary citizen of Athens. Hamilton established her reputation as a scholar with her book *The Greek Way,* which was an interpretation of the Greek mind and spirit. She is also famed for her best-selling collection of myths called *Mythology.*

PREREADING

1. **BUILDING ON PRIOR KNOWLEDGE.** Aeneas leaves Troy at the end of the ten-year Trojan War to found a new homeland. In many ways, his journey is similar to that of Odysseus, described in Homer's *Odyssey.* Odysseus, however, is simply trying to get home. They both face terrible monsters, natural hardships (which are often caused by the enmities of the gods and goddesses), and numerous other obstacles. Both men finally achieve their goals. (Portions of the *Odyssey* are included in *Elements of Literature: Third Course.*)

2. **ESTABLISHING A PURPOSE.** While reading the story about Aeneas, try to determine what makes him continue on his journey.

3. **PREREADING JOURNAL.** Ask students to briefly name some of the hardships that Aeneas might encounter on his journey. Remind them that he has nothing with him, he is carrying his father on his shoulders, and he has a small son to care for. How will he travel? Will he meet any more Greeks?

A. Theme
It is important to note that Aeneas brings his father and son and the household gods with him when he leaves Troy. Protection and love of the father and son are an extremely important theme in this story and in the concept of *pietas.* In one account of Aeneas, the Greek warriors let him leave the burning city of Troy safely because the Greeks respected the devotion Aeneas showed to his father.

B. Plot
This reveals the plot structure of the *Aeneid.* Notice that here, as in the *Iliad,* (see text page 512), a dream reveals a character's destiny.

AENEAS

Retold by Jay Macpherson

Aeneas (i·nē′əs) was the legendary founding father of Rome, and was considered a national hero. His story is told by the Roman poet Virgil in the *Aeneid*—a long poem that was left unfinished at the poet's death in 19 B.C. Virgil's goal was to present Aeneas as a model of what the Romans called *pietas*. As you read, take note of Aeneas's attitudes toward the gods, toward his family and friends, and toward his sense of destiny. What do you think the Romans meant by *pietas*?

Homonyms. Homonyms are words that sound alike but have different spellings and meanings. In "Aeneas," an example of a pair of homonyms is *new* and *knew*. As you read, try to detect other words that are homonyms.

Another story of the aftermath of Troy, though not exactly a "return," is that of the wanderings of one of the Trojan princes, Aeneas, the son of the goddess Aphrodite and a mortal man, Anchises, with whom she fell in love while he was tending his flock on the slopes of Mount Ida. Her passion for him was sent by Zeus, in revenge for the many humiliations that she and her prankish son Eros had inflicted on him and the other gods. Anchises later was so foolish as to boast of his remarkable conquest, and Zeus, seeing that the joke was getting out of hand, loosed a thunderbolt at him. Aphrodite interposed her marvelous girdle and saved his life, but he was never able to walk again.

A Protected by his divine mother, Aeneas escaped from the flames of Troy, bearing his old father on his back and the figures of his household gods in his arms, accompanied by a few friends and his little son Ascanius. He had been told in a dream that it was his destiny to found a nation in a country lying far to the west, Italy, to which divine guidance would eventually bring them. A prophet advised them how to direct their journey: they must take a roundabout way in order to avoid certain perils they would not be strong enough to overcome. Many years of wandering lay before them, at the end of which they would reach their new home. B

Landscape of Aeneas at Delos by Claude Lorraine (1672). Oil.

For a detailed lesson plan on this myth, see Teacher's Manual pages 174–175. A biography of Jay Macpherson appears on page 471.

Supplementary Support Material
1. Vocabulary Activity Sheet
2. Reading Check Test blackline master
3. Selection Test (page 201 of Test Book)
4. Connections Between Reading and Writing worksheet
5. Reader's Response Journal
6. Workbook (page 151)

Developing Vocabulary
The following words appear on a test in the Test Book, page 202. (See also the Vocabulary Activity Sheet.)

aftermath	resolved
mortal	divert
humiliation	trifling
accompanied	helm
destiny	pitiful

A

A. Humanities Connection: Responding to the Fine Art Claude Lorraine (1600–1682) was a French painter who founded the European landscape tradition. He often painted the Roman countryside with light slanting across fields. He was interested in the effects of the changing light as the sun moved across the sky. This painting shows Aeneas at Delos, an island among the Cyclades Islands in the Mediterranean. Delos was said to be the birthplace of Apollo. In the *Aeneid,* the king of Delos gave Aeneas and his father, Anchises, some valuable advice about their voyage.

B. Recalling
Why did Hera hate the Trojans? (Because Paris, who was a Trojan, chose Aphrodite over herself and Athena as the most beautiful)

Passing Sicily, where lived the monster Polyphemus, who shouted terrible threats after them from the shore, they were met by a fearful storm
B sent by Hera, who hated all the Trojans but especially Aeneas, and had resolved that he should never reach Italy. He with his small fleet came safely through the storm, however, and landed near the city of Carthage in North Africa. Carthage was under the protection of Hera, who knew that the city the Trojans were destined to found would in later times go to war against Carthage, raze it to the ground, and lay waste all the surrounding territory; so she devised a plan to divert Aeneas from his course. The hero was to fall in

Reading Check Test

1. Aeneas was the son of Anchises and ________. *Aphrodite*
2. The goddess ________ tried to keep Aeneas from getting to Italy. *Hera*
3. In order to safely visit the underworld, Aeneas had to bring the Sibyl the ________. *golden bough*
4. In the underworld, Aeneas got advice from ________. *his father*
5. Aeneas finally became the father of the ________ people. *Roman*

Closure

Divide students into groups of four and have them briefly define the term *pietas*. Ask them to explain why Aeneas had this virtue.

A. Interpreting Zeus is the most powerful god, so we know that his will is going to prevail over Hera's.

B. Expansion In many of the ancient stories, people visited the underworld. Odysseus visits the underworld in the *Odyssey* to seek advice from the dead prophet Teiresias.

C. Expansion It was believed that Charon had to be paid to take the dead across the river Styx to Hades. Therefore, the dead were buried with coins under their tongues.

D. Expansion The Trojans took the name and the language of the Latins when they settled, and the Latins agreed to worship the Trojan's household gods, which Aeneas had carried with him from Troy. Rome was founded many centuries later by Romulus, a descendant of Aeneas.

★ **Texas Essential Elements/(a) English Language Arts: 1B** Purpose and audience; **3C** Literary traditions; **3D** Folklore/legends/myths. **(c) Reading: 1B** Structural analysis; **3A** Main ideas/details

love with Dido, the beautiful early-widowed Carthaginian queen, and settle quietly down as her consort. His mother Aphrodite was willing to help entangle Aeneas in this love affair, knowing what Hera did not know, that Zeus had sworn her son should fulfill his destiny and become the founder of the greatest empire on earth. A

For a time Aeneas lived at Carthage, happy in Dido's love. But when he and his men were thoroughly rested and refreshed from the long campaign at Troy and their wanderings since, the gods decided to end this trifling. Hermes, sent from Zeus, arrived one day to remind Aeneas of his duty. Ashamed of his luxurious idleness, Aeneas immediately ordered his men to prepare for departure, heedless of Dido's pleading and laments. That very night the ships set sail, and that same night Dido had raised a high funeral pyre, on which she stabbed herself to death, calling on the gods to avenge her fate. From this harsh return for her generosity is supposed to have sprung the enmity between Carthage and the race of Aeneas, later the Roman people.

Leaving Carthage behind, Aeneas held his course toward Italy. The fleet had again left Sicily behind when he lost his valued and experienced pilot, Palinurus, who one night fell asleep at the helm and slid into the sea. Aeneas, awake while his men slept, saw that the ship had lost its pilot and was drifting. He took the helm himself and guided the ship all that night, grieving for his friend: "Alas, Palinurus, you trusted too much in the sky and the quiet sea: Now you will lie unburied on an unknown shore."

Passing the Sirens' rock, Aeneas landed on the west coast of Italy. There he sought out the Sibyl of Cumae, the prophetic priestess of Apollo, to enquire the will of the gods about his journey. She gave him no advice herself, but promised to guide him to the underworld where he could consult the ghost of his old father Anchises, who had died on the way in Sicily. B The path to the lower world was hard and dangerous, and to undertake it in safety Aeneas must carry in his hand the mysterious golden bough, sacred to Persephone, the queen of the dead. Guided by two doves sent by his mother, Aeneas saw the golden bough glimmering in the dark grove surrounding Lake Avernus, where the underworld pathway began, and breaking it off he carried it back to the Sibyl. She, after sacrificing to Hecate, led him in the night down the steep road to Tartarus.

Five rivers encircle and wind through the abode of the dead: Styx or the Hateful, the river by which Zeus swears, Acheron the Sorrowful, Phlegethon the Fiery, Cocytus or Lamentation, and Lethe, the river of Forgetfulness. Their banks are crowded with pitiful wailing souls, waiting for Charon the infernal ferryman to row them over in his creaky boat. C The golden bough was sufficient passport for Aeneas and his guide, who quickly reached the farther shore, where they placated the three-headed watchdog Cerberus by throwing him small cakes brought for the purpose. Among the fields of the dead they met the pale shade of Dido, who passed them without a look or word, pale with anger and bleeding from her mortal wound. At last they found Anchises, who greeted his son affectionately, instructed him where he should settle and how he should proceed, and prophesied to him the future glory of Rome.

Back on the Italian shore, Aeneas with his men made his way to Latium, the district around the mouth of the Tiber where Rome was eventually to be founded. There Hera stirred up trouble for them among the inhabitants. Coming in peace and asking only for a place to settle, they met armed resistance and had to make war for the right to stay. At length Aeneas put down all his enemies, and he married Lavinia, the daughter of Latinus the friendly king of Latium; and from them sprang the Roman people. D

ANALYZING THE MYTH

Identifying Facts

1. His mother is Aphrodite and his father is Anchises, who cannot walk.

Zeus loosed a thunderbolt at him for boasting of his relationship with Aphrodite.

2. Aeneas escapes from Troy protected by his mother, Aphrodite.

He takes his father, the figures of his household gods, his son Ascanius, and a few friends.

3. He had been told that it was his destiny to found a nation in Italy to which he would be led by divine guidance.

4. Dido is the widowed queen of Carthage.

Aeneas spends his time happily.

5. Hermes reminds Aeneas of his duty.

Aeneas is ashamed and orders his men to prepare to leave immediately.

6. Palinurus is Aeneas's pilot.

Aeneas takes the helm himself and guides the ship all night.

7. She is the prophetic prietess of Apollo.

He wants to know the will of the gods concerning his journey.

She leads him to the underworld to consult his dead father.

8. His father, who tells him what to do.

Interpreting Meanings

9. His behavior is characterized by love and devotion.

He carries his lame father on his back; he grieves over the loss of Palinurus.

10. Aeneas honors and respects the gods.

He carries his household gods out of Troy; he leaves Carthage as soon as Hermes reminds him of his duty.

11. He may have acted improperly, but it was proper for him to leave Dido at some stage.

They valued above all else a man's duty to his gods, his family, and his country.

Applying Meanings

12. They mean that someone is not necessarily trustworthy just because he or she gives you something.

13. It comes from Latium, which is close to where Rome was built.

14. Aeneas no longer had a home to which he could return.

Responding to the Myth

Analyzing the Myth

Identifying Facts

1. Who are Aeneas's parents? What handicap does his father have? How did he come by it?
2. Tell how Aeneas escapes from Troy. What and whom does he take along with him?
3. What had Aeneas been told in a dream?
4. Who is Dido? How does Aeneas spend his time with her?
5. When Hermes is sent by Zeus to Carthage, of what does he remind Aeneas? How does Aeneas respond to the god's message?
6. Who is Palinurus? Tell what Aeneas does when he discovers him missing.
7. Who is the Sibyl of Cumae? What does Aeneas wish to learn from her? How does she help him?
8. Whom does Aeneas consult in the underworld? What does this person tell Aeneas?

Interpreting Meanings

9. How would you **characterize** Aeneas's behavior toward his family and friends? Find evidence in the story to support your opinion.
10. Describe Aeneas's attitude toward the gods. Find incidents to support your opinion.
11. Considering Aeneas's "destiny," do you think he acted properly when he left Dido despite her "pleading and laments"? Why might an ancient Roman citizen have thought he acted properly?

Applying Meanings

12. What do people mean today when they warn someone, "Beware of Greeks bearing gifts!"?
13. What do you learn from this story about the origin of the word *Latin*?
14. In what way was Aeneas a "displaced person"? What people today have been, like Aeneas, "displaced people" who have had to strike out for a new country?

Writing About the Myth

A Creative Response

1. **Writing a Hymn of Praise.** Imagine that you are a Roman citizen and that Aeneas is your favorite hero. Write a hymn of praise addressed to Aeneas. Your hymn should be about twelve lines long. You might, for example, briefly describe Aeneas's journey to the underworld and then praise his bravery and devotion to duty.

A Critical Response

2. **Supporting an Opinion.** In a paragraph or two, explain how Aeneas displays the Roman virtue of *pietas,* or duty to family, religion, and country. Support your opinion by citing examples of Aeneas's behavior that display *pietas.* Consider his attitudes toward the gods, his family and friends, and his country. Include in your essay a statement telling whether or not you think people today share Aeneas's values.

See Teacher's Manual page 176.

Analyzing Language and Vocabulary

Homonyms

Homonyms are words that sound alike but have different spellings and meanings. For example, *new* and *knew* are homonyms. Using the homonyms listed below, choose the correct word for each blank in the following sentences.

night/knight	new/knew	sea/see
blue/blew	there/their	him/hymn

1. Aeneas sang a ______ to his mother.
2. Aeneas and his family left Troy in the middle of the ______.
3. They began a long journey to a ______ home.
4. During a fierce storm, the wind ______ them to Carthage.
5. Aphrodite ______ that Zeus would help Aeneas.
6. When they left Carthage, the sky was a beautiful ______ and the ______ was calm.
7. Dido was heartbroken at ______ departure.
8. Then and ______ Dido killed herself, but Aeneas did not ______ her do it.

For answers, see Teacher's Manual page 176.

★ Texas Essential Elements/(a) English Language Arts: 1B Purpose and audience; 3C Literary traditions; 3D Folklore/legends/myths; 4D Cause/effect. (c) Reading: 3A Main ideas/details; 3C Cause/effect

Review: Exercises in Reading Myths

NORSE MYTHOLOGY

The people living on the Scandinavian peninsula developed a whole body of mythology of their own. In some respects these myths are similar to the Greek myths; in other respects, they are very different. Here is the opening of the myth explaining the creation of the race of heroes.

In the beginning of ages there lived a cow, whose breath was sweet, and whose milk was bitter. This cow was called Audhumla, and she lived all by herself on a frosty, misty plain, where there was nothing to be seen but heaps of snow and ice piled strangely over one another. Far away to the north it was night, far away to the south it was day; but all around where Audhumla lay a cold, gray twilight reigned. By and by a giant came out of the dark north, and lay down upon the ice near Audhumla. "You must let me drink of your milk," said the giant to the cow; and though her milk was bitter, he liked it well, and for him it was certainly good enough.

After a little while the cow looked all round her for something to eat, and she saw a very few grains of salt sprinkled over the ice; so she licked the salt, and breathed with her sweet breath, and then long golden locks rose out of the ice, and the southern day shone upon them, which made them look bright and glittering.

The giant frowned when he saw the glitter of the golden hair; but Audhumla licked the pure salt again, and a head of a man rose out of the ice. The head was more handsome than could be described, and a wonderful light beamed out of its clear blue eyes. The giant frowned still more when he saw the head; but Audhumla licked the salt a third time, and then an entire man arose—a hero majestic in strength and marvelous in beauty.

Now, it happened that when the giant looked full in the face of that beautiful man, he hated him with his whole heart, and, what was still worse, he took a terrible oath, by all the snows of Ginnungagap, that he would never cease fighting until either he or Buri, the hero, should lie dead upon the ground. And he kept his vow; he did not cease fighting until Buri had fallen beneath his cruel blows. I cannot tell how it could be that one so wicked should be able to conquer one so majestic and so beautiful; but so it was, and afterward, when the sons of the hero began to grow up, the giant and his sons fought against them too, and were very near conquering them many times.

But there was of the sons of the heroes one of very great strength and wisdom, called Odin, who, after many combats, did at last slay the great old giant, and pierced his body through with his keen spear, so that the blood swelled forth in a mighty torrent, broad and deep, and all the hideous giant brood were drowned in it excepting one, who ran away panting and afraid.

After this Odin called round him his sons, brothers, and cousins, and spoke to them thus: "Heroes, we have won a great victory; our enemies are dead, or have run away from us. We cannot stay any longer here, where there is nothing evil for us to fight against."

The heroes looked round them at the words of Odin. North, south, east, and west there was no one to fight against them anywhere, and they called out with one voice, "It is well spoken, Odin; we follow you."

"Southward," answered Odin, "heat lies, and northward night. From the dim east the sun begins his journey westward home."

"Westward home!" shouted they all; and westward they went.

—from *The Heroes of Asgaard,*
retold by A. and E. Keary

Answers to Questions
1. In the beginning there was a cow called Audhumea.
2. The cow licked three times at a few grains of salt on the ice and an entire man arose.
3. The giant and his sons are the enemy of the heroes.
4. Odin was one of the sons of the heroes. He was very strong and wise.
5. He killed the giant with his spear and so destroyed the brood of giants.
6. Their mission is to fight evil.
7. The references to ice, the frosty plain, and the heaps of snow reflect the place where the mythmakers lived. In addition, the references to the dark north and the gray twilight reflect their location.
8. Evil arose from the conflict between the giant and the first man. When the man and his race defeat the giant, he tells his family that they must seek evil to fight against. The fighting, we assume, continues.

Review: Exercises in Reading Myths/*cont.*

1. According to this myth, what existed in the beginning?
2. How does it explain the creation of the heroes?
3. Who is going to be the enemy of the heroes?
4. Who is Odin?
5. What did Odin do?
6. What is the mission of Odin and his family?
7. What details in this myth reflect the place where the myth-makers lived?
8. Does this myth suggest the cause of evil and suffering in the human world? Explain.

Writing

1. **Comparing Myths.** In a paragraph or more, tell how the Norse myth of beginnings is like, and unlike, the Greek origin myth. Consider these elements in the myths before you write:
   a. What existed in the beginning
   b. The creation of man (and woman)
   c. The source of evil
   d. The battle between good and evil
2. **Extending the Myth.** Suppose you were Audhumla, the cow. Write a paragraph in which you tell what you think as you exist all by yourself on the misty, frosty plain. What do you see? What do you think as the handsome man rises out of the ice? What eventually happens to you?
3. **Describing a Mythical Character.** One of the hideous brood of giants escaped and ran away. In a paragraph, describe what this giant offspring might have looked like. In your description, take into account the place these characters come from: the far reaches of the North.

For evaluation strategies, see Teacher's Manual page 177.

Illustrated by Charles E. Brock.

★ **Texas Essential Elements/(a) English Language Arts: 1A** Composing process; **1B** Purpose and audience; **1C** Synthesize information; **1H** Proofread; **1I** Spelling generalizations; **2B** Parts of speech

Exercises in Critical Thinking and Writing

For teaching and evaluation strategies, see Teacher's Manual page 177.

SRW p. 47

MAKING AND SUPPORTING GENERALIZATIONS

Writing Assignment

Write a brief report that includes at least two generalizations about the ancient Greeks and their myths. You may use information from the introductions in this unit and from reference books, as well as the myths themselves. Write four or five paragraphs.

Background

A **generalization** makes a statement that applies to a whole group of people or things.

All cows are green.
People need oxygen to breathe.

These are generalizations because they make statements about *all* cows and *all* human beings.

The statement about green cows, however, is an example of a **false generalization.** It is a generalization (because it makes a statement about all cows), but it isn't true. A **valid** (true) generalization is based on a great many observations and experiences, and it must be true for every specific individual within the group. The statement about people and their need for oxygen is a valid generalization.

When you make a generalization, you need to support it with **evidence**—facts, examples, and quotations from experts. The evidence that you provide shows why you think the generalization is true. For example, here is the outline for a paragraph showing a generalization and the evidence to support it. What other evidence can you think of to support this generalization?

GENERALIZATION The Greek gods and goddesses showed human emotions.

EVIDENCE

EXAMPLE Myths of Zeus's love affairs and Hera's jealousy.

QUOTATION Quotation from Edith Hamilton's *Mythology* about Hera's jealousy.

EXAMPLE Myth of Hades's love for Persephone and of Demeter's grief.

Prewriting

1. Before you begin your research, think about these two questions:
   a. What do the ancient Greek myths tell us about the Greek people?
   b. What can you say in general about Greek mythology?

   Keep these questions in mind as you do your research.
2. Reread the introductions in this unit, and do some additional research by reading encyclopedia articles (look up Greek Mythology or Ancient Greek Literature or Mythology) and the introductions to books about Greek mythology. Take notes on topics that you think you might want to write about.

The following passage is from the introduction to *Mythology* by Edith Hamilton. If you wish, you may use information from it in your report. Notice that the passage contains some generalizations supported by evidence.

> Human gods naturally made heaven a pleasantly familiar place. The Greeks felt at home in it. They knew just what the divine inhabitants did there, what they ate and drank and where they banqueted, and how they amused themselves. Of course, they were to be feared; they were very powerful and very dangerous when angry. Still, with proper care a man could be quite fairly at

Exercises in Critical Thinking and Writing/*cont.*

ease with them. He was even perfectly free to laugh at them. Zeus, trying to hide his love affairs from his wife and invariably shown up, was a capital figure of fun. The Greeks enjoyed him and liked him all the better for it. Hera was that stock character of comedy, the typical jealous wife, and her ingenious tricks to discomfit her husband and punish her rival, far from displeasing the Greeks, entertained them as much as Hera's modern counterpart does us today. Such stories made for a friendly feeling. Laughter in the presence of an Egyptian sphinx or an Assyrian bird-beast was inconceivable; but it was perfectly natural in Olympus, and it made the gods companionable.

On earth, too, the deities were exceedingly and humanly attractive. In the form of lovely youths and maidens they peopled the woodland, the forest, the rivers, the sea, in harmony with the fair earth and the bright waters.

That is the miracle of Greek mythology—a humanized world, men freed from the paralyzing fear of an omnipotent Unknown. The terrifying incomprehensibilities which were worshiped elsewhere, and the fearsome spirits with which earth, air, and sea swarmed, were banned from Greece. It may seem odd to say that the men who made the myths disliked the irrational and had a love for facts; but it is true, no matter how wildly fantastic some of the stories are. Anyone who reads them with attention discovers that even the most nonsensical takes place in a world which is essentially rational and matter-of-fact. Hercules, whose life was one long combat against preposterous monsters, is always said to have had his home in the city of Thebes. The exact spot where Aphrodite was born of the foam could be visited by any ancient tourist; it was just offshore from the island of Cythera. The winged steed Pegasus, after skimming the air all day, went every night to a comfortable stable in Corinth. A familiar local habitation gave reality to all the mythical beings. If the mixture seems childish, consider how reassuring and how sensible the solid background is as compared with the Genie who comes from nowhere when Aladdin rubs the lamp and, his task accomplished, returns to nowhere.

—from *Mythology,*
Edith Hamilton

3. Based on your research and on the myths in the unit, try stating two generalizations that you think are true about the ancient Greek people or about their myths. Here are some ideas for generalizations:
   - **a.** How the Greeks regarded nature
   - **b.** What kinds of relationships the Greeks believed they had with their gods
   - **c.** How the Greeks believed the gods influenced their lives
   - **d.** What the Greeks thought about fate or destiny
   - **e.** What human character traits and behavior the Greeks valued
   - **f.** What human character traits and behavior the Greeks thought of as harmful or dangerous
4. Gather evidence (from your notes and from the myths you have read) to support each generalization. As evidence, you can summarize a myth or simply refer to it. If you quote from a reference book, be sure to mention the book's title and author.

Writing

Follow this outline for your report:

Paragraph 1: Introductory paragraph includes a **thesis statement**—a sentence that summarizes the report's main ideas.

Paragraphs 2–3: Body of the report consists of two (or three) paragraphs. Each paragraph begins with a generalization that is supported by examples from the myths and/or quotations from reference works.

★ **Texas Essential Elements/(c) Reading: 3D** Generalizations; **4A** Follow directions

Exercises in Critical Thinking and Writing/*cont.*

Paragraph 4: Concluding paragraph summarizes or restates the main ideas or makes an additional comment on the main ideas.

Here is a model opening paragraph based on the outline.

The Greeks thought of their gods and goddesses as very much like human beings with human emotions. The gods were as prone to fall in love as humans were. Zeus, for example, was always falling in love with mortal women, and his wife Hera was jealous and sharp-tongued. The myth of Echo shows Hera's fierce anger and her desire for revenge. When Hera realized that the talkative nymph Echo was distracting her to protect Zeus, she punished Echo by taking away her ability to speak. In her discussion of Hera in *Mythology*, Edith Hamilton says that Hera's main occupation was punishing the women Zeus fell in love with even if they were innocent. "Her implacable anger followed them and their children too. She never forgot an injury." Hades, too, god of the Underworld, was a victim of love. He fell passionately in love with Demeter's daughter Persephone and kidnapped the unwilling girl. Demeter, goddess of grain and fertility, suffered such grief when she realized what had happened that she neglected her duties and let the earth be barren in every way. Eventually, Zeus had to intervene to calm Demeter and save life on earth. Many other myths tell of the gods' jealousy, anger, love, or grief; the gods suffered and behaved in a way that humans could understand.

Revising and Proofreading Self-Check

1. Does the introductory paragraph contain a thesis statement?
2. Does the body contain at least two generalizations? Are the generalizations valid?
3. Is each generalization supported with enough examples and quotations? Does each paragraph have at least four sentences?
4. Are quotations punctuated properly? Have I cited the source (title and author) of each quotation?
5. Does every sentence start with a capital letter and end with a period or other end punctuation mark?
6. Are my ideas clearly expressed? Have I said everything I wanted to say?

Partner Check

1. Are there any spelling errors?
2. Are sentences punctuated correctly?
3. Are paragraphs fully developed (at least four sentences long) and indented?
4. Are any sentences or ideas unclear?
5. What do I like best about this paper? What needs improvement?

THE ELEMENTS OF A NOVEL

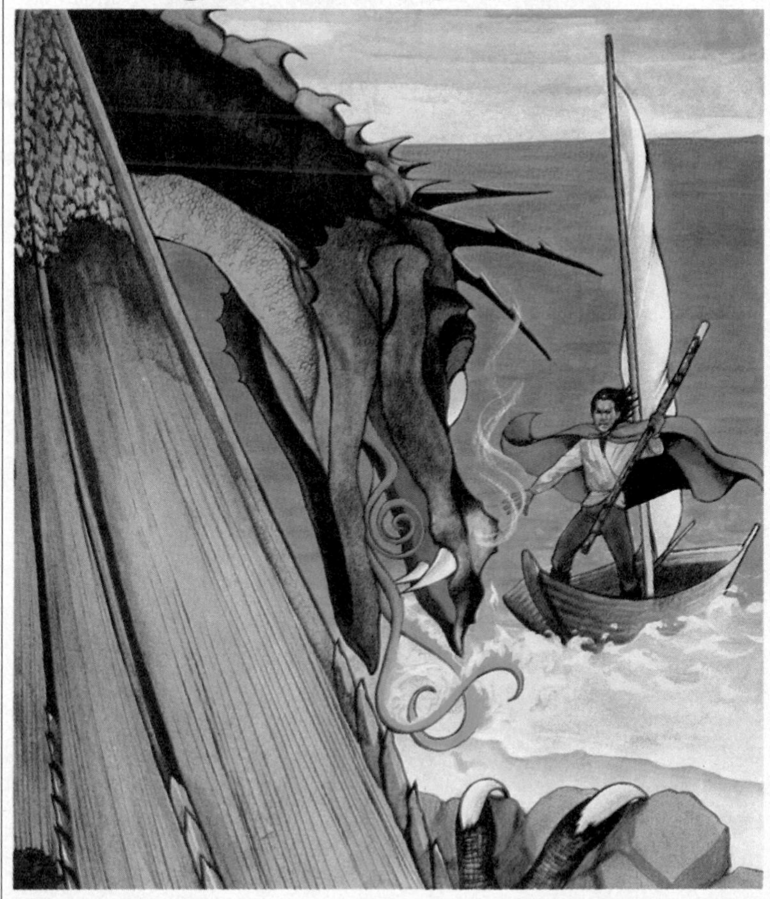

UNIT NINE **John Leggett**

Responding to the Illustration

Tell students that this illustration is a scene from the novel they are going to read next.

? Is this illustration a photograph or an artist's drawing? How do you know? What does the illustration contain that tells you that the novel is a fantasy? (A dragon) What do you think the person in the boat is about to do? (Probably attack the dragon since his expression is pretty fierce) Does the conflict seem to be an equal one? Who do you think will win? The man in the boat has a secret weapon. As you read the novel, you will find out what this secret weapon is.

Teaching the Novel

This unit presents students with an opportunity to study in depth a single long work of fiction. The size of the task should not be overwhelming, as the novel is divided into five sections consisting of two chapters each, and the story is one that is sure to hold students spellbound. It is an adventure fantasy whose young hero is a wizard engaged in a quest against an evil power that threatens to destroy him.

Students who are unfamiliar with the genre of fantasy should understand that a fantasy presents an imaginary world. The writer of a fantasy asks us to suspend disbelief as we enter into a world of strange lands, creatures, and events. Readers are able to do this because, in a well-constructed fantasy, everything makes sense within the world the writer has created.

You may approach study of this unit by explaining that a novel has the same elements as a short story: plot, character, setting, theme, and point of view. Of course, the novel is much longer, and usually involves more characters, more themes, and several subplots that are related to the main plot.

The questions and exercises that follow each section of *A Wizard of Earthsea* will help students explore the major literary elements of the novel. The exercises in each section call for an understanding of the development of the plot and character to that point. An understanding of the important themes is also built up gradually through the course of the novel. Following the final chapter, exercises help students see the novel as a whole, as they analyze how the setting, characters, and actions work together to create a story with a strong central theme.

If your class is reading the novel in sections over a period of time, you might have students predict what will happen in the next section when they are finished with the exercises. You can review these predictions after the next section is read.

Objectives of the Unit

1. To improve reading proficiency and expand vocabulary knowledge
2. To gain exposure to a notable author and her work
3. To identify and analyze the elements of the novel: plot, character, setting, theme, point of view
4. To identify and define foreshadowing, symbolism, and irony
5. To interpret and respond to fiction orally and in writing
6. To practice the following critical thinking and writing skills:
   - **a.** Analyzing a novel's theme
   - **b.** Evaluating the story's ending
   - **c.** Analyzing methods of characterization
   - **d.** Supporting an opinion
   - **e.** Responding to a novel as a whole

SUPPLEMENTARY SUPPORT MATERIAL: UNIT NINE

1. Author photograph on *A Gallery of Authors* poster
2. Poster of illustration for *A Wizard of Earthsea*
3. Audiocassette recording (excerpt from Chapter 2)
4. Connections Between Reading and Writing worksheet
5. Reader's Response Journal
6. Word Analogies Test (page 223 of Test Book)
7. Unit Review Test (page 225 of Test Book)
8. Critical Thinking and Writing Test (page 229 of Test Book)
9. Study Guides to *Where the Red Fern Grows, Treasure Island,* and *Roll of Thunder, Hear My Cry*
10. Understanding a Novel (Study and Reinforcement Worksheet, page 9)
11. Instructional Overhead Transparencies

Unit Outline

THE ELEMENTS OF A NOVEL

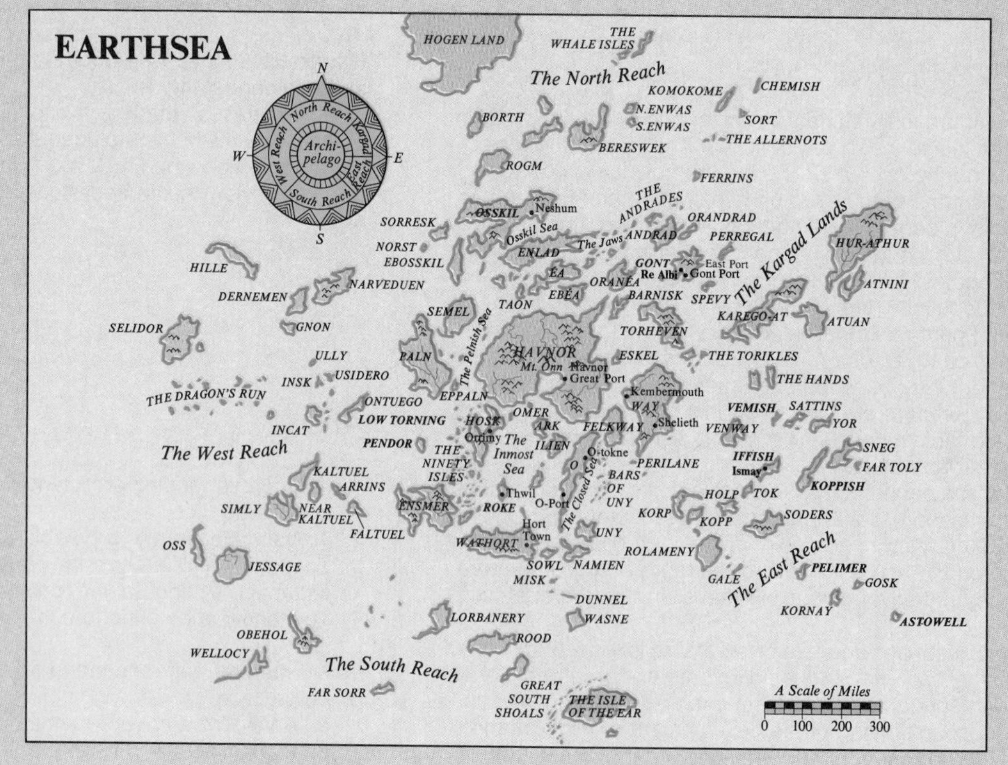

SUPPLEMENTARY SUPPORT MATERIAL
1. Reading Check Test blackline master
2. Introduction/Understanding Elements of the Novel Test (page 211 of Test Book)

Texas Essential Elements/(a) English Language Arts: 4B Main idea; 4H Point of view.
(c) Reading: 3A Main ideas/details; 3F Purpose/point of view/opinion

There have been great societies that did not use the wheel, but there have been no societies that did not tell stories.

—Ursula K. Le Guin

SRW p. 49

A

The Elements of a Novel

Written storytelling at its simplest takes the form of a short story. A short story is a dozen or so pages long, it usually focuses on a single character, and it follows one plot line.

Alongside a novel, the short story seems like a one-room cottage overshadowed by a mansion. A novel is likely to weigh a pound or more and to run on for hundreds of pages. A **novel** is a long fictional story that follows the adventures of several characters and that often has more than one plot.

However, both the short story and the novel are made of the same elements. They are both built of plot, character, setting, theme, and point of view.

The Building Blocks of Fiction

In your study of the short story in this book (page 189), you learned about these basic building blocks of fiction:

1. **Plot** tells us "what happened." SRW p. 67

2. The people the events happen to are the **characters.** Writers help us to know characters in several ways: they tell us how they look, they let us hear them speak, and they let us watch them in action. They also let us watch how other people in the story react to a character. Sometimes the writer will tell us directly what a character is like: *Lilly is painfully shy.*

3. The **setting** is where the story takes place. A setting can be the real world or it can be a place that has never existed. Setting can be a time in the misty past, or a time in the distant future. If a setting is well described, the writer has succeeded in helping us feel "we are there." SRW p. 79

4. **Theme** is the truth about our lives that is revealed by the novel's events. Because they are long, most novels have several themes—but one is usually the most important. SRW p. 87

5. The **point of view** is the vantage point from which the story is told. Most stories are told by an **omniscient narrator:** this is the voice of someone who is not in the story and who knows everything about all the characters. Other stories are told by a **first-person narrator.** This means that someone who refers to himself or herself as *I* (the first-person pronoun) tells the story. In **the limited third-person point of view,** an omniscient narrator zooms in on just one character and tells the story through that person's eyes. It makes us feel as if we get to know this one character very, very well—often better than the person knows himself, or herself.

SRW p. 69

Illustration by Edmund Dulac of Scheherazade, the heroine of *The Thousand and One Nights.*

B

A. Responding to the Quotation
The quotation is from an essay that Le Guin wrote for *The Living Light* magazine. Earlier in the essay Le Guin states that people who have never heard a story would know little about "what it is to be human." You can tell students that the wheel dates back to 3000 B.C., but cave drawings telling stories have been found that date back to as early as 5000 B.C.

? Why do you think people have such a need to tell stories?

B. Humanities Connection: Responding to the Illustration
Edmund Dulac (1882–1953) was a French artist. His paintings for *The Thousand and One Nights* (see page 413) made him famous throughout Europe. (Another painting by Dulac is on page 415.) Notice how Dulac repeats the design and shape of the peacock's tail in Scheherazade's trailing gown.

? What do you think she might be holding?

533

A. Responding
? Have you ever seen a movie or watched a play on television (or on stage) that made you cry, or feel angry, or feel wonderful? What in the production made you feel this way?

What Is the Novel's Purpose?

People sometimes ask what possible use a novel has to a person's life. Why, they ask, in the course of a busy life, would someone want to leave time for the reading of novels?

One answer lies in the novelist's intent. The novelist's hope is to give us pleasure. Only by entertaining us, will the writer capture our attention and keep us interested in reading to the story's end.

If the novelist is a good entertainer, we will be drawn into the story. The story may even become more interesting than what is actually going on around us. We may be so moved by the story that we laugh, or cry, or even get angry over it. If we are moved in some way, the novelist has triumphed, and so have we.

The novelist may have a second purpose in writing a novel, which is to share some experience that enlarges our understanding of what it means to be alive on this earth. The novelist's story might even tell us something about another part of the world or some other time in history.

A Reading novels can be similiar to going to movies or watching television programs. You won't enjoy everything you try. But when you do enjoy a novel, it can be a terrific experience, like making a new friend. You and the novelist can share a fresh understanding of how people live. Sometimes, that understanding can even help you decide how you want to live your own life.

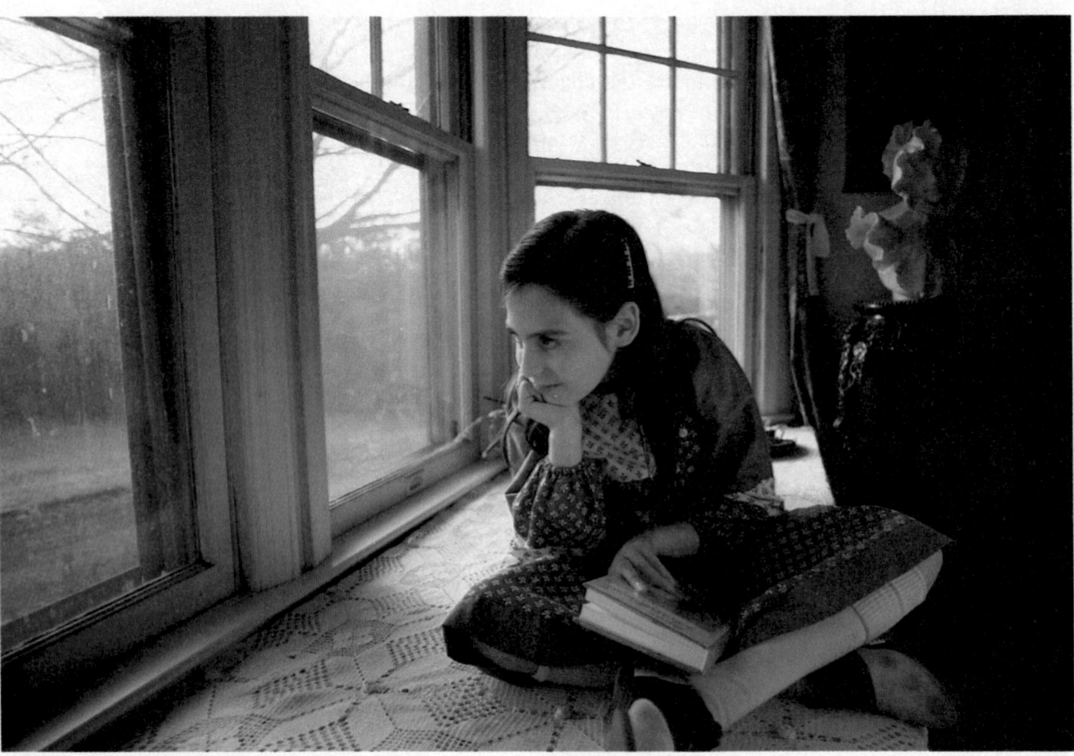

Magic and Science

You may want to emphasize that in our world, educated people, including Le Guin, do not believe in magic. In fact, our world, with its emphasis on the power of science, is very different from Earthsea. It is the dramatic difference between the two worlds, as much as their similarities, that make this novel exciting to read as well as an important work of literature.

READING CHECK TEST

1. Short stories and novels are made up of the same elements. *(True)*
2. A novel is shorter than a short story. *(False)*
3. Many novelists hope to entertain their readers. *(True)*
4. No one in Earthsea believes in the power of magic. *(False)*
5. *A Wizard of Earthsea* takes place in a world that is more technically advanced than ours. *(False)*

A Wizard of Earthsea

It is not surprising that Ursula Le Guin is a champion among writers of fantasy and science fiction. In this short novel, *A Wizard of Earthsea,* she wins her audience at once. She provides a young hero who is about to be launched on an interesting career. Ged is to become a sorcerer, and he has already shown a talent for his profession.

A

B

Here we watch Ged as he learns the true use of his superhuman powers. It might occur to you that Ged is like many heroes of folk tales, myths, and fantasy, who have found dependable ways of winning out over a stubborn environment. Superman and Wonder Woman have "super" powers. So do Merlin, the marvelous magician in the King Arthur stories, and Gandalf, the great magician in J. R. R. Tolkien's *The Lord of the Rings.*

C

But the appeal of this novel probably comes from more than the hero's adventures as a magician. The appeal comes from its **setting,** the world in which Ged's adventures take place. Earthsea is a magical place, a watery world of great beauty, scattered with various climates, peoples, and islands. The time is not our own. There are no engines, people travel by boat, rooms are lighted by candles, and everyone has a deep faith in the power of magic.

Another appeal comes from the story's **theme.** Ged's story is essentially a story of growing into adulthood. As such, it is a story that everyone can identify with. Though Earthsea is a world apart, it has much in common with our own world. The magic academy Ged attends on Roke is in many ways like schools everywhere. And, like most of us, Ged gets some important education outside the classroom. He learns about the importance of friendship, for one thing, and about the danger of using his powers for evil ends.

But the most important aspect of the novel has to do with the lesson Ged learns when he reaches manhood. It is a lesson that centers on the mystical importance of knowing a person's real name and thereby knowing that person's real being. This central theme of the novel suggests that your worst enemy lies within yourself; and that to really know yourself is to reach your full power. That, the story implies, is as good as magic any day.

A. Pronunciation
"Ged" should be pronounced with a hard "g" like the "g" in "get."

B. Vocabulary
sorcerer: one who has magic powers
? Find two synonyms for *sorcerer* on this page. (*Wizard* and *magician*)

C. Expansion
Refer students to the painting of Gandalf as an old man on text page 387. If some of your advanced students have read any of the books that make up the trilogy *The Lord of the Rings,* ask them to tell the class about the characters and settings. An excerpt from *The Hobbit,* which introduces the trilogy, appears on page 386. You might show Tolkien's wonderful maps of Middle-Earth. In most editions they are at the beginning of each book in the trilogy.

Prereading

1. **Building on Prior Knowledge.** You might find a map of Earth and reduce or enlarge it so that the map of Earthsea (page 532) and the map of Earth are approximately the same size. Ask students to compare the two maps. How are they different? How are they alike? Ask students if they can find an "archipelago"—a group of many islands—on Earth. (Hawaii and Malay Archipelago are examples.) Ask students to identify the important "boundary" areas on the Earthsea map, which are indicated in the Earthsea "compass rose": North Reach, Kargad Lands, East Reach, South Reach, West Reach. Explain that Le Guin uses the word "reach" to mean a great stretch at each "end" of the world as the people of Earthsea knew it.

2. **Establishing a Purpose.** Read the five lines from the Creation of Éa. (You may want to introduce the word "epigraph," a beginning quotation that foreshadows important events or ideas.) This epigraph is like a riddle. When students finish the novel, they will know what these lines mean, but there are clues

Earthsea Vocabulary

Refer to the top of the side columns throughout the novel unit for a section called "Earthsea Vocabulary" which lists Le Guin's invented words. You might have students create their own Earthsea dictionary. Encourage them to illustrate their dictionary.

★ **Texas Essential Elements/(a) English Language Arts: 1B** Purpose and audience; **1D** Direct quotations; **1E** Formal/informal language; **3A** Plot/character; **3B** Figurative language; **4B** Main idea; **4E** Predict

A WIZARD OF EARTHSEA

For a detailed lesson plan on the novel, see Teacher's Manual pages 179–190. A biography of Ursula Le Guin appears on text page 617.

Ursula K. Le Guin

even in this opening chapter. As they read, have them look for references to silence, dark, light, bright, and hawk.

3. PREREADING JOURNAL. Ask students to write three sentences predicting what the novel will be about. They should base their prediction on the five lines.

Summary: Chapter 1

A boy named Duny lives on the mountainous island of Gont. When at seven Duny shows signs of having magical powers, his aunt, who is a witch, teaches him the spells she knows. These are relatively minor spells used for working weather and calling animals. One day the savage Kargads attack the island. Duny saves his village and becomes a hero when he creates a mist that the Kargs cannot see through, but through which the villagers can counterattack. Hearing of the boy's feat, Ogion, the great mage of Gont, offers to take Duny as apprentice when he is thirteen and receives his true name. When the time comes, Ogion names him Ged, and the two go off together.

★ **Texas Essential Elements/(c) Reading: 1A** Context clues; **1B** Structural analysis; **1C** Dictionaries; **2A** Word meaning; **3A** Main ideas/details; **3H** Predict; **3I** Draw conclusions

This is a fantasy, a story set in an imaginary world that, so far as we know, has never existed. It is the story of a young boy who foolishly and recklessly misuses his powers and so lets a terrible shadow loose on the world.

As you read, you might want to refer to the map of Earthsea on page 532. But the best picture of this enchanted world will exist in your own imagination.

Invented and Uncommon Words. Earthsea, the setting of this novel, resembles our world in many ways. However, much of its geography, plants, animals, and people were invented by the writer. When inventing names for these things and people, the writer had to make them sound as if they all came from the same imaginary Earthsea language. The novel also contains some unfamiliar English words (including compound words) that may seem made up. Footnotes and context clues will help you figure out the meanings of many words. Read some of these words aloud: They add to the story's magical effect.

Only in silence the word,
only in dark the light,
only in dying life:
bright the hawk's flight
on the empty sky.
—*The Creation of Éa*

Chapter 1
Warriors in the Mist

The island of Gont, a single mountain that lifts its peak a mile above the storm-racked Northeast Sea, is a land famous for wizards. From the towns in its high valleys and the ports on its dark narrow bays many a Gontishman has gone forth to serve the Lords of the Archipelago in their cities as wizard or mage, or, looking for adventure, to wander working magic from isle to isle of all Earthsea. Of these some say the greatest, and surely the greatest voyager, was the man called Sparrowhawk, who in his day became both dragonlord and Archmage. His life is told of in the *Deed of Ged* and in many songs, but this is a tale of the time before his fame, before the songs were made.

He was born in a lonely village called Ten Alders, high on the mountain at the head of the Northward Vale. Below the village the pastures and plowlands of the Vale slope downward level below level toward the sea, and other towns lie on the bends of the River Ar; above the village only forest rises ridge behind ridge to the stone and snow of the heights.

The name he bore as a child, Duny, was given him by his mother, and that and his life were all she could give him, for she died before he was a year old. His father, the bronzesmith of the village, was a grim unspeaking man, and since Duny's six brothers were older than he by many years and went one by one from home to farm the land or sail the sea or work as smith in other towns of the Northward Vale, there was no one to bring the child up in tenderness. He grew wild, a thriving weed, a tall, quick boy, loud and proud and full of temper. With the few other children of the village he herded goats on the steep meadows above the river-springs; and when he was strong enough to push and pull the long bellows-sleeves,[1] his father made him work as smith's boy, at a high cost in blows and whippings. There was not much work to be got out of Duny. He was always off and away; roaming deep in the forest, swimming in the pools of the River Ar that like all Gontish rivers runs very quick and cold, or climbing by cliff and scarp to the heights above the forest, from which he could see the sea, that broad northern ocean where, past Perregal, no islands are.

A sister of his dead mother lived in the village. She had done what was needful for him as a baby, but she had business of her own and once he could look after himself at all she paid no more heed to him. But one day when the boy was seven years old, untaught and knowing nothing of the arts and powers that are in the world, he heard his aunt crying out words to a goat which had jumped up onto the thatch of a hut and would not come down: but it came jumping when she cried a certain rhyme to it. Next day herding the longhaired goats on the meadows of High Fall, Duny shouted to them the words he had heard, not knowing their use or meaning or what kind of words they were:

Noth hierth malk man
hiolk han merth han!

1. **bellows-sleeves:** a device that blows air onto a fire when its two sides are pressed together.

Earthsea Vocabulary
dragonlord
Archmage
Old Speech

A. Protagonist
The protagonist, or main character, in this novel has three names. What are they? (Duny, Sparrowhawk, Ged)

B. Character
What words tell you about Duny's character and personality? ("Tall," "quick," "loud," "proud," "full of temper"; "there was not much work to be got out of Duny") What circumstances in his life may have made him this kind of person? (His mother died when he was a baby; his six brothers are much older than he; his father is a "grim, unspeaking man" who makes him work hard and beats him.)

SUPPLEMENTARY SUPPORT MATERIAL: CHAPTERS 1 AND 2

1. Vocabulary Activity Sheet
2. Reading Check Test blackline Master
3. Selection Test (page 213 of Test Book)
4. Workbook (page 153)

DEVELOPING VOCABULARY

The following words appear on a test in the Test Book, page 214. (See also the Vocabulary Activity Sheet.)

scarp	rankle
enchantment	jargon
dubious	uncanny
humbug	mocking
smolder	abate

Earthsea Vocabulary
rushwash
paramal
kingsfoil
clovenfoot

A. Earthsea Map
? You might have students locate Gont on this detail of the Earthsea map, and also on the larger map, page 532.

B. Atmosphere
? What is the atmosphere inside the witch's hut? (Quiet and mysterious. The fact that children fear the hut gives it a sense of foreboding.) Have students list details of the taste, smell, and feel of the hut.

C. Character
? What does this fact tell about Duny's character? (It shows his pride and competitive spirit.)

D. Point of View
? Is the point of view third-person omniscient or third-person limited? How do you know? (Third-person omniscient; we know the aunt's thoughts and feelings as well as Duny's.)

He yelled the rhyme aloud, and the goats came to him. They came very quickly, all of them together, not making any sound. They looked at him out of the dark slot in their yellow eyes.

Duny laughed and shouted it out again, the rhyme that gave him power over the goats. They came closer, crowding and pushing round him. All at once he felt afraid of their thick, ridged horns and their strange eyes and their strange silence. He tried to get free of them and to run away. The goats ran with him keeping in a knot around him, and so they came charging down into the village at last, all the goats going huddled together as if a rope were pulled tight round them, and the boy in the midst of them weeping and bellowing. Villagers ran from their houses to swear at the goats and laugh at the boy. Among them came the boy's aunt, who did not laugh. She said a word to the goats, and the beasts began to bleat and browse and wander, freed from the spell.

"Come with me," she said to Duny.

B She took him into her hut where she lived alone. She let no child enter there usually, and the children feared the place. It was low and dusky, windowless, fragrant with herbs that hung drying from the crosspole of the roof, mint and moly and thyme, yarrow and rushwash and paramal, kingsfoil, clovenfoot, tansy, and bay. There his aunt sat cross-legged by the firepit, and looking sidelong at the boy through the tangles of her black hair she asked him what he had said to the goats, and if he knew what the rhyme was. When she found that he knew nothing, and yet had spellbound the goats to come to him and follow him, then she saw that he must have in him the makings of power.

As her sister's son he had been nothing to her, but now she looked at him with a new eye. She praised him, and told him she might teach him rhymes he would like better, such as the word that makes a snail look out of its shell, or the name that calls a falcon down from the sky.

"Aye, teach me that name!" he said, being clear over the fright the goats had given him, and puffed up with her praise of his cleverness.

The witch said to him, "You will not ever tell that word to the other children, if I teach it to you."

"I promise."

She smiled at his ready ignorance. "Well and good. But I will bind your promise. Your tongue will be stilled until I choose to unbind it, and even then, though you can speak, you will not be able to speak the word I teach you where another person can hear it. We must keep the secrets of our craft."

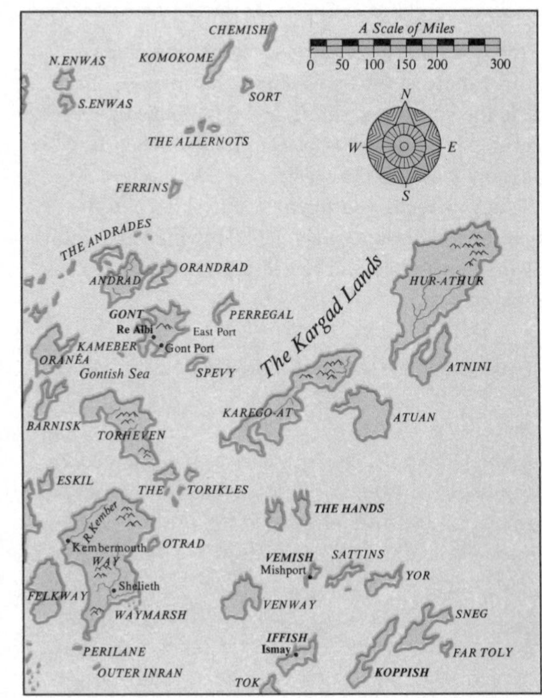

A

"Good," said the boy, for he had no wish to tell the secret to his playmates, liking to know and do what they knew not and could not. C

He sat still while his aunt bound back her uncombed hair, and knotted the belt of her dress, and again sat cross-legged throwing handfuls of leaves into the firepit, so that a smoke spread and filled the darkness of the hut. She began to sing. Her voice changed sometimes to low or high as if another voice sang through her, and the singing went on and on until the boy did not know if he waked or slept, and all the while the witch's old black dog that never barked sat by him with eyes red from smoke. Then the witch spoke to Duny in a tongue he did not understand, and made him say with her certain rhymes and words until the enchantment came on him and held him still.

"Speak!" she said to test the spell.

The boy could not speak, but he laughed.

Then his aunt was a little afraid of his strength, for this was as strong a spell as she knew how to weave: She had tried not only to gain control of his speech and silence, but to bind him at the same time to her service in the craft of sorcery. Yet even as the spell bound him, he had laughed. She said nothing. She threw clear water on the fire till the smoke cleared away, and gave the boy water to drink, and when the air was clear and he could D

Motifs in the Novel

Ask students to look for images and words that recur throughout the novel. Recognizing these repetitions as patterns or motifs in the design of the work will deepen their understanding of the novel's theme. The important motifs are mentioned in the lines from *The Creation of Éa: silence; words* (standing also for names); *dark* (standing also for shadow); *light; dying* (death); *living* (life); *bright, hawk,* and *sky.* Several of these words are woven into every page of the novel. For instance, you might have students look for the repetition of the following words on this page: "word" (three times); "name" (three times).

speak again she taught him the true name of the falcon, to which the falcon must come.

This was Duny's first step on the way he was to follow all his life, the way of magery, the way that led him at last to hunt a shadow over land and sea to the lightless coasts of death's kingdom. But in those first steps along the way, it seemed a broad, bright road.

When he found that the wild falcons stooped down to him from the wind when he summoned them by name, lighting with a thunder of wings on his wrist like the hunting birds of a prince, then he hungered to know more such names and came to his aunt begging to learn the name of the sparrowhawk and the osprey and the eagle. To earn the words of power he did all the witch asked of him and learned of her all she taught, though not all of it was pleasant to do or know. There is a saying on Gont, *Weak as woman's magic,* and there is another saying, *Wicked as woman's magic.* Now the witch of Ten Alders was no black sorceress, nor did she ever meddle with the high arts or traffic with Old Powers; but being an ignorant woman among ignorant folk, she often used her crafts to foolish and dubious ends. She knew nothing of the Balance and the Pattern which the true wizard knows and serves, and which keep
A him from using his spells unless real need demands. She had a spell for every circumstance, and was forever weaving charms. Much of her lore was mere rubbish and humbug, nor did she know the true spells from the false. She knew many curses, and was better at causing sickness, perhaps, than at curing it. Like any village witch she could brew up a love potion, but there were other, uglier brews she made to serve men's jealousy and hate. Such practices, however, she kept from her young prentice,[2] and as far as she was able she taught him honest craft.

At first all his pleasure in the art-magic was, childlike, the power it gave him over bird and beast, and the knowledge of these. And indeed that pleasure stayed with him all his life. Seeing him in the high pastures often with a bird of prey about him, the other children called him Sparrowhawk, and so he came by the name that he kept in later life as his use-name, when his true name was not known.

As the witch kept talking of the glory and the
B riches and the great power over men that a sorcerer could gain, he set himself to learn more useful lore. He was very quick at it. The witch praised him and the children of the village began to fear him, and he himself was sure that very soon he would become great among men. So he went on from word to word and from spell to spell with the witch till he was twelve years old and had learned from her a great part of what she knew: not much, but enough for the witchwife of a small village, and more than enough for a boy of twelve. She had taught him all her lore in herbals and healing, and all she knew of the crafts of finding, binding, mending, unsealing, and revealing. What she knew of chanters' tales and the great Deeds she had sung him, and all the words of the True Speech that she had learned from the sorcerer that taught her, she taught again to Duny. And from weatherworkers and wandering jugglers who went from town to town of the Northward Vale and the East Forest he had learned various tricks and pleasantries, spells of Illusion.[3] It was with one of these light spells that he first proved the great power that was in him.

In those days the Kargad Empire was strong. Those are four great lands that lie between the Northern and the Eastern Reaches: Karego-At, Atuan, Hur-at-Hur, Atnini. The tongue they speak there is not like any spoken in the Archipelago or the other Reaches, and they are a savage people, white-skinned, yellow-haired, and fierce, liking the sight of blood and the smell of burning towns. Last year they had attacked the Torikles and the strong island Torheven, raiding in great force in fleets of red-sailed ships. News of this came north to Gont, but the Lords of Gont were busy with their piracy and paid small heed to the woes of the other lands. Then Spevy fell to the Kargs and was looted[4] and laid waste, its people taken as slaves, so that even now it is an isle of ruins. In lust of conquest the Kargs sailed next to Gont, coming in a host, thirty great longships, to East Port. They fought through that town, took it, burned it; leaving their ships under guard at the mouth of the River Ar they went up the Vale wrecking and looting, slaughtering cattle and men. As they went they split into bands, and each of these bands plundered where it chose. Fugitives brought warning to the villages of the heights. Soon the people of Ten Alders saw smoke darken the eastern sky, and that night those who climbed the High Fall looked down on the Vale all hazed and red-streaked with fires where fields ready for harvest had been set ablaze, and orchards burned, the fruit roasting on the blazing boughs, and barns and farmhouses smoldered in ruin.

Some of the villagers fled up the ravines and

2. **prentice** (pren'tis): apprentice, or person who is learning a trade or craft from a master craftsperson.

3. **illusion:** unreal or misleading image.

4. **looted:** stripped of everything valuable.

A. Making Inferences

What do the "ignorant folk" of Gont think about women's magic, or witches? (Witches are not as powerful as sorcerers, and they also can practice black, or evil, magic.)

B. Character's Motivation

What seems to be Duny's motivation for learning his aunt's magic? (He is having fun; however, the underlying reason is his desire for power and fame.) Tell students to watch for examples of Duny's pride in the early parts of the novel.

Epic Style

In *A Wizard of Earthsea* Le Guin uses several devices that are typical of ancient epic poetry. Alliteration (repeating consonant sounds, most often at the beginning of words that occur close together), compound forms (two nouns or a noun and an adjective written as one word or connected by a hyphen), and wise sayings (proverbs) occur frequently throughout the novel. You might want to elicit a definition and examples of each of these. (See notes A, B, and C below.)

A. Alliteration

Notice Le Guin's frequent use of alliteration in this paragraph; for example, "handles of hoes"; "sockets and shaft."

? Find two examples of alliteration in the next paragraph. ("Huts and houses"; "straggling street"; "distances and dangers")

B. Compound Forms

? Notice the unusual compound "fog-dew." Find other unusual compounds on this page. (There are many; possible answers: fogweaving, new-forged, forge-bellows, binding spell)

C. Wise Sayings

Notice the proverbial saying here. Have students watch for others in the following pages.

D. Character

? What do you learn about Duny from his reaction to the attack? (He is brave; he knows his own power; he thinks quickly.)

hid in the forest, and some made ready to fight for their lives, and some did neither but stood about lamenting. The witch was one who fled, hiding alone in a cave up in the Kapperding Scarp and sealing the cave mouth with spells. Duny's father the bronzesmith was one who stayed, for he would not leave his smelting pit and forge where he had worked for fifty years. All that night where he labored beating up what ready metal he had there into spearpoints, and others worked with him binding these to the handles of hoes and **A** rakes, there being no time to make sockets and shaft them properly. There had been no weapons in the village but hunting bows and short knives, for the mountain folk of Gont are not warlike; it is not warriors they are famous for, but goat thieves, sea pirates, and wizards.

With sunrise came a thick white fog, as on many autumn mornings in the heights of the island. Among their huts and houses down the straggling street of Ten Alders the villagers stood waiting with their hunting bows and new-forged spears, not knowing whether the Kargs might be far off or very near, all silent, all peering into the fog that hid shapes and distances and dangers from their eyes.

With them was Duny. He had worked all night at the forge-bellows, pushing and pulling the two long sleeves of goathide that fed the fire with a blast of air. Now his arms so ached and trembled from that work that he could not hold out the spear he had chosen. He did not see how he could fight or be of any good to himself or the villagers. It rankled at his heart that he should die, spitted on a Kargish lance, while still a boy: that he should go into the dark land without ever having known his own name, his true name as a man. He looked **B** down at his thin arms, wet with cold fog-dew, and raged at his weakness, for he knew his strength. There was power in him, if he knew how to use it, and he sought among all the spells he knew for some device that might give him and his companions an advantage, or at least a chance. But need **C** alone is not enough to set power free: There must be knowledge.

The fog was thinning now under the heat of the sun that shone bare above on the peak in a bright sky. As the mists moved and parted in great drifts and smoky wisps, the villagers saw a band of warriors coming up the mountain. They were armored with bronze helmets and greaves[5] and breastplates of heavy leather and shields of wood and bronze, and armed with swords and the long Kargish lance. Winding up along the steep bank of the Ar they came in a plumed, clanking, straggling line, near enough already that their white faces could be seen, and the words of their jargon heard as they shouted to one another. In this band of the invading horde there were about a hundred men, which is not many; but in the village were only eighteen men and boys.

Now need called knowledge out: Duny, seeing the fog blow and thin across the path before the Kargs, saw a spell that might avail him. An old weatherworker of the Vale, seeking to win the boy as prentice, had taught him several charms. One of these tricks was called fogweaving, a binding-spell that gathers the mists together for a while in one place; with it one skilled in illusion can shape the mist into fair ghostly seemings, which last a little and fade away. The boy had no such skill, but his intent was different, and he had the strength to turn the spell to his own ends. Rapidly and aloud he named the places and the boundaries of the village, and then spoke the fogweaving charm, but in among its words he enlaced the words of a spell of concealment, and last he cried the word that set the magic going.

Even as he did so his father coming up behind him struck him hard on the side of the head, knocking him right down. "Be still, fool! Keep your blattering mouth shut, and hide if you can't fight!"

Duny got to his feet. He could hear the Kargs now at the end of the village, as near as the great yew-tree by the tanner's yard. Their voices were clear, and the clink and creak of their harness and arms, but they could not be seen. The fog had closed and thickened all over the village, graying the light, blurring the world till a man could hardly see his own hands before him.

"I've hidden us all," Duny said, sullenly, for his head hurt from his father's blow, and the working of the doubled incantation[6] had drained his strength. "I'll keep up this fog as long as I can. **D** Get the others to lead them up to High Fall."

The smith stared at his son who stood wraithlike[7] in that weird, dank mist. It took him a minute to see Duny's meaning, but when he did he ran at once, noiselessly, knowing every fence and corner of the village, to find the others and tell them what to do. Now through the gray fog bloomed a blur of red, as the Kargs set fire to the thatch of a house. Still they did not come up into

5. **greaves** (grēvz): leg armor.

6. **incantation** (in'kan·tā'shən): chanting of magical words to cast a spell.

7. **wraithlike** (rāth'līk): ghostlike.

the village, but waited at the lower end till the mist should lift and lay bare their loot and prey.

The tanner, whose house it was that burned, sent a couple of boys skipping right under the Karg's noses, taunting and yelling and vanishing again like smoke into smoke. Meantime the older men, creeping behind fences and running from house to house, came close on the other side and sent a volley of arrows and spears at the warriors, who stood all in a bunch. One Karg fell writhing with a spear, still warm from its forging, right through his body. Others were arrow-bitten, and all enraged. They charged forward then to hew down their puny attackers, but they found only the fog about them, full of voices. They followed the voices, stabbing ahead into the mist with their great, plumed, bloodstained lances. Up the length of the street they came shouting, and never knew they had run right through the village, as the empty huts and houses loomed and disappeared again in the writhing gray fog. The villagers ran scattering, most of them keeping well ahead since they knew the ground; but some, boys or old men, were slow. The Kargs stumbling on them drove their lances or hacked with their swords, yelling their war cry; the names of the White Godbrothers of Atuan:

A

"Wuluah! Atwah!"

Some of the band stopped when they felt the land grow rough underfoot, but others pressed right on, seeking the phantom village, following dim wavering shapes that fled just out of reach before them. All the mist had come alive with these fleeting forms, dodging, flickering, fading on every side. One group of the Kargs chased the wraiths straight to the High Fall, the cliff's edge above the springs of Ar, and the shapes they pursued ran out onto the air and there vanished in a thinning of the mist, while the pursuers fell screaming through fog and sudden sunlight a hundred feet sheer to the shallow pools among the rocks. And those that came behind and did not fall stood at the cliff's edge, listening.

Now dread came into the Kargs' hearts and they began to seek one another, not the villagers, in the uncanny mist. They gathered on the hillside,

B

and yet always there were wraiths and ghost-shapes among them, and other shapes that ran and stabbed from behind with spear or knife and vanished again. The Kargs began to run, all of them, downhill, stumbling, silent, until all at once they ran out from the gray blind mist and saw the river and the ravines below the village all bare and bright in morning sunlight. Then they stopped, gathering together, and looked back. A wall of wavering, writhing gray lay blank across the path, hiding all that lay behind it. Out from it burst two or three stragglers, lunging and stumbling along, their long lances rocking on their shoulders. Not one Karg looked back more than that once. All went down, in haste, away from the enchanted place.

Farther down the Northward Vale those warriors got their fill of fighting. The towns of the East Forest, from Ovark to the coast, had gathered their men and sent them against the invaders of Gont. Band after band they came down from the hills, and that day and the next the Kargs were harried back down to the beaches above East Port, where they found their ships burnt; so they fought with their backs to the sea till every man of them was killed, and the sands of Armouth were brown with blood until the tide came in.

But on that morning in Ten Alders village and up on the High Fall, the dank gray fog had clung a while, and then suddenly it blew and drifted and melted away. This man and that stood up in the windy brightness of the morning, and looked about him wondering. Here lay a dead Karg with yellow hair long, loose, and bloody; there lay the village tanner, killed in battle like a king.

Down in the village the house that had been set afire still blazed. They ran to put the fire out, since their battle had been won. In the street, near the great yew, they found Duny the bronzesmith's son standing by himself, bearing no hurt, but speechless and stupid like one stunned. They were well aware of what he had done, and they led him into his father's house and went calling for the witch to come down out of her cave and heal the lad who had saved their lives and their property, all but four who were killed by the Kargs, and the one house that was burnt.

No weapon-hurt had come to the boy, but he would not speak nor eat nor sleep; he seemed not to hear what was said to him, not to see those who came to see him. There was none in those parts wizard enough to cure what ailed him. His aunt said, "He has overspent his power," but she had no art to help him.

While he lay thus dark and dumb, the story of the lad who wove the fog and scared off Kargish swordsmen with a mess of shadows was told all down the Northward Vale, and in the East Forest, and high on the mountain and over the mountain even in the Great Port of Gont. So it happened that on the fifth day after the slaughter at Armouth a stranger came into Ten Alders village, a man neither young nor old, who came cloaked and bareheaded, lightly carrying a great staff of oak that was as tall as himself. He did not come up the course of the Ar like most people, but down, C

A. Novel by the Same Author
The fierce Kargs are the villains of the second book in the Earthsea trilogy, *The Tombs of Atuan,* which tells how a young priestess escapes from a dark maze in the land of Atuan. You might assign this novel for independent reading.

B. Conflict
? What is the turning point in the battle? (When some of the Kargs fall over the cliff. The Kargs then realize that they are battling a spell that cannot be broken and will eventually defeat them.)

C. Character
? How can someone be "neither young nor old"? What does this suggest about the character we are going to meet? (The phrase implies that he is ageless. We assume that he has magic powers—perhaps he will be someone who can cure Duny.)

Summary: Chapter 2

Though Ged respects Ogion, he finds the methods of the quiet and contemplative mage frustrating, for he is eager to learn showy tricks. Ogion tries to teach the proud, impetuous boy the importance of silence and the responsibilities that go with power. While gathering herbs, Ged meets a girl who knows about his powers. She challenges him to transform himself into an animal, and he goes home determined to learn the necessary spells. Opening Ogion's Lore-Books, Ged is drawn to a spell that can summon spirits. As he reads the spell, he feels and then sees a shadow in the room that reaches for him. Suddenly Ogion returns, and in a blaze of light, sends the spirit back. Ogion tells Ged that the girl is the daughter of an enchantress, who may have caused Ged to read the spell; he reminds Ged that sorcery is not a game. Ogion then asks Ged if he wishes to continue as his apprentice, or if he would rather go to the School of Roke and study there. Ged chooses to go to Roke.

Earthsea Vocabulary

healall

Sunreturn (a winter feast celebrating the solstice, December 21 or 22 on Earth, when the sun is farthest south and "turns" back to the north)

A. Conflict

? Why was the conflict between the Kargs and Duny important to the future course of Duny's life? (Duny proved his tremendous power; Ogion heard of it, and came to name Duny.)

B. Foreshadowing

? Identify the phrases that foreshadow problems ahead for Duny. (". . . clouds crossed the sun's face and great shadows slid . . . over the water . . .") Water in literature often symbolizes life.

C. Vocabulary

rune (rōōn): a mark used in ancient Scandinavia, which was believed to have been given by the gods. Magic spells were written in runes so that their meaning was kept secret.

out of the forests of the higher mountainside. The village goodwives saw well that he was a wizard, and when he told them that he was a healall, they brought him straight to the smith's house. Sending away all but the boy's father and aunt the stranger stooped above the cot where Duny lay staring into the dark, and did no more than lay his hand on the boy's forehead and touch his lips once.

Duny sat up slowly looking about him. In a little while he spoke, and strength and hunger began to come back into him. They gave him a little to drink and eat, and he lay back again, always watching the stranger with dark wondering eyes.

The bronzesmith said to that stranger, "You are no common man."

"Nor will this boy be a common man," the other answered. "The tale of his deed with the fog has come to Re Albi, which is my home. I have come here to give him his name, if as they say he has not yet made his passage into manhood."

The witch whispered to the smith, "Brother, this must surely be the Mage of Re Albi, Ogion the Silent, that one who tamed the earthquake—"

"Sir," said the bronzesmith who would not let a great name daunt him, "my son will be thirteen this month coming, but we thought to hold his Passage at the feast of Sunreturn this winter."

"Let him be named as soon as may be," said the mage, "for he needs his name. I have other business now, but I will come back here for the day you choose. If you see fit I will take him with me when I go thereafter. And if he prove apt I will keep him as prentice, or see to it that he is schooled as fits his gifts. For to keep dark the mind of the mageborn, that is a dangerous thing." **A**

Very gently Ogion spoke, but with certainty, and even the hardheaded smith assented to all he said.

On the day the boy was thirteen years old, a day in the early splendor of autumn while still the bright leaves are on the trees, Ogion returned to the village from his rovings over Gont Mountain, and the ceremony of Passage was held. The witch took from the boy his name Duny, the name his mother had given him as a baby. Nameless and naked he walked into the cold springs of the Ar where it rises among rocks under the high cliffs. As he entered the water clouds crossed the sun's face and great shadows slid and mingled over the water of the pool about him. **B** He crossed to the far bank, shuddering with cold but walking slow and erect as he should through that icy, living water. As he came to the bank Ogion, waiting, reached out his hand and clasping the boy's arm whispered to him his true name: Ged.

Thus was he given his name by one very wise in the uses of power.

The feasting was far from over, and all the villagers were making merry with plenty to eat and beer to drink and a chanter from down the Vale singing the *Deed of the Dragonlords,* when the mage spoke in his quiet voice to Ged: "Come, lad. Bid your people farewell and leave them feasting."

Ged fetched what he had to carry, which was the good bronze knife his father had forged him, and a leather coat the tanner's widow had cut down to his size, and an alder-stick his aunt had becharmed for him: that was all he owned besides his shirt and breeches. He said farewell to them, all the people he knew in all the world, and looked about once at the village that straggled and huddled there under the cliffs, over the river-springs. Then he set off with his new master through the steep slanting forests of the mountain isle, through the leaves and shadows of bright autumn.

Chapter 2

The Shadow

Ged had thought that as the prentice of a great mage he would enter at once into the mystery and mastery of power. He would understand the language of the beasts and the speech of the leaves of the forest, he thought, and sway the winds with his word, and learn to change himself into any shape he wished. Maybe he and his master would run together as stags, or fly to Re Albi over the mountain on the wings of eagles.

But it was not so at all. They wandered, first down into the Vale and then gradually south and westward around the mountain, given lodging in little villages or spending the night out in the wilderness, like poor journeyman sorcerers, or tinkers, or beggars. They entered no mysterious domain. Nothing happened. The mage's oaken staff that Ged had watched at first with eager dread was nothing but a stout staff to walk with. Three days went by and four days went by and still Ogion had not spoken a single charm in Ged's hearing, and had not taught him a single name or rune or spell. **C**

Though a very silent man he was so mild and calm that Ged soon lost his awe of him, and in a day or two more he was bold enough to ask his master, "When will my apprenticeship begin, Sir?"

"It has begun," said Ogion.

There was a silence, as if Ged was keeping back

Comment from a Critic
Eleanor Cameron, in her review of *A Wizard of Earthsea* for *Horn Book* magazine, writes that the attitudes of an anthropologist color Le Guin's work. It is Le Guin's "curiosity about people different from one's own kind, interest in languages . . . a sense of kinship across seas and centuries; a love of strangeness; a love of exactness . . . which enrich the quality, the texture, and the spirit of *A Wizard of Earthsea.*"

The Influence of Anthropology
Le Guin's writing is distinctive in its attention to details of setting, customs, and language that reveal her interest and background in anthropology. (See Reading About the Writer, page 617.) An anthropology professor, her father was a specialist in American Indian languages. Her mother published collections of myths and wrote anthropology books for children.

Earthsea Vocabulary
fourfoil
Runebook

A. Interpreting
? In your own words, tell what Ogion means when he says, "You've drawn too much water from that well." ("You've used that gift too often. You need to learn more about other things before you work spells.")

B. Proverbs
? Find and list two "wise sayings" on this page. ("Manhood is patience." "Mastery is nine times patience." "To hear, one must be silent.") These wise sayings, like proverbs in folk literature, convey the important values and attitudes of Earthsea culture.

C. Making Inferences
? Why do you think Ogion smiles here? (He probably knows exactly what Ged is thinking—he knows that Ged is impatient to be a wizard.)

something he had to say. Then he said it: "But I haven't learned anything yet!"

"Because you haven't found out what I am teaching," replied the mage, going on at his steady, long-legged pace along their road, which was the high pass between Ovark and Wiss. He was a dark man, like most Gontishmen, dark copper-brown; gray-haired, lean and tough as a hound, tireless. He spoke seldom, ate little, slept less. His eyes and ears were very keen, and often there was a listening look on his face.

Ged did not answer him. It is not always easy to answer a mage.

A "You want to work spells," Ogion said presently, striding along. "You've drawn too much water from that well. Wait. Manhood is patience. Mastery is nine times patience. What is that herb by the path?"

"Strawflower."

"And that?"

"I don't know."

"Fourfoil, they call it." Ogion had halted, the coppershod foot of his staff near the little weed, so Ged looked closely at the plant, and plucked a dry seedpod from it, and finally asked, since Ogion said nothing more, "What is its use, Master?"

"None I know of."

B Ged kept the seedpod a while as they went on, then tossed it away.

"When you know the fourfoil in all its seasons root and leaf and flower, by sight and scent and seed, then you may learn its true name, knowing its being: which is more than its use. What, after all, is the use of you? Or of myself? Is Gont Mountain useful, or the Open Sea?" Ogion went on a halfmile or so, and said at last, "To hear, one must be silent."

The boy frowned. He did not like to be made to feel a fool. He kept back his resentment and impatience, and tried to be obedient, so that Ogion would consent at last to teach him something. For he hungered to learn, to gain power. It began to seem to him, though, that he could have learned more walking with any herb-gatherer or village sorcerer, and as they went round the mountain westward into the lonely forests past Wiss he wondered more and more what was the greatness and the magic of this great Mage Ogion. For when it rained Ogion would not even say the spell that every weatherworker knows, to send the storm aside. In a land where sorcerers come thick, like Gont or the Enlades, you may see a raincloud blundering slowly from side to side and place to place as one spell shunts it on to the next, till at last it is buffeted out over the sea where it can rain in peace. But Ogion let the rain fall where it would. He found a thick fir tree and lay down beneath it. Ged crouched among the dripping bushes wet and sullen, and wondered what was the good of having power if you were too wise to use it, and wished he had gone as prentice to that old weatherworker of the Vale, where at least he would have slept dry. He did not speak any of his thoughts aloud. He said not a word. His master smiled, and fell asleep in the rain. C

Along towards Sunreturn when the first heavy snows began to fall in the heights of Gont they came to Re Albi, Ogion's home. It is a town on the edge of the high rocks of Overfell, and its name means Falcon's Nest. From it one can see far below the deep harbor and the towers of the Port of Gont, and the ships that go in and out the gate of the bay between the Armed Cliffs, and far to the west across the sea one may make out the blue hills of Oranéa, easternmost of the Inward Isles.

The mage's house, though large and soundly built of timber, with hearth and chimney rather than a firepit, was like the huts of Ten Alders village: all one room, with a goatshed built onto one side. There was a kind of alcove in the west wall of the room, where Ged slept. Over his pallet was a window that looked out on the sea, but most often the shutters must be closed against the great winds that blew all winter from the west and north. In the dark warmth of that house Ged spent the winter, hearing the rush of rain and wind outside or the silence of snowfall, learning to write and read the Six Hundred Runes of Hardic. Very glad he was to learn this lore, for without it no mere rote-learning of charms and spells will give a man true mastery. The Hardic tongue of the Archipelago, though it has no more magic power in it than any other tongue of men, has its roots in the Old Speech, that language in which things are named with their true names: and the way to the understanding of this speech starts with the Runes that were written when the islands of the world first were raised up from the sea.

Still no marvels and enchantments occurred. All winter there was nothing but the heavy pages of the Runebook turning, and the rain and the snow falling; and Ogion would come in from roaming the icy forests or from looking after his goats, and stamp the snow off his boots, and sit down in silence by the fire. And the mage's long, listening silence would fill the room, and fill Ged's mind, until sometimes it seemed he had forgotten what words sounded like: and when Ogion spoke at last it was as if he had, just then and for the first time, invented speech. Yet the words he spoke were no great matters but had to do only with the simple things, bread and water and weather and sleep.

Metamorphoses

Changing spells are spells that change the shape of something or someone. Magical changes, called metamorphoses, are common in the folklore and mythology of most cultures. In "The First Anemones" (text page 492) the goddesses Aphrodite and Persephone take pity on the miserable Smyrna and change her into a tree. In Jewish legends, the golem is an artificial being made out of clay. When brought to life, it becomes a monster who destroys its creator. The Shangani tribe of South Africa tells of a water serpent that love and courage transform into a handsome king.

? What changes in nature may have given people the idea that magical changes were possible even in the human world? (Possible answers: a caterpillar into a butterfly; winter into spring; an apparently "dead" tree into a blossoming tree)

As the spring came on, quick and bright, Ogion often sent Ged forth to gather herbs on the meadows above Re Albi, and told him to take as long as he liked about it, giving him freedom to spend all day wandering by rainfilled streams and through the woods and over wet green fields in the sun. Ged went with delight each time, and stayed out till night; but he did not entirely forget the herbs. He kept an eye out for them, while he climbed and roamed and waded and explored, and always brought some home. He came on a meadow between two streams where the flower called white hallows grew thick, and as these blossoms are rare and prized by healers, he came back again next day. Someone else was there before him, a girl, whom he knew by sight as the daughter of the old Lord of Re Albi. He would not have spoken to her, but she came to him and greeted him pleasantly: "I know you, you are the Sparrowhawk, our mage's adept.[1] I wish you would tell me about sorcery!"

He looked down at the white flowers that brushed against her white skirt, and at first he was shy and glum and hardly answered. But she went on talking, in an open, careless, willful way that little by little set him at ease. She was a tall girl of about his own age, very sallow, almost white-skinned; her mother, they said in the village, was from Osskil or some such foreign land. Her hair fell long and straight like a fall of black water. Ged thought her very ugly, but he had a desire to please her, to win her admiration, that grew on him as they talked. She made him tell all the story of his tricks with the mist that had defeated the Kargish warriors, and she listened as if she wondered and admired, but she spoke no praise. And soon she was off on another tack: "Can you call the birds and beasts to you?" she asked.

A

"I can," said Ged.

He knew there was a falcon's nest in the cliffs above the meadow, and he summoned the bird by its name. It came, but it would not light on his wrist, being put off no doubt by the girl's presence. It screamed and struck the air with broad barred wings, and rose up on the wind.

"What do you call that kind of charm, that made the falcon come?"

"A spell of Summoning."

"Can you call the spirits of the dead to come to you, too?"

He thought she was mocking him with this question, because the falcon had not fully obeyed his summons. He would not let her mock him. "I might if I chose," he said in a calm voice.

1. **adept:** expert.

"Is it not very difficult, very dangerous, to summon a spirit?"

"Difficult, yes. Dangerous?" He shrugged.

This time he was almost certain there was admiration in her eyes.

"Can you make a love charm?"

"That is no mastery."

"True," says she, "any village witch can do it. Can you do Changing spells? Can you change your own shapes, as wizards do, they say?"

Again he was not quite sure that she did not ask the question mockingly, and so again he replied, "I might if I chose." B

She began to beg him to transform himself into anything he wished—a hawk, a bull, a fire, a tree. He put her off with short secretive words such as his master used, but he did not know how to refuse flatly when she coaxed him; and besides he did not know whether he himself believed his boast, or not. He left her, saying that his master the mage expected him at home, and he did not come back to the meadow the next day. But the day after he came again, saying to himself that he should gather more of the flowers while they bloomed. She was there, and together they waded barefoot in the boggy grass, pulling the heavy white hallow-blooms. The sun of spring shone, and she talked with him as merrily as any goatherd lass of his own village. She asked him again about sorcery, and listened wide-eyed to all he told her, so that he fell to boasting again. Then she asked him if he would not work a Changing spell, and when he put her off, she looked at him, putting back the black hair from her face, and said, "Are you afraid to do it?"

"No, I am not afraid."

She smiled a little disdainfully and said, "Maybe you are too young." C

That he would not endure. He did not say much, but he resolved that he would prove himself to her. He told her to come again to the meadow tomorrow, if she liked, and so took leave of her, and came back to the house while his master was still out. He went straight to the shelf and took down the two Lore-Books, which Ogion had never yet opened in his presence.

He looked for a spell of self-transformation, but being slow to read the runes yet and understanding little of what he read, he could not find what he sought. These books were very ancient, Ogion having them from his own master Heleth Farseer, and Heleth from his master the Mage of Perregal, and so back into the times of myth. Small and strange was the writing, overwritten and interlined by many hands, and all those hands were dust now. Yet here and there Ged understood some-

A. Reading Aloud
Ask three students to prepare to read this scene aloud in class. You will need a Narrator, the Girl, and Ged.

B. Interpreting
? Do you agree with Ged when he thinks the girl is mocking him? (Ged is proud and sensitive; he is probably misinterpreting a challenge as an insult.)

C. Character
? What impression does the girl make on you? If you could advise Ged at this point, what advice about his new friend might you give him? Do you think he would listen?

Ogion's Oaken Staff

Sir James George Frazer in the classic anthropological study *The Golden Bough* states that the people of ancient Europe worshiped the oak tree as a holy tree of great power. The oak was thought to be the sacred tree of Diana, goddess of fertility, and Jupiter, the father of the gods. The Druids of prehistoric Britain also worshiped the oak tree. They believed that the oak was the original source of fire, from lightening sent down by the sky-god.

A. Interpreting

? Why is Ged still afraid even after Ogion got rid of the shadow? (Because he has never seen Ogion, his quiet and sensible teacher, use his wizardly powers and appear as a true mage.)

B. Paraphrasing

? What does Ogion mean when he says, "Before you speak or do you must know the price that is to pay." (Either good or evil will follow any use of supernatural power. Before he acts, Ged must be sure that good will follow his action. He must also be aware that his power can be dangerous.)

C. Conflict

? What conflict does Ged feel now? (His love for Ogion vs. his pride and eagerness to learn)

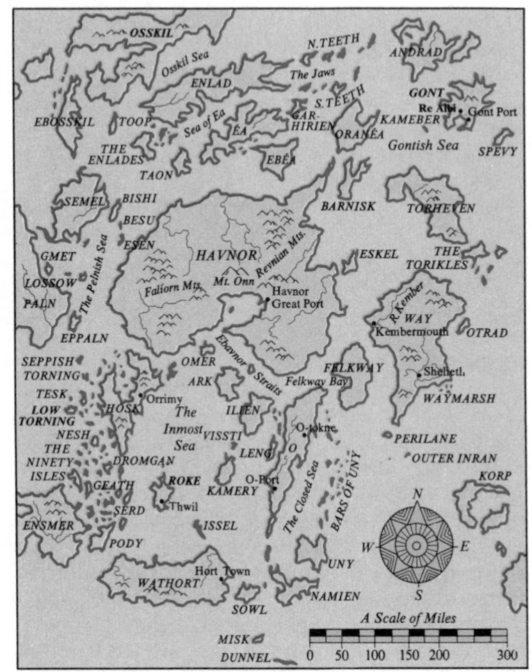

thing of what he tried to read, and with the girl's questions and her mockery always in his mind, he stopped on a page that bore a spell of summoning up the spirits of the dead.

As he read it, puzzling out the runes and symbols one by one, a horror came over him. His eyes were fixed, and he could not lift them till he had finished reading all the spell.

Then raising his head he saw it was dark in the house. He had been reading without any light, in the darkness. He could not now make out the runes when he looked down at the book. Yet the horror grew in him, seeming to hold him bound in his chair. He was cold. Looking over his shoulder he saw that something was crouching beside the closed door, a shapeless clot of shadow darker than the darkness. It seemed to reach out toward him, and to whisper, and to call to him in a whisper: but he could not understand the words.

The door was flung wide. A man entered with a white light flaming about him, a great bright figure who spoke aloud, fiercely and suddenly. The darkness and the whispering ceased and were dispelled.

A The horror went out of Ged, but still he was mortally afraid, for it was Ogion the Mage who stood there in the doorway with a brightness all about him, and the oaken staff in his hand burned with a white radiance.

Saying no word the mage came past Ged, and lighted the lamp, and put the books away on their shelf. Then he turned to the boy and said, "You will never work that spell but in peril of your power and your life. Was it for that spell you opened the books?"

"No, Master," the boy murmured, and shamefully he told Ogion what he had sought, and why.

"You do not remember what I told you, that that girl's mother, the Lord's wife, is an enchantress?"

Indeed Ogion had once said this, but Ged had not paid much attention, though he knew by now that Ogion never told him anything that he had not good reason to tell him.

"The girl herself is half a witch already. It may be the mother who sent the girl to talk to you. It may be she who opened the book to the page you read. The powers she serves are not the powers I serve: I do not know her will, but I know she does not will me well. Ged, listen to me now. Have you never thought how danger must surround power as shadow does light? This sorcery is not a game we play for pleasure or for praise. Think of this: that every word, every act of our Art is said and is done either for good, or for evil. Before you speak or do you must know the price that is to B pay!"

Driven by his shame Ged cried, "How am I to know these things, when you teach me nothing? Since I lived with you I have done nothing, seen nothing—"

"Now you have seen something," said the mage. "By the door, in the darkness, when I came in."

Ged was silent.

Ogion knelt down and built the fire on the hearth and lit it, for the house was cold. Then still kneeling he said in his quiet voice, "Ged, my young falcon, you are not bound to me or to my service. You did not come to me, but I to you. You are very young to make this choice, but I cannot make it for you. If you wish, I will send you to Roke Island, where all high arts are taught. Any craft you undertake to learn you will learn, for your power is great. Greater even than your pride, I hope. I would keep you here with me, for what I have is what you lack, but I will not keep you against your will. Now choose between Re Albi and Roke."

Ged stood dumb, his heart bewildered. He had come to love this man Ogion who had healed him C with a touch, and who had no anger: He loved him, and had not known it until now. He looked at the oaken staff leaning in the chimney-corner, remembering the radiance of it that had burned out evil from the dark, and he yearned to stay with Ogion, to go wandering through the forests with him, long and far, learning how to be silent. Yet other cravings were in him that would not be stilled, the wish for glory, the will to act. Ogion's seemed a long road toward mastery, a slow bypath to follow, when he might go sailing before the seawinds straight to the Inmost Sea, to the Isle of the Wise, where the air was bright with enchantments and the Archmage walked amidst wonders.

"Master," he said, "I will go to Roke."

So a few days later on a sunny morning of spring Ogion strode beside him down the steep road from the Overfell, fifteen miles to the Great Port of Gont. There at the landgate between carven dragons the guards of the City of Gont, seeing the mage, knelt with bared swords and welcomed him. They knew him and did him honor by the Prince's order and their own will, for ten years ago Ogion had saved the city from earthquake that would have shaken the towers of the rich down to the ground and closed the channel of the Armed Cliffs with avalanche. He had spoken to the Mountain of Gont, calming it, and had stilled the trembling precipices of the Overfell as one soothes a frightened beast. Ged had heard some talk of this, and now, wondering to see the armed guardsmen kneel to his quiet master, he remembered it. He glanced up almost in fear at this man who had stopped an earthquake; but Ogion's face was quiet as always.

They went down to the quays, where the Harbormaster came hastening to welcome Ogion and ask what service he might do. The mage told him, and at once he named a ship bound for the Inmost Sea aboard which Ged might go as passenger. "Or they will take him as windbringer," he said, "if he has the craft. They have no weatherworker aboard."

"He has some skill with mist and fog, but none with seawinds," the mage said, putting his hand lightly on Ged's shoulder. "Do not try any tricks with the sea and the winds of the sea, Sparrowhawk; you are a landsman still. Harbormaster, what is the ship's name?"

A "*Shadow,* from the Andrades, bound to Hort Town with furs and ivories. A good ship, Master Ogion."

B The mage's face darkened at the name of the ship, but he said, "So be it. Give this writing to the Warden of the School on Roke, Sparrowhawk. Go with a fair wind. Farewell!"

That was all his parting. He turned away, and went striding up the street away from the quays. Ged stood forlorn and watched his master go.

"Come along, lad," said the Harbormaster, and took him down the waterfront to the pier where *Shadow* was making ready to sail.

It might seem strange that on an island fifty miles wide, in a village under cliffs that stare out forever on the sea, a child may grow to manhood never having stepped in a boat or dipped his finger in salt water, but so it is. Farmer, goatherd, cattleherd, hunter, or artisan, the landsman looks at the ocean as at a salt unsteady realm that has nothing to do with him at all. The village two days' walk from his village is a foreign land, and the island a day's sail from his island is mere rumor, misty hills seen across the water, not solid ground like that he walks on.

So to Ged who had never been down from the heights of the mountain, the Port of Gont was an awesome and marvelous place, the great houses and towers of cut stone and waterfront of piers and docks and basins and moorages, the seaport where half a hundred boats and galleys rocked at quayside or lay hauled up and overturned for repairs or stood out at anchor in the roadstead with furled sails and closed oarports, the sailors shouting in strange dialects and the longshoremen running heavy-laden amongst barrels and boxes and coils of rope and stacks of boards, the bearded merchants in furred robes conversing quietly as C they picked their way along the slimy stones above the water, the fishermen unloading their catch, coppers pounding and shipmakers hammering and clam-sellers singing and shipmasters bellowing, and beyond all the silent, shining bay. With eyes and ears and mind bewildered he followed the Harbormaster to the broad dock where *Shadow* was tied up, and the Harbormaster brought him to the master of the ship.

With a few words spoken the ship's master agreed to take Ged as passenger to Roke, since it was a mage that asked it; and the Harbormaster left the boy with him. The master of the *Shadow* was a big man, and fat, in a red cloak trimmed with pellawi-fur such as Andradean merchants wear. He never looked at Ged but asked him in a mighty voice, "Can you work weather, boy?"

"I can."

"Can you bring the wind?"

He had to say he could not, and with that the master told him to find a place out of the way and stay in it.

The oarsmen were coming aboard now, for the ship was to go out into the roadstead before night fell, and sail with the ebb tide near dawn. There was no place out of the way, but Ged climbed up as well as he could onto the bundled, lashed, and hide-covered cargo in the stern of the ship, and clinging there watched all that passed. The oars-

Earthsea Vocabulary
pellawi-fur

A. Earthsea Map
You might have students locate Re Albi, Roke, the Inmost Sea, Great Port of Gont, the Andrades, Hort Town.

B. Foreshadowing
? How does the name of the ship foreshadow trouble? (The name *Shadow* reminds us, and Ogion, of the shadow that appeared when Ged read the spell that summons spirits.)

C. Style
Ask students to notice how Le Guin describes sights and sounds to convey Ged's feeling of bewilderment; for example, "great houses and towers of cut stone and waterfront of piers and docks." Ask them to find other examples in this paragraph.

A. Personification
Personification is a figure of speech that gives human qualities to inanimate objects. Notice that the ship is compared to someone eager to be off.

Reading Check Test: Chapters 1 and 2

1. Duny lives in the village of Ten Alders. (*True*)
2. The enemies who invade the island are Gontishmen. (*False*)
3. Ogion teaches Ged not by talking, but by showing. (*True*)
4. Ged reads a spell that puts him in danger. (*True.*)
5. Ged stays with Ogion to learn more about magic. (*False*)

B. Character
? How old is Ged? (Thirteen) What does his behavior aboard the ship tell you about him? (He is not afraid of hard work; he can be sociable. With others, he has always seemed distant, aloof, and eager to impress. Here he acts naturally and the crew respects him.)

C. Earthsea Map
You might want to have students trace the voyage: Gontish Sea, Barnisk, Torheven, Havnor, Way, Kembermouth, Felkway Bay, O Island, Ebavnor Straits, Inmost Sea, Ark, Ilien, Borilous Rocks, Kamery, Roke, and Thwil Bay.

D. Expansion
Ask students if any of them know what the purpose of the drum is here. (When ships were propelled by rowers, one person would keep the crew rowing together by hitting a drum in a regular rhythm.)

men came leaping aboard, sturdy men with great arms, while longshoremen rolled water barrels thundering out the dock and stowed them under the rowers' benches. The well-built ship rode low with her burden, yet danced a little on the lapping shore waves, ready to be gone. Then the steersman took his place at the right of the sternpost, looking forward to the ship's master, who stood on a plank let in at the jointure of the keel with the stem, which was carved as the Old Serpent of Andrad. The master roared his orders hugely, and *Shadow* was untied and towed clear of the docks by two laboring rowboats. Then the master's roar was "Open ports!" and the great oars shot rattling out, fifteen to a side. The rowers bent their strong backs while a lad up beside the master beat the stroke on a drum. Easy as a gull oared by her wings the ship went now, and the noise and hurlyburly of the City fell away suddenly behind. They came out in the silence of the waters of the bay, and over them rose the white peak of the Mountain, seeming to hang above the sea. In a shallow creek in the lee of the southern Armed Cliff the anchor was thrown over, and there they rode the night.

Of the seventy crewmen of the ship some were like Ged very young in years, though all had made their passage into manhood. These lads called him over to share food and drink with them, and were friendly though rough and full of jokes and jibes. They called him Goatherd, of course, because he was Gontish, but they did not go further than that. He was as tall and strong as the fifteen-year-olds, and quick to return either a good word or a jeer; so he made his way among them and even that first night began to live as one of them and learn their work. This suited the ship's officers, for there was no room aboard for idle passengers.

There was little enough room for the crew, and no comfort at all, in an undecked galley crowded with men and gear and cargo; but what was comfort to Ged? He lay that night among corded rolls of pelts from the northern isles and watched the stars of spring above the harbor waters and the little yellow lights of the City astern, and he slept and waked again full of delight. Before dawn the tide turned. They raised anchor and rowed softly out between the Armed Cliffs. As sunrise reddened the Mountain of Gont behind them they raised the high sail and ran southwestward over the Gontish Sea.

Between Barnisk and Torheven they sailed with a light wind, and on the second day came in sight of Havnor, the Great Island, heart and hearth of the Archipelago. For three days they worked along its eastern coast, but they did not come to shore. Not for many years did Ged set foot on that land or see the white towers of Havnor Great Port at the center of the world.

They lay over one night at Kembermouth, the northern port of Way Island, and the next at a little town on the entrance of Felkway Bay, and the next day passed the northern cape of O and entered the Ebavnor Straits. There they dropped sail and rowed, always with land on either side and always within hail of other ships, great and small, merchants and traders, some bound in from the Outer Reaches with strange cargo after a voyage of years and others that hopped like sparrows from isle to isle of the Inmost Sea. Turning southward out of the crowded Straits they left Havnor astern and sailed between the two fair islands Ark and Ilien, towered and terraced with cities, and then through rain and rising wind began to beat their way across the Inmost Sea to Roke Island.

In the night as the wind freshened to a gale they took down both sail and mast, and the next day, all day, they rowed. The long ship lay steady on the waves and went gallantly, but the steersman at the long steering-sweep in the stern looked into the rain that beat the sea and saw nothing but the rain. They went southwest by the pointing of the magnet, knowing how they went, but not through what waters. Ged heard men speak of the shoal waters north of Roke, and of the Borilous Rocks to the east; others argued that they might be far out of course by now, in the empty waters south of Kamery. Still the wind grew stronger, tearing the edges of the great waves into flying tatters of foam, and still they rowed southwest with the wind behind them. The stints at the oars were shortened, for the labor was very hard; the younger lads were set two to an oar, and Ged took his turn with the others as he had since they left Gont. When they did not row they bailed, for the seas broke heavy on the ship. So they labored among the waves that ran like smoking mountains under the wind, while the rain beat hard and cold on their backs, and the drum thumped through the noise of the storm like a heart thumping.

A man came to take Ged's place at the oar, sending him to the ship's master in the bow. Rainwater dripped from the hem of the master's cloak, but he stood stout as a winebarrel on his bit of decking and looking down at Ged he asked, "Can you abate this wind, lad?"

"No, sir."

"Have you craft with iron?"

He meant, could Ged make the compass needle point their way to Roke, making the magnet follow not its north but their need. That skill is a secret of the Seamasters, and again Ged must say no.

ANALYZING CHAPTERS 1 AND 2
Identifying Facts
1. When Duny shouts the rhyme, the goats immediately gather close around him. When his aunt sees that he is able to bind the goats to him, she realizes that he has great power, and will become a sorcerer.
2. Duny speaks two spells that cause a thick fog to gather around the village, concealing it and its inhabitants from view. He then instructs his father to have the villagers lead the Kargs to the High Fall. Some Kargs fall to their deaths, and the rest run away in terror.
3. The stranger, a mage named Ogion, says that he has come to give Duny his true name. He also offers to take the boy as his apprentice.
4. On his thirteenth birthday, Duny walks naked through the icy waters of the river Ar to the opposite shore, where Ogion awaits him. Ogion clasps his arms and whispers to him his true name: Ged.
5. He is disappointed because he feels he isn't being taught anything. He wants to learn magic spells and have adventures, but Ogion teaches him only through silence and example.
(Answers continue on page 550.)

"Well then," the master bellowed through the wind and rain, "you must find some ship to take you back to Roke from Hort Town. Roke must be west of us now, and only wizardry could bring us there through this sea. We must keep south."

Ged did not like this, for he had heard the sailors talk of Hort Town, how it was a lawless place, full of evil traffic, where men were often taken and sold into slavery in the South Reach. Returning to his labor at the oar he pulled away with his companion, a sturdy Andradean lad, and heard the drum beat the stroke and saw the lantern hung on the stern bob and flicker as the wind plucked it about, a tormented fleck of light in the rain-lashed dusk. He kept looking to westward, as often as he could in the heavy rhythm of pulling the oar. And as the ship rose on a high swell he saw for a moment over the dark smoking water a light between clouds, as it might be the last gleam of sunset: but this was a clear light, not red.

His oarmate had not seen it, but he called it out. The steersman watched for it on each rise of the great waves, and saw it as Ged saw it again, but shouted back that it was only the setting sun. Then Ged called to one of the lads that was bailing to take his place on the bench a minute, and made his way forward again along the encumbered aisle between the benches, and catching hold of the carved prow to keep from being pitched overboard he shouted up to the master, "Sir! that light to the west is Roke Island!"

"I saw no light," the master roared, but even as he spoke Ged flung out his arm pointing, and all saw the light gleam clear in the west over the heaving scud and tumult of the sea.

Not for his passenger's sake, but to save his ship from the peril of the storm, the master shouted at once to the steersman to head westward toward the light. But he said to Ged, "Boy, you speak like a Seamaster, but I tell you if you lead us wrong in this weather I will throw you over to swim to Roke!"

Now instead of running before the storm they must row across the wind's way, and it was hard: Waves striking the ship abeam pushed her always south of their new course, and rolled her, and filled her with water so that bailing must be ceaseless, and the oarsmen must watch lest the ship rolling should lift their oars out of water as they pulled and so pitch them down among the benches. It was nearly dark under the storm clouds, but now and again they made out the light to the west, enough to set course by, and so struggled on. At last the wind dropped a little, and the light grew broad before them. They rowed on, and they came as it were through a curtain, between one oarstroke and the next running out of the storm into a clear air, where the light of after-sunset glowed in the sky and on the sea. Over the foam-crested waves they saw not far off a high, round, green hill, and beneath it a town built on a small bay where boats lay at anchor, all in peace. A

The steersman leaning on his long sweep turned his head and called, "Sir! Is this true land or a witchery?"

"Keep her as she goes, you witless wooden-head! Row, you spineless slave-sons! That's Thwil Bay and the Knoll of Roke, as any fool could see! Row!"

So to the beat of the drum they rowed wearily into the bay. There it was still, so that they could hear the voices of people up in the town, and a bell ringing, and only far off the hiss and roaring of the storm. Clouds hung dark to north and east and south a mile off all about the island. But over Roke stars were coming out one by one in a clear and quiet sky.

A. Mood
? How is the weather at Roke different from the weather outside the bay? (It is clear and quiet at Roke; it is windy and stormy outside.) Notice how the sudden change in the weather creates a magical feeling of peace and beauty as the ship arrives.

Responding to the Novel

Analyzing Chapters 1 and 2

Identifying Facts

1. The novel's action begins when its main **character,** Duny, is a young boy. What happens when Duny shouts his aunt's rhyme to the goats? What does his aunt realize about him?
2. Describe how Duny protects the village when the Kargs invade Gont.
3. Duny is ill after the defeat of the Kargs, and a stranger saves him. What does the stranger say he has come to do?
4. How is the boy's name changed from Duny to Ged?

(Answers begin on page 549.)

Ogion says "Manhood is patience. Mastery is nine times patience."

6. Ged finds that he is unable to lift his eyes from the spell, and is forced to read to the end of it. As he finishes, he is filled with a sense of horror. He looks up to find that darkness has descended and that beside the door crouches a shadow darker than the darkness. It whispers and reaches out for him. At that moment, Ogion returns and dispels the darkness.

7. The weather on Roke is peaceful and calm, while on the seas a fierce storm rages.

Interpreting Meanings

8. The setting of the story is in the distant past of the planet Earthsea. The land surfaces of the planet are islands—many small ones and some very large ones. Gont is nearer to the eastern edge of the islands, closer to the Kargad Empire than to Roke.

9. Most students will reply that they are more interested in the hero, for the hints whet their appetites for more information about what happens to him.

10. From the encounter with the Kar-

(Answers continue in left-hand column.)

(Continued from top.)

gads, we learn that Ged is creative, resourceful, and brave. From the encounter with the daughter of Re Albi, we learn that he is vain and impatient and boastful. When Ged speaks with Ogion after the shadow has been dispelled, we find that he is honest.

11. Ged chooses to go to Roke because he wants to have adventure, see new places, and learn more quickly about magic.

Answers will vary.

5. Why is Ged disappointed during his first days with Ogion? When Ged complains, what does Ogion tell Ged about manhood and mastery?
6. When Ged tries to win the admiration of the daughter of the old Lord of Re Albi, he looks through Ogion's Lore-Books. Describe what happens when he starts reading from the page that tells how to summon spirits.
7. On the way to the island of Roke, Ged's boat hits a furious storm. How does the weather on Roke compare to the weather on the seas around it?

Interpreting Meanings

SRW p. 79

8. Use the maps to help you understand the novel's imaginary **setting**—the time and place in which the events occur. Is Earthsea made up of large or small bodies of land? Is Gont, Ged's home island, at the center or at the edge of this world? Is Gont closer to the dangerous Kargads or to the magical isle of Roke?
9. A **flashback** is a scene in a narrative that interrupts the present action to "flash backward" and tell what happened at an earlier time. The first paragraph of the novel suggests that the story will be one long flashback from a much later time. Do these hints about the eventual fate of the hero make you more interested or less interested in him? Explain.
10. A **conflict** is a struggle between two opposing forces. In these two chapters, Ged has several important conflicts. The way a character overcomes a conflict can give you insight into his or her personality. What do you learn about Ged from the following three confrontations: with the Kargads, with the daughter of the old Lord of Re Albi, and with Ogion (when Ogion returns home and finds Ged reading the dangerous spell)?
11. Ged chooses to go to the school on Roke rather than to stay with Ogion. Explain Ged's reasons for his choice. Would you have made the same choice if you were in Ged's situation? Why or why not?

Writing About the Novel

A Creative Response

Predicting the Outcome. Pretend you have a power even the wizards of Earthsea don't have: You can predict the future. Look into your crystal ball, and tell the fortune of Ged on the isle of Roke. What will happen to him there? Will he succeed and become a wizard? Will the shadow he saw in Ogion's home return? Will Ged resent the rule of the masters of Roke, just as he sometimes resented Ogion's? What new powers will he acquire? Use your imagination and write two paragraphs that answer these questions.

See Teacher's Manual page 184.

Analyzing Language and Vocabulary

Imaginary Words

Many herbs grow on the Earthsea islands. Some of them are real and some have been made up by the writer. You have read that Duny's aunt, the witch, collects "mint and moly and thyme, yarrow and rushwash and paramal, kingsfoil, clovenfoot, tansy, and bay." Ogion shows Ged "strawflower" and "fourfoil." Guess which of these herbs are real and which ones are made up. Then answer the following questions.

1. Use a good dictionary to look up the herbs' names. Were you surprised to find that some that sounded invented are actually real? Which others, if any, sound real but are not?
2. One of the herbs is not real, but Le Guin did not invent it—it appears in many myths. This herb is *moly.* What mythical characteristics does it have?
3. Some of the imaginary herb names suggest what the plants look like, what they are used for, or what some of their other characteristics are. Pick three of the imaginary herbs, and tell how you think an Earthsea dictionary would describe them.
4. Invent two imaginary herbs of your own, and list the qualities of each one.

For answers, see Teacher's Manual page 184.

Summary: Chapter 3

At the School Ged develops an intense rivalry with a more advanced student named Jasper. Another advanced student, Vetch, becomes Ged's close friend. Ged excels as a student, soon outdistancing his classmates. Eager to learn advanced arts, Ged asks the Master Hand to teach him the spells of transformation. The mage refuses, saying that wizards must be careful with their knowledge, for their actions can change the balance of the world and Ged is not ready for that yet. Ged is dissatisfied but accepts the Master Hand's decision, and goes to study the thousands of true names that a wizard needs to know. In this world, knowledge of an object's true name gives a person power over that thing. Once again Ged displays his abilities, learning what he needs to know several months before his classmates.

Chapter 3
The School for Wizards

Ged slept that night aboard *Shadow,* and early in the morning parted with those first sea-comrades of his, they shouting good wishes cheerily after him as he went up the docks. The town of Thwil is not large, its high houses huddling close over a few steep narrow streets. To Ged, however, it seemed a city, and not knowing where to go he asked the first townsman of Thwil he met where he would find the Warder of the School on Roke. The man looked at him sidelong a while and said, "The wise don't need to ask, the fool asks in vain," and so went on along the street. Ged went uphill till he came out into a square, rimmed on three sides by the houses with their sharp slate roofs and on the fourth side by the wall of a great building whose few small windows were higher than the chimneytops of the houses: a fort or castle it seemed, built of mighty gray blocks of stone. In the square beneath it market booths were set up and there was some coming and going of people. Ged asked his question of an old woman with a basket of mussels, and she replied, "You cannot always find the Warder where he is, but sometimes you find him where he is not," and went on crying her mussels to sell.

In the great building, near one corner, there was a mean little door of wood. Ged went to this and knocked loud. To the old man who opened the door he said, "I bear a letter from the Mage Ogion of Gont to the Warder of the School on this island. I want to find the Warder, but I will not hear more riddles and scoffing!" A B

"This is the School," the old man said mildly. "I am the doorkeeper. Enter if you can."

Ged stepped forward. It seemed to him that he had passed through the doorway: yet he stood outside on the pavement where he had stood before.

Once more he stepped forward, and once more he remained standing outside the door. The doorkeeper, inside, watched him with mild eyes.

Ged was not so much baffled as angry, for this seemed like a further mockery to him. With voice and hand he made the Opening spell which his aunt had taught him long ago; it was the prize among all her stock of spells, and he wove it well now. But it was only a witch's charm, and the power that held this doorway was not moved at all.

A. Vocabulary
Here the word *mean* means unimposing.

B. Character
? What seems to be Ged's attitude when he greets the old man? (Arrogant and impatient) Why do you think he has this attitude? (He mistakenly believes that the townspeople are mocking him. Because he feels uncomfortable in a new situation, he is sensitive to the reactions of others.)

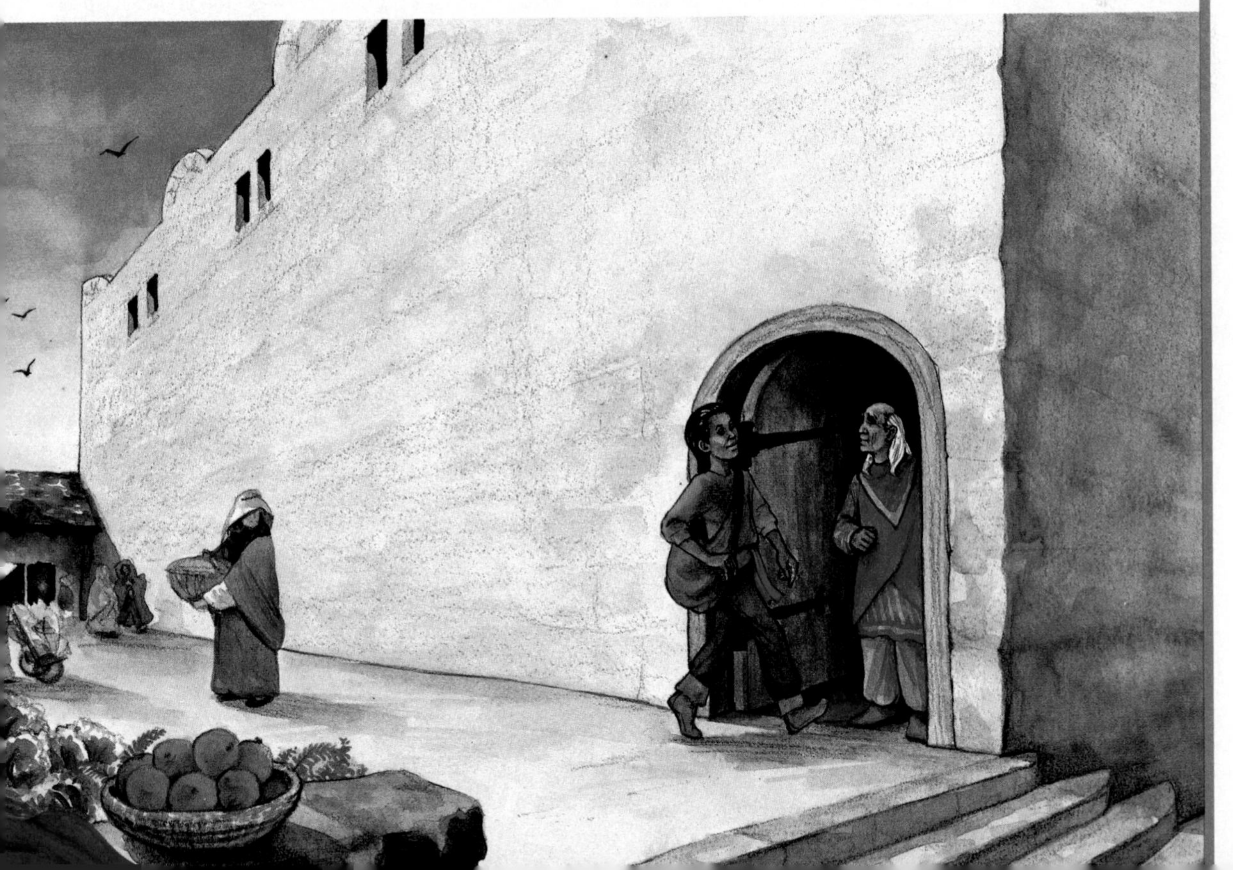

A. Character

? What does the doorkeeper cause Ged to realize? (He cannot enter without the doorkeeper's help.) What qualities in Ged does the doorkeeper test? (Humility—Ged must ask for help; trust—Ged must say his true name.)

SUPPLEMENTARY SUPPORT MATERIAL: CHAPTERS 3 AND 4

1. Vocabulary Activity Sheet
2. Reading Check Test blackline master
3. Selection Test (page 215 of Test Book)
4. Workbook (page 155)

DEVELOPING VOCABULARY

The following words appear on a test in the Test Book, page 216. (See also the Vocabulary Activity Sheet.)

scoff	intricate
quaver	perilous
disdain	humiliate
quench	benign
condescend	haggard

B. Foreshadowing

? What is the bad omen here? (The light is behind Ged, but a shadow follows him inside.)

C. Expansion

Important to the creation of Earthsea, the "thousand-leaved tree" is borrowed from Norse mythology. The World-Tree of Yggdrasill (ig′ drə·sil) was a giant ash tree whose roots held the universe together.

D. Setting and Atmosphere

Have students pick out the images that appeal to the senses in this paragraph. What atmosphere do these details create? (A mood of magic, wonder, peace, and happiness)

E. Responding

? Why is this a good rune for Ogion? (Because he is a quiet, but wise, mage)

When that failed Ged stood a long while there on the pavement. A At last he looked at the old man who waited inside. "I cannot enter," he said unwillingly, "unless you help me."

The doorkeeper answered, "Say your name."

Then again Ged stood still a while; for a man never speaks his own name aloud, until more than his life's safety is at stake.

B "I am Ged," he said aloud. Stepping forward then he entered the open doorway. Yet it seemed to him that though the light was behind him, a shadow followed him in at his heels.

He saw also as he turned that the doorway through which he had come was not plain wood as he had thought, but ivory without joint or seam: It was cut, as he knew later, from a tooth of the Great Dragon. The door that the old man closed behind him was of polished horn, through which the daylight shone dimly, and on its inner face was C carved the Thousand-Leaved Tree.

"Welcome to this house, lad," the doorkeeper said, and without saying more led him through halls and corridors to an open court far inside the walls of the building. The court was partly paved with stone, but was roofless, and on a grass plot a fountain played under young trees in the sunlight. There Ged waited alone some while. He stood still, and his heart beat hard, for it seemed to him that he felt presences and powers at work unseen about him here, and he knew that this place was built not only of stone but of magic stronger than stone. He stood in the innermost room of the House of the Wise, and it was open to the sky. Then suddenly he was aware of a man clothed in white who watched him through the falling water of the fountain.

D As their eyes met, a bird sang aloud in the branches of the tree. In that moment Ged understood the singing of the bird, and the language of the water falling in the basin of the fountain, and the shape of the clouds, and the beginning and end of the wind that stirred the leaves: It seemed to him that he himself was a word spoken by the sunlight.

Then that moment passed, and he and the world were as before, or almost as before. He went forward to kneel before the Archmage, holding out to him the letter written by Ogion.

The Archmage Nemmerle, Warder of Roke, was an old man, older it was said than any man then living. His voice quavered like the bird's voice when he spoke, welcoming Ged kindly. His hair and beard and robe were white, and he seemed as if all darkness and heaviness had been leached out of him by the slow usage of the years, leaving him white and worn as driftwood that has been a century adrift. "My eyes are old, I cannot read what your master writes," he said in his quavering voice. "Read me the letter, lad."

So Ged made out and read aloud the writing, which was in Hardic runes, and said no more than this: *Lord Nemmerle! I send you one who will be greatest of the wizards of Gont, if the wind blow true*. This was signed, not with Ogion's true name which Ged had never yet learned, but with Ogion's rune, the Closed Mouth. E

"He who holds the earthquake on a leash has sent you, for which be doubly welcome. Young Ogion was dear to me, when he came here from Gont. Now tell me of the seas and portents[1] of your voyage, lad."

"A fair passage, Lord, but for the storm yesterday."

"What ship brought you here?"

"*Shadow,* trading from the Andrades."

"Whose will sent you here?"

"My own."

The Archmage looked at Ged and looked away, and began to speak in a tongue that Ged did not understand, mumbling as will an old old man whose wits go wandering among the years and islands. Yet in among his mumbling there were words of what the bird had sung and what the water had said falling. He was not laying a spell and yet there was a power in his voice that moved Ged's mind so that the boy was bewildered, and for an instant seemed to behold himself standing in a strange vast desert place alone among the shadows. Yet all along he was in the sunlit court, hearing the fountain fall.

A great black bird, a raven of Osskil, came walking over the stone terrace and the grass. It came to the hem of the Archmage's robe and stood there all black with its dagger beak and eyes like pebbles, staring sidelong at Ged. It pecked three times on the white staff Nemmerle leaned on, and the old wizard ceased his muttering, and smiled. "Run and play, lad," he said at last as to a little child. Ged knelt again on one knee to him. When he rose, the Archmage was gone. Only the raven stood eyeing him, its beak outstretched as if to peck the vanished staff.

It spoke, in what Ged guessed might be the speech of Osskil. "Terrenon ussbuk!" It said croaking. "Terrenon ussbuk orrek!" And it strutted off as it had come.

Ged turned to leave the courtyard, wondering where he should go. Under the archway he was met by a tall youth who greeted him very cour-

1. **portents:** signs or warnings of an event that is about to occur.

teously, bowing his head. "I am called Jasper, Enwit's son of the Domain of Eolg on the Havnor Isle. I am at your service today, to show you about the Great House and answer your questions as I can. How shall I call you, Sir?"

A Now it seemed to Ged, a mountain villager who had never been among the sons of rich merchants and noblemen, that this fellow was scoffing at him with his "service" and his "Sir" and his bowing and scraping. He answered shortly, "Sparrowhawk, they call me."

The other waited a moment as if expecting some more mannerly response, and getting none straightened up and turned a little aside. He was two or three years older than Ged, very tall, and he moved and carried himself with stiff grace, posing (Ged thought) like a dancer. He wore a gray cloak with hood thrown back. The first place he took Ged was the wardrobe room, where as a student of the school Ged might find himself another such cloak that fitted him, and any other clothing he might need. He put on the dark gray cloak he had chosen, and Jasper said, "Now you are one of us."

Jasper had a way of smiling faintly as he spoke which made Ged look for a jeer hidden in his polite words. "Do clothes make the mage?" he answered, sullen.

"No," said the old boy. "Though I have heard that manners make the man. Where now?"

"Where you will. I do not know the house."

Jasper took him down the corridors of the Great House showing him the open courts and the roofed halls, the Room of Shelves where the books of lore and rune-tomes were kept, the great Hearth Hall where all the school gathered on festival days, and upstairs, in the towers and under the roofs, the small cells where the students and Masters slept. Ged's was in the South Tower, with a window looking down over the steep roofs of Thwil town to the sea. Like the other sleeping-cells it had no furniture but a straw-filled mattress in the corner. "We live very plain here," said Jasper. "But I expect you won't mind that."

"I'm used to it." Presently, trying to show himself an equal of this polite disdainful youth, he added, "I suppose you weren't, when you first came."

Jasper looked at him, and his look said without words, "What could you possibly know about what I, son of the Lord of the Domain of Eolg on the Isle of Havnor, am or am not used to?" What Jasper said aloud was simply, "Come on this way."

A gong had been rung while they were upstairs, and they came down to eat the noon meal at the Long Table of the refectory,[2] along with a hundred or more boys and young men. Each waited on himself, joking with the cooks through the window-hatches of the kitchen that opened into the refectory, loading his plate from great bowls of food that steamed on the sills, sitting where he pleased at the Long Table. "They say," Jasper told Ged, "that no matter how many sit at this table, there is always room." Certainly there was room both for many noisy groups of boys talking and eating mightily, and for older fellows, their gray cloaks clasped with silver at the neck, who sat more quietly by pairs or alone, with grave, pondering faces, as if they had much to think about. Jasper took Ged to sit with a heavyset fellow called Vetch, who said nothing much but shoveled in his food with a will. He had the accent of the East Reach, and was very dark of skin, not red-brown like Ged and Jasper and most folk of the Archipelago, but black-brown. He was plain, and his manners were not polished. He grumbled about the dinner when he had finished it, but then turning to Ged said, "At least it's not illusion, like so much around here; it sticks to your ribs." Ged did not know what he meant, but he felt a certain liking for him, and was glad when after the meal he stayed with them. B

They went down into the town, that Ged might learn his way about it. Few and short as were the streets of Thwil, they turned and twisted curiously among the high-roofed houses, and the way was easy to lose. It was a strange town, and strange also its people, fishermen and workmen and artisans[3] like any others, but so used to the sorcery that is ever at play on the Isle of the Wise that they seemed half sorcerers themselves. They talked (as Ged had learned) in riddles, and not one of them would blink to see a boy turn into a fish or a house fly up into the air, but knowing it for a schoolboy prank would go on cobbling shoes or cutting up mutton, unconcerned.

Coming up past the Back Door and around through the gardens of the Great House, the three boys crossed the clear-running Thwilburn on a wooden bridge and went on northward among woods and pastures. The path climbed and wound. They passed oak groves where shadows lay thick for all the brightness of the sun. There was one grove not far away to the left that Ged could never quite see plainly. The path never reached it, though it always seemed to be about to. He could not even make out what kind of trees they were. Vetch, seeing him gazing, said softly,

---

2. **refectory** (ri·fek'tər·ē): dining hall.
3. **artisans** (är'tə·z'nz): skilled workers or craftspeople.

A. Conflict
Ask students to notice the beginning of this important conflict between Ged, the protagonist of the novel, and Jasper, the most important human antagonist.
? Who do you think starts the conflict? Is Ged correct in feeling that Jasper is mocking him?

B. Character
? Why do you think Ged likes Vetch but not Jasper? (Vetch is plain and unrefined, more like Ged. Jasper is overly polite and polished. However, so far, Jasper has given Ged no real reason to dislike him. Ged dislikes him because he feels intimidated by him.)

Earthsea Vocabulary
sparkweed
werelight

A. Allusion
Have students note this reference to Earthsea's past. Such allusions give a fictional work the feeling and flavor of a true story.

B. Making Inferences
? What might be Ogion's opinion of Jasper? (Ogion would think Jasper a fool since Ogion believes that magic should be used sparingly, never for sport.)

C. Interpreting
? Whose words are these? (Ogion's)

D. Character
? What do you think Ged may learn from Vetch? (Friendship and kindness)

"That is the Immanent[4] Grove. We can't come there, yet. . . ."

In the hot sunlit pastures yellow flowers bloomed. "Sparkweed," said Jasper. "They grow where the wind dropped the ashes of burning Ilien, when Erreth-Akbe defended the Inward Isles from the Firelord." He blew on a withered flowerhead, and the seeds shaken loose went up on the wind like sparks of fire in the sun. **A**

The path led them up and around the base of a great green hill, round and treeless, the hill that Ged had seen from the ship as they entered the charmed waters of Roke Island. On the hillside Jasper halted. "At home in Havnor I heard much about Gontish wizardry, and always in praise, so that I've wanted for a long time to see the manner of it. Here now we have a Gontishman; and we stand on the slopes of Roke Knoll, whose roots go down to the center of the earth. All spells are strong here. Play us a trick, Sparrowhawk. Show us your style." **B**

Ged, confused and taken aback, said nothing.

"Later on, Jasper," Vetch said in his plain way. "Let him be a while."

"He has either skill or power, or the doorkeeper wouldn't have let him in. Why shouldn't he show it, now as well as later? Right, Sparrowhawk?"

"I have both skill and power," Ged said. "Show me what kind of thing you're talking about."

"Illusions, of course—tricks, games of seeming. Like this!"

Pointing his finger Jasper spoke a few strange words, and where he pointed on the hillside among the green grasses a little thread of water trickled, and grew, and now a spring gushed out and the water went running down the hill. Ged put his hand in the stream and it felt wet, drank of it and it was cool. Yet for all that it would quench no thirst, being but illusion. Jasper with another word stopped the water, and the grasses waved dry in the sunlight. "Now you, Vetch," he said with his cool smile.

Vetch scratched his head and looked glum, but he took up a bit of earth in his hand and began to sing tunelessly over it, molding it with his dark fingers and shaping it, pressing it, stroking it: And suddenly it was a small creature like a bumblebee or furry fly, that flew humming off over Roke Knoll, and vanished.

Ged stood staring, crestfallen. What did he know but mere village witchery, spells to call goats, cure warts, move loads, or mend pots?

"I do no such tricks as these," he said. That was enough for Vetch, who was for going on; but Jasper said, "Why don't you?"

"Sorcery is not a game. We Gontishmen do not play it for pleasure or praise," Ged answered haughtily. **C**

"What do you play it for," Jasper inquired, "—money?"

"No!" But he could not think of anything more to say that would hide his ignorance and save his pride. Jasper laughed, not ill-humoredly, and went on, leading them on around Roke Knoll. And Ged followed, sullen and sore-hearted, knowing he had behaved like a fool, and blaming Jasper for it.

That night as he lay wrapped in his cloak on the mattress in his cold unlit cell of stone, in the utter silence of the Great House of Roke, the strangeness of the place and the thought of all the spells and sorceries that had been worked there began to come over him heavily. Darkness surrounded him, dread filled him. He wished he were anywhere else but Roke. But Vetch came to the door, a little bluish ball of werelight nodding over his head to light the way, and asked if he could come in and talk a while. He asked Ged about Gont, and then spoke fondly of his own home isles of the East Reach, telling how the smoke of village hearthfires is blown across that quiet sea at evening between the small islands with funny names: Korp, Kopp, and Holp, Venway and Vemish, Iffish, Koppish, and Sneg. When he sketched the shapes of those lands on the stones of the floor with his finger to show Ged how they lay, the lines he drew shone dim as if drawn with a stick of silver for a while before they faded. Vetch had been three years at the School, and soon would be made Sorcerer; he thought no more of performing the lesser arts of magic than a bird thinks of flying. Yet a greater, unlearned skill he possessed, which was the art of kindness. That night, and always from then on, he offered and gave Ged friendship, a sure and open friendship which Ged could not help but return. **D**

Yet Vetch was also friendly to Jasper, who had made Ged into a fool that first day on Roke Knoll. Ged would not forget this, nor, it seemed, would Jasper, who always spoke to him with a polite voice and a mocking smile. Ged's pride would not be slighted or condescended to. He swore to prove to Jasper, and to all the rest of them among whom Jasper was something of a leader, how great his power really was—someday. For none of them, for all their clever tricks, had saved a village by wizardry. Of none of them had Ogion written that he would be the greatest wizard of Gont.

So bolstering up his pride, he set all his strong will on the work they gave him, the lessons and

4. **immanent** (im'ə·nənt): living or remaining within.

crafts and histories and skills taught by the gray-cloaked Masters of Roke, who were called the Nine.

A Part of each day he studied with the Master Chanter, learning the Deeds of heroes and the Lays of wisdom, beginning with the oldest of all songs, *The Creation of Éa*. Then with a dozen other lads he would practice with the Master Windkey at arts of wind and weather. Whole bright days of spring and early summer they spent out in Roke Bay in light catboats, practicing steering by word, and stilling waves, and speaking to the world's wind, and raising up the magewind. These are very intricate skills, and frequently Ged's head got whacked by the swinging boom as the boat jibed under a wind suddenly blowing backwards, or his boat and another collided though they had the whole bay to navigate in, or all three boys in his boat went swimming unexpectedly as the boat was swamped by a huge, unintended wave. There were quieter expeditions ashore, other days, with the Master Herbal who taught the ways and properties of things that grow; and the Master Hand taught sleight and jugglery and the lesser arts of Changing.

At all these studies Ged was apt, and within a month was bettering lads who had been a year at Roke before him. Especially the tricks of illusion came to him so easily that it seemed he had been born knowing them and needed only to be reminded. The Master Hand was a gentle and lighthearted old man, who had endless delight in the wit and beauty of the crafts he taught; Ged soon felt no awe of him, but asked him for this spell and that spell, and always the Master smiled and showed him what he wanted. But one day, having it in mind to put Jasper to shame at last, Ged said to the Master Hand in the Court of Seeming, "Sir, all these charms are much the same; knowing one, you know them all. And as soon as the spell-weaving ceases, the illusion vanishes. Now if I make a pebble into a diamond"—and he did so with a word and a flick of his wrist—"what must I do to make that diamond remain diamond? How is the changing-spell locked, and made to last?"

The Master Hand looked at the jewel that glittered on Ged's palm, bright as the prize of a dragon's hoard. The old Master murmured one word, "*Tolk,*" and there lay the pebble, no jewel but a rough gray bit of rock. The Master took it and held it out on his own hand. "This is a rock; *tolk* in the True Speech," he said, looking mildly up at Ged now. "A bit of the stone of which Roke Isle is made, a little bit of the dry land on which men live. It is itself. It is part of the world. By the Illusion-Change you can make it look like a diamond—or a flower or a fly or an eye or a flame." The rock flickered from shape to shape as he named them, and returned to rock. "But that is mere seeming. Illusion fools the beholder's senses; it makes him see and hear and feel that the thing is changed. But it does not change the thing. To change this rock into a jewel, you must change its true name. And to do that, my son, even to so small a scrap of the world, is to change the world. It can be done. Indeed it can be done. It is the art of the Master Changer, and you will learn it, when you are ready to learn it. But you must not change one thing, one pebble, one grain of sand, until you know what good and evil will follow on that act. The world is in balance, in Equilibrium.[5] A wizard's power of Changing and of Summoning can shake the balance of the world. It is dangerous, that power. It is most perilous. It must follow knowledge, and serve need. To light a candle is to cast a shadow. . . ."

He looked down at the pebble again. "A rock is a good thing, too, you know," he said, speaking less gravely. "If the Isles of Earthsea were all made of diamond, we'd lead a hard life here. Enjoy illusions, lad, and let the rocks be rocks." He smiled, but Ged left dissatisfied. Press a mage for his secrets and he would always talk, like Ogion, about balance, and danger, and the dark. But surely a wizard, one who had gone past these childish tricks of illusion to the true arts of Summoning and Change, was powerful enough to do what he pleased, and balance the world as seemed best to him, and drive back darkness with his own light. B

In the corridor he met Jasper, who, since Ged's accomplishments began to be praised about the School, spoke to him in a way that seemed more friendly, but was more scoffing. "You look gloomy, Sparrowhawk," he said now, "did your juggling-charms go wrong?"

Seeking as always to put himself on equal footing with Jasper, Ged answered the question ignoring its ironic tone. "I'm sick of juggling," he said, "sick of these illusion-tricks, fit only to amuse idle lords in their castles and Domains. The only true magic they've taught me yet on Roke is making werelight, and some weatherworking. The rest is mere foolery."

"Even foolery is dangerous," said Jasper, "in the hands of a fool."

At that Ged turned as if he had been slapped, and took a step toward Jasper; but the older boy smiled as if he had not intended any insult, nodded his head in his stiff, graceful way, and went on.

5. **equilibrium:** state of balance between opposing forces.

Earthsea Vocabulary
magewind
windkey
tolk

A. Allusion
? What allusion do you find here? Where did it appear previously? (*The Creation of Éa.* See page 537.)

B. Foreshadowing
? How does Ged's reaction to the speech of the Master Hand foreshadow later events? (Even though the words of the Master Hand are logical, and echo what Ogion has told him, Ged dismisses them in his impatience. This foreshadows his attempt to cast a changing spell—one that will be driven by his pride and may actually tilt the balance between good and evil.)

Earthsea Vocabulary
spellboat

A. Inference
? Why might Jasper now hate Ged? (Ged is younger but he learns quickly and seems to have more power than most of the other boys on Roke. Jasper feels threatened by Ged's progress.)

B. Character
? What characteristic gives him the most trouble and causes him to be at war with his own better nature? (Pride) Point out that pride or "hubris" was the "tragic flaw" that caused the downfall of heroes in Greek tragedy. Ged's pride is excessive. He has always craved power; he hopes one day to be powerful enough to "balance the world as seemed best to him."

C. Word Choice
Refer to "The Founding of Earthsea," on page 614, where Le Guin tells the reader that she chose the name "Kurremkarmerruk" because she meant it to look formidable. Why do you think Le Guin chose a "formidable" name for the Master Namer? (The task of learning the true name of everything was difficult but very important. The task was as endless and formidable as the teacher's name.)

Standing there with rage in his heart looking after Jasper, Ged swore to himself to outdo his rival, and not in some mere illusion-match but in a test of power. He would prove himself, and humiliate Jasper. He would not let the fellow stand there looking down at him, graceful, disdainful, hateful.

A Ged did not stop to think why Jasper might hate him. He only knew why he hated Jasper. The other prentices had soon learned they could seldom match themselves against Ged either in sport or in earnest, and they said of him, some in praise and some in spite, "He's a wizard born, he'll never let you beat him." Jasper alone neither praised him nor avoided him, but simply looked down at him, smiling slightly. And therefore Jasper stood alone as his rival, who must be put to shame.

B He did not see, or would not see, that in this rivalry, which he clung to and fostered as part of his own pride, there was anything of the danger, the darkness, of which the Master Hand had mildly warned him.

When he was not moved by pure rage, he knew very well that he was as yet no match for Jasper, or any of the older boys, and so he kept at his work and went on as usual. At the end of summer the work was slackened somewhat, so there was more time for sport: spellboat races down in the harbor, feats of illusion in the courts of the Great House, and in the long evenings, in the groves, wild games of hide-and-seek where hiders and seeker were both invisible and only voices moved laughing and calling among the trees, following and dodging the quick, faint werelights. Then as autumn came they set to their tasks afresh, practicing new magic. So Ged's first months at Roke went by fast, full of passions and wonders.

In winter it was different. He was sent with seven other boys across Roke Island to the farthest northmost cape, where stands the Isolate Tower. There by himself lived the Master Namer, who was called by a name that had no meaning in any language, Kurremkarmerruk. No farm or C dwelling lay within miles of the Tower. Grim it stood above the northern cliffs, gray were the clouds over the seas of winter, endless the lists and ranks and rounds of names that the Namer's eight pupils must learn. Amongst them in the Tower's high room Kurremkarmerruk sat on a high seat, writing down lists of names that must be learned before the ink faded at midnight leaving the parchment blank again. It was cold and half-dark and always silent there except for the scratching of the Master's pen and the sighing, maybe, of a student who must learn before midnight the name of every cape, point, bay, sound, inlet, channel, harbor, shallows, reef, and rock of

The Importance of Names

Throughout the ancient world names had magical significance. In India, China, and Egypt, and among many North American Indian tribes, people had at least two names, one by which they were generally known, and a secret name. Those who knew a person's secret name were thought to have magical power over that person. Among many tribes the secret name is given in an initiation ceremony when the child reaches puberty. As a child, Le Guin first learned about the importance of names from Lady Frazer's *Leaves from the Golden Bough* (1924), a children's edition of *The Golden Bough* which Le Guin has listed as an early influence on her work.

the shores of Lossow, a little islet of the Pelnish Sea. If the student complained the Master might say nothing, but lengthen the list; or he might say, "He who would be Seamaster must know the true name of every drop of water in the sea."

Ged sighed sometimes, but he did not complain. He saw that in this dusty and fathomless matter of learning the true name of every place, thing, and being, the power he wanted lay like a jewel at the bottom of a dry well. For magic consists in this, the true naming of a thing. So Kurremkarmerruk had said to them, once, their first night in the Tower; he never repeated it, but Ged did not forget his words. "Many a mage of great power," he had said, "has spent his whole life to find out the name of one single thing—one single lost or hidden name. And still the lists are not finished. Nor will they be, till world's end. Listen, and you will see why. In the world under the sun, and in the other world that has no sun, there is much that has nothing to do with men and men's speech, and there are powers beyond our power. But magic, true magic, is worked only by those beings who speak the Hardic tongue of Earthsea, or the Old Speech from which it grew.

"That is the language dragons speak, and the language Segoy spoke who made the islands of the world, and the language of our lays and songs, spells, enchantments, and invocations.[6] Its words lie hidden and changed among our Hardic words. We call the foam on waves *sukien*: that word is made from two words of the Old Speech, *suk,* feather, and *inien,* the sea. Feather of the sea, is foam. But you cannot charm the foam calling it *sukien;* you must use its own true name in the Old Speech, which is *essa*. Any witch knows a few of these words in the Old Speech, and a mage knows many. But there are many more, and some have been lost over the ages, and some have been hidden, and some are known only to dragons and to the Old Powers of Earth, and some are known to no living creature; and no man could learn them all. For there is no end to that language.

"Here is the reason. The sea's name is *inien,* well and good. But what we call the Inmost Sea has its own name also in the Old Speech. Since no thing can have two true names, *inien* can mean only 'all the sea except the Inmost Sea.' And of course it does not mean even that, for there are seas and bays and straits beyond counting that bear names of their own. So if some Mage-Seamaster were mad enough to try to lay a spell of storm or calm over all the ocean, his spell must say not only that word *inien,* but the name of every stretch and bit and part of the sea through all the Archipelago and all the Outer Reaches and beyond to where names cease. Thus, that which gives us the power to work magic, sets the limits of that power. A mage can control only what is near him, what he can name exactly and wholly. And this is well. If it were not so, the wickedness of the powerful or the folly of the wise would long ago have sought to change what cannot be changed, and Equilibrium would fail. The unbalanced sea would overwhelm the islands where we perilously dwell, and in the old silence all voices and all names would be lost."

Ged thought long on these words, and they went deep in his understanding. Yet the majesty of the task could not make the work of that long year in the Tower less hard and dry; and at the end of the year Kurremkarmerruk said to him, "You have made a good beginning." But no more. Wizards speak truth, and it was true that all the mastery of Names that Ged had toiled to win that year was the mere start of what he must go on learning all his life. He was let go from the Isolate Tower sooner than those who had come with him, for he had learned quicker; but that was all the praise he got.

He walked south across the island alone in the early winter, along townless empty roads. As night came on it rained. He said no charm to keep the rain off him, for the weather of Roke was in the hands of the Master Windkey and might not be tampered with. He took shelter under a great pendick tree, and lying there wrapped in his cloak he thought of his old master Ogion, who might still be on his autumn wanderings over the heights of Gont, sleeping out with leafless branches for a roof and falling rain for housewalls. That made Ged smile, for he found the thought of Ogion always a comfort to him. He fell asleep with a peaceful heart, there in the cold darkness full of the whisper of water. At dawn waking he lifted his head; the rain had ceased; he saw, sheltered in the folds of his cloak, a little animal curled up asleep which had crept there for warmth. He wondered, seeing it, for it was a rare strange beast, an otak. **A**

These creatures are found only on four southern isles of the Archipelago, Roke, Ensmer, Pody, and Wathort. They are small and sleek, with broad faces, and fur dark brown or brindle, and great bright eyes. Their teeth are cruel and their temper fierce, so they are not made pets of. They have no call or cry or any voice. Ged stroked this one, and it woke and yawned, showing a small brown tongue and white teeth, but it was not afraid.

6. **invocations** (in'və·kā'shənz): calling on spirits in acts of conjuring.

Earthsea Vocabulary
sukien
suk
inien
essa
pendick tree
otak

A. Personality Change
Point out that Ged's experiences in the Tower seem to have quieted him and made him feel more at peace with himself. He also seems to have gained a new appreciation for nature.

Nonhuman Companions
In many ancient and contemporary quest stories, the hero has a nonhuman companion who often teaches the hero about friendship, loyalty, and trust. Science fantasy films also use this device, which is most appealing to children and young adolescents. Ask your students for examples of human/nonhuman friendships in films and cartoons.

Earthsea Vocabulary
hoeg

A. Vocabulary
In the seventeenth century on Earth, those who were accused of witchcraft were said to have kept "familiars" or demons in the form of an animal.

B. Long Dance
This is like our midsummer festival, celebrated (like winter solstice) with bonfires, dancing, and feasting. Midsummer Day is the longest day of sunlight, June 21 or 22 in the northern hemisphere.

C. Similes
Notice how Le Guin brings this magical scene to life by using similes (comparisons using "like" or "as") to create images. ("A bird . . . all white with a tail like a fall of snow.") Ask students to find additional similes in this scene.

"Otak," he said, and then remembering the thousand names of beasts he had learned in the Tower he called it by its true name in the Old Speech, "Hoeg! Do you want to come with me?"

The otak sat itself down on his open hand, and began to wash its fur.

He put it up on his shoulder in the folds of his hood, and there it rode. Sometimes during the day it jumped down and darted off into the woods, but is always came back to him, once with a woodmouse it had caught. He laughed and told it to eat the mouse, for he was fasting, this night being the Festival of Sunreturn. So he came in the wet dusk past Roke Knoll, and saw bright werelights playing in the rain over the roofs of the Great House, and he entered there and was welcomed by his Masters and companions in the firelit hall.

It was like a homecoming to Ged, who had no home to which he could ever return. He was happy to see so many faces he knew, and happiest to see Vetch come forward to greet him with a wide smile on his dark face. He had missed his friend this year more than he knew. Vetch had been made sorcerer this fall and was a prentice no more, but that set no barrier between them. They fell to talking at once, and it seemed to Ged that he said more to Vetch in the first hour than he had said during the whole long year at the Isolate Tower.

The otak still rode his shoulder, nestling in the fold of his hood as they sat at dinner at long tables set up for the festival in the Hearth Hall. Vetch marveled at the little creature, and once put up his hand to stroke it, but the otak snapped its sharp teeth at him. He laughed. "They say, Sparrowhawk, that a man favored by a wild beast is a man to whom the Old Powers of stone and spring will speak in human voice."

A "They say Gontish wizards often keep familiars," said Jasper, who sat on the other side of Vetch. "Our Lord Nemmerle has his raven, and songs say the Red Mage of Ark led a wild boar on a gold chain. But I never heard of any sorcerer keeping a rat in his hood!"

At that they all laughed, and Ged laughed with them. It was a merry night and he was joyful to be there in the warmth and merriment, keeping festival with his companions. But, like all Jasper ever said to him, the jest set his teeth on edge.

That night the Lord of O was a guest of the school, himself a sorcerer of renown. He had been a pupil of the Archmage, and returned sometimes to Roke for the Winter Festival or the Long Dance
B in summer. With him was his lady, slender and young, bright as new copper, her black hair crowned with opals. It was seldom that any woman sat in the halls of the Great House, and some of the old Masters looked at her sidelong, disapproving. But the young men looked at her with all their eyes.

"For such a one," said Vetch to Ged, "I could work vast enchantments. . . ." He sighed, and laughed.

"She's only a woman," Ged replied.

"The Princess Elfarran was only a woman," said Vetch, "and for her sake all Enlad was laid waste, and the Hero-Mage of Havnor died, and the island Soléa sank beneath the sea."

"Old tales," says Ged. But then he too began to look at the Lady of O, wondering if indeed this was such mortal beauty as the old tales told of.

The Master Chanter had sung the *Deed of the Young King,* and all together had sung the Winter Carol. Now when there was a little pause before they all rose from the tables, Jasper got up and went to the table nearest the hearth, where the Archmage and the guests and Masters sat, and he spoke to the Lady of O. Jasper was no longer a boy but a young man, tall and comely,[7] with his cloak clasped at the neck with silver; for he also had been made sorcerer this year, and the silver clasp was the token of it. The lady smiled at what he said and the opals shone in her black hair, radiant. Then, the Masters nodding benign consent, Jasper worked an illusion-charm for her. A white tree he made spring up from the stone floor. Its branches touched the high roofbeams of the hall, and on every twig of every branch a golden apple shone, each a sun, for it was the Year Tree. A bird flew among the branches suddenly, all white with a tail like a fall of snow, and the golden apples dimming turned to seeds, each one a drop of crystal. These falling from the tree with a sound like rain, all at once there came a sweet fragrance, while the tree, swaying, put forth leaves of rosy C
fire and white flowers like stars. So the illusion faded. The Lady of O cried out with pleasure, and bent her shining head to the young sorcerer in praise of his mastery. "Come with us, live with us in O-tokne—can he not come, my lord?" she asked, childlike, of her stern husband. But Jasper said only, "When I have learned skills worthy of my Masters here and worthy of your praise, my lady, then I will gladly come, and serve you ever gladly."

So he pleased all there, except Ged. Ged joined his voice to the praises, but not his heart. "I could have done better," he said to himself, in bitter envy; and all the joy of the evening was darkened for him, after that.

---

7. **comely:** attractive.

Summary: Chapter 4

During the school's summer celebration, Ged challenges Jasper to a contest, and they go to Roke Knoll to stage their duel of sorcery. Ged summons a spirit from the dead, a great act of magic, but with that spirit comes a dreadful shadow that attacks Ged. The Archmage drives off the shadow, but dies as a result of his effort. It is many months before Ged can walk or talk. When he meets with the new Archmage to discuss his future, it is decided that Ged will continue his studies at Roke. Until he is ready to leave, the power of the island will protect him from the shadow, which has hidden itself in the world. His pride and impatience replaced by fear and humility, Ged continues his studies and is rewarded with the wizard's staff. He leaves Roke to become the wizard of the remote isle of Low Torning, where the people desire protection from dragons.

Earthsea Vocabulary

spellsmiths
spellwrights

Chapter 4

The Loosing of the Shadow

That spring Ged saw little of either Vetch or Jasper, for they being sorcerers studied now with the Master Patterner in the secrecy of the Immanent Grove, where no prentice might set foot. Ged stayed in the Great House, working with the Masters at all the skills practiced by sorcerers, those who work magic but carry no staff: windbringing, weatherworking, finding, and binding, and the arts of spellsmiths and spellwrights, tellers, chanters, healalls, and herbalists. At night alone in his sleeping-cell, a little ball of werelight burning above the book in place of lamp or candle, he studied the Further Runes and the Runes of Éa, which are used in the Great Spells. All these crafts came easy to him, and it was rumored among the students that this Master or that had said that the Gontish lad was the quickest student that had ever been at Roke, and tales grew up concerning the otak, which was said to be a disguised spirit who whispered wisdom in Ged's ear, and it was even said that the Archmage's raven had hailed Ged at his arrival as "Archmage to be." Whether or not they believed such stories, and whether or not they liked Ged, most of his companions admired him, and were eager to follow him when the rare wild mood came over him and he joined them to lead their games on the lengthening evenings of spring. But for the most part he was all work and pride and temper, and held himself apart. Among them all, Vetch being absent, he had no friend, and never knew he wanted one.

He was fifteen, very young to learn any of the High Arts of wizard or mage, those who carry the staff; but he was so quick to learn all the arts of illusion that the Master Changer, himself a young man, soon began to teach him apart from the others, and to tell him about the true Spells of Shaping. He explained how, if a thing is really to be changed into another thing, it must be renamed for as long as the spell lasts, and he told how this affects the names and natures of things surrounding the transformed thing. He spoke of the perils of changing, above all when the wizard transforms his own shape and thus is liable to be caught in his own spell. Little by little, drawn on by the boy's sureness of understanding, the young Master began to do more than merely tell him of these mysteries. He taught him first one and then another of the Great Spells of Change, and he gave
A him the Book of Shaping to study. This he did
B without knowledge of the Archmage, and unwisely, yet he meant no harm.

Ged worked also with the Master Summoner now, but that Master was a stern man, aged and hardened by the deep and somber wizardry he taught. He dealt with no illusion, only true magic, the summoning of such energies as light, and heat, and the force that draws the magnet, and those forces men perceive as weight, form, color, sound: real powers, drawn from the immense fathomless energies of the universe, which no man's spells or uses could exhaust or unbalance. The weatherworker's and seamaster's calling upon wind and water were crafts already known to his pupils, but it was he who showed them why the true wizard uses such spells only at need, since to summon up such earthly forces is to change the earth of which they are a part. "Rain on Roke may be drought in Osskil," he said, "and a calm in the East Reach may be storm and ruin in the West, unless you know what you are about."

As for the calling of real things and living people, and the raising up of spirits of the dead, and the invocations of the Unseen, those spells which are the height of the Summoner's art and the mage's power, those he scarcely spoke of to them. Once or twice Ged tried to lead him to talk a little of such mysteries, but the Master was silent, looking at him long and grimly, till Ged grew uneasy C
and said no more.

Sometimes indeed he was uneasy working even such lesser spells as the Summoner taught him. There were certain runes on certain pages of the Lore-Book that seemed familiar to him, though he did not remember in what book he had ever seen them before. There were certain phrases that must be said in spells of Summoning that he did not like D
to say. They made him think, for an instant, of shadows in a dark room, of a shut door and shadows reaching out to him from the corner by the door. Hastily he put such thoughts or memories aside and went on. These moments of fear and darkness, he said to himself, were the shadows merely of his ignorance. The more he learned, the less he would have to fear, until finally in his full power as Wizard he needed fear nothing in the world, nothing at all.

In the second month of that summer all the school gathered again at the Great House to celebrate the Moon's Night and the Long Dance, which that year fell together as one festival of two nights, which happens but once in fifty-two years. All the first night, the shortest night of full moon of the year, flutes played out in the fields, and the narrow streets of Thwil were full of drums and torches, and the sound of singing went out over the moonlit waters of Roke Bay. As the sun rose next morning the Chanters of Roke began to sing

A. Making Inferences

? Why did the Master Changer not tell the Archmage what he was teaching Ged? (Ged is too young to learn such spells.)

B. Suspense

? What word in this passage does the most to increase your suspense? ("Unwisely")

C. Interpreting

? Why do you think the Master Summoner doesn't answer Ged's question and stares grimly at him? (He is probably worried about Ged's intense curiosity about the serious spells. The Master Summoner knows that Ged is too young and inexperienced to use these spells correctly.)

D. Making Inferences

? What do these runes remind Ged of? (The spell that he read from Ogion's Lore-Book. The runes are probably similar because the spell that created the shadow was also a spell of summoning.)

A. Earthsea's Past
Éa, we learn, is the "Old Island." Have students locate the Sea of Éa, West Reach, Selidor, and Havnor.

B. Atmosphere
? What atmosphere or feeling does Le Guin build here? (One of fun, magic, wildness) Notice the contrast as she moves to the confrontation between Ged and Jasper.

C. Oral Reading
Have five students prepare a reading of this scene. You will need a Narrator, Jasper, Ged, Vetch, and a Younger Boy. Wherever possible, the readers should omit dialogue tags used only to identify the speaker.

D. Making Inferences
? Which boy do you think is more to blame for the duel—Jasper or Ged? Why?

the long *Deed of Erreth-Akbe,* which tells how the white towers of Havnor were built, and of Erreth-Akbe's journeys from the Old Island, Éa, through all the Archipelago and the Reaches, until at last in the uttermost West Reach on the edge of the **A** Open Sea he met the dragon Orm; and his bones in shattered armor lie among the dragon's bones on the shore of lonely Selidor, but his sword set atop the highest tower of Havnor still burns red in the sunset above the Inmost Sea. When the chant was finished the Long Dance began. Townsfolk and Masters and students and farmers all together, men and women, danced in the warm dust down all the roads of Roke to the sea beaches, to the beat of drums and drone of pipes and flutes. Straight out into the sea they danced, under the moon one night past full, and the music was lost in the breakers' sound. As the east grew light they came back up the beaches and the roads, the drums silent and only the flutes playing soft and shrill. So it was done on every island of the Archipelago that night: one dance, one music binding together the sea-divided lands.

When the Long Dance was over most people slept the day away, and gathered again at evening to eat and drink. There was a group of young fellows, prentices and sorcerers, who had brought their supper out from the refectory to hold private feast in a courtyard of the Great House: Vetch, Jasper, and Ged were there, and six or seven others, and some young lads released briefly from the Isolate Tower, for this festival had brought even Kurremkarmerruk out. They were all eating and laughing and playing such tricks out of pure frolic as might be the marvel of a king's court. One boy had lighted the court with a hundred stars of werelight, colored like jewels, that swung in a slow netted procession between them and the real stars; and a pair of boys were playing bowls with balls of green flame and bowling pins that leaped and hopped away as the ball came near; and all the while Vetch sat cross-legged, eating roast chicken, up in mid-air. One of the younger boys tried to pull him down to earth, but Vetch merely drifted up a little higher, out of reach, and sat calmly smiling on the air. Now and then he tossed away a chicken bone, which turned to an owl and flew hooting among the netted star-lights. Ged shot breadcrumb arrows after the owls and brought them down, and when they touched the ground there they lay, bone and crumb, all illusion **B** gone. Ged also tried to join Vetch up in the middle of the air, but lacking the key of the spell he had to flap his arms to keep aloft, and they were all laughing at his flights and flaps and bumps. He kept up his foolishness for the laughter's sake, laughing with them, for after those two long nights of dance and moonlight and music and magery he was in a fey and wild mood, ready for whatever might come.

He came lightly down on his feet just beside Jasper at last, and Jasper, who never laughed **C** aloud, moved away saying, "The Sparrowhawk that can't fly . . ."

"Is jasper a precious stone?" Ged returned, grinning. "O Jewel among sorcerers, O Gem of Havnor, sparkle for us!"

The lad that had set the lights dancing sent one down to dance and glitter about Jasper's head. Not quite as cool as usual, frowning, Jasper brushed the light away and snuffed it out with one gesture. "I am sick of boys and noise and foolishness," he said.

"You're getting middle-aged, lad," Vetch remarked from above.

"If silence and gloom is what you want," put in one of the younger boys, "you could always try the Tower."

Ged said to him, "What is it you want, then, Jasper?"

"I want the company of my equals," Jasper said. "Come on, Vetch. Leave the prentices to their toys."

Ged turned to face Jasper. "What do sorcerers have that prentices lack?" he inquired. His voice was quiet, but all the other boys suddenly fell still, for in his tone as in Jasper's the spite between them now sounded plain and clear as steel coming out of a sheath. **D**

"Power," Jasper said.

"I'll match your power act for act."

"You challenge me?"

"I challenge you."

Vetch had dropped down to the ground, and now he came between them, grim of face. "Duels in sorcery are forbidden to us, and well you know it. Let this cease!"

Both Ged and Jasper stood silent, for it was true they knew the law of Roke, and they also knew that Vetch was moved by love, and themselves by hate. Yet their anger was balked, not cooled. Presently, moving a little aside as if to be heard by Vetch alone, Jasper spoke, with his cool smile: "I think you'd better remind your goatherd friend again of the law that protects him. He looks sulky. I wonder, did he really think I'd accept a challenge from him? A fellow who smells of goats, a prentice who doesn't know the First Change?"

"Jasper," said Ged, "What do you know of what I know?"

For an instant, with no word spoken that any heard, Ged vanished from their sight, and where he had stood a great falcon hovered, opening its hooked beak to scream: for one instant, and then Ged stood again in the flickering torchlight, his dark gaze on Jasper.

Jasper had taken a step backward, in astonishment; but now he shrugged and said one word: "Illusion."

The others muttered. Vetch said, "That was not illusion. It was true change. And enough. Jasper,
A listen—"

"Enough to prove that he sneaked a look in the Book of Shaping behind the Master's back: What then? Go on, Goatherd. I like this trap you're building for yourself. The more you try to prove yourself my equal, the more you show yourself for what you are."

At that, Vetch turned from Jasper, and said very softly to Ged, "Sparrowhawk, will you be a man and drop this now—come with me—"

B Ged looked at his friend and smiled; but all he said was, "Keep Hoeg for me a little while, will you?" He put into Vetch's hands the little otak, which as usual had been riding on his shoulder. It had never let any but Ged touch it, but it came to Vetch now, and climbing on his arm cowered on his shoulder, its great bright eyes always on its master.

"Now," Ged said to Jasper, quietly as before, "what are you going to do to prove yourself my superior, Jasper?"

"I don't have to do anything, Goatherd. Yet I will. I will give you a chance—an opportunity. Envy eats you like a worm in an apple. Let's let out the worm. Once by Roke Knoll you boasted that Gontish wizards don't play games. Come to Roke Knoll now and show us what it is they do instead. And afterward, maybe I will show you a little sorcery."

"Yes, I should like to see that," Ged answered. The younger boys, used to seeing his black temper break out at the least hint of slight or insult, watched him in wonder at his coolness now. Vetch watched him not in wonder, but with growing fear. He tried to intervene again, but Jasper said, "Come, keep out of this, Vetch. What will you do with the chance I give you, Goatherd? Will you show us an illusion, a fireball, a charm to cure goats with the mange?"

"What would you like me to do, Jasper?"

The older lad shrugged, "Summon up a spirit from the dead, for all I care!"

"I will."

"You will not." Jasper looked straight at him, rage suddenly flaming out over his disdain. "You will not. You cannot. You brag and brag—"

"By my name, I will do it!"

They all stood utterly motionless for a moment.

Breaking away from Vetch who would have held him back by main force, Ged strode out of the courtyard, not looking back. The dancing werelights overhead died out, sinking down. Jasper hesitated a second, then followed after Ged. And the rest came straggling behind, in silence, curious and afraid.

The slopes of Roke Knoll went up dark into the darkness of summer night before moonrise. The presence of that hill where many wonders had been worked was heavy, like a weight in the air about them. As they came onto the hillside they thought of how the roots of it were deep, deeper than the sea, reaching down even to the old, blind, secret fires at the world's core. They stopped on the east slope. Stars hung over the black grass above them on the hill's crest. No wind blew.

Ged went a few paces up the slope away from the others and turning said in a clear voice, "Jasper! Whose spirit shall I call?"

"Call whom you like. None will listen to you." Jasper's voice shook a little, with anger perhaps. Ged answered him softly, mockingly, "Are you afraid?"

He did not even listen for Jasper's reply, if he made one. He no longer cared about Jasper. Now that they stood on Roke Knoll, hate and rage were gone, replaced by utter certainty. He need envy no one. He knew that his power, this night, on this dark enchanted ground, was greater than it had ever been, filling him till he trembled with the sense of strength barely kept in check. He knew now that Jasper was far beneath him, had been sent perhaps only to bring him here tonight, no rival but a mere servant of Ged's destiny. Under his feet he felt the hillroots going down and down into the dark, and over his head he saw the dry, far fires of the stars. Between, all things were his to order, to command. He stood at the center of the world.

"Don't be afraid," he said, smiling. "I'll call a woman's spirit. You need not fear a woman. Elfarran I will call, the fair lady of the *Deed of Enlad.*"

"She died a thousand years ago, her bones lie afar under the Sea of Éa, and maybe there never was such a woman."

"Do years and distances matter to the dead? Do the Songs lie?" Ged said with the same gentle mockery, and then saying, "Watch the air between my hands," he turned away from the others and stood still.

In a great slow gesture he stretched out his

A. Suspense
Ask students to notice that the events in this scene become more and more exciting and suspenseful until they reach a peak on page 562.

B. Interpreting
? How is suspense created when Ged gives the otak to Vetch? (The spell of summoning he is about to work will be dangerous—he doesn't want his pet to get hurt.) How does the otak's behavior increase the suspense? (The otak, normally fierce, comes willingly to Vetch—it is scared of Ged.)

Comment from a Critic
Francis Molson in his essay "The Earthsea Trilogy: Ethical Fantasy for Children" writes that Ged summons Elfarran when he refuses to grow up, although Vetch has begged him to ". . . be a man and drop this now . . ." (page 561). Good and evil motives struggle in Ged, but evil wins out when he "sinks to a display of naked power . . . Ironically, instead of the integrated personality that accompanies maturity, he has produced a monstrous symbol. . . ." According to Molson, the shadow is the embodiment of Ged's "arrogance and immaturity."

A. Imagery
? What images of touch help you feel what is happening? ("They shivered a little"; "straining hands and arms"; "so heavy that he shook with effort"; "the hot wind whined")

B. Metaphor
? What metaphor does the author use to describe the night world? (A piece of fabric)

C. Climax
? This is the climactic event of this episode—but not of the entire novel. How is it both a victory and a tragedy for Ged? (A victory because he does summon a spirit from the dead, but tragic because he lets a terrible evil into the world.) Note that the expression on the spirit's face foreshadows the evil that is behind her.

D. Figurative Language
Le Guin describes the shadow as "clambering." What image does this word evoke? (That of a beast)

arms, the gesture of welcome that opens an invocation. He began to speak.

He had read the runes of this Spell of Summoning in Ogion's book, two years and more ago, and never since had seen them. In darkness he had read them then. Now in this darkness it was as if he read them again on the page open before him in the night. But now he understood what he read, speaking it aloud word after word, and he saw the markings of how the spell must be woven with the sound of the voice and the motion of body and hand.

A The other boys stood watching, not speaking, not moving unless they shivered a little: for the great spell was beginning to work. Ged's voice was soft still, but changed, with a deep singing in it, and the words he spoke were not known to them. He fell silent. Suddenly the wind rose roaring in the grass. Ged dropped to his knees and called out aloud. Then he fell forward as if to embrace earth with his outstretched arms, and when he rose he held something dark in his straining hands and arms, something so heavy that he shook with effort getting to his feet. The hot wind whined in the black tossing grasses on the hill. If the stars shone now none saw them.

The words of the enchantment hissed and mumbled on Ged's lips, and then he cried out aloud and clearly, "Elfarran!"

Again he cried the name, "Elfarran!"

The shapeless mass of darkness he had lifted split apart. It sundered, and a pale spindle of light gleamed between his opened arms, a faint oval reaching from the ground up to the height of his raised hands. In the oval of light for a moment there moved a form, a human shape: a tall woman looking back over her shoulder. Her face was beautiful, and sorrowful, and full of fear.

Only for a moment did the spirit glimmer there. Then the sallow oval between Ged's arms grew bright. B It widened and spread, a rent in the darkness of the earth and night, a ripping open of the fabric of the world. Through it blazed a terrible brightness. And through that bright misshapen breach clambered something like a clot of black shadow, quick and hideous, and it leaped straight out at Ged's face.

C Staggering back under the weight of the thing, Ged gave a short, hoarse scream. The little otak watching from Vetch's shoulder, the animal that had no voice, screamed aloud also and leaped as if to attack.

Ged fell, struggling and writhing, while the bright rip in the world's darkness above him widened and stretched. The boys that watched fled, and Jasper bent down to the ground hiding his eyes from the terrible light. Vetch alone ran forward to his friend. So only he saw the lump of shadow that clung to Ged, tearing at his flesh. It was like a black beast, the size of a young child, though it seemed to swell and shrink; and it had no head or face, only the four taloned[1] paws with which it gripped and tore. Vetch sobbed with horror, yet he put out his hands to try to pull the thing away from Ged. Before he touched it, he was bound still, unable to move.

The intolerable brightness faded, and slowly the torn edges of the world closed together. Nearby a voice was speaking as softly as a tree whispers or a fountain plays.

Starlight began to shine again, and the grasses of the hillside were whitened with the light of the moon just rising. The night was healed. Restored and steady lay the balance of light and dark. The shadow-beast was gone. Ged lay sprawled on his back, his arms flung out as if they yet kept the wide gesture of welcome and invocation. His face was blackened with blood and there were great black stains on his shirt. The little otak cowered by his shoulder, quivering. And above him stood an old man whose cloak glimmered pale in the moonrise: the Archmage of Nemmerle.

The end of Nemmerle's staff hovered silvery above Ged's breast. Once gently it touched him over the heart, once on the lips, while Nemmerle whispered. Ged stirred, and his lips parted gasping for breath. Then the old Archmage lifted the staff, and set it to earth, and leaned heavily on it with bowed head, as if he had scarcely strength to stand.

Vetch found himself free to move. Looking around, he saw that already others were there, the Masters Summoner and Changer. An act of great wizardry is not worked without arousing such men, and they had ways of coming very swiftly when need called, though none had been so swift as the Archmage. They now sent for help, and some who came went with the Archmage, while others, Vetch among them, carried Ged to the chambers of the Master Herbal.

All night long the Summoner stayed on Roke Knoll, keeping watch. Nothing stirred there on the hillside where the stuff of the world had been torn open. No shadow came crawling through moonlight seeking the rent through which it might clamber back into its own domain. D It had fled from Nemmerle, and from the mighty spell-walls that surround and protect Roke Island, but it was in the world now. In the world, somewhere, it hid. If Ged had died that night it might have tried to

1. **taloned:** clawed.

Comment from Critics

Robert Scholes and Eric Rabkin in their critical history of science fiction say that the magical power in Earthsea is in many ways analagous to scientific power on Earth. They comment that the number of things in the Earthsea world and "the difficulty of discovering their names set limits to magical power, even as the boundaries of scientific knowledge set limits to the power of science." One of the many important ideas for our time that can be learned from *A Wizard of Earthsea* is that anyone who is gifted enough to acquire great knowledge and power must wield these gifts with utmost care to preserve the beauty and balance in the world.

Earthsea Vocabulary
perriot

A. Interpreting
Ged indirectly causes the death of Nemmerle.
? What does this indicate about Ged's power? (His power must be great, since he created an evil spirit that took all of the Archmage's strength to defeat.)

B. Making Inferences
? Why do you think Ged wept when he saw sunlight? (The opening of the shutters and the light that comes through represents life and the outside world, which Ged must now join. He probably cries in shame, for he no longer can hide in the darkness, away from the truth of what he has done.)

C. Character Change
? Ged's wounds have finally healed, but his meeting with the shadow has changed his character. How is he different? (His pride and arrogance are replaced with uncertainty and shame.)

D. Making Inferences
? Why does Gensher refuse to accept Ged's fealty? (He doesn't yet know whether Ged is cured of the evil inside him. He isn't sure that Ged will not attempt another foolish spell.)

find the doorway he had opened, and follow him into death's realm, or slip back into whatever place it had come from; for this the Summoner waited on Roke Knoll. But Ged lived.

They had laid him abed in the healing-chamber, and the Master Herbal tended the wounds he had on his face and throat and shoulder. They were deep, ragged, and evil wounds. The black blood in them would not stanch, welling out even under the charms and the cobweb-wrapped perriot leaves laid upon them. Ged lay blind and dumb in fever like a stick in a slow fire, and there was no spell to cool what burned him.

Not far away, in the unroofed court where the fountain played, the Archmage lay also unmoving, but cold, very cold: Only his eyes lived, watching the fall of moonlit water and the stir of moonlit leaves. Those with him said no spells and worked no healing. Quietly they spoke among themselves from time to time, and then turned again to watch their Lord. He lay still, hawk nose and high forehead and white hair bleached by moonlight all to the color of bone. To check the ungoverned spell and drive off the shadow from Ged, Nemmerle had spent all his power, and with it his bodily strength was gone. He lay dying. But the death of a great mage, who has many times in his life walked on the dry steep hillsides of death's kingdom, is a strange matter: for the dying man goes not blindly, but surely, knowing the way. Then Nemmerle looked up through the leaves of the tree, those with him did not know if he watched the stars of summer fading in daybreak, or those other stars, which never set above the hills that see no dawn. A

The raven of Osskil that had been his pet for thirty years was gone. No one had seen where it went. "It flies before him," the Master Patterner said, as they kept vigil.

The day came warm and clear. The Great House and the streets of Thwil were hushed. No voice was raised, until along toward noon iron bells spoke out aloud in the Chanter's Tower, harshly tolling.

On the next day the Nine Masters of Roke gathered in a place somewhere under the dark trees of the Immanent Grove. Even there they set nine walls of silence about them, that no person or power might speak to them or hear them as they chose from amongst the mages of all Earthsea him who would be the new Archmage. Gensher of Way was chosen. A ship was sent forth at once across the Inmost Sea to Way Island to bring the Archmage back to Roke. The Master Windkey stood in the stern and raised up the magewind into the sail, and quickly the ship departed, and was gone.

Of these events Ged knew nothing. For four weeks of that hot summer he lay blind, and deaf, and mute, though at times he moaned and cried out like an animal. At last, as the patient crafts of the Master Herbal worked their healing, his wounds began to close and the fever left him. Little by little he seemed to hear again, though he never spoke. On a clear day of autumn the Master Herbal opened the shutters of the room where Ged lay. Since the darkness of that night on Roke Knoll he had known only darkness. Now he saw daylight, and the sun shining. He hid his scarred face in his hands and wept. B

Still when winter came he could speak only with a stammering tongue, and the Master Herbal kept him there in the healing-chambers, trying to lead his body and mind gradually back to strength. It was early spring when at last the Master released him, sending him first to offer his fealty[2] to the Archmage Gensher. For he had not been able to join all the others of the School in this duty when Gensher came to Roke.

None of his companions had been allowed to visit him in the months of his sickness, and now as he passed some of them asked one another, "Who is that?" He had been light and lithe and strong. Now, lamed by pain, he went hesitantly, and did not raise his face, the left side of which was white with scars. He avoided those who knew him and those who did not, and made his way straight to the court of the Fountain. There where once he had awaited Nemmerle, Gensher awaited him. C

Like the old Archmage the new one was cloaked in white; but like most men of Way and the East Reach Gensher was black-skinned, and his look was black, under thick brows.

Ged knelt and offered him fealty and obedience. Gensher was silent a while.

"I know what you did," he said at last, "but not what you are. I cannot accept your fealty." D

Ged stood up, and set his hand on the trunk of the young tree beside the fountain to steady himself. He was still very slow to find words. "Am I to leave Roke, my lord?"

"Do you want to leave Roke?"

"No."

"What do you want?"

"To stay. To learn. To undo . . . the evil. . . ."

"Nemmerle himself could not do that. No, I would not let you go from Roke. Nothing protects you but the power of the Masters here and the defenses laid upon this island that keep the creatures of evil away. If you left now, the thing you

2. **fealty** (fē′əl·tē): loyalty; duty.

Earthsea Vocabulary

gebbeth

A. Vocabulary

Gebbeth is a made-up word, but the prefix *geb-* means "born."

? How does this meaning relate to the shadow? (The shadow was "born" out of Ged's pride and arrogance.)

B. Character Change

Have students examine these passages for other changes in Ged.

C. Reading Aloud

This scene between Ged and Vetch is one of the most moving in the novel. You may want to have two students (Ged and Vetch) and a Narrator prepare it and read it aloud in class. The scene continues to the end of the sixth paragraph, page 566.

D. Character's Motivation

? Why do you think he is considering working with the Master Namer in the future? (He wants to stay on Roke. He worries that the shadow will use him to work evil after he leaves the protection of Roke; he also now fears his own power.)

loosed would find you at once, and enter into you, and possess you. You would be no man but a

A *gebbeth,* a puppet doing the will of that evil shadow which you raised up into the sunlight. You must stay here, until you gain strength and wisdom enough to defend yourself from it—if ever you do. Even now it waits for you. Assuredly it waits for you. Have you seen it since that night?"

"In dreams, lord." After a while Ged went on, speaking with pain and shame, "Lord Gensher, I do not know what it was—the thing that came out of the spell and cleaved to me—"

"Nor do I know. It has no name. You have great power inborn in you, and you used that power wrongly, to work a spell over which you had no control, not knowing how that spell affects the balance of light and dark, life and death, good and evil. And you were moved to do this by pride and by hate. Is it any wonder the result was ruin? You summoned a spirit from the dead, but with it came one of the Powers of unlife. Uncalled it came from a place where there are no names. Evil, it wills to work evil through you. The power you had to call it gives it power over you: You are connected. It is the shadow of your arrogance, the shadow of your ignorance, the shadow you cast. Has a shadow a name?"

Ged stood sick and haggard. He said at last, "Better I had died."

"Who are you to judge that, you for whom Nemmerle gave his life? You are safe here. You will live here, and go on with your training. They tell me you were clever. Go on and do your work. Do it well. It is all you can do."

So Gensher ended, and was suddenly gone, as is the way of mages. The fountain leaped in the sunlight, and Ged watched it a while and listened to its voice, thinking of Nemmerle. Once in that court he had felt himself to be a word spoken by the sunlight. Now the darkness also had spoken: a word that could not be unsaid.

He left the court, going to his old room in the South Tower, which they had kept empty for him. He stayed there alone. When the gong called to

B supper he went, but he would hardly speak to the other lads at the Long Table, or raise his face to them, even those who greeted him most gently. So after a day or two they all left him alone. To be alone was his desire, for he feared the evil he might do or say unwittingly.

Neither Vetch nor Jasper was there, and he did not ask about them. The boys he had led and lorded over were all ahead of him now, because of the months he had lost, and that spring and summer he studied with lads younger than himself. Nor did he shine among them, for the words of any spell, even the simplest illusion-charm, came halting from his tongue, and his hands faltered at their craft.

In autumn he was to go once again to the Isolate Tower to study with the Master Namer. This task which he had once dreaded now pleased him, for silence was what he sought, and long learning where no spells were wrought, and where that power which he knew was still in him would never be called upon to act.

The night before he left for the Tower a visitor came to his room, one wearing a brown traveling cloak and carrying a staff of oak shod with iron. Ged stood up, at sight of the wizard's staff.

"Sparrowhawk—"

At the sound of the voice, Ged raised his eyes: C

It was Vetch standing there, solid and foursquare as ever, his black blunt face older but his smile unchanged. On his shoulder crouched a little beast, brindle-furred and bright-eyed.

"He stayed with me while you were sick, and now I'm sorry to part with him. And sorrier to part with you, Sparrowhawk. But I'm going home. Here, Hoeg! go to your true master!" Vetch patted the otak and set it down on the floor. It went and sat on Ged's pallet, and began to wash its fur with a dry brown tongue like a little leaf. Vetch laughed, but Ged could not smile. He bent down to hide his face, stroking the otak.

"I thought you wouldn't come to me, Vetch," he said.

He did not mean any reproach, but Vetch answered, "I couldn't come to you. The Master Herbal forbade me; and since winter I've been with the Master in the Grove, locked up myself. I was not free, until I earned my staff. Listen: When you too are free, come to the East Reach. I will be waiting for you. There's good cheer in the little towns there, and wizards are well received."

"Free . . ." Ged muttered, and shrugged a little, trying to smile.

Vetch looked at him, not quite as he had used to look, with no less love but more wizardry, perhaps. He said gently, "You won't stay bound on Roke forever."

"Well . . . I have thought, perhaps I may come D

to work with the Master in the Tower, to be one of those who seek among the books and the stars for lost names, and so . . . so do no more harm, if not much good. . . ."

"Maybe," said Vetch. "I am no seer, but I see before you, not rooms and books, but far seas, and the fire of dragons, and the towers of cities, and all such things a hawk sees when he flies far and high."

A. Making Inferences

How does Ged answer his own question? (He throws his shadow on the wall behind him—he is saying to Vetch that the shadow, or evil, he created will always follow him.)

B. Language

Compare Vetch's use-name with his true name. Why do you think they are so different in sound? (The beautiful combination of sounds in "Estarriol," which contains and thus suggests the word "star," reflects Vetch's true nature; the use-name "Vetch" is the sign of his "outer man," a bit heavy, blunt, and awkward.)

C. Responding

Why is this such a great gift? (We have learned that people only tell their true names to those that they completely trust. Vetch has given Ged the gift of trust and faith.)

D. Plot

In what way is the exchange of names a turning point in Ged's recovery? (Because of Vetch's trust in him, he begins again to have faith in himself.)

A "And behind me—what do you see behind me?" Ged asked, and stood up as he spoke, so that the werelight that burned overhead between them sent his shadow back against the wall and floor. Then he turned his face aside and said, stammering, "But tell me where you will go, what you will do."

"I will go home, to see my brothers and the sister you have heard me speak of. I left her a little child and soon she'll be having her Naming—it's strange to think of! And so I'll find me a job of wizardry somewhere among the little isles. Oh, I would stay and talk with you, but I can't, my ship goes out tonight and the tide is turned already. Sparrowhawk, if ever your way lies East, come B to me. And if ever you need me, send for me, call on me by my name: Estarriol."

At that Ged lifted his scarred face, meeting his friend's eyes.

"Estarriol," he said, "my name is Ged."

Then quietly they bade each other farewell, and Vetch turned and went down the stone hallway, and left Roke.

Ged stood still a while, like one who has received great news, and must enlarge his spirit to C receive it. It was a great gift that Vetch had given him, the knowledge of his true name.

No one knows a man's true name but himself and his namer. He may choose at length to tell it to his brother, or his wife, or his friend, yet even those few will never use it where any third person may hear it. In front of other people they will, like other people, call him by his use-name, his nickname—such a name as Sparrowhawk, and Vetch, and Ogion which means "fir-cone." If plain men hide their true name from all but a few they love and trust utterly, so much more must wizardry men, being more dangerous, and more endangered. Who knows a man's name, holds that man's life in his keeping. Thus to Ged who had D lost faith in himself, Vetch had given that gift only a friend can give, the proof of unshaken, unshakable trust.

Ged sat down on his pallet and let the globe of werelight die, giving off as it faded a faint whiff of marsh gas. He petted the otak, which stretched comfortably and went to sleep on his knee as if it had never slept anywhere else. The Great House was silent. It came to Ged's mind that this was the eve of his own Passage, the day on which Ogion had given him his name. Four years were gone since then. He remembered the coldness of the mountain spring through which he had walked naked and unnamed. He fell to thinking of other bright pools in the River Ar, where he had used to swim; and of Ten Alders village under the great slanting forests of the mountain; of the shadows of morning across the dusty village street, the fire leaping under bellow-blast in the smith's smelting pit on a winter afternoon, the witch's dark fragrant hut where the air was heavy with smoke and wreathing spells. He had not thought of these things for a long time. Now they came back to him, on this night he was seventeen years old. All the years and places of his brief broken life came within mind's reach and made a whole again. He knew once more, at last, after this long, bitter, wasted time, who he was and where he was.

But where he must go in the years to come, that he could not see; and he feared to see it.

Next morning he set out across the island, the otak riding on his shoulder as it had used to. This time it took him three days, not two, to walk to the Isolate Tower, and he was bone-weary when he came in sight of the Tower above the spitting, hissing seas of the northern cape. Inside, it was dark as he remembered, and cold as he remembered, and Kurremkarmerruk sat on his high seat writing down lists of names. He glanced at Ged and said without welcome, as if Ged had never been away, "Go to bed; tired is stupid. Tomorrow you may open the Book of the Undertakings of the Makers, learning the names therein."

At winter's end he returned to the Great House. He was made sorcerer then, and the Archmage Gensher accepted at that time his fealty. Thenceforth he studied the high arts and enchantments, passing beyond arts of illusion to the works of real ınagery, learning what he must know to earn his wizard's staff. The trouble he had had in speaking spells wore off over the months, and skill returned into his hands: yet he was never so quick to learn as he had been, having learned a long hard lesson from fear. Yet no ill portents or encounters followed on his working even of the Great Spells of Making and Shaping, which are most perilous. He came to wonder at times if the shadow he had loosed might have grown weak, or fled somehow out of the world, for it came no more into his dreams. But in his heart he knew such hope was folly.

From the Masters and from ancient lore-books Ged learned what he could about such beings as this shadow he had loosed; little was there to learn. No such creature was described or spoken of directly. There were at best hints here and there in the old books of things that might be like the shadow-beast. It was not a ghost of human man, nor was it a creature of the Old Powers of Earth, and yet it seemed it might have some link with these. In the *Matter of the Dragons,* which Ged read very closely, there was a tale of an ancient

Reading Check Test: Chapters 3 and 4

1. The island to which Ged goes to study is called ______. (*Roke*)
2. Ged is allowed to enter the school after he ______. (*says his true name*)
3. ______ is the name of Ged's rival at the school. (*Jasper*)
4. On Roke Knoll, Ged tries to summon ______. (*Elfarran, a spirit of the dead*)
5. The evil that Ged releases is in the form of a ______. (*shadow*)

A Dragonlord who had come under the sway of one of the Old Powers, a speaking stone that lay in a far northern land. "*At the Stone's command,*" said the book, "*he did speak to raise up a dead spirit out of the realm of the dead, but his wizardry being bent awry by the Stone's will there came with the dead spirit also a thing not summoned, which did devour him out from within and in his shape walked, destroying men.*" But the book did not say what the thing was, nor did it tell the end of the tale. And the Masters did not know where such a shadow might come from: From unlife, the Archmage had said; from the wrong side of the world, said the Master Changer; and the Master Summoner said, "I do not know." The Summoner had come often to sit with Ged in his illness. He was grim and grave as ever, but Ged knew now his compassion, and loved him well. "I do not know. I know of the thing only this: That only a great power could have summoned up such a thing, and perhaps only one power—only one voice—your voice. But what in turn that means, I do not know. You will find out. You must find out, or die, and worse than die. . . ." He spoke softly and his eyes were somber as he looked at Ged. "You thought, as a boy, that a mage is one who can do anything. So I thought, once. So did we all. And the truth is that as a man's real power grows and his knowledge widens, ever the way he can follow grows narrower: until at last he chooses nothing, but does only and wholly what he *must do*. . . ."

The Archmage sent Ged, after his eighteenth birthday, to work with the Master Patterner. What is learned in the Immanent Grove is not much talked about elsewhere. It is said that no spells are worked there, and yet the place itself is an enchantment. Sometimes the trees of that Grove are seen, and sometimes they are not seen, and they are not always in the same place and part of Roke Island. It is said that the trees of the Grove themselves are wise. It is said that the Master Patterner learns his supreme magery there within the Grove, and if ever the trees should die so shall his wisdom die, and in those days the waters will rise and drown the islands of Earthsea which Segoy raised from the deeps in the time before myth, all the lands where men and dragons dwell.

But all this is hearsay; wizards will not speak of it.

The months went by, and at last on a day of spring Ged returned to the Great House, and he had no idea what would be asked of him next. At the door that gives on the path across the fields to Roke Knoll an old man met him, waiting for him in the doorway. At first Ged did not know him, and then putting his mind to it recalled him as the one who had let him into the School on the day of his coming, five years ago.

The old man smiled, greeting him by name, and asked, "Do you know who I am?"

Now Ged had thought before of how it was always said, the Nine Masters of Roke, although he knew only eight: Windkey, Hand, Herbal, Chanter, Changer, Summoner, Namer, Patterner. It seemed that people spoke of the Archmage as the ninth. Yet when a new Archmage was chosen, nine Masters met to choose him.

"I think you are the Master Doorkeeper," said Ged.

"I am. Ged, you won entrance to Roke by saying your name. Now you may win your freedom of it by saying mine." So said the old man smiling, and waited. Ged stood dumb.

He knew a thousand ways and crafts and means for finding out names of things and of men, of course; such craft was a part of everything he had learned at Roke, for without it there could be little useful magic done. But to find out the name of a Mage and Master was another matter. A mage's name is better hidden than a herring in the sea, better guarded than a dragon's den. A prying charm will be met with a stronger charm, subtle devices will fail, devious inquiries will be deviously thwarted, and force will be turned ruinously back upon itself. B

"You keep a narrow door, Master," said Ged at last. "I must sit out in the fields here, I think, and fast till I grow thin enough to slip through."

"As long as you like," said the Doorkeeper, smiling.

So Ged went off a little way and sat down under an alder on the banks of the Thwilburn, letting his otak run down to play in the stream and hunt the muddy banks for creek crabs. The sun went down, late and bright, for spring was well along. Lights of lantern and werelight gleamed in the windows of the Great House, and down the hill the streets of Thwil town filled with darkness. Owls hooted over the roofs and bats flitted in the dusk air above the stream, and still Ged sat thinking how he might, by force, ruse, or sorcery, learn the Doorkeeper's name. The more he pondered the less he saw, among all the arts of witchcraft he had learned in these five years on Roke, any one that would serve to wrest such a secret from such a mage.

He lay down in the field and slept under the stars, with the otak nestling in his pocket. After the sun was up he went, still fasting, to the door of the House and knocked. The Doorkeeper opened.

A. Allusion
Note the allusion here to the Old Powers that existed in Earthsea long ago. One old Power is a "speaking stone" which Ged will meet in Chapter 7. The belief that certain stones had magic power is common among ancient cultures.

B. Comparisons
? Why are these comparisons effective? Why are they also appropriate to Earthsea? (To find one small herring in the sea is nearly impossible; Earthsea is a world mostly made up of seas. Dragons fiercely guard their hoards; dragons exist in Earthsea.)

Analyzing Chapters 3 and 4

Identifying Facts

1. He must speak his true name.

2. To Ged, Jasper seems haughty, false, and condescending. He smiles disdainfully, and seems "jeering behind politeness."

3. The Master Hand warns Ged that the powers of changing and of summoning can shake the balance of the world. He says that the power is very dangerous, that its use must "follow knowledge and serve need," and that every action has a consequence.

4. Ged boasts that he can summon the spirits of the dead.

5. Ged summons the spirit of Elfarran, but along with Elfarran comes a strange, hideous, black shadow.

The Archmage dies after using all of his power to save Ged from the shadow. With his power drained, he can no longer survive.

6. Ged must guess the Master's true name.

Interpreting Meanings

7. The conflict between Ged and the shadow is the major one in the chapters. *(Answers continue on left-hand column.)*

(Continued from top.)
(See Teacher's Manual page 185 for reasons.)

8. Ged's knowledge that it is dangerous to use magic without knowing consequences and his desire to do good are struggling with his pride and his desire for power.

9. After saving his village, Ged became proud and impatient, which led him to behave foolishly. After Ged's struggle with the shadow he loses his pride and impatience. He shows his new humility when he talks with the Archmage Gensher.

10. The most valuable lesson Ged learns is that evil can come from the misuse of the sorcerer's powers.

Applying Meanings

11. Students might mention atomic energy (electricity and nuclear arms), natural gas (warmth and explosions), automobiles (transportation and collisions), and so on.

"Master," said Ged, "I cannot take your name from you, not being strong enough, and I cannot trick your name from you, not being wise enough. So I am content to stay here, and learn or serve, whatever you will: unless by chance you will answer a question I have."

"Ask it."

"What is your name?"

The Doorkeeper smiled, and said his name: and Ged, repeating it, entered for the last time into that House.

When he left it again he wore a heavy dark-blue cloak, the gift of the township of Low Torning, whereto he was bound, for they wanted a wizard there. He carried also a staff of his own height, carved of yew-wood, bronze-shod. The Doorkeeper bade him farewell opening the door of the Great House for him, the door of horn and ivory, and he went down the streets of Thwil to a ship that waited for him on the bright water in the morning.

Responding to the Novel

Analyzing Chapters 3 and 4

Identifying Facts

1. To enter the School on Roke, what does Ged have to do?
2. One of the first people Ged meets is Jasper, another student at the school. What makes Ged dislike him almost immediately?
3. Ged longs to attain enough power to prove himself to Jasper, but his masters give him many warnings. How does the Master Hand warn about the powers of changing and summoning?
4. When Ged first arrives at the School, he refuses a challenge on Roke Knoll from Jasper. Later, again on Roke Knoll, what dangerous boast does Ged make to Jasper?
5. What two things arise from the underworld when Ged uses the summoning spell? Explain how the Archmage dies as a result of Ged's abuse of his power.
6. In order to leave the School, what must Ged tell the Master Doorkeeper?

Interpreting Meanings

7. An **external conflict,** or struggle, involves a character and another character (or characters) or a natural force. Which of the following do you feel is the most important external conflict in these two chapters: the conflict between Ged and Jasper, between Ged and the shadow, or between Ged and the Masters? Give reasons for your choice.
8. An **internal conflict** is a conflict that takes place within a character's own mind. It involves opposing emotions or ideas. Describe the internal conflict Ged experiences that leads to his dangerous loosing of the shadow. That is, which of Ged's desires or emotions are struggling with each other?
9. Ged **changes** significantly during these two chapters. What changes can you see in his behavior or personality since he saved his village from the Kargs (Chapter 1)? Has he become more or less brave, wise, proud, patient? Give evidence from the novel for your opinion.
10. Ever since Ged was first taught by the village witch on Gont, he has tried to get greater power. After his experience on Roke, do you think his greatest lesson was learning new powers, or learning the evil that can come from the misuse of these powers? Explain the reasons for your answer.

Applying Meanings

11. On Roke, Ged begins to understand that magic powers can be dangerous if they are misused. Our world is not controlled by magic and wizards, but it does contain powers that can be both beneficial and dangerous. Electricity, for example, can provide light and warmth, but it can also cause a deadly shock. What other beneficial powers in our world can you think of that are potentially dangerous?

Summary: Chapter 5
On Low Torning, Ged's closest friend is a fisherman named Pechvarry. To save the life of Pechvarry's son, Ged sends his spirit after the boy's to try to keep it from reaching the realm of the dead. By mistake, he crosses over into the dead world, and meets the shadow. He uses his staff to ward off the shadow and through great effort, returns to the world of the living. Knowing that he is useless to the people of Low Torning if he must worry about the shadow, Ged decides to fulfill his obligation to them and search out the Dragon of Pendor. He sails to Pendor, and kills five of the eight young dragons. He calls out the great dragon, and defeats him by calling him by his true name—Yevaud. He forces the dragon to swear never to fly to the Archipelago. The threat to the islanders is ended.

Chapter 5
The Dragon of Pendor

West of Roke in a crowd between the two great lands Hosk and Ensmer lie the Ninety Isles. The nearest to Roke is Serd, and the farthest is Seppish, which lies almost in the Pelnish Sea; and whether the sum of them is ninety is a question never settled, for if you count only isles with freshwater springs you might have seventy, while if you count every rock you might have a hundred and still not be done; and then the tide would change. Narrow run the channels between the islets, and there the mild tides of the Inmost Sea, chafed and baffled, run high and fall low, so that where at high tide there might be three islands in one place, at low there might be one. Yet for all that danger of the tide, every child who can walk can paddle, and has his little rowboat; housewives row across the channel to take a cup of rushwash tea with the neighbor; peddlers call their wares in rhythm with the stroke of their oars. All roads there are salt water, blocked only by nets strung from house to house across the straits to catch the small fish called turbies, the oil of which is the wealth of the Ninety Isles. There are few bridges, and no great towns. Every islet is thick with farms and fishermen's houses, and these are gathered into townships each of ten or twenty islets. One such was Low Torning, the westernmost, looking not on the Inmost Sea but outward to empty ocean, that lonely
A corner of the Archipelago where only Pendor lies, the dragon-spoiled isle, and beyond it the waters of the West Reach, desolate.

A house was ready there for the township's new wizard. It stood on a hill among green fields of barley, sheltered from the west wind by a grove of pendick trees that now were red with flowers. From the door one looked out on other thatched roofs and groves and gardens, and other islands with their roofs and fields and hills, and amongst them all the many bright winding channels of the sea. It was a poor house, windowless, with earthen floor, yet a better house than the one Ged was born in. The Isle-Men of Low Torning, standing in awe of the wizard from Roke, asked pardon for its humbleness. "We have no stone to build with," said one, "We are none of us rich, though none starve," said another, and a third, "It will be dry at least, for I saw to the thatching myself, Sir." To Ged it was as good as any palace. He thanked the leaders of the township frankly, so that the eighteen of them went home, each in his own rowboat to his home isle, to tell the fishermen and housewives that the new wizard was a strange

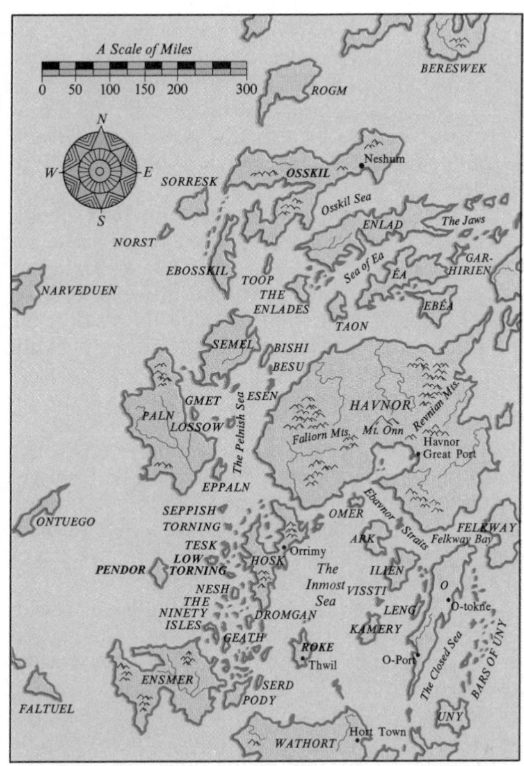

young grim fellow who spoke little, but he spoke fairly, and without pride. B

There was little cause, perhaps, for pride in this first magistry of Ged's. Wizards trained on Roke went commonly to cities or castles, to serve high lords who held them in high honor. These fishermen of Low Torning in the usual way of things would have had among them no more than a witch or a plain sorcerer, to charm the fishing nets and sing over new boats and cure beasts and men of their ailments. But in late years the old Dragon of C Pendor had spawned:[1] Nine dragons, it was said, now laired in the ruined towers of the Sealords of Pendor, dragging their scaled bellies up and down the marble stairs and through the broken doorways there. Wanting food on that dead isle, they would be flying forth some year when they were grown and hunger came upon them. Already a flight of four had been seen over the southwest shores of Hosk, not alighting but spying out the sheepfolds, barns, and villages. The hunger of a dragon is slow to wake, but hard to sate.[2] So the Isle-Men of Low Torning had sent to Roke beg-

1. **spawned:** produced eggs.
2. **sate:** satisfy.

Earthsea Vocabulary
turbies

A. Earthsea Map
You might have students locate: Hosk, Insmer, the Ninety Isles, Serd, Seppish, Pelnish Sea, Low Torning, Pendor, West Reach.

B. Making Inferences
? Why do the Low Torning leaders like Ged? (He liked the house they made for him; he is not proud.) This lack of pride is worth noting: what a difference in character from when we first met Ged!

C. Setting
? Where is Low Torning located in relation to Pendor? (Most westward and therefore closest to Pendor) What effect does this setting have on the plot? (It creates suspense—we know that Ged will have to fight the dragon soon.)

Supplementary Support Material: Chapters 5 and 6

1. Vocabulary Activity Sheet
2. Reading Check Test blackline master
3. Selection Test (page 217 of Test Book)
4. Reader's Response Journal
5. Workbook (page 157)

Developing Vocabulary

The following words appear on a test in the Test Book, page 218. (See also the Vocabulary Activity Sheet.)

somber	talon
jetty	subtle
scant	avert
bewilder	portent
ashen	dominion

Earthsea Vocabulary
corlyroot
redfever

A. Language
The word *wizard* has the same root as *wisdom.* Note also that Le Guin avoids using the word "magician"; she prefers "mage." The Magi were a priestly caste in Persia, said to have supernatural power. The three wise men who bore gifts to the Christ child were Magi. Le Guin chooses her words carefully, not just for what they denote, that is, what they mean, but for what they connote, that is, what they suggest.

B. Foreshadowing
The wise Archmage's words foreshadow Ged's confrontation with the shadow, or the evil that haunts him.

C. Character
? What qualities in Ged does his friendship with Pechvarry show? (Humility, tact, willingness to learn, need for friendship, ability to make a friend)

A ging for a wizard to protect their folk from what boded over the western horizon, and the Archmage had judged their fear well founded.

"There is no comfort in this place," the Archmage had said to Ged on the day he made him wizard, "no fame, no wealth, maybe no risk. Will you go?"

"I will go," Ged had replied, not from obedience only. Since the night on Roke Knoll his desire had turned as much against fame and display as once it had been set on them. Always now he doubted his strength and dreaded the trial of his power. Yet also the talk of dragons drew him with a great curiosity. In Gont there have been no dragons for many hundred years; and no dragon would ever fly within scent or sight or spell of Roke, so that there also they are a matter of tales and songs only, things sung of but not seen. Ged had learned all he could of dragons at the School, but it is one thing to read about dragons and another to meet them. The chance lay bright before him, and heartily he answered, "I will go."

The Archmage Gensher had nodded his head, but his look was somber. "Tell me," he said at last, "do you fear to leave Roke? Or are you eager to be gone?"

"Both, my lord."

B Again Gensher nodded. "I do not know if I do right to send you from your safety here," he said very low. "I cannot see your way. It is all in darkness. And there is a power in the North, something that would destroy you, but what it is and where, whether in your past or on your forward way, I cannot tell: It is all shadowed. When the men from Low Torning came here, I thought at once of you, for it seemed a safe place and out of the way, where you might have time to gather your strength. But I do not know if anyplace is safe for you, or where your way goes. I do not want to send you out into the dark. . . ."

It seemed a bright enough place to Ged at first, the house under the flowering trees. There he lived, and watched the western sky often, and kept his wizard's ear tuned for the sound of scaly wings. But no dragon came. Ged fished from his jetty, and tended his garden patch. He spent whole days pondering a page or a line or a word in the Lore-Books he had brought from Roke, sitting out in the summer air under the pendick trees, while the otak slept beside him or went hunting mice in the forests of grass and daisies. And he served the people of Low Torning as healall and weatherworker whenever they asked him. It did not enter his head that a wizard might be ashamed to perform such simple crafts, for he had been a witch-child among poorer folk than these. They, however, asked little of him, holding him in awe, partly because he was a wizard from the Isle of the Wise, and partly on account of his silence and his scarred face. There was that about him, young as he was, that made men uneasy with him.

Yet he found a friend, a boatmaker who dwelt on the next islet eastward. His name was Pechvarry. They had met first on his jetty, where Ged stopped to watch him stepping the mast of a little catboat. He had looked up at the wizard with a grin and said, "Here's a month's work nearly finished. I guess you might have done it in a minute with a word, eh, Sir?"

"I might," said Ged, "but it would likely sink the next minute, unless I kept the spells up. But if you like . . ." He stopped.

"Well, Sir?"

"Well, that is a lovely little craft. She needs nothing. But if you like, I could set a binding-spell on her, to help keep her sound; or a finding-spell, to help bring her home from the sea."

He spoke hesitantly, not wanting to offend the craftsman, but Pechvarry's face shone. "The little boat's for my son, Sir, and if you would lay such charms on her, it would be a mighty kindness and a friendly act." And he climbed up onto the jetty to take Ged's hand then and there and thank him.

After that they came to work together often, Ged interweaving his spellcrafts with Pechvarry's handwork on the boats he built or repaired, and in return learning from Pechvarry how a boat was built, and also how a boat was handled without aid of magic: for this skill of plain sailing had been somewhat scanted on Roke. Often Ged and Pechvarry and his little son Ioeth went out into the channels and lagoons, sailing or rowing one boat or another, till Ged was a fair sailor, and the friendship between him and Pechvarry was a settled thing. C

Along in late autumn the boatmaker's son fell sick. The mother sent for the witchwoman of Tesk Isle, who was a good hand at healing, and all seemed well for a day or two. Then in the middle of a stormy night came Pechvarry hammering at Ged's door, begging him to come save the child. Ged ran down to the boat with him and they rowed in all haste through dark and rain to the boatmaker's house. There Ged saw the child on his pallet-bed, and the mother crouching silent beside him, and the witchwoman making a smoke of corlyroot and singing the Nagian Chant, which was the best healing she had. But she whispered to Ged, "Lord Wizard, I think this fever is the redfever, and the child will die of it tonight."

When Ged knelt and put his hands on the child, he thought the same, and he drew back a moment.

In the latter months of his own long sickness the Master Herbal had taught him much of the healer's lore, and the first lesson and the last of all that lore was this: Heal the wound and cure the illness, but let the dying spirit go.

The mother saw his movement, and the meaning of it, and cried out aloud in despair. Pechvarry stooped down by her saying, "The Lord Sparrowhawk will save him, wife. No need to cry! He's here now. He can do it."

Hearing the mother's wail, and seeing the trust
A Pechvarry had in him, Ged did not know how he could disappoint them. He mistrusted his own judgment, and thought perhaps the child might be saved, if the fever could be brought down. He said, "I'll do my best, Pechvarry."

He set to bathing the little boy with cold rainwater that they brought new-fallen from out of doors, and he began to say one of the spells of feverstay. The spell took no hold and made no whole, and suddenly he thought the child was dying in his arms.

B Summoning his power all at once and with no thought for himself, he sent his spirit out after the child's spirit, to bring it back home. He called the child's name, "Ioeth!" Thinking some faint answer came in his inward hearing he pursued, calling once more. Then he saw the little boy running fast and far ahead of him down a dark slope, the side of some vast hill. There was no sound. The stars above the hill were no stars his eyes had ever seen. Yet he knew the constellations by name: the Sheaf, the Door, the One Who Turns, the Tree. They were those stars that do not set, that are not paled by the coming of any day. He had followed the dying child too far.

Knowing this he found himself alone on the dark hillside. It was hard to turn back, very hard.

A. Interpreting
Notice the emphasis on rules. No wizard is all-powerful.

B. Character Change
This is the third summoning spell that Ged has used. ? How is his present motive different from his previous motives? (First, he wanted to impress a girl; next, he wanted to show his power; now he acts out of love.)

A. Point of View
The story is told from the third-person omniscient point of view, but mostly through the eyes of Ged. Sometimes you see an event through the eyes of a different character; here you are told what Pechvarry, his wife and the witch saw. We could not have learned what happened to Ged from him, since he became unconscious from the strain of using his power.

B. Responding
? This is the third time Ged becomes tranced from expending his power. What were the other two times? (When Ged saved his village from the Kargs by creating fog, and when Ged met the shadow on Roke Knoll.)

He turned slowly. Slowly he set one foot forward to climb back up the hill, and then the other. Step by step he went, each step willed. And each step was harder than the last.

The stars did not move. No wind blew over the dry steep ground. In all the vast kingdom of the darkness only he moved, slowly, climbing. He came to the top of the hill, and saw the low wall of stones there. But across the wall, facing him, there was a shadow.

The shadow did not have the shape of man or beast. It was shapeless, scarcely to be seen, but it whispered at him, though there were no words in its whispering, and it reached out toward him. And it stood on the side of the living, and he on the side of the dead.

Either he must go down the hill into the desert lands and lightless cities of the dead, or he must step across the wall back into life, where the formless evil thing waited for him.

His spirit-staff was in his hand, and he raised it high. With that motion, strength came into him. As he made to leap the low wall of stones straight at the shadow, the staff burned suddenly white, a blinding light in that dim place. He leaped, felt himself fall, and saw no more.

A Now what Pechvarry and his wife and the witch saw was this: The young wizard had stopped midway in his spell, and held the child a while motionless. Then he had laid little Ioeth gently down on the pallet, and had risen, and stood silent, staff in hand. All at once he raised the staff high and it blazed with white fire as if he held the lightning-bolt in his grip, and all the household things in the hut leaped out strange and vivid in that momentary fire. When their eyes were clear from the dazzlement they saw the young man lying huddled forward on the earthen floor, beside the pallet where the child lay dead.

To Pechvarry it seemed that the wizard also was dead. His wife wept, but he was utterly bewildered. But the witch had some hearsay knowledge concerning magery and the ways a true wizard may go, and she saw to it that Ged, cold and lifeless as he lay, was not treated as a dead man B but as one sick or tranced. He was carried home, and an old woman was left to watch and see whether he slept to wake or slept forever.

The little otak was hiding in the rafters of the house, as it did when strangers entered. There it stayed while the rain beat on the walls and the fire sank down and the night wearing slowly along left the old woman nodding beside the hearthpit. Then the otak crept down and came to Ged where he lay stretched stiff and still upon the bed. It began to lick his hands and wrists, long and patiently, with its dry leaf-brown tongue. Crouching beside his head it licked his temple, his scarred cheek, and softly his closed eyes. And very slowly under that soft touch Ged roused. He woke, not knowing where he had been or where he was or what was the faint gray light in the air about him, which was the light of dawn coming to the world. Then the otak curled up near his shoulder as usual, and went to sleep.

Later, when Ged thought back upon that night, he knew that had none touched him when he lay thus spirit-lost, had none called him back in some way, he might have been lost for good. It was only the dumb instinctive wisdom of the beast who licks his hurt companion to comfort him, and yet in that wisdom Ged saw something akin to his own power, something that went as deep as wizardry. From that time forth he believed that the wise man is one who never sets himself apart from other living things, whether they have speech or not, and in later years he strove long to learn what can be learned, in silence, from the eyes of animals, the flight of birds, the great slow gestures of trees.

He had now made unscathed, for the first time, that crossing-over and return which only a wizard can make with open eyes, and which not the greatest mage can make without risk. But he had returned to a grief and a fear. The grief was for his friend Pechvarry, the fear was for himself. He knew now why the Archmage had feared to send him forth, and what had darkened and clouded even the mage's foreseeing of his future. For it was darkness itself that had awaited him, the unnamed thing, the being that did not belong in the world, the shadow he had loosed or made. In spirit, at the boundary wall between death and life, it had waited for him these long years. It had found him there at last. It would be on his track now, seeking to draw near to him, to take his strength into itself, and suck up his life, and clothe itself in his flesh.

Soon after, he dreamed of the thing like a bear with no head or face. He thought it went fumbling about the walls of the house, searching for the door. Such a dream he had not dreamed since the healing of the wounds the thing had given him. When he woke he was weak and cold, and the scars on his face and shoulder drew and ached.

Now began a bad time. When he dreamed of the shadow or so much as thought of it, he felt always that same cold dread: Sense and power drained out of him, leaving him stupid and astray. He raged at his cowardice, but that did no good. He sought for some protection, but there was none: The thing was not flesh, not alive, not spirit, unnamed, having no being but what he himself had given it—a terrible power outside the laws of the sunlit world. All he knew of it was that it was drawn to him and would try to work its will through him, being his creature. But in what form it could come, having no real form of its own as yet, and how it would come, and when it would come, this he did not know.

He set up what barriers of sorcery he could about his house and about the isle where he lived. Such spell-walls must be ever renewed, and soon he saw that if he spent all his strength on these defenses, he would be of no use to the islanders. What could he do, between two enemies, if a dragon came from Pendor?

Again he dreamed, but this time in the dream the shadow was inside his house, beside the door, reaching out to him through the darkness and whispering words he did not understand. He woke in terror, and sent the werelight flaming through the air, lighting every corner of the little house till he saw no shadow anywhere. Then he put wood on the coals of his firepit, and sat in the firelight hearing the autumn wind fingering at the thatch
A roof and whining in the great bare trees above; and he pondered long. An old anger had awakened in his heart. He would not suffer this helpless waiting, this sitting trapped on a little island mut-
B tering useless spells of lock and ward. Yet he could not simply flee the trap: to do so would be to break his trust with the islanders and to leave them to the imminent dragon, undefended. There was but one way to take.

C The next morning he went down among the fishermen in the principal moorage of Low Torning, and finding the Head Isle-Man there said to him, "I must leave this place. I am in danger, and I put you in danger. I must go. Therefore I ask your leave to go out and do away with the dragons on Pendor, so that my task for you will be finished and I may leave freely. Or if I fail, I should fail also when they come here, and that is better known now than later."

The Isle-Man stared at him all dropjawed. "Lord Sparrowhawk," he said, "there are nine dragons out there!"

"Eight are still young, they say."

"But the old one—"

"I tell you, I must go from here. I ask your leave to rid you of the dragon-peril first, if I can do so."

"As you will, Sir," The Isle-Man said gloomily. All that listened there thought this a folly or a crazy courage in their young wizard, and with sullen faces they saw him go, expecting no news of him again. Some hinted that he meant merely to sail back by Hosk to the Inmost Sea, leaving them in the lurch; others, among them Pechvarry, held that he had gone mad, and sought death.

For four generations of men all ships had set their course to keep far from the shores of Pendor Island. No mage had ever come to do combat with the dragon there, for the island was on no traveled sea road and its lords had been pirates, slave-takers, warmakers, hated by all that dwelt in the southwest parts of Earthsea. For this reason none had sought to revenge the Lord of Pendor, after the dragon came suddenly out of the west upon him and his men where they sat feasting in the tower, and smothered them with the flames of his mouth, and drove all the townsfolk screaming into the sea. Unavenged, Pendor had been left to the dragon, with all its bones, and towers, and jewels stolen from long-dead princes of the coasts of Paln and Hosk.

All this Ged knew well, and more, for ever since he came to Low Torning he had held in mind and pondered over all he had ever learned of dragons. As he guided his small boat westward—not rowing now nor using the seaman's skill Pechvarry had taught him, but sailing wizardly with the magewind in his sail and a spell set on prow and keel to keep them true—he watched to see the dead isle rise on the rim of the sea. Speed he wanted, and therefore used the magewind, for he feared what was behind him more than what was before him. But as the day passed, his impatience turned from fear to a kind of glad fierceness. At last he sought this danger of his own will; and the nearer he came to it the more sure he was that, for this time at least, for this hour perhaps before his death, he was free. The shadow dared not follow him into a dragon's jaws. The waves ran white-tipped on the gray sea, and gray clouds streamed overhead on the north wind. He went west with the quick magewind in his sail, and came in sight of the rocks of Pendor, the still streets of the town, and the gutted, falling towers.

At the entrance of the harbor, a shallow crescent bay, he let the windspell drop and stilled his little boat so it lay rocking on the waves. Then he summoned the dragon: "Usurper[3] of Pendor, come defend your hoard!"

His voice fell short in the sound of breakers beating on the ashen shores; but dragons have keen ears. Presently one flitted up from some roofless ruin of the town like a vast black bat, thin-winged and spiny-backed, and circling into the north wind came flying toward Ged. His heart swelled at the sight of the creature that was a myth

3. **usurper** (yōō·surp′ər): someone who takes another's power or position by force.

A. Personification
Point out the use of personification—giving human qualities to ideas, objects, animals, or aspects of nature—in this line: ". . . the autumn wind fingering at the thatch roof and whining in the great bare trees above . . ."
? Find another example of personification in this paragraph. ("An old anger had awakened . . .")

B. Vocabulary
ward: guard. Remind students that Nemmerle and Gensher have the title "Warder of Roke."
? Against what do they guard Roke? (Evil forces)

C. Conflict
? What internal conflict does Ged resolve when he decides to do away with the dragon? (His fear of the shadow versus his responsibility to the islanders)

Dragons

The dragon is the best known of all the monsters of fantasy. Stories were told about dragons long before people discovered that dinosaurs once walked the earth. Yet dragons resemble dinosaurs more than any living creature! The Bible mentions dragons several times, often by the name "Leviathan." In Chinese mythology, dragons were thought to be of divine origin. Oriental dragons aided humans unless the humans angered them. Oriental dragons were thought to control the weather; people tried to please dragons so they would have good luck. In Western mythology, dragons are usually evil. In many legends, dragons guard a hoard of treasure that they have stolen from their victims. David Rees in his essay "Earthsea Revisited" states that Le Guin elevates dragons to "a position in the scheme of things that is superior to that of any other beast. Dangerous and unpredictable they may be, but their primitive majesty is awe-inspiring. . . ."

Analyzing Style
A Reader's Guide to Science Fiction describes Le Guin's writing style as "beautiful . . . both evocative and unobtrusive." The third complete paragraph in the right-hand column is a good one for your advanced students to study closely. Ask them to find examples of compound words, simile, metaphor, and alliteration. Have them note the wonderful combination of simile and alliteration in the sentence that begins "Lean as a hound. . . ." This sentence is also, like so much of Le Guin's writing, perfectly balanced, with "lean as a hound" having the same structure as "huge as a hill." Ask students also to notice that the author varies the length of her sentences, using a short sentence such as "Ged stared in awe" for emphasis.

to his people, and he laughed and shouted, "Go tell the Old One to come, you wind-worm!"

For this was one of the young dragons, spawned there years ago by a she-dragon from the West Reach, who had set her clutch of great leathern eggs, as they say she-dragons will, in some sunny broken room of the tower and had flown away again, leaving the Old Dragon of Pendor to watch the young when they crawled like baneful[4] lizards from the shell.

The young dragon made no answer. He was not large of his kind, maybe the length of a forty-oared ship, and was worm-thin for all the reach of his black membranous wings. He had not got his growth yet, nor his voice, nor any dragon-cunning. Straight at Ged in the small rocking boat he came, opening his long, toothed jaws as he slid down arrowy from the air: so that all Ged had to do was bind his wings and limbs stiff with one sharp spell and send him thus hurtling aside into the sea like a stone falling. And the gray sea closed over him.

Two dragons like the first rose up from the base of the highest tower. Even as the first one they came driving straight at Ged, and even so he caught both, hurled both down, and drowned them; and he had not yet lifted up his wizard's staff.

Now after a little time there came three against him from the island. One of these was much greater, and fire spewed curling from its jaws. Two came flying at him rattling their wings, but the big one came circling from behind, very swift, to burn him and his boat with its breath of fire. No binding spell would catch all three, because two came from north and one from south. In the instant that he saw this, Ged worked a spell of Changing, and between one breath and the next flew up from his boat in dragon-form.

Spreading broad wings and reaching talons out, he met the two head on, withering them with fire, and then turned to the third, who was larger than he and armed also with fire. On the wind over the gray waves they doubled, snapped, swooped, lunged, till smoke roiled about them red-lit by the
A glare of their fiery mouths. Ged flew suddenly upward and the other pursued, below him. In
B midflight the dragon Ged raised wings, stopped, and stooped as the hawk stoops, talons outstretched downward, striking and bearing the other down by neck and flank. The black wings flurried and black dragon-blood dropped in thick drops into the sea. The Pendor dragon tore free and flew low and lamely to the island, where it hid, crawling into some well or cavern in the ruined town.

At once Ged took his form and place again on the boat, for it was most perilous to keep that dragon-shape longer than need demanded. His hands were black with the scalding wormblood, and he was scorched about the head with fire, but this was no matter now. He waited only till he had his breath back and then called, "Six I have seen, five slain, nine are told of: Come out, worms!"

No creature moved nor voice spoke for a long while on the island, but only the waves beat loudly on the shore. Then Ged was aware that the highest tower slowly changed its shape, bulging out on one side as if it grew an arm. He feared dragon-magic, for old dragons are very powerful and guileful in a sorcery like and unlike the sorcery of men: but a moment more and he saw this was no trick of the dragon, but of his own eyes. What he had taken for a part of the tower was the shoulder of the Dragon of Pendor as he uncurled his bulk and lifted himself slowly up.

When he was all afoot his scaled head, spike-crowned and triple-tongued, rose higher than the broken tower's height, and his taloned forefeet rested on the rubble of the town below. His scales were gray-black, catching the daylight like broken stone. Lean as a hound he was and huge as a hill. Ged stared in awe. There was no song or tale could prepare the mind for this sight. Almost he stared into the dragon's eyes and was caught, for one cannot look into a dragon's eyes. He glanced away from the oily green gaze that watched him, and held up before him his staff, that looked now like a splinter, like a twig. C

"Eight sons I had, little wizard," said the great dry voice of the dragon. "Five died, one dies: enough. You will not win my hoard by killing them."

"I do not want your hoard."

The yellow smoke hissed from the dragon's nostrils: That was his laughter.

"Would you not like to come ashore and look at it, little wizard? It is worth looking at."

"No, dragon." The kinship of dragons is with wind and fire, and they do not fight willingly over the sea. That had been Ged's advantage so far and he kept it; but the strip of seawater between him and the great gray talons did not seem much of an advantage anymore.

It was hard not to look into the green, watching eyes.

"You are a very young wizard," the dragon said, "I did not know men came so young into D their power." He spoke, as did Ged, in the Old Speech, for that is the tongue of dragons still.

4. **baneful:** causing distress, death, or ruin.

A. Responding
? What mistakes cause the young dragons' downfall? (They underestimate Ged and dive straight at him.) Ged, even in his borrowed dragon-form, is more clever than the dragons, who have never fought before.

B. Language
? Find examples of strong verbs that help you see the action. ("Spewed," "tore," "lunged")

C. Oral Reading
Have three students prepare and read the rest of this chapter to the class. You will need a Narrator, Ged, and the Dragon.

D. Conflict
Notice that the conflict with the young dragons is physical, but the conflict with the old dragon is a battle of wits.
? How does the dragon try to trick Ged? (He tries to get Ged to come ashore; he tries to make Ged look at him.)

A. Expansion
Ask students to notice that Ged mocked the young dragons but he treats the old one with respect. The Dragon of Pendor appears again in *The Farthest Shore,* the final book in the Earthsea trilogy. There, Ged saves the dragon from extinction and the dragon, in gratitude, later saves Ged's life.

B. Character
? What qualities does the encounter with the dragon reveal in Ged? (His power, cleverness, courage, wisdom, ability to duel in words and to command respect, sense of responsibility to the people of Low Torning)

C. Language
? What do you think of the sound of the dragon's name? Do you agree with critic Eleanor Cameron in her *Horn Book* review of the novel that it is a perfect choice for a dragon's name? What are some other names that might be suitable for a dragon?

D. Symbol
In medieval art, dragons were used as symbols of evil and sin.
? Do you think that Le Guin's dragons stand for evil? Why or why not?

Although the use of the Old Speech binds a man to truth, this is not so with dragons. It is their own language, and they can lie in it, twisting the true words to false ends, catching the unwary hearer in a maze of mirrorwords each of which reflects the truth and none of which leads anywhere. So Ged had been warned often, and when the dragon spoke he listened with an untrustful ear, all his doubts ready. But the words seemed plain and clear: "Is it to ask my help that you have come here, little wizard?"

"No, dragon."

"Yet I could help you. You will need help soon, against that which hunts you in the dark."

Ged stood dumb.

"What is it that hunts you? Name it to me."

"If I could name it—" Ged stopped himself.

Yellow smoke curled above the dragon's long head, from the nostrils that were two round pits of fire.

"If you could name it you could master it, maybe, little wizard. Maybe I could tell you its name, when I see it close by. And it will come close, if you wait about my isle. It will come wherever you come. If you do not want it to come close you must run, and run, and keep running from it. And yet it will follow you. Would you like to know its name?"

Ged stood silent again. How the dragon knew of the shadow he had loosed, he could not guess, nor how it might know the shadow's name. The Archmage had said that the shadow had no name. Yet dragons have their own wisdom; and they are an older race than man. Few men can guess what a dragon knows and how he knows it, and those few are the Dragonlords. To Ged, only one thing was sure: that, though the dragon might well be speaking truth, though he might indeed be able to tell Ged the nature and name of the shadow-thing and so give him power over it—even so, even if he spoke truth, he did so wholly for his own ends.

A "It is very seldom," the young man said at last, "that dragons ask to do men favors."

"But it is very common," said the dragon, "for cats to play with mice before they kill them."

"But I did not come here to play, or to be played with. I came to strike a bargain with you."

Like a sword in sharpness but five times the length of any sword, the point of the dragon's tail arched up scorpion-wise over his mailed back, above the tower. Drily he spoke: "I strike no bargains. I take. What have you to offer that I cannot take from you when I like?"

"Safety. Your safety. Swear that you will never fly eastward of Pendor, and I will swear to leave you unharmed."

A grating sound came from the dragon's throat like the noise of an avalanche far off, stones falling among mountains. Fire danced along his three-forked tongue. He raised himself up higher, looming over the ruins. "You offer me safety! You threaten me! With what?"

"With your name, Yevaud."

Ged's voice shook as he spoke the name, yet he spoke it clear and loud. At the sound of it, the old dragon held still, utterly still. A minute went by, and another; and then Ged, standing there in his rocking chip of a boat, smiled. He had staked his venture and his life on a guess drawn from old histories of dragon-lore learned on Roke, a guess that this Dragon of Pendor was the same that had spoiled the west of Osskil in the days of Elfarran and Morred, and had been driven from Osskill by a wizard, Elt, wise in names. The guess had held.

"We are matched, Yevaud. You have the strength: I have your name. Will you bargain?"

Still the dragon made no reply.

Many years had the dragon sprawled on the island where golden breastplates and emeralds lay scattered among dust and bricks and bones; he had watched his black lizard-brood play among crumbling houses and try their wings from the cliffs; he had slept long in the sun, unwaked by voice or sail. He had grown old. It was hard now to stir, to face this mage-lad, this frail enemy, at the sight of whose staff Yevaud, the old dragon, winced.

"You may choose nine stones from my hoard," he said at last, his voice hissing and whining in his long jaws. "The best: Take your choice. Then go!"

"I do not want your stones, Yevaud."

"Where is men's greed gone? Men loved bright stones in the old days in the North. . . . I know what it is you want, wizard. I, too, can offer you safety, for I know what can save you. I know what alone can save you. There is a horror follows you. I will tell you its name."

Ged's heart leaped in him, and he clutched his staff, standing as still as the dragon stood. He fought a moment with sudden, startling hope. B

It was not his own life that he bargained for. One mastery, and only one, could he hold over the dragon. He set hope aside and did what he must do.

"That is not what I ask for, Yevaud." C

When he spoke the dragon's name it was as if he held the huge being on a fine, thin leash, tightening it on his throat. He could feel the ancient malice and experience of men in the dragon's gaze that rested on him, he could see the steel talons each as long as a man's forearm, and the stone- D

Summary: Chapter 6
Ged returns to Low Torning a hero. The people there want him to stay, but he decides to go back to Roke where he feels he will be safer from the shadow. The Roke-wind, which keeps all evil influences away from Roke Island, makes it impossible for his boat to land. Stranded on another island, Ged talks to a stranger who tells him to go to the Court of the Terrenon in Osskil to get help to fight the shadow. Ged sails there and meets a shipmate named Skiorh, whom he distrusts. When they arrive in Osskil, Skiorh guides him to the Court. Traveling for hours over a wasteland, Ged finally confronts Skiorh, and finds that Skiorh's body has been taken over by the shadow. The shadow calls Ged by his true name, stripping him of his powers. Ged barely escapes, falling through the gates of the Court of the Terrenon.

A hard hide, and the withering fire that lurked in the dragon's throat: and yet always the leash tightened, tightened.

He spoke again: "Yevaud! Swear by your name that you and your sons will never come to the Archipelago."

Flames broke suddenly bright and loud from the dragon's jaws, and he said, "I swear it by my name!"

Silence lay over the isle then, and Yevaud lowered his great head.

When he raised it again and looked, the wizard was gone, and the sail of the boat was a white fleck on the waves eastward, heading towards the fat bejeweled islands of the inner seas. Then in rage the old Dragon of Pendor rose up breaking the tower with the writhing of his body, and beating his wings that spanned the whole width of the ruined town. But his oath held him, and he did not fly, then or ever, to the Archipelago.

Chapter 6
Hunted

As soon as Pendor had sunk under the sea-rim behind him, Ged looking eastward felt the fear of the shadow come into his heart again; and it was hard to turn from the bright B danger of the dragons to that formless, hopeless horror. He let the magewind drop, and sailed on with the world's wind, for there was no desire for speed in him now. He had no clear plan even of what he should do. He must run, as the dragon had said; but where? To Roke, he thought, since C there at least he was protected, and might find counsel among the wise.

First, however, he must come to Low Torning once more and tell his tale to the Isle-Men. When word went out that he had returned, five days from his setting forth, they and half the people of the township came rowing and running to gather round him, and stare at him, and listen. He told this tale, and one man said, "But who saw this wonder of dragons slain and dragons baffled? What if he—"

"Be still!" the Head Isle-Man said roughly, for he knew, as did most of them, that a wizard may have subtle ways of telling the truth, and may keep the truth to himself, but that if he says a thing the thing is as he says. For that is his mastery. So they wondered, and began to feel that their fear was lifted from them, and then they began to rejoice. They pressed round their young wizard and asked for the tale again. More islanders came, and asked for it again. By nightfall he no longer had to tell it. They could do it for him, better. Already the village chanters had fitted it to an old tune, and were singing the *Song of the Sparrowhawk*. Bonfires were burning not only on the isles of Low Torning but in townships to the south and east. Fishermen shouted the news from boat to boat, from isle to isle it went: Evil is averted, the dragons will never come from Pendor!

That night, that one night, was joyous for Ged. No shadow could come near him through the brightness of those fires of thanksgiving that burned on every hill and beach, through the circles of laughing dancers that ringed him about, singing his praise, swinging their torches in the gusty autumn night so that sparks rose thick and bright and brief upon the wind.

The next day he met with Pechvarry, who said, "I did not know you were so mighty, my lord." There was fear in that because he had dared make Ged his friend, but there was reproach in it also. Ged had not saved a little child, though he had slain dragons. After that, Ged felt afresh the unease and impatience that had driven him to Pendor, and drove him now from Low Torning. The next day, though they would have kept him gladly the rest of his life to praise and boast of, he left the house on the hill, with no baggage but his books, his staff, and the otak riding on his shoulder.

He went in a rowboat with a couple of young fishermen of Low Torning, who wanted the honor of being his boatmen. Always as they rowed on among the craft that crowd the eastern channels of the Ninety Isles, under the windows and balconies of houses that lean out over the water, past the wharves of Nesh, the rainy pastures of Dromgan, the malodorous oilsheds of Geath, word of his deed had gone ahead of him. They whistled the *Song of the Sparrowhawk* as he went by, they vied to have him spend the night and tell his dragon-tale. When at last he came to Serd, the ship's master of whom he asked passage out to Roke bowed as he answered, "A privilege to me, Lord Wizard, and an honor to my ship!"

So Ged turned his back on the Ninety Isles; but even as the ship turned from Serd Inner Port and raised sail, a wind came up hard from the east against her. It was strange, for the wintry sky was clear and the weather had seemed settled mild that morning. It was only thirty miles from Serd to Roke, and they sailed on; and when the wind still rose, they still sailed on. The little ship, like most traders of the Inmost Sea, bore the high fore-and-aft sail that can be turned to catch a headwind, and her master was a handy seaman, proud of his

D E

A. Figure of Speech
? What is the "leash" that Ged uses to force a promise from Yevaud? (His knowledge of the dragon's true name)

B. Vocabulary
? What does "bright" mean here? (Clear, visible)

C. Heroism
? Do you think this decision is wise? Does Ged's fear of the shadow and his longing for safety make him heroic or more like a real human being?

D. Earthsea Map
You might have the students locate Nesh, Dromgan and Geath.

E. Vocabulary
malodorous: bad smelling

A. Vocabulary
jibing: shifting backward or sideways instead of ahead.

B. Invented Word Le Guin invented the word *ragefully.* ? Why do you think she invented "ragefully" when "angrily" would have had a similar meaning? ("Ragefully" implies a fury that "angrily" does not. Also, she wanted the alliteration with "roared.")

C. Compound Word Notice the compound "Dragon-tamer," used instead of the name "Ged." Tell students that this is an example of a "kenning," a metaphorical phrase or compound word used instead of the name of a person or thing. Kennings are characteristic of Anglo-Saxon poetry.

D. Recalling ? At what other time did the otak show its fear? (On Roke Knoll, when it gladly went to Vetch, seeking protection from Ged)

E. Repetition ? What words does Le Guin repeat here to create an atmosphere of fear and uncertainty? ("Doom," "shadow")

skill. So tacking now north now south they worked eastward. Clouds and rain came up on the wind, which veered and gusted so wildly that there was a considerable danger of the ship jibing. "Lord Sparrowhawk," said the ship's master to the young man, whom he had beside him in the place of honor in the stern, though small dignity could be kept up under that wind and rain that wet them all to a miserable sleekness in their sodden cloaks—"Lord Sparrowhawk, might you say a word to this wind, maybe?"

"How near are we to Roke?"

"Better than half way. But we've made no headway at all this past hour, Sir."

Ged spoke to the wind. It blew less hard, and for a while they went on fairly enough. Then sudden great gusts came whistling out of the south, and meeting these they were driven back westward again. The clouds broke and boiled in the sky, and the ship's master roared out ragefully, "This fool's gale blows all ways at once! Only a magewind will get us through this weather, Lord."

Ged looked glum at that, but the ship and her men were in danger for him, so he raised up the magewind into her sail. At once the ship began to cleave straight to the east, and the ship's master began to look cheerful again. But little by little, though Ged kept up the spell, the magewind slackened, growing feebler, until the ship seemed to hang still on the waves for a minute, her sail drooping, amid all the tumult of the rain and gale. Then with a thundercrack the boom came swinging round and she jibed and jumped northward like a scared cat.

Ged grabbed hold of a stanchion, for she lay almost over on her side, and shouted out, "Turn back to Serd, master!"

The master cursed and shouted that he would not: "A wizard aboard, and I the best seaman of the Trade, and this the handiest ship I ever sailed—turn back?"

Then, the ship turning again almost as if a whirlpool had caught her keel, he too grabbed hold of the sternpost to keep aboard, and Ged said to him, "Leave me at Serd and sail where you like. It's not against your ship this wind blows, but against me."

"Against you, a wizard of Roke?"

"Have you never heard of the Roke-wind, master?"

"Aye, that keeps off evil powers from the Isle of the Wise, but what has that to do with you, a Dragon-tamer?"

"That is between me and my shadow," Ged answered shortly, as a wizard will; and he said no more as they went swiftly, with a steady wind and under clearing skies, back over the sea to Serd.

There was a heaviness and a dread in his heart as he went up from the wharves of Serd. The days were shortening into winter, and dusk came soon. With dusk Ged's uneasiness always grew, and now the turning of each street seemed a threat to him, and he had to steel himself not to keep looking back over his shoulder at what might be coming behind him. He went to the Sea-House of Serd, where travelers and merchants ate together of good fare provided by the township, and might sleep in the long raftered hall: Such is the hospitality of the thriving islands of the Inmost Sea.

He saved a bit of meat from his dinner, and by the firepit afterward he coaxed the otak out of the fold of his hood where it had cowered all that day, and tried to get it to eat, petting it and whispering to it, "Hoeg, hoeg, little one, silent one. . . ." But it would not eat, and crept into his pocket to hide. By that, by his own dull uncertainty, by the very look of the darkness in the corners of the great room, he knew that the shadow was not far from him.

No one in this place knew him: They were travelers, from other isles, who had not heard the *Song of the Sparrowhawk.* None spoke to him. He chose a pallet at last and lay down, but all night long he lay with open eyes there in the raftered hall among the sleep of strangers. All night he tried to choose his way, to plan where he should go, what he should do: but each choice, each plan was blocked by a foreboding of doom. Across each way he might go lay the shadow. Only Roke was clear of it: and to Roke he could not go, forbidden by the high, enwoven, ancient spells that kept the perilous island safe. That the Roke-wind had risen against him was proof the thing that hunted him must be very close upon him now.

That thing was bodiless, blind to sunlight, a creature of a lightless, placeless, timeless realm. It must grope after him through the days and across the seas of the sunlit world, and could take visible shape only in dream and darkness. It had as yet no substance or being that the light of the sun would shine on; and so it is sung in the *Deed of Hode,* "Daybreak makes all earth and sea, from shadow brings forth form, driving dream to the dark kingdom." But if once the shadow caught up with Ged it could draw his power out of him, and take from him the very weight and warmth and life of his body and the will that moved him.

That was the doom he saw lying ahead on every road. And he knew that he might be tricked toward that doom; for the shadow, growing stronger always as it was nearer him, might even now have strength enough to put evil powers or evil men to its own use—showing him false portents, or speaking with a stranger's voice. For all he knew, in one of these men who slept in this corner or that of the raftered hall of the Sea-House tonight, A the dark thing lurked, finding a foothold in a dark soul and there waiting and watching Ged and feeding, even now, on his weakness, on his uncertainty, on his fear.

It was past bearing. He must trust to chance, and run wherever chance took him. At the first cold hint of dawn he got up and went in haste under the dimming stars down to the wharves of Serd, resolved only to take the first ship outward bound that would have him. A galley was loading turbie-oil; she was to sail at sunrise, bound for Havnor Great Port. Ged asked passage of her master. A wizard's staff is passport and payment on most ships. They took him aboard willingly, and within that hour the ship set forth. Ged's spirits lifted with the first lifting of the forty long oars, and the drumbeat that kept the stroke made a brave music to him.

And yet he did not know what he could do in Havnor, or where he would run from there. Northward was as good as any direction. He was a Northerner himself; maybe he could find some ship to take him on to Gont from Havnor, and he might see Ogion again. Or he might find some ship going far out into the Reaches, so far the shadow would lose him and give up the hunt. Beyond such vague ideas as these, there was no plan in his head, and he saw no one course that he must follow. Only he must run. . . .

Those forty oars carried the ship over a hundred and fifty miles of wintry sea before sunset of the second day out from Serd. They came in to port at Orrimy on the east shore of the great land Hosk, for these trade-galleys of the Inmost Sea keep to B the coasts and lie overnight in harbor whenever they can. Ged went ashore, for it was still daylight, and he roamed the steep streets of the port town, aimless and brooding.

Orrimy is an old town, built heavily of stone and brick, walled against the lawless lords of the interior of Hosk Island; the warehouses on the docks are like forts, and the merchants' houses are towered and fortified. Yet to Ged wandering through the streets those ponderous mansions seemed like veils, behind which lay an empty dark; and people who passed him, intent on their business, seemed not real men but voiceless shadows of men. As the sun set he came down to the wharves again, and even there in the broad red light and wind of the day's end, sea and land alike to him seemed dim and silent.

"Where are you bound, Lord Wizard?"

So one hailed him suddenly from behind. Turning he saw a man dressed in gray, who carried a staff of heavy wood that was not a wizard's staff. The stranger's face was hidden by his hood from the red light, but Ged felt the unseen eyes meet his. Starting back he raised his own yew-staff between him and the stranger.

Mildly the man asked, "What do you fear?"

"What follows behind me."

"So? But I'm not your shadow."

Ged stood silent. He knew that indeed this man, whatever he was, was not what he feared: He was no shadow or ghost or gebbeth-creature. Amidst the dry silence and shadowiness that had come over the world, he even kept a voice and some solidity. He put back his hood now. He had a strange, seamed, bald head, a lined face. Though age had not sounded in his voice, he looked to be an old man.

"I do not know you," said the man in gray, "yet I think perhaps we do not meet by chance. I heard a tale once of a young man, a scarred man, who won through darkness to great dominion, even to kingship. I do not know if that is your tale. But I will tell you this: Go to the Court of the Terrenon, if you need a sword to fight shadows with. A staff of yew-wood will not serve your need."

Hope and mistrust struggled in Ged's mind as he listened. A wizardly man soon learns that few indeed of his meetings are chance ones, be they for good or for ill.

"In what land is the Court of the Terrenon?"

"In Osskil."

At the sound of that name Ged saw for a moment, by a trick of memory, a black raven on green grass who looked up at him sidelong with an eye like polished stone, and spoke; but the words were forgotten. C

"That land has something of a dark name," Ged said, looking ever at the man in gray, trying to judge what kind of man he was. There was a manner about him that hinted of the sorcerer, even of the wizard; and yet boldly as he spoke to Ged, there was a queer beaten look about him, the look D almost of a sick man, or a prisoner, or a slave.

"You are from Roke," he answered. "The wizards of Roke give a dark name to wizardries other than their own."

"What man are you?"

"A traveler; a trader's agent from Osskil; I am here on business," said the man in gray. When Ged asked him no more he quietly bade the young

A. Foreshadowing

? What clues prepare you for what will happen later in this chapter? (The shadow might be strong enough to find a "foothold in a dark soul.")

B. Setting

Notice how Ged's aimless, brooding mood causes him to see Orrimy as a hostile, dark and shadowy town.

C. Interpreting

This refers to the words of the Archmage Nemmerle's raven on page 552.

D. Making Inferences

? Do you think this stranger is someone that Ged can trust? What details give you this opinion? (Although he gives Ged advice, we are not sure he can be trusted. Osskil has "something of a bad name"; the man has a "queer, beaten look"; he advises Ged to go to a place that Roke might call a "dark wizardry.")

Earthsea Vocabulary
loto-shell

A. Motivation
? Why do you think Ged decides to go to Osskil? (As night approaches, his fear and desperation intensifies.) Is this a rational decision? (No, it is an emotional decision based on feelings.)

B. Vocabulary
dory: a small boat

C. Earthsea Map
You might have students locate Osskil, Semel, the Enlades.

D. Understatement
? What does Le Guin mean: "Gold is a great thing in Osskil. But it is not a source of good fellowship there, or amongst the dragons, who also prize it highly." (This is an example of understatement: Le Guin means that gold makes enemies of people who prize it too highly.)

E. Onomatopoeia
? Is "Skiorh" a name that Le Guin would give to a villain or a hero? Explain. (It is an unpleasant sound, so it suits a villain. It sounds a little like "skewer.")

man good night, and went off up the narrow stepped street above the quays.

Ged turned, irresolute[1] whether to heed this sign or not, and looked to the north. The red light was dying out fast from the hills and from the windy sea. Gray dusk came, and on its heels the night.

A Ged went in sudden decision and haste along the quays to a fisherman who was folding his nets down in his dory, and hailed him: "Do you know any ship in this port bound north—to Semel, or the Enlades?"

B "The longship yonder's from Osskil, she might be stopping at the Enlades."

C In the same haste Ged went on to the great ship the fisherman had pointed to, a longship of sixty oars, gaunt as a snake, her high bent prow carven and inlaid with disks of loto-shell, her oarport-covers painted red, with the rune Sifl sketched on each in black. A grim, swift ship she looked, and all in sea-trim, with all her crew aboard. Ged sought out the ship's master and asked passage to Osskil of him.

"Can you pay?"

"I have some skill with winds."

"I am a weatherworker myself. You have nothing to give? No money?"

In Low Torning the Isle-Men had paid Ged as best they could with the ivory pieces used by traders in the Archipelago; he would take only ten pieces, though they wanted to give him more. He offered these now to the Osskilian, but he shook his head. "We do not use those counters. If you have nothing to pay, I have no place aboard for you."

"Do you need arms? I have rowed in a galley."

"Aye, we're short two men. Find your bench then," said the ship's master, and paid him no more heed.

So, laying his staff and his bag of books under the rowers' bench, Ged became for ten bitter days of winter an oarsman of that Northern ship. They left Orrimy at daybreak, and that day Ged thought he could never keep up his work. His left arm was somewhat lamed by the old wounds in his shoulder, and all his rowing in the channels about Low Torning had not trained him for the relentless pull and pull and pull at the long galley-oar to the beat of the drum. Each stint at the oars was of two or three hours, and then a second shift of oarsmen took the benches, but the time of rest seemed only long enough for all Ged's muscles to stiffen, and then it was back to the oars. And the second day of it was worse; but after that he hardened to the labor, and got on well enough.

There was no such comradeship among this crew as he had found aboard *Shadow* when he first went to Roke. The crewmen of Andradean and Gontish ships are partners in the trade, working together for a common profit, whereas traders of Osskil use slaves and bondsmen or hire men to row, paying them with small coins of gold. Gold is a great thing in Osskil. But it is not a source of good fellowship there, or amongst the dragons, who also prize it highly. D Since half this crew were bondsmen, forced to work, the ship's officers were slavemasters, and harsh ones. They never laid their whips on the back of an oarsman who worked for pay or passage; but there will not be much friendliness in a crew of whom some are whipped and others are not. Ged's fellows said little to one another, and less to him. They were mostly men from Osskil, speaking not the Hardic tongue of the Archipelago but a dialect of their own, and they were dour men, pale-skinned with black drooping mustaches and lank hair. *Kelub*, the red one, was Ged's name among them. Though they knew he was a wizard they showed him no regard, but rather a kind of cautious spitefulness. And he himself was in no mood for making friends. Even on his bench, caught up in the mighty rhythm of the rowing, one oarsman among sixty in a ship racing over void gray seas, he felt himself exposed, defenseless. When they came into strange ports at nightfall and he rolled himself in his cloak to sleep, weary as he was he would dream, wake, dream again: evil dreams, that he could not recall waking, though they seemed to hang about the ship and the men of the ship, so that he mistrusted each one of them.

All the Osskilian freemen wore a long knife at the hip, and one day as his oar-shift shared their noon meal one of these men asked Ged, "Are you slave or oathbreaker, Kelub?"

"Neither."

"Why no knife, then? Afraid to fight?" said the man, Skiorh, jeering. E

"No."

"Your little dog fight for you?"

"Otak," said another who listened. "No dog, that is otak," and he said something in Osskilian that made Skiorh scowl and turn away. Just as he turned Ged saw a change in his face, a slurring and shifting of the features, as if for a moment something had changed him, looking out through his eyes sidelong at Ged. Yet the next minute Ged saw him fullface, and he looked as usual, so that Ged told himself that what he had seen was his own fear, his own dread reflected in the other's eyes. But that night as they lay in port in Esen he dreamed, and Skiorh walked in his dream. After-

1. **irresolute** (ir·rez′ə·lōot′): indecisive.

ward he avoided the man as best he could, and it seemed also that Skiorh kept away from him, and no more words passed between them.

The snow-crowned mountains of Havnor sank away behind them southward, blurred by the mists of early winter. They rowed on past the mouth of the Sea of Éa where long ago Elfarran was drowned, and past the Enlades. They lay two days in port at Berila, the City of Ivory, white above its bay in the west of myth-haunted Enlad. At all ports they came to, the crewmen were kept aboard the ship, and set no foot on land. Then as a red sun rose they rowed out on the Osskil Sea, into the northeast winds that blow unhindered from the islandless vastness of the North Reach. Through that bitter sea they brought their cargo safe, coming the second day out of Berila into port at Neshum, the trade-city of Eastern Osskil.

A Ged saw a low coast lashed by a rainy wind, a gray town crouching behind the long stone breakwaters that made its harbor, and behind the town treeless hills under a snow-darkened sky. They had come far from the sunlight of the Inmost Sea.

Longshoremen of the Sea-Guild of Neshum came aboard to unload the cargo—gold, silver, jewelry, fine silks and Southern tapestries, such precious stuff as the lords of Osskil hoard—and the freemen of the crew were dismissed. Ged stopped one of them to ask his way; up until now the distrust he felt of all of them had kept him from saying where he was bound, but now, afoot and alone in a strange land, he must ask for guidance. The man went on impatiently saying he did not know, but Skiorh, overhearing, said, "The Court of the Terrenon? On the Keksemt Moors. I go that road."

Skiorh's was no company Ged would have chosen, but knowing neither the language nor the way he had small choice. Nor did it much matter, he thought; he had not chosen to come here. He had
B been driven, and now was driven on. He pulled his hood up over his head, took up his staff and bag, and followed the Osskilian through the streets of the town and upward into the snowy hills. The little otak would not ride on his shoulder, but hid in the pocket of his sheepskin tunic, under his cloak, as was its wont in cold weather. The hills stretched out into bleak rolling moorlands as far as the eye could see. They walked in silence and the silence of winter lay on all the land.

"How far?" Ged asked after they had gone some miles, seeing no sight of village or farm in any direction, and thinking that they had no food with them. Skiorh turned his head a moment, pulling up his own hood, and said, "Not far."

It was an ugly face, pale, coarse, and cruel, but Ged feared no man, though he might fear where such a man would guide him. He nodded, and they went on. Their road was only a scar through the waste of thin snow and leafless bushes. From time to time other tracks crossed it or branched from it. Now that the chimney-smoke of Neshum was hidden behind the hills in the darkening afternoon there was no sign at all of what way they should go, or had gone. Only the wind blew always from the east. And when they had walked for several hours Ged thought he saw, away off on the hills in the northwest where their way tended, a tiny scratch against the sky, like a tooth, white. But the light of the short day was fading, and on the next rise of the road he could make C out the thing, tower or tree or whatever, no more clearly than before.

"Do we go there?" he asked, pointing.

Skiorh made no answer but plodded on, muffled in his coarse cloak with its peaked, furred Osskilian hood. Ged strode on beside him. They had come far, and he was drowsy with the steady pace of their walking and with the long weariness of hard days and nights in the ship. It began to seem to him that he had walked forever and would walk forever beside this silent being through a silent darkening land. Caution and intention were dulled in him. He walked as in a long, long dream, going no place.

The otak stirred in his pocket, and a little vague fear also woke and stirred in his mind. He forced himself to speak. "Darkness comes, and snow. How far, Skiorh?"

After a pause the other answered, without turning, "Not far."

But his voice sounded not like a man's voice, but like a beast, hoarse and lipless, that tries to speak.

Ged stopped. All around stretched empty hills in the late, dusk light. Sparse snow whirled a little falling. "Skiorh!" he said, and the other halted, and turned. There was no face under the peaked hood.

Before Ged could speak spell or summon power, the gebbeth spoke, saying in its hoarse voice, "Ged!"

Then the young man could work no transformation, but was locked in his true being, and must face the gebbeth thus defenseless. Nor could he summon any help in this alien land, where nothing and no one was known to him and would come at his call. He stood alone, with nothing between him and his enemy but the staff of yew-wood in his right hand.

The thing that had devoured Skiorh's mind and possessed his flesh made the body take a step

A. Personification
Ask students to find examples of personification in this passage. ("Coast lashed by a rainy wind"; "town crouching behind the long stone breakwaters")

B. Making Inferences
? What does Ged think has driven him to this place? (The shadow)

C. Setting
? What details of the setting create a mood of gloom? ("bleak, rolling moorland"; "the silence of winter lay on all the land"; "the road was only a scar through the waste of thin snow"; "he saw . . . a tiny scratch . . . like a tooth")

A. Making Inferences

? Why do you think the shadow "would cast aside the husk of Skiorh and enter into Ged"? (Ged has more power than Skiorh and the shadow could use it to work greater evil. It also seeks to destroy Ged.)

READING CHECK TEST: CHAPTERS 5 AND 6

1. What do the people of Low Torning fear? *(Dragons)*

2. How does Ged almost die? *(He sends his spirit into the land of the dead and almost doesn't return.)*

3. How does Ged defeat the dragon? *(He says its true name.)*

4. What happens when Ged tries to return to Roke? *(The Roke-wind blows against him and turns back his ship.)*

5. What happens to Skiorh while he is leading Ged to the Court of the Terrenon? *(He is taken over by the shadow and becomes a gebbeth.)*

B. Irony

A situation is ironic when it is just the opposite of what you might expect.

? What is ironic about the burns Ged gets on his hand? (His magic staff burns his hand, but his magic does him no good, because the shadow has stripped him of his powers by calling him Ged.)

C. Onomatopoeia

Notice the repeated use of words containing "n," "m," and "s" sounds to convey the sound of whispering and mumbling that Ged hears.

D. Symbolism

? What does the long, dim slope represent? (Death; it reminds the reader of the slope Ged struggled to climb after he sent his spirit after the dying child's spirit—see page 571.)

toward Ged, and the arms came groping out toward him. A rage of horror filled Ged and he swung up and brought down his staff whistling on the hood that hid the shadow-face. Hood and cloak collapsed down nearly to the ground under the fierce blow as if there was nothing in them but wind, and then writhing and flapping stood up again. The body of a gebbeth has been drained of true substance and is something like a shell or a vapor in the form of a man, an unreal flesh clothing the shadow which is real. So jerking and billowing as if blown on the wind the shadow spread
A its arms and came at Ged, trying to get hold of him as it had held him on Roke Knoll: and if it did it would cast aside the husk of Skiorh and enter into Ged, devouring him out from within, owning him, which was its whole desire. Ged struck at it again with his heavy, smoking staff, beating it off, but it came again and he struck again, and then dropped the staff that blazed and
B smoldered, burning his hand. He backed away, then all at once turned and ran.

He ran, and the gebbeth followed a pace behind him, unable to outrun him yet never dropping behind. Ged never looked back. He ran, he ran, through that vast dusk land where there was no hiding place. Once the gebbeth in its hoarse whistling voice called him again by name, but though it had taken his wizard's power thus, it had no power over his body's strength, and could not make him stop. He ran.

Night thickened about the hunter and the hunted, and snow blew fine across the path that Ged could no longer see. The pulse hammered in his eyes, the breath burned in his throat, he was no longer really running but stumbling and staggering ahead: and yet the tireless pursuer seemed unable to catch up, coming always just behind C
him. It had begun to whisper and mumble at him, calling to him, and he knew that all his life that whispering had been in his ears, just under the threshold of hearing, but now he could hear it, and he must yield, he must give in, he must stop. Yet he labored on, struggling up a long, dim slope. D

ANALYZING CHAPTERS 5 AND 6
Identifying Facts
1. The people of Low Torning are threatened by the dragon of Pendor.
2. Ged must decide whether to stay in the land of the dead, into which his spirit has followed the boy's spirit, or to return to the land of the living and face his shadow.
3. Ged senses that the shadow is near, and he wants to escape before it attacks him again. He knows that he can't protect the islanders from the dragon if he is at the same time protecting himself from the shadow.
4. As the boat Ged is traveling on approaches Roke, a fierce gale turns it back. This is the Roke-wind, which keeps evil away from the island. The wind arises against Ged because he is being followed by the evil shadow.
5. Skiorh, a fellow oarsman aboard the ship that brought Ged to Osskil, agrees to guide Ged to the Court. Along the way, his body is taken over by the shadow and transformed into a gebbeth—a vapor of a man who has been drained of true substance.

Interpreting Meanings
6. Ged refuses the dragon's offer because he has undertaken this mission for the people of Low Torning, not for himself. Also, he knows that dragons twist words, so what the dragon tells him may result in evil anyway. This shows that Ged has learned to care about other people before himself, and that he understands his responsibilities as a wizard.
7. Ged's power is shown in his ability to bring his spirit back from the land of the dead and in his conquest of the dragon of Pendor.
The enemy's power is shown to be just as strong as Ged's by the fact that it can follow Ged anywhere, and that it can neutralize Ged's power (as happens in Osskil).
The shadow appears to be stronger, since it is the one who is chasing Ged. Students may realize that Ged's fear is what makes him weaker than the shadow.

He thought there was a light somewhere before him, and he thought he heard a voice in front of him, above him somewhere, calling, "Come! Come!"

He tried to answer but he had no voice. The pale light grew certain, shining through a gateway straight before him: He could not see the walls, but he saw the gate. At the sight of it he halted, and the gebbeth snatched at his cloak, fumbled at his sides trying to catch hold of him from behind. With the last strength in him Ged plunged through that faint-shining door. He tried to turn to shut it behind him against the gebbeth, but his legs would not hold him up. He staggered, reaching for support. Lights swam and flashed in his eyes. He felt himself falling, and he felt himself caught even as he fell; but his mind, utterly spent, slid away into the dark.

Responding to the Novel

Analyzing Chapters 5 and 6

Identifying Facts

1. Why does Low Torning need a wizard?
2. Trying to save the child of his friend Pechvarry, Ged takes a risky journey in which he meets his enemy, the shadow. What horrifying choice must he make?
3. What are Ged's reasons for leaving Low Torning to fight the dragon of Pendor?
4. After Ged leaves Pendor and Low Torning, he decides to return to Roke Island. Explain what prevents him from returning to Roke, and why.
5. Ged follows a stranger's advice and goes to Osskil. Who offers to take him to the Court of Terrenon? What does that guide transform into?

Interpreting Meanings

6. The dragon offers to tell Ged the name of that which pursues him. Why do you think Ged refuses this invaluable offer, and instead makes the dragon promise not to attack the Archipelago? What does this decision reveal about Ged's **character,** or personality, and how it has changed since he was a student on Roke?
7. In the first four chapters of the novel, Ged has developed his powers, but he has also called into being a strong enemy against whom he may be powerless. Which events in this section show the strength of Ged's power? Which events suggest that the enemy's power might be just as strong, if not stronger? Tell who you think is stronger at this point. Give evidence for your views.

Writing About the Novel

A Critical Response

SRW p. 87

Analyzing a Theme of the Novel. The **theme** of a work is the idea it reveals about life or human nature. Theme is not the same as a novel's subject; it is an idea *about* the subject. A novel may have several themes. Having read half of *A Wizard of Earthsea,* what do you think is its most important theme? (Think about what Ged's adventures so far have told you about the balance of good and evil, and about growing up and maturing.) Explain which characters or events point to this theme.

See Teacher's Manual page 186.

Analyzing Language and Vocabulary

Inventing Imaginary Names

Earthsea is composed of many peoples speaking different languages. As a result, not all the names the author makes up sound the same. Le Guin herself, when asked how she thinks up these names, answered "that I find them, that I hear them . . . I can offer no explanation." Try inventing some names of your own for the following imaginary people, places, and things. If they sound good to you, you've probably found the "right" ones.

1. A large lake with a rocky shore
2. The tallest mountain in the universe
3. The most evil of villains
4. The greatest of heroines
5. A small, furry, cuddly, three-tailed creature sometimes kept as a pet

For answers, see Teacher's Manual page 186.

Summary: Chapter 7

Ged awakens in a luxurious room in a tower of the Court of the Terrenon. The Court is ruled by the old Lord Benderesk and his beautiful but deceitful wife Serret, who is the enchantress's daughter Ged had met on Gont when he was studying under Ogion. Serret tries to persuade Ged to touch and talk to the magical Stone of Terrenon. She tells him it will help him overcome the shadow, and that when the Stone is his slave, she and Ged will rule together. Feeling that the Stone holds a great and ancient evil, Ged resists. Benderesk overhears Serret and knows she would betray him. Before he can cast a spell on her, Ged stops him, and he and Serret flee. Benderesk unleashes the servants of the Stone, who kill Serret. Ged, changing himself into a falcon, flies to Ogion's home on Gont. Ogion transforms Ged back into a man and counsels him to confront the shadow. Ged leaves his master's house to search for it.

A. Responding
Serret is someone whom Ged has met before. Tell students to look for clues that show who she is. (She is the girl from Gont, who first led Ged to read the summoning spell.)

B. Vocabulary
keep: a fort or castle

C. Word Study
? Does the name "Serret" suggest something pleasant or unpleasant? (Despite its silvery sound, "Serret" sounds a bit like "ferret," a sharp toothed weasel!)

D. Constrast
? What phrase in this paragraph is a dramatic contrast to Serret's sweetness in the previous paragraph? ("The tower that rose like a sharp tooth")

Chapter 7

The Hawk's Flight

Ged woke, and for a long time he lay aware only that it was pleasant to wake, for he had not expected to wake again, and very pleasant to see light, the large plain light of day all about him. He felt as if he were floating on that light, or drifting in a boat on very quiet waters. At last he made out that he was in bed, but no such bed as he had ever slept in. It was set up on a frame held by four tall carven legs, and the mattresses were great silk sacks of down, which was why he thought he was floating, and over it all a crimson canopy hung to keep out drafts. On two sides the curtain was tied back, and Ged looked out at a room with walls of stone and floor of stone. Through three high windows he saw the moorland, bare and brown, snow-patched here and there, in the mild sunlight of winter. The room must be high above the ground, for it looked a great way over the land.

A coverlet of downfilled satin slid aside as Ged sat up, and he saw himself clothed in a tunic of silk and cloth-of-silver like a lord. On a chair beside the bed, boots of glove-leather and a cloak lined with pellawi-fur were laid ready for him. He sat a while, calm and dull as one under an enchantment, and then stood up, reaching for his staff. But he had no staff.

His right hand, though it had been salved and bound, was burned on palm and fingers. Now he felt the pain of it, and the soreness of all his body.

He stood without moving a while again. Then he whispered, not aloud and not hopefully, "Hoeg . . . hoeg . . ." For the little fierce loyal creature too was gone, the little silent soul that once had led him back from death's dominion. Had it still been with him last night when he ran? Was that last night, was it many nights ago? He did not know. It was all dim and obscure in his mind, the gebbeth, the burning staff, the running, the whispering, the gate. None of it came back clearly to him. Nothing even now was clear. He whispered his pet's name once more, but without hope of answer, and tears rose in his eyes.

A little bell rang somewhere far away. A second bell rang in a sweet jangle just outside the room. A door opened behind him, across the room, and a woman came in. "Welcome, Sparrowhawk," she said smiling.

She was young and tall, dressed in white and silver, with a net of silver crowning her hair that fell straight down like a fall of black water.

Stiffly Ged bowed.

A "You don't remember me, I think."

"Remember you, Lady?"

He had never seen a beautiful woman dressed to match her beauty but one in his life: that Lady of O who had come with her Lord to the Sunreturn festival at Roke. She had been like a slight bright candle-flame, but this woman was like the white new moon.

"I thought you would not," she said, smiling. "But forgetful as you may be, you're welcome here as an old friend."

"What place is this?" Ged asked, still stiff and slow-tongued. He found it hard to speak to her and hard to look away from her. The princely clothes he wore were strange to him, the stones he stood on were unfamiliar, the very air he breathed was alien; he was not himself, not the self he had been.

"This keep is called the Court of Terrenon. My lord, who is called Benderesk, is sovereign of this land from the edge of the Keksemt Moors north to the Mountains of Os, and keeper of the precious stone called Terrenon. As for myself, here in Osskil they call me Serret, Silver in their language. And you, I know, are sometimes called Sparrowhawk, and were made wizard in the Isle of the Wise." B C

Ged looked down at his burned hand and said presently, "I do not know what I am. I had power, once. I have lost it, I think."

"No! You have not lost it, or only to regain it tenfold. You are safe here from what drove you here, my friend. There are mighty walls about this tower and not all of them are built of stone. Here you can rest, finding your strength again. Here you may also find a different strength, and a staff that will not burn to ashes in your hand. An evil way may lead to a good end, after all. Come with me now, let me show you our domain."

She spoke so sweetly that Ged hardly heard her words, moved by the promise of her voice alone. He followed her.

His room was high up indeed in the tower that rose like a sharp tooth from its hilltop. Down winding stairs of marble he followed Serret, through rich rooms and halls, past high windows that looked north, west, south, east over the low brown hills that went on, Houseless and treeless and changeless, clear to the sun-washed winter sky. Only far to the north small white peaks stood sharp against the blue, and southward one could guess the shining of the sea. D

Servants opened doors and stood aside for Ged and the lady; pale, dour Osskilians they were all. She was light of skin, but unlike them she spoke Hardic well, even, it seemed to Ged, with the accent of Gont. Later that day she brought him

SUPPLEMENTARY SUPPORT MATERIAL: CHAPTERS 7 AND 8

1. Vocabulary Activity Sheet
2. Reading Check Test blackline master
3. Selection Test (page 219 of Test Book)
4. Workbook (page 159)

DEVELOPING VOCABULARY

The following words appear on a test in the Test Book, page 220. (See also the Vocabulary Activity Sheet.)

salve	frail
obscure	solitude
desolation	doggedly
covetous	usurper
endure	lunge

before her husband Benderesk, Lord of the Terrenon. Thrice her age, bone-white, bone-thin, with clouded eyes, Lord Benderesk greeted Ged with grim cold courtesy, bidding him stay as guest however long he would. Then he had little more to say, asking Ged nothing of his voyages or of the enemy that had hunted him here; nor had the Lady Serret asked anything of these matters.

A If this was strange, it was only part of the strangeness of this place and of his presence in it. Ged's mind never seemed quite to clear. He could not see things plainly. He had come to this tower-keep by chance, and yet the chance was all design; or he had come by design and yet all the design had merely chanced to come about. He had set out northward; a stranger in Orrimy had told him to seek help here; an Osskilian ship had been waiting for him; Skiorh had guided him. How much of this was the work of the shadow that hunted him? Or was none of it; had he and his hunter both been drawn here by some other power, he following that lure and the shadow following him, and seizing on Skiorh for its weapon when the moment came? That must be it, for certainly the shadow was, as Serret had said, barred from the Court of the Terrenon. He had felt no sign or threat of its lurking presence since he wakened in the tower. But what then had brought him here? For this was no place one came to by chance; even in the dullness of his thoughts he began to see that. No other stranger came to these gates. The tower stood aloof and remote, its back turned on the way to Neshum that was the nearest town. No man came to the keep, none left it. Its windows looked down on desolation.

B From these windows Ged looked out, as he kept by himself in his high tower-room, day after day, dull and heartsick and cold. It was always cold in the tower, for all the carpets and the tapestried hangings and the rich furred clothing and the broad marble fireplaces they had. It was a cold that got into the bone, into the marrow, and would not be dislodged. And in Ged's heart a cold shame settled also and would not be dislodged, as he thought always how he had faced his enemy and been defeated and had run. In his mind all the Masters of Roke gathered, Gensher the Archmage frowning in their midst, and Nemmerle was with them, and Ogion, and even the witch who had taught him his first spell: All of them gazed at him and he knew he had failed their trust in him. He would plead, saying, "If I had not run away the shadow would have possessed me: It had already Skiorh's strength, and part of mine, and I could not fight it: It knew my name. I had to run away. A wizard-gebbeth would be a terrible power for evil and ruin. I had to run away." But none of those who listened in his mind would answer him. And he would watch the snow falling, thin and ceaseless, on the empty lands below the window, and feel the dull cold grow within him, till it seemed no feeling was left to him except a kind of weariness.

So he kept to himself for many days out of sheer misery. When he did come down out of his room, he was silent and stiff. The beauty of the Lady of the Keep confused his mind, and in this rich, seemly, orderly, strange Court, he felt himself to be a goatherd born and bred.

They let him alone when he wanted to be alone, and when he could not stand to think his thoughts and watch the falling snow any longer, often Serret met with him in one of the curving halls, tapestried and firelit, lower in the tower, and there they would talk. There was no merriment in the Lady of the Keep, she never laughed though she often smiled; yet she could put Ged at ease almost with one smile. With her he began to forget his stiffness and his shame. Before long they met every day to talk, long, quietly, idly, a little apart from the serving-women who always accompanied Serret, by the fireplace or at the window of the high rooms of the tower.

The old lord kept mostly in his own apartments, coming forth mornings to pace up and down the snowy inner courtyards of the castle-keep like an old sorcerer who has been brewing spells all night. When he joined Ged and Serret for supper he sat silent, looking up at his young wife sometimes with a hard, covetous glance. Then Ged pitied her. She was like a white deer caged, like a white bird wing-clipped, like a silver ring on an old man's finger. She was an item of Benderesk's hoard. When the lord of the keep left them Ged stayed with her, trying to cheer her solitude as she had cheered his.

"What is this jewel that gives your keep its name?" he asked her as they sat talking over their emptied gold plates and gold goblets in the cavernous, candlelit dining hall.

"You have not heard of it? It is a famous thing."

"No. I know only that the lords of Osskil have famous treasuries."

"Ah, this jewel outshines them all. Come, would you like to see it?"

She smiled, with a look of mockery and daring, as if a little afraid of what she did, and led the young man from the hall, out through the narrow corridors of the base of the tower, and downstairs underground to a locked door he had not seen before. This she unlocked with a silver key, looking up at Ged with that same smile as she did so,

A. Making Inferences

? Why do you think Ged's mind doesn't clear? (He is under some sort of spell.) In the second paragraph of Chapter 7, "dull as one under an enchantment" foreshadows this.

B. Setting and Atmosphere

The setting of the Court of the Terrenon is vivid and mood-provoking. Tell students to watch for details of cold, loneliness, and darkness. Ask them to describe the mood of the place—is it evil or benign?

About Stones
Large stones, trees, and water are thought to have been the first objects of worship. In many parts of the world, people considered pieces of meteorite to be sacred. Small stones of unusual shape and color were used as amulets (magic charms) and were worn or carried to protect against evil. Some people believed that evil, in the form of disease, infertility, or cowardice, could be magically transferred to a stone which would then be thrown away. Such stones were said to keep the quality that had been given to them, and would harm anyone who picked them up.

A. Making Inferences
From the three doors that Serret must unlock, and her attitude, what might you conclude about the stone? (It is very precious. From her "look of daring" we get the feeling that it is also dangerous.) For earlier references to this stone, see pages 567 and 570.

B. Responding
What wiles does Serret use to trap Ged? (She flatters him, tempts him with great knowledge and power, even tries to shame him by suggesting that he fears the stone.)

A

as if she dared him to come on with her. Beyond the door was a short passage and a second door, which she unlocked with a gold key, and beyond that again a third door, which she unlocked with one of the Great Words of unbinding. Within that last door her candle showed them a small room like a dungeon cell: floor, walls, ceiling all rough stone, unfurnished, blank.

"Do you see it?" Serret asked.

As Ged looked round the room his wizard's eye caught one stone of those that made the floor. It was rough and dank as the rest, a heavy unshapen paving stone: yet he felt the power of it as if it spoke to him aloud. And his breath caught in his throat, and a sickness came over him for a moment. This was the foundingstone of the tower. This was the central place, and it was cold, bitter cold; nothing could ever warm the little room. This was a very ancient thing: an old and terrible spirit was prisoned in that block of stone. He did not answer Serret yes or no, but stood still, and presently, with a quick curious glance at him, she pointed out the stone. "That is the Terrenon. Do you wonder that we keep so precious a jewel locked away in our deepest hoardroom?"

Still Ged did not answer, but stood dumb and wary. She might almost have been testing him; but he thought she had no notion of the stone's nature, to speak of it so lightly. She did not know enough of it to fear it. "Tell me of its powers," he said at last.

"It was made before Segoy raised the islands of the world from the Open Sea. It was made when the world itself was made, and will endure until the end of the world. Time is nothing to it. If you lay your hand upon it and ask a question of it, it will answer, according to the power that is in you. It has a voice, if you know how to listen. It will speak of things that were, and are, and will be. It told of your coming, long before you came to this land. Will you ask a question of it now?"

"No."

"It will answer you."

"There is no question I would ask it."

"It might tell you," Serret said in her soft voice, "how you will defeat your enemy."

Ged stood mute.

B

"Do you fear the stone?" she asked as if unbelieving; and he answered, "Yes."

In the deadly cold and silence of the room encircled by wall after wall of spellwork and of stone, in the light of the one candle she held, Serret glanced at him again with gleaming eyes. "Sparrowhawk," she said, "you are not afraid."

"But I will not speak with that spirit," Ged replied, and looking full at her spoke with a grave boldness: "My lady, that spirit is sealed in a stone, and the stone is locked by binding-spell and blinding-spell and charm of lock and ward and triple fortress-walls in a barren land, not because it is precious, but because it can work great evil. I do not know what they told you of it when you came here. But you who are young and gentlehearted should never touch the thing, or even look on it. It will not work you well."

"I have touched it. I have spoken to it, and heard it speak. It does me no harm."

She turned away and they went out through the doors and passages till in the torchlight of the broad stairs of the tower she blew out her candle. They parted with few words.

That night Ged slept little. It was not the thought of the shadow that kept him awake; rather that thought was almost driven from his mind by the image, ever returning, of the Stone on which this tower was founded, and by the vision of Serret's face bright and shadowy in the candlelight, turned to him. Again and again he felt her eyes on him, and tried to decide what look had come into those eyes when he refused to touch the Stone, whether it had been disdain or hurt. When he lay down to sleep at last the silken sheets of the bed were cold as ice, and ever he wakened in the dark thinking of the Stone and of Serret's eyes.

Next day he found her in the curving hall of gray marble, lit now by the westering sun, where often she spent the afternoon at games or at the weaving loom with her maids. He said to her, "Lady Serret, I affronted[1] you. I am sorry for it."

"No," she said musingly, and again, "No. . . ." She sent away the serving-women who were with her, and when they were alone she turned to Ged. "My guest, my friend," she said, "you are very clear-sighted, but perhaps you do not see all that is to be seen. In Gont, in Roke they teach high wizardries. But they do not teach all wizardries. This is Osskil, Ravenland: It is not a Hardic land: Mages do not rule it, nor do they know much of it. There are happenings here not dealt with by the loremasters of the South, and things here not named in the Namers' lists. What one does not know, one fears. But you have nothing to fear here in the Court of the Terrenon. A weaker man would, indeed. Not you. You are one born with the power to control that which is in the sealed room. This I know. It is why you are here now."

"I do not understand."

"That is because my lord Benderesk has not been wholly frank with you. I will be frank. Come, sit by me here."

1. **affronted:** insulted or offended.

Comment from a Critic

George E. Slusser suggests that the Stone of Terrenon, like the Old Dragon, is a "dark power" of Earthsea, "but these are primeval, inhuman powers; beside these and over them man has built up civilization. . . . In order to exist, man must strike a balance with them. . . . They cannot be conquered but they must be contained." Ged forces a promise from the dragon that contains it, and previous mages have sealed the Stone in the fortress. These dark powers must not be served, concludes Slusser because "in seeking to rule these forces, man enslaves himself to them. . . ."

A. Setting

? What details of setting create a mood of foreboding? ("Dying sunlight . . . in which there was no warmth," "snow. . . a dull white pall over the earth")

B. Responding

Ged thought that Fate or the shadow had driven him to the Court; he finds out otherwise here.

? Who brought Ged to the Court of the Terrenon? (The powers of the Stone, including Serret and her husband)

C. Plot

? Where is the turning point in this conflict between Serret and Ged? (Serret goes too far when she tells him that he will rule and she will rule with him. He realizes that her motivation is power, not a desire to help him. Also, Ged is highly moral: He dislikes the suggestion that Serret will leave or do away with Lord Benderesk and put Ged in his place.)

D. Making Inferences

? Why do you think Benderesk was listening behind the door? (He did not trust Serret.)

A He sat down beside her on the deep, cushioned window ledge. The dying sunlight came level through the window, flooding them with a radiance in which there was no warmth; on the moorlands below, already sinking into shadow, last night's snow lay unmelted, a dull white pall over the earth.

She spoke now very softly. "Benderesk is Lord and Inheritor of the Terrenon, but he cannot use the thing, he cannot make it wholly serve his will. Nor can I, alone or with him. Neither he nor I has the skill and power. You have both."

"How do you know that?"

"From the Stone itself! I told you that it spoke of your coming. It knows its master. It has waited for you to come. Before ever you were born it waited for you, for the one who could master it. And he who can make the Terrenon answer what he asks and do what he wills, has power over his own destiny: strength to crush any enemy, mortal or of the other world: foresight, knowledge, wealth, dominion, and a wizardry at his command that could humble the Archmage himself! As much of that, as little of that as you choose, is yours for the asking."

Once more she lifted her strange bright eyes to him, and her gaze pierced him so that he trembled as if with cold. Yet there was fear in her face, as if she sought his help but was too proud to ask it. Ged was bewildered. She had put her hand on his as she spoke; its touch was light, it looked narrow and fair on his dark, strong hand. He said, pleading, "Serret! I have no such power as you think—what I had once, I threw away. I cannot help you, I am no use to you. But I know this, the Old Powers of earth are not for men to use. They were never given into our hands, and in our hands they work only ruin. Ill means, ill end. I was not drawn here, but driven here, and the force that drove me works to my undoing. I cannot help you."

"He who throws away his power is filled sometimes with a far greater power," she said, smiling, as if his fears and scruples were childish ones. "I may know more than you of what brought you here. Did not a man speak to you in the streets of Orrimy? He was a messenger, a servant of the Terrenon. He was a wizard once himself, but he
B threw away his staff to serve a power greater than any mage's. And you came to Osskil, and on the moors you tried to fight a shadow with your wooden staff; and almost we could not save you, for that thing that follows you is more cunning than we deemed, and had taken much strength from you already. . . . Only shadow can fight shadow. Only darkness can defeat the dark. Listen, Sparrowhawk! What do you need, then, to defeat that shadow, which waits for you outside these walls?"

"I need what I cannot know. Its name."

"The Terrenon, that knows all births and deaths and beings before and after death, the unborn and undying, the bright world and the dark one, will tell you that name."

"And the price?"

"There is no price. I tell you it will obey you, serve you as your slave."

Shaken and tormented, he did not answer. She held his hand now in both of hers, looking into his face. The sun had fallen into the mists that dulled the horizon, and the air too had grown dull, but her face grew bright with praise and triumph as she watched him and saw his will shaken within him. Softly she whispered, "You will be mightier than all men, a king among men. You will rule, and I will rule with you—" C

Suddenly Ged stood up, and one step forward took him where he could see, just around the curve of the long room's wall, beside the door, the Lord of the Terrenon who stood listening and smiling a little.

Ged's eyes cleared, and his mind. He looked down at Serret. "It is light that defeats the dark," D
he said stammering—"light."

As he spoke he saw, as plainly as if his own words were the light that showed him, how indeed he had been drawn here, lured here, how they had used his fear to lead him on, and how they would, once they had him, have kept him. They had saved him from the shadow, indeed, for they did not want him to be possessed by the shadow until he had become a slave of the Stone. Once his will was captured by the power of the Stone, then they would let the shadow into the walls, for a gebbeth was a better slave even than a man. If he had once touched the Stone, or spoken to it, he would have been utterly lost. Yet, even as the shadow had not quite been able to catch up with him and seize him, so the Stone had not been able to use him—not quite. He had almost yielded, but not quite. He had not consented. It is very hard for evil to take hold of the unconsenting soul.

He stood between the two who had yielded, who had consented, looking from one to the other as Benderesk came forward.

"I told you," the Lord of the Terrenon said dry-voiced to his lady, "that he would slip from your hands, Serret. They are clever fools, your Gontish sorcerers. And you are a fool too, woman of Gont, thinking to trick him and me, and rule us both by your beauty, and use the Terrenon to your own ends. But I am the Lord of the Stone, I, and this I do to the disloyal wife: *Ekavroe ai oelwantar*—"

Earthsea Vocabulary
banefire
magefire

A. Character
What does Serret say and do that shows Ged the kind of person she really is? (She calls the guards "filth" and puts a horrid spell on them that kills them.) Why do you think that up until now, Ged has underestimated Serret's evil nature? (He has been under her spell; he has also had little experience with women, and associates beauty with goodness.)

B. Making Inferences
Why do you think Serret cannot find the gate? (A spell has been put on it to keep her inside.)

C. Responding
What does the presence of the one wild blade of grass in the middle of a wintery, barren land symbolize? (The otak represents good and love in this evil land; again, it helps save Ged's life. From its body comes a living thing that Ged is able to use to fight his enemy.)

It was a spell of Changing, and Benderesk's long hands were raised to shape the cowering woman into some hideous thing, swine or dog or driveling hag. Ged stepped forward and struck the lord's hands down with his own, saying as he did so only one short word. And though he had no staff, and stood on alien ground and evil ground, the domain of a dark power, yet his will prevailed. Benderesk stood still, his clouded eyes fixed hateful and unseeing upon Serret.

"Come," she said in a shaking voice, "Sparrowhawk, come, quick, before he can summon the Servants of the Stone—"

As if in echo a whispering ran through the tower, through the stones of the floor and walls, a dry trembling murmur, as if the earth itself should speak.

Seizing Ged's hand Serret ran with him through the passages and halls, down the long twisted stairs. They came out into the courtyard where a last silvery daylight still hung above the soiled, trodden snow. Three of the castle-servants barred their way, sullen and questioning, as if they had been suspecting some plot of these two against their master. "It grows dark, Lady," one said, and another, "You cannot ride out now."

"Out of my way, filth!" Serret cried, and spoke in the sibilant[2] Osskilian speech. The men fell back from her and crouched down to the ground, writhing, and one of them screamed aloud.

"We must go out by the gate, there is no other way out. Can you see it? Can you find it, Sparrowhawk?"

A She tugged at his hand, yet he hesitated. "What spell did you set on them?"

"I ran hot lead in the marrow of their bones, they will die of it. Quick, I tell you, he will loose the Servants of the Stone, and I cannot find the gate—there is a great charm on it. Quick!"

B Ged did not know what she meant, for to him the enchanted gate was as plain to see as the stone archway of the court through which he saw it. He led Serret through the one, across the untrodden snow of the forecourt, and then, speaking a word of Opening, he led her through the gate of the wall of spells.

She changed as they passed through that doorway out of the silvery twilight of the Court of the Terrenon. She was not less beautiful in the dreary light of the moors, but there was a fierce witch-look to her beauty; and Ged knew her at last—the daughter of the Lord of the Re Albi, daughter of a sorceress of Osskil, who had mocked him in the green meadows above Ogion's house, long ago, and had sent him to read that spell which loosed the shadow. But he spent small thought on this, for he was looking about him now with every sense alert, looking for that enemy, the shadow, which would be waiting for him somewhere outside the magic walls. It might be gebbeth still, clothed in Skiorh's death, or it might be hidden in the gathering darkness, waiting to seize him and merge its shapelessness with his living flesh. He sensed its nearness, yet did not see it. But as he looked he saw some small dark thing half buried in snow, a few paces from the gate. He stooped, and then softly picked it up in his two hands. It was the otak, its fine short fur all clogged with blood and its small body light and stiff and cold in his hands.

"Change yourself! Change yourself, they are coming!" Serret shrieked, seizing his arm and pointing to the tower that stood behind them like a tall white tooth in the dusk. From slit windows near its base dark creatures were creeping forth, flapping long wings, slowly beating and circling up over the walls toward Ged and Serret where they stood on the hillside, unprotected. The rattling whisper they had heard inside the keep had grown louder, a tremor and moaning in the earth under their feet.

Anger welled up in Ged's heart, a hot rage of hate against all the cruel deathly things that tricked him, trapped him, hunted him down. "Change yourself!" Serret screamed at him, and she with a quick-gasped spell shrank into a gray gull, and flew. But Ged stooped and plucked a blade of wild grass that poked up dry and frail out of the snow where the otak had lain dead. This blade he held up, and as he spoke aloud to it in C
the True Speech it lengthened, and thickened, and when he was done he held a great staff, a wizard's staff, in his hand. No banefire burned red along it when the black, flapping creatures from the Court of the Terrenon swooped over him and he struck their wings with it: It blazed only with the white magefire that does not burn but drives away the dark.

The creatures returned to the attack: botched beasts, belonging to ages before bird or dragon or man, long since forgotten by the daylight but recalled by the ancient, malign,[3] unforgetful power of the Stone. They harried Ged, swooping at him. He felt the scythe-sweep of their talons about him and sickened in their dead stench. Fiercely he parried and struck, fighting them off with the fiery staff that was made of his anger and a blade of wild grass. And suddenly they all rose up like ravens frightened from carrion and wheeled away,

2. **sibilant** (sib′′l·ənt): having or making a hissing sound.

3. **malign** (mə·līn′): evil.

About Hawks
The Pilgrim Falcon and the sparrowhawk are both species of hawks. The sparrowhawk, one of the smallest hawks, is commonly seen in open and semi-open country; it eats mostly insects. The Pilgrim (also known as the peregrine) falcon is a rare, large hawk that is seen in woods, mountains, and coastal areas. It preys mostly on birds and can fly at speeds of up to 175 miles per hour.

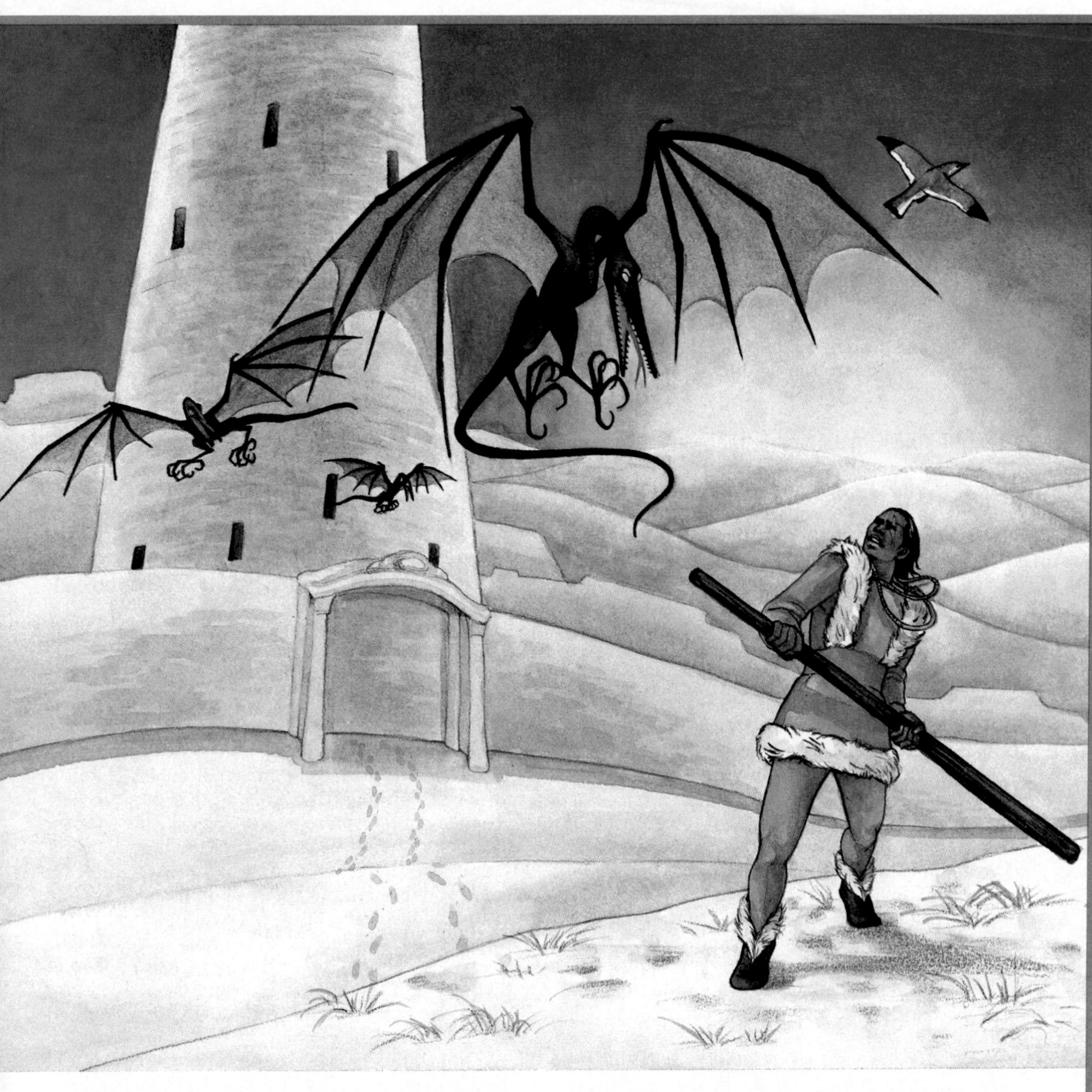

A. Vocabulary
barred: here, stripes that look like bars

B. Figurative Language
? Find one example of simile and one example of metaphor on this page. (Similes: "like arrow, like thought," "as waterdrops scatter from a cast pebble." Metaphors: "black clot," "ashy gleam," "iron beaks")

flapping, silent, in the direction that Serret in her gull-shape had flown. Their vast wings seemed slow, but they flew fast, each downbeat driving them mightily through the air. No gull could long outmatch that heavy speed.

Quick as he had once done at Roke, Ged took the shape of a great hawk: not the sparrowhawk they called him but the Pilgrim Falcon that flies A like arrow, like thought. On barred, sharp, strong wings he flew, pursuing his pursuers. The air darkened and among the clouds stars shone brightening. Ahead he saw the black ragged flock all driving down and in upon one point in mid-air. Beyond that black clot the sea lay, pale with last ashy gleam of day. Swift and straight the hawk-Ged shot toward the creatures of the Stone, and B they scattered as he came amongst them as waterdrops scatter from a cast pebble. But they had caught their prey. Blood was on the beak of this one and white features stuck to the claws of another, and no gull skimmed beyond them over the pallid sea.

Already they were turning on Ged again, coming quick and ungainly with iron beaks stretched out agape. He, wheeling once above them, screamed the hawk's scream of defiant rage, and then shot on across the low beaches of Osskil, out over the breakers of the sea.

A. Making Inferences

? Why do you think Ogion did not speak to the Lord of the Isle? (The Lord of Gont was asking his aid in the type of enterprise that Ogion would never approve of because he believes that magic should be used only rarely, and then only in great need.)

B. Vocabulary
sere: dry and withered.

C. Earthsea Map
You might have students trace the hawk's flight from Osskil to Gont.

The creatures of the Stone circled a while croaking, and one by one beat back ponderously inland over the moors. The Old Powers will not cross over the sea, being bound each to an isle, a certain place, cave or stone or welling spring. Back went the black emanations[4] to the tower-keep, where maybe the Lord of the Terrenon, Benderesk, wept at their return, and maybe laughed. But Ged went on, falcon-winged, falcon-mad, like an unfalling arrow, like an unforgotten thought, over the Osskil Sea and eastward into the wind of winter and the night.

Ogion the Silent had come home late to Re Albi from his autumn wanderings. More silent, more solitary than ever he had become as the years went on. The new Lord of Gont down in the city below had never got a word out of him, though he had climbed clear up to the Falcon's Nest to seek the help of the mage in a certain piratic venture toward the Andrades. Ogion who spoke to spiders on their webs and had been seen to greet trees courteously never said a word to the Lord of the Isle, who went away discontented. There was perhaps some discontent or unease also in Ogion's mind, for he had spent all summer and autumn alone up on the mountain, and only now near Sunreturn was come back to his hearthside.

A

The morning after his return he rose late, and wanting a cup of rushwash tea he went out to fetch water from the spring that ran a little way down the hillside from his house. The margins of the spring's small lively pool was frozen, and the sere moss among the rocks were traced with flowers of frost. It was broad daylight, but the sun would not clear the mighty shoulder of the mountain for an hour yet: All western Gont, from sea beaches to the peak, was sunless, silent, and clear in the winter morning. As the mage stood by the spring looking out over the falling lands and the harbor and the gray distances of the sea, wings beat above him. He looked up, raising one arm a little. A great hawk came down with loud-beating wings and lighted on his wrist. Like a trained hunting bird it clung there, but it wore no broken leash, no band or bell. The claws dug hard in Ogion's wrist; the barred wings trembled; the round, gold eye was dull and wild.

B

"Are you messenger or message?" Ogion said gently to the hawk. "Come on with me—" As he spoke the hawk looked at him. Ogion was silent a minute. "I named you once, I think," he said, and then strode to his house and entered, bearing the bird still on his wrist. He made the hawk stand on the hearth in the fire's heat, and offered it water. It would not drink. Then Ogion began to lay a spell, very quietly, weaving the web of magic with his hands more than with words. When the spell was whole and woven he said softly—"Ged"—not looking at the falcon on the hearth. He waited some while, then turned, and got up, and went to the young man who stood trembling and dull-eyed before the fire.

Ged was richly and outlandishly dressed in fur and silk and silver, but the clothes were torn and stiff with sea-salt, and he stood gaunt and stooped, his hair lank about his scarred face.

Ogion took the soiled, princely cloak off his shoulders, led him to the alcove-room where his prentice once had slept and made him lie down on the pallet there, and so with a murmured sleep-charm left him. He had said no word to him, knowing that Ged had no human speech in him now.

As a boy, Ogion like all boys had thought it would be a very pleasant game to take by art-magic whatever shape one liked, man or beast, tree or cloud, and so to play at a thousand beings. But as a wizard he had learned the price of the game, which is the peril of losing one's self, playing away the truth. The longer a man stays in a form not his own, the greater this peril. Every prentice-sorcerer learns the tale of the wizard Bordger of Way, who delighted in taking bear's shape, and did so more and more often until the bear grew in him and the man died away, and he became a bear, and killed his own little son in the forests, and was hunted down and slain. And no one knows how many of the dolphins that leap in the waters of the Inmost Sea were men once, wise men, who forgot their wisdom and their name in the joy of the restless sea.

Ged had taken hawk-shape in fierce distress and rage, and when he flew from Osskil there had been but one thought in his mind: to outfly both Stone and shadow, to escape the cold treacherous lands, to go home. The falcon's anger and wildness were like his own, and had become his own, and his will to fly had become the falcon's will. Thus he had passed over Enlad, stooping down to drink at a lonely forest pool, but on the wing again at once, driven by fear of the shadow that came behind him. So he had crossed the great sea lane called the Jaws of Enlad, and gone on and on, east by south, the hills of Oranéa faint to his right and the hills of Andrad fainter to his left, and before him only the sea; until at last, ahead there rose up out of the waves one unchanging wave, towering always higher, the white peak of Gont. In all the

C

4. **emanations** (em'ə·nā'shənz): things that come forth from a source.

The Taoist Influence

Several critics believe that Taoism has had the greatest influence on Le Guin's writing. Introduced in the 3rd or 4th century B.C., Taoism is an ancient Chinese philosophy that is based on the ideas of simplicity and selflessness. Charlotte Spivack in her book on Le Guin comments that Le Guin has been interested in Taoism since she was a young child. Spivack explains that the word "Tao" refers to the Way, the basic law underlying all of nature and human behavior. "One of the principles of Taoism," she states, "is the doctrine of inaction. . . . This asserts the superior value of . . . passivity over aggression, of patience over initiative."

The Roke mages, like the Tao Te Ching, teach the importance of acting, speaking, and using power only when they are absolutely essential. Ogion is very much like a Taoist wise man: he lives according to Taoist ideals, especially in his respect for living and nonliving things. Perhaps the dominant Taoist belief in the novel is the inseparability of opposites. Spivack explains, "Taoism asserts the mutual interdependence of light and darkness . . . male and female . . . visually depicted in the yin-yang symbol of interlocking dark and light semicircles."

sunlight and the dark of that great flight he had worn the falcon's wings, and looked through the falcon's eyes, and forgetting his own thoughts he had known at last only what the falcon knows: hunger, the wind, the way he flies.

He flew to the right haven. There were few on Roke and only one on Gont who could have made him back into a man.

He was savage and silent when he woke. Ogion never spoke to him, but gave him meat and water and let him sit hunched by the fire, grim as a great, weary, sulking hawk. When night came he slept. On the third morning he came in to the fireside where the mage sat gazing at the flames, and said "Master. . . ."

"Welcome, lad," said Ogion.

A "I have come back to you as I left: a fool," the young man said, his voice harsh and thickened. The mage smiled a little and motioned Ged to sit across the hearth from him, and set to brewing them some tea.

A. Character ? Do you think this is true? (Ged is no longer a fool. When he left Ogion, he was full of pride and impatience; these foolish qualities produced a fearsome enemy that now hunts him. Ogion's smile shows that he knows that Ged is no longer a fool; Ged has learned wisdom through painful experience.)

Snow was falling, the first of the winter here on the lower slopes of Gont. Ogion's windows were shuttered fast, but they could hear the wet snow as it fell soft on the roof, and the deep stillness of snow all about the house. A long time they sat there by the fire, and Ged told his old master the tale of the years since he had sailed from Gont aboard the ship called *Shadow.* Ogion asked no questions, and when Ged was done he kept silent for a long time, calm, pondering. Then he rose, and set out bread and cheese and wine on the table, and they ate together. When they had done and had set the room straight, Ogion spoke.

"Those are bitter scars you bear, lad," he said.

"I have no strength against the thing," Ged answered.

Ogion shook his head but said no more for a time. At length, "Strange," he said: "You had strength enough to outspell a sorcerer in his own domain, there in Osskil. You had strength enough to withstand the lures and fend off the attack of the servants of an Old Power of Earth. And at Pendor you had strength enough to stand up to a dragon."

"It was luck I had in Osskil, not strength," Ged replied, and he shivered again as he thought of the dreamlike deathly cold of the Court of the Terrenon. "As for the dragon, I knew his name. The evil thing, the shadow that hunts me, has no name."

"*All* things have a name," said Ogion, so certainly that Ged dared not repeat what the Archmage Gensher had told him, that such evil forces as he had loosed were nameless. The Dragon of Pendor, indeed, had offered to tell him the shadow's name, but he put little trust in the truth of that offer, nor did he believe Serret's promise that the Stone would tell him what he needed to know.

"If the shadow has a name," he said at last, "I do not think it will stop and tell it to me. . . ."

"No," said Ogion. "Nor have you stopped and told it your name. And yet it knew it. On the moors in Osskil it called you by your name, the name I gave you. It is strange, strange. . . ."

He fell to brooding again. At last Ged said, "I came here for counsel, not for refuge, Master. I will not bring this shadow upon you, and it will soon be here if I stay. Once you drove it from this very room—"

"No; that was but the foreboding[5] of it, the shadow of a shadow. I could not drive it forth, now. Only you could do that."

"But I am powerless before it. Is there any place . . ." His voice died away before he had asked the question.

"There is no safe place," Ogion said gently. "Do not transform yourself again, Ged. The shadow seeks to destroy your true being. It nearly did so, driving you into hawk's being. No, where you should go, I do not know. Yet I have an idea of what you should do. It is a hard thing to say to you."

Ged's silence demanded truth, and Ogion said at last, "You must turn around."

"Turn around?"

"If you go ahead, if you keep running, wherever you run you will meet danger and evil, for it drives you, it chooses the way you go. You must choose. You must seek what seeks you. You must hunt the hunter."

Ged said nothing.

"At the spring of the River Ar I named you," the mage said, " a stream that falls from the mountain to the sea. A man would know the end he goes to, but he cannot know it if he does not turn, and return to his beginning, and hold that beginning in his being. If he would not be a stick whirled and whelmed in the stream, he must be the stream itself, all of it, from its spring to its sinking in the sea. You returned to Gont, you returned to me, Ged. Now turn clear round, and seek the very source, and that which lies before the source. There lies your hope of strength." B

B. Interpreting ? What does Ogion mean here? (That Ged must search for the source that created the shadow. Only by discovering the origin of the shadow will he be able to conquer it.) What do you think the source of the shadow is?

"There, Master?" Ged said with terror in his voice—"Where?"

Ogion did not answer.

"If I turn," Ged said after some time had gone by, "if as you say I hunt the hunter, I think the

5. **foreboding** (fôr·bōd'iŋ): prediction or feeling that something bad will happen.

Summary: Chapter 8

Ged travels over the seas in search of his shadow, which now has the shape of a man, and flees from Ged. Just as Ged thinks he is about to catch the shadow, it disappears, and Ged's boat crashes on the rocks of a barren isle. He finds a hut and meets the old couple who live there. They do not speak the same language, so all communication is through signs. Ged stays there for three days, fixing his boat, and then sets off again in pursuit of the shadow. Sensing that he is close to it, Ged turns around in his boat, and the shadow is there behind him. He grabs the shadow, they wrestle, and it tears away and flees.

A. Foreshadowing

? What foreshadowing of Ged's future life do you find here? (Ogion recognizes the strength of Ged's power and foresees that Ged will become a great mage.)

B. Making Inferences

? Why does Ged decide to buy a boat instead of sailing on a fishing or trading ship? (Now that Ged has made his decision to hunt the shadow, he is eager to start his journey; he cannot wait for a boat to take him. However, the description of the weather shows that it might not be a wise choice.)

C. Vocabulary

clinkerbuilt: made with overlapping boards

hunt will not be long. All its desire is to meet me face to face. And twice it has done so, and twice defeated me."

"Third time is the charm," said Ogion.

Ged paced the room up and down, from fireside to door, from door to fireside. "And if it defeats me wholly," he said, arguing perhaps with Ogion perhaps with himself, "it will take my knowledge and my power, and use them. It threatens only me, now. But if it enters into me and possesses me, it will work great evil through me."

"That is true. If it defeats you."

"Yet if I run again, it will as surely find me again. . . . And all my strength is spent in the running." Ged paced on a while, and then suddenly turned, and kneeling down before the mage he said, "I have walked with great wizards and have lived on the Isle of the Wise, but you are my true master, Ogion." He spoke with love, and with a somber joy.

A "Good," said Ogion. "Now you know it. Better now than never. But you will be my master, in the end." He got up, and built up the fire to a good blaze, and hung the kettle over it to boil, and then pulling on his sheepskin coat said, "I must go look after my goats. Watch the kettle for me, lad."

When he came back in, all snow-powdered and stamping snow from his goatskin boots, he carried a long, rough shaft of yew-wood. All the end of the short afternoon, and again after their supper, he sat working by lampfire on the shaft with knife and rubbing-stone and spellcraft. Many times he passed his hands along the wood as if seeking any flaw. Often as he worked he sang softly. Ged, still weary, listened, as he grew sleepy he thought himself a child in the witch's hut in Ten Alders village, on a snowy night in the firelit dark, the air heavy with herb-scent and smoke, and his mind all adrift on dreams as he listened to the long soft singing of spells and deeds of heroes who fought against dark powers and won, or lost, on distant islands long ago.

"There," said Ogion, and handed the finished staff to him. "The Archmage gave you yew-wood, a good choice and I kept to it. I meant the shaft for a longbow, but it's better this way. Good night, my son."

As Ged, who found no words to thank him, turned away to his alcove-room, Ogion watched him and said, too soft for Ged to hear, "O my young falcon, fly well!"

In the cold dawn when Ogion woke, Ged was gone. Only he had left in wizardly fashion a message of silver-scrawled runes on the hearthstone, that faded even as Ogion read them: "Master, I go hunting."

Chapter 8

Hunting

Ged had set off down the road from Re Albi in the winter dark before sunrise, and before noon he came to the Port of Gont. Ogion had given him decent Gontish leggings and shirt and vest of leather and linen to replace his Osskilian finery, but Ged had kept for his winter journey the lordly cloak lined with pellawi-fur. So cloaked, empty-handed but for the dark staff that matched his height, he came to the Land Gate, and the soldiers lounging against the carven dragons there did not have to look twice at him to see the wizard. They drew aside their lances and let him enter without question, and watched him as he went on down the street.

On the quays and in the House of the Sea-Guild he asked of ships that might be going out north or west to Enlad, Andrad, Oranéa. All answered him that no ship would be leaving Gont Port now, so near Sunreturn, and at the Sea-Guild they told him that even fishingboats were not going out through the Armed Cliffs in the untrusty weather.

They offered him dinner at the buttery there in the Sea-Guild; a wizard seldom has to ask for his dinner. He sat a while with those longshoremen, shipwrights, and weatherworkers, taking pleasure in their slow, sparse conversation, their grumbling Gontish speech. There was a great wish in him to stay here on Gont, and foregoing all wizardry and venture, forgetting all power and horror, to live in peace like any man on the known, dear ground of his home land. That was his wish; but his will was other. He did not stay long in the Sea-Guild, nor in the city, after he found there would be no ships out of port. He set out walking along the bay shore till he came to the first of the small villages that lie north of the City of Gont, and there he asked B among the fishermen till he found one that had a boat to sell.

The fisherman was a dour old man. His boat, twelve foot long and clinker-built, was so warped C and sprung as to be scarce seaworthy, yet he asked a high price for her: the spell of sea-safety for a year laid on his own boat, himself, and his son. For Gontish fishermen fear nothing, not even wizards, only the sea.

That spell of sea-safety which they set much store by in the Northern Archipelago never saved a man from storm-wind or storm-wave, but, cast by one who knows the local seas and the ways of a boat and the skills of the sailor, it weaves some daily safety about the fisherman. Ged made the charm well and honestly, working on it all that night and the next day, omitting nothing, sure and patient, though all the while his mind was strained with fear and his thoughts went on dark paths seeking to imagine how the shadow would appear to him next, and how soon, and where. When the spell was made whole and cast, he was very weary. He slept that night in the fisherman's hut in a whale-gut hammock, and got up at dawn smelling like a dried herring, and went down to the cover under Cutnorth Cliff where his new boat lay.

He pushed it into the quiet water by the landing, and water began to well softly into it at once. Stepping into the boat light as a cat Ged set straight the warped boards and rotten pegs, working both with tools and incantations, as he had used to do with Pechvarry in Low Torning. The people in the village gathered in silence, not too close, to watch his quick hands and listen to his soft voice. This job too he did well and patiently until it was done and the boat was sealed and sound. Then he set up his staff that Ogion had made him for a mast, stayed it with spells, and fixed across it a yard of sound wood. Downward from this yard he wove on the wind's loom a sail of spells, a square sail white as the snows on Gont peak above. At this the women watching sighed with envy. Then standing by the mast Ged raised up the magewind lightly. The boat moved out upon the water, turning toward the Armed Cliffs across the great bay. When the silent watching fishermen saw that leaky rowboat slip out under sail as quick and neat as a sandpiper taking wing, then they raised a cheer, grinning and stamping in the cold wind on the beach; and Ged looking back a moment saw them there cheering him on, under the
A dark jagged bulk of Cutnorth Cliff, above which the snowy fields of the Mountain rose up into cloud.

He sailed across the bay and out between the Armed Cliffs onto the Gontish Sea, there setting his course northwestward to pass north of Oranéa, returning as he had come. He had no plan or strategy in this but the retracing of his course. Following his falcon-flight across the days and winds from Osskil, the shadow might wander or might come straight, there was no telling. But unless it had withdrawn again wholly into the dream-realm, it should not miss Ged coming openly, over open sea, to meet it.

On the sea he wished to meet it, if meet it he must. He was not sure why this was, yet he had a terror of meeting the thing again on dry land. Out of the sea there rise storms and monsters, but
B no evil powers: Evil is of earth. And there is no sea, no running of river or spring, in the dark land where once Ged had gone. Death is the dry place. Though the sea itself was a danger to him in the hard weather of the season, that danger and change and instability seemed to him a defense and chance. And when he met the shadow in this final end of his folly, he thought, maybe at least he could grip the thing even as it gripped him, and drag it with the weight of his body and the weight of his own death down into the darkness of the deep sea, from which, so held, it might not rise again. So at least his death would put an end to the evil he had loosed by living.

He sailed a rough chopping sea above which clouds drooped and drifted in vast mournful veils. He raised no magewind now but used the world's wind, which blew keen from the northwest; and so long as he maintained the substance of his spell-woven sail often with a whispered word, the sail itself set and turned itself to catch the wind. Had he not used that magic he would have been hard put to keep the crank little boat on such a course, on that rough sea. On he went, and kept keen lookout on all sides. The fisherman's wife had given him two loaves of bread and a jar of water, and after some hours, when he was first in sight of Kameber Rock, the only isle between Gont and C
Oranéa, he ate and drank, and thought gratefully of the silent Gontishwoman who had given him the food. On past the dim glimpse of land he sailed, tacking more westerly now, in a faint dank drizzle that over land might be a light snow. There was no sound at all but the small creaking of the boat and light slap of waves on her bow. No boat or bird went by. Nothing moved but the ever-moving water and the drifting clouds, the clouds that he remembered dimly as flowing all about him as he, a falcon, flew east on this same course he now followed to the west; and he had looked down on the gray sea then as now he looked up at the gray air.

Nothing was ahead when he looked around. He stood up, chilled, weary of this gazing and peering into empty murk. "Come then," he muttered, "come on, what do you wait for, Shadow?" There was no answer, no darker motion among the dark mists and waves. Yet he knew more and more surely now that the thing was not far off, seeking blindly down his cold trail. And all at once he shouted out aloud, "I am here, I Ged the Sparrowhawk, and I summon my shadow!"

The boat creaked, the waves lisped, the wind hissed a little on the white sail. The moments went by. Still Ged waited, one hand on the yew-wood mast of his boat, staring into the icy drizzle that slowly drove in ragged lines across the sea from the north. The moments went by. Then, far off in

A. Interpreting
We take the cheering of the villagers as a good omen for Ged's trip.

B. Recalling
Remind students that the Servants of the Stone, or Old Powers of the Earth, are from earth and will not cross over the sea.

C. Earthsea Map
You might have students locate Kameber Rock and Oranéa.

Quotation from the Author
"Fantasy is the natural . . . language of the recounting of the spritual journey and the struggle of good and evil in the soul."
—Ursula Le Guin

You might want to discuss this quote with students. What spiritual journey is Ged making? What is the good and evil in his soul? Do you agree with what Le Guin says here?

A. Irony
Irony, in this case, is the surprising difference between what is expected to happen and what really does happen.
? What is ironic about what happens here? (You expect the shadow to grab Ged but, instead, it runs away.) This is an important turning point in the conflict between Ged and the shadow, because this is the first time the shadow flees from Ged. Note Le Guin's use of a one-sentence paragraph for emphasis.

B. Earthsea Map
You might have students trace the flight of the shadow.

C. Foreshadowing
? How does the setting foreshadow trouble for Ged? (The storm and the mist prevent Ged from seeing the shadow, or anything else, clearly. We wonder where the shadow is leading him, and we fear that Ged won't be able to see any obstacles in his blind pursuit.)

the rain over the water, he saw the shadow coming.

It had done with the body of the Osskilian oarsman Skiorh, and not as gebbeth did it follow him through the winds and over sea. Nor did it wear that beast-shape in which he had seen it on Roke Knoll, and in his dreams. Yet it had a shape now, even in the daylight. In its pursuit of Ged and in its struggle with him on the moors it had drawn power from him, sucking it into itself: and it may be that his summoning of it, aloud in the light of day, had given to it or forced upon it some form and semblance. Certainly it had now some likeness to a man, though being shadow it cast no shadow. So it came over the sea, out of the Jaws of Enlad toward Gont, a dim ill-made thing pacing uneasy on the waves, peering down the wind as it came; and the cold rain blew through it.

Because it was half blinded by the day, and because he had called it, Ged saw it before it saw him. He knew it, as it knew him, among all beings, all shadows.

In the terrible solitude of the winter sea Ged stood and saw the thing he feared. The wind seemed to blow it farther from the boat, and the waves ran under it bewildering his eye, and ever and again it seemed closer to him. He could not tell if it moved or not. It had seen him, now. Though there was nothing in his mind but horror and fear of its touch, the cold black pain that drained all his life away, yet he waited, unmoving. Then all at once speaking aloud he called the magewind strong and sudden into his white sail, and his boat leapt across the gray waves straight at the lowering thing that hung upon the wind.

A In utter silence the shadow, wavering, turned and fled.

Upwind it went, northward. Upwind Ged's boat followed, shadow-speed against mage-craft, the rainy gale against them both. And the young man yelled to his boat, to the sail and the wind and the waves ahead, as a hunter yells to his hounds when the wolf runs in plain sight before them, and he brought into that spell-woven sail a wind that would have split any sail of cloth and that drove his boat over the sea like a scud of blown foam, closer always to the thing that fled.

Now the shadow turned, making a half-circle, and appearing all at once more loose and dim, less like a man more like mere smoke blowing on the wind, it doubled back and ran downwind with the gale, as if it made for Gont.

With hand and spell Ged turned his boat, and it leaped like a dolphin from the water, rolling, in that quick turn. Faster than before he followed, but the shadow grew ever fainter to his eyes. Rain, mixed with sleet and snow, came stinging across his back and his left cheek, and he could not see more than a hundred yards ahead. Before long, as the storm grew heavier, the shadow was lost to sight. Yet Ged was sure of its track as if he followed a beast's track over snow, instead of a wraith fleeing over water. Though the wind blew his way now he held the singing magewind in the sail, and flake-foam shot from the boat's blunt prow, and she slapped the water as she went.

For a long time hunted and hunter held their weird, fleet course, and the day was darkening fast. Ged knew that at the great pace he had gone these past hours he must be south of Gont, heading past it toward Spevy or Torheven, or even past these islands out into the open Reach. He could not tell. He did not care. He hunted, he followed, and fear ran before him. B

All at once he saw the shadow for a moment and far from him. The world's wind had been sinking, and the driving sleet of the storm had given way to a chill, ragged, thickening mist. Through this mist he glimpsed the shadow, fleeing somewhat to the right of his course. He spoke to wind and sail and turned the tiller and pursued, C though again it was a blind pursuit: The fog thickened fast, boiling and tattering where it met with the spellwind, closing down all round the boat, a featureless pallor[1] that deadened light and sight. Even as Ged spoke the first word of a clearing-charm, he saw the shadow again, still to the right of his course but very near, and going slowly. The fog blew through the faceless vagueness of its head, yet it was shaped like a man, only deformed and changing, like a man's shadow. Ged veered the boat once more, thinking he had run his enemy to ground: In that instant it vanished, and it was his boat that ran aground, smashing up on shoal rocks that the blowing mist had hidden from his sight. He was pitched nearly out, but grabbed hold on the mast-staff before the next breaker struck. This was a great wave, which threw the little boat up out of water and brought her down on a rock, as a man might lift up and crush a snail's shell.

Stout and wizardly was the staff Ogion had shaped. It did not break, and buoyant as a dry log it rode the water. Still grasping it Ged was pulled back as the breakers streamed back from the shoal, so that he was in deep water and saved, till the next wave, from battering on the rocks. Salt-blinded and choked, he tried to keep his head up and to fight the enormous pull of the sea. There was sand beach a little aside of the rocks, he glimpsed this a couple of times as he tried to swim

1. **pallor:** unnatural paleness.

A free of the rising of the next breaker. With all his strength and with the staff's power aiding him he struggled to make for that beach. He got no nearer. The surge and recoil of the swells tossed him back and forth like a rag, and the cold of the deep sea drew warmth fast from his body, weakening him till he could not move his arms. He had lost sight of rocks and beach alike, and did not know what way he faced. There was only a tumult of water around him, under him, over him, blinding him, strangling him, drowning him.

A wave swelling in under the ragged fog took him and rolled him over and over and flung him up like a stick of driftwood on the sand.

There he lay. He still clutched the yew-wood staff with both hands. Lesser waves dragged at him, trying to tug him back down the sand in their outgoing rush, and the mist parted and closed above him, and later a sleety rain beat on him.

After a long time he moved. He got up on hands and knees, and began slowly crawling up the beach, away from the water's edge. It was black night now, but he whispered to the staff, and a little werelight clung about it. With this to guide him he struggled forward, little by little, up toward the dunes. He was so beaten and broken and cold that this crawling through the wet sand in the whistling, sea-thundering dark was the hardest thing he had ever had to do. And once or twice it seemed to him that the great noise of the sea and
B the wind all died away and the wet sand turned to dust under his hands, and he felt the unmoving gaze of strange stars on his back: but he did not lift his head, and he crawled on, and after a while he heard his own gasping breath, and felt the bitter wind beat the rain against his face.

The moving brought a little warmth back into him at last, and after he had crept up into the dunes, where the gusts of rainy wind came less hard, he managed to get up on his feet. He spoke a stronger light out of the staff, for the world was utterly black, and then leaning on the staff he went on, stumbling and halting, half a mile or so inland. Then on the rise of a dune he heard the sea, louder again, not behind him but in front: The dunes sloped down again to another shore. This was no island he was on but a mere reef, a bit of sand in the midst of the ocean.

He was too worn out to despair, but he gave a kind of sob and stood there, bewildered, leaning on his staff, for a long time. Then doggedly he turned to the left, so the wind would be at his back at least, and shuffled down the high dune,
C seeking some hollow among the ice-rimed, bowing sea-grass where he could have a little shelter. As he held up the staff to see what lay before him, he caught a dull gleam at the farthest edge of the circle of werelight: a wall of rain-wet wood.

It was a hut or shed, small and rickety as if a child had built it. Ged knocked on the low door with his staff. It remained shut. Ged pushed it open and entered, stooping nearly double to do so. He could not stand up straight inside the hut. Coals lay red in the firepit, and by their dim glow Ged saw a man with white, long hair, who crouched in terror against the far wall, and another, man or woman he could not tell, peering from a heap of rags or hides on the floor.

"I won't hurt you," Ged whispered.

They said nothing. He looked from one to the other. Their eyes were blank with terror. When he laid down his staff, the one under the pile of rags hid whimpering. Ged took off his cloak that was heavy with water and ice, stripped naked and huddled over the firepit. "Give me something to wrap myself in," he said. He was hoarse, and could hardly speak for the chattering of his teeth and long shudders that shook him. If they heard him, neither of the old ones answered. He reached out and took a rag from the bed-heap—a goathide, it might have been years ago, but it was now all tatters and black grease. The one under the bed-heap moaned with fear, but Ged paid no heed. He rubbed himself dry and then whispered, "Have you wood? Build up the fire a little, old man. I come to you in need, I mean you no harm." D

The old man did not move, watching him in a stupor of fear.

"Do you understand me? Do you speak no Hardic?" Ged paused, and then asked, "Kargad?"

At that word, the old man nodded all at once, one nod, like a sad old puppet on strings. But as it was the only word Ged knew of the Kargish language, it was the end of their conversation. He found wood piled by one wall, built up the fire himself, and then with gestures asked for water, for swallowing seawater had sickened him and now he was parched with thirst. Cringing, the old man pointed to a great shell that held water, and pushed toward the fire another shell in which were strips of smoke-dried fish. So, cross-legged close by the fire, Ged drank, and ate a little, and as some strength and sense began to come back into him, he wondered where he was. Even with the magewind he could not have sailed clear to the Kargad Lands. This islet must be out in the Reach, E
east of Gont but still west of Karego-At. It seemed strange that people dwelt on so small and forlorn a place, a mere sandbar; maybe they were castaways; but he was too weary to puzzle his head about them then.

A. Suspense
? What details make this description suspenseful? (Ged "got no nearer"; the cold weakens him "till he could not move his arms"; "he had lost sight of rocks and beach alike" and it seems as if he will drown.)

B. Responding
? What terrible climb does the author cause you to recall here? (Ged's climb from the land of the dead. We can infer that Ged is battling death here.)

C. Vocabulary
ice-rimed: ice-coated

D. Imagery
? Find details on this page that appeals to these senses: sight, sound, taste, and touch. (Sight: "a mere reef"; sound: "sea-thundering dark"; taste: "swallowing seawater had sickened him"; touch: "long shudders . . . shook him")

E. Earthsea Map
Students might study the map and guess where Ged has landed.

A. Interpreting
? How did the shadow trick him? (It led Ged through the storm and fog to crash upon the rocks that he could not see.)

He kept turning his cloak to the heat. The silvery pellawi-fur dried fast, and as soon as the wool of the facing was at least warm, if not dry, he wrapped himself in it and stretched out by the firepit. "Go to sleep, poor folk," he said to his silent hosts, and laid his head down on the floor of sand, and slept.

Three nights he spent on the nameless isle, for the first morning when he woke he was sore in every muscle and feverish and sick. He lay like a log of driftwood in the hut by the firepit all that day and night. The next morning he woke still stiff and sore, but recovered. He put back on his salt-crusted clothes, for there was not enough water to wash them, and going out into the gray windy A morning looked over this place whereto the shadow had tricked him.

It was a rocky sandbar a mile wide at its widest and a little longer than that, fringed all about with shoals and rocks. No tree or bush grew on it, no plant but the bowing sea grass. The hut stood in a hollow of the dunes, and the old man and woman lived there alone in the utter desolation of the empty sea. The hut was built, or piled up rather, of driftwood planks and branches. Their water came from a little brackish well beside the hut; their food was fish and shellfish, fresh or dried, and rockweed. The tattered hides in the hut, and a little store of bone needles and fishhooks, and the sinew for fishlines and firedrill, came not from goats as Ged had thought at first, but from spotted seal; and indeed this was the kind of place where the seal will go to raise their pups in summer. But no one else comes to such a place. The old ones feared Ged not because they thought him a spirit, and not because he was a wizard, but only because he was a man. They had forgotten that there were other people in the world.

The old man's sullen dread never lessened. When he thought Ged was coming close enough to touch him, he would hobble away, peering back with a scowl around his bush of dirty white hair. At first the old woman had whimpered and hidden under her rag pile whenever Ged moved, but as he had lain dozing feverishly in the dark hut, he saw her squatting to stare at him with a strange,

A. Interpreting

? Why do you think the old woman looks at Ged "with that same craving look in her eyes"? (She probably yearns to talk with him; perhaps she yearns for the son she never had.)

B. Theme

Ged believes that the shadow is evil and that it wants him to do evil.

? What good has come out of the shadow's tricking Ged onto the island? (He finds the old people and receives a part of history—the ring. He will seek the other half of the ring in the next book in the Earthsea trilogy, *The Tombs of Atuan.* He also does a good deed: He creates an everlasting freshwater spring on the isle.)

? What might Le Guin be suggesting about the shadow? (Perhaps that, just as Ged said on page 587, "it is very hard for evil to take hold of the unconsenting soul")

C. Character

Ged used to be almost helpless with fear and depression when he thought of the shadow.

? How has his attitude toward the shadow changed? (He feels in control. The shadow now is running from him.)

dull, yearning look; and after a while she had brought him water to drink. When he sat up to take the shell from her she was scared and dropped it, spilling all the water, and then she wept, and wiped her eyes with her long whitish-gray hair.

Now she watched him as he worked down on the beach, shaping driftwood and planks from his boat that had washed ashore into a new boat, using the old man's crude stone adze and a binding-spell. This was neither a repair nor a boat-building, for he had not enough proper wood, and must supply all his wants with pure wizardry. Yet the old woman did not watch his marvelous work so much as she watched him, with that same craving look in her eyes. After a while she went off, and came back presently with a gift: a handful of mussels she had gathered on the rocks. Ged ate them as she gave them to him, sea-wet and raw, and thanked her. Seeming to gain courage, she went to the hut and came back with something again in her hands, a bundle wrapped up in a rag. Timidly, watching his face all the while, she unwrapped the thing and held it up for him to see.

It was a little child's dress of silk brocade stiff with seed pearls, stained with salt, yellow with years. On the small bodice the pearls were worked in a shape Ged knew: the double arrow of the God-Brothers of the Kargad Empire, surmounted by a king's crown.

The old woman, wrinkled, dirty, clothed in an ill-sewn sack of sealskin, pointed at the little silken dress and at herself, and smiled: a sweet, unmeaning smile, like a baby's. From some hiding place sewn in the skirt of the dress she took a small object, and this was held out to Ged. It was a bit of dark metal, a piece of broken jewelry perhaps, the half-circle of a broken ring. Ged looked at it, but she gestured that he take it, and was not satisfied until he took it; then she nodded and smiled again; she had made him a present. But the dress she wrapped up carefully in its greasy rag-coverings, and she shuffled back to the hut to hide the lovely thing away.

Ged put the broken ring into his tunic-pocket with almost the same care, for his heart was full of pity. He guessed now that these two might be children of some royal house of the Kargad Empire; a tyrant or usurper who feared to shed kingly blood had sent them to be cast away, to live or die, on an uncharted islet far from Karego-At. One had been a boy of eight or ten, maybe, and the other a stout baby princess in a dress of silk and pearls; and they had lived, and lived on alone, forty years, fifty years, on a rock in the ocean, prince and princess of Desolation.

But the truth of this guess he did not learn until, years later, the quest of the Ring of Erreth-Akbe led him to the Kargad Lands, and to the Tombs of Atuan.

His third night on the isle lightened to a calm, pale sunrise. It was the day of Sunreturn, the shortest day of the year. His little boat of wood and magic, scraps and spells, was ready. He had tried to tell the old ones that he would take them to any land, Gont or Spevy or the Torikles; he would have left them even on some lonely shore of Karego-At, had they asked it of him, though Kargish waters were no safe place for an Archipelagan to venture. But they would not leave their barren isle. The old woman seemed not to understand what he meant with his gestures and quiet words; the old man did understand, and refused. All his memory of other lands and other men was a child's nightmare of blood and giants and screaming: Ged could see that in his face, as he shook his head and shook his head.

So Ged that morning filled up a sealskin pouch with water at the well, and since he could not thank the old ones for their fire and food, and had no present for the old woman as he would have liked, he did what he could, and set a charm on that salty unreliable spring. The water rose up through the sand as sweet and clear as any mountain spring in the heights of Gont, nor did it ever fail. Because of it, that place of dunes and rocks is charted now and bears a name; sailors call it Springwater Isle. But the hut is gone, and the storms of many winters have left no sign of the two who lived out their lives there and died alone.

They kept hidden in the hut, as if they feared to watch, when Ged ran his boat out from the sandy south end of the isle. He let the world's wind, steady from the north, fill his sail of spell-cloth, and went speedily forth over the sea.

Now this sea-quest of Ged's was a strange matter, for as he well knew, he was a hunter who knew neither what the thing was that he hunted, nor where in all Earthsea it might be. He must hunt it by guess, by hunch, by luck, even as it had hunted him. Each was blind to the other's being, Ged as baffled by impalpable[2] shadows as the shadow was baffled by daylight and by solid things. One certainty only Ged had: that he was indeed the hunter now and not the hunted. For the shadow, having tricked him onto the rocks, might have had him at its mercy all the while he lay half-dead on the shore and blundered in darkness in the stormy dunes; but it had not waited

2. **impalpable** (im·pal′pə·b'l): something that cannot be felt by touching; intangible.

A. Interpreting You might have students consider, and discuss, the idea that the mist Ged created to save his village was a foreshadowing of the evil shadow that is now tormenting him.

B. Personification ? Can you find two examples of personification in this paragraph? ("Forest-crowned cliffs"; "the sea, confined, was restless and fretted . . .")

C. Suspense On this page, Ged is alone with his thoughts, sailing in search of the shadow. ? How does the author build suspense in these descriptive paragraphs? (By telling you Ged's thoughts and moving him closer and closer to the thing he is seeking.)

for that chance. It had tricked him and fled away at once, not daring now to face him. In this he saw that Ogion had been right: The shadow could not draw on his power, so long as he was turned against it. So he must keep against it, keep after it, though its track was cold across these wide seas, and he had nothing at all to guide him but the luck of the world's wind blowing southward, and a dim guess or notion in his mind that south or east was the right way to follow.

Before nightfall he saw away off on his left hand the long, faint shoreline of a great land, which must be Karego-At. He was in the very sea roads of those white barbaric folk. He kept a sharp watch out for any Kargish longship or galley; and he remembered, as he sailed through red evening, that morning of his boyhood in Ten Alders village, the plumed warriors, the fire, the mist. And think- A ing of that day he saw all at once, with a qualm at his heart, how the shadow had tricked him with his own trick, bringing that mist about him on the sea as if bringing it out of his own past, blinding him to danger and fooling him to his death.

He kept his course to the southeast, and the land sank out of sight as night came over the eastern edge of the world. The hollows of the waves all were full of darkness while the crests shone yet with a clear ruddy reflection of the west. Ged sang aloud the Winter Carol, and such cantoes of the *Deed of the Young King* as he remembered, for those songs are sung at the Festival of Sunreturn. His voice was clear, but it fell to nothing in the vast silence of the sea. Darkness came quickly, and the winter stars.

All that longest night of the year he waked, watching the stars rise upon his left hand and wheel overhead and sink into far black waters on the right, while always the long wind of winter bore him southward over an unseen sea. He could sleep for only a moment now and then, with a sharp awakening. This boat he sailed was in truth no boat but a thing more than half charm and sorcery, and the rest of it mere planks and driftwood which, if he let slack the shaping-spells and the binding-spell upon them, would soon enough lapse and scatter and go drifting off as a little flotsam on the waves. The sail too, woven of magic and the air, would not long stay against the wind if he slept, but would turn to a puff of wind itself. Ged's spells were cogent and potent, but when the matter on which such spells work is small, the power that keeps them working must be renewed from moment to moment: so he slept not that night. He would have gone easier and swifter as falcon or dolphin, but Ogion had advised him not to change his shape, and he knew the value of Ogion's advice. So he sailed southward under the west-going stars, and the long night passed slowly, until the first day of the new year brightened all the sea.

Soon after the sun rose he saw land ahead, but he was making little way toward it. The world's wind had dropped with daybreak. He raised a light magewind into his sail, to drive him toward that land. At the sight of it, fear had come into him again, the sinking dread that urged him to turn away, to run away. And he followed that fear as a hunter follows the signs, the broad, blunt, clawed tracks of the bear, that may at any moment turn on him from the thickets. For he was close now: He knew it.

It was a queer-looking land that loomed up over the sea as he drew nearer and nearer. What had from afar seemed to be one sheer mountain wall, was split into several long steep ridges, separate isles perhaps, between which the sea ran in narrow sounds or channels. Ged had pored over many charts and maps in the Tower of the Master Namer on Roke, but those had been mostly of the Archipelago and the inner seas. He was out in the East Reach now, and did not know what this island might be. Nor had he much thought for that. It was fear that lay ahead of him, that lurked hiding from him or waiting for him among the slopes and forests of the island, and straight for it he steered.

Now the dark forest-crowned cliffs gloomed and towered high over his boat, and spray from the waves that broke against the rocky headlands blew spattering against his sail, as the magewind bore him between two great capes into a sound, a sea lane that ran on before him deep into the island, no wider than the length of two galleys. B The sea, confined, was restless and fretted at the steep shores. There were no beaches, for the cliffs dropped straight down into the water that lay darkened by the cold reflection of their heights. It was windless, and very silent.

The shadow had tricked him out onto the moors in Osskil, and tricked him in the mist onto the rocks, and now would there be a third trick? Had he driven the thing here, or had it drawn him here, into a trap? He did not know. He knew only the torment of dread, and the certainty that he must go ahead and do what he had set out to do: hunt down the evil, follow his terror to its source. Very cautiously he steered, watching before him and behind him and up and down the cliffs on either hand. He had left the sunlight of the new day behind him on the open sea. All was dark here. The opening between the headlands seemed a remote, bright gateway when he glanced back. The C

Reading Check Test: Chapters 7 and 8

1. The stone of Terrenon is evil. *(True)*
2. Ged rescues Serret from Lord Benderesk's evil spell. *(True)*
3. Ged escapes from Osskil by turning himself into a hawk and flying away. *(True)*
4. Ogion advises Ged to hunt the shadow. *(True)*
5. When Ged meets the shadow on the sea, he runs from it in terror. *(False)*

---

cliffs loomed higher and ever higher overhead as he approached the mountain-root from which they sprang, and the lane of water grew narrower. He peered ahead into the dark cleft, and left and right up the great, cavern-pocked, boulder-tumbled slopes where trees crouched with their roots half in the air. Nothing moved. Now he was coming to the end of the inlet, a high blank wrinkled mass
A of rock against which, narrowed to the width of a little creek, the last sea-waves lapped feebly. Fallen boulders and rotten trunks and the roots of gnarled trees left only a tight way to steer. A trap: a dark trap under the roots of the silent mountain, and he was in the trap. Nothing moved before him or above him. All was deathly still. He could go no further.

He turned the boat around, working her carefully round with spell and with makeshift oar lest she knock up against the underwater rocks or be entangled in the outreaching roots and branches, till she faced outward again; and he was about to raise up a wind to take him back as he had come, when suddenly the words of the spell froze on his lips, and his heart went cold within him. He looked back over his shoulder. The shadow stood
B behind him in the boat.

Had he lost one instant, he had been lost; but he was ready, and lunged to seize and hold the thing which wavered and trembled there within arm's reach. No wizardry would serve him now but only his own flesh, his life itself, against the unliving. He spoke no word, but attacked, and the boat plunged and pitched from his sudden turn and lunge. And a pain ran up his arms into his breast, taking away his breath, and an icy cold filled him, and he was blinded: yet in his hands that seized the shadow there was nothing—darkness, air.

He stumbled forward, catching the mast to stay his fall, and light came shooting back into his eyes. He saw the shadow shudder away from him and shrink together, then stretch hugely up over him, over the sail, for an instant. Then like black smoke on the wind it recoiled and fled, formless, down the water toward the bright gate between the cliffs.

Ged sank to his knees. The little spell-patched boat pitched again, rocked itself to stillness, drifting on the uneasy waves. He crouched in it, numb, unthinking, struggling to draw breath, until at last cold water welling under his hands warned him that he must see to his boat, for the spells binding it were growing weak. He stood up, holding onto the staff that made the mast, and rewove the binding-spell as best he could. He was chilled and weary; his hands and arms ached sorely, and there was no power in him. He wished he might lie down there in that dark place where sea and mountain met and sleep, sleep on the restless rocking water.

He could not tell if this weariness were a sorcery laid on him by the shadow as it fled, or came of the bitter coldness of its touch, or was from mere hunger and want of sleep and expense of strength; but he struggled against it, forcing himself to raise up a light magewind into the sail and follow down the dark seaway where the shadow had fled.

All terror was gone. All joy was gone. It was a chase no longer. He was neither hunted nor hunter, now. For the third time they had met and touched: He had of his own will turned to the shadow, seeking to hold it with living hands. He had not held it, but he had forged between them a bond, a link that had no breaking point. There was no need to hunt the thing down, to track it, nor would its flight avail it. Neither could escape. When they had come to the time and place of their last meeting, they would meet.

But until that time, and elsewhere than that place, there would never be any rest or peace for Ged, day or night, on earth or sea. He knew now, and the knowledge was hard, that his task had never been to undo what he had done, but to finish what he had begun.

He sailed out from between the dark cliffs, and on the sea was broad, bright morning, with a fair C
wind blowing from the north.

He drank what water he had left in the sealskin pouch, and steered around the westernmost headland until he came into a wide strait between it and a second island lying to the west. Then he knew the place, calling to mind sea-charts of the East Reach. These were the Hands, a pair of lonely isles that reach their mountain-fingers D
northward toward the Kargad Lands. He sailed on between the two, and as the afternoon darkened with storm clouds coming up from the north he came to shore, on the southern coast of the west isle. He had seen there was a little village there, above the beach where a stream came tumbling down to the sea, and he cared little what welcome he got if he could have water, fire's warmth, and sleep.

The villagers were rough shy people, awed by a wizard's staff, wary of a strange face, but hospitable to one who came alone, over sea, before a storm. They gave him meat and drink in plenty, and the comfort of firelight and the comfort of human voices speaking his own Hardic tongue, and last and best they gave him hot water to wash the cold and saltness of the sea from him, and a bed where he could sleep.

A. Setting
? How does the setting affect the plot here? (Ged has steered between two cliffs into an opening that he realizes is a trap.)

B. Irony
? Why is this situation ironic? (Because, although the suspense has been building up, neither Ged nor the reader expected the shadow to appear so soon)

C. Symbol
? What might the change in setting symbolize? (Ged has come out of the dark of ignorance, and into the light of his new knowledge concerning his conflict with the shadow.)

D. Earthsea Map
You might have students locate the Hands.

ANALYZING CHAPTERS 7 AND 8
Identifying Facts

1. Ged thinks that either the shadow lured him there, or that both he and the shadow were drawn there by some other power.
2. Serret tries to persuade Ged by telling him that if he touches the Stone he will gain great power. She tells him that the Stone can tell him the name of his enemy and that he will become "a king among men," and that she will rule with him. Ged realizes that the Stone is evil and that if he touches it or speaks to it he will be its slave.
3. Ogion advises Ged to turn on the shadow—to be the pursuer instead of the pursued. If he does not, he will always be fearful wherever he goes. He also shows Ged that Ged is at least as powerful as the shadow, and should not fear it.
4. Instead of a shapeless mass, the shadow takes the general shape of a man.
5. Ged thinks the old man and woman may have been children of a royal family of the Kargad Empire who were abandoned on the deserted island by *(Answers continue in left-hand column.)*

(Continued from top.)
tyrants who took over the Empire. As a gift, he leaves them a spring of fresh water.
6. He learns that his task is not to undo what he did on Roke Knoll, but to complete what he had begun.

Interpreting Meanings

7. Details of luxury are mattresses made of silk and down; Ged's silk and silver tunic; his glove-leather boots. Bleak details include the stone walls and floors; the bare moorland; the tower standing remote and aloof, with its back to the nearest town. For more details, see Teacher's Manual page 187.
8. Serret is basically dishonest, cruel, and powerful. For details, see Teacher's Manual page 187.
9. At first, Ged was terrified of the shadow. He fled from it until Ogion advised to turn and face it, or to confront his fear. Now that Ged is pursuing the shadow, it turns and flees from him.

Responding to the Novel

Analyzing Chapters 7 and 8

Identifying Facts

1. Ged finds his arrival at the Court of the Terrenon puzzling. What two possible explanations does he think of for why he was drawn to the Court?
2. The day after Serret shows Ged the Stone, she tells him that he alone has the power to become its master. How does she try to persuade him to touch the Stone? Explain why Ged refuses.
3. After Ged escapes the Servants of the stone, he flees to Ogion's cottage. Summarize Ogion's advice about how to resolve his struggle.
4. Out on the sea, Ged summons the shadow. How has it changed since the last time they met?
5. When Ged crashes on a sandbar, he meets two people. Who does he think they are? Although he has brought nothing to the island, what present does he leave them?
6. When he leaves the sandbar, Ged encounters the shadow one more time. What new knowledge does he gain about his task after this meeting?

Interpreting Meanings

7. The **setting** of the Court of the Terrenon is described in very particular detail. List some descriptive details describing the castle and the landscape surrounding it that emphasize luxury and wealth. Then list some details that emphasize cold and grayness. Explain whether you feel this setting creates an overall feeling that is inviting and secure, or one that is bleak and forbidding.
8. Serret turns out to be someone who first appeared in Chapter 2—the daughter of the old Lord of Re Albi, on Gont. Think about her action on both Gont and Osskil. Do they reveal her to be honest or dishonest, kind or cruel, weak or powerful? Give evidence from the novel.
9. As Chapter 7 opens, Ged has been hunted and almost defeated by his shadow. Explain how the balance of power between Ged and the shadow shifts in Chapters 7 and 8. That is, compare how Ged felt and behaved toward the shadow earlier in the novel to how he feels and behaves toward it now. How did the shadow behave toward Ged earlier, and how does it behave now?

Analyzing Language and Vocabulary

Exotic Words

In order to give her story the feeling of a magical, far-distant world, Le Guin uses many exotic, unfamiliar English words. She uses words that are **archaic**—that is, once common but rarely used today. For example, *mage* is an archaic word for *magician.* She also uses words that refer to legends, history, and fairy tales. For instance, the word *greaves,* meaning "armor for the legs," is frequently used in stories about knights. And she uses words that are usually found in poetry, such as *lest,* which means "in case" or "for fear that."

The author also creates exotic words by combining other ordinary English words. For example, she uses *sea-rim* to mean "rim of the sea," or "horizon." All of these types of words, together with the novel's invented words, can give you the sense that you are reading a language that is rich, exotic, mysterious, and yet understandable.

Use a dictionary to help you answer the questions about the words from the novel listed below.

rune	drear
prentice	tower-keep
mage-craft	wraith
Sunreturn	carven
magewind	spellsmith

1. Which are archaic words? What words would be used instead today?
2. Which words are often used in history, legends, or fairy tales?
3. Which words are ordinarily used only in poetry? For each of these, list one or two words with the same meaning that are more commonly used in prose or everyday speech.
4. Which words are combinations of other words? You will not find these words in the dictionary. Examine the parts of each of these words, and explain what you think each of these words means.
5. See if you can write a paragraph that uses all ten words in the list above. Write about a world that you make up yourself.

For answers, see Teacher's Manual page 187.

Summary: Chapter 9
Ged stops at a village in the Hands to ready a new boat. His next stop is Vemish. He learns that the shadow has just been there, and that it now looks like him. He sails to Ismay where he meets the island's wizard, his friend Vetch. Ged meets Vetch's family—his younger brother and younger sister Yarrow. Vetch decides to go with Ged on his quest so that he can either warn the Archipelago if Ged fails or make up a song celebrating Ged's conquest. The two friends set out together.

Earthsea Vocabulary
Simn
Pirr

A. Vocabulary
cataracts: eye disease

B. Expansion
Le Guin foreshadows far jouneys for Ged's new boat. He uses this boat for the rest of his life. It takes him to the Kargad Lands in *The Tombs of Atuan* and to the South Reach in *The Farthest Shore.*

C. Character
? What character traits are revealed by Ged's actions in the village of West Hand? (Kindness, understanding, helpfulness)

Chapter 9
Iffish

Ged spent three days in that village of the West Hand, recovering himself, and making ready a boat built not of spells and seawrack but of sound wood well pegged and caulked,[1] with a stout mast and sail of her own, that he might sail easily and sleep when he needed. Like most boats of the North and the Reaches she was clinker-built, with planks overlapped and clenched one upon the other for strength in the high seas; every part of her was sturdy and well-made. Ged reinforced her wood with deep-inwoven charms, for he thought he might go far in that boat. She was built to carry two or three men, and the old man who owned her said that he and his brothers had been through high seas and foul weather with her and she had ridden all gallantly.[2]

Unlike the shrewd fisherman of Gont, this old man, for fear and wonder of his wizardry, would have given the boat to Ged. But Ged paid him for A it in sorcerers' kind, healing his eyes of the cataracts that were in the way of blinding him. Then the old man, rejoicing, said to him, "We called the boat *Sanderling,* but do you call her *Lookfar,* and paint eyes aside her prow, and my thanks will look out of that blind wood for you and keep you B from rock and reef. For I had forgotten how much light there is in the world, till you gave it back to me."

Other works Ged also did in his days in that village under the steep forests of the Hand, as his power came back into him. These were such people as he had known as a boy in the Northward Vale of Gont, though poorer even than those. With them he was at home, as he would never be in the courts of the wealthy, and he knew their bitter wants without having to ask. So he laid charms of heal and ward on children who were lame or sickly, and spells of increase on the villagers' scrawny flocks of goats and sheep; he set the rune Simn on the spindles and looms, the boat's oars and tools of bronze and stone they brought him, that these might do their work well; and the rune Pirr he wrote on the rooftrees of the huts, which protects the house and its folk from fire, wind, C and madness.

When his boat *Lookfar* was ready and well stocked with water and dried fish, he stayed yet one more day in the village, to teach to their young chanter the *Deed of Morred* and the *Havnorian Lay.* Very seldom did any Archipelagan ship touch at the Hands: Songs made a hundred years ago were news to those villagers, and they craved to hear of heroes. Had Ged been free of what was laid on him he would gladly have stayed there a week or a month to sing them what he knew, that the great songs might be known on a new isle. But he was not free, and the next morning he set sail, going straight south over the wide seas of the Reach. For southward the shadow had gone. He need cast no finding-charm to know this: He knew it, as certainly as if a fine unreeling cord bound him and it together, no matter what miles and seas and lands might lie between. So he went certain, unhurried, and unhopeful on the way he must go, and the wind of winter bore him to the south.

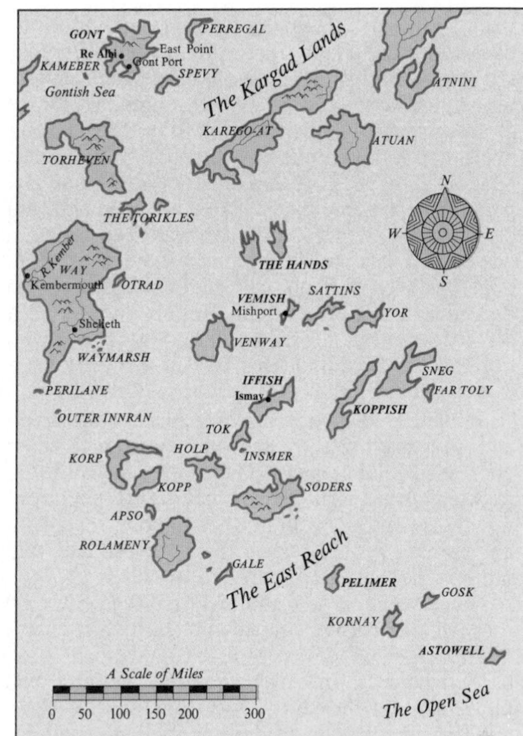

He sailed a day and a night over the lonesome sea, and on the second day he came to a small isle, which they told him was called Vemish. The people in the little port looked at him askance,[3] and soon their sorcerer came hurrying. He looked hard at Ged, and then he bowed, and said in a voice that was both pompous and wheedling,

1. **caulked:** made watertight by filling the seams and cracks.
2. **gallantly:** bravely and nobly.
3. **askance:** with suspicion or disapproval.

Supplementary Support Material: Chapters 9 and 10

1. Vocabulary Activity Sheet
2. Reading Check Test blackline master
3. Selection Test (page 221 of Test Book)
4. Workbook (page 161)

Developing Vocabulary

The following words appear on a test in the Test Book, page 222. (See also the Vocabulary Activity Sheet.)

pompous	comely
linger	odorous
reluctant	respite
decorously	unheeding
vanquish	insolent

A. Making Inferences

Who do you think this strange person might be? (The shadow) What can we infer from this sighting? (That the shadow has taken strength from Ged, because it now goes in his form)

B. Interpreting

Why do you think Ged won't admit to himself that he is sad? (Probably because he knows that if he gives in to his emotion, he will be tempted to give up his hunt. The shadow would then conquer him.)

"Lord Wizard! forgive my temerity, and honor us by accepting of us anything you may need for your voyage—food, drink, sailcloth, rope—my daughter is fetching to your boat at this moment a brace of fresh-roasted hens—I think it prudent, however, that you continue on your way from here as soon as it meets your convenience to do so. The people are in some dismay. For not long ago, the day before yesterday, a person was seen crossing our humble isle afoot from north to south, and no boat was seen to come with him aboard it nor no boat was seen to leave with him aboard it, and it did not seem that he cast any shadow. Those who saw this person tell me that he bore some likeness to yourself." **A**

At that, Ged bowed his own head, and turned and went back to the docks of Vemish and sailed out, not looking back. There was no profit in frightening the islanders or making an enemy of their sorcerer. He would rather sleep at sea again, and think over this news the sorcerer had told him, for he was sorely puzzled by it.

The day ended, and the night passed with cold rain whispering over the sea all through the dark hours, and gray dawn. Still the mild north wind carried *Lookfar* on. After noon the rain and mist blew off, and the sun shone from time to time; and late in the day Ged saw right athwart[4] his course the low blue hills of a great island, brightened by that drifting winter sunlight. The smoke of hearthfires lingered blue over the slate roofs of little towns among those hills, a pleasant sight in the vast sameness of the sea.

Ged followed a fishing fleet in to their port, and going up the streets of the town in the golden winter evening he found an inn called *The Harrekki,* where firelight and ale and roast ribs of mutton warmed him body and soul. At the tables of the inn there were a couple of other voyagers, traders of the East Reach, but most of the men were townsfolk come there for good ale, news, and conversation. They were not rough timid people like the fisherfolk of the Hands, but true townsmen, alert and sedate. Surely they knew Ged for a wizard, but nothing at all was said of it, except that the innkeeper in talking (and he was a talkative man) mentioned that this town, Ismay, was fortunate in sharing with other towns of the island the inestimable treasure of an accomplished wizard trained at the School of Roke, who had been given his staff by the Archmage himself, and who, though out of town at the moment, dwelt in his ancestral home right in Ismay itself, which, therefore, stood in no need of any other practitioner of the High Arts. "As they say, *two staffs in one town must come to blows,* isn't it so, Sir?" said the innkeeper, smiling and full of cheer. So Ged was informed that as journeyman-wizard, one seeking a livelihood from sorcery, he was not wanted here. Thus he had got a blunt dismissal from Vemish and a bland one from Ismay, and he wondered at what he had been told about the kindly ways of the East Reach. This isle was Iffish, where his friend Vetch had been born. It did not seem so hospitable a place as Vetch had said.

And yet he saw that they were, indeed, kindly faces enough. It was only that they sensed what he knew to be true: that he was set apart from them, cut off from them, that he bore a doom upon him and followed after a dark thing. He was like a cold wind blowing through the firelit room, like a black bird carried by on a storm from foreign lands. The sooner he went on, taking his evil destiny with him, the better for these folk.

"I am on a quest," he said to the innkeeper. "I will be here only a night or two." His tone was bleak. The innkeeper, with a glance at the great yew-staff in the corner, said nothing at all for once, but filled up Ged's cup with brown ale till the foam ran over the top.

Ged knew that he should spend only the one night in Ismay. There was no welcome for him there, or anywhere. He must go where he was bound. But he was sick of the cold empty sea and the silence where no voice spoke to him. He told himself he would spend one day in Ismay, and on the morrow go. So he slept late; when he woke a light snow was falling, and he idled about the lanes and byways of the town to watch the people busy at their doings. He watched children bundled in fur capes playing at snow-castle and building snowmen; he heard gossips chatting across the street from open doors, and watched the bronzesmith at work with a little lad red-faced and sweating to pump the long bellows-sleeves at the smelting pit; through windows lit with a dim ruddy gold from within as the short day darkened he saw women at their looms, turning a moment to speak or smile to child or husband there in the warmth within the house. Ged saw all these things from outside and apart, alone, and his heart was very heavy in him, though he would not admit to himself that he was sad. **B** As night fell he still lingered in the streets, reluctant to go back to the inn. He heard a man and a girl talking merrily as they came down the street past him toward the town square, and all at once he turned, for he knew the man's voice.

He followed and caught up with the pair, coming up beside them in the late twilight lit only by

4. **athwart:** across.

distant lantern-gleams. The girl stepped back, but the man stared at him and then flung up the staff he carried, holding it between them as a barrier to ward off the threat or act of evil. And that was somewhat more than Ged could bear. His voice shook a little as he said, "I thought you would know me, Vetch."

Even then Vetch hesitated for a moment.

"I do know you," he said, and lowered the staff and took Ged's hand and hugged him round the shoulders—"I do know you! Welcome, my friend, welcome! What a sorry greeting I gave you, as if you were a ghost coming up from behind—and I have waited for you to come, and looked for you—"

"So you are the wizard they boast of in Ismay? I wondered—"

"Oh, yes, I'm their wizard; but listen, let me tell you why I didn't know you, lad. Maybe I've looked too hard for you. Three days ago—were you here three days ago, on Iffish?"

"I came yesterday."

"Three days ago, in the street in Quor, the village up there in the hills, I saw you. That is, I saw a presentment of you, or an imitation of you, or maybe simply a man who looks like you. He was ahead of me, going out of town, and he turned a bend in the road even as I saw him. I called and got no answer, I followed and found no one; nor any tracks; but the ground was frozen. It was a queer thing, and now seeing you come up out of the shadows like that I thought I was tricked again. I am sorry, Ged." He spoke Ged's true name softly, so that the girl who stood waiting a little way behind him would not hear it. A

Ged also spoke low, to use his friend's true name: "No matter, Estarriol. But this is myself, and I am glad to see you. . . ." B

Vetch heard, perhaps, something more than simple gladness in his voice. He had not yet let go of Ged's shoulder, and he said now, in the True Speech, "In trouble and from darkness you come,

A. Making Inferences
? Who was the figure that Vetch saw? (The shadow)

B. Interpreting
? Why do you think Vetch and Ged call each other by their true names here? (As a sign of the trust and friendship they share)

603

Earthsea Vocabulary

harekki: (This is both the name of Yarrow's pet and the name of the inn where Ged stayed.)

Earthsea Names

You may want to point out some of Le Guin's methods for inventing names. She may begin with a word that suggests good ("star" in "Estarriol") or evil ("kill" abbreviated to "kil" in "Osskil"); then she places a letter or two in front of or at the end of the English word. In the case of "Serret," she changed the first letter of the word "ferret." She suggests terror by beginning "Terrenon" with the same first syllable as "terror." Suggest that students use some of Le Guin's methods to invent names for a pleasant place, an evil monster, a good person. Le Guin gives a hint about Yarrow when she writes ". . . she answered him straight"; Yarrow is as direct as an arrow. She is honest and open, unlike Serret, who was secretive and deceptive.

A. Paraphrasing

? Explain in your own words two meanings of Vetch's statement to Ged, "it's time to get in out of the dark!" ("It's night so it's time to go home. It's time to be with friends; you've been alone too long.")

B. Character

Beginning with his first words to her, Ged's attitude toward Yarrow is different from his attitude toward anyone else.

? How would you describe this attitude? (He is almost flirtatious; here he flatters her by suggesting that she is brave. He is showing the side of him that is easygoing, friendly, and teasing.)

C. Irony

? Why is Jasper's fate ironic? (We would have thought that Jasper's skill and power—of which Ged was so jealous—would have led him to do great deeds. As it is, he didn't even win his wizard's staff. It brings home Ged's original foolish pride and jealousy of such a person which caused such evil.)

A Ged, yet your coming is joy to me." Then he went on in his Reach-accented Hardic, "Come on, come home with us, we're going home, it's time to get in out of the dark! This is my sister, the youngest of us, prettier than I am as you see, but much less clever: Yarrow she's called. Yarrow, this is the Sparrowhawk, the best of us and my friend."

"Lord Wizard," the girl greeted him, and decorously she bobbed her head and hid her eyes with her hands to show respect, as women did in the East Reach; her eyes when not hidden were clear, shy, and curious. She was perhaps fourteen years old, dark like her brother, but very slight and slender. On her sleeve there clung, winged and taloned, a dragon no longer than her hand.

B They set off down the dusky street together, and Ged remarked as they went along, "In Gont they say Gontish women are brave, but I never saw a maiden there wear a dragon for a bracelet."

This made Yarrow laugh, and she answered him straight, "This is only a harrekki, have you no harrekki on Gont?" Then she got shy for a moment and hid her eyes.

"No, nor no dragons. Is not the creature a dragon?"

"A little one, that lives in oak trees, and eats wasps and worms and sparrows' eggs—it grows no greater than this. So, Sir, my brother has told me often of the pet you had, the wild thing, the otak—do you have it still?"

"No. No longer."

Vetch turned to him as if with a question, but he held his tongue and asked nothing till much later, when the two of them sat alone over the stone firepit of Vetch's house.

Though he was the chief wizard in the whole island of Iffish, Vetch made his home in Ismay, this small town where he had been born, living with his youngest brother and sister. His father had been a sea trader of some means, and the house was spacious and strong-beamed, with much homely wealth of pottery and fine weaving and vessels of bronze and brass on carven shelves and chests. A great Taonian harp stood in one corner of the main room, and Yarrow's tapestry loom in another, its tall frame inlaid with ivory. There Vetch for all his plain quiet ways was both a powerful wizard and a lord in his own house. There were a couple of old servants, prospering along with the house, and the brother, a cheerful lad, and Yarrow, quick and silent as a little fish, who served the two friends their supper and ate with them, listening to their talk, and afterward slipped off to her own room. All things there were well-founded, peaceful, and assured; and Ged looking about him at the firelit room said, "This is how a man should live," and sighed.

"Well, it's one good way," said Vetch. "There are others. Now, lad tell me if you can what things have come to you and gone from you since we last spoke, two years ago. And tell me what journey you are on, since I see well that you won't stay long with us this time."

Ged told him, and when he was done Vetch sat pondering for a long while. Then he said, "I'll go with you, Ged."

"No."

"I think I will."

"No, Estarriol. This is no task or bane of yours. I began this evil course alone, I will finish it alone, I do not want any other to suffer from it—you least of all, you who tried to keep my hand from the evil act in the very beginning, Estarriol—"

"Pride was ever your mind's master," his friend said smiling, as if they talked of a matter of small concern to either. "Now think: It is your quest, assuredly, but if the quest fail, should there not be another there who might bear warning to the Archipelago? For the shadow would be a fearful power then. And if you defeat the thing, should there not be another there who will tell of it in the Archipelago, that the Deed may be known and sung? I know I can be of no use to you; yet I think I should go with you."

So entreated Ged could not deny his friend, but he said, "I should not have stayed this day here. I knew it, but I stayed."

"Wizards do not meet by chance, lad," said Vetch. "And after all, as you said yourself, I was with you at the beginning of your journey. It is right that I should follow you to its end." He put new wood on the fire, and they sat gazing into the flames a while.

"There is one I have not heard of since that night on Roke Knoll, and I had no heart to ask any at the School of him: Jasper I mean."

"He never won his staff. He left Roke that same summer, and went to the Island of O to be sorcerer in the Lord's household at O-tokne. I know no more of him than that." **C**

Again they were silent, watching the fire and enjoying (since it was a bitter night) the warmth on their legs and faces as they sat on the broad coping of the firepit, their feet almost among the coals.

Ged said at last, speaking low, "There is a thing that I fear, Estarriol. I fear it more if you are with me when I go. There in the Hands in the dead end of the inlet I turned upon the shadow, it was within my hands' reach, and I seized it—I tried to seize it. And there was nothing I could hold. I could

Comment from a Critic
Critic Rollin A. Lasseter states that "Ged's attraction to . . . Yarrow completes Ged's . . . humanization. It awakens his feelings for women, as the cold witch-beauty of Osskil could not, and allows him to trust her with his spontaneous jests and gentleness."

A. Responding
? Do you think the shadow has a name? If so, what is it?

not defeat it. It fled, I followed. But that may happen again, and yet again. I have no power over the thing. There may be neither death nor triumph to end this quest; nothing to sing of; no end. It may be I must spend my life running from sea to sea and land to land on an endless vain venture, a shadow-quest."

"Avert!" said Vetch, turning his left hand in the gesture that turns aside the ill chance spoken of. For all his somber thoughts this made Ged grin a little, for it is rather a child's charm than a wizard's; there was always such village innocence in Vetch. Yet also he was keen, shrewd, direct to the center of a thing. He said now, "That is a grim thought and I trust a false one. I guess rather that what I saw begin, I may see end. Somehow you will learn its nature, its being, what it is, and so hold and bind and vanquish it. Though that is a hard question: what is it. . . . There is a thing that worries me, I do not understand it. It seems the shadow now goes in your shape, or a kind of likeness of you at least, as they saw it on Vemish and as I saw it here in Iffish. How may that be, and why, and why did it never do so in the Archipelago?"

"They say, *Rules change in the Reaches*."

"Aye, a true saying, I can tell you. There are good spells I learned on Roke that have no power here, or go all awry; and also there are spells worked here I never learned on Roke. Every land has its own powers, and the farther one goes from the Inner Lands, the less one can guess about those powers and their governance. But I do not think it is only that which works this change in the shadow."

"Nor do I. I think that, when I ceased to flee from it and turned against it, that turning of my will upon it gave it shape and form, even though the same act prevented it from taking my strength from me. All my acts have their echo in it; it is my creature."

"In Osskil it named you, and so stopped any wizardry you might have used against it. Why did it not do so again, there in the Hands?"

"I do not know. Perhaps it is only from my weakness that it draws the strength to speak. Almost with my own tongue it speaks: for how did it know my name? How did it know my name? I have racked my brains on that over all the seas since I left Gont, and I cannot see the answer. Maybe it cannot speak at all in its own form or formlessness, but only with borrowed tongue, as a gebbeth. I do not know."

"Then you must beware meeting it in gebbeth-form a second time."

"I think," Ged replied, stretching out his hands to the red coals as if he felt an inward chill, "I think I will not. It is bound to me now as I am to it. It cannot get so far free of me as to seize any other man and empty him of will and being, as it did Skiorh. It can possess me. If ever I weaken again, and try to escape from it, to break the bond, it will possess me. And yet, when I held it with all the strength I had, it became mere vapor, and escaped from me. . . . And so it will again, and yet it cannot really escape, for I can always find it. I am bound to the foul cruel thing, and will be forever, unless I learn the word that masters it: its name."

Brooding his friend asked, "Are there names in the dark realms?" **A**

"Gensher the Archmage said there are not. My master Ogion said otherwise."

"*Infinite are the arguments of mages,*" Vetch quoted, with a smile that was somewhat grim.

"She who served the Old Power on Osskil swore that the Stone would tell me that shadow's name, but that I count for little. However there was also a dragon, who offered to trade that name for his own, to be rid of me; and I have thought that, where mages argue, dragons may be wise."

"Wise, but unkind. But what dragon is this? You did not tell me you had been talking with dragons since I saw you last."

They talked together late that night, and though always they came back to the bitter matter of what lay before Ged, yet their pleasure in being together overrode all; for the love between them was strong and steadfast, unshaken by time or chance. In the morning Ged woke beneath his friend's roof, and while he was still drowsy he felt such well-being as if he were in some place wholly defended from evil and harm. All day long a little of this dream-peace clung to his thoughts, and he took it, not as a good omen, but as a gift. It seemed likely to him that leaving this house he would leave the last haven he was to know, and so while the short dream lasted he would be happy in it.

Having affairs he must see to before he left Iffish, Vetch went off to other villages of the island with the lad who served him as prentice-sorcerer. Ged stayed with Yarrow and her brother, called Murre, who was between her and Vetch in age. He seemed not much more than a boy, for there was no gift or scourge of mage-power in him, and he had never been anywhere but Iffish, Tok, and Holp, and his life was easy and untroubled. Ged watched him with wonder and some envy, and exactly so he watched Ged: To each it seemed very queer that the other, so different, yet was his own age, nineteen years. Ged marveled how one who had lived nineteen years could be so carefree.

A. Tone
? How would you describe the tone of this conversation between Ged and Yarrow? (Gently teasing, kind, mutually respectful and admiring)

B. Vocabulary
zealous: hard-working or devoted to one's craft

C. Interpreting
? From Ged's tone, what do you think his thoughts are? (Probably that there is the sad possibility that he may never come back. He wants to protect Yarrow from this thought.)

Admiring Murre's comely, cheerful face he felt himself to be all lank and harsh, never guessing that Murre envied him even the scars that scored his face, and thought them the track of a dragon's claws and the very rune and sign of a hero.

The two young men were thus somewhat shy with each other, but as for Yarrow she soon lost her awe of Ged, being in her own house and mistress of it. He was very gentle with her, and many were the questions she asked of him, for Vetch, she said, would never tell her anything. She kept busy those two days making dry wheatcakes for the voyagers to carry, and wrapping up dried fish and meat and other such provender to stock their boat, until Ged told her to stop, for he did not plan to sail clear to Selidor without a halt.

"Where is Selidor?"

"Very far out in the Western Reach, where dragons are as common as mice."

"Best stay in the East then, our dragons are as small as mice. There's your meat, then; you're sure that's enough? Listen, I don't understand: You and my brother both are mighty wizards, you wave your hand and mutter and the thing is done. Why do you get hungry, then? When it comes suppertime at sea, why not say, *Meatpie!* and the meatpie appears, and you eat it?"

"Well, we could do so. But we don't much wish to eat our words, as they say. *Meatpie!* is only a
A word, after all. . . . We can make it odorous, and savorous, and even filling, but it remains a word. It fools the stomach and gives no strength to the hungry man."

"Wizards, then, are not cooks," said Murre, who was sitting across the kitchen hearth from Ged, carving a box-lid of fine wood; he was a
B woodworker by trade, though not a very zealous one.

"Nor are cooks wizards, alas," said Yarrow on her knees to see if the last batch of cakes baking on the hearth-bricks was getting brown. "But I still don't understand, Sparrowhawk. I have seen my brother, and even his prentice, make light in a dark place only by saying one word: and the light shines, it is bright, not a word but a light you can see your way by!"

"Aye," Ged answered. "Light is a power. A great power, by which we exist, but which exists beyond our needs, in itself. Sunlight and starlight are time, and time is light. In the sunlight, in the days and years, life is. In a dark place life may call upon the light, naming it. But usually when you see a wizard name or call upon some thing, some object to appear, that is not the same, he calls upon no power greater than himself, and what appears is an illusion only. To summon a thing that is not there at all, to call it by speaking its true name, that is a great mastery, not lightly used. Not for mere hunger's sake. Yarrow, your little dragon has stolen a cake."

Yarrow had listened so hard, gazing at Ged as he spoke, that she had not seen the harrekki scuttle down from its warm perch on the kettle-hook over the hearth and seize a wheatcake bigger than itself. She took the small scaly creature on her knee and fed it bits and crumbs, while she pondered what Ged had told her.

"So then you would not summon up a real meatpie lest you disturb what my brother is always talking about—I forget its name—"

"Equilibrium," Ged replied soberly, for she was very serious.

"Yes. But, when you were shipwrecked, you sailed from the place in a boat woven mostly of spells, and it didn't leak water. Was it illusion?"

"Well, partly it was illusion, because I am uneasy seeing the sea through great holes in my boat, so I patched them for the looks of the thing. But the strength of the boat was not illusion, nor summoning, but made with another kind of art, a binding-spell. The wood was bound as one whole, one entire thing, a boat. What is a boat but a thing that doesn't leak water?"

"I've bailed some that do," said Murre.

"Well, mine leaked, too, unless I was constantly seeing to the spell." He bent down from his corner seat and took a cake from the bricks, and juggled it in his hands. "I too have stolen a cake."

"You have burned fingers, then. And when you're starving on the waste water between the far isles you'll think of that cake and say, *Ah! had I not stolen that cake I might eat it now, alas!*— I shall eat my brother's, so he can starve with you—"

"Thus is Equilibrium maintained," Ged remarked, while she took and munched a hot, half-toasted cake; and this made her giggle and choke. But presently looking serious again she said, "I wish I could truly understand what you tell me. I am too stupid."

"Little sister," Ged said, "it is I that have no skill explaining. If we had more time—"

"We will have more time," Yarrow said. "When my brother comes back home, you will come with him, for a while at least, won't you?"

"If I can," he answered gently. C

There was a little pause; and Yarrow asked, watching the harrekki climb back to its perch, "Tell me just this, if it is not a secret: What other great powers are there beside the light?"

"It is no secret. All power is one in source and

Summary: Chapter 10

Ged and Vetch sail to the south, and on beyond Lastland into the Open Sea. For three days they follow the shadow. Finally Ged knows that they have reached their destination, and they begin rowing. The water beneath the boat becomes sluggish; Ged stops rowing, and to Vetch's amazement, walks over the sea. The shadow comes to meet Ged, and they each call the other by their one true name—Ged. At that, Ged and the shadow become one; Ged is free. Vetch and Ged return joyously to Vetch's home.

A end, I think. Years and distances, stars and candles, water and wind and wizardry, the craft in a man's hand and the wisdom in a tree's root: They all arise together. My name, and yours, and the true name of the sun, or a spring of water, or an unborn child, all are syllables of the great word that is very slowly spoken by the shining of the stars. There is no other power. No other name."

Staying his knife on the carved wood, Murre asked, "What of death?"

The girl listened, her shining black head bent down.

B "For a word to be spoken," Ged answered slowly, "there must be silence. Before, and after." Then all at once he got up, saying, "I have no right to speak of these things. The word that was mine to say I said wrong. It is better that I keep still; I will not speak again. Maybe there is no true power but the dark." And he left the fireside and the warm kitchen, taking up his cloak and going out alone into the drizzling cold rain of winter in the streets.

"He is under a curse," Murre said, gazing somewhat fearfully after him.

"I think this voyage he is on leads him to his death," the girl said, "and he fears that, yet he goes on." She lifted her head as if she watched, through the red flame of the fire, the course of a boat that came through the seas of winter alone, and went on out into empty seas. Then her eyes filled with tears a moment, but she said nothing.

Vetch came home the next day, and took his leave of the notables of Ismay, who were most unwilling to let him go off to sea in midwinter on a mortal[5] quest not even his own; but though they might reproach him, there was nothing at all they could do to stop him. Growing weary of old men who nagged him, he said, "I am yours, by parentage and custom and by duty undertaken toward you. I am your wizard. But it is time you recalled that, though I am a servant, I am not your servant. When I am free to come back I will come back: till then farewell."

At daybreak, as gray light welled up in the east from the sea, the two young men set forth in *Lookfar* from the harbor of Ismay, raising a brown, strong-woven sail to the north wind. On the dock Yarrow stood and watched them go, as sailor's wives and sisters stand on all shores of all Earthsea watching their men go out on the sea, and they do not wave or call aloud, but stand still in hooded cloak of gray or brown, there on the shore that dwindles smaller and smaller from the boat while the water grows wide between.

5. **mortal:** causing death.

Chapter 10

The Open Sea

The haven now was sunk from sight and *Lookfar*'s painted eyes, wave-drenched, looked ahead on seas ever wider and more desolate. In two days and nights the companions made the crossing from Iffish to Soders Island, a hundred miles of foul weather and contrary winds. They stayed in port there only briefly, long enough to refill a waterskin, and to buy a tar-smeared sailcloth to protect some of their gear in the undecked boat from seawater and rain. They had not provided this earlier, because ordinarily a wizard looks after such small conveniences by way of spells, the very least and commonest kind of spells, and indeed it takes little more magic to freshen seawater and to save the bother of carrying fresh water. But Ged seemed most unwilling to use his craft, or to let Vetch use his. He said only, "It's better not," and his friend did not ask or argue. For as the wind first filled their sail, both had felt a heavy foreboding, cold as that winter wind. Haven, harbor, peace, safety, all that was behind. They had turned away. They went now a way in which all events were perilous, and no acts were meaningless. On the course on which they were embarked, the saying of the least spell might change chance and move the balance of power and of doom: for they went now toward the very center of that balance, toward the place where light and darkness meet. Those who travel thus say no word carelessly. C

Sailing out again and coasting round the shores of Soders, where white snowfields faded up into foggy hills, Ged took the boat southward again, and now they entered waters where the great traders of the Archipelago never come, the outmost fringes of the Reach.

Vetch asked no question about their course, knowing that Ged did not choose it but went as he must go. As Soders Island grew small and pale behind them, and the waves hissed and smacked under the prow, and the great gray plain of water circled them all round clear to the edge of the sky, Ged asked, "What lands lie ahead this course?"

"Due south of Soders there are no lands at all. Southeast you go a long way and find little: Pelimer, Kornay, Gosk, and Astowell which is also called Lastland. Beyond it, the Open Sea."

"What to the southwest?"

"Rolameny, which is one of our East Reach isles, and some small islets round about it; then nothing till you enter the South Reach: Rood, and Toom, and the Isle of the Ear where men do not go." D

A. Paraphrasing
? Ask students to paraphrase this beautifully written passage. (Answers will differ but should express the idea that there is one source for all the beauty, skill, wisdom, and power in the world.)

B. Symbols
? What do "word" and "silence" symbolize here? ("Word": life; "silence": nothingness)

C. Theme
? Why is Ged unwilling to use magic when he pursues the shadow? (He fears that the use of magic may disturb the balance of light and dark in the world. The shadow, he thinks, is at the center of the balance.)

D. Earthsea Map
You might have students locate Kornay, Gosk, Astowell, Rolameny, Rood, Toom, Isle of the Ear.

A. Making Inferences

What does Ged think will happen to him when he finds the shadow? (He will die.)

B. Symbolism

What three represent evil or lost opportunity for Ged? (Power, shadow, dark)

"We may," Ged said wryly.

"I'd rather not," said Vetch—"that is a disagreeable part of the world, they say, full of bones and portents. Sailors say that there are stars to be seen from the waters by the Isle of the Ear and Far Sorr that cannot be seen anywhere else, and that have never been named."

"Aye, there was a sailor on the ship that brought me first to Roke who spoke of that. And he told tales of the Raftfolk in the far South Reach, who never come to land but once a year, to cut the great logs for their rafts, and the rest of the year, all the days and months, they drift on the currents of ocean, out of sight of any land. I'd like to see those raft-villages."

"I would not," said Vetch grinning. "Give me land, and landfolk; the sea in its bed and I in mine. . . ."

A "I wish I could have seen all the cities of the Archipelago," Ged said as he held the sail-rope, watching the wide gray wastes before them. "Havnor at the world's heart, and Éa where the myths were born, and the Shelieth of the Fountains on Way; all the cities and the great lands. And the small lands, the strange lands of the Outer Reaches, them too. To sail right down the Dragons' Run, away in the west. Or to sail north into the ice floes, clear to Hogen Land. Some say that is a land greater than all the Archipelago, and others say it is mere reefs and rocks with ice between. No one knows. I should like to see the whales in the northern seas. . . . But I cannot. I must go where I am bound to go, and turn my back on the bright shores. I was in too much haste, B and now have no time left. I traded all the sunlight and the cities and the distant lands for a handful of power, for a shadow, for the dark." So, as the mageborn will, Ged made his fear and regret into song, a brief lament, half-sung, that was not for himself alone; and his friend replying spoke the hero's words from the *Deed of Erreth-Akbe,* "O may I see the earth's bright heart once more, the white towers of Havnor. . . ."

So they sailed their narrow course over the wide forsaken[1] waters. The most they saw that day was a school of silver pannies swimming south, but

1. **forsaken:** abandoned; desolate.

A never a dolphin leapt nor did the flight of gull or murre or tern break the gray air. As the east darkened and the west grew red, Vetch brought out food and divided it between them and said, "Here's the last of the ale. I drink to the one who thought to put the keg aboard for thirsty men in cold weather: my sister Yarrow."

At that Ged left off his bleak thoughts and his gazing ahead over the sea, and he saluted Yarrow more earnestly, perhaps, than Vetch. The thought of her brought to his mind the sense of her wise and childish sweetness. She was not like any person he had known. (What young girl had he ever known at all? But he never thought of that.) "She is like a little fish, a minnow, that swims in a clear creek," he said, "—defenseless, yet you cannot catch her."

At this Vetch looked straight at him, smiling. "You are a mage born," he said. "Her true name

B is Kest." In the Old Speech, *kest* is minnow, as Ged well knew, and this pleased him to the heart. But after a while he said in a low voice. "You should not have told me her name, maybe."

But Vetch, who had not done so lightly, said, "Her name is safe with you as mine is. And, besides, you knew it without my telling you. . . ."

Red sank to ashes in the west, and ash-gray sank to black. All the sea and sky were wholly dark. Ged stretched out in the bottom of the boat to sleep, wrapped in his cloak of wool and fur. Vetch, holding the sail-rope, sang softly from the *Deed of Enlad,* where the song tells how the mage Morred the White left Havnor in his oarless longship, and coming to the island Soléa saw Elfarran in the orchards in the spring. Ged slept before the song came to the sorry end of their love, Morred's death, the ruin of Enlad, the sea waves, vast and bitter, whelming the orchards of Soléa. Towards midnight he woke, and watched again while Vetch slept. The little boat ran sharp over choppy seas, fleeing the strong wind that leaned on her sail, running blind through the night. But the overcast had broken, and before dawn the thin moon shining between brown-edged clouds shed a weak light on the sea.

"The moon wanes to her dark," Vetch murmured, awake in the dawn, when for a while the cold wind dropped. Ged looked up at the white half-ring above the paling eastern waters, but said nothing. The dark of the moon that follows first after Sunreturn is called the Fallows, and is the contrary pole of the days of the Moon and the

C Long Dance in summer. It is an unlucky time for travelers and for the sick; children are not given their true name during the Fallows, and no Deeds are sung, nor swords nor edge-tools sharpened, nor oaths sworn. It is the dark axis of the year, when things done are ill done.

Three days out from Soders they came, following seabirds and shore-wrack, to Pelimer, a small isle humped high above the high gray seas. Its people spoke Hardic, but in their own fashion, strange even to Vetch's ears. The young men came ashore there for fresh water and a respite from the sea, and at first were well received, with wonder and commotion. There was a sorcerer in the main town of the island, but he was mad. He would talk only of the great serpent that was eating at the foundations of Pelimer so that soon the island must go adrift like a boat cut from her moorings, and slide out over the edge of the world. At first he greeted the young wizards courteously, but as he talked about the serpent he began to look askance at Ged: and then he fell to railing at them there in the street, calling them spies and servants of the Sea Snake. The Pelimerians looked dourly at them after that, since though mad he was their sorcerer. So Ged and Vetch made no long stay, but set forth again before nightfall, going always south and east.

In these days and nights of sailing Ged never spoke of the shadow, nor directly of his quest; and the nearest Vetch came to asking any question was (as they followed the same course farther and farther out and away from the known lands of Earthsea)—"Are you sure?"—To this Ged answered only, "Is the iron sure where the magnet lies?" Vetch nodded and they went on, no more being said by either. But from time to time they talked of the crafts and devices that mages of old days had used to find out the hidden name of baneful powers and beings: how Nereger of Paln had learned the Black Mage's name from overhearing the conversation of dragons, and how Morred had seen his enemy's name written by falling raindrops in the dust of the battlefield of the Plains of Enlad. They spoke of finding-spells, and invocations, and those Answerable Questions which only the Master Patterner of Roke can ask. But often Ged would end by murmuring words which Ogion had said to him on the shoulder of Gont Mountain in an autumn long ago: "To hear, one must be silent. . . ." And he would fall silent, and ponder, hour by hour, always watching the sea ahead of the boat's way. Sometimes it seemed to Vetch that his friend saw, across the waves and miles and gray days yet to come, the thing they followed and the dark end of their voyage.

They passed between Kornay and Gosk in foul weather, seeing neither isle in the fog and rain, and knowing they had passed them only on the next day when they saw ahead of them an isle of

Earthsea Vocabulary
kest
Fallows

A. Vocabulary
murre: a sea bird. (This was also the name of Vetch's brother.)

B. Names
Note that the name *Yarrow* evokes the meaning of the true-name *Kest*—minnow.

C. Explanation
Le Guin compares the year to a circle with Long Dance (summer solstice) at one end, and Sunreturn (winter solstice) at the other end.

? What mood is set by the fact that they are traveling during the Fallows? (A grim one)

A. Foreshadowing
Remind students that "death is the dry place" (page 593). Ged seems to be implying that he will meet the shadow in death.

B. Vocabulary
wattle: made with sticks and branches

C. Vocabulary
coracles: boats made of material stretched over a wicker frame

D. Interpreting
? Usually, when Ged stops at an island where he is given friendly treatment, he is tempted to linger. Why do you think that here, amid the warmth and good company—and little hope of land ahead of him—he is so impatient to be off? (He only has one goal in mind—to catch the shadow. Perhaps he feels he is close to reaching his goal, and is impatient to have his fate decided.)

pinnacled cliffs above which sea-gulls wheeled in huge flocks whose mewing clamor could be heard from far over the sea. Vetch said, "That will be Astowell, from the look of it. Lastland. East and south of it the charts are empty."

"Yet they who live there may know of farther lands," Ged answered.

"Why do you say so?" Vetch asked, for Ged had spoken uneasily; and his answer to this again was halting and strange. "Not there," he said, gazing at Astowell ahead, and past it, or through it—"Not there. Not on the sea. Not on the sea but on dry land: What land? Before the springs of the open sea, beyond the sources, behind the gates of daylight—" A

Then he fell silent, and when he spoke again, it was in an ordinary voice, as if he had been freed from a spell or a vision, and had no clear memory of it.

The port of Astowell, a creek-mouth between rocky heights, was on the northern shore of the isle, and all the huts of the town faced north and west; it was as if the island turned its face, though from so far away, always toward Earthsea, toward mankind.

Excitement and dismay attended the arrival of strangers, in a season when no boat had ever braved the seas round Astowell. The women all stayed in the wattle huts, peering out the door, B hiding their children behind their skirts, drawing back fearfully into the darkness of the huts as the strangers came up from the beach. The men, lean fellows ill-clothed against the cold, gathered in a solemn circle about Vetch and Ged, and each one held a stone hand-ax or a knife of shell. But once their fear was past they made the strangers very welcome, and there was no end to their questions. Seldom did any ship come to them even from Soders or Rolameny, they having nothing to trade for bronze or fine wares; they had not even any wood. Their boats were coracles woven of reed, C and it was a brave sailor who would go as far as Gosk or Kornay in such a craft. They dwelt all alone here at the edge of all the maps. They had no witch or sorcerer, and seemed not to recognize the young wizards' staffs for what they were, admiring them only for the precious stuff they were made of, wood. Their chief or Isle-Man was very old, and he alone of his people had ever before seen a man born in the Archipelago. Ged, therefore, was a marvel to them; the men brought their little sons to look at the Archipelagan, so they might remember him when they were old. They had never heard of Gont, only of Havnor and Éa, and took him for a Lord of Havnor. He did his best to answer their questions about the white city he had never seen. But he was restless as the evening wore on, and at last he asked the men of the village, as they sat crowded round the firepit in the lodgehouse in the reeking warmth of the goat-dung and broom-faggots that were all their fuel, "What lies eastward of your land?"

They were silent, some grinning, others grim. The old Isle-Man answered, "The sea."

"There is no land beyond?"

"This is Lastland. There is no land beyond. There is nothing but water till world's edge."

"These are wise men, father," said a younger man, "seafarers, voyagers. Maybe they know of a land we do not know of."

"There is no land east of this land," said the old man, and he looked long at Ged, and spoke no more to him.

The companions slept that night in the smoky warmth of the lodge. Before daylight Ged roused his friend, whispering, "Estarriol, wake. We cannot stay, we must go."

"Why so soon?" Vetch asked, full of sleep. D

"Not soon—late. I have followed too slow. It has found the way to escape me, and so doom me. It must not escape me, for I must follow it however far it goes. If I lose it I am lost."

"Where do we follow it?"

"Eastward. Come. I filled the waterskins."

So they left the lodge before any in the village was awake, except a baby that cried a little in the darkness of some hut, and fell still again. By the vague starlight they found the way down to the creek mouth, and untied *Lookfar* from the rock cairn where she had been made fast, and pushed her out into the black water. So they set out eastward from Astowell into the Open Sea, on the first day of the Fallows, before sunrise.

That day they had clear skies. The world's wind was cold and gusty from the northeast, but Ged had raised the magewind: the first act of magery he had done since he left the Isle of the Hands. They sailed very fast due eastward. The boat shuddered with the great, smoking, sunlit waves that hit her as she ran, but she went gallantly as her builder had promised, answering the magewind as true as any spell-enwoven ship of Roke.

Ged spoke not at all that morning, except to renew the power of the wind-spell or to keep a charmed strength in the sail, and Vetch finished his sleep, though uneasily, in the stern of the boat. At noon they ate. Ged doled their food out sparingly, and the portent of this was plain, but both of them chewed their bit of salt fish and wheaten cake, and neither said anything.

All afternoon they cleaved eastward never turning nor slackening pace. Once Ged broke his si-

Comment from the Author
In her essay "The Child and the Shadow," Le Guin tells how the idea of writing about the shadow came to her. A Hans Christian Anderson fairy tale called "The Shadow" fascinated her when she read it as a child. In Anderson's tale, a kind youth longs to visit a lovely maiden. When he notices that his shadow reaches her balcony, he jokingly suggests that his shadow go to her; he is appalled when his shadow leaves him and enters the maiden's house. Years later, the man meets his shadow again and is ruled by it. When they meet a princess, the shadow convinces her that he is the real person, and that the man is his shadow! The shadow marries the princess and has the man killed. This is a cruel story, Le Guin admits, but it is great fantasy, because it speaks to the unconscious. The man represents the civilized, decent artist while the shadow symbolizes the "dark side of his soul," the greeds and passions that he suppressed to become an adult. According to Le Guin, Anderson is saying that the shadow is part of the man and "cannot be denied. "If the artist tries to ignore evil, he will never attain greatness."
After students have read the novel, you might discuss with them the similarities between Anderson's fairy tale and the struggle between Ged and his shadow.

A lence, saying, "Do you hold with those who think the world is all landless sea beyond the Outer Reaches, or with those who imagine other Archipelagoes or vast undiscovered lands on the other face of the world?"

"At this time," said Vetch, "I hold with those who think the world has but one face, and he who sails too far will fall off the edge of it."

Ged did not smile; there was no mirth left in him. "Who knows what a man might meet, out there? Not we, who keep always to our coasts and shores."

"Some have sought to know, and have not returned. And no ship has ever come to us from lands we do not know."

Ged made no reply.

All that day, all that night they went driven by the powerful wind of magery over the great swells of ocean, eastward. Ged kept watch from dusk till dawn, for in darkness the force that drew or drove him grew stronger yet. Always he watched ahead, though his eyes in the moonless night could see no more than the painted eyes aside the boat's blind prow. By daybreak his dark face was gray with weariness, and he was so cramped with cold that he could hardly stretch out to rest. He said whispering, "Hold the magewind from the west, Estarriol," and then he slept.

There was no sunrise, and presently rain came beating across the bow from the northeast. It was no storm, only the long, cold winds and rains of winter. Soon all things in the open boat were wet through, despite the sailcloth cover they had bought; and Vetch felt as if he too were soaked clear to the bone; and Ged shivered in his sleep. In pity for his friend, and perhaps for himself, Vetch tried to turn aside for a little that rude ceaseless wind that bore the rain. But though, following Ged's will, he could keep the magewind strong and steady, his weatherworking had small power here so far from land, and the wind of the Open Sea did not listen to his voice.

And at this a certain fear came into Vetch, as he began to wonder how much wizardly power would be left to him and Ged if they went on and on away from the lands where men were meant to live.

Ged watched again that night, and all night held the boat eastward. When day came the world's wind slackened somewhat, and the sun shone fitfully; but the great swells ran so high that *Lookfar* must tilt and climb up them as if they were hills, and hang at the hillcrest and plunge suddenly, and climb up the next again, and the next, and the next, unending.

In the evening of that day Vetch spoke out of long silence. "My friend," he said, "you spoke once as if sure we would come to land at last. I would not question your vision but for this, that it might be a trick, a deception made by that which you follow, to lure you on farther than a man can go over ocean. For our power may change and weaken on strange seas. And a shadow does not tire, or starve, or drown."

They sat side by side on the thwart, yet Ged looked at him now as if from a distance, across a wide abyss. His eyes were troubled, and he was slow to answer.

At last he said, "Estarriol, we are coming near."

Hearing his words, his friend knew them to be true. He was afraid, then. But he put his hand on Ged's shoulder and said only, "Well, then, good; that is good." B

Again that night Ged watched, for he could not sleep in the dark. Nor would he sleep when the third day came. Still they ran with that ceaseless, light, terrible swiftness over the sea, and Vetch wondered at Ged's power that could hold so strong a magewind hour after hour, here on the Ocean Sea where Vetch felt his own power all weakened and astray. And they went on, until it seemed to Vetch that what Ged had spoken would come true, and they were going beyond the sources of the sea and eastward behind the gates of daylight. Ged stayed forward in the boat, looking ahead as always. But he was not watching the ocean now, or not the ocean that Vetch saw, a waste of heaving water to the rim of the sky. In Ged's eyes there was a dark vision that overlapped and veiled the gray sea and the gray sky, and the darkness grew, and the veil thickened. None of this was visible to Vetch, except when he looked at his friend's face; then he too saw the darkness for a moment. They went on, and on. And it was as if, though one wind drove them in one boat, Vetch went east over the world's sea, while Ged went alone into a realm where there was no east or west, no rising or setting of the sun, or of the stars. C

Ged stood up suddenly in the prow, and spoke aloud. The magewind dropped. *Lookfar* lost headway, and rose and fell on the vast surges like a chip of wood. Though the world's wind blew strong as ever straight from the north now, the brown sail hung slack, unstirred. And so the boat hung on the waves, swung by their great slow swinging, but going no direction.

Ged said, "Take down the sail," and Vetch did so quickly, while Ged unlashed the oars and set them in the locks and bent his back to rowing.

Vetch, seeing only the waves heaving up and down clear to the end of sight, could not under-

A. Making Inferences
? What evidence can you find here that Vetch and Ged know that Earthsea must be a planet that can be circumnavigated? (Vetch speaks ironically here; he knows that Earthsea is round, but suggests the opposite to make Ged smile; Ged speaks of lands "on the other face of the world.")

B. Character
? Explain why Vetch tells Ged, "Well, then, good; that is good," even though he is afraid and thinks they should turn back. (He knows that Ged will find peace only when he meets the shadow; he values Ged's peace more than his own life.)

C. Symbolism
? What realm is this? (The land of the dead)

Comment from Critics: The Shadow
Rollin A. Lasseter suggests that the light of Ged's staff stands for his self-knowledge. Ged sees "all the spoiled or self-demanding relationships that littered his past, and now in the clear light of self-vision he sees it in its only true shape, no longer terrible and paralyzing but almost pathetic and pitiable. He reaches out and takes hold of his shadow . . . " as it reaches out to him.

Robert Scholes writes, "To become whole, [Ged] had to face it, name it with his own name, and accept it as part of himself. Thus by restoring the balance in himself, he helped to restore the balance of the world."

A. Suspense
Ask students to notice how Le Guin builds suspense up to the climax of the novel. The conflict between protagonist Ged and his antagonist shadow becomes more and more exciting, rising to its highest peak of suspense on this page.

B. Interpreting
? What land do you think this is? What details suggest it? (Probably the land of the dead: "nothing moved in the dark sky or on that dry unreal ground"; "darkness . . . as far as the eye could see." Also, we remember that "death is a dry place.")

C. Interpreting
? What does each form represent about Ged's past? (His father–hate, submission; Jasper—pride, jealousy; the bloated face of Pechvarry—probably his guilt in not being able to save the child Ioeth's life; Skiorh—fear)

stand why they went now by oars; but he waited, and presently he was aware that the world's wind was growing faint and the swells diminishing. The climb and plunge of the boat grew less and less, till at last she seemed to go forward under Ged's strong oarstrokes over water that lay almost still, as in a landlocked bay. And though Vetch could not see what Ged saw, when between his strokes he looked ever and again over his shoulder at what lay before the boat's way—though Vetch could not see the dark slopes beneath unmoving stars, yet he began to see with his wizard's eye a darkness that welled up in the hollows of the waves all around the boat, and he saw the billows grow low and sluggish as they were choked with sand.

If this were an enchantment of illusion, it was powerful beyond belief; to make the Open Sea seem land. Trying to collect his wits and courage, Vetch spoke the Revelation-spell, watching between each slow-syllabled word for change or tremor of illusion in this strange drying and shallowing of the abyss[2] of ocean. But there was none. Perhaps the spell, though it should affect only his own vision and not the magic at work about them, had no power here. Or perhaps there was no illusion, and they had come to world's end.

Unheeding, Ged rowed always slower, looking over his shoulder, choosing a way among channels or shoals and shallows that he alone could see. The boat shuddered as her keel dragged. Under that keel lay the vast deeps of the sea, yet they were aground. Ged drew the oars up rattling in their locks, and that noise was terrible, for there was no other sound. All sounds of water, wind, wood, sail, were gone, lost in a huge profound silence that might have been unbroken forever. The boat lay motionless. No breath of wind moved. The sea had turned to sand, shadowy, unstirred. Nothing moved in the dark sky or on that dry unreal ground that went on and on into gathering darkness all around the boat as far as eye could see.

Ged stood up, and took his staff, and lightly stepped over the side of the boat. Vetch thought to see him fall and sink down in the sea, the sea that surely was there behind this dry, dim veil that hid away water, sky, and light. But there was no sea anymore. Ged walked away from the boat. The dark sand showed his footprints where he went, and whispered a little under his step.

His staff began to shine, not with the werelight but with a clear white glow, that soon grew so bright that it reddened his fingers where they held the radiant wood.

He strode forward, away from the boat, but in no direction. There were no directions here, no north or south or east or west, only toward and away.

To Vetch, watching, the light he bore seemed like a great slow star that moved through the darkness. And the darkness about it thickened, blackened, drew together. This also Ged saw, watching always ahead through the light. And after a while he saw at the faint outermost edge of the light a shadow that came toward him over the sand.

At first it was shapeless, but as it drew nearer it took on the look of a man. An old man it seemed, gray and grim, coming toward Ged; but even as Ged saw his father the smith in that figure, he saw that it was not an old man but a young one. It was Jasper: Jasper's insolent handsome young face, and silver-clasped gray cloak, and stiff stride. Hateful was the look he fixed on Ged across the dark intervening air. Ged did not stop, but slowed his pace, and as he went forward he raised his staff up a little higher. It brightened, and in its light the look of Jasper fell from the figure that approached, and it became Pechvarry. But Pechvarry's face was all bloated and pallid like the face of a drowned man, and he reached out his hand strangely as if beckoning. Still Ged did not stop, but went forward, though there were only a few yards left between them now. Then the thing that faced him changed utterly, spreading out to either side as if it opened enormous thing wings, and it writhed, and swelled, and shrank again. Ged saw in it for an instant Skiorh's white face, and then a pair of clouded, staring eyes, and then suddenly a fearful face he did not know, man or monster, with writhing lips and eyes that were like pits going back into black emptiness.

At that Ged lifted up the staff high, and the radiance of it brightened intolerably, burning with so white and great a light that it compelled and harrowed even that ancient darkness. In that light all form of man sloughed off the thing that came toward Ged. It drew together and shrank and blackened, crawling on four short taloned legs upon the sand. But still it came forward, lifting up to him a blind unformed snout without lips or ears or eyes. As they came right together it became utterly black in the white mage-radiance that burned about it, and it heaved itself upright. In silence, man and shadow met face to face, and stopped.

Aloud and clearly, breaking that old silence, Ged spoke the shadow's name and in the same moment the shadow spoke without lips or tongue, saying the same word: "Ged." And the two voices were one voice.

2. **abyss** (ə·bis′): bottomless depths.

Comment from a Critic: Taoism and Opposites

According to Charlotte Spivack, an important principle of philosophical Taoism is the relativity and interpendence of opposites, rather than the struggle between them. The lines from *The Creation of Éa* suggest a "reconciliation of opposites" that is at the heart of *A Wizard of Earthsea:* Silence balanced against the Word; dark against light; death against life. "The name *Earthsea* itself," Spivack points out, "suggests a reconciliation of opposites, a balance of conscious (Earth) and unconscious (Sea)."

Reading Check Test: Chapters 9 and 10

1. Who is the wizard of Iffish? *(Vetch)*

2. When Vetch hears Ged's plans, what does he decide to do? *(To accompany Ged on his quest)*

3. Who prepared the food for Vetch and Ged's journey? *(Vetch's sister, Yarrow)*

4. Where do the two friends sail to find the shadow? *(Beyond Lastland, into the Open Sea)*

5. What is the shadow's name? *(Ged)*

Closure

Divide the class into four or five groups. Ask each group to write one sentence expressing what it considers to be the central theme of *A Wizard of Earthsea.* At the end of ten minutes, ask each group to have one person read the statement of theme aloud.

A. Theme

? What happens to the shadow? (It merges with Ged.) What idea might Le Guin be suggesting about Ged and his shadow? (They are different parts of the same person.)

B. Interpreting

? What does the land turning back into water represent? (The emergence from death's realm to the land of the living)

C. Symbol

? What might the shadow symbolize? (The feelings and ideas people try to deny in themselves.)

D. Meaning of the Epigraph

? What meaning does the epigraph of the novel have for you now? (The hawk represents Ged; the "empty sky" stands for life, with its infinite possibilities. The lines from *The Creation of Éa* are a poetic expression of the "truth" that Vetch has just realized.)

A Ged reached out his hands, dropping his staff, and took hold of his shadow, of the black self that reached out to him. Light and darkness met, and joined, and were one.

But to Vetch, watching in terror through the dark twilight from far off over the sand, it seemed that Ged was overcome, for he saw the clear radiance fail and grow dim. Rage and despair filled him, and he sprang out on the sand to help his friend or die with him, and ran toward the small fading glimmer of light in the empty dusk of the dry land. B But as he ran the sand sank under his feet, and he struggled in it as in quicksand, as through a heavy flow of water: until with a roar of noise and a glory of daylight, and the bitter cold of winter, and the bitter taste of salt, the world was restored to him and he floundered in the sudden, true, and living sea.

Nearby the boat rocked on the gray waves, empty. Vetch could see nothing else on the water; the battering wave tops filled his eyes and blinded him. No strong swimmer, he struggled as best he could to the boat, and pulled himself up into her. Coughing and trying to wipe away the water that streamed from his hair, he looked about desperately, not knowing now which way to look. And at last he made out something dark among the waves, a long way off across what had been sand and now was wild water. Then he leapt to the oars and rowed mightily to his friend, and catching Ged's arms helped and hauled him up over the side.

Ged was dazed and his eyes stared as if they saw nothing, but there was no hurt to be seen on him. His staff, black yew wood, all radiance quenched, was grasped in his right hand, and he would not let go of it. He said no word. Spent and soaked and shaking he lay huddled up against the mast, never looking at Vetch who raised the sail and turned the boat to catch the northeast wind. He saw nothing of the world until, straight ahead of their course, in the sky that darkened where the sun had set, between long clouds in a bay of clear blue light, the new moon shone: a ring of ivory, a rim of horn, reflected sunlight shining across the ocean of the dark.

Ged lifted his face and gazed at that remote bright crescent in the west.

He gazed for a long time, and then he stood up erect, holding his staff in his two hands as a warrior holds his long sword. He looked about at the sky, the sea, the brown swelling sail above him, his friend's face.

"Estarriol," he said, "look, it is done. It is over." He laughed. "The wound is healed," he said, "I am whole, I am free." Then he bent over and hid his face in his arms, weeping like a boy.

Until that moment Vetch had watched him with an anxious dread, for he was not sure what had happened there in the dark land. He did not know if this was Ged in the boat with him, and his hand had been for hours ready to the anchor, to stave in the boat's planking and sink her there in midsea, rather than carry back to the harbors of Earthsea the evil thing that he feared might have taken Ged's look and form. Now when he saw his friend and heard him speak, his doubt vanished. C And he began to see the truth, that Ged had neither lost nor won but, naming the shadow of his death with his own name, had made himself whole: a man: who, knowing his whole true self, cannot be used or possessed by any power other than himself, and whose life therefore is lived for life's sake and never in the service of ruin, or pain, or hatred, or the dark. D In the *Creation of Éa,* which is the oldest song, it is said, "Only in silence the word, only in dark the light, only in dying life: bright the hawk's flight on the empty sky." That song Vetch sang aloud now as he held the boat westward, going before the cold wind of the winter night that blew at their backs from the vastness of the Open Sea.

Eight days they sailed and eight again, before they came in sight of land. Many times they had to refill their waterskin with spell-sweetened water of the sea; and they fished, but even when they called out fisherman's charms they caught very little, for the fish of the Open Sea do not know their own names and pay no heed to magic. When they had nothing left to eat but a few scraps of smoked meat Ged remembered what Yarrow had said when he stole the cake from the hearth, that he would regret his theft when he came to hunger on the sea; but hungry as he was the remembrance pleased him. For she had also said that he, with her brother, would come home again.

The magewind had borne them for only three days eastward, yet sixteen days they sailed westward to return. No men have ever returned from so far out on the Open Sea as did the young wizards Estarriol and Ged in the Fallows of winter in their open fishing boat. They met no great storms, and steered steadily enough by the compass and by the star Tolbegren, taking a course somewhat northward of their outbound way. Thus they did not come back to Astowell, but passing by Far Toly and Sneg without sighting them, first raised land off the southernmost cape of Koppish. Over the waves they saw cliffs of stone rise like a great fortress. Seabirds cried wheeling over the break-

ANALYZING CHAPTERS 9 AND 10
Identifying Facts
1. The sorcerer is protecting the people of Vemish, who are frightened because they saw a man who resembled Ged crossing the island, although no one saw him arrive on or leave the island and he seemed to cast no shadow.
2. Vetch points out that if Ged fails in his quest there should be someone who will bring warning to the Archipelago. If he succeeds, there should be someone who can sing a song about it.
3. A magic meatpie is a work whose shape, flavor, and taste are illusion.

Ged says he believes the source of all power is a single, great word—of which the names of all other things are syllables—spoken by the shining stars.
4. They avoid using spells because they have embarked on a quest in which all events are perilous and none are meaningless. The saying of any spell might change chance and move the power of doom, or upset the balance.
5. Vetch thinks that the shadow may be leading them farther than man can sail on the ocean, to strange seas where they will have no power.
(Answers continue on page 616.)

ers, and smoke of the hearthfires of small villages drifted blue on the wind.

From there the voyage to Iffish was not long. They came in to Ismay harbor on a still, dark evening before snow. They tied up the boat *Lookfar* that had borne them to the coasts of death's kingdom and back, and went up through the narrow streets to the wizard's house. Their hearts were very light as they entered into the firelight and warmth under that roof; and Yarrow ran to meet them, crying with joy.

. . .

If Estarriol of Iffish kept his promise and made a song of that first great deed of Ged's, it has been lost. There is a tale told in the East Reach of a boat that ran aground, days out from any shore, over the abyss of ocean. In Iffish they say it was Estarriol who sailed that boat, but in Tok they say it was two fishermen blown by a storm far out on the Open Sea, and in Holp the tale is of a Holpish fisherman, and tells that he could not move his boat from the unseen sands it grounded on, and so wanders there yet. So of the song of the Shadow there remain only a few scraps of legend, carried like driftwood from isle to isle over the long years. But in the *Deed of Ged* nothing is told of that voyage nor of Ged's meeting with the shadow, before ever he sailed the Dragon's Run unscathed, or brought back the Ring of Erreth-Akbe from the Tombs of Atuan to Havnor, or came at last to Roke once more, as Archmage of all the islands of the world. **A**

A. Making Inferences
? Why do you think the *Deed of Ged* might not include anything about the shadow? (The meeting with the shadow involves the solution of a personal problem—it was important to his coming-of-age. The other deeds are heroic ones and performed for the benefit of others.)

Responding to the Novel

Analyzing Chapters 9 and 10

Identifying Facts

1. Why is the sorcerer of Vemish reluctant to welcome Ged?
2. Though Ged is reluctant to allow it, Vetch insists on going along on the journey. What two reasons does Vetch give for wanting to accompany Ged?
3. In a talk about magic and meatpies, Ged explains many things to Vetch's sister, Yarrow. Explain why a magic meatpie provides no nourishment, according to Ged. What does Ged tell Yarrow is the source of all power?
4. Explain why Ged and Vetch avoid using spells on their journey from Iffish.
5. As Ged and Vetch sail past the Lastland, what trick does Vetch think the shadow may be playing on them? What seems to happen to the sea as they approach the shadow?
6. When Vetch hears Ged speak after the battle with the shadow, he realizes an important truth. Explain what this truth is.

Interpreting Meanings

7. We get a sense of **irony** when something happens that is the opposite of what we were expecting. The innkeeper of Iffish says: "Two staffs in one town must come to blows." Explain why this statement is ironic when we find out who the "staff" (wizard) of Iffish is.
8. Compare the **characters** of Yarrow and Serret. Which young woman is more intelligent? Kinder? Stronger? More understanding? Tell which you like better, and explain why.
9. At the end, when the sea turns into land, does the **setting** foreshadow victory or failure for Ged? What did you think was going to happen?
10. Throughout the novel Ged develops his powers, which call into being an enemy who pursues him and whom Ged in turn pursues. Does the novel's ending mark Ged's victory over that enemy, or do Ged and the shadow finish as equals? Explain your opinion.

SRW p. 79

(*Answers begin on page 615.*)

The sea becomes flat and calm, appearing to turn into sand.

6. Vetch realizes that Ged neither lost nor won, but that in naming the shadow—Ged—he made himself a whole person, who in knowing his good and his bad side cannot be used or possessed by any other power.

Interpreting Meanings

7. The irony is that the wizard of Iffish is Vetch, Ged's best friend from the School of Roke.

8. Both women are intelligent, though Serret knows sorcery and Yarrow does not. However, Yarrow is kind and good, while Serret is evil.

9. The setting, with its eerie land, darkness, and unmoving stars, seems to foreshadow failure or death for Ged. However, most students will see that despite the setting Ged will be victorious, as they already know that Ged will go on to perform greater deeds.

10. Since the shadow turns out to be a part of Ged, there is no real victory, and they are not really equals. They are both parts of one whole, although the good part controls the evil part.

Analyzing the Novel as a Whole

1. Did you suspect what the shadow's name was before Ged spoke it? How do you suppose Ged figured out the shadow's name? (Think about which events, advice, and other details throughout the novel might have **foreshadowed,** or hinted at, the shadow's name.) SRW p. 43
2. Do you think this novel's most important **conflict,** or struggle, is the **external conflict** between Ged and the shadow, or Ged's **internal conflict** over how to cope with the shadow? Explain the reasons for your opinion. (Before answering, think about whether you are more interested in Ged's actions or in his thoughts and feelings.)
3. The novel's female characters include Ged's aunt, Serret, the old woman on the sandbar, and Yarrow. Think about the number of male and female characters, and about their strengths, weaknesses, and other personal qualities. What position do women have in Earthsea and in the novel, compared to men? Do you think the author presents a fair picture of women?
4. One way of looking at *A Wizard of Earthsea* is to see it as the story of a young man's education. In your opinion, what is the most important thing Ged learns? Discuss the following possible answers and any others you think important: to cast spells, to change his form, to be silent, to respect Equilibrium, to be a whole person.
5. Ged, after much contemplation, realizes that the shadow's name is his own. If the shadow is a part of him that he unloosed, what do you think it stands for, or **symbolizes**? In other words, what part of Ged—a part that he must come to accept in order to conquer—could the shadow represent? (Think of the circumstances in which Ged first unloosed the shadow.)
6. A novel's main idea about life or human nature is its **theme.** Although this novel is set in a land of magic, castles, and dragons, it contains messages that apply to life and human nature in the real world. You have now read the entire novel. Think about what the novel and its resolution seem to be saying about these subjects:

   a. Good and evil
   b. Growing up
   c. Power

   In a sentence, what would you say the novel's principle theme is? Support your answer by citing events and characters that suggest this theme.

   SRW p. 87
7. Which character in the novel, if any, did you **identify** with? That is, which one seemed most like yourself? Explain your answer.
8. Pick a hero of an adventure story from a novel, a movie, TV, or a selection from this book. Compare the **character** of Ged to that of the hero you picked. Which one is wiser? Stronger? Kinder? Who learns more lessons? Is one a better human being than the other?

Writing About the Novel

A Creative Response

1. **Writing a Sequel.** *A Wizard of Earthsea* ends with some hints about the rest of Ged's life. In one or two paragraphs, write a summary of the sequel, or the next installment, to this novel. You can make up anything you like, including events not mentioned in the last paragraph of the book. You can even change that last paragraph if you think your version of Ged's life is more interesting than the one Le Guin suggests.
2. **Describing an Imaginary World.** In at least two or three paragraphs, invent an imaginary world. You will have to describe these elements of the world: climate, geographical features, animals, and human inhabitants. You might also want to tell where people live, how they get around, and what kinds of food they like. You might also want to describe the enemies of your imaginary land. Finally, give your world a name.
3. **Making Up Names.** Make up names that could be used for the following characters in a fantasy. Try to find sounds that seem to suggest the characters' natures (sweet, sharp, and so on):

   a. A hero and heroine
   b. An enemy
   c. An evil animal and a good animal
   d. A wise old man or woman
   e. A mysterious stranger

A Critical Response

4. **Evaluating an Ending.** At the novel's end, Ged joins together with the shadow instead of destroying it. How satisfying do you find this ending? Would you have preferred a clearer victory for one side? Do you think the ending the author uses is exactly right? Do you find it completely wrong? Or are there some things you like about it and other things you don't like? Write two

ANALYZING THE NOVEL AS A WHOLE

1. Some students may have guessed that the shadow was really a part of Ged and therefore carried his name. There are foreshadowing clues early in the novel, for instance when Ged sails to Roke on the ship *Shadow.* (For examples of more clues, see Teacher's Manual page 188.)

2. Students should understand that the central conflict is Ged's internal struggle over how to cope with the shadow. The physical struggles with the shadow are brief, and always lead back to the internal struggle. Most of the novel is concerned with Ged's thoughts and inner struggles.

3. There are many more male characters than female characters in the novel, and the women are generally shy and retiring. Women are referred to in a slighting way—"Weak as women's magic." The male characters seem to hold the greatest power and take the important actions. The one woman with strong powers, Serret, is evil. Students should see that, according to our standards, the women of Earthsea are not treated fairly. However, this may be a fair treatment by Earthsea's standards.

4. Ged learns all these things, and they are all important to the plot, but students should understand that casting spells is the least important, while learning to be a whole person is the most important.

5. The shadow represents the part of Ged that is unkind, cruel, or evil—the dark side. It comes into being when Ged is being vain, angry, arrogant, and ignorant.

6. A sample thematic statement is: "Good and bad exist side by side within each person, and wisdom comes from recognizing this fact so one may act responsibly."

7. Answers will vary, depending on students' personalities.

8. Help students brainstorm for possible heroes to compare with Ged.

paragraphs explaining your opinion. Be sure to support your ideas with evidence from the story.

5. **Analyzing a Quotation.** The quotation from *The Creation of Éa* at the beginning of the novel might have seemed hard to understand, or even meaningless, when you first read it. However, now that you have finished the novel, you may have some ideas about the meaning of these five lines. Reread the quotation and write two paragraphs analyzing it. In the first paragraph, explain what you think the quotation means. In the second paragraph, discuss how the quotation applies to the novel's main character and its events. (For example, does the quotation **foreshadow,** or hint at, events to come? Does it sum up the lesson the hero learns? Does it point to the novel's principle **theme,** or main idea?)

See Teacher's Manual page 189.

Analyzing Language and Vocabulary

Context Clues

The novel contains many unfamiliar words invented by the writer. Invented words, however, may not be the only words that are unfamiliar to you in this novel. When you're not sure of a word's meaning, you can often guess it from clues in the word's **context**—the other words and phrases surrounding the word. You can do this for both invented and English words.

For example, look at the beginning of Chapter 7. Ged awakes in a strange room. What is the bed's "canopy"? Even if you don't know what the word means, you can guess that it's some sort of covering because it is "hung to keep out drafts." In the next sentence, it is referred to as a "curtain." Therefore, a *canopy* must be a protective curtain hung around the bed.

Use the context to discover the meanings of the words in italics. When you are finished, tell which of the italicized words were invented by the author.

1. "Through three high windows he saw the *moorland,* bare and brown, snow-patched here and there. . . ."
2. ". . . he saw himself clothed in a *tunic* of silk and cloth-of-silver like a lord."
3. ". . . a cloak lined with *pellawi*-fur [was] laid ready for him."
4. " 'He who throws away his power is filled sometimes with a far greater power,' she said, smiling, as if his fears and *scruples* were childish ones."
5. "She kept busy those two days making dry wheatcakes for the voyagers to carry, and wrapping up dried fish and meat and other such *provender* to stock their boat . . . ."
6. "The most they saw that day was a school of silver *pannies* swimming south, but never a dolphin leapt . . . ."

For answers, see Teacher's Manual page 189.

Reading About the Writer

Ursula K. Le Guin (1929–) is the daughter of the well-known writer Theodora Kroeber and the distinguished anthropologist Alfred Kroeber. She was born in Berkeley, California, and grew up in that university community. She furthered her education in the East, at Radcliffe College and at Columbia University.

While studying in Paris on a Fulbright grant, she met and married the historian Charles Le Guin. With their children, the Le Guins now make their home in Portland, Oregon.

Le Guin says that her father used to tell her American Indian myths and legends. She thought they were impressive and mysterious stories. But she never realized that "grown-up" people could still make up their own myths today. Then one day when she was twelve years old, she read a book called *A Dreamer's Tales.* "The moment was decisive," she later said. "I had discovered my native country."

Le Guin has written poetry, short stories, novels, and children's books. Her fiction has won many awards: *A Wizard of Earthsea* won the Boston *Globe* Horn Book Award for Excellence. The next two books in the trilogy (series of three books) also won awards: *The Tombs of Atuan* won the Newbery Award, and *The Farthest Shore* won the National Book Award for Children's Books. Her novel *The Dispossessed* won the Nebula Award.

FURTHER READING

FOR TEACHERS

The Left Hand of Darkness (1969). An outer space novel about sexual roles; considered Le Guin's best work.

Ursula Le Guin (Twentieth-Century Views), ed. by Harold Bloom.

FOR STUDENTS

The two other books in the Earthsea trilogy: *The Tombs of Atuan* and *The Furthest Shore.*

Rocannon's World by Ursula Le Guin (1966). An outer space novel based on a Norse myth.

The Word for World Is Forest by Ursula Le Guin (1976). The destruction of a planet due to lack of concern for ecology.

The Narnia Series by C. S. Lewis

The Lord of the Rings by J. R. R. Tolkien

A Wrinkle in Time by Madeleine L'Engle

Focusing on Background

The Founding of Earthsea

Ursula Le Guin was asked how she planned the Earthsea world. She responded: "But I didn't plan anything, I found it . . . in my subconscious." Here, she talks about the beginnings of the book in which she "found" the world of Earthsea:

"For some weeks or months I let my imagination go groping around in search of what was wanted, in the dark. It stumbled over the Islands, and the magic employed there. Serious consideration of magic, and of writing for kids, combined to make me wonder about wizards. Wizards are usually elderly or ageless Gandalfs[1] . . . But what were they before they had white beards? How did they learn what is obviously an erudite[2] and dangerous art? Are there colleges for young wizards? And so on.

"The story of the book is essentially a voyage, a pattern in the form of a long spiral. I began to see the places where the young wizard would go. Eventually I drew a map. Now that I knew where everything was, now was the time for cartography.[3] Of course a great deal of it only appeared above water, as it were, in drawing the map.

"Three small islands are named for my children, their baby names; one gets a little jovial and irresponsible, given the freedom to create a world out of nothing at all. (Power corrupts.) None of the other names "means" anything that I know of, though their sound is more or less meaningful to me.

"People often ask how I think of names in fantasies, and again I have to answer that I find them, that I hear them. This is an important subject in this context. From that first story on, *naming* has been the essence of the art-magic as practiced in Earthsea. For me, as for the wizards, to know the name of an island or a character is to know the island or the person. Usually the name comes of itself, but sometimes one must be very careful: as I was with the protagonist, whose true name is Ged. I worked (in collaboration with a wizard named Ogion) for a long time trying to 'listen for' his name, and making certain it really was his name. This all sounds very mystical and indeed there are aspects of it I do not understand, but it is a pragmatic business too, since if the name had been wrong the character would have been wrong—misbegotten, misunderstood.

"A man who read the ms.[4] . . . thought 'Ged' was meant to suggest 'God.' That shook me badly. I considered changing the name in case there were other such ingenious minds waiting to pounce. But I couldn't do so. The fellow's name was Ged and no two ways about it.

"It isn't pronounced Jed, by the way. That sounds like a mountain moonshiner to me. I thought the analogy with 'get' would make it clear, but a lot of people have asked. One place I do exert deliberate control in name-inventing is in the area of pronounce-ability. I try to spell them so they don't look too formidable (unless, like Kurremkarmerruk, they're meant to look formidable), and they can be pronounced either with the English or the Italian vowels. I don't care which.

"Much the same holds for the bits of invented languages in the text of the trilogy.

"There are words, like rushwash tea, for which I can offer no explanation. They simply drink rushwash tea there; that's what it's called, like lapsang soochong or Lipton's here. Rushwash is a Hardic word, of course. If you press me, I will explain that it comes from the rushwash bush, which grows both wild and cultivated everywhere south of Enlad, and bears a small round leaf which when dried and steeped yields a pleasant brownish tea. I did not know this before I wrote the foregoing sentence. Or did I know it, and simply never thought about it? What's in a name? A lot, that's what."

—Ursula Le Guin

1. **Gandalf:** the good wizard in J.R.R. Tolkien's trilogy *The Lord of The Rings.*
2. **erudite:** learned, scholarly.
3. **cartography:** the art of making maps.
4. **ms.:** abbreviation for manuscript.

A. Expansion
An excerpt from *The Adventures of Tom Sawyer* appears on pages 88–101.

★ **Texas Essential Elements/(a) English Language Arts: 1B** Purpose and audience; **1H** Proofread; **1I** Spelling generalizations; **2B** Parts of speech; **2D** Grammar/punctuation/spelling

Review: Exercises in Reading Fiction

SRW pp. 21, 23

CHARACTER

Writers of fiction can use several different methods of **characterization.** Some might use physical description to suggest what a character is like. Or a character's actions might tell what kind of person he or she is. Sometimes a reader learns about a character from comments made by other characters in the story. And sometimes the writer will simply tell the reader that a character is smart or brave, evil or trustworthy.

Now think about a story that is told by a first-person narrator. How does the writer of such a story reveal the character of the narrator? None of the methods named above will work, because everything the reader learns comes from the character telling the story.

Here is a passage from *The Adventures of Huckleberry Finn,* a book narrated by the main character. See how much you learn about Huck and his friend,
A Tom Sawyer.

Huck is a simple boy who believes (wrongly) that just about everyone is smarter than he is. In this passage, he argues with Tom, an avid reader of adventure stories. Tom has just warned Huck about the danger of running into someone with magical powers during an adventure.

"Why," said he, "a magician could call up a lot of genies, and they would hash you up like nothing before you could say Jack Robinson. They are as tall as a tree and as big around as a church."

"Well," I says, "s'pose we got some genies to help *us*—can't we lick the other crowd then?"

"How you going to get them?"

"I don't know. How do *they* get them?"

"Why, they rub an old tin lamp or an iron ring, and then the genies come tearing in, with the thunder and lightning a-ripping around and the smoke a-rolling, and everything they're told to do they up and do it. They don't think nothing of pulling a shot-tower up by the roots, and belting a Sunday-school superintendent over the head with it—or any other man."

"Who makes them tear around so?"

"Why, whoever rubs the lamp or the ring. They belong to whoever rubs the lamp or the ring, and they've got to do whatever he says. If he tells them to build a palace forty miles long out of di'monds, and fill it full of chewing-gum, or whatever you want, and fetch an emperor's daughter from China for you to marry, they've got to do it—and they've got to do it before sun-up next morning, too. And more: they've got to waltz that palace around over the country wherever you want it, you understand."

"Well," says I, "I think they are a pack of flatheads for not keeping the palace themselves 'stead of fooling them away like that. And what's more—if I was one of them I would see a man in Jericho before I would drop my business and come to him for the rubbing of an old tin lamp."

"How you talk, Huck Finn. Why, you'd *have* to come when he rubbed it, whether you wanted to or not."

"What! and I as high as a tree and as big as a church? All right, then; I *would* come; but I lay I'd make that man climb the highest tree there was in the country."

"Shucks, it ain't no use to talk to you, Huck Finn. You don't seem to know anything, somehow—perfect saphead."

I thought all this over for two or three days, and then I reckoned I would see if there was anything in it. I got an old tin lamp and an iron ring, and went out in the woods and rubbed and rubbed till I sweat like an Injun, calculating to build a palace and sell it; but it warn't no use, none of the genies come. So then I judged that all that stuff was only just one of Tom Sawyer's lies. I reckoned he believed in the Arabs and the elephants, but as for me I think different. It had all the marks of a Sunday school.

—from *The Adventures of Huckleberry Finn,* Mark Twain

Answers to Questions

1. Words describing Huck might include *practical, intelligent, earnest, down-to-earth,* while Tom might be *gullible, imaginative,* and *naive.* Students should support their descriptions with appropriate evidence from the excerpt.

2. Through Huck's words and thoughts, we see that he questions the far-fetched, improbable things that Tom romantically accepts.

3. Huck's actions show that he does not dismiss things as false simply because he has never heard of them. He is intelligent and open-minded, and he verifies things. Huck probably does not judge himself as being as intelligent as Tom, because he does not read the way Tom does. We learn about his intelligence and curiosity because Twain allows us to know his thoughts.

★ **Texas Essential Elements/(a) English Language Arts (continued): 3A** Plot/character; **4I** Follow directions. **(c) Reading: 4A** Follow directions

Review: Exercises in Reading Fiction/*cont.*

For evaluation strategies, see Teacher's Manual page 190.

1. Think of one or two words or phrases you could use to describe Huck Finn's **character.** Then do the same for Tom Sawyer. Mention specific parts of the passage that show these descriptions to be accurate.
2. Because of his reading, Tom clearly knows more than Huck does. In spite of that, Twain makes us realize that Huck is more intelligent. How does Twain do that?
3. Reread the last paragraph of the excerpt. What does Huck do? What does this tell you about his character? From what you have read, do you think he knows this about himself? If not, how can readers know it, since they have only Huck's narration to work with?

Writing

1. **Creating a Character.** Invent a character who does not understand much about himself or herself. (You might want to consider inventing a child.) Write a list of words or phrases that describe important aspects of this character's personality.
2. **Writing the Beginning of a Story.** Write the beginning of a story narrated by your character. Your goal is to tell your reader something about the character that the character doesn't realize. Before you write, decide what you want to reveal about your character: perhaps that he or she is ignorant, prejudiced, etc. Then write a brief narration in which the character reveals this quality to the reader without realizing it.

Here are some other opinions that students may want to support with an essay:

1. Fantasies are more (or less) valuable for children to read than stories based completely in the real world.
2. To write interesting books, a novelist should have (or doesn't need) many different kinds of experiences.
3. Except for his supernatural powers, Ged is very much like a modern teenager.
4. Even without his supernatural powers, Ged is not at all like a modern teenager.

 **Texas Essential Elements/(a) English Language Arts: 1A** Composing process

Exercises in Critical Thinking and Writing

For teaching and evaluation strategies on this exercise see Teacher's Manual page 191.

SRW p. 37

SUPPORTING AN OPINION

Writing Assignment

In a brief essay, support one of the following opinions with reasons and evidence from the novel:

1. Because *A Wizard of Earthsea* is a fantasy, it cannot possibly tell us anything about people and life in the real world.
2. Even though *A Wizard of Earthsea* is a fantasy, it conveys the writer's insights about people and life in the real world.

Background

Opinions are different from facts. A **fact** is a statement that can be proved to be true.

Facts Ursula Le Guin was born in 1929.
A Wizard of Earthsea is the first book in a trilogy.

Another kind of fact is the result of an agreed-upon definition.

Facts *A Wizard of Earthsea* is a fantasy.
A Wizard of Earthsea tells the story of a hero's quest (search).

Unlike facts, **opinions** cannot be proved. The closest you can come to "proving" an opinion is to support it with reasons and evidence. A **reason** is a statement that explains why you hold an opinion. **Evidence** consists of facts, examples, quotations, and details used to back up a reason. The following paragraph outline gives three reasons to support the opinion.

Opinion: *A Wizard of Earthsea* is an excellent novel.

Reasons

1. Its plot involves a series of exciting conflicts.
2. It is filled with suspense and mystery.
3. Its main character is believable and likable; we care what happens to him.

To support each of these reasons, you would give as evidence specific incidents, details, and examples from the story.

Prewriting

1. Before you decide which of the two statements in the Writing Assignment to support, define what you think a *fantasy* is.
2. Review the discussion of *theme* on page 191. What are the themes of *A Wizard of Earthsea*?
3. Now you're ready to make up your mind which statement of opinion to support—1 or 2 in the Writing Assignment. The one you choose will be your essay's **thesis statement.**
4. Write down all of the reasons you can think of that might possibly support your opinion. For example, which of the following reasons do you think could be used to support opinion 1, and which ones could be used to support opinion 2?
   a. Although they are from a strange universe, the characters show human traits.
   b. The characters in the novel have experiences that human beings can never have.
   c. The novel says something about pride and true friendship.
   d. The novel is set in a fantastic world full of magic, demons, dragons. This world is extremely unlike the world we live in.
   e. The hero of the novel is not even typical of the people in his universe; he is unique.
5. Look for evidence (examples, incidents, quotations) in the novel to back up each of the reasons that you think of. Try to find at least one piece of evidence for each reason; the more evidence, the better. To help plan your essay, fill in a chart such as the following:

Opinion:	
Reasons	**Evidence**
1.	
2.	
3. etc.	

Exercises in Critical Thinking and Writing/*cont.*

Think of your opinion as being literally supported (held up) by the reasons and evidence.

Writing

Look carefully at your Prewriting chart, and choose the two reasons you think are best. (Make sure that you are giving two separate reasons, not just restating the same reason twice.) Follow this plan for your essay:

Paragraph 1: Introductory paragraph. Mention title, author; include thesis statement (opinion).

Paragraph 2: Give first reason to support your opinion. Include evidence (details from the novel) to support first reason.

Paragraph 3: Give second reason to support your opinion. Include evidence.

Paragraph 4: Concluding paragraph. Summarize reasons and restate your opinion.

Here is an example of an introductory paragraph for an essay that supports the following opinion: "*A Wizard of Earthsea* is an excellent novel."

A Wizard of Earthsea by Ursula Le Guin is the first in a trilogy, a series of three fantasies set in a made-up world called Earthsea. The hero of the novel is a young man with mysterious powers who is destined to become a great wizard. But first the young man must embark on a long and perilous quest that takes him beyond the edges of the known world. I think that *A Wizard of Earthsea* is an excellent novel.

Mentions title and author.

Summarizes plot briefly.

States thesis (opinion).

Revising and Proofreading Self-Check

1. Does the introductory paragraph contain a thesis statement that states my opinion?
2. Does the essay contain at least two reasons to support my opinion?
3. Is each reason supported with evidence (specific incidents, details, and examples from the novel)?
4. Does every sentence start with a capital letter and end with a period or other end punctuation marks?
5. Are my ideas clearly expressed? Have I said everything I wanted to say?

Partner Check

1. Are there any spelling errors?
2. Are sentences punctuated correctly?
3. Are paragraphs fully developed (at least four sentences long) and indented?
4. Are there any sentences or ideas that are unclear?
5. What do I like best about this paper?
6. What needs improvement?

WRITING ABOUT LITERATURE

The Writing Process

One of the things you learn in English class is how to write about literature. Your teacher might ask you to analyze a poem, to compare two short stories, to show how two characters differ from each other, or to give your opinion of something you have read.

A good paragraph or essay, like any other superior product, doesn't come about by accident. It's the result of thought, planning, attention to detail, revisions, and last-minute polishing. Good writers think of writing as a *process*—a series of steps that lead to a finished product they are satisfied with.

The writing process is made up of three main stages: **prewriting, writing,** and **revising.** If you take the time to give careful attention to each stage of the process, you're likely to find that writing good essays is not as difficult as you thought.

Prewriting

During the **prewriting** stage, your first goal is to come up with ideas. You might discuss the assignment with someone in your class. Or you might work alone, jotting down what comes to mind as you think about the assignment. The next step during this stage is to narrow your topic. It will help to write several **thesis statements**—sentences that could serve as the main idea of the essay you are planning. You will eventually use only one of these statements in your essay.

Writing

The prewriting material becomes the basis of what you do during the **writing** stage. First, choose the thesis statement you think best. It becomes the key to your essay and will help keep you from wandering away from your topic. Second, concentrate on getting your ideas on paper. Don't worry too much about grammar, spelling, or punctuation. Just say all that you want to say. Be sure to say it as clearly as possible so that readers will understand your points.

Revising

During the third stage—**revising**—your job is to mold the essay into final form. This is the time to look for errors in spelling, punctuation, capitalization, and sentence structure. It is also the time to decide whether you have said everything you want to say. In addition, you'll want to read your essay over as if you were your own audience to make sure everything is expressed as clearly as possible. When you have rewritten the essay with all necessary changes, you have finished the last stage of the writing process.

The whole writing process need not take a lot of time. In some cases, for example, you will decide immediately what you want to say in your essay. The prewriting stage could then take only a few minutes. If you are very good at expressing yourself in writing, the same could be true for revising. The time you spend on each stage is up to you. The key thing to understand is the importance of going through all three steps.

The following material will help you apply the three steps in the writing process to typical assignments in literature class. You'll probably find the material helpful for assignments in other classes as well.

Writing Answers to Essay Questions

When you write an answer to an essay question, your success will depend on two things. First, you must understand what the question asks. Second, you must complete the three stages of the writing process.

Understanding Essay Questions

Before you begin the prewriting stage, think about the question and make sure you understand what it asks you to do. In most questions, the key word is the verb. The following verbs show up in many questions. If you understand them, your essay answers are likely to be good.

- **Analyze.** When you analyze something, you take it apart to see how it works. If a question asks you to analyze a whole literary work, try to focus on the elements of the work. Sometimes a question will ask you to analyze just one element. In this case, you'll have to show how the element affects the selection as a whole.

  Question: Analyze the setting in the story "Three Skeleton Key."
  Possible Strategy: Go through the story and find the key descriptions of the setting. Make a note of each example. Then review the ways setting can be important to a story. Do any of these apply to the setting in "Three Skeleton Key"?

- **Compare.** When you compare two things, you show how they are alike. If a question asks you to compare two pieces of writing, look for as many similarities as you can find. *Note:* Sometimes when a question asks you to compare, it really means that you should look for similarities *and* differences. Your teacher will clarify this for you.

Question: Compare the poem "Hector the Collector" with any of the poems of Ogden Nash.
Possible Strategy: Examine the poems carefully to see how they might be alike. Think about the elements of a poem: rhyme, meter, and other sound effects, subject, tone. Then make a list. Include as many similarities as you can find, even if you don't expect to write about all of them.

• **Contrast.** When you contrast two things, you show how they differ from each other. If a question asks you to contrast two pieces of writing, look for as many differences as you can find.

Question: Contrast the use of imaginary characters in "Charles" and "A Mother in Mannville."
Possible Strategy: Look over both stories to see how they use imaginary characters. Then make a list of all the ways the imaginary characters are different.

• **Describe.** When you describe something or someone, you paint a picture with words. Description is usually based mostly on details that someone can see. However, you could also include details such as sounds, tastes, and aromas that appeal to other senses.

Question: Describe the settings in *A Wizard of Earthsea.*
Possible Strategy: Review all the settings in the novel. Then list the descriptive details that help you visualize those settings (or smell them, taste them, hear their sounds).

• **Discuss.** When you discuss a topic, you examine it in a general way and make comments on it.

Question: Discuss the mood, or atmosphere, of "The Listeners."
Possible Strategy: Look over the poem and decide what mood the writer was trying to create. Then list the details in the poem that help create that mood.

• **Evaluate.** When you evaluate a work of literature, you make a judgment about how effective it is. An evaluation is an expression of opinion backed up by references to specific details in the work.

Question: Write an evaluation of "The Fun They Had."
Possible Strategy: First, list the characteristics you think a good short story should have. Then reread "The Fun They Had" with those characteristics in mind. Decide how well it measures up to the standards you are using. Begin your essay by naming the characteristics of a good short story. Then write several paragraphs explaining how Asimov's story does or does not meet each of the standards you named.

• **Explain.** When you explain something, you make it clear or easier to understand.

Question: Explain what eventually will happen to Charlie in "Flowers for Algernon."
Possible Strategy: Decide first how to answer the question. Then list your reasons for answering as you did.

• **Illustrate.** When you illustrate something, you provide examples that support a certain position.

Question: How do the Greek and Roman gods and goddesses reveal human qualities? Use examples to illustrate your answer.
Possible Strategy: Look over the myths you have read and list the gods and goddesses. Next to each name, describe his or her human qualities. In a short essay, you will not be able to write about all these gods and goddesses. Select at least three that you find interesting and use your examples to illustrate how each behaves in a human way.

Writing Essays About Literature

Prewriting

Choosing a Topic. If you are planning an essay that responds to a question, your topic has already been chosen. Sometimes, however, your teacher will ask you to choose a topic. In that case, keep three things in mind. (1) Library research is a good way to find topics to write about. For instance, you can look up what critics say about a particular work and thereby find a topic. (2) The narrower and more specific your topic is, the easier it will be to write about. (3) You can always find a topic if you think about the elements of literature you've studied in this book.

Gathering Information. If you do library research, the prewriting stage should include taking notes about what you read. Most people use index cards, with only one piece of information on each card. Each notecard should also include the title of the work in which you found the information, its author, its publisher and copyright date, and the page number on which the information appears.

If you are working on an assigned topic, prewriting might consist of anything that will help you get some ideas on paper. For example, you might make a list of everything you think of as you reread the literary work. (See the reader's notes in the sections called "Responding" in the front of several units in this book.) You might talk to a friend who has read the work and share some ideas about it. You might even simply begin writing, putting down anything that comes into your head. This is called **free writing,** and some people find it an effective way of discovering ideas to write about.

Writing a Thesis Statement. A thesis statement is a sentence (or more) that states the central idea of your essay. There are two good reasons for having a thesis statement when you begin the writing stage. First, the thesis statement will almost certainly appear in the early part of the essay you are planning. Second, it can help you stick to your topic. *Note:* It often will be helpful to start by writing several thesis statements. Look them over and choose the best one for your essay.

Writing

There are many ways to organize an essay; when you are more experienced at writing, you may want to experiment with different methods of organization. For now, though, it would be a good idea to write all your essays according to the following three-part plan.

Introduction. The first paragraph of your essay should mention the title and author of the work you are writing about. It should also tell what your essay will be about. In most cases, the best way to do that is by using the thesis statement you have already written. The introduction might also mention some of the details you will refer to in supporting the thesis statement.

Body. The body of your essay should be *at least* one paragraph long. Each paragraph should include one or more examples to support your thesis statement. A paragraph consists of a topic sentence and evidence that supports that sentence. Whenever possible, use quotations from the work you are writing about.

Conclusion. The last paragraph of your essay might do one of three things. It could (1) restate the thesis statement in other words; (2) summarize the main points of the essay; or (3) give your personal response to the work you have written about.

Revising

Revising means making changes in the first draft of an essay. There are several kinds of changes you might make. Because of this, some writers read their essays several times. During each reading, they concentrate on only one kind of change.

Reading for Content. During one reading of your essay, you should think about nothing but content. Did you include a thesis statement? Does it say what you want it to say? Does each paragraph in the body of the essay support your thesis statement? Does your concluding paragraph do what you intended it to do?

Reading for Style. You should also reread your essay to see if you can improve the writing style. Does it read as smoothly as you want it to? Would some long sentences be easier to understand if they were broken into two or three shorter sentences? Would some short sentences be better if they were combined? Do you find unnecessary words or phrases that could be cut? Are your ideas clear and easy to follow?

Proofreading for Errors. Proofreading involves looking for mistakes in grammar, spelling, punctuation, capitalization, and sentence structure. During this reading, remember that the title of a poem, a short story, or an essay should be enclosed in quotation marks; the title of a play, a novel, or any other book should be in italics. (In handwriting and typing, you underline anything that should be in italics.)

Use the following proofreader's symbols to correct errors in spelling, capitalization, and punctuation.

Symbol	Meaning of Symbol	Example
≡	Capitalize a lower-case letter.	Robert frost (≡ under f)
/	Change a capital letter to lower case.	"Going /To Norway"
^	Insert a word or phrase.	"The Glove and ^the Lions"
ℊ	Delete (take out) one or more letters and close up the space.	"Rikki-Tikki-Tavyi"

^	Insert a letter.	Rudyad Kipling
⊙	Add a period.	O Henry
^,	Add a comma.	stories, poems and novels
^"	Insert quotation marks.	Cat & the Weather"
∽	Change the order of the letters.	*Brain's Song*
¶	Begin a new paragraph.	"The Monkey's Paw" is a scary story.

A Model Essay

Here is a draft of an essay based on library research. The essay includes revisions the writer made during the final stage of the writing process.

A Comparison of Two Plots

INTRODUCTION
Gives titles and author.
States thesis.

Mark Twain wrote two novels based on his boyhood. They were *The Adventures of Tom Sawyer* and *The Adventures of Huckleberry Finn* in which twain gave very different views of the town where he grew up.

BODY
States topic sentence.
Identifies source of quote.
Adds supporting details.

Mark Twain called *The Adventures of Tom Sawyer* "a hymn to boyhood (Baldanza, page 103). In this book, the small Missouri town where Tom lives is a kind of paradise he and his friends spend most of their time lazing around or playing games, swimming, they trade marbles, and they form secret societies to make their lives feel exciting.

States another topic sentence.

The plot of the novel invoes an adventure that puts Tom and his friends into some danger and everything turns out well in the end.

626

Tom and Huck even wind up with thousands of dollars in reward money. Its the kind of ending you expect when your watching a family movie on TV.

Adds supporting details.

The plot of *The Adventures of Huckleberry Finn* is filled with danger and death. Huck is kidnapped by his drunken father, he beats him and makes fun of him for wanting to learn how to read and write. Later he fakes his own murder in order to run away without being followed. The plot of this story is about an adventure that could send Huck to jail. In fact, he thinks it could send him to hell. It involves helping an escaped slave to run away, a fact that is against the law. While they are traveling, they meet up with some of the worse types of people you can imagine. The story ends up with Huck back in town. But he decides to take off again, because he can't stand being "sivil-ized." In the end Huck prefers the river and its freedom to life on the shore.

States another topic sentence.

Adds supporting details.

Both stories are about Tom, Huck, and their friends. But they present contrasting views of the same period in Twain's life, the two books may even present two different sides of Twain's personality (Baldanza, page 111). Maybe Tom Sawyers story shows St. Petersburg as Twain wanted to remember his boyhood, maybe Huck Finn's story shows it as it really was.

CONCLUSION

Summarizes the main idea.

Identifies source of information.

Presents an interesting interpretation.

Identifying Your Sources

Whenever you do research for an essay, identify your sources of information. (In the essay you just read, there are two references, with page numbers, to a writer named Baldanza.) At the end of your essay, include a bibliography—a list of books and articles used in writing the essay. List your sources alphabetically by the author's last names. Here is a sample bibliography.

Baldanza, Frank. *Mark Twain: An Introduction and Interpretation.* New York: Barnes & Noble, Inc., 1961.

Smith, Henry Nash. *Mark Twain: The Development of an Author.* Cambridge, Mass.: The Belknap Press of Harvard University Press, 1962.

Additional Terms
Genre 631
Folk tale 631

A HANDBOOK OF LITERARY TERMS

For more information about a topic, turn to the page(s) in this book indicated on a separate line at the end of the entries. To learn more about **Allusion,** for example, turn to pages 502–503.

On another line are cross-references to entries in this Handbook that provide closely related information. For instance, **Autobiography** contains a cross-reference to *Biography*. It usually will help to look up all the cross-references mentioned at an entry.

ALLITERATION The repetition of the same, or very similar, consonant sounds in words that are close together in a poem, or other type of writing. While alliteration usually occurs at the beginning of words, it can also occur within or at the end of words. Alliteration can do many things, such as help establish a mood, emphasize words, and serve as a memory aid. In the following example, the "s" sound is repeated at the beginning of the words *silken* and *sad*, and within the words *uncertain* and *rustling*.

And the silken sad uncertain rustling of each
  purple curtain
—from "The Raven,"
Edgar Allan Poe

SRW p. 11 See pages 271, 276.

ALLUSION A reference to something, such as a statement, person, place, or event, that is known from fields like literature, history, religion, mythology, politics, sports, or science. Allusions enrich the reading experience. Writers expect readers to recognize allusions and to think almost at the same time about the literary work and the allusions contained in it. The following lines describing a tunnel in the snow contain an allusion to Aladdin, a character in *The Thousand and One Nights*.

With mittened hands, and caps drawn low,
To guard our necks and ears from snow,
We cut the solid whiteness through.
And, where the drift was deepest, made
A tunnel walled and overlaid
With dazzling crystal: we had read
Of rare Aladdin's wondrous cave,
And to our own his name we gave.
—from "Snow-Bound,"
John Greenleaf Whittier

The cave in the tale contained a magic lamp that enabled Aladdin to acquire vast riches. By alluding to Aladdin's cave, Whittier shows that the icy tunnel in the snow seemed a magical, fairy-tale place.

SRW p. 13 See pages 502–503.

ATMOSPHERE The overall mood or emotion of a work of literature. A work's atmosphere can often be described in one or two adjectives, such as scary, dreamy, happy, sad, or nostalgic. Atmosphere is created through a writer's use of words to create images, sounds, and descriptions that convey a particular feeling. The following poem establishes a mysterious, dark, lonesome atmosphere.

The Horse

Under pared moons
it walks around,
a horse once killed
on a battleground.

Its ghostly hoofs . . .
it shudders, slips,
and darkly neighs
to distant whips.

At the leaden bend
of the barricade,
with hollow eyes,
it stops, afraid.

And later its slow
step retreats
through ruined squares,
desolate streets.

—José Maria Eguren
(translated by Cheli Durán)

SRW p. 15

AUTOBIOGRAPHY An account of the writer's own life, or part of it. *The Diary of a Young Girl*, a journal kept by Anne Frank as she and her family hid from the Nazis during World War II, is a well-known autobiographical work. So is the *Autobiography* of Benjamin Franklin.

SRW p. 17 See also *Biography.*

BIOGRAPHY An account of a person's life, or part of it, written or told by another person. A classic American biography is Carl Sandburg's life of Abraham Lincoln. Another well-known biography is Joseph Lash's *Helen and Teacher*, the story of Helen Keller and her teacher Annie Sullivan. In a library or bookstore you can find biographies of movie stars, television personalities, politicians, sports figures, self-made millionaires, even underworld figures. Biographies are among the most popular forms of contemporary literature.

SRW p. 17 See also *Autobiography*.

CHARACTER A person, animal, or thing in a story, play, or other literary work. In some works, such as Aesop's fables, a character is an animal. In other works, such as fairy tales, a natural force like the wind may be a character. In still other works, a character is a god or a hero, as are Zeus and Prometheus in "Prometheus" (page 467). But most often a character is an ordinary human being, such as Jerry in "A Mother in Mannville" (page 209).

The process of revealing the personality of a character in a story is called **characterization.** A writer can reveal a character in the following ways:

1. by letting us hear the character speak
2. by describing how the character looks and dresses
3. by letting us listen to the character's inner thoughts and feelings
4. by revealing what other people in the story think or say about the character
5. by showing us what the character does—how he or she acts.
6. by telling us directly what the character's personality is like (cruel, kind, sneaky, brave, and so on)

When a writer uses the first five ways to reveal a character we must use our judgment to decide what the character is like, based on the evidence the writer gives us. When a writer uses the sixth method, however, we don't decide for ourselves. We are told directly what kind of person the character is.

Characters can be classified as static or dynamic. A **static character** is one who does not change much in the course of a work. The twins in "The Lost Beach" (page 57) are static characters. By contrast, a **dynamic character** changes as a result of the story's events. Roger Clark in "Miss Awful" (page 160) is a dynamic character.

See pages 71–73, 123–126, 338–339, 619–620.
See also *Protagonist*. SRW p. 21

CONFLICT A struggle or clash between opposing characters, or between opposing forces. In an **external conflict,** a character struggles against some outside force. This outside force might be another character, or society as a whole, or a natural force. "Three Skeleton Key" (page 7) concerns the characters' external conflict with a swarm of sea-rats. An **internal conflict,** on the other hand, takes place within the character's own mind. It is a struggle between opposing needs or desires or emotions. In "After Twenty Years" (page 194), Officer Wells must resolve an internal conflict over whether to arrest an old friend.

SRW p. 25 See pages 3–4, 65–68, 183–184, 338.

CONNOTATION A meaning, association, or emotion that a word suggests. For example, *tiny, cramped,* and *compact* all have roughly the same dictionary definition, or denotation. But they have different connotations. A maker of small cars would be careful not to describe its product as tiny or cramped. Instead, it might say its cars are compact. To grasp a writer's full meaning, it is important to pay attention not just to the literal definitions of words, but also to their connotations. Connotations can be especially important in poetry.

SRW p. 27 See pages 182, 266.

DENOTATION The literal, dictionary definition of a word.

See page 182.
SRW p. 27 See also *Connotation.*

DESCRIPTION Writing intended to create a mood or emotion, or to recreate a person, a place, a thing, an event, or an experience. Description works through images that appeal to the senses of sight, smell, taste, hearing, or touch. Writers use description in all forms of fiction, nonfiction, and poetry. Here is a description of a city street by the noted writer James Baldwin. Baldwin's descriptive images not only give you a clear picture of the street, but also establish a mood.

> The avenue . . . was very long and silent. Somehow, it seemed old, like a picture in a book. It stretched straight before me, endless, and the streetlights did not so much illuminate it as prove how dark it was. The familiar buildings were now merely dark, silent shapes, great masses of wet rock; men stood against the walls or the stoops, made faceless by the light in the hallway behind them. The rain was falling harder. Cars sloshed by, sending up sheets of water and bobbing like boats; from the bars I heard music faintly, and many voices.
>
> —from "These Saturday Afternoons," James Baldwin

SRW p. 29 See pages 214–215.

DIALECT A way of speaking characteristic of a particular region or of a particular group of people. Dialects may have a distinct vocabulary, pronunciation system, and grammar. In a sense, we all speak dialects. One dialect usually becomes dominant in a country or culture, however, and is accepted as the standard way of speaking. In the United States, for example, the formal written language is known as Standard English. (You usually hear it spoken by newscasters on television.) Writers often reproduce regional dialects, or those that reveal a person's economic or social class, in order to give a story local color. For example, the characters in "Lassie Come-Home" (page 104) speak a dialect of Yorkshire, England. The poem "Madam and the Rent Man" (page 327) includes dialect spoken in some black communities.

SRW p. 31 See pages 88, 103, 105, 116, 328.

DIALOGUE Conversation between two or more characters. Most stage dramas consist entirely of dialogue, together with stage directions. (Screenplays and television dramas sometimes also include an unseen narrator.) The dialogue in a drama must move the plot along and reveal character almost singlehandedly. Dialogue is also an important element in most stories and novels, as well as in some poems and nonfiction. It is one of the most effective ways for a writer to show what a character is like. It can also add realism and humor.

In the written form of a play, dialogue appears without quotation marks. In prose or poetry, however, dialogue is normally enclosed in quotation marks.

A **monologue,** or **soliloquy,** is a part of a drama in which one character speaks alone.

SRW p. 33 See pages 379–380.

DRAMA A story written to be acted in front of an audience. (A drama can be appreciated and enjoyed in written form, however.) The action of a drama is usually driven by a character who wants something very much and takes steps to get it. The stages of drama are often described as **introduction, complications, climax,** and **resolution.**

See pages 337–339, 341, 377.
See also *Dialogue.*

FABLE A very brief story in prose or verse that teaches a moral or a practical lesson about how to get along in life. The characters of most fables are animals that behave and speak like human beings. Some of the most popular fables are those attributed to Aesop, who supposedly was a slave in ancient Greece. The poem "The Boy and the Wolf" (page 322) is a retelling in verse of one of Aesop's fables.

SRW p. 35 See pages 251–252.

FANTASY Imaginative writing that carries the reader into an invented, unrealistic world. In fantasy worlds, supernatural forces are often at play. Characters may wave magic wands, cast magical spells, or appear and disappear at will. These characters may seem almost like ordinary human beings—or they may be witches, Martians, elves, giants, or fairies. To take characters or readers into a fantasy world, the writer often uses some kind of magic carpet—a time machine, a magical looking glass, a mysterious door, even a Kansas tornado. Some of the oldest fantasy stories, such as "The Water of Life" (page 391), are called **fairy tales.** A newer type of fantasy, which deals with the changes that science may bring in the future, is called **science fiction.** *A Wizard of Earthsea* (page 536) is a fantasy novel set in the imaginary land of Earthsea.

See pages 385, 447.
See also *Science Fiction.*

Additional Terms

GENRE A type or species of literature. Examples of genre are fiction, nonfiction, drama, and poetry.

FOLK TALE A story with no known author, which originally was passed on from one generation to another by word of mouth. Most folk tales reflect the values of the society in which they were told. "The Water of Life" by the Grimms Brothers (page 391) and "The Story of the Fisherman" from *The Arabian Nights* (page 413) are folktales.

FICTION A prose account that is basically made-up rather than factually true. The term *fiction* usually refers to novels and short stories. Fiction may be based on a writer's actual experiences or on historical events, but characters, events, or other details are altered or added by the writer to create a desired effect. The excerpt from *A Tree Grows in Brooklyn* (page 52) is a fictional account of an episode in the writer's childhood.

See also *Fantasy, Nonfiction, Science Fiction.*

FIGURE OF SPEECH A word or phrase that describes one thing in terms of another and is not meant to be understood as literally true. Figures of speech always involve some sort of imaginative comparison between seemingly unlike things.

Some 250 different types of figures of speech have been identified. The most common by far are the **simile** ("The stars were like diamonds"), the **metaphor** ("My soul is an enchanted boat"), and **personification** ("The sun smiled down on the emerald-green fields").

See pages 309–310, 331–332.
See also *Metaphor, Personification, Simile.*

FLASHBACK Interruption in the present action of a plot to flash backward and tell what happened at an earlier time. A flashback breaks the normal movement of the narrative from one point in time forward to another point. A flashback can also be placed at the very beginning of a work. It usually gives background information needed to understand the present action. The first paragraph of "The Saddest Day the Summer Had" (page 171) makes clear that the narrator is speaking some time after the events of the story took place. Almost the entire story, then, is a flashback to an earlier time. Flashbacks are common in stories, novels, and movies and sometimes appear in stage plays and poems.

A break in the movement of a plot to an episode in the future is known as a **flash forward.**

FORESHADOWING The use of clues or hints suggesting events that will occur later in the plot. Foreshadowing is used to build suspense or anxiety in the reader or viewer. In a drama, a gun found in a bureau drawer in Act I is likely to foreshadow violence later in the play. In "Wine on the Desert" (page 220), Tony's description of how people die from thirst in the desert foreshadows Durante's death.

SRW p. 43 See page 4.

FREE VERSE Poetry without a regular meter or a rhyme scheme. Poets writing in free verse try to capture the natural rhythms of ordinary speech. Free verse may use **internal rhyme, repetition, alliteration, onomatopoeia,** and other musical devices. Free verse also frequently makes use of vivid imagery. The following poem in free verse effectively uses images and the repetition of words to describe the effects of a family's eviction for not paying rent.

The 1st

What I remember about that day
is boxes stacked across the walk
and couch springs curling through the air
and drawers and tables balanced on the curb
and us, hollering,
leaping up and around
happy to have a playground;

nothing about the emptied rooms
nothing about the emptied family

—Lucille Clifton

SRW p. 45 See pages 270, 308.

IMAGERY Language that appeals to the senses. Most images are visual—that is, they create pictures in the reader's mind by appealing to the sense of sight. Images can also appeal to the senses of sound, touch, taste, or smell, or to several senses at once. While imagery is an element in all types of writing, it is especially important in poetry. The following lines contain images that let us see, hear, and even smell what the speaker experiences as she spends time with someone she loves.

We were very tired, we were very merry—
We had gone back and forth all night on the ferry.
It was bare and bright, and smelled like a stable—
But we looked into a fire, we leaned across a table,
We lay on a hilltop underneath the moon;
And the whistles kept blowing, and the dawn came soon.

—from "Recuerdo,"
Edna St. Vincent Millay

SRW p. 51 See pages 296–297, 390.

INVERSION The reversal of the normal word order of a sentence. The normal word order of an English sentence is subject-verb-complement. When a writer or speaker inverts the word order, one (or more) of these elements is used in a different place in the sentence. For example, instead of saying "You are right," someone might want to emphasize the word *right* and say "Right you are!" Poets often invert word order to fit the demands of their rhymes or rhythms. In these famous lines from a little song by William Shakespeare, you'll find two inverted sentences. (The speaker is talking to someone whose father is thought to be drowned in a shipwreck.)

Full fathom five thy father lies:
  Of his bones are coral made;
Those are pearls that were his eyes;
  Nothing of him that doth fade
But doth suffer a sea-change
Into something rich and strange.
Sea nymphs hourly ring his knell:
                    Ding-dong.
Hark! now I hear them—ding-dong, bell.

—from *The Tempest* (Act One, Scene 2), William Shakespeare

If we were to rewrite these first three lines in normal English word order, we'd get something like this:

Your father lies full fathom five;
His bones are made of coral;
Those are pearls that were his eyes . . .

SRW p. 55

IRONY A contrast between what appears to be true and what is really true or between expectation and reality. Irony can create powerful effects, from humor to strong emotion.

The following are three common types of irony.

1. **Verbal irony** involves a contrast between what is said or written and what is really meant. If you call someone who has just failed a test "Einstein," you are using verbal irony.

2. **Situational irony** occurs when what happens is very different from what we expected would happen. The surprise ending of "After Twenty Years" (page 194) involves situational irony.

3. **Dramatic irony** occurs when the audience or the reader knows something that a character does not know. In the excerpt from *Tom Sawyer* (page 87) we feel an amused sense of irony when Tom brags to his Aunt Polly about whitewashing the fence. Although Aunt Polly doesn't know the truth, we know that Tom actually tricked his friends into doing the job for him.

SRW p. 57

See page 421.

METAMORPHOSIS A marvelous change from one shape or form to another one. In myths and other stories, the change is usually from human or god to animal, from animal to human, or from human to plant. Greek and Roman myths contain many examples of metamorphosis. The myth of Narcissus (page 488) tells how the vain youth Narcissus pines away from love of his own reflection, and is finally changed into a flower.

See pages 434–435.

METAPHOR A comparison between two unlike things in which one thing becomes another thing. A metaphor is an important type of figure of speech. Metaphors are used in all forms of writing and are common in ordinary speech. When you say someone has a heart of gold, you do not mean that the person's heart is made of metal. You mean that the person is warm and caring.

Metaphors differ from similes, which use specific words (notably *like, as, than,* and *resembles*) to state comparisons. William Wordsworth's famous comparison, "I wandered lonely as a cloud," is a simile because it uses *as.* If Wordsworth had written, "I was a lonely, wandering cloud," he would have been using a metaphor.

In the following lines from William Shakespeare's tragedy *Othello,* the words *jewel, trash,* and *slave* are used metaphorically. Can you find another metaphor? (The lines are spoken in the play by Iago to Othello. "Immediate" means most valuable.)

Good name in man and woman, dear my lord,
Is the immediate jewel of their souls.
Who steals my purse steals trash—'tis something, nothing,
'Twas mine, 'tis his, and has been slave to thousands—
But he that filches from me my good name
Robs me of that which not enriches him
And makes me poor indeed.

—from *Othello* (Act Three, Scene 3), William Shakespeare

See pages 309–310, 434–435.
See also *Figure of Speech, Personification, Simile.*

SRW p. 61

MYTH A story that explains something about the world and typically involves gods or other supernatural beings. Myths reflect the traditions and beliefs of the culture that produced them. Almost every culture has **creation myths,** stories that explain how the world came to exist, or how human beings were created. Myths may also explain many other aspects of life and the natural world. The ancient Roman myth of Ceres and Proserpine (page 481) explains the change of seasons. Most myths are very old and were handed down orally before being put in written form. The exact origin of most myths is not known. **Legends** and **folk tales** are also stories handed down orally from generation to generation, but they are different from myths in important ways. Legends have some basis in history (such as the legends of the Trojan War, see pages 510–525). Folk tales are imaginary and not about gods. Fairy tales are examples of folk literature (see pages 391 and 413).

See pages 453–457, 480, 486–487, 500, 510, 526–527

NONFICTION Prose writing that deals with real people, events, and places without changing any facts. Popular forms of nonfiction are the **autobiography,** the **biography,** and the **essay.** Other examples of nonfiction include newspaper stories, magazine articles, historical writing, scientific reports, and even personal diaries and letters.

See also *Autobiography, Biography, Fiction.*

NOVEL A long fictional story, whose length is normally somewhere between one hundred and five hundred book pages. A novel uses all the elements of storytelling—plot, character, setting, theme, and point of view. It usually has more characters, settings, and themes and a more complex plot than a short story. Modern writers sometimes do not pay much attention to one or more of the novel's traditional elements. Some novels today are basically character studies, with only the barest story lines. Other novels don't look much below the surface of their characters and concentrate instead on plot and setting. A novel can deal with almost anything. The novel in this book, *A Wizard of Earthsea* (page 536), is a fantasy about an imaginary place and people.

See pages 533–534.

ONOMATOPOEIA The use of a word whose sound imitates or suggests its meaning. Onomatopoeia is so natural to us that we begin using it instinctively at a very early age. *Buzz, rustle, boom, tick-tock, tweet,* and *bark* are all examples of onomatopoeia. Onomatopoeia is an important element in creating the music of poetry. In the following lines, the poet creates a frenzied mood by choosing words that imitate the sounds of alarm bells.

> Oh, the bells, bells, bells!
> What a tale their terror tells
> Of Despair!
> How they clang, and clash, and roar!
> What a horror they outpour
> On the bosom of the palpitating air!
> Yet the ear, it fully knows
> By the twanging
> And the clanging
> How the danger ebbs and flows
>
> —from "The Bells,"
> Edgar Allan Poe

See pages 50, 159, 272, 283, 313.
SRW p. 63 See also *Alliteration.*

PARAPHRASE A restatement of a poem or a story, in which the meaning is expressed in other words. Students are frequently asked to paraphrase a work of literature to be sure they have understood exactly what it says. When you paraphrase a poem, you should tell what it says, line by line, in your own words. When you paraphrase a work, you should give a brief summary of the main points. Here is a paraphrase of these opening lines by Thomas Jefferson. Notice that the paraphrase is not as elegant or interesting as the original.

> When, in the course of human events, it becomes necessary for one people to dissolve the political bands which have connected them with another, and to assume, among the powers of the earth, the separate and equal station to which the laws of nature and of nature's God entitle them, a decent respect to the opinions of mankind requires that they should declare the causes which impel them to the separation.
>
> —The Preamble to *The Declaration of Independence*

At times, in life, it becomes necessary for one society to break its political ties with another country, and to establish a separate and equal nation. This is a right that comes from natural law and from God's law. Because of a respect toward others, the society should declare the reasons for its separation.

PERSONIFICATION A special kind of metaphor in which a nonhuman thing or quality is talked about as if it were human. In the following lines sleep is spoken of as having hands.

> The soft gray hands of sleep
> Toiled all night long
> To spin a beautiful garment
> Of dreams
>
> —from "Forgotten Dreams,"
> Edward Silvera

See page 310.
SRW p. 65 See also *Figure of Speech, Metaphor.*

PLOT The series of related events that make up a story. Plot is what happens in a short story, novel, play, or narrative poem. Most plots are built on these bare bones: An **introduction,** or **exposition,** tells us who the characters are and, usually, what their conflict is. **Complications** arise as the characters take steps to resolve the conflict. Eventually, the plot reaches a **climax,** the most exciting moment in the story, when the outcome is decided one way or another. The final part of a story is the **resolution.** This is when the characters' problems are solved and the story is closed.

Not all works of fiction or drama have a traditional plot structure. Modern writers sometimes experiment with plot, eliminating at times some or nearly all of the parts of a traditional plot in order to focus on other elements, such as character, point of view, or mood.

See pages 189–190, 253–254, 337–338.
SRW p. 67

POETRY A kind of rhythmic, compressed language that uses figures of speech and imagery designed to appeal to our emotions and imaginations. Poetry is usually arranged in lines. It often has a regular pattern of rhythm, and may have a regular rhyme scheme. Free verse is poetry that has no regular pattern of rhythm or rhyme, though it generally is arranged in lines. The major forms of poetry are the **lyric,** the **epic,** and the **ballad.** Beyond this, it is difficult to define poetry, though many readers feel it is easy to recognize it. Emily Dickinson once explained how she recognized poetry:

> If I read a book and it makes my whole body so cold that no fire can ever warm me, I know that it is poetry. If I feel physically as if the top of my head were taken off, I know that it is poetry.

See pages 257–260, 318, 331–334.
See also *Alliteration, Figure of Speech, Free Verse, Imagery, Refrain, Rhyme, Rhythm, Speaker, Stanza.*

POINT OF VIEW The vantage point from which a story is told. The most common points of view are the **omniscient,** the **third-person limited,** and the **first person.**

1. In the *omniscient*, or *all-knowing, point of view*, the narrator knows everything about the characters and their problems. This all-knowing narrator can tell us about the past, the present, and the future of the characters. This narrator can even tell us what the characters are thinking or what is happening in other places or parts of the world. But the narrator is not in the story. Rather, this kind of narrator stands above the action like a god. The omniscient is a very familiar point of view; we hear it in fairy tales from the time we are very young. "The Water of Life" (page 391) is told from the omniscient point of view: "There was once a king who had an illness, and no one believed that he would come out of it with his life."

2. In the *third-person limited point of view,* the narrator focuses on the thoughts and feelings of just one character. With this point of view, we feel we are observing the action through the eyes and with the feelings of only one of the characters in the story. "Beware of the Dog" (page 199) is told from the third-person limited point of view: "He realized that he was no longer feeling good, that he was sick and giddy. . . . But he knew that he was flying the Spitfire. He could feel the handle of the stick between the fingers of his right hand."

3. In the *first-person point of view,* one of the characters is actually telling the story, using the personal pronoun "I." We become very familiar with the narrator, but we can know only what this person knows, observe only what this person observes. All our information about the story must come from this one person. In some cases the information is incorrect. "The Fifty-Yard Dash" (page 144) is told from the first-person point of view: "After a certain letter came to me from New York the year I was twelve, I made up my mind to become the most powerful man in my neighborhood."

SRW p. 69
See pages 190–191.

PROTAGONIST The main character in a work of literature. The protagonist is involved in the work's central conflict. If there is another character opposing the protagonist, that character is called the **antagonist.** In the story "Rikki-Tikki-Tavi" (page 39) the mongoose Rikki-tikki is the protagonist, and his cobra enemies Nag and Nagaina are the antagonists.

See pages 338–339.

PUN A play (1) on the multiple meanings of a word or (2) on two words that sound alike but have different meanings. Most often puns are used for their humorous effects; they turn up in jokes all the time. *"What makes a tree noisy?" Answer: "Its bark."* This pun is called a **homographic pun;** it is based on a word (*bark*) that has two meanings ("the outer covering of a tree" and "the noise a dog makes"). *"Why can't you trust an Asian leopard?" Answer: "Because it's a cheetah."* This pun is called a **homophonic pun;** it is based on words that sound alike but are spelled differently (*cheater* and *cheetah*).

SRW p. 71
See pages 134, 143.

REFRAIN A repeated sound, word, phrase, line, or group of lines. Refrains are usually associated with songs and poems, but they are also used in speeches and other forms of literature. Refrains are most often used to build rhythm, but they may also provide emphasis or commentary, create suspense, or help hold a work together. Refrains may be repeated with small variations in a work in order to fit a particular context or to create a special effect. The line "O bury me not on the lone prairie" is used as a refrain in the song on page 265.

See page 260.

RHYME The repetition of accented vowel sounds and all sounds following them, in words that are close together in a poem. *Mean* and *screen* are rhymes, as are *crumble* and *tumble*. The many purposes of rhymes in poetry include building rhythm, lending a songlike quality, emphasizing ideas, organizing the poem (for instance, into stanzas or couplets), providing humor or delight for the reader, and aiding memory.

End-rhymes are rhymes at the ends of lines. In the following stanza, *walls/calls/falls* form end-rhymes, as do *hands/sands*.

Darkness settles on roofs and walls,
But the sea, the sea in the darkness calls;
The little waves, with their soft, white hands,
Efface the footprints in the sands,
And the tide rises, the tide falls.

—from "The Tide Rises, the Tide Falls,"
Henry Wadsworth Longfellow

Internal rhymes are rhymes within lines. The following line has an internal rhyme (*turning/burning*):

Back into the chamber turning, all my soul within
me burning

—from "The Raven,"
Edgar Allan Poe

Rhyming sounds need not be spelled the same way; for instance, *gear/here* forms a rhyme. Rhymes can involve more than one syllable or more than one word; *poet/know it* is an example. Rhymes involving sounds that are similar but not exactly the same are called **approximate rhymes** (or **near rhymes** or **slant rhymes**). *Leave/live* is an example of an approximate rhyme. Poets writing in English often use approximate rhymes because English is not a very rhymable language. It has many words that rhyme with no other word, or just one other word (*mountain/fountain*, for instance). Poets interested in how a poem looks on the printed page sometimes use **eye-rhymes,** or **visual rhymes**—"rhymes" involving words that are spelled similarly but are pronounced differently. *Tough/cough* is an eye-rhyme. (*Tough/rough* is a "real" rhyme.)

The pattern of end-rhymes in a poem is called a **rhyme scheme.** To indicate the rhyme scheme of a poem, use a separate letter of the alphabet for each rhyme. For example, the rhyme scheme of Longfellow's stanza above is *aabba*.

SRW p. 75 See pages 271, 323, 331–332.

SRW p. 73

RHYTHM A musical quality produced by the repetition of stressed and unstressed syllables or by the repetition of certain other sound patterns. Rhythm occurs in all language—written and spoken—but it is particularly important in poetry.

The most obvious kind of rhythm is the regular repetition of stressed and unstressed syllables found in some poetry. In the following lines describing a cavalry charge, the rhythm echoes the galloping of the attacking horses.

The Assyrian came down like the wolf on the fold,
And his cohorts were gleaming in purple and gold;
And the sheen of their spears was like stars on the sea,
When the blue wave rolls nightly on deep Galilee.

—from "The Destruction of Sennacherib,"
George Gordon, Lord Byron

Marking the stressed (´) and unstressed (˘) syllables in a line is called **scanning** the line. Lord Byron's lines are scanned for you, showing that they have a rhythm pattern in which two unstressed syllables are followed by a stressed syllable. Read the lines aloud and listen to this rhythmic pattern. Also notice how the poem's end-rhymes help create the rhythm.

Writers can also create rhythm by repeating words and phrases, or even by repeating whole lines and sentences. The following passage by Walt Whitman is written in free verse and does not follow a regular pattern of rhythm or rhyme. Yet the lines are rhythmical because of Whitman's repeated use of certain sentence structures, words, and sounds:

I hear the sound I love, the sound of the human voice,
I hear all sounds running together, combined, fused,
or following,
Sounds of the city and sounds out of the city, sounds
of the day and night,
Talkative young ones to those that like them, the loud
laugh of work-people at their meals . . .

—from "Song of Myself,"
Walt Whitman

SRW p. 77 See pages 260, 270–271, 287, 332.

SCIENCE FICTION A kind of fantasy usually based on changes that science may bring in the future. Some science fiction deals with the past, especially prehistoric times. While science fiction creates imaginary worlds—often on other planets or in Earth's future—it typically makes use of physical laws as we know them. It is realistic, except that it is set in another place or time and presents imaginary scientific discoveries or developments. Classic early science fiction novels include Jules Verne's *Twenty Thousand Leagues Under the Sea* and H. G. Wells's *The War* of the Worlds. "The Fun They Had" (page 418) is a science fiction story set on earth in the year 2155.

See pages 385–386, 448.
See also *Fantasy*.

SETTING The time and place of a story or play. Most often the setting of a narrative is described early in the story. For example, "A Mother in Mannville" (page 209) begins with "The orphanage is high in the Carolina mountains. . . ." Setting often contributes to a story's emotional effect. In "Wine on the Desert" (page 220), the bleak desert setting helps build a tense, grim mood. Setting frequently plays an important role in a story's plot, especially when a conflict is between a character and nature. In "Survive the Savage Sea" (page 17), for example, the shipwrecked Robertson family struggles against the sea. Some stories are closely tied to a particular setting, and it is difficult to imagine them taking place elsewhere. Other stories could just as easily take place in a variety of settings.

SRW p. 79 See page 533.

SHORT STORY A short fictional prose narrative that usually makes up about ten to twenty book pages. Short stories were first written in the nineteenth century. Early short-story writers include Sir Walter Scott and Edgar Allan Poe. Short stories are usually built on a plot that consists of at least these bare bones: the **introduction** or **exposition, complications, climax,** and **resolution.** Short stories are more limited than novels. They usually have only one or two major characters and one important setting.

See pages 189–191.
See also *Fiction, Plot*.

SIMILE A comparison between two unlike things, using a word such as *like, as, resembles,* or *than.* The simile is an important type of figure of speech. In the following lines a simile creates a clear image of moths in the evening air.

When the last bus leaves, moths stream toward lights
like litter in wind.

—from "Depot in Rapid City,"
Roberta Hill

This example shows that similes can have strong emotional impact. By choosing to compare the moths to litter, the poet not only creates a picture in your mind, but also establishes a lonely, dreary mood.

See pages 64, 226–227, 309.
SRW p. 81 See also *Figure of Speech, Metaphor*.

SPEAKER The voice talking to us in a poem. Sometimes the speaker is identical to the poet, but often the speaker and the poet are not the same. The poet may be speaking as a child, a woman, a man, a whole people, an animal, or even an object. SRW p. 85

STANZA A group of consecutive lines in a poem that form a single unit. A stanza in a poem is something like a paragraph in prose; it often expresses a unit of thought. A stanza may consist of one line, or two, three, four, or any number of lines beyond that. The word *stanza* is an Italian word for "stopping place" or "place to rest." "A Word" (page 319) consists of two three-line stanzas, each expressing a separate idea. In some poems each stanza has the same rhyme scheme.

See pages 257–258.

SUSPENSE The uncertainty or anxiety we feel about what will happen next in a story. In "Three Skeleton Key" (page 7), our curiosity is hooked in the very first sentences, as the narrator hints he is about to describe his "most terrifying experience." Our suspense is heightened when the narrator recounts the chilling incident that gave the island of Three Skeleton Key its name. When the island is invaded by killer rats, suspense reaches a peak, as we seek to find out whether the narrator and his friends defeat the invaders.

See pages 4, 189.
See also *Plot*.

THEME A main idea of a work of literature. A theme is not the same as a subject. The subject of a work can usually be expressed in a word or two: love, childhood, death. The theme is the idea the writer wishes to convey *about* that subject. The theme must be expressed in a statement or sentence. A work can have more than one theme. For example, one theme of *A Wizard of Earthsea* (page 536) might be stated, "True wisdom can only be acquired through experience." A work's themes usually are not stated directly. The reader has to think about all the elements of the work and use them to make an inference, or educated guess, about what the themes are.

SRW p. 87 See page 191.

TONE The attitude a writer takes toward the audience, a subject, or a character. Tone is conveyed through the writer's choice of words and detail. The poem "Hector the Collector" (page 284) is light and humorous in tone. On the other hand, the story "Christmas" (page 179) is serious and sad in tone.

SRW p. 89

GLOSSARY

The glossary below is an alphabetical list of difficult words found in the selections in this book. Use this glossary just as you use a dictionary—to find out the meanings of unfamiliar words. (A few technical, foreign, or more obscure words in this book are not listed here but are defined instead in footnotes that accompany the selections.)

Many words in the English language have more than one meaning. This glossary gives the meanings that apply to the words as they are used in the selections in this book. Words closely related in form and meaning are usually listed together in one entry (*aimless* and *aimlessly*), and the definition is given for the first form.

The following abbreviations are used:

adj. adjective   **n.** noun   **v.** verb
adv. adverb   **pl.** plural form

Unless a word is very simple to pronounce, its pronunciation is given in parentheses. A guide to the pronunciation symbols appears at the bottom of each right-hand glossary page.

For more information about the words in this glossary, or about words not listed here, consult a dictionary.

abscond (əb·skänd′) ***v.*** To run away and hide, especially in order to escape the law.
accost (ə·kôst′) ***v.*** To approach and speak to, especially in an intrusive way.
affiliate (ə·fil′ē·āt′) ***v.*** To connect or associate with.
agape (ə·gāp′) ***adv., adj.*** With the mouth open, as in surprise or wonder.
aghast (ə·gast′) ***adj.*** Terrified; horrified.
aimless (ām′ləs) ***adj.*** Having no aim or purpose. **—aimlessly *adv.***
alacrity (ə·lak′rə·tē) ***n.*** Eager willingness or readiness, often shown by quick, lively action.
allege (ə·lej′) ***v.*** To assert positively, or declare.
amorous (am′ər·əs) ***adj.*** Full of or showing love. **—amorousness *n.***
anguish (an′gwish) ***n.*** Great suffering.
annihilate (ə·nī′ə·lāt′) ***v.*** To destroy completely.
apathetic (ap′ə·thet′ik) ***adj.*** Feeling little or no emotion. **—apathetically *adv.***
apathy (ap′ə·thē) ***n.*** Lack of emotion or interest; indifference.
apparition (ap′ə·rish′ən) ***n.*** Anything that appears unexpectedly or in an extraordinary way.
appease (ə·pēz′) ***v.*** To pacify or quiet, especially by giving in to the demands of.
aromatic (ar′ə·mat′ik) ***adj.*** Smelling sweet or spicy; fragrant.
array (ə·rā′) ***v.*** To dress in fine or showy clothes.
arrogance (ar′ə·gəns) ***n.*** Overbearing pride or self-importance.
ascend (ə·send′) ***v.*** To rise upward.
ascribe (ə·skrīb′) ***v.*** To assign (to a supposed cause).
asphalt (as′fôlt) ***n.*** A brown or black tarlike substance.
assault (ə·sôlt′) ***n.*** A violent attack, either physical or verbal.
assent (ə·sent′) ***v.*** To agree.
astray (ə·strā′) ***adv.*** Off the right path.
attentive (ə·ten′tiv) ***adj.*** Paying attention to; observant.
audible (ô′də·b′l) ***adj.*** Loud enough to be heard.
avaricious (av′ə·rish′əs) ***adj.*** Greedy for riches.
avenge (ə·venj′) ***v.*** To get revenge for (an injury, wrong).
avert ***v.*** To turn away.
awesome (ô′səm) ***adj.*** Causing a mixed feeling of fear and wonder, as by the power, size, or majesty of.

baffle ***v.*** To confuse so as to keep from understanding; puzzle.
banish ***v.*** To send into exile.
bedlam (bed′ləm) ***n.*** Any condition of noise and confusion.

---

fat, āpe, cär; ten, ēven; is, bīte; gō, hôrn, tōōl, look; **oi**l, **ou**t; up, f**u**r; get; joy; yet; **ch**in; **sh**e; **th**in, ***th*en**; **zh,** leisure; **ŋ,** ring; ə for *a* in *ago, e* in *agent, i* in *sanity, o* in *comply, u* in *focus;* ′ as in *able* (ā′b′l).

---

bellow *v.* To cry out loudly.
benign (bi·nīn′) *adj.* Good-natured; kindly.
besiege (bi·sēj′) *v.* To hem in with armed forces.
bewilder (bi·wil′dər) *v.* To confuse hopelessly; puzzle. **—bewilderment** *n.*
bilious (bil′yəs) *adj.* **1.** Resulting from an ailment of the liver. **2.** A yellowish, sickly color.
blunder *v.* To make a foolish or stupid mistake.
bluster *v.* **1.** To blow stormily. **2.** To speak or behave in a noisy and bullying manner.
bode *v.* To be an omen of.
bombard (bäm·bärd′) *v.* To attack as with artillery.
brandish *v.* To wave or shake in a challenging way; flourish.
breach *n.* A failure to observe the terms, as of a law or promise.
bungalow (buŋ′gə·lō′) *n.* A small, low house or cottage.
buoy (boi) *v.* To lift up or keep up in spirits.
buoyant (boi′ənt) *adj.* Able to keep afloat.
burrow (bur′ō) *n.* A hole dug in the ground by an animal.

cadence (kād′′ns) *n.* A rhythmic flow of sound.
calamitous (kə·lam′ə·təs) *adj.* Causing great trouble or misery.
calisthenics (kal′əs·then′iks) *n. pl.* Simple gymnastics.
cavernous (kav′ər·nəs) *adj.* Characteristic of a cave; hollow.
chafe *v.* To wear away by rubbing.
chisel (chiz′′l) *n.* A sharp tool used to cut or shape metal or wood. —*v.* To cut or shape with or as if with a chisel.
clannish (klan′ish) *adj.* Tending to associate closely with one's own group and avoid others.
clarion (klar′ē·ən) *adj.* Clear, sharp, and ringing.
coagulate (kō·ag′yo͞o·lāt′) *v.* To cause a liquid to become a soft solid.
cogent (kō′jənt) *adj.* Forceful; compelling.
commend *v.* **1.** To praise. **2.** To transmit the kind regards of.
commotion (kə·mō′shən) *n.* A noisy rushing about; bustle.
compassion (kəm·pash′ən) *n.* Deep sympathy; pity.
compel (kəm·pel′) *v.* To force to do something.
compensation (käm′pən·sa′shən) *n.* Anything given to make up for a loss, damage, unemployment, etc.
compliance (kəm·plī′əns) *n.* Giving in to a request or demand.
composure (kəm·pō′zhər) *n.* Calmness of mind or manner; self-possession.
conceited (kən·sēt′id) *adj.* Having an exaggerated opinion of oneself; vain.
condescend (kän′də·send′) *v.* To treat others in a proud way.
confirmation (kän′fər·mā′shən) *n.* Proof; verification.
conglomeration (kən·gläm′ə·rā′shən) *n.* A collection or mixture of different things.
congregate (käŋ′grə·gāt′) *v.* To gather into a crowd; assemble.
conjecture (kən·jek′chər) *n.* Guesswork.
consent *v.* To agree to do something.
console (kən·sōl′) *v.* To make feel less sad or disappointed; comfort. **—consolingly** *adv.*
consort (kän′sôrt) *n.* A spouse, especially of a king or queen.
conspicuous (kən·spik′yoo·wəs) *adj.* Easy to see or perceive.
consult (kən·sult′) *v.* To seek an opinion from; ask advice.
contempt (kən·tempt′) *n.* The feeling of a person toward someone or something that he or she considers worthless; scorn.
contort (kən·tôrt′) *v.* To twist or wrench out of its usual form into one that is grotesque.
convenience (kən·vēn′yəns) *n.* Personal well-being; comfort.
converse (kən·vurs′) *v.* To hold a conversation; talk.
convey (kən·vā′) *v.* To make known.
convivial (kən·viv′ē·əl) *adj.* Sociable; jovial.
convulsion (kən·vul′shən) *n.* A violent, involuntary contraction or spasm of the muscles.
copious (kō′pē·əs) *adj.* Very plentiful.
cordial (kôr′jəl) *adj.* Warm and friendly; hearty.
corroborate (kə·räb′ə·rāt) *v.* To confirm; support.
corrupt (kə·rupt′) *adj.* Depraved, wicked, or dishonest.
courteous (kur′tē·əs) *adj.* Polite and well-mannered. **—courteously** *adv.*
covet (kuv′it) *v.* To want greatly, especially something that another person has.
cowardice (kou′ərd·is) *n.* Lack of courage.
cower (kou′ər) *v.* To crouch or huddle up, as from fear or cold.
cunning *adj.* Skillful in deception; sly.

daunt *v.* To make afraid; intimidate.
decorous (dek′ər·əs) *adj.* Showing good taste in behavior. **—decorously** *adv.*
delirious (di·lir′ē·əs) *adj.* **1.** Temporarily out of one's mind; wild (often caused by fever). **2.** Extremely excited.
derelict (der′ə·likt′) *n.* A property abandoned by the owner.
derisive (di·rī′siv) *adj.* Ridiculing.
desolate (des′ə·lāt′) *v.* To rid of inhabitants. —*adj.* (des′ə·lit) Left alone; lonely; solitary.
desolation (des′ə·lā′shən) *n.* **1.** Loneliness. **2.** A deserted place.
despondency (di·spän′dən·sē) *n.* Loss of courage or hope.

destiny (des'tə·nē) ***n.*** The outcome or fate that is bound to come; one's lot.
desultory (des''l·tôr'ē) ***adj.*** Passing from one thing to another in an aimless way; disconnected; random.
deteriorate (di·tir'ē·ə·rāt') ***v.*** To make or become worse; lower in quality or value. **—deterioration *n.***
devour *v.* **1.** To eat up hungrily. **2.** To consume or destroy with devastating force.
diminution (dim'ə·nyo͞o'shən) ***n.*** A decrease.
disclaim *v.* To refuse to accept responsibility.
disclose *v.* To reveal; make known.
disdainful (dis·dān'fəl) ***adj.*** Treating as unworthy; scornful. **—disdainfully *adv.***
dismay (dis·mā') ***v.*** To make afraid; fill with apprehension.
disparage (dis·par'ij) ***v.*** To speak of as having little importance or value.
divert (də·vʉrt') ***v.*** To distract the attention of.
dogged (dôg'id) ***adj.*** Not giving in; stubborn. **—doggedly *adv.***
dominion (də·min'yən) ***n.*** Rule or power to rule; authority.
doughty (dout'ē) ***adj.*** Brave.
dour *adj.* Sullen; gloomy.
dramatic (drə·mat'ik) ***adj.*** Filled with action, emotion, or exciting qualities; striking. **—dramatically *adv.***
dubious (do͞o'bē·əs) ***adj.*** Feeling doubt; hesitating.
duplicity (do͞o·plis'ə·tē) ***n.*** Cunning; double-dealing.

effusion (e·fyo͞o'zhən) ***n.*** Unrestrained or emotional expression in speaking or writing.
elaborate (i·lab'ər·it) ***adj.*** **1.** Highly ornamented; complicated. **2.** Painstaking. **—elaborately *adv.***
elope *v.* To run away secretly, especially to get married.
emblem *n.* A visible symbol that stands for something else.
embrace (im·brās') ***v.*** To hug, as an expression of affection.
encumber (in·kum'bər) ***v.*** To hold back the motion of, as with a burden.
endow (in·dou') ***v.*** To provide with some talent or quality.
endure (in·door') ***v.*** **1.** To hold up under; stand. **2.** To remain.
engrossing (in'grōs'iŋ) ***adj.*** Taking one's entire attention.
enigmatic (en·ig·mat'ik) ***adj.*** Perplexing; baffling.
enthrall *v.* To hold as if in a spell; fascinate.
entreat (in·trēt') ***v.*** To ask earnestly; beg.
eternal (i·tʉr'n'l) ***adj.*** Everlasting.
evacuate (i·vak'yoo·wāt') ***v.*** To remove inhabitants from a place for protection.
exaltation (eg'zôl·tā'shən) ***n.*** A feeling of great joy; elation.
exasperation (ig·zas'pə·rā'shən) ***n.*** Great irritation or annoyance.
exceedingly (ik·sēd'iŋ·lē) ***adv.*** Extremely; to a great degree.
excessive (ik·ses'iv) ***adj.*** Being too much or too great.
exempt (ig·zempt') ***adj.*** Not bound by a rule or obligation applying to others.
exertion (ig·zʉr'shən) ***n.*** Active use of strength; exercise.
expiration (ek'spə·rā'shən) ***n.*** A coming to an end; close.
exuberant (ig·zo͞o'bər·ənt) ***adj.*** Characterized by high spirits; full of life; uninhibited. **—exuberantly *adv.***
exult (ig·zult') ***v.*** To rejoice greatly.

facade (fə·säd') ***n.*** A false or artificial appearance or effect.
famine *n.* An acute shortage of food during a period of time.
fathom *v.* To understand thoroughly.
fatigue (fə·tēg') ***n.*** Weariness.
feckless *adj.* Weak; ineffective.
feeble *adj.* Weak; without force or effectiveness.
festoon (fes·to͞on') ***n.*** A wreath or garland of flowers, leaves, or paper, etc. hanging in a loop or curve. ***—v.*** To adorn or hang with festoons.
fetid (fet'id) ***adj.*** Having a bad smell, as of decay; stinking.
fidget (fij'it) ***n.*** The state of being restless or nervous.
flourish (flʉr'ish) ***v.*** To grow vigorously; thrive.
foreboding (fôr·bōd'iŋ) ***n.*** A feeling that something bad is going to happen.
forfeit (fôr·fit) ***v.*** To lose or give up as a penalty for an offense or fault.
forlorn (fər·lôrn') ***adj.*** In pitiful condition; miserable.
frivolous (friv'ə·ləs) ***adj.*** Not properly serious; silly.
frolic *v.* To play or romp about in a happy, carefree way.
furtive (fʉr'tiv) ***adj.*** Done or acting in a sneaky manner.
futile (fyo͞ot''l) ***adj.*** Useless; vain; hopeless.

gait *n.* Way of walking or running.
gossamer (gäs'ə·mər) ***n.*** A filmy cobweb. ***—adj.*** Light, thin, and filmy.
grimace (gri·mās') ***n.*** A twisting or distortion of the face, as in an expression of pain or disgust.

fat, āpe, cär; ten, ēven; is, bīte; gō, hôrn, to͞ol, look; oil, out; up, fʉr; get; joy; yet; chin; she; thin, *th*en; zh, leisure; ŋ, ring; ə for *a* in *ago, e* in *agent, i* in *sanity, o* in *comply, u* in *focus;* ' as in *able* (ā'b'l).

guile (gīl) ***n.*** Slyness and cunning in dealing with others; craftiness. **—guileful** ***adj.***
gyrate (jī'rāt) ***v.*** To move in a circular path; whirl.

habitat (hab'ə·tat') ***n.*** The region where an animal or plant naturally grows or lives; native environment.
habitual (hə·bich'oo·wəl) ***adj.*** Doing a certain thing by habit.
haggard ***adj.*** Having a wild, wasted, worn look; drawn.
harrow (har'ō) ***v.*** To torment; vex.
harry (har'ē) ***v.*** To torment or worry; harass.
hasten (hās''n) ***v.*** To move or act swiftly; hurry.
haughty (hôt'ē) ***adj.*** Showing great pride in oneself and scorn for others; proud. **—haughtily** ***adv.***
haven (hā'vən) ***n.*** Any sheltered, safe place.
hoard (hôrd) ***n.*** A supply stored up and hidden.
homicide (häm'ə·sīd') ***n.*** Murder.
horde ***n.*** A large, moving crowd; swarm.
hospitable (häs'pi·tə·b'l) ***n.*** Friendly and kind toward guests.
humiliate (hyo͞o·mil'ē·āt') ***v.*** To hurt the pride of by causing to seem foolish.
hysteria (his·tir'ē·ə) ***n.*** An outbreak of uncontrolled excitement or feeling.

ignorant (ig'nər·ənt) ***adj.*** Having little knowledge, education, or experience.
illiteracy (i·lit'ər·ə·sē) ***n.*** Lack of education or culture; especially, an inability to read or write.
immense (i·mens') ***adj.*** **1.** Very large; vast. **2.** Excellent.
imminent (im'ə·nənt) ***adj.*** Likely to happen without delay; threatening.
impair (im·per') ***v.*** To make worse, less, or weaker.
impale (im·pāl') ***v.*** To pierce through with something pointed.
impassive (im·pas'iv) ***adj.*** Not feeling or showing emotion.
impel (im·pel') ***v.*** To force or drive to an action.
imperious (im·pir'ē·əs) ***adj.*** Overbearing; arrogant.
impersonal (im·pʉr's'n·əl) ***adj.*** Without connection or reference to any particular person.
implore (im·plôr') ***v.*** To ask or beg earnestly.
impostor (im·päs'tər) ***n.*** A person who deceives others, especially by pretending to be someone he or she is not.
impound ***v.*** To take and hold in legal custody.
improbable (im·präb'ə·b'l) ***adj.*** Unlikely to happen or be true.
inaudible (in·ô'də·b'l) ***adj.*** That cannot be heard.
incessant (in·ses''nt) ***adj.*** Without stopping; constant. **—incessantly** ***adv.***
incision (in·sizh'ən) ***n.*** The act of cutting.
incredulity (in·krə·do͞o'lə·tē) ***n.*** Doubt; disbelief.
incredulous (in·krej'oo·ləs) ***adj.*** Showing doubt or disbelief. **—incredulously** ***adv.***
indignation (in'dig·nā'shən) ***n.*** Anger or scorn resulting from injustice or meanness; righteous anger.
inertia (in·ʉr'shə) ***n.*** Not moving or acting.
inferior (in·fir'ē·ər) ***adj.*** Low or lower in order or status.
infernal (in·fʉr'n'l) ***adj.*** Of the ancient mythological world of the dead.
infiltrate (in·fil'trāt) ***v.*** To pass through; penetrate.
ingenious (in·jēn'yəs) ***adj.*** Clever, original, and inventive.
initiate (i·nish'ē·āt') ***v.*** **1.** To set up or start going. **2.** To admit as a member of a club, usually with a secret ceremony.
insatiable (in·sā'shə·b'l) ***adj.*** Constantly wanting more; greedy.
insignia (in·sig'nē·ə) ***n. pl.*** Badges or emblems.
insolent (in'sə·lənt) ***adj.*** Boldly disrespectful in speech or behavior. **—insolently** ***adv.***
intercept (in'tər·sept') ***v.*** To stop or interrupt; cut off.
interminable (in·tʉr'mi·nə·b'l) ***adj.*** Endless.
interpose (in'tər·pōz') ***v.*** To introduce or interrupt.
intervene (in'tər·vēn') ***v.*** To come between.
intimidate (in·tim'ə·dāt') ***v.*** To make timid; make afraid.
intricate (in'tri·kit) ***adj.*** Full of elaborate detail.
introspection (in'trə·spek'shən) ***n.*** A looking into one's own mind or feelings. **—introspective** ***adj.***
invocation (in'və·kā'shən) ***n.*** A conjuring of evil spirits.
irascible (i·ras'ə·b'l) ***adj.*** Easily angered; quick-tempered.

jar ***v.*** To make a harsh sound; grate.
jargon (jär'gən) ***n.*** **1.** A language or dialect unknown to one so that it seems incomprehensible. **2.** Specialized vocabulary of a profession.
jeer ***v.*** To mock or taunt in a rude manner.
jostle (jäs''l) ***v.*** To bump or push, as in a crowd.

laborious (lə·bôr'ē·əs) ***adj.*** Calling for much hard work.
lament ***v.*** To mourn; grieve.
lavish (lav'ish) ***adj.*** **1.** More than enough; very abundant. **2.** Very generous or liberal in giving or spending.
liability (lī'ə·bil'ə·tē) ***n.*** Being legally bound or obligated.
linger ***v.*** To continue to stay because of a reluctance to leave.
lithe (lī*th*) ***adj.*** Bending easily; flexible.
loathe (lō*th*) ***v.*** To hate; detest.
loathsome (lō*th*'səm) ***adj.*** Disgusting; detestable.
lofty (lôf'tē) ***adj.*** Haughty; overproud; arrogant.
lope ***v.*** To move along easily, with a long, swinging stride.
lurid (loor'id) ***adj.*** Vivid in a shocking way; startling.
lurk ***v.*** To stay hidden, ready to spring out or attack.

malevolent (mə·lev'ə·lənt) ***adj.*** Wishing evil or harm to others.
malign (mə·līn') ***adj.*** Showing ill will.
mammoth (mam'əth) ***adj.*** Enormous.
maneuver (mə·no͞o'vər) ***v.*** To move skillfully. ***n.*** Any skillful move or action.
maniacal (mə·nī'ə·k'l) ***adj.*** Wildly insane; raving.
meander (mē·an'dər) ***n.*** An aimless wandering; rambling.
meditation (med'ə·tā'shən) ***n.*** Deep, continued thought.
melancholy (mel'ən·käl'e) ***n.*** Sadness and depression of spirits.
menace (men'is) ***n.*** Anything threatening harm or evil.
merchandise (mʉr'chən·dīz') ***n.*** Things bought and sold; goods.
modest (mäd'ist) ***adj.*** Not vain or boastful; unassuming.
molten (mōl't'n) ***adj.*** Melted or liquefied by heat.
monarch (män'ərk) ***n.*** The single or sole ruler of a state.
monotonous (mə·nät''n·əs) ***adj.*** Going on in the same way without variation.
monstrosity (män·sträs'ə·tē) ***n.*** The quality of being greatly different from the natural or normal, as in form or looks.
morale (mə·ral') ***n.*** Moral or mental condition.
morose (mə·rōs') ***adj.*** Ill-tempered; gloomy.
mortify (môr'tə·fī') ***v.*** To cause to feel shame or humiliation.
motley (mät'lē) ***adj.*** Composed of many different elements.
mottle ***v.*** To mark with blotches, streaks, and spots of different colors or shades.
motto ***n.*** A rule adopted as a principle of behavior.
mutilate (myo͞o't'l·āt') ***v.*** To cut off or damage a limb or other important part of a person or animal.

nebulous (neb'yə·ləs) ***adj.*** Unclear; vague; indefinite.
negotiate (ni·gō'shē·āt') ***v.*** **1.** To discuss with view to reaching an agreement. **2.** To succeed in crossing.
neutral (no͞o'trəl) ***adj.*** Without strongly marked characteristics.
nonchalant (nän'shə·länt') ***adj.*** Casually indifferent.

objective (əb·jek'tiv) ***adj.*** Free from personal opinions or feelings; detached.
oblivious (ə·bliv'ē·əs) ***adj.*** Forgetful or unmindful.
obscenity (əb·sen'ə·tē) ***n.*** The state or quality of being offensive to accepted moral standards.
obscure (əb·skyoor') ***v.*** To conceal.
ominous (äm'ə·nəs) ***adj.*** Threatening; sinister.
omit ***v.*** To fail to include; leave out.
oppressive (ə·pres'iv) ***adj.*** Weighing heavily on the mind, spirits, or senses; distressing.
outlandish ***adj.*** Strange; bizarre. **—outlandishly** ***adv.***

pallid ***adj.*** Pale.
pantomime (pan'tə·mīm') ***n.*** Actions or gestures without words as means of expression.
parry ***v.*** To ward off or deflect (a blow, etc.).
passport (pas'pôrt') ***n.*** **1.** Anything that enables one to be accepted or admitted. **2.** An official document that identifies a citizen and gives the right to travel abroad.
peril ***n.*** Danger.
perilous (per'əl·əs) ***adj.*** Dangerous. **—perilously** ***adv.***
perish ***v.*** **1.** To be destroyed or ruined. **2.** To die.
permissive (pər·mis'iv) ***adj.*** Allowing freedom; especially, tolerant of behavior or practices disapproved of by others.
perpetual (pər·pech'oo·wəl) ***adj.*** Lasting forever; permanent.
perturb (pər·tʉrb') ***v.*** To cause to be alarmed or agitated.
pervade (pər·vād') ***v.*** To pass through; spread throughout.
pestilential (pes'tə·len'shəl) ***adj.*** Causing infection.
pine ***v.*** To waste (away) through grief, longing, etc.
pinnacle (pin'ə·k'l) ***n.*** **1.** A slender, pointed formation, as at the top of certain mountains. **2.** The highest point.
placard (plak'ärd) ***n.*** A small card or plaque.
placid (plas'id) ***adj.*** Undisturbed; tranquil; calm; quiet.
plague (plāg) ***v.*** To trouble; torment; harass.
plausible (plô'zə·b'l) ***adj.*** Seemingly true, acceptable: often implying disbelief.
plunder ***v.*** To rob or despoil (a person or place) by force, especially in warfare.
pompous (päm'pəs) ***adj.*** Self-important.
ponder ***v.*** To think deeply about; consider carefully.
ponderous (pän'dər·əs) ***adj.*** That seems heavy; bulky; massive. **—ponderously** ***adv.***
potent (pōt''nt) ***adj.*** **1.** Effective or powerful in action. **2.** Having authority or power; mighty.
precedence (pres'ə·dəns) ***n.*** The right or condition of being ahead in place, time, or rank.
precipitate (pri·sip'ə·tāt') ***v.*** **1.** To cause to happen before expected. **2.** To condense and cause to fall as rain or snow.
precocious (pri·kō'shəs) ***adj.*** Developed or matured to a point beyond that which is normal for the age.
predicate (pred'ə·kāt') ***v.*** To affirm as a quality or property of a person or thing.

fat, **ā**pe, c**ä**r; t**e**n, **ē**ven; **i**s, b**ī**te; g**ō**, h**ô**rn, t**o͞o**l, l**oo**k; **oi**l, **ou**t; **u**p, f**ʉ**r; **g**et; **j**oy; **y**et; **ch**in; **sh**e; **th**in, ***th*en**; **zh,** leisure; **ŋ,** ring; ə for *a* in *ago, e* in *agent, i* in *sanity, o* in *comply, u* in *focus;* ' as in *able* (ā'b'l).

predominate (pri·däm'ə·nāt') *adj.* To have dominating influence over others.
preliminaries (pri·lim'ə·ner'ēs) *n. pl.* Introductory steps.
preoccupy *v.* To occupy the thoughts of to the exclusion of almost all other matters; absorb.
preposterous (pri·päs'tər·əs) *adj.* So contrary to nature or reason as to be absurd; ridiculous.
presumptuous (pri·zump'choo·wəs) *adj.* Too bold or forward; taking too much for granted.
prey *n.* **1.** An animal hunted or killed for food by another animal. **2.** The mode of living by preying on others.
primeval (prī·mē'v'l) *adj.* Of the earliest times or ages.
profanity (prə·fan'ə·tē) *n.* **1.** Treating with disrespect or abuse. **2.** Bad language.
progeny (präj'ə·nē) *n.* Children or descendants.
propaganda (präp'ə·gan'də) *n.* A widespread promotion of ideas or practices.
prophecy (präf'ə·sē) *n.* Prediction of the future under the influence of divine guidance; act of a prophet.
prosaic (prō·zā'ik) *adj.* Matter-of-fact; commonplace.
prospective (prə·spek'tiv) *adj.* Looking toward the future.
providence (präv'ə·dəns) *n.* **1.** A preparation for the future. **2.** The care or guidance of God or nature.
provisions (prə·vizh'əns) *n. pl.* A stock of food and other supplies assembled for future need.
prudent (pro͞od''nt) *adj.* Wise.
pulsate (pul'sāt) *v.* To vibrate; quiver.
pungent (pun'jənt) *adj.* Producing a sharp taste and smell.

quaver (kwā'vər) *v.* To shake or tremble.
quest *n.* A seeking; hunt; pursuit.
quizzical (kwiz'i·k'l) *adj.* **1.** Odd; comical. **2.** Perplexed; questioning. **—quizzically** *adv.*

radiant (rā'dē·ənt) *adj.* **1.** Sending out rays of light. **2.** Showing pleasure, love, well-being, etc.
radiate (rā'dē·āt') *v.* To send out rays of heat or light.
radical (rad'i·k'l) *adj.* Favoring extreme change.
rambunctious (ram·buŋk'shəs) *adj.* Wild, disorderly, unruly.
rankle *v.* To cause long-lasting anger.
rapturous (rap'chər·əs) *adj.* Feeling or showing great delight or ecstasy. **—rapturously** *adv.*
rationalize (rash'ən·ə·līz') *v.* To explain in a way that is false but that seems reasonable.
raucous (rô'kəs) *adj.* Loud and rowdy.
ravine (rə·vēn') *n.* A long, deep hollow in the earth's surface.
realm (relm) *n.* A region; area.
rebellious (ri·bel'yəs) *adj.* Resisting authority; defiant.
recede (ri·sēd') *v.* To go or move back.
recoil (ri·koil') *v.* To draw back; fall back.
reconnaissance (ri·kän'ə·səns) *n.* An exploratory survey.
reconvene (rē·kən·vēn') *v.* To gather together again.
redeem (ri·dēm') *v.* **1.** To get back by paying a fee. **2.** To make amends for; atone.
reflective (ri·flek'tiv) *adj.* Thoughtful. **—reflectively** *adv.*
reformation (ref'ər·mā'shən) *n.* An improvement in character and conduct.
reiterate (rē·it'ə·rāt') *v.* To repeat; say or do again repeatedly. **—reiterative** *adj.*
remnant (rem'nənt) *n.* A small remaining part.
remonstrate (ri·män'strāt) *v.* To present and urge reasons in objection or protest.
remote (ri·mōt') *adj.* Far off; far away.
render *v.* To give.
renounce (ri·nouns') *v.* **1.** To give up, usually by a formal public statement. **2.** To cast off or disown; refuse.
repress (ri·pres') *v.* To keep down or hold back; restrain.
reprimand (rep'rə·mand') *n.* A severe or formal rebuke.
reproach (ri·prōch') *v.* To accuse of and blame for a fault.
reproachful (ri·prōch'fəl) *adj.* Expressing blame.
resentment (ri·zent'mənt) *n.* Bitter hurt or indignation.
reside (ri·zīd') *v.* To live in.
residual (ri·zij'oo·wəl) *adj.* Left at the end of a process; remaining.
resignation (rez'ig·nā'shən) *n.* Passive acceptance.
resolution (rez'ə·lo͞o'shən) *n.* **1.** Process of resolving something or breaking it up into elements. **2.** Determination.
resound *v.* To be filled with sound.
revel (rev''l) *v.* To make merry; be noisily festive.
reverberate (ri·vur'bə·rāt') *v.* To cause (a sound) to re-echo.
rhapsody (rap'sə·dē) *n.* Great delight; ecstasy.
rivalry (rī'v'l·rē) *n.* Competition.
rivet (riv'it) *v.* To hold the eyes or attention of firmly.
roam *v.* To wander over or through.
rote *n.* A fixed mechanical way of doing something; routine.
ruthless *adj.* Pitiless.

sabotage (sab'ə·täzh') *v.* Destruction of machinery as by enemy agents or by an underground resistance.
salvage (sal'vij) *v.* To save or rescue from shipwreck or some other form of damage, destruction, or waste.
saunter *v.* To walk idly; stroll.
savor (sā'vər) *v.* To enjoy with appreciation.
savorous (sā'vər·əs) *adj.* Tasty.
scanty *adj.* Insufficient; not enough.
scoff *v.* To show mocking or scorn.
scornful *adj.* Showing contempt. **—scornfully** *adv.*
scourge (skurj) *n.* Any cause of serious trouble.
scruple *n.* A qualm about something that one thinks is wrong.

scrupulous (skrōō'pyə·ləs) ***adj.*** Characterized by careful attention to what is right or proper.
scrutinize (skrōōt''n·īz') ***v.*** To examine closely.
sedate (si·dāt') ***adj.*** Composed; unemotional.
semblance (sem'bləns) ***n.*** Outward form or appearance.
servile (sur'v'l) ***adj.*** Like that of slaves or servants.
shrewd (shrōōd) ***adj.*** Keen-witted; clever.
siege (sēj) ***n.*** Any persistent attempt to gain control or overcome opposition.
simultaneous (sī'm'l·tā'nē·əs) ***adj.*** Occurring, done, existing, etc. together or at the same time. **—simultaneously *adv.***
singe *v.* To burn slightly.
sinister (sin'is·tər) ***adj.*** Threatening harm, evil, or misfortune.
skeptical (skep'ti·k'l) ***adj.*** Not easily persuaded; doubting.
slacken (slak''n) ***v.*** To reduce the intensity or severity of.
smolder *v.* To burn and smoke without flame.
sober (sō'bər) ***adj.*** Serious; calm; thoughtful. **—soberly *adv.***
solitary (säl'ə·ter'ē) ***adj.*** Characterized by loneliness or lack of companions.
solitude (säl'ə·tōōd') ***n.*** The state of being alone; isolation.
sorcery (sôr'sər·ē) ***n.*** Witchcraft; black magic.
sparse *adj.* Thinly distributed; not crowded. **—sparsely *adv.***
speculate (spek'yə·lāt') ***v.*** To think about the various aspects of a subject; ponder.
spinster *n.* An unmarried woman; especially, an elderly woman who has never married.
spite *n.* A mean and evil feeling toward someone; malice.
stalwart (stôl'wərt) ***adj.*** Strong and well-built; sturdy.
stamina (stam'ə·nə) ***n.*** The resistance to fatigue, illness, or hardship; endurance.
stammer *v.* To speak with involuntary pauses; stutter.
stoic (stō'ik) ***adj.*** Indifferent to pleasure or pain.
stratagem (strat'ə·jəm) ***n.*** A trick, scheme, or plan.
strategic (strə·tē'jik) ***adj.*** Well-planned. **—strategically *adv.***
subdue (səb·dōō') ***v.*** To make less intense; reduce; soften.
submerge (səb·murj') ***v.*** To place under cover; plunge, as into water.
submission (səb·mish'ən) ***n.*** The act of surrendering.
subtle (sut''l) ***adj.*** Not open or direct; crafty.
successive (sək·ses'iv) ***adj.*** Following one after another in sequence. **—successively *adv.***
sufficient (sə·fish''nt) ***adj.*** As much as is needed; enough.
sulk *v.* To show resentment and ill humor by sullen behavior.
sullen *adj.* Gloomy; glum; sad. **—sullenly *adv.***
summon *v.* To order to come or appear; call or send for.
surmount (sər·mount') ***v.* 1.** To get the better of; conquer. **2.** To be or lie at the top of.
surreptitious (sur'əp·tish'əs) ***adj.*** Done, got, made, etc. in a secret, stealthy way. **—surreptitiously *adv.***
syndrome (sin'drōm) ***n.*** A number of symptoms occurring together and characterizing a specific disease or condition.

tamper *v.* To interfere with or meddle with.
tangible (tan'jə·b'l) ***adj.*** That can be touched or felt.
tapering *adj.* Gradually decreasing in thickness.
taunt *v.* To jeer at; mock.
tenement (ten'ə·mənt) ***n.*** An apartment house that is poorly built or maintained, usually overcrowded.
tentative (ten'tə·tiv) ***adj.*** Indicating hesitancy or uncertainty.
terminology (tur'mə·näl'ə·jē) ***n.*** The terms used in a specific science or art.
terrain (tə·rān') ***n.*** Ground or a tract of ground.
torment (tôr·ment') ***v.*** To annoy, harrass, or tease.
torrent (tôr'ənt) ***n.*** A swift stream, especially of water.
tranquil (traŋ'kwəl) ***adj.*** Free from disturbance or agitation; calm; peaceful. **—tranquilly *adv.***
traverse (tra·vurs') ***v.*** To pass or move across; cross.
treacherous (trech'ər·əs) ***adj.*** Giving a false appearance of safety; untrustworthy.
tremulous (trem'yōō·ləs) ***adj.*** Trembling; quivering. **—tremulously *adv.***
trepidation (trep'ə·da'shən) ***n.*** Fearful uncertainty; anxiety.
trespass (tres'pəs) ***v.* 1.** To go beyond the limits of what is considered right or moral. **2.** To go on another's land or property.

uncanny (un·kan'ē) ***adj.*** Mysterious or unfamiliar.
unceasing (un·sēs·iŋ) ***adj.*** Unending.
undulate (un'joo·lāt') ***v.*** To move in waves. **—undulation *n.***
unintelligible (un·in·tel'ij·ə·b'l) ***adj.*** That cannot be understood. **—unintelligibly *adv.***
unkempt *adj.* Not tidy, neat, or groomed; slovenly.
unrequited (un·ri·kwīt'id) ***adj.*** Not returned in kind.

fat, āpe, cär; ten, ēven; is, bīte; gō, hôrn, tōōl, look; oil, out; up, fur; get; joy; yet; chin; she; thin, *th*en; zh, leisure; ŋ, ring; ə for *a* in *ago, e* in *agent, i* in *sanity, o* in *comply, u* in *focus;* ' as in *able* (ā'b'l).

unscathed (un·ska*th*d′) ***adj.*** Not hurt; uninjured.
unsurpassed (un·sər·pas′d) ***adj.*** Not improved upon or exceeded.

vacant (vā′kənt) ***adj.*** **1.** Empty. **2.** Showing emptiness of mind or lack of intelligence. **—vacantly *adv.***
vacate (vā′kāt) ***v.*** To cause to be unfilled or unoccupied.
valiant (val′yənt) ***adj.*** Full of courage; brave.
vanquish (vaŋ′kwish) ***v.*** To conquer; defeat.
vengeful (venj′fəl) ***adj.*** Seeking to inflict an injury for an injury; vindictive.
venture (ven′chər) ***n.*** A risky or dangerous undertaking.
veritable (ver′i·tə·b′l) ***adj.*** Being such truly; actual.
vermilion (vər·mil′yən) ***adj.*** A bright red or scarlet.
vexation (vek·sā′shən) ***n.*** Being annoyed or irritated.
vicinity (və·sin′ə·tē) ***n.*** **1.** The state of being near or close by. **2.** Neighborhood.
vigorous (vig′ər·əs) ***adj.*** Forceful or powerful. **—vigorously *adv.***
volunteer (väl′ən·tir′) ***v.*** To enter or offer to enter into any service of one's own free will.

wallow (wäl′ō) ***v.*** To roll about or flounder.
wane ***v.*** To grow gradually less, said of the moon.
wary (wer′ē) ***adj.*** Cautious; on one's guard. **—warily *adv.***
whimsical (wim′zi·k′l) ***adj.*** Oddly out of the ordinary; fanciful; freakish.
wistful ***adj.*** Expressing vague yearnings. **—wistfully *adv.***
wither ***v.*** To dry up; shrivel.

yield (yēld) ***v.*** To give in; surrender.

zenith (zē′nith) ***n.*** The highest point; peak.

SUPPLEMENTARY SUPPORT MATERIAL
1. Previewing the Anthology: Using the Indexes (page 3 of Workbook)
2. Study and Reinforcement Worksheets, numbers 1–46

INDEX OF SKILLS

LITERARY SKILLS

LANGUAGE AND VOCABULARY SKILLS

Most of the page numbers listed below refer to discussions that appear in the Analyzing Language and Vocabulary exercises. Additional page references for some terms can be found in the Literary Skills index.

SPEAKING AND LISTENING SKILLS

COMPOSITION SKILLS

Writing: A Creative Response

Writing: A Critical Response

CRITICAL THINKING SKILLS

The page numbers in italics refer to critical thinking skills covered in the Exercises in Critical Thinking and Writing.

Analysis

Comparison and Contrast

Evaluation and Response

Interpretation

Synthesis

[All of the writing activities listed in the Composition Skills index require synthesis.]

INDEX OF FEATURES

Focusing on Background

Responding to Literature

ORGANIZATION OF CONTENTS BY THEME

INDEX OF FINE ART

PICTURE CREDITS

Page: 3, Granger Collection; 4, Geoffrey Clifford/Wheeler Pictures; 6, Stephen Brown/The Stock Market; 12, (detail) #2864(2), Photo O. Bauer/J. Beckett; Courtesy Department of Library Services, American Museum of Natural History; 17, Ron and Valerie Taylor/Bruce Coleman; 20–21, Michael Yamashita/Woodfin Camp; 23, Drawing by Pam Littlewood © 1973 Elek Books Limited/Grafton Books; 25, Kashiwa Yoshito/E. T. Archive; 33, Costa Manos/Magnum; 39, 41, 44, 47, 50, from *The Jungle Book* by Rudyard Kipling. Macmillan and Co., London and New York 1894. Courtesy of Rare Books and Manuscripts Division, The New York Public Library, Astor, Lenox and Tilden Foundations; 52, Brooklyn Historical Society; 63, Photo Melvin Adelglass; 65, Robert Semenuik/The Stock Market; 71, Richard Hutchings/Photo Researchers; 72, The Bettmann Archive; 73, Granger Collection; 76, Photo Ernest Coppolino; 83, Walter Harvey/Photo Researchers; 84, Robert Bornemann/Photo Researchers; 87, 93, 96, 101, from *The Adventures of Tom Sawyer* © 1938 Jane Brehm, © 1917 Clara Gabrilowitsch. Reprinted by permission of Harper & Row, Inc. Courtesy of New York Public Library at Lincoln Center, Children's Library; 90, The Bettmann Archive; 104, from *Lassie Come-Home* by Eric Knight, illustrated by Marguerite Kirmse. Copyright 1940 by the John C. Winston Company. Reprinted by permission of Henry Holt and Company, Inc.; 108–109, from *Lassie Come-Home* by Eric Knight, illustrated by Cyrus LeRoy Baldridge. Copyright 1940, © 1968 by Jere Knight. Reprinted by permission of Henry Holt and Company, Inc. New York Public Library, Central Children's Room, Donnell Library Center; 113, Reprinted from *The Saturday Evening Post* © 1954 The Curtis Publishing Co.; 132, Catherine Ursillo/Photo Researchers; 144, Reprinted from *The Saturday Evening Post* © 1922 The Curtis Publishing Co.; 151, Joe McDonald/Bruce Coleman; 163, Peter Miller/The Image Bank; 167, Arthur d'Arazien/The Image Bank; 175, Frank Whitney/The Image Bank; 181, Joe McNally/Wheeler Pictures; 189, Culver Pictures; 190, Granger Collection; 196, Courtesy Charles Roth; 201, Bettmann/BBC Hulton Picture Library; 210, Michael Melford/Wheeler Pictures; 217, Martha Cooper; 227, F. Gohier/Photo Researchers; 228, 231, 234, Kobal Collection; 240, Movie Star News; 243, 247, 249, Kobal Collection; 257, Art Resource; 258, Joe McNally/Wheeler Pictures; 259, Jay Lurie/Bruce Coleman; 264–265, R. S. Uzzel/Woodfin Camp; 270, 271, The Bettmann Archive; 272, Björn Bolstead/Peter Arnold; 286, Culver Pictures; 288, Private Collection; 296, J. Wright/Bruce Coleman; 299, E. R. Degginger/Bruce Coleman; 300, Nicholas Devore/Bruce Coleman; 302, R. L. Zentmaier/Photo

Researchers; 304, Granger Collection; 307, Merlin D. Tuttle/Photo Researchers; 310, Marmel Studios/The Stock Market; 316, D. Hershkowitz/Bruce Coleman; 322, New York Public Library Picture Collection; 335, Jeffrey Smith/Woodfin Camp; 340, The Bettmann Archive; 341, Courtesy *Variety,* photo Bob Rubic; 342, Courtesy Chicago Bears; 345, Courtesy Columbia Pictures; 349, from *Brian Piccolo: A Short Season* © 1971 by Rand McNally and Company; 352, Courtesy Columbia Pictures; 358–359, UPI/Bettmann Newsphotos; 363, Cleveland Press; 368, 375, Courtesy Columbia Pictures; 376, Courtesy Chicago Bears; 385, Culver Pictures; 387, Tim Kirk. © 1972 Rufus Publications, Inc.; 389, Anthony Howarth/Woodfin Camp; 415 and 417, from *Stories from the Arabian Nights,* retold by Lawrence Housman, New York Charles Scribner's Sons, 1907. Courtesy of the Oriental Division, New York Public Library, Astor, Lenox and Tilden Foundations; 447, Michael Radigan/The Stock Market; 451, Farrell Grehan/Photo Researchers; 453, Harvey Lloyd/Peter Arnold; 454, Scala/Art Resource; 455, (t) Michael Holford; (b) John Kelly/The Image Bank; 456; NASA Science Source/Photo Researchers; 457, 458, 459, Granger Collection; 461, Ronald Royer/Science Photo Library/Photo Researchers; 464, 465, Granger Collection; 466, Kavaler/Art Resource; 469, The Bettmann Archive; 472–473, Erich Lessing/Magnum; 476–477, Bruckmann; 480, Pat and Tom Leeson/Photo Researchers; 482, Scala/Art Resource; 486, William Hubbell/Woodfin Camp; 487, Chuck O'Rear/Woodfin Camp; 488, Granger Collection; 490, Yvonne Freund/Photo Researchers; 493, Wayne Estep/The Stock Market; 499, Gianni Tortoli/Photo Researchers; 500, 503, 504, Granger Collection; 508, The Bettmann Archive; 509, Illustration by Steele Savage from *Stories of Gods and Heroes* by Sally Benson. © 1940 by Sally Benson. Reprinted by permission of Doubleday, a division of Bantam, Doubleday, Dell Publishing Group, Inc.; 511, William Kennedy/The Image Bank; 513, 516, Scala/Art Resource; 518–519 and 522–523, Granger Collection; 527, Illustration by C. E. Brock from *The Heroes of Asgard* by A. & E. Keary. Reprinted by permission of Macmillan, London and Basingstoke; 533, from *Stories from the Arabian Nights,* retold by Lawrence Housman, New York Charles Scribner's Sons, 1907. Courtesy of the Oriental Division, New York Public Library, Astor, Lenox and Tilden Foundations; 534, Joe McNally/Wheeler Pictures; 620, Granger Collection.

INDEX OF AUTHORS AND TITLES

Page numbers in italic type refer to the pages on which author biographies appear.

Pronunciation Guide for Selected Authors

Beatriz Badikian (bē·ə·trēz' ba·dē'kē·ən)
Charles Boer (bo͞or)
Arthur Cavanaugh (ka'vä·nô)
Anton Chekhov (chek'ôf)
Sandra Cisneros (sis·nā'rōs)
Roald Dahl (rōld däl)
Walter de la Mare (dē lä mâr')
Jose Maria Éguren (hō·sā' mä·rē'ə ā'go͞o·ren)
Richard Garcia (gär·sē'ə)
Roger Lancelyn (lan'slin) Green
Hesiod (hē'sē·əd)
Joyce Hovelsrud (hov'əls·rəd)
Leigh (lē) Hunt
Randall Jarrell (ran'd'l jär'əl)
Daniel Keyes (kēz)
Jamaica Kincaid (kin·kād')
Robin Kinkead (kin·kēd')
Felicia Lamport (läm·pôrt')
Vachel Lindsay (vā'chəl lin'zē)
Don Marquis (mär'kwis)
Edna St. Vincent Millay (mi·lā')
Nicholasa Mohr (nē·kō·lä'sä môr)
Alfred Noyes (noiz)
Ovid (äv'id)
Marjorie Kinnan Rawlings (rô'liŋs)
Dougal (do͞o'g'l) Robertson
William Saroyan (sä·rō'yän)
Shel Silverstein (sil'vər·stēn)
J. R. R. Tolkien (tol'kēn)
George G. Toudouze (to͞o·do͞oz')
Louis Untermeyer (un'tər·mī'ər)
Judith Viorst (vyôrst)
William Butler Yeats (yāts)
Jane Yolen (yō'lin)